BUILDINGS, CLIMATE AND ENERGY

BUILDINGS, CLIMATE AND ENERGY

T.A. MARKUS
MA, MArch(MIT), RIBA
Professor of Building Science
University of Strathclyde

E.N. MORRIS
BSc, MSc, FIWSc
Reader in Building Science
University of Strathclyde

with chapters by
P.A. REED BA, RIBA (11)
W.D. McGEORGE MSc, ARICS, AIQS (12)
P.P. YANESKE BSc, PhD, MIOA (13)

PITMAN

PITMAN PUBLISHING LIMITED
39 Parker Street, London WC2B 5PB

North American Editorial Office
1020 Plain Street, Marshfield, Massachusetts

Associated Companies
Fearon Pitman Publishers Inc, San Francisco
Copp Clark Pitman, Toronto
Pitman Publishing New Zealand Ltd, Wellington
Pitman Publishing Pty Ltd, Melbourne

© T A Markus & E N Morris 1980

LIBRARY OF CONGRESS CATALOGING IN PUBLICATION DATA
Markus, Thomas A.
Buildings, Climate and Energy
Bibliography: p.
Includes index
1. Architecture and climate 2. Architecture and solar energy
I. Morris, Edwin N., joint author II. Title
NA 2541.M37   720   79−4141

ISBN 0 273 00266 X hardcover
ISBN 0 273 00268 6 flexicover

Printed in Great Britain by Spottiswoode Ballantyne Ltd.,
Colchester and London

CONTENTS

Preface   ix

Acknowledgements   xi

Symbols   xii

1 **Shelter**   1
   References   17

2 **The System**   19
   References   32

3 **People's Response to the Thermal Environment**   33
   3.1 Basic principles   33
   3.2 Previous work   37
   3.3 Survival   40
   3.4 Thermal comfort   46
   3.5 Performance   70
   3.6 Health   ·71
   3.7 Psychological, social and economic factors   72
   3.8 General design consequences of thermal response characteristics   72
   References   73
   Appendix 3A: Heat balance and comfort equations
                      Operative temperature charts   76
   Appendix 3B: Thermal comfort charts   84

4 **Climate**   140
   4.1 Introduction   140
   4.2 General Concepts   142
   4.3 The climate-built form interaction; some examples   158
   4.4 Elements of climate   165
   4.5 Microclimate   207
   References   217
   Appendix 4A: Sunpath charts and Overlays   218
   Appendix 4B: Tables of R-values   262

5 **Heat Loss from a Building under Steady-state Conditions**   268
   5.1 Introduction   268
   5.2 Thermal conductivity   268

5.3 Thermal resistance 271
5.4 Thermal transmittance — U-values 274
5.5 Temperature gradient through an element 281
5.6 Condensation 285
5.7 Heat loss by fabric 297
5.8 Heat loss by ventilation 297
5.9 Energy consumption during heating periods 302
References 303
Appendix 5: Tables of U-values 303

6 **Heat Gains due to Solar Radiation — Steady-state and Cyclic Conditions** 310
6.1 Influence of solar radiation 310
6.2 Absorption 310
6.3 Emissivity 311
6.4 Sol-air temperature 313
6.5 Heat flow through fabric due to solar radiation 318
6.6 Transmission of solar radiation through glass 327
6.7 Effect of solar radiation on the building — cyclic heat inputs 334
References 343

7 **Intermittent Heating of a Building — Winter Conditions** 344
7.1 Intermittent heating — temperature swings 344
7.2 Intermittent heating — energy consumption 351
References 357

8 **Air Infiltration into Buildings by Natural Means** 358
8.1 Air infiltration 358
8.2 Calculation of infiltration 358
8.3 Pressure due to wind flow 359
8.4 Air flow through openings 364
8.5 Temperature difference — stack effect 366
8.6 Combined wind and stack effect 368
8.7 Air infiltration around windows 368
8.8 Total infiltration rate 369
8.9 Use of ventilation for cooling 370
References 371

9 **Shape of Building** 373
9.1 Variables 373
9.2 Relationship between surface area and volume 373
9.3 'Thermal cube' 377
9.4 Fabric heat loss, ventilation loss and volume 385
9.5 Relationship between heat flow, window area and orientation
for buildings in a temperate climate 387
9.6 Relationship between shape of building and solar radiation
heat gain 390
References 396

10 **Experimental Methods** 397
10.1 Data required 397

10.2 Temperature measurement 398
10.3 Humidity 400
10.4 Air velocity 401
10.5 The heliodon 401
10.6 Use of electrical analogs 406
10.7 Use of models 413
References 414

11 Engineering Services 415
11.1 Flow systems 415
11.2 Distribution in systems 420
11.3 Conversion in systems 430
11.4 Storage in systems 442
11.5 Complementary systems 450
11.6 Sizing of systems 455
11.7 Control of systems 460
11.8 Services as building sub-systems 466
References 478

12 Energy Accounting — Methods of Analysis 479
12.1 Introduction 479
12.2 Measurement of resources 479
12.3 Building resource allocation model 480
12.4 Life-cycle costing 481
12.5 Life-cycle costing using market prices 481
12.6 Life-cycle costing using prime energy accounting 493
12.7 Energy analysis 496
12.8 Life-cycle costing using energy analysis 497
12.9 General summary 499
References 500
Appendix 12A—E: Interest tables 500

13 Natural Sources, Heat Pumps and Heat Recovery 507
13.1 Solar power and buildings 507
13.2 Wind power and buildings 515
13.3 Heat Pumps 520
13.4 Heat recovery within buildings 527
References 532

Index 535

PREFACE

Although a few reliable books on the topics covered by the present volume have always been available, since the 'energy crisis' of 1973 with all its environmental, political and economic implications, the rate of publication of such books has substantially increased. As in other fields where interest arises relatively suddenly, this publication spate has had both its advantages and disadvantages. The advantages are that there are now a host of journals, reports and textbooks which deal with the energy implications of building design, and the subject is under continuous development at research institutes. The disadvantages are that for the teacher, or student, and for the professional designer in the building industry, the subject has become somewhat fragmented and, even within a given section of it, there is a wide range of techniques and formulations often inconsistent or in conflict with one another.

The present volume is based on a model of the interactions between climate and the internal environment of buildings which is explained in Chapter 2. The model is basically simple. It says that one object of buildings is to provide comfortable internal conditions in an economic way. It is therefore possible to prescribe and specify the limits of internal environment within which various human activities and mechanical processes can take place. The major area of knowledge required for this in the thermal field (that is, omitting the visual and acoustic environments) is physiology and its application to thermal comfort. In order to specify the characteristics of the building and its services required to provide this range of environments, it is necessary to have a reasonably accurate picture of the climatic and microclimatic characteristics of the areas in which the building is located. So climatology is a second major area of interest. The intervening system between the climate and the internal environment consists of the building itself and of the energy services used to complement the performance of the building fabric. So design (in both the architectural and the building science senses) and the study of engineering systems are two further areas which have to be covered. In addition, the fifth area, which is covered in summary form only, is that of new energy sources. Finally, all these aspects are linked together through economic techniques in which good or 'optimum' solutions are sought.

In every one of these six topics there are major textbooks and a large body of recent research literature. It was therefore found necessary to steer a middle course between either producing bulky and detailed material in each of these areas, which would have resulted in a totally unweildy book, or summarizing them so briefly that the resulting descriptions and techniques would have given neither a fundamental grasp nor practical design techniques to the reader. We believe that the frequently used phrase 'understanding of principles' is sometimes confused with understanding of a general and superficial kind. We further believe that there is a level of detail which has to be achieved in order that one may have an understanding of the principles, and this has been the guideline which we have followed in writing this book.

Because much of the work in this field has been done by the physiologists, climatologists, physicists and economists, the architectural design implications have sometimes been ignored. The book therefore starts with a brief historical review in which the attitudes and achievements of designers of both the remote and recent past are analysed. Included are some of the lessons which can be learned from the climatic and thermal design of vernacular buildings in which professional designers played no role, but in which design and building techniques tested and developed over a long period of time were used.

Although the book is addressed to anyone involved in making design decisions about buildings, its primary use will be to architects and building scientists who, between them, often have to make the strategic decisions about building form and construction. The treatment of the engineering services is at the conceptual and systems level, which is all-important in relating the performance of the overall design to the climate and internal environment. The further development of engineering services design to the actual specification of the hardware of engineering systems has clearly not been possible and is not desirable in the present framework. There are plenty of good textbooks available on the subject and it is, in any case, an area in which decisions will ultimately be made by the heating or mechanical engineer rather than the architect or building scientist. Nevertheless, we hope and believe that the present volume should be of interest to engineers working in this field, because it lays out the general pattern of relationships on the basis of which the various specialists can proceed with their own detailed design work.

The production of a book like this takes two to three years from inception to publication. During that time, many changes in techniques and calculation methods have occurred in this subject. We do not believe that these changes have outdated the basic techniques presented. No doubt, however, here and there, more up-to-date cost, technical or design data have become available during the production of the book. In particular, the reader's attention is drawn to the change in name of the Institute of Heating and Ventilating Engineers to the Chartered Institute of Building Services. Therefore, the *IHVE Guide* has become the *CIBS Guide*, and is now published as a series of 33 books instead of the original three volumes. In so far as this has occurred, we ask the reader's indulgence and express our hope that he may easily assimilate the recent techniques and fit them into the framework which he finds here.

T.A. Markus   Glasgow
E.N. Morris   March 1979

ACKNOWLEDGEMENTS

The authors thank a number of people who, by discussion, contribution, advice or assistance with the preparation of the manuscript, have helped.

Professor A.P. Gagge and Dr. R. Gonzalez of the John B. Pierce Laboratory at Yale University, gave substantial help and advice in connection with Chapter 3, and allowed the basic design data in that chapter to be based on their experimental work. The thermal comfort charts were plotted on the basis of print-outs from their computer programs, which they kindly provided. They have given invaluable comment, advice and corrections on several drafts of Chapter 3.

Similarly, the authors acknowledge comments and advice from Professor P.O. Fanger of the Technical University of Denmark; Dr. D.A. McIntyre of the Electricity Council Research Centre, Capenhurst; M.A. Humphreys of the Building Research Establishment, Garston. The authors, nevertheless, accept full responsibility for the interpretation of the work and advice of these research workers.

The Building Research Establishment's permission to use the charts and overlays in Chapter 4 is acknowledged elsewhere but special thanks are due to Peter Petherbridge of BRE for his advice and help.

The production of three chapters by three of the co-authors' colleagues is acknowledged in its place, but special thanks are also due to Peter Reed for useful comments on the systems aspects in Chapter 2; and Paul Yaneske for useful advice and data, especially for Chapter 4.

Iain Forrest is thanked for his substantial help in the drawing of the thermal comfort charts, and Margaret Ling and Margaret I. Morris for typing the manuscript.

All references to published and unpublished work, and all sources of illustrations are acknowledged where they occur.

One of the authors, Thomas A. Markus, wishes to express his thanks to the Carnegie Trust for the Universities of Scotland for their generous help in making a grant available which assisted with travel expenses in connection with the preparation of the manuscript.

Finally, but not least, the authors have to acknowledge a debt to their families, which can only be fully understood by married authors.

SYMBOLS

A	=	area *or* end-of-period payment (or receipt — according to text)
A_{DU}	=	Dubois surface area of body
$A(\theta)$	=	across variable
a	=	surface absorptivity *or* constant (according to text)
a_i, a_o	=	constants for solar altitude
B	=	breadth
b	=	constant
C	=	heat loss by convection from outer surface of clothed body to environment *or* capital cost
C_c	=	contact coefficient
C_{res}	=	dry heat loss from body by respiration
C_v	=	ventilation conductance or loss
CET	=	corrected effective temperature
COP	=	coefficient of performance
COPh	=	coefficient of performance for heating
C_1, C_2	=	cost coefficients
c	=	specific heat *or* constant (according to text)
clo	=	clothing insulation unit
D	=	diffusivity
DCF	=	discounted cash flow
DISC	=	degree of discomfort scale
DV	=	design or desired value
d	=	declination *or* temperature difference for degree day calculation *or* constant *or* diameter of circular channel (according to text)
$d(\theta)$	=	demand rate
E	=	emissivity
E_{diff}	=	heat loss from the body by water diffusion through skin
E_e	=	extractable electrical energy
E_{res}	=	latent heat loss from the body by respiration
E_{rsw}	=	heat loss from the body by evaporation of regulatory sweat secretion from skin
ET	=	effective temperature
ET*	=	new effective temperature
e	=	fixed rate of price escalation
F	=	irradiance factor *or* configuration factor *or* future sum of money (according to text)
f	=	decrement factor *or* correction factor for infiltration (according to text)

f_{cl}	=	ratio of clothed surface of body to nude body surface area
f_g	=	globe temperature correction factor
f_r	=	retransmission factor
G	=	rate of vapour flow
GER	=	gross energy requirements
H	=	height
H_{Gs}	=	global irradiation on sloping surface
H_{GV}	=	global irradiation on vertical surface
H_{met}	=	body heat production
H_w	=	windchill index (body heat loss)
$\hat{H}$	=	hour angle
$\bar{H}\downarrow$	=	monthly mean daily global irradiation on horizontal surface
$\bar{H}_D\downarrow$	=	monthly mean daily direct irradiation on horizontal surface
$\bar{H}_{Dh}\downarrow$	=	mean hourly direct irradiation on horizontal surface
$\bar{H}_d\downarrow$	=	monthly mean daily diffuse irradiation on horizontal surface
$\bar{H}_{dh}\downarrow$	=	mean hourly diffuse irradiation on horizontal surface
$\bar{H}_{Dhs}$	=	mean hourly direct irradiation on sloping surface
$\bar{H}_{dhs}$	=	mean hourly sky diffuse irradiation on sloping surface
$\bar{H}_{Ghs}$	=	mean hourly global irradiation on sloping surface
$\bar{H}_{ghs}$	=	mean hourly ground reflected diffuse irradiation on sloping surface
$\bar{H}_h\downarrow$	=	mean hourly global irradiation on horizontal surface
$\bar{H}_o\downarrow$	=	monthly mean daily global irradiation outside atmosphere
h_a	=	air conductance
h_b	=	body height
h_c	=	convection coefficient
h_{co}	=	external convection coefficient
h_r	=	radiation coefficient
I	=	electrical current
I_{cl}	=	insulation of clothing in clo units
I_D	=	direct solar irradiance
$I_D\downarrow$	=	direct solar irradiance on horizontal surface
I_d	=	diffuse (sky) irradiance
$I_d\downarrow$	=	diffuse (sky) irradiance on horizontal surface
I_{DN}	=	normal incident direct solar irradiance
I_{Ds}	=	direct solar irradiance on sloping surface
I_{ds}	=	diffuse (sky) irradiance on sloping surface
I_{DV}	=	direct solar irradiance on vertical surface
I_{dV}	=	diffuse (sky) irradiance on vertical surface
$I_{(d\,+\,g)s}$	=	total (sky + ground) diffuse irradiance on sloping surface
$I_{(d\,+\,g)V}$	=	total (sky + ground) diffuse irradiance on vertical surface
$I_G\downarrow$	=	global irradiance on horizontal surface
I_G	=	global irradiance
$\bar{I}_G$	=	mean global irradiance
$\tilde{I}_G$	=	alternating global irradiance
I'_G	=	peak global irradiance
I_{Gs}	=	global irradiance on sloping surface
$\bar{I}_{Gs}$	=	monthly mean global irradiance on sloping surface
I_{GV}	=	global irradiance on vertical surface

I_g	=	reflected direct and diffuse irradiance from the ground
I_{gs}	=	diffusely reflected irradiance from the ground on sloping surface
I_{gV}	=	diffusely reflected irradiance from the ground on vertical surface
I_L	=	long-wave radiation
I_0	=	normal incidence direct solar irradiance outside atmosphere (=solar constant)
I_N^*	=	direct normal incidence solar irradiance in aerosol-free atmosphere
i	=	angle of incidence *or* interest rate *or* flow (according to text)
K	=	heat transfer from skin to outer surface of clothed body
k	=	conductivity *or* constant (according to text)
L	=	Latitude *or* length (according to text)
L_R	=	crack length
l	=	thickness
M	=	metabolic rate
m	=	air mass *or* days in the month
N	=	number of interest periods
$\bar{N}_0$	=	daylength in hours
n	=	number of air changes per hour
$\bar{n}$	=	mean daily hours of bright sunshine
P	=	present sum of money
P_v	=	vapour pressure
P_{vdp}	=	vapour pressure at dew-point temperature
P_w	=	wind pressure
p	=	power or pressure
Q	=	rate of heat flow
Q_a	=	rate of air flow
Q_f	=	fabric heat loss
Q_m	=	monthly solar energy receipt
Q_v	=	ventilation heat loss
Q_x	=	maximum heat input
$\bar{Q}$	=	mean heat input
$\bar{Q}_f$	=	mean heat flow through the fabric
$\tilde{Q}$	=	alternating heat gain
$\tilde{Q}_f$	=	alternating mean heat flow through the fabric
q	=	rate of fluid flow
$\tilde{q}$	=	alternating heat flow per unit area
R	=	heat loss by radiation from outer surface of clothed body to environment *or* resistance *or* slope correction factor (according to text)
R_{cl}	=	thermal resistance of clothing
R_h	=	correction factor
R_{si}	=	internal surface resistance
R_{so}	=	external surface resistance
R_V	=	vapour resistance
RH	=	relative humidity
r	=	surface reflectivity *or* radius of a conductor *or* ratio (according to text)

S	=	solar gain factor
SET	=	Standard Effective Temperature
S_a	=	alternating solar gain factor
s	=	slope angle of a tilted surface from horizontal *or* specific heat *or* standard deviation (according to text)
s_V	=	specific heat (volumetric)
$s(\theta)$	=	rate of supply
T	=	absolute temperature (°K)
TSENS	=	termal sensation scale
T_{df}	=	thermal damping factor
$T(\theta)$	=	through variable
$\tilde{t}$	=	peak amplitude *or* temperature swing
t_a	=	air temperature
t_{ai}	=	internal air temperature
t_{ao}	=	external air temperature
$\bar{t}_{ao}$	=	mean external air temperature
$\tilde{t}_{ao}$	=	alternating external air temperature
t_{cl}	=	temperature of clothing surface
t_{dp}	=	dew point temperature
t_{ei}	=	environmental temperature
$\bar{t}_{ei}$	=	mean environmental temperature
t'_{ei}	=	peak environmental temperature
$\tilde{t}_{ei}$	=	peak-to-mean environmental temperature swing
t_{eo}	=	sol-air temperature
$\bar{t}_{eo}$	=	mean sol-air temperature
t_{eq}	=	equivalent temperature (Bedford)
t_g	=	globe temperature
t_{mrt}	=	mean radiant temperature
t_o	=	operative temperature
t_{oh}	=	humid operative temperature
t_s	=	surface temperature
t_{si}	=	inside surface temperature
t_{sk}	=	skin temperature
t_{so}	=	outside surface temperature
t_1, t_2	=	temperatures
U	=	thermal transmittance coefficient
V	=	air flow rate *or* voltage (according to text)
Vol	=	volume
v	=	velocity
v_p	=	vapour permeability
Wk	=	work
w	=	skin wettedness
w_b	=	body weight
X	=	constant *or* unknown quantity
x	=	constant
Y	=	admittance factor
y	=	constant
z	=	zenith
a	=	ratio
β	=	solar altitude; ratio

γ	=	wall solar azimuth
Δ_p	=	pressure difference
Δ_t	=	temperature difference
δ	=	horizontal shadow angle
ϵ	=	vertical shadow angle
η	=	efficiency
θ	=	time
λ	=	wavelength *or* amplitude decrement factor
μ	=	mean
ρ	=	density
σ	=	Stefan's constant
τ	=	transmittance factor
τ_a	=	turbidity coefficient
ϕ	=	solar altitude
χ	=	constant
ψ	=	time lag

1
SHELTER

Since the idea that buildings, settlements and cities are forms of shelter is both natural and rather obvious, not surprisingly it forms a central concept even in the earliest Classical writings about architecture, building and medicine. Vitruvius, drawing on earlier work, discusses the concept together with its necessary counterpart – the elements from which shelter is required – the climate. Users of his work in the Middle Ages may have been influenced by this discussion; certainly the theme recurs continuously in the commentaries which proliferate from the 15th Century onwards and in the theories which are developed therein. Rykwert [1] has shown that, in many of these writings, the notion of the primitive house, or primeval shelter, and speculation about its source, form and construction, are curiously persistent and its potency is no less diminished in the early 20th Century writings of the architectural pioneers.

However, interest in the primitive built form has arisen from other directions than architectural theory and its critique. Historical studies of vernacular buildings, and the discoveries of archeology and anthropology, are helping in the development of a new kind of planning and architectural theory – concerned not with monumental planning and design, but with the pattern of cities, settlements and buildings as expressive of the structural relationship between technological, social, symbolic and natural forces – that is, a cultural theory of form. This theory attempts to unravel the meaning of patterns found in primitive or vernacular creations of the past and, by studying the processes and forms of still active authentic societies, to draw conclusions for design today. A notable recent addition to this type is said to be the squatter housing movement in cities of the developing world.

These new orientations in theory and history are limited to more or less scholarly work and, by themselves, could not have much impact on either the conservation of existing, or the creation of new, environments. However, they have become reinforced by a group of economic, political and popular forces which may, in the long run, be more influential. These reached a climactic expression immediately after the Arab–Israeli conflict of October 1973, with the consequent reappraisal, throughout the world, of the availability and uses of the globe's fossil fuel reserves. It may turn out that this war and its political consequences will be seen by future historians of our environment as having created changes as significant as those brought about by the industrial revolution and the urbanization of rural populations. It is pertinent to later discussion to list this group of influences or what might be called pragmatic forces; and a very heterogeneous group it is.

(i) *Energy conservation*. Reference has already been made to the events which brought this issue in front of the public and politicians in a most dramatic manner. Scientists and economists had, of course, been issuing warnings of increasing urgency over the previous quarter century, but, for the most part, these went unheeded, certainly in so far as they related to the environmental uses of energy. There were some isolated pockets of research on energy, both fossil and natural; there were improvements in building standards, notably in Scandinavian countries, and some increase in plant efficiencies. However, most of the Western world, and the developing countries too, remained unaffected.

(ii) *Building, land and nature conservation*. This is itself the confluence of miscellaneous trends. One is concerned with ecology, agriculture, land use and natural resources. Another is based on an appreciation of the cultural and historical value of urban and rural survivals from the past – not only the well-known monumental examples, but also the humbler, anonymous ones, existing in their thousands but disappearing, for a variety of reasons, at an accelerating rate. Economic arguments now often support conservation of existing structures. This movement has been exploited or not according to its usefulness to the politicians in power. Occasionally some major issue – a new airport or trunk route proposal, or a major industrial development in a nature conservancy – brings a more broadly-based popular support for conservation, which soon vanishes once the threat disappears or a particular battle is lost. The booming holiday trade to remote areas of the world and 'unspoilt' European villages, as well as the flourishing business of buying and restoring or converting old (mainly rural) houses, testifies to the public's desire for contact with roots as it perceives them – often in a highly romantic light. Nevertheless, a genuine shift towards environmental concerns has taken place both in the public's, and in governments' thinking.

(iii) *Waste and pollution*. The widespread concern about these, and increasingly effective legislative action, is now also linked to the interest in the recycling and energy potential of waste material.

(iv) *Developing countries*. There is an awareness of the plight of these, especially the non-oil-producing ones. Industrialization, urbanization and increasing standards of living – all of which cause exponential rises in energy demand – require them to increase the import of energy at a time when they can no longer afford to pay the new prices even for their existing consumption.

(v) *Materials shortages*. Shortages of raw materials, and increased transport (energy) costs, are causing a renewed interest in indigenous materials, and the production of renewable ones such as timber and grasses.

(vi) *Urban blight*. The public and professional outcry against the monotony, inhumanity and vast scale of much new planning and housing is causing a reaction against megalithic, large-scale solutions and a search for variety, complexity and smaller-scale forms.

(vii) *Participation*. There is a persistent demand for greater involvement of the public in environmental decisions at national, regional and local scales. Some political acceptance and corresponding machinery exists; but the movement is in its infancy.

So, some important economic, political and popular forces are focusing attention on the same type of precedent and solution which the scholarly work indicates: small-scale, varied, economic development, in tune with technology and nature and expressive of cultural patterns. Whether this will ever again be an achievable aim is open to question; however, it explains the relative success of conservation, some discernible changes in the planning and design processes and the tolerance, and even support, for squatter housing in many countries. It also highlights the fact that not only are the theoretical and pragmatic forces tending towards similar types of solution, but that they both need access to similar types of analytical data. One of the astonishing aspects of the historical—theoretical studies referred to earlier is that, though shelter is a central concept, the system against which shelter is being provided — namely the climatic system — is only discussed in the most general, superficial way. We discuss below how this has come about; but first it will be useful to examine briefly why climatic analysis might also perform a useful function in resolving some of the pragmatic problems outlined above.

It goes without saying that the energy consumption in buildings is related to the energy system, i.e. the climate, in which buildings are located as well as to the properties of the shelter itself. Much of this book is concerned with explaining these relationships in a manner which leads to design guidance. The conservation of existing building stock often hinges on the ability to resist or delay the effects of climate on the fabric. Although this is a matter outside our scope, it is nevertheless one that requires analysis of many of the same features of the environment as those with which we are concerned. The dispersion of wastes and pollution, especially in air and water, is a climate-dependent phenomenon. The energy problems of developing countries require especially close attention to climatic features so that industry, technology and urbanization use them to positive advantage, whilst, at the same time, comfort and health standards can be raised. Materials shortages will demand climatic understanding, first, so that indigenous or other materials chosen are suited to the particular conditions they will meet and, second, so that production of the most appropriate local materials (for instance timber, bamboo or grasses) can be undertaken.

Whether it is reasonable to hope that design based on a better climatic understanding will change and improve the quality of built forms really awaits an answer from later sections of this chapter and other parts of the book. It is sufficient to note here that many designers believe that the variety, complexity and cultural meaningfulness of much that we admire from the past was partly the outcome of a rational and sensitive relationship to the land and its climate, a relationship which we should seek to re-establish. In reviewing vernacular and primitive settlements, Oliver [2] suggests their essential quality:

> '. . . they are shelters of societies whose social patterns require of their buildings specific forms to accord with their material, spiritual and kinaesthetic needs, resolved through available resources and conditioned by factors of economy, environment, climate and site. They are shelters built from within the community as essential to its life and as a direct expression of it, and not to the plans and specifications of appointed specialists.'

He, thus, also raises the last of our contemporary issues — the question of whether climatic analysis may relate to the attitudes which go under the general label of 'participation'. There are three reasons why the answer to this question might be in the affirmative. The first is that one of the underlying problems in any move in this direction is the absence of uniformity of values and culture once possessed by the homogeneous societies whose work Oliver is discussing. In pluralistic societies the breakdown of traditional cultures, social and economic conflicts between individuals, groups and classes, the divided interests of individuals, families and small entrepreneurial businesses, all militate against the acceptance of a common spatial expression of the older type. Nevertheless, the shelter aspects of built form, because they are based on the realities of (an often harsh) climate and of a universal human response, has allowed wide agreement on certain environmental issues and concomitant acceptance of constraints within nations, cities and groups. Much of the planning and building control legislation of the last century was based on such a consensus about health and welfare. Today, agreement about energy and resource issues may once more become the basis of communal design policies.

A second reason relates to common justice. In English law there exists a unique provision for 'Rights of Light' – the continued enjoyment of daylight once a building owner has had it available for a period of time. Related to such legal safeguards are planning tools [3] used for determining the space–height relationships between buildings in a way such that the future rights of adjacent landowners are protected. So far laws or regulations dealing with microclimatic rights are limited. For instance, no country in the world at the moment has a legal system which would allow one to sue a developer for so changing the wind microclimate around an existing building as to cause increased velocity, heat loss, noise and dust. Nor is there a legal right to a minimum amount of solar radiation. However, once these effects are fully understood we can, and should, in the opinion of one recent study [4], expect adequate legal and planning controls whose basic aim will be environmental justice and freedom. When that time comes, a large area of legally protected consensus for participatory design will have been created which in earlier days was the outcome of accepted custom and tradition.

There is yet a third reason, related to the second, why climatic analysis may introduce criteria for acceptable shared values into environmental design. All space costs something to build and maintain. In cold or hot climates this maintenance can be a major burden on occupants and there is evidence that the old, the poor and those with large families – the deprived – are the sections of the community whose sparse resources allow them to achieve only less than acceptable standards of climate control. In Britain, lighting, fuel and power expenditure typically represents 10 per cent of family income for the poorest families but only 3 per cent for the wealthiest [5]. Now, the type and location of dwelling in which someone finds him- or herself is largely a matter of chance; yet one may find that the cost of heating it, per unit volume of space, is up to 30 per cent more than that of a neighbouring dwelling; for example, the end flat on the top floor of a block in comparison with the middle flat on a lower floor. Some countries already control thermal standards by methods which ensure equal rates of heat loss, irrespective of the severity of region or the exposure of the house; in France, for instance, thermal requirements are expressed in terms of the 'G coefficient', which relates not only to the climatic region but volume, thermal transmittance, ratio of heat-losing surfaces to floor area and ventilation [6]. These points are discussed in Chapter 7. It may well be that such systems of environmental equity will become accepted not only within countries but in larger regions such as the European Common Market area.

The achievement of any of these objectives will require a scientific analysis of climate which will be brought about only by a continuous reminder, by and to all concerned, of the shelter function of buildings. Before the necessary measurement and theoretical methods were developed, the application of climatic knowledge to building design was based, by the theorists and architects, on the classical theories of the elements, on personal observation and, to some extent, the living, vernacular tradition which the authors observed. Vernacular climatic building design, on the other hand, was entirely based on the availability of well-tried models and on personal experience in which climate, materials, form and comfort were integrated. The gaps between 'architecture' and the vernacular, and between the architects' own theories and their actual practice, were quite large in this pre-scientific age and exist today as much as they did then. Contemporary critique of the vernacular forms is largely devoid of anything but the most simple climatic generalizations. The brief examination of these attitudes at various times, which follows, may help in the understanding of the theoretical standpoint within which the design principles and aids which form the bulk of this book can be placed.

The interest by architects and historians in the primitive and vernacular form is, according to Rykwert [1] a universal manifestation of a search for roots. It is a validation of what we do, in terms both of what has gone before and of where we are going; . . . 'Paradise is a promise as well as a memory'. Certainly Vitruvius shows this interest. He describes the beginnings of the house as being connected with the discovery of fire and, indeed, of language. A storm causes the branches of trees to rub together; they catch fire and cause a forest conflagration; on its subsidence the savage creatures drew near, found comfort both in the fire and in each other's company; developed language and, soon, the first houses. At first these were in caves, bent boughs and even nests (in imitation of birds). Soon they set up forked stakes, connected with twigs and covered in mud, for the walls. The flat roofs were inadequate to keep out the rain so they were pitched and had eaves; reeds and leaves were used as a cover. Vitruvius finds confirmation of his theory in the survival of such huts in various parts of Europe. He notes the pit dwellings of the Phrygians (dug into the soil, on account of the lack of forests and, hence, timber, but nevertheless having roofs of logs covered with reeds and brushwood; from where?). Other roofs he notes are of mud and he then goes on to describe the beginnings of 'real' houses, with proper foundations, using brick or stone walls and roofs of timber with tiles. 'From wondering and uncertain judgements' the builders now proceed to 'the assured method of symmetry' [7]. So architecture was born from an elaboration of the elemental shelter.

Vitruvius's work is deeply influenced by climatic awareness and advice. This starts from principles of site choice and town layout — to avoid the funnelling of prevailing winds; the avoidance of south winds and heat, as well as of excessive humidity, in the choice of sites as well as a whole chapter devoted to the climate as a determinant of the style of the house [8]. Houses should conform to diversity of climate, being of southerly exposure, and roofed, in the north and of northerly exposure, and more open, in the south. There follows a short discourse on how the pitch of human voice changes with Latitude — the southerners have high and shrill voices, the northerners speaking in heavier tones. Bodies and minds correspond to these climatic effects too — the northerners being of vast height, fair and grey-eyed, unable to withstand heat or fever but brave; the southerners more stocky, robust in heat but timid. Those in central Latitudes, such as his own Rome, combined ideal features of voice, mind and physique. Of course Vitruvius was aware of the Greek writers' views on health, city planning and building – particularly the work of Aristotle, Xenophon and Hippocrates. He must have seen Aristotle's recipes for laying out a town so that it faces East, or is sheltered from the North [9] ; Xenophon's advice to provide porticoes for shade against high summer sun but allowing low-angle, winter sun to penetrate deeply [10] and for making the south side loftier and the north lower, 'to keep out the cold winds'.

There is not a lot of evidence that the advice of these Mediterranean architects and scientists was followed by Roman architects in any precise detail. Of course climatic conditions in the Mediterranean, in spite of local variations, were generally favourable in both summer and winter and so 'failure' was relative and, as a result of great redundancy in the buildings, easily tolerated. Nevertheless, it is interesting to see that Roman structures, such as villas, amphitheatres and baths, had forms and constructions which were basically similar whether in North Africa or in central Gaul, some 15° Latitude further north. This indicates that the uniformity and anonymity of modern architecture, often blamed on the spread of big business, technology and international stylistic fads, is a recent version of something quite ancient; the tendency for political and military power, in empires, to diffuse certain central images and technologies, which partially or totally override the local, particular and specific needs and traditions. The professional designers were often not only employed, but also educated, in systems which were attached to this central imperial power.

Vitruvius may have been read, and the practical aspects of his work used, during the Middle Ages. But it is in the 15th Century that the series of great theories, many of them commentaries on, or critiques of, Vitruvius starts with the publication of Alberti's *Ten Books on Architecture* in 1485. His picture of the beginnings of architecture is simpler and more general than Vitruvius's:

> 'In the beginning men looked out for settlements in some secure country; and having found a convenient spot suitable to their occasions, they made themselves a habitation so contrived, that private and public matters might not be confounded together in the same place; but that they might have one part for sleep, another for their kitchen, and others for their other necessary uses. They then began to think of a covering to defend them from sun and rain; and in order thereto, they erected walls to place this covering upon. By this means they knew they should be more completely sheltered from piercing colds, and stormy winds. Lastly, in the sides of the walls, from top to bottom, they opened passages and windows, for going in and out, and letting in light and air, and for the conveniency of discharging any wet, or gross vapours which might chance to get into the house.' [11]

From this he goes on to describe the evolution of more complex, specialized buildings. His work, like Vitruvius's, devotes substantial parts to the selection of the site, microclimate, suitable materials for keeping space warm or cold and protection against sun and wind. He gives one of the earliest descriptions of advection and frost hollows:

> '. . . a city standing at the foot of a hill, and looking towards the setting sun, is accounted unhealthy, more for this reason than any other, that it feels too suddenly the cold chilling breezes of the night.'

He warns against valley currents and eddies, reflected solar radiation from land or water (whereby a house suffers a 'double sun') in hot climates and also deals with lightweight linings to walls, in the form of wool and flax, for insulating and rapid cooling. So the picture of the primitive shelter and of more refined, architectural ways of controlling climate and achieving comfort emerges strongly.

Alberti's example was followed by others. Palladio refers to Vitruvius's description of the original hut and elaborates on the change from flat to pitched roofs. He too advises against valley sites, on account of humidity, wind and the reflection of the sun's rays creating excessive heat [12]. He believes the private house to have been the progenitor of villages, cities and public buildings and has his own, pedimented classical interpretation of what it must have been like. Rykwert considers his villas to be formal expressions of this 'primitive ancient house' [1], and traces the idea of the primitive hut through the Italian, Spanish and French theorists and commentators on Vitruvius. Notably he shows that whilst the theories of Laugier, Claude Perrault, Chambers and others on the origins of the elementary form and construction conflict, in all cases its shelter function as primary is taken for granted. Viollet le Duc develops this picture in greater detail. In the British tradition Ruskin and Morris extol the virtues of simplicity, natural use of materials and ornament, and the importance of following natural influences rather than imitating – amongst these influences climate being an important one.

In practice, however, the Renaissance, 17th and 18th Century architects did

Fig. 1.1 (a) Plan and elevation of Chiswick house, begun 1725 (British Architectural Library) (b) Plan of Palladio's Villa Rotonda

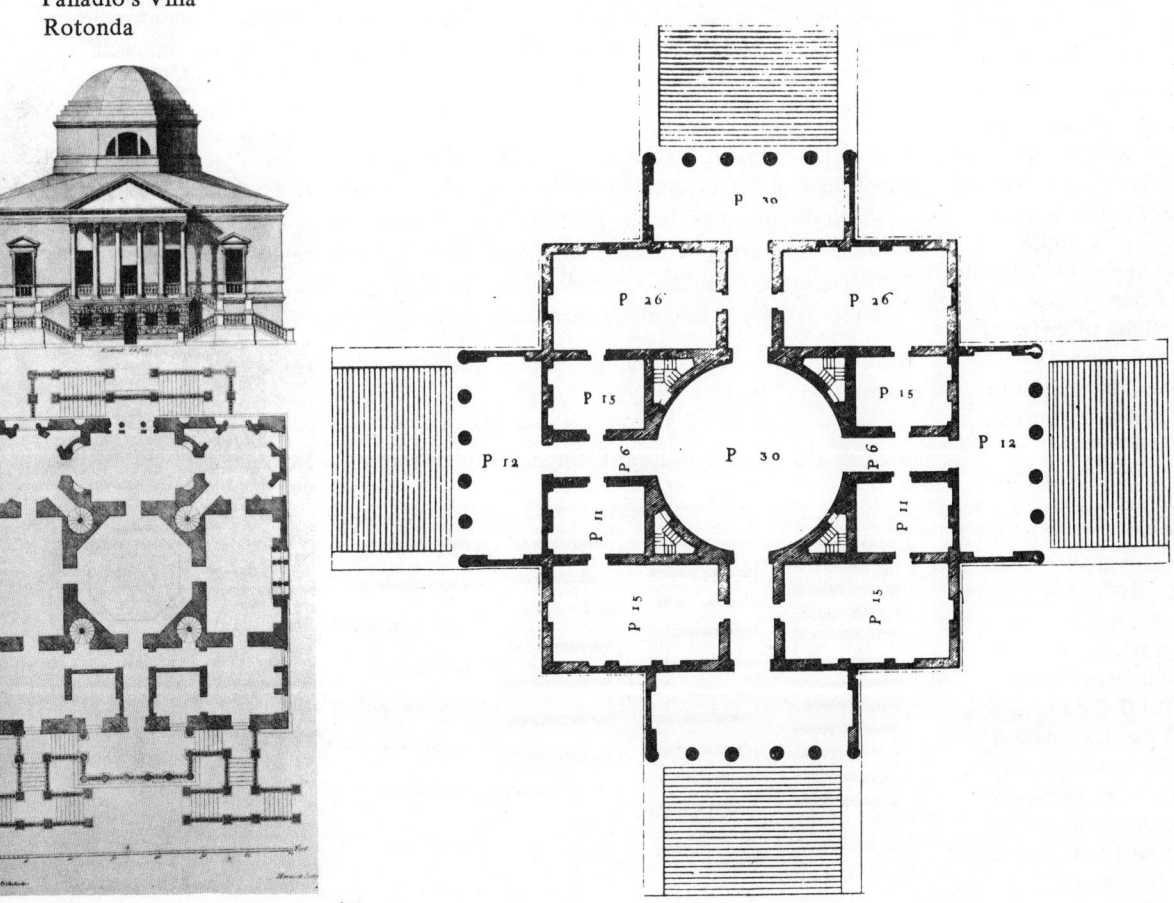

(a)   (b)

not realize to the full the implications of their climatic differentiation theories any more than the Roman architects had before them. This is not to say the buildings were environmentally or climatically unsound – far from it. Generally of massive construction, with limited window areas, they had achieved a technology which had the universal merit of thermal mass, limited heat loss and gain through windows and reasonable thermal resistance of walls and roofs. This served well in both Western and cold climates and against diurnal swings – and internal thermal standards and expectations were, by all accounts, fairly low. Nevertheless, it is surprising to find that a Palladian villa in Lombardy and in London uses the same plan form, window pattern and volumetric relationships (Fig. 1.1). This lack of differentiation, or universality, is in striking contrast to the variety found in vernacular building even within a limited area such as Provence, Tuscany or the Black Sea coast. We have commented earlier on the phenomenon of the uniform force of professional style and technology.

Rykwert shows that the preoccupation, obsession perhaps, with the primitive hut runs through the 19th and the first half of the 20th Centuries. Loos, the Futurist Sant' Elia, Mendelsohn, Frank Lloyd Wright, Corbusier, Gropius and Neutra each in his way returned to the purity and harmony of this natural source. But the descriptions are now more in terms of landscape, unselfconscious forms and honest use of materials than of climatic factors.

It must be emphasized that climatic principles, as they saw them, deeply influenced the thought and work of these architects. To refer merely to the last four in the list: Wright used solar geometry in a number of houses; notable is the Sturges house, Los Angeles, where the varying projections of the eaves on each elevation was related to solar angles. Gropius put climate as foremost in basic design conception:

'. . . true regional character cannot be found through sentimental or imitative approach by incorporating either old emblems or the newest local fashions which disappear as they appear. But if you take . . . the basic difference imposed on architectural design by the climatic conditions . . . diversity of expression can result . . . if the architect will use the utterly contrasting indoor–outdoor relations . . . as focus for design conception.'[13]

Much of his housing and planning design was based on angles suitable for sun penetration (Fig. 1.2).

Corbusier, from the 1920's onwards, was deeply concerned in his design research and writing to use the sun and wind as formative influences in city

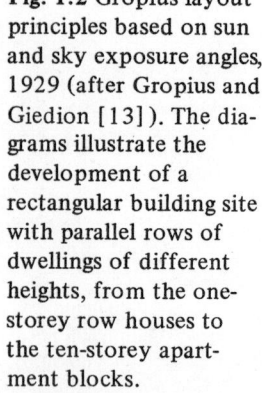

Fig. 1.2 Gropius layout principles based on sun and sky exposure angles, 1929 (after Gropius and Giedion [13]). The diagrams illustrate the development of a rectangular building site with parallel rows of dwellings of different heights, from the one-storey row houses to the ten-storey apartment blocks.

On the same site, slablike, ten-storey buildings result in much broader green spaces between buildings than the narrow spaces between walk-ups or row houses.

(a) If the site area and the illumination angle (sun exposure) remain the same, the number of rooms increases with the number of storeys.

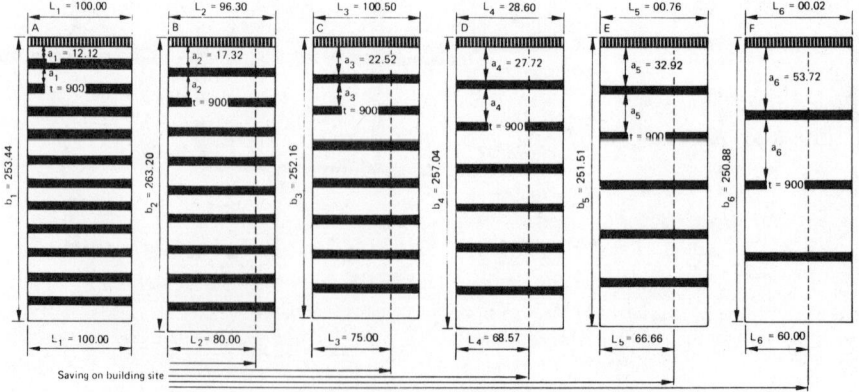

(b) If the illumination angle and the number of rooms remain the same, the site area diminishes as the number of storeys increases.

(c) and (d) If the site area and number of rooms remains the same, the illumination angle diminishes and the sun exposure improves with the number of storeys.

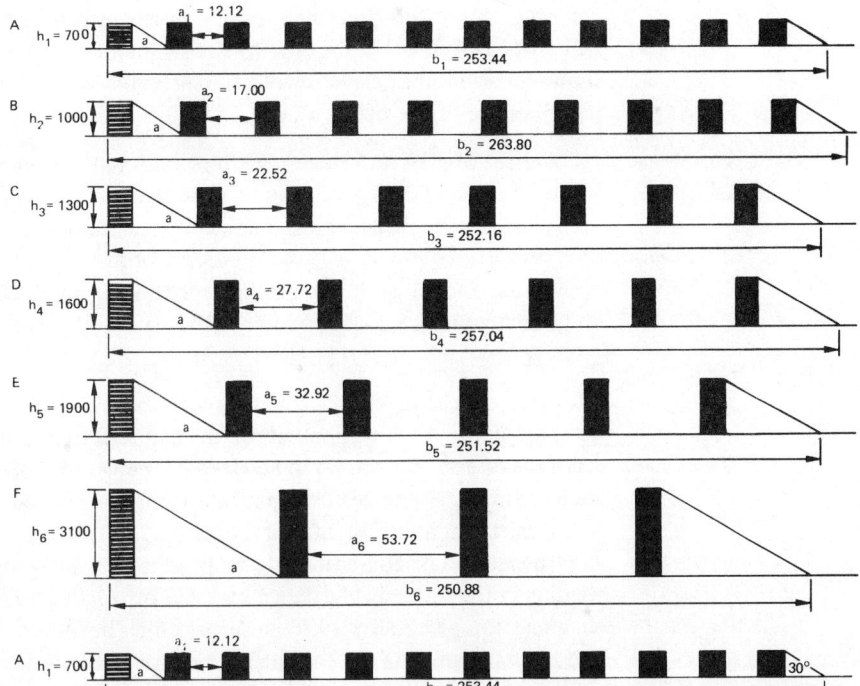

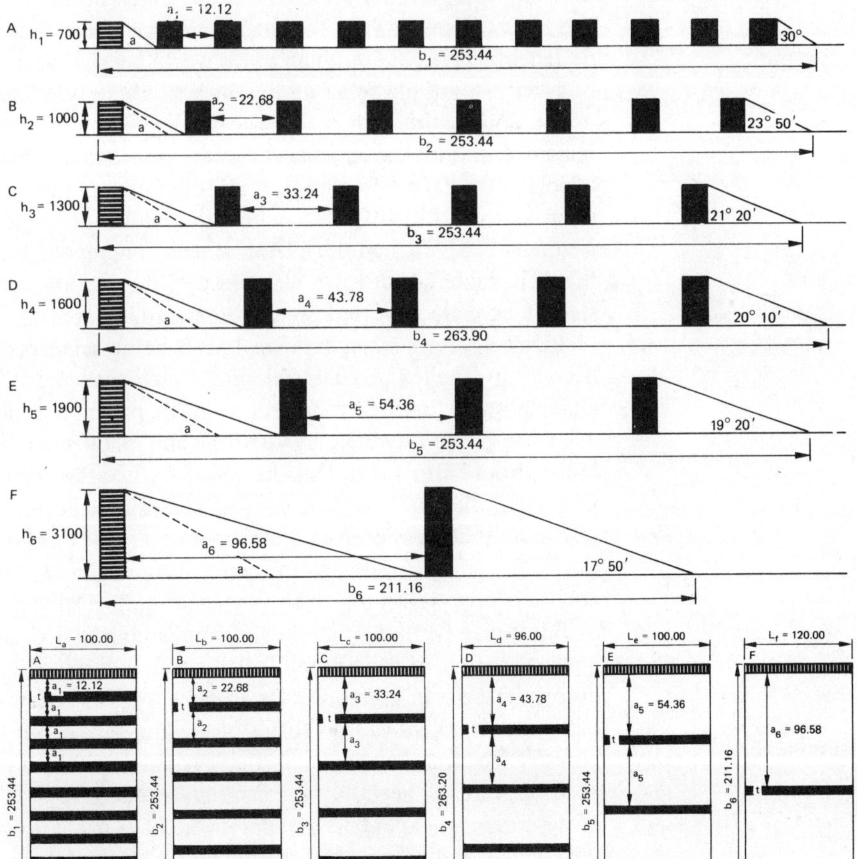

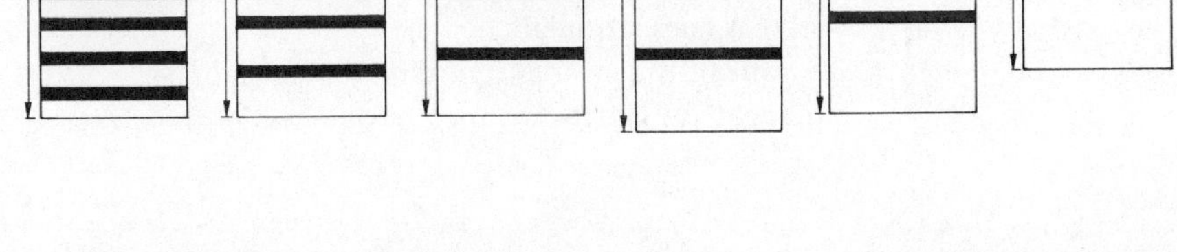

planning. But at this time the idea of climatic influence on building design was still unformed. In 1922 his cruciform tower block of 'Une ville contemporaire' shows no attempt at elevational differentiation or solar control. In 1929 he describes the future office block:

'A sheet of glass and three partition walls make an ideal office: this type of construction holds good when a thousand have to be provided. So from top to bottom the facades of the new city's office buildings form unbroken expanses of glass . . . . These translucent prisms that seem to float in the air without anchorage to the ground – flashing in summer sunshine, softly gleaming under the grey winter skies, magically glittering at nightfall – one huge block of offices.'[14]

Although he was vaguely becoming aware that this really could not work, the abstract picture became concrete in the hands of hundreds of hack designers from the late 1940's on. So in all cities of the world there are now acres of just such – climatically uncontrollable catastrophes – curtain wall facades.

Corbusier himself saw that in summer '. . . l'entrée catastrophique du soleil' [15] needed to be combatted. In 1928 he is already experimenting with sun shading in the house at Carthage; by 1933 his Algiers housing has more complete shading strategy; and by 1936 he suggests the 'brise-soleil' to Oscar Niemeyer and his associates for the National Education and Public Health Building in Rio de Janeiro. This, like so much of his work, became a fashion which for a quarter of a century was plastered on buildings in a variety of climates, irrespective of orientation, Latitude or shading principles. Corbusier's own solar studies always remained simple – often consisting of no more than a few sketches or the note of solar altitude in mid-winter or mid-summer on a particular orientation at noon, or the notion of the 'axe héliothermique' explored in his plans for Nemours [16]. He had the CIAM Athens Congress of 1933 adopt his principle that 'The materials of town planning are: the sun, the space, the vegetation, steel and concrete, in that precise order and hierarchy.'

Richard Neutra often expressed his belief in science; he wants his architect to become an 'applied physiologist' and a 'biological realist' [17]. '. . . there are annually some hundred thousand scientific papers that penetrate profoundly in what was guessed wrongly by Aristotle and many great seekers that followed him'. 'From Vitruvius to Palladio geometry was the great science'. How he failed to notice the scientific basis of this work is deeply puzzling; although he does note that we cannot operate any more (as Vitruvius and Palladio did) on 'earth, fire, air and water' as the concepts of elements. This 'biologically-inclined architect' now has to return to an ancient biological tradition.

But it may be that Aristotle's town planning advice, and the design science of 'seekers' such as Vitruvius and Palladio were more than guesswork compared to his own efforts. In his studies for the Los Angeles Hall of Records he notes sun-paths and examines various forms of shading device; but finally the choice of movable, vertical louvres, controlled automatically by a roof-sensor of the sun's position, will still need '. . . the carefully studied research and recommendations of the foremost experienced experts who have made proven installations'; his own understanding may be signified by his belief that Los Angeles is at '120°W (sic) latitude'!

One of the most extraordinary aspects of early 20th Century architectural thought and practice is the unawareness of the effects of scale and size. Some experience of tall buildings had already been obtained in the late 19th Century in North American cities, but they were generally in streets and of limited height. Now the new towers and slabs were designed as simple proportional enlargements of traditional, smaller, structures. In terms of solar geometry this worked – but only within the limits that shading angles remained unaltered. Vast areas of open ground between the blocks were more or less permanently deprived of sunlight, and substantial parts of skylight too, with consequent loss of energy for photosynthesis in grass and plants. Moreover, the white concrete building surfaces – later to be replaced by even more effective specular mirrors of curtain walling – reflected solar energy so that even north-facing facades and windows in the Northern hemisphere were now receiving substantial solar heat gains. Even Alberti, who had conceived of no buildings of this scale, was nevertheless aware of this 'double sun' effect, from south-facing valley slopes. The tall buildings also experienced a new wind climate; higher velocities, eddies and turbulence and rain flowing *up* a building facade under the pressure of wind. In turn, they altered the climate around their base – often to wind- and rain-swept wastes and wind tunnels under the buildings raised on their newly fashionable *pilotis*. This breakdown or suspension of physical imagination was, of course, parallelled by an analogous breakdown in visual sensibility; so the pattern for more than half a century of worldwide development of soulless high-rise flats and offices was set.

The remarkable aspect of the 18th and 19th Century Beaux Arts writings we have referred to above, and of the theories and practices of the 'modern masters', is the simplistic view of climate. The most obvious, and easily handled was solar geometry – it involved graphics, shadows could be projected and drawn on plan, section and elevation, or better still, on racy perspective sketches, and spatial rules deduced from sun paths. But it was mainly pictorially handled and there was little of any greater analytic depth. This was all the more remarkable as the growth of scientific climatology and meteorological instrumentation from the mid-18th Century made available theoretical and empirical data of immensely greater power than the Renaissance writers could draw upon.

The two basic parameters were temperature and pressure, made measurable by Galileo's development of the thermometer in 1593 and his pupil Torricelli's invention of the mercury barometer in 1643. The quantification of regional climate, by the amassing of meteorological measurements, was well on the way in the 17th and 18th Centuries – with weather observations encouraged by the Royal Society after 1660 and the setting up of national meteorological networks in France in the 1770's and Prussia in 1817. As long ago as 1818, Howard published the results of measurements commenced in 1806 at Somerset House and other sites around London showing the existence of an urban micro-climate [18]. This scientific work appears to have been as uniformly ignored by the theorists of the 'Schools' as by Corbusier and other leading critics of these very institutions in the first half of this century. Indeed the contemporary students of the primitive and vernacular adopt, on the whole, an equally cavalier attitude.

Rapoport makes a useful distinction between primitive and vernacular buildings [19]. The first he defines as buildings, usually dwellings, built in societies with little specialization; where diffuse knowledge is possessed by everyone and where there is no technical vocabulary, but rather a model which persists for long periods of time. Vernacular he sees as a pre-industrial technique where tradesmen and specialist craftsmen have appeared and where the model is continually adjusted according to the needs of each individual family, this resulting in far greater variety but still a common type or style. Both are distinguished from the monumental buildings with a specialized function – churches, palaces and tombs – usually the work of an individual, or team of professional designers. These are the buildings to which standard histories of architecture are devoted – and have been since Fergusson to whom '. . . Shelter is easily provided, but monumental and ornamental shelter, in other words, architecture, is one of the most prominent of the fine arts.'[20]

A substantial portion of Rapoport's work is devoted to disposing of theories which see the physical environment of climate or site, or the technological forces of societies, as being the determining or even the most powerful influences on form. He quotes numerous examples to show that climatically inappropriate forms are often used where cultural, symbolic or social factors are the potent, crucial ones. The technical ones may act as mediating filters, or 'possibilistic' influences. He illustrates a number of cases where migrations from one climate to another have not resulted in a change of form or even of construction (although new materials may have to be used to build in the old methods); the survival in the same climate of entirely different forms side by side – an outstanding example of which is the Pueblo Indian group dwelling and the Navajo Hogan. Nevertheless, he sees various house types as 'responding to climate very well'. However, from time to time there seems to be a curious contradiction in his analysis which reduces the force of his own argument. For instance, he quotes the Eskimo igloo, with a central space with rooms arranged radially round it, as 'not the most efficient climatically'; quoting Carpenter, he refers to the fact that the form is far from the most compact which could be devised and which would be climatically desirable. Yet further, after a detailed description of the same dwelling in the context of compact or subterranean dwellings of extreme-cold climates, it is said that '. . . the attempt [in all these cases] is to offer least resistance to wind and provide a maximum volume with a minimum surface area. The hemisphere of the Igloo does that perfectly, as well as being the most efficiently heated by a seal-oil lamp, a point source of radiant heat which helps to focus at the centre'. (The excellent thermal performance of the igloo is described in Chapter 4.) This makes his position along the scale of determinism to 'possibilism' difficult to locate.

In any case, the conflict to which he devotes considerable effort seems to be rather an artificial one, and he has to erect some straw men to knock them down again. For one thing, the so-called climatic and technological determinists are difficult to find. In evidence of the former he quotes Archer's work on *systematic design methods* [21] and an obscure article in the *Naturalist* of 1889. For the latter view, specifically that materials have 'determined' the character of buildings, the Austrian theorist Abraham, probably writing about *1880(?)* is quoted. His view is said to be both popular and to have roots that '. . . go far back in time'. But even those scientific architects who have written in the greatest detail about climate, construction and architecture, such as the Olgyay brothers, Aronin, Givoni and Pleijel [22], have made no such exaggerated claims. The Renaissance theorists who have been briefly quoted certainly do not (or how far back in time does one have to go?); nor does Corbusier nor other early modern architectural writers. Even the more modest claims they do make are partially denied by their own practice.

The debate is analogous to those on the practical as opposed to the symbolic significance of clothes or whether eating meals is a nutritional or cultural activity. These, and the house form debate, arise from a functional view of behaviour which is quite opposed to the structuralist view to which, in the end, Rapoport himself adheres. According to this view, human language and behaviour have a structure in which the complex net of physical and symbolic forces is patterned according to certain recognizable rules. To the structural anthropologist, the form of a shelter is but part of the totality of social structures and signs. We can see in Lévi-Strauss's work that this integration reinforces (rather than diminishes) the significance of village plans and house forms, since they are now seen as deeply related to every other aspect of life [23].

The deep relationship between topography, climate, culture and house or settlement form is nowhere better shown than in Chinese and Japanese systems governing siting and construction. According to the Feng Shui system, layout has to be harmonized with forces that flow from the hills, through fields and woods and, of course, through the house itself. Room layout, roof shapes, the placing of kitchens and toilets, furniture arrangement and even the orientation of graves in cemeteries are governed by these force lines. As far as we know no adequate analysis of the climatic correlates of these rules has been made, but it is quite likely that solar and wind advantages will be found to reside deep within them [24].

In Japanese house building there are complex rules about orientation. Houses have to face down a hill – an entrance on the uphill side brings ill fortune (and the cold air of night-time advection currents!); south and east are preferred as cheerful orientations. Imaginary lines running north east–south west and north west–south east cross in the centre of the house. The north east 'ki-mon' (devil's gate) should have no openings – a wall or closet should be built on that side. Each of the other three 'gates' is associated with wind, earth and man and there is little doubt but that the resulting layout gave the most sheltered and sunny solution in the cold, hill areas of Japan [25].

It is clearly impossible here to develop further the numerous examples of cosmological ideas in house design in various times and places. The climatic good sense of many of the solutions seems to be beyond doubt: the desert courtyard house, narrow streets and massive walls and roof; the light timber-framed structure of the Malay house on stilts with open screen walls; the stone and timber houses of the Turkish Black Sea region set deeply in the hill slopes of hazelnut orchards.

If the rules governing the creation, growth and use of built space have the characteristic of a language, as Hillier and Leaman have proposed [26], then the concept of shelter must certainly form an essential root. The language of space must also elaborate the elementary notion of inside–outside, and the continuity of these areas through openings will be expressed in it. We do indeed find that these openings are overlaid with layers of functions and meanings. Doors and gates for entrance and exits are charged with symbolism of royalty, entrance to a future life, contact points with settled communities and as places for defence or encounter and reception. Windows are frequently mentioned in this book in connection with their physical performance in the admission of solar energy, sun and daylight and air. But, as Markus shows in an earlier work [27, 28], windows are *meta*physical elements too. They may be sun-oriented to admit sunlight on to a sacred spot on a significant date; they express social relationships (Fig. 1.3),

Fig. 1.3 Windows as social filters and connectors (Markus's collection).

since through them one sees others and can be seen, and various cultures use them in different ways according to the significance of the concept of privacy. A small window-like opening appears carved in the frieze of the Florentine building sheltering the Madonna in Crivelli's 'Annunciation' (Fig. 1.4) in order to admit the Holy Spirit, in the form of a dove, to settle upon her.

The use of elements in this meaningful way – as a functional and symbolic language – depends on a living tradition of 'speaking' and 'listening'. That is, the ability to create space and form, and to enter into an active relationship with it, and the ability to understand the meaning of space that is being used. In no small degree this active and receptive use of space has always depended on experience of climate, its daily and seasonal changes, its extremes, and of the effects of familiar materials and forms in modifying it. This familiarity has disappeared, with mass-produced materials, non-involvement in design and building and uniform, artificial climates within buildings maintained by engineering services. In Lévi-Strauss's terms, our way of life, including our settlements, are no longer 'authentic'. He pinpoints intermediaries such as written documents and administrative machinery which prevent authenticity – he might well have added the building 'intermediaries' of professionals and a highly industrialized building industry.

Scientific analysis of climate, buildings and people's thermal responses is not a complete substitute for learnt and understood experience. But experience is impossible to obtain at the rate of change and settlement in many parts of the world; so it is certainly a big step forward from the normal planning and architectural methods of today – which lack both such experience and science. The idea that a piece of ground, in a place, can be adequately represented by a contoured site plan and a North point, would seem equally absurd to a peasant-builder or to Alberti. We have had to come through professionalization, functionalism and the scientific revolution to arrive at a point where such a procedure is daily, placidly accepted as a norm! The approach has undoubtedly led to catastrophe; vast amounts of wasted energy; serious discomfort and unpleasant living and working conditions for millions; great capital expenditure on unnecessary heating and cooling plant; condensation and a host of other defects. The fabric is generally regarded as an inert lump; although César Daly as early as 1857 in his comments on the Reform Club makes the analogy with bodily functions as the quotation in Chapter 2 shows. Fitch [29] traces this idea through American architecture and Markus [30] shows how the change from solid walled structures to framed ones can usefully be seen as an analogy of the differences between exo- and endo-skeleton animals. Scientific analysis may help to resensitize designers to the rich variety of solutions which they should explore. Moreover, such analysis also needs to be applied in retrospect. For a

Fig. 1.4 Apertures as metaphysical symbols (Trustees of the National Gallery, London. *See also* [28]).

proper understanding of the role of climate both in the primitive and vernacular types, and in the monumental architecture, we await thorough observation and measurement. It is not surprising if commentators on the first and historians of the second limit themselves to vague generalizations. They refer to the sunlitness of facades or courtyards; heavy and light walls; sizes of openings, roof shapes and colours. But, whilst Rapoport would be appalled to comment on the cultural significance of a Pueblo courtyard without close observation of what actually goes on, and thorough reading of all relevant literature on the mythology and customs of the Pueblo Indians, he goes on to report that:

> '. . . the building works extremely well both in summer and winter, [having] . . . maximum volume with minimum surface area, mutual shading of surfaces and a vast mass, with the resultant high time-lag of the building fabric;'.

All this may be true; he may in fact have observed it. But has anyone recorded, over a summer and winter season, the temperatures and the external climate? Do the dwellings at the back behave as those on the front? What *is* the decrement and time-lag of the structure? Has a model been studied on a heliodon? Of the few measurements recorded in various climates, almost all are on experimental (and architecturally and culturally meaningless) buildings. In Chapter 4 we illustrate some of the recorded results, including temperature measurements in an igloo, and thermal measurements in various Malaysian village houses made by one of the authors and students. But, in general, Rapoport and others cannot be blamed for their unsupported generalizations; the data is simply not there. To gather it would involve a vast, and fascinating, field research programme.

We are in a similar difficulty with regard to monumental buildings. In structural performance at long last some thorough analyses — such as Mainstone's — are becoming available [31]. But do we know the thermal performance of Byzantine domed churches? Or Florentine palaces, Palladian villas, Corbusier blocks of flats at Marseilles, or indeed of any major monument?

For lack of this type of proper analysis, the authors will proceed as those who have gone before them, in making such deductions as appear to be justified. There is not the time, nor is this the place, for such analysis — but it is desperately needed. So, throughout the book, wherever vernacular or monumental examples occur which seem to illustrate a particular point, we shall use it, on the assumption that with science and common sense combined, a number of aspects of climatic behaviour can, and will have to be guessed. And this general *apologia* for such treatment will have to suffice.

Whether shelter is regarded as an object which is symbolic of myth, or as one capable of scientific or cultural analysis, it is clear that we are in the presence of a system continuous in space and time. A system of energy and mass moving over the globe, forming a specific environment for both people and their shelters; the shelters may nullify or change the energy and mass flow to give a new environment between which and the natural climate there are not only many connections but also people continuously moving in and out. The responses of these people are in part physiological — but psychological and cultural factors may strongly modify behaviour and perception. So, in the next chapter, an attempt is made to explain these relationships as a series of related systems.

References

1 Rykwert, J., *On Adam's House in Paradise; The Idea of the Primitive Hut in Architectural History*. Museum of Modern Art, New York, 1972.

2 Oliver, P., *Shelter and Society*. Barrie and Jenkins, London, 1969, 28.

3 British Standards Institution, *BS Code of Practice CP3*, Chap. 1, Part 1, Daylighting, 1964 encoded much earlier British work on access to daylight. *See* for instance: Allen, W. A. and Crompton, D.H., A form of control of building development in terms of daylighting, *Journal of the Royal Institute of British Architects*, **54** (491), 3–11, 1947; and *Post-War Building Studies No. 12, The Lighting of Buildings*. HMSO, London, 1964. Some of this work had its roots in 19th Century thinking and techniques related to photographic and geometrical daylight prediction techniques.

4 UK Branch, International Solar Energy Society. *Solar Energy: A U.K. Assessment*. UK ISES, London, 1975. In Chap. 11, one recommendation reads: 'The legal implications of the wider use of solar energy should be studied. We attach particular importance to the legal protection of rights of sunlight. Appropriate legislation should be formulated to encourage wider use of solar energy.' (328.).

5 Department of Employment. *Family Income and Expenditure Survey, 1975*. HMSO, London, 1976, Table A, Appendix 6. The poorest families listed are in the categories: family income under £15 per week and £25 to £30 per week. The wealthiest category is over £150 per week.

6 Aldous, J., How France is improving structural insulation standards, *Building Services Engineer*, **43**, A26–A27, April 1975.

7 Vitruvius, *Of Architecture; The Ten Books*, translated by F. Granger. Heinemann, London and Cambridge, Mass., 1970, 2 volumes, Book II, Chap. 1.

8 Vitruvius, *op. cit*. Book I, Chaps. 4 and 6, Book IV, Chap. 1.

9 Aristotle, *Politics*, translated by T. A. Sinclair. Penguin Books, London, 1962, Book VII, Chap. 11.

10 Xenophon, *Memorabilia*, translated by E. C. Marchant, Loeb Classics, Heinemann, London, 1923, Book III, Chap. 8, Section 9.

11 Alberti, L. B., *Ten Books of Architecture*, translated into Italian by C. Bartoli and from Italian into English by J. Leoni, facsimile of 1755 edition (Rykwert, J., ed.). Tiranti, London, 1955, Book I, Chap. 2.

12 Palladio, A., *The Four Books of Architecture*, translated by I. Ware, facsimile of 1738 edition. Dover Publications, New York, 1965, Book II, Chap. 12.

13 Gropius, W., *Scope of Total Architecture*. Allen and Unwin, London, 1956; also Die Wohnformen, Flach- Mittel- oder Hochnau in *Neues Berlin* (M. Wagner and A. Behne, eds), April 1929, quoted in Giedion, S., *Walter Gropius: Work and Teamwork*. The Architectural Press, London, 1954, 79 and Figs. 255 to 258, 204.

14 Le Corbusier and Jeanneret, P., *Oeuvre complète de 1910–1929*. Boesiger and Stonorov, Zürich, 1946, 118; reprint of article 'La Rue' in *L'Intransigeant*, May 1929.

15 Le Corbusier, *Oeuvre complète 1938–1946* (Boesiger, W., ed.). Boesiger, Zürich, 1946, 103–113.

16 Le Corbusier and Jeanneret, P., *Oeuvre complète 1934–1938*, 7th ed. Bill, Zürich, 1964, 26–29.

17   Boesiger, W. (ed.), *Richard Neutra; Buildings and Projects*, 4th ed. Boesiger, Zürich, 1966, Introduction and 190, 191.

18   Howard, L., *The Climate of London,* Vol. I, W. Phillips, London, 1818; Vol. II, 1820.

19   Rapoport, A., *House Form and Culture*, Prentice Hall, New Jersey, 1969.

20   Fergusson, J., *A History of Architecture in All Countries from the Earliest Times to the Present Day*. Murray, London, 1874, Vol. 1, 4.

21   Archer, L. B., Systematic method for designers, reprinted from *Design*, 1963–1964 (Nos. 172, 173, 174, 176, 181 and 188) with revisions, Part 2, 2.

22   Olgyay, V. and Olgyay, A., quoted in Olgyay, V., *Design with Climate*. Princeton University Press, Princeton, N.J., 1963, Chap. 1, References; Aronin, J. E., *Climate and Architecture*. Reinhold, New York, 1953; Givoni, B., *Man, Climate and Architecture*. Elsevier, Amsterdam, 1969; Pleijel, G., *The Computation of Natural Radiation in Architecture and Town Planning*. State Committee for Building Research, Stockholm, 1954.

23   Levi-Strauss, C., *Structural Anthropology*, translated by Claire Jacobsen. Penguin Books, London, 1968.

24   Needham, J., *Science and Civilization in China*, Vol. 1. Cambridge University Press, Cambridge, 1956, 359–363; and Vol. 4. Cambridge University Press, Cambridge, 1971, *especially* Chap. 28(d), Building technology.

25   Harada, Jiro, *The Lesson of Japanese Architecture*. The Studio, London, 1936, 46–48.

26   Hillier, W. and Leaman, A., How is design possible?, *Journal of Architectural Research* 3(1), 4–11, January 1974.

27   Markus, T. A., The function of windows: a re-appraisal, *Building Science,* 2, 97–112, 1967.

28   Markus, T. A., in Turner, D. P. (ed.), *Windows and Environment Guide,* Pilkington Bros., St. Helens, 1969.

29   Fitch, J.M., *American Building 2; The Environmental Forces that Shape It*, 2nd revised enlarged edition. Houghton Mifflin, New York, 1972.

30   Markus, T.A., Windows and insulation. *Insulation*, September/November 1961, March, May, June 1962.

31   Mainstone, R.J., *Developments in Structural Form*. Allen Lane, London, 1975 and references at end of Chap. 7.

2
THE SYSTEM

We have seen that, in the history of the concept of the building as shelter, the notion of the fabric as a modifier between the exterior and interior climates crops up from time to time. Hillier and Leaman have put this function forward as one of four functions which explain the *raison d'être* for buildings [1]. The behaviour of the buildings as a modifier between these two environments, and the response of people to the modified environment, was of interest to Vitruvius as to his Renaissance disciples. It is true that these responses were seen mainly in terms of a few notional categories of health, and the climate too in terms of discontinuous categories, such as Vitruvius's principal wind directions. His rules as to the layout of cities with respect to these winds were as often broken as observed [2]; to the architects of the Italian Renaissance the climatic principles were generally overridden by the requirements of proportion, symmetry and the correct use of the Orders. Nevertheless, the four elements – outside climate, internal environment, people's responses and the building fabric – were dimly seen as parts of an interconnected whole; but the idea of these four interacting in a complex way, as parts of one or more system, awaited the influence of general systems theory in the present century.

However, the idea that the shelter itself was a dynamic, reactive system, having some features of an organic system is not new. In 1857 César Daly, commenting on Barry's London Reform Club, noted that

> '. . . the building is not an inert mass of stone, brick and iron; it is almost a living body, with its blood circulation and nervous systems. In these walls, which appear so immobile, there circulate gases, vapours, fluids, liquids; in examining them closely one discovers flues, pipes and wires – the arteries, veins and nerves of a new, organised being – through which heat is conducted in winter, fresh air in summer, and throughout the year, light, hot water, cold water, bodily nourishment and all the numerous accessories of a high civilization'. [3]

The combination of the structure of buildings with energy services, rather than with a non-load-bearing skin, is of course, an ancient technique – at least as old as the Korean *ondol* and the Roman hypocaust (Fig. 2.1) [4]. In the early days of the industrial revolution iron buildings gave a new fillip to these ideas, as in Jeremy Bentham's Panopticon (Fig. 2.2) 1791, where rainwater was conducted through hollow iron columns, and in Neil Snodgrass's 1806 Patent for a mill steam heating system where the iron columns were to carry steam [5]. However, it was Daly's view which emerged as the truly prophetic one – for it was skin and services rather than structure and services which became the engineering

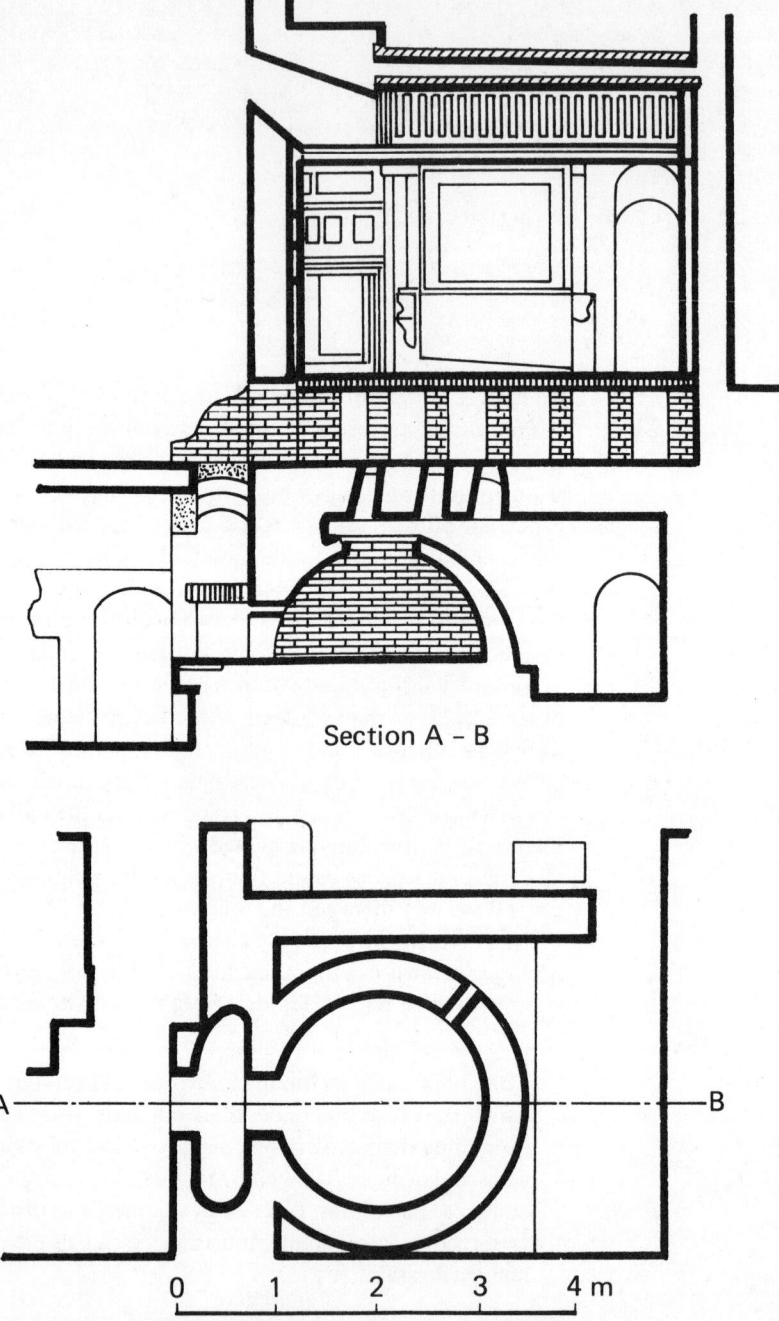

Fig. 2.1 Plan of the calidarium, the hypocaust and the heating furnace, together with a section of the furnace in the House of Menander at Pompeii (after Iorio [4]).

Section A – B

0   1   2   3   4 m

combination to be widely used in much large-scale urban architecture of the 20th Century in the form of lightweight cladding and curtain walling which incorporates electrical, water and air conditioning services. Fitch, in a seminal analysis of American building design up to the end of World War 2, in 1947 drew attention to the skin and skeleton nature of much American building [6]. Prior to the development of structural framing in iron, steel and concrete, and non-load-bearing external walls, the external wall was 'undifferentiated' as opposed to the 'specialization' of 'contemporary structure'. Fitch's book was not only

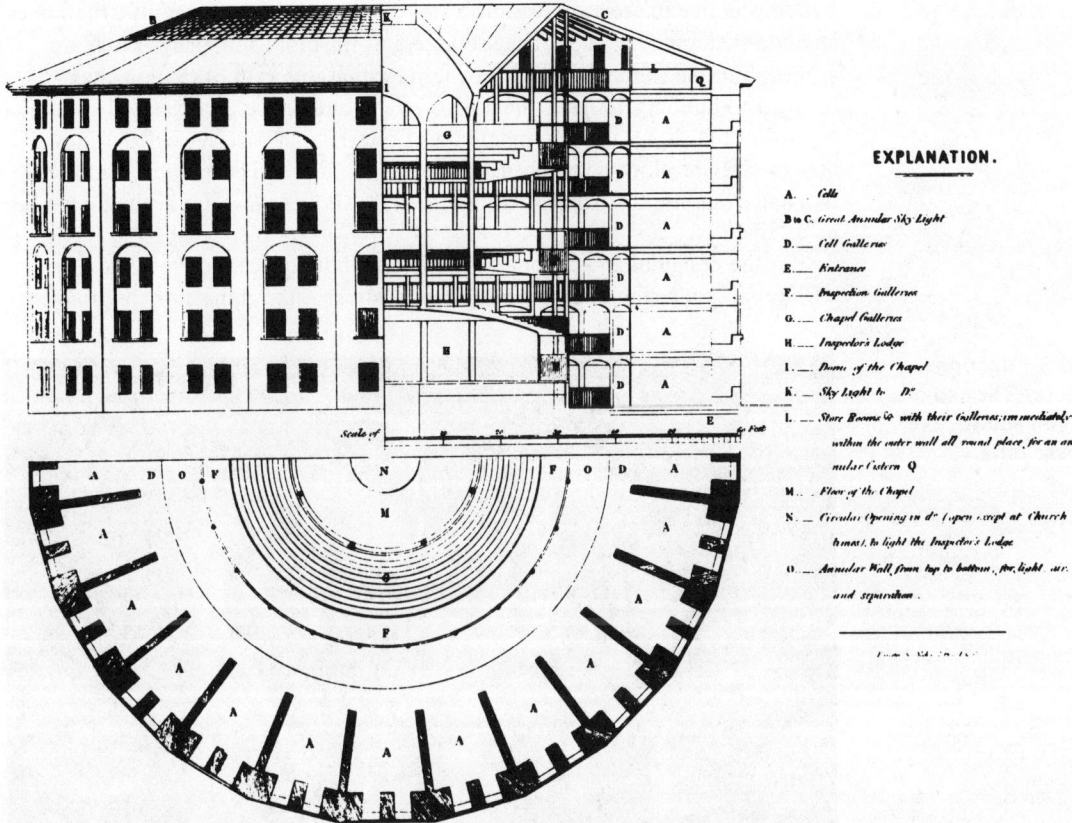

A General Idea of a PENITENTIARY PANOPTICON in an Improved, but as yet (Jan.ʸ 23ᵈ 1791) Unfinished State.
See Postscript References to Plan, Elevation, & Section (being Plate referred to as N.º 2).

EXPLANATION.

A. — Cells
B to C. — Great Annular Sky Light
D. — Cell Galleries
E. — Entrance
F. — Inspection Galleries
G. — Chapel Galleries
H. — Inspector's Lodge
I. — Dome of the Chapel
K. — Sky Light to Dº
L. — Store Rooms &c with their Galleries; immediately within the outer wall all round place, for an annular Cistern Q
M. — Floor of the Chapel
N. — Circular Opening in dº (open except at Church times), to light the Inspector's Lodge
O. — Annular Wall from top to bottom, for light, air, and separation.

Fig. 2.2 Jeremy Bentham's 'Panopticon' prison, 1791.

seminal but also prophetic; even as he was writing, the UN Secretariat Building in New York was under construction; to be followed by 30 years of curtain-walled structures in every part of the globe. These structures were, and are, nothing short of environmental catastrophes, both in regard to their interior conditions and to their effects on their immediate external, urban microclimate. Internally they are excessively cold in winter and hot in summer; they freely admit street noise; they have problems of direct radiation and glare for occupants; the peripheral areas are almost uncontrollable for working conditions; they are difficult to clean and keep waterproof (wind-driven rain travels *up* the facades and enters downward sloping condensation tubes); they are expensive in plant and energy consumption; they can act as blinding mirrors in the approaching streets; sources of minor waterfalls over pavements from their impermeable façades; creators of wind turbulence around their bases; reflectors of traffic noise; and, as if these technical problems were not enough, they have been a major source of loss of scale, and creators of urban monotony and of the bureaucratization of the mid-20th Century city. Their failure is total – technical, economic, aesthetic, symbolic. Fitch saw all this before it happened, and when he returns to his theme 25 years later [7] he draws together eminently sensible conclusions derived, basically, from his first analysis.

Markus [8] extended the biological analogy to an analogy of the traditional building as an exo-skeleton organism and the frame and curtain-wall structure as an endo-skeleton (Fig. 2.3). The usefulness of the biological analysis may be argued; but one of the undoubted benefits which this kind of thinking has brought to building design is the notion of the building as an organised system or organism; that is, having a complete set of interrelated parts and subsystems, controls, feedback devices, means for energy storage and generation, and the dynamic response to change such that desirable *homeostasis* (as in the body) can be attained.

But the design of an economic and pleasant building cannot be achieved without an understanding of the adjacent systems — the climate or environment

Fig. 2.3 Functional skins. (a) The exo-skeleton and (b) the endoskeleton.

(a)

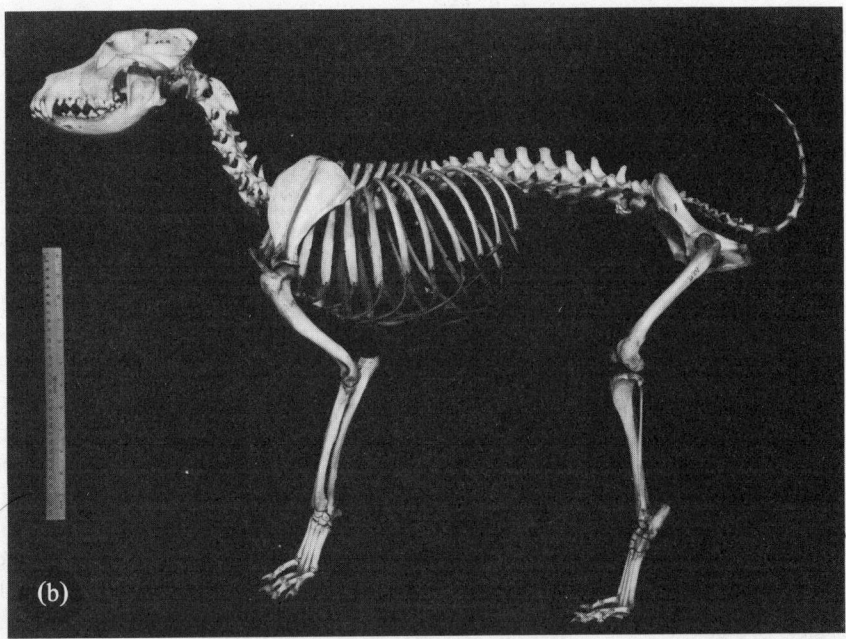

(b)

and the human response systems. As most of this book is devoted to these three systems it will help to indicate the network of relationships, influences and interaction which link them together. This will be done by using a model of connected systems.

However, it has been usual to treat the exterior climate as one system, the building hardware (fabric and services) as another, modifying, one; the internal environment as a third and the human being and his responses as a fourth. There is a problem with this view: conceptually the notion of 'exterior' and 'interior' is useful, and is used in this book; the distinction cannot, however, be rigorously made. First, where should one place the many spaces which are in various ways intermediate, such as covered arcades, terraces, balconies, loggias, paved and landscaped areas? In all these the air mass is modified by adjacent surfaces – sometimes simultaneously 'external' ones such as trees or grass and 'internal' ones such as floors, openings to interior rooms and walls. Even where there is no continuity of air mass – as, for instance, in the case of a hermetically sealed building – the flow of energy through the fabric gives the environment on the two sides a continuity which is not usefully divided by the artificial concept of exterior/interior; and even a hermetically sealed building would need openings to allow entry and exit.

Another factor in the continuity of environment is the spatial mobility of people. As they move around in a building, from open window and sun to an internal corridor or through the intermediate spaces to open country, the continuity of their experience and response makes quite unreal the usual distinction. The very making of the distinction may be either causal or symptomatic of one of the most serious defects of modern design – the absence of finely graded, intermediate space. A typical Malay house, for instance, (*see* Fig. 4.17) is set amongst palms and other trees. The steps lead to a covered porch or terrace; from there through a relatively open family room to interior bedrooms. These spaces are not only graded socially along the public, semi-public/semi-private, family and private dimension, but also in their thermal environment. The thermal gradient from outside to inside slopes gently and the performance specification required of spaces and elements is correspondingly unexacting. Even more marked examples occur in many large, public buildings, with landscaped courtyards, porches, terraces, outer and inner rooms. Typical examples are the Topkapi Palace in Instanbul and the Alhambra in Granada, both with a series of linked pavilions, arcades, courtyards, water surfaces and controlled planting. In contrast, many recent buildings in the tropics are set in open, sun-lit and exposed sites, with the outer skin as an abrupt barrier between an inhospitable climate and a fully air-conditioned, bland interior, with a correspondingly steep thermal gradient across the building fabric.

The main systems have each, in the past, been the province of a different branch of science, each of which has its own history of development, instrumental method and theoretical formulation. The external climate is the area of climatology and meteorology. More recently agricultural climatologists such as Geiger [9] have specialized in the microclimate near the ground. Observation and instrumentation has traditionally been concerned with recording and much of the data is spatially and temporally averaged, thus masking variation and the differences between locations. The responses of the human body have been studied by physiologists and biologists. Concentration has been on careful measurement of metabolic and sweat rates, skin temperatures, activity levels and clothing. The variations introduced as a result of work and movement in buildings, uneven environments and psycho-physical factors have been relatively ignored. The study of the behaviour of the building's fabric has been the province of architects and building scientists; much of the work has assumed simplified models; for instance, steady-state heat transfer, sine-wave variation in external conditions, and heat flow at right angles to the plane of an element. The study of the internal environment has been, equally, the province of architects, building scientists and environmental engineers. Even within this system there has been a variety of standpoints, according to discipline. So it is not surprising if the overall system model is inadequate, lacks unity of concept and measurement, and fails to bring out the essential continuity of the internal and external environments. A telling example of the disjointedness of the treatment of the whole subject is the manner of treating heat exchange at surfaces — a process governed by laws of radiation exchange and convective transfer between solids and fluids (or gases). In micro-climatology, solar radiant heat transfer at ground level is discussed in terms of 'albedo', referring to the reflective properties of the ground. In building science, calculations of heat transfer at surfaces is dealt with either by means of a combined radiation/convection coefficient or by means of two separate coefficients. The effect of short-wave (solar) radiation on opaque surfaces is dealt with by means of the useful fiction of 'sol-air' temperature. Physiologists on the other hand, have devised their own methods of dealing with heat transfer coefficients at the skin. These include techniques for allowing for clothing, hair, sweat evaporation and body radiation configuration.

Another example of the difficulty of bringing together the various systems is the treatment of thermal comfort. The environmental factors which combine to determine thermal comfort — air temperature, air velocity, radiation and humidity — are all present both indoors and out. Yet the indices used for the two situations, for no apparent reason, vary. We shall see that indoors air velocity is allowed for by means of adjustment to the convective heat exchange; whereas outdoors, at least in cold climate conditions, the 'windchill' index is used. Though Koenigsberger *et al.*[10] use *corrected effective temperature* for both indoors and out, and Olgyay [11] used his 'bioclimatic' chart, in both cases differences in clothing and activity level are not systematically accounted for, and, of course, clothing adjustment is the chief means of personal adaptation to the changes of environment resulting from movement in or out of buildings.

So a useful general model is based, first, on the concept of the continuity of space. This space has thermal (and other) characteristics which vary in both time and space. (There could be a semantic difficulty here in the use of 'space' both as describing the connective tissue between concrete elements and as the *locational* aspects of points of reference within this tissue. Provided this inevitable, and necessary, overlap of meaning is understood it should cause no difficulties.) Any point in space has conditions resulting from mass and energy flow determined by the radiative and convective characteristics of its location. It will be subject to direct short-wave radiation from sun, sky, and electric or other high-temperature sources and reflected short-wave radiation from surfaces (including those consisting of particulates such as dust and water droplets – i.e. clouds); and long-wave radiation from low-temperature surfaces such as sky, ground, building surfaces and some heating appliances. It will be immersed in air moving at speeds and directions determined by climatic factors and the nature of the terrain, natural or man-made objects, building surfaces and openings and at temperatures determined both by climatic factors and the presence of the above objects.

Once the point in space is not infinitely small, but has its own mass and heat absorbing or generative properties it, too, exerts an influence on the space in which it is immersed and on the surrounding surfaces. The human body is a special type of 'object' in space; it exerts an influence in two ways; first, by the very fact of its presence; and second, by deliberate or unintentional alteration of the energy and mass state of the space – directly or by the creation of new objects. Thus this body radiates energy; it impedes air flow; it opens or shuts windows and turns control knobs; in groups, it plants trees and vegetation, builds lakes and dams, cities, villages and houses; it releases gases and pollutants into air, water and soil. All these activities will affect its environment and, hence, comfort, efficiency and pleasure.

So the second characteristic of the model is that the systems within it are *inter*active and that at all levels they will tend, on account of the second law of thermodynamics, towards increased entropy – an increasingly random and stable condition. The input of energy into the system – from the sun, burning of fossil fuels, generation of nuclear energy and the consumption of food – 'pushes against' entropy; and human intervention, by creation of artificial controls – landscape, building, clothes and engineering services – can be seen as a method of maintaining stability without paying the price for stability which, in physical terms, is entropy. All organic systems of energy conversion in plants and animals have this same characteristic and the organic ('natural') system which will be of most interest in this book is that which regulates the thermal behaviour of the body.

The psychological and social forces which, equally, drive individuals and groups to create 'artificial' systems for environmental stability together with differentiation within the environmental system, have been sparsely studied in so far as they influence the thermal and energy strategies of design and construction. That they are potent is certain; but they are also so closely interwoven with symbolic, cultural, technological and social factors that there is great difficulty in identifying them. For instance, the whole concept of the building fabric can be seen as a way of introducing environmental differentiation of an almost step-function type between the internal and external environments, whilst keeping the interior as stable as possible and independent of the semi-random temporal changes of weather and the systematic diurnal and seasonal cycles. But this fabric also defines property and territory; space has social as well as environmental gradations, from public to semi-public, semi-private and private; it has openings which attempt both to differentiate and separate and at the same time link and unite, the most notable being the window.

The building of walls around a town for defence and territorial marking is surrounded with ritual and sacred significance. Rykwert [2] describes the Etruscan cosmological creation rites associated with the founding of a city and the marking of its walls. Not only were the walls themselves but even the trenches ploughed for their foundations sacred; the plough was lifted when it crossed the ground where the gates were later to perforate the walls. But Vitruvius shows how these gates, and the main streets leading from them, were oriented with due regard to wind shelter. Outer space, the unspoilt country outside the city, is today seen as the ultimate in 'natural' systems; in primitive civilizations and in the Middle Ages space outside the walls represented the desert, wilderness, primal chaos. Between this and the most controlled, 'artificial' space, is a whole gradation of spaces having different mixtures of natural and artificial — random forces and human control. These spaces are environmentally graded and differentiated; and have corresponding social and symbolic meanings. These meanings correspond to environmental states; so that an environment was judged as appropriate not merely on some abstract and generalized criterion of, say, physiological comfort, but in the degree to which it reinforced the significance of the place. Corresponding to this sense of appropriateness there is a psychological process of adaptation, acceptance and expectation which results in a wide range of environments being judged acceptable or desirable. This idea of people's response is further explored in the next chapter.

The development of a model of climate, building shelter and people sufficiently complete to include social and psychological factors is beyond the scope of the present work and awaits substantial further research. We can, however, give an outline descriptive sketch of its boundaries, systems, elements and links and indicate the main feedback and control paths.

The simplest way to build up this sketch model is to start with the (physically) simplest and unreal situation of a point in space or the upper atmosphere and gradually add to it until we arrive at the most complete and perhaps equally unreal situation of a point inside a hermetically sealed, fully conditioned and controlled building. Fitch [7] makes the interesting point that in the first of the above situations, as in other similar extreme environments such as the deep-sea one, the clothes become highly specialized, serviced and controlled and, in fact, have the systems characteristics of the shelter in the second situation — the fully specialized, serviced and controlled fabric/services system. In the normal terrestrial world of everyday life such clothes are not necessary, efficient, pleasant or meaningful.

In building up the model in this way, a useful mode of distinguishing between the situation is in terms of the amount and rate of spatial environmental variation. The environmental variation can be in terms of any significant element – say air or globe temperature, air speed or humidity – or in terms of any of the numerous indices, such as *standard effective temperature*, which combine these elements. By observing the variation in space, as measured by horizontal or vertical gradients for instance, the magnitude of the variation is shown by peaks and troughs and the rate of change by the slope of the curve. A classical example of rapid rate of change is shown by the vertical gradients immediately above the ground shown in Fig. 4.58.

So we start by taking the simplest case, that of a point in outer space, subject only to radiation from the sun and other planets, or in the outer atmosphere where energy is also contained in the surrounding medium (Fig. 2.4). The climatic system which influences such a point is the generalized, extraterrestrial

Fig. 2.4 The system – a point in space.

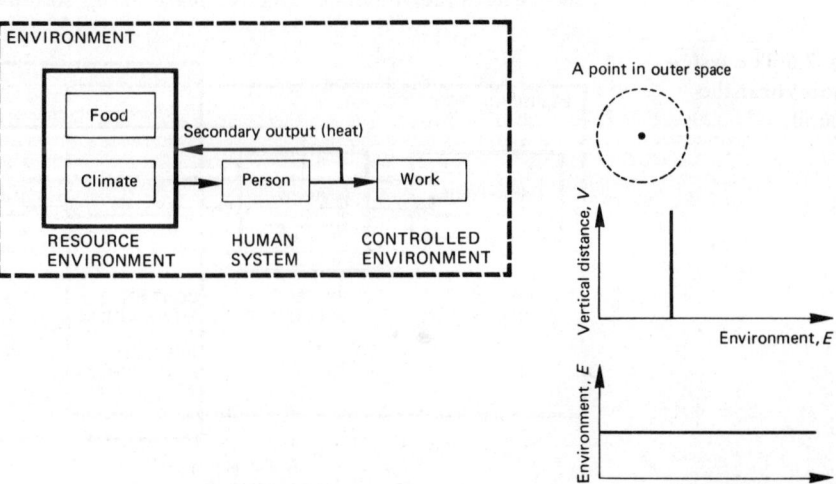

one of interplanetary space so that division into global, regional, topo- and microclimate is meaningless until one approaches sufficiently closely to a surface – say the earth's – to be in the presence of radiation or convection gradients. Movement vertically, horizontally or in any other direction results in no environmental change. An astronaut at this point is exposed to a uniform environment which acts upon him; there is no intervening shelter system between him and his resource environment – the climate – other than his clothes which we shall regard throughout as if they were part of his body, a kind of extended skin. He is thus intimately associated with this general environment which acts as an input upon him.

The energy from this climate, and food, are the *resource environment* which the person, the *human system*, takes in, uses, modifies, and, as a consequence produces an output into the *controlled environment*.* The output is work and the controlled environment which this creates can be thought of as any of the

*The systems terminology used here is more fully explained in Chapter 11.

personal, social or public activities which sustain individuals and societies. A *secondary* output of the human system is heat which, once we reach a resource environment such as the modified climate inside a building, will affect that in a significant way. In this first case, of outer space, this effect is insignificant. Figure 2.4 also shows food as an intake to the human system; this is accepted in the further development of the model and omitted from the later figures.

If we now take a big step towards everyday reality, we can imagine a point near the earth's surface over, say, *grass*-covered ground. This point is in a microclimate determined by the full range of climates from global, through regional to topoclimates. These may be regarded as the general, unspecific environments of the system. The microclimate is also determined by reflected radiation from the ground; evaporation from the grass which is transevaporating moisture from the soil; and the ground's retarding and turbulence effects on the moving air stream. Thus the ground generates a modified climate. This is both the output of the first system and the input (resource environment) to the second, the human system (Fig. 2.5). A person at this point is exposed to this microclimate and, in turn, causes radiant and convective heat transfer to it and also will distort the

Fig. 2.5 The system — a point near the ground.

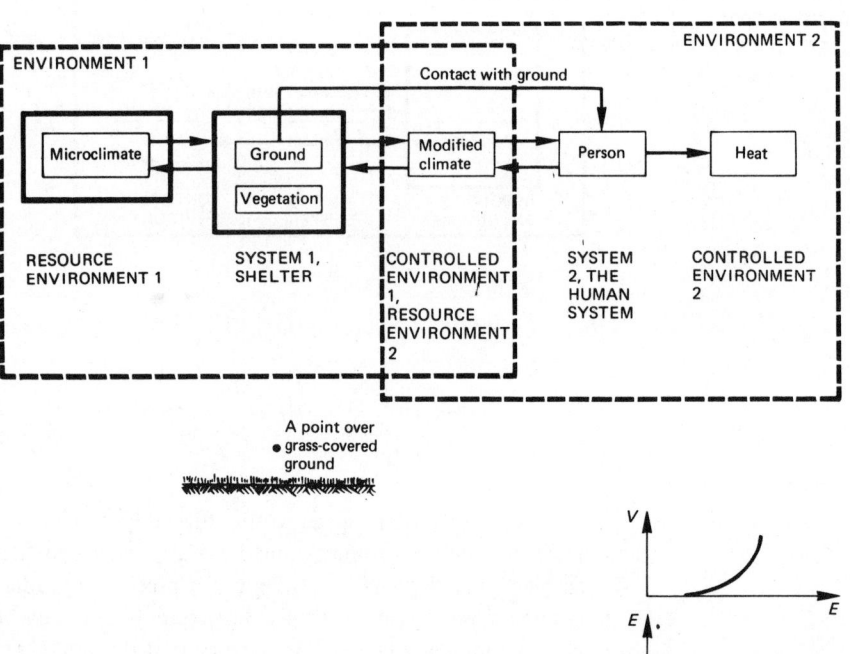

wind flow around him. His feet, if in direct contact with the grass-covered ground, will exchange energy by direct conduction without the intermediary of the microclimatic space. Therefore, a direct link, crossing the two systems, is indicated. The vertical environmental gradient changes smoothly but rapidly; the horizontal one stays uniform.

The next stage is to cover a piece of the ground with a roof — which shades the ground from sun and sky radiation; shields it from cold, clear sky so that the ground reradiates less long-wave radiation and, thus, remains cooler during the day and warmer at night than the adjacent, open ground. It also shields the ground from rain and, thus, alters the vegetation; and so on. We can now represent the grass-covered ground and the roof as two components of the shelter system which is, in some parts of the world, an actual dwelling (Fig. 2.6). The horizontal gradient will now also vary, with a steep gradient where the effect of the roof edge becomes apparent.

Fig. 2.6 The system — a point in an open shelter.

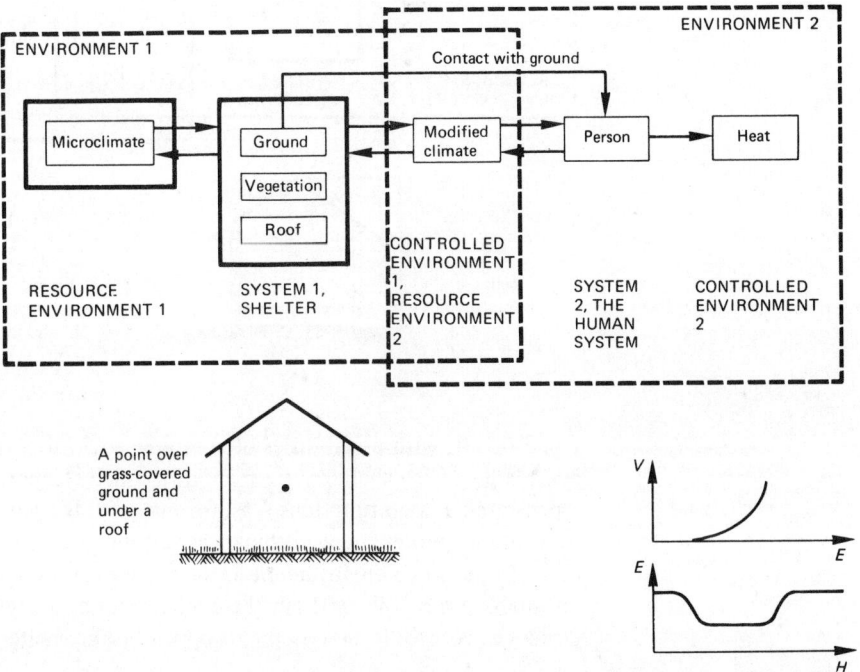

If, next, the structure is completed with walls and windows — elements to be added to the shelter system — the model is as before but increased in complexity. The ground, vegetation, roof, walls, windows and contents interact with each other as well as with microclimate 'outside' and the modified environment 'inside'. For convenience, the roof, walls, windows and contents are lumped together as the 'fabric' subsystem of shelter (Fig. 2.7).

For reasons explained before, the microclimate and the modified climate are only nominally 'outside' and 'inside', respectively; for that distinction in architectural terms is often meaningless. An 'outside' area sheltered by a tree or rise in the ground is part of the modified environment; and, therefore, all impact of the microclimate on the person is modelled as coming through the modified environment — even when the shelter system has certain elements which do not alter a climatic input, so that the output is equal to the input. This would be the case, for instance, with solar radiation falling on a person through an open window, whose presence in no way modifies it. If amongst the activities, or 'work' output of the human system, there is an action upon the shelter system designed to improve the modified environment — such as opening or shutting a window — this can be represented as a negative feedback control action, actuated by the thermal sensing mechanism of the body and the central nervous system. Such a control path is shown on Fig. 2.7.

The vertical and horizontal environmental gradients are similar to those in

Fig. 2.7 The system — a point in an unserviced building.

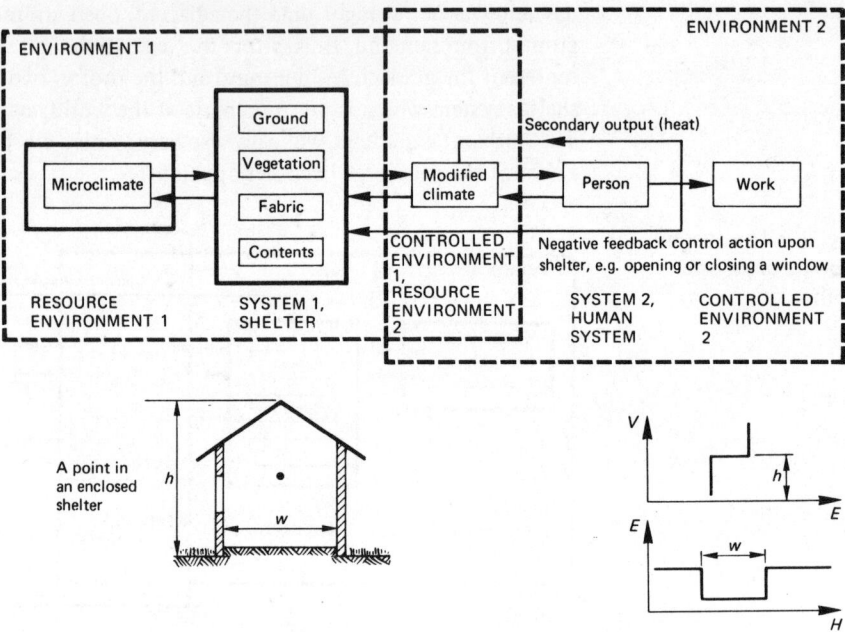

Fig. 2.6, but, with possibilities of complete enclosure, the gradients across the boundaries of the shelter system are now much steeper. They can even be represented as step functions – as, for instance, the temperature gradient across a wall (if one ignores the wall thickness and the gradient across it).

If the modified environment in the shelter is now assumed to become unsuitable for people without the expenditure of energy through special thermal devices to control it, new elements appear in the shelter; the services subsystems.

Fig. 2.8 The system — a point in a serviced building.

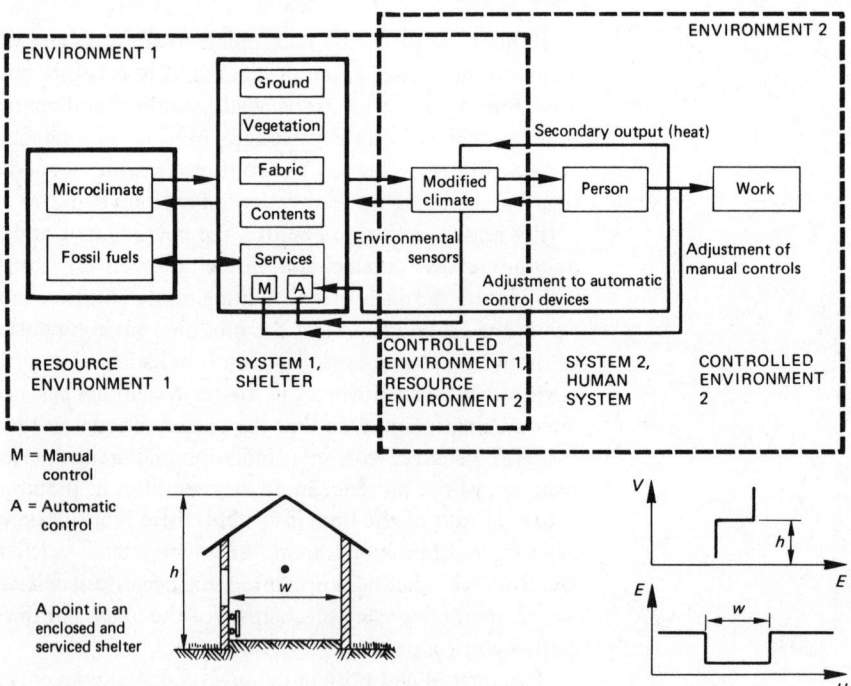

They may take in, store, and use energy from sources separate from the micro-climate system we have been considering – say fossil or nuclear fuel – which are nevertheless part of the resource environment; or from 'natural' sources immediately available in the microclimate – say solar or wind energy, or low-grade air or ground heat upgraded through a heat pump, itself using some 'external' energy. We now have a more or less complete model of an isolated, rural building (Fig. 2.8).

The control mechanisms now available to people include operating the controls of the services and the control of the consumption of 'natural' or 'external' energy sources for fuel. Chapter 11 deals with the service subsystems as systems in their own right, with manual or automatic control. In the latter case, human action is indirect, through the adjustment of such devices as thermo-stats, and the services require sensing feedback from the modified environment to actuate the automatic control devices.

Finally, our model can be considered at the larger scale of groups of buildings. In an urban agglomeration, these now interact with each other and the ground between them, affecting wind flow, temperature, sunlight and radiation. Such an agglomerate can be regarded as a large shelter system producing its own form of modified environment – the urban microclimate – which is discussed in Chapter 4. People within this urban fabric not only have the modified environment of individual buildings, shown in the earlier models, but that of the town. Within this they work, travel, move about and pursue their productive, social and recreational activities (Fig. 2.9). The vertical environmental gradients, on the urban scale, again change rapidly but smoothly; the horizontal ones will be infinitely varied but with fewer step-function-type discontinuities. The urban shelter system also has its secondary outputs such as, for instance, pollution.

Fig. 2.9 The system – a point in an urban setting.

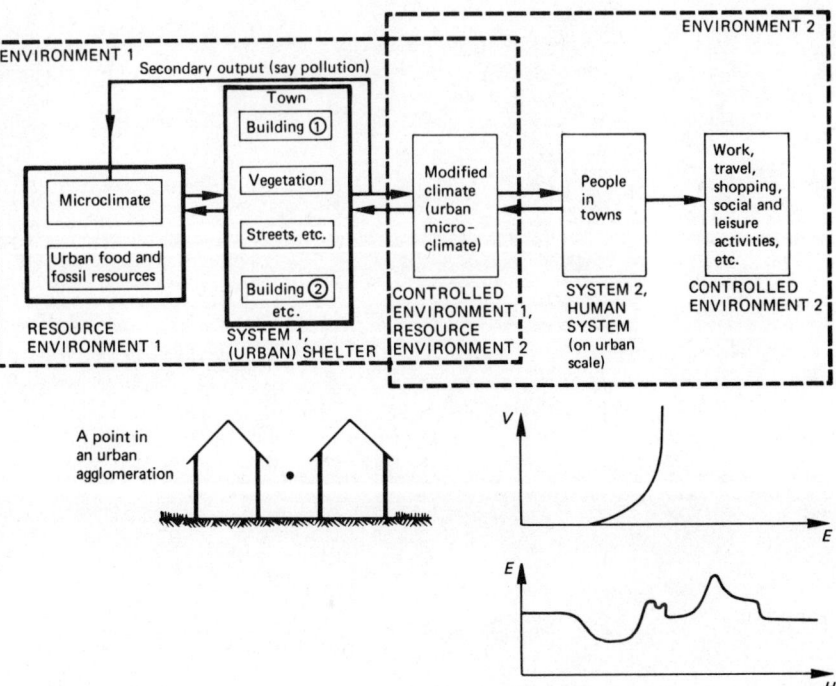

References

1   Hillier, W. and Leaman, A., Architecture as a discipline. *Journal of Architectural Research*, **5** (1), 28–32, March 1974.

2   Rykwert, J., The idea of a town. In *Lectura Architectonica*. van Saane, Hilversum, 1963.

3   Daly, C. (ed.), *Revue de l'architecture et des travaux publics.* Paris, 1857, Vol. 15, 346–348.

4   Iorio, A., System of heating in the ancient baths of Pompeii, Parts 1 and 2. *Building Services Engineer*, **41**, A18–A19, January 1974 and **41**, A24–A30, February 1974 translated by M. Oliver from *Termotechnica* **27**, 142 *et seq.*, 1973.

5   Neil Snodgrass's patent is described fully in *Trans. Roy. Soc. Arts,* XXIV, 1806, 118.

6   Fitch, J.M., *American Building; The Forces that Shape It.* Batsford, London, 1947.

7   Fitch, J.M., *American Building 2; The Environmental Forces that Shape It.* 2nd revised enlarged edition. Houghton Mifflin, Boston, 1972.

8   Markus, T.A., Windows and insulation. *Insulation*, September/November 1961 and March, May and July 1962.

9   Geiger, R., *The Climate near the Ground.* Harvard University Press, Cambridge, Mass., 1965.

10 Koenigsberger, O. H., Ingersoll, T. G., Mayhew, A. and Szokolay, S. V., *Manual of Tropical Housing and Building, Part I, Climatic Design.* Longman, London, 1974.

11 Olgyay, V., *Design with Climate.* Princeton University Press, Princeton, N.J., 1963.

3
PEOPLE'S RESPONSE TO THE THERMAL ENVIRONMENT

3.1 Basic principles

So far we have described some historical and more recent notions of buildings as shelters; i.e. structures which intervene by acting as barriers and as responsive filters between the natural or urban environment and the range of environments required for human activities. The line of argument has been that buildings serve many purposes – the four which are commonly recognized being functional, social, symbolic and artistic. These are interwoven in the language of built form – that is, in both design of buildings and in the use and experience of buildings. But separation of the purposes can be useful in analysis and the separation of the climate/shelter strand is necessary for the theme of this book. But, whilst this aspect is usually presented as merely functional, we shall note, from time to time, that even at this specific level the creation or use of space in a thermally meaningful way is closely related to the other three purposes of buildings.

The need for shelter arises, of course, from the basic objectives which a building is designed to attain. Their attainment needs a pattern of activities, and these take place within an environment which is the outcome of the performance of the building's hardware system. This hardware, i.e. the fabric, the services and the contents of a building, continuously affects the physical and, more specifically, the thermal environment, variations in which, both in space and in time, may be needed not only for different activities, but also to provide stimulation and perhaps aesthetic experiences based on thermal sensations.

The specification of an appropriate thermal environment and tolerances on its achievement, and the appraisal of the degree to which it has been achieved, depends upon an adequate definition of activities. This involves not only an understanding of the people carrying out the activities – age, sex, clothing, eating and rest habits, cultural and social factors about behaviour and clothes – but also a knowledge of the energy requirements for their work, any associated problems of attention, fatigue and boredom and, possibly, knowledge of their customary indoor and outdoor thermal experience.

The above information will often be inexact; the use of a building or of any particular space in it may change, perhaps in an unpredictable way; people have a wide range of physiological and personal adaptation mechanisms; and the research in many areas – for example on the effect of thermal transients – is sketchy in the extreme. Moreover, economic forces such as energy prices can and do alter people's thermal judgments and behaviour. In the light of these uncertainties and latitudes the need for, and the usefulness of, a reasonably accurate understanding of the physiology and psychology of thermal response may be questioned. The answer lies in the actual thermal performance of buildings and people's judgments of them, despite their adaptive powers and tolerance of a range of conditions.

We then find, at one extreme, regularly reported cases of old people and infants dying of hypothermia in houses in winter [1] and deaths in overheated rooms. Complaints of summer overheating and winter chill, stuffiness, dryness, condensation, draughts, cold floors and of excessive energy costs in meeting even these, inadequate, thermal conditions, occur as one of the most common responses to buildings completed in the last 25 years. That the energy costs are excessive is not only measurable by the level of complaint about costs, and by the obvious method of monitoring the amounts actually expended, but by such apparently irrational and wasteful behaviour as the opening of windows in winter in cold climates and heated buildings; or in air-conditioned buildings in the tropics; the shedding of all but minimal clothes in winter, indoors in cold and temperate climates; the donning of extra clothes on entering an air-conditioned building in the tropics. Such comment, expenditure and behaviour indicate conditions outside the range which normal response and notions of acceptability indicate. What has gone wrong?

In the design—build—occupy process characteristic of vernacular buildings, the learnt experience, established technology and continuous feedback linked to simple means of control, combine to avoid these deficiencies, even though the buildings are at least as varied and variable as the professionally designed ones of today and the thermal requirements at least as wide-ranging. So perhaps the answer lies in the fact that the variability and range of conditions which are achieved with the more remote professional design processes are of the wrong *kind*; rather than look for further precision one might look for a more appropriate variability and range. However, to do this requires some precision in our understanding of thermal sensations, although this understanding will not necessarily lead to more precise solutions.

An important factor is the variety of criteria which can be used to judge the quality of a thermal environment in relation to human activity, health or well-being; and whilst each individual criterion may allow considerable latitude, the set of criteria may not necessarily lie, as Wyon [2] points out, in topologically concentric sets. The criteria, which are discussed in later parts of this chapter, can be summarized as follows:

(i) *Survival*. The maintenance of deep tissue temperature at or near 37 °C when at rest is the principal object of the body's complex thermoregulatory system. Activity raises this temperature, even under comfort conditions by about 0.1°C met^{-1} (see later for definition of 'met'). A deviation by up to 2 °C above or below this can be tolerated for a short time — but over longer durations, or a greater deviation, results in health hazards or death. A wide variety of environmental conditions will allow this narrowly defined condition to be achieved, and control of activity levels and clothing are used as additional mechanism to achieve this *homeostasis*.

(ii) *Comfort*. Within the range of conditions necessary for survival lies a smaller range which is judged as comfortable (that is, neither too warm nor too cold; or thermally neutral). In these conditions the strain on the body's thermo-regulatory mechanisms is minimal.

(iii) *Performance*. Whilst there is some evidence that thermal conditions will affect levels of arousal, vigilance, fatigue, attention and boredom, the precise effects are relatively little understood. Nevertheless it is known that, through these effects, performance of both mental and physical tasks will be affected by thermal conditions, and there is some evidence that conditions for optimum performance may not coincide with those for comfort; they may be a more restricted set; or wider, and only partially or perhaps even not at all overlapping the comfort set.

(iv) *Health.* For persons in normal health, thermal conditions are unlikely to affect well-being, even under conditions of discomfort, until extreme conditions of cold or heat occur. But for those who are sick, or who, through age or debility, are particularly prone to suffer from chest, heart, circulatory and other ailments, the thermal environment can have serious effects both on the occurrence of, and the recovery rate from, sickness. There is a known correlation in northern climates between seasonal weather variations and morbidity and mortality [3]. It is probable that this is caused by the aggravating effects of cold, pollution and moisture; and there is evidence that there is a link between conditions within poorly heated buildings and these health statistics. Similar evidence suggests a link between hot weather, excessively warm buildings, and heat-induced disease and death. There is little information on the coincidence or otherwise of health and comfort conditions; it is likely that the latter set lies totally within the former.

(v) *Psychological, social and economic factors.* Survival, comfort, performance and health are responses to thermal environment which have been widely studied. Far less is known about responses which may be dependent on personal, social, cultural and economic variables. Many of these are matters which the good designer appreciates from experience and observation and, provided he is dealing with traditional situations, he is likely to make well-informed guesses or hypotheses. Traditional situations are those in which the occupiers of the building and their lifestyles, values and social structures are familiar, and the building form and arrangement of its immediate surrounds are also formally and technically well-tried. In many situations today, however, this no longer applies: for instance, designers work in regions of the world outside their own experience; for populations about whom they know little, not even their traditional mode of dressing; for jobs or organizations where there is little precedent (e.g. oil platforms, computer suites, teaching-machine laboratories); in materials and with technologies outside their experience; and in unfamiliar climates. In these circumstances more formal predictive knowledge, based on empirical research is required, but is, today, very sparse indeed. Some of the interesting questions to which answers are needed include:

the effect of spatial and temporal transients — that is local or short-term variation in conditions;

the conscious and unconscious adaptation processes in adjustments to clothing, level and mode of activity and social customs;

the effect of social status on expectations and hence on perceived and reported sensations;

the 'meaning' or appropriateness of thermal environments related to function, culture and past experience (For instance, is a church in a Mediterranean summer climate expected to feel 'cool'? What are one's expectations and hopes for environments in a restaurant, a theatre foyer, a Turkish bath and on the roof of a seaside villa? If they are different, can these differences be explained solely in physiological terms of activity, clothing and transients or are there deeper, symbolic matters involved?);

the effect of economic constraints, operating, for instance, through fuel prices, not only on choice (for instance of room temperature) but also on perceived and reported levels of satisfaction;

the interaction between the thermal environment – itself multi-dimensional – and other aspects of environment such as the visual scene, movement, acoustic conditions, tactile experience and such ergonomic factors as postural comfort.

About some of these factors there are some findings – which will be discussed below. About most, our information is scanty or non-existent. This should not make designers despair; rather, awareness of the questions themselves will cause them to reflect, introspect, speculate, observe more carefully, and make conscious efforts to envisage alternative possible responses. These are powerful techniques which complement knowledge derived from more formal research.

Wyon [4] has spoken of the 'topology of environmental criteria'. By this he meant that environment, or more specifically, thermal environment, is the outcome of a number of parameters, and can, therefore, be defined as a point in

Fig. 3.1 The topology of the thermal environment (after Wyon [2]).

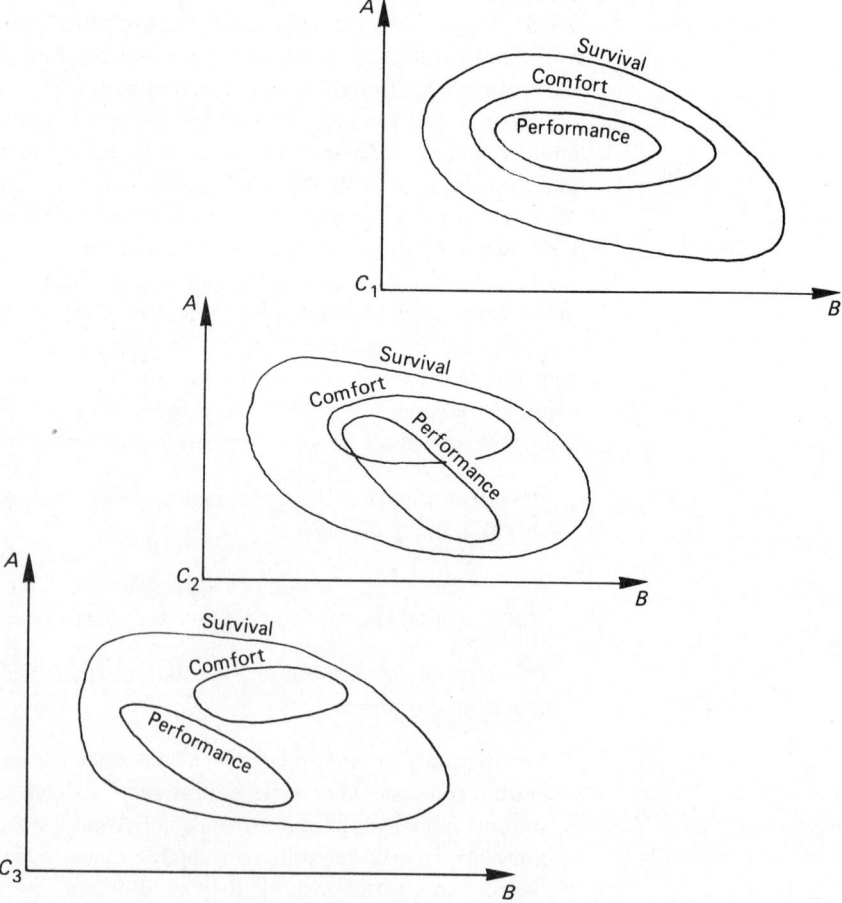

multi-dimensional space. If boundaries for tolerable, or good, conditions are then drawn, the way in which these overlap, are concentric, identical or discrete, will tell the designer which are the critical criteria and when he has to make a deliberate choice between satisfying one rather than another. These topological relationships may change as one moves along any particular dimension of the multi-dimensional space. To simplify and illustrate this idea, Wyon assumes that thermal conditions might be defined by three parameters, A, B and C, and, to draw this three-dimensional space in two dimensions, he illustrates various combinations of A and B at three chosen levels of C, C_1, C_2 and C_3 (Fig. 3.1). He further assumes three criteria – survival, comfort and performance. At C_1 these are concentric and in that order – therefore performance presents the most critical conditions. At C_2 performance and comfort criteria only partially overlap, both of course lying in the survival boundary – as they have to do in all cases. At C_3 they are totally discrete, thus presenting a designer with a conscious choice of optimization in conditions where the best overall solution may not be optimal for either of the two constituent criteria.

In actuality there are at least six parameters which give dimensions to any unique thermal condition; two of these, activity level and clothing, are specific to an individual, and the other four are properties of the environment itself – air temperature, humidity, air velocity and radiation. Thus, the topological solid is actually six-dimensional and can only be represented by means of matrices – but the three-dimensional simplification demonstrates the principle. A further condition, C_4, has not been illustrated; it would be that in which the comfort zone was wholly within the performance zone, the implication of which, Wyon believes, is so unlikely as to make further consideration unnecessary; it would indicate that comfort is only possible under optimum performance conditions.

3.2 Previous work

Before considering in detail the physiological and psychological mechanisms which explain how the various criteria might be met, it is useful to review briefly earlier work and approaches to this subject.

Work on thermal comfort is one of the oldest areas of building science. Bedford gave a useful summary of the history of early theoretical and experimental work in 1961 [5] which is summarized here, and in which further references can be found. The work advanced simultaneously with developments in medicine and thermometry in the 18th and 19th Centuries. As long ago as 1733, Arbuthnot pointed out the chilling effects of wind by dispersing the layer of warm, moist air around the body. Sir John Leslie used an alcohol thermometer in 1804 to measure air velocity by observing the cooling of the heated thermometer. Heberden drew attention to the shortcomings of the thermometer as an indicator of cold in 1826, and devised a method basically similar to Kata thermometry, in which a thermometer is heated to well above ambient air temperature and its rate of cooling against time is carefully observed, from which the 'cooling power' of the environment is assessed. With the Kata this gives a measure of air velocity if the air temperature is known, and the technique is described in detail in Chapter 10.

With regard to radiation effects, Tredgold in 1824 already described the lower air temperatures required for people exposed to a radiant source; and as early as 1857 the Commissioners appointed by the General Board of Health to enquire into the heating and ventilation of houses recommended that the wall temperatures of a room should be at least as high as the general temperature of the room. To meet this requirement was as difficult then as it is today, when it is still regarded as a criterion of a good environment. By 1887 the principle of the black globe thermometer to measure radiation had been established by Aitken – although his use of the instrument, for obtaining both radiation and wind speed data, was limited to meteorological purposes.

By the early 19th Century the importance of humidity control was recognized, both excessively dry and excessively humid atmospheres being considered inadvisable.

Although by the 18th Century the effect of overheating in crowded rooms was recognized as a cause of discomfort, in the 19th Century, under the influence of Lavoisier, carbon dioxide came to be held as a contributing factor and, in 1862, Pettenkofer introduced the idea of organic material exhaled from the skin as a major contributory cause. This 'anthropotoxin' theory was argued throughout the latter half of the century and it was not until 1913 that it was finally abandoned and the effects of the four main variables recognized for what they were. Hill introduced the Kata thermometer; and, in the same year, giving evidence before a select Committee of the House of Commons, recommended cool heads, warm feet, varying radiant heat, variable breezes and a medium relative humidity. Throughout the First World War he continued his work, in connection with munitions workers and other tasks and further refined his criteria.

In the 1920's and 1930's, Hill, Vernon, Bedford and Warner in England continued their work, both of a fundamental kind, and with many industrial applications.

At the same time, significant laboratory studies were proceeding in the USA. From 1923 onwards an important series of papers began to appear by Houghten, Yaglou and their colleagues, in which they described the combined effects of air temperature, humidity and velocity and derived, for the engineer, the first *effective temperature* scale (ET). In this, the three variables are combined in such a way that equal values of ET give equal sensations of temperature, later re-defined as 'comfort' (or 'discomfort') as judged by subjects in the laboratory. The subjects were at or near rest, and the reference temperature used was that of saturated and still air. Thus, a combination of conditions judged to have an ET of, say, 18 °C is equivalent in sensation to saturated (100 per cent relative humidity) air at, say, a velocity of 0.1 m s^{-1} (equivalent to the air velocity caused simply by the convection over the warm body surface) at 18 °C. Zones of winter and summer comfort in terms of ET (differing on account of seasonal differences in clothing insulation) were established and had far-reaching influence in air-conditioning design in the USA, Britain and later Australia and tropical countries.

The ET scale ignored the effects of thermal radiation, which, in most indoor conditions, is not significant. However, where warm ceilings, floors or walls are concerned, and when high-temperature local radiant sources, or direct sunshine, or large cold surfaces such as windows are present, it cannot be ignored. From 1930 onwards, Vernon, in Britain, developed the globe thermometer for radiation measurements, based on the earlier work by Aitken. Bedford and others were now using the black globe as a field survey instrument and valuable data began to emerge from which the effects of radiant heat or cold were capable of statistical analysis, through Barker's concept, in 1926, of the *mean radiant temperature*, i.e. the uniform temperature of a complete black enclosure at which a black body would radiate with an intensity equal to the mean observed. In 1932, Vernon and Warner [6] used the globe temperature, with a correction for the wet bulb temperature, in calculating the ET, and in 1946 Bedford published the same proposal, without correction, and called the resultant temperature the *corrected effective temperature* (CET). Because of its simplicity, this has been, and still is, one of the most widely used indices; it is important to realize that it relates to a particular amount of clothing and a level of activity; whilst it exaggerates the effect of humidity at lower temperatures, and does not fully allow for the beneficial effects of air movement at high values of CET when the humidity is also high, it has nevertheless been a reasonable predictor of comfort under normal indoor conditions, activity levels and types of clothing.

The search for an index which would adequately express the warmth of an environment in a general way, independently of the activity level or clothing of an occupant, caused Dufton in 1929 to develop his eupatheostat, a thermostat which allowed for radiation, and in 1932 the eupatheoscope, a heated instrument similar to the globe thermometer, in which the internal temperature was set at a level which gave, on the surface of the sphere, a temperature of about 24 °C, the average surface temperature of a clothed person in normal surroundings. The heat loss was taken as the equivalent of the heat input and was measured on a thermometer scaled in *equivalent temperature* (t_{eq}). In 1936, Dufton adjusted the surface temperature to correspond more closely to that of a clothed person; and all readings are referred back to a still air environment. We shall refer later to Madsen's 'Comfytest' meter, developed over 40 years later, but basically measuring the same factors and, thus, describing the dry heat loss from the body. In conditions where evaporation is not too critical – i.e. moderate environments – t_{eq} is reasonably representative of response; in the Comfytest meter corrections for ambient humidity are also made.

The calculation of t_{eq} from analysis of Bedford's and other data, gives the equation:

$$t_{eq} = 0.522\, t_a + 0.478\, t_{mrt} - 0.21(37.8 - t_a)\sqrt{v}, \qquad (3.1)$$

where t_a = air temperature, t_{mrt} = mean radiant temperature (both in degrees Centigrade) and v = air velocity (in metres per second).

In conditions where humidity effects can be ignored (i.e. about 30 to 60 per cent relative humidity) it was a useful concept, which allowed any combination of the three variables to be described as that uniform (i.e. equal t_a and t_{mrt}) temperature at zero air velocity which would give the same dry heat loss (and sensation of comfort) as the actual combination present. For winter heating this index was used for many years in Britain.

At this time, the first of a series of experiments were being carried out and published in the USA by Winslow, Herrington and Gagge at the John B. Pierce Laboratory in Yale University, which carries on to this day, with Gagge and his colleagues systematically producing a wealth of data on all the six variables; data which has become the basis of the comfort criteria of the American Society of Heating, Refrigeration and Airconditioning Engineers (ASHRAE) over decades of its *ASHRAE Handbook of Fundamentals*. One of the first valuable indices they developed was that of *operative temperature* (t_o) – similar in concept to the equivalent temperature but referring to a uniform environment which is equivalent to the actual combination of air temperature and radiation but at the *same* velocity as the actual, and not still, air. We shall be using t_o later.

More recently, ASHRAE has produced a new index, the *new effective temperature* (ET*) scale, which takes all the six major parameters into account and is a rationally derived index – that is, one based on fundamental heat transfer and physiological principles. Finally, this has been extended to the *standard effective temperature* (SET). As we shall be using it later it can be defined later too; it should be noted here that it is based on the work of Gagge *et al.* at the Pierce Laboratory, and Nevins *et al.* at the ASHRAE Laboratory at Kansas State University and, thus, makes a direct link to the earlier, now historical, work.

Recent work by Fanger in Denmark and Humphreys *et al.* in Britain, will be referred to in later sections.

3.3 Survival

The organs of the body, its chemical processes and the functions of its physiological mechanisms, such as the nervous, muscular, circulatory and breathing systems, all operate optimally within a narrow temperature range. This temperature is maintained by a thermoregulatory system which establishes balance, or *homeostasis*, within a wide range of environmental conditions. Deviations from the narrow range of optimal deep-tissue temperature cause first, stress, then temporary or permanent damage and finally death. The deep-tissue, or core, temperature is about 37 °C; during heavy work or exercise it rises by a few tenths of a degree. Under extreme activity it may rise as high as 39.5 °C for short durations – but above this, whilst the thermoregulatory system still operates to some extent, various other systems may be damaged, and once the temperature reaches 42 to 43 °C the thermoregulatory system itself breaks down, starting a vicious circle in the other systems and causing death. Temperatures of about 42 °C are sometimes experienced in severe fevers and can be survived for short periods.

In the downward direction chilling of deep tissue to 36 °C is possible without damage; below this muscular weakness, exposure and then death results. (Although, under carefully controlled conditions, temperatures as low as 30 °C and less can be survived, for instance under surgical hypothermia.)

Since normal deep-tissue temperature varies only slightly around 37 °C, and since the conditions under which people survive range from arctic temperatures combined with high wind and the absence of solar radiation, to desert temperatures with intense radiation levels and air movement which, at air temperatures above skin temperature, *increase* the heat gain to the body, the thermoregulatory systems must be, and indeed are, extremely powerful to enable this constancy in the clothed body to be maintained against such high variations. The effect of these systems is to achieve a condition of heat balance – where the rate of heat generation in the body is equal to the rate of heat loss from it. This heat balance is the underlying and fundamental condition of survival and, as we shall see later, comfort. The heat balance equation below (equation (3.2)) expresses this equality. When it is satisfied, the deep-tissue temperature remains constant. If inequality occurs, there will be a raising or lowering of body temperature, since the body is a heat store; such changes in it can only be tolerated within the narrow limits and for the short durations indicated above.

The general form of the double heat balance equation using Fanger's formulation [7] is

$$H_{met} - E_{diff} - E_{rsw} - E_{res} - C_{res} = K = R + C, \qquad (3.2)$$

where H_{met} = the internal heat production of the body; E_{diff} = the heat loss by water diffusion through the skin; E_{rsw} = the heat loss by evaporation of regulatory sweat secretion from the skin; E_{res} = latent heat loss by respiration; C_{res} = dry heat loss by respiration; K = heat transfer from the skin to outer surface of clothed body; R = heat loss by radiation from the outer surface of the clothed body to its environment; C = heat loss by convection from the outer surface of the clothed body to its environment. In survivable conditions H_{met} is always positive; E_{diff}, E_{rsw} and E_{res} are zero or positive; K, R, C_{res} and C are positive, zero or negative.

The rate of heat generation and heat loss by each of the mechanisms can be evaluated and Fanger shows that the only three physiological variables which enter into the heat balance equation are skin temperature t_{sk}, the rate of sweat secretion E_{rsw} and the metabolic rate M (which determines body heat production H_{met}). The first two will be shown later also to be the two variables upon which comfort sensation depends.

The control of skin temperature and sweat secretion are the two basic mechanisms used in the thermoregulatory system, and both are controlled by the hypothalamus.

The oxygen which is inspired is absorbed into the bloodstream within the lungs and distributed to the body tissues where it is used to break down food; from that reaction, heat and mechanical energy for the muscles are produced. The rate of total energy production is known as the metabolic rate, M. The energy converted to external mechanical power is dependent on the mechanical efficiency of a particular activity (Wk/M); this is generally low, often zero. Even for such activities as the heavy building site work of lifting or pushing it is only 0.2, and for most activities all or most of the metabolic energy becomes heat energy to be dissipated by heat loss mechanisms.

In order to maintain the body heat balance, the heat losses must increase as the internal heat production increases and, conversely, decrease as it falls. At a given activity level the total heat losses by radiation, convection and evaporation must remain constant, in spite of variations in the environmental factors. The first regulatory mechanism is that which increases or decreases the thermal resistance of skin tissues. At a given activity level, as the thermal environment becomes cooler, the blood vessels under the surface of the skin constrict (vasoconstriction), reduce the flow of blood and, thus, reduce the surface temperature of the body and, hence, the rate of heat loss. Similarly, as the environment becomes warmer, the blood vessels expand (vasodilation), the skin temperature rises, the heat loss increases and this represents a decrease in the thermal resistance of the skin tissue. Additional effects occur as the environment cools or heats up further.

In cold environments, when the limit of control by vasoconstriction has been reached, goose pimples form – which corresponds to the raising of the hair on the skin to provide extra insulation, but this is a mechanism which is not particularly effective on the human body with its sparse hair cover. Also, shivering occurs – a form of spontaneous muscular skin activity which generates heat. In warm environments, the chief additional physiological effect is the actuation of the sweat glands which produce moisture for evaporative cooling at the skin surface; this is in addition to the normal evaporation which takes place under all circumstances by skin diffusion, and by evaporation in the lungs and respiratory tract. Further cooling below the shivering region will cause a drop in body temperature; further heating above the level at which the whole body surface is covered with unevaporated sweat will cause body heating. Both, ultimately, lead to damage of tissue and death.

Clearly, these physiological mechanisms are affected by the general environment and also by the level of activity and the nature of clothing worn. The general environment can be characterized by four main variables, each of which will be considered in detail in other later parts of the book. The first is air temperature; this will affect the convective heat transfer from skin and clothing surfaces and also the dry respiration heat loss. The second is air velocity; this affects both convective heat loss and the rate of evaporation from the body surface and, hence, the evaporative heat loss. The third is the mean radiant temperature of the environment, which affects the radiation heat loss from the body. The fourth is the moisture content of the ambient air; this affects the rate of evaporation from the skin and, hence, the evaporative heat loss, as well as the rates of evaporation from the lungs and of vapour diffusion through the skin. It will be seen that the effects of all four will be modified by the amount and type of clothing which is worn. Inside buildings, or in urban or rural outdoor environments, the four environmental variables are affected by the properties of building fabric, ground, topography and planting and other natural or artificial features. These are the chief subjects of this book.

The evaluation of each of the eight terms in the general heat balance equation (equation (3.2)) requires a detailed physiological treatment. Several thorough ones are available; the present treatment is in summary form and is based on Fanger's formulation, to which reference can be made for a complete treatment [7].

3.3.1 Internal Heat Production, H_{met}

The energy released by the oxidation process, known as the metabolic energy, M, is partly converted to heat, H_{met} and partly to work, Wk.

$M = H_{met} + Wk$ (in watts per square metre).

If the external mechanical efficiency η is defined as $\eta = Wk/M$, then

$$H_{met} = M(1 - \eta). \tag{3.3}$$

Usually this is expressed per unit area of body surface, thus allowing for people of different size and shape.

A very good estimate of the body surface area is given by the Dubois equation; for the Dubois area (A_{DU}):

$$A_{DU} = w_b^{0.425} \times h_b^{0.725} \times 0.2024,$$

where A_{DU} = Dubois surface area (in square metres); w_b = body weight (in kilogrammes); h_b = body height (in metres). Typical values for adult males and females range from 1.65 to 2.00 m^2; with 1.8 m^2 as a reasonable single figure adult average. Expressing equation (3.3) in terms of unit body area,

$$H_{met}/A_{DU} = (M/A_{DU})(1 - \eta). \tag{3.4}$$

Values of M/A_{DU} are characteristic of different activities; Table 3.1 gives some typical ones. They range from 41 W m^{-2} for sleeping to 200 W m^{-2} and over for prolonged heavy physical work or athletics. Walking slowly on the level has a value of 116 W m^{-2}; sitting, 58 W m^{-2}; standing 70 W m^{-2}. The 'sitting' rate is used later in this chapter as the basic unit of activity, and is equivalent to 1 'met'. Any activity, of X W m^{-2}, is equivalent to $X/58$ in met units.

Table 3.1 *Metabolic rate of different activities with mechanical efficiency and relative still air velocity – i.e. velocity induced by the activity itself (based on Fanger [7] and ASHRAE [3])*

Activity	Metabolic rate, M/A_{DU} (W m^{-2})	Mechanical efficiency, η	Relative velocity in still air (m s^{-1})
Sleeping	41	0	0
Reclining	47	0	0
Sitting	58	0	0
Standing, relaxed	70	0	0
Walking, level, at 3.2 km h^{-1}	116	0	0.9
Walking, level, at 4.8 km h^{-1}	151	0	1.3
Walking, level, at 6.4 km h^{-1}	221	0	1.8
Walking, 15° upward slope, at 3.2 km h^{-1}	267	0.1	0.9
House cleaning	116−198	0−0.1	0.1−0.3
Typing	70−81	0	0.05
Gymnastics	175−233	0−0.1	0.5−2.0
Dancing	140−256	0	0.2−2.0
Sawing by hand	232−280	0.1−0.2	0.1−0.2
Heavy machine work (e.g. steel forming)	204−262	0−0.1	0−0.2

The value of η depends on the mechanical efficiency of the activity. Table 3.1 also gives a typical range. It will be seen that for many common activities it is 0 or low; it never exceeds 0.2. Thus, for, say, standing, with $\eta = 0$, the total metabolic heat to be dissipated for a person is

$$H_{met} = 70 \times 1.77 = 124 \text{ W}$$

3.3.2 Heat Loss by Skin Diffusion, E_{diff}

There is continuous diffusion of water vapour through the skin; this is not controlled by the sweat glands and, hence, is not part of the thermoregulatory process. The rate of diffusion is proportional to the difference between the saturated vapour pressure at the skin and the partial vapour pressure of the air. It can be evaluated if the latter is known, as well as the skin temperature. In conditions when there is no sweating, skin diffusion still takes place.

3.3.3 Heat Loss by Evaporation of Sweat Secretion, E_{rsw}

The rate of sweat secretion depends not only on the ambient environmental conditions and, hence, how much body heat is lost by convection and radiation, but also on activity and clothing – including the thermal resistance and the vapour permeability of the clothes. Whatever cannot be lost by convection and radiation, and the other, non-sweating evaporative processes, will be lost by sweating, until such time as the whole skin is covered by a film of unevaporated sweat ('skin wettedness', $w = 1.0$). Heating of the body beyond this point will result in raising of deep tissue temperature and health hazards. The actual rate of sweat secretion will certainly affect sensations of comfort – as will be seen later. So, for the present, the heat lost by sweat secretion and evaporation will simply be stated in unit terms of body area as E_{rsw}/A_{DU} W m^{-2}.

3.3.4 Latent Respiration Heat Loss, E_{res}

Whilst the air reaching the lungs is saturated at deep-tissue temperatures, as it is moved out again, on breathing out, some heat and water is transferred back to the body, but on balance there is still more heat and moisture in the expired air than in that breathed in. Thus, there is both a latent and a dry heat loss in normal environments due to breathing.

It can be shown that E_{res} is a function of two variables – the activity level and the absolute vapour pressure of the ambient air.

The average person loses about 12 W m^{-2} by evaporation through the combined processes of skin diffusion and latent respiration heat loss. This amount of moisture is equivalent to 6 per cent of the body surface being covered with a film of moisture; i.e. w, skin wettedness, = 0.06 with no sweating.

3.3.5 Dry Respiration Heat Loss, C_{res}

This is the heat loss due to the temperature difference between the inspired and expired air. It can be shown that C_{res} can be expressed as a function of the metabolic rate M and the ambient air temperature, t_a.

3.3.6 Heat Conduction through the Clothing, K

The process is itself quite complex, involving transfer through air spaces, conduction through solid material and radiation exchange across gaps between layers and fibres. As a simplification, the properties of the clothes can be considered in terms of their total thermal resistance – and Gagge *et al.* introduced the unit 'clo', which is a dimensionless expression for the thermal insulation of clothing, measured from the skin to the outer surface of the clothes, but excluding the external surface resistance, as the term K, which is being evaluated here, is from the skin to the *outer* clothing surface.

The standard clo unit = 0.155 m^2 $^\circ$C W^{-1} and this represents approximately the thermal resistance, R_{cl}, of a lounge suit with normal underwear. If R_{cl} for any particular clothing ensemble is known, from measurements, expressed in terms of the Dubois area, then its insulation value in clo units will be

$$I_{cl} = R_{cl}/0.155.$$

Typical values in clo units are given in Table 3.2; it will be seen that these range from 0, for nude conditions, to about 4.0 for heavy Arctic uniform. Normal outdoor winter clothes will range from 1.5 to 2.0; whilst the light clothes likely to be worn in the warm tropics will range from about 0.3 to 0.5.

If the clothing insulation I_{cl} is known, then the heat transfer from skin to outer surface, per unit (Dubois) area of body, will be proportional to the temperature difference between the skin and the outer clothing surface. (In both temperatures the area–weighted mean values are used.)

If a person sits in a chair or lies on a couch, the effective insulation of the clothing, as given in Table 3.2 of I_{cl} values, will be increased and an appropriate adjustment in the value of I_{cl} should be made.

3.3.7 Heat Loss by Radiation, R

The Stefan Bolzmann radiation law (in terms of the difference between the fourth power of the absolute temperatures of two surfaces) expresses the rate of radiation exchange between the human body and its environment. In order to compute the rate of radiation, the effective radiation area of the body, the emissivity of its surface, its surface temperature and the mean radiant temperature of its environment need to be known. The effective radiation area is a function, amongst other factors, of the ratio f_{cl} between the surface area of the clothed body to that of the nude body. Table 3.2 gives typical values of f_{cl} for a few clothing assemblies.

Table 3.2   *Values of I_{cl} and f_{cl} for various clothing ensembles (from Fanger [7], ASHRAE [3] and estimated)*

Clothing ensemble	Insulation, I_{cl}	Ratio of surface area of the clothed body to surface area of nude body, f_{cl}
Nude	0	1.0
Shorts	0.1	1.0
Tropical ensemble (shorts, open-neck short-sleeved shirt, light socks, sandals or women's equivalent)	0.3–0.4	1.05
Men's light summer clothing (long lightweight trousers, open-neck short-sleeved shirt)	0.5	1.1
Typical men's business suit (+ cotton underwear, long-sleeved shirt, tie, woollen socks, shoes)	1.0	1.15
Men's heavy three-piece business suit (+ cotton underwear, long-sleeved shirt, tie, woollen socks, shoes)	1.5	1.15–1.2
Women's indoor ensemble (skirt, long-sleeved blouse and jumper, normal underwear, stockings, shoes)	0.7–0.9	1.1–1.15
Men's heavy suit as above + woollen overcoat	2.0–2.5	1.2–1.3

Typically the effective radiation area of the body is about 0.71 times the actual body area, due to re-entrant angles, concavities, etc.

3.3.8 Heat Loss by Convection, C

The convection loss from the clothed body is proportional to the temperature difference between its surface and that of the ambient air, which is multiplied by a convection coefficient, whose value depends on air velocity.

3.3.9 Heat Balance Equation

Appendix 3A gives the detailed heat balance equation (3.5) according to Fanger, in which each of the eight factors above, evaluated and combined, is taken into account. Inspection of the equation shows that only three independent physiological measures are included – skin temperature, sweat rate and metabolic rate.

The satisfaction of the equation means that the body heat generated equals the total heat lost and there is no lowering or raising of body temperature; thus healthy survival is possible. This does not mean that any combination of conditions which satisfy the equation will be judged as *comfortable*; the conditions for comfort are more stringent and will now be discussed in detail.

3.4 Thermal comfort

3.4.1 Comfort Equation

It has already been stated that whilst there is a wide range of conditions within which the deep-tissue temperature can be maintained at or near 37 °C, by thermoregulatory processes, there is only a narrow one within which people will feel, and express, a comfortable sensation. We have seen that only three physiological variables – skin temperature t_{sk}, sweat rate E_{rsw} and metabolic rate M – are involved in the heat balance equation. Therefore, the comfort range should be definable in terms of these three variables. Fanger suggests the following two equations, based on regression analysis of experiments in which subjects at different activity levels had skin temperatures and sweat secretion monitored, and they also expressed, at various levels, their sensations of comfort. These results are in close agreement with those by Gagge [8], Nevins and McNall [9], and others.

Limits on skin temperature as a function of activity are given by

$$t_{sk} = 35.7 - 0.0276\, M \,^{\circ}C \tag{3.6}$$

and on sweat secretion as a function of activity by

$$E_{rsw} = 0.42\,(M-58)\,\mathrm{W\,m^{-2}}, \tag{3.7}$$

where M = the metabolic rate per unit (Dubois) body surface area in watts per square metre.

By substitution of equations (3.6) and (3.7) into the general double heat balance equation (3.5) given in Appendix 3A, Fanger obtained equation (3.8) in Appendix 3A, which defines the envelope of conditions within which optimum comfort judgments would be made. A similar, physiological, treatment of comfort conditions has been carried out by Gagge *et al.* whose *standard effective temperature* (SET) we shall use as a general index of the thermal environment [8].

Below, we discuss the meaning of 'optimum' and the ways in which this can be established by obtaining people's responses to various environments. A simple definition for thermal comfort is that state in which a person will judge the environment to be neither too cold nor too warm – a kind of neutral point defined by the absence of any feeling of discomfort.

Equations (3.6) and (3.7) show several interesting features. First, as activity level, M, increases, the skin temperature required for comfort drops; from about 34 °C at rest ($M = 58$ W m^{-2}) to about 30.5 °C under very active conditions ($M = 200$ W m^{-2}). Sweat rate varies from 0 to 60 W m^{-2} at the same two levels – that is, it increases with activity level. Adding 12 W m^{-2} for the more or less constant evaporative heat loss due to diffusion and respiration latent heat loss, the total evaporative loss is seen to be about $0.3M$ to $0.4M$. So the idea that sweating is a cause of discomfort as such is shown not to be the case – at higher activity levels some sweating appears to be desirable for comfort (quite apart, of course, from its heat balance function).

Closer inspection of the thermal comfort equation (3.8) in Appendix 3A shows it contains three types of terms:

(i) Those which are of a function of clothing (I_{cl} and f_{cl}) which define the insulation value of the clothing and the proportion of the body which is clothed.

(ii) Those which are a function of activity (M/A_{DU}, η and v), that is the activity level, the mechanical efficiency of the activity and air velocity. The presence of v in this group may be surprising, but it is due to the fact that many activities induce an air flow which is additional to the velocity caused by wind or thermal currents. Table 3.1 includes typical values for activity-induced velocities.

(iii) Those which are a function of the environment (t_a, p_a, v and t_{mrt}), air temperature, ambient humidity, air velocity and mean radiant temperature of the environment.

Several points have to be noted about any equation purporting to define comfort, such as equation (3.8) in Appendix 3A. First, it is based on steady-state conditions; where there are rapid transients, as when people from one environment move into a noticeably warmer or colder one, other factors also affect comfort and these will be discussed later. Second, it gives the optimum conditions for one person, whose activity level and clothing can be defined. But there will be differences between individuals in a group due to clothing and activity variations and, as will be shown later, no set of conditions can optimally satisfy 100 per cent of the members of a group.

Four main questions remain to be answered under the general theme of thermal comfort:

(i) Using the comfort equation and methods of assessing discomfort, can a family of predictive tools be produced which give a designer a thermal index which can reasonably accurately predict the consequences of any unique combination of the four environmental variables and the two personal ones of clothing and activity?

(ii) How can *dis*comfort be assessed? Such assessment will clearly have to express not only the degree of discomfort (warm or cold) felt, but also its duration and the number of people in a group who are affected by it.

(iii) Is there a practical general index of the environment itself, which, adequately accounting for activity and clothing, can give the designer a measure of the general quality of the environment? This index would have to be one which, in terms of the ideas of the spatial and temporal unity of so-called 'indoors' and 'outdoors' climate explained in Chapter 2, can express both in uniform terms.

(iv) Finally, what is known about the special factors which may influence comfort assessments – age, sex, state of health, sleep, transients, subjective judgments such as 'freshness' and 'stuffiness' and others?

The next four sections deal with each of these questions in turn.

3.4.2 A Thermal Index

We have seen that there have been a number of attempts in the past to develop a temperature index which, in a single number, combines the effect of all the environmental variables. Usually they involve making assumptions about a standard activity and standard clothing and their applicability to other levels of these two variables, in a range of environments, is limited.

In the present book we have decided to use the *standard effective temperature* of Gagge and his colleagues, which is a rational, physiologically-based index of comfort, already widely used by engineers throughout the world as a result of its adoption by the ASHRAE, and supported by widescale experimental and theoretical work. Over a large part of the range of real conditions its results agree closely with those of Fanger and his colleagues.

Its definition requires first the definition of two other terms. The first is the *operative temperature, t_o*. This is defined as the uniform temperature (i.e. $t_a = t_{mrt}$) of an imaginary enclosure in which man will exchange the same dry heat by radiation and convection as in the actual environment. Thus,

$$t_o = (h_r t_{mrt} + h_c t_a)/(h_r + h_c), \tag{3.9}$$

where h_r and h_c are the radiation and convection coefficients, respectively.

With a suitably sized and coloured globe thermometer, whose convection and radiation coefficients are in the same ratio as that for the body, t_o can be equated with the globe temperature, t_g. It can be seen from equation (3.9) that the measured or computed value of t_o will depend on air velocity – since this will change the value of h_c. The higher the velocity the nearer the value of t_o will lie to that of t_a.

t_o determines the dry heat loss from the body, and, since the relative effects of air temperature and mean radiant temperature will change with different air velocities, it is necessary to compute t_o for each of the five values of v which are used for the *thermal comfort charts*. In Appendix 3B a number of charts are given for finding the *Standard effective temperature* (see below) at any one of 55 combinations of these five variables. In Appendix 3A is another series of charts for finding the value of t_o over the *same* range of air velocities v.

To calculate t_{mrt} from a measured value of t_g, a correction needs to be made for air velocity. The diameter of the globe should be such that the radiation and convection losses from it are in the same ratio as in the human body. For low air speeds, Humphreys [10] has shown that 40 mm gives this result. However, diameters from 25 mm to 150 mm (the traditional 6-in globe) will give acceptable results. An approximate correction is given by

Fig. 3.2 The response to air temperature t_a and mean radiant temperature t_{mrt} of globe thermometers of diameter 20 to 150 mm for air speeds of 0.1 to 1.0 m s^{-1}. The shaded zone indicates the human response at low air movement (after Humphreys [10]).

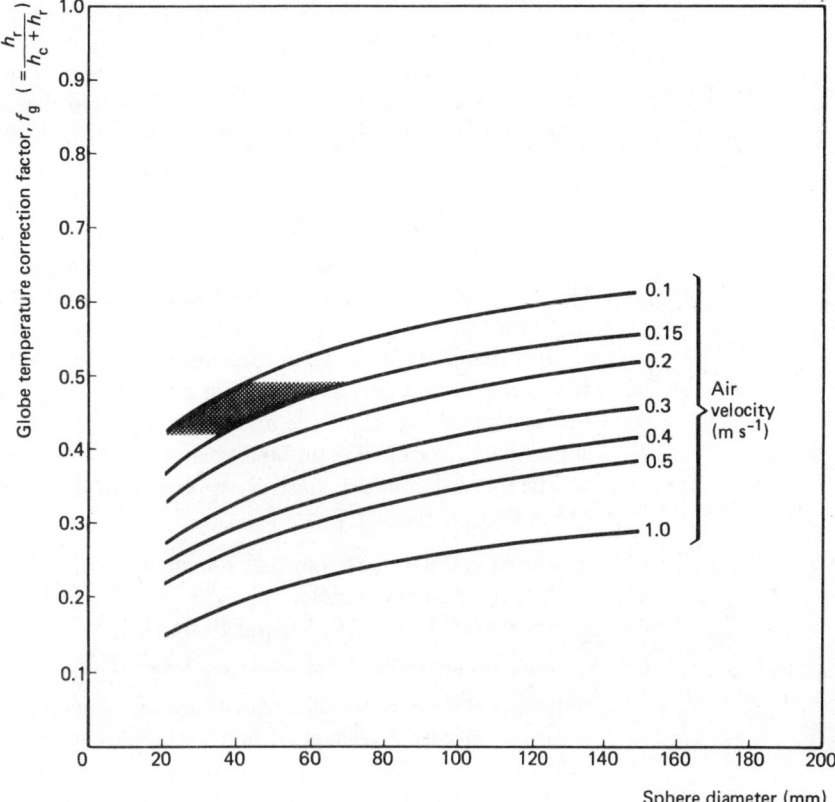

$$t_g = t_a + f_g(t_{mrt} - t_a), \tag{3.10}$$

where f_g is a globe temperature correction factor whose value depends on both air velocity, v and on the diameter of the globe. Values of f_g are given in Fig. 3.2 up to $v = 1$ m s^{-1}. The derivation of equation (3.10) is shown in Chapter 10.

The second term to be defined is analogous, but also deals with the humidity of the environment. It is the *humid operative temperature*, t_{oh}, which now not only weights t_a and t_{mrt} by appropriate coefficients, but also the dewpoint temperature t_{dp} by an appropriate coefficient. It is defined as the uniform temperature of an imaginary enclosure at 100 per cent relative humidity in which man will exchange the same total heat, by radiation, convection and evaporation, at the same mean skin temperature (t_{sk}) and skin wettedness (w), which occur in the actual environment.

The *new effective temperature*, ET* of Gagge *et al.* [11] has an analogous definition, but in terms of a standard environment at 50 per cent relative humidity rather than at the 100 per cent of t_{oh}. Thus, it is defined as the uniform temperature of an imaginary enclosure at 50 per cent relative humidity in which man will exchange the same total heat by radiation, convection and evaporation, at the same skin temperature and skin wettedness, which occur in the actual environment. Thus ET* is a single temperature measure thermally equivalent to the air temperature, radiation and humidity actually existing; the air velocities in the real environment and in ET* are the same.

The *standard effective temperature*, SET [8] is a further development of ET*, in which any environment, clothing and activity level is expressed in terms of a uniform environment ($t_a = t_{mrt}$) standardized at 50 per cent relative humidity, air velocity at 0.125 m s^{-1} ('still' air conditions in a room), activity of 1 met (which is equivalent to sedentary metabolic rate at 58 W m^{-2} and zero external work) and intrinsic clothing at 0.6 clo (equivalent to normal, lightweight, indoor clothing). Thus, if for any combination of the four environmental variables, and of clothing and activity, SET is, for example, 5 °C, this would mean that the thermal sensation would be the same as for a sitting person, dressed in indoor clothes, in 'still' air, in a uniform environment of 5 °C and at a relative humidity of 50 per cent.

This standard environment, described above, is familiar and easy to imagine and, hence, meaningful as a means of comparing the thermal sensation, discomfort and physiological effects of a whole range of environments, clothing levels and activities – including unfamiliar and extreme combinations of conditions.

The thermal comfort charts in Appendix 3B show SET for 55 combinations of variables, as follows:

Clothing, 0.0 (nude), 0.6, 0.9, 2.4 and 4.0 clo;
Activity, 1, 3 and 5 met;
Velocity, 0.1, 0.5, 2.0, 5.0 and 10.0 m s^{-1}.

Combinations of 3 and 5 met activity with clothing over 0.9 clo have not been shown, as at these levels such heavy clothing would be impractical.

On the charts, the degree of skin wettedness w is marked; this represents the equivalent percentage of the body which is covered with moisture. When no sweating occurs, $w = 0.06$; this amount of moisture being that due to skin diffusion. As w increases above about 0.2, the discomfort level increases; at $w = 1.0$ the limit of tolerance is reached; any conditions warmer than this will lead to body heating, damage and death. At a skin temperature of 34 °C, $w = 0.06$; at conditions cooler than this, as skin temperature drops and w remains at this value, body cooling takes place, the body protecting itself first by vasoconstriction and then by shivering. In the cold conditions, lines of constant SET are parallel to skin temperature lines; in the warm, approximately to lines of constant w; but above $w = 1.00$ the SET lines are again parallel to the (raised) skin temperature lines. These latter are not drawn on the charts for the sake of clarity.

Also marked on the curves is a broad area of comfort, and varying degrees of cold and warm discomfort; as well as DISC, on the 10-point scale; this is described in the next section. The lines for DISC = +0.5 and −0.5 are the upper and lower boundaries of the optimum range of conditions for the variables combined in each chart, and this represents the zone of acceptability by about 80 per cent of the population. Between ±1.0, the equivalent percentage is about 70 per cent.

The abscissa can either be used for the air temperature t_a or, where significantly different radiation effects are present, for the operative temperature t_o. This can be found by use of one of the seven auxiliary t_o charts.

For a full physiological treatment of SET and the related indices the original references should be consulted. But some characteristics of the charts are worth commenting on briefly.

First, it will be seen that at low temperatures and activity levels, lines of SET,

DISC and w are nearly vertical – that is, the influence of environmental humidity is minimal; this is because evaporative cooling by sweating is of little significance here. Second, at warm conditions and light activity levels, lines of DISC crowd together. This indicates that discomfort is now primarily a function of body temperature rather than increasing sweat rate since, although values of w may be only in the region of about 0.5, another limit on sweating has been passed – that is, that for an average-sized person the maximum possible sweat rate is about 500 g m^{-2} h^{-1}. The sharp curvature of the DISC curves at higher humidities in these conditions emphasizes the great increase in discomfort if limits on evaporation of sweat take place. Third, at the higher activity levels of 3 and 5 met, and low air velocities of 0.1 and 0.5 m s^{-1}, the convection caused by the activity, rather than the air velocity, determines the convection loss. Hence, using the t_o charts 6 or 7 at these combinations, the value of t_o is found. The appropriate thermal comfort chart for the *nominal* value of v is then used, but the SET and other values given make the appropriate allowance for the fact that the true convection is higher.

So, the process of predicting thermal comfort and discomfort using SET is as follows:

(i) Knowing the activity, air temperature, mean radiant temperature and air velocity, find the operative temperature t_o by using the appropriate t_o chart in Appendix 3A. If the mean radiant temperature is not known, but the globe temperature has been measured, this can be taken as being the operative temperature provided that its surface has similar absorption to short-wave radiation and the air velocity is below about 4 m s^{-1}. At higher velocities, equation (3.10) can be used.

(ii) Having found the value of t_o from (i) above, select the appropriate thermal comfort chart in Appendix 3B for the air velocity, and the combination of clothing and activity under consideration. Then find the point given by the value of t_o on the x-axis and the value of P_v, vapour pressure, on the y-axis. This point will lie on a line of SET and w, and also the DISC can be obtained. From the DISC an indication of the degree of cold or warm discomfort is obtained as indicated.

Example 3.1   Find SET, w and DISC for RH = 20 per cent, t_a = 25 °C, t_{mrt} = 20 °C, v = 2 m s^{-1}, clo = 0.9, activity = 1 met.

First, using t_o chart 3 for v = 2 m s^{-1}, t_o = 23.5° (by interpolation).

Second, using thermal comfort chart 33 for the same values of met and v and for clo = 0.9, and entering t_o = 23.5° on the x-axis, read off the following values:

SET = 20 °C, w = 0.06,   DISC = −0.7.

Example 3.2   Find SET, w and DISC for RH = 80 per cent, t_a = 1.5 °C, t_{mrt} = 40 °C, v = 0.5 m s^{-1}, clo = 0.6, activity = 5 met.

In this case the activity level creates convection higher than the velocity of 0.5 m s^{-1}; therefore, t_o chart 7 for 5 met and v = < 1.29 m s^{-1} is used. t_o is read off as 22.5 °C (by interpolation).

Using this value of t_o, thermal comfort chart 27 for v = 0.5 m s^{-1}, clo = 0.6 and met = 5.0 is used; entering t_o = 22.5°C on the x-axis, read off the following values:

SET = 33 °C, w = 0.55,   DISC = +1.5.

3.4.3 Assessment of Discomfort

This is the second of the four factors listed at the end of the introductory section on thermal comfort (*page* 47). So far, we have listed the factors that affect comfort conditions and in the previous section we presented techniques for predicting SET at any combination of the six relevant variables. However, since most real environments are not exactly optimal – even for a single individual – they will be to some extent too warm or too cool for the actual clothing and activity level. If there is a group of people concerned, then there is no condition, as we shall see, which can be optimal for every member of the group, due to individual variation. So one must have some measure of discomfort, which involves determining the degree of discomfort, the number of people affected, and the duration of the discomfort.

The discussion of and research into human thermal comfort has a long history. The results are illuminating but far from unambiguous. In all cases, at least of the more thorough work, the authors have had to limit and qualify their conclusions. Sometimes they hold only for a limited range of environments; or a special group of people (in terms of age, ethnic group, acclimatization or work conditions); and usually they involve acceptance of a theoretical standpoint with regard to the definition, and hence the measurement, or even the measurability, of 'comfort' itself.

Several approaches towards this definition have been used. The two main ones are semantic and behavioural. The latter include measures such as those of sweat rate, oxygen consumption, activity adjustment, analysis of clothing worn and observation of people's choices in setting thermal controls, opening windows and so on. These methods are complex; the observation of physiological (or autonomous) behaviour, which is outside conscious control, is suited specially for the laboratory. Observation of the other types of behaviour is ideally suited for field studies, and involves no interference with the normal routines of life; in fact, if carefully done, it can be carried out by totally unobtrusive methods. Most of the laboratory and field results are, however, based on the simpler semantic techniques, in which people are asked to express their feelings about an environment in words. These expressions are quantified by scaling and then correlated to variations in the environment and in clothing and activity levels.

The analysis may be based on words people use naturally, in unsolicited situations such as daily conversations, essays about general topics or newspaper articles. Or they may be responses to open-ended interviews or questionnaires where people are asked to comment on a wide range of topics, upon which their attention has been more or less focused. In either case, solicited or not, their comments can only be usefully analysed by grouping them into categories or classes and recording the frequency of items occurring in the different groups. Further analysis may enable the categories to be arranged in some sort of continuum, or, strictly speaking, dimension. There are usually several underlying dimensions beneath the concepts people have about environment or, for that matter, any other complex and rich experience. One aim in dimensional analysis, as for instance by factor analysis, is to discover what these underlying dimensions are and to explain them as 'parsimoniously' – that is, by as few dimensions – as possible. It is also an aim to discover dimensions which are relatively independent of each other.

In thermal comfort work a commonly used semantic approach is to ask people to express their impressions of the environment on a linear scale in which numbers are fitted to phrases. One such scale is that used by Bedford [12].

Thermal sensation scales

Bedford		ASHRAE	
Much too warm	1	Cold	1
Too warm	2	Cool	2
Comfortably warm	3	Slightly cool	3
Comfortable	4	Neutral	4
Comfortably cool	5	Slightly warm	5
Too cool	6	Warm	6
Much too cool	7	Hot	7

Fanger*		Rohles and Nevins*	
Cold	−3	Very cold	−4
Cool	−2	Cold	−3
Slightly cool	−1	Cool	−2
Neutral	0	Slightly cool	−1
Slightly warm	+1	Neutral	0
Warm	+2	Slightly warm	+1
Hot	+3	Warm	+2
		Hot	+3
		Very hot	+4
		Painful	+5

A similar one is that used by ASHRAE [3] on a 1–7 scale, but with 'cold' at one end, 1, and 'hot' at the other, 7. The midpoint 4 is labelled 'neutral'. Fanger [7] uses the same scale but, for convenience, numbers the midpoint 0 and one end −3 and the other +3. Rohles and Nevins' TSENS is a 10-point scale, all of which correspond to Fanger's, with one extra point at the cold end and two at the hot [13]. Other workers have used variants of such scales. One important difference between the Bedford and the Fanger scales and the Rohles and Nevins TSENS is the semantic of the midpoint. In the first it is 'comfortable' a positive affective statement. It corresponds roughly with the ASHRAE definition as 'that condition of mind which expresses satisfaction with the thermal environment' [3]. In the latter two, a descriptive term, 'neutral' is used — and this is a relatively value-free concept defined as that condition in which a person does not know whether he or she would prefer a warmer or a colder environment. It is basically a point of *in*decision. The affective and descriptive judgments may conceptually and emotionally express slightly different physiological and environmental conditions.

Humphreys [14] has recently analysed data from more than 30 field studies of thermal comfort from various parts of the world. We shall be referring to this work later — but his suggestion should be noted here, that preferred conditions may lie to one side or the other of the thermally neutral conditions, perhaps slightly warmer in cold climates and slightly cooler in warm ones. This emphasizes the importance of semantic clarity and accuracy in all such work. The word used by a questioner and the same word used by a respondent are linked by the understanding (cognitive) processes of both. If these are different, then the answers from different respondents do not necessarily mean exactly the

* These scales are called TSENS.

same thing – a point to which little attention has been paid in classical thermal comfort work. When this point is considered, some explanations of anomalous results may be forthcoming.

The results of such scale judgments, which assume that the intervals between the statements are equal, and hence merit equal numerical intervals of unity, indicate the degree of departure from the optimal conditions; either on the warm or the cold side. However, different individuals, under the same conditions, vary slightly in their evaluations of thermal (and other) environments. So any given condition will give a *range* of responses. This range can be analysed by examining the frequency distribution of a given response to a range of environments or of the range of responses to a given environment.

Thus, using, say, a seven-point scale, for instance, it is possible to find out the proportions of respondents who fall into each of the categories at a particular environmental condition – say temperature. On this basis six cumulative frequency curves of the type shown in Fig. 3.3 can be drawn; each represents the boundary between two scale judgments. This shows the percentages of judgements falling into the various categories at each condition. If any particular zone is taken – say between –1 and +1 – a frequency distribution curve like the one in Fig. 3.4 can be drawn – which shows the percentage of people making judgments within these points on the scale; as the temperature increases, the percentage increases at first, rising to a maximum at the peak of the curve, and then begins to fall off again.

Fig. 3.3 Cumulative frequencies of thermal judgments.

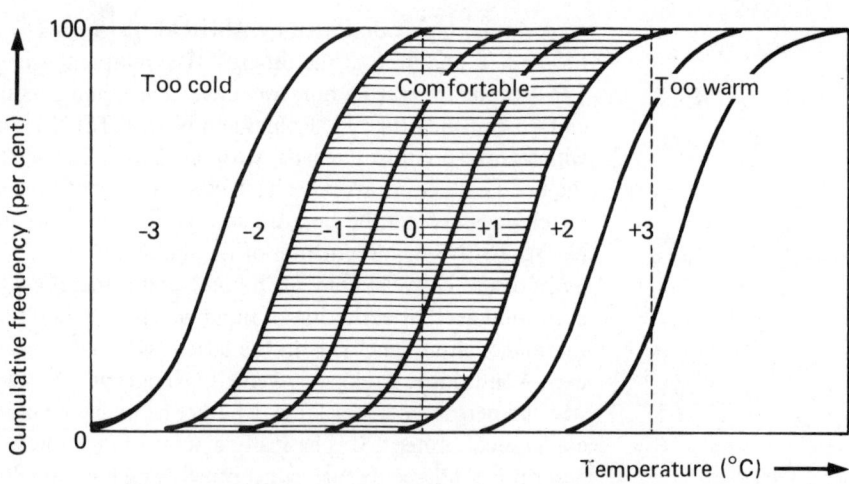

Fig. 3.4 Frequency distribution of judgments (−1 to +1 in Fig. 3.3).

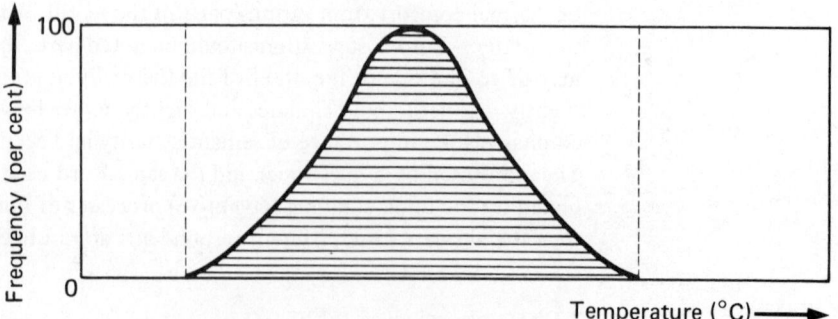

Instead of temperature on the *x*-axis, what is required is a thermal index which takes *all* the variables of both the environment and of activity and clothing into account. Such an index is a person's judgment of the environment. When the comfort equation is satisfied, for a large group of persons a vote of 0, or thermal neutrality, will be obtained. The problem is to predict what the vote will be if the conditions deviate to one side or the other of the neutral condition.

Fanger proposes to measure the degree of discomfort in terms of the thermal load placed on a person in a given environment. The thermal load is defined as the difference between the internal heat production and the heat loss to the actual environment for a man hypothetically kept at the comfort values of the mean skin temperature and the sweat secretion at the actual activity level. He calculates this load, and then establishes a relationship between the predicted vote, on the seven-point scale, and the load. Finally he computes the predicted *mean* vote (PMV) for a large group of persons, from experimental data. PMV then becomes the combined thermal index which expresses, on the seven-point scale previously described, the thermal discomfort in a given environment.

The question then arises as to what a particular value of PMV really means; if, for instance, the PMV is on the cold side, −2, how many people, and to what extent, will feel dissatisfied with their environment? Fanger proposes a rather gross simplification; that all those judging between −1 and +1 should be called 'satisfied' and all those above and below these limiting values 'dissatisfied'. The satisfied group are, therefore, those represented by the shaded area in Fig. 3.3 above, and that area is re-represented in the frequency distribution in Fig. 3.4. If, instead of drawing the distribution of 'satisfied', the inverse distribution of 'dissatisfied' is shown, as in Fig. 3.5, the PMV can be directly related to the percentage of people expected to be dissatisfied (the actual statistical technique

Fig. 3.5 Predicted percentage of dissatisfied (PDD) as a function of predicted mean vote (PMV) (after Fanger [7]).

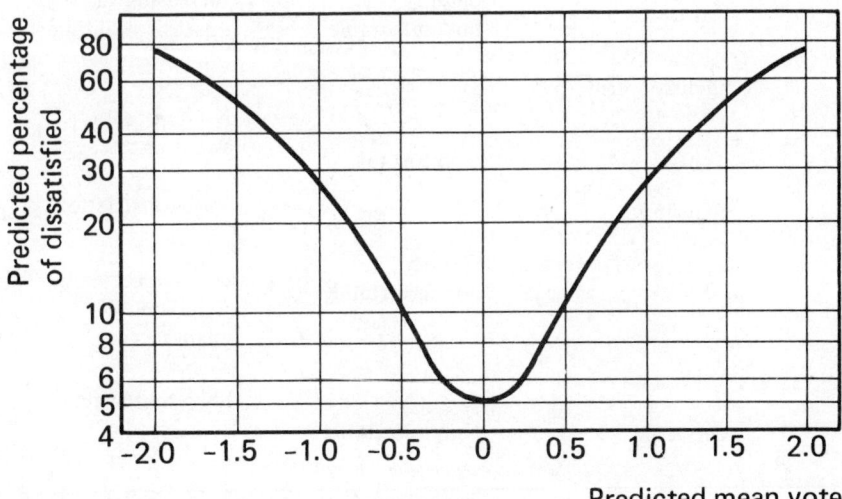

for obtaining the relationship shown is explained in the reference). Any numerical comfort/discomfort scale can have the same technique applied; and the percentage of persons satisfied or dissatisfied at a given mean vote determined.

A scale similar in type to PMV is Gagge's DISC, with thermal neutrality at zero, with negative values in the cold and positive ones in the warm [8] and it has been selected as the index of discomfort in the present book. Values can be obtained from the charts in Appendix 3B for any combination of the four environmental and the two personal variables described earlier. Section 3.4.4 deals in more detail with the various uses to which the DISC scale can be put. DISC has certain advantages; first, it has been validated over a wide range of conditions and not merely the normal 'room' conditions. Second, unlike the thermal *sensation* scales such as those listed on *page* 53 (including TSENS), it expresses judgments in degrees of *discomfort* and thus equivalences can be found between cold and warm conditions in terms of a common response. Between DISC −0.5 and +0.5, 80 per cent of the population will be satisfied; between −1.0 and +1.0 this drops to 70 per cent.

The relationship between thermal sensation (which can be measured by TSENS), discomfort (which can be measured by DISC), the physiologically-based temperature index standard effective temperature, SET, with which we have dealt above, and the state of health is shown in Table 3.3.

Table 3.3 *Human thermal responses to the standard effective temperature (SET) (after Gagge et al.* [8] *)*

SET (°C)	Temperature sensation	Discomfort	Regulation of body temperature	Health
		Limited tolerance	Failure of free skin evaporation	↑
40	Very hot	Very uncomfortable		
	Hot	Uncomfortable	↑	Increasing danger of heat-stroke
35				
	Warm	Slightly uncomfortable	Increasing vaso-dilation sweating	
30	Slightly warm			
25	Neutral	Comfortable	No registered sweating	Normal health
			¦	
20	Slightly cool		Vasoconstriction	
	Cool	Slightly uncomfortable	↓	Complaints from dry mucosa
15			Behavioural changes	Impairment peripheral circulation
	Cold		Shivering begins	
10	Very cold	Uncomfortable		↓

We have seen that SET is based on standard conditions of:

clo　　　　 = 0.6,
activity　　 = 1 met (sedentary),
air velocity = 0.125 m s^{-1}.

Under these conditions the numerical value TSENS of thermal sensation judgment in Table 3.3, and listed on *page* 53, is related to the environmental conditions by:

$$\text{TSENS} = 0.245\, t_a \text{ (or } t_o) + 0.000247\, P_{vdp} -6.471, \qquad (3.11)$$

where t_a = air temperature, t_o = operative temperature and P_{vdp} = vapour pressure at dewpoint temperature t_{dp} (in pascals).

DISC, in warm conditions, is a function of skin wettedness w and is obtained from

$$\text{DISC} = 5.0\, (w -0.06), \qquad (3.12)$$

giving DISC = 0 when w = 0.06, i.e. before the onset of sweating. At about 41 °C TSENS $\simeq$ DISC = 4.7.

From equation (3.7) we have seen that a moderate amount of sweating is required for comfort and, hence, on the thermal comfort charts in Appendix 3B the optimum comfort zone for moderate activity of met = 1.0 to 1.2 is indicated as lying in conditions of w = 0.06 to about w = 0.2. Above w = 1.0, DISC and TSENS are both a function of skin temperature.

DISC, in cold conditions, is a function of skin temperature and is numerically equal to TSENS, which is obtained from equation (3.11).

3.4.4 A General Index of the Environment

This relates to the third of the questions raised at the end of Section 3.1.1. We have seen in Chapter 2 that there is a real need for a general index of the thermal environment which describes the degree of stress or thermal discomfort which people will experience. We have also argued that the traditional division between external climate and internal environment is not meaningful, since people freely move between the two, and in any case many spaces are marginal and do not clearly fall into either category. It is, therefore, necessary to have an index of the thermal environment which is valid throughout the building and all the spaces around it.

We have also shown that traditional indices, which combine mean radiant temperature, air temperature, air velocity and humidity, cannot be used since the combined effect of these depends both on the clothing and on the activity of the person. For instance, the effect of air movement depends both on the amount and on the permeability of the clothing; the effect of humidity, in limiting evaporation, depends on the activity – since at high rates of activity sweating becomes more significant and, hence, so does environmental humidity.

The SET index takes all these effects into account – but by itself, in referring to the thermal environment of the 'standard' conditions, leaves quite a lot to the imagination. DISC, on the other hand, gives a direct comparison between any combinations of conditions not in terms of a thermal index but in terms of degrees of cold or warm discomfort people will feel at any combination of the six main variables. So by using the charts in Appendix 3B, SET, w and DISC for any place and time can be found, even making allowances for such matters as the donning of an outer garment when leaving the building. Contours of equivalent DISC, or zones of uniform DISC, can be plotted. Thus, for instance, two spaces may have precisely the same physical environment, but in moving from one to the other activity changes – say from a classroom to a gymnasium. The DISC figure will show the change in comfort level which occurs with raised activity and also indicates what changes in either clothing or the environment would be required to bring back conditions to comfort. Figures 3.6 and 3.7 show two examples of the use of DISC contours as a general environmental index.

Figure 3.6 (a) shows the environment around a 2 m high shelter wall on a cold, sunny day, with $t_a = -5°C$, wind velocities as shown, and RH = 50 per cent. The effect of the shadow cast by the wall can be seen on the DISC value in the shade in Figure 3.6 (b). The area sheltered from the wind is also in shade, thus depressing the value of t_o and, similarly, the resultant DISC value, to the extent that the warmest spot is seen to be on the windward (and sunny) side of the wall.

Figure 3.7 shows the SET contours of Fig. 4.11, in the next chapter, presented in terms of DISC. DISC charts of this kind can be drawn for any climatic data, and will show the seasonal and diurnal comfort sensation of a

Fig. 3.6 (a) Velocity isopleths and (b) DISC isopleths in wind on the sunny and shady sides of a shelter wall. Clothing, 2.4 clo; activity, 1.0 met (= 58 W m^{-2}); $t_a = -5.0°C$; t_o (in sun) = +5.0 °C, t_o (in shade) = t_a.

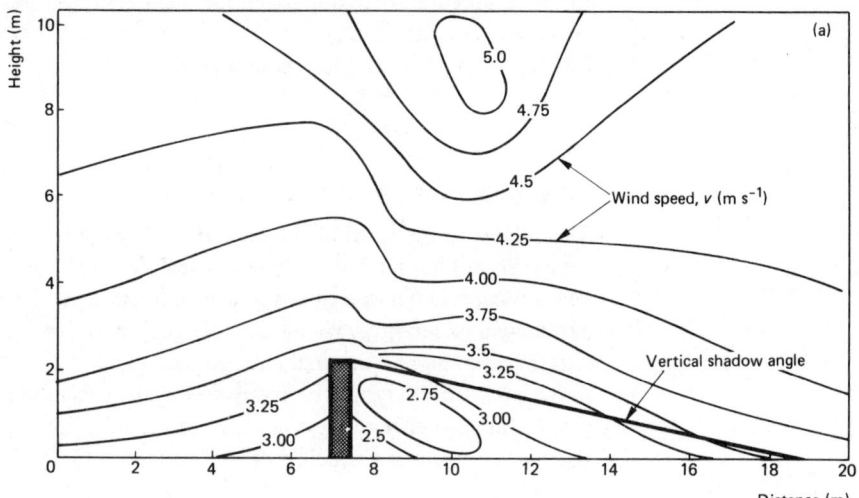

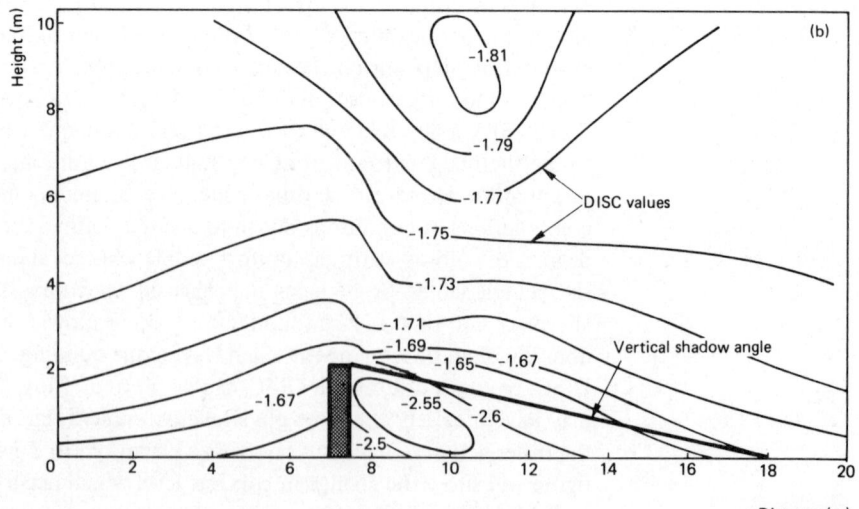

Fig. 3.7 DISC values based on meteorological conditions and SET values in Fig. 4.11. Clothing 0.6 clo; activity, 1 met. N.B. DISC lines do not follow exactly the shapes of SET lines in Fig. 4.11, as wind velocity, v, varies.

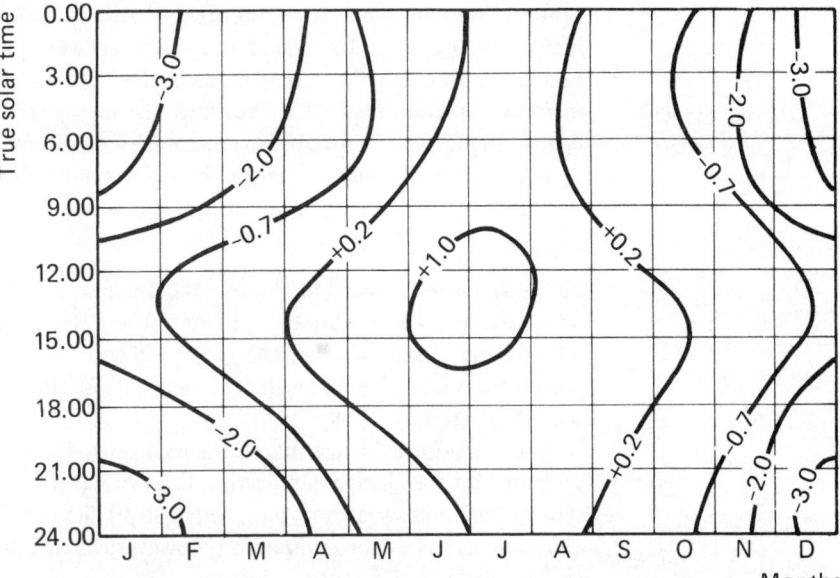

person dressed at an assumed level and carrying out an assumed activity. Changes in clothing, between day and night or summer and winter, would be reflected in the DISC values; so if the intention is to present a picture of the natural micro-climate it is better to hold these two variables constant.

3.4.5 Special Factors

The general comfort equation, the thermal indices, and the psychrometric charts for prediction, all deal with a model which assumes certain basic physiological processes. Whilst such a model, and techniques based upon it, go a long way towards explaining people's responses, there are a number of special circumstances and factors which will now be considered.

3.4.5.1 Humidity

The psychrometric charts show that, at high temperatures, evaporation becomes increasingly important and, naturally, the humidity of the atmosphere, as this will determine the ease of evaporation. They also show that, other things being equal, under these conditions, air velocity plays an increasingly important role, in increasing the rate of evaporation. This will be seen, for instance, by comparing operative temperature charts 16 and 19 for velocities of 0.1 and 5.0 m s^{-1}, showing that, under the latter condition, the SET is substantially lower for the same combinations of t_o and vapour pressure.

Air velocity has little effect on evaporation at low humidities, where it takes place readily in any case, although it is, of course, of great importance in hot, dry conditions in affecting the convection transfer. At very high ones, again its effect is limited (but important) due to the atmosphere's inability to absorb moisture readily. Therefore, it is in the medium/high conditions, typical of the humid tropics, that air velocity is of the greatest importance.

It has often been said that extreme conditions of humidity, low or high, should be avoided. There is no evidence, from the thermal comfort point of view itself, that this is the case — and it will be seen that, on the charts, the neutral or optimal line runs from 20 to 100 per cent RH. Extreme conditions can, however, lead to other undesirable side effects – such as 'wettedness' sensation at high humidities, and dehydration of mucous membranes at low ones. A recent experiment by Andersen *et al.* [15] indicates that relative humidities as low as 9 per cent were judged comfortable over long periods of time.

In any case, it is quite clear that in warm, humid climates, especially for active situations, the importance of air movement is very great.

3.4.5.2 Transients

So far the heat balance and comfort factors have been considered for people under steady-state conditions. However, where there are thermal transients – due either to the conditions themselves varying with time, or the movement of a person from one place to another – then the sensations and comfort judgment will be different.

There is some evidence that in the change from a neutral to a cold or warm environment the change in sensation follows approximately the change in skin temperature and sweat rate, and, hence, is predictable from the comfort equation. In the opposite direction, however, when a cold or warm environment changes towards the neutral, the sensation seems faster – that is, comfort appears to be felt before the necessary physiological changes have been fully established. Gagge *et al.* [16] explain this as being due to the *rate* of change which is sensed rather than the physiological state itself, and this anticipatory 'assessment' by the body leads to a smoothing out of reactions in response to changing environment by utilizing a hysteresis delay.

Other work, by McIntyre and Griffiths for instance [17], indicates another effect; when subjects in an initial cold or warm discomfort condition are asked to adjust the environment to achieve comfort, the adjustments overshoot the neutral conditions, but the cycles decrease in amplitude and gradually a stable near-neutral adjustment is made.

There is some work to suggest that since there is an important relationship between the thermal environment and levels of arousal, and since arousal is related to performance of certain (mainly mental) tasks, variations in conditions which maintain arousal and avoid fatigue and monotony could affect performance. This aspect is discussed further under Section 3.5 but it is worth noting here that changes in any aspect of the environment, including the thermal, might be beneficial in the narrow, or specifically measurable, sense of performance. Moreover, in the broader sense of stimulation and interest there is a generally held view that some variation is beneficial. Certainly, in most practical circumstances, it is in any case inevitable, due simply to moving around in space, or between indoor and outdoor environments, or the continuously changing conditions out-of-doors. But, as Fanger points out [7], since even at a given, fixed condition, it is impossible to meet the optimum judgment of 100 per cent of the members of a group, under conditions which change outside certain limits, the PMV, or group assessment, is bound to express greater dissatisfaction.

Wyon *et al.* [18] suggest that even though large swings appear to have a stimulative effect compared to small ones, neither are preferable to steady, optimal conditions.

So, the critical question to be answered is 'What is known about acceptable variation and its limits?' Variation can be described by two parameters – its size and time features, or, more technically, amplitude and frequency. Sprague and McNall [19] studied variations in t_a and t_{mrt}, effectively in t_o, and found that acceptable variations could be defined by

$$[\; \tilde{t}_a^2 \times (c.p.h.) \;] < 4.6°C\, h^{-1},$$

where $\tilde{t}_a$ = peak-to-peak amplitude of air temperature (in degrees Centigrade) and c.p.h. = frequency in cycles per hour.

The concept of 'freshness' is related to the question of transients. This appears to be a desirable assessment more or less at the opposite end of the scale to 'stuffiness'; it seems to be unrelated to sensation of warmth or cold but more associated with transients, air movement and perhaps humidity. Vernon and Manley [20] reported that with the same mean air velocity and temperature, an increase of 14 per cent in the amplitude of air movement variation raised the 'freshness' judgments by one unit on the appropriate subjective scale.

Wyon *et al.* [21] have carried out experiments in which subjects were free to adjust the amplitude and frequency of temperature swings within velocities of 0 to 1.0 m s^{-1} and amplitudes of 0 to 8 °C. It was found that the swings they accepted were much greater than those that are implicit in many current regulations, such as those of ASHRAE. For fast frequencies, greater amplitudes were acceptable than for slow ones; and for resting, smaller amplitudes than for working conditions at the same frequencies. Figure 3.8 shows the results (circles). It would seem that unwanted stimuli are more easily tolerated when attention is not concentrated upon them and this raises, of course, the classical problem of 'over-sensitivity' to environmental effects when people are concentrating their attention on these in laboratory studies.

Figure 3.8 also shows (crosses) the frequencies selected by subjects carrying

Fig. 3.8 The amplitude and frequency of acceptable temperature swings (after Wyon *et al.* [21]).

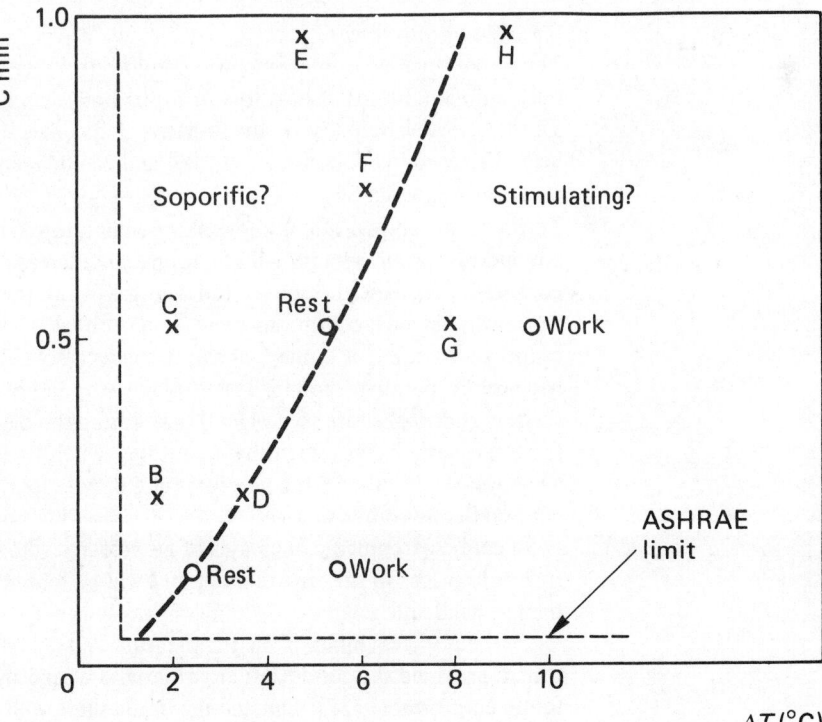

out an arithmetical task at four amplitudes. Points D, G and H show a significantly higher performance than the other five; and all this leads Wyon to suggest a boundary condition as shown on the figure by the dotted line. To the left of this, variations were imperceptible and produced a soporific environment; to the right, they were noticeable and produced a stimulating environment, described by the subjects as 'fresher'. On the same figure the ASHRAE limits on amplitude and frequency are also shown and are seen to be not only too tight, but also to exclude many perfectly satisfactory combinations.

So, the findings all indicate that both for comfort and for performance (dealt with later) some limited variation is acceptable and even desirable. In real buildings, and out of doors, as has been shown, there is continuous variation in space and time. This is not only caused by climatic changes and by built form, but also by activity, posture and adjustments to clothing. These are a part of normal experience and in fact contribute to the infinitely varied experiences which result from the complexity of all environments. They may correspond to a genuine desire for complexity in the human mind and feelings. Cities, buildings, clothes and engineering systems serve to eliminate certain extreme combinations of conditions but, in general, by so doing, also reduce the range of variation experienced *between* the eliminated extremes. Thus, putting on an overcoat not only avoids excessive chilling on going out into the winter weather, but also reduces the apparent differences between those conditions which, without the overcoat might have been not only within the tolerable but even within the comfortable range. Thus, environmental controls will cause a tendency towards greater uniformity as well as the (desirable) avoidance of extremes – the former a danger of which many designers have not become aware. The control of natural variation in space and time – by intermediate zones and thermal mass, for instance – may be more important than its total elimination, often at great cost.

3.4.5.3 Air movement

The importance of air movement in conditions where evaporative cooling is the only, or main, means of heat loss from the body has already been pointed out. The effect of air velocity on the radiative and convective heat loss has already been discussed in Sections 3.3 and 3.4 and can be seen in the thermal comfort charts in Appendix 3B.

Where air temperature is above skin temperature – say about 34 °C – then any increase in air velocity will, of course, by increasing the convection coefficient, increase the convection heat gain from the environment. It can be shown that in such conditions there is an optimal air velocity – below this evaporative cooling is limited, above it convective heat gain more than counterbalances evaporative cooling. This explains why in hot, desert conditions, both shelters and clothes are so designed that during the day they protect the body from excessive air movement by enclosures which fit loosely, thus allowing local air movement in 'shade' temperatures and easy evaporation, and which have a white reflective outer surface.

In cold environments, increases of air velocity will, conversely, increase the rate of heat loss to the environment and will be sensed first as cold draughts and then as windchill.

Figure 3.9 gives limits of air temperature and air velocity combinations which, provided the conditions are otherwise within the comfort zone, will be found comfortable [22]. Outside the limits there will be complaints of draughts.

Fig. 3.9 Limits in air movement (after IHVE).

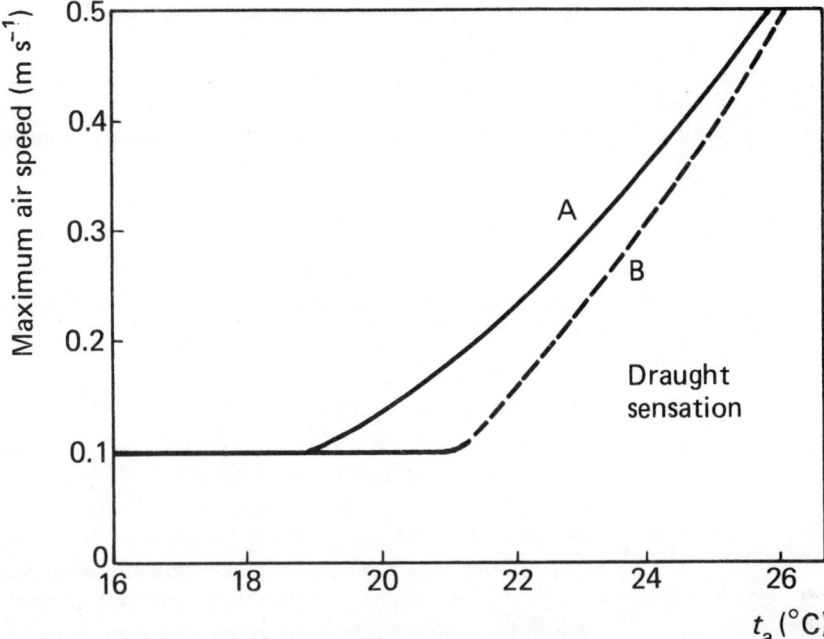

Two lines are given: A for normal conditions, B for those when the particularly sensitive back of the neck is exposed to the direction of the air flow. Other sensitive areas for chilling are the forehead and ankles; on the former, air movement is often sensed as a welcome cooling effect, on the latter as a draught.

Where little or no clothing is worn, and even more so where the body is wet, as in baths, showers and swimming pools, the limits are much tighter, and air movement should not exceed 0.1 m s^{-1} (natural convection speeds) for normal temperatures. Conversely, under active athletic, or leisure conditions (e.g. dancing) much higher speeds are permissible; the comfort charts indicate this.

Gagge *et al* [8] have shown how SET can be used as a windchill index.

For more severe outdoor conditions, the SET may not fully reflect the cold

Fig. 3.10 (a) Comfort conditions for strolling in full sun. (b) Comfort conditions for strolling in the shade (after Penwarden [24]).

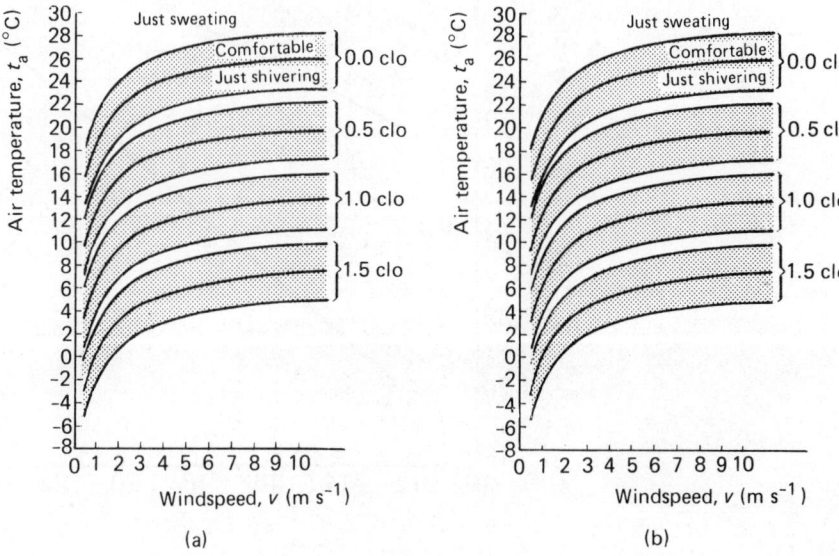

discomfort taking place. A frequently used index is Siple and Passel's windchill index, H_W [23] obtained from

$$H_W = (33 - t_a)(12.1 + 11.6v^{0.5} - 1.16v) \text{ W m}^{-2}, \qquad (3.13)$$

where H_W = heat loss from body per unit area, t_a = air temperature and v = wind velocity. The relationship was obtained from sub-freezing Arctic conditions, ranging from $-9\,°C$ to $-56\,°C$ and with windspeeds from 0 to 12 m s^{-1}. Its use for more moderate conditions is of doubtful value. Penwarden [24] has discussed methods of relating discomfort to windspeed in the sun or shade, and to activity and clothing. Figure 3.10 (a) and (b) shows his results for one activity – strolling ($M = 100$ W m^{-2}).

3.4.5.4 Asymmetry

The discussion of comfort has, up to now, assumed that the body is uniformly and symmetrically heated and cooled. Of course, in practice, this can never be the case. Clothing itself causes differential effects over various parts; furniture, such as an upholstered chair, increases this further. The skin temperatures of various parts of the body are not uniform, as will be seen from Fig. 3.11; the shape of the body itself results in differential convective and radiation coefficients. On top of all this, the external environment is usually non-uniform – due to the presence of radiant sources, local winds and perhaps warm or cold contact surfaces (such as floors).

With regard to unilateral radiation there is no general agreement on limits. On

Fig. 3.11 Average skin temperature in relation to air temperature (after Croome-Gale and Roberts [25] and Bedford [26]).

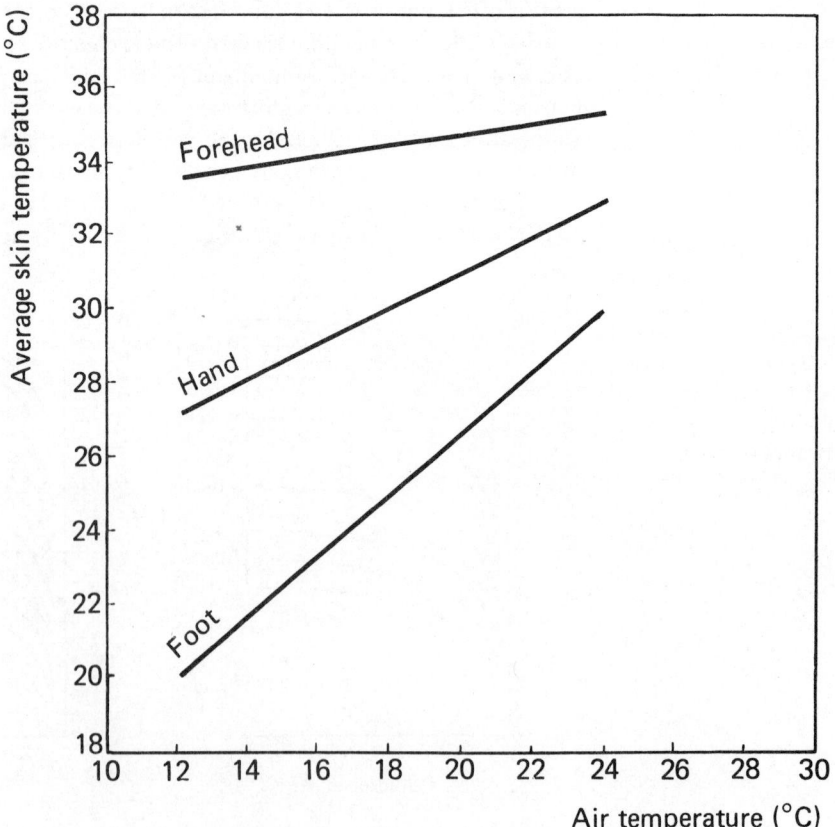

the one hand it is common experience that even near-nude persons can be comfortable when sunbathing in relatively low air temperatures, receiving radiation only on one side of the body. Similar experiences when sitting in front of a radiant fire occur. Moreover Gagge *et al.* [27] have shown similarly acceptable conditions for even nude persons in air temperatures as low as 10 °C when they could adjust the intensity of local radiant heaters. For a comfortable value of t_o of, say, 28°C, they found that $t_{mrt} - t_a < 13$°C gave acceptable conditions. Whilst, on the one hand, Chrenko [28], as the result of experimental work on radiant ceiling panels, recommends a maximum increase of 2 °C in the radiation temperature on the head over the mean radiant temperature; on the other hand, in an extensive series of tests by McNall *et al.* [29] substantial asymmetries caused no discomfort, and Olesen *et al.* [30] have put forward limits to asymmetrical radiation for still air conditions.

McIntyre and Griffiths [31] also indicate higher tolerances than those given by Chrenko. They also show that the body does not fully integrate asymmetrical thermal sensations and that the warming effect of directional radiant sources is less than would be predicted on a physical basis (e.g. by measurement with a globe thermometer).

Local air movement effects can cause draught complaints, as discussed in Section 3.4.5.2. People who already feel cold are likely to complain of draughts if the coldness of the environment is in part due to velocity effects. In a group, some people will always complain of draughts on the cooler side of neutral conditions since normal room velocities vary from 0 to 0.3 m s^{-1}. This question also relates to clothing, for people with sensitive areas such as ankles exposed will suffer first; hence, normal clothing is more likely to cause draught complaints by women than for men in Western style clothes.

Floor temperatures are also an important aspect of asymmetry. The warmth or coldness of floors which will cause discomfort when wearing footwear depends on the insulating properties of the footwear; Nevins *et al.* [32] indicate that upper and lower comfort limits may be 29 °C and 17 °C; European work, by Chrenko, for instance [33], indicates rather narrower limits. Work is currently proceeding at the Technical University of Denmark which may lead to more rational design criteria. For bare feet the picture is more certain; here the sensation of comfort, or pain, will depend on the contact coefficient C_c which is a function of three properties of the flooring material – its conductivity, density and specific heat. It is defined as

$$C_c = k \rho c, \tag{3.14}$$

where k = conductivity, ρ = density, and c = specific heat. The lower the contact coefficient the greater the range of comfortable surface temperatures; thus, for cork it is about 5 to 42 °C, whilst for concrete it is only 29 to 32 °C. Table 3.4, based on rough calculations by Fanger [7], gives a few comfort and pain ranges for six common flooring materials.

3.4.5.5 Sleep
An area which has received little attention is that of comfort conditions for sleep. It would be specially important if it could be shown, as is almost certainly the case, that there is a relationship between depth of sleep and thermal comfort.

Another related question is whether, due to the circadian rhythm, day/night variations in comfort requirements exist. Fanger *et al.* have found no significant effect.

Table 3.4   *Temperature limits for different flooring materials, bare feet (after Fanger [7])*

Flooring material (without surface finishing)	Contact coefficient, C_c	Comfort range of floor temperature (°C)	Pain limits	
			Lower (°C)	Upper (°C)
Steel	209	29–32	14	45
Concrete	29	27–34	4	54
Linoleum, rubber	10.5	24–35	−12	67
Oak wood	8.0	22–35	−20	74
Pine wood	4.7	17–39	−53	84
Cork	2.3	5–42	−140	150

Using an appropriate metabolic rate, say of about 42 W m^{-2}, the thermal comfort charts in Appendix 3B give reasonable guidance if the insulation value of the bedding and night attire combined are known. For instance, for an SET of 24 °C a clo value for the bedding of about 1.7 is required. It appears that adjustments to the heat loss at night are continuously made by controlling the surface area of skin which is exposed – by uncovering greater or lesser areas of skin on face, neck, shoulders, arms, wrists and hands. Under tropical conditions of high temperatures and high humidity, air movement and cold radiating surfaces are essential for comfort and both, of course, require more or less exposed skin surfaces for maximum efficiency. Out of doors under tropical conditions, long-wave radiation loss to clear, night skies can be of significant benefit where temperatures are high and even more so when this is combined with high humidity; but under the latter conditions the sky conditions are usually sufficiently turbid and dense for the apparent temperature to be higher than under desert conditions and, hence, less effective for radiative cooling.

3.4.5.6 Age, sex, ethnic grouping and body build
Fanger [7] has discussed these effects in detail and shown that there is little evidence that they have a significant effect once differences in clothing and activity level have been adequately accounted for.

3.4.5.7 Other environmental factors
One of the most widely held beliefs is that the colour of a space enclosure influences people's thermal comfort responses. Investigations going back to 1961 (Berry [34]), and including recent studies by Fanger *et al.* [35], indicate effects which are so slight as to be negligible. Similar relationships with noise (<85 dBA) have been investigated and shown to be insignificant. Interactions with regard to *performance*, due to arousal and 'sensory overload' do, of course, occur, and are briefly referred to in Section 3.5.

3.4.5.8 Calculations and laboratory studies compared with field studies
One of the most interesting results of thermal studies is that whilst laboratory work carried out in different centres and over a long period of time shows reasonable agreement, field studies show a much greater variation. Humphreys [14], in an important recent paper, has re-analysed the results of over 30 field studies carried out since 1935 and covering over 200 000 individual observations. In all these, some physical measures were recorded, most commonly air

temperature, together with some subjective assessment of comfort sensation. The analysis of these results, in terms of air temperature as the environmental variable, indicates that people's judgments of neutral, or optimal, temperature tends to shift in the same direction as their general thermal experience. 'Thermal experience' is interpreted as the mean temperature of the environment during the observations; but it could be computed from data which takes a weighted mean of the outdoor, domestic and work temperatures. This is shown in Fig. 3.12, where the mean values of the neutral air or globe temperatures are plotted against the mean air or globe temperatures in the place where the study was carried out during the period of observations.

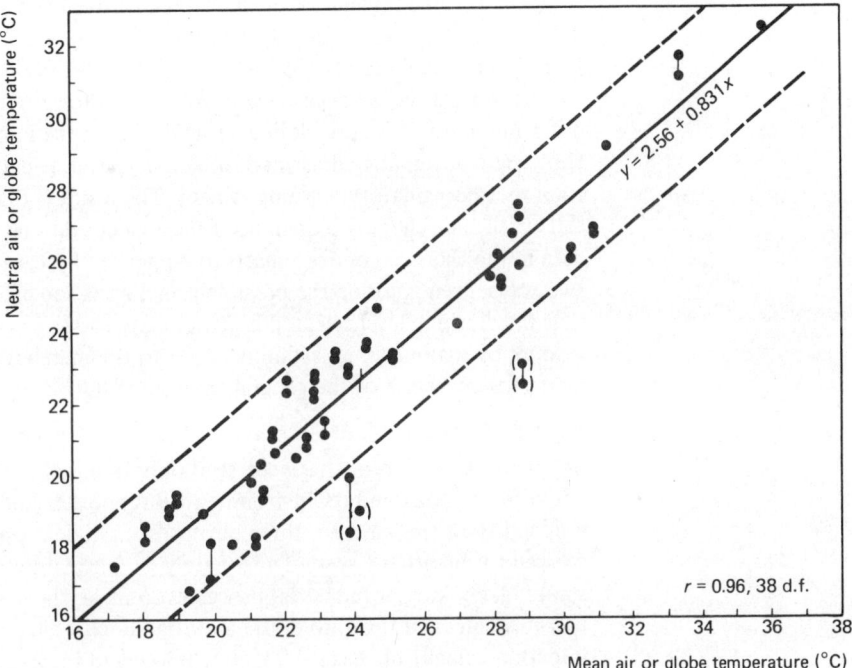

Fig. 3.12 Scatter diagram of mean temperature and neutral temperature (after Humphreys [14]).

The upward 'drift' is quite striking, as the neutral temperatures range from 17 to 33 °C. The upper figure becomes, effectively, 30 °C if an appropriate air velocity correction is made. Part of this difference can be accounted for by known differences in clothing – but this still leaves a range of 6 °C to explain. A variable which is not recorded in the studies is the metabolic rate. It is possible that in warmer climates the actual energy expenditure for carrying out specific activities, such as walking, typing, or merely sitting, are lower and, hence, correspond to lower metabolic rates than in cooler climates. This would correspond with the experience of those who have lived in such climates, where it seems that people move in a slower, more relaxed way with less associated muscular tension. This slowing down in pace is one way of adapting to tropical climates. At the lower metabolic rate the heat to be lost is diminished and, hence, a higher neutral temperature will be chosen.

A third effect may be an acclimatization one. Edholm [36], Bedford [37] and others have described detailed experiments and acclimatization programmes which show that repeated exposure to gradually increasing thermal stress can achieve what, in fact, people achieve naturally in any case over a longer time span – a long-term adaptation to the change in their environment. The process appears to be associated mainly with increased ability to regulate by sweating, under warm conditions. Although such acclimatization enables a person to endure extremes better (that is, with less danger of heat stress or death, or less extreme discomfort) Fanger [7] suggests that the neutral or optimal temperature remains remarkably static. Moreover, he has shown with Olesen [38] that downward acclimatization, to cold environments, which does not involve the retraining of the sweat mechanism, occurs only to the extent of a shift of about 1 °C, too small to be of practical significance.

There is some evidence that for resting people little seasonal acclimatization in thermal sensation judgments occur; but for those at higher levels of activity there is a noticeable shift [39].

The exact effect of acclimatization on the choice of neutral temperature is not known; but it is possible that, together with the known effects of clothing choice and automatic adjustment of activity level, it plays a small role in the total thermoregulatory learning system. The result is that comfort requirements shift with the generally experienced thermal conditions which means that the data in the thermal comfort charts in Appendix 3B can now be interpreted in two ways, even ignoring the possible acclimatization effect. First, by making sure that the clothing level selected is appropriate to the known conditions; and second, by making a modest adjustment to the metabolic rate assumed in the light of the warmth of the general environment.

3.4.5.9 Fresh air

So far, thermal comfort has been seen only in terms of the heat exchange between the body and its environment. But another important factor is the availability of fresh air, for three purposes: first, to supply an adequate level of oxygen for breathing; second adequately to dilute odours arising from bodies, smoking, cooking or industrial processes to make them acceptable or unnoticeable; and third, to dilute air vitiated with bacteria sufficiently to make infection a negligible hazard. Much window and louvre design, ventilation and air conditioning and fan design is aimed at achieving these objectives without

Table 3.5 *Minimum ventilation rates where density of occupation is known (after IHVE)*

Air space per person (m^3)	Fresh air supply per person (l s^{-1})		
		Recommended minima	
	Minimum	Smoking not permitted	Smoking permitted
3	11.3	17.0	22.6
6	7.1	10.7	14.2
9	5.2	7.8	10.4
12	4.0	6.0	8.0

The statutory minimum volume per person in factories and offices is 11.5 m³. The corresponding minimum fresh air supply is 4.72 l s⁻¹ per person.

causing draughts and with as little loss of heat in the process of air change as possible.

Recommendations for minimum fresh air requirements are normally set out in terms of volumes per unit time, say litres per second, according to the volume of the space per person and to the nature of the contamination (e.g. smoking). Table 3.5 is reproduced from the *IHVE Guide* and is typical of such recommendations. Other air-conditioning guides give approximately similar guidance – but the estimation of exact requirements requires the advice of an air-conditioning consultant. Clearly the level that is chosen will have several significant effects:

(i) It will cause heat loss or heat gain, according to the direction and magnitude of the inside/outside temperature difference.

(ii) It will require inlets and outlets, and proper mixing in the occupied spaces, without causing excessive movement giving rise to draughts, disturbance of papers and other unwanted local effects. Where high velocity, small area inlets or outlets are involved, there are also acoustic problems to be avoided.

The achievement of the required natural ventilation rate is a question of careful design of openings, adjustable for a variety of wind and temperature conditions, so that the two basic processes of air exchange can be used:

(i) Pressure differentials due to wind.

(ii) Stack effects, due to the lower density of warm air, causing it to rise and hence encouraging the entry of low-level, cooler air.

Both effects are described in further detail in Chapter 8.

3.4.5.10 Comfort and behaviour

We have indicated that our knowledge of thermal comfort can be based on three types of data: physiological, semantic and behavioural. It has been shown that the physiological approach, in which the optimum condition is equated with the minimum load on the body's thermoregulatory system, gives results which closely correspond to laboratory studies in which semantic scales for comfort are used.

Another source of data is non-verbal behaviour. Careful observation of this, especially in the field, may lead to knowledge on areas where the analytic approach has not given sufficient guidance. The factors which would be observed are the actual adjustments to personal behaviour which takes place in occupied space. We have already seen that adjustments to clothing and muscular effort are processes which take place consistently in response to changes in the environment. Other data of interest are the degree and type of adjustments which people make to thermal controls – radiator valves, thermostats, opening and shutting windows, use of blinds and curtains and moving of personal work-place (for instance, out of the sun). Wyon [40] and Humphreys [41] have studied changes in schoolchildren's clothing under various conditions. Pallot [42] has shown the changes in the percentage of open windows on a London office block with weather conditions.

This is, however, a field where designers and users of buildings, by systematic observation, measurement and recording of data could add a unique dimension to thermal comfort research. The 'field laboratory' is in fact the whole built environment and within it a wealth of information remains to be uncovered.

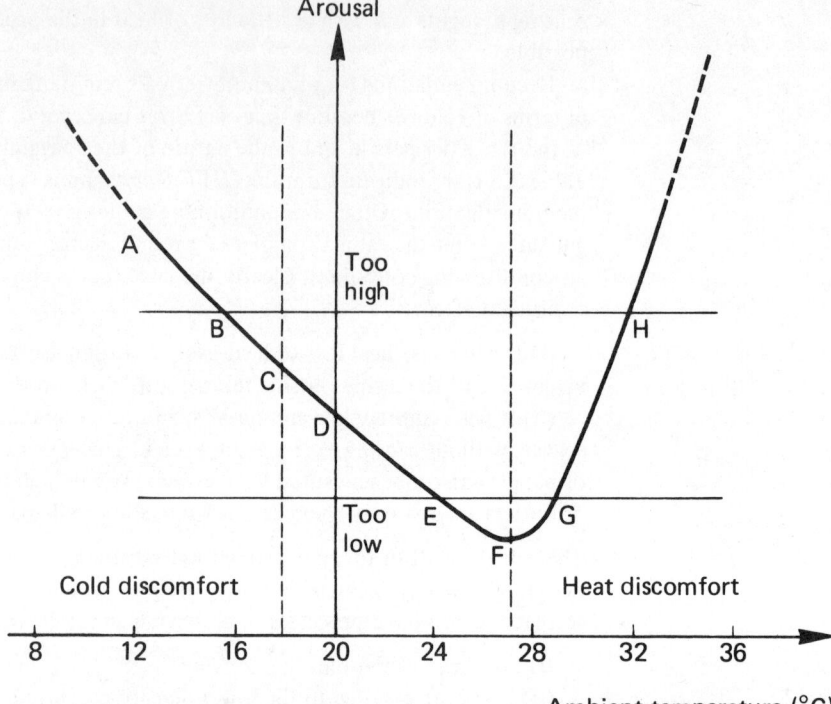

Fig. 3.13 Temperature and arousal (after Wyon [2]).

3.5 Performance

It was mentioned in Section 3.1.3 that criteria for optimal performance and optimal comfort were not necessarily coincident.

Wyon [2] puts forward the following general relationship, graphically explained in Fig. 3.13. He maintains that the most important intervening variable between thermal environment as measured, say, by ambient temperature, and task performance, is the level of arousal. The underlying theory is that for every activity there is an appropriate level of arousal – a specific psychological term, for whose measurement there are some physiological tools – and that levels above or below this tend to depress performance. Thus activities requiring high concentration and vigilance probably require higher arousal levels to be maintained than those involving memory or creative ability, unless the activity provides its own arousal. The relationships expressed in Fig. 3.13 indicates that the optimum level of arousal for an activity, half way between too high and too low, may occur at about 20 °C. Moderate rises in warmth, but still within the comfort zone, cause a drop in arousal; at about the upper limit of comfort (say DISC = +1) arousal levels suddenly rise again, but at the cost of considerable warm discomfort, and the levels are probably rather unstable. Similarly, within the cold limit of comfort, arousal increases as the temperature drops, for a small range; then any increase is accompanied by cold discomfort.

Wyon explains the interactions as follows. Environments which change the level of arousal may have features which distract or cause irritation due to the discomfort they cause. These effects may cause motivation and the will to exert effort to drop, and, hence, performance declines. So it seems that combinations of environmental factors which create appropriate levels of arousal for the task, and allow the right amount of attention and effort, will be judged positively; whilst those which involve the expenditure of extra effort to maintain arousal and attention will be judged negatively. Therefore, perhaps environments of the first type will be judged as having a positive quality rather than merely the neutral property which thermal comfort criteria indicate, and will not be coincident with the neutral point of a thermal-comfort-based scale. As Wyon points out, however, there is too little research to give practical design guidance on performance-based thermal criteria, as this involves not only the six variables so far considered, but personality, age, sex, job motivation and perhaps a host of other factors.

Wyon *et al*. have also shown [43] that two conditions of equal thermal comfort, but achieved with very different combinations of clothing and temperatures (one light clothing, warm environment; the other heavy clothing, cold environment) led to no difference in the performance of a wide range of mental tasks. Thus, whatever the relationship between comfort and performance may be, it is probable that different means of achieving the same comfort state do not result in different performance.

As far as physical work is concerned, it is established that increasing metabolic rate causes the production of greater body heat and a rise in body temperature; this will result either in heat stress or in the need for more frequent rest pauses. More usually, the rate of working is deliberately or unconsciously adjusted to the opposite direction, to involve a lower metabolic rate, and hence a slower performance.

3.6 Health

Apart from comfort and performance, health is the remaining criterion for selection of a thermal environment.

The main factors are survival and, related to it, cold and heat stress; the effect of heat and cold on the morbidity and mortality rate of certain diseases; and the relationship between air conditions and bacterial infection.

As for survival and heat stress, this has been discussed in detail in Section 3.3. What is not generally recognized is that low-temperature exposure can and does often take place indoors as well as out – particularly in the houses of the single, poor and old. Hypothermia is that condition where the body cools a few degrees below the normal; it will thus trigger off a number of illnesses, including pneumonia, bronchitis, heart attacks and other chest complaints. In Great Britain alone it is estimated that between 60 000 and 80 000 more old people die in winter than in summer, and although many of the causes of death are recorded under one of the above disease categories, it is strongly suspected that these are cold-related if not actually cases of hypothermia. Young infants are similarly at risk and, since their body storage is so small, slight drops over quite short periods can be fatal. Again, exact statistics are difficult to come by, but there is plenty of evidence that there is a relationship between infant mortality and deprivation, including housing environment.

The fact that many diseases show seasonal patterns is well known; in the US for instance, many heart and chest ailments reach crises in hot weather spells as well as during extreme cold. Certainly in well heated, or cooled buildings these seasonal fluctuations are reduced – but many buildings follow external conditions closely due to poor design of fabric and services.

Experiments on cross-infection due to airborne viruses and bacteria travelling on droplets or dust are definitive. The movement of infected air to sterile areas is carefully avoided in hospitals – but in other buildings, such as offices, no particular attention is paid to this and there is evidence of considerable cross-infection, especially when common colds, influenza and respiratory infections are widespread in winter.

3.7 Psychological, social and economic factors

Much of what has been described so far is based on laboratory studies, with few, and carefully controlled, variables. An even more important fact is that people in such studies are usually out of 'context' – the social, family, work and economic pressures and inducements normally present in all buildings are absent.

The basic fact is that the thermal environment is one of many characteristics of spaces; and spaces, according to their function and the expectation of a person, have a meaning. Thus, an environment may be physiologically optimal, but have the wrong association or meaning. Research in this area is as yet limited – but already the work of Wools, Canter and others [44] has demonstrated that certain physical features are closely associated with function and people. For instance, a space can be made to look more or less friendly by the presence or absence of a sloping ceiling. Similarly, certain thermal environments are associated, traditionally and functionally, with certain types of spatial experience. For example, the interior of a baroque church in a Mediterranean town, in summer, is expected to feel cool, both to the touch (cold marble) and to the body in general. The sensation is associative and quite specific and different from, say, the sensation in a house or shop.

Similarly, much money is paid for the sensation of a Turkish bath, or a sauna; conditions which, in a laundry, would in most countries contravene the laws governing factory work! The pleasure of climatic extremes on the beach, on a snowfield, climbing mountains, swimming in cold lakes, are all real and much valued – yet many are far outside any physiologically determined comfort zones. They have associations with danger, status (the money to go far afield in search of them) and perhaps cultural factors.

There is evidence of the preference for radiant heating sources, even though room conditions with them are often far below the standard which can be achieved with ducted warm air [45]. So the form of a heating appliance, and the characteristic thermal environment associated with it – for instance small-area high-intensity radiation – may be as important an influence on responses as the physical parameters.

Another factor seems to colour people's sense of satisfaction with the thermal environment. This is their economic freedom. There is evidence that those of limited means not only put up with poorer conditions – say colder – but judge these as less poor than those from a better socioeconomic background would. Thus, when insulation standards are improved, instead of the energy-saving accruing to the occupants, only some savings are made, the rest of the improvement being in achieving higher thermal standards – such as, under previous hardship, were considered unnecessary and unreachable [46]. It is not far-fetched to suggest that even judgment of neutral temperature may be influenced by what one is accustomed to pay for environmental energy and what has become the normal experience. But hard evidence on such influences is at present lacking.

3.8 General design consequences of thermal response characteristics

It now remains to summarize the design consequences of what we know about human response to the thermal environment.

If the definition of design includes two key factors – first, that its product is *for* people; second, that resources are always limited – then the best design is that which divides these resources so as to give the maximum satisfaction to those affected by the design. So people and economy are at the centre of good decisions about the thermal environment. This implies that in the trade-offs which have to be made, response itself, and particularly dissatisfaction, have to be evaluated in a way which makes it possible to set them against investment and benefit. In Chapter 12 we shall be dealing with cost benefit and other techniques which can be used to yield good solutions; but, to use them, the human responses described in this chapter will have to be translated into money or other units commensurate with resource investment. This involves assigning to a measurable amount of dissatisfaction – say the PPD – some value. Study of what people actually pay to achieve comfort, and how much they negotiate in the free market situation for discomfort (e.g. in the union-agreed rates for danger, inconvenience or discomfort) may give guidance on appropriate values.

The main design consequences in terms of town and building form will be developed in later chapters. But a few simple facts emerge immediately.

First, that it should be possible to devise pleasant and comfortable conditions in most climates, by a proper gradation of spaces between the inside and outside, with a graded set of experiences and activities.

Second, that control, both human and automatic, over conditions is a vital part of economy, so that quick response to change is possible.

Third, that as energy to achieve comfort is becoming a major item of public and personal expenditure, careful thought has to be given on the cheapest combinations of the six main variables. One suggestion is that clothing should be more effectively used, indoors and out, for thermal control. Another, that radiant methods of heating (and cooling) may yield substantial economies. Attention to fine detail such as the elimination of draughts, cold floor and window surfaces, and direct radiation on and through windows (in hot climates), and the maintenance of a reasonable balance between air temperature and the warmth of surrounding surface can all produce tangible economic benefits.

Perhaps the most important factor is the scope of human adaptability, in the widest sense. This statement may seem inconsistent with the rather narrow comfort limits described in this chapter, but it is meant to be all-embracing. That is, to emphasize that those narrow comfort limits can be attained in a wide variety of ways – by adjustment of clothing, deliberate and unconscious control over activity; choice of workplace (region, town, location in a building); continuous adjustment to fabric and services controls; using the variability of individual response to allow a self-selection procedure in the choice of environments; allowing 'free trade' in environments, so that anyone having to, or choosing to, put up with less than optimal conditions reaps the benefits in other tangible ways; and by careful integration of the thermal with other aspects of environment so that the benefit of interactions and psychological factors is obtained.

References

1 *The Times*, 6th February 1976, 2.

2 Wyon, D.P., The role of the environment in buildings today: thermal aspects (factors affecting the choice of a suitable room temperature). *Building International*, (6), 39–54, 1973.

3 *American Society of Heating, Refrigeration and Air-Conditioning Engineers, Handbook of Fundamentals.* ASHRAE, New York, 1972. Chapter 7, 143–145 and References gives a good recent review of the relevant literature.

4 Wyon, D. P., *op. cit.*

5   Bedford, T., Researches on thermal comfort. *Ergonomics*, **4**, (4), 280–310, 1961. The references to earlier work in this chapter will be found in Bedford's paper.

6   Vernon, H. M. and Warner, C. G., The influence of the humidity of the air on capacity for work at high temperatures. *Journal of Hygiene*, Cambridge, **32**, 431, 1932.

7   Fanger, P. O., *Thermal Comfort; Analysis and Applications in Environmental Engineering*. McGraw–Hill Book Company, New York, 1973.

8   Gagge, A. P., Nishi, Y. and Gonzalez, R. R. Standard effective temperature – a single index of temperature sensation and thermal discomfort. In *Proceedings of the CIB Commission W45 (Human Requirements) Symposium at the Building Research Station, 13th–15th September, 1972. Building Research Establishment Report 2*. HMSO, London, 1973, 229–250.

9   Nevins, R. G. and McNall, P.E., Jr. ASHRAE thermal comfort standards as performance criteria for buildings. In *BRE Symposium* as in ref. 8, 217–227.

10   Humphreys, M. A., The optimum diameter for a globe thermometer. *Building Research Establishment Note PD 30/75*, 1975; and private communication, Adjustment to globe thermometer temperature to allow for air movement, December 1974.

11   Gagge, A. P. and Nishi, Y., A psychometric chart for graphical prediction of comfort and heat tolerance. *American Society of Heating, Refrigeration and Air-Conditioning Engineers Transactions;* **80**, 115–130, 1974.

12   Chrenko, F. A. (ed.). *Bedford's Basic Principles of Ventilation and Heating*. H. K. Lewis, London, 1974.

13   Rohles, F. H. and Nevins, R. G., The nature of thermal comfort for sedentary man. *American Society of Heating, Refrigeration and Air-Conditioning Engineers Transactions*, 77(1) 239–246, 1971.

14   Humphreys, M. A., Field studies of thermal comfort compared and applied. *Building Research Establishment Current Paper 76/75*; also presented at Symposium on Physiological Requirements of the Microclimate. Prague, 8th–10th September, 1975.

15   Andersen, I., Lundquist, G. R., Jensen, P. L. and Proctor, D. F., Human response to 78 hour exposure to dry air. *Archives of Environmental Health*, **29**, 319–324, 1974.

16   Gagge, A. P., Stolwijk, J. A. J. and Hardy, J.D., Comfort and thermal sensations and associated physiological responses at various ambient temperatures. *Environmental Research*, **1**, 1–20, 1967.

17   McIntyre, D. A., Determination of individual preferred temperatures. *American Society of Heating, Refrigeration and Air-Conditioning Engineers Transactions*, **81**(2), 131–139, 1975.

18   Wyon, D. P., The effects of ambient temperature swings on comfort performance and behaviour. *Archives des Sciences Physiologiques*, **27**(4), 441–458, 1973.

19   Sprague, C. H. and McNall, P. E., The effects of fluctuating temperatures and relative humidity on the thermal sensation (thermal comfort) of sedentary subjects. *American Society of Heating, Refrigeration and Air-Conditioning Engineers Transactions*, **76**(1), 146–156, 1970.

20   Vernon, M. D. and Manley, J. J., The measurement of variations in the

velocity and temperature of air currents. *Special Report Series. Medical Research Council* No. 100, Part 1, 1926 (reference on page 421 of Bedford [12]).

21   Wyon, D. P., Breum, N-O., Olesen, S., Kjerulf-Jensen, P. and Fanger, P.O., Factors affecting the subjective tolerance of ambient temperature swings. In *Proceedings of the 5th International Congress for Heating, Ventilating and Air-Conditioning, Copenhagen, 1971*, Vol. 1, 87–107.

22   *IHVE Guide, Book A*. Institution of Heating and Ventilating Engineers, London, 1970, A1–A6.

23   Siple, P. A. and Passel, C. F., Measurements of dry atmospheric cooling in subfreezing temperatures. *Proceedings of the American Philosophical Society*, **89**, 177, 1945.

24   Penwarden, A. D., Acceptable wind speeds in towns. *Building Science*, **8**, 259–267, 1973.

25   Croome-Gale, D. G. and Robert, B. M., *Air-Conditioning and Ventilation of Buildings*. Pergamon Press, Oxford, 1975.

26   Bedford, T., The warmth factor in comfort at work. *Industrial Health Research Board, London, Report no. 76*, 1936.

27   Gagge, A. P., Hardy, J. D. and Rapp, G. M., Exploratory study of comfort for high temperature sources of radiant heat. *American Society of Heating, Refrigeration and Air-Conditioning Engineers Transactions*, **71**(2), 19–26, 1965; Gagge, A. P., Rapp, G. M. and Hardy, J. D., The effective radiant field and operative temperature necessary for comfort with radiant heating. *Ibid.*, **73**(1), 1, 1967.

28   Chrenko, F. A., Heated ceilings and comfort. *Journal of the Institution of Heating and Ventilating Engineers*, **23**, 385, 1956.

29   Schlegel, J. C. and McNall, P. E., The effect of asymmetric radiation on thermal and comfort sensations of sedentary subjects. *American Society of Heating, Refrigeration and Air-Conditioning Engineers Transactions*, **74**(2), 144–154, 1968. McNall, P. E. and Biddison, R. E., Thermal comfort sensations of sedentary persons exposed to asymmetric radiant fields. *Ibid.*, **76**(1), 123–136, 1970.

30   Olesen, S., Fanger, P. O., Jensen, P. B. and Nielsen, O. J., Comfort limits for man exposed to asymmetric thermal radiation. In *BRE Symposium* as in ref. 8, 133–148.

31   McIntyre, D. A. and Griffiths, I. D., Radiant temperature and comfort. In *CIB symposium on Thermal Comfort and Moderate Heat Stress*. HMSO, London, 1973, 113–132.

32   Nevins, R. G., Michaels, K. B. and Feyerherm, A. M., The effect of floor surface temperatures on comfort: I, College-age males; II, College-age females; and IV, Cold floors. *American Society for Heating, Refrigeration and Air-Conditioning Engineers Transactions*, **70**, 29, 1964; **70**, 37, 1964; **73**(2), III.2.1.–III.2.8, 1967.

33   Chrenko, F. A., Heated floors and comfort. *Journal of the Institution of Heating and Ventilating Engineers*, **23**, 385, 1956.

34   Berry, P. C., Effect of colored illumination upon perceived temperature. *Journal of Applied Psychology*, **45**(4), 248–250, 1961.

35   Fanger, P. O., Breum, N.-O. and Jerking, E., Can colour and noise influence man's thermal comfort? Paper submitted for publication in *Ergonomics*, Technical University of Denmark, November, 1975.

36   Edholm, O. G., *The Biology of Work*. World University Library, London, 1967, Chapter 4.

37   Bedford, T., *Basic Principles of Ventilation and Heating*, H. K. Lewis, London, 1964, Chapter 21.

38   Olesen, S. and Fanger, P. O., Can man be adapted to prefer a lower ambient temperature? In *Proceedings of the 5th International Congress for Heating, Ventilating and Air Conditioning, Copenhagen, 1971*, Vol. 1, 27–40.

39   McIntyre, D. A. and Gonzalez, R. R., Man's thermal sensitivity during temperature changes at two levels of clothing and activity. *American Society for Heating, Refrigeration and Air-Conditioning Engineers Transactions*, 82(2), 219–233, 1976.

40   Wyon, D. P. and Holmberg, I., Systematic observation of classroom behaviour during moderate heat stress. In *BRE Symposium* as in ref. 8, 19–33.

41   Humphreys, M. A., Classroom temperature, clothing and thermal comfort – a study of secondary school children in summertime. *Building Services Engineer*, 41, 191–202, December 1973.

42   Pallot, A. C., Window opening in an office building. In *The Yearbook of the Heating and Ventilating Industry, 1962–63*, 4–22.

43   Wyon, D. P., Fanger, P. O., Olesen, B. W. and Pedersen, C. J. K., The mental performance of subjects clothed for comfort at two different air temperatures. *Ergonomics*, 18(4), 359–374, 1975.

44   Wools, R. and Canter, D., The effect of the meaning buildings on behaviour. *Applied Ergonomics*, 1(3), 144–150, 1970.

45   Lee, K. H. and Markus, T. A., Heating forms and living room usage. *Journal of Architectural Research*, 5(1), 4–13, 1976.

46   Fisk, D. J., Microeconomics and the demand for space heating. *Energy*, 2, (4), 391–405, 1977. Cornish, J. P., The effect of thermal insulation on the energy consumption in houses. *Proceedings of the CIB Symposium on Energy Consumption in the Built Environment, London, 6th–8th April 1976*. Construction Press, Lancaster, 1976. Markus, T. A., Building and services design options. CIBS Symposium, *Man, Environment and Buildings*. Loughborough University, 28th September 1978. (To be published).

APPENDIX 3A: Heat balance and comfort equations

Operative temperature charts

Heat Balance Equation (3.5)

$$(M/A_{DU})(1 - \eta) - 2.6 \times 10^{-3}(256\, t_{sk} - 3370 - P_v)$$
$$- E_{rsw}/A_{DU} - 1.72 \times 10^{-5} \times (M/A_{DU})(5800 - P_v)$$
$$- 0.0014\,(M/A_{DU})(34 - t_a)$$
$$= (t_{sk} - t_{cl})/0.155\, I_{cl}$$
$$= 3.96 \times 10^{-8} f_{cl}\,[(t_{cl} + 273)^4$$
$$- (t_{mrt} + 273)^4] + f_{cl}h_c(t_{cl} - t_a)$$

Comfort Equation (3.8)

$$(M/A_{DU})(1 - \eta) - 2.6 \times 10^{-3}[5770 - 7.16(M/A_{DU})(1 - \eta) - P_v]$$
$$- 0.42[(M/A_{DU})(1 - \eta) - 58] - 1.72 \times 10^{-5}(M/A_{DU})(5800 - P_v)$$
$$- 0.0014(M/A_{DU})(34 - t_a)$$
$$= [35.7 - 0.028(M/A_{DU})(1 - \eta) - t_{cl}]/0.155 I_{cl}$$
$$= 3.96 \times 10^{-8}f_{cl}[(t_{cl} + 273)^4 - (t_{mrt} + 273)^4]$$
$$+ f_{cl} h_c (t_{cl} - t_a)$$

Operative temperature chart 1

After Fanger [7]. All symbols as listed on pp. xii–xvi.

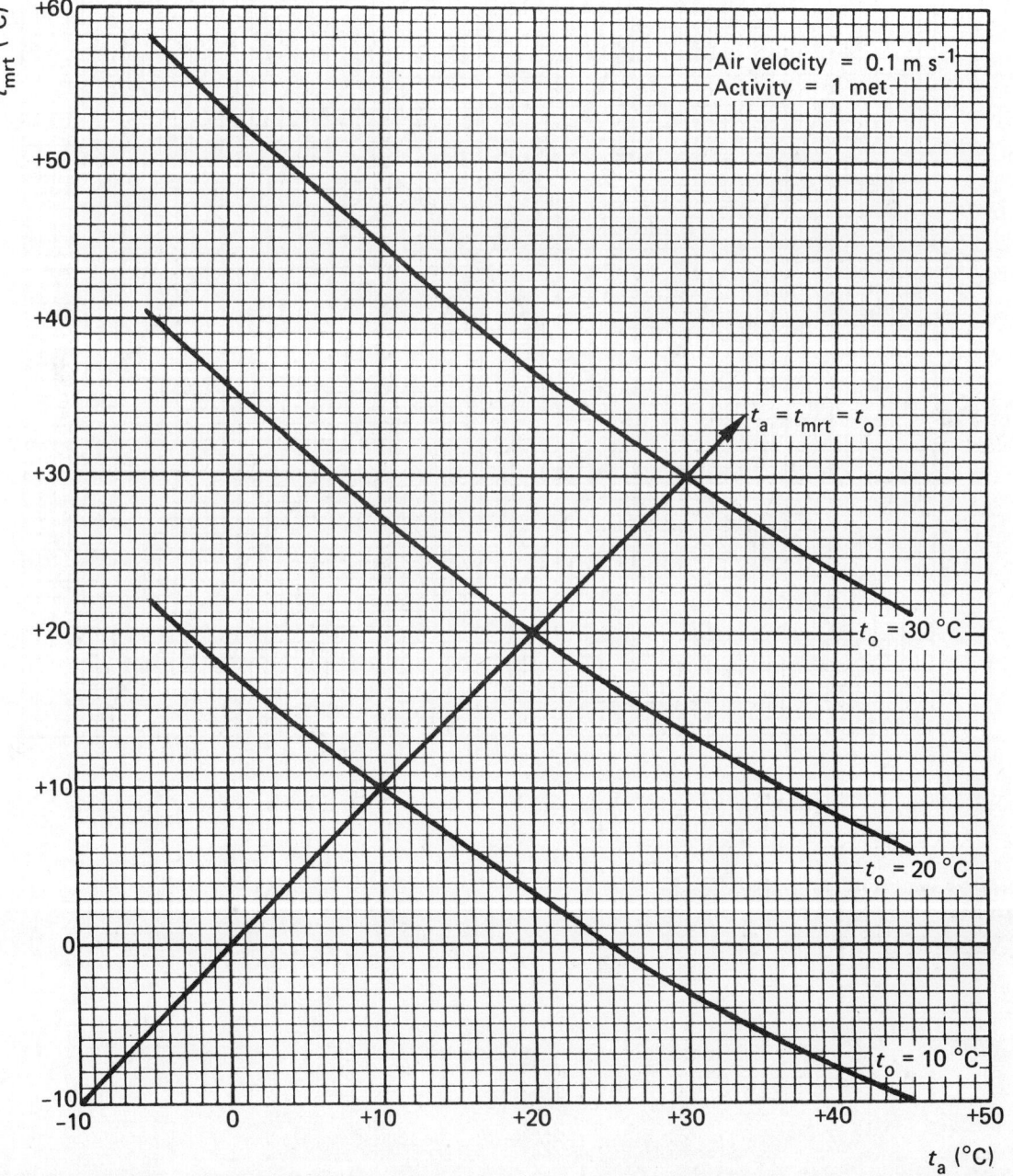

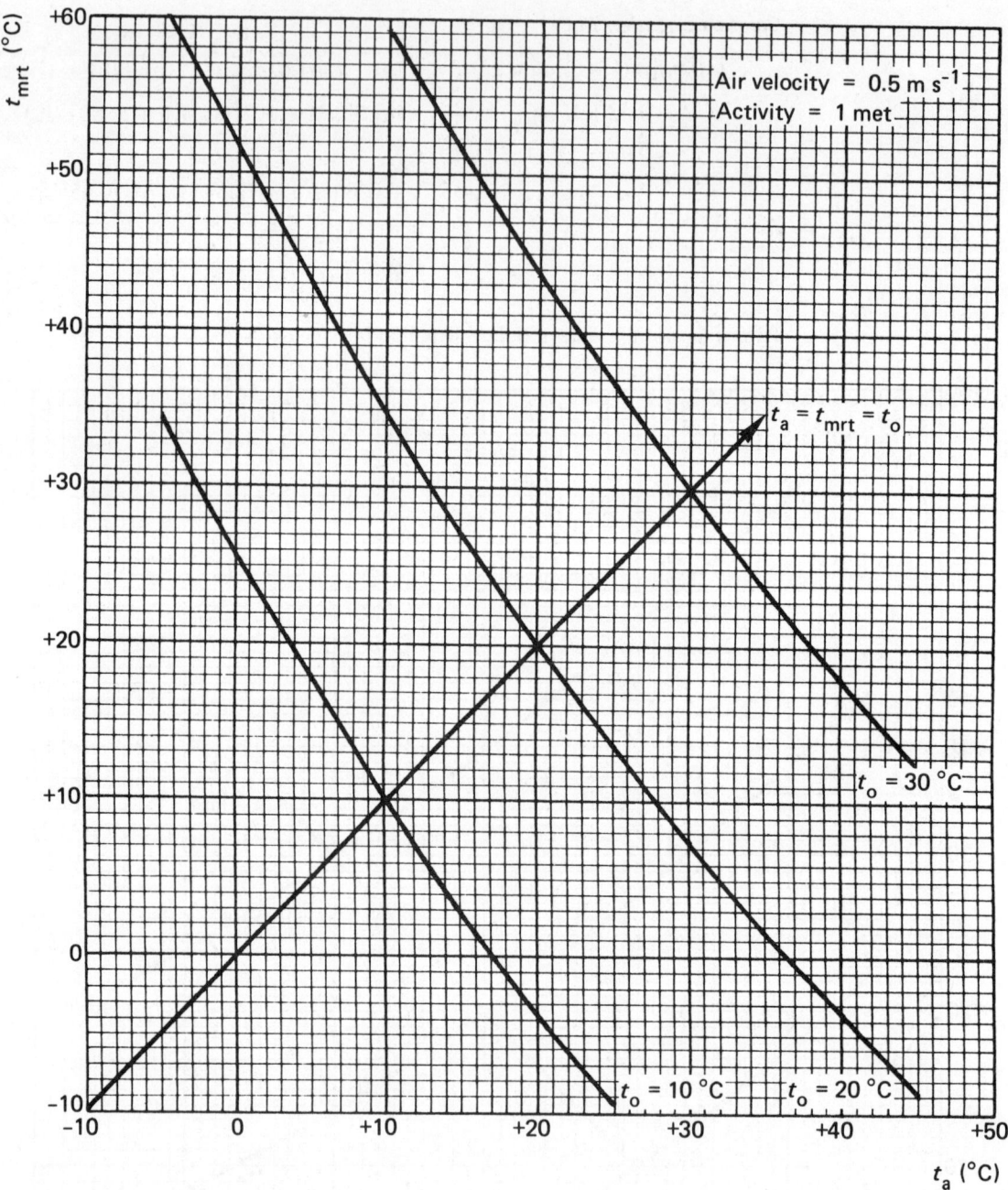

Operative temperature
chart 2

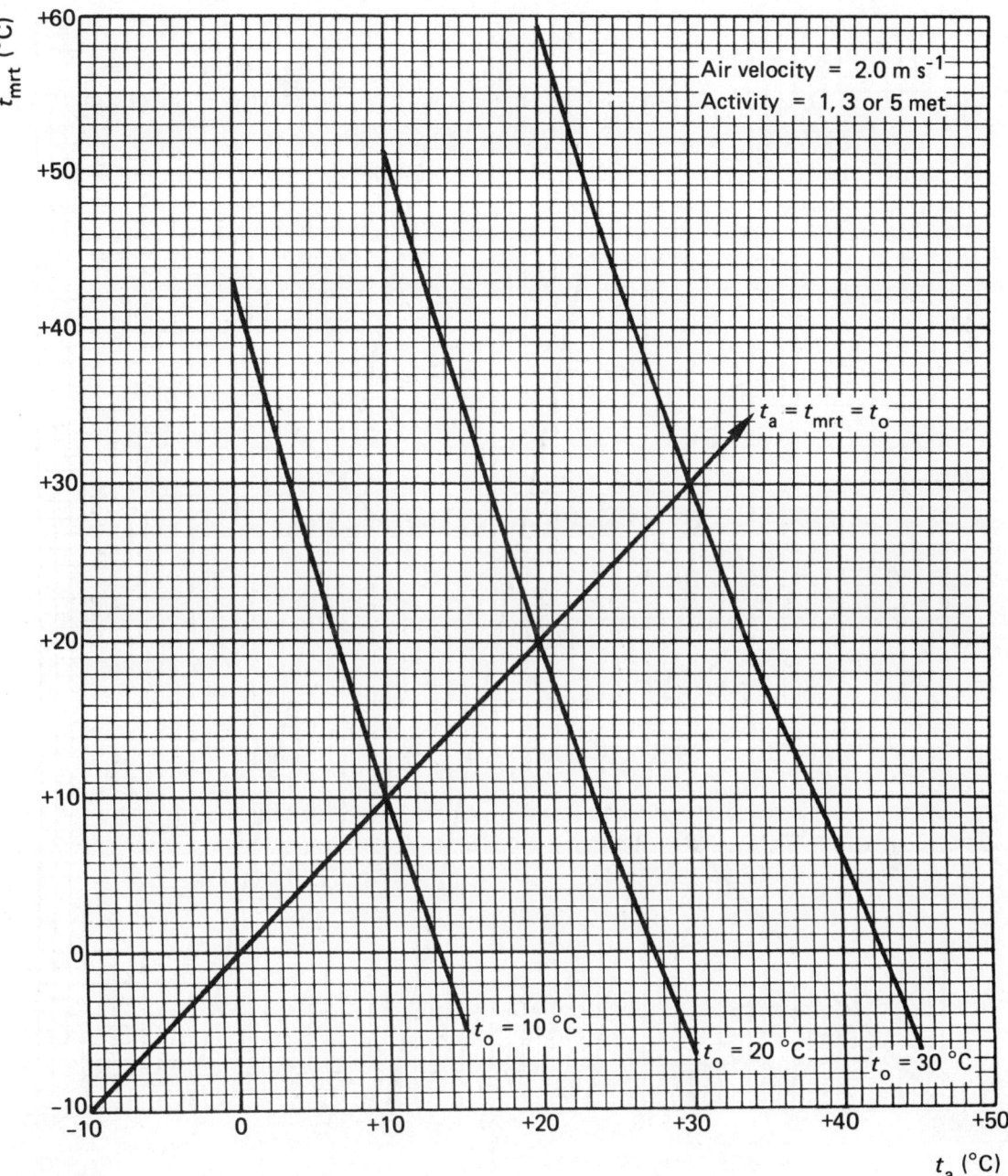

Operative temperature
chart 3

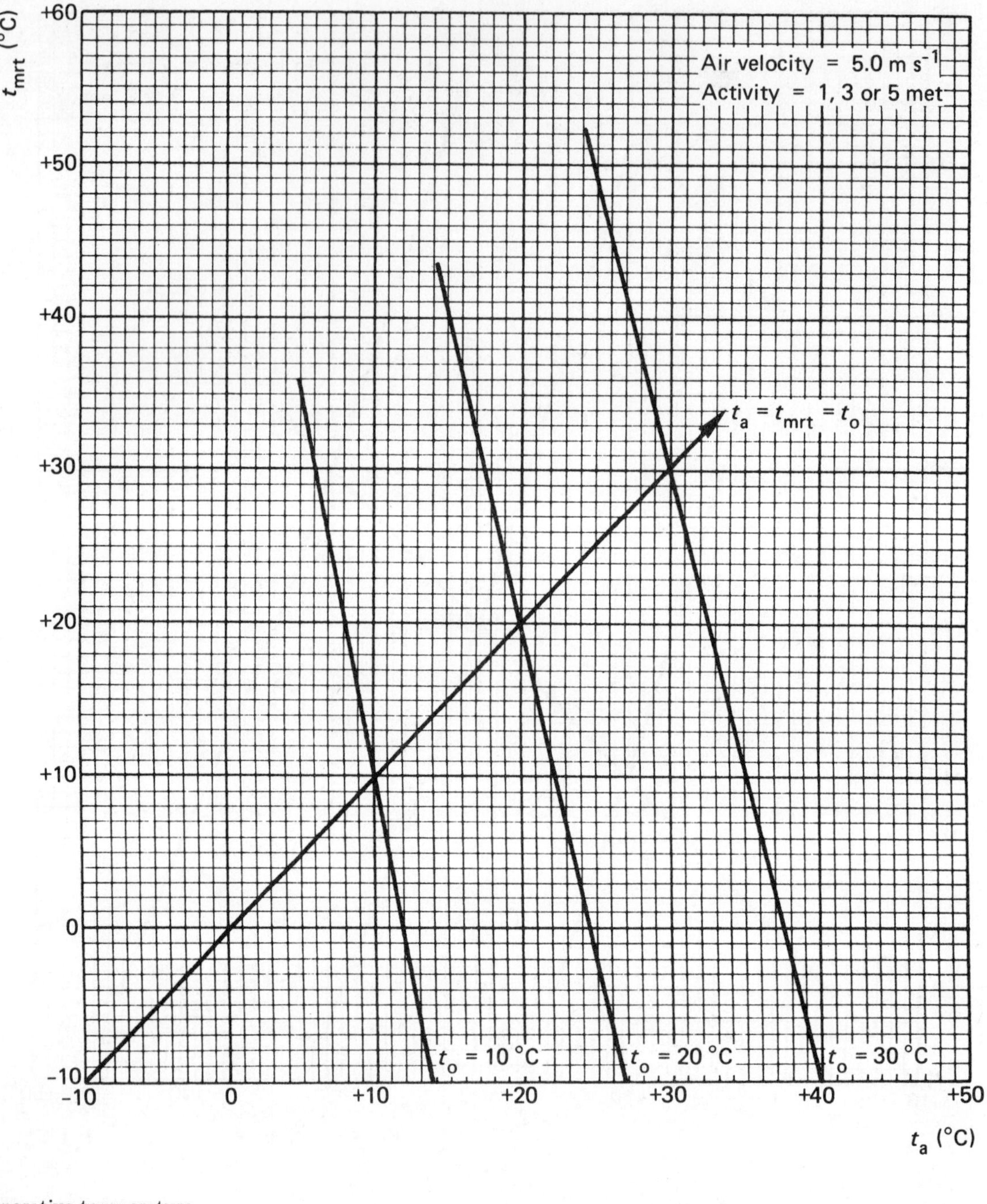
t_{mrt} (°C)
+60
+50
+40
+30
+20
+10
0
-10
Air velocity = 5.0 m s^{-1}
Activity = 1, 3 or 5 met
$t_a = t_{mrt} = t_o$
t_o = 10 °C
t_o = 20 °C
t_o = 30 °C
-10
0
+10
+20
+30
+40
+50
t_a (°C)

Operative temperature
chart 4

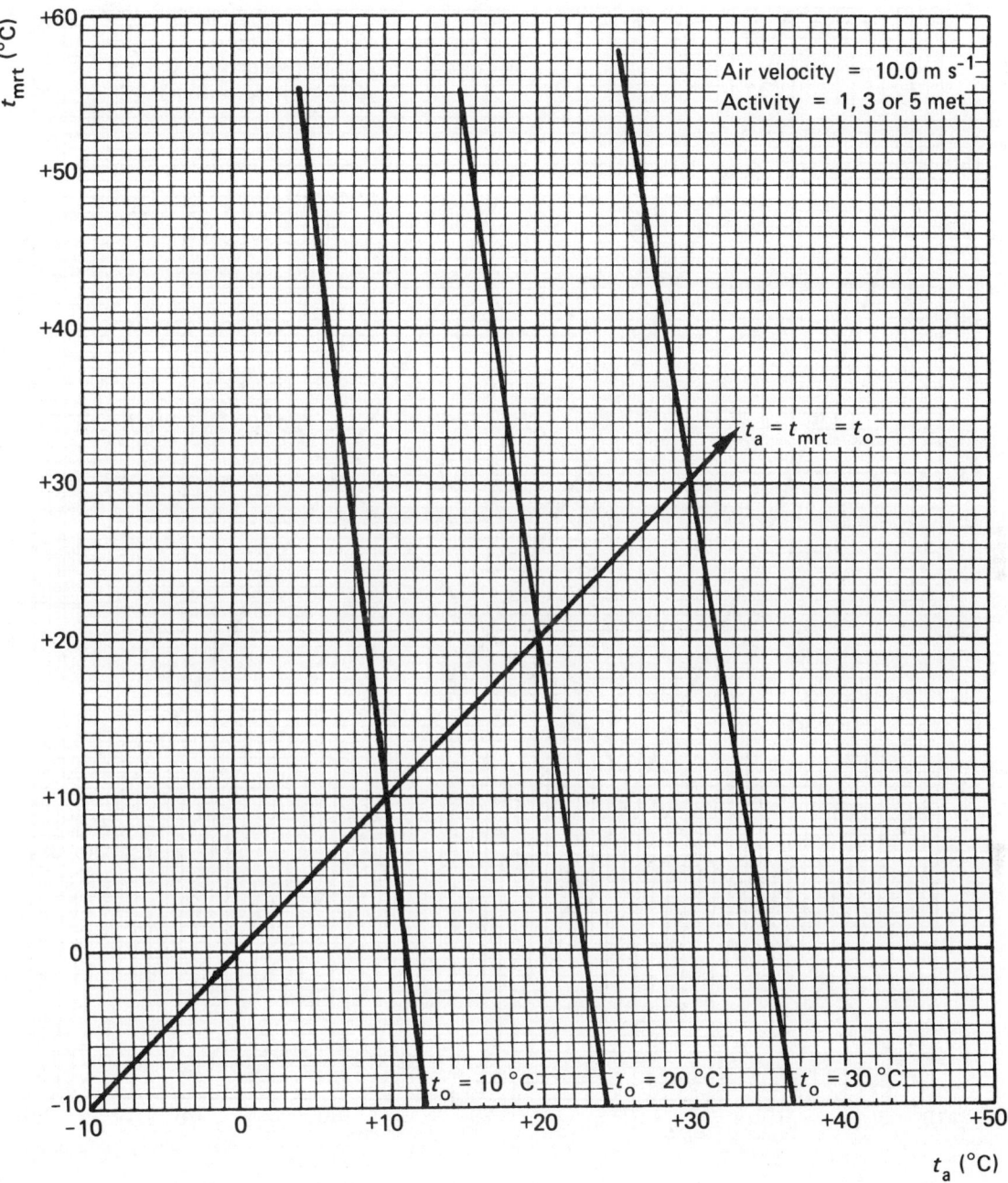

Operative temperature
chart 5

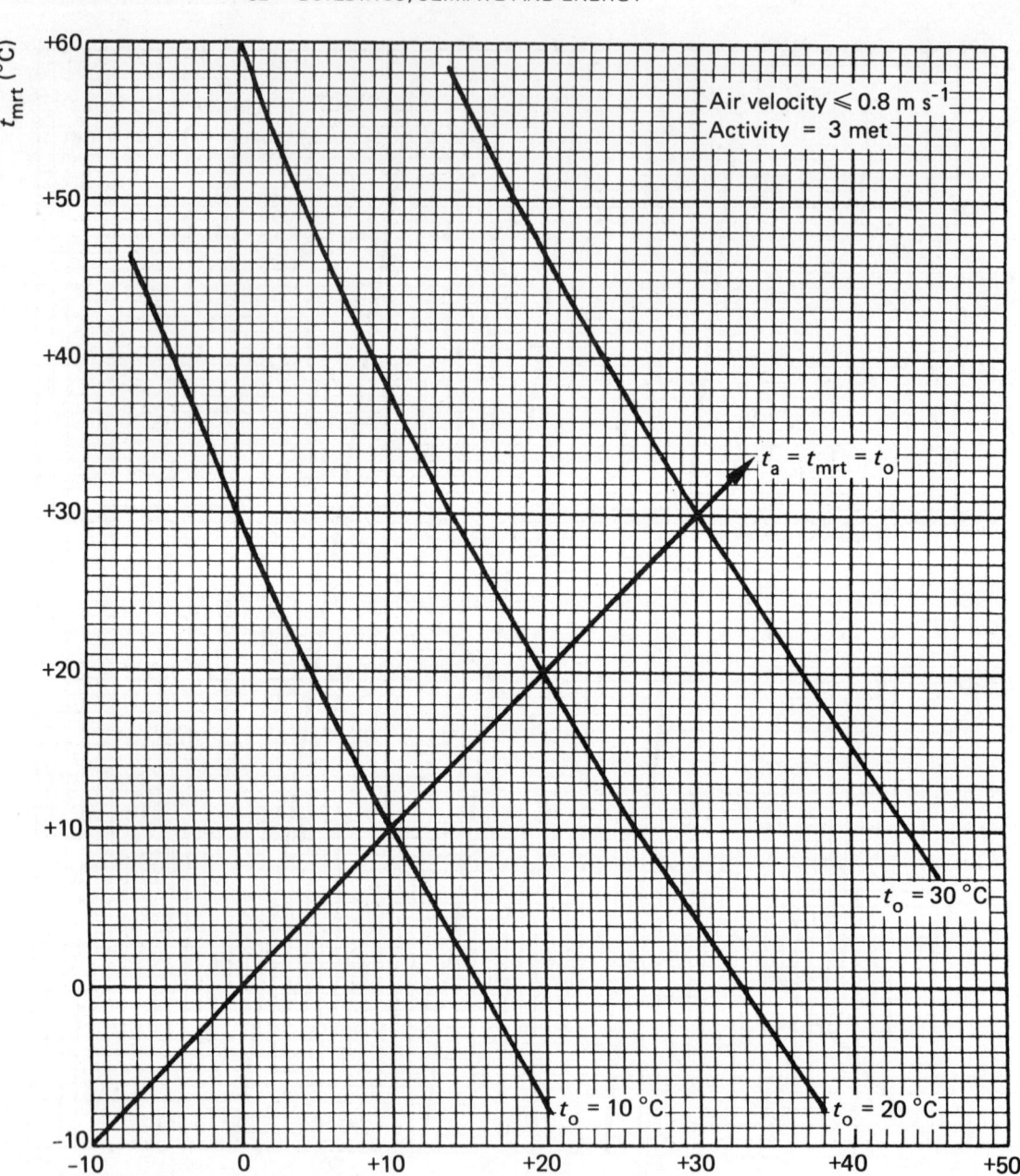

Operative temperature
chart 6

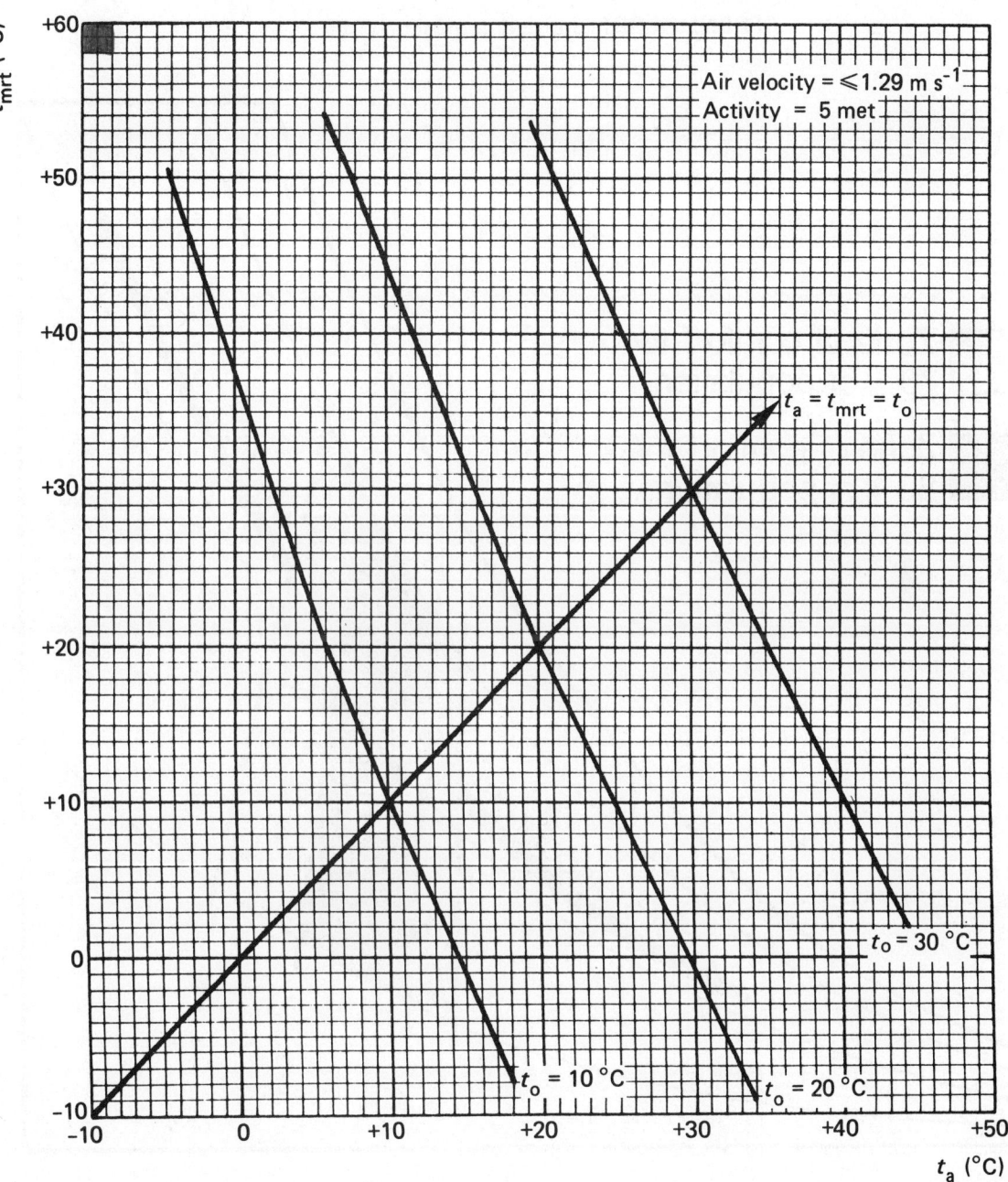

Operative temperature
chart 7

APPENDIX 3B: Thermal comfort charts

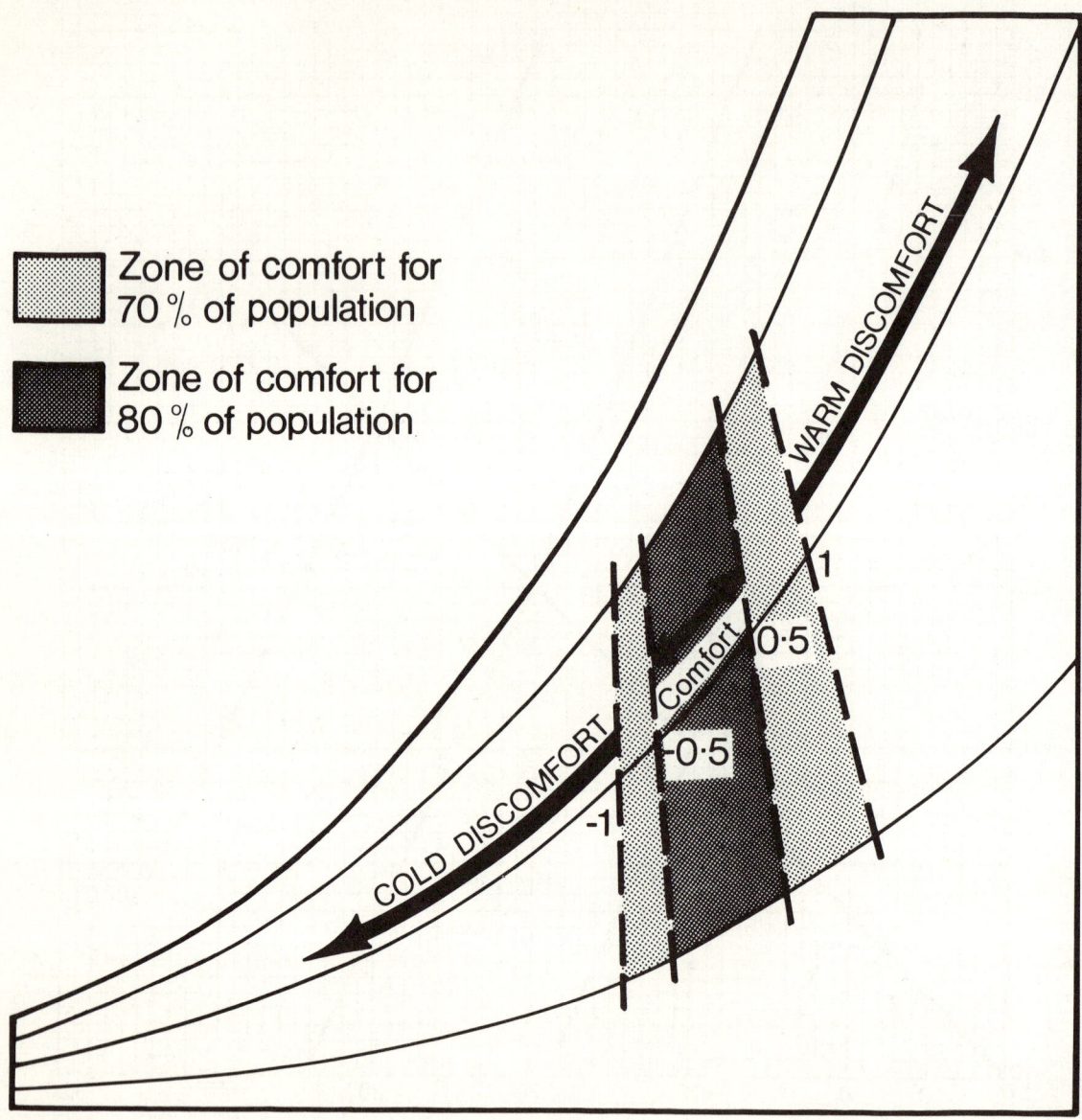

Zone of comfort for 70 % of population

Zone of comfort for 80 % of population

WARM DISCOMFORT

COLD DISCOMFORT

Comfort

1

0·5

-0·5

-1

Key chart

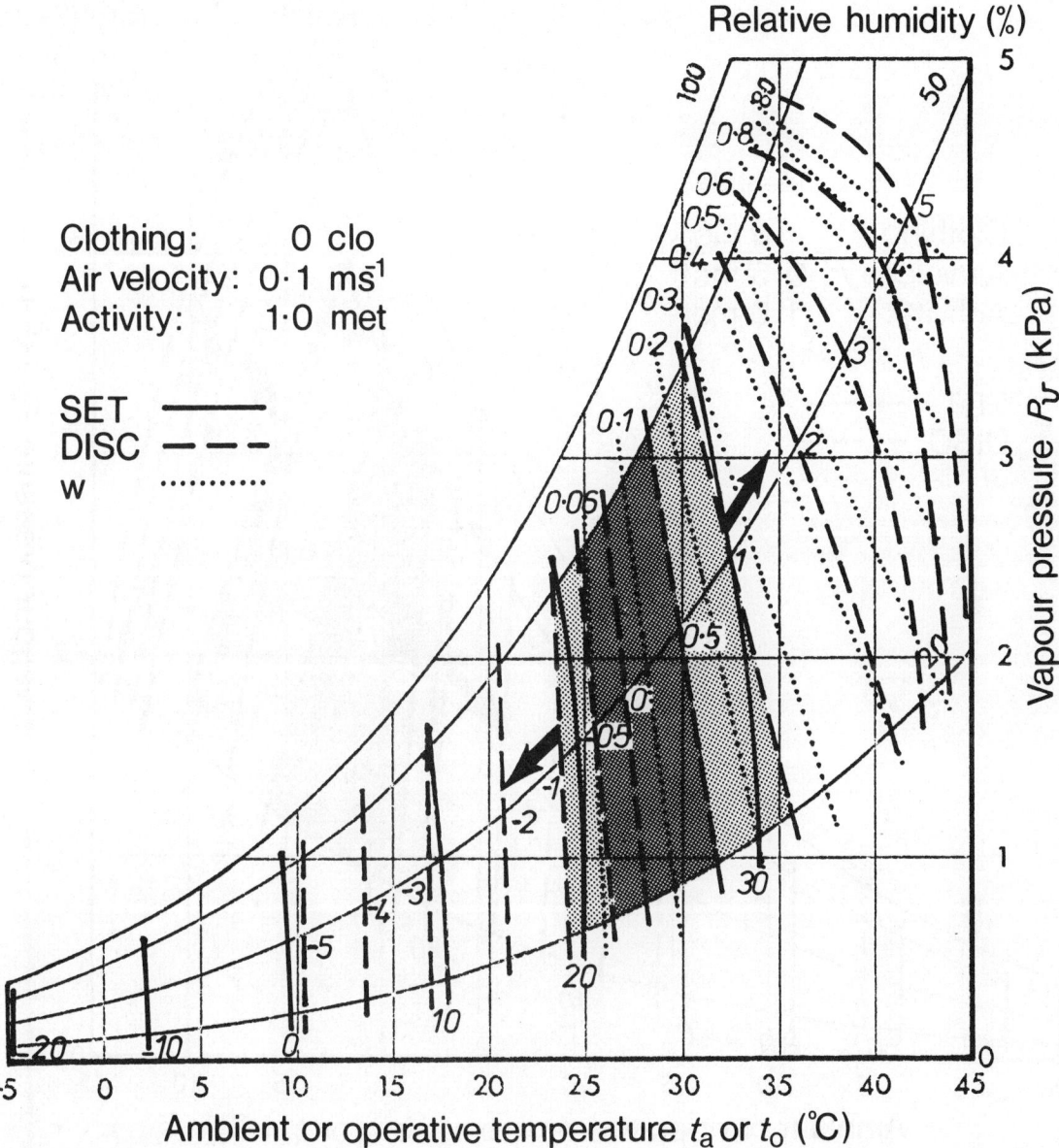

Thermal comfort
chart 1

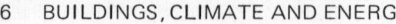

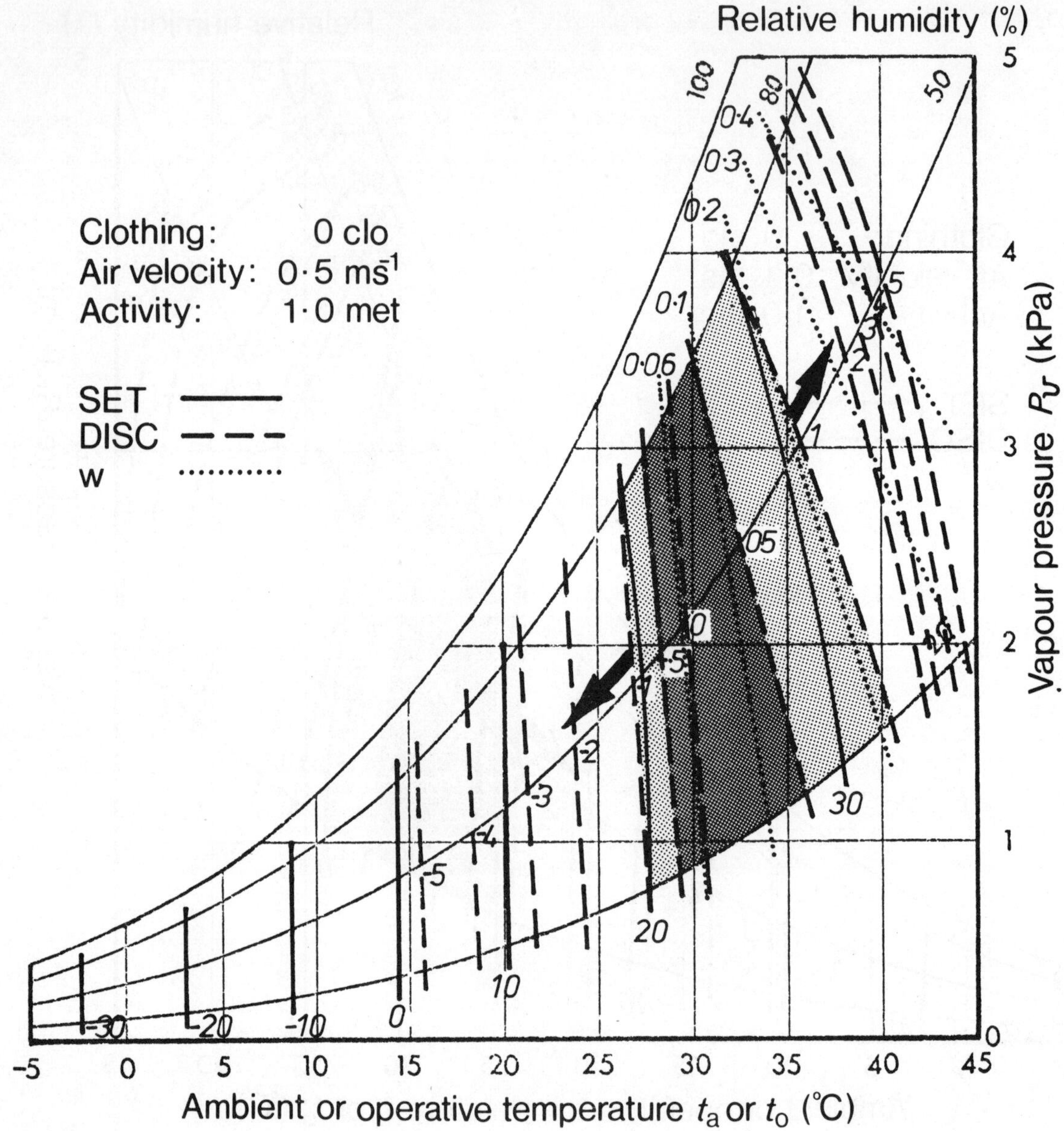
Relative humidity (%)
100
80
50
Clothing: 0 clo
Air velocity: 0·5 ms⁻¹
Activity: 1·0 met
SET
DISC
w
0·4
0·3
0·2
0·1
0·06
Vapour pressure P_v (kPa)
5
4
3
2
1
0
-30
-20
-10
0
10
20
30
-5
-4
-3
-2
-1
-·5
0
·05
1
2
3
4
5
-5 0 5 10 15 20 25 30 35 40 45
Ambient or operative temperature t_a or t_o (°C)

Thermal comfort
chart 2

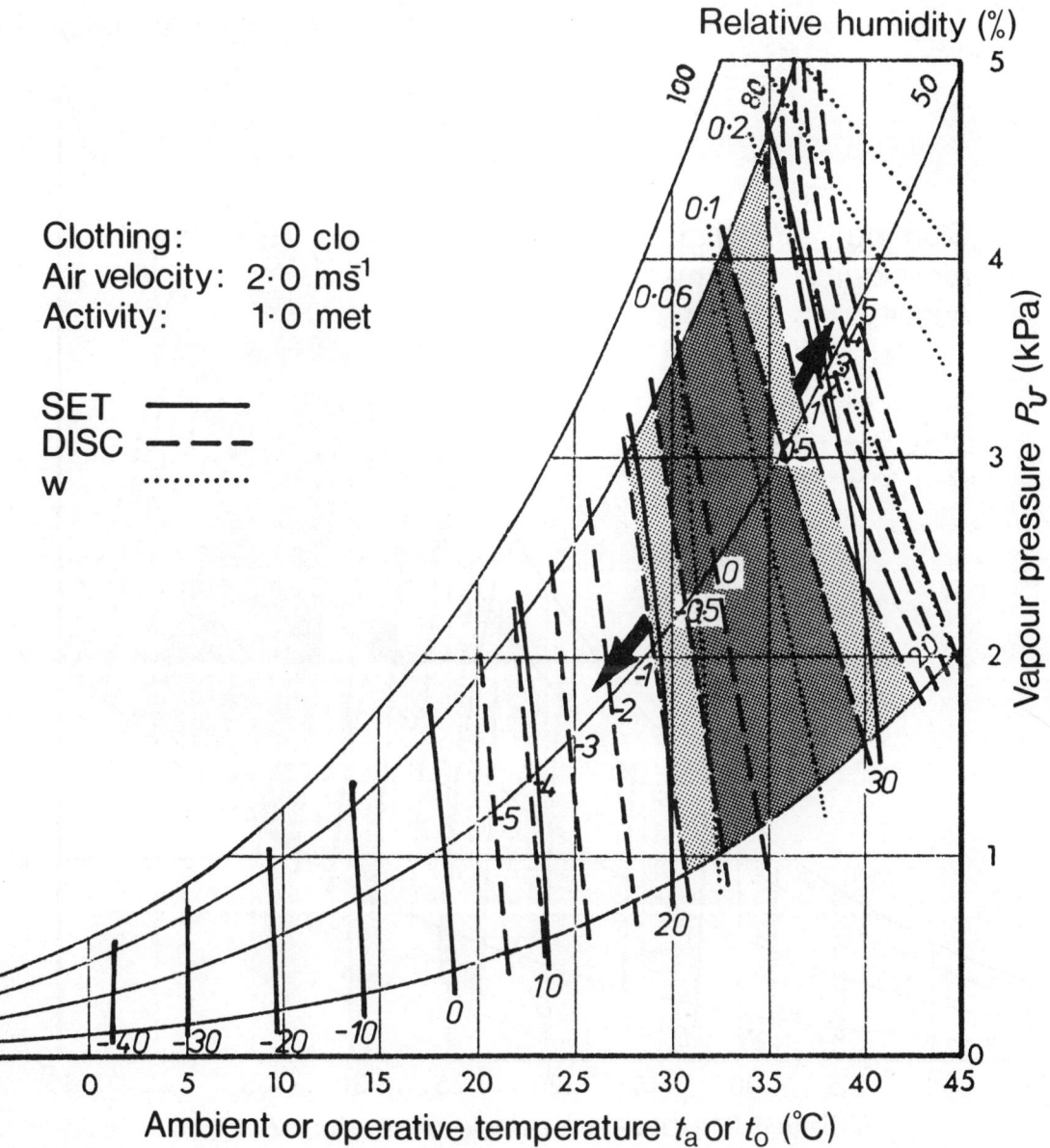

Relative humidity (%)

Clothing: 0 clo
Air velocity: 2·0 ms⁻¹
Activity: 1·0 met

SET ———
DISC – – –
w ·············

Ambient or operative temperature t_a or t_o (°C)

Thermal comfort
chart 3

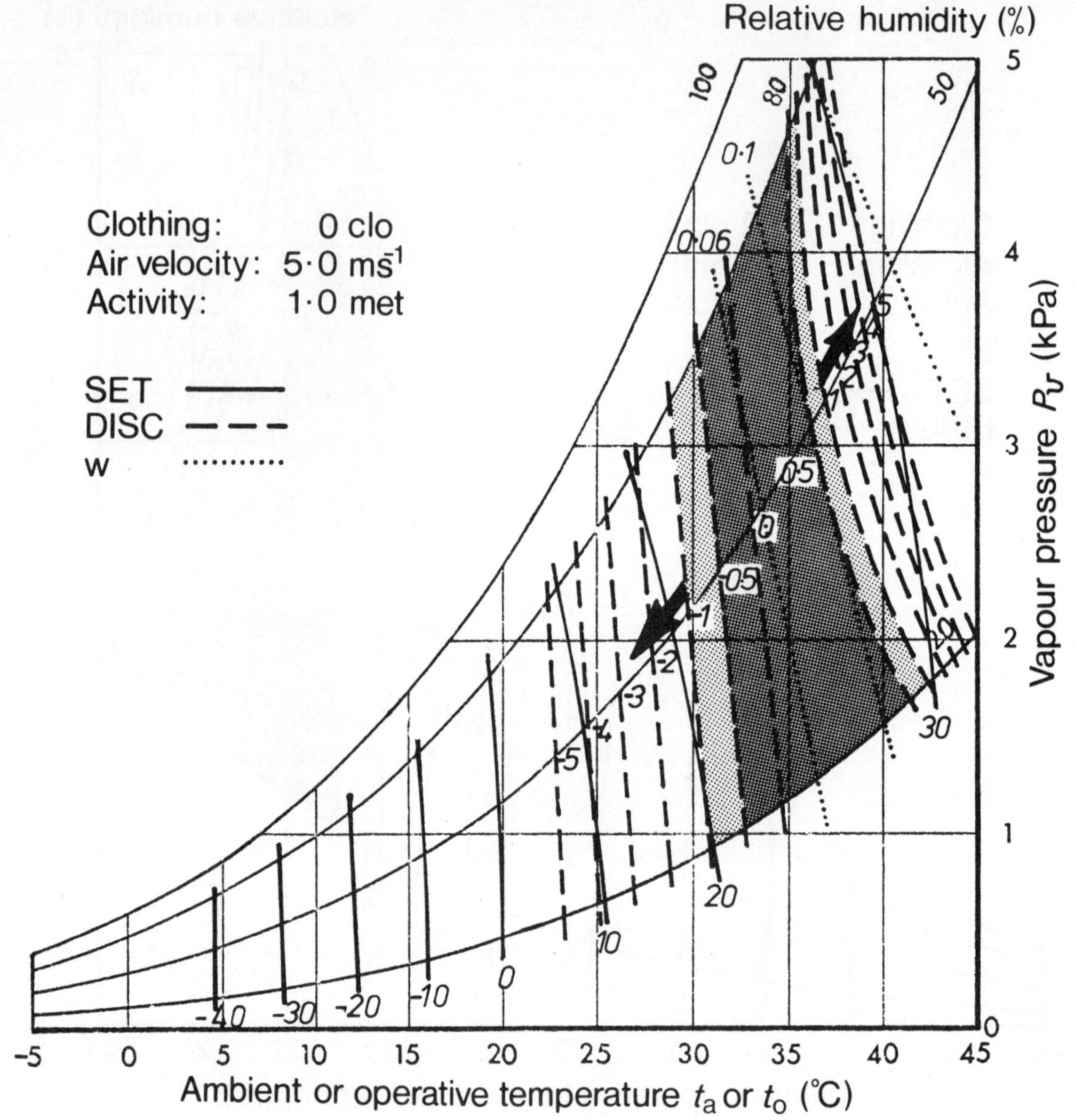

Relative humidity (%)

Clothing: 0 clo
Air velocity: 5·0 ms^{-1}
Activity: 1·0 met

SET ————
DISC — — —
W ············

Vapour pressure P_{v} (kPa)

Ambient or operative temperature t_{a} or t_{o} (℃)

Thermal comfort
chart 4

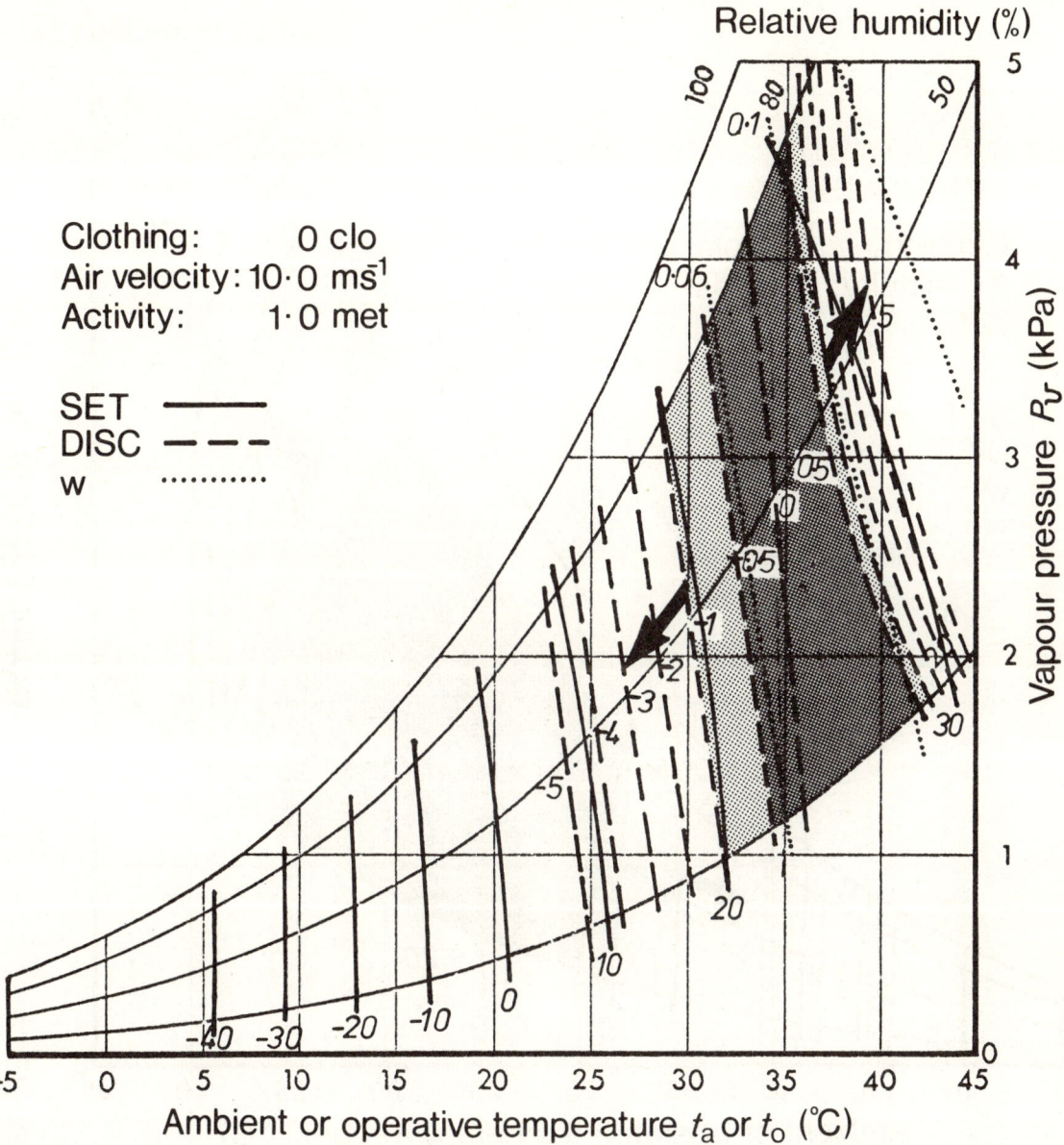

Clothing: 0 clo
Air velocity: 10·0 ms⁻¹
Activity: 1·0 met

SET ——————
DISC – – – – –
w ·············

Thermal comfort
chart 5

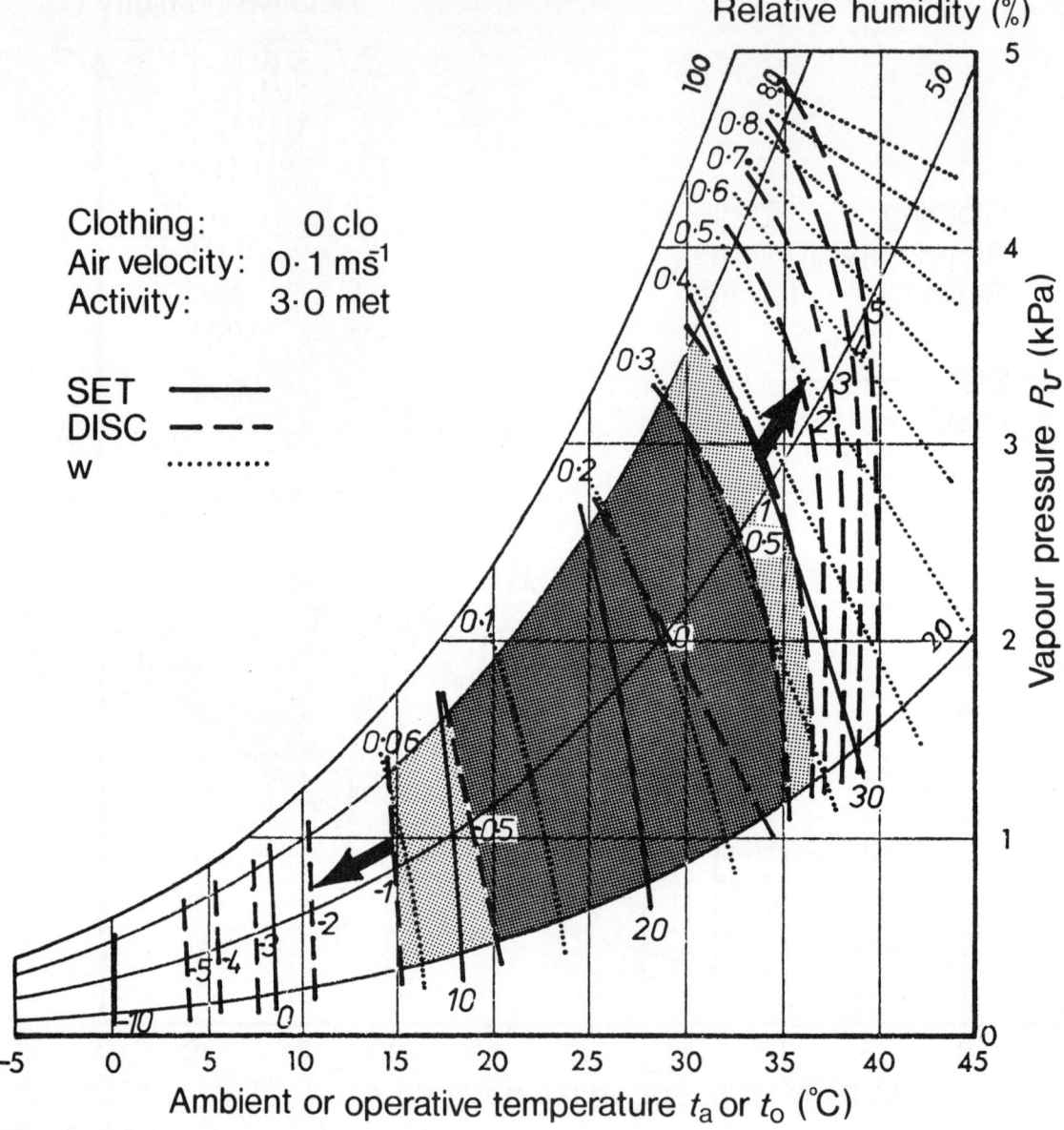

Thermal comfort
chart 6

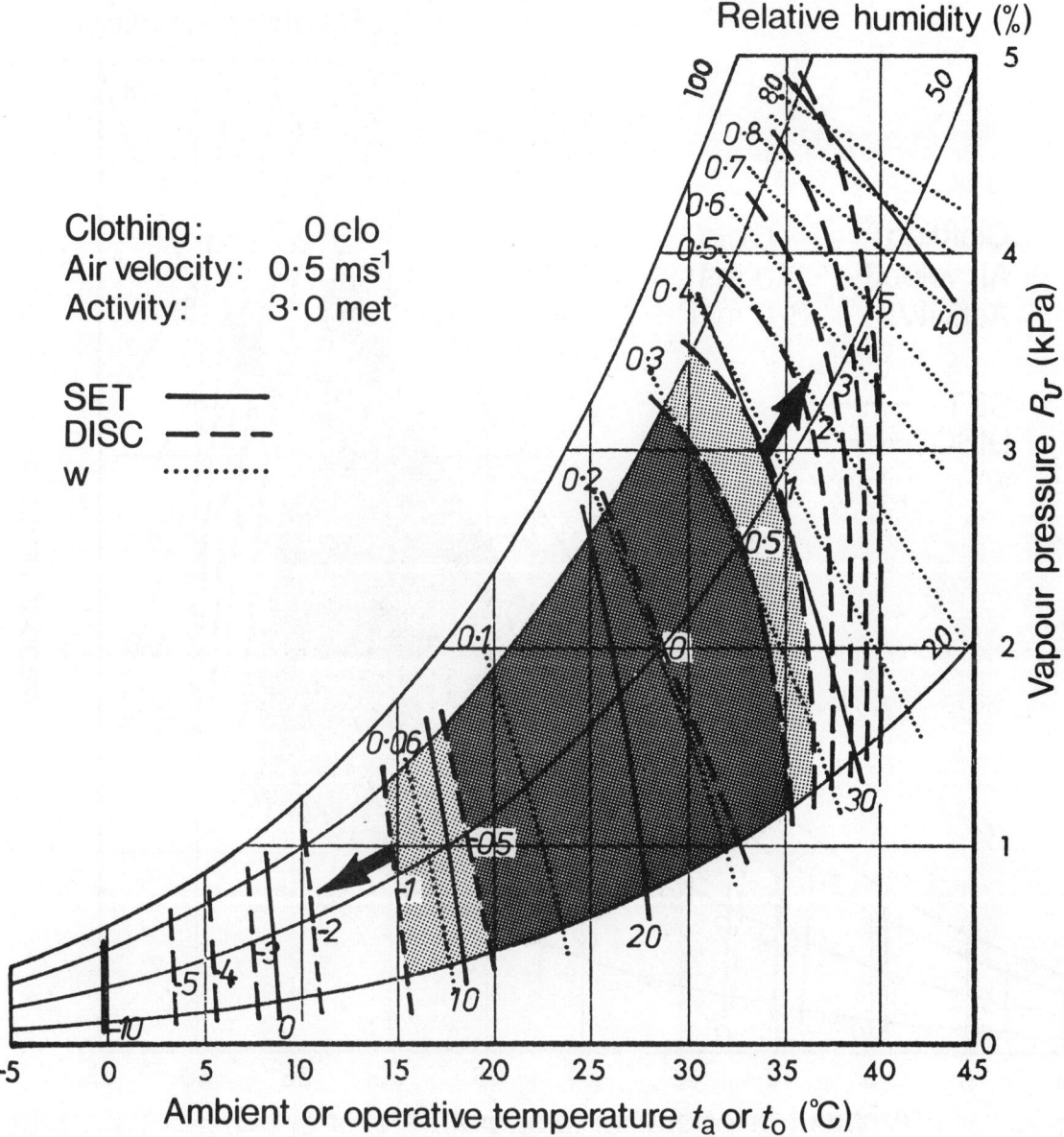

Thermal comfort
chart 7

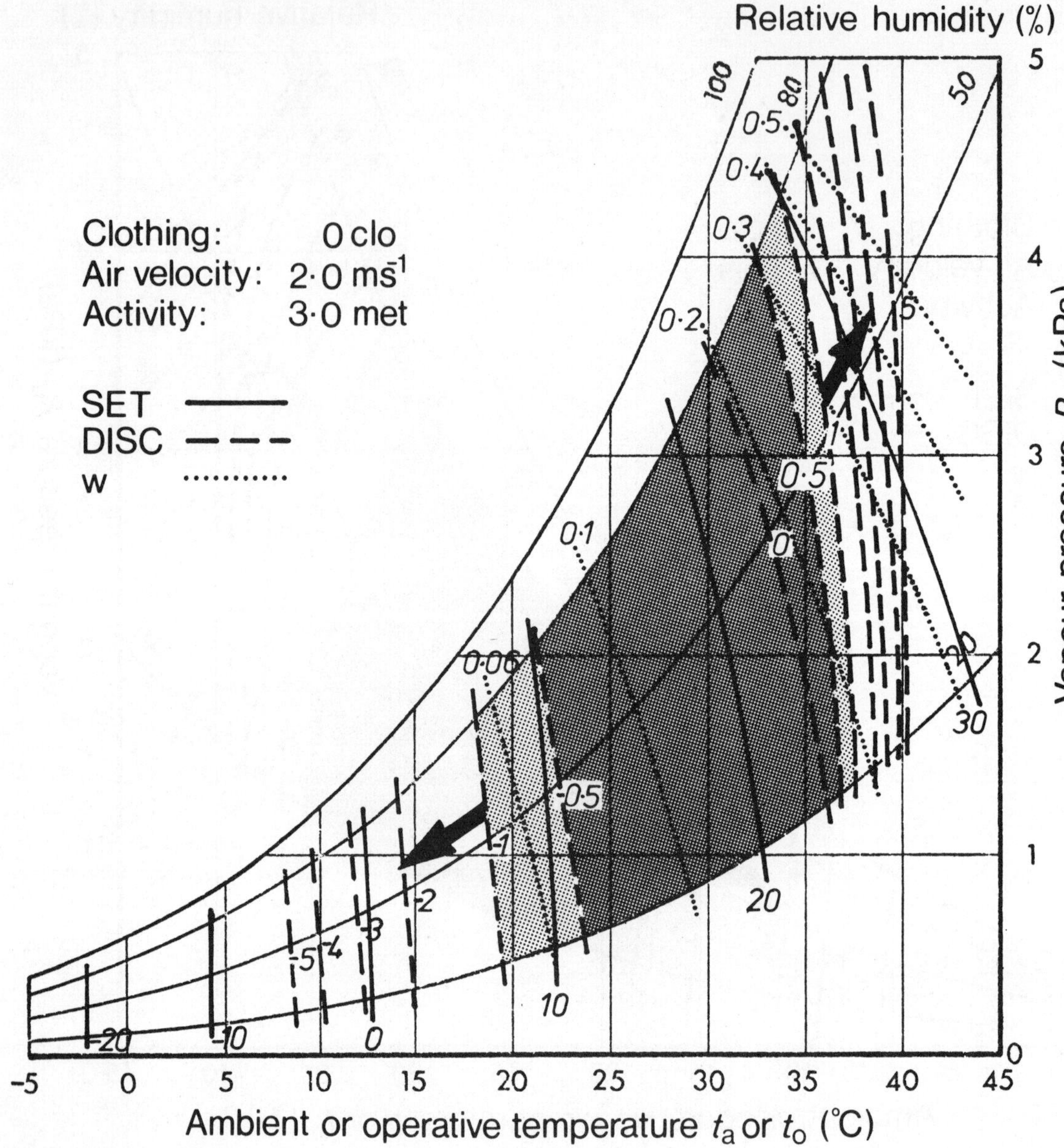

Relative humidity (%)
100
80
50
Clothing: 0 clo
Air velocity: 2·0 ms⁻¹
Activity: 3·0 met
SET
DISC
w
0·5
0·4
0·3
0·2
0·1
0·06
0·5
0
-0·5
-1
-2
-3
-4
-5
1
5
20
30
20
10
0
-10
-20
Vapour pressure P_v (kPa)
5
4
3
2
1
0
-5
0
5
10
15
20
25
30
35
40
45
Ambient or operative temperature t_a or t_o (°C)

Thermal comfort
chart 8

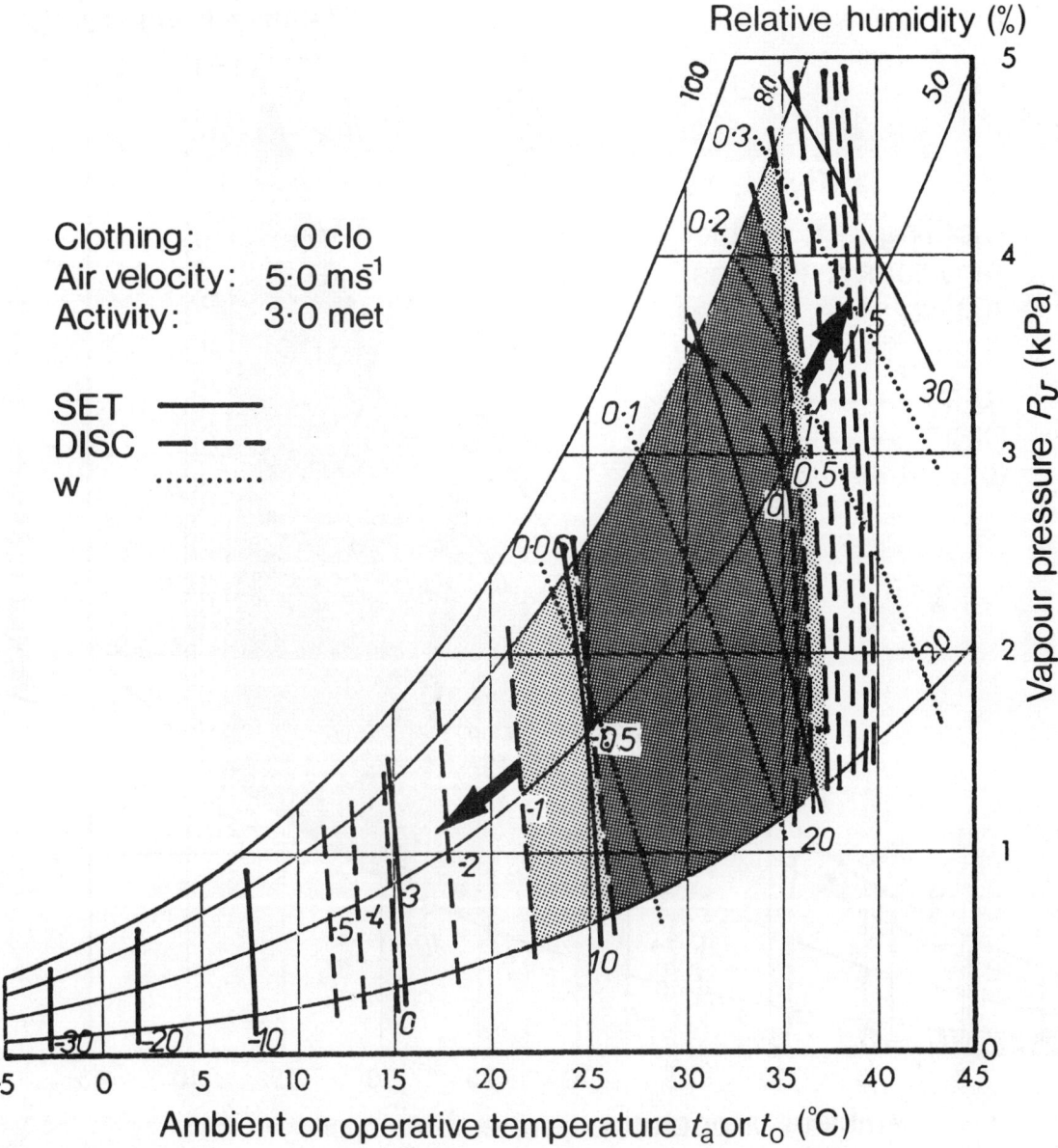

Clothing: 0 clo
Air velocity: 5·0 ms⁻¹
Activity: 3·0 met

SET   ———————
DISC   — — — —
W   ··············

Thermal comfort
chart 9

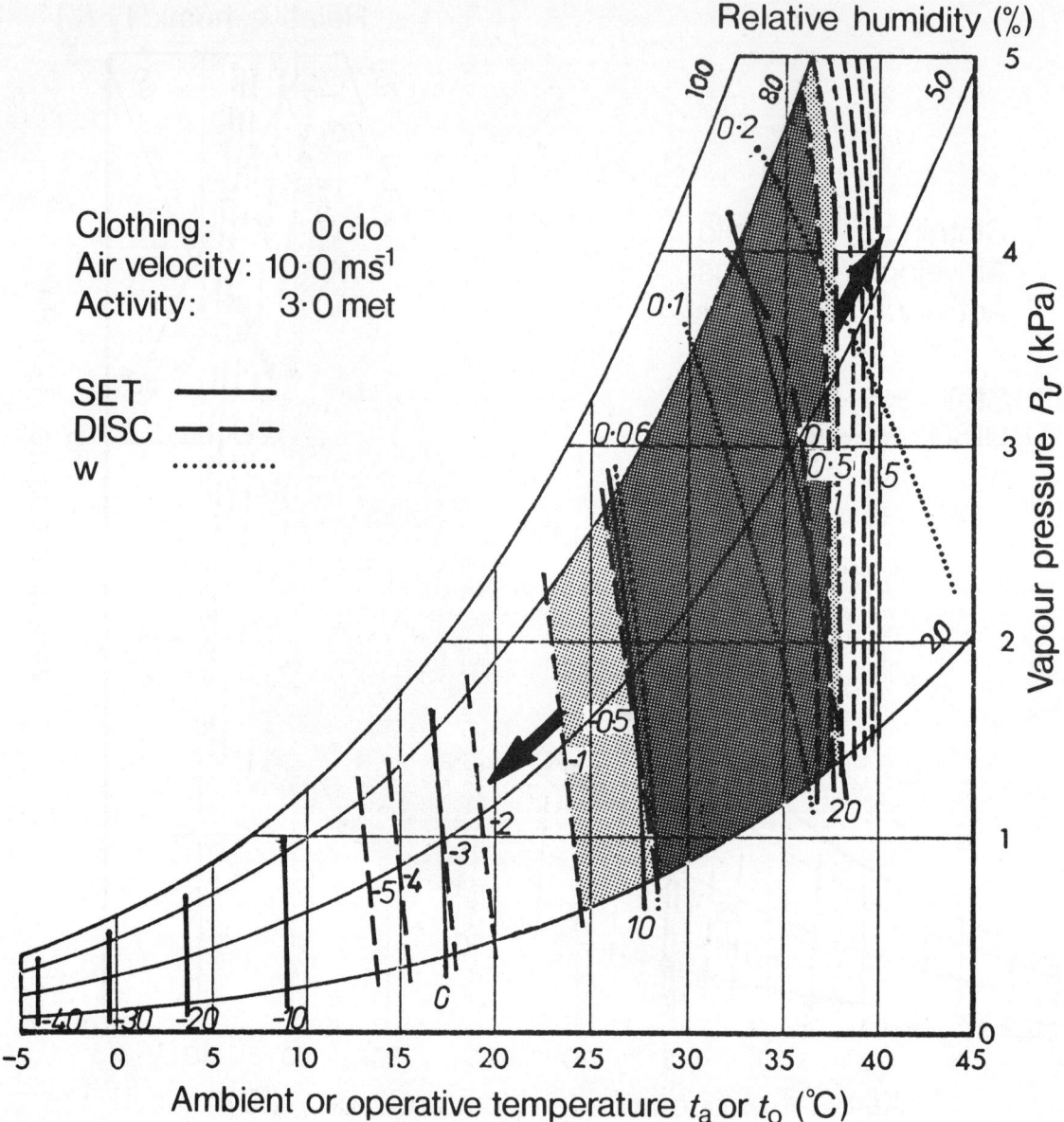

Clothing: 0 clo
Air velocity: 10·0 ms^{-1}
Activity: 3·0 met

SET ———
DISC – – –
w ·············

Relative humidity (%)

Vapour pressure P_v (kPa)

Ambient or operative temperature t_a or t_o (°C)

Thermal comfort
chart 10

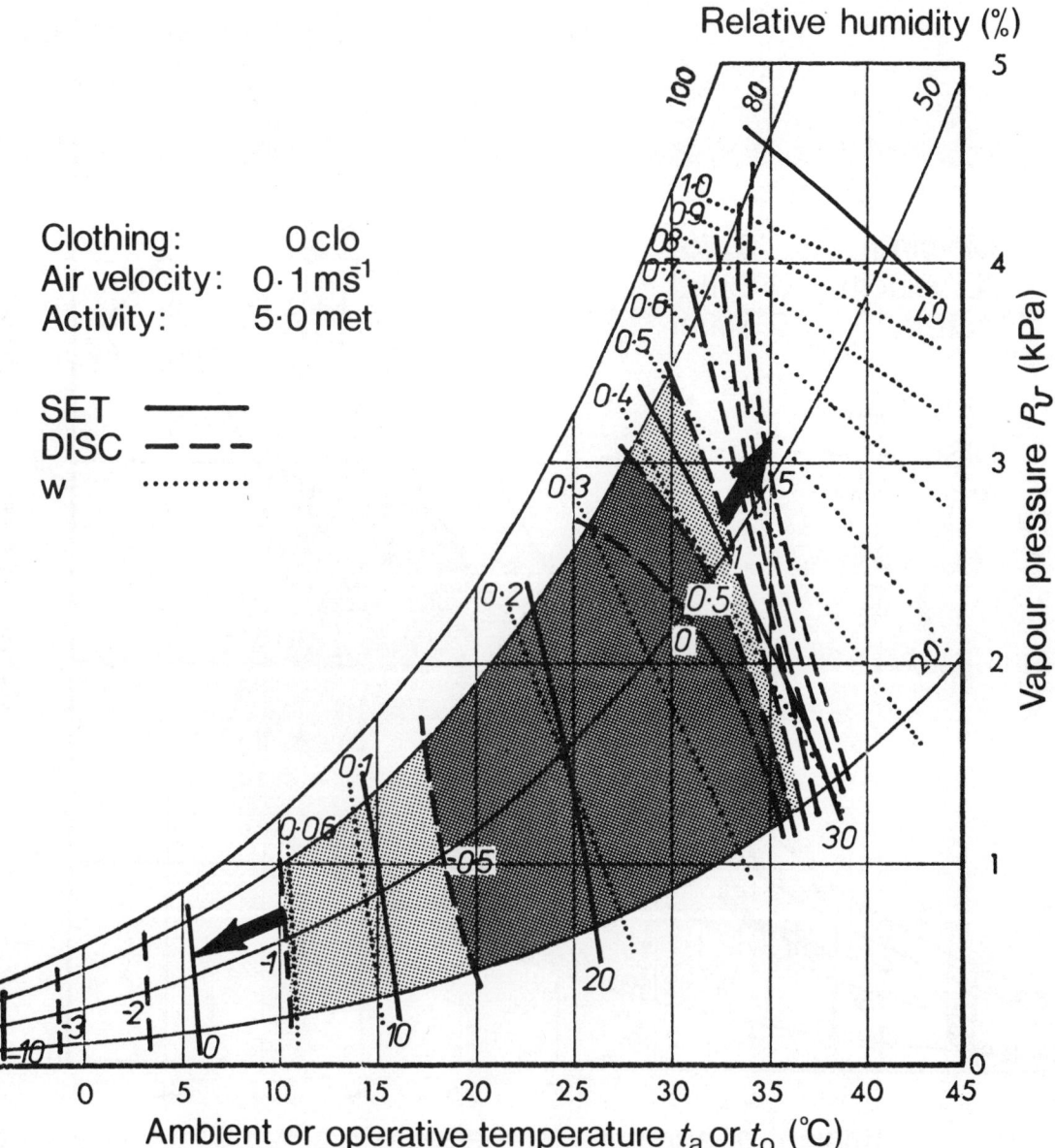

Thermal comfort
chart 11

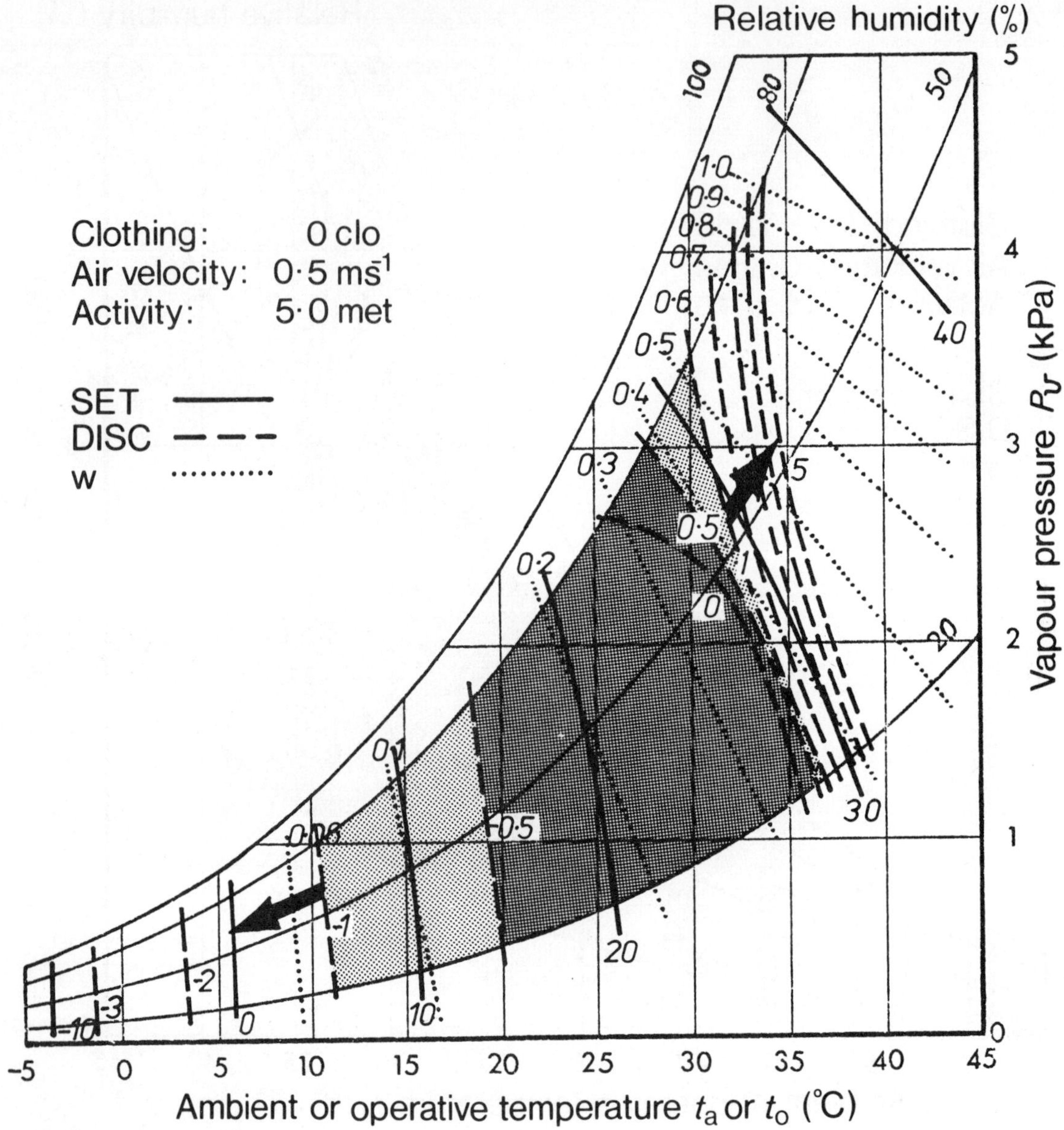

Relative humidity (%)

Clothing: 0 clo
Air velocity: 0·5 ms⁻¹
Activity: 5·0 met

SET ————
DISC – – –
w ·············

Vapour pressure P_U (kPa)

Ambient or operative temperature t_a or t_o (°C)

Thermal comfort
chart 12

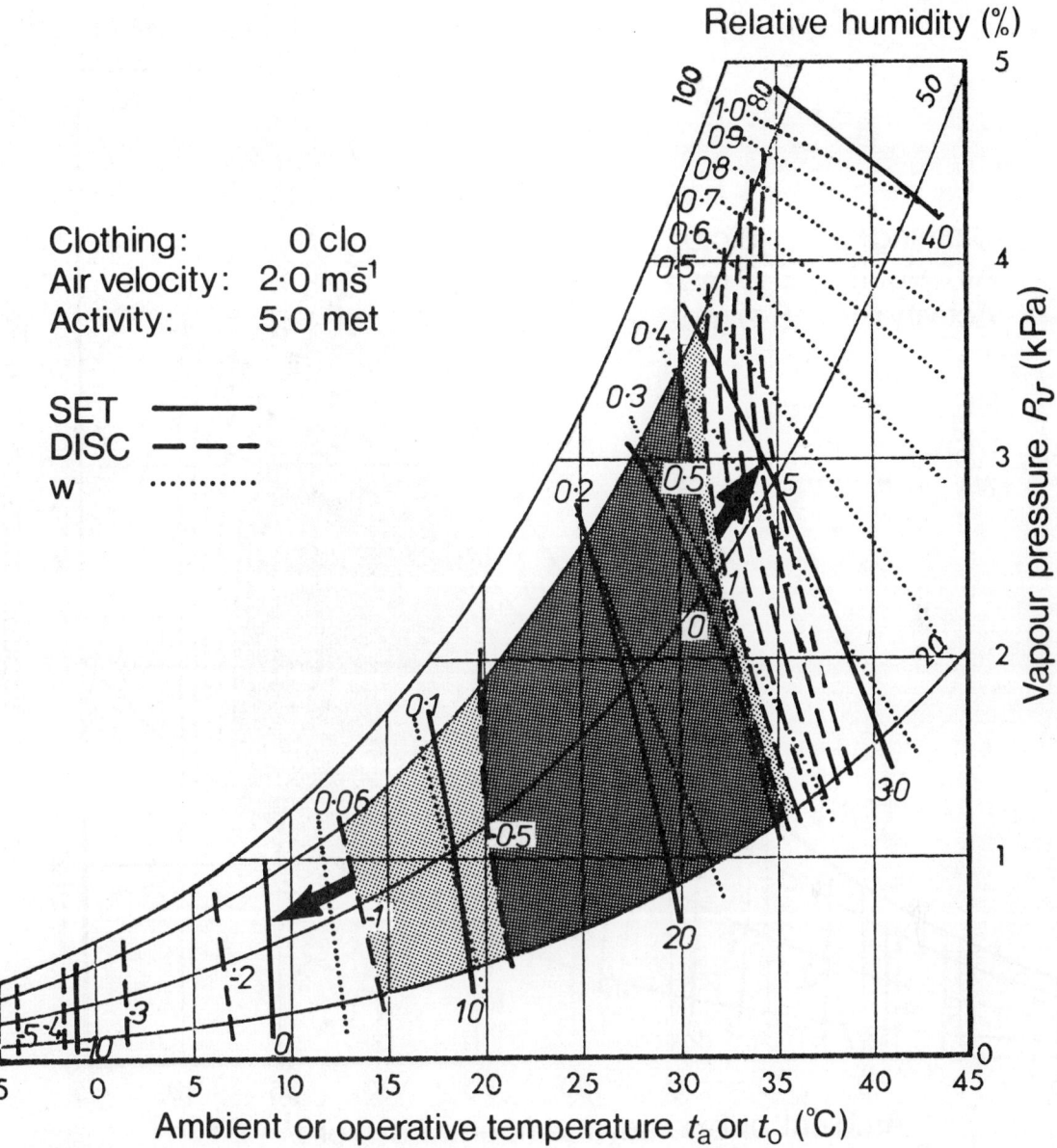

Clothing: 0 clo
Air velocity: 2·0 ms⁻¹
Activity: 5·0 met

SET ———
DISC — — —
w ·············

Relative humidity (%)

Vapour pressure P_{sf} (kPa)

Ambient or operative temperature t_a or t_o (°C)

Thermal comfort
chart 13

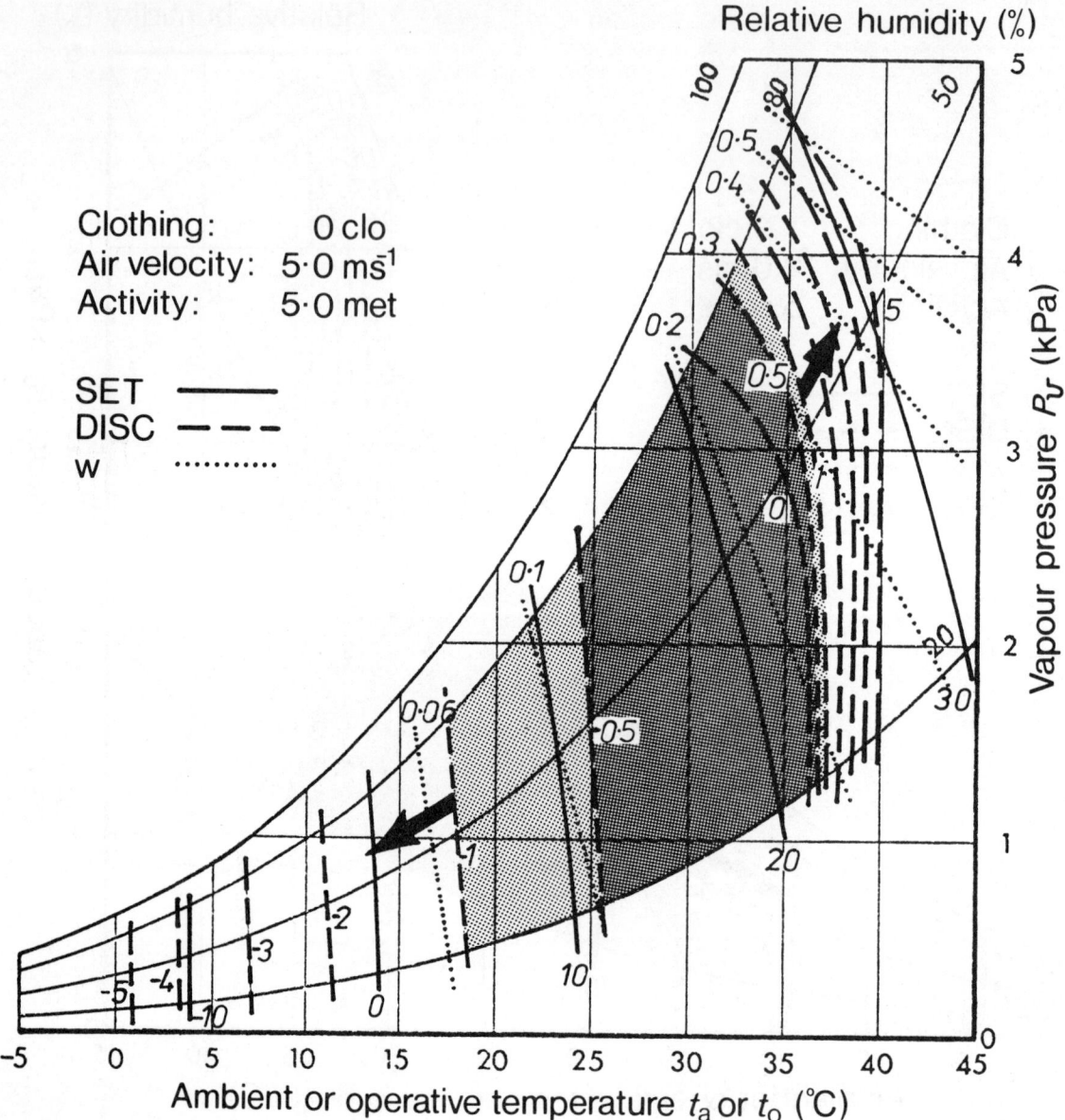

Relative humidity (%)

Clothing: 0 clo
Air velocity: 5·0 ms⁻¹
Activity: 5·0 met

SET ———
DISC — — —
w ··········

Vapour pressure P_v (kPa)

Ambient or operative temperature t_a or t_o (°C)

Thermal comfort
chart 14

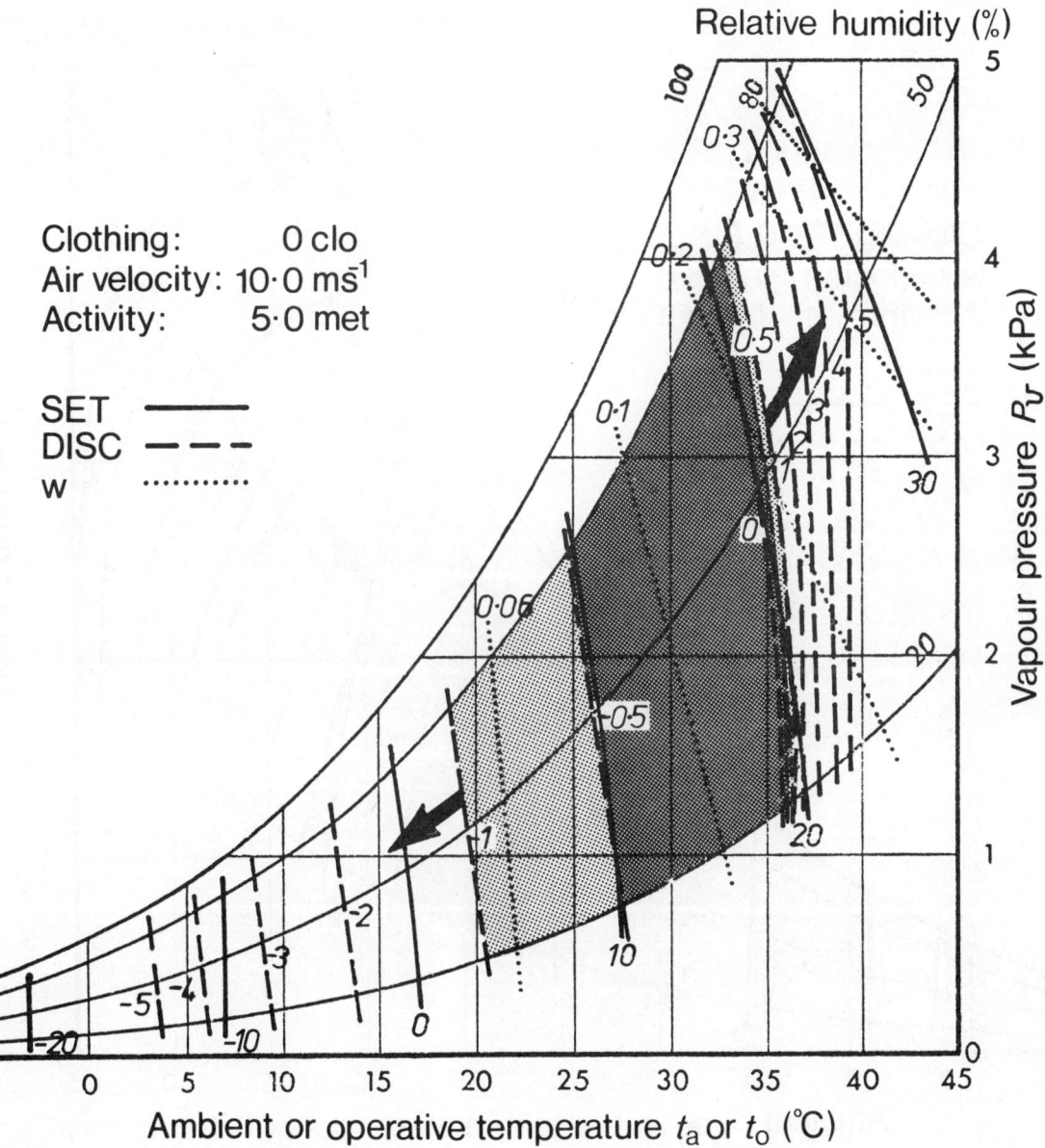

Thermal comfort
chart 15

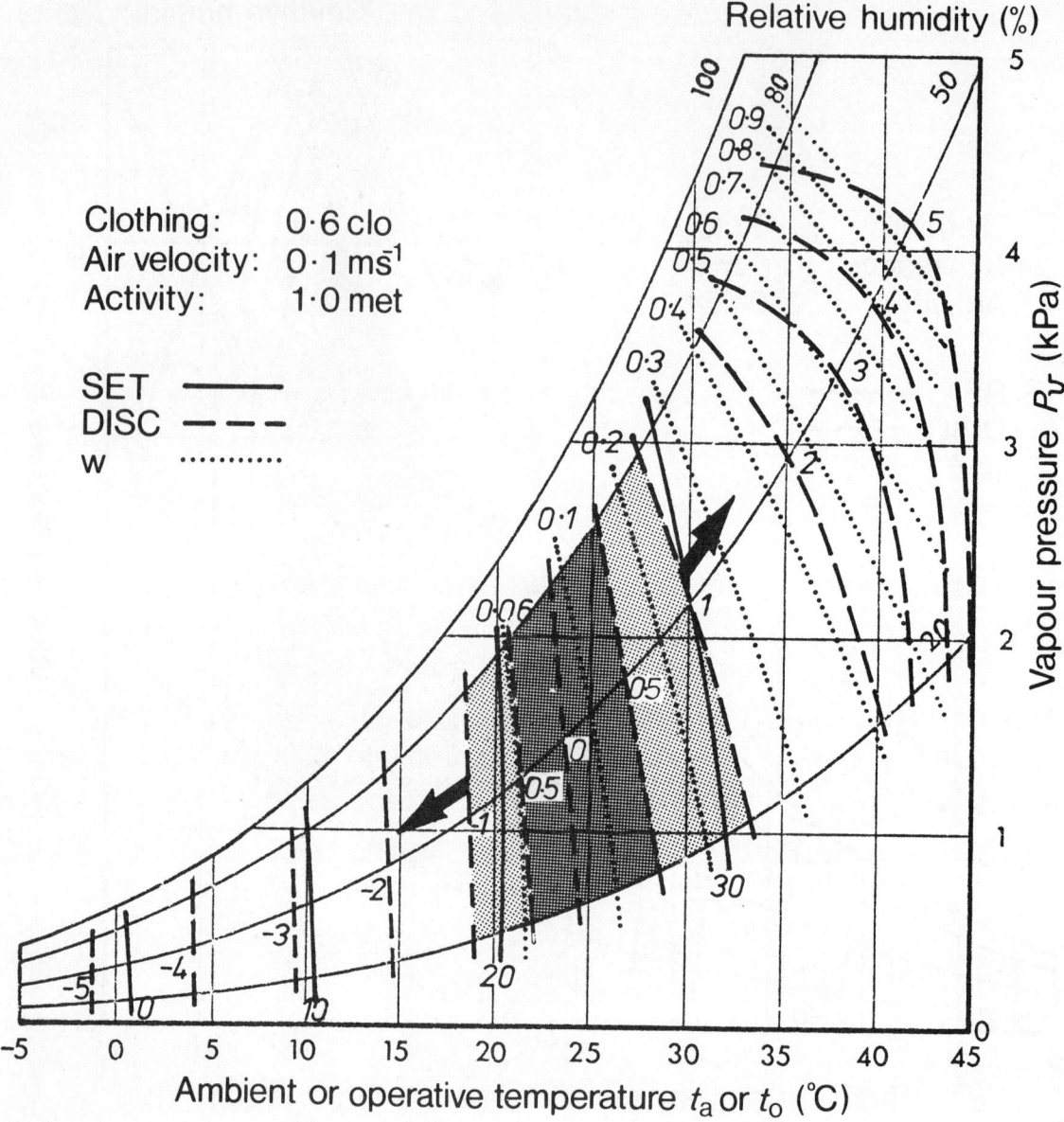

Relative humidity (%)

Clothing: 0·6 clo
Air velocity: 0·1 ms⁻¹
Activity: 1·0 met

SET ———
DISC — — —
w ·············

Vapour pressure P_v (kPa)

Ambient or operative temperature t_a or t_o (°C)

Thermal comfort
chart 16

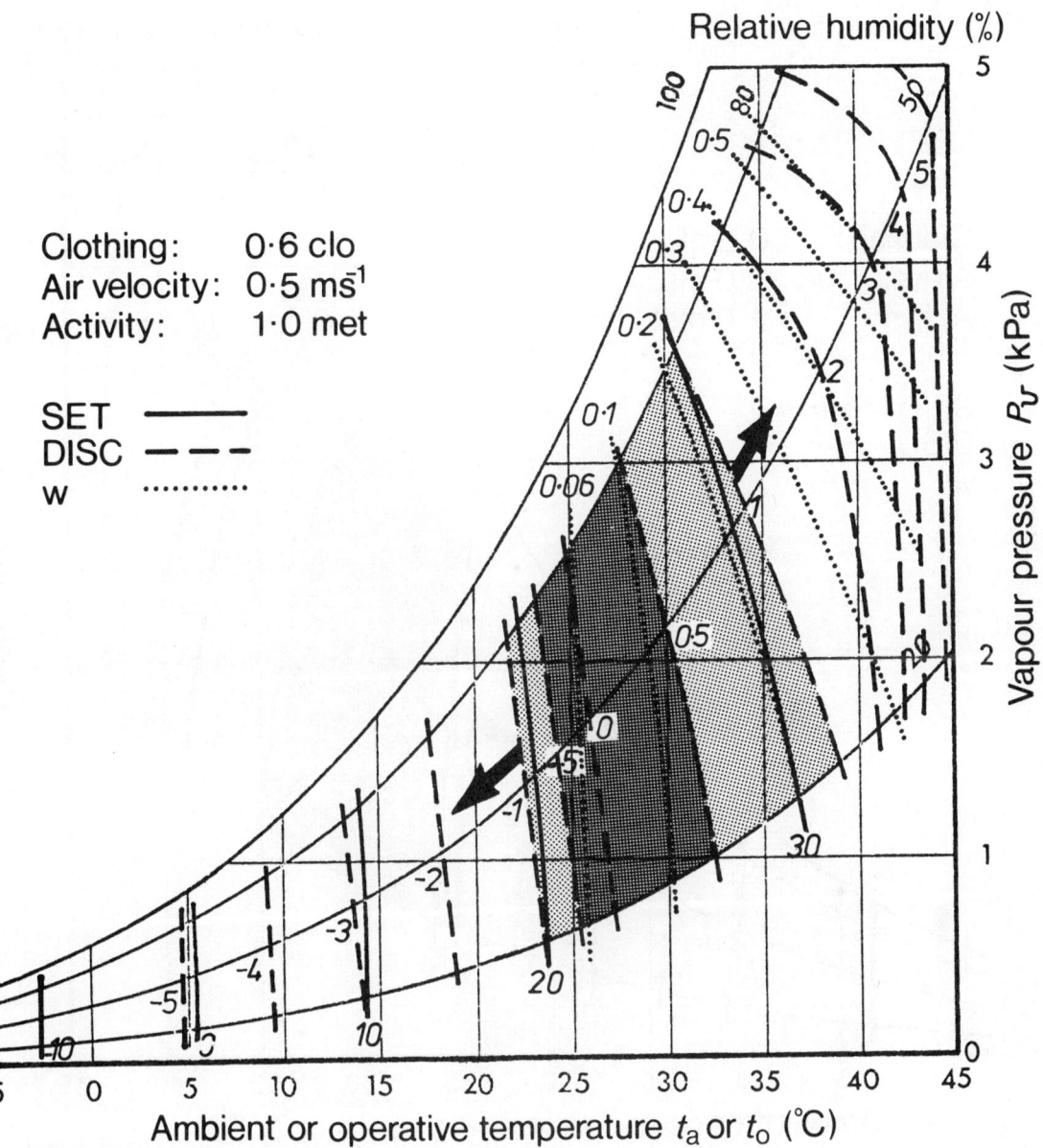

Thermal comfort
chart 17

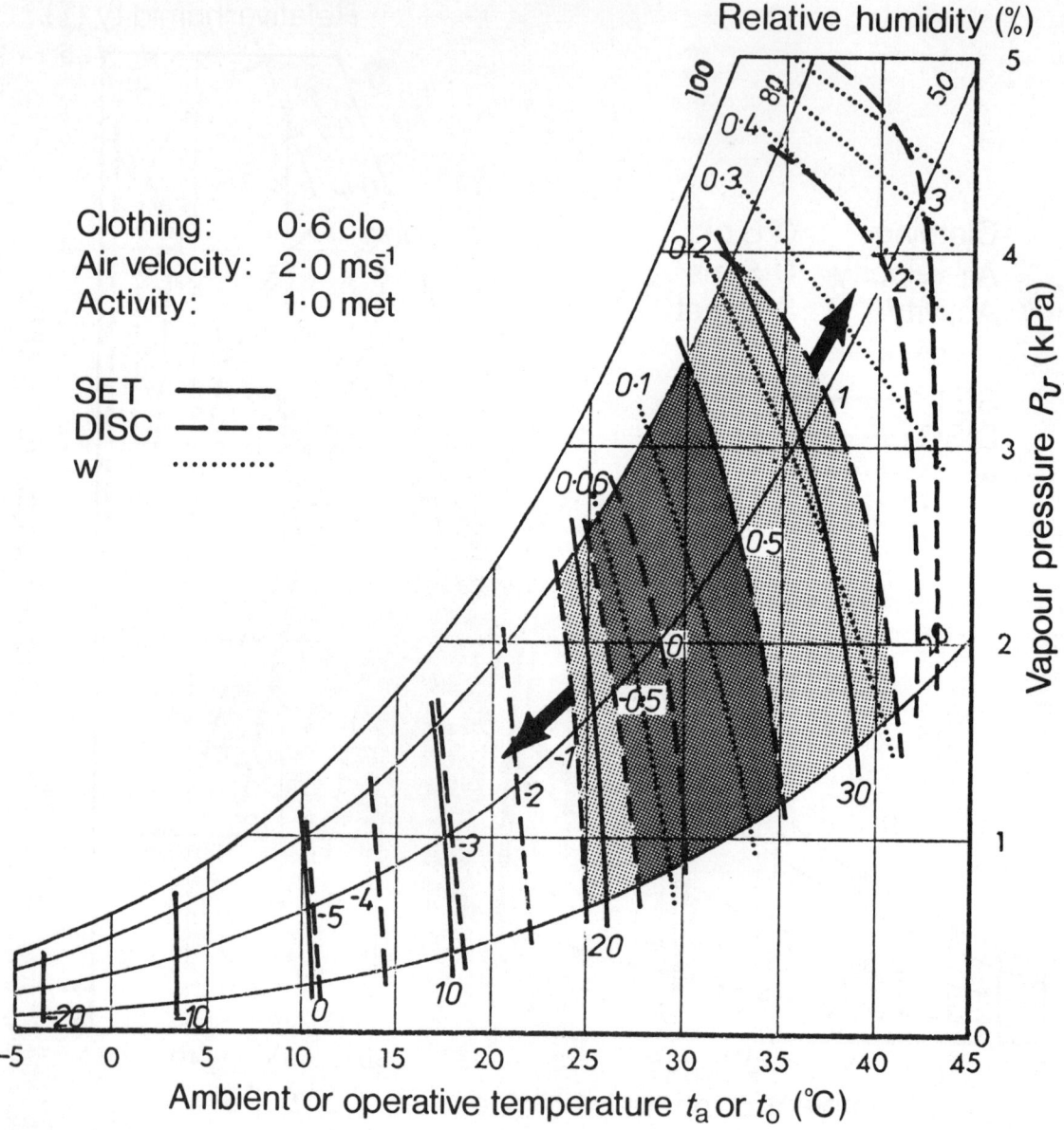

Thermal comfort
chart 18

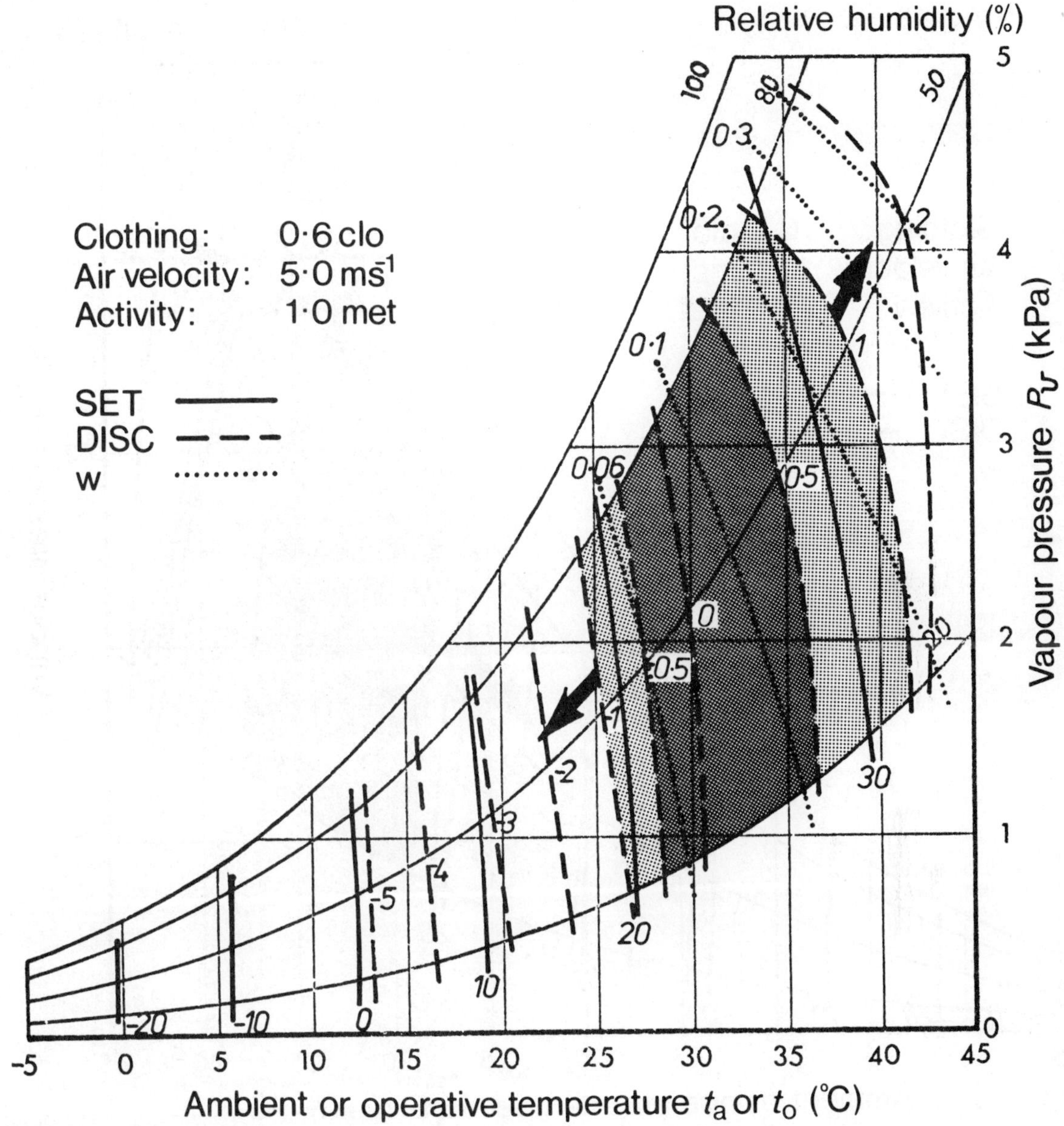

Relative humidity (%)

Clothing: 0·6 clo
Air velocity: 5·0 ms⁻¹
Activity: 1·0 met

SET   ——————
DISC   — — — —
w   ············

Vapour pressure $P_{\rm U}$ (kPa)

Ambient or operative temperature $t_{\rm a}$ or $t_{\rm o}$ (°C)

Thermal comfort
chart 19

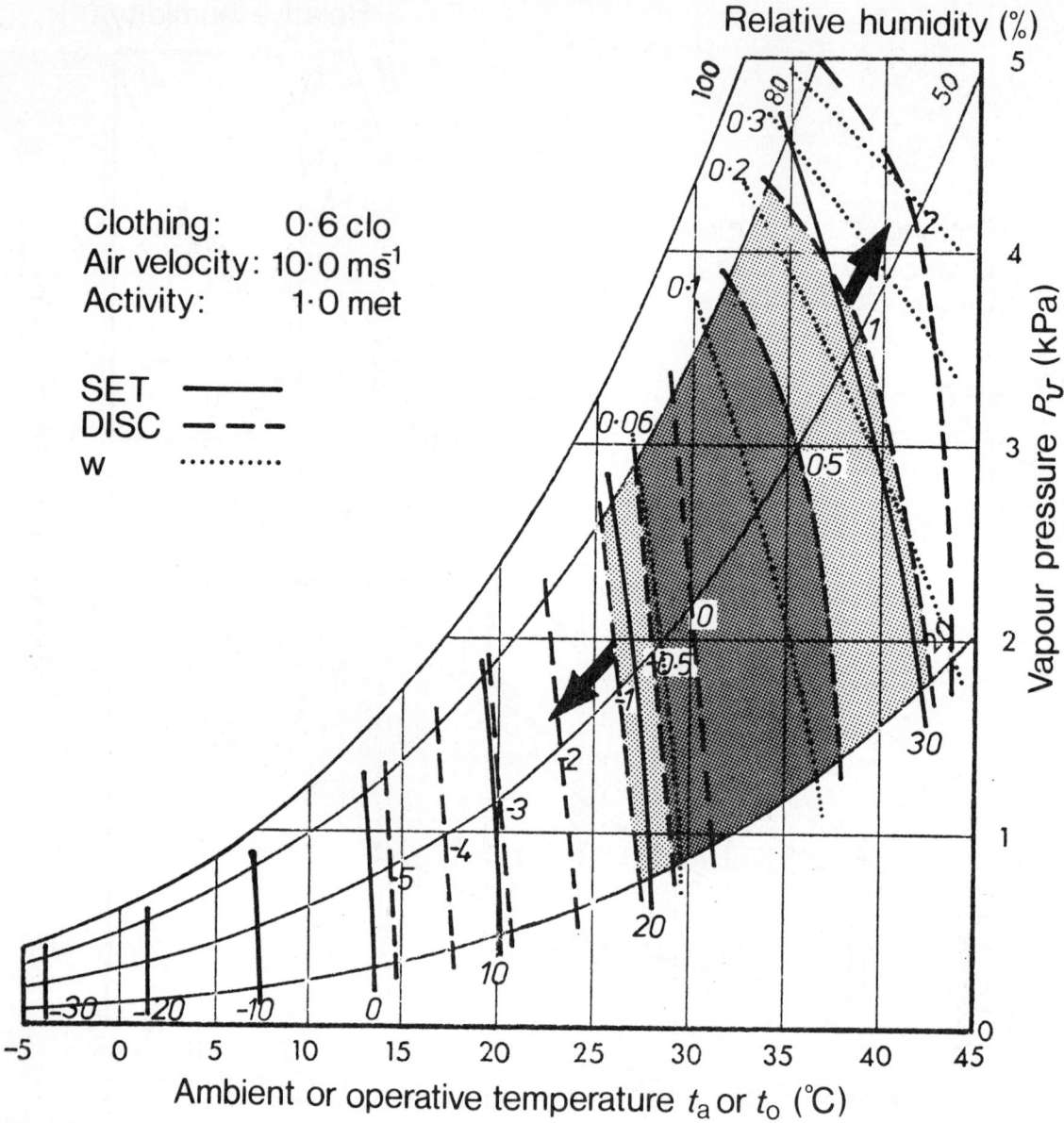

Relative humidity (%)

Clothing: 0·6 clo
Air velocity: 10·0 ms⁻¹
Activity: 1·0 met

SET ———
DISC — — —
w ··········

Ambient or operative temperature t_a or t_o (°C)

Thermal comfort
chart 20

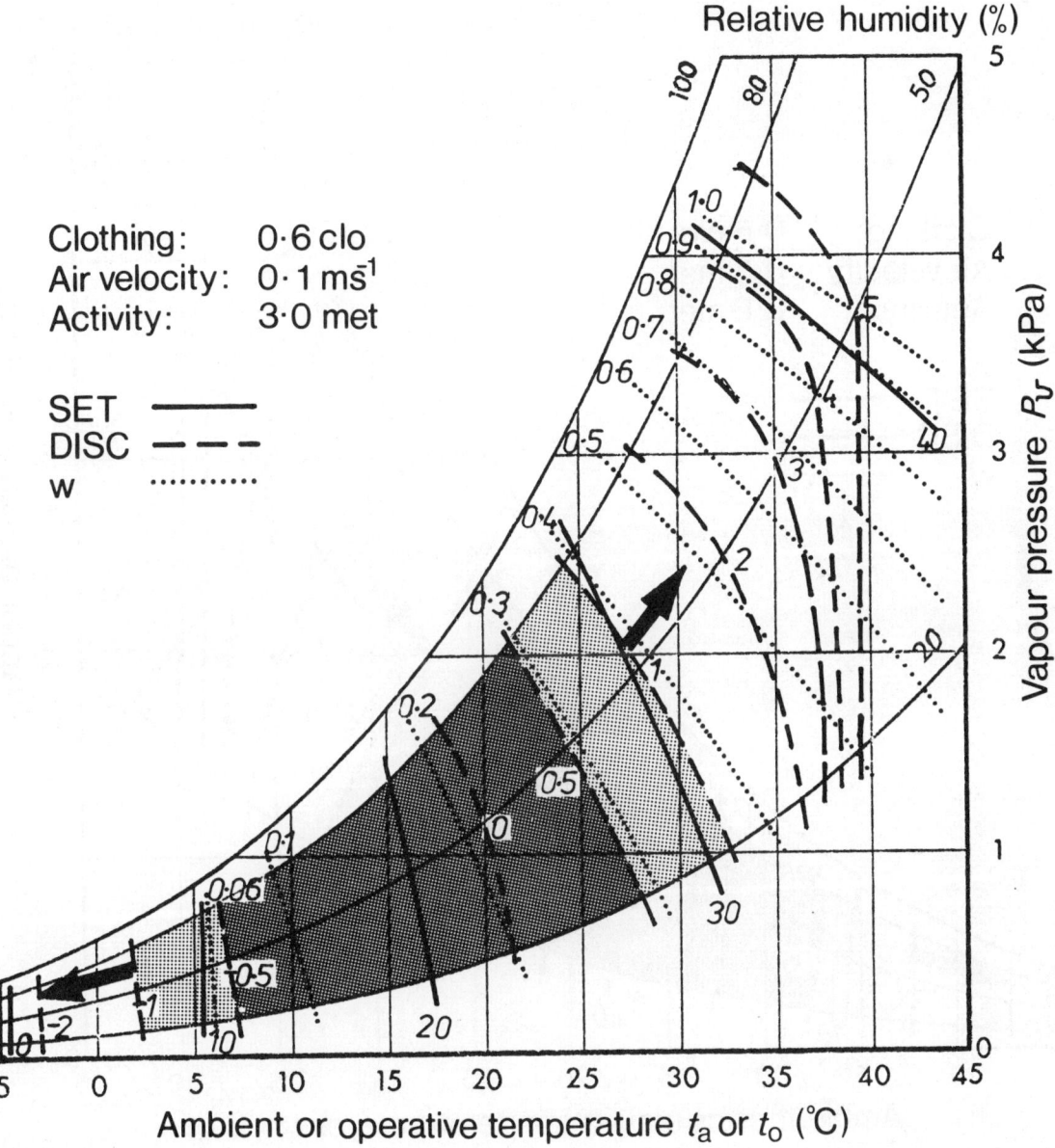

Thermal comfort
chart 21

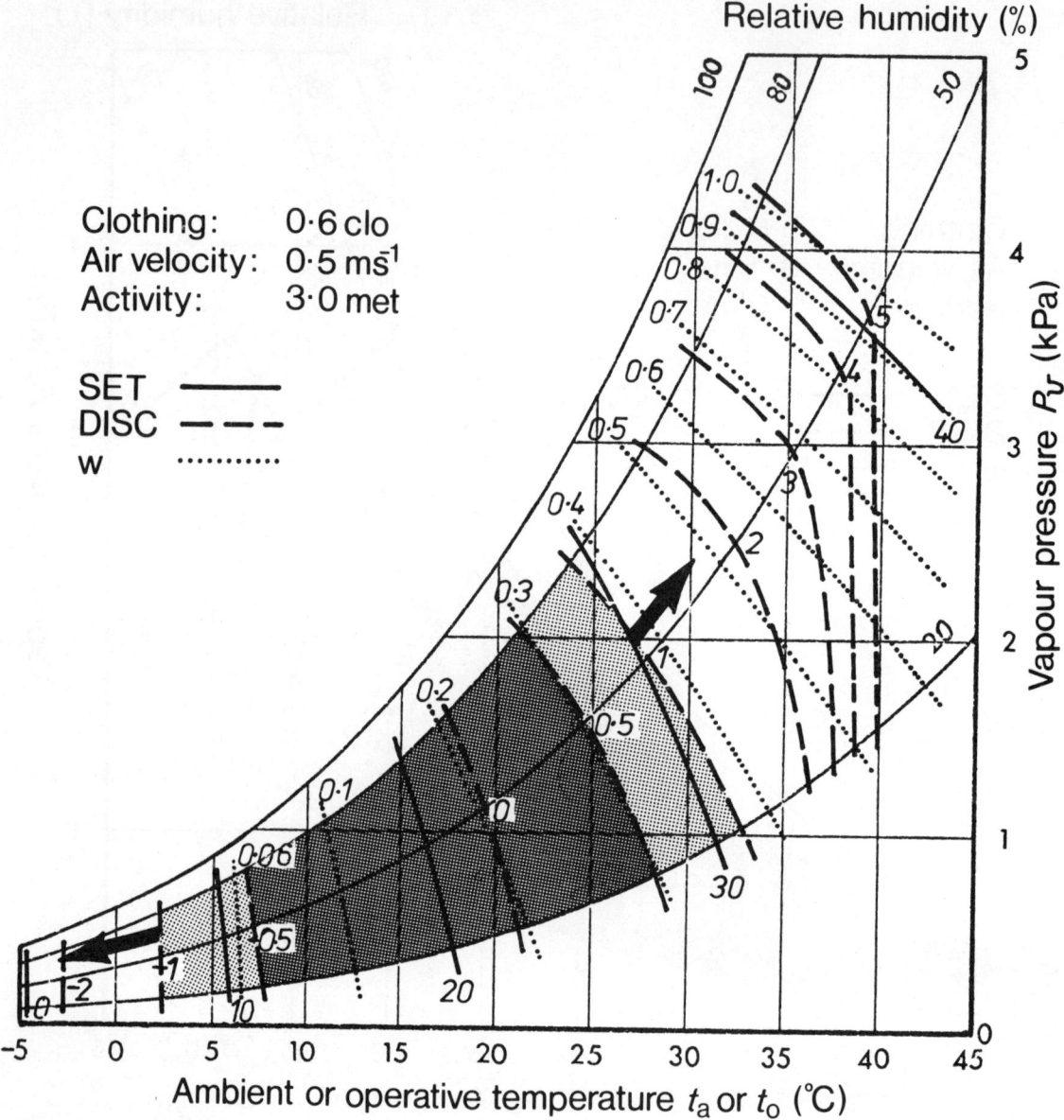

Clothing: 0·6 clo
Air velocity: 0·5 ms⁻¹
Activity: 3·0 met

SET ———————
DISC — — — —
w ·················

Relative humidity (%)

Vapour pressure P_v (kPa)

Ambient or operative temperature t_a or t_o (°C)

Thermal comfort
chart 22

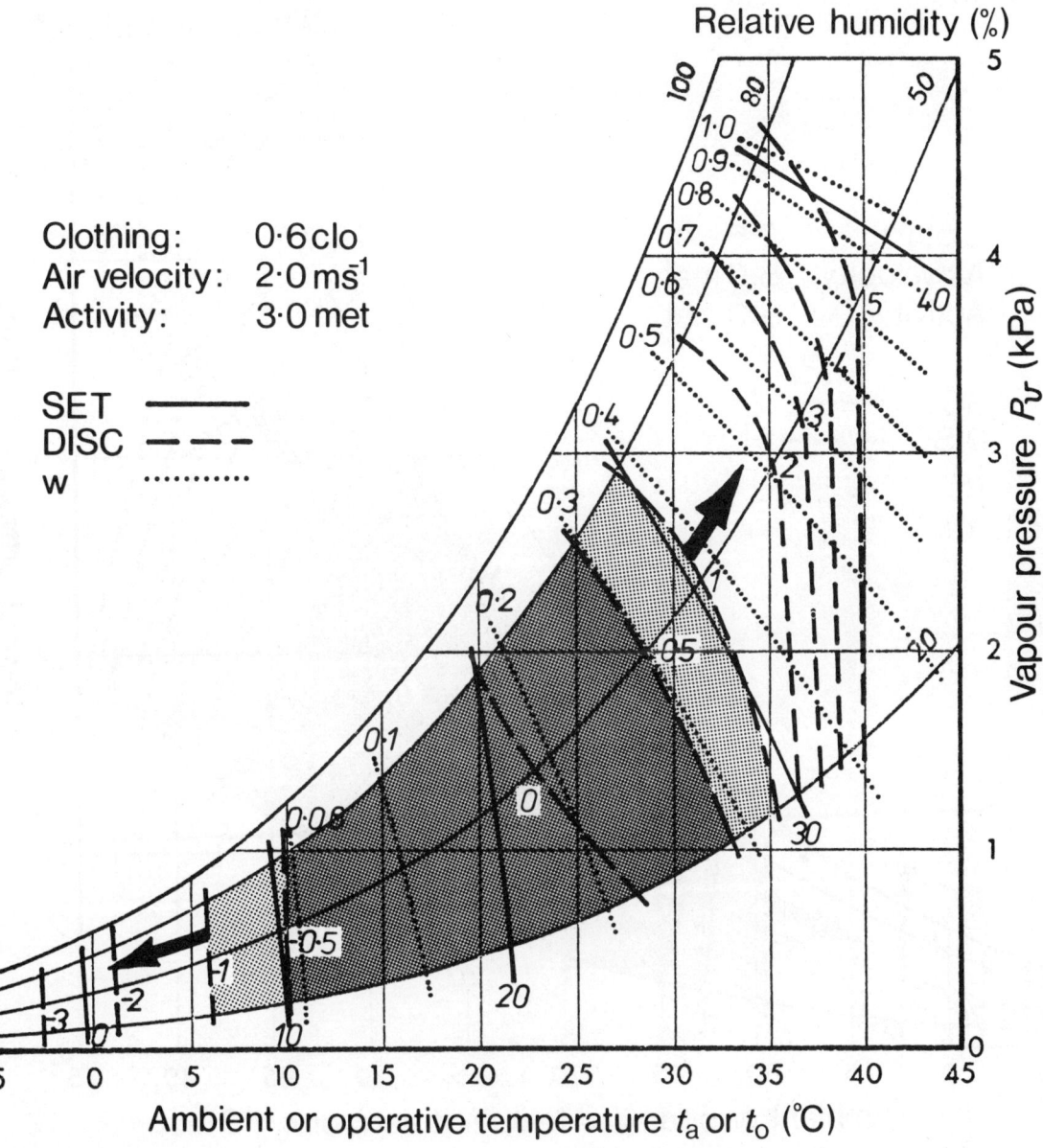

Clothing: 0·6 clo
Air velocity: 2·0 ms^{-1}
Activity: 3·0 met

SET ———————
DISC – – – – –
w ···············

Thermal comfort
chart 23

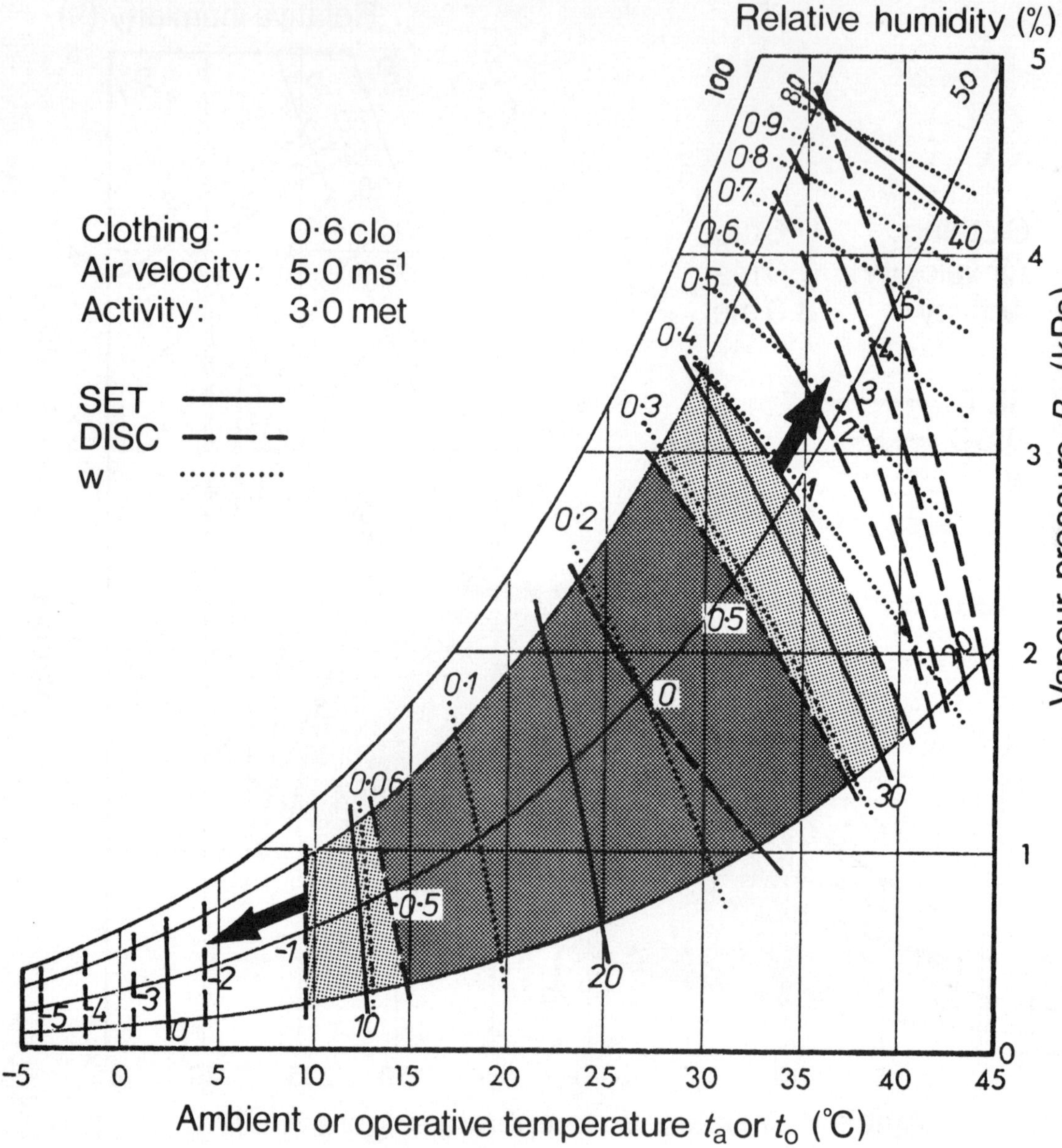

Relative humidity (%)

Clothing: 0·6 clo
Air velocity: 5·0 ms⁻¹
Activity: 3·0 met

SET ———
DISC — — —
W ....

Vapour pressure P_v (kPa)

Ambient or operative temperature t_a or t_o (°C)

Thermal comfort
chart 24

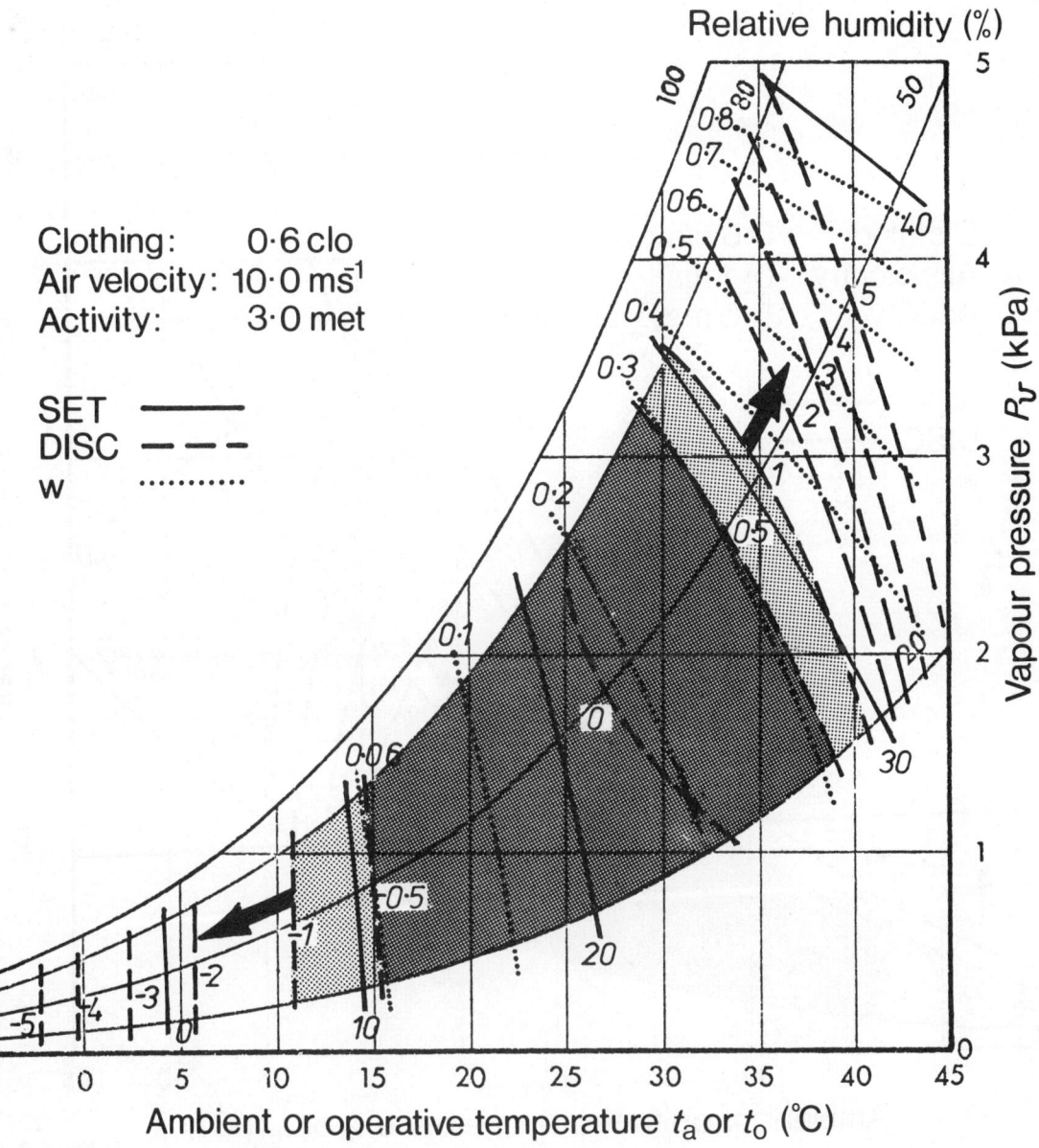

Clothing: 0·6 clo
Air velocity: 10·0 ms⁻¹
Activity: 3·0 met

SET ————
DISC – – –
w   ············

Thermal comfort
chart 25

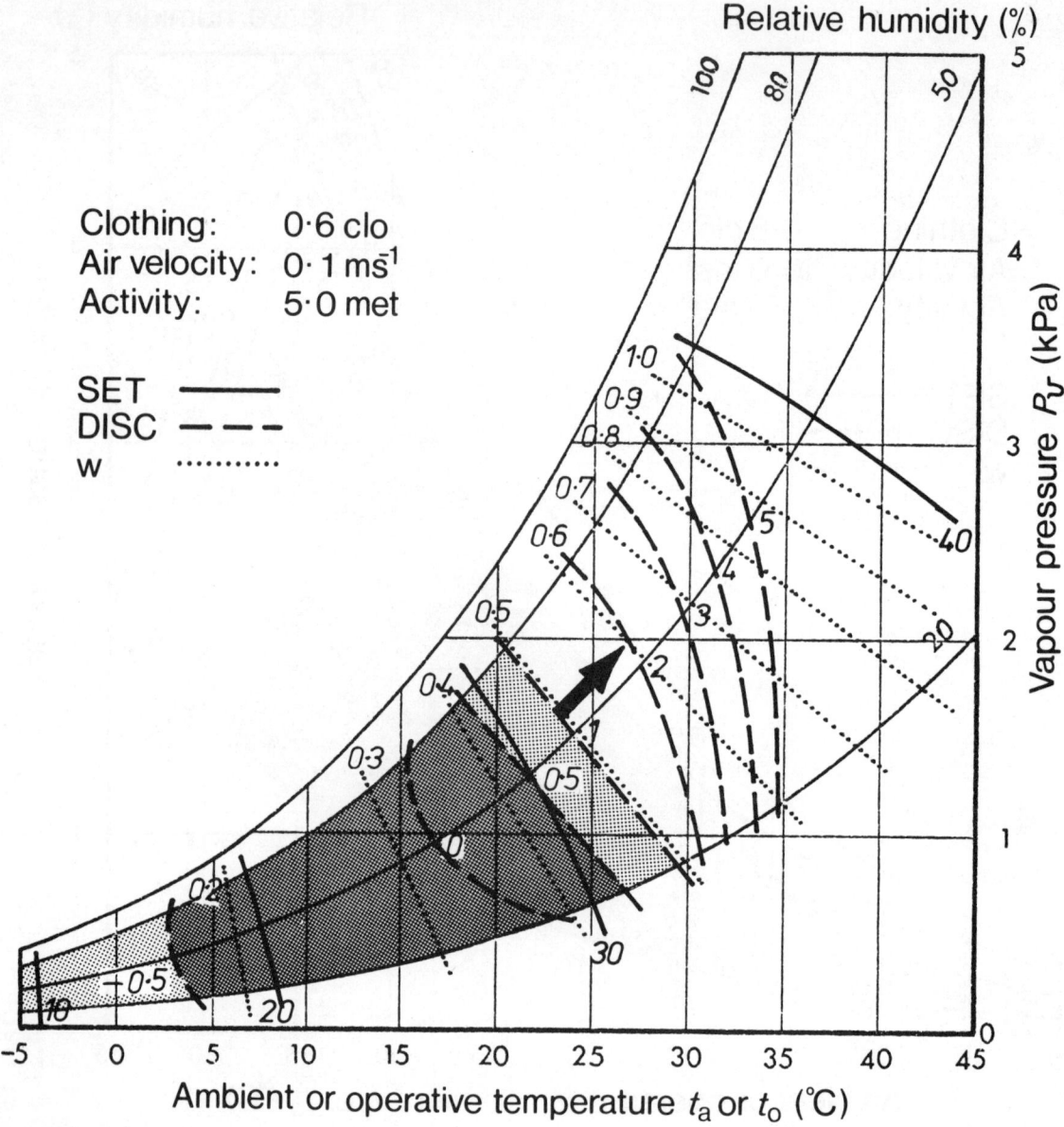

Clothing: 0·6 clo
Air velocity: 0·1 ms⁻¹
Activity: 5·0 met

SET ———
DISC – – –
w ....

Thermal comfort
chart 26

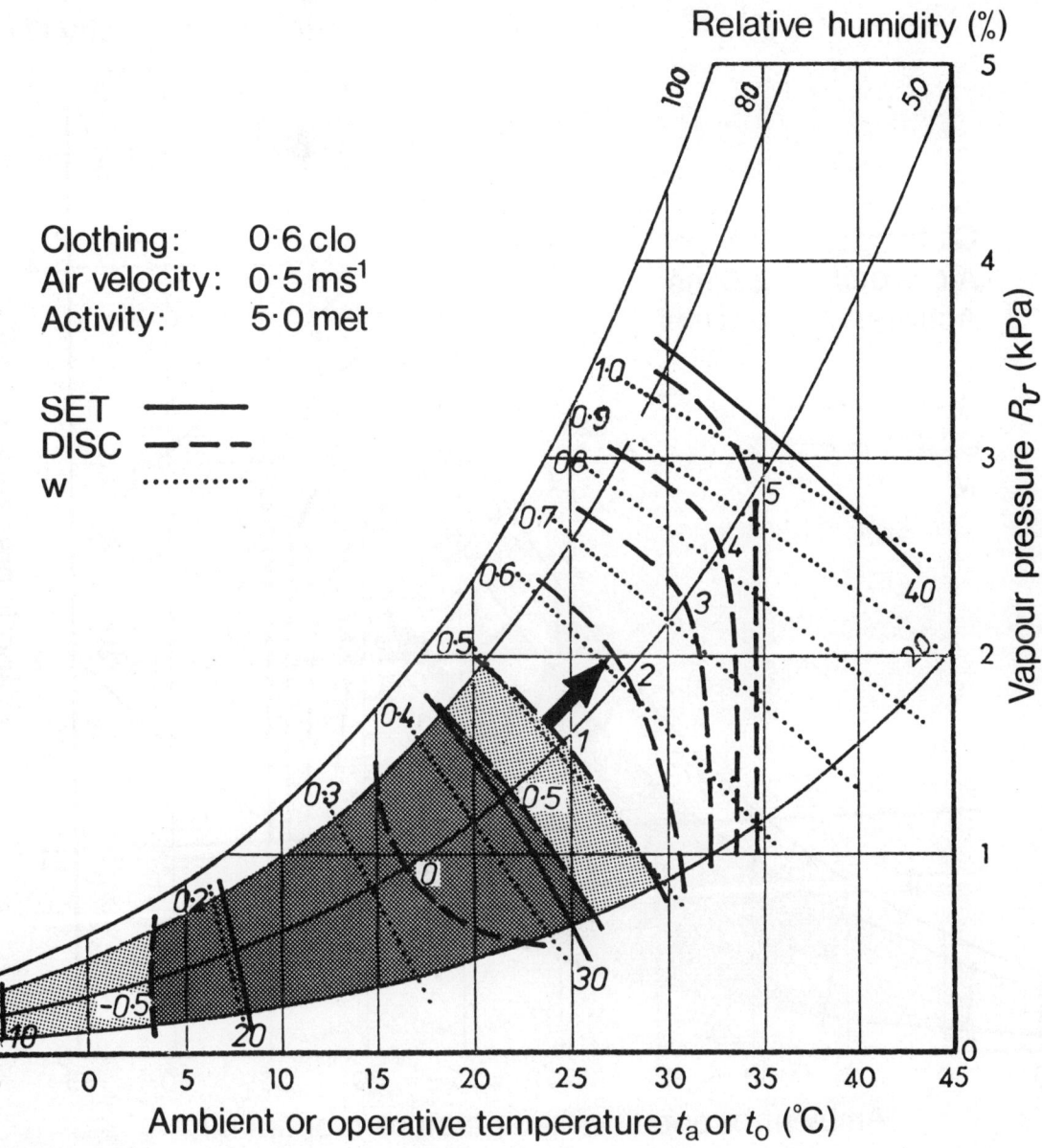

Clothing: 0·6 clo
Air velocity: 0·5 ms⁻¹
Activity: 5·0 met

SET ———
DISC — — —
w ············

Relative humidity (%)

Vapour pressure P_U (kPa)

Ambient or operative temperature t_a or t_o (°C)

Thermal comfort
chart 27

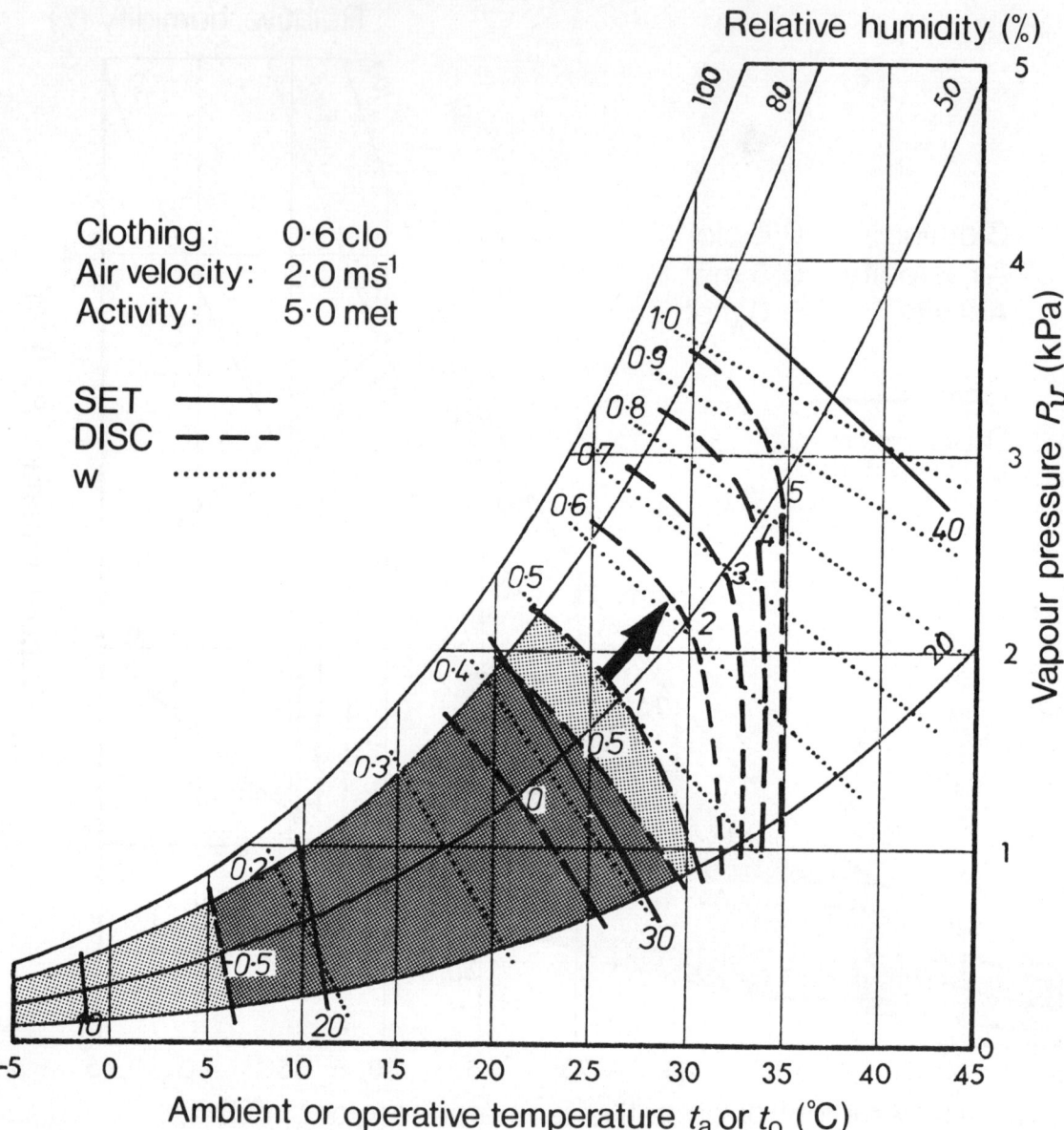

Clothing: 0·6 clo
Air velocity: 2·0 ms⁻¹
Activity: 5·0 met

SET ——————
DISC — — —
w ....

Thermal comfort
chart 28

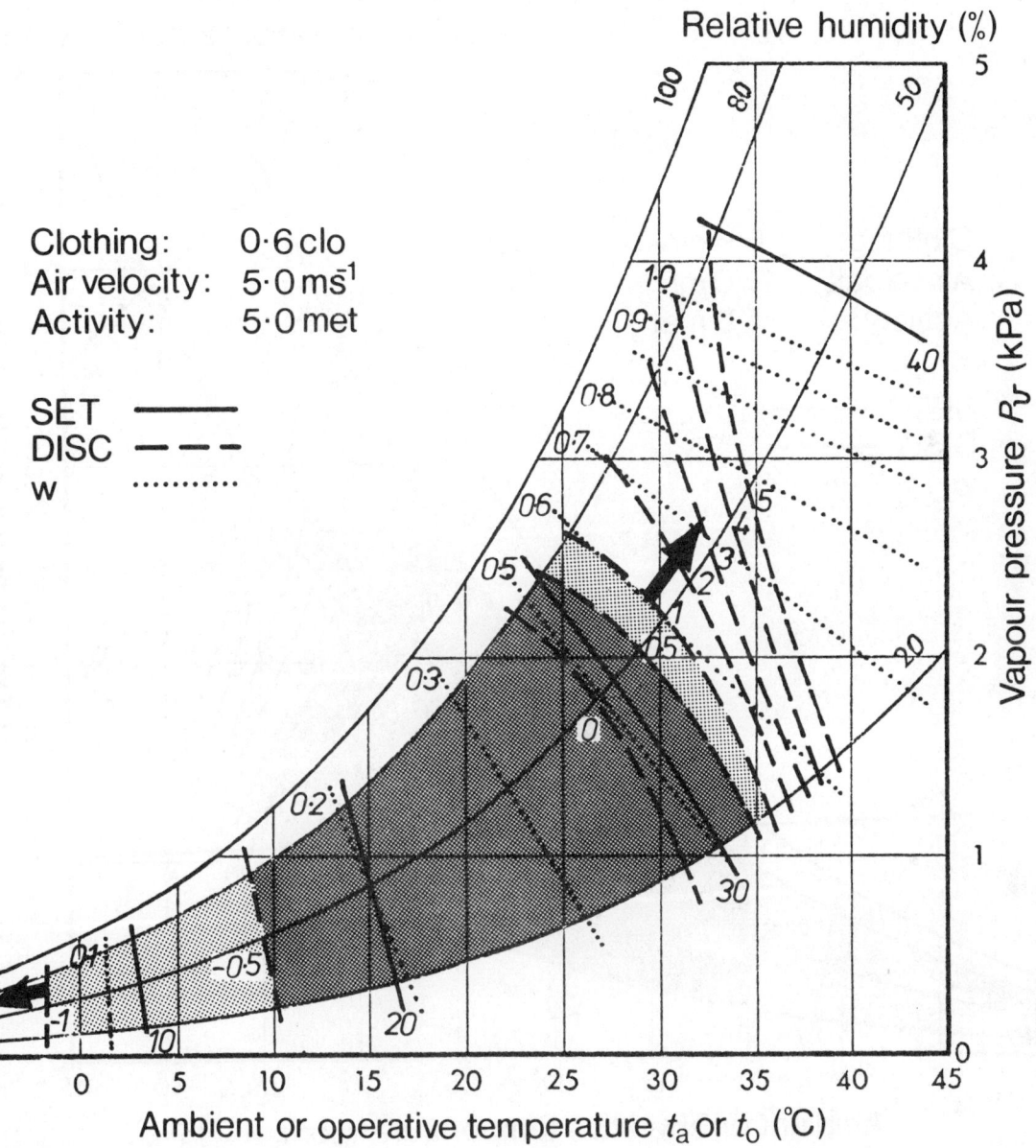

Thermal comfort
chart 29

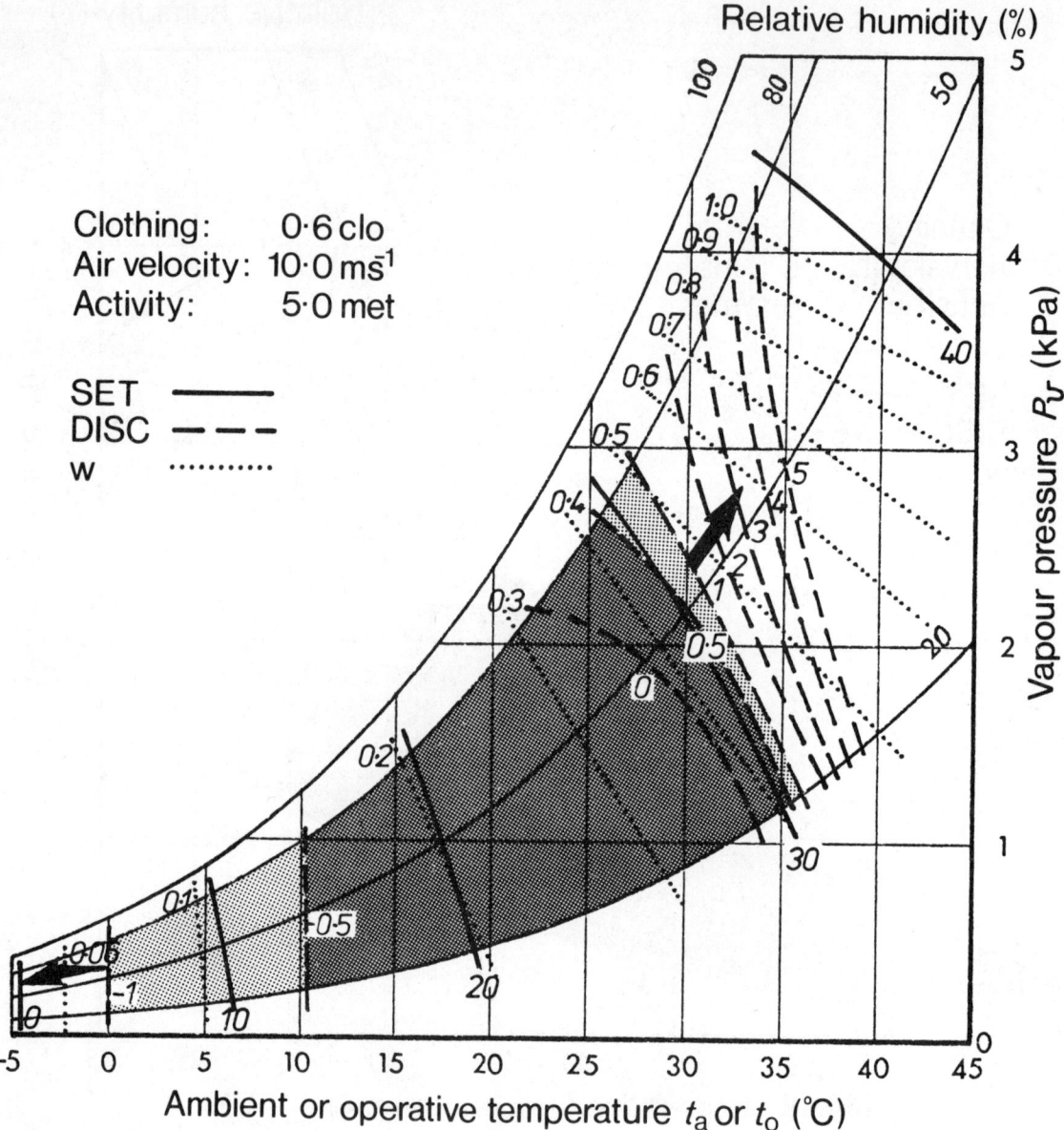

Thermal comfort
chart 30

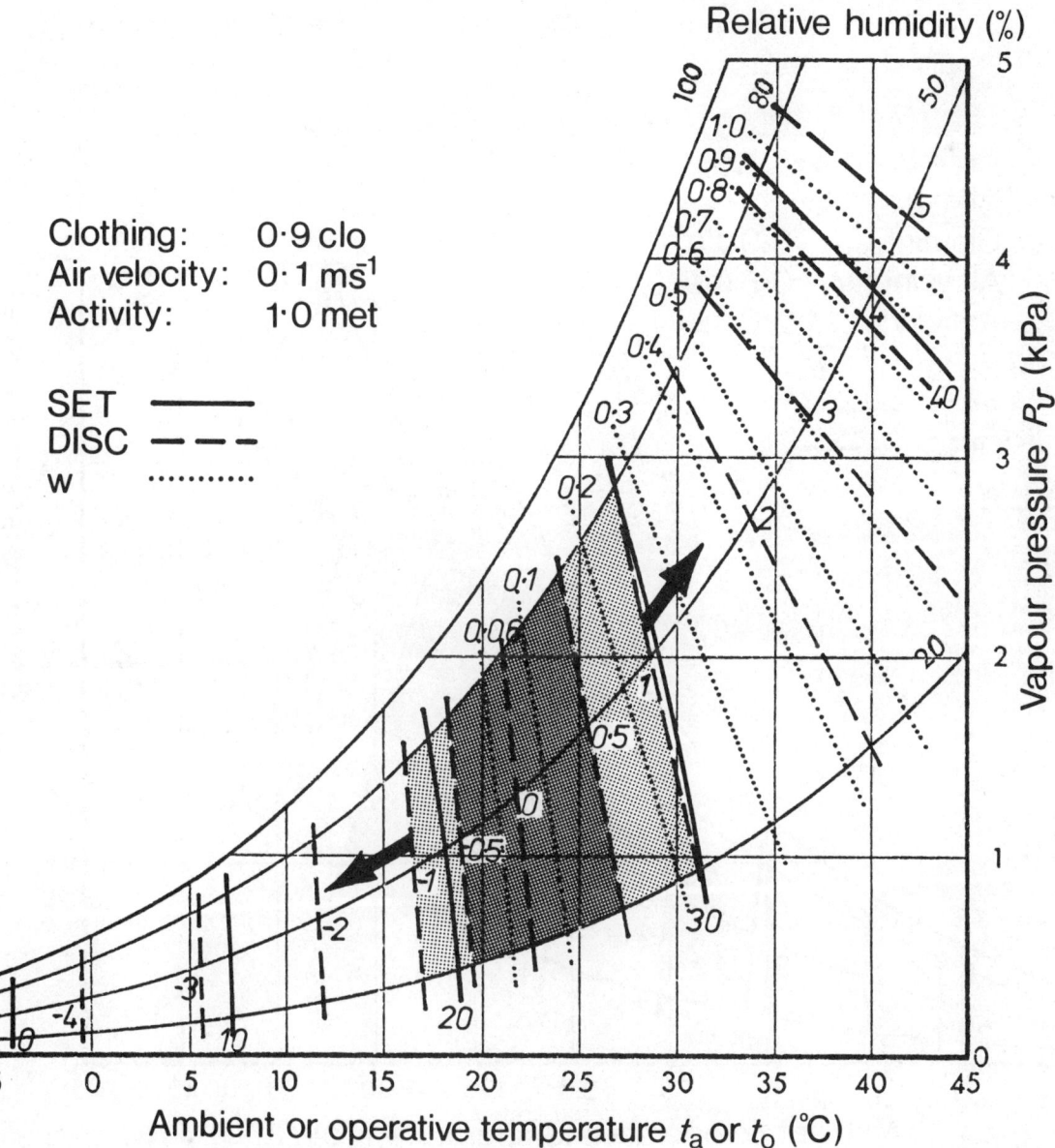

Clothing: 0·9 clo
Air velocity: 0·1 ms⁻¹
Activity: 1·0 met

SET ———
DISC ‑ ‑ ‑
w   ············

Relative humidity (%)

Vapour pressure P_J (kPa)

Ambient or operative temperature t_a or t_o (°C)

Thermal comfort
chart 31

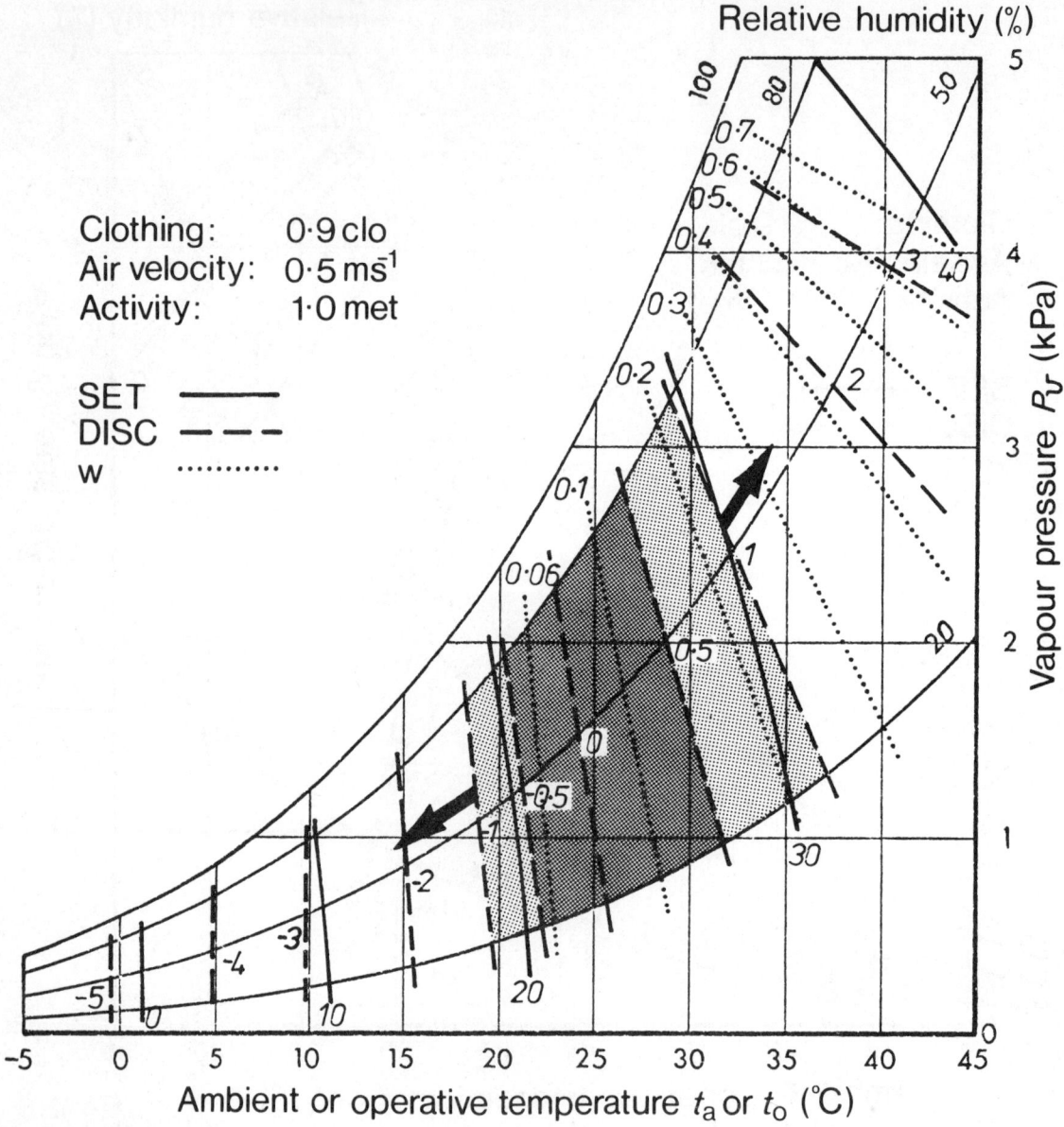

Relative humidity (%)

Clothing: 0·9 clo
Air velocity: 0·5 ms⁻¹
Activity: 1·0 met

SET ——————
DISC — — — —
w   ··············

Vapour pressure P_v (kPa)

Ambient or operative temperature t_a or t_o (°C)

Thermal comfort
chart 32

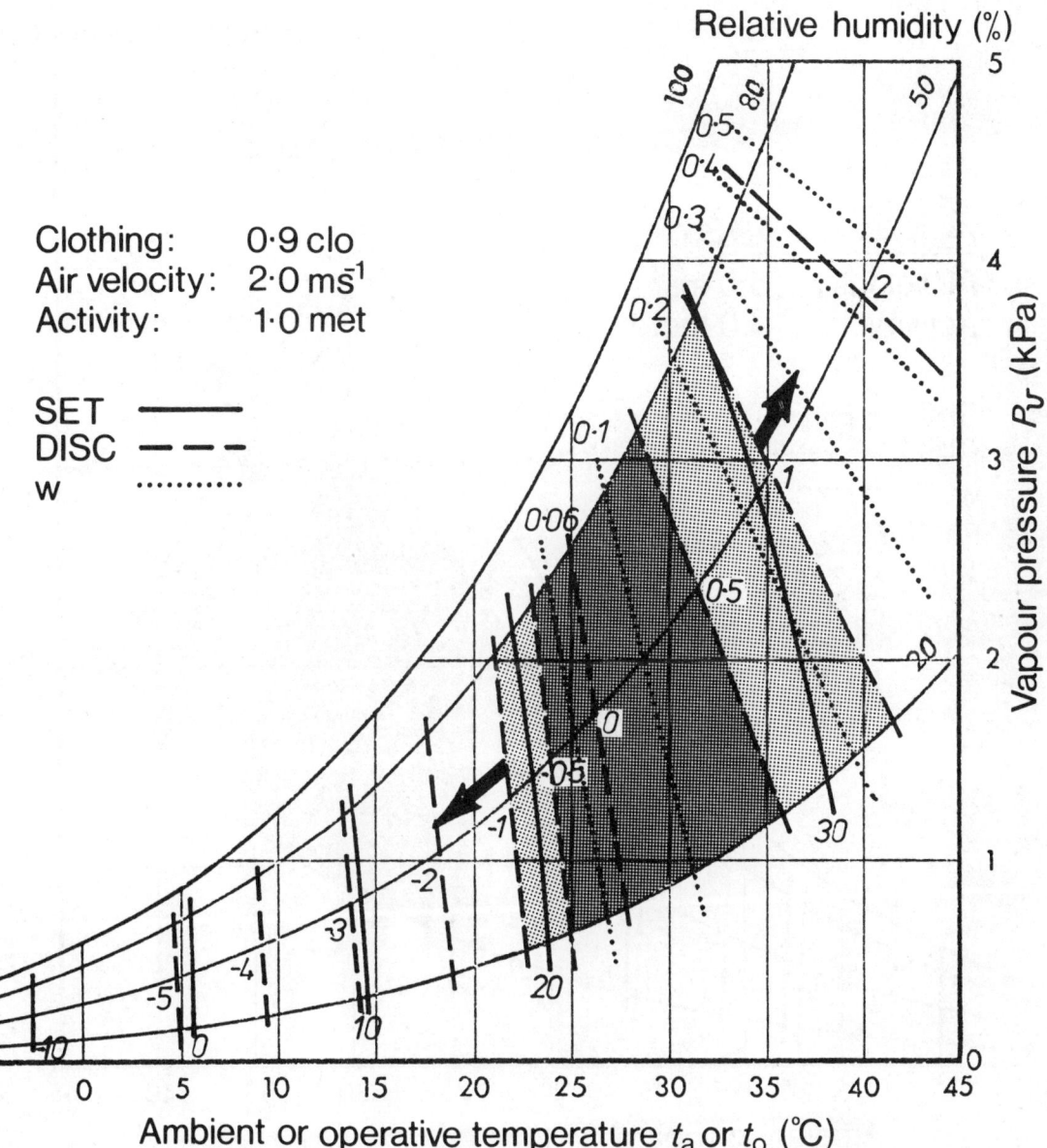

Thermal comfort
chart 33

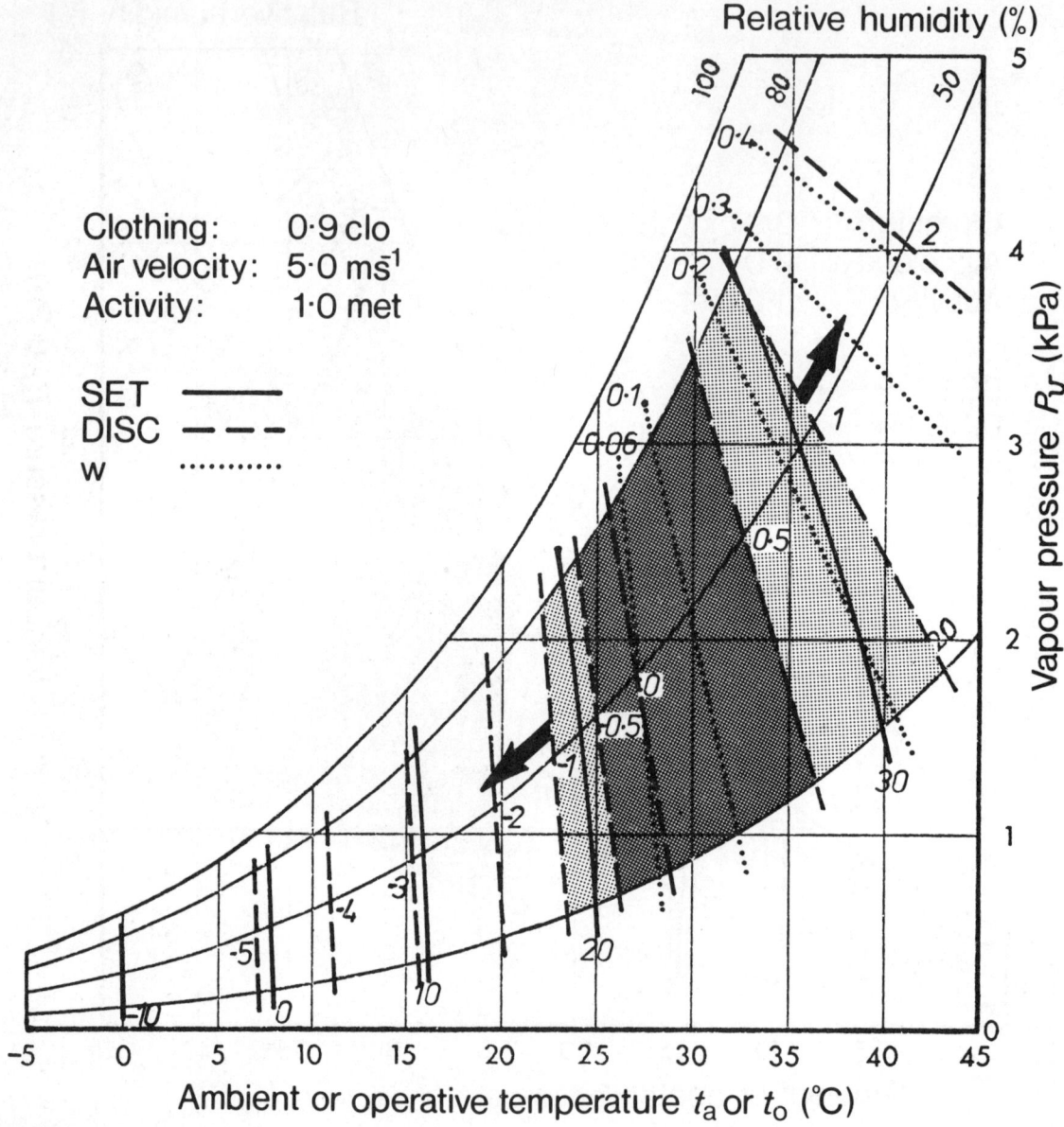

Clothing: 0·9 clo
Air velocity: 5·0 ms⁻¹
Activity: 1·0 met

SET ————
DISC – – – –
w ·············

Thermal comfort
chart 34

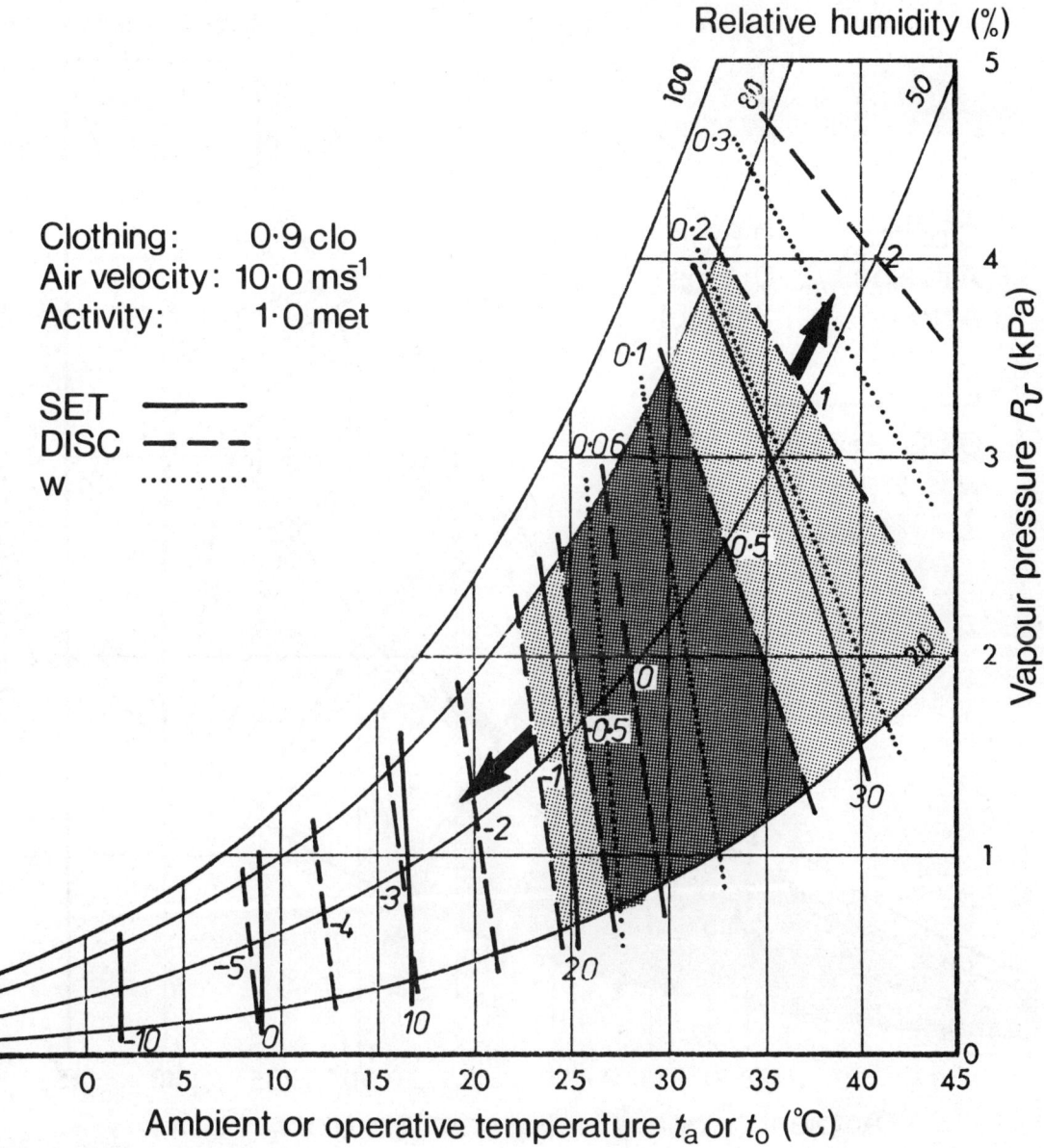

Clothing: 0·9 clo
Air velocity: 10·0 ms⁻¹
Activity: 1·0 met

SET ——————
DISC — — —
w   ⋯⋯⋯⋯⋯⋯

Relative humidity (%)

Vapour pressure P_v (kPa)

Ambient or operative temperature t_a or t_o (°C)

Thermal comfort
chart 35

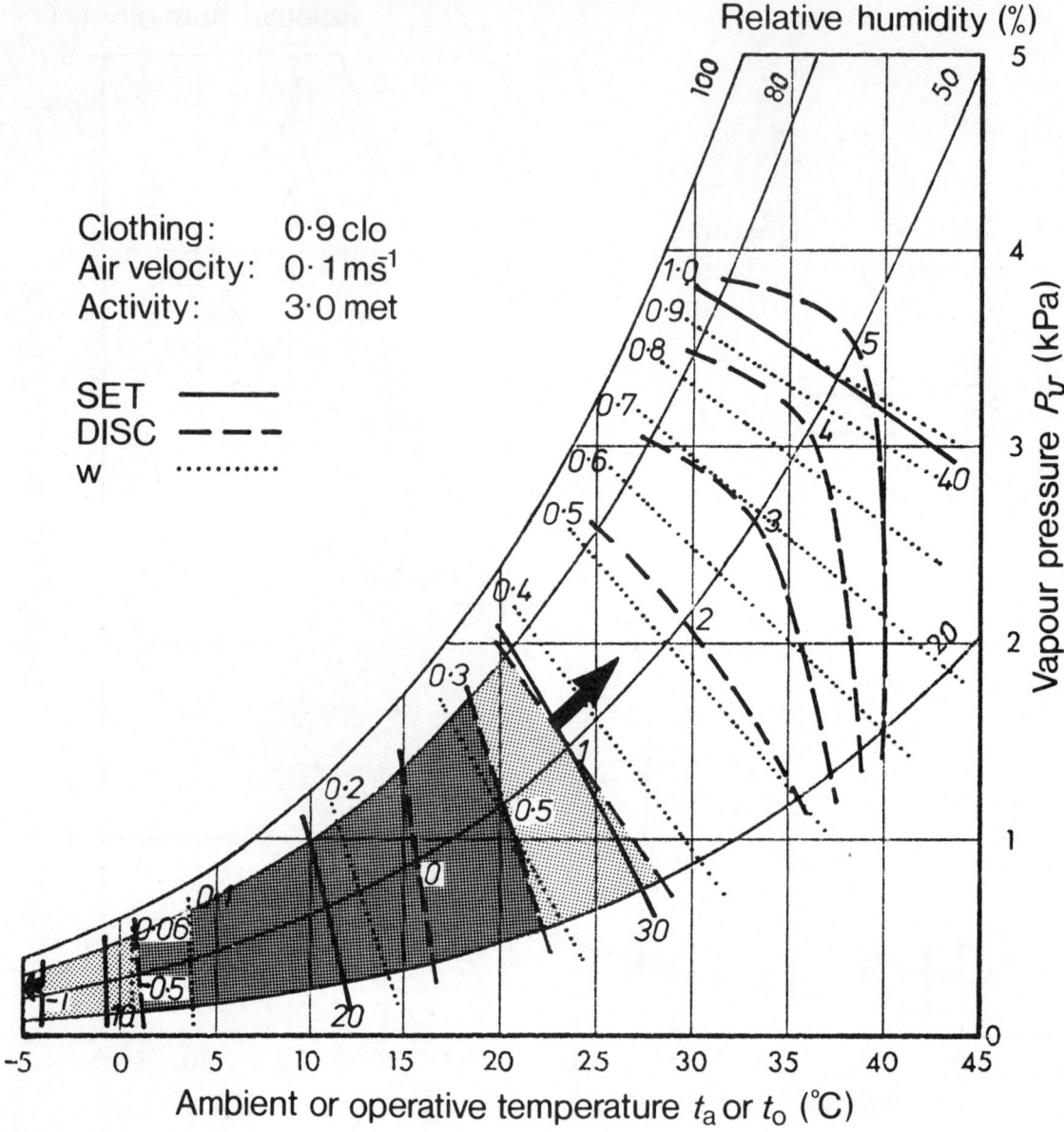

Relative humidity (%)

Clothing: 0·9 clo
Air velocity: 0·1 ms⁻¹
Activity: 3·0 met

SET ——
DISC ─ ─ ─
w ···········

Vapour pressure P_v (kPa)

Ambient or operative temperature t_a or t_o (°C)

Thermal comfort
chart 36

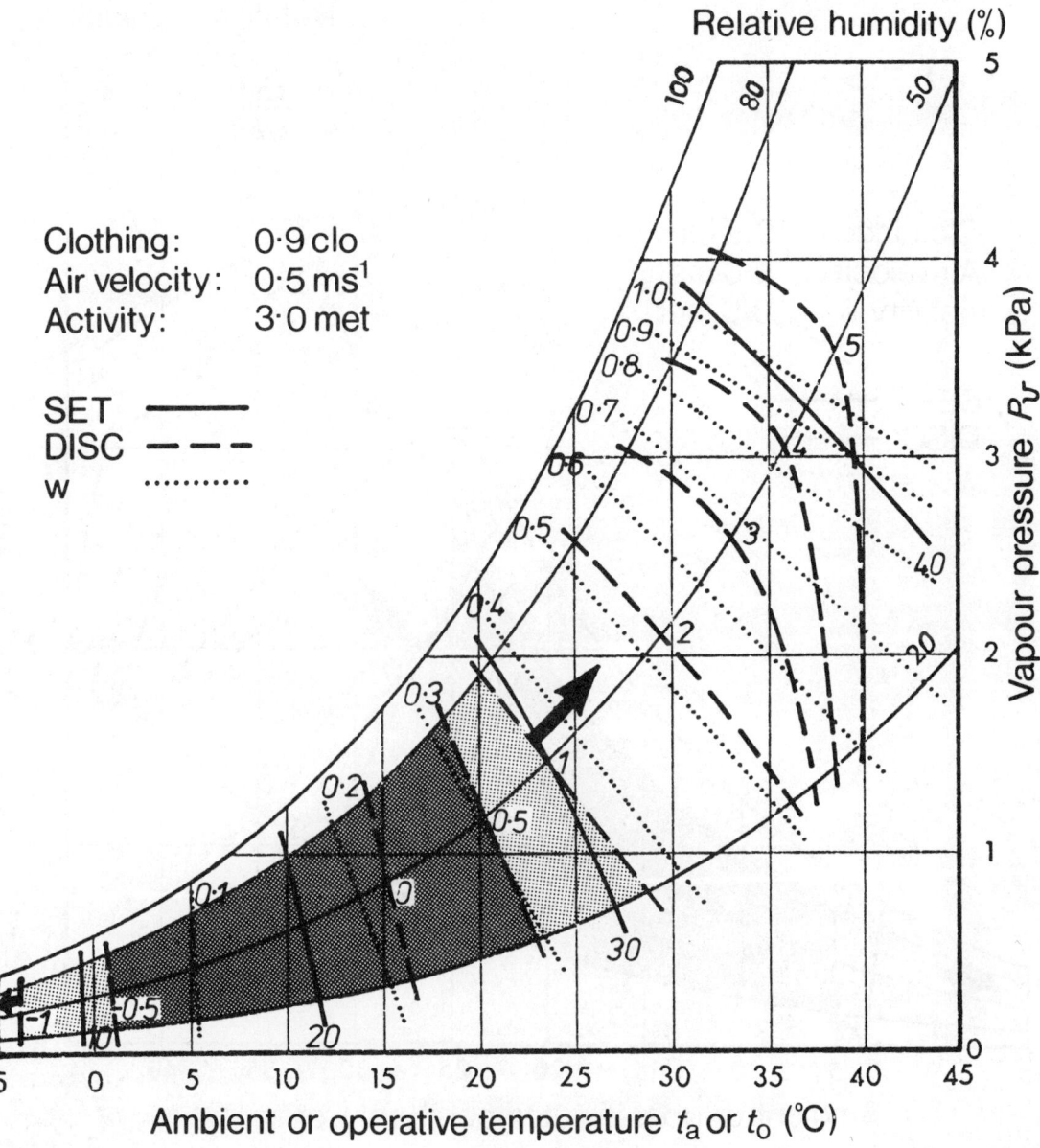

Clothing: 0·9 clo
Air velocity: 0·5 ms⁻¹
Activity: 3·0 met

SET ——————
DISC — — —
w   ....

Thermal comfort
chart 37

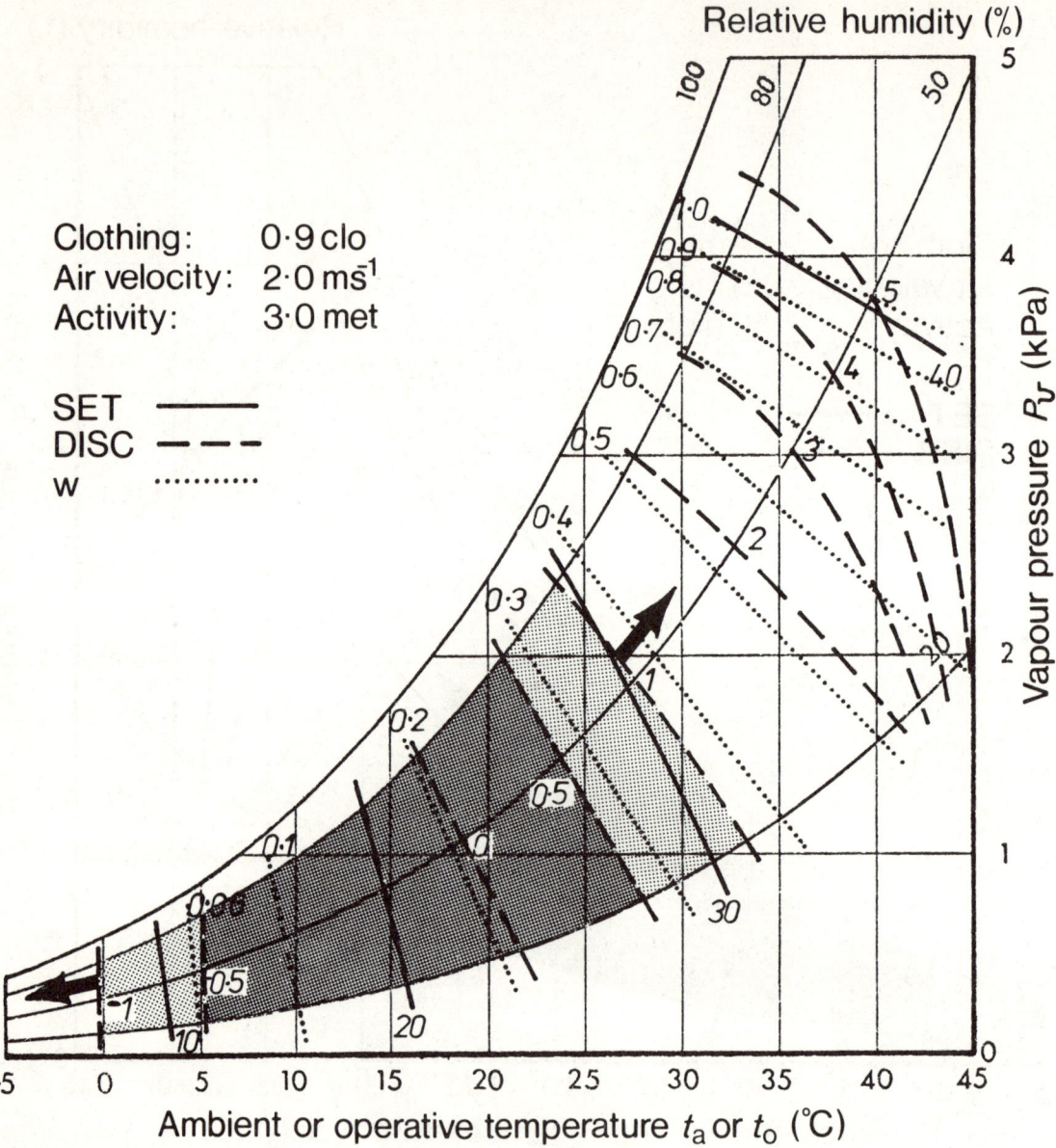

Relative humidity (%)

Clothing: 0·9 clo
Air velocity: 2·0 ms⁻¹
Activity: 3·0 met

SET ———
DISC – – –
W ·············

Vapour pressure P_J (kPa)

Ambient or operative temperature t_a or t_o (°C)

Thermal comfort
chart 38

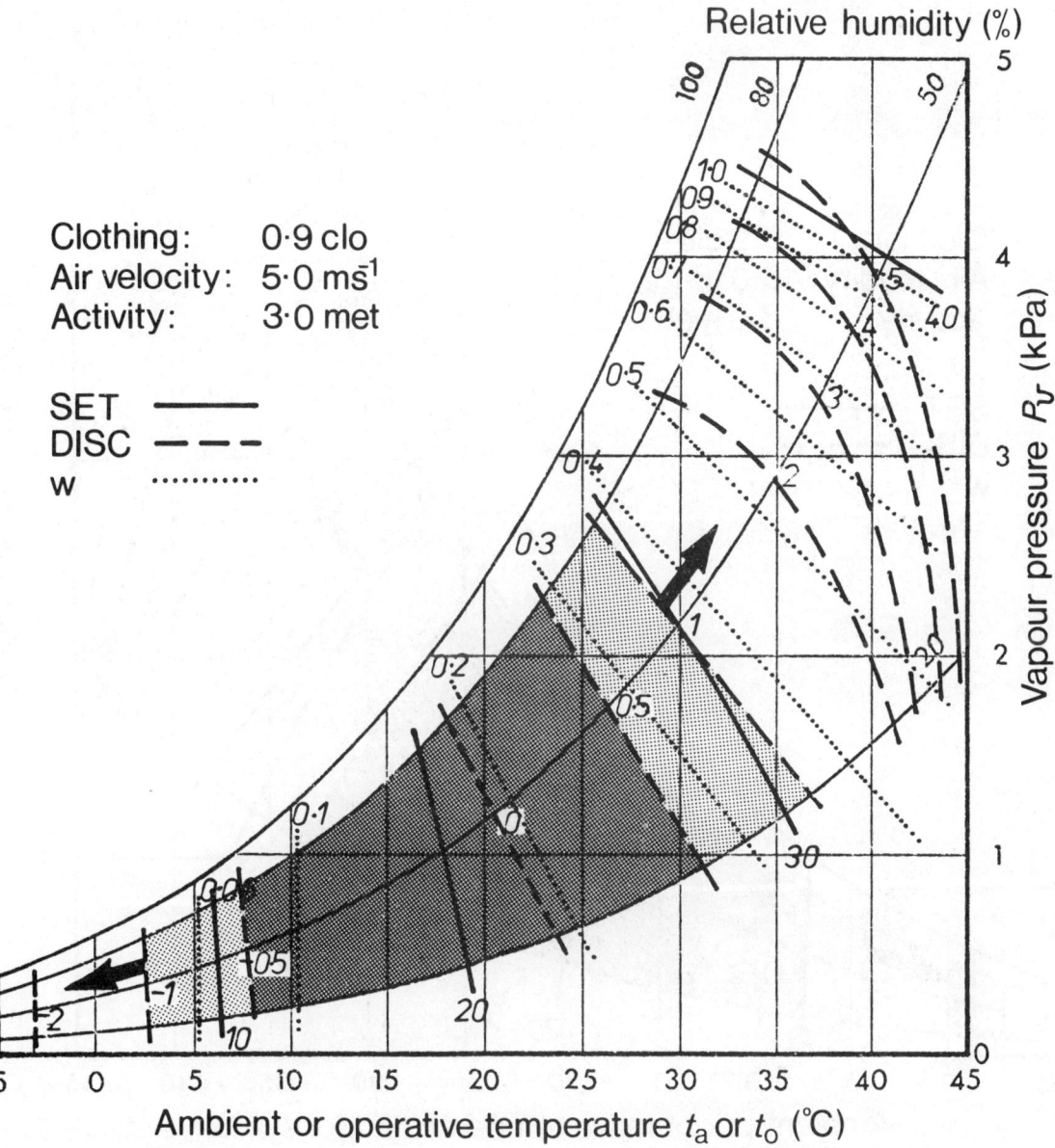

Clothing: 0·9 clo
Air velocity: 5·0 ms⁻¹
Activity: 3·0 met

SET ——————
DISC — — — —
w ··············

Relative humidity (%)

Vapour pressure P_U (kPa)

Ambient or operative temperature t_a or t_o (°C)

Thermal comfort
chart 39

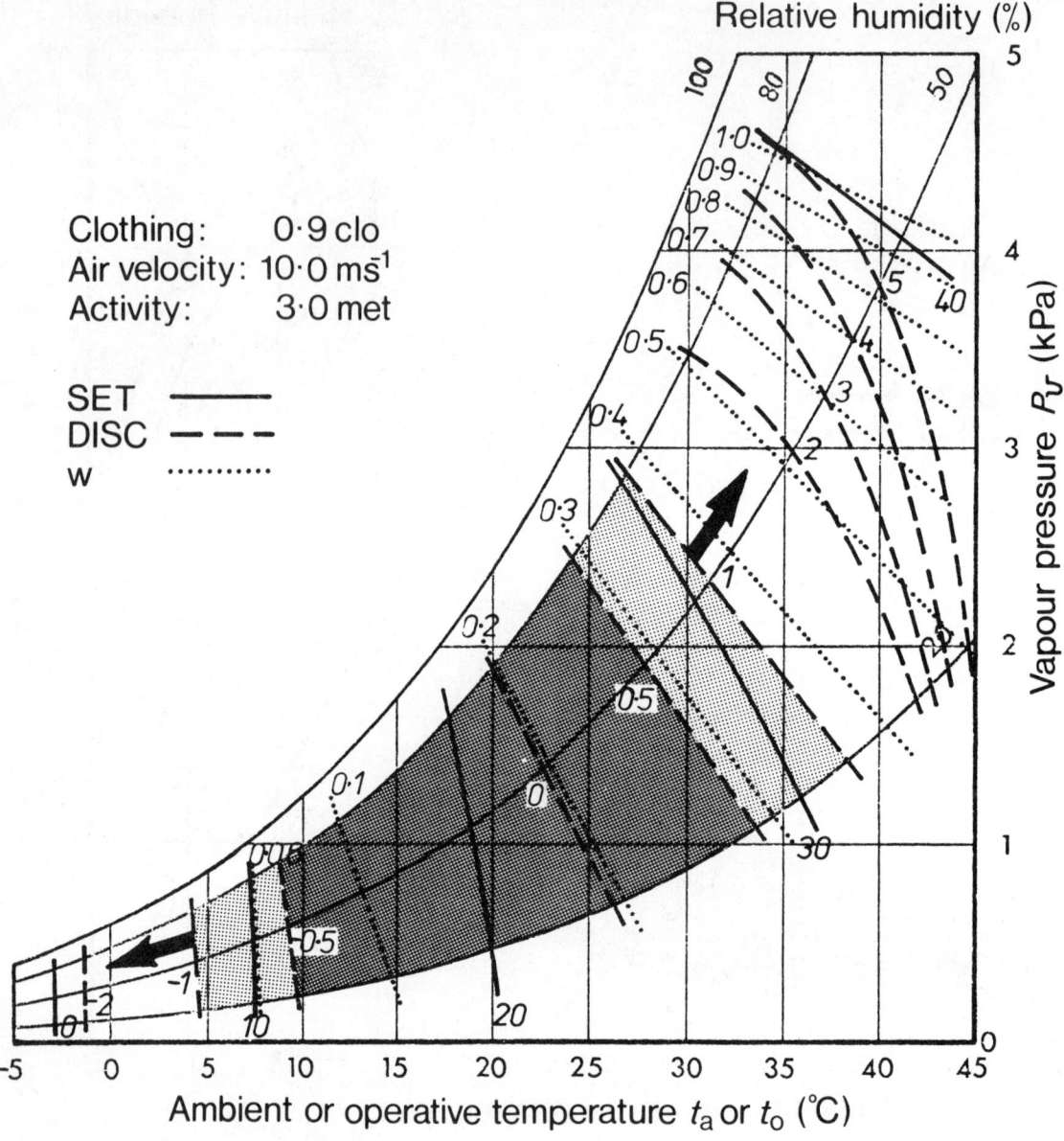

Clothing: 0·9 clo
Air velocity: 10·0 ms⁻¹
Activity: 3·0 met

SET ———
DISC – – –
w ··········

Relative humidity (%)

Vapour pressure P_v (kPa)

Ambient or operative temperature t_a or t_o (°C)

Thermal comfort
chart 40

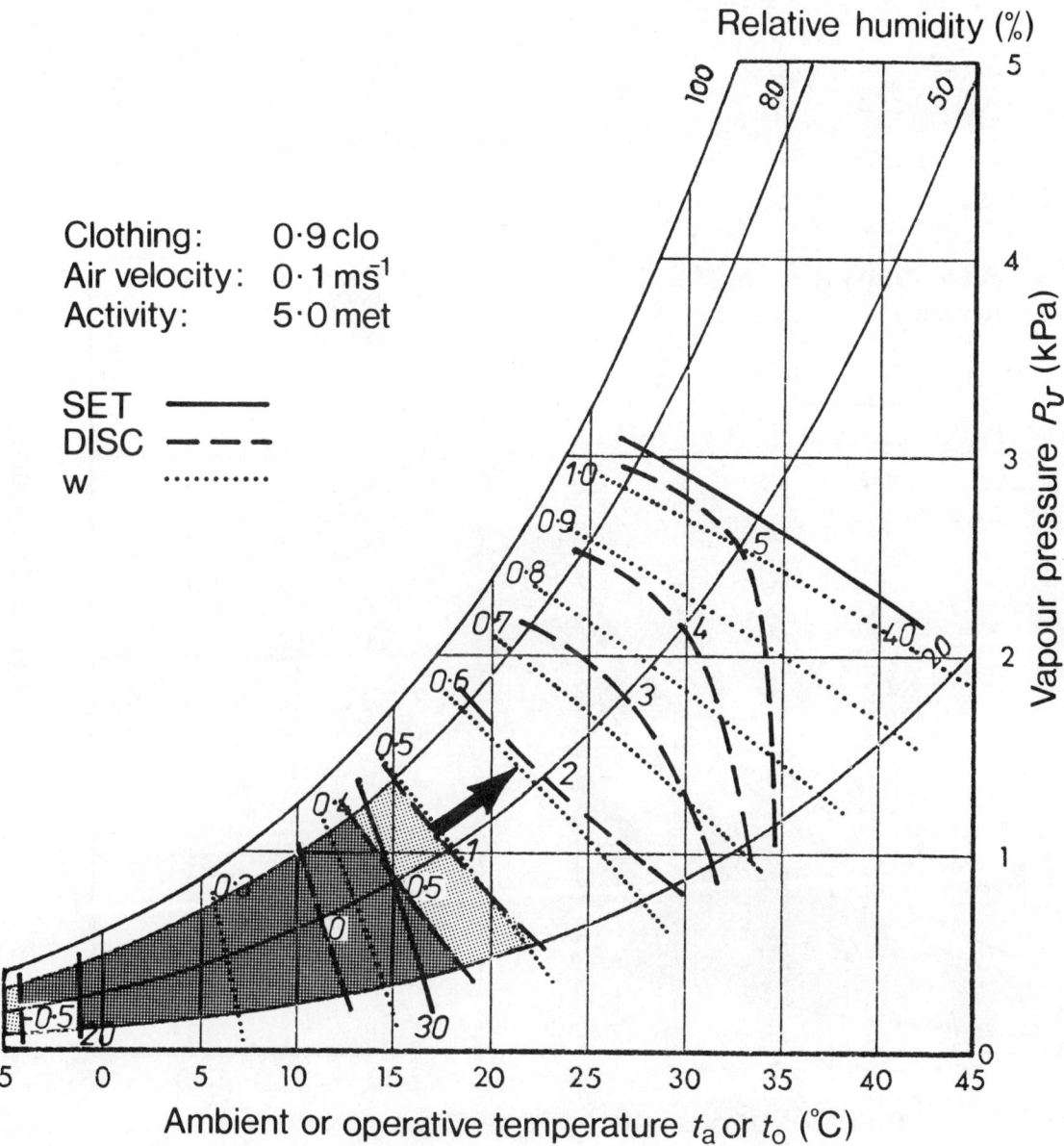

Clothing: 0·9 clo
Air velocity: 0·1 ms^{-1}
Activity: 5·0 met

SET ——————
DISC — — —
W   ··············

Thermal comfort
chart 41

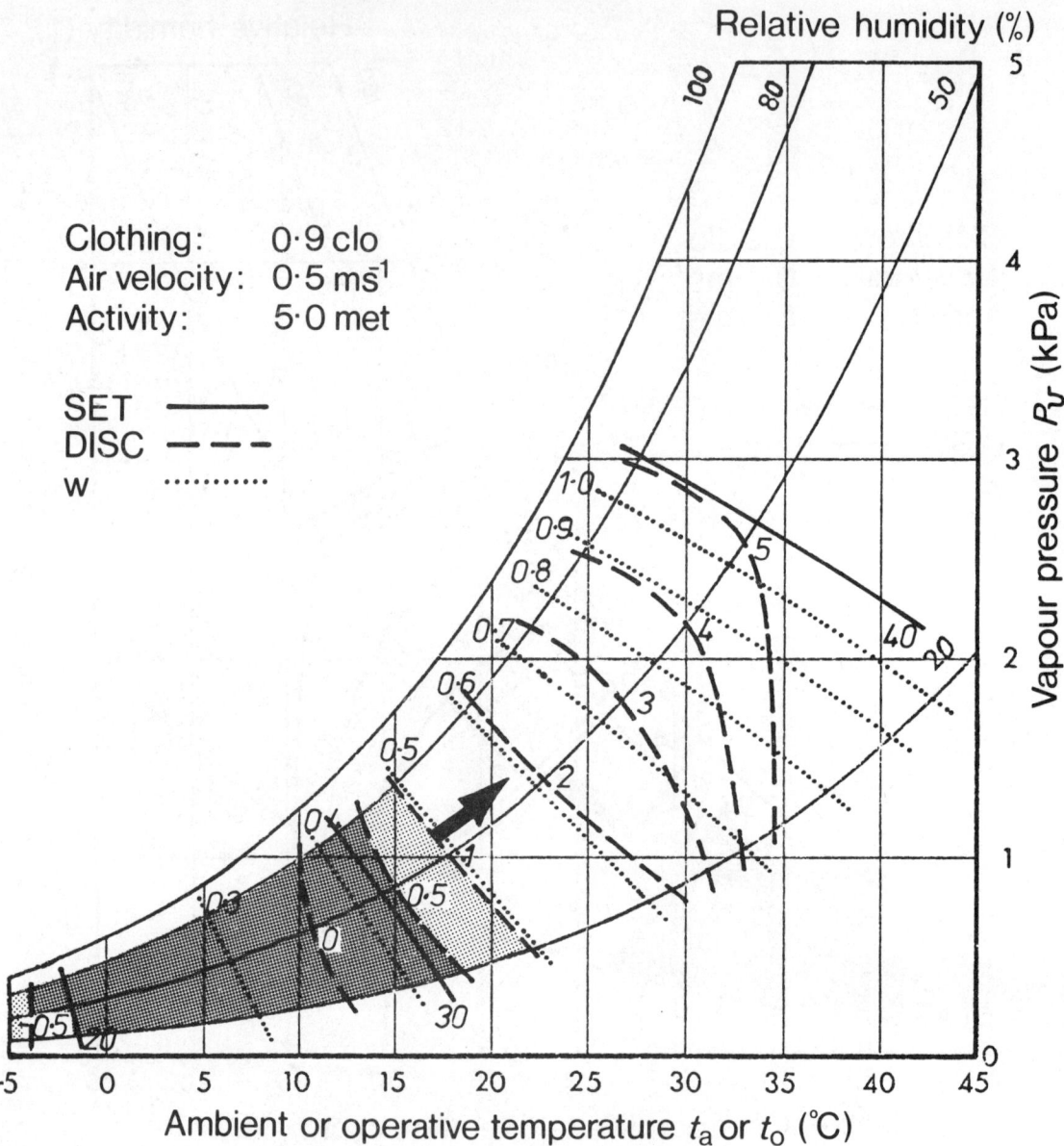

Clothing: 0·9 clo
Air velocity: 0·5 ms⁻¹
Activity: 5·0 met

SET   ———
DISC — — —
w   ··········

Relative humidity (%)

Vapour pressure P_v (kPa)

Ambient or operative temperature t_a or t_o (°C)

Thermal comfort
chart 42

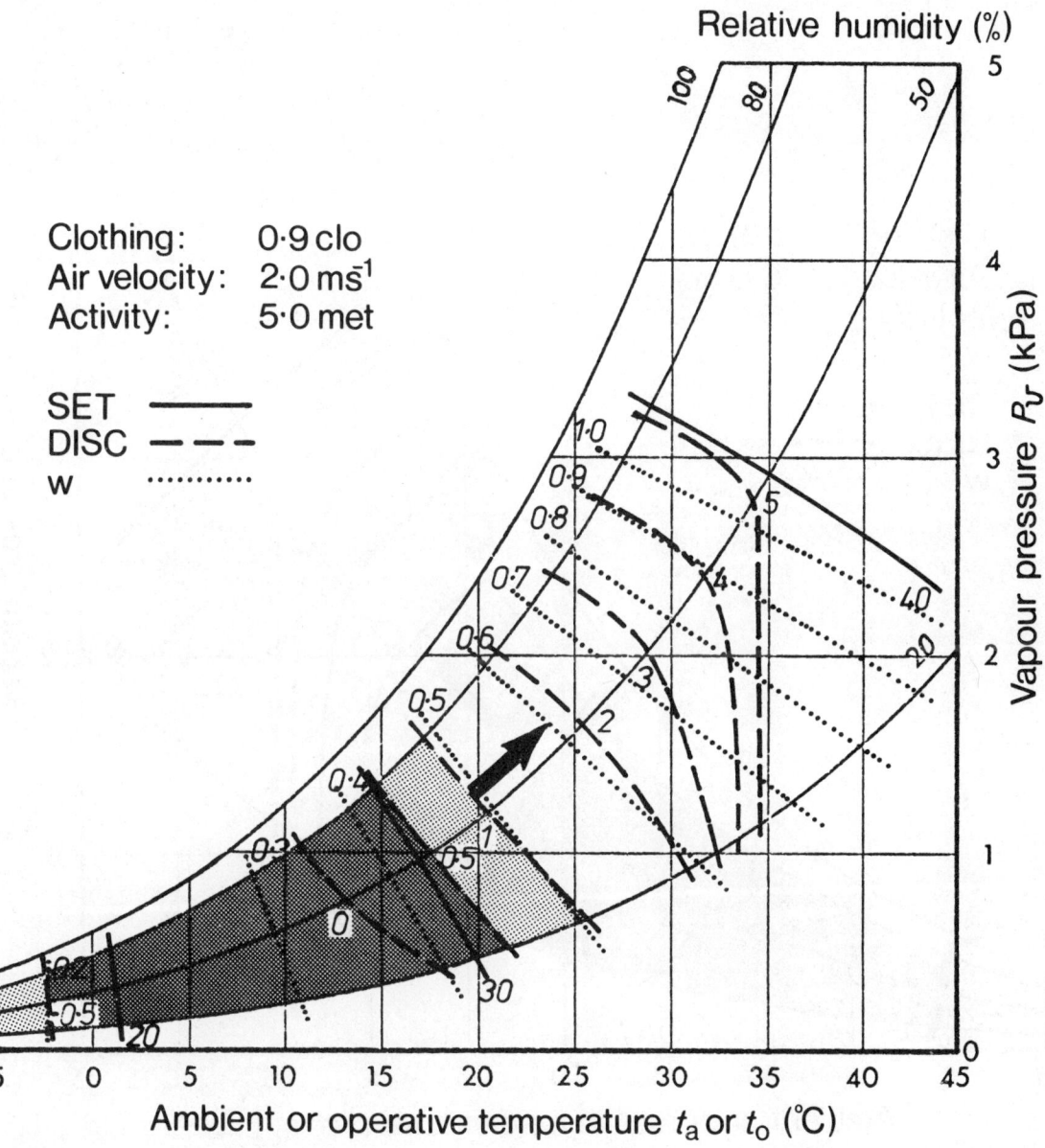

Clothing: 0·9 clo
Air velocity: 2·0 ms⁻¹
Activity: 5·0 met

SET ———
DISC – – –
w ·············

Thermal comfort
chart 43

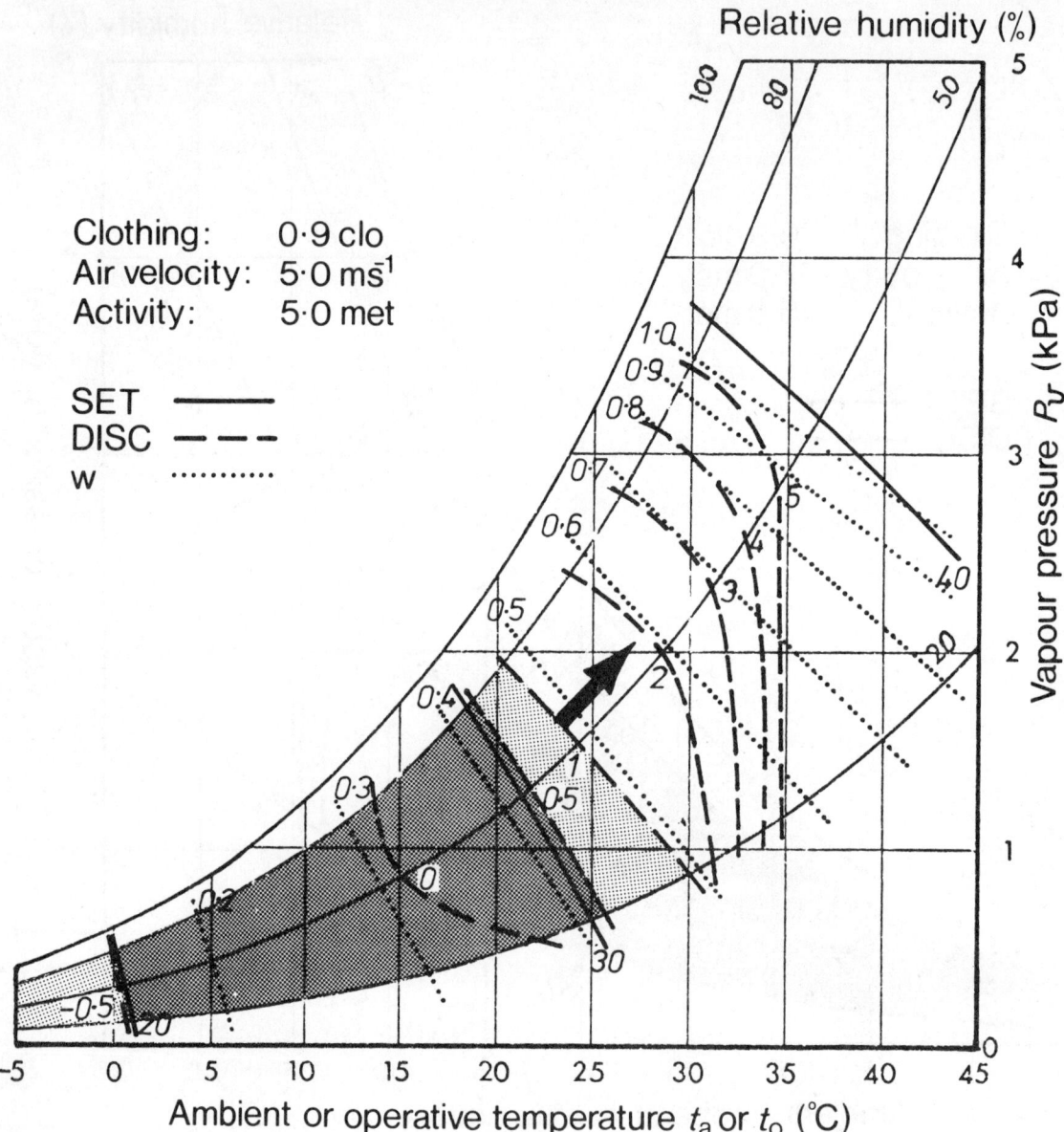

Relative humidity (%)

Clothing: 0·9 clo
Air velocity: 5·0 ms⁻¹
Activity: 5·0 met

SET ——
DISC – – –
w ·········

Vapour pressure P_v (kPa)

Ambient or operative temperature t_a or t_o (°C)

Thermal comfort
chart 44

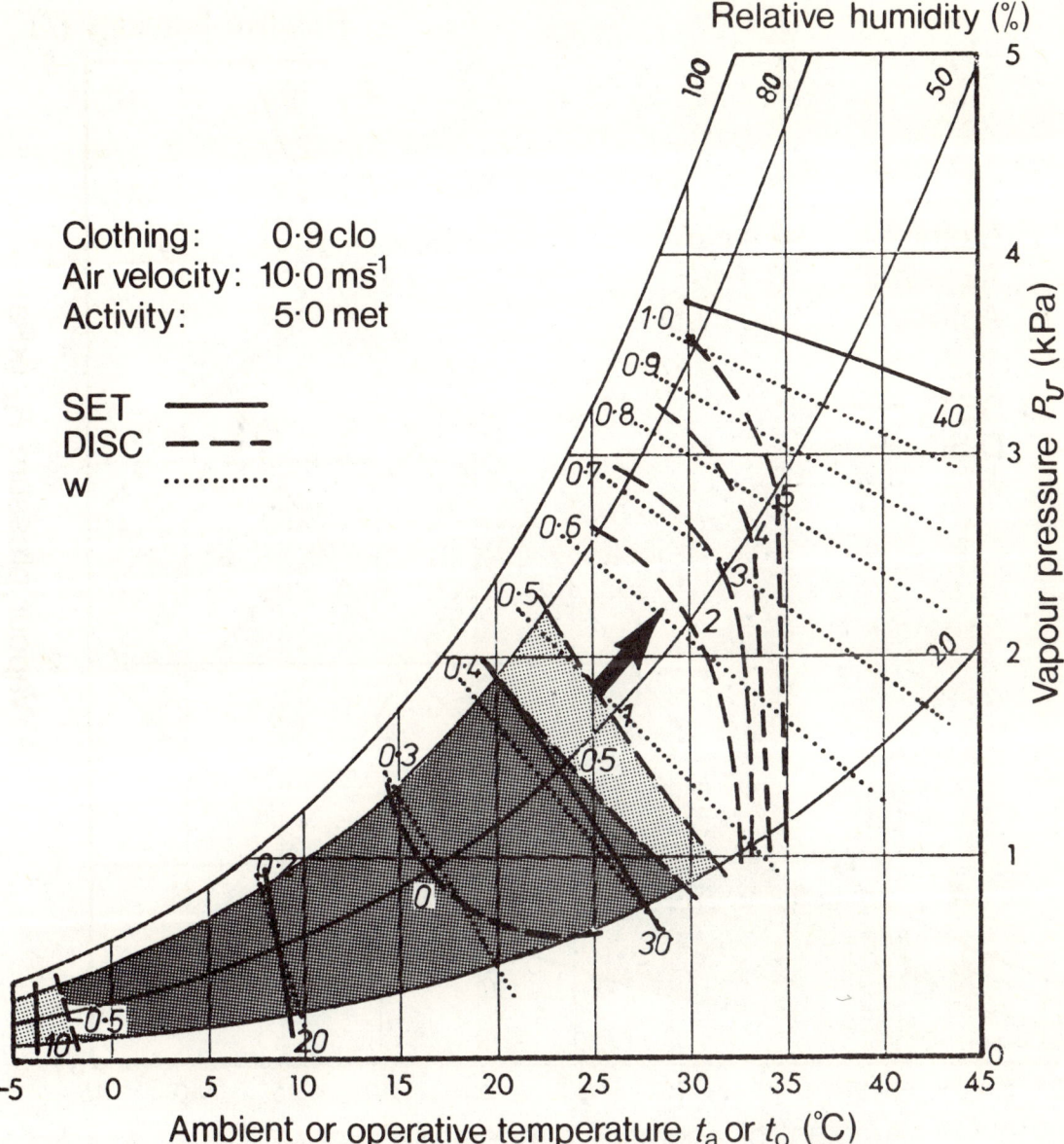

Thermal comfort
chart 45

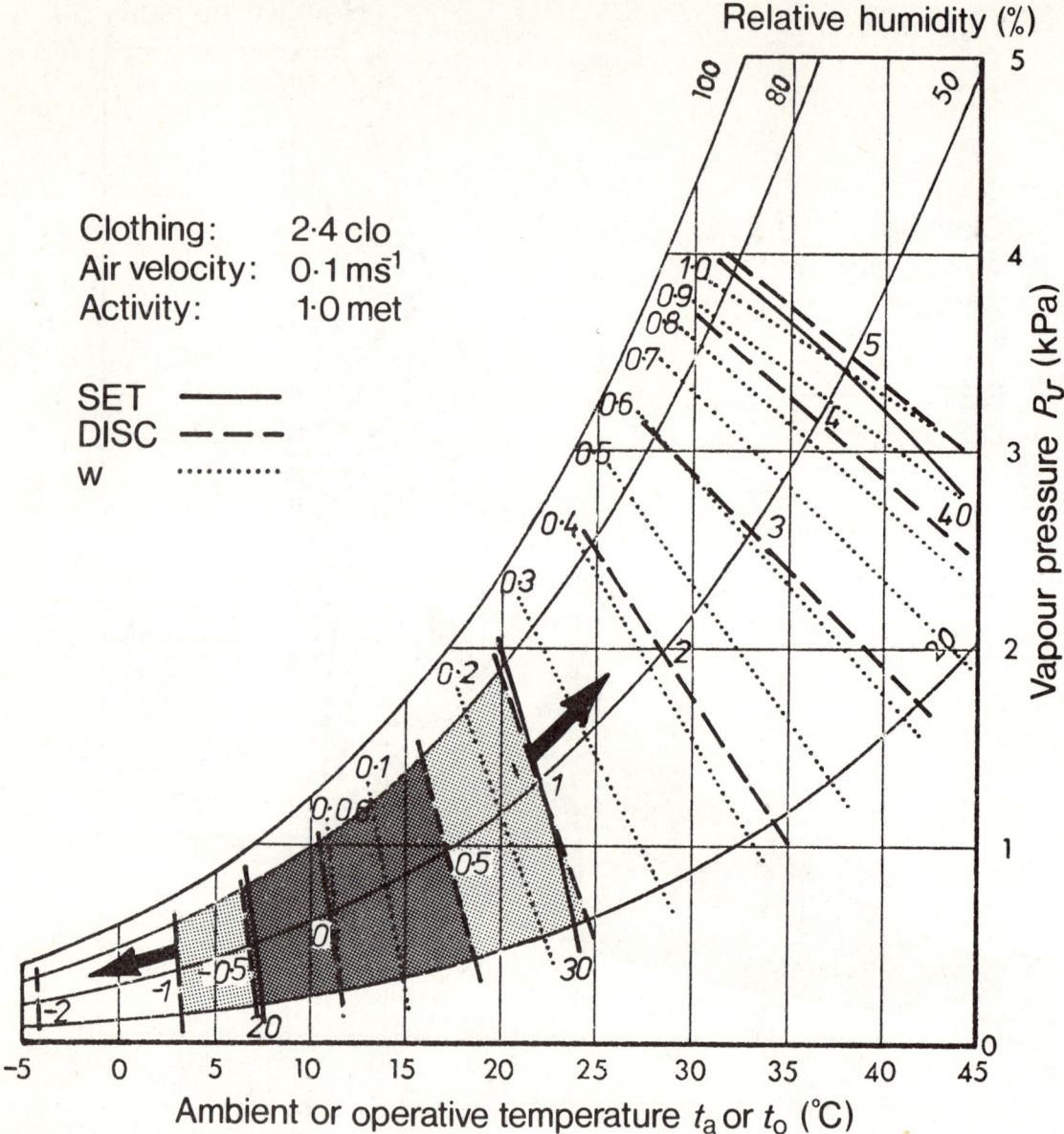

Relative humidity (%)

Clothing: 2·4 clo
Air velocity: 0·1 ms⁻¹
Activity: 1·0 met

SET ———
DISC – – –
W ·············

Vapour pressure P_v (kPa)

Ambient or operative temperature t_a or t_o (°C)

Thermal comfort
chart 46

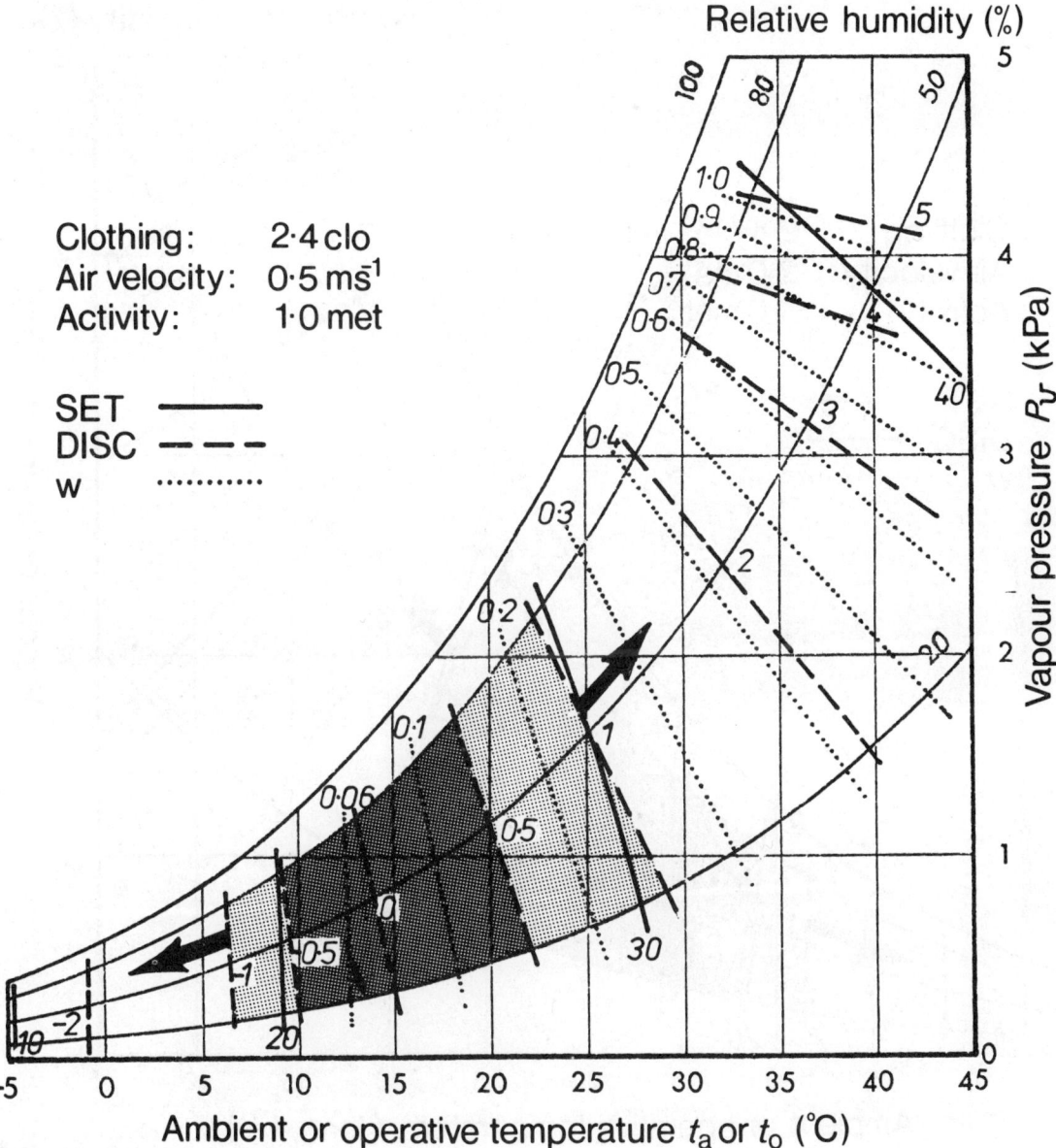

Clothing: 2·4 clo
Air velocity: 0·5 ms⁻¹
Activity: 1·0 met

SET   ———
DISC — — —
w   ···········

Relative humidity (%)

Vapour pressure P_V (kPa)

Ambient or operative temperature t_a or t_o (°C)

Thermal comfort
chart 47

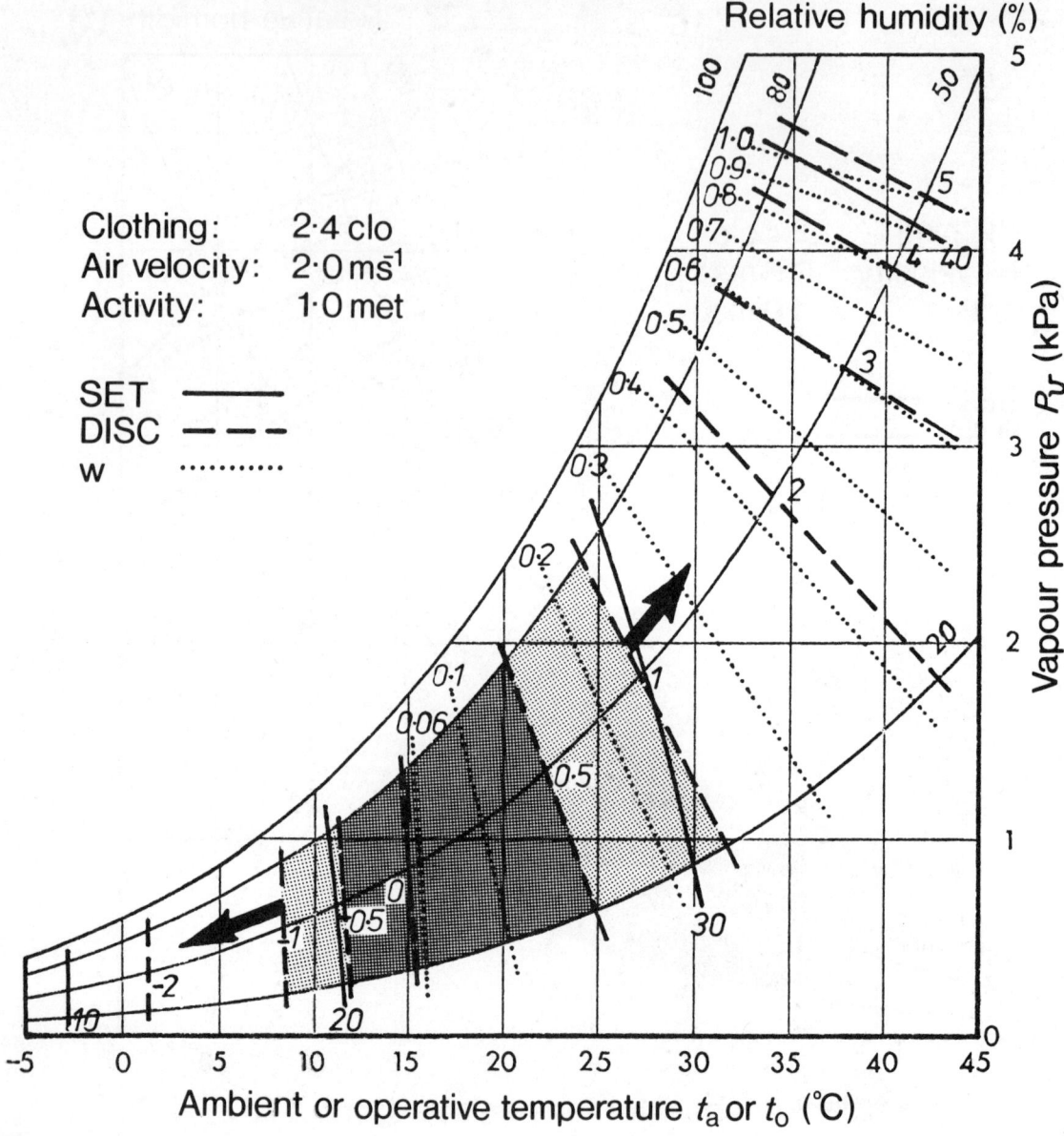

Clothing: 2·4 clo
Air velocity: 2·0 ms⁻¹
Activity: 1·0 met

SET ———
DISC — — —
w ·············

Relative humidity (%)

Vapour pressure P_v (kPa)

Ambient or operative temperature t_a or t_o (°C)

Thermal comfort
chart 48

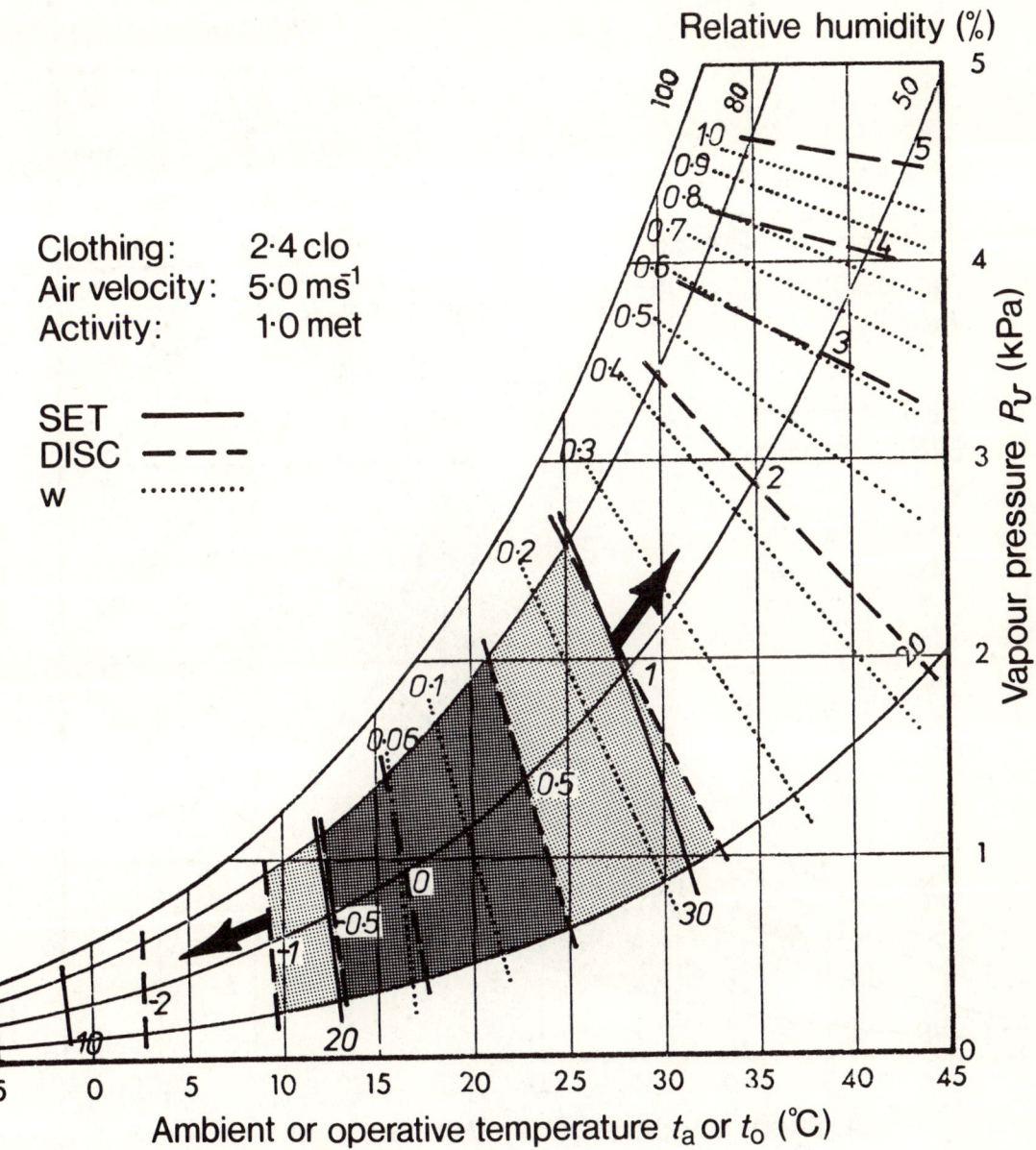

Clothing: 2·4 clo
Air velocity: 5·0 ms^{-1}
Activity: 1·0 met

SET   ⸺⸺⸺
DISC ⸺ ⸺ ⸺
w   ·············

Relative humidity (%)

Vapour pressure P_v (kPa)

Ambient or operative temperature t_a or t_o (°C)

Thermal comfort
chart 49

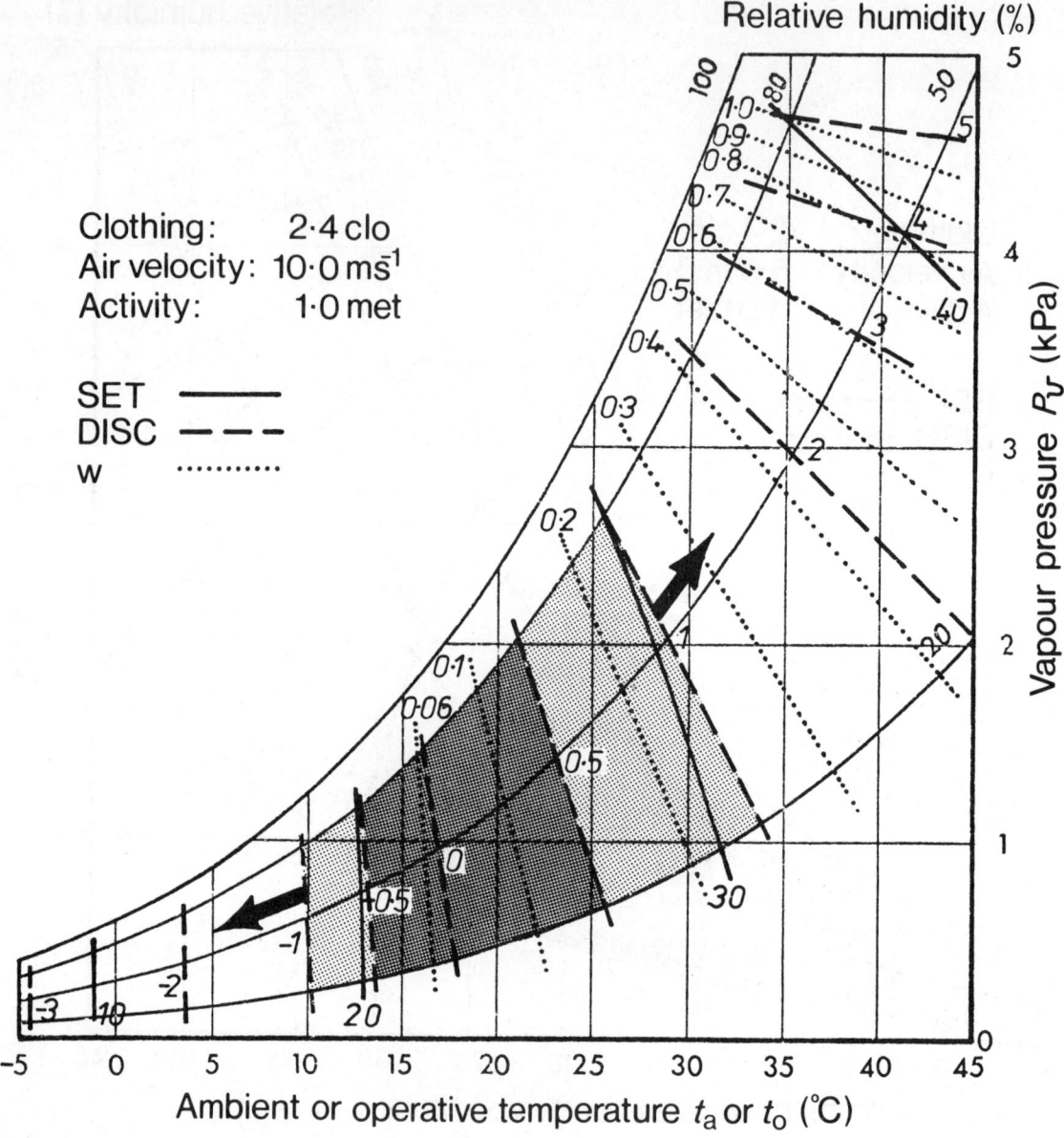

Relative humidity (%)

Clothing: 2·4 clo
Air velocity: 10·0 ms⁻¹
Activity: 1·0 met

SET ——————
DISC ———
w ···········

Vapour pressure P_v (kPa)

Ambient or operative temperature t_a or t_o (°C)

Thermal comfort
chart 50

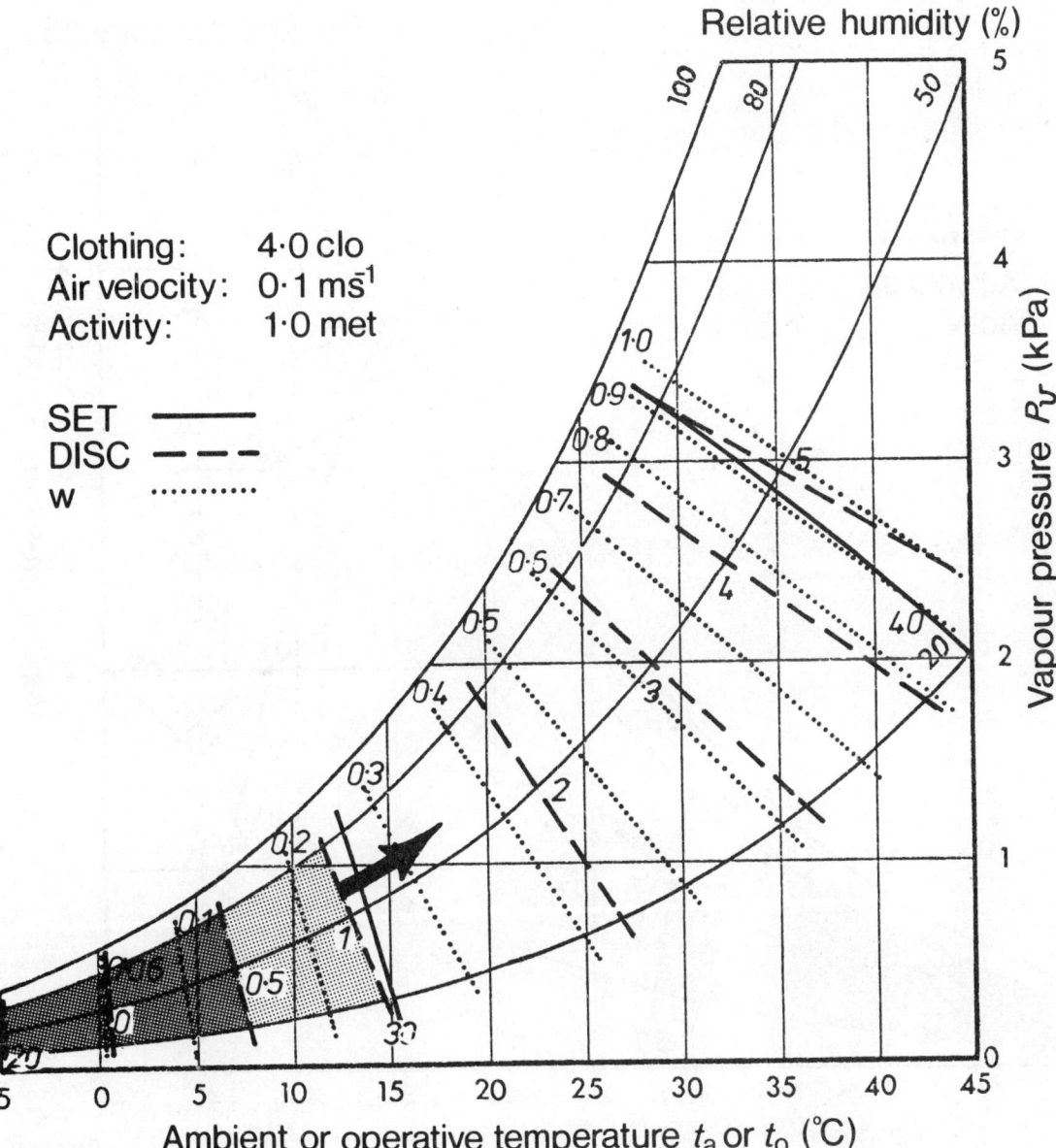

Thermal comfort
chart 51

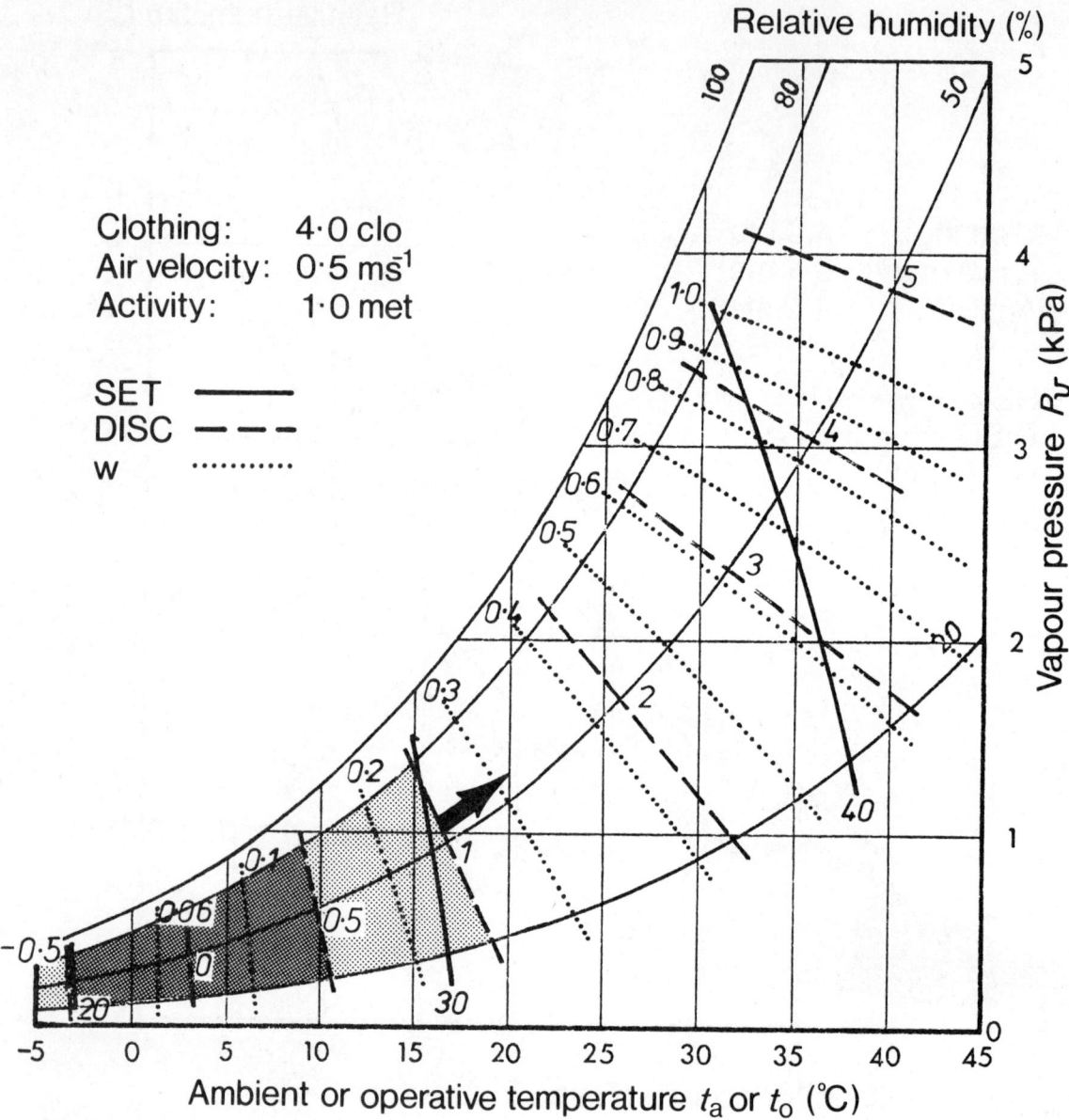

Relative humidity (%)

Clothing: 4·0 clo
Air velocity: 0·5 ms⁻¹
Activity: 1·0 met

SET ⎯⎯⎯⎯
DISC ⎯ ⎯ ⎯
w ·············

Vapour pressure P_v (kPa)

Ambient or operative temperature t_a or t_o (°C)

Thermal comfort
chart 52

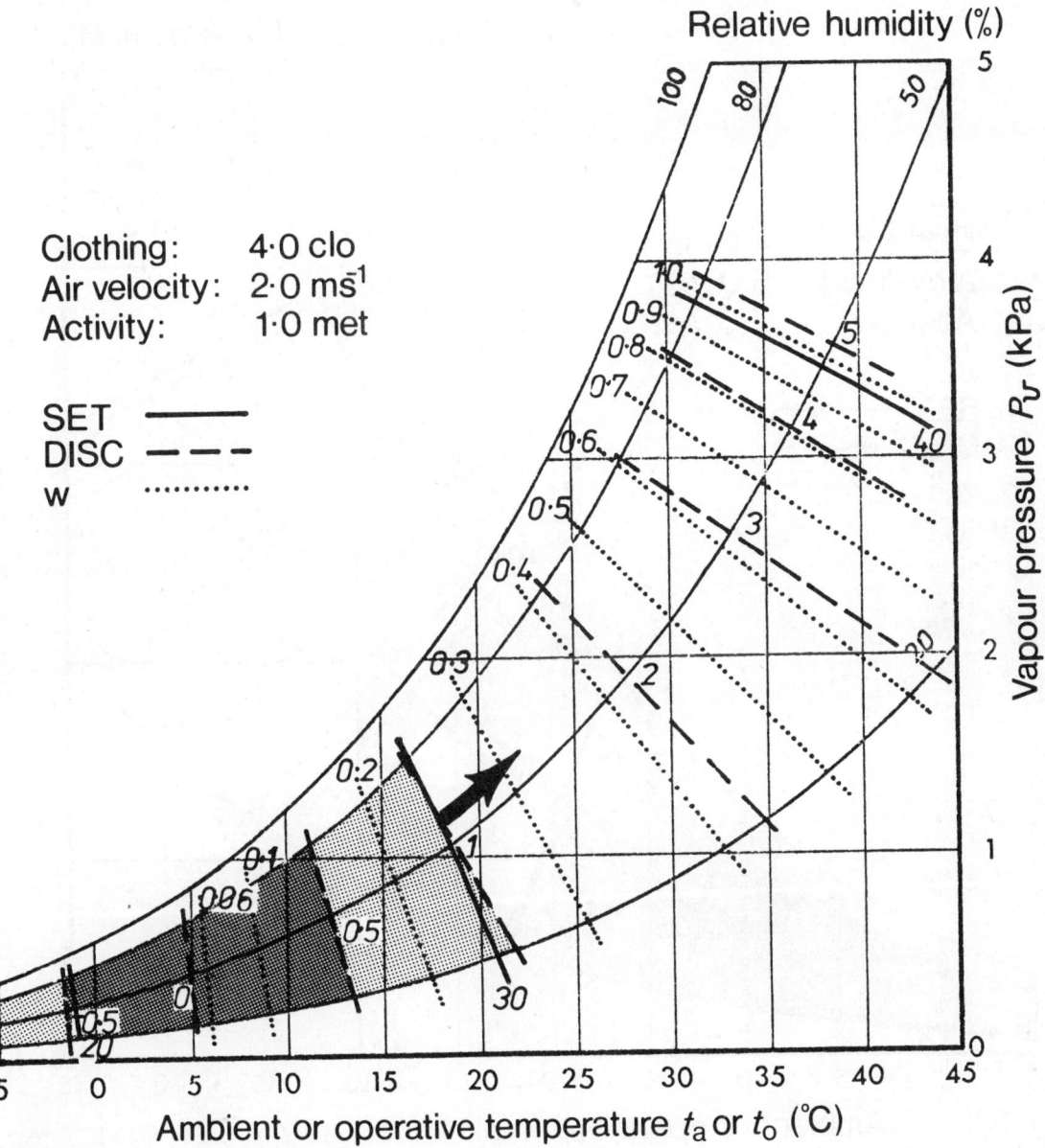

Clothing: 4·0 clo
Air velocity: 2·0 ms⁻¹
Activity: 1·0 met

SET ——————
DISC — — —
W   ···············

Thermal comfort
chart 53

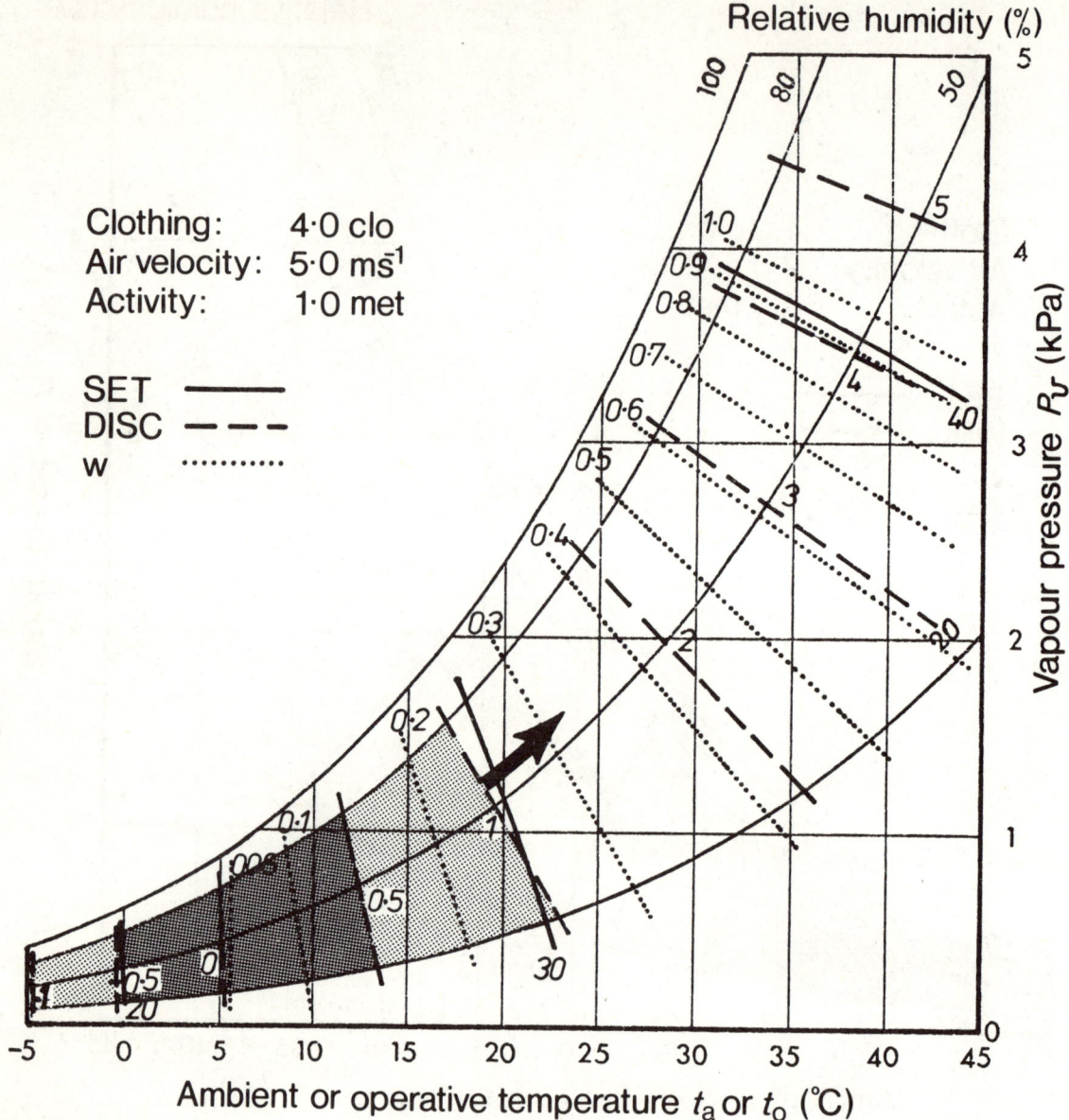

Relative humidity (%)

Clothing: 4·0 clo
Air velocity: 5·0 ms⁻¹
Activity: 1·0 met

SET   ———
DISC — — —
w   ·········

Vapour pressure P_v (kPa)

Ambient or operative temperature t_a or t_o (°C)

Thermal comfort
chart 54

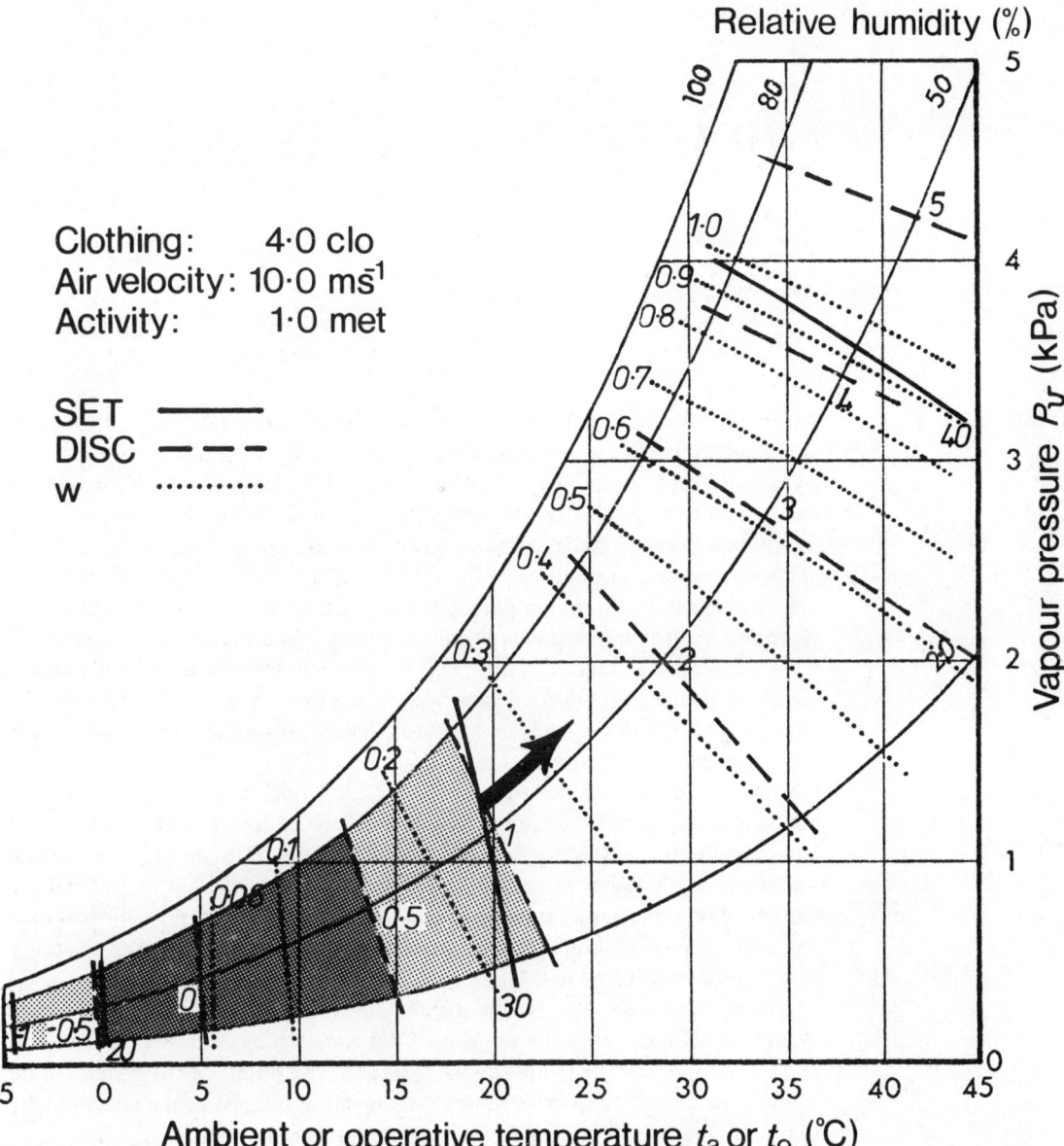

Clothing: 4·0 clo
Air velocity: 10·0 ms⁻¹
Activity: 1·0 met

SET ———
DISC – – –
w ·············

Thermal comfort
chart 55

4
CLIMATE

4.1 Introduction

In line with the view developed so far, the external climate of a building is seen as a medium which surrounds it, penetrates it through openings and by heat transfer through non-permeable membranes, and is continuous with the internal environment which surrounds the occupants of the building. The complex and interlinked global climatic system is powered by the sun's energy, heating land and water masses. The convection of air masses over these, the associated evaporative and precipitation processes, the shifts of air masses caused by variations in air temperature, atmospheric pressure and the earth's rotation — all these make up the climatic system which is characterized by spatial and temporal variations. Many of these are regular and predictable — such as the daily and seasonal cycles, and longer-term cycles of climatic change, including those which take thousands of years, such as the advancing and receding of glaciers. Similarly, the spatial variations of climate over the earth's surface have many known, predictable and regular variations, which enable us to classify the climate of a region by its chief seasonal characteristics. Other variations are of a random kind — which makes weather forecasting a less than exact science; but in much of building design the actual time when an event occurs is less important than its probable frequency. And the actual place where it will occur, in terms of storey height or orientation of facade, is often highly predictable.

The physical forces involved in the climate system are completely interlinked. Therefore, to understand the working of the system they, and their relationship to each other, have to be understood. Moreover, the results of the system, in the form of the actually experienced weather, are all of interest to the climatologist. For building designers, too, all aspects of weather are relevant — for instance, wind, air temperature, sunshine, radiation and humidity from the thermal point of view; rain, frost and humidity because of their effects on materials, problems of decay, corrosion and breakdown of finishes; wind and snow on account of the structural load they impose; rain, since drainage for it has to be designed; thermal changes, since they affect movement of joints and panels. In this book we are concerned only with the thermal design of buildings for comfort and energy economy and hence only those climatic features which affect the thermal regime will be described in detail. However, since the causative systems are interlinked, a brief description of the whole system is given below before the more specific and detailed aspects are discussed.

Whilst the climatic determinism of Huntington [1] and other 19th and early 20th Century geographers is no longer acceptable, it is quite clear that climate, ethnic characteristics, land-use, culture and built form are closely related. We have already discussed the arguments against climatic determinism in the interpretation of built form – and very similar ones apply in the interpretation of these other factors. The climate-built form interaction on a global or regional scale will make itself felt on the thermal design of buildings in the following ways.

First, climate clearly affects the use of land, the type of crop that can be grown or animal husbandry that can be practised. These variations in the use of land can cause regional climatic changes – such as the spread of desert conditions due to deforestation – and also microclimatic variations caused by the presence of trees, grass and water (entering the environment through transevaporation and evaporation); ground reflecting surfaces; and artificial topographical features affecting wind flow, sunshine and hence temperature patterns.

Second, the occurrence of many natural or artificial materials is not only geologically, but also climatically, dependent. Thus, the massive flat roofs of high thermal capacity characteristic of many desert climates are supported on timber, brushwoods, palm trunks and twigs according to the availability of materials. Lightweight, portable structures of nomadic people are made of skins, fabrics or felts dependent on the availability of livestock which in turn is, in part at least, climatically limited by the type of vegetation (Fig. 4.1). The outstanding example is, of course, the use of ice and snow for Eskimo igloo building (Fig. 4.2).

The climatic influences on agriculture, livestock raising, and hunting, especially in the case of nomadic peoples, may give rise to two distinct types of dwelling, suited to two phases of the climate and sometimes two entirely different terrains and materials resources. Thus the Eskimo summer and winter houses are quite different; on the other hand, in other cases the need for transportability, related to the same climatic and cultural forces, requires structures such as the Mongolian *yurt* with its lightweight, collapsible framework covered by two layers of heavy felt (Fig. 4.3).

Fig. 4.1 A flat-roofed building characteristic of desert climates (after Fitch and Branch [12]).

Fig. 4.2 Exterior and interior views of an Eskimo igloo (after Fitch and Branch [12]).

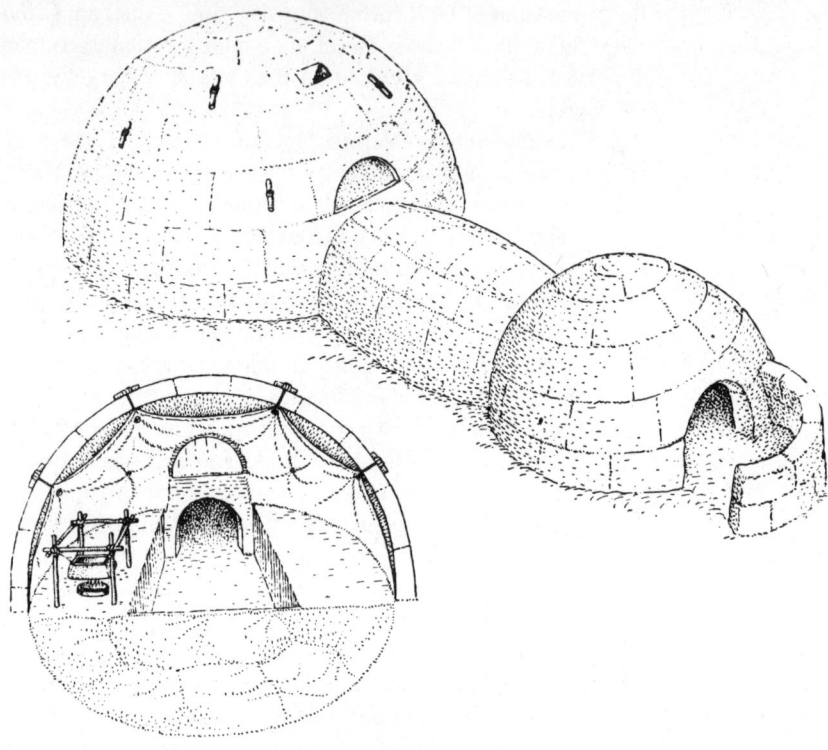

Fig. 4.3 A Mongolian yurt (after Fitch and Branch [12]).

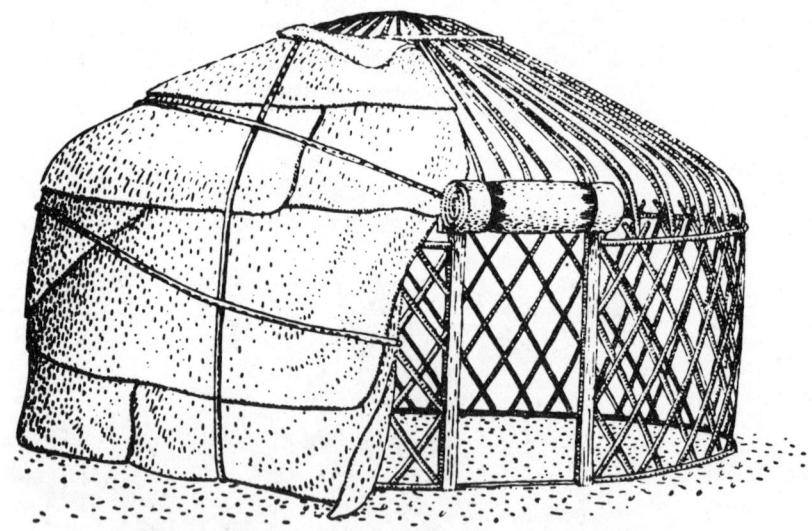

Apart from these indirect influences of climate, the direct ones are reasonably well known in principle, but the climatic performance of most vernacular and primitive structures has hardly been studied in detail. Section 4.3 below gives a few detailed examples.

4.2 General concepts

4.2.1 Scale

One of the most interesting and at the same time complicating factors about building climatology is that of scale. Climate can be considered at a variety of spatial and time scales – from the globe to the leaf on a plant, and from major climatic cycles lasting thousands of years to changes over a few minutes or hours. Of course the divisions are not hard and fast and the effects are continuous from one scale to another – for in reality the scale divisions are quite arbitrary ones in a totally integrated physical system. The question of scale has received some attention recently and Barry [2] has proposed a general system of categories which are quite widely accepted and useful, and will be used here (Table 4.1).

Table 4.1   *Spatial systems of climate (after Barry [2])*

System	Approximate characteristic dimensions		
	Horizontal scale (km)	Vertical scale (km)	Time scale
Global wind belts	2×10^3	3 to 10	1 to 6 months
Regional macroclimate	5×10^2 to 10^3	1 to 10	1 to 6 months
Local (topo) climate	1 to 10	10^{-2} to 10^{-1}	1 to 24 h
Microclimate	10^{-1}	10^{-2}	24 h

The global climate is explicable in terms of the movement of air masses, and associated wind belts, resulting from temperature and pressure changes which in turn follow the variations in radiation input. This is the result of the tilt of the earth's axis in relation to the ecliptic (the plane drawn through the sun and the earth's centre around which the earth rotates annually), the earth's rotation itself, the differential radiation absorption and reflection of large land and sea masses and major evaporative processes which utilize much of the sun's incident energy. The global climatic features are largely independent of minor surface topography and changes in surface cover. To a lesser extent, this is also true of regional climate, on a horizontal scale up to 1000 km, although here these features begin to have some role. At the next scale, the topoclimate, with variations up to 10 km horizontally and vertical effects up to 1 km in depth being of interest, land features, including the effects of human activity such as building towns which emit heat and pollutants, and agricultural patterns, begin to have a marked effect and cause significant and measurable differences in local climate.

Finally, the microclimate, with limits of about 1 km horizontally and up to 100 m vertically, is the one of prime importance for the building designer. In fact, the actual dimensions of concern are often smaller – the difference between orientations on the same building; the variations between the ground and an upper floor; the effect of walls and trees on windflow patterns. The agricultural climatologists have been used to studying at this fine scale, which plants inhabit – generally up to a height of 1 m. Outstanding amongst this work has been that of Geiger [4], whose contributions are now finding considerable applications in building and planning. The Russians have carried out work in this field for over a century – Vitkevich gives a useful historical summary [4]. What characterizes agricultural climatology is the painstaking nature of the observations, coupled with the avoidance of generalization; the awareness that accurate data may be, literally, a question of life or death, and certainly is vital for productivity and profit; and an interest in the modifications introduced by human activity mainly, of course, in the sphere of planting, soil conditioning and irrigation. But the data and the methods have great usefulness to building designers and in the micro-climate section below we shall rely on them quite substantially.

The location of measuring stations is related to the question of scale – for they are usually chosen deliberately to be as free as possible from microclimatic influences.

Whilst tremendous progress has been made in the last decade in obtaining weather information from artificial and manned satellites, which has given a much better understanding of global climatic processes and energy balances, the location of traditional meteorological sites has been, on the whole, of relatively little value for topo- or microclimatic information for the designer. Most are on open flat sites, often airfields, some distance from urban centres; some on top of tall buildings or high mountains; others on remote islands or weather ships. Some aspects of climate which are vital for designers, mainly data on solar radiation, are measured at few stations and of these a very small number are in urban locations.

4.2.2 Probability

One problem which faces the designer is the quantity and nature of the data. In some senses there is too much information; a mass of hourly, daily, monthly and annual figures for all meteorological variables, available from a world-wide network of thousands of major and minor stations; measured with internationally standardized instruments, the results expressed in internationally agreed units. Much of this data are in tabular or graphical form, showing variations over time. Searching through it, and calculating averages, peak values and combinations of certain events – for instance, low temperatures accompanied by a certain wind direction and speed – is laborious without a computer accompanied by suitable programs and systems for the transformation of the data into a form which can be handled in the computer. Moreover, most of the information is in the form of averages, and means, measured over different units of time (1 h, 24 h, a month or a year) and averaged over different periods of time (1 year, 30 years, etc.).

For most purposes, annual or monthly mean values are too gross to be of much value. The information should be on the basis of frequencies of hourly values in each class of the range – e.g. the hourly mean temperature for, say, 17.00 to 18.00 hours in November, for the site, in each class at, say, 1 °C intervals; i.e. $-3.0°C$ to $-2.1°C$; $-2.0°C$ to $-1.1°C$; $-1.0°C$ to $-0.1°C$; $0.0°C$ to $0.9°C$; $1.0°C$ to $1.9°C$; etc. From such data the hourly means can easily be cal-culated; but, more significantly, the frequency distributions can be plotted as in Fig. 4.4, showing the percentage of the time over, say, 30 years, that the temperature occurred in certain classes. The same data can be replotted, as in Fig. 4.5, on a cumulative frequency basis. On both figures not only can the mean hourly value be read off, but also such questions answered, as for instance, 'What temperature does it fall below 90% of the time?' (In the example the answer is $4.0°C$.) The principle can be applied to any other climatic variable, to any class interval, and to any time period – instead of hours say days or months. But from the hourly values the corresponding values for longer periods are, of course, easily computed.

With the application of digital recording, or the transfer of the older records into digital form, many countries in the world have now available computerized

Fig. 4.4 Histogram of the frequency distribution of air temperature.

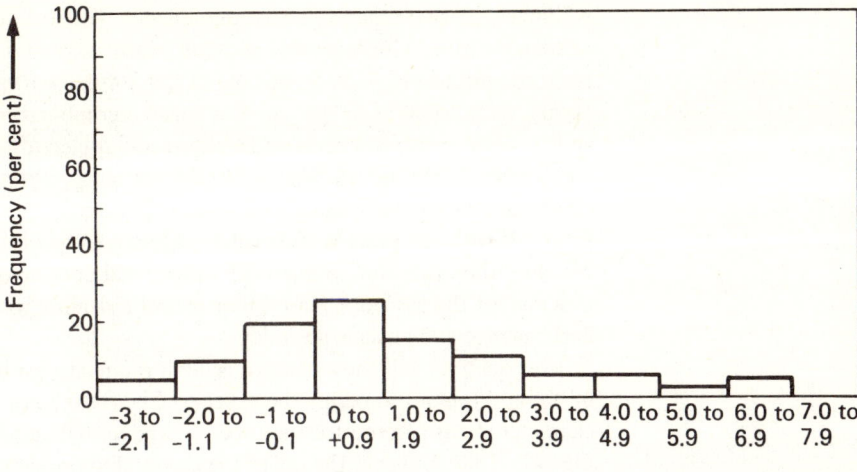

Fig. 4.5 Graph of the cumulative frequency distribution of air temperature.

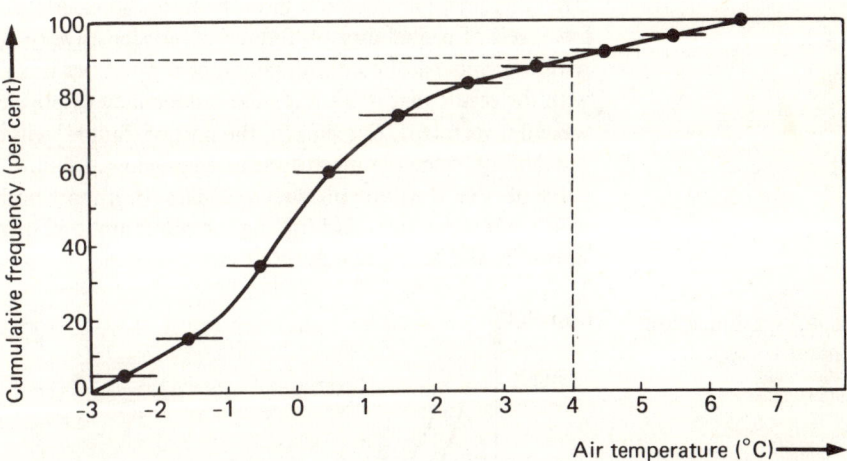

systems, which are able to produce on demand the records in any form desired – for instance, monthly means for hours or days, or annual means, or mean peak values. However, for many design purposes it will be necessary to make intelligent use of tabulated published data; and in either case, it will still be the designer who will have to decide the level of probability of a certain condition occurring in the building which he is willing to accept. This decision on probability or risk of 'failure' (*see* Chapters 11 and 12 for a further development of this idea) depends both on the magnitude and duration of the condition under consideration, and on the relationship between costs – both initial and continuing – and the control of the effects.

We have already shown in Chapter 3 that, for any specified thermal condition, one can predict approximately the degree of thermal discomfort. The actual thermal condition in a space will be predictable from a knowledge of the climatic conditions, and the nature of the fabric and service systems. Having decided on an acceptable level of discomfort – say DISC = −0.5 to +0.5 – and an acceptable duration during which conditions must remain within these limits — say 95 per cent of the days or working hours— and having the climatic data as a 'given', the designer can then select a combination of fabric and services which will meet the two criteria most economically. The second criterion — of time — will enable him to look for the extreme (warm or cold) conditions which exist for those durations — i.e. 5 per cent of the normal working hours in this example. Having established these, he can now select a combination of hardware (fabric and services) systems which, under those climatic conditions, just give internal conditions within the acceptable discomfort range. The selected climatic conditions will be his 'design' conditions. Of course the total costs of alternative solutions with the same performance will have to be obtained, and almost certainly the optimum, or a good solution, will only be obtained by an iterative process; for this purpose a computer program dealing with climate, thermal performance and costs is desirable.

Cost analysis will show that, in general the relationship between probability of 'failure' (i.e. not meeting the set thermal criteria) and costs obeys a law whose characteristic is to produce the type of exponential curve shown by curve A in Fig. 4.6. That is to say, the lower the acceptable probability is set the steeper the slope of the curve becomes and, hence, the greater the cost increase for a given incremental reduction in probability. So clearly a decision at these very low levels of probability of 'failure' is very sensitive to costs and has to be made with the greatest of care. In many recent buildings this care has not been taken, with the result that there is a great redundancy of physical plant and consequent wasted investment. Conversely, the cost of 'failure' will decrease with decreasing probability, since the magnitude or frequency of failure will decrease; and a curve of type B will be produced. If data to support both curves is available, it is worth summing them and finding the optimum level of probability of failure as shown by the zero-slope point of curve C.

Fig. 4.6 Optimization of plant costs.

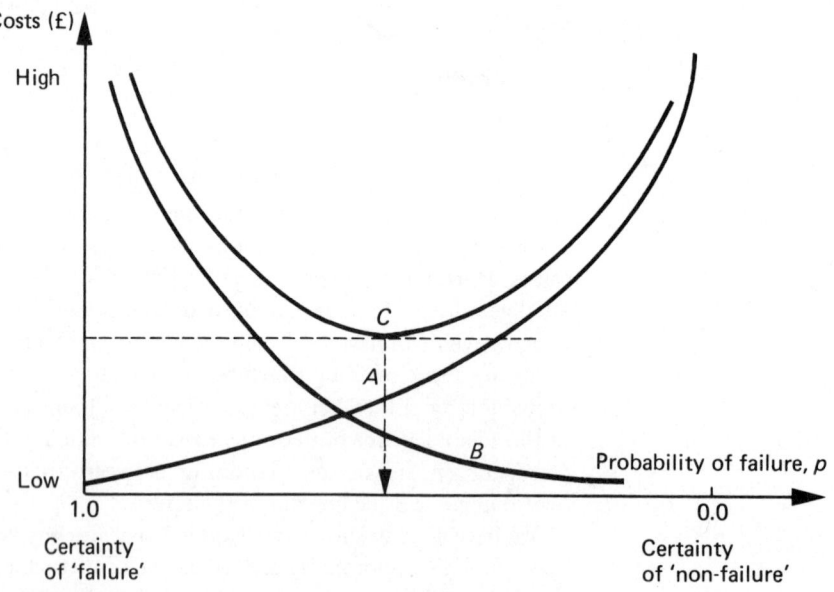

So the selection of the appropriate climatic data for thermal design has two objectives: the design of the building and its services to cope with extreme conditions, and the reasonably accurate prediction of annual energy consumption.

For plant design, having found an acceptable probability of extremes,

Fig. 4.7 Cold weather data in Aberdeen, Scotland, based on records for 1925-6 to 1949-50 (after *IHVE Guide* [5]).
Curve A represents the average frequency of occurrence of days per heating season falling in periods of *two* or more consecutive days with mean temperatures below the value shown. Curve B is analogous to curve A except that a period of *one* or more consecutive days is examined. Points C represent the maximum number of consecutive days in the 25-year period with mean daily temperatures below the value shown.

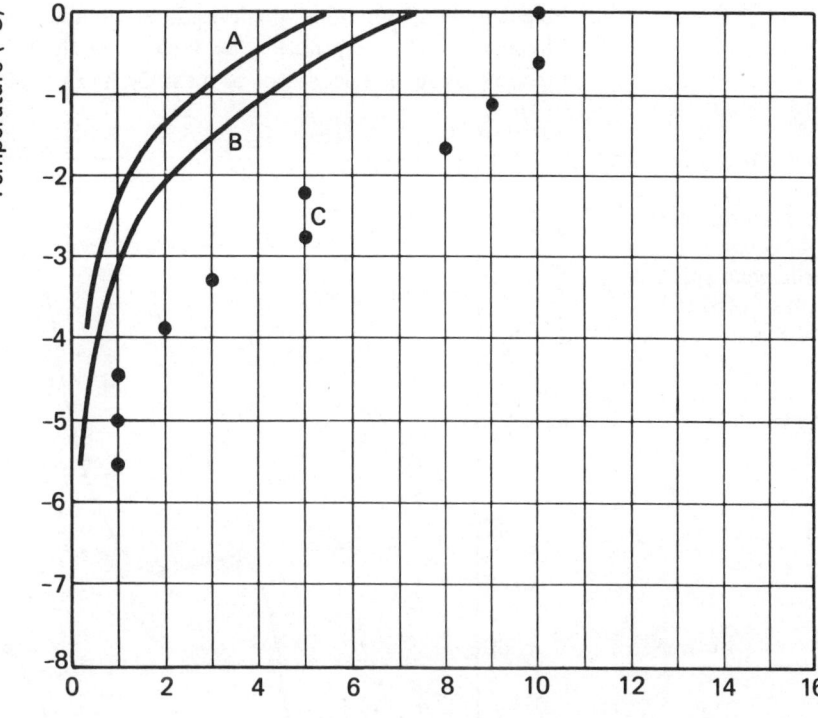

Frequency for curves A and B
Number of days for points C

reference to meteorological data or design guides will show the appropriate values to use. For instance, the *IHVE Guide* [5] gives data in suitable form for both British and world conditions. This data takes into account the size and thermal inertia of the building, as well as the critical factor of the overload capacity (redundancy) in the size of the plant. Heavy buildings have a less severe outdoor condition assigned to them, on the assumption that in short spells of severe weather the plant can also be continuously operated and the building will cushion some of the severity by its storage effects. Buildings with oversized plant are also assigned less severe outdoor design data, since they can more easily cope with these spells and can also effectively cope with heating up (or cooling down) periods during intermittent operation. (The actual sizing of plant is briefly discussed in Chapter 11 and the effects of intermittent heating in Chapter 7).

The *IHVE Guide* also gives data for a variety of British locations of the number of days of continuous cold spells below stated temperatures, based on 25 years' records. Figure 4.7 is one, typical, diagram from a set of eight, showing the average frequency of days per season falling into the classes of daily mean temperatures for two or more consecutive days; also the same data for single days; and, finally, the maximum number of consecutive days at stated mean daily temperatures which have occurred in the whole 25-year period — that is, the most severe, near-unique circumstances. (If the heating season is taken to be 180 days, then 5 per cent of the most severe days are the nine coldest ones.)

Such curves are *daily* means, and for lightweight, intermittently used buildings represent less than the full severity of the weather. The daily means hide day—night variations which result in maximum heating loads at night (and of course cooling loads during the day). Mean night-time values occur with about the same frequency per season as mean 24-h values of about 1 °C higher;

Fig. 4.8 Wind speed and temperature at Heathrow, London (after *IHVE Guide* [7].
(a) 6h, wind speed ⩾ 2.5 m s⁻¹. (b) 12 h, wind speed ⩾ 2.5 m s⁻¹. (c) 18 h, wind speed ⩾ 2.5 m s⁻¹. (d) 24 h, wind speed ⩾ 2.5 m s⁻¹.

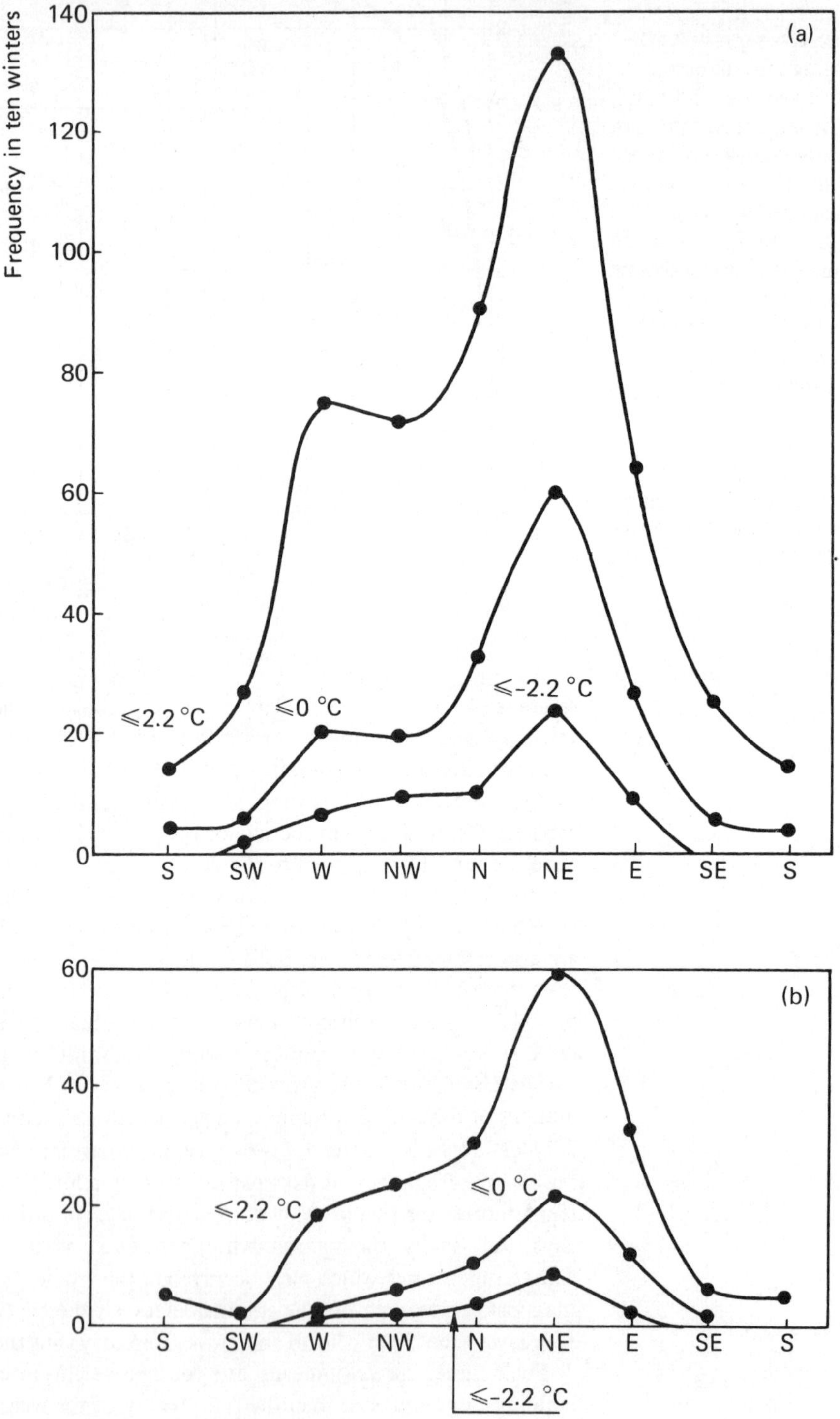

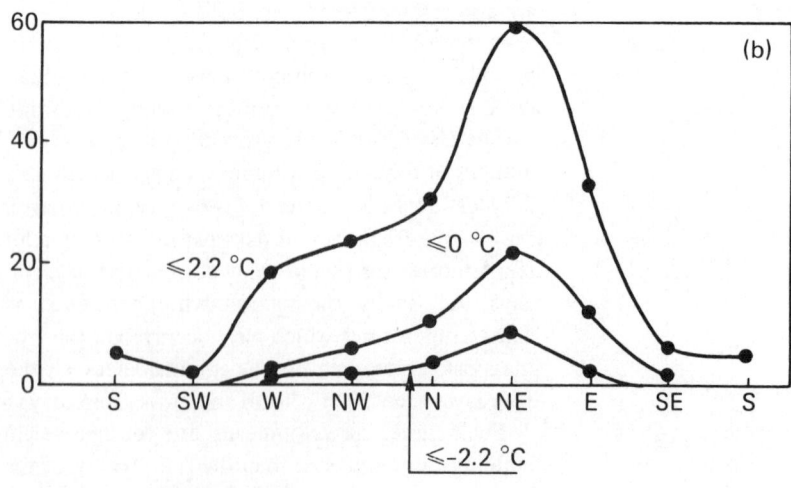

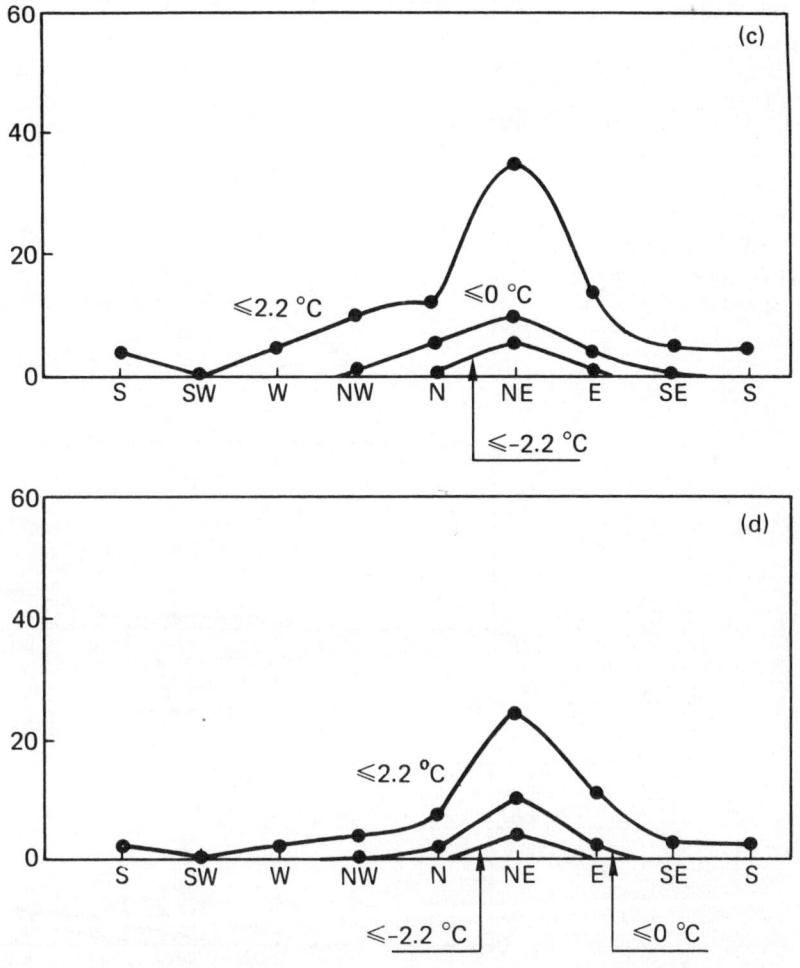

similarly, mean daytime values with the same frequency as mean 24-h values about 1 °C lower [6]. Sometimes the low temperatures will be accompanied by high winds; these will have two effects. First, they will lower the surface resistance of external surfaces, and hence increase the transmittance of the structure (*see* Section 5.2) and, second, they will increase the wind-induced air change rate and, hence, heat loss. So these combinations can be said to represent the most severe design conditions for heating and, if they are accompanied by clear night skies, will also increase the long-wave radiation loss from the structure to the sky. Figures 4.8 and 4.9 show combinations of air temperature and wind speeds from one station (Heathrow, London), analysed by continuous coincident values of the two for periods of 6, 12, 18 and 24 h, at three wind-speeds − $\geqslant 2.5$, $\geqslant 5.0$ and $\geqslant 7.5$ m s^{-1}.

For warm weather conditions, similar design principles apply to the selection of suitable climatic data for plant sizing. For instance, *IHVE Guide* [7] suggests the selection, from tables, of dry and wet bulb temperatures which are reached or exceeded for only 1 per cent of the hours in summer, from June to September in Britain − that is 29 h in total. If a less rigorous criterion is to apply (2.5 per cent is suggested), the corresponding value is 73 h. As an alternative, for calculating the peak temperatures reached *within* buildings under warm weather

Fig. 4.9 Wind speed and temperature at Heathrow, London (after *IHVE Guide* [7].
(a) 6h, wind speed $\geqslant 5$ m s^{-1}. (b) 12 h, wind speed $\geqslant 5$ m s^{-1}. (c) 18 h, wind speed $\geqslant 5$ m s^{-1}. (d) 24 h, wind speed $\geqslant 5$ m s^{-1}. (e) 6 h, wind speed $\geqslant 7.5$ m s^{-1}.

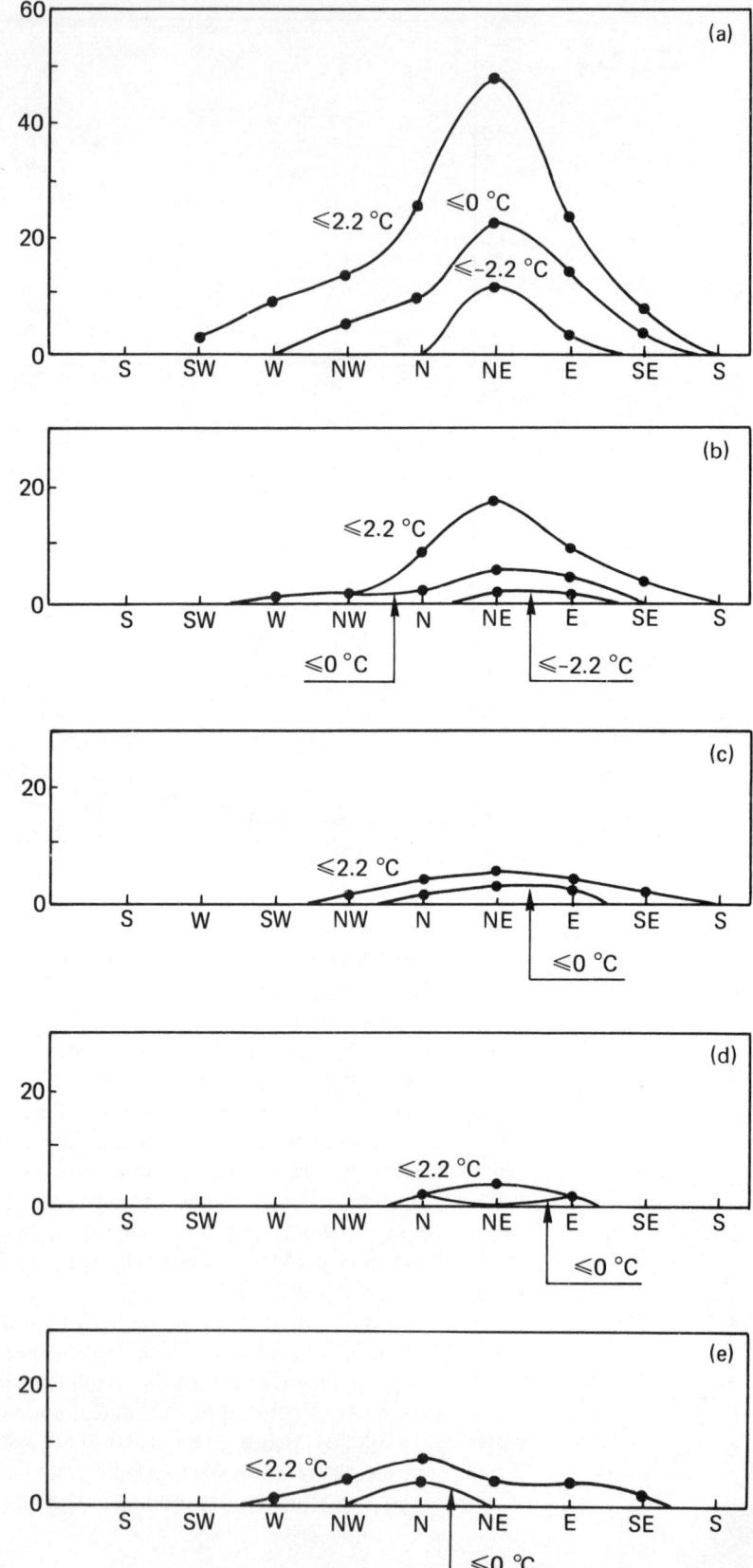

conditions, the *IHVE Guide* suggests values of external air temperatures which occur on the 5 per cent of days of highest solar radiation.

So the choice of suitable extreme design conditions, whether for heating or cooling, involves making decisions about the probability of the combined occurrence of the critical variables. For instance, if the probability of a certain · value of each of two variables is known separately, and one is p_1 and the other p_2, the combined probability of the two occurring simultaneously is $p_1 p_2$ provided that they are totally independent of each other, that is, completely unrelated. If they are completely correlated, the combined probability is the same as that of either of the two individual ones, p_1 or p_2. In the real world, the likelihood is that the probability will lie between $p_1 p_2$ and p_1 (or p_2).

These climatic estimations involve dynamic, cyclic variations of one or more variables – over periods of hours and days – and covariations of several, possibly related, variables. The durations to be chosen depend on the thermal response of the fabric and the services systems. Extreme values have to be obtained from long-term meteorological records. All this is really too complex a task for the designer to solve *ab initio* on each occasion from raw data. What are required are model design periods – say for five continuous days – selected according to agreed probabilities – for each particular location or district. Such model days can be represented graphically, or simulated on an analogue computer or, of course, stored as inputs in any computer program. A start has been made by various workers and organizations [8] and data for various European and other Continental locations are becoming available.

The choice of data for predicting energy consumption is somewhat simpler. Here it is *average* conditions which are of concern. For a fully controlled and conditioned building, maintained at continuously uniform levels throughout the year – say the bedroom block of an air-conditioned hotel – one single seasonal average under a heating regime and one under a cooling regime will suffice. From such an average outdoor temperature, knowing the (constant) indoor temperature, the average temperature difference can be obtained and, hence, the heat loss or gain using normal structural heat transfer and air infiltration heat exchange calculation methods (*see* Chapters 5 and 8). Solar and incidental heat gains also, of course, enter in the prediction of energy consumption.

One method of dealing with seasonal heat losses is the 'degree-day' method. This is based on observations that an unheated building on average maintains an indoor temperature higher than the outdoor temperature as a result of casual heat gains. The difference (d) is about 3 °C for traditional construction. For heavier or lighter buildings the temperature differences are as suggested in Table 4.2. Thus, in theory, the building will only need heating when the outdoor temperature falls by more than the tabulated amount below the required indoor temperature. The outdoor temperature which is below the indoor design temperature by this tabulated amount, is known as the 'base' temperature. For a 3 °C difference and an internal design temperature of 18.5 °C, the base temperature is 15.5 °C – a value commonly adopted in Britain. For a day when the mean daily temperature is 1 °C below the base temperature this difference of 1 °C can be used in the heat loss and energy consumption calculations and such a day gives '1 degree-day'. A day with a 2 °C drop below base, or two days with a 1 °C drop, will give 2 degree-days and so on. Thus, the number of degree-days of a locality give an indication of its climatic severity and degree-day maps such as that in Fig. 4.10 and tables such as that in Table 4.3 are published.

Fig. 4.10 Map of
annual degree-days for
the period 1921–50,
below a base
temperature of 15.6°C
(after Shellard [33]
and Lacy [34]).

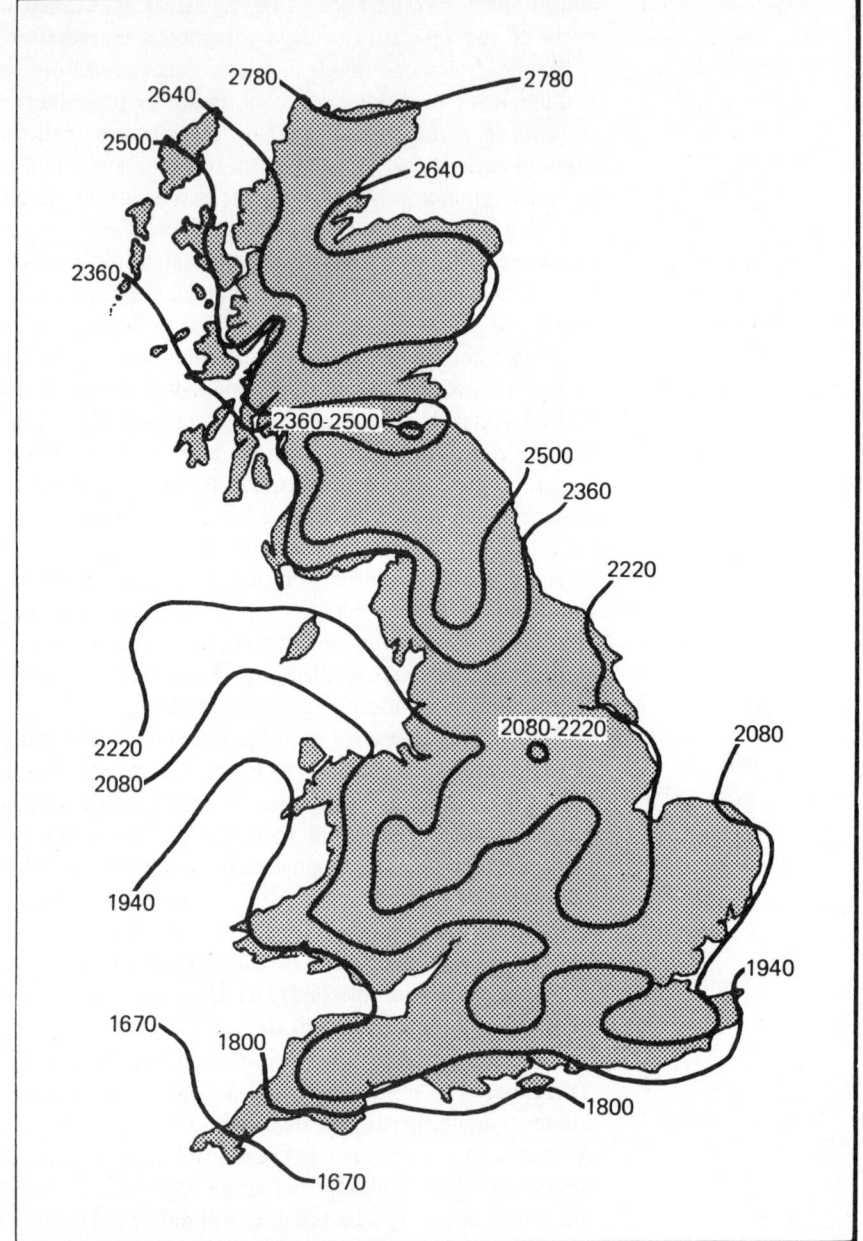

The problem arises if the indoor conditions are not constant with time, as
happens in the case of intermittent heating. Knight and Cornell and others [9]
have suggested factors which can be applied to the 24-h degree-days to obtain
other daily, weekly and seasonal heating patterns and these are detailed in the
IHVE Guide. Chapter 5 shows some typical heat loss calculations using the
degree-day method.

Another simplified method, devised by the Building Research Station for
dwelling calculations [10], uses average temperature differences between inside
and outside, making assumptions about the length of the heating season and

Table 4.2   *Values of d for various classes of building (after IHVE Guide)*

Class of building	Building structure	d (°C)
1	Building with large area of external glazing, much internal heat-producing equipment (unless separately allowed for in the design heat loss) and densely populated	5 to 6
2	Buildings with one or two of the above factors	4 to 5
3	'Traditional' buildings with normal glazing, equipment and occupancy	3 to 4
4	Sparsely occupied buildings with little or no heat-producing equipment and small glazed area	2 to 3
5	Dwellings	5 to 8

Add 1 °C for single-storey buildings.

Table 4.3   *British degree-days from 1st September to 31st May (after IHVE Guide)*

Area	Degree-days*
West Scotland	2496
North Eastern	2463
East Scotland	2435
South-east Scotland	2394
North Western	2334
Yorkshire	2298
South Eastern	2277
Midland	2248
Lancashire	2243
Eastern	2211
Severn Valley	2110
Thames Valley	2012
Southern	1930
Western	1794
Average	2231

outdoor conditions based on Outer London. It must be clear from Table 4.3 that for other locations quite significant adjustments will have to be made.

It has already been mentioned above that where an analogue or digital computer simulation of an 'extreme' condition, lasting perhaps several days, is available, the choice of appropriate climatic data becomes simpler in that the effect of choosing different levels of probability of severity is seen in the output – the required plant capacity or fabric properties. Similarly, for energy consumption, where a design year, or typical day or set of days for each month

*Base temperature 15.5 °C. The *IHVE Guide* gives a technique for finding the degree-days for other base temperatures (from 10 °C to 18 °C).

can be simulated, on an hour-by-hour basis, the somewhat gross inaccuracies involved in the various climatic assumptions discussed are avoided.

Nevertheless, even probabilistic climatic data is required in a form which enables the spatial and temporal variations to be plotted so as to express the relative degree of stress caused by the climate. The stress is of two kinds; first, as discussed earlier, on the physiological responses of people. To establish this, an index is required which combines the four environmental variables of the climate and the two personal ones of clothing and activity. Making sensible assumptions about these, and using real climatic data, the SET, as presented in Chapter 3, can express all the climatic factors in a single figure index. For instance, for a given site, the records indicate that for a given 3-h period – say 12.00 to 15.00 hours – on a given date – say April 10th – the following probabilistic meteorological conditions will be observed:

Mean air temperature (t_a) $= 25\,^\circ$C;
Mean wind speed (v) $= 0.1$ m s^{-1} (still air);
Mean relative humidity (RH) $= 50$ per cent.

Assuming shade conditions, sedentary activity (1 met, i.e. 58 W m^{-2}) and light clothing (0.6 clo), Thermal Chart 16 in Appendix 3B shows that SET $\simeq 25^\circ$C. If conditions in the sun were of interest, it would be necessary to compute, or measure, t_{mrt}. The simplest way would be to measure t_g with a suitably-sized and coloured globe thermometer and either assume that it was equal to t_o, the operative temperature, or calculate t_{mrt}, and, hence, find t_o from Operative Temperature Chart 1, as shown in Chapter 3. Then using the t_o value in place of the previous t_a, the same chart is used to find a new value of SET.

By repeating this process for each 3-h period for each of the 12 months, a diagram of SET such as that shown in Fig. 4.11 can be produced. This same data

Fig. 4.11 Shade values of SET based on meteorological data for v, t_a and RH (clo = 0.6, met = 58 W m^{-2}).

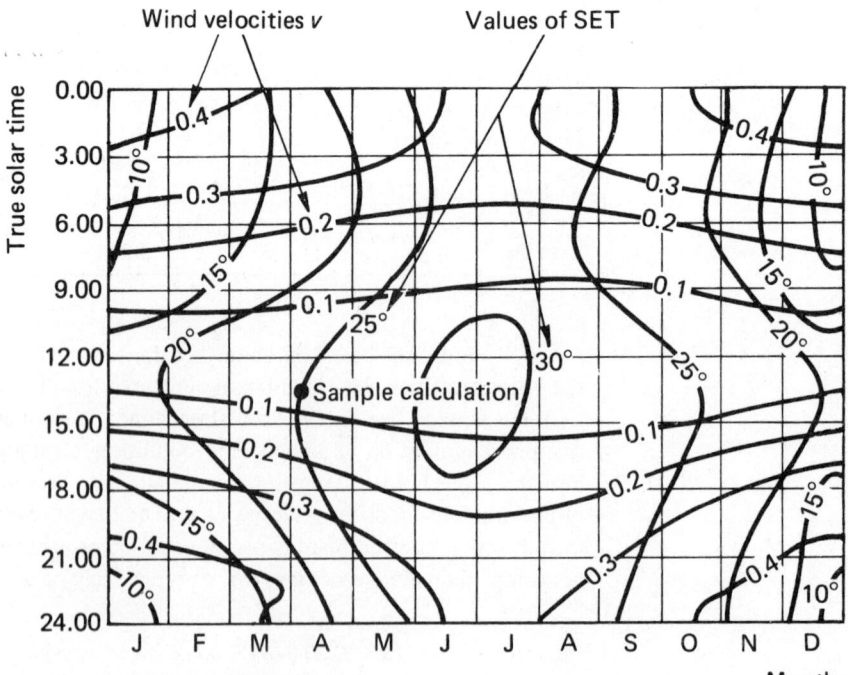

Fig. 4.12 (a) An aerial view of part of central Baghdad, which is largely composed of traditional courtyard houses (Aerofilms Ltd). (b) Section and plans of a typical Baghdad house (after (Al-Azzawi [11]).

(a)

Prevailing wind ⟶

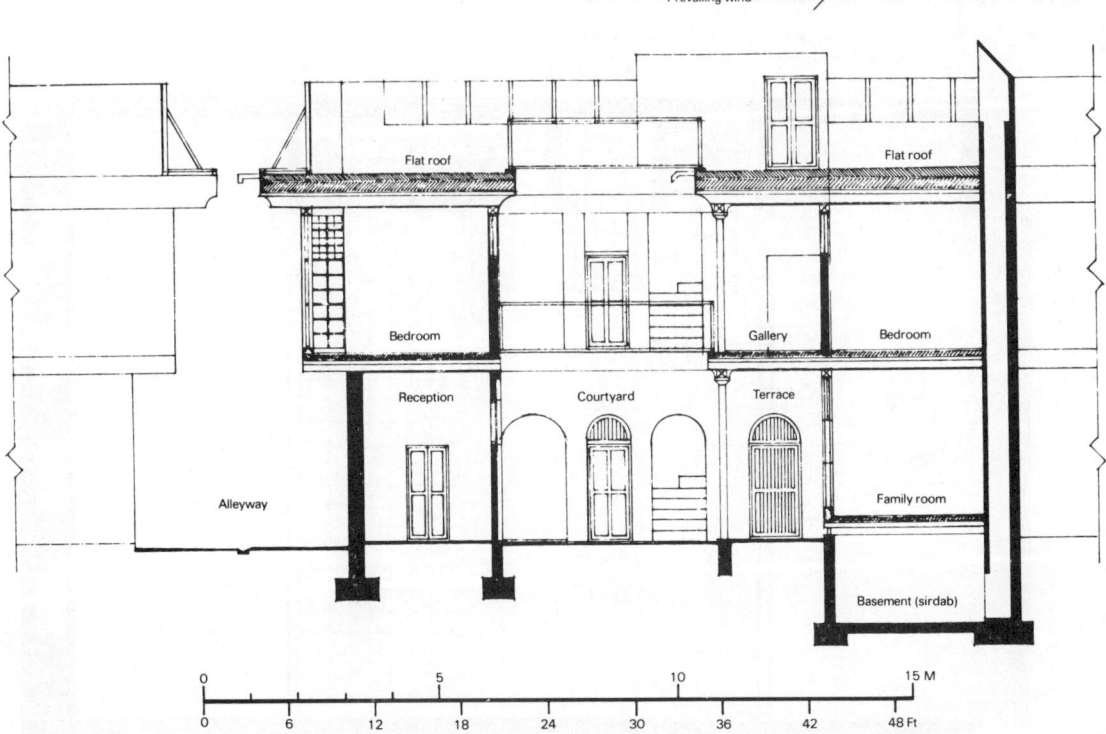

Flat roof   Flat roof

Bedroom   Gallery   Bedroom

Reception   Courtyard   Terrace

Alleyway   Family room

Basement (sirdab)

0   5   10   15 M
0   6   12   18   24   30   36   42   48 Ft

4.12 (b) i   North-West—South-East Section

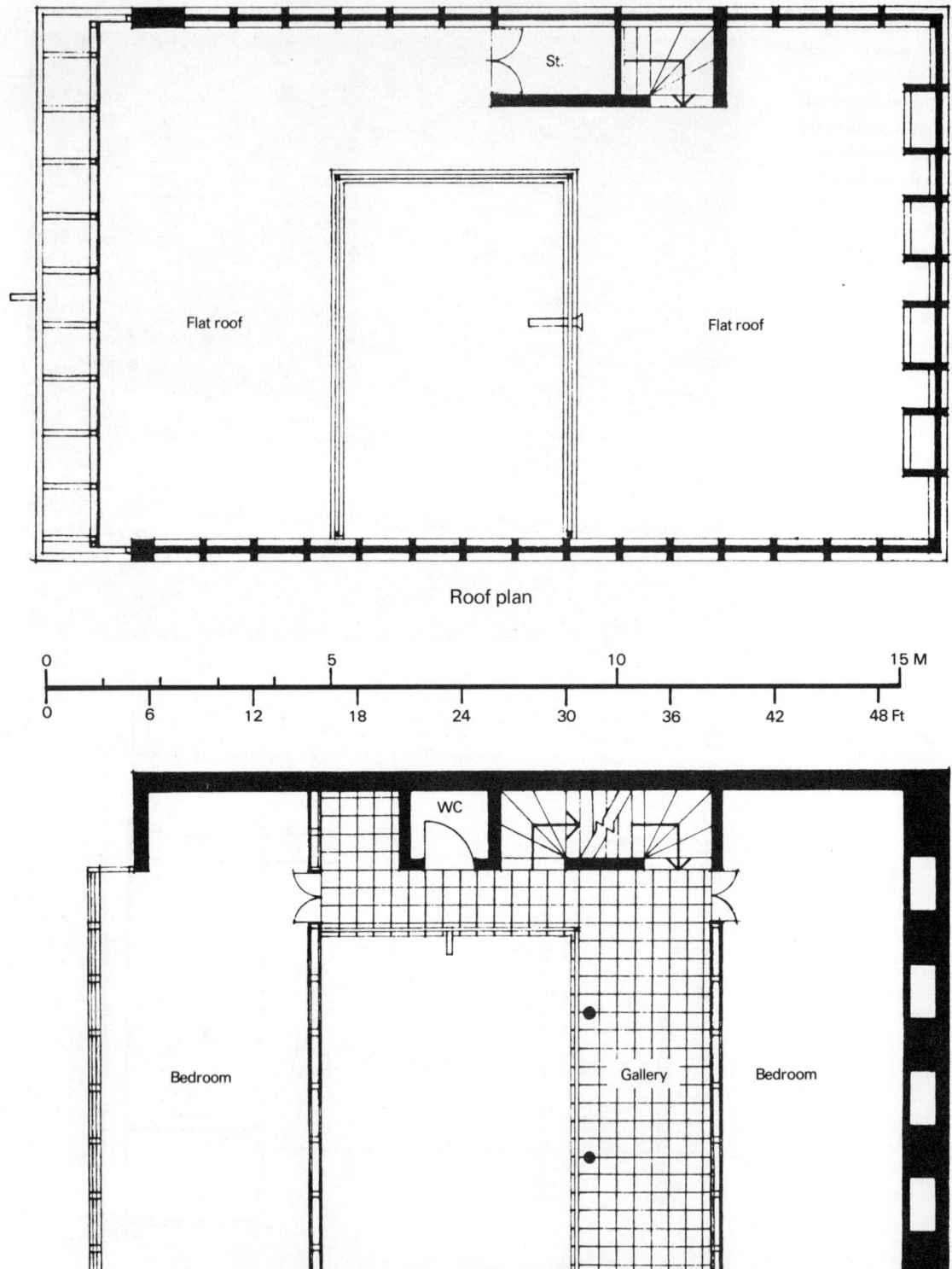

Roof plan

First floor plan

4.12(b) ii

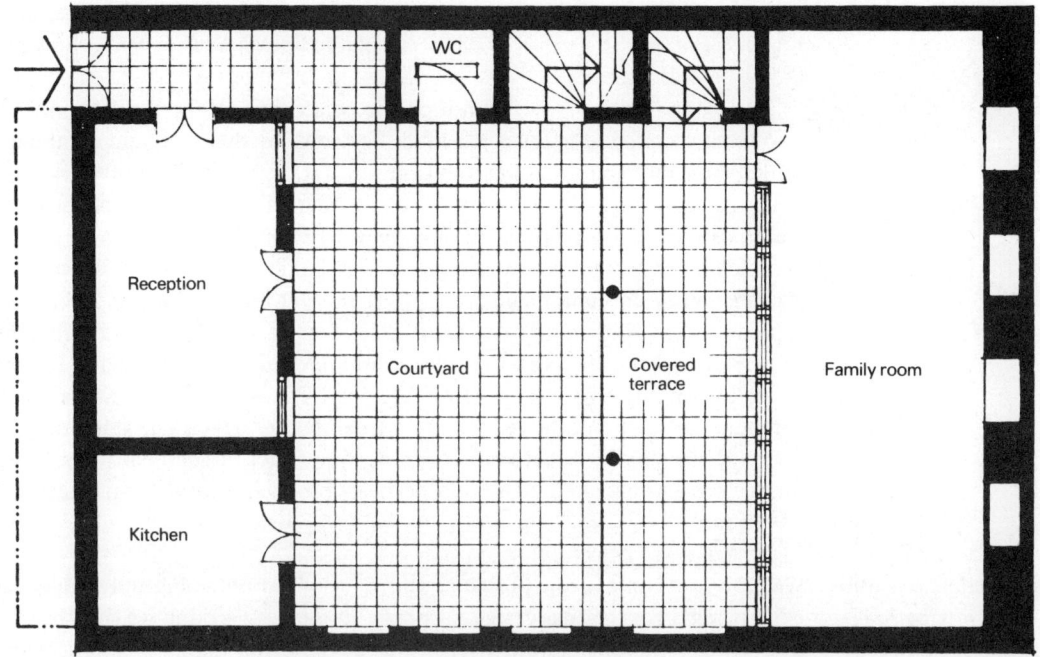

Ground floor plan

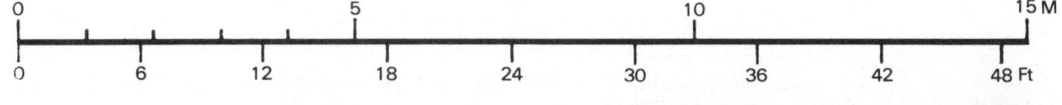

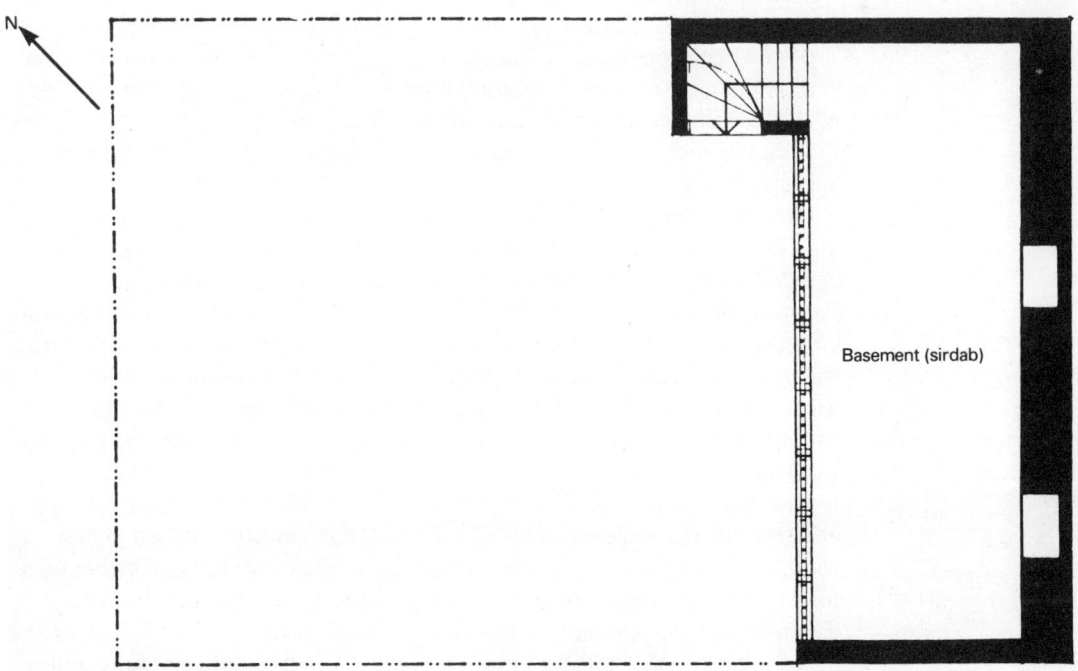

Basement plan

4.12 (b) iii

was used in Chapter 3 for the preparation of the equivalent DISC values in Fig. 3.7. For the SET value of 25 °C calculated above, DISC = +0.2, showing there is no discomfort.

The second form of stress is not on the person but on the building. An analogous compound index is required. For cold weather it should combine air velocity, air temperature, radiation (long- and short-wave), humidity and precipitation (both of which may affect the thermal insulation of porous materials). The degree-day index only deals with air temperature. Any more complex index would have to assume certain building properties – shape, height, glazing, colour, insulation and mass. It has not yet been developed and is just as difficult a task as obtaining a comfort index free of activity and clothing effects.

For warm days, the same variables would have to be combined and the same limitation on building properties would apply. The 'solair' temperature – which combines air temperature and radiation (*see* Chapter 6) – is one standard method, but only deals with effects on opaque structures and has to assume surface absorption and emission properties with regard to short- and long-wave radiation.

4.3 The climate – built form interaction; some examples

We have seen some of the problems and solutions in obtaining and sifting climatic data for thermal design purposes. In the next section we shall be describing in more detail the mechanisms of the major relevant climatic elements, and giving typical data for design use. A good way of linking these two sections is to study in some detail a few examples of buildings which have been designed and constructed in rather extreme climates, without the benefit of scientific analysis, professional designers or recorded meteorological data. To see the gradual evolution of design features, materials and details to cope with these extremes, without the use of any energy-consuming services other than the localized combustion of solid fuel or oil, will help to focus attention on the most relevant aspects of climate.

It must be re-emphasized that one is not dealing with climatic determinism; even in the most extreme conditions a variety of solutions have been used, not all of them in fact equally good in climatic terms; so we accept Rapoport's view that the cultural factors are often dominant. However, we refer to climatic appropriateness.

The first example is one which shows a remarkable unity between city planning, house form and constructional technology. It is the Middle Eastern, courtyard town house as found in most of the older urban areas, typically in Baghdad. Houses of this type have a long history – courtyard houses of a similar kind are found at Ur, dating back 4000 years; in central Anatolia, North Africa and numerous sites of Mesopotamia. The houses in Baghdad lie on either sides of narrow streets, with the 'bent' entrance, taking a 90° turn, from the street entrance, and the back and sides adjoining each other or separated by narrow alleyways (Fig. 4.12).

The width of the streets is such that even with the high-altitude sun which occurs at this Latitude of 33°N (80° at noon, midsummer, and even in mid-winter 33°) little direct sun strikes the facades. The courtyards are higher than their width and length – the houses being generally two storeys high, with a basement and a raised parapet around a flat roof. Al-Azzawi [11] describes one of these houses. The walls and roof are massive – 340 to 450 mm walls, and 460 mm roof – and thus provide the thermal time-lag required in a climate with

Fig. 4.13 Diurnal temperature-difference chart for Baghdad. Average highest and lowest monthly temperatures (after *Air Ministry Meteorological Office Tables of Temperature, Relative Humidity and Precipitation for the World*, HMSO, London, 1960, Part V, p. 490).

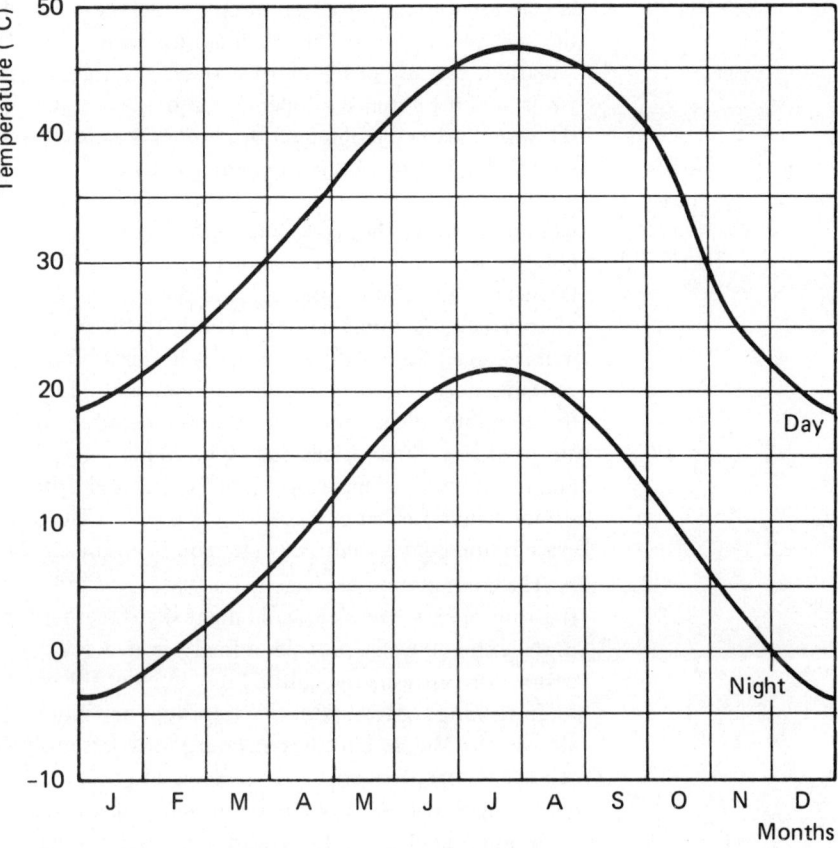

Fig. 4.14 A typical Middle Eastern 'wind scoop'.

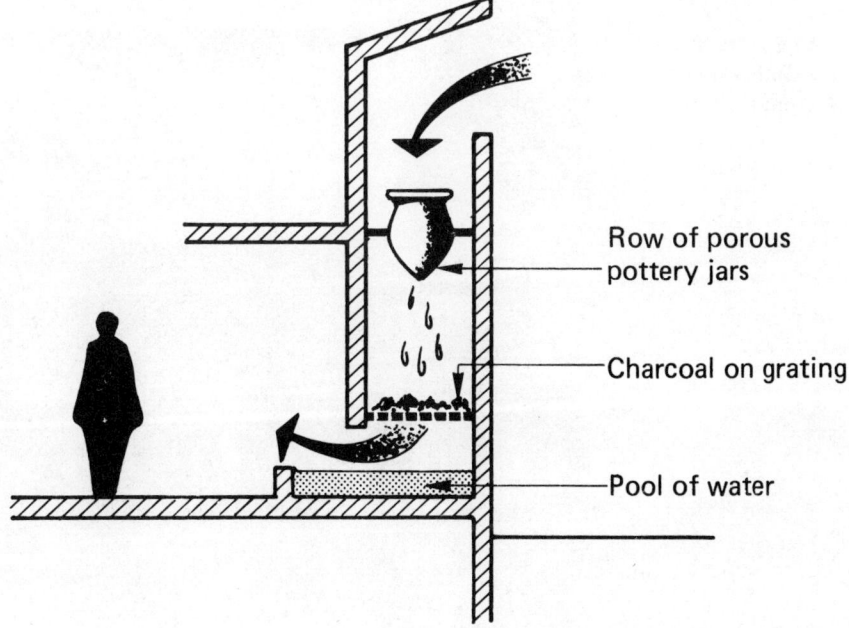

large diurnal temperature variations, as shown in Fig. 4.13. At night, much of
the heat gained by the courtyard during the day is lost to the sky by long-wave
radiation. Because of the narrow streets and the tall proportion of the courtyards, and the absence of openings in the external walls, the cooling effects of
the wind have to be obtained by another means. This is the characteristic 'wind
scoop' (Fig. 4.14). This is an opening with a 45° roof, facing the prevailing
north-westerly wind, projecting above roof level and conducting the trapped
wind downwards through ducts measuring about 900 to 1200 mm wide by
600 mm deep into the basement 'sirdab' – a family rest room used mostly during
the heat of the afternoon. The wind pressure, as well as the convection current
of air which, on coming into contact with the permanently shaded massive party
wall is cooled, causes the air to drop. In the shaft, earthenware drinking-water
containers are cooled by the flow of cool air and by evaporation, which cause
the humidity of the ventilating air to be raised in what is, otherwise, a very dry
atmosphere – rarely exceeding 20 to 30 per cent relative humidity. In some
Middle Eastern regions water from the jars also drips on to porous charcoal over
a pool, where further evaporation takes place. The latent heat required for the
evaporation comes from the water and from the air, thus cooling both.

The combination of shaded courtyard, covered open terrace, cool rooms, and
flat roof open to the clear, cold night sky, together with the absence of openings
in the external walls, provides a finely graded and cooled environment which, of
course, also answers the cultural requirement for family privacy.

In striking contrast with this tradition, new housing in Baghdad, and in fact
all over the Middle East, has no courtyards, has unshaded external walls, with
relatively large, Western-style windows and thin concrete or metal roofs. Not
surprisingly, without full air-conditioning, these houses are far less comfortable.

A useful contrast to this essentially desert climate is that of the humid, warm
tropics. Typically, the traditional Malay timber house represents a climatically
responsive house in this environment. It is lightweight – being basically of
timber framing, with timber boarded floors and palm thatch ('nipa' or 'atap') roof.

Fig. 4.15 A traditional Malay timber house with complex gables.

Fig. 4.16 A traditional Malay timber house with simple gables.

The house is raised on stilts; the gables whether of the complex type illustrated in Fig. 4.15 or of the simpler form in Fig. 4.16 have ventilation apertures in them which open into the void between roof and ceiling. The side walls are constructed of a variety of open timber screens, slatting, boarding and woven panels (Fig. 4.17).

The light weight of the structure and roof result in negligible thermal storage – a property which would be not only useless, since the diurnal temperature variation (Fig. 4.18) is so small that little daytime relief could be obtained from night-time cooling of the structure as in the previous hot-dry climate; but, moreover, it would actually be damaging, in that the continuously warm structure would take longer to cool down on the short occasions when a cooling breeze *is* available.

The main defence in this climate is shade, and air movement to assist in sweat

Fig. 4.17 Side wall of a traditional Malay timber house.

evaporation, which is made the more difficult by the generally high ambient humidity (Fig. 4.19). Shade is provided for the walls by the relatively large overhang of eaves and the planting of coconut palm and other trees around the house. Shade under the house provides a permanently cooler space, with lower ground surface temperatures, which assists in below-floor cooling both by radiation and cooling the air under the house.

Under pressures from Western notions of adequacy, and seeking 'status', a number of these old Malay houses have been re-roofed in corrugated, galvanized iron ('zinc'). Figure 4.20 shows *corrected effective temperature* measurements made by Markus and some of his students in one such house (curve A), compared to the palm roof ('atap') type (curve C). Both houses were unshaded by palms and show a significant effect due to the roofing material, the use of 'atap' having

Fig. 4.18 Temperature isopleths of Butterworth, west coast of Malaysia (after Markus *et al.* [35]), based on records by the Malaysian Meteorological Service.

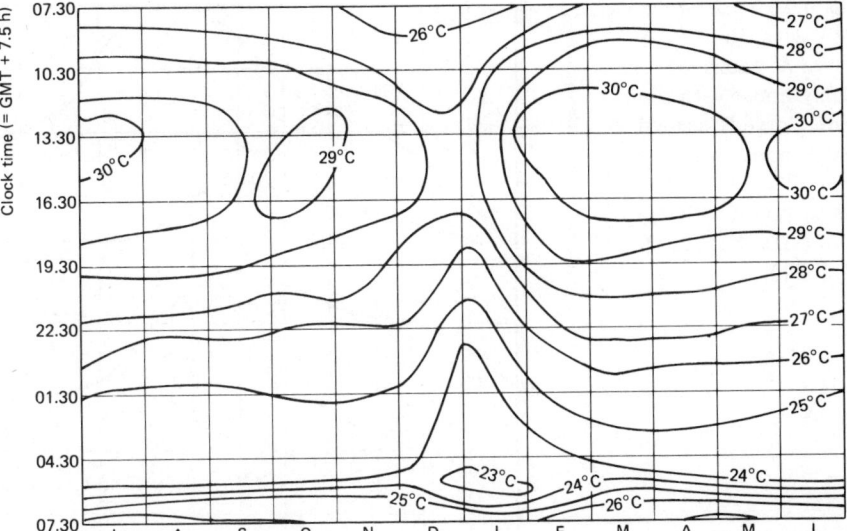

Fig. 4.19 Relative humidity isopleths of Butterworth, west coast of Malaysia (after Markus *et al.* [35]), based on records by the Malaysian Meteorological Service. Values are given as percentage relative humidity.

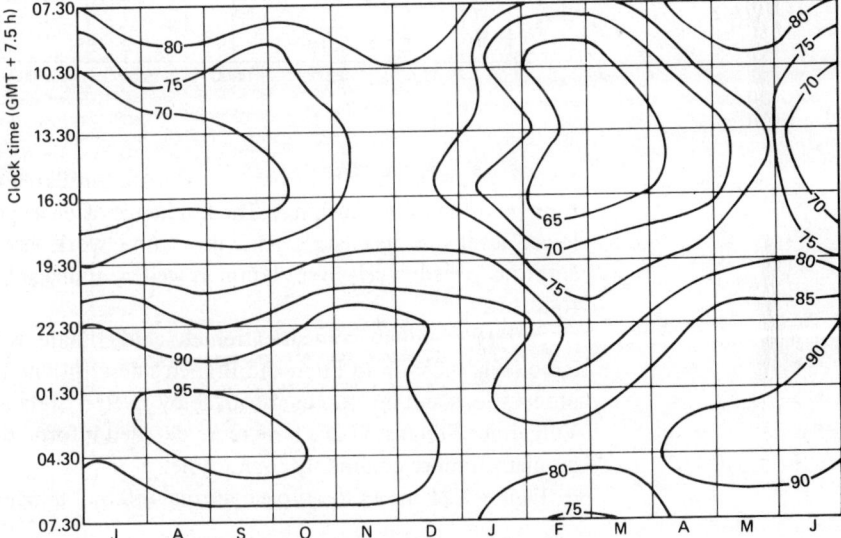

an even greater cooling effect than is achieved by shading a 'zinc' roof with palms (curve B). Corrected effective temperature (CET) – an older index whilst not recommended or discussed in detail in this book, gives a reasonably true comparative statement of comfort, including the effects of air and mean radiant temperatures, air velocity and humidity.

One of the most characteristic features of the house is the gradation of environment between the inside and outside. Between the sunlit fields and the house there are groups of palms and broad-leaved trees, such as banana and low shrubs. These shield not only the roof but also the walls of the house and the ground – and provide multidirectional shielding which is important since, with the humid atmosphere and high turbidity, a substantially greater proportion of the total radiation is in diffuse form than in the hot-dry, desert climate and, hence, is non-directional. Entry up some steps will usually lead to a covered terrace or porch, from which an outer living room is reached. The internal,

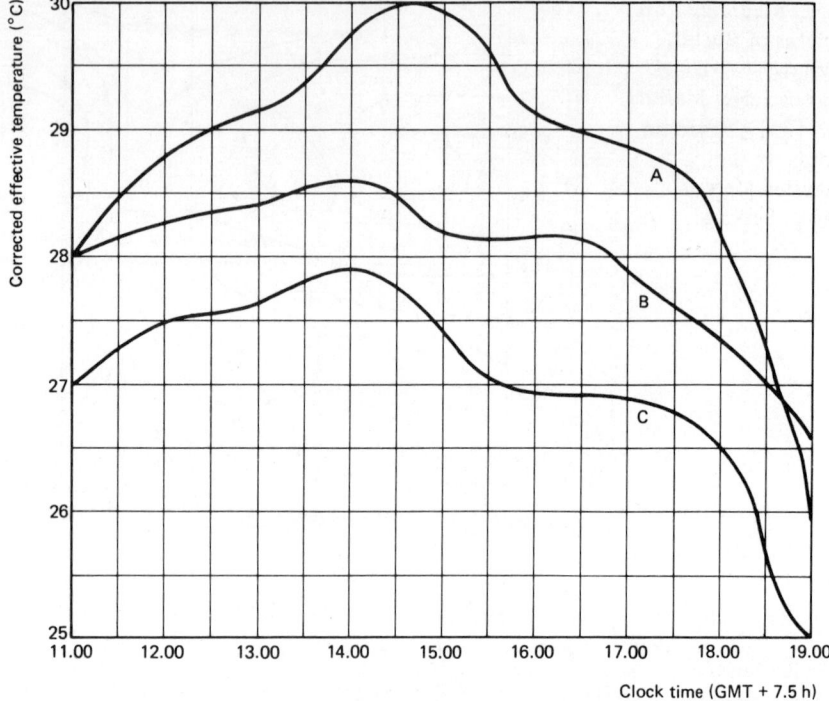

Fig. 4.20 Variation of CET with time of day. Curve A, unshaded Malay house with 'zinc' roof. Curve B, shaded Malay house with 'zinc' roof. Curve C, unshaded Malay house with 'atap' roof (after Markus *et al.* [35]).

family spaces, are entered from here and are ventilated through the outer living room and their own openings. The kitchen is often at ground, or at least a lower, level with its characteristic projecting 'work shelf', which is open-slatted and thus gives low-level ventilation as well as drainage for pots, pans and foodstuffs.

A third example, from an extremely cold climate, is the well-known Eskimo igloo (Fig. 4.2). From Fitch and Branch's descriptions [12], based on observations and measurements made by Evelyn Stefansson, wife of the explorer Vilhjalmur Stefansson, we have more detailed information on this structure than on many a more commonly found type.

Figure 4.21 shows the typical diurnal internal temperatures at ceiling, sleeping

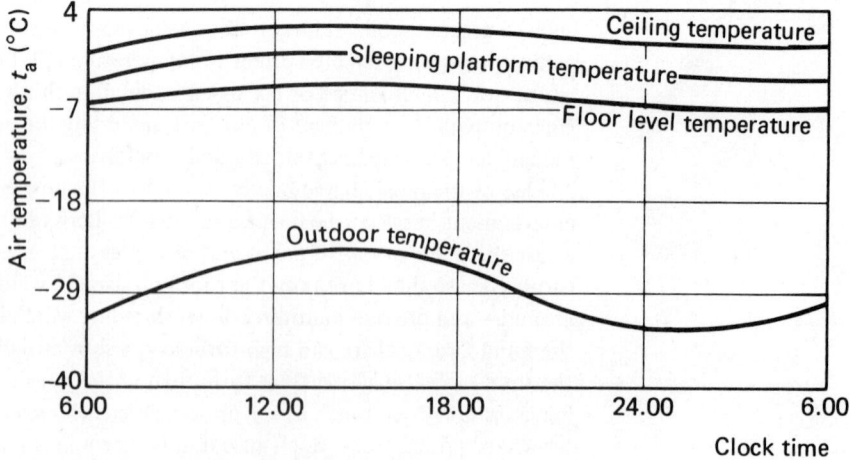

Fig. 4.21 Igloo temperatures (after Fitch and Branch [12]).

platform and floor levels; together with the outdoor temperature. The interior, heated (and lit) by a few oil lamps and the body heat of the occupants, is maintained as much as $26°C$ above the exterior at floor level. The walls, of dry snow, offer relatively good insulation in the thickness, 500 mm, in which they are built. The form of the igloo is ideal for the conditions, offering the minimum surface per unit volume, as well as an aerodynamic shape which offers low resistance to wind and, hence, a higher surface resistance to heat flow. A point source of radiant heat is capable of heating it uniformly, and it, with the body heat of the occupants, melts the inner surface which then forms a glaze of ice, which not only seals the porous structure of the snow, but to some extent acts as a reflective surface. The inner surfaces of the dome and the floor are usually covered in furs and skins, thus adding a lightweight, quick-response layer, which not only increases the insulation but also provides a relatively higher surface temperature and, thus, reduces radiant body heat losses. Limited ventilation is provided by a small opening near the top of the dome, facing away from the prevailing wind direction. When the outside temperature rises to about $-6°C$, the inside walls begin to melt and when it rises fractionally above freezing point the igloo collapses. But by then the Eskimos are ready to move to a different territory where a different, summer dwelling is built.

These three examples from severe climates indicate the important effect of radiation (direct and diffuse), wind and temperature as climatic 'basics'. These are the three main factors we shall consider in the next section.

4.4 Elements of climate

Since we are concerned with the thermal design of buildings, the aspects of climate of immediate interest are thermal – primarily radiation, temperature, humidity and wind. These, together with precipitation, are linked into a global system which is the result of the constant radiation of energy from the sun and the 24-h rotation of the earth about its axis and the 12-month rotation around the sun. Thus radiation and planetary movement in the solar system are the prime movers of the earth's system of mass and energy flow.

Outside the earth's atmosphere the intensity of solar radiation is approximately 1.4 kW m^{-2} at normal incidence to the solar beam. This is known as the solar constant. About 50 per cent of this radiation penetrates the earth's atmosphere and is absorbed at the earth's surface. Since the atmosphere is, however, almost opaque to the long-wave radiation emitted by the earth, this is largely absorbed in the atmosphere and continuously re-radiated to outer space. Figure 4.22 shows the annual radiation budget at the earth's surface, separately for both short and long-wave radiation.

The global radiation, direct and diffuse, received on a horizontal surface at the earth's surface is shown in Fig. 4.23, based on data from Budyko [13]. This radiation is reflected back to the atmosphere in quantities dependent on the reflectance ('albedo') of the earth's surface – varying a good deal with water, vegetation cover, snow and ice. The mean albedo is about 30 per cent, but more accurate values are becoming available from spacecraft and satellite data.

The earth's surface loses heat by long-wave radiation; by turbulent heat exchange due to convective losses caused by air flow; and by evaporation from land and sea, as well as transevaporation through plants. As a result of all these modes of gain and loss a picture of the net heat balance at the earth's surface can be obtained such as in Fig. 4.24.

The differential radiation balance on the surface, varying with Latitude, is

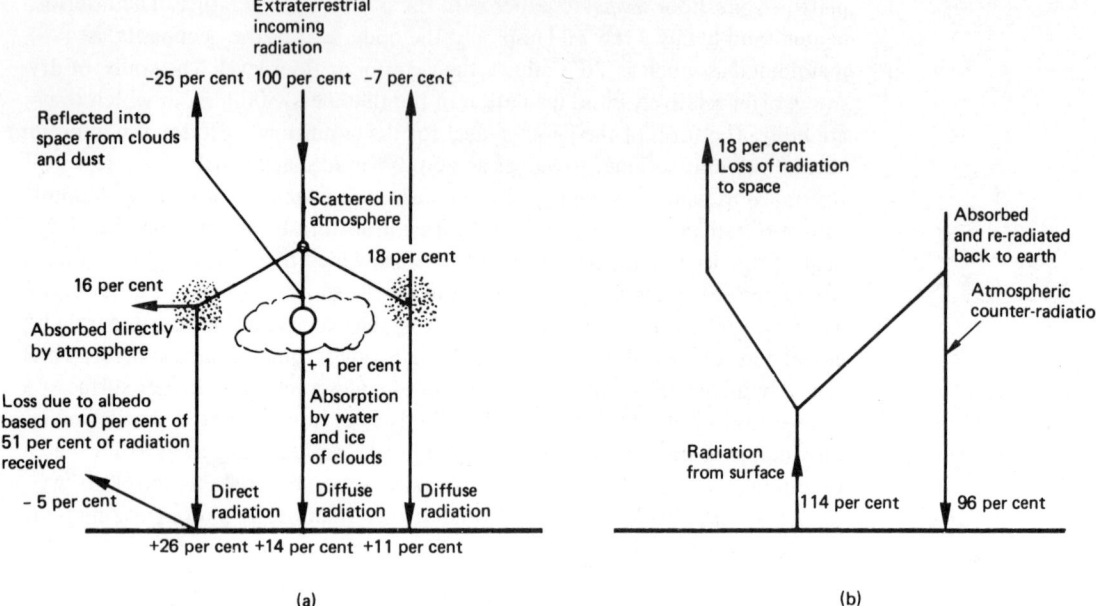

(a)   (b)

Fig. 4.22 The annual radiation budget of the planet earth. The exchanges are referred to 100 units of incoming solar radiation at the top of the atmosphere. (a) Short-wave solar radiation. (b) Long-wave terrestrial radiation (after Flohn [29]).

one of the major causes of the general circulation of the air. In the absence of the effect of the rotation of the earth, the circulation would take the simple form of a rising cell over the equator and a falling one over the poles.

However, the earth's rotation introduces two other forces on the thermal, and hence pressure-induced, convective movements of air. The first force is the so-called Coriolis acceleration, which is the apparent acceleration of the air by virtue of the earth's rotation. It results in the apparent deflection of a parcel of air to the right in the northern and the left in the southern hemisphere as it moves from the poles outwards towards the equator. The other force is that of angular momentum — as a result of which a parcel of air, which tends to conserve its velocity, will appear to move faster than the earth as it moves towards the poles, creating effectively an apparent wind. This has an apparent clockwise rotation in the northern hemisphere and anticlockwise in the southern. The combination of all these forces gives rise to the global wind patterns which are displayed in Fig. 4.25.

Fig. 4.23 Average annual global radiation. Isolines at intervals of 20 kcal cm^{-2} year^{-1} (after Budyko [13]). 1 kcal cm^{-2} year^{-1} = 11.6 kW h m^{-2} year^{-1}.

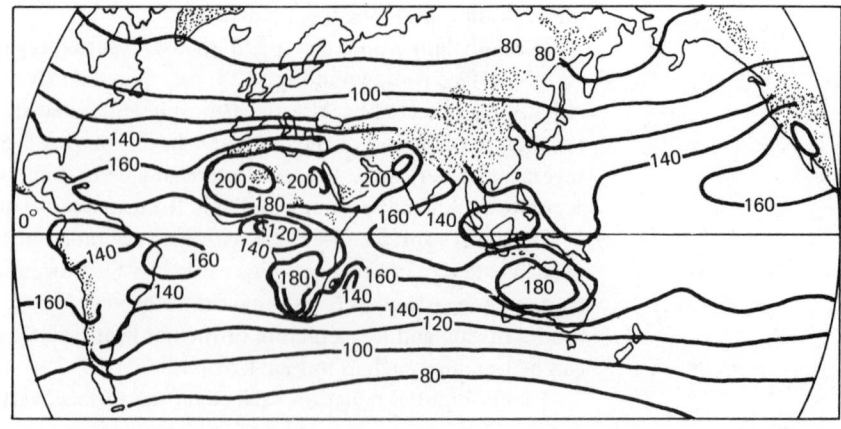

Fig. 4.24 Geographical distribution of annual net radiation balance of the surface–atmosphere system. Isolines at intervals of 20 kcal cm^{-2} $year^{-1}$ (after Budyko and Kondratyev [13]). 1 kcal cm^{-2} $year^{-1}$ = 11.6 kW h m^{-2} $year^{-1}$.

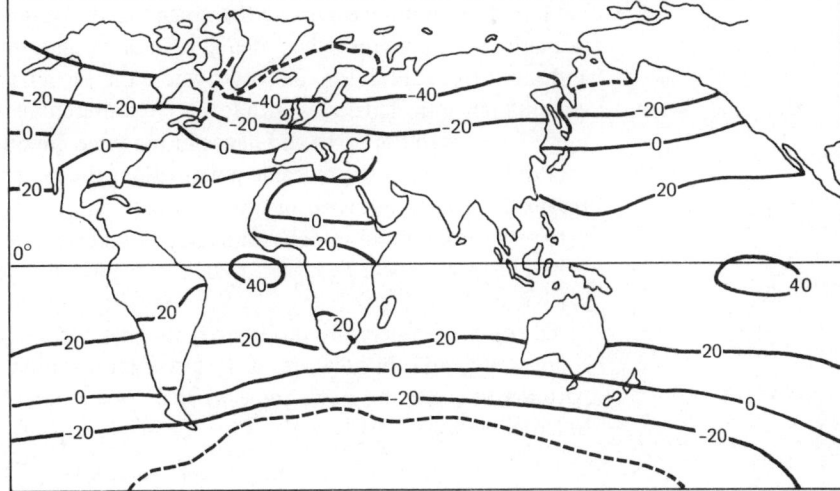

Fig. 4.25 Global wind patterns.

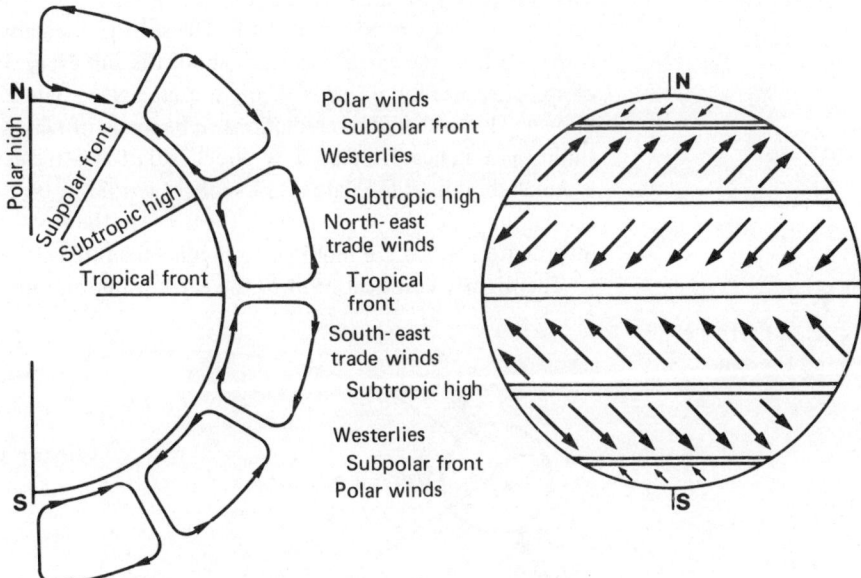

At the equator, warm air moves upwards, and drops as cooler air in the subtropical high-pressure zones. At the same time it divides here, flowing towards both the equator and the poles, to rise again in the low-pressure subpolar zones, flowing up and in both directions again. The rotational forces, plus the frictional and gravitational forces so far not considered, result in the atmosphere exerting a drag on the earth; this means that, in order to maintain the rate of rotation constant, the drag forces must alternate eastwards and westwards, and this indeed is the pattern seen in Fig. 4.25. The tropical zones have the characteristic northeasterly and south-easterly trade winds, in the northern and southern hemispheres respectively; at about the two tropics winds are typically light and variable in the high-pressure zone.

These trade winds are primarily the result of the Coriolis force, causing the winds to blow in a direction opposite to the rotation of the earth. Beyond the subtropical high-pressure areas, up to about 60° Latitude, the westerlies predominate (south-westerly in the north, north-westerly in the south) now primarily under the influence of angular momentum, since the air moving north and south from about 30° Latitude, where the earth has a high velocity at the circumference, to Latitudes with lower circumferential velocity, will appear to move faster than the earth and hence in the same direction as the earth's rotation. Finally, in the extreme polar regions the movement is again primarily thermally dominated, with air moving away from the poles at low level; starting with a circumferential velocity of nearly zero at the poles and gradually 'lagging' behind; hence, appearing, again, to be moving in a direction opposite to the earth's rotation.

Of course, temperature difference over land and sea, day/night variations, topography and other features will cause significant local variations of these patterns, in space and time. Some we shall look at later in more detail under 'microclimate'.

4.4.1 Sun Movement

The apparent movement of the sun through the sky is the result of the earth's rotation on its own axis every 24 h. The shift in the daily path from day to day is the result of the earth's rotation about the sun every 365 days. For many design purposes the position of the sun on a given date at a given time has to be known. This will enable predictions to be made of which faces of a building are sunlit (and, hence, irradiated by direct radiation); to calculate the shadows cast around a building; the patches of sunlight within it, on floors and walls; and to fix the sun's altitude and azimuth (bearing) in the sky – two pieces of information which are required to predict the intensity of solar radiation.

The slightly elliptical orbit of the earth round the sun is illustrated in

Fig. 4.26 Earth's orbit around the sun.

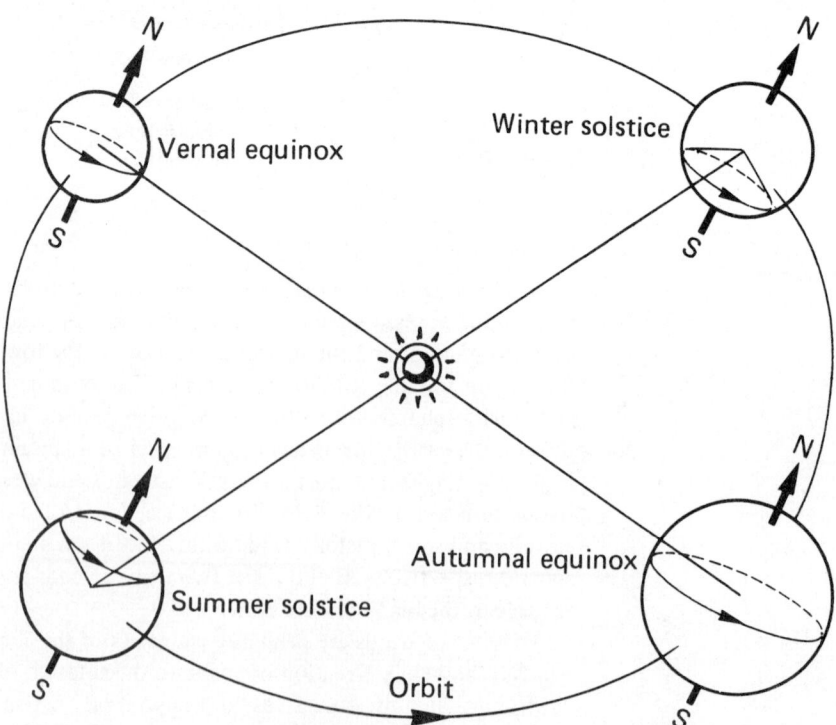

Fig. 4.27 A section through the sun, the ecliptic plane and the earth in two directions.

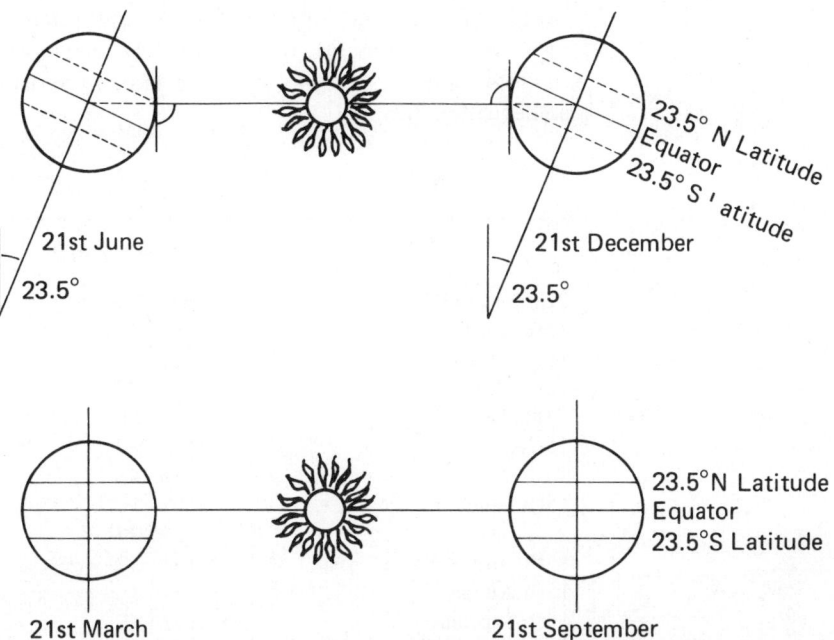

Fig. 4.26. The axis of the earth is tilted with respect to the plane which passes through the sun and the equator at 23.5°. This tilt accounts for the changes of radiation, length of day, and climate with season; if the axis were at right angles to this plane (the 'ecliptic') there would be uniform conditions throughout the year. Figure 4.27 shows a section through the sun, the ecliptic plane and the earth in two directions; one represents the equinoxes (March 21st and September 21st) and the other the two solstices (June 21st and December 21st).

The sun describes an apparent path in the sky each day; it moves through the zenith (90° altitude) at noon at the equator on September 21st and March 21st (the 'equinoxes' – i.e. equal night and day of 12 h each); and on the 21st June (the summer solstice) at the tropic of Cancer (23.5°N Latitude) and, equally, on 21st December (the winter solstice) at the tropic of Capricorn (23.5°S Latitude). It will be seen from Fig. 4.27 that this is the case on account of the 23.5° tilt of the earth's axis.

The Equinoxes exist at all Latitudes — and on these two dates all places on the earth have a 12-h day and a 12-h night; with sunrise exactly due east and sunset exactly due west.

The length of day increases from December to June and decreases from June to December in the northern hemisphere, and vice versa in the southern.

The angle between the earth–sun line and the earth's equatorial plane is known as the angle of declination. Clearly this varies with the date; and the orbital velocity of the earth travelling around the ecliptic plane also varies slightly. Thus, a clock, adjusted to run at a uniform rate, will show slight deviations from *true solar time** as determined, for instance, by a sundial. The positive or negative correction is known as the *equation of time*; an amount that

---

*   In astronomical and nautical calculations, true solar time is usually known as *local apparent time* (LAT); however, this terminology is not suitable for our purpose and has not been adopted in this text.

has to be added to or subtracted from the uniform *mean solar time* as indicated by a clock, to obtain the true solar time (i.e. one in which noon occurs as the sun is due South). Table 4.4 shows the monthly variations of both declination and equation of time.

Table 4.4   *Monthly variations of solar declination and the equation of time*

Date	Solar declination, d	Equation of time
21st December	$-23°\ 27'$	$+\ 1'\ 32''$
15th January	$-21°\ 17'$	$-\ 9'\ 00''$
15th February	$-12°\ 58'$	$-14'\ 30''$
15th March	$-\ 2°\ 23'$	$-\ 9'\ 30''$
21st March	$0°\ 00'$	$-\ 7'\ 19''$
15th April	$+\ 9°\ 33'$	$-\ 0'\ 30''$
15th May	$+18°\ 44'$	$+\ 4'\ 00''$
15th June	$+23°\ 17'$	$0'\ 00''$
21st June	$+23°\ 27'$	$-\ 1'\ 48''$
15th July	$+21°\ 37'$	$-\ 5'\ 30''$
15th August	$+14°\ 15'$	$-\ 4'\ 30''$
15th September	$+\ 3°\ 17'$	$+\ 4'\ 30''$
21st September	$0°\ 00'$	$+\ 7'\ 30''$
15th October	$-\ 8°\ 18'$	$+14'\ 00''$
15th November	$-18°\ 20'$	$+15'\ 30''$
15th December	$-23°\ 15'$	$+\ 5'\ 00''$

There is a further time correction to make between mean solar time and clock time at any spot. The world is divided into time zones, each one of which has a reference Longitude where mean solar time and clock time are the same. Any spot east or west of this reference Longitude, but within the same time zone, must have a correction made which amounts to 4 min per degree of Longitude (since it takes 24 h to revolve through $360°$). If the locality lies to the west of the reference Longitude, the amount has to be added to the clock time to obtain mean solar time and, if to the east, it has to be subtracted. Naturally, if further clock corrections have been made (such as special summer times, etc.), these also have to be allowed for in obtaining the mean solar time from clock time.

For example, to calculate the clock time in Singapore when true solar time noon occurs, on January 15th, the following steps are required:

(i) Singapore clock time is based on time zone Longitude $112°\ 30'$ ($112.5°$) east of Greenwich (Longitude $= 0°$).

(ii) Therefore, Singapore clock time is $112.5 \times \frac{4}{60}$ h ahead of GMT $= 7.5$ h ahead of GMT.

(iii) Actual Longitude of Singapore $= 103°\ 50'$ E.

(iv) Therefore, Singapore is $8°\ 40'$ W of standard Longitude upon which its clock time is based.

(v) Hence, mean solar time at Singapore is $(4 \times 8°\ 40')$ min later than clock time, $= 4 \times 8\frac{2}{3}$ min $= 34$ min 40 s.

(vi) So, mean solar time noon $= 12 + 34$ min 40 s clock time $= 12.34.\ 40$ clock time.

(vii) From Table 4.4, equation of time correction for January 15 = −9.0 min.

(viii) Therefore, true solar time noon = mean solar time noon + 9 min.

(ix) Hence, true solar time noon = 12.34. 40 + 9 min clock time.

(x) So, true solar time noon = (say) 12.44 clock time.

For most purposes, true solar time is acceptable as a basis of calculation. It gives a daily symmetry about noon, and is used in this book in the solar overlays, etc. Where more accurate data is required — for instance in relation to working hours — then the above corrections must be applied.

The two angles that completely describe the sun's position are the solar altitude β, measured from $0°$ to $90°$ above the horizon, and the solar azimuth ϕ, measured from $0°$ to $180°$ from the south with positive sign eastwards and negative sign westwards. To determine these two angles from data on Latitude, date and time, the following calculation is carried out.

Instead of being expressed in time units, true solar time can be expressed in angular terms related to the earth's rotation as the *hour angle, $\hat{H}$,* where

$$\hat{H} = 0.25 \times \text{(Number of minutes from true solar time noon)},$$

since in *one* minute the earth rotates $0.25°$. Values a.m. are +ve and p.m. −ve. Then,

$$\sin \beta = \cos L \cos d \cos \hat{H} + \sin L \sin d \tag{4.1}$$

and

$$\sin \phi = \frac{\cos d \sin \hat{H}}{\cos \beta}, \tag{4.2}$$

where L = Latitude, degrees, d = declination, degrees (northern hemisphere = +ve, southern hemisphere = −ve).

Values of β and ϕ are tabulated in a number of almanacs, guides and other publications. Graphical techniques for finding them are also available, including the use of stereographic projection given in this book.

For example, let us find the solar altitude and azimuth at 14.00 true solar time on June 22nd at $55°$N Latitude.

$$\hat{H} = (−0.25 \times 120) = −30°,$$

d (from Table 4.4) for June 21st = $+23.5°$ and so, using equation (4.1),

$$\begin{aligned} \sin \beta &= \cos 55 \cos 23.5 \cos 30 + \sin 55 \sin 23.5 \\ &= 0.574 \times 0.917 \times 0.866 + 0.819 \times 0.399 \\ &= 0.456 + 0.326 \\ &= 0.782. \end{aligned}$$

Hence, $\beta = 51.5°$. Using equation (4.2),

$$\begin{aligned} \sin \phi &= \frac{\cos 23.5 \sin −30}{\cos 51.5} \\ &= \frac{0.917 \times −0.500}{0.623} \\ &= −0.736. \end{aligned}$$

Therefore, $\phi = −47.4°$ (W of south). Both altitude and azimuth angles can be confirmed by using Overlay 6 over the $55°$ sunpath chart in Appendix 4A.

The altitude and azimuth bearings of the sun enable some further important sets of angles to be computed. The first is the angle of incidence, i. This, it will be seen, is a vital piece of information, for the intensity of direct irradiance is a function of the angle of incidence, being a maximum at $0°$ (the angle of incidence is always measured from the *normal* to the surface), and dropping off as the cosine of the angle of incidence, until it reaches zero at $90°$ incidence.

The second are the shadow angles, that is the angle the sun makes on section (the vertical shadow angle ϵ) and on plan (the horizontal shadow angle δ). These angles enable the shadows cast and the patches of sunlight on surfaces inside and outside buildings to be predicted and plotted on sections and plans.

The third is the wall solar azimuth, γ, of a vertical or tilted surface, which describes the angle between its orientation and the sun's bearing (solar azimuth, ϕ).

The relationships between these angles is illustrated in Figs. 4.28 and 4.29. To calculate the angle of incidence i on any plane, including the horizontal, the following equation may be used:

$$\cos i = \cos \beta \cos \gamma \sin s + \sin \beta \cos s, \tag{4.3}$$

where s = slope angle of surface from horizontal. For a vertical surface, when $s = 90°$,

$$\cos i = \cos \beta \cos \gamma. \tag{4.4}$$

For a horizontal surface, when $s = 0°$,

$$\cos i = \sin \beta. \tag{4.5}$$

To avoid calculations which can be quite tedious without a computer program, many graphical prediction devices are available which allow altitude, azimuth, vertical and horizontal shadow angles, and angles of incidence on any

Fig. 4.28 Solar angles for vertical, sloping and horizontal surfaces. Solar altitude $\beta = \angle QOH$; solar azimuth $\phi = \angle SOH$; zenith angle $z = \angle QOV = 90 - \beta$; incident angle $i = \angle QOP$; wall azimuth $\psi = \angle SOP$; wall–solar azimuth $\gamma = \angle HOP$.

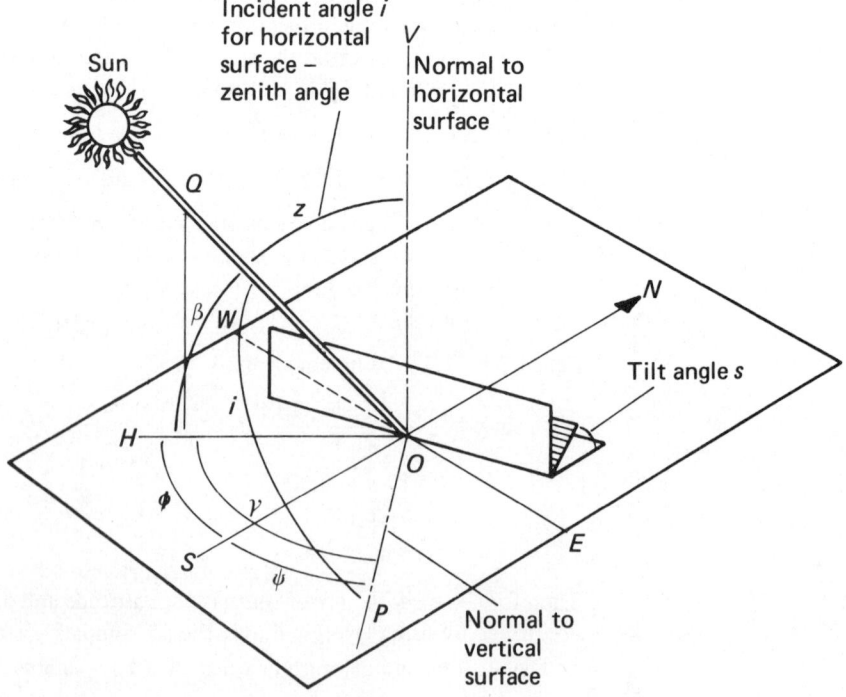

Fig. 4.29 (a) The angle of incidence i; $\cos i =$ $\cos \delta \cos \beta$. (b) The horizontal shadow angle δ. (c) The vertical shadow angle ϵ; $\tan \epsilon =$ $\tan \beta \sec \delta$.

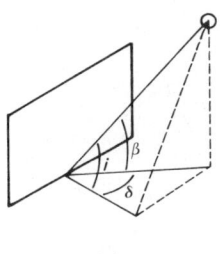
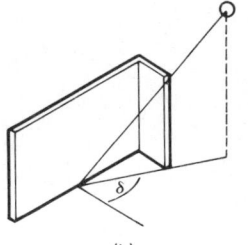
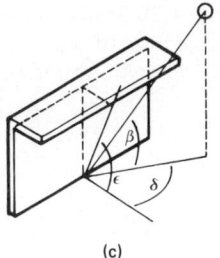

(a)   (b)   (c)

plane, to be found. A related set of graphical tools allow prediction of direct and diffuse solar radiation intensities on surfaces, and we shall deal with these in Section 4.4.2 below.

The graphical technique adopted here is stereographic projection, whose principles are explained in Fig. 4.30.

Any point on the surface of a hemisphere is connected to the sphere's nadir – equivalent to viewing the inside surface of the upper hemisphere from the nadir as the eye's position. These connecting, or sight, lines cut the equatorial plane of the sphere; this plane can represent the horizon. On to this plane, at the intersections of the sight lines, every point on the surface of the hemisphere can be projected. This yields a two-dimensional projection, with the horizon forming the outer circle and the zenith the centre of the hemisphere's surface. On such a projection the paths of the sun can be plotted as they would appear to pass over the imaginary sky hemisphere; the altitudes can be represented by a series of concentric rings and the azimuths by a scale from 0° to 180° along the periphery. Hence, the altitude and azimuth of the sun at any date and time can be read off directly. Each such diagram will be correct for one Latitude; by reversal of the dating, each diagram will also serve for the equivalent Latitude in the other hemisphere. Charts 1 to 18 in Appendix 4A give sunpath diagrams from 1° to 65° Latitude at 4° intervals; each is labelled for the northern hemisphere, but the dates and orientations, printed upside down on each diagram, enable it to be turned the other way up and be used for the same southern hemisphere Latitude. 55° Latitude has been included, in addition, for greater accuracy in the British Isles.

The sunpath diagrams also have hour lines plotted on them (again one set of labels for the northern and the other set, upside down, for the southern hemispheres). All these times are in true solar time; that is the sun is due south (in the northern hemisphere) at noon. It will be seen that the equinox sunpaths at all Latitudes show sunrise exactly due east and sunset due west, at 6.00 and 18.00 hours, respectively.

To obtain the solar altitude, β and the solar azimuth ϕ, Overlay 6 is laid over the sunpath chart for the Latitude and the values of β and ϕ read at the intersection of a date line and an hour line.

To obtain the angle of incidence i on a surface one overlay for every slope angle s is required and Overlays 1 to 5 show these for vertical surfaces and for surfaces tilted at 15°, 30°, 45° and 60° to the horizontal.

To find the vertical and horizontal shadow angles, ϵ and δ, Overlay 6, including a 'protractor', is placed over the sunpath diagram. The former angle, ϵ, is read off one of the arcs, 90° at the centre and 0° at the outer periphery; the latter angle, δ, on the periphery of the protractor. The protractor has to be

Fig. 4.30 Stereographic projection of 0°, 30°, 60° and 90° altitudes.

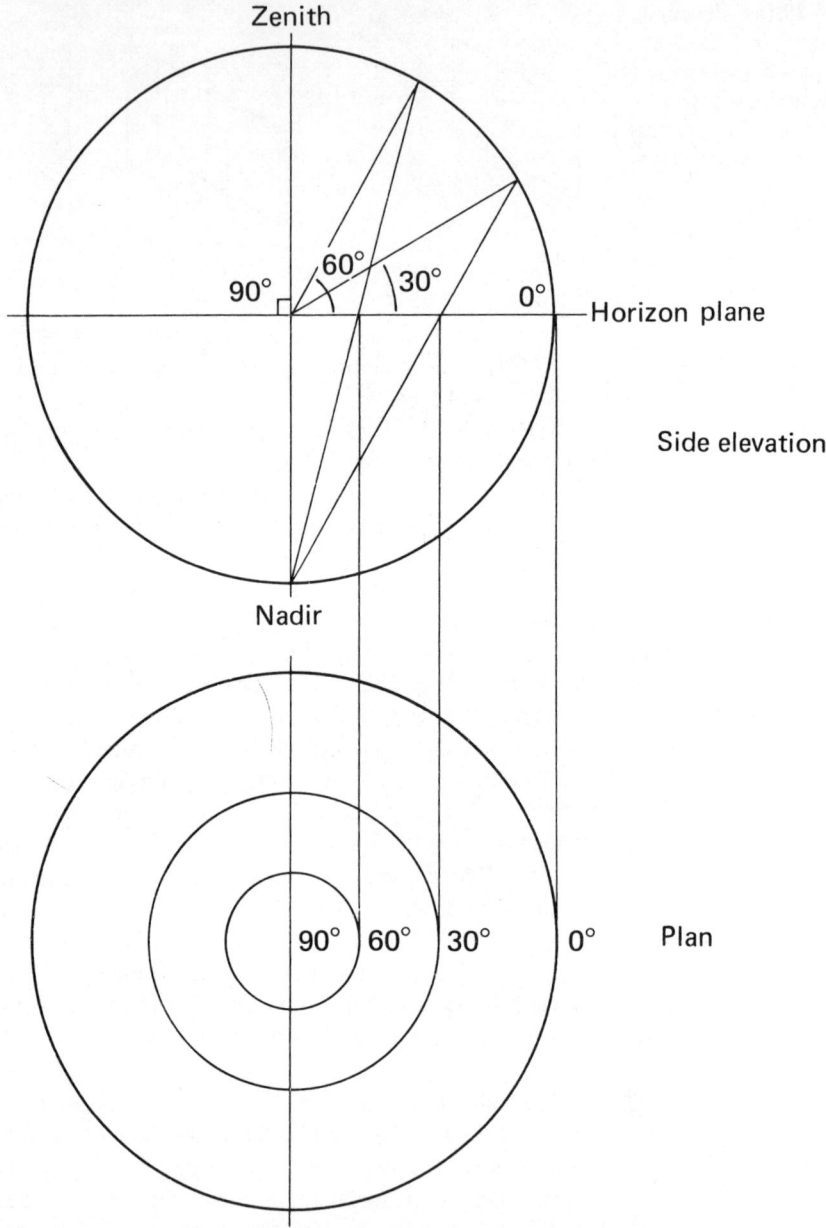

placed on the sunpath diagram with the base line, representing the plane of a vertical or sloping surface on plan, facing in the correct orientation — that is with the *normal* to this surface having the azimuth bearing of the surface. Fig. 4.31 illustrates the use of the protractor for a south-west-facing vertical surface at Latitude 55°N for the sun at 14.00 solar time on the equinox, giving

$$\epsilon = 31° \text{ and } \delta = 9°.$$

The use of the shadow angle protractors enables shading masks to be drawn, which show the shading effect of any object. Fig. 4.32 shows some examples of overhangs and shading devices and how the angles they produce on plan and section can be transferred on to the shadow angle protractor to produce the

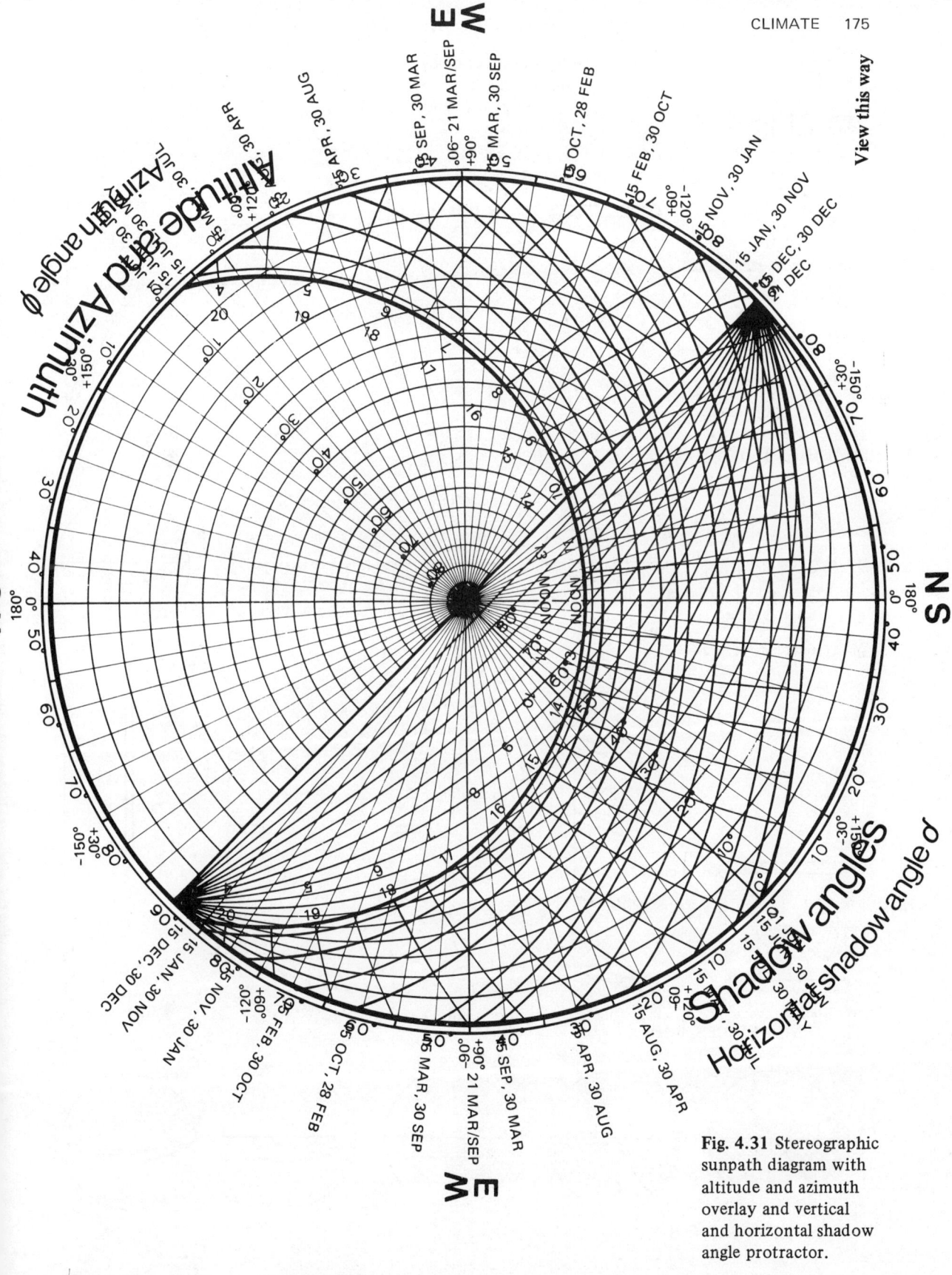

Fig. 4.31 Stereographic sunpath diagram with altitude and azimuth overlay and vertical and horizontal shadow angle protractor.

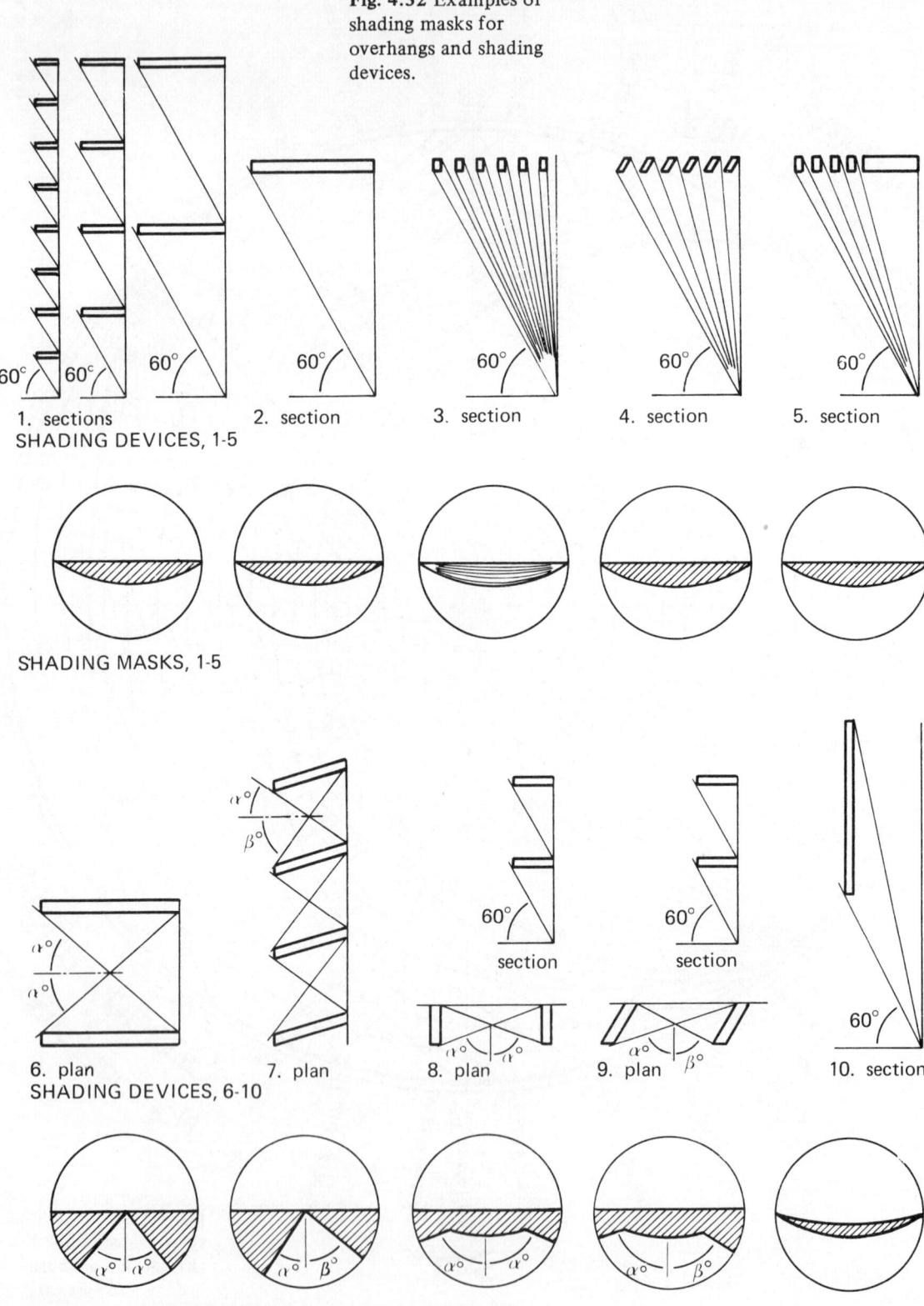

Fig. 4.32 Examples of shading masks for overhangs and shading devices.

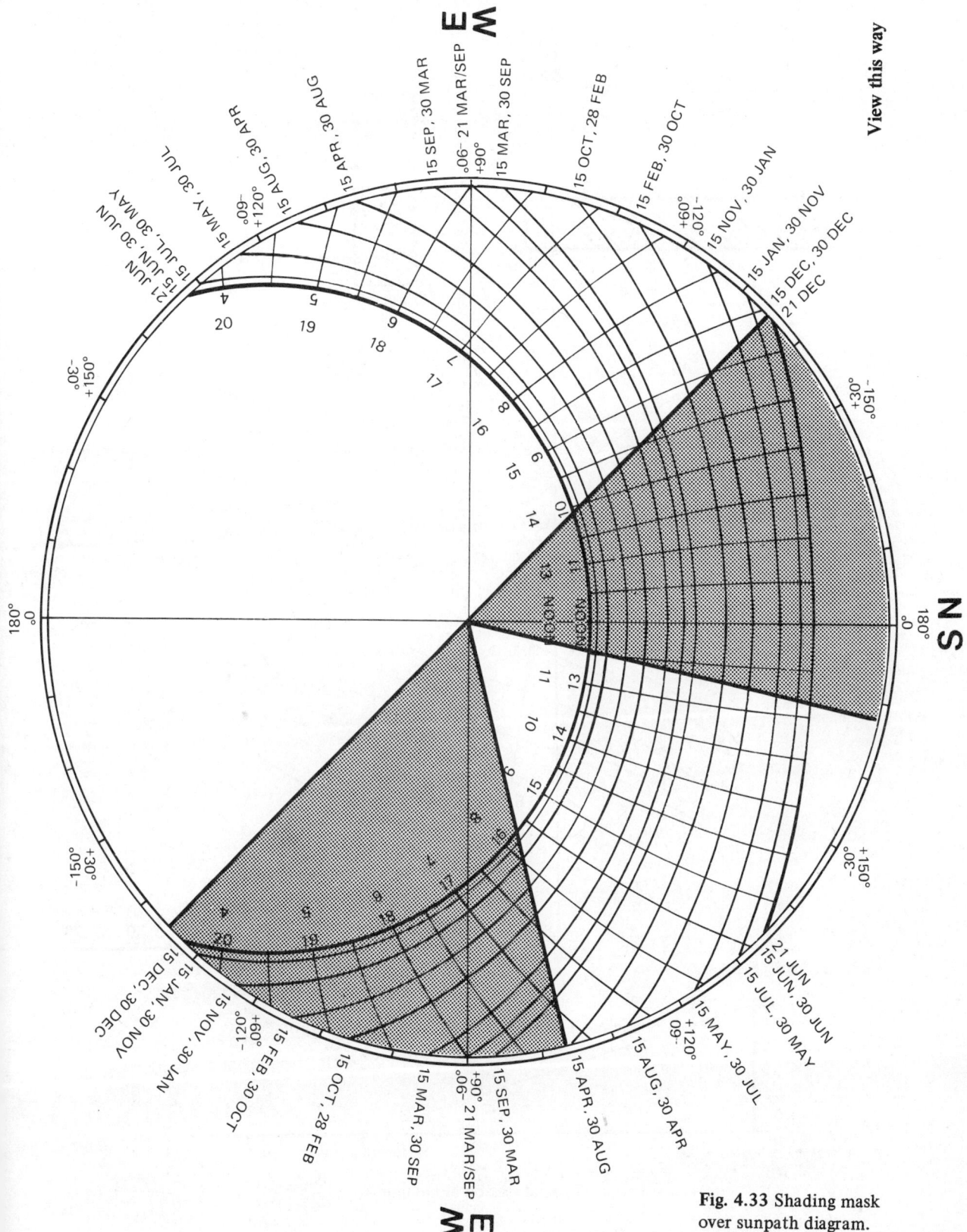

Fig. 4.33 Shading mask over sunpath diagram.

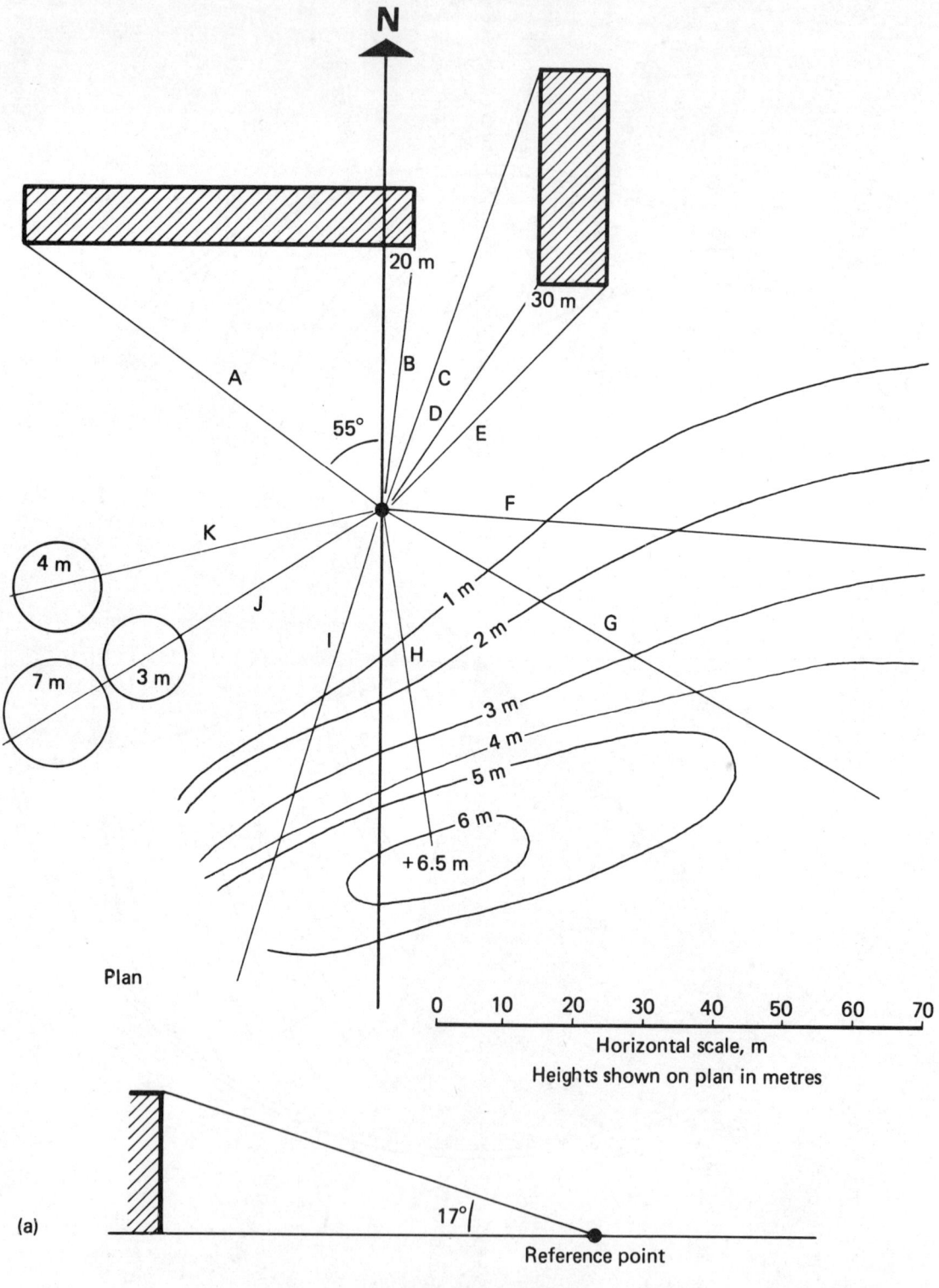

N

20 m

30 m

A

B

C

D

E

55°

F

K

4 m

J

1 m

2 m

G

I

H

7 m

3 m

3 m

4 m

5 m

6 m

+6.5 m

Plan

| 0 | 10 | 20 | 30 | 40 | 50 | 60 | 70 |

Horizontal scale, m

Heights shown on plan in metres

17°

(a)

Reference point

Typical section along line A

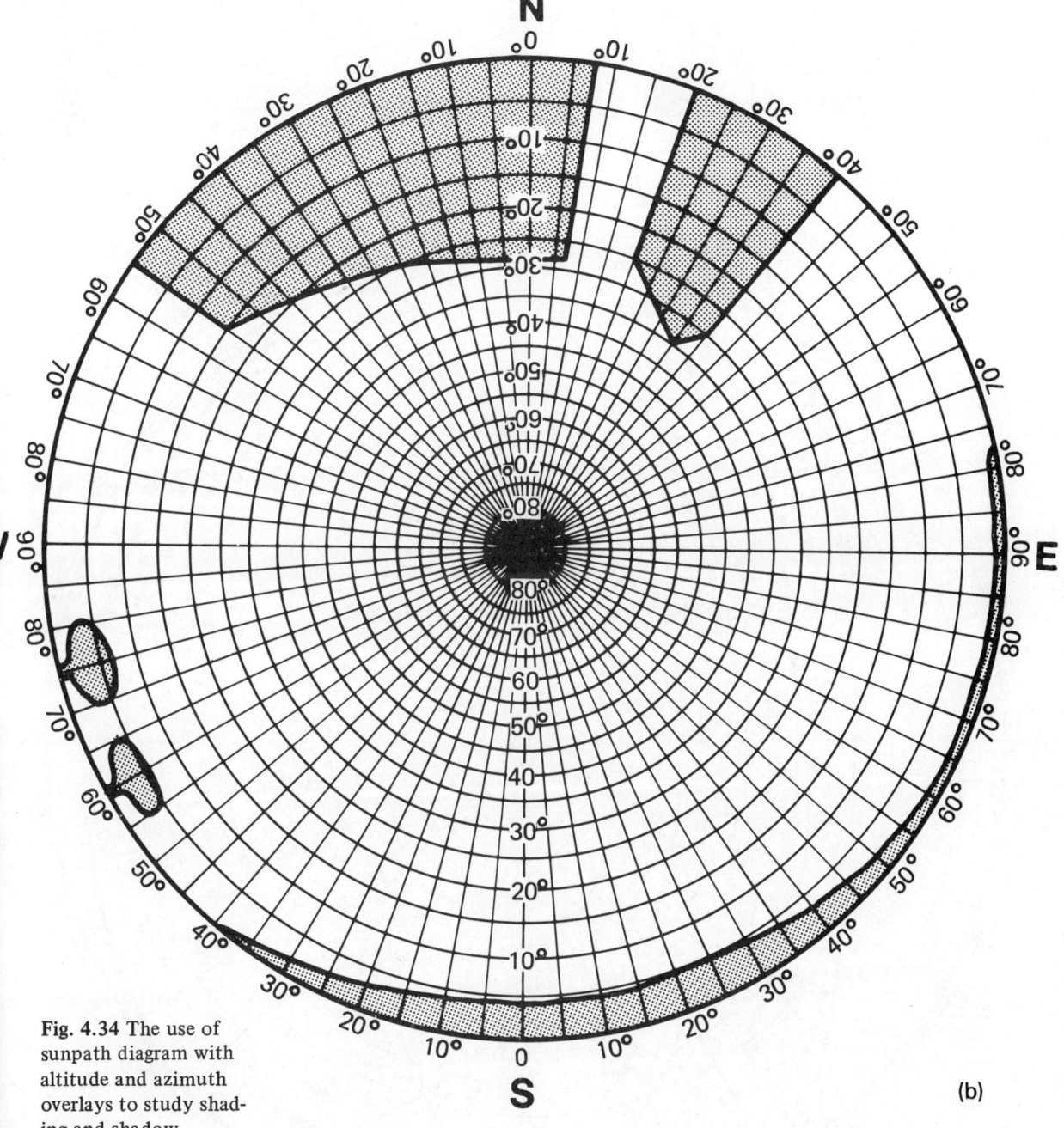

Fig. 4.34 The use of sunpath diagram with altitude and azimuth overlays to study shading and shadow patterns on a building site. (a) Site plan with heights. (b) Shading mask. (c) Shading mask superimposed over sunpath chart. (d) Stereographic photograph with sunpath chart superimposed.

(b)

shading mask. This in turn can be superimposed on to the sunpath and will indicate the times and dates when the sun is obscured from a surface – that is when the sunpaths are covered by any part of the mask, as in the example in Fig. 4.33. Shading mask 6 from Fig. 4.32 is superimposed on the sunpath diagram for 55°N Latitude (Chart 15, Appendix 4A) for a south-west-facing facade. The *un*obscured sunpaths give the dates and times when the sun will penetrate this device.

The sunpath charts and altitude and azimuth overlay can also be used to

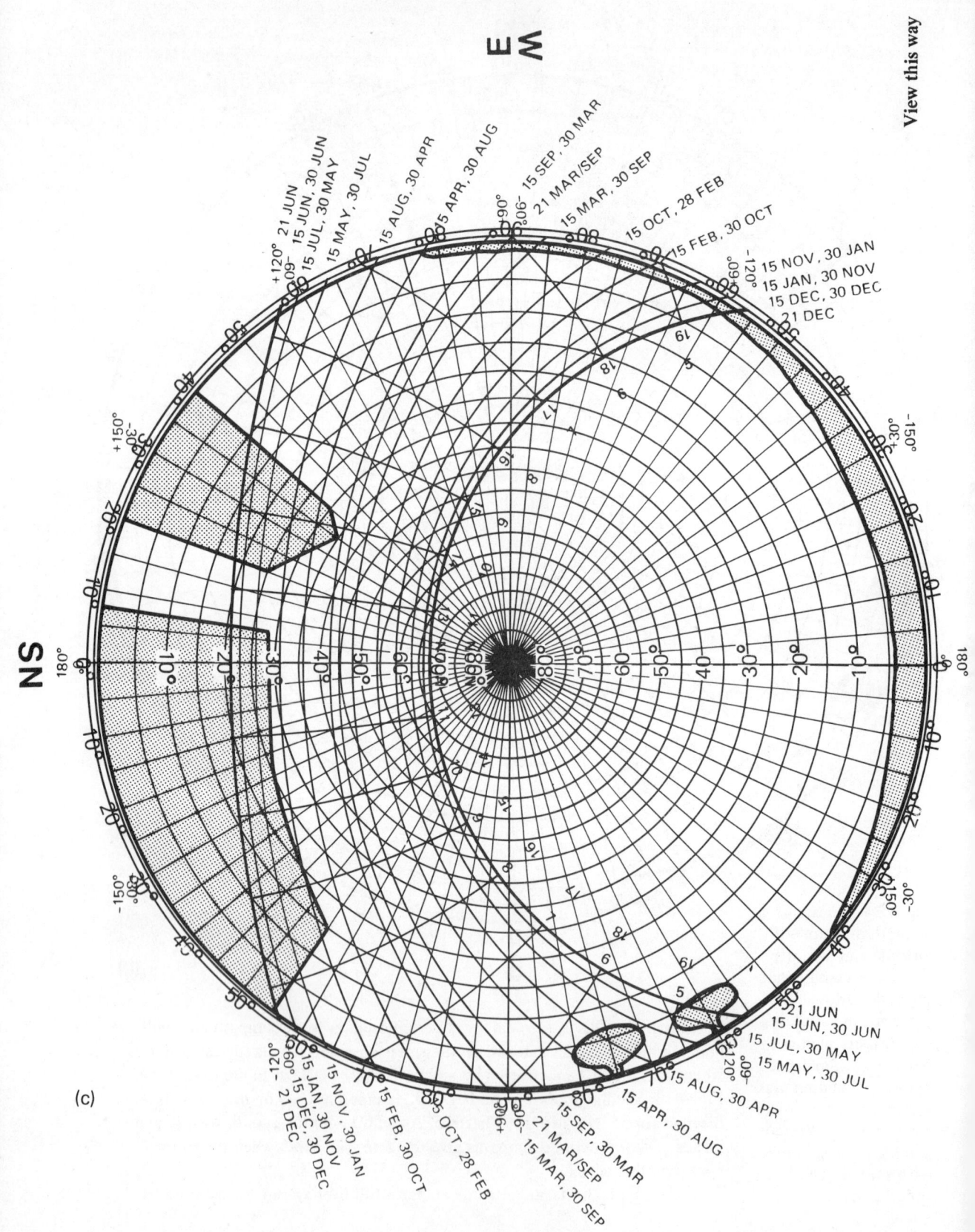

(c)

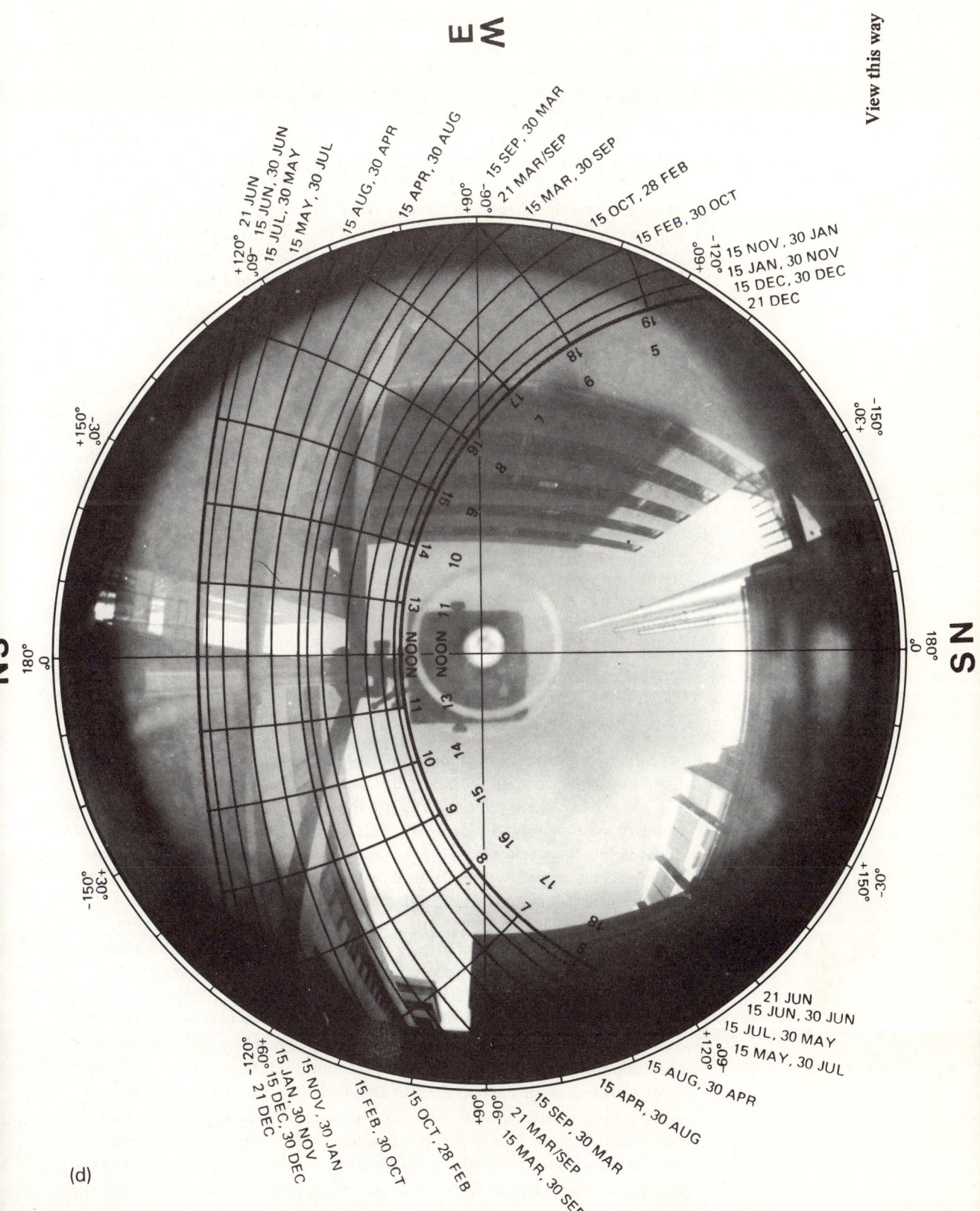

(d)

study the shading and shadow patterns on a building site. Fig. 4.34(a) shows a site plan, on which the heights of all buildings, trees and land contours have been marked. The section, along line A, shows how the altitude of an obstruction with respect to a reference point is measured. By doing this along each of the lines A to K marked on the plan, a stereographic shading mask of the type shown in Fig. 4.34(b) is produced. If this is drawn on transparent or translucent film, it can be laid over the appropriate sunpath chart, as in Fig. 4.34(c), where the 45°S chart is used. A similar effect can be produced photographically by photographing the image of the site as reflected in a parabolic reflector, enlarging the print to the same diameter as that of the sunpath chart, and laying the latter (drawn on transparent or translucent film) over the photograph as shown in Fig. 4.34(d). Figure 4.34(c) and (d) enable the dates and times when the sun is obstructed from central point to be predicted.

4.4.2 Solar Radiation

The prediction of the maximum clear sky irradiance values (Section 4.4.2.1) is primarily of interest for computing maximum cooling loads, or maximum internal temperatures in buildings without cooling, or maximum heating benefit which can be expected from solar radiation during the heating season. For the prediction of mean total irradiation, for any day, month, season or year, needed for prediction of energy consumption for heating or cooling, and also for estimating the useful energy which can be collected from a solar energy collection device, Section 4.4.2.2 gives methods of estimation of mean total irradiation which include allowances for cloudiness.

4.4.2.1 Maximum values under clear sky conditions

Under clear sky conditions there are three sources of radiation:

(i) Direct irradiance from the sun I_D;
(ii) Diffuse irradiance from the clear sky I_d;
(iii) Reflected direct and diffuse irradiance from the ground I_g.

(a) *Direct normal incidence solar irradiance* I_{DN} It has been pointed out above that outside the earth's atmosphere the normal incidence direct irradiance, known as the solar constant, I_0 is about 1.4 kW m^{-2}; the precise figure used in standard calculations is 1353 W m^{-2}. This, in fact, varies by a few per cent between the two solstices and the two equinoxes due to the variation in sun–earth distance caused by the elliptical orbit of the earth around the sun. This variation will be ignored in the present text.

On its passage through the earth's atmosphere, radiation is attenuated, scattered and partially reflected back to outer space. The atmosphere absorbs and scatters the radiation in different degrees at its various wavelengths.

Fig. 4.35 shows the solar spectrum outside the earth's atmosphere – indicating an almost smooth curve, obeying the radiation laws for a 'black' body at a radiation temperature of about 5900 K. The figure also indicates the spectrum of the direct irradiance which is transmitted through the atmosphere – having an air mass of 1 (equivalent to a solar altitude of 90°) and having a typical composition of water vapour, ozone, carbon dioxide and dust, as might be found in summer in a temperate climate. It will be seen that after transmission through the atmosphere, very little ultraviolet energy reaches the earth; it is in the longer (B) waveband, of about 300 to 380 nm. The visible portion of

Fig. 4.35 Spectral irradiance curves for direct sunlight extra-terrestrially and at sea level. Shaded areas indicate absorption due to atmospheric constituents, mainly H_2O, CO_2 and O_3 (after Page [15]).

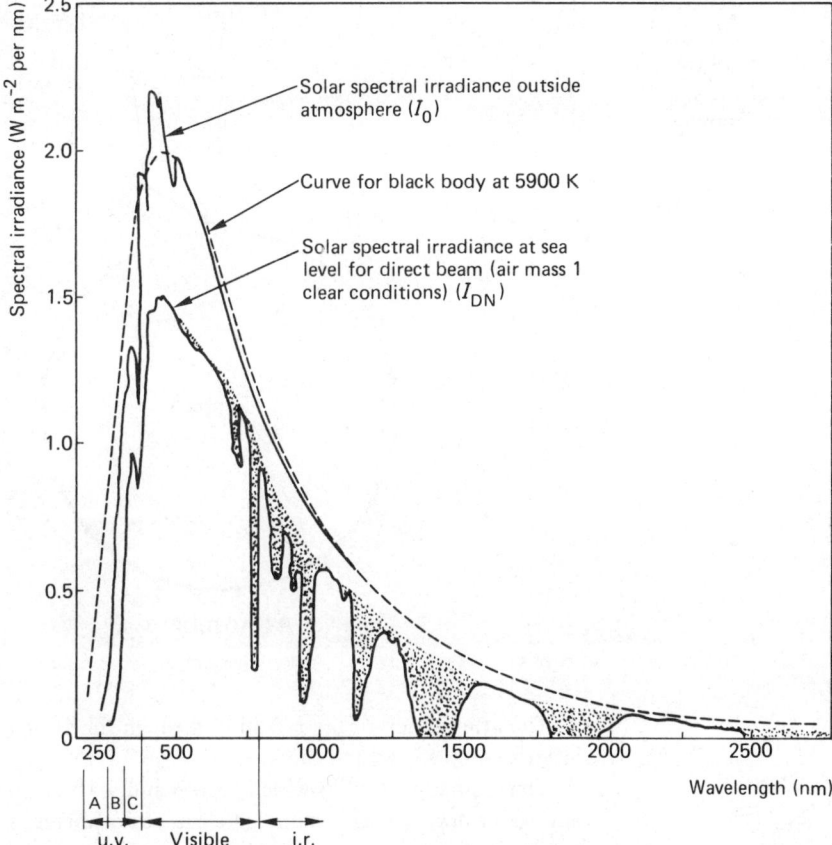

Fig. 4.36 Spectral composition of global irradiance for clear sky $I_G\downarrow$, direct irradiance $I_D\downarrow$, diffuse irradiance from clear sky $I_d\downarrow_{(i)}$ and diffuse irradiance from cloudy sky $I_d\downarrow_{(ii)}$ as calculated for a horizontal plane. The curves apply to a solar elevation of about $30°$ above the horizon (after Pleijel [15].

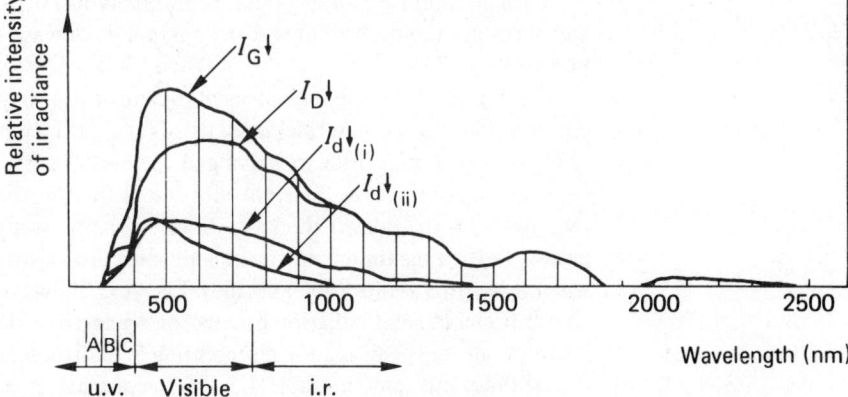

the spectrum, from 380 to 780 nm, has a peak at between 500 and 600 nm that is in the yellow–green region. The spectrum continues into the short-wave infra-red region, finally being extinguished at about 2500 nm. It will be seen that about half the energy lies in the visible and half in the short-wave infra-red regions. Fig. 4.36 indicates the relative spectral intensity of direct irradiance at air mass 2 (= solar altitude, β, of $30°$), and diffuse irradiance from a clear sky, and from a cloudy sky. In this figure the absorption bands have been omitted to give a clearer comparison, and the spectrum of global irradiance is also shown.

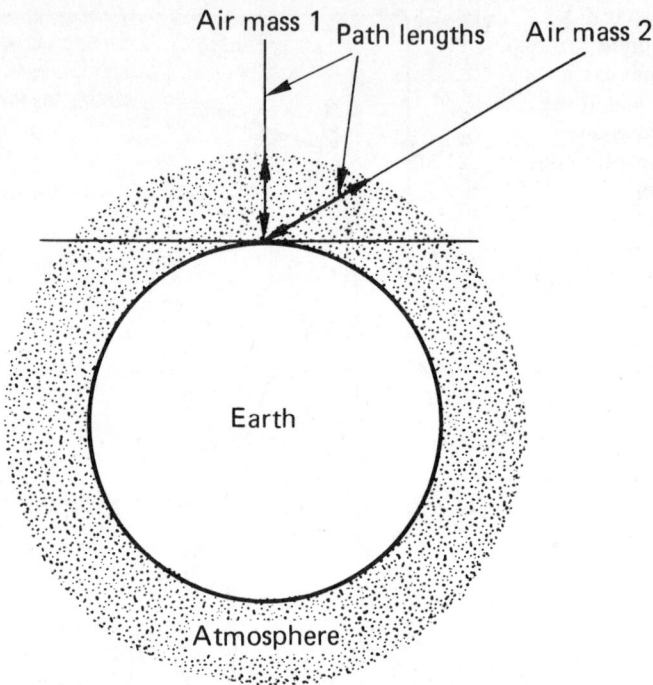

The attenuation of the radiation through the atmosphere depends on the latter's composition and thickness.

The main constituents which absorb and scatter radiation are water vapour and water droplets, and ozone, in clean atmospheres; and in addition, the presence of aerosols (dust, grit, natural aerosols over vegetated areas) also causes scatter of radiation. 'Turbidity' describes this property of the atmosphere.

It is a common assumption that of the radiation scattered by gases, droplets and aerosols, about one half is scattered in a downward direction and one half upwards.

The degree of atmospheric absorption and scatter depends not only on composition, but also on thickness, that is the path length through which the radiation has to pass prior to arriving at the earth's surface. This path length depends on two factors. First, the altitude of the sun above the horizon – clearly the lower it is the thicker the layer of atmosphere through which the solar beam passes – with a maximum at sunrise and sunset (0° altitude) and a minimum when it is at the zenith (90° altitude). Fig. 4.37 shows this effect. It is conventional in solar radiation calculation to describe this altitude effect in terms of 'air mass'; air mass 1 representing 90° altitude, and air masses 2 to 5 the altitudes indicated in Table 4.5. The second effect is that of altitude above sea level; clearly the higher this is, the less the effective atmospheric thickness.

Table 4.5   *Solar altitudes represented by air masses 1 to 6*

	Air mass, m						
	1	1.5	2	3	4	5	6
Solar altitude β (degrees)	90	42	30	20	14.5	11.5	9.6

We shall now proceed to deal, in turn, with each effect:

(i) *Air mass*   If the solar constant is assumed to be 1353 W m^{-2}, and if it is assumed that there is a constant ozone content, equivalent to a 3 mm thickness of condensed matter, then Rodgers and Souster [14] have shown that the normal incidence direct irradiance I_N^* varies with water content and air mass as shown in Table 4.6; the same data is presented graphically in Fig. 4.38. These values (without further correction) are higher than those used for I_{DN} in Overlay 7, Appendix 4A, of the present book, which are those of the Building Research Establishment, in turn based on the standard radiation curves published by Moon in 1940 [15]. The overlay values were computed on the Moon values, which for many types of atmosphere are too high; but also included by the Building Research Establishment was an allowance for a small part of the diffuse sky irradiance, that intense part immediately around the sun (the 'circumsolar irradiance').

By including this part of the diffuse sky irradiance with the direct component (and suitably diminishing the value of the total diffuse sky irradiance) the combined total corresponds with sufficient accuracy to measured values in temperate climates. Such values include, of course, the effects of atmospheric turbidity, which are excluded from the values in Table 4.6 and Fig. 4.38; hence these are higher than the overlay values. If, however, turbidity corrections are applied to the above table and figure values, in the way described below, the two will be found to correspond reasonably well if a turbidity coefficient τ_a of 0.15 and water vapour of 20 mm is assumed.

Use of Overlay 7 for normal incidence irradiance I_{DN} and all the derived ones (8 to 11 and 13) for vertical, horizontal and sloping surfaces, will be reasonably accurate for sky conditions corresponding to the two assumptions given above; a precipitable water content of 20 mm and a turbidity coefficient of about 0.15. Where other water vapour and turbidity conditions apply, appropriate values from Table 4.6 or Fig. 4.38 can be found; then corrected by the appropriate turbidity coefficient according to (iii) below. Whilst under such conditions the

Fig. 4.38 Graph showing the variation of solar irradiance normal to the solar beam I_N^* with air mass and precipitable water content of the atmosphere (after Rodgers and Souster [14]).

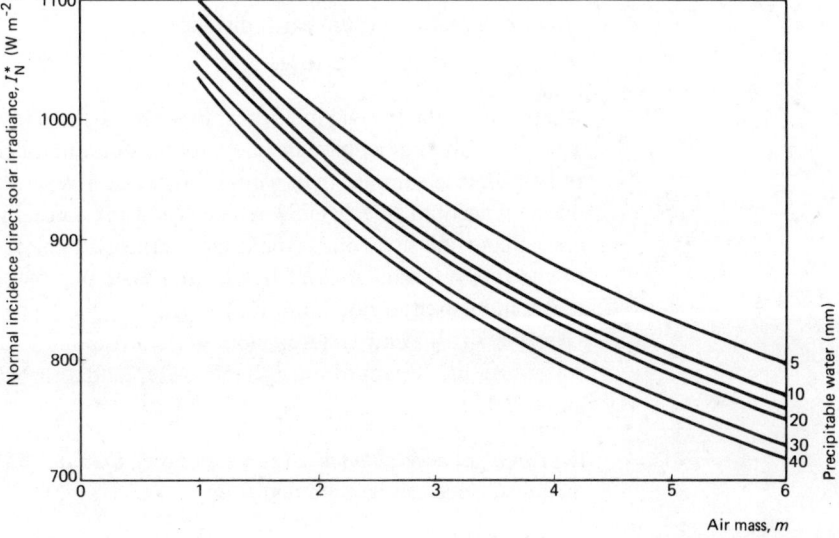

Table 4.6 *Values of I_N^* (W m^{-2}), the irradiance of the solar beam at normal incidence at mean solar distance below an aerosol-free atmosphere, as a function of air mass and precipitable water content of the atmosphere (after Rodgers and Souster [14]).*

Precipitable water, mm	Air mass, m						
	1	1.5	2	3	4	5	6
	Solar altitude, β						
	$90°$	$42°$	$30°$	$20°$	$14.5°$	$11.5°$	$9.6°$
5	1100	1055	1010	940	885	835	800
10	1090	1035	990	915	860	810	775
15	1080	1020	975	900	845	800	760
20	1065	1010	960	890	835	790	750
30	1050	990	945	870	820	770	730
40	1035	980	930	860	805	755	720

overlay values will no longer be accurate in *absolute* terms, for *comparative* studies of the effect of time, orientation or season, they will nevertheless yield useful data.

(ii) *Altitude above sea level*   The values of irradiance in Overlays 7 to 11 of Appendix 4A and in Table 4.6 and Fig. 4.38 will be approximately correct for altitudes of 0 to 300 m above sea level. Above these the air mass, m, corresponding to a specified solar altitude β, should be corrected by a factor which makes allowance for reduced atmospheric thickness, and, hence, increased irradiance. This correction can be made using Fig. 4.39. It gives a factor, greater than unity, by which the direct solar irradiance values given by the Overlays 7 to 11 in Appendix 4A, Table 4.6 and Fig. 4.38 should be multiplied.

(iii) *Turbidity*   The values of I_N^* in Table 4.6 and Fig. 4.38 are for an aerosol-free atmosphere; this is never actually the case, and we have already seen that values for an aerosol-free atmosphere are too high, and require correction. Unsworth [16] suggests a correction which is a function of the turbidity coefficient, τ_a. The correction to the aerosol-free values of I_N^* (ignoring the effect of variation in sun–earth distance) is

$$I_{DN} = I_N^* \exp\left(-\tau_a m\right) \text{W m}^{-2}, \tag{4.6}$$

where I_{DN} is the normal incidence direct irradiance, taking turbidity effects into account. Values of τ_a have been computed for a number of locations; they tend to be higher in summer than winter; higher over vegetated rural sites than arid ones, on account of vegetable aerosols; and substantially higher over large urban areas than rural sites, due to pollutant aerosols. Typical values range from 0.12 to about 0.4. If data are available from a particular meteorological station then they can be used; if not, an informed estimate has to be made. The values in the Overlays 7 to 11 and 13 (Appendix 4A) correspond to average conditions of water vapour, 20 mm of precipitable water, and a turbidity coefficient τ_a of about 0.15.

(b) *Direct solar irradiance on surfaces other than normal, I_{DS}*   Irradiance, I_{DS}, on any surface can be obtained from

$$I_{DS} = I_{DN} \cos i, \tag{4.7}$$

Fig. 4.39 Variation in solar irradiance with height above sea level (after *IHVE Guide*).

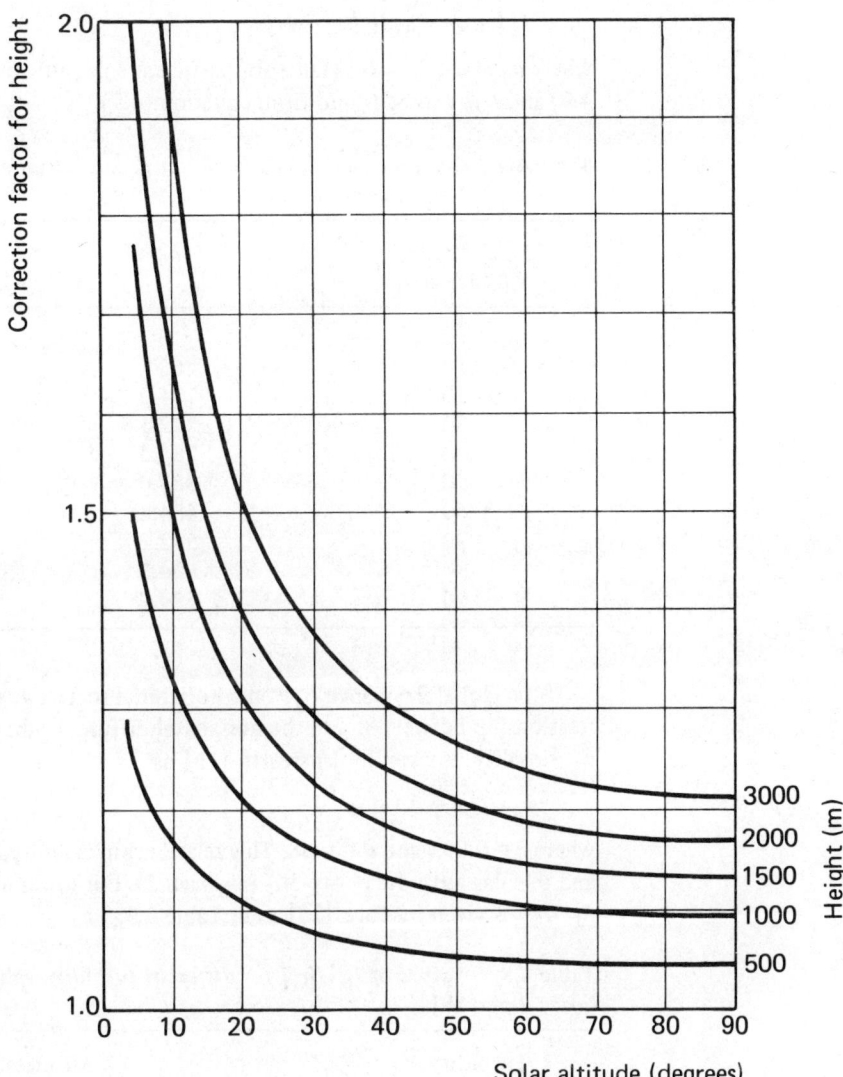

where I_{DN} = the normal incidence intensity, and i = the angle of incidence; on a horizontal surface this intensity (written $I_D\downarrow$) is equivalent to

$$I_{DS} = I_D\downarrow = I_{DN} \sin \beta$$

where β = solar altitude. Intensities on vertical (I_{DV}), horizontal ($I_D\downarrow$), and various sloping surfaces (I_{DS}), are given by the use of Overlays 7 to 11 (Appendix 4A) without further computation.

(c) *Clear sky diffuse irradiance and reflected ground irradiance*   We have already shown in (a) the typical spectral composition of clear sky irradiance. The intensity is a function of both solar altitude and the composition of the atmosphere. In general, the lower the direct component the higher, through the same cause, the diffuse component.

The relationship between $I_d\downarrow$ (diffuse irradiance on a horizontal surface) and $I_D\downarrow$ (direct irradiance on a horizontal surface) is given by Parmelee [17] as

$$I_d\downarrow = a_0 - a_1 I_D\downarrow, \tag{4.8}$$

where a_0 and a_1 are constants for particular solar altitudes (tabulated in Table 4.7) and $I_D\downarrow$ can be found from equation (4.7).

Table 4.7   *Values of a_0 and a_1 at various solar altitudes (after Rodgers and Souster [14] and Parmelee [17])*

Solar altitude, β (degrees)	a_0	a_1
0	0	0.290
10	63.1	0.295
20	134.9	0.314
30	222.1	0.360
40	284.3	0.362
50	383.0	0.424
60	484.6	0.492
70	552.1	0.520
80	604.3	0.545
90	624.7	0.560

If the global irradiance $I_G\downarrow$ on a horizontal surface is known, the general relationship between it and the horizontal diffuse irradiance $I_d\downarrow$, as a function of turbidity, is given by Unsworth [16] as

$$I_d\downarrow/I_G\downarrow = c + d\,(\tau_a), \tag{4.9}$$

where $c = 0.097$ and $d = 0.68$. This relationship is limited to temperate climates, and to solar altitudes above $30°$ (air mass 2). For lower altitudes the ratio of $I_d\downarrow/I_G\downarrow$ is given by Page [18] as in Table 4.8.

Table 4.8   *Values of $I_d\downarrow/I_G\downarrow$ for different turbidity values and solar altitudes (after Page [18])*

Turbidity, τ_a	Air mass, m					
	1.5	2	3	4	5	6
	Solar altitude, β					
	42	30	20	14.5	11.5	9.6
0.05	0.092	0.13	0.17	0.22	0.25	0.28
0.10	0.12	0.17	0.24	0.29	0.34	0.39
0.20	0.19	0.24	0.33	0.42	0.50	0.57
0.30	0.24	0.32	0.45	0.56	0.65	0.72
0.40	0.30	0.41	0.55	0.67	0.77	0.83

If $I_d\downarrow$ is assumed to be of uniform intensity over the sky hemisphere then vertical surface values of diffuse sky irradiance I_{dV} will be one half of $I_d\downarrow$.

Overlay 12 (Appendix 4A) from the work of the Building Research Establishment gives similar values for clear sky diffuse irradiance. Here, too, the assumption is that the distribution is uniform, and that therefore the values on a horizontal surface, $I_d\downarrow$, are twice those on a vertical as given by the overlay.

The values correspond closely to those published in the *IHVE Guide*.

Overlay 12 also gives values for clear sky diffuse reflected irradiance from the ground under clear sky conditions on vertical surfaces, I_{gV}. The assumption is a ground reflectance, to both direct and diffuse irradiance, of 20 per cent. The use of these values without correction for other altitudes, water vapour contents and turbidities will not result in serious error.

(d) *Clear sky diffuse and reflected ground irradiance on surfaces other than vertical $I_{(d+g)s}$*   To obtain the combined diffuse and reflected irradiance $I_{(d+g)s}$ on surfaces other than vertical the following equation is used (using the vertical surface values obtained from Overlay 12, Appendix 4A or using equation (4.8) for $I_{d\downarrow}$):

$$I_{(d+g)s} = I_{dV} \times (1 + \cos s) + I_{gV} \times (1 - \cos s), \tag{4.10}$$

where I_{dV} = diffuse sky irradiance on vertical surface, I_{gV} = diffuse ground irradiance (reflected) on vertical surface, s = inclination of sloping surface to horizontal.

(e) *Global clear sky irradiance on any surface I_{Gs}*   From the previous sections, the global irradiance I_{Gs} on any surface can be computed by adding the direct and the diffuse (including reflected) components:

$$I_{Gs} = I_{Ds} + I_{(d+g)s}.$$

Overlay 13 (Appendix 4A) gives values of $I_G\downarrow$ on a horizontal surface (the special case when $s = 0°$).

The 1-h irradiation follows and, by cumulative summation, the daily total values ΣH_{Gs} are found. ΣH_{Gs} divided by the total insolation per day (in hours) gives the *mean* global hourly irradiation value $\bar{H}_{Gs}$ with which Section 4.4.2.2 is concerned.

4.4.2.2 Monthly mean daily values of clear sky irradiation

The previous section dealt with the prediction of peak irradiance on days of clear sky. Such data will be mainly used in calculating peak indoor temperatures (*see* Chapter 6) and for sizing of air-conditioning plant. For estimation of energy requirements, either for cooling, or the reduction of heating energy which can be made on account of available solar energy, or for the estimation of the performance of solar energy collection devices, what is required is an accurate prediction of average energy availability. If sophisticated computer simulations of climate are available, of the type mentioned above, then for any time of the year and length of period – day, week, month – a complete simulation can be set up, making allowances for typical cloudiness, asymmetries about solar noon (which will have important effects on building shape and orientation) and full geometrical data on shading.

Without such programs it is customary to work on estimation of monthly means based on sunshine hours and Latitude.

(a) Mean global irradiation on a horizontal surface   For a horizontal surface, a number of workers have derived a regression equation of the type:

$$\bar{H}\downarrow = \bar{H}_0\downarrow(a + b\bar{n}/\bar{N}_0), \tag{4.11}$$

where $\bar{H}\downarrow$ is the monthly mean daily global irradiation on a horizontal surface at a location, $\bar{H}_0\downarrow$ is the same, in the absence of any atmosphere (i.e. outside the earth's atmosphere) at the same location, $\bar{n}$ is the mean daily hours of bright sunshine for the given month, $\bar{N}_0$ is the mean daily number of hours between sunrise and sunset for the given month, or day length in hours. a and b are climatically determined constants, unique to a particular location. Page [19] gives appropriate values for a number of places in the world, some of which are shown in Table 4.9.

Table 4.9   *Values of a and b in equation* (4.11) (*after Page* [19])

Location	Latitude	Altitude above sea level (m)	a	b
Nairobi	1° 16′ S	437	0.25	0.41
Singapore	1° 18′ S	120	0.22	0.45
Trinidad	10° 38′ N	20	0.28	0.51
Pretoria	24° 45′ S	1369	0.28	0.47
Capetown	33° 54′ S	17	0.21	0.61
Versailles	48° 08′ N	49	0.24	0.52
Kew	51° 05′ N	19	0.15	0.68
Rothamstead	51° 08′ N	128	0.16	0.57
Cambridge*	52° 12′ N	12	0.15	0.72
Garston, Herts	51° 42′ N	78	0.14	0.68
Aberporth*	52° 08′ N	133	0.16	0.78
Aldegrove	54° 39′ N	81	0.18	0.67
Eskdalemuir*	55° 19′ N	242	0.14	0.78
Lerwick*	60° 08′ N	78	0.18	0.76
Valentia (Eire)	51° 56′ N	9	0.24	0.62
Kingsway (London)	51° 31′ N	23	0.12	0.70

*Average of two or more workers' measurements.

For Britain, the Kew values of 0.15 and 0.68 for a and b, respectively, are often used, although, as Table 4.9 shows, even within the small geographical limits of the British Isles, considerable variation in the values exists.

Values of $\bar{H}_0\downarrow$ can be found from Fig. 4.40, based on the work of Duffie and Beckman [20].

Values of $\bar{n}$ for any month and location are readily available from local meteorological records of mean monthly sunshine hours; values of $\bar{N}_0$ from almanacs, or from the sunpath charts in Appendix 4A, by simply adding the hours (and fractions of hours after sunrise and before sunset) as indicated by the hour lines.

Alternatively, values of $\bar{N}_0$ can be obtained from Fig. 4.41, from the work of Whillier [21], for any Latitude and date.

(b) Mean diffuse irradiation on a horizontal surface $\bar{H}_d\downarrow$ The global irradiation on a horizontal surface is composed of a direct and a diffuse component. In order to estimate mean global irradiation on vertical and other inclined surfaces, the value of $\bar{H}\downarrow$, on a horizontal surface, can be used but it must first be split into its two components; the direct irradiation, $\bar{H}_D\downarrow$ and the diffuse irradiation, $\bar{H}_d\downarrow$.

Diffuse irradiation, as a fraction of global, clearly will increase with increasing

Fig. 4.40 Values of $\bar{H}_0\downarrow$ at various Latitudes and times of year (after Duffie and Beckman [20]).

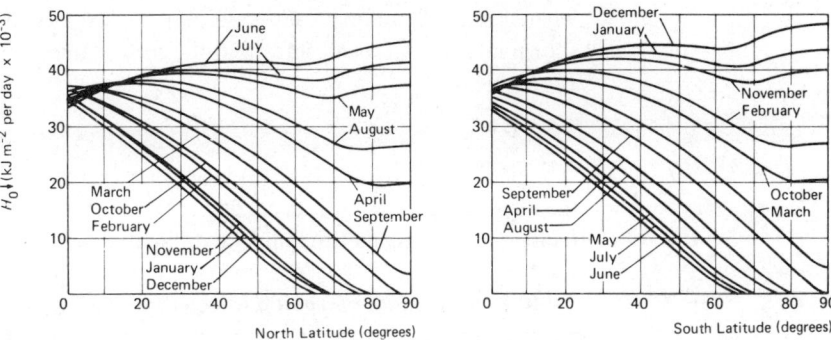

Fig. 4.41 Estimation of day length $\bar{N}_0$ (after Whillier [21]).

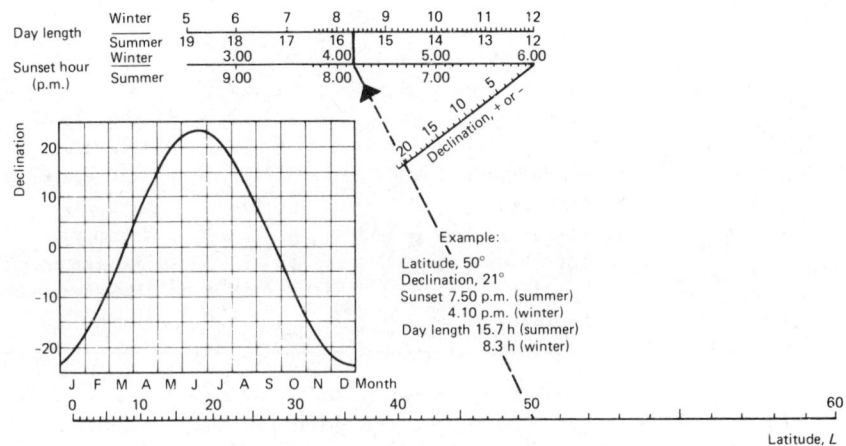

cloudiness. So, as the direct irradiation falls, the diffuse increases. Fig. 4.42 (after Liu and Jordan [22]) shows this non-linear relationship; as the ratio of global to extraterrestrial irradiation approaches unity (increasing clarity) the ratio of diffuse to global irradiation approaches zero. Page expresses this relationship in the form of a linear regression equation:

$$\bar{H}_d\downarrow/\bar{H}\downarrow = c + d\,(\bar{H}\downarrow/\bar{H}_0\downarrow), \tag{4.12}$$

Fig. 4.42 Estimation of diffuse irradiation $\bar{H}_d\downarrow$ (after Liu and Jordan [22]).

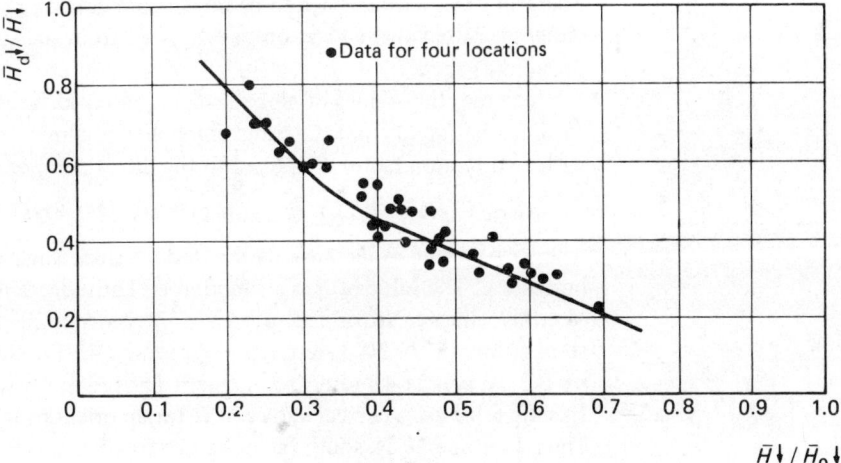

where c and d are climatically determined constants. He gives a range of values shown in Table 4.10 and finds that the mean values for ten locations in the world, are:

$$c = 1.00,$$
$$d = -1.13,$$

the highest values of both occurring in hot-humid climates, the lowest in temperate, and high-altitude hot-dry climates.

Table 4.10   *Values of c and d in equation* 4.12 *(after Page* [19])

Location	Latitude	Type of climate	c	d
Kingsway (London)	51° 31′ N	Temperate	0.990	−1.103
Kew	51° 05′ N	Temperate	0.980	−1.026
Cambridge	52° 12′ N	Temperate	0.937	−0.841
Belfast	54° 39′ N	Temperate	0.901	−0.717
Eskdalemuir	55° 19′ N	Temperate	0.809	−0.515
Lerwick	60° 08′ N	Temperate	1.078	−1.14
Blue Hill (Mass., USA)	42° 13′ N	Temperate	0.72	−0.67
Capetown	33° 54′ S	Mediterranean	1.07	−1.26
Pretoria	25° 45′ S	Hot-dry	0.98	−1.16
Leopoldville	4° 22′ S	Hot-humid	1.08	−1.21

Using equation 4.12 and Table 4.10, or Fig. 4.42, the mean monthly horizontal diffuse irradiation $\bar{H}_d\downarrow$ can be found, and, from it, the mean monthly horizontal direct irradiation $\bar{H}_D\downarrow$ by subtraction, for

$$\bar{H}_D\downarrow = \bar{H}\downarrow - \bar{H}_d\downarrow. \tag{4.13}$$

(c) Mean irradiation on a tilted (including vertical) surface   Meteorological records of global, direct, diffuse and ground reflected irradiation on tilted (and vertical) surfaces are even more scarce than those for horizontal surfaces. Yet for most building design purposes, such as the estimation of cooling loads arising from radiation incident on walls or transmitted through windows, or for the prediction of the performance of solar collectors, this is the information required. Therefore, estimations have to be made from data on horizontal irradiation – either measured at the location or estimated from sunshine records as shown in Section (*a*) above.

Mean monthly values of global irradiation on surfaces other than horizontal, $\bar{H}_{Gs}$, can be found from the three components, direct, diffuse and reflected, with a correction factor R applied to the direct component, from

$$\bar{H}_{Gs} = (\bar{H}\downarrow - \bar{H}_d\downarrow) \times R + \bar{H}_d\downarrow(1 + \cos s)/2 + r\bar{H}\downarrow(1 - \cos s)/2, \tag{4.14}$$

where r = ground reflectance factor, and s = slope angle of surface from horizontal. The value of R is a function of Latitude, date and slope of surface. Monthly values of R for Latitudes in 5° steps from 20° to 60° and slopes in 15° steps (from 15° to 90°) are given in Appendix 4B for eight orientations assuming $r = 0.2$. Appendix 4B refers to northern Latitudes; for southern Latitudes any specific table gives correct values of R for an orientation 180° to that stated. Thus, Latitude 20°N, south-facing values are identical to Latitude 20°S, north-facing [23].

4.4.2.3 Hourly values of irradiation

(a) Horizontal hourly irradiation values It is sometimes necessary, or useful, to have irradiation data on an hourly rather than daily basis. To obtain these for a horizontal surface Liu and Jordan's relationship [22], illustrated in Fig. 4.43, should be used, solid lines for global and the dotted lines for diffuse irradiation. (As before, the direct component can be obtained by subtraction.) Thus, having found $\bar{H}\downarrow$ as shown in (a) or $\bar{H}_d\downarrow$ as shown in (b), Fig. 4.43 indicates the ratio of the hourly to the monthly value ($\bar{H}_{dh}\downarrow/\bar{H}_d\downarrow$ or $\bar{H}_h\downarrow/\bar{H}\downarrow$), on a horizontal surface, as a function of day length N_0 and time of day (expressed in 'hours from solar noon').

Fig. 4.43 Estimation of hourly irradiation (after Liu and Jordan [22] and Duffie and Beckman [20]).

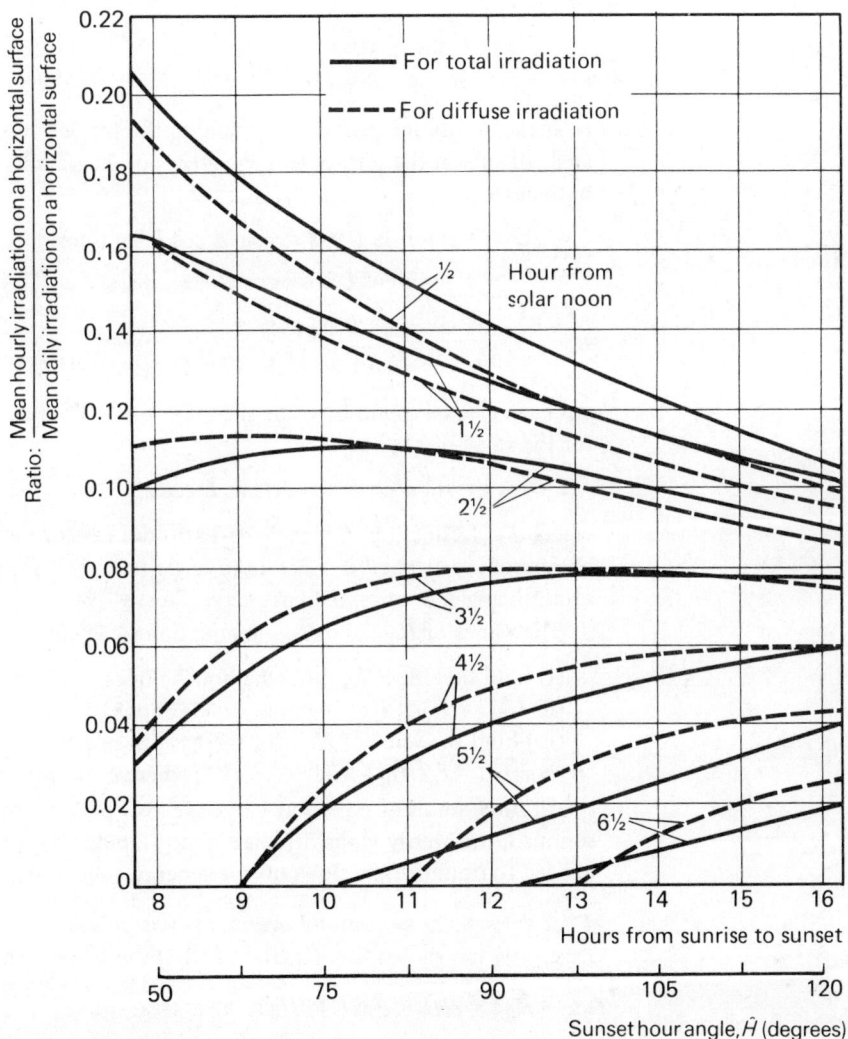

(b) Hourly irradiation values on sloping surfaces We have shown a method for obtaining the *daily* tilted (and vertical) surface irradiation intensities from horizontal *daily* values; and also a method for obtaining the *hourly* horizontal values from the *daily* horizontal values. All that remains is to show how to

obtain *hourly* tilted (and vertical) values from the *hourly* horizontal ones, by using an analogous correction factor, R_h.

If $\bar{H}_{Ghs}$ = mean hourly global irradiation on a sloping surface, $\bar{H}_{Dhs}$ = mean hourly direct irradiation on a sloping surface, $\bar{H}_{dhs}$ = mean hourly diffuse (sky) irradiation on a sloping surface, $\bar{H}_{ghs}$ = mean hourly ground-reflected irradiation on a sloping surface and $\bar{H}_{Dh}\downarrow$ = mean hourly direct irradiation on a horizontal surface, then

$$\bar{H}_{Ghs} = \bar{H}_{Dhs} + \bar{H}_{dhs} + \bar{H}_{ghs} \tag{4.15}$$

and

$$\bar{H}_{Dhs} = \bar{H}_{Dh}\downarrow \times R_h, \tag{4.16}$$

where

$$R_h = \frac{\bar{H}_{Dhs}}{\bar{H}_{Dh}\downarrow} = \frac{\cos i}{\cos z},$$

i = mean hourly incident angle of sun on the surface and z = mean hourly zenith angle of sun on the surface (*see* Fig. 4.28 for diagrammatic representation of both angles).

$$\cos i = \sin d \sin L \cos s - \sin d \cos L \sin s \cos \gamma$$
$$+ \cos d \cos L \cos s \cos H$$
$$+ \cos d \sin L \sin s \cos \gamma$$
$$+ \cos d \sin s \sin H \sin \gamma.$$

$\cos i$ can also be found by using the appropriate Overlay 1 to 5 (Appendix 4A) for the value of s (slope).

$$\cos z = \sin d \sin L + \cos d \cos L \cos H$$

where d = declination, L = angle of Latitude, s = slope angle (between surface and horizontal; vertical = $90°$), H = hour angle (a.m. = +ve, p.m. = −ve), γ = surface azimuth angle, South = $0°$, East = +ve, West = −ve.

The values of $\bar{H}_{dhs}$ and $\bar{H}_{ghs}$ in equation (4.15) are obtained as follows:

(i) Find the value $H_{dh}\downarrow$ for the hour in question from Fig. 4.43.
(ii) $\bar{H}_{dhs} = \bar{H}_{dh}\downarrow$ (for the hour) $\times (1 + \cos s)/2$.
(iii) Find the value of $\bar{H}_h\downarrow$ for the hour in question from Fig. 4.43.
(iv) $\bar{H}_{ghs} = r \times \bar{H}_h\downarrow \times (1 - \cos s)/2$, where r = ground reflectance factor.

All three terms of equation 4.15 have now been estimated to give, when summed, the hourly global irradiation on sloping surfaces such as might be needed to optimize the slope of solar energy collectors.

4.4.2.4 Partially and wholly overcast sky irradiation

Page [19] has shown that equation (4.12) can be rearranged as follows:

$$\bar{H}_d\downarrow = c\bar{H}\downarrow + d\,(\bar{H}\downarrow)^2/\bar{H}_0\downarrow. \tag{4.17}$$

This is a parabolic function whose maximum value, by differentiation, occurs when $\bar{H}\downarrow/\bar{H}_0\downarrow = -c/2d$. When $c = 0.94$ and $d = -1.03$, $\bar{H}\downarrow/\bar{H}_0\downarrow = 0.46$. Using this ratio, and values of $a = 0.14$ and $b = 0.66$ in equation (4.11) gives a value of $\bar{n}/N_0 = 0.49$. That is to say, maximum short-term irradiations are likely to occur on days when the daily sunshine hours are about half the possible total. The explanation for this lies in the fact that for the clear sky, and for the totally overcast, diffuse irradiations are both relatively low.

However, on partially clouded days during a sunny spell not only is there a substantial, direct irradiation, but also high intensities of diffuse, reflected from the clouds, more so if these are of the vertical, cumulus kind. The most intense areas are around the sun and a region opposite the sun. On such days the short-term global irradiance can exceed the solar constant.

4.4.2.5 Summary

We have seen, therefore, that prediction of peak (clear sky) irradiance values can be carried out if time, date, altitude above sea level, Latitude, water vapour content and turbidity of the atmosphere are known.

For mean daily values of irradiation, we need to find the irradiation outside the earth's atmosphere for the Latitude and month; we also need meteorological records for mean daily sunshine hours and the mean length of day between sunrise and sunset for the month.

We have seen how to estimate irradiation on surfaces other than horizontal, and also how to obtain hourly values for any time of day on any day of the month from the daily values.

The examples which follow show some typical calculations. These are then followed by a sample of graphical presentations of the type of data which a designer might use for general investigations – showing radiation variation with Latitude, season, time and slope. The calculation and graphical techniques of this section can be used to produce any of these, or similar, plots. Clearly, how-ever, this is extremely laborious without a computer program.

4.4.2.6 Examples of radiation calculations

Example 4.1 Global clear sky irradiance, using overlays   Find the global, clear sky irradiance I_{GV} on a south-facing vertical surface at Latitude 55°N, on March 21st at 14.00. Assume sea-level altitude, a turbidity of $\tau_a = 0.15$; and a precipitable water vapour content of 20 mm.

As shown in Section 4.4.2.1 (a) (i), for the turbidity and water vapour given, the values of I_{DV} given in Overlay 7 (Appendix 4A) can be used without further correction. Placing this overlay over the sunpath diagram for 55°N Latitude, the value of direct irradiance I_{DV} is read off as 520 W m^{-2}. Using Overlay 12 for diffuse and ground reflected irradiance, $I_{(d + g)V}$ is read off as 80 W m^{-2}.

$$I_{GV} = I_{DV} + I_{(d + g)V}$$
$$= 520 + 80$$
$$= 600 \text{ W m}^{-2}.$$

Example 4.2 Global clear sky irradiance using tables   For the Latitude, date and time given in Example 4.1 above, assume an altitude above sea-level of 500 m, a precipitable water vapour content of 40 mm and a turbidity of $\tau_a = 0.325$.

Direct irradiance, I_{DV}   Under these conditions the assumptions used in the construction of the overlay no longer apply and the values from Fig. 4.38 have to be used.

Altitude correction   From Overlay 6 placed over sunpath Chart 15 (Appendix 4A) for 55°N Latitude, on March 21st at 14.00, $\beta = 30°$. From Table 4.5, m for $\beta = 30°$, = 2.0. From Fig. 4.39, at $\beta = 30°$ and altitude above sea level

= 500 m, the direct irradiance must be multiplied by a correction factor of 1.08.

Water vapour correction   Using Fig. 4.38, for air mass 2 and precipitable water vapour = 40 mm, $I_N^* = 925$ W m^{-2}. Corrected by the altitude correction, $I_N^* = 925 \times 1.08$ W m^{-2} = 999 W m^{-2}.

Turbidity correction   From equation 4.6,

$$I_{DN} = I_N^* \exp(-\tau_a \times m)$$
$$= 999 \times e^{(-0.325 \times 2.0)}$$
$$= 999 \times 2.7^{-0.65}$$
$$= 999 \times 1/2.7^{0.65}$$
$$= 525 \text{ W m}^{-2}.$$

Conversion from normal incidence   Using Overlay 1 over the sunpath Chart 15 gives $i = 45°$ (this can be verified by calculating i from equation (4.4)). From equation (4.7), $I_{DS} = I_{DN} \cos i$. For the special case where $s = 90°$ (i.e. $I_{DS} = I_{DV}$),

$$I_{DV} = I_{DN} \cos i$$
$$= 525 \times 0.707$$
$$= 371 \text{ W m}^{-2}.$$

This compares with the 520 W m^{-2} Overlay 12 values in Example 4.1, showing the effect of increased altitude above sea-level, and doubling of the precipitable water vapour content and turbidity values.

Vertical diffuse irradiance I_{dV} and vertical global irradiance I_{GV}   Equation (4.8) shows the relationship between $I_d\!\downarrow$ and $I_D\!\downarrow$. To compute $I_D\!\downarrow$ for the present case, we use equation (4.7), $I_{Ds} = I_{DN} \cos i$, which, for a horizontal surface, becomes

$$I_D\!\downarrow = I_{DN} \sin \beta$$

In this case,

$$I_D\!\downarrow = 525 \times 0.500$$
$$= 262.5 \text{ W m}^{-2}.$$

From Table 4.7 for a solar altitude, $\beta = 30°$, the constant $a_0 = 222.1$ and $a_1 = 0.360$. From equation 4.8,

$$I_d\!\downarrow = a_0 - a_1 I_D\!\downarrow$$
$$= 222.1 - 0.360 \times 262.5$$
$$= 221.1 - 94.5$$
$$= 126.6 \text{ W m}^{-2},$$
$$I_{dV} = 0.5 \times I_d\!\downarrow,$$

therefore

$$I_{dV} = 63.3 \text{ W m}^{-2} \text{ (say 63 W m}^{-2}).$$

Assuming that the intensity of ground reflected irradiance I_{gV} is as given by Overlay 12, which is 42 W m^{-2}, then

$$I_{GV} = 371 + 63 + 42$$

$$= 476 \text{ W m}^{-2}.$$

This compares with $I_{GV} = 600 \text{ W m}^{-2}$ in Example 4.1.

Example 4.3 Global irradiation on a sloping surface   A roof of $30°$ slope to the horizontal, facing south-east, at $40°N$ Latitude, is to have a solar collector panel fitted. Taking 15th October as representing the mean length of day for the month, and the mean October daily hours of bright sunshine to be 6, calculate the global daily irradiation which can be expected to fall upon the collector in October. Assume that the values of a and b in regression equation (4.11) for the location are 0.24 and 0.52, respectively. Assume a ground reflectance of 0.2. Also, calculate the 1-h irradiation between 10.00 and 11.00.

The monthly mean daily global irradiation on a horizontal surface $\bar{H}\downarrow$
Using equation (4.11),

$$\bar{H}\downarrow = \bar{H}_0\downarrow (a + b\bar{n}/\bar{N}_0).$$

From Fig. 4.40, for $40°N$ latitude on 15th October,

$$\bar{H}_0\downarrow = 23 \text{ kJ m}^{-2} \text{ per day} \times 10^{-3}$$

$$= (23/3.6) \text{ kW h m}^{-2} \text{ per day}$$

$$= 6.39 \text{ kW h m}^{-2} \text{ per day}.$$

From Fig. 4.41, or from the sunpath Chart for $41°N$ (an error of $1°$ Latitude), the day length N_0 for 15th October $= 11$ h. Therefore,

$$\bar{H}\downarrow = 6.39 \times (0.24 + 0.52 \times 6/11)$$

$$= 3.34 \text{ kW h m}^{-2} \text{ per day}.$$

The monthly mean daily diffuse irradiation on a horizontal surface $\bar{H}_d\downarrow$
The ratio

$$\bar{H}\downarrow/\bar{H}_0\downarrow = 3.34/6.39$$

$$= 0.523.$$

Reading from the curve on Fig. 4.42, the value of $\bar{H}_d\downarrow/\bar{H}\downarrow = 0.36$. Therefore,

$$\bar{H}_d\downarrow = 3.34 \times 0.36$$

$$= 1.20 \text{ kW h m}^{-2} \text{ per day}.$$

As a check, use equation (4.12),

$$\bar{H}_d\downarrow/\bar{H}\downarrow = c + d(\bar{H}\downarrow/\bar{H}_0\downarrow),$$

with the average values of $c = 1.0$ and $d = -1.13$. Hence,

$$\bar{H}_d\downarrow/3.34 = 1.0 - 1.13 \times 0.523,$$

$$\bar{H}_d\downarrow = 1.37 \text{ kW h m}^{-2} \text{ per day}.$$

It is worth noting that this is less than a 15 per cent error on the Fig. 4.42 value.

The monthly mean daily global irradiation on a sloping surface $\bar{H}_{Gs}$ First, $\bar{H}\downarrow$ requires to be split into its three components, each corrected for slope, and the three (corrected) components recombined according to equation (4.14):

$$\bar{H}_{Gs} = (\bar{H}\downarrow - \bar{H}_d\downarrow) R + \bar{H}_d\downarrow (1 + \cos s)/2 + r\bar{H}\downarrow (1 - \cos s)/2.$$

From the tables in Appendix 4B, for $40°N$ Latitude, south-east orientation and

$s = 30°$ in October, $R = 1.291$. Therefore,

$$\bar{H}_{Gs} = (3.34 - 1.20) \times 1.291 + 1.20 \times (1 + \cos 30)/2$$
$$+ 0.2 \times 3.34 \times (1 - \cos 30)/2$$
$$= 2.76 + 1.12 + 0.045$$
$$= 3.925 \text{ kW h m}^{-2} \text{ per day.}$$

The hourly meal global irradiation on a horizontal surface $\bar{H}_h\downarrow$ To find the 1-h irradiation from 10.00 to 11.00, use Fig. 4.43 with the 10.30 value. The day length is 11 h; the time from solar noon $\doteq$ 1.5 h. From Fig. 4.43 the ratio $\bar{H}_h\downarrow/\bar{H}\downarrow$ for 1.5 h from solar noon is given by

$$\bar{H}_h\downarrow/\bar{H}\downarrow \quad = 0.135.$$
$$\bar{H}_{dh}\downarrow/\bar{H}_d\downarrow = 0.128.$$

Hence,

$$\bar{H}_h\downarrow = 3.34 \times 0.135$$
$$= 0.450 \text{ kW h m}^{-2}$$

and

$$\bar{H}_{dh}\downarrow = 1.20 \times 0.128$$
$$= 0.154 \text{ kW h m}^{-2}.$$

Since $\bar{H}_{Dh}\downarrow = \bar{H}_h\downarrow - \bar{H}_{dh}\downarrow$,

$$\bar{H}_{Dh}\downarrow = 0.450 - 0.154$$
$$= 0.296 \text{ kW h m}^{-2}.$$

It is worth comparing the mean value of $\bar{H}_h\downarrow$ with the 1-h irradiation under clear sky conditions. Using Overlay 7 (Appendix 4A) over the $41°N$ sunpath chart, 1 the horizontal direct irradiance $I_D\downarrow$ at 10.30 on 15th October = 500 W m^{-2}. Using Overlay 12 (and mulitplying the vertical value I_{dV} by 2), the horizontal diffuse irradiance, $I_d\downarrow$ = 80 W m^{-2}. Therefore global irradiance on a horizontal surface $I_G\downarrow$ = 580 W m^{-2} and 1-h clear sky global irradiation, $H_h\downarrow$ = 0.58 kW h m^{-2}; this is approximately 30 per cent higher than the 1-h daily *mean* irradiation $\bar{H}_h\downarrow$ over the same period.

The hourly mean global irradiation on a sloping surface $\bar{H}_{Ghs}$ To convert the hourly irradiation on the horizontal to values of hourly irradiation on a south-east facing slope of $s = 30°$, we use equation (4.15),

$$\bar{H}_{Ghs} = \bar{H}_{Dhs} + \bar{H}_{dhs} + \bar{H}_{ghs}.$$

From equation (4.16),

$$\bar{H}_{Dhs} = \bar{H}_{Dh}\downarrow R_h,$$
$$R_h \quad = \bar{H}_{Dhs}/\bar{H}_{Dh}\downarrow = \cos i/\cos z.$$

Using Overlay 3 (Appendix 4A) for a slope of $30°$ ($s = 30°$) over the sunpath chart for $41°N$ Latitude,

$$i = 24°,$$
$$z = 90° - \beta.$$

Using Overlay 6 over the same sunpath chart gives

$$\beta = 38°.$$

Hence,

$$z = (90-38)°$$
$$= 52°.$$

Therefore,

$$R_h = \cos 24°/\cos 52° = 0.914/0.616$$
$$= 1.48$$

and so

$$\bar{H}_{Dhs} = \bar{H}_{Dh}\downarrow \times 1.48$$
$$= 0.296 \times 1.48$$
$$= 0.438 \text{ kW h m}^{-2},$$

$$\bar{H}_{dhs} = \bar{H}_{dh}\downarrow \text{ (for the hour)} \times (1 + \cos s)/2$$
$$= 0.154 \times (1 + 0.866)/2$$
$$= 0.144 \text{ kW h m}^{-2},$$

$$\bar{H}_{ghs} = r \bar{H}_h\downarrow (1 - \cos s)/2$$
$$= 0.2 \times 0.450 \times (1 - 0.866)/2$$
$$= 0.090 \times 0.067$$
$$= 0.006 \text{ kW h m}^{-2}$$

and

$$\bar{H}_{Ghs} = 0.438 + 0.144 + 0.006$$
$$= 0.588 \text{ kW h m}^{-2}.$$

It is worth noting that this compares with 0.450 kW h m^{-2} on a horizontal surface, showing that the slope of 30° increases the available incident energy at this time by 31 per cent.

4.4.2.7 Examples of radiation graphical plots

Using the techniques in Section 4.4.2 and the associated sunpath charts and overlays, or, preferably, appropriate computer programs, radiation data for any given combination of variables can be produced. To make such data useful the *pattern* of variation in radiation intensity needs to be displayed. The following five examples illustrate a few of the possibilities.

Example 4.4   Fig. 4.44 shows the extraterrestrial irradiation on various surfaces at 0° to 90° Latitude and the relative daily irradiation [24] (after Hottel) (1.0 = solar constant × 24).

Example 4.5   Fig. 4.45(a) shows design peak solar irradiance intensities (direct + sky diffuse + ground-reflected) at Latitude 51.7°N (after Loudon [25]).

Example 4.6   Fig. 4.45(b) shows design daily amounts of global solar irradiation (direct + sky diffuse + ground-reflected) at Latitude 51.7°N (after Loudon [25]).

Fig. 4.44 Extra-terrestrial irradiation on various surfaces at 0° to 90° Latitude and the relative daily irradiation (after Hottel [24]) (1.0 = solar constant × 24).

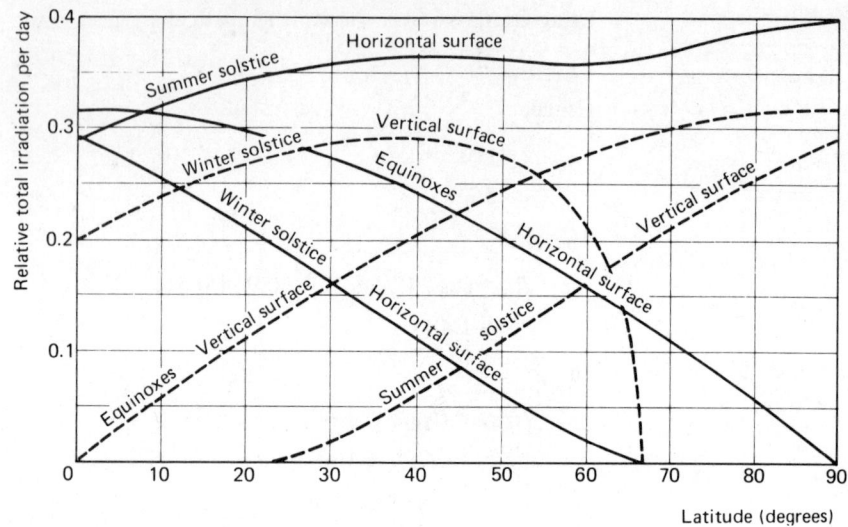

Fig. 4.45 (a) Design peak solar irradiance intensities (direct + sky diffuse + ground-reflected) at Latitude 51.7°N. (b) Design daily amounts of global solar irradiation (direct + sky diffuse + ground-reflected) at Latitude 51.7°N (after Loudon [25]).

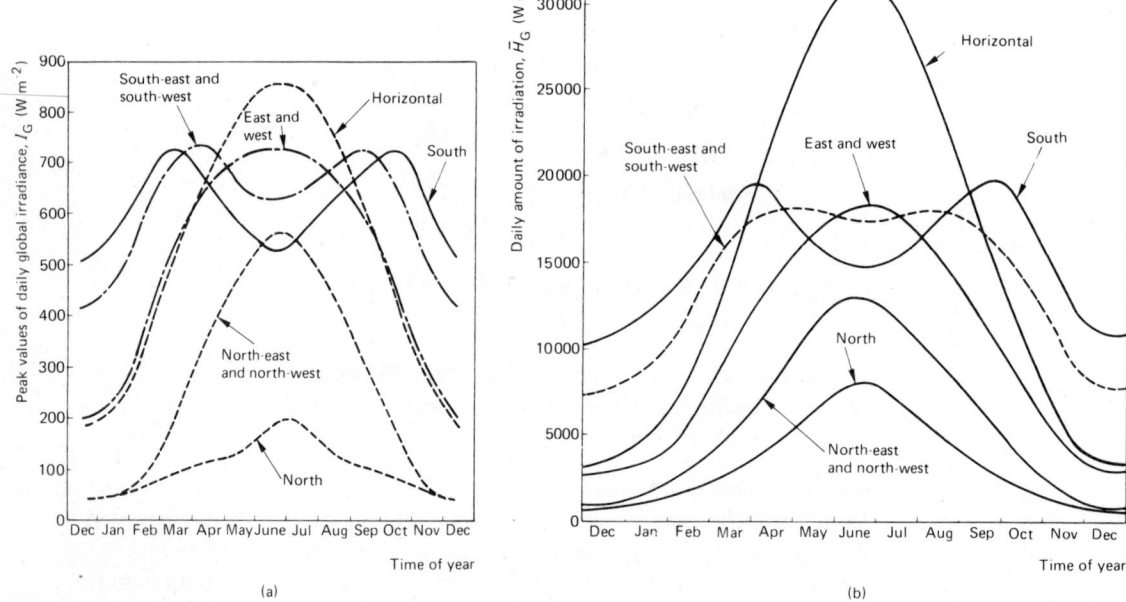

Example 4.7   Fig. 4.46 shows clear sky solar global irradiance I_G intensities for Latitude 33°S (Sydney) – calculated values (after Koenigsberger *et al.* [26]).

Example 4.8   Fig. 4.47 shows annual total irradiation polar diagrams for North and Central America (after Olgyay [27]).

4.4.3 Temperature

A knowledge of the air temperature is necessary as it is the most important of the four variables which determine thermal comfort, as we have seen in Chapter 3. Extreme values of temperature are required for the design of heating or cooling plant. We have seen earlier in the chapter that the notion of 'extreme' is

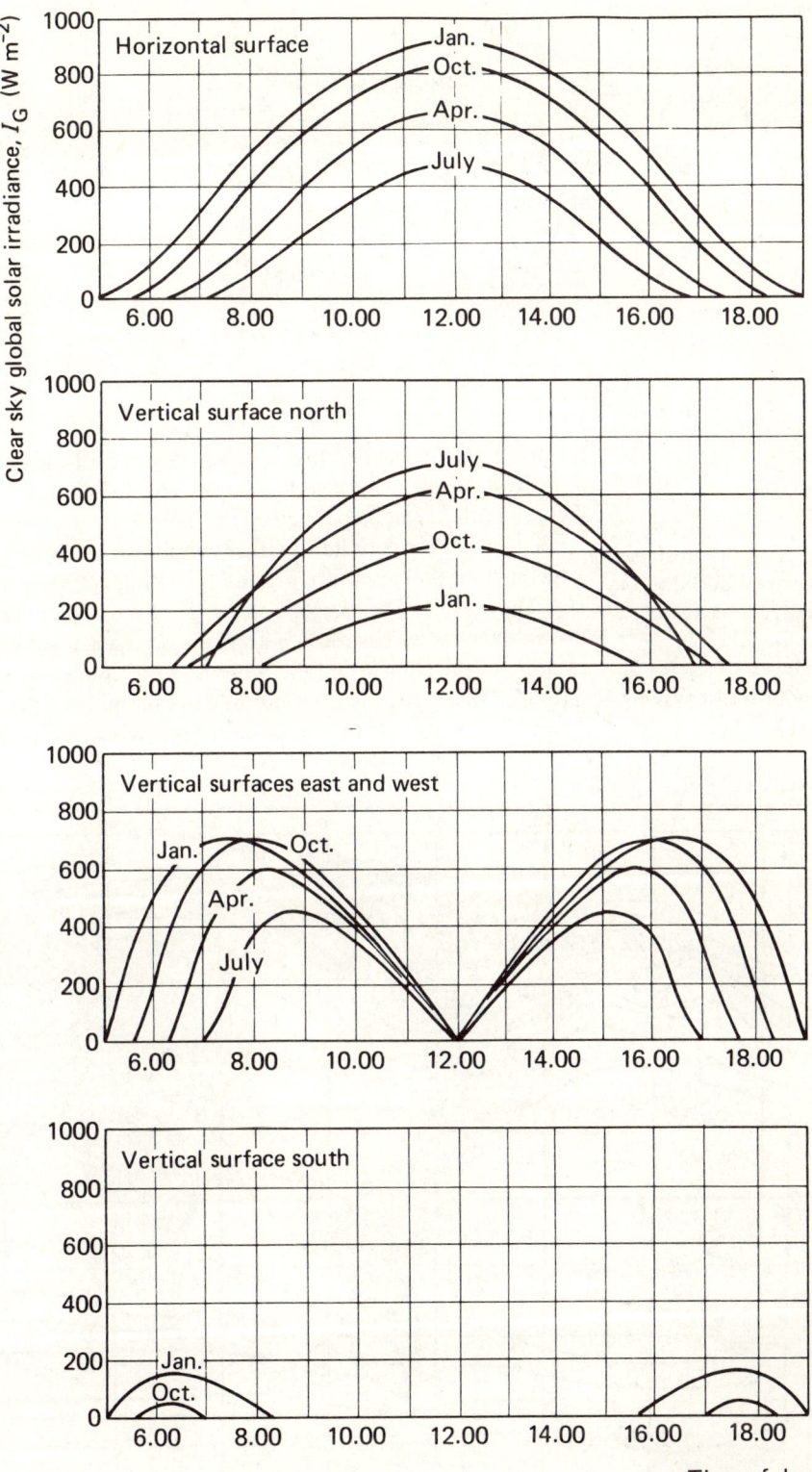

Fig. 4.46 Clear sky solar global irradiance I_G intensities for Latitude 33°S (Sydney) — Calculated values (after Koenigsberger *et al.* [26]).

Fig. 4.47 Annual total irradiation polar diagrams for North and Central America (after Olgyay [27]).

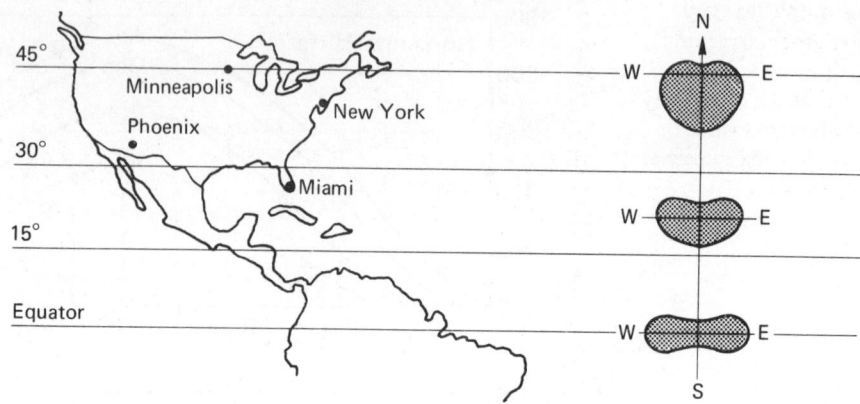

a probabilistic one, and that values have to be selected according to the use to be made of the data. Average values also have to be known in order that energy consumptions can be predicted. The diurnal swings need to be known to calculate peak indoor hot weather conditions in relation to the thermal mass of the building and intermittent heating or cooling patterns.

Fig. 4.48 (a) Mean isotherms (reduced to sea level), January. (b) Mean isotherms (reduced to sea level), July (after Kendrew [28]).

The output of heating or cooling plant is based on design temperatures which are chosen, as we have seen before, on a statistical basis, bearing in mind the nature of the climate and the response of the building. Temperature data in the form of frequency distributions of daily means, monthly maxima and minima, two or more successive days above or below a stated temperature, etc., are

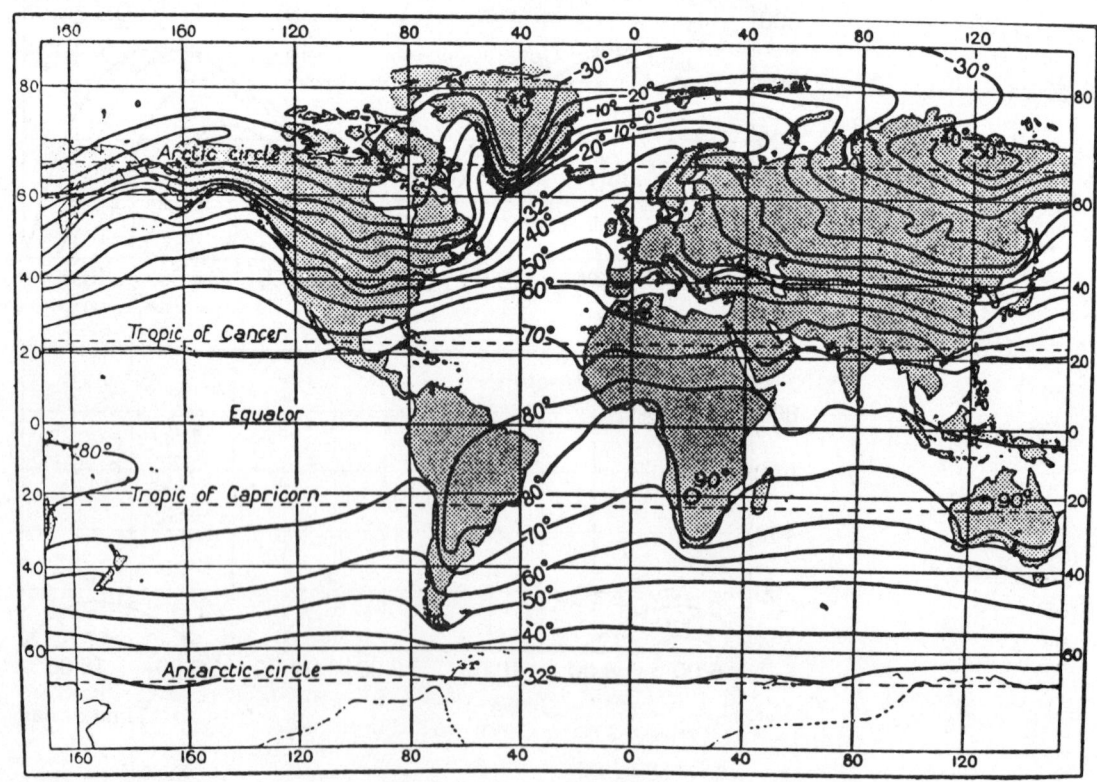

(a)

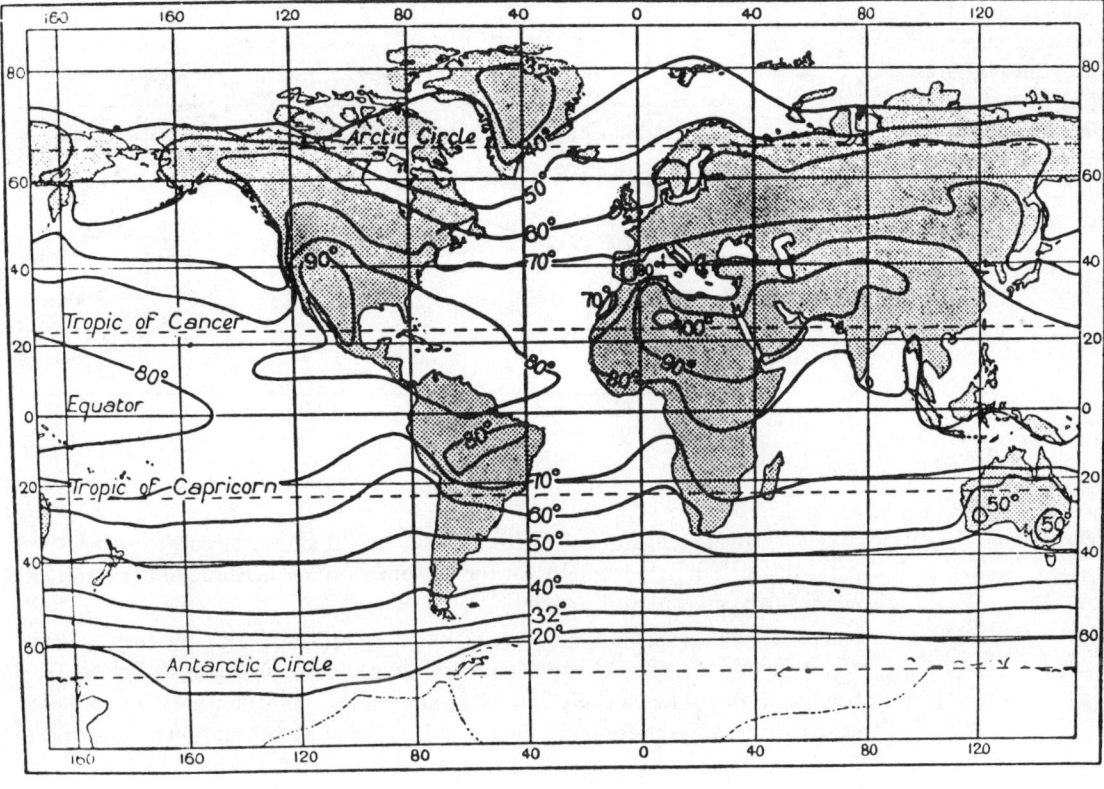

(b)

available. To obtain a representation of the spatial distribution of temperature the most commonly used method is to draw isotherms. These are lines connecting points at which the temperatures are equal – and these can be selected on any time basis – hourly, daily, monthly or other mean, or extreme values, as for instance the mean January and July isotherms of the earth shown in Fig. 4.48.

However, as Kendrew [28] points out, isotherms, just because of their graphic power, may give erroneous impressions. For instance, the Orkneys and the Aegean lie on the same January isotherm! The Orkneys have a small diurnal variation; warm south-westerlies during the day, little radiation to the sky at night – since it is mostly overcast – and little sunshine. In the Aegean on the other hand there will be both clear days, with sun, during the day, and clear nights, with radiation loss to the sky and cold air over the ground surface. The air is dry, and frequently cold continental air masses descend from the north, bringing snow and frost with them.

The variation in time, at a particular place, can of course be expressed in the form of standard curves (such as in Fig. 4.49) for monthly means, mean monthly maxima and minima and extreme values of monthly maxima and minima. More usefully, the diurnal as well as monthly pattern can be displayed on isotherms. We have already seen in Section 4.2.2 that such diagrams can show more than just air temperature – SET for instance as in Fig. 4.11; or as in Fig. 4.50(b) ET for Butterworth, Malaysia, taking into account air temperature, and humidity (illustrated earlier in Figs. 4.18 and 4.19), and wind speed (Fig. 4.50(a)).

Fig. 4.49 Standard temperature curves for monthly means, mean monthly maxima and minima and extreme values of monthly maxima and minima.

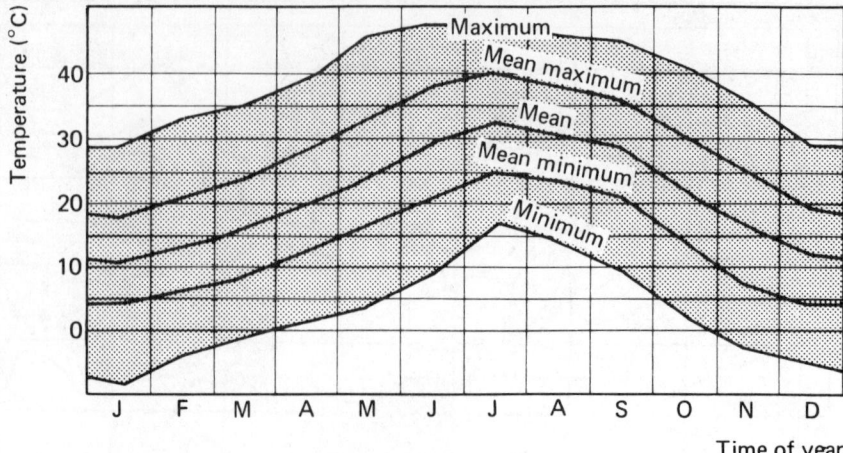

The vertical gradient of temperature with height above the earth's surface – a pattern which in part accounts for the movement of air masses and the resultant winds – is as shown in Fig. 4.51.

All weather occurs in the lowest 15 km of the atmosphere – the troposphere – where, under normal conditions, temperature decreases with height. Under conditions of cold, especially with clear night skies and little wind, this gradient can be reversed, as the air near the ground is cooled by it, and flows towards the lowest point, in valley bottoms or is retained in plains surrounded by hills or mountains. Such conditions are known as 'temperature inversions' and often lead to periods of hours or even days of static conditions, with no vertical mixing of air and layers of mist or fog lying low above the earth's surface.

The more local effects of frost hollows, which are really nothing more than local temperature inversions, will be described under Section 4.5 below.

For energy calculations the cumulative difference between the outside and inside temperatures needs to be known – neither extreme values nor averages giving a sufficiently accurate picture. The concept of 'degree days' has already been mentioned (*page* 151) as one common measure. Maps of degree days for regions or countries are published and a typical example was given in Fig. 4.10.

Although it is quite a good measure of severity of the climate, the degree-day clearly should vary with the heating type and regime (e.g. convective or radiant); 24-h or 8-h; with thermal insulation and mass of the building; its wind and sunshine exposure – which in turn will be affected by its shape and orientation – and other factors. A winter and summer 'severity index', perhaps based on a building of standard properties and shape, or a range of standard types, would be a most useful design tool.

4.4.4 Wind

Wind force and direction will affect the thermal regime of a building in two ways; it will determine the external surface resistance and hence the insulation of the shell; and it will affect the air change rate due to infiltration through openings, and hence the total heat balance.

The *IHVE Guide* and other design guides tabulate the *U*-values of constructions with variable external surface resistances according to exposure

Fig. 4.50 (a) Wind speed isopleths of Butterworth, west coast of Malaysia, in metres per second. (b) ET isopleths of Butterworth, west coast of Malaysia, in degrees Centigrade (after Markus *et al.* based on records from the Malaysian Meteorological Service).

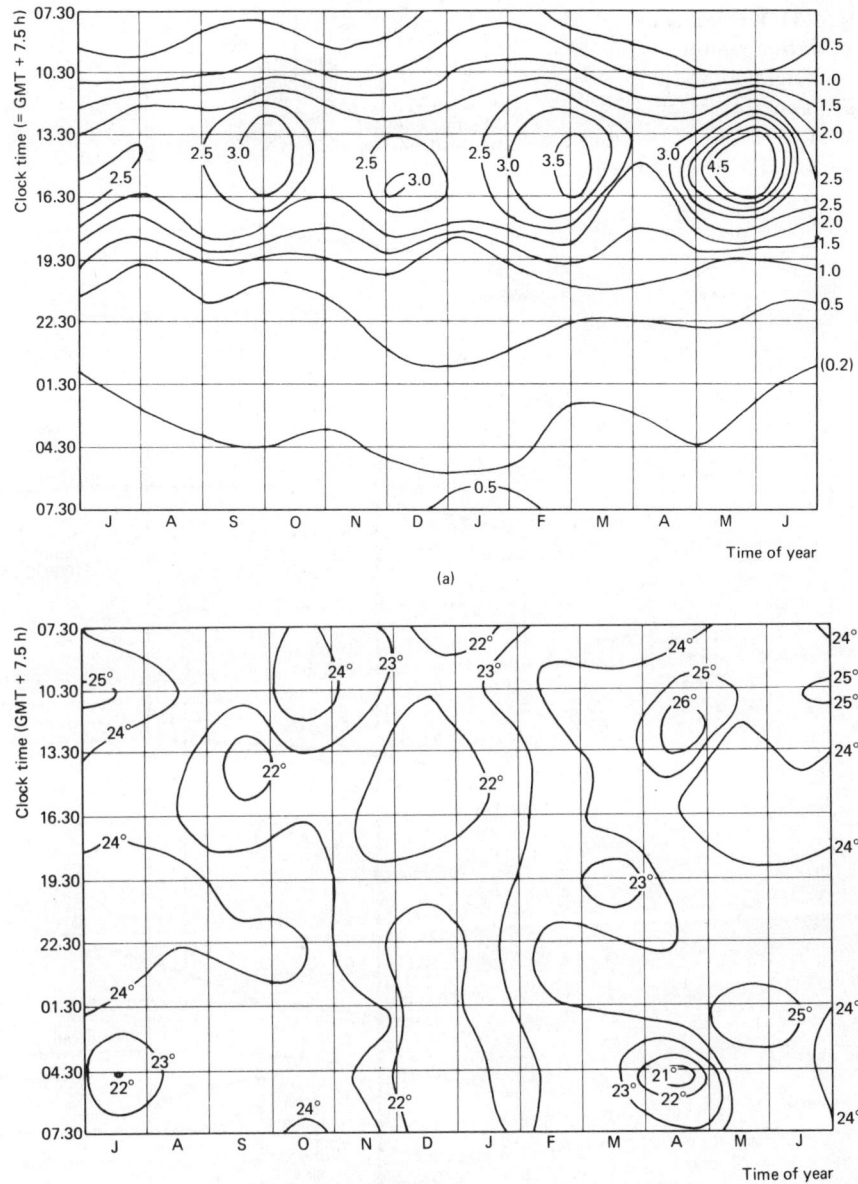

(a)

(b)

to wind, and we follow this in Chapter 5. For the prediction of energy consumption this is a reasonable procedure, provided the mean windspeed for the period in question is known from meteorological data. Mean daily wind speeds for each month would be an adequate measure of exposure for selection of the mean U-value, using for each speed an appropriate convection coefficient as indicated in Chapter 5.

For selection of an appropriate value of the maximum U-value, for design of the plant capacity for maximum load, one might for instance select that velocity which is exceeded for 1 per cent of the time (in hours) at the location in question. Whilst low wind speeds are likely to occur more or less randomly, from any direction, the higher speeds are likely to come from a preferred direction –

Fig. 4.51 Vertical gradient of temperature with height above the earth's surface (after Flohn [29]).

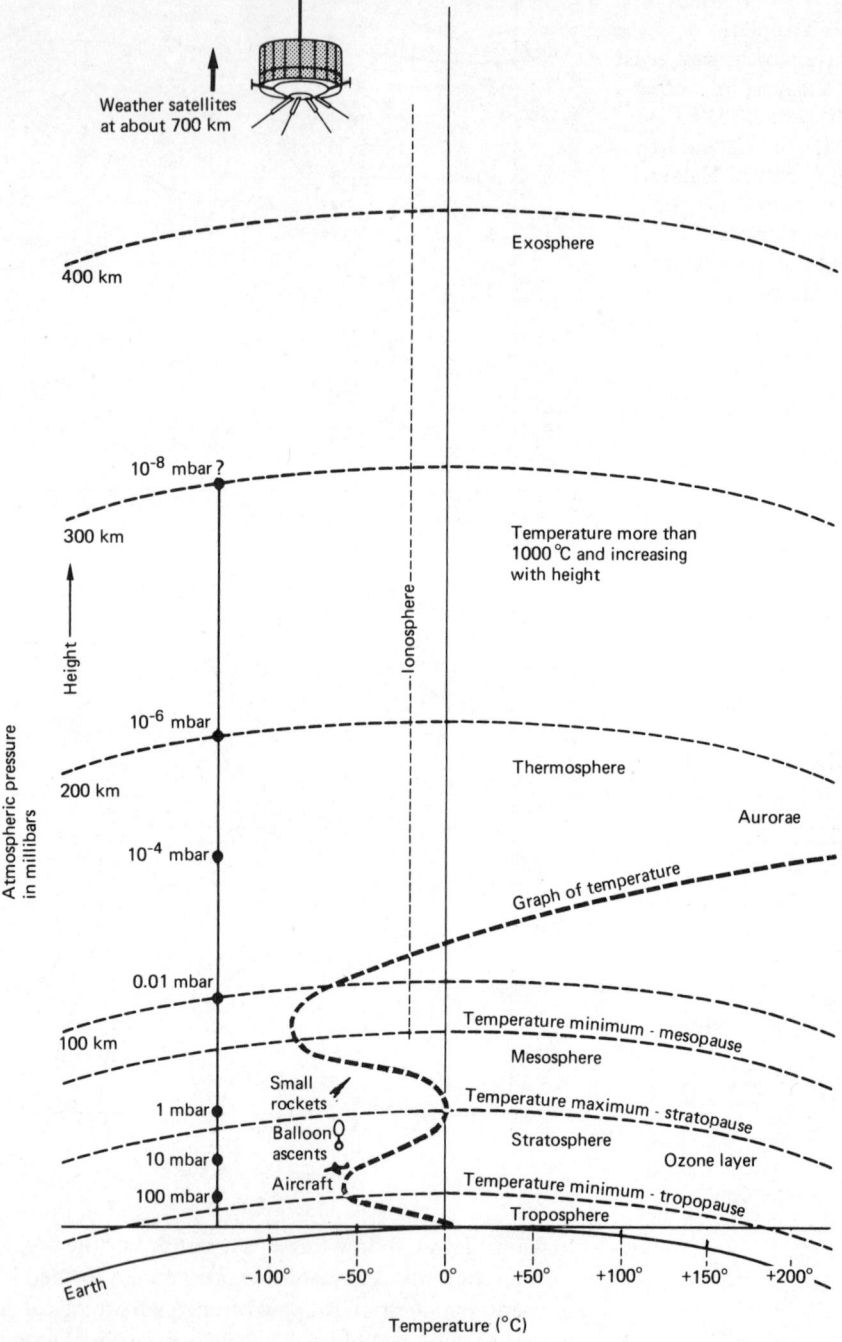

and this is a further refinement that could be introduced by selecting different velocities, and hence surface coefficients, for different orientations. Moreover, prevailing direction in the coldest, or hottest, months of the year may not be the same as the annual prevailing direction. For instance, over much of Britain the prevailing annual direction is west to south-west, but the coldest spells occur during east to north-east prevailing wind periods.

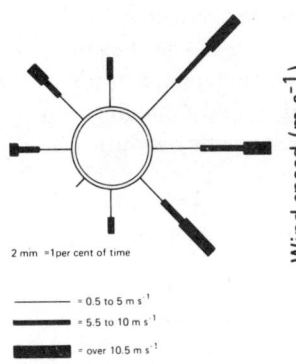

Fig. 4.52 A wind rose.

Fig. 4.53 Hourly wind-speed and direction frequencies at London Airport, Heathrow, for period 1950-59. The data from which this diagram was drawn are divided into 30° direction classes 350-010°, 020-040°, and so on, at 5° intervals, and into speed classes on the Beaufort scale (right-hand axis), although the speeds are also plotted on a uniform scale of metres per second (left-hand axis). The contours are percentage frequencies of occurrences in the grid rectangles. The zero frequency contour shows the highest wind speeds reported in the period from each direction (after Lacy [30]).

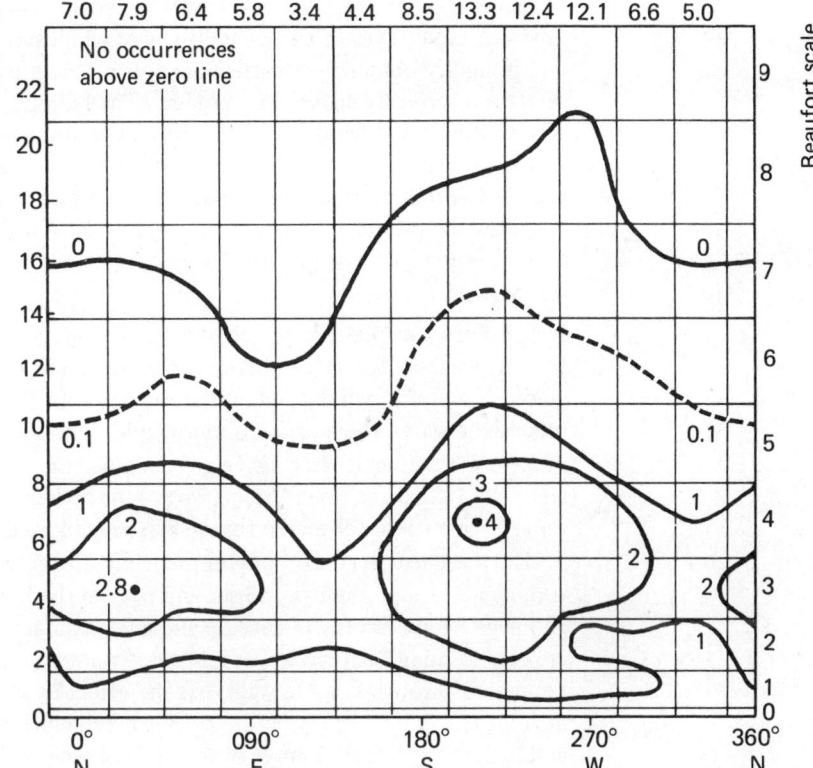

Wind roses, giving direction and percentage of time when certain speeds are exceeded for each compass point, of the type shown in Fig. 4.52 are a useful way of presenting design data for such purposes. They should, preferably, be on a monthly basis as shown.

A more refined presentation of wind data is shown in Fig. 4.53, where the mean annual hourly values of speed and direction are shown, for London Airport. Similar data can be presented on a monthly basis.

For wind speed data for ventilation and infiltration calculations, exactly the same conditions apply. That is, it is necessary to choose sensible mean values, for energy prediction, and peak values for plant design. In Britain, 9 m s^{-1} is currently adopted in the *IHVE Guide*; for maximum speeds, again, the values exceeded 1 per cent of the time might be selected, based on Lacy's suggestion on measurements averaged over 5-min periods of measurement [30].

4.4.5 Humidity

Changes in atmospheric humidity affect thermal comfort – in the ways described in Chapter 3. As far as the thermal response of the building is concerned, the chief effect will be in alteration of the moisture content, and hence the conductivity, of porous materials.

Almost all meteorological records will give hourly, daily and monthly mean values of dry bulb and wet bulb temperatures, from which relative humidity or other humidity parameters can easily be computed.

4.5 Microclimate

Finally, in design, the conditions that matter both for the transfer of energy

across or through the building fabric, and for determining the thermal sensation
of people, are the specific, local ones – generally classed under the heading of
'microclimate'. These are the conditions of wind, sun, radiation, temperature
and humidity obtaining at particular spots on the ground around a building, and
on its roof or wall and window surfaces. The building itself, causing a bluff
obstruction to the wind flow, and casting shadows on the ground and on other
buildings, will change this microclimate by its presence. One of the designer's
tasks is to predict, from a knowledge of the general and the microclimate of a
site, how the placing of a particular building on it will alter that microclimate.

4.5.1 Wind

Wind velocity increases with height above the ground, as frictional effects
become weaker. The rate of increase with height is known as the velocity
gradient, and this will depend on the roughness of the ground. Thus, over flat
ground, or water, the increase is more rapid than over forests, or cities with a
variety of building heights. Three typical gradients are shown in Fig. 4.54. It is
seen that, height for height, velocities will be higher on buildings standing in
smooth, open country than on those surrounded by trees or other buildings.

   The presence of a bluff body in the wind stream will cause 'rolls' and
turbulence around the base, edges, and roof of the building. Areas of positive
and negative pressures will develop and a few characteristic pressure distributions
are illustrated in Chapter 8. The release of wind below buildings which are raised
on legs, or through holes in walls, has the effect of smoothing out the flow both
in front and behind the structure; a similar principle is often employed in fences
and hedges on the lower edges of orchards or vineyards on a hill slope. Here, on
cold clear nights, the cool air will sink to the bottom of the slope, where a solid
obstruction would hold it and form a 'cold lake' and plants in it would suffer
frost damage. By piercing the obstruction and letting cold air flow through it,
this is avoided.

   Windbreaks in the form of walls, screens and tree belts can be useful, but will
increase turbulence where the airstream that has been forced upwards hits the
ground again and once again reaches its original velocity; the distance where this

Fig. 4.54 Three typical
wind velocity gradients.

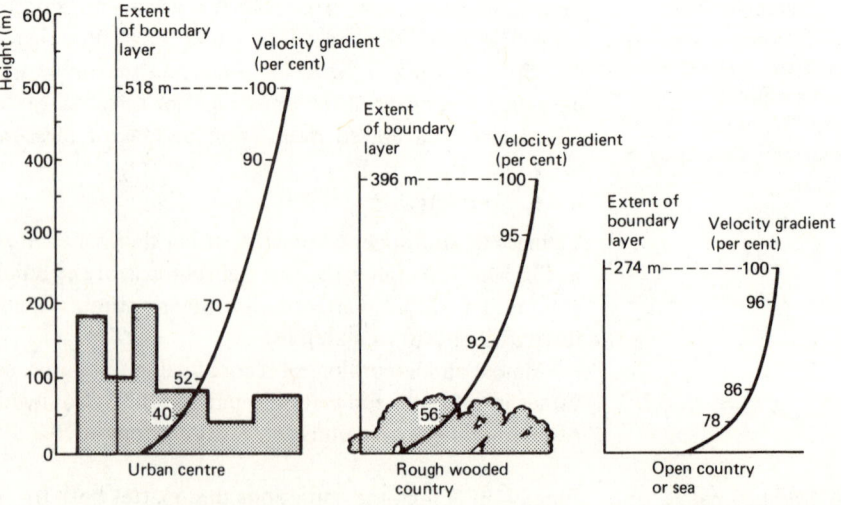

Fig. 4.55 The effect of a shelterbelt as a function of its penetrability (after Geiger and Nägeli [3]).

Fig. 4.56 Some effects of air flow through openings. Note that a velocity increase is indicated by *narrowing* of the arrow stem (after Koenigsberger *et al* [26]).

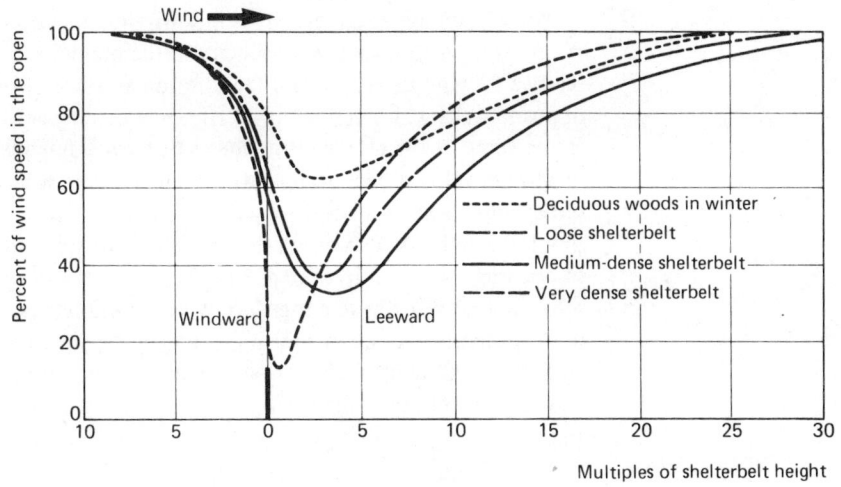

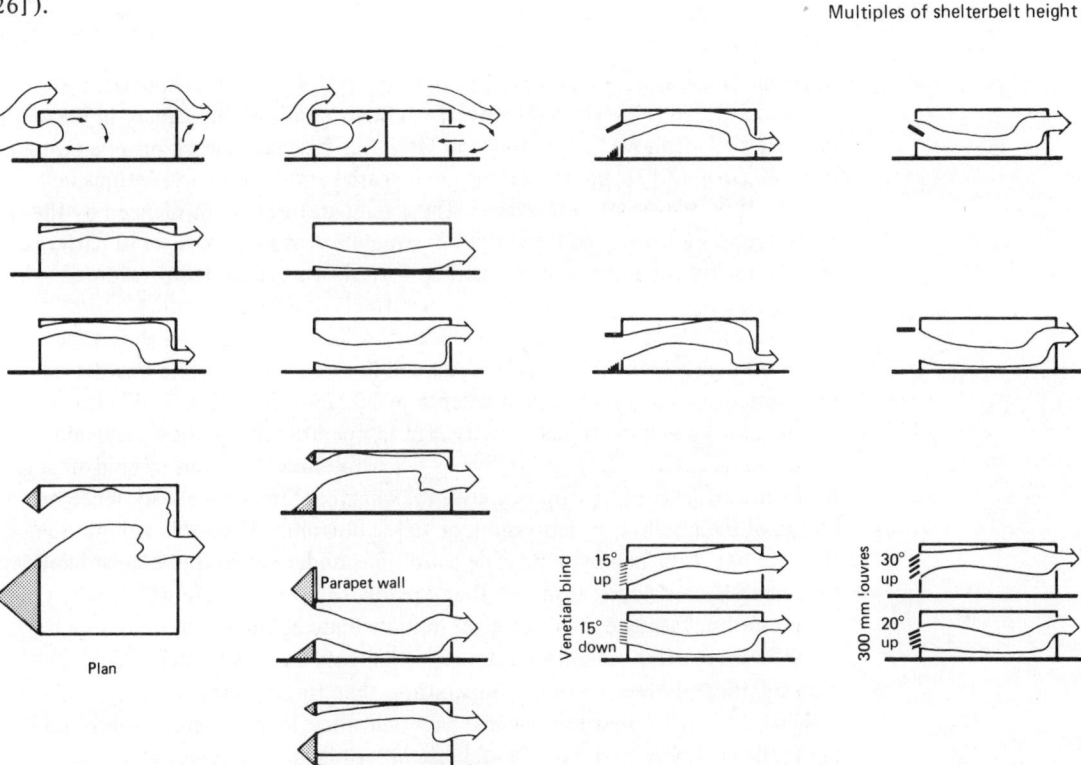

will happen depends on the height of the screen, as shown in Fig. 4.55. Thus, the height, density and distance of a shelter screen will all affect its efficacy.

The difference in pressure between the inside and the outside of a building, under windy conditions, will cause air to flow into the building through holes, cracks, gaps and openings such as windows and doors, on the windward, pressure side, and out on the leeward, suction side. Such air flow will be a cause of heat loss (or heat gain when the external air is warmer than the internal) and may also negate the effects of mechanical ventilation controlled by fans and dampers, through ducts, at constant pressures.

When openings are designed, as in warm humid tropical climates, to obtain the maximum air change and velocity inside buildings, then their position relative to wind direction, and the position and size of openings in adjacent or opposite walls will determine the efficiency of the ventilation system. Fig. 4.56 shows some of the effects. It indicates that, with unequal openings, the maximum velocity will occur near the smaller one, whether it is an inlet or outlet, but for maximum through ventilation the sizes of the two openings should be equal. It also shows the advantages of solid areas of wall adjacent to openings, which trap wind and deflect some of it into the opening; thus a solid parapet wall above a top floor window will increase the wind flow through it, in comparison to a flat roof projecting above the same opening. Overhangs and blinds will reduce the flow and change its direction as shown.

Chapter 8 shows some examples of the local wind effects of various forms and groupings of buildings.

4.5.2 Temperature

Vertical temperature gradients exist not only on the gross, atmospheric, scale but also at the microscale. Agricultural scientists consider the climate in the layer up to 1 m above the ground, and Geiger, in his classic work on *The Climate near the Ground* [3], has shown the great spatial and temporal variations in temperature that occur in this layer. These temperatures are influenced by the reflectivity and density of the soil; by the radiation at night; and wind patterns and shelter from buildings or plants; Fig. 4.57 shows typical temperature variations over grass and concrete and the effects of a nearby wall.

Similar kinds of effects are noted in soil; for instance Fig. 4.58 shows the effect of alteration of the reflectivity of soil (by spreading a white powder on the surface) showing that even at a depth of 200 mm the effect is still clear.

The best known microscale variation of temperature is the local inversion which, in its extreme form, is known as a 'frost hollow'. Streams of cold air sink to the lowest level of the topography and, when contained by a wall, fence or hedge, or by a hollow or depression, or valley bottom, lie in pools as long as they are not disturbed by wind. The conditions under which this is most likely to happen is on cold, clear nights; then the low sky temperature will rapidly cool the ground surface and, hence, the air in immediate contact with it, and such conditions are often calm. Buildings or settlements on sites in such hollows will have significantly lower winter temperatures than those on surrounding land, especially at night; their total degree days will, thus, increase and, correspondingly, the energy required to maintain the interiors at a given temperature. A similar effect may be found for ground floors or semi-basements which have an excavated area outside them and which lie below the general site level (Fig. 4.59).

The change in the direction of local winds between day and night is a feature most marked in valleys and on sea and lake coasts. In valleys, there is generally an upvalley and upslope wind during the day and downvalley and downslope wind at night. The former is the result of heated parcels of rising air during the day creating not only upslope movements but also requiring replacement from lower parts of the valley; the latter the result of the downward flow of cold night air as previously described.

The shore wind effects are due to surface temperature differences between

Fig. 4.57 The transitional climate of a landing strip and meadow on an airfield (after Geiger and Knochenhauer [3]).

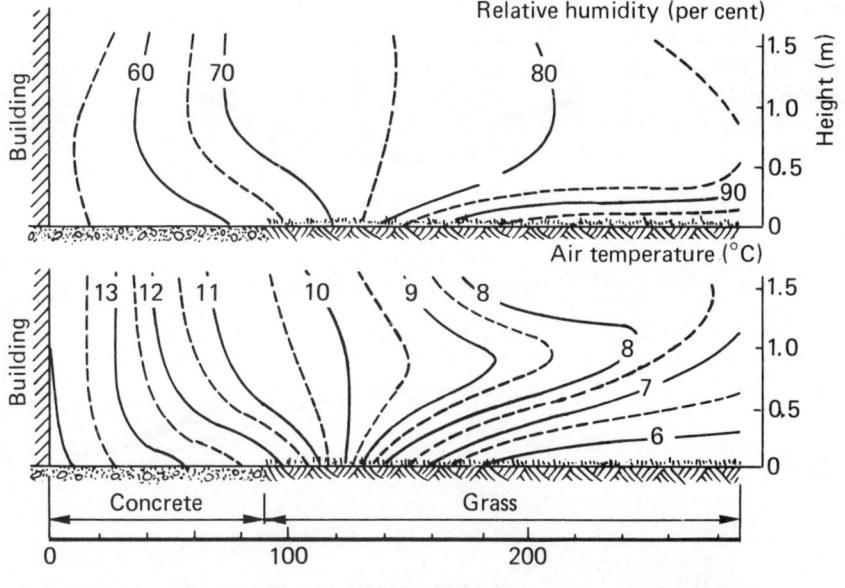

Fig. 4.58 Changes in soil temperature caused by whitening the surface, from an experiment in India (after Geiger [3]). The arrows labelled A and B indicate the two days on which the spreading of the white powder was started and finished, respectively.

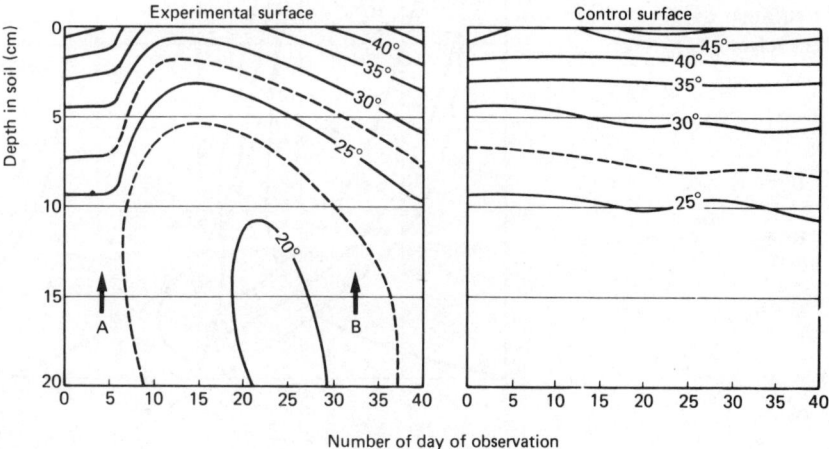

water and land during the day and at night. In the day-time the land, especially in warm climates, heats up to a temperature considerably above that of the water; hence, the rising air current above it will be replaced by cooler air coming in over the sea, causing the on-shore day-time breeze. At night the situation is reversed – the rapidly cooling land giving surface temperatures below that of the adjacent water, and the off-shore night breeze. In tropical climates, especially humid ones, the value of these winds can be fully exploited by orientation of openings across the breeze direction; and by selecting the freshest indoor and outdoor locations for sleeping and day-time resting.

4.5.3 Humidity

Variations in atmospheric humidity with time or in space will affect the thermal design of buildings in three ways:

Fig. 4.59 'Frost hollow' effect on buildings with floors below the general site level and in depressions in a general site level.

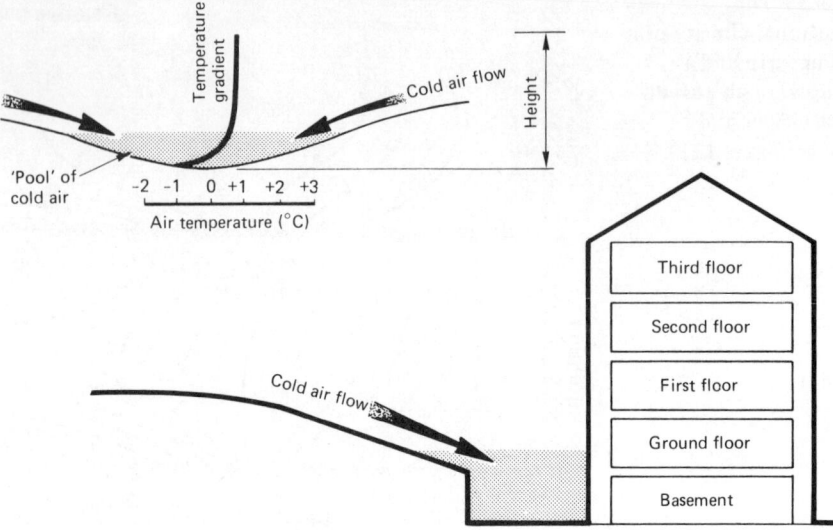

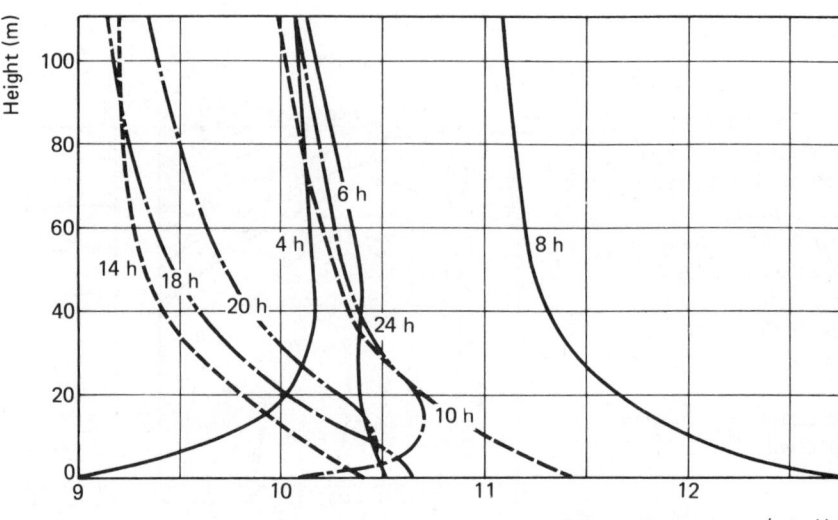

Fig. 4.60 Water vapour pressure stratification in the lowest 100 m on clear summer days (after Geiger [3]).

(i) We have seen from Chapter 3 that humidity, especially in warm conditions, affects people's thermal responses, both physically and psychologically.

(ii) The humidity of the atmosphere will affect the probability of condensation occurring on the surface of or within the building fabric.

(iii) The moisture content of porous materials will affect their thermal insulation properties.

The humidity gradient with height above the ground can be positive or negative, according to the type of climate and time of day. Fig. 4.60 shows a typical pattern, where the night-time and early morning humidity decreases towards the ground; whilst after sunset, the humidity increases towards the ground. Thus the type of diurnal profile, at three heights, shown in Fig. 4.61 is obtained.

Much, of course, depends on ground cover. Where there is rich vegetation, atmospheric humidity is chiefly the result of evaporation from the soil and

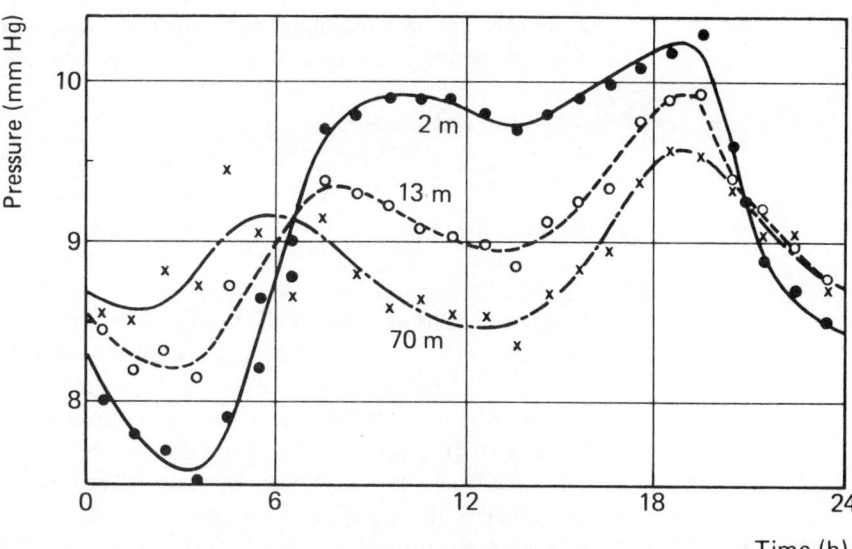

Fig. 4.61 Diurnal variation of water vapour pressure at Quickborn, U.S.A., on clear July days (after Frankenberger and Geiger [3]).

transevaporation through the leaves of plants. Thus, after a period of rainfall, ground-held water will continue to humidify the atmosphere for a considerable time; whilst in cities, with hard, non-absorbent surfaces and a rapid drain-off of surface water, much lower humidities will be found even quite a short while after the cessation of rain.

Thus, the planting of grass and vegetation around a building will ensure a

Fig. 4.62 (a) Sunlight patterns in a room. (b) Shadow patterns in a housing layout (after Markus [36]).

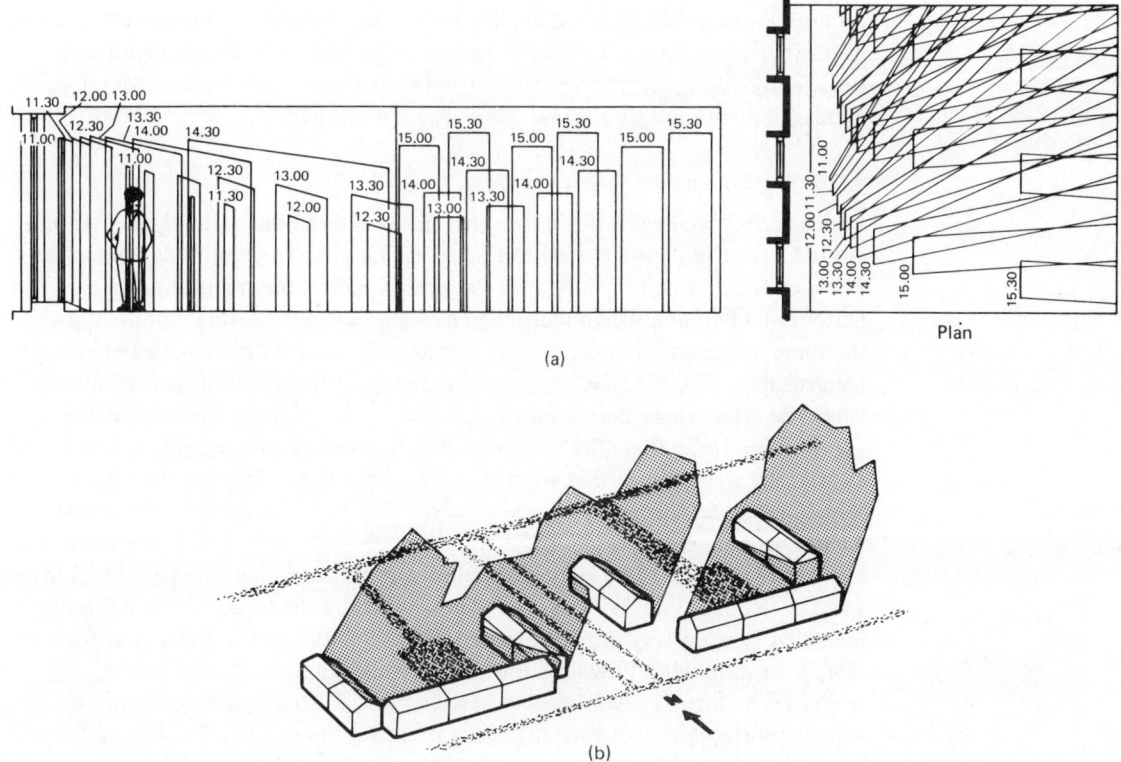

more constant local humidity; and, of course, the presence of open water will do the same as well as increase the overall average moisture of the air.

4.5.4 Sun and Shade

The movement of patches of sunlight and patches of shadow around a building, both as determined by the built form itself and by the presence of topographical features, trees or other solid objects, will have a critical effect on the changing microclimate of the building and its immediate surroundings. The sunpaths described in Section 4.4.1 will enable these movements to be studied, and the hourly positions of shadows and sunlight patches to be plotted on both plans and elevations. Fig. 4.62(a) shows a typical plot of this kind with the half-hourly sunlight patterns in a room marked for the winter solstice. Similarly, Fig. 4.62(b) shows the shadow pattern in a housing layout.

Chapter 10 describes the construction and use of helidons – sun simulators – with which a continuous visual impression of sun patterns is achieved. If these are filmed or photographed then a permanent study record becomes available.

Clearly the incidence of sunshine and, hence, direct radiation, on to building surfaces and through the glazed areas has to be determined for any energy predictions to be made. However, the incidence of sunshine on to the ground surrounding the building is too often ignored, and is equally important. It will determine the suitability of areas for children's play, sitting areas, clothes drying and, above all, the likelihood of strong grass and plant growth. In many housing schemes in Northern Europe, the shape and orientation of houses or blocks of flats have been so carefully contrived to ensure maximum penetration *into* the houses, especially in winter, that the buildings become louvers over the ground, shielding the ground for much of the day from adequate sunshine. This can result in levels of radiation inadequate for photosynthesis, with consequent loss of plant growth; thus, grass subject to pedestrian wear is unable to maintain sufficiently strong growth for renewal and large areas of mud quickly develop. Similarly, plants and shrubs may die or become stunted.

4.5.5 The Climate of Towns and Cities

In this section we have already seen that in and around the building surfaces and ground a relatively large spatial and temporal variation in conditions takes place. These effects can significantly alter the energy consumption and thermal response pattern of a building. When multiplied by the presence of several hundred or thousand buildings – in urban clusters – the effects are more marked and give recognizably different climates to the urban region from that of its rural hinterland. The effects have been studied for some years – perhaps the outstanding contribution being Chandler's study of the climate of London [31].

We have already seen that wind velocity gradients are different over the 'rough' urban terrain and over open country. Although, in general, lower mean wind speeds are experienced in the city, because of the nature of building blocks, streets and squares, there is a great deal of complex turbulence, especially at the bases of tall buildings. Wind deflected downward by the facades of buildings joins that flowing horizontally to create high velocities and turbulence at the side, downward wind flow on the windward side and upward flow on the leeward side. Streets often become wind funnels, collecting spillage from adjacent surfaces and creating high velocities near the ground. These conditions will often create conditions of considerable discomfort, dust and, in low temperatures, windchill.

Another major urban effect is on the radiation and temperature budget. The buildings and surfaces between them are generally of higher reflectivity than those in rural areas; but on the other hand, the radiation they do absorb is more slowly released by these high thermal capacity materials. The protection from wind and the emission of heating, air-conditioning and other forms of energy from buildings all combine to create the well-studied 'heat island' of cities. This is particularly marked at night, and in cold weather, when the mean city temperature may be as much as 4 °C above that of the suburbs and country outside. Figures 4.63 and 4.64 show some typical heat islands in Washington and London and many similar records from other cities exist. The depth of the island effect is probably up to about 150 m above ground but will vary with topography and wind conditions.

Radiation and sunshine hours in cities are substantially less than outside them, due to the extra turbidity caused by smoke, dust and other pollutants. The decrease can be in the order of 20 per cent, even in summer, although in cities with smokeless zone programmes this percentage is decreasing to the order of 10 per cent. In winter the decrease is far greater. Fig. 4.65 indicates this effect in London.

So, in cold climates, in spite of decreased sun and radiation, city climate is likely to be more temperate than rural – in degree-day terms (and hence in terms of energy consumption for space heating) the difference is about 10 per cent according to Chandler [31].

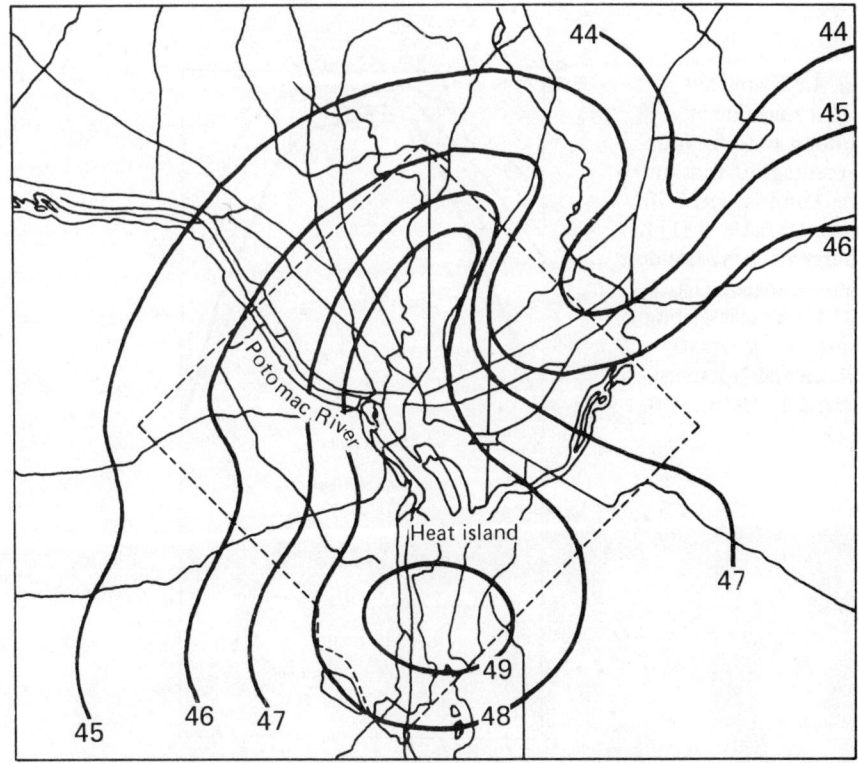

Fig. 4.63 Annual temperature record of Washington D.C., and its environs giving the average annual minimum temperatures for the period 1946-1960. The areas inside closed isotherms constitute what is known as the heat island. Here, as in other cities, the island is associated with the most densely built-up part of the urban complex. This map is based on data obtained by Clarence A. Woollum of the U.S. Weather Bureau. Note that the temperatures are in degrees Fahrenheit (after Lowry [32]).

Fig. 4.64 Degree-days in London. Distribution of annual accumulated temperature below 15.6°C in London 1951–60 (Centigrade degree-days) (after Chandler [31] and Lacy [34]).

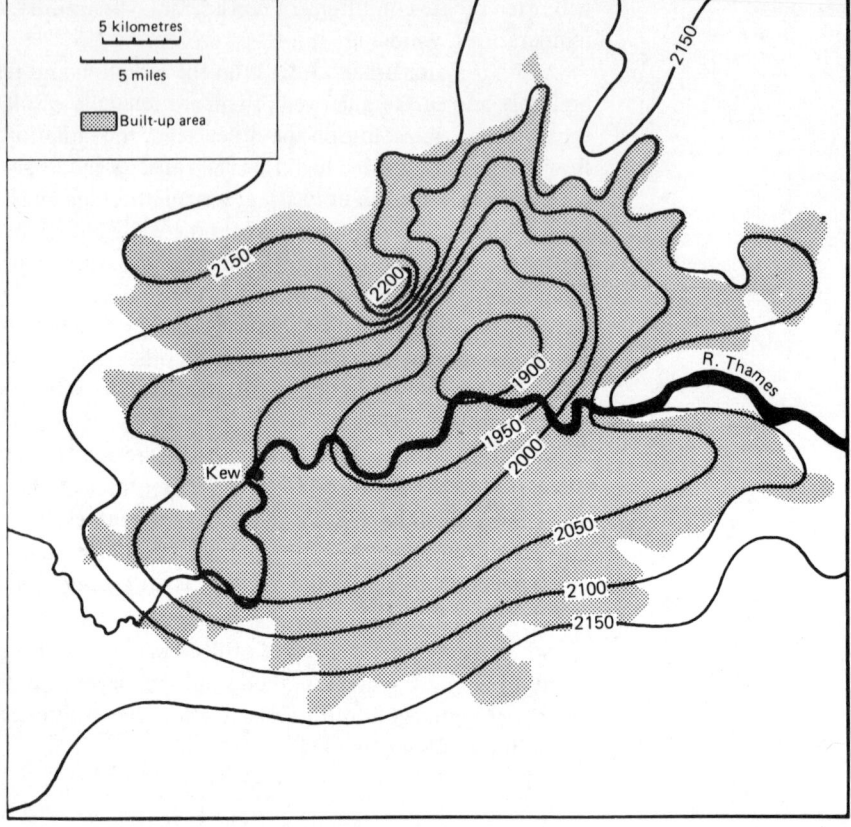

Fig. 4.65 Monthly bright sunshine at London stations as a percentage of that outside London, 1921-50 (after Chandler [31]). Source of data: London Meteorological Office 1953 Averages of bright sunshine for Great Britain and Northern Ireland 1921 to 1950, M.O. 572.

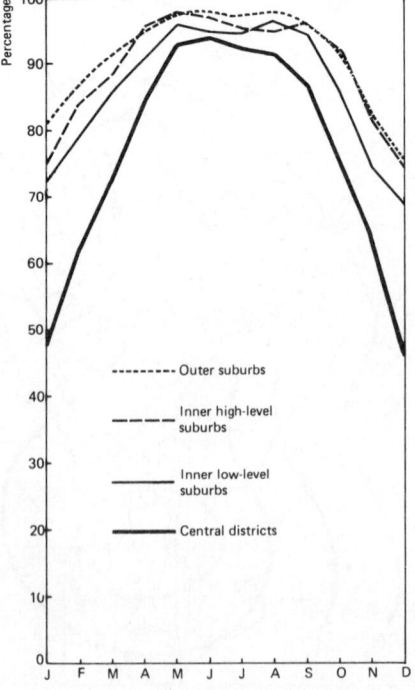

References

1   Huntington, E., *Civilization and Climate*. Yale University Press, New Haven, Conn., 1915.

2   Barry, R. G., A framework of climatological research with particular reference to scale concepts. *Transactions of the Institute of British Geography,* **49**, 61–70, 1970.

3   Geiger, R., *The Climate near the Ground*. Harvard University Press, Cambridge, Mass., 1965.

4   Vitkevitch, V. I., *Agricultural Meteorology*. Israel Program for Scientific Translations, Jerusalem, 1963 (translated from Russian).

5   *IHVE Guide*, Vol. A. Institution of Heating and Ventilating Engineers, London, 1970.

6   *IHVE Guide*, Vol. A, Table A2.4.

7   *IHVE Guide*, Vol. A, Figs. A2.11 and A2.12.

8   Clarke, J. A., Environmental systems performance. Ph.D. thesis, University of Strathclyde, 1977.

9   Knight, J. C. and Cornell, A. A., Degree days and fuel consumption for office buildings. *Journal of the Institution of Heating and Ventilating Engineers*, **26**, 309, 1959.

10   *Building Research Station Digest No. 94*, November 1956.

11   Al-Azzawi, S. H., Oriental houses in Iraq. In *Shelter and Society* (P. Oliver, ed.). Barrie and Jenkins, London, 1969, 91–102.

12   Fitch, J. M. and Branch, D. P., Primitive architecture and climate. *Scientific American,* **203**, 138, December 1960.

13   Budyko, M. I. and Kondratyev, K. Ya., The heat balance of the earth. *Research in Geophysics,* **2**, MIT, Cambridge, Mass., 1964.

14   Rodgers, G. G. and Souster, C. G. S., The development of an interactive computer program for the calculation of solar irradiances and daily irradiations on horizontal surfaces on cloudless days for given conditions of sky clarity and atmospheric water content. *Department of Building Science, Faculty of Architectural Studies, University of Sheffield, Report BS28*, August 1976.

15   Pleijel, G., The computation of natural radiation in architecture and town-planning. State Committee for Building Research, *Stockholm Report 25*, 1954. Moon, P., Proposed standard solar-radiation curves for engineering use. *Journal of the Franklin Institute,* **230**(5), 583–617, 1940. Page, J.K. (ed.), *Solar Energy: a UK Assessment*. International Solar Energy Society, UK Section, London, 1976.

16   Unsworth, M. H., In *Proceedings of Conference on UK Meteorological Data and Solar Energy Applications*. International Solar Energy Society, UK Section, London, 1975, 18–36.

17   Parmelee, G. V., Irradiation on vertical and horizontal surfaces by diffuse solar radiation from cloudless skies. *American Society of Heating, Refrigeration and Air-Conditioning Engineers Transactions,* **60**(1510), 341–356, 1954.

18   Page, J. K., In *Proceedings of Conference on UK Meteorological Data and Solar Energy Applications*. International Solar Energy Society, UK Section, London, 1975, 37–39.

19   Page, J. K., The estimation of monthly mean values of daily short wave irradiation on vertical and inclined surfaces from sunshine records for Latitudes 60°N to 40°S. *University of Sheffield, Department of Building*

Science, Report BS32, July 1976.

20   Duffie, J. A. and Beckman, W. A., *Solar Energy Thermal Processes.* Wiley-Interscience, New York and London, 1974.

21   Whillier, A., Solar radiation graphs. *Solar Energy,* 9(3), 164–165, 1965.

22   Liu, B. Y. H. and Jordan, R. C., The interrelationship and characteristic distribution of direct, diffuse and total solar radiation. *Solar Energy,* 4(3), 1–19, 1960.

23   I am indebted to my colleague Paul Yaneske for computing the *R*-values in and for suggesting the method of obtaining *hourly* tilted values given in Section 4.4.2.3(b).

24   Hottel, H. C., Introductory lecture at the Space Heating and Solar Energy Symposium. Massachussetts Institute of Technology, Boston, Mass., 1954.

25   Loudon, A. G., The interpretation of solar radiation measurements for building problems. In *Sunlight in Buildings.* CIB, Rotterdam, 1967, 111–118.

26   Koenigsberger, O. H., Ingersoll, T. G., Mayhew, A. and Szokolay, S. V., *Manual of Tropical Housing and Building, Part I: Climatic Design.* Longman, London, 1974.

27   Olgyay, V., *Design with Climate.* Princeton University Press, Princeton, N.J., 1963.

28   Kendrew, W. K., *Climatology.* Oxford University Press, Oxford, 1957.

29   Flohn, H., *Climate and Weather.* World University Library, London, 1969.

30   Lacy, R. E., The analysis of climatological data for the building industry. *CIB Report No. 39.* CIB, Rotterdam, 1972.

31   Chandler, T. J., *The Climate of London.* Hutchinson, London, 1965.

32   Lowry, W.P., The climate of cities. *Scientific American,* 217, 15–23, August 1967.

33   Shellard, H. C., Monthly averages of accumulated temperature above and below various base temperatures for stations in Great Britain and Northern Ireland, 1921–50. Meteorological Office, *Clim. Mem.,* 5, Bracknell, 1956.

34   Lacy, R. E., *Climate and Building in Britain.* HMSO, London, 1977.

35   Markus, T. A. *et al.* Unpublished reports on student projects, University of Science, Penang, 1974.

36   Markus, T. A., The function of windows — a re-appraisal. *Building Science,* 2, 97–121, 1967.

APPENDIX 4A: Sunpath Charts 1–18; Overlays 1–13

Charts 1 to 18 are positioned so that the North point for use in the Northern Hemisphere is in the left-hand side of every page. Turn the book clockwise through 90° to get North in its conventional position.

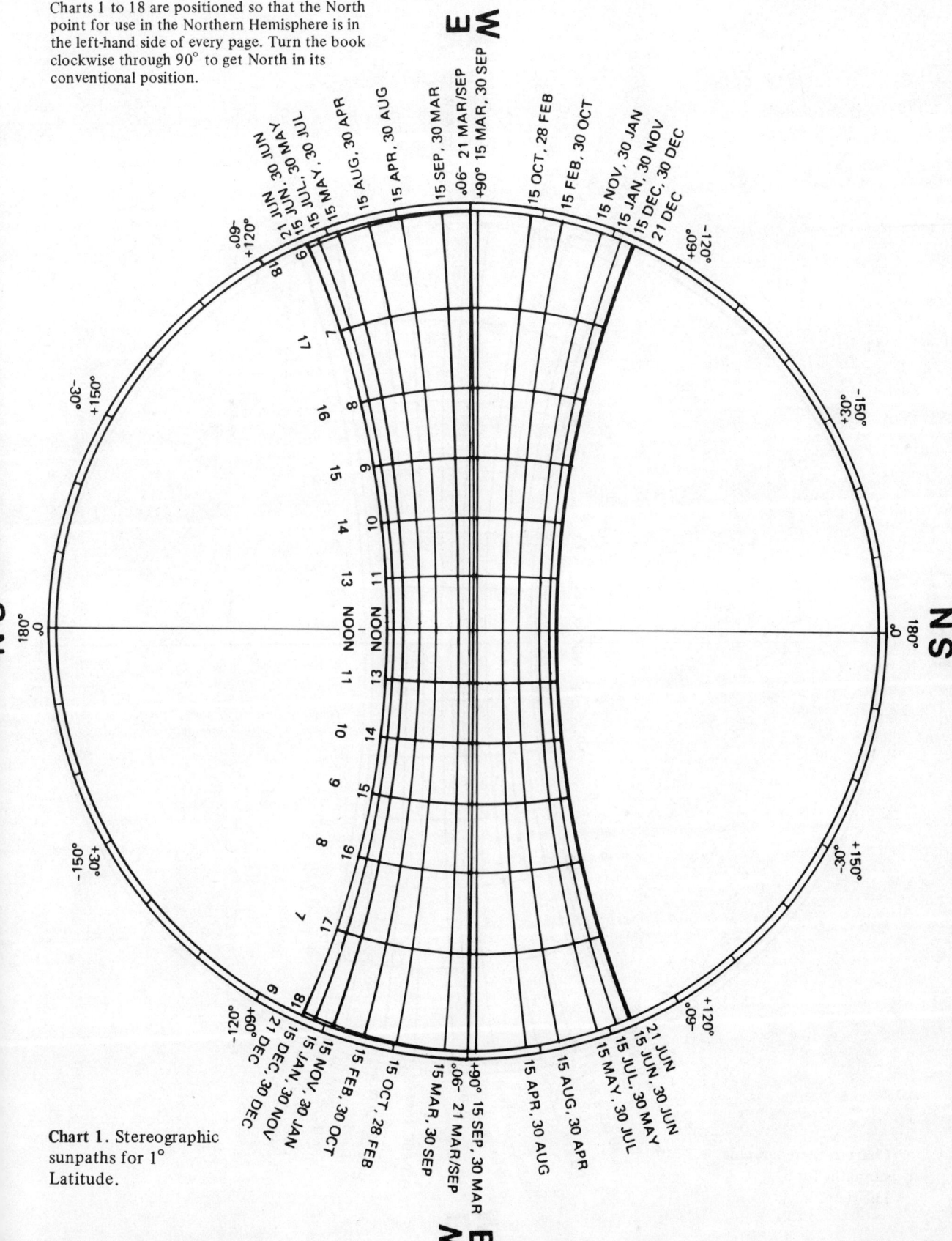

Chart 1. Stereographic sunpaths for 1° Latitude.

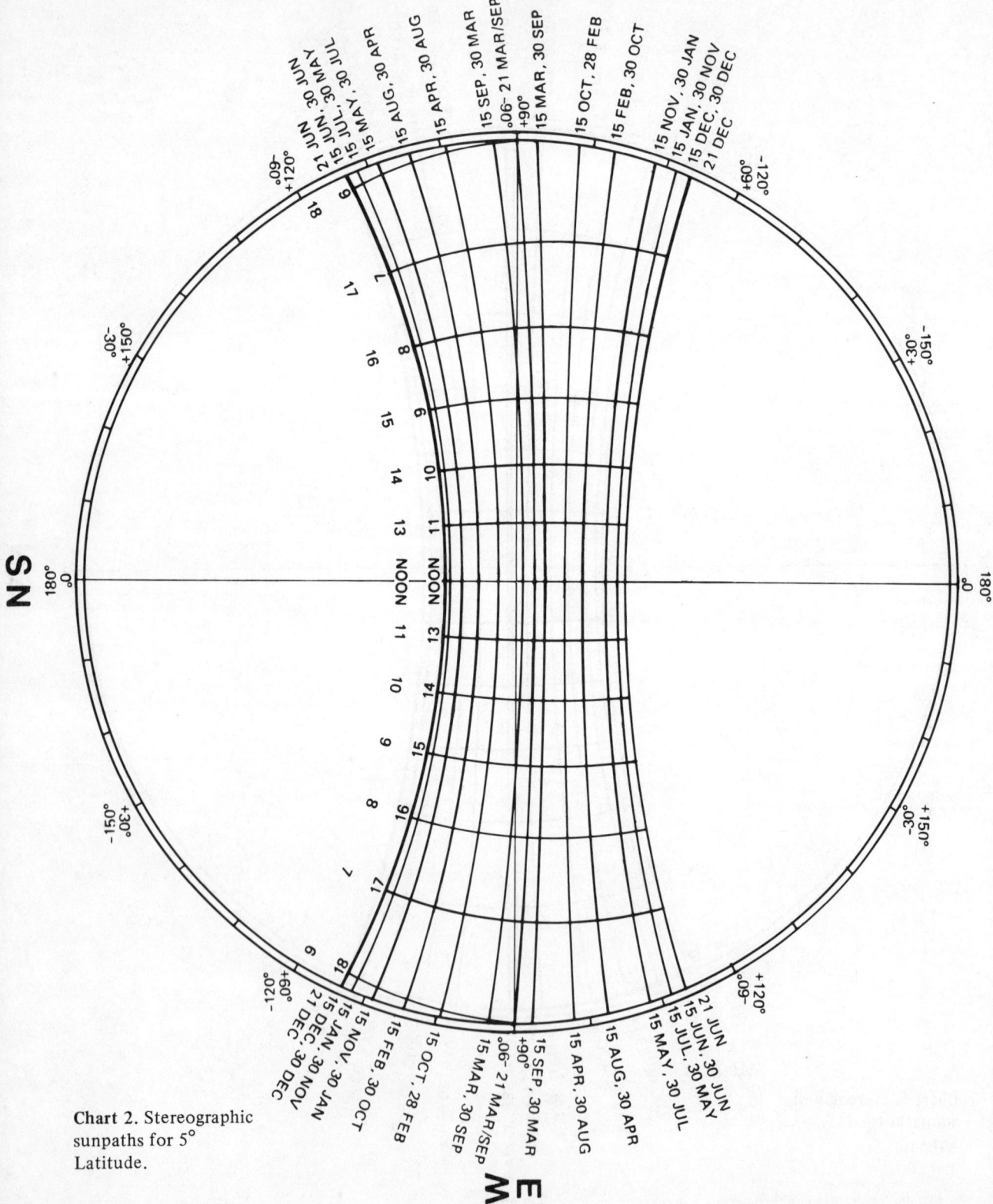

Chart 2. Stereographic sunpaths for 5° Latitude.

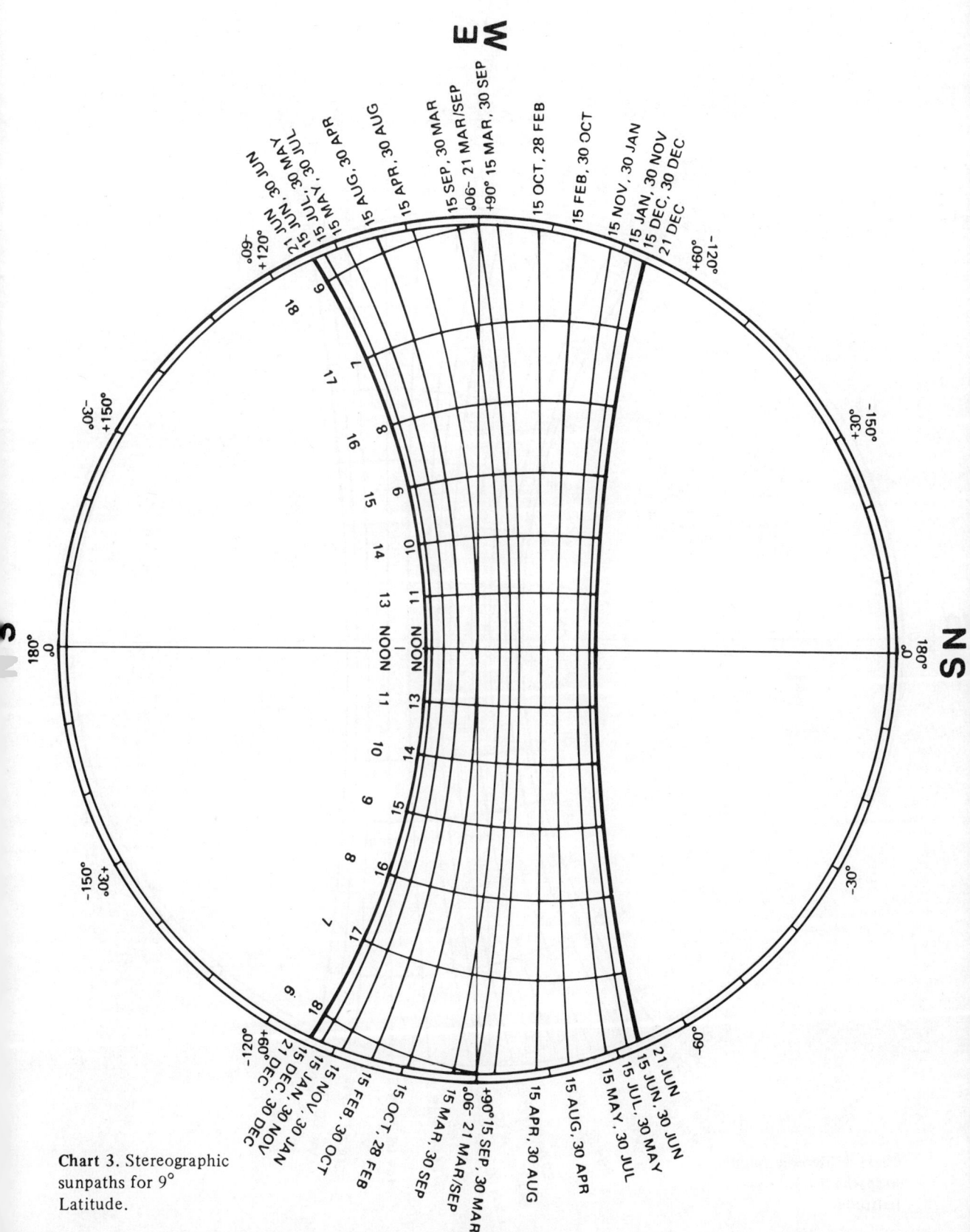

Chart 3. Stereographic sunpaths for 9° Latitude.

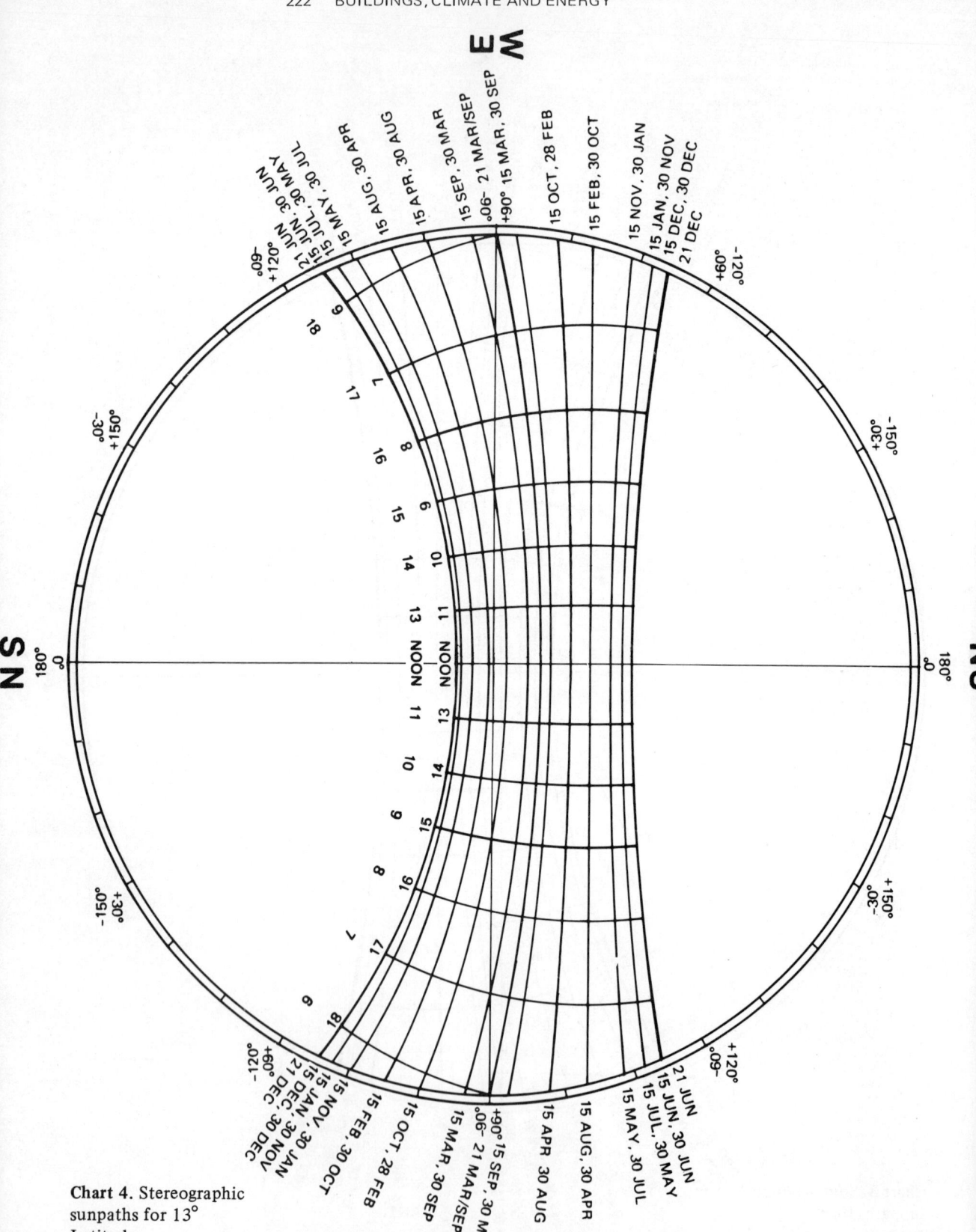

Chart 4. Stereographic sunpaths for 13° Latitude.

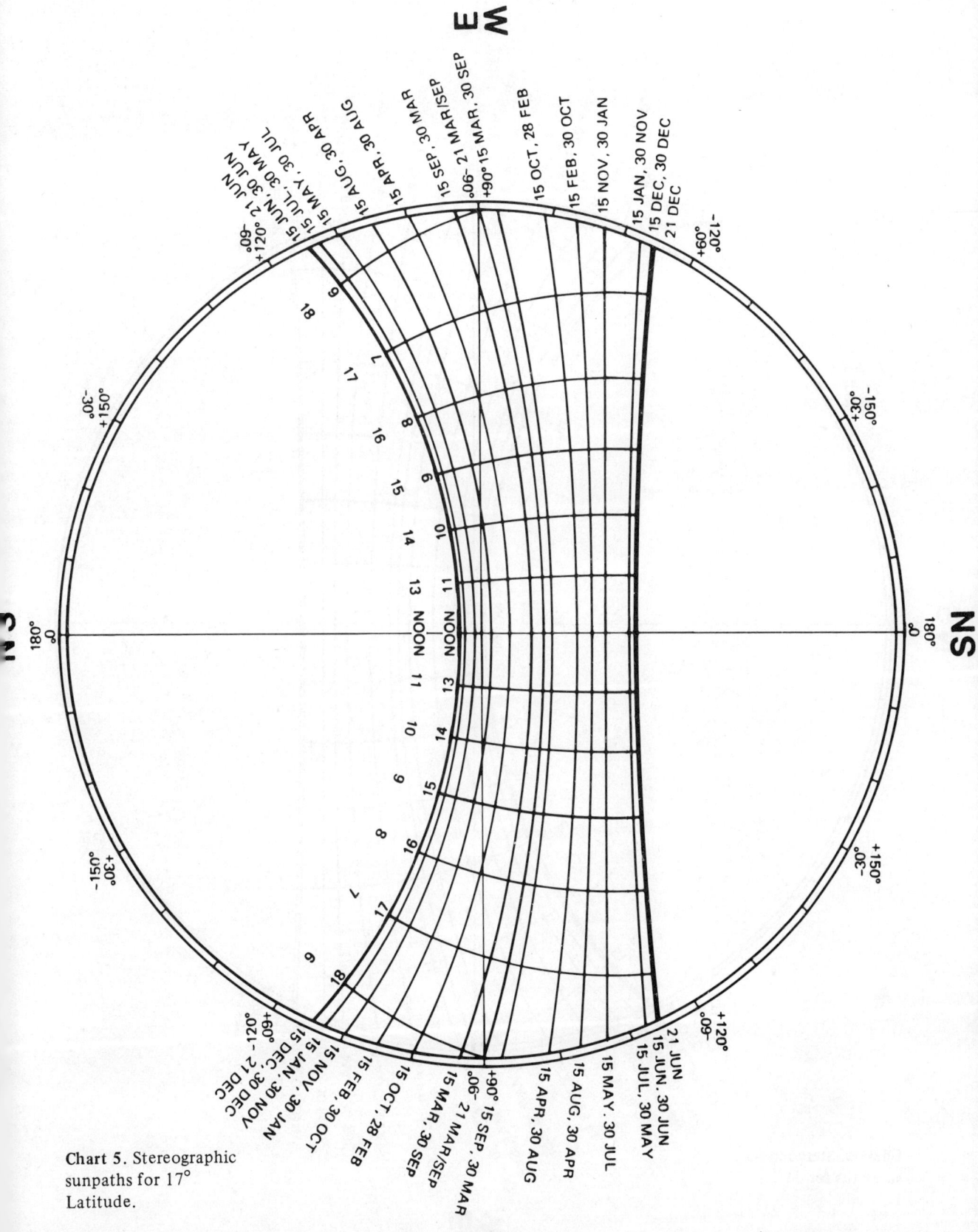

Chart 5. Stereographic sunpaths for 17° Latitude.

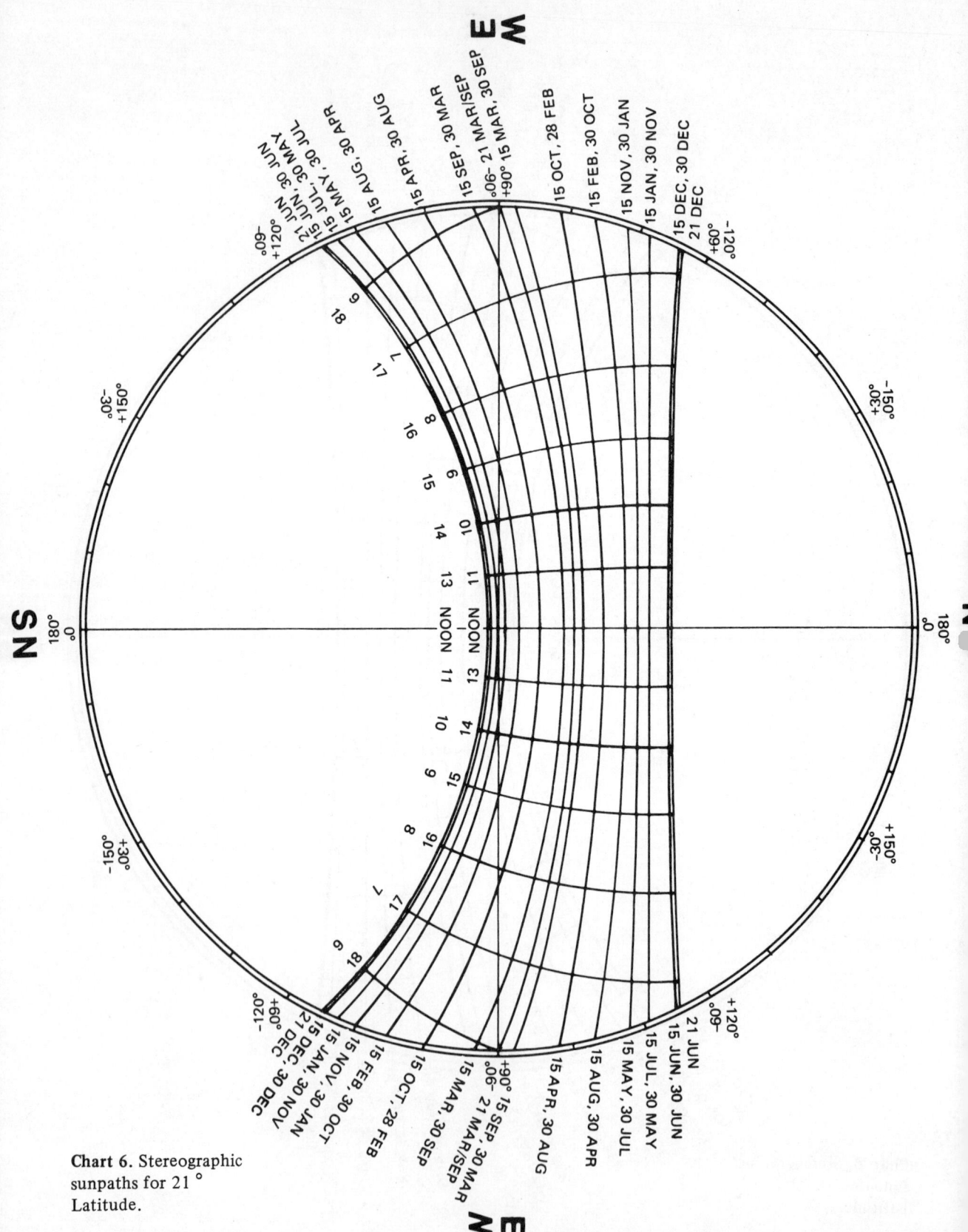

Chart 6. Stereographic sunpaths for 21 ° Latitude.

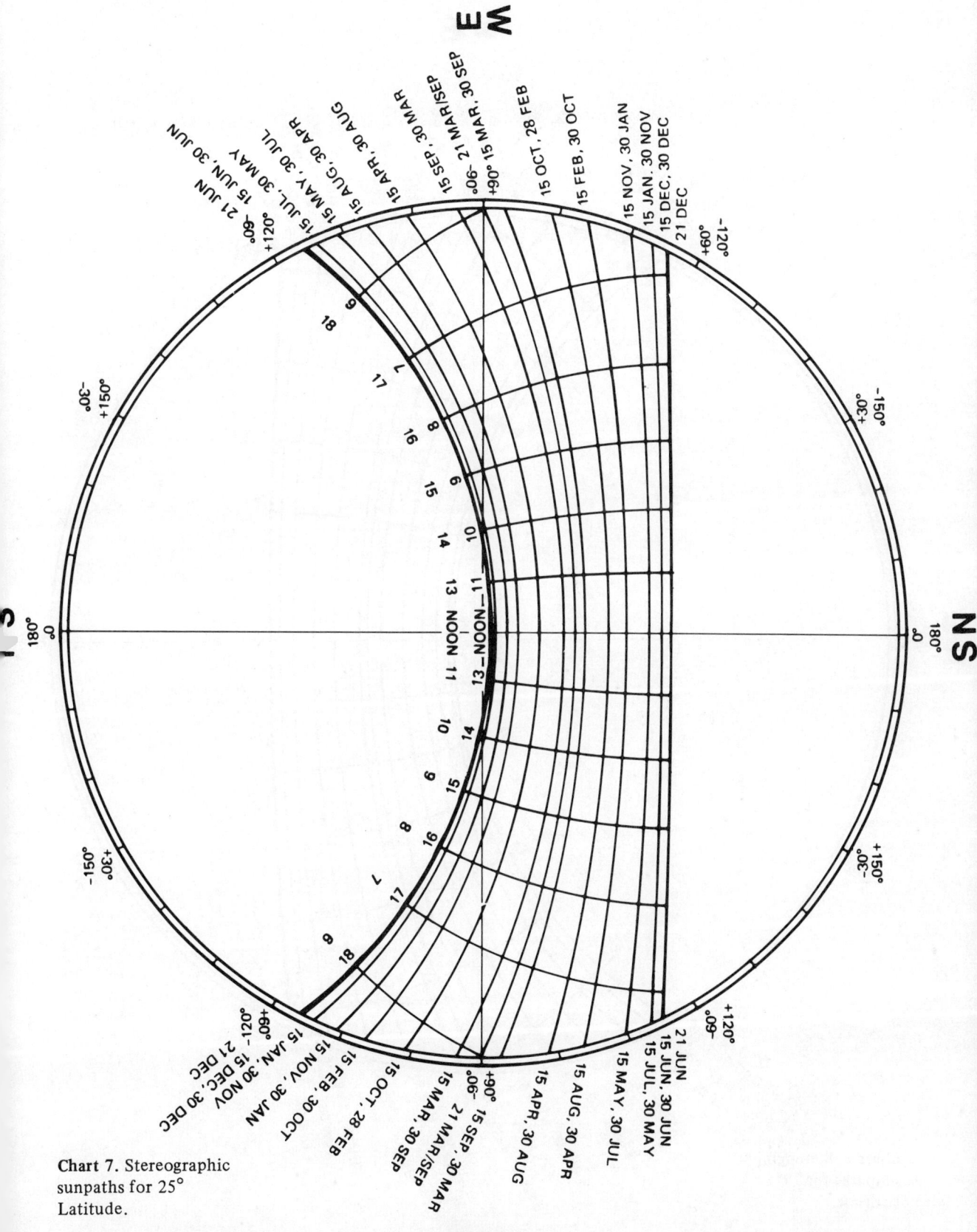

Chart 7. Stereographic sunpaths for 25° Latitude.

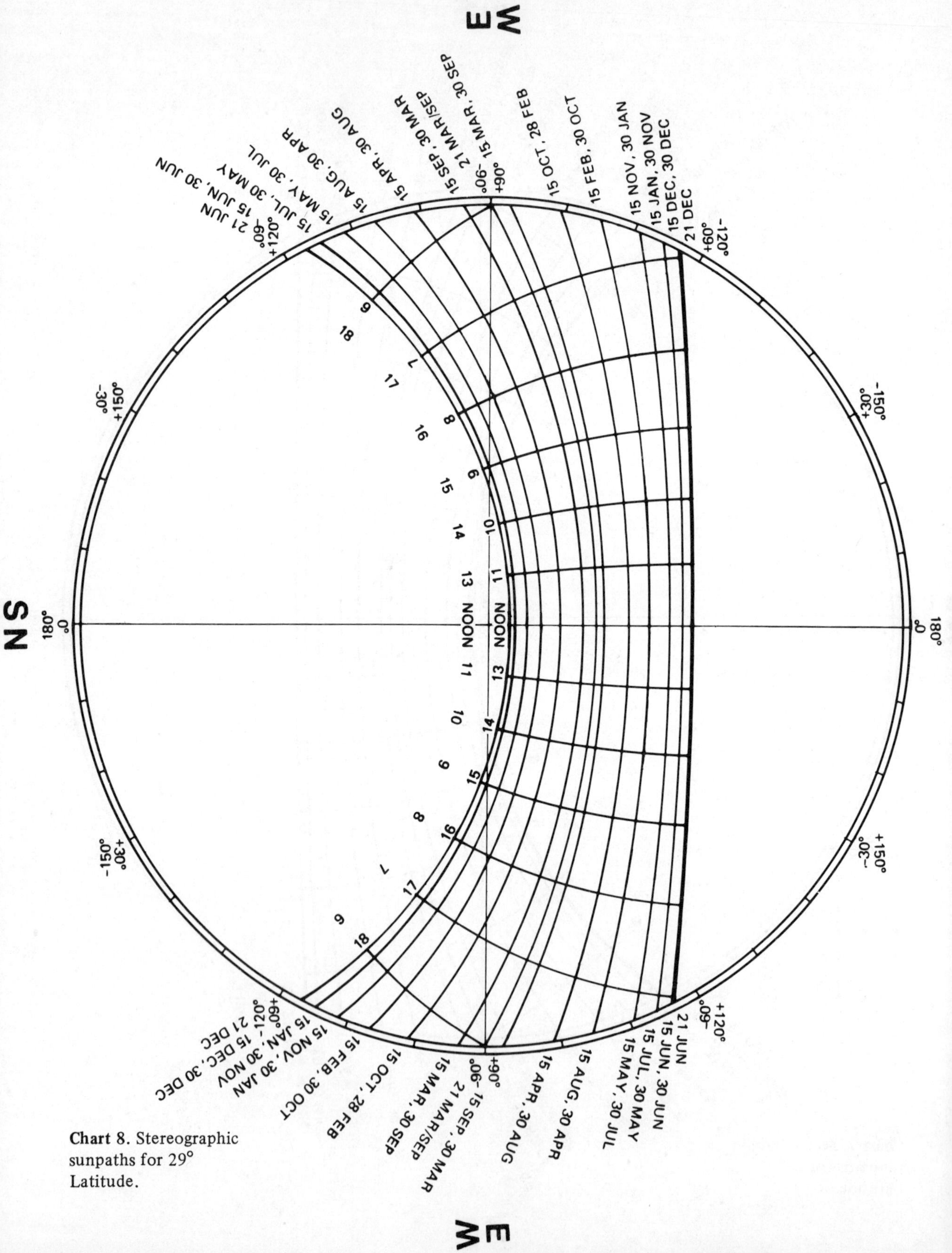

Chart 8. Stereographic sunpaths for 29° Latitude.

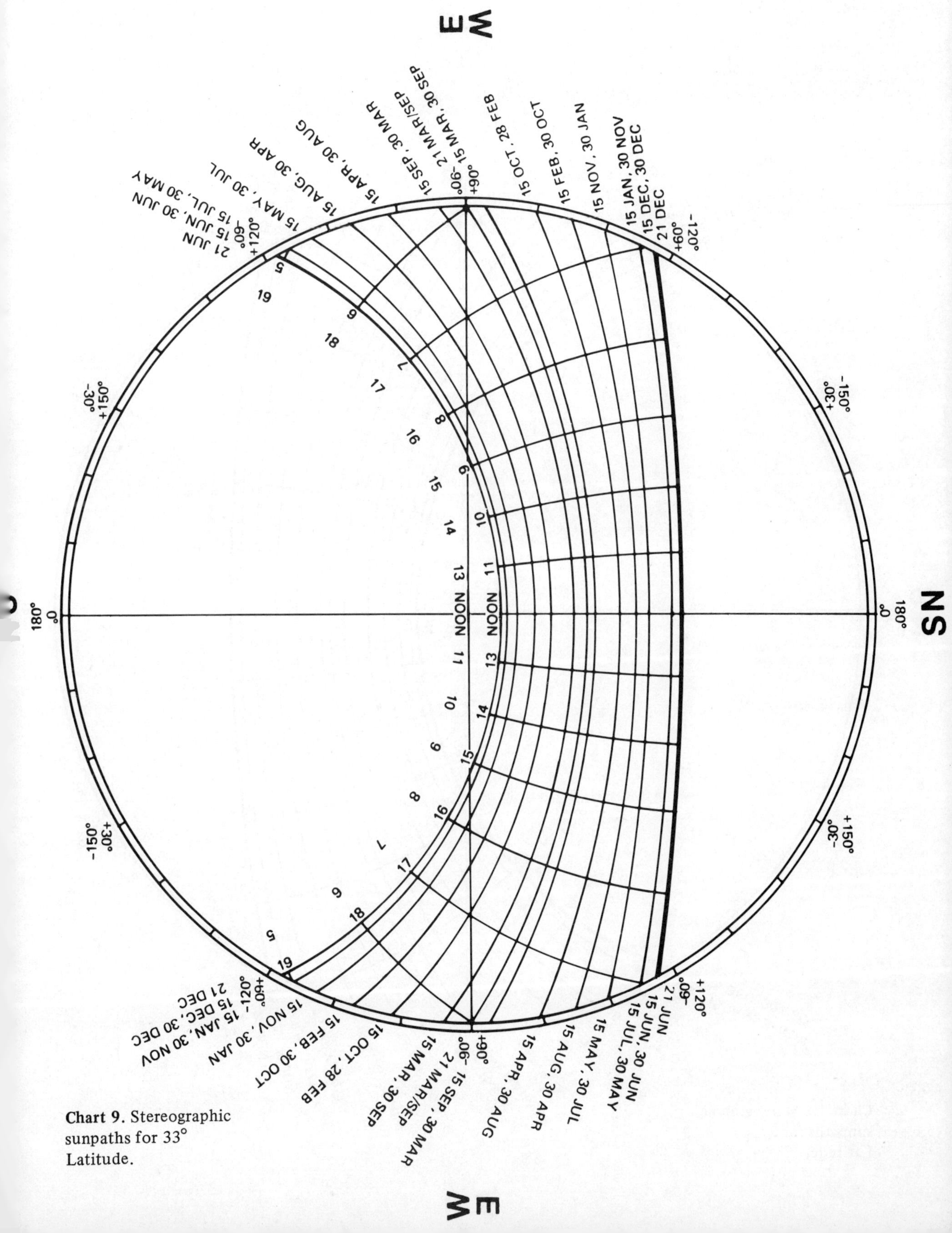

Chart 9. Stereographic
sunpaths for 33°
Latitude.

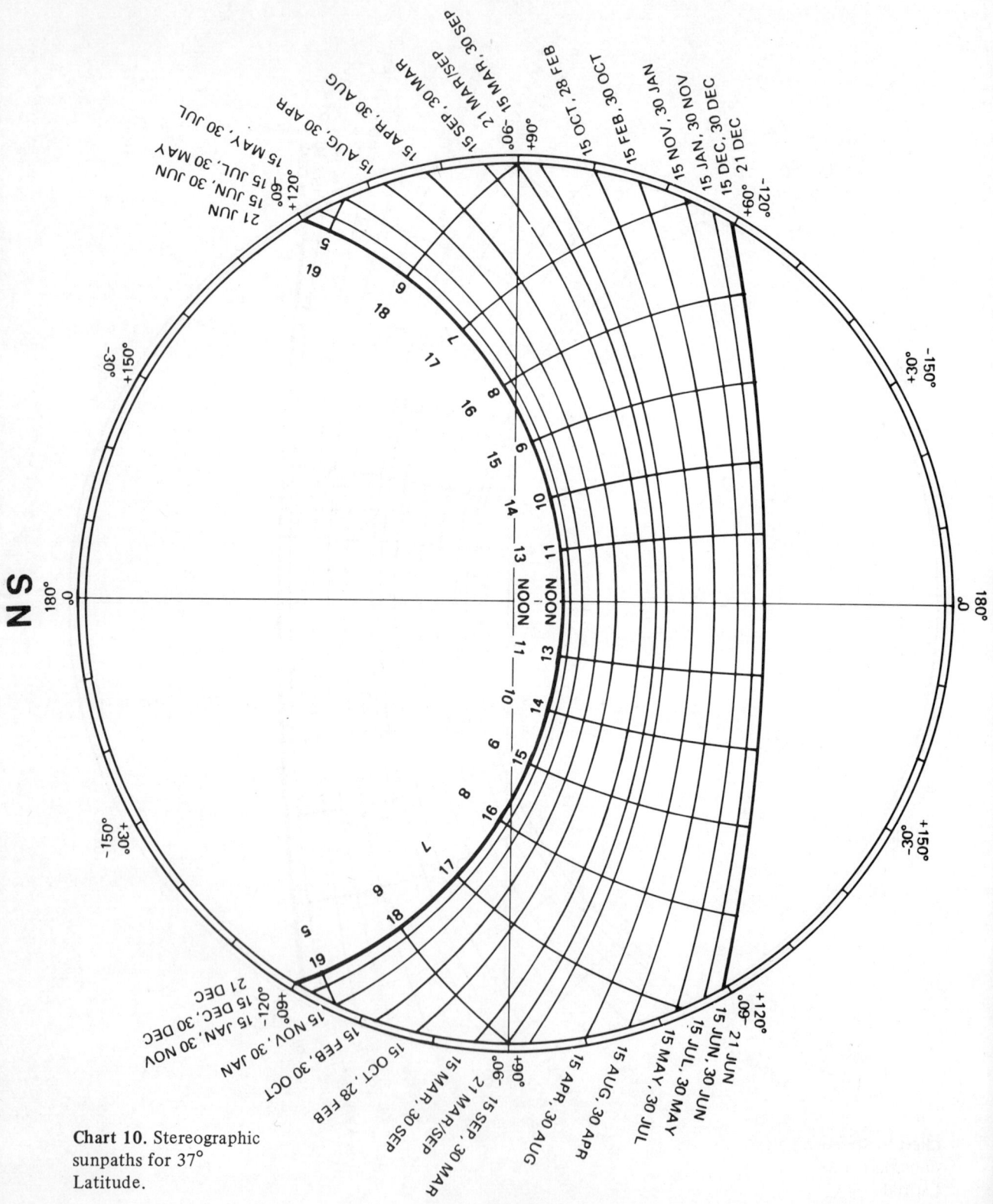

Chart 10. Stereographic sunpaths for 37° Latitude.

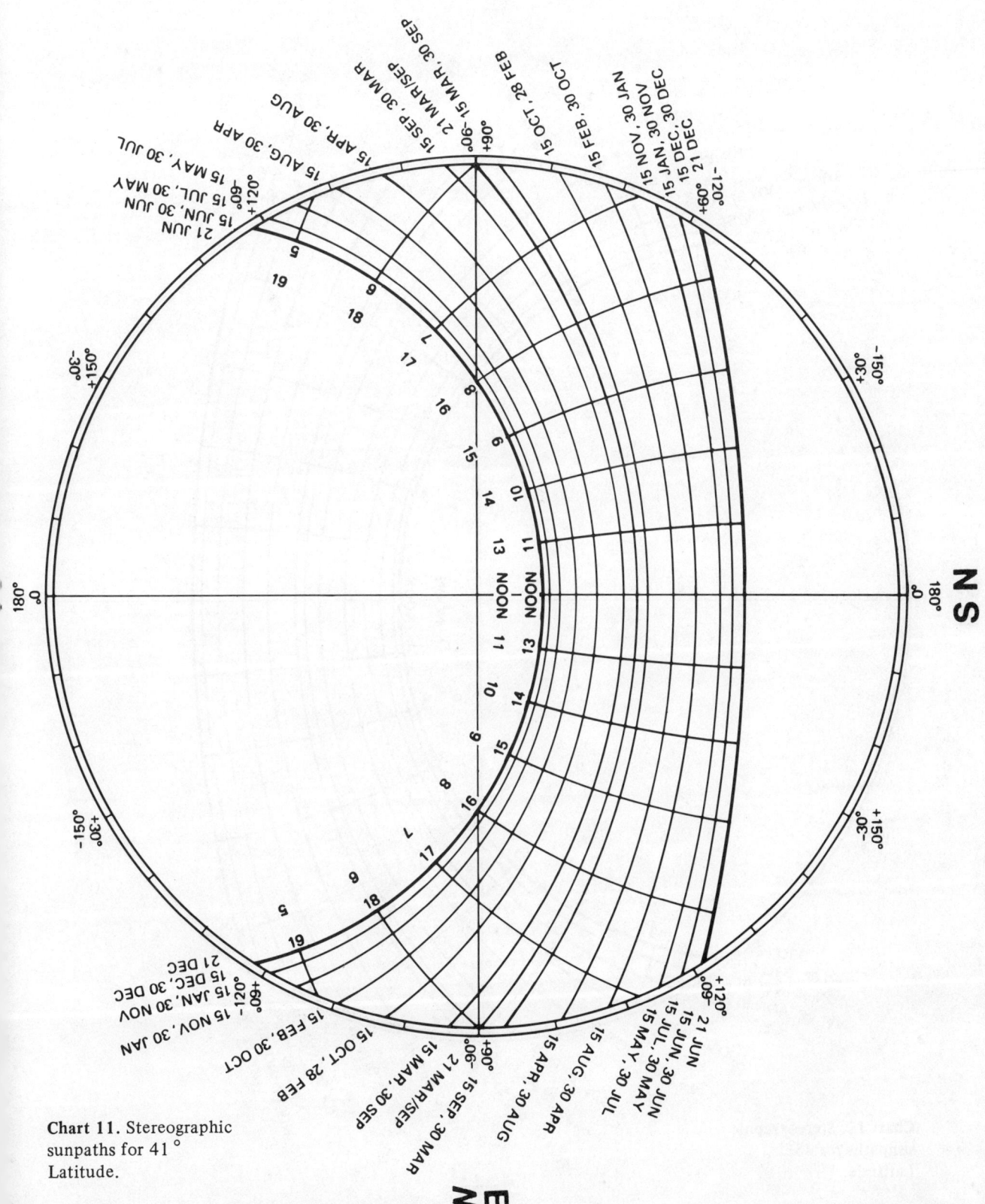

Chart 11. Stereographic sunpaths for 41° Latitude.

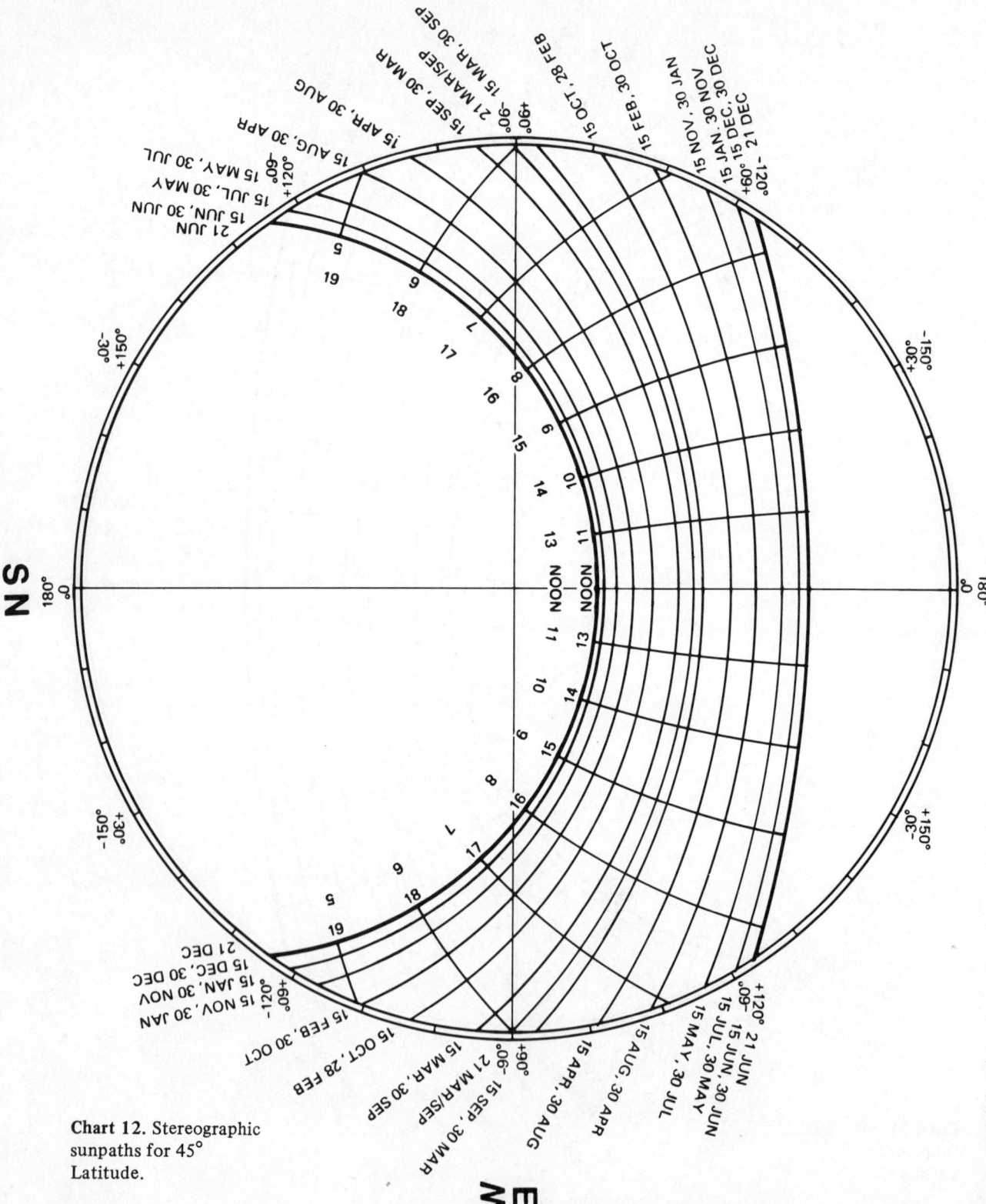

Chart 12. Stereographic
sunpaths for 45°
Latitude.

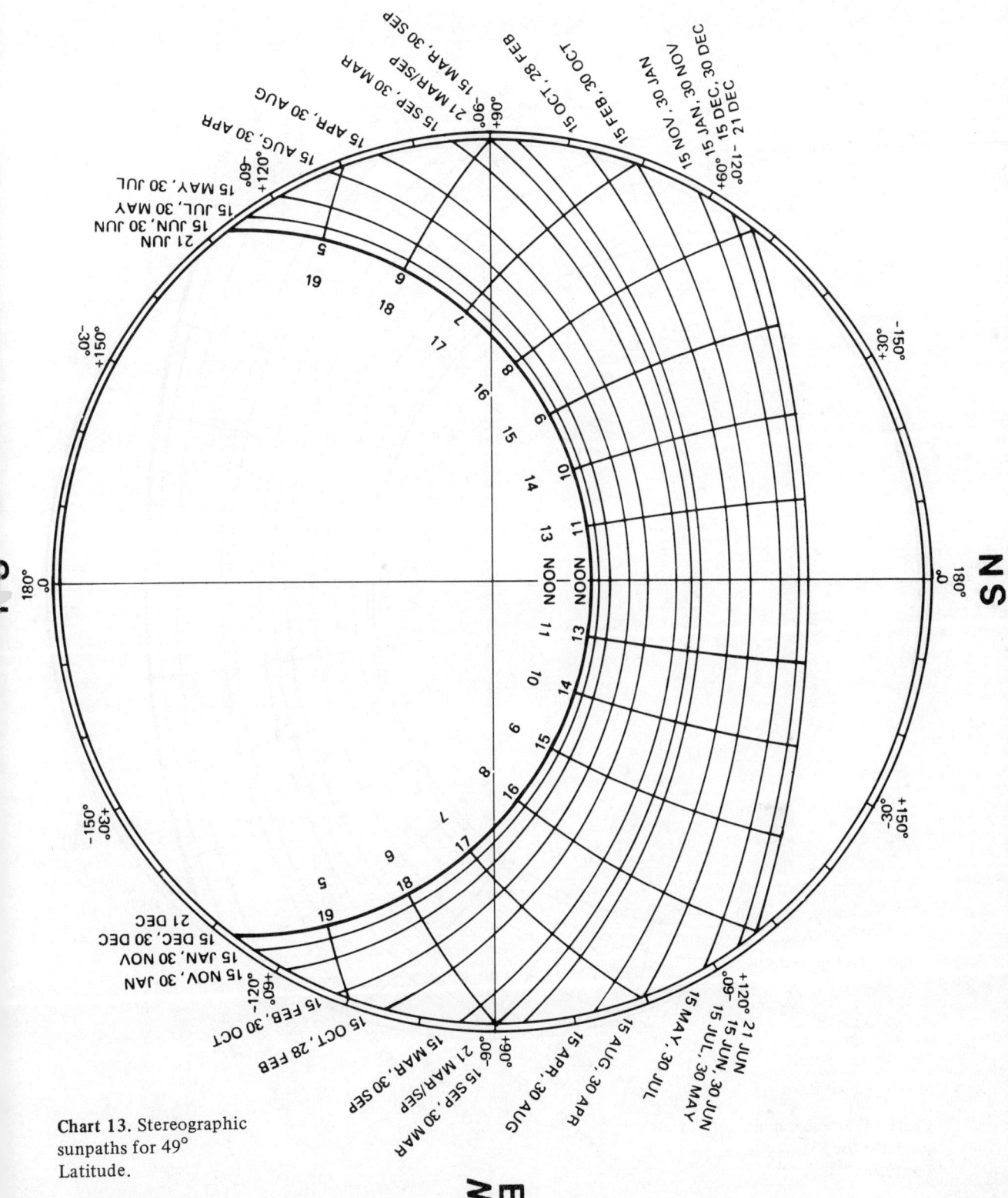

Chart 13. Stereographic sunpaths for 49° Latitude.

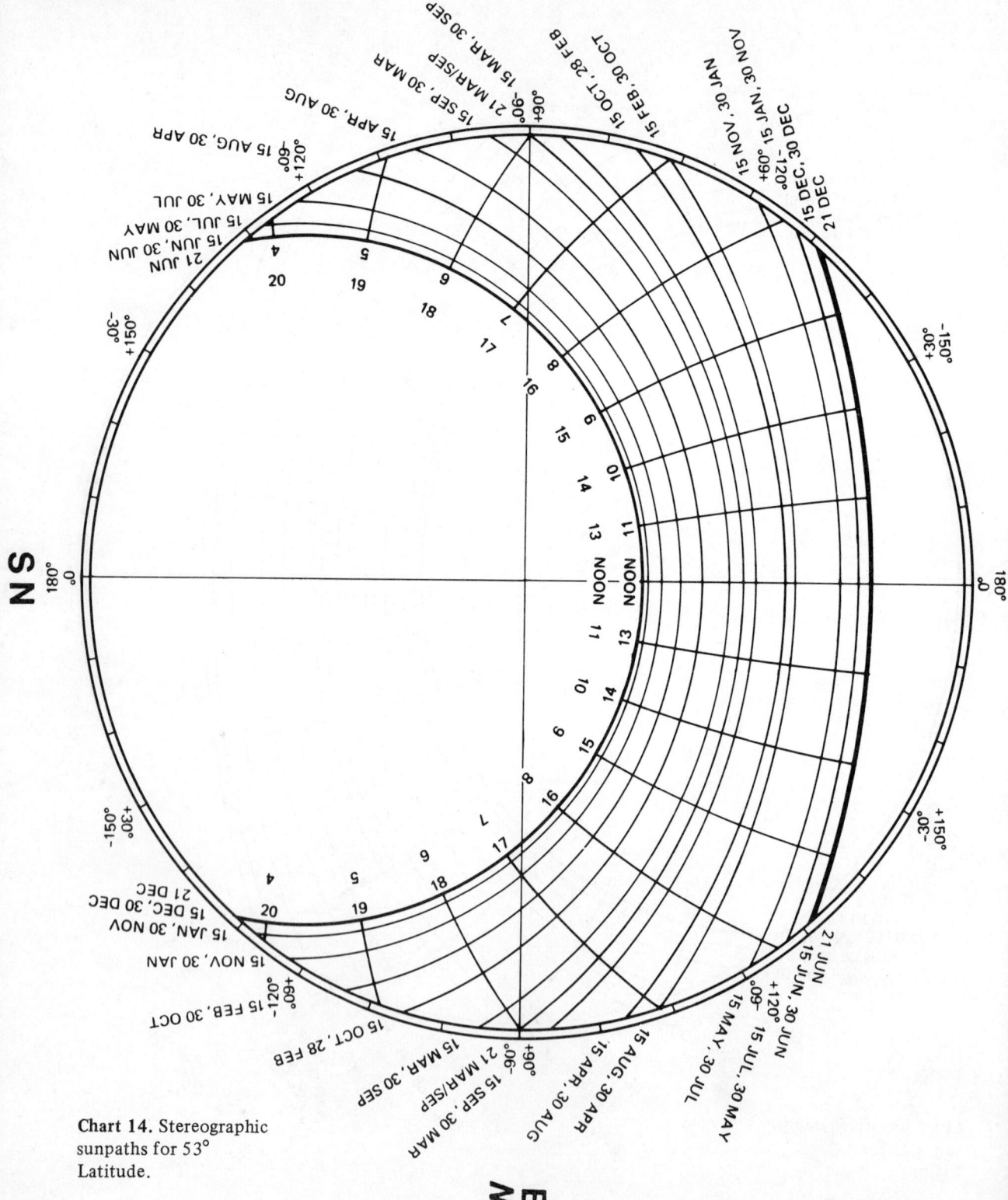

Chart 14. Stereographic sunpaths for 53° Latitude.

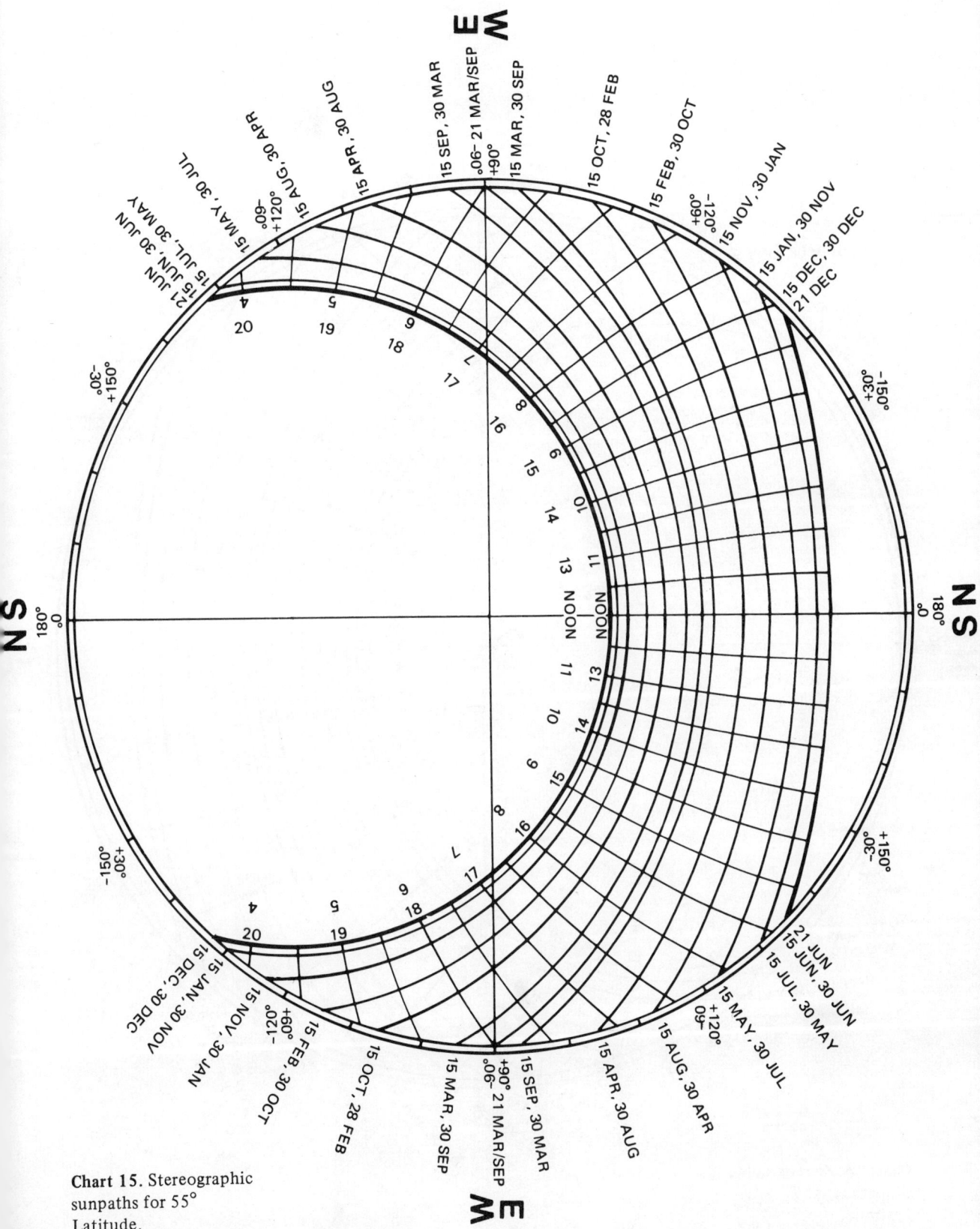

Chart 15. Stereographic sunpaths for 55° Latitude.

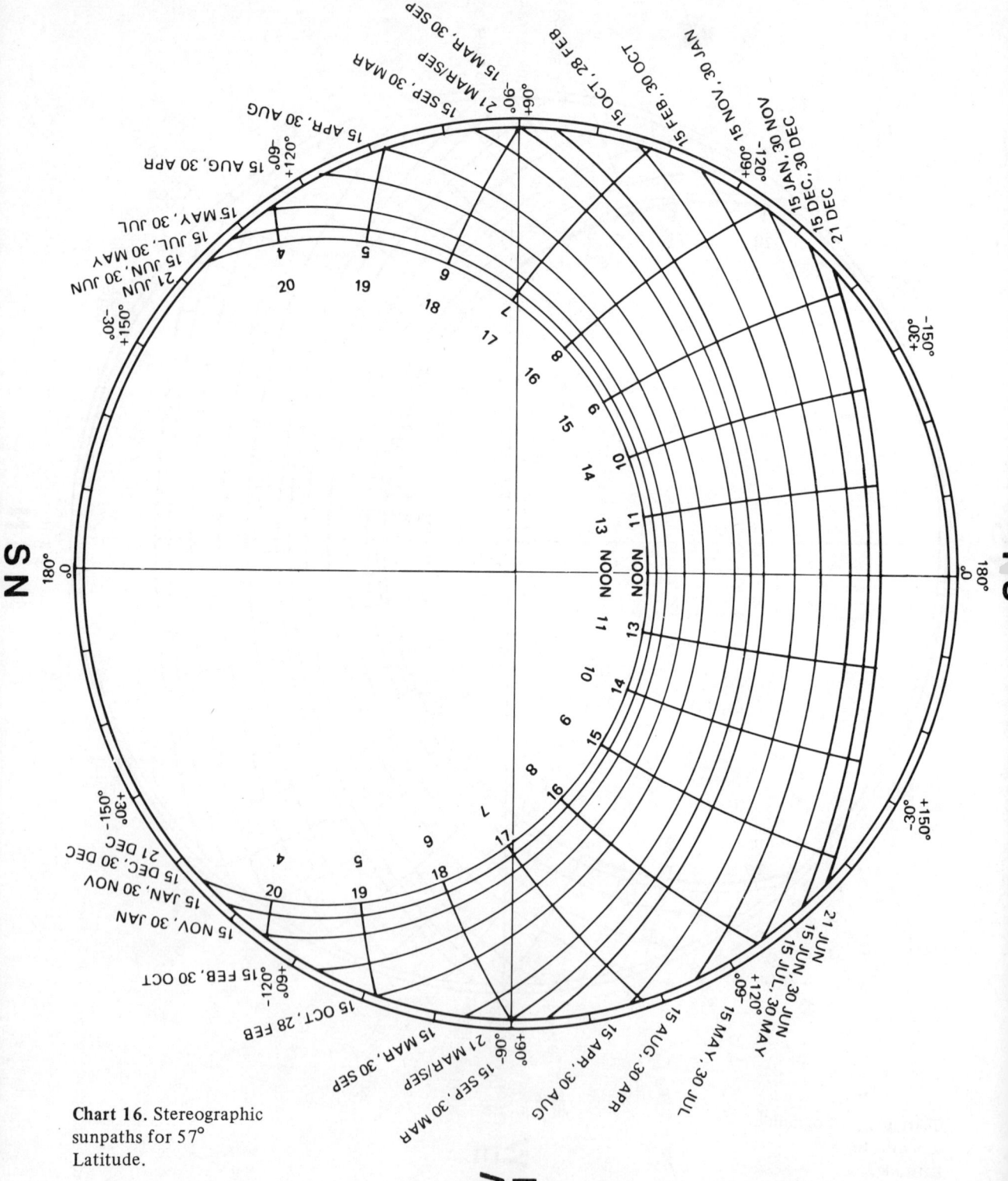

Chart 16. Stereographic sunpaths for 57° Latitude.

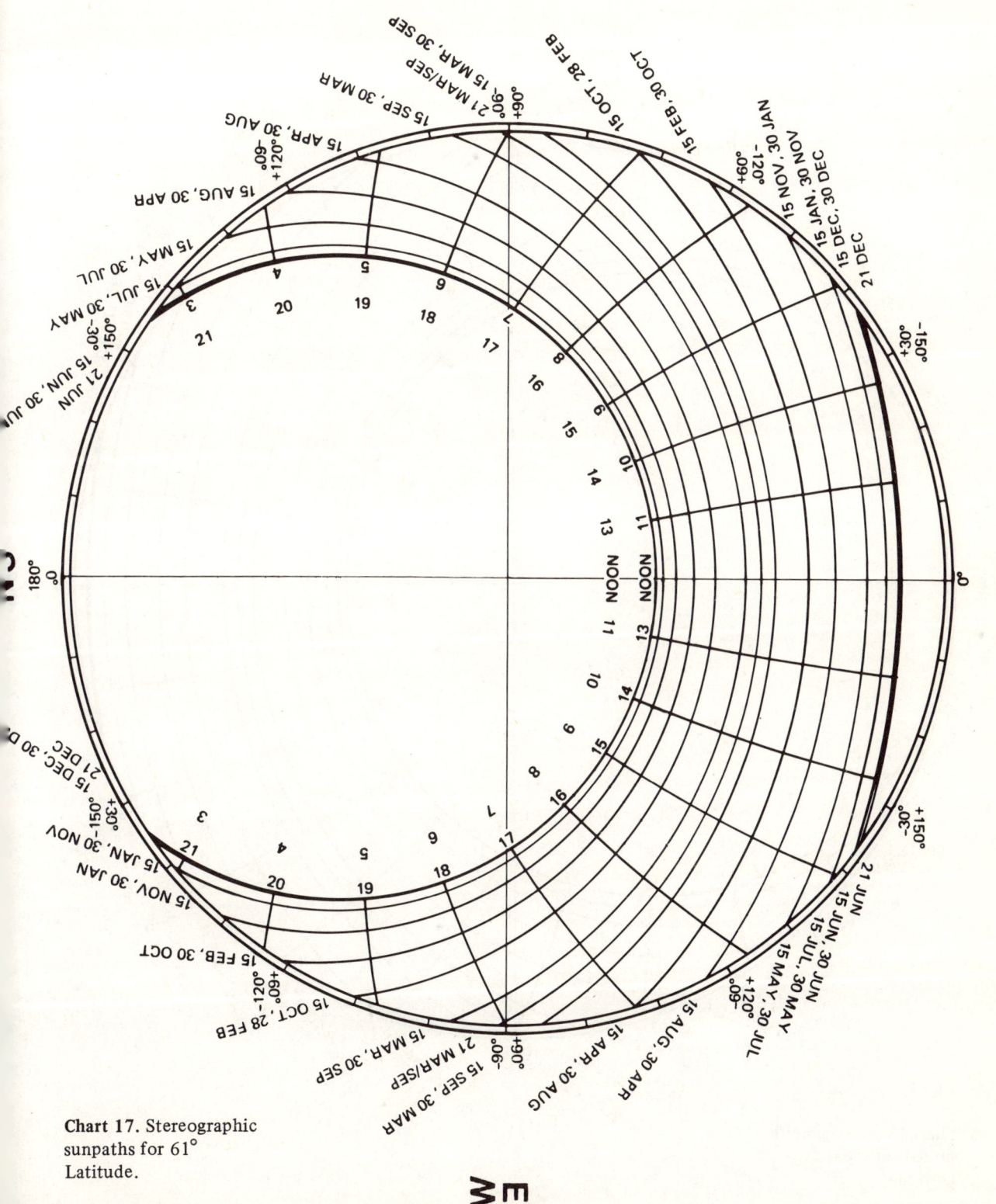

Chart 17. Stereographic
sunpaths for 61°
Latitude.

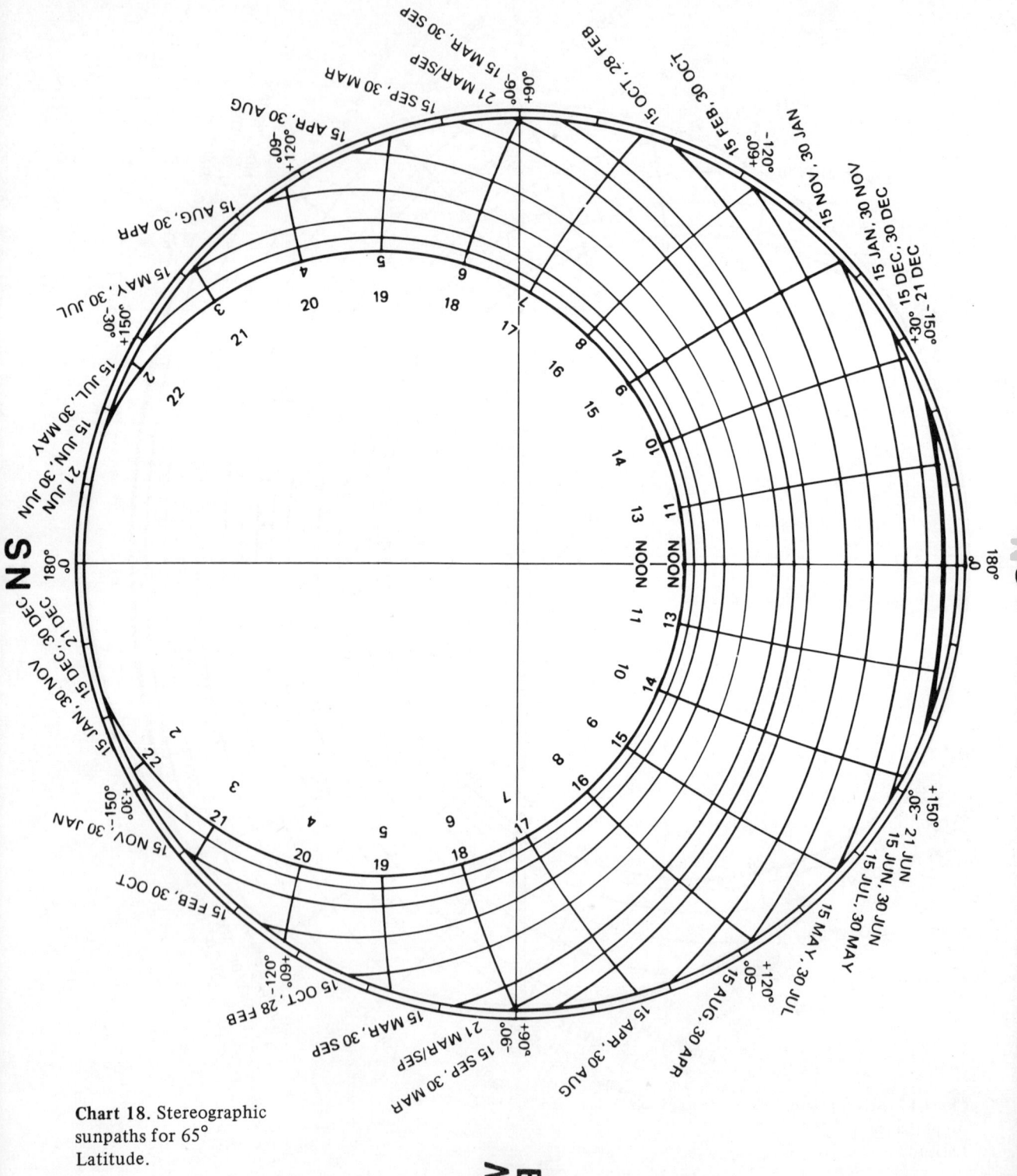

Chart 18. Stereographic sunpaths for 65° Latitude.

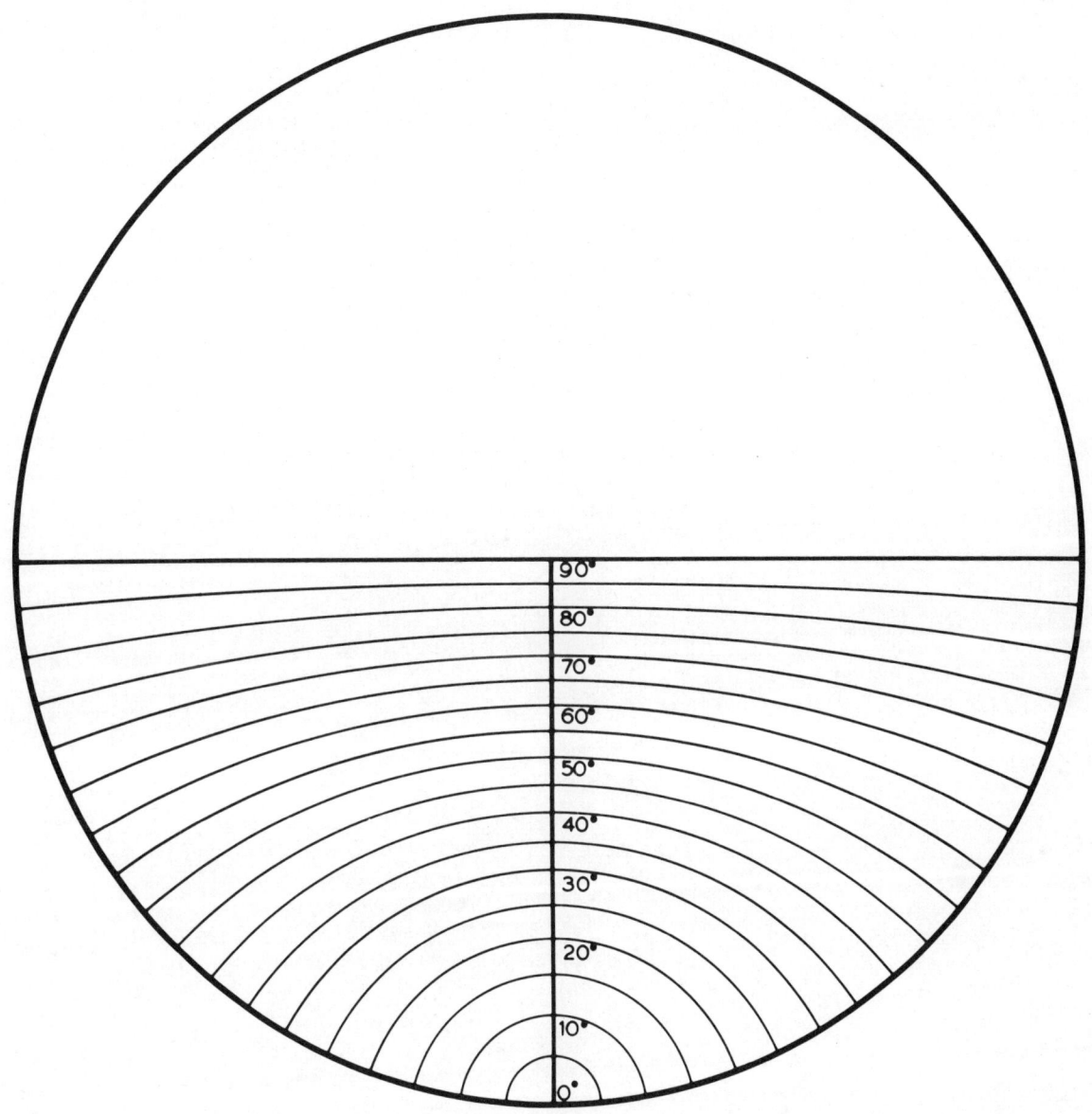

90°
80°
70°
60°
50°
40°
30°
20°
10°
0°

Overlay 1. Stereo-
graphic sunpath overlay
giving angle of
incidence *i* of direct
solar irradiance on
vertical surface.

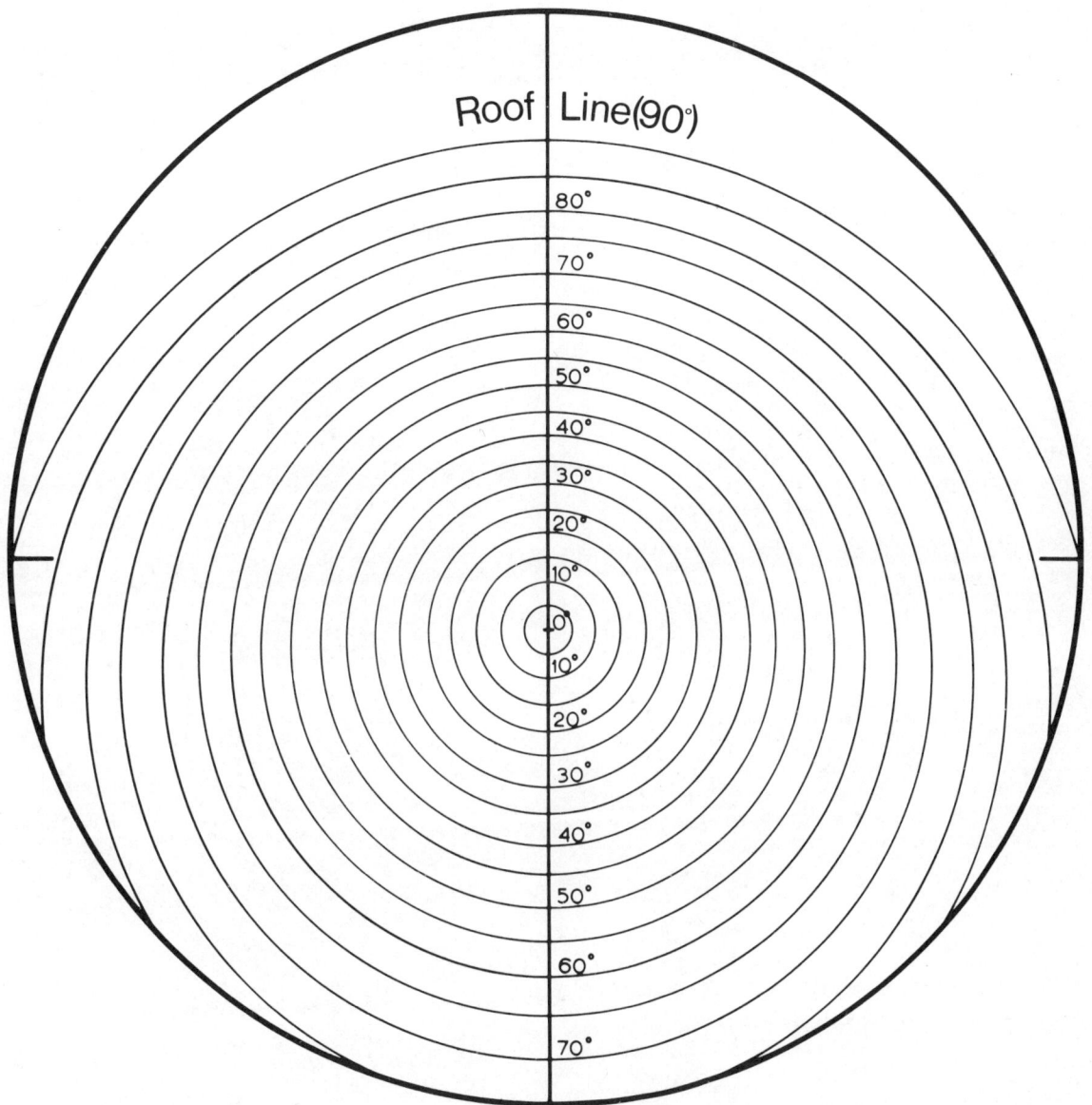

Overlay 2. Stereographic sunpath overlay giving angle of incidence *i* of direct solar irradiance on surface 15° to the horizontal.

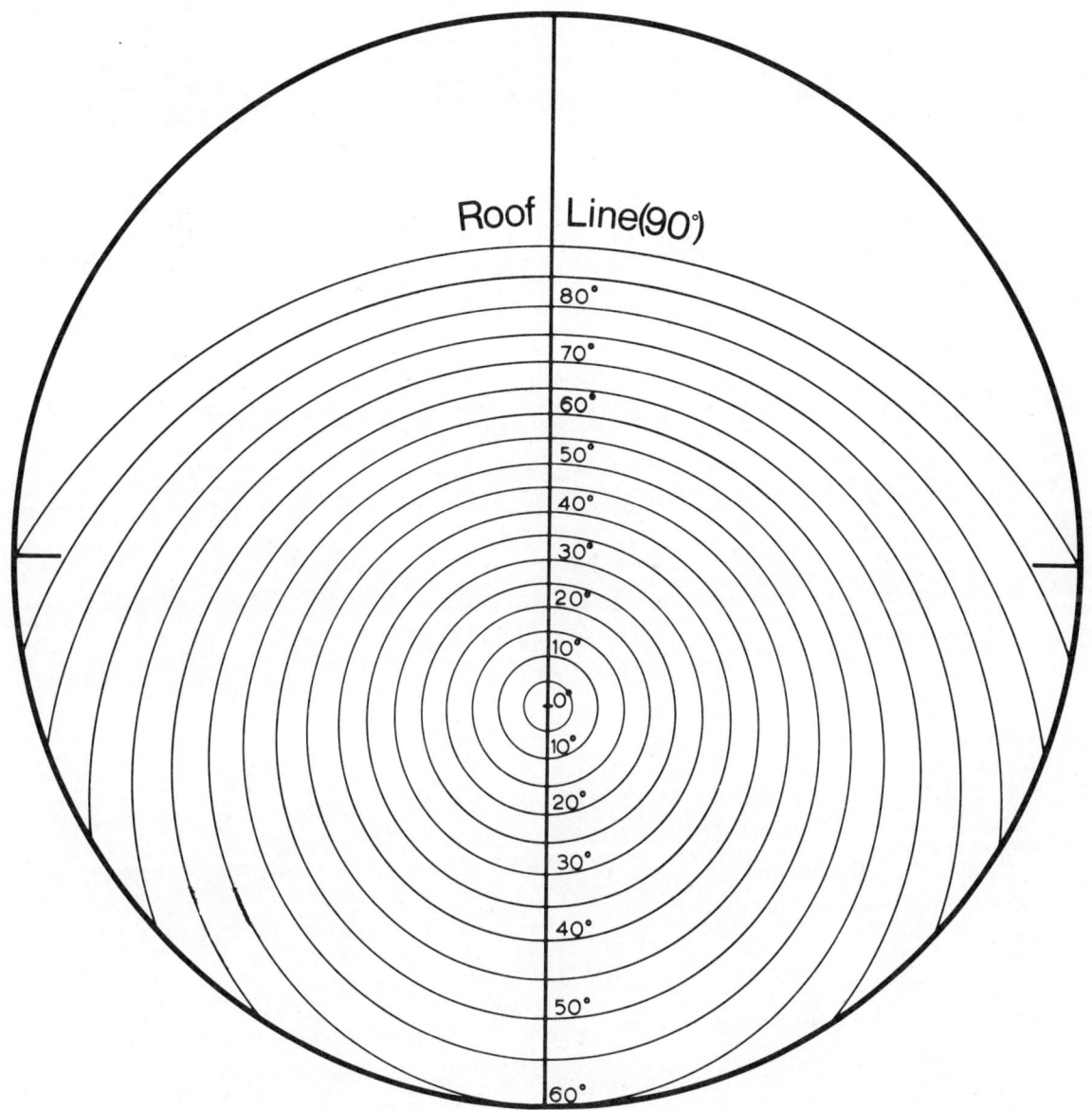

Roof Line(90°)

Overlay 3. Stereographic sunpath overlay giving angle of incidence *i* of direct solar irradiance on surface 30° to the horizontal.

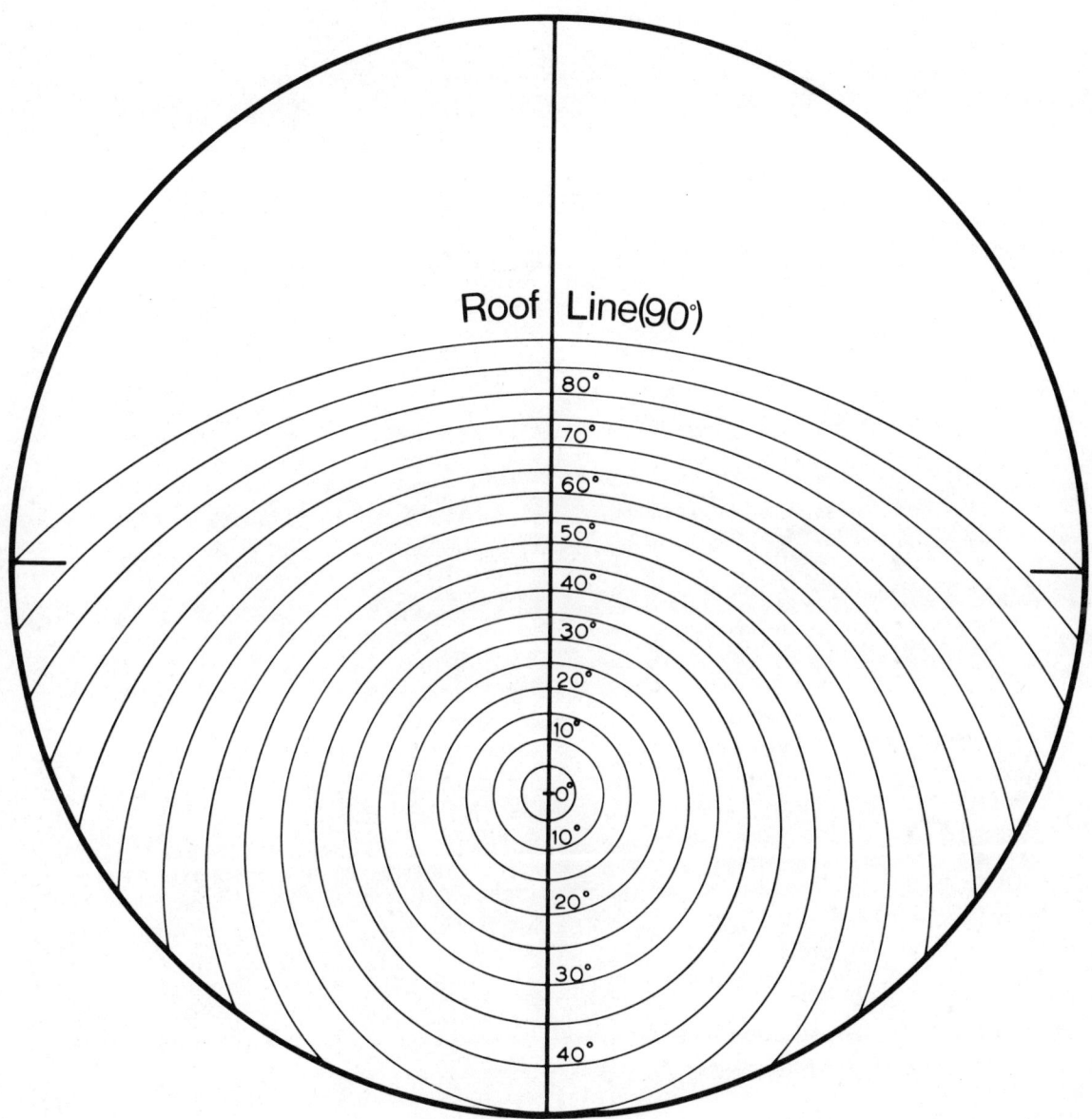

Overlay 4. Stereographic sunpath overlay giving angle of incidence *i* of direct solar irradiance on surface 45° to the horizontal.

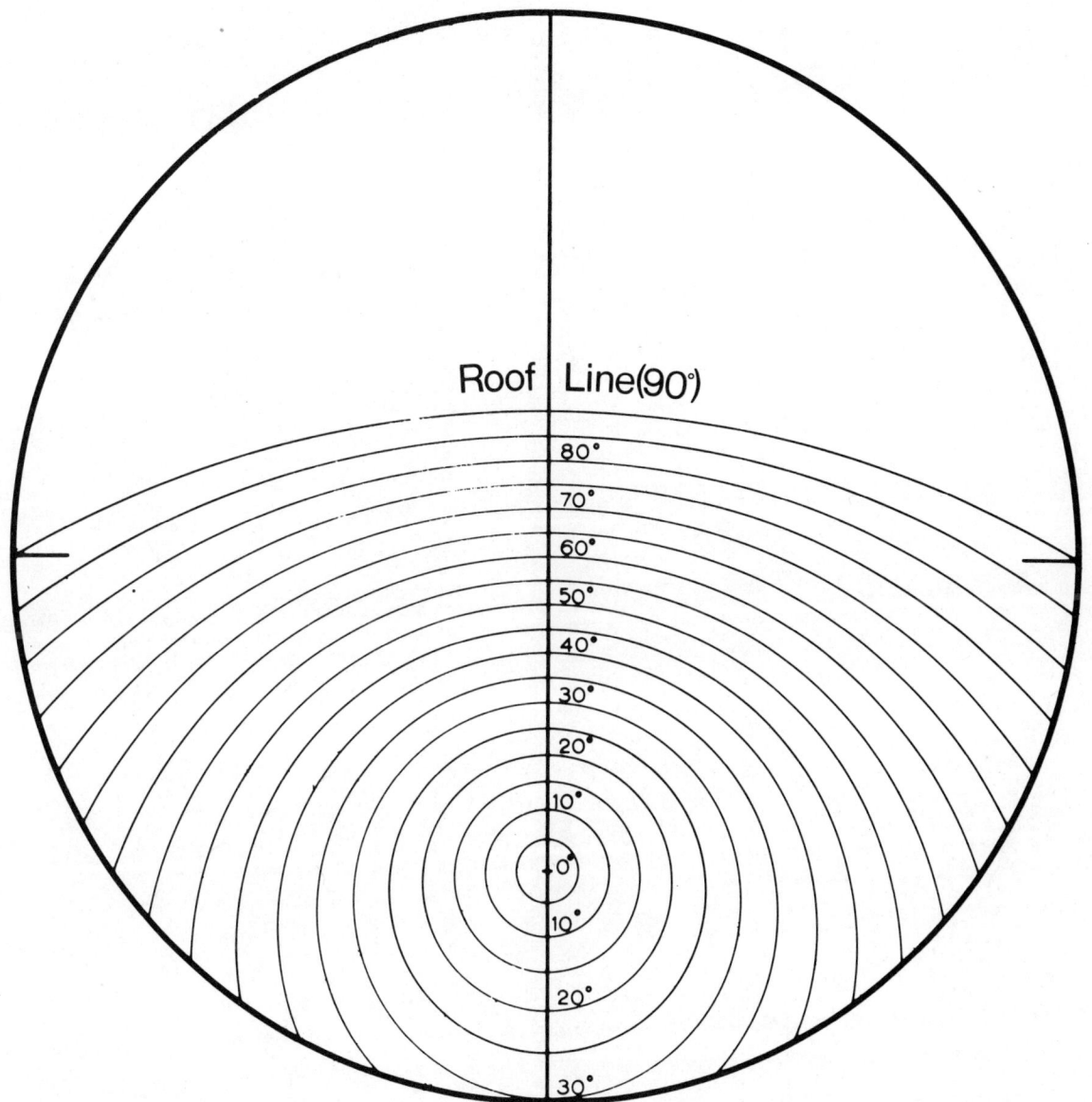

Roof | Line(90°)

80°
70°
60°
50°
40°
30°
20°
10°
0°
10°
20°
30°

Overlay 5. Stereographic sunpath overlay giving angle of incidence *i* of direct solar irradiance on surface 60° to the horizontal.

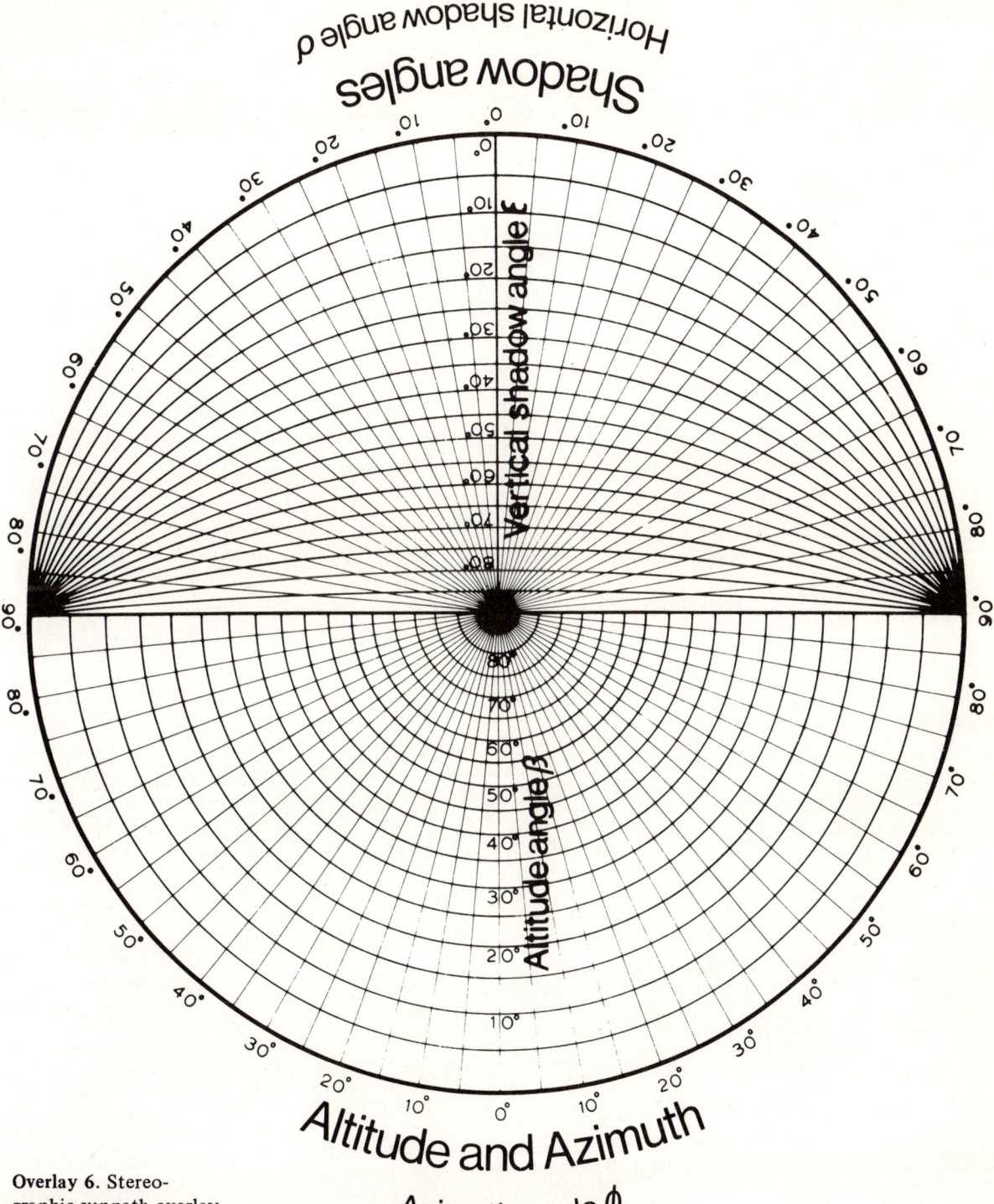

Shadow angles

Horizontal shadow angle δ

Vertical shadow angle ε

Altitude and Azimuth

Altitude angle β

Azimuth angle φ

Overlay 6. Stereographic sunpath overlay giving altitude β and azimuth φ and protractor for vertical and horizontal shadow angles ε and δ.

Normal intensity I_{DN}

Horizontal intensity $I_D\downarrow$

100
300
500
700
800
850
900
930
900
850
800
700
600
500
400
300
200
100

100
200
300
400
500
600
700
800
850
900
930

Vertical intensity I_{DV}

100
200
300
400
500
550
600

600
550
500
400
300
200
100

Overlay 7. Stereographic sunpath overlay giving direct solar irradiance on horizontal ($I_D\downarrow$) and vertical (I_{DV}) surfaces and on surfaces normal (I_{DN}) to the sun's rays. (All values are in watts per square metre.)

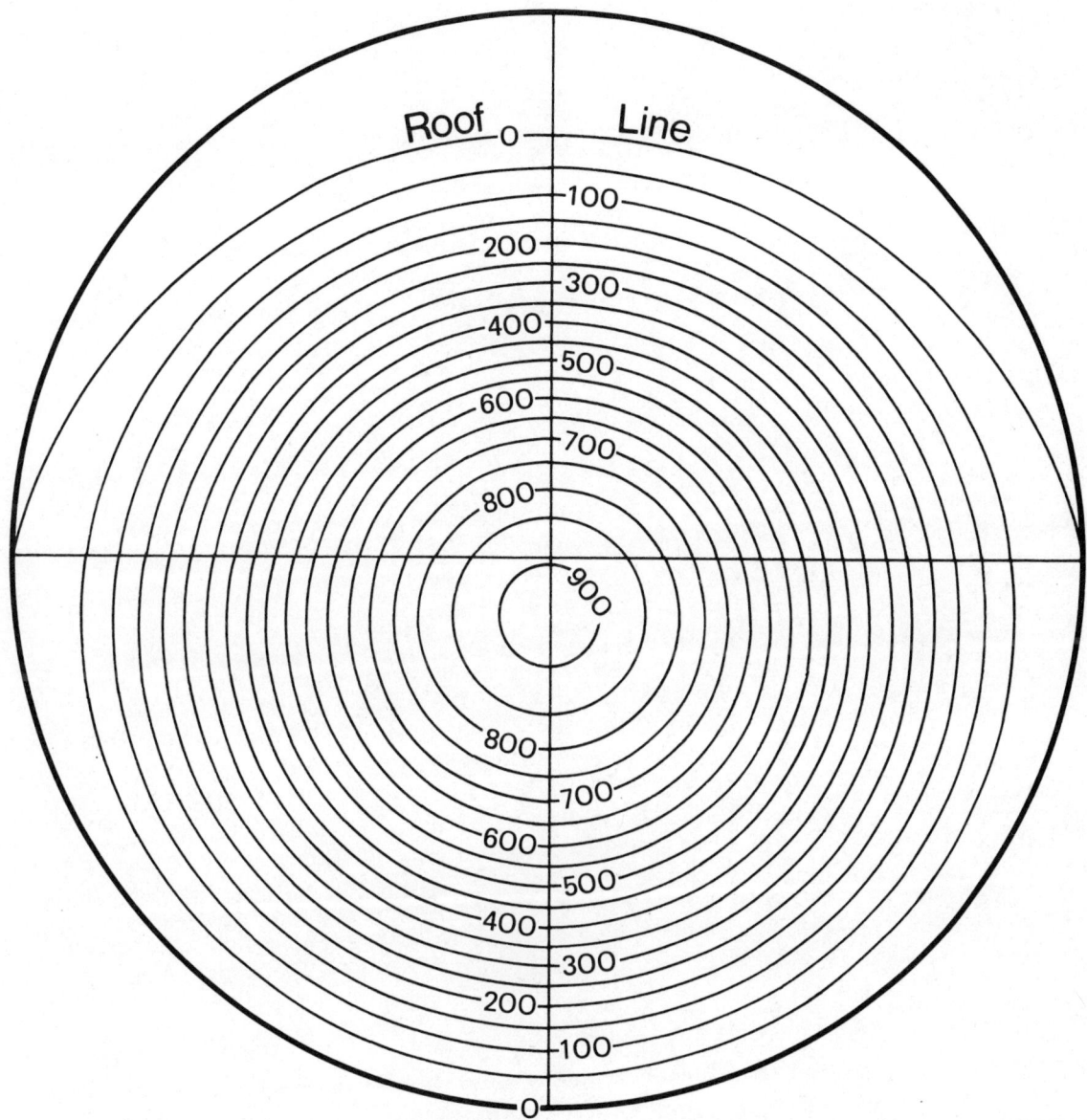

Overlay 8. Stereographic sunpath overlay giving direct solar irradiance (I_{Ds}) on a surface 15° to the horizontal (in watts per square metre).

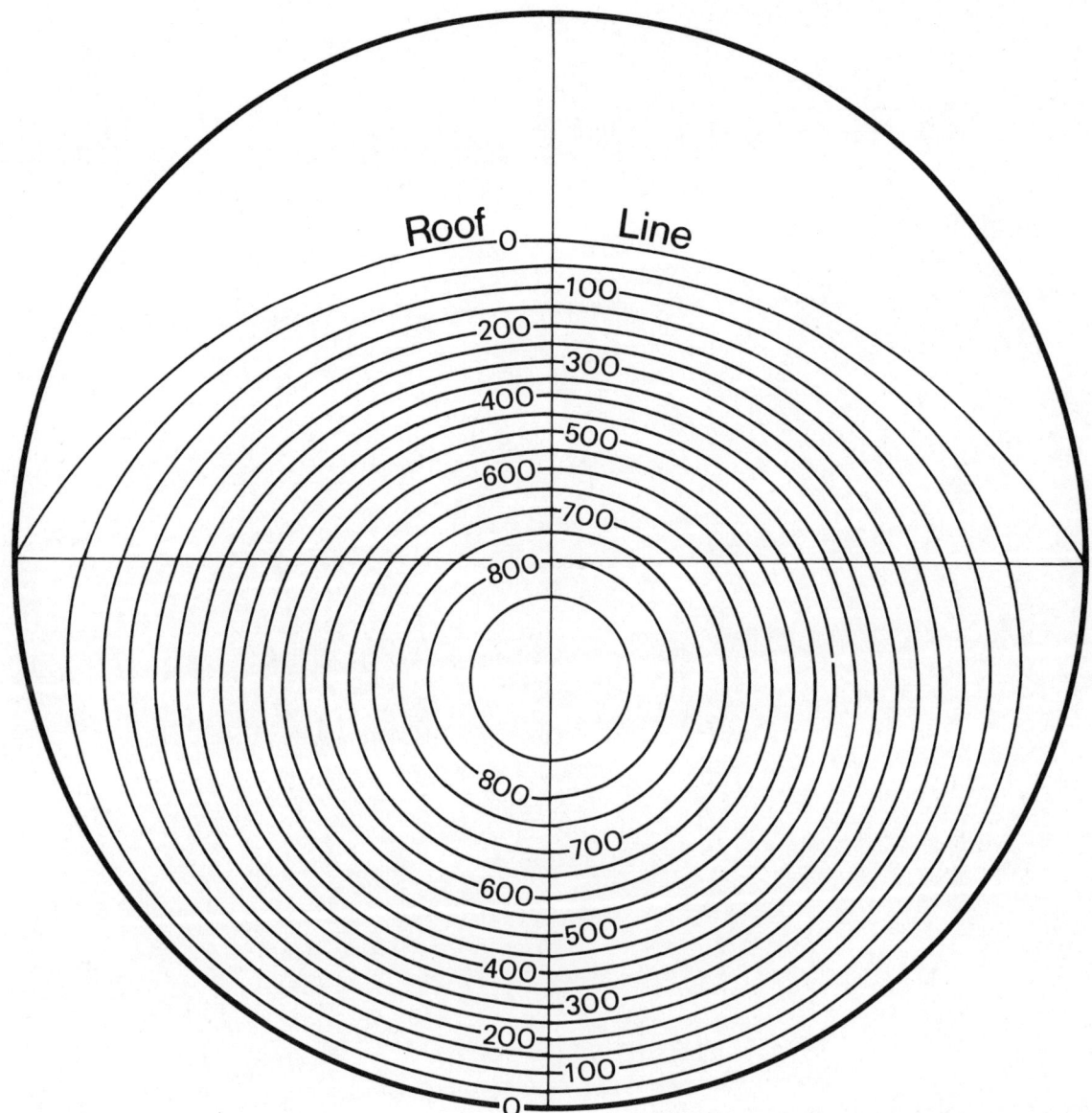

Overlay 9. Stereographic sunpath overlay giving direct solar irradiance (I_{Ds}) on a surface 30° to the horizontal (in watts per square metre).

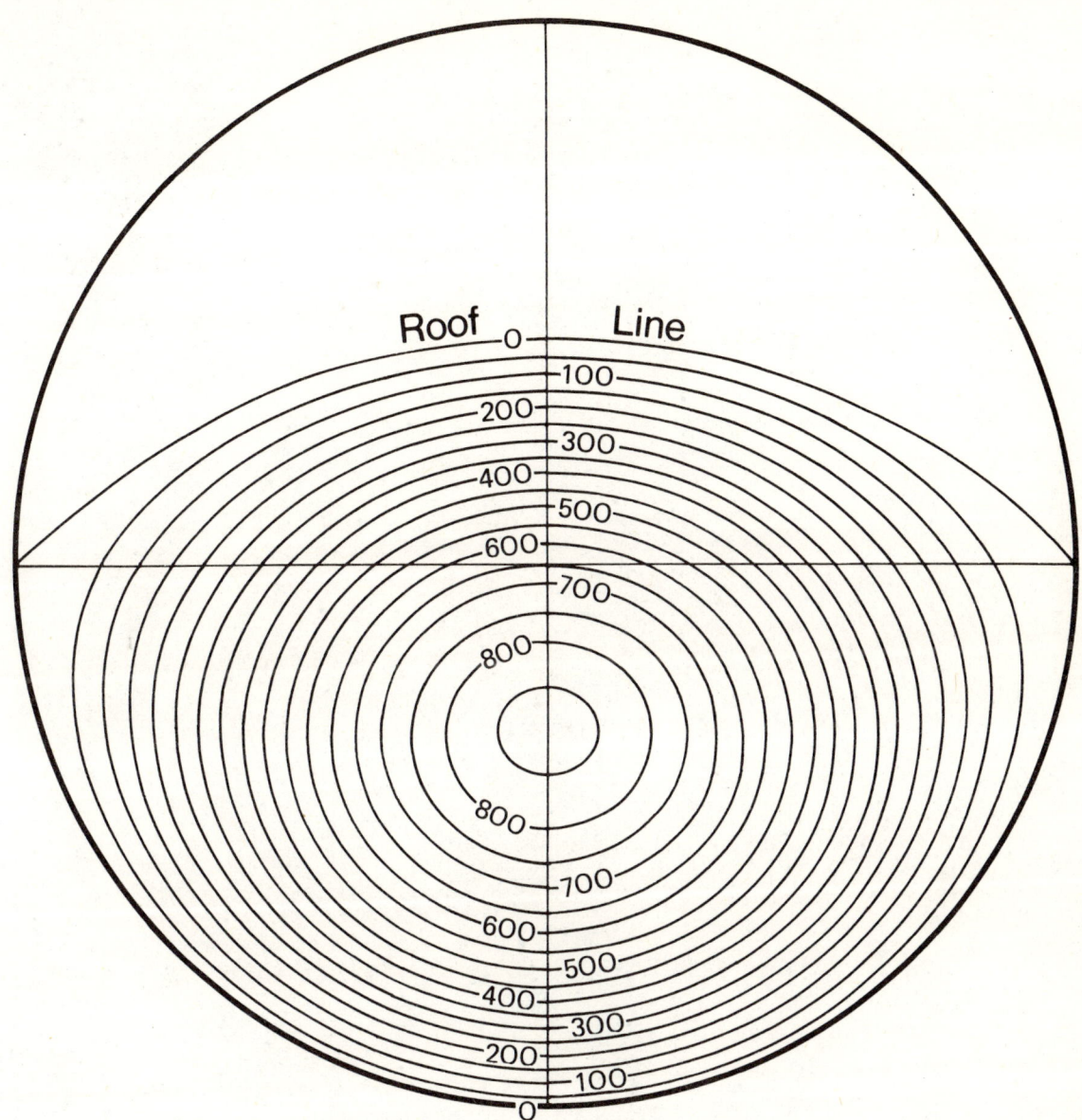

Overlay 10. Stereographic sunpath overlay giving direct solar irradiance (I_{Ds}) on a surface 45° to the horizontal (in watts per square metre).

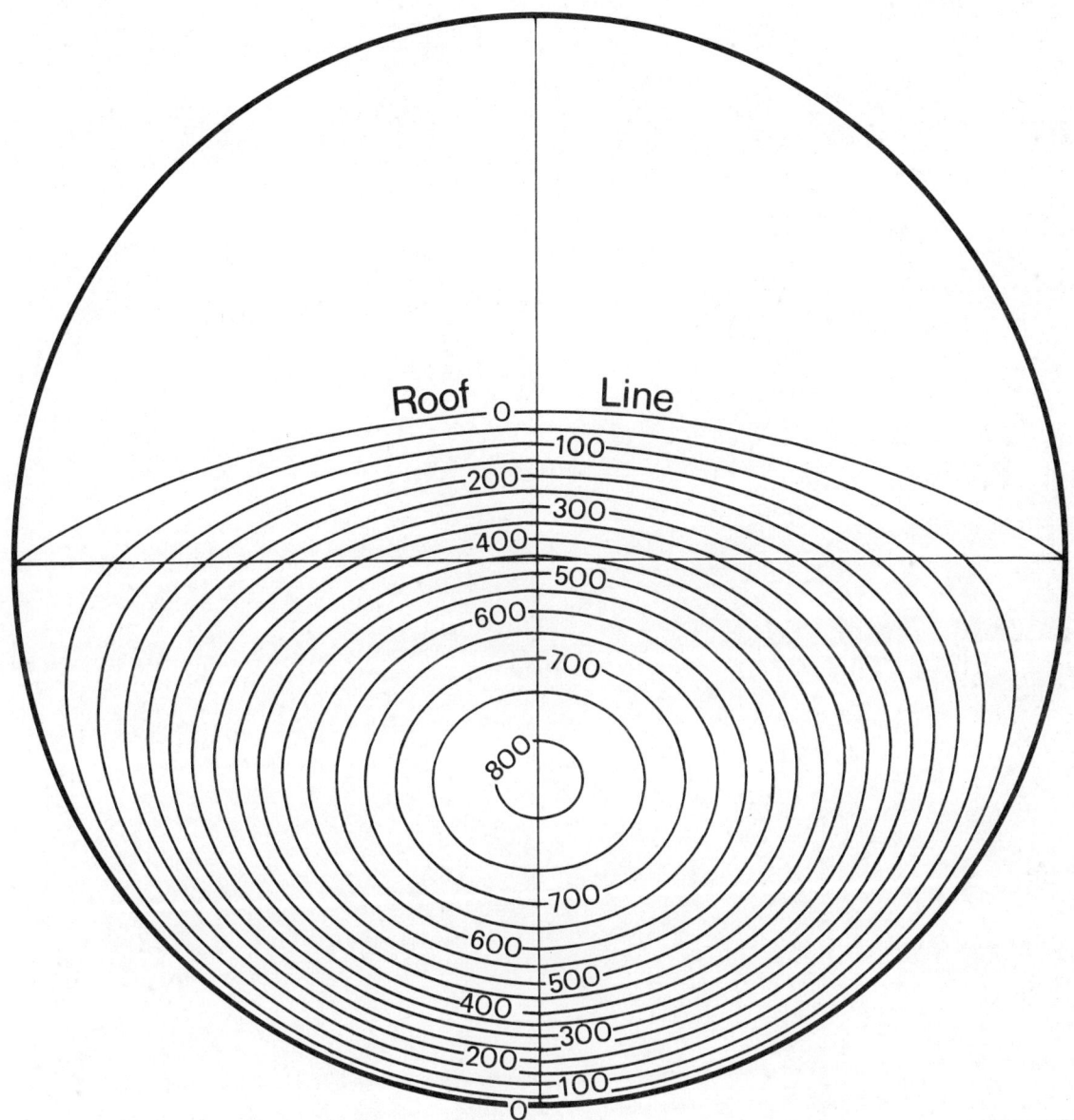

Roof 0 Line
100
200
300
400
500
600
700
800
700
600
500
400
300
200
100
0

Overlay 11. Stereographic sunpath overlay giving direct solar irradiance (I_{Ds}) on a surface 60° to the horizontal (in watts per square metre).

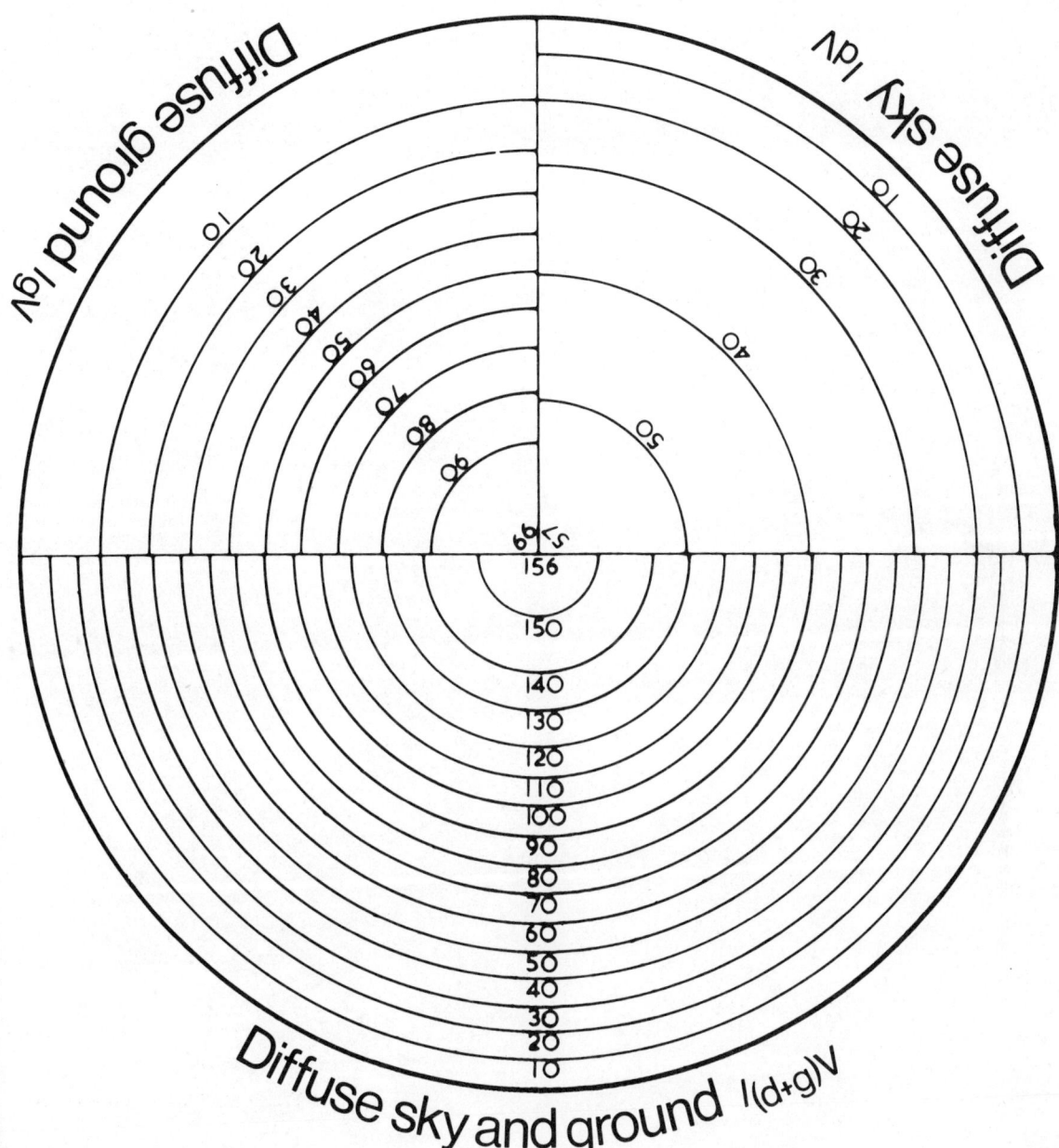

Overlay 12. Stereographic sunpath overlay giving diffuse irradiance on a vertical surface from uniform sky and ground (in watts per square metre) at 20 per cent ground reflectance.

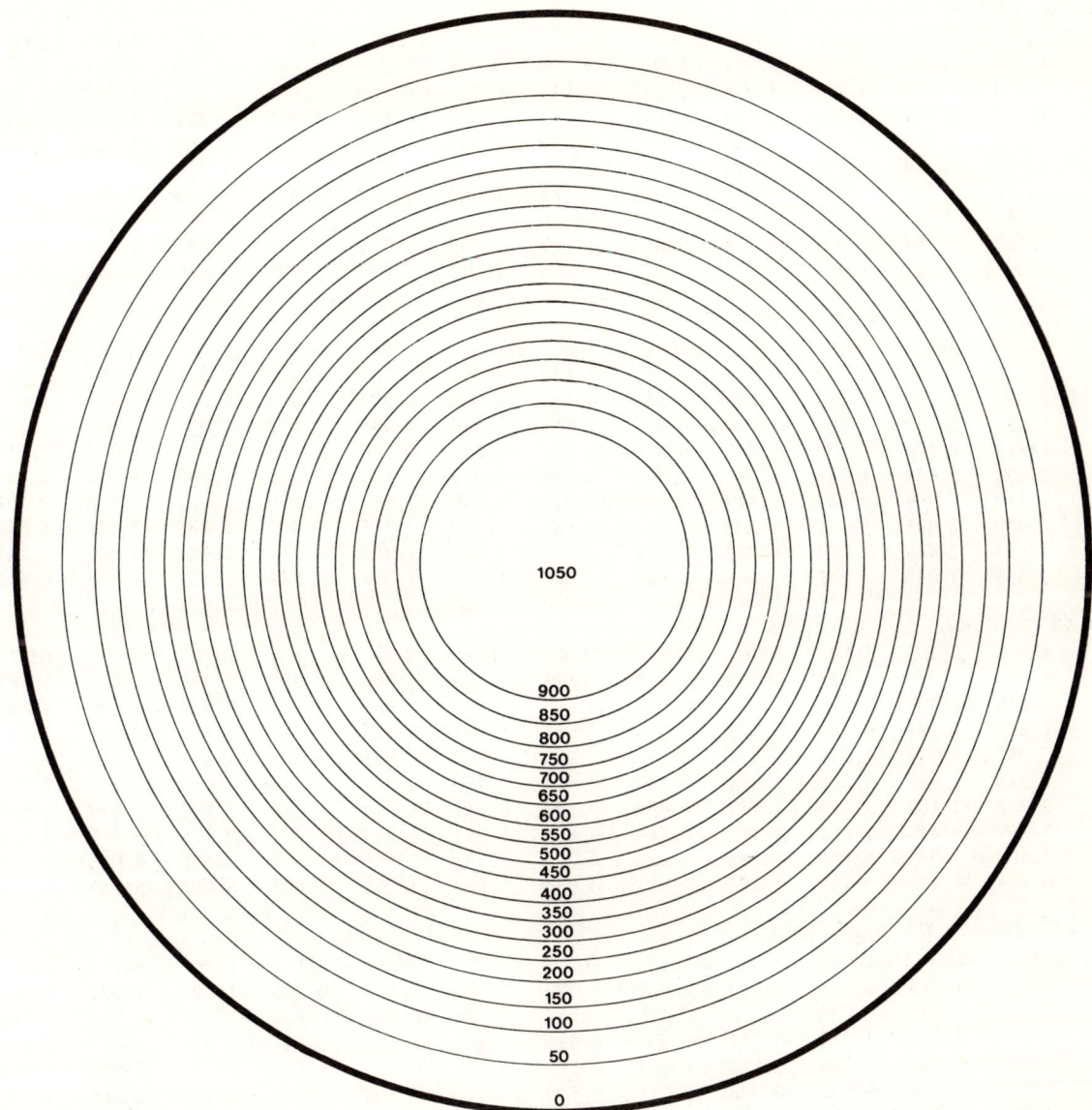

1050

900
850
800
750
700
650
600
550
500
450
400
350
300
250
200

150

100

50

0

Overlay 13. Stereo-graphic sunpath overlay giving global solar irradiance $I_G\!\downarrow$ on a horizontal surface (in watts per square metre).

APPENDIX 4B: Tables of R-values

Slope, 15°; azimuth, 0.0; south facing

LAT	JAN	FEB	MAR	APR	MAY	JUN	JLY	AUG	SEP	OCT	NOV	DEC
20	1.262	1.180	1.080	0.989	0.923	0.894	0.908	0.962	1.045	1.146	1.241	1.290
25	1.314	1.219	1.109	1.011	0.944	0.914	0.928	0.983	1.071	1.181	1.289	1.347
30	1.377	1.264	1.140	1.034	0.964	0.934	0.947	1.004	1.098	1.221	1.348	1.418
35	1.458	1.320	1.175	1.058	0.983	0.952	0.966	1.026	1.128	1.268	1.421	1.509
40	1.566	1.389	1.216	1.083	1.002	0.969	0.984	1.049	1.162	1.326	1.517	1.634
45	1.718	1.478	1.264	1.111	1.021	0.985	1.002	1.072	1.200	1.399	1.650	1.816
50	1.951	1.602	1.323	1.140	1.039	1.000	1.018	1.096	1.245	1.496	1.848	2.105
55	2.357	1.785	1.398	1.173	1.056	1.011	1.032	1.121	1.300	1.632	2.177	2.643
60	3.245	2.087	1.501	1.210	1.071	1.018	1.042	1.147	1.370	1.840	2.836	3.981

Slope, 30°; azimuth, 0.0; south facing

LAT	JAN	FEB	MAR	APR	MAY	JUN	JLY	AUG	SEP	OCT	NOV	DEC
20	1.439	1.279	1.087	0.912	0.791	0.739	0.763	0.861	1.019	1.214	1.398	1.493
25	1.538	1.354	1.142	0.955	0.831	0.778	0.802	0.903	1.068	1.281	1.491	1.602
30	1.661	1.442	1.202	1.000	0.870	0.815	0.840	0.945	1.122	1.359	1.603	1.739
35	1.817	1.549	1.270	1.047	0.908	0.851	0.877	0.987	1.180	1.450	1.745	1.916
40	2.025	1.683	1.348	1.096	0.946	0.886	0.913	1.031	1.245	1.562	1.931	2.157
45	2.319	1.856	1.441	1.149	0.984	0.920	0.949	1.077	1.319	1.703	2.188	2.507
50	2.770	2.095	1.555	1.208	1.022	0.951	0.983	1.126	1.407	1.889	2.570	3.067
55	3.554	2.448	1.702	1.272	1.059	0.980	1.016	1.177	1.513	2.152	3.205	4.107
60	5.268	3.032	1.899	1.345	1.094	1.003	1.044	1.231	1.648	2.555	4.479	6.691

Slope, 45°; azimuth, 0.0; south facing

LAT	JAN	FEB	MAR	APR	MAY	JUN	JLY	AUG	SEP	OCT	NOV	DEC
20	1.517	1.291	1.020	0.775	0.613	0.544	0.575	0.706	0.924	1.199	1.459	1.593
25	1.658	1.397	1.097	0.837	0.668	0.598	0.630	0.765	0.994	1.294	1.590	1.748
30	1.831	1.522	1.182	0.900	0.723	0.651	0.684	0.824	1.069	1.404	1.750	1.941
35	2.052	1.673	1.278	0.966	0.778	0.703	0.737	0.885	1.151	1.534	1.950	2.192
40	2.348	1.862	1.369	1.036	0.833	0.753	0.790	0.948	1.243	1.691	2.213	2.533
45	2.762	2.107	1.521	1.112	0.889	0.803	0.841	1.014	1.349	1.891	2.577	3.028
50	3.399	2.445	1.682	1.195	0.944	0.851	0.893	1.084	1.473	2.154	3.117	3.820
55	4.508	2.945	1.889	1.288	1.000	0.896	0.943	1.158	1.623	2.526	4.016	5.290
60	6.933	3.771	2.169	1.394	1.055	0.936	0.989	1.239	1.814	3.096	5.817	8.944

Slope, 60°; azimuth, 0.0; south facing

LAT	JAN	FEB	MAR	APR	MAY	JUN	JLY	AUG	SEP	OCT	NOV	DEC
20	1.492	1.215	0.883	0.589	0.402	0.327	0.361	0.509	0.766	1.103	1.421	1.586
25	1.665	1.345	0.978	0.663	0.469	0.391	0.426	0.580	0.852	1.219	1.582	1.775
30	1.877	1.498	1.082	0.741	0.536	0.455	0.491	0.652	0.944	1.354	1.777	2.011
35	2.147	1.683	1.200	0.822	0.603	0.517	0.556	0.726	1.045	1.512	2.023	2.318
40	2.508	1.914	1.335	0.908	0.671	0.580	0.621	0.804	1.157	1.705	2.345	2.736
45	3.017	2.215	1.497	1.002	0.739	0.642	0.685	0.885	1.286	1.949	2.790	3.343
50	3.797	2.629	1.694	1.104	0.810	0.703	0.750	0.972	1.438	2.272	3.452	4.312
55	5.155	3.241	1.948	1.219	0.881	0.762	0.815	1.065	1.623	2.727	4.552	6.113
60	8.125	4.252	2.290	1.350	0.953	0.818	0.877	1.166	1.858	3.426	6.759	10.588

Slope, 75°; azimuth, 0.0; south facing

LAT	JAN	FEB	MAR	APR	MAY	JUN	JLY	AUG	SEP	OCT	NOV	DEC
20	1.365	1.056	0.686	0.367	0.182	0.115	0.145	0.285	0.557	0.931	1.286	1.470
25	1.558	1.202	0.792	0.449	0.252	0.178	0.211	0.362	0.652	1.061	1.465	1.681
30	1.794	1.372	0.908	0.535	0.323	0.244	0.279	0.441	0.755	1.211	1.683	1.945
35	2.096	1.579	1.039	0.625	0.396	0.311	0.349	0.523	0.867	1.388	1.957	2.267
40	2.498	1.836	1.191	0.721	0.471	0.379	0.420	0.609	0.993	1.603	2.316	2.752
45	3.066	2.172	1.370	0.825	0.548	0.448	0.492	0.701	1.137	1.875	2.813	3.430
50	3.937	2.633	1.591	0.940	0.627	0.517	0.566	0.798	1.307	2.236	3.551	4.511
55	5.451	3.316	1.874	1.070	0.709	0.586	0.641	0.904	1.513	2.743	4.778	6.519
60	8.764	4.444	2.256	1.217	0.793	0.653	0.715	1.019	1.775	3.523	7.239	11.511

Slope, 90°; azimuth, 0.0; south facing

LAT	JAN	FEB	MAR	APR	MAY	JUN	JLY	AUG	SEP	OCT	NOV	DEC
20	1.145	0.826	0.443	0.134	0.007	0.0	0.0	0.069	0.312	0.696	1.063	1.254
25	1.345	0.976	0.552	0.213	0.052	0.008	0.026	0.137	0.410	0.831	1.249	1.472
30	1.590	1.153	0.673	0.299	0.112	0.052	0.077	0.213	0.516	0.986	1.475	1.745
35	1.902	1.366	0.808	0.390	0.180	0.109	0.140	0.294	0.632	1.169	1.758	2.099
40	2.318	1.633	0.965	0.489	0.253	0.173	0.208	0.381	0.762	1.392	2.130	2.582
45	2.906	1.980	1.151	0.597	0.331	0.240	0.280	0.475	0.911	1.674	2.644	3.283
50	3.807	2.458	1.379	0.716	0.413	0.311	0.356	0.576	1.087	2.047	3.409	4.402
55	5.375	3.165	1.672	0.850	0.499	0.383	0.434	0.687	1.300	2.572	4.679	6.481
60	8.805	4.333	2.068	1.005	0.588	0.456	0.514	0.808	1.571	3.379	7.227	11.649

Slope, 15°; azimuth, 45.0; south-west and south-east facing

LAT	JAN	FEB	MAR	APR	MAY	JUN	JLY	AUG	SEP	OCT	NOV	DEC
20	1.131	1.089	1.039	0.992	0.958	0.943	0.950	0.978	1.021	1.072	1.120	1.145
25	1.159	1.110	1.055	1.005	0.969	0.953	0.961	0.990	1.035	1.091	1.146	1.175
30	1.193	1.135	1.072	1.018	0.980	0.964	0.971	1.002	1.051	1.113	1.178	1.214
35	1.237	1.166	1.092	1.031	0.991	0.974	0.982	1.015	1.068	1.140	1.218	1.263
40	1.295	1.204	1.115	1.046	1.002	0.984	0.992	1.028	1.088	1.172	1.270	1.330
45	1.377	1.254	1.143	1.063	1.014	0.993	1.003	1.042	1.111	1.213	1.342	1.427
50	1.501	1.322	1.178	1.082	1.025	1.002	1.013	1.057	1.138	1.268	1.449	1.580
55	1.716	1.423	1.224	1.103	1.037	1.009	1.022	1.074	1.172	1.344	1.624	1.862
60	2.179	1.588	1.285	1.129	1.047	1.013	1.029	1.093	1.217	1.461	1.970	2.557

Slope, 30°; azimuth, 45.0; south-west and south-east facing

LAT	JAN	FEB	MAR	APR	MAY	JUN	JLY	AUG	SEP	OCT	NOV	DEC
20	1.201	1.123	1.031	0.945	0.883	0.855	0.868	0.920	0.998	1.092	1.181	1.227
25	1.256	1.165	1.062	0.970	0.905	0.876	0.889	0.943	1.026	1.130	1.232	1.287
30	1.323	1.215	1.097	0.996	0.926	0.896	0.910	0.967	1.057	1.174	1.294	1.361
35	1.409	1.276	1.137	1.024	0.949	0.917	0.932	0.992	1.092	1.227	1.373	1.458
40	1.522	1.351	1.184	1.055	0.973	0.938	0.954	1.020	1.132	1.291	1.475	1.588
45	1.681	1.450	1.242	1.090	0.997	0.959	0.976	1.051	1.180	1.373	1.616	1.776
50	1.923	1.585	1.313	1.131	1.024	0.980	1.000	1.085	1.237	1.481	1.823	2.072
55	2.336	1.782	1.405	1.178	1.051	1.000	1.023	1.123	1.308	1.633	2.162	2.614
60	3.226	2.103	1.531	1.235	1.079	1.016	1.045	1.167	1.401	1.863	2.828	3.946

Slope, 45°; azimuth, 45.0; south-west and south-east facing

LAT	JAN	FEB	MAR	APR	MAY	JUN	JLY	AUG	SEP	OCT	NOV	DEC
20	1.204	1.039	0.975	0.861	0.779	0.741	0.759	0.827	0.931	1.057	1.177	1.240
25	1.282	1.159	1.019	0.895	0.808	0.769	0.787	0.859	0.971	1.111	1.250	1.325
30	1.377	1.230	1.069	0.932	0.839	0.798	0.817	0.893	1.015	1.174	1.338	1.430
35	1.499	1.316	1.127	0.973	0.871	0.828	0.848	0.930	1.066	1.249	1.450	1.566
40	1.660	1.424	1.195	1.019	0.906	0.858	0.880	0.971	1.124	1.342	1.595	1.751
45	1.885	1.565	1.278	1.070	0.943	0.890	0.914	1.016	1.193	1.459	1.794	2.016
50	2.226	1.757	1.381	1.130	0.983	0.923	0.951	1.067	1.276	1.614	2.087	2.433
55	2.808	2.037	1.515	1.201	1.027	0.956	0.988	1.126	1.381	1.830	2.565	3.195
60	4.058	2.491	1.697	1.287	1.073	0.986	1.026	1.194	1.517	2.158	3.502	5.068

Slope, 60°; azimuth, 45.0; south-west and south-east facing

LAT	JAN	FEB	MAR	APR	MAY	JUN	JLY	AUG	SEP	OCT	NOV	DEC
20	1.141	1.019	0.876	0.745	0.652	0.610	0.629	0.707	0.826	0.970	1.110	1.183
25	1.235	1.091	0.929	0.786	0.686	0.642	0.662	0.744	0.873	1.035	1.198	1.286
30	1.351	1.178	0.989	0.830	0.722	0.675	0.697	0.785	0.927	1.112	1.305	1.414
35	1.499	1.283	1.060	0.879	0.761	0.710	0.734	0.830	0.988	1.204	1.441	1.580
40	1.696	1.415	1.144	0.916	0.800	0.748	0.773	0.879	1.060	1.317	1.618	1.804
45	1.970	1.587	1.246	1.000	0.850	0.788	0.816	0.936	1.145	1.461	1.861	2.127
50	2.385	1.822	1.373	1.075	0.901	0.829	0.862	1.000	1.248	1.651	2.218	2.635
55	3.094	2.165	1.539	1.164	0.957	0.873	0.911	1.074	1.378	1.916	2.800	3.563
60	4.617	2.719	1.764	1.273	1.017	0.913	0.961	1.161	1.547	2.317	3.943	5.847

Slope, 75°; azimuth, 45.0; south-west and south-east facing

LAT	JAN	FEB	MAR	APR	MAY	JUN	JLY	AUG	SEP	OCT	NOV	DEC
20	1.018	0.890	0.742	0.608	0.514	0.471	0.491	0.569	0.690	0.839	0.985	1.061
25	1.120	0.968	0.798	0.650	0.547	0.502	0.523	0.607	0.740	0.909	1.080	1.173
30	1.247	1.062	0.863	0.697	0.585	0.536	0.558	0.649	0.797	0.993	1.198	1.314
35	1.410	1.178	0.940	0.750	0.626	0.573	0.597	0.697	0.864	1.093	1.348	1.497
40	1.627	1.324	1.033	0.811	0.671	0.612	0.639	0.751	0.943	1.218	1.543	1.744
45	1.930	1.514	1.145	0.882	0.722	0.656	0.686	0.813	1.037	1.377	1.812	2.101
50	2.389	1.774	1.287	0.965	0.778	0.702	0.737	0.885	1.152	1.588	2.207	2.663
55	3.175	2.154	1.471	1.065	0.841	0.751	0.792	0.968	1.297	1.883	2.851	3.691
60	4.865	2.769	1.722	1.188	0.910	0.798	0.849	1.066	1.487	2.328	4.118	6.227

Slope, 90°; azimuth, 45.0; south-west and south-east facing

LAT	JAN	FEB	MAR	APR	MAY	JUN	JLY	AUG	SEP	OCT	NOV	DEC
20	0.846	0.725	0.586	0.462	0.376	0.338	0.356	0.426	0.538	0.677	0.815	0.888
25	0.948	0.801	0.639	0.500	0.405	0.364	0.383	0.460	0.585	0.745	0.909	0.999
30	1.075	0.895	0.703	0.544	0.439	0.393	0.414	0.500	0.640	0.827	1.027	1.140
35	1.239	1.010	0.779	0.595	0.476	0.426	0.449	0.545	0.705	0.928	1.177	1.325
40	1.459	1.158	0.871	0.655	0.520	0.463	0.489	0.597	0.783	1.053	1.375	1.577
45	1.768	1.351	0.985	0.725	0.569	0.505	0.534	0.658	0.878	1.215	1.649	1.941
50	2.238	1.617	1.129	0.809	0.625	0.550	0.584	0.730	0.995	1.430	2.053	2.516
55	3.044	2.006	1.317	0.911	0.689	0.599	0.640	0.814	1.143	1.732	2.714	3.572
60	4.783	2.637	1.575	1.037	0.759	0.647	0.698	0.916	1.338	2.189	4.017	6.165

Slope, 15°; azimuth, 90.0; east and west facing

LAT	JAN	FEB	MAR	APR	MAY	JUN	JLY	AUG	SEP	OCT	NOV	DEC
20	0.862	0.893	0.932	0.969	0.996	1.008	1.003	0.980	0.946	0.906	0.870	0.851
25	0.843	0.879	0.921	0.959	0.987	1.000	0.994	0.971	0.936	0.893	0.853	0.831
30	0.822	0.863	0.909	0.950	0.979	0.991	0.986	0.962	0.925	0.879	0.833	0.807
35	0.796	0.844	0.897	0.941	0.971	0.984	0.978	0.953	0.914	0.863	0.809	0.778
40	0.763	0.822	0.883	0.931	0.963	0.977	0.971	0.945	0.902	0.844	0.779	0.740
45	0.720	0.795	0.867	0.921	0.956	0.971	0.964	0.936	0.889	0.822	0.741	0.690
50	0.659	0.762	0.849	0.912	0.950	0.966	0.958	0.928	0.875	0.794	0.689	0.617
55	0.568	0.717	0.829	0.902	0.945	0.963	0.955	0.920	0.860	0.760	0.613	0.500
60	0.410	0.654	0.806	0.893	0.942	0.964	0.954	0.914	0.843	0.715	0.489	0.282

Slope, 30°; azimuth, 90.0; east and west facing

LAT	JAN	FEB	MAR	APR	MAY	JUN	JLY	AUG	SEP	OCT	NOV	DEC
20	0.724	0.775	0.838	0.899	0.945	0.967	0.957	0.918	0.861	0.796	0.737	0.707
25	0.698	0.754	0.821	0.883	0.929	0.950	0.941	0.902	0.845	0.777	0.713	0.680
30	0.670	0.732	0.804	0.868	0.915	0.936	0.926	0.888	0.829	0.757	0.686	0.649
35	0.639	0.709	0.787	0.854	0.901	0.922	0.913	0.874	0.813	0.736	0.657	0.614
40	0.602	0.684	0.770	0.841	0.890	0.911	0.901	0.861	0.798	0.714	0.624	0.572
45	0.559	0.656	0.753	0.830	0.880	0.902	0.891	0.851	0.784	0.691	0.585	0.522
50	0.505	0.627	0.738	0.821	0.873	0.895	0.885	0.843	0.772	0.668	0.539	0.456
55	0.433	0.594	0.726	0.815	0.870	0.893	0.882	0.839	0.763	0.644	0.480	0.363
60	0.317	0.557	0.719	0.818	0.874	0.899	0.888	0.842	0.761	0.621	0.392	0.201

Slope, 45°; azimuth, 90.0; east and west facing

LAT	JAN	FEB	MAR	APR	MAY	JUN	JLY	AUG	SEP	OCT	NOV	DEC
20	0.596	0.655	0.729	0.801	0.857	0.883	0.871	0.824	0.756	0.679	0.611	0.577
25	0.573	0.635	0.711	0.784	0.838	0.863	0.851	0.806	0.739	0.661	0.589	0.553
30	0.550	0.617	0.695	0.768	0.821	0.845	0.834	0.790	0.723	0.644	0.567	0.528
35	0.527	0.599	0.682	0.755	0.807	0.830	0.820	0.777	0.710	0.628	0.546	0.501
40	0.503	0.584	0.671	0.746	0.797	0.820	0.809	0.767	0.701	0.614	0.524	0.473
45	0.477	0.570	0.665	0.741	0.791	0.813	0.803	0.762	0.695	0.604	0.502	0.442
50	0.447	0.560	0.664	0.742	0.792	0.813	0.804	0.763	0.696	0.598	0.478	0.402
55	0.404	0.552	0.672	0.753	0.802	0.823	0.813	0.774	0.706	0.598	0.448	0.339
60	0.319	0.547	0.693	0.778	0.826	0.847	0.837	0.798	0.729	0.606	0.391	0.205

Slope, 60°; azimuth, 90.0; east and west facing

LAT	JAN	FEB	MAR	APR	MAY	JUN	JLY	AUG	SEP	OCT	NOV	DEC
20	0.484	0.540	0.613	0.686	0.743	0.770	0.757	0.709	0.641	0.565	0.498	0.465
25	0.469	0.527	0.600	0.671	0.725	0.749	0.738	0.693	0.627	0.552	0.484	0.449
30	0.456	0.517	0.591	0.660	0.710	0.734	0.723	0.681	0.617	0.542	0.471	0.435
35	0.444	0.510	0.585	0.653	0.701	0.723	0.713	0.673	0.611	0.536	0.461	0.422
40	0.435	0.507	0.585	0.651	0.697	0.717	0.708	0.670	0.611	0.534	0.454	0.409
45	0.426	0.508	0.591	0.657	0.700	0.719	0.710	0.675	0.617	0.538	0.448	0.395
50	0.415	0.515	0.605	0.671	0.712	0.730	0.722	0.688	0.632	0.548	0.443	0.375
55	0.393	0.528	0.631	0.697	0.737	0.754	0.746	0.714	0.659	0.567	0.433	0.333
60	0.327	0.544	0.673	0.742	0.780	0.797	0.789	0.758	0.703	0.598	0.398	0.213

Slope, 75°; azimuth, 90.0; east and west facing

LAT	JAN	FEB	MAR	APR	MAY	JUN	JLY	AUG	SEP	OCT	NOV	DEC
20	0.385	0.435	0.499	0.565	0.616	0.640	0.629	0.585	0.524	0.456	0.397	0.369
25	0.379	0.429	0.493	0.554	0.601	0.623	0.613	0.574	0.516	0.450	0.392	0.362
30	0.376	0.428	0.490	0.549	0.593	0.613	0.603	0.567	0.513	0.449	0.389	0.358
35	0.375	0.430	0.493	0.549	0.589	0.608	0.599	0.566	0.515	0.451	0.389	0.356
40	0.377	0.437	0.501	0.556	0.593	0.609	0.602	0.571	0.523	0.459	0.393	0.355
45	0.380	0.449	0.517	0.570	0.605	0.620	0.613	0.585	0.538	0.474	0.399	0.354
50	0.383	0.468	0.542	0.594	0.626	0.640	0.634	0.608	0.564	0.496	0.407	0.347
55	0.375	0.494	0.580	0.632	0.662	0.675	0.669	0.645	0.602	0.528	0.411	0.320
60	0.323	0.526	0.636	0.689	0.717	0.731	0.724	0.701	0.660	0.573	0.390	0.212

Slope, 90°; azimuth, 90.0; east and west facing

LAT	JAN	FEB	MAR	APR	MAY	JUN	JLY	AUG	SEP	OCT	NOV	DEC
20	0.298	0.338	0.390	0.443	0.485	0.505	0.496	0.460	0.410	0.355	0.308	0.285
25	0.298	0.339	0.389	0.439	0.476	0.494	0.486	0.454	0.408	0.355	0.309	0.285
30	0.302	0.343	0.393	0.439	0.473	0.489	0.482	0.453	0.410	0.360	0.312	0.288
35	0.308	0.352	0.401	0.445	0.476	0.490	0.483	0.458	0.418	0.369	0.320	0.293
40	0.317	0.365	0.415	0.457	0.485	0.497	0.492	0.469	0.432	0.383	0.330	0.300
45	0.329	0.384	0.437	0.477	0.502	0.513	0.508	0.487	0.453	0.403	0.344	0.307
50	0.340	0.410	0.468	0.506	0.529	0.539	0.534	0.516	0.484	0.432	0.360	0.310
55	0.342	0.444	0.512	0.550	0.570	0.579	0.575	0.558	0.528	0.471	0.374	0.294
60	0.303	0.484	0.574	0.612	0.631	0.641	0.636	0.620	0.592	0.524	0.364	0.201

Slope, 15°; azimuth, 135.0; north-west and north-east facing

LAT	JAN	FEB	MAR	APR	MAY	JUN	JLY	AUG	SEP	OCT	NOV	DEC
20	0.680	0.757	0.852	0.944	1.012	1.043	1.029	0.972	0.887	0.789	0.700	0.655
25	0.632	0.719	0.824	0.922	0.992	1.024	1.009	0.951	0.862	0.754	0.654	0.602
30	0.573	0.675	0.793	0.900	0.973	1.005	0.990	0.930	0.835	0.715	0.599	0.538
35	0.500	0.622	0.759	0.876	0.954	0.988	0.973	0.909	0.805	0.669	0.532	0.457
40	0.407	0.557	0.719	0.851	0.936	0.972	0.956	0.887	0.772	0.614	0.447	0.353
45	0.286	0.475	0.671	0.824	0.919	0.959	0.941	0.865	0.733	0.545	0.336	0.217
50	0.129	0.368	0.613	0.796	0.904	0.948	0.928	0.842	0.689	0.456	0.191	0.050
55	0.008	0.225	0.540	0.765	0.892	0.944	0.920	0.820	0.634	0.339	0.041	0.000
60	0.000	0.072	0.443	0.731	0.886	0.951	0.921	0.799	0.566	0.185	0.000	0.000

Slope, 30°; azimuth, 135.0; north-west and north-east facing

LAT	JAN	FEB	MAR	APR	MAY	JUN	JLY	AUG	SEP	OCT	NOV	DEC
20	0.342	0.473	0.648	0.825	0.956	1.015	0.988	0.878	0.715	0.530	0.374	0.301
25	0.260	0.403	0.594	0.782	0.917	0.977	0.949	0.838	0.666	0.466	0.295	0.215
30	0.167	0.324	0.535	0.738	0.879	0.942	0.913	0.797	0.613	0.394	0.205	0.119
35	0.068	0.234	0.469	0.692	0.843	0.909	0.879	0.756	0.556	0.311	0.106	0.025
40	0.005	0.133	0.394	0.644	0.809	0.879	0.847	0.714	0.492	0.216	0.022	0.000
45	0.000	0.041	0.306	0.593	0.776	0.852	0.817	0.671	0.419	0.112	0.000	0.000
50	0.000	0.002	0.204	0.537	0.746	0.832	0.793	0.627	0.334	0.034	0.000	0.000
55	0.000	0.000	0.104	0.477	0.723	0.823	0.777	0.584	0.235	0.002	0.000	0.000
60	0.000	0.000	0.038	0.412	0.712	0.836	0.779	0.543	0.137	0.000	0.000	0.000

Slope, 45°; azimuth, 135.0; north-west and north-east facing

LAT	JAN	FEB	MAR	APR	MAY	JUN	JLY	AUG	SEP	OCT	NOV	DEC
20	0.049	0.181	0.403	0.648	0.834	0.918	0.879	0.725	0.495	0.250	0.077	0.018
25	0.004	0.100	0.329	0.588	0.779	0.864	0.825	0.667	0.426	0.169	0.016	0.000
30	0.000	0.032	0.249	0.526	0.726	0.814	0.774	0.609	0.352	0.086	0.000	0.000
35	0.000	0.002	0.163	0.461	0.675	0.768	0.725	0.551	0.273	0.028	0.000	0.000
40	0.000	0.000	0.083	0.393	0.626	0.725	0.680	0.492	0.187	0.002	0.000	0.000
45	0.000	0.000	0.033	0.320	0.580	0.688	0.638	0.431	0.107	0.000	0.000	0.000
50	0.000	0.000	0.013	0.244	0.538	0.659	0.604	0.369	0.056	0.000	0.000	0.000
55	0.000	0.000	0.008	0.186	0.504	0.646	0.581	0.310	0.037	0.000	0.000	0.000
60	0.000	0.000	0.007	0.166	0.489	0.665	0.584	0.280	0.034	0.000	0.000	0.000

Slope, 60°; azimuth, 135.0; north-west and north-east facing

LAT	JAN	FEB	MAR	APR	MAY	JUN	JLY	AUG	SEP	OCT	NOV	DEC
20	0.000	0.002	0.144	0.428	0.655	0.758	0.710	0.522	0.244	0.025	0.000	0.000
25	0.000	0.000	0.074	0.354	0.588	0.693	0.644	0.451	0.165	0.003	0.000	0.000
30	0.000	0.000	0.031	0.278	0.523	0.631	0.582	0.380	0.094	0.000	0.000	0.000
35	0.000	0.000	0.013	0.202	0.461	0.574	0.522	0.309	0.049	0.000	0.000	0.000
40	0.000	0.000	0.008	0.142	0.401	0.522	0.466	0.239	0.031	0.000	0.000	0.000
45	0.000	0.000	0.006	0.110	0.344	0.477	0.416	0.189	0.025	0.000	0.000	0.000
50	0.000	0.000	0.006	0.103	0.305	0.442	0.375	0.172	0.023	0.000	0.000	0.000
55	0.000	0.000	0.005	0.109	0.311	0.436	0.375	0.180	0.023	0.000	0.000	0.000
60	0.000	0.000	0.006	0.128	0.360	0.503	0.434	0.210	0.027	0.000	0.000	0.000

Slope, 75°; azimuth, 135.0; north-west and north-east facing

LAT	JAN	FEB	MAR	APR	MAY	JUN	JLY	AUG	SEP	OCT	NOV	DEC
20	0.000	0.000	0.013	0.183	0.432	0.547	0.494	0.283	0.045	0.000	0.000	0.000
25	0.000	0.000	0.008	0.121	0.357	0.474	0.420	0.207	0.028	0.000	0.000	0.000
30	0.000	0.000	0.006	0.087	0.285	0.405	0.350	0.151	0.021	0.000	0.000	0.000
35	0.000	0.000	0.005	0.074	0.228	0.341	0.285	0.124	0.017	0.000	0.000	0.000
40	0.000	0.000	0.004	0.069	0.205	0.294	0.250	0.115	0.016	0.000	0.000	0.000
45	0.000	0.000	0.004	0.070	0.204	0.287	0.247	0.116	0.016	0.000	0.000	0.000
50	0.000	0.000	0.004	0.076	0.219	0.306	0.264	0.126	0.017	0.000	0.000	0.000
55	0.000	0.000	0.004	0.089	0.253	0.353	0.305	0.147	0.019	0.000	0.000	0.000
60	0.000	0.000	0.005	0.113	0.319	0.448	0.385	0.186	0.023	0.000	0.000	0.000

Slope, 90°; azimuth, 135.0; north-west and north-east facing

LAT	JAN	FEB	MAR	APR	MAY	JUN	JLY	AUG	SEP	OCT	NOV	DEC
20	0.000	0.000	0.004	0.060	0.192	0.298	0.245	0.102	0.015	0.000	0.000	0.000
25	0.000	0.000	0.004	0.052	0.159	0.234	0.197	0.087	0.013	−0.000	0.000	0.000
30	0.000	0.000	0.003	0.048	0.144	0.208	0.177	0.080	0.012	−0.000	0.000	0.000
35	0.000	0.000	0.003	0.047	0.139	0.199	0.170	0.078	0.011	0.000	0.000	0.000
40	0.000	0.000	0.003	0.049	0.142	0.201	0.173	0.081	0.011	0.000	0.000	0.000
45	0.000	0.000	0.003	0.053	0.154	0.216	0.186	0.088	0.012	0.000	0.000	0.000
50	0.000	0.000	0.003	0.061	0.176	0.246	0.212	0.101	0.014	0.000	0.000	0.000
55	0.000	0.000	0.004	0.075	0.214	0.299	0.258	0.124	0.016	0.000	0.000	0.000
60	0.000	0.000	0.004	0.098	0.282	0.398	0.341	0.163	0.021	0.000	0.000	0.000

Slope, 15°; azimuth, 180.0; north facing

LAT	JAN	FEB	MAR	APR	MAY	JUN	JLY	AUG	SEP	OCT	NOV	DEC
20	0.816	0.859	0.912	0.962	1.000	1.017	1.009	0.978	0.931	0.877	0.827	0.802
25	0.790	0.839	0.896	0.949	0.988	1.005	0.997	0.965	0.917	0.859	0.803	0.774
30	0.760	0.816	0.880	0.936	0.976	0.994	0.986	0.953	0.902	0.838	0.774	0.740
35	0.722	0.789	0.862	0.923	0.965	0.984	0.975	0.941	0.886	0.814	0.740	0.698
40	0.674	0.757	0.841	0.909	0.954	0.974	0.965	0.928	0.868	0.787	0.697	0.643
45	0.611	0.717	0.818	0.895	0.944	0.966	0.956	0.916	0.849	0.754	0.641	0.570
50	0.524	0.666	0.791	0.880	0.935	0.959	0.948	0.903	0.828	0.713	0.565	0.465
55	0.394	0.598	0.759	0.864	0.927	0.955	0.942	0.891	0.803	0.660	0.454	0.303
60	0.186	0.503	0.720	0.848	0.923	0.957	0.941	0.880	0.775	0.589	0.283	0.045

Slope, 30°; azimuth, 180.0; north facing

LAT	JAN	FEB	MAR	APR	MAY	JUN	JLY	AUG	SEP	OCT	NOV	DEC
20	0.637	0.707	0.795	0.881	0.946	0.976	0.962	0.907	0.827	0.736	0.654	0.613
25	0.598	0.676	0.769	0.858	0.924	0.954	0.940	0.885	0.803	0.707	0.618	0.572
30	0.555	0.642	0.743	0.836	0.903	0.933	0.919	0.863	0.779	0.676	0.578	0.526
35	0.506	0.604	0.715	0.814	0.883	0.914	0.899	0.842	0.754	0.643	0.532	0.471
40	0.449	0.563	0.687	0.792	0.864	0.896	0.881	0.822	0.728	0.606	0.479	0.408
45	0.381	0.517	0.657	0.771	0.847	0.881	0.865	0.803	0.703	0.567	0.418	0.331
50	0.300	0.465	0.627	0.752	0.833	0.869	0.852	0.786	0.677	0.524	0.345	0.238
55	0.200	0.407	0.597	0.735	0.823	0.861	0.843	0.772	0.654	0.477	0.257	0.122
60	0.079	0.339	0.570	0.725	0.820	0.862	0.842	0.765	0.635	0.427	0.147	0.006

Slope, 45°; azimuth, 180.0; north facing

LAT	JAN	FEB	MAR	APR	MAY	JUN	JLY	AUG	SEP	OCT	NOV	DEC
20	0.480	0.560	0.664	0.768	0.848	0.886	0.869	0.800	0.703	0.595	0.500	0.454
25	0.443	0.529	0.636	0.740	0.820	0.857	0.840	0.773	0.675	0.564	0.465	0.415
30	0.405	0.497	0.609	0.715	0.794	0.830	0.814	0.748	0.650	0.535	0.428	0.374
35	0.365	0.465	0.584	0.692	0.771	0.807	0.790	0.725	0.625	0.505	0.391	0.331
40	0.323	0.434	0.560	0.672	0.752	0.787	0.771	0.705	0.604	0.477	0.352	0.284
45	0.277	0.403	0.540	0.657	0.737	0.772	0.756	0.690	0.586	0.451	0.310	0.233
50	0.226	0.372	0.525	0.647	0.728	0.764	0.748	0.681	0.573	0.427	0.265	0.173
55	0.160	0.341	0.516	0.646	0.730	0.766	0.749	0.681	0.569	0.405	0.209	0.094
60	0.070	0.304	0.517	0.659	0.747	0.786	0.768	0.696	0.576	0.385	0.131	0.005

Slope, 60°; azimuth, 180.0; north facing

LAT	JAN	FEB	MAR	APR	MAY	JUN	JLY	AUG	SEP	OCT	NOV	DEC
20	0.356	0.433	0.535	0.639	0.722	0.762	0.744	0.673	0.574	0.466	0.375	0.331
25	0.329	0.409	0.512	0.614	0.694	0.732	0.714	0.647	0.550	0.443	0.349	0.304
30	0.304	0.387	0.492	0.593	0.670	0.706	0.689	0.625	0.530	0.422	0.325	0.277
35	0.280	0.368	0.476	0.577	0.651	0.686	0.670	0.607	0.514	0.404	0.302	0.250
40	0.255	0.351	0.464	0.566	0.639	0.672	0.656	0.596	0.503	0.390	0.280	0.222
45	0.229	0.337	0.458	0.562	0.633	0.666	0.651	0.592	0.499	0.379	0.257	0.191
50	0.196	0.325	0.459	0.566	0.638	0.670	0.655	0.596	0.502	0.372	0.230	0.150
55	0.148	0.312	0.468	0.583	0.656	0.689	0.674	0.614	0.515	0.369	0.193	0.888
60	0.069	0.294	0.489	0.617	0.694	0.730	0.713	0.650	0.543	0.369	0.128	0.005

Slope, 75°; azimuth, 180.0; north facing

LAT	JAN	FEB	MAR	APR	MAY	JUN	JLY	AUG	SEP	OCT	NOV	DEC
20	0.263	0.329	0.418	0.511	0.586	0.622	0.605	0.541	0.452	0.358	0.279	0.243
25	0.248	0.315	0.403	0.493	0.563	0.596	0.581	0.521	0.436	0.344	0.265	0.227
30	0.235	0.304	0.392	0.480	0.546	0.577	0.563	0.507	0.425	0.334	0.252	0.213
35	0.223	0.296	0.386	0.472	0.536	0.565	0.551	0.498	0.419	0.327	0.242	0.199
40	0.211	0.291	0.385	0.471	0.533	0.560	0.547	0.496	0.419	0.323	0.231	0.184
45	0.196	0.288	0.390	0.478	0.538	0.565	0.552	0.503	0.425	0.324	0.220	0.164
50	0.175	0.288	0.402	0.494	0.554	0.581	0.568	0.519	0.439	0.329	0.205	0.134
55	0.138	0.287	0.424	0.522	0.584	0.612	0.599	0.548	0.464	0.337	0.179	0.082
60	0.067	0.279	0.457	0.569	0.636	0.668	0.653	0.597	0.505	0.348	0.123	0.005

Slope, 90°; azimuth, 180.0; north facing

LAT	JAN	FEB	MAR	APR	MAY	JUN	JLY	AUG	SEP	OCT	NOV	DEC
20	0.193	0.245	0.316	0.391	0.452	0.482	0.468	0.416	0.344	0.268	0.206	0.177
25	0.187	0.239	0.309	0.381	0.438	0.465	0.452	0.404	0.336	0.262	0.200	0.170
30	0.182	0.236	0.306	0.376	0.429	0.454	0.442	0.397	0.332	0.260	0.196	0.164
35	0.178	0.236	0.308	0.376	0.426	0.450	0.439	0.397	0.334	0.260	0.192	0.159
40	0.173	0.238	0.314	0.382	0.431	0.453	0.443	0.402	0.340	0.264	0.190	0.151
45	0.166	0.242	0.325	0.395	0.443	0.465	0.455	0.415	0.353	0.271	0.186	0.139
50	0.153	0.248	0.344	0.417	0.466	0.487	0.477	0.438	0.373	0.283	0.179	0.118
55	0.124	0.254	0.371	0.452	0.503	0.525	0.515	0.473	0.404	0.298	0.160	0.074
60	0.062	0.255	0.410	0.504	0.560	0.587	0.574	0.528	0.450	0.316	0.114	0.004

5

HEAT LOSS FROM A BUILDING UNDER STEADY-STATE CONDITIONS

5.1 Introduction

In Chapter 4 it was shown how climatic data can be used to define the external environment for design purposes. By applying the procedure described in Chapter 3 it will be found that there are many situations where this external environment is unsuitable from the point of view of comfort and, hence, the building has to act as a modifier. The fabric of the building can be considered as functioning as a filter or barrier between the external and internal environment and in this and subsequent chapters we shall consider how the fabric behaves in relation to the flow of heat and moisture.

5.2 Thermal conductivity

Consider an element under steady-state conditions such that the temperature difference $t_1 - t_2$ between the two faces is constant. Let the area of the element be A mm^2 and its thickness be l mm.

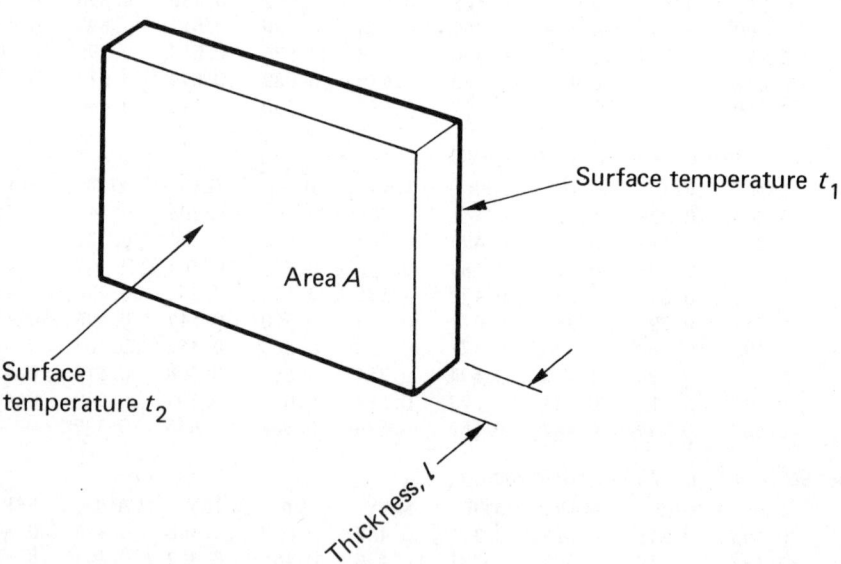

If Q = rate of heat flow between the two surfaces (in joules per second or watts), then

Q varies directly as the temperature difference, $(t_1 - t_2)$ (°C),
Q varies directly as the area, A (mm^2),
Q varies inversely as the thickness, l (mm).

Hence,

$$Q = \frac{k\,A}{l}\,(t_1 - t_2)\, \text{J s}^{-1} \text{ or W,}$$

where k is a constant:

$$k = \text{coefficient of thermal conductivity} = Ql/A(t_1 - t_2)\, \text{W m}^{-1}\, \text{K}^{-1}.$$

Tables giving the values of thermal conductivity for various building materials are published in the *ASHRAE Handbook of Fundamentals* the *IHVE Guide,* and various official specifications, and values can also be found in some Building Research Establishment publications.

5.2.1 Factors Affecting Thermal Conductivity

The value of the thermal conductivity is affected by both the density and the moisture content of the material. As a general rule, materials with a low density tend to have a low value for k, although there are exceptions. The main reason for lightweight materials having a low value for thermal conductivity is due to the presence of air-filled pores in their structure. Fig. 5.1, which is based upon data in the *IHVE Guide*, shows how the value of k for concrete changes with density; many other building materials would give similar curves.

Since water is a better conductor of heat than air, it will be seen that as the material becomes wet, i.e. the pores become filled with water, there will be a corresponding increase in the thermal conductivity.

These factors were considered in papers by Loudon [1] and by Arnold [2] and much of the information which was discussed in these papers is now included in the *IHVE Guide*, with particular reference to the effect of moisture content. It will be appreciated that this aspect could be of importance when considering building units which are likely to be subjected to rain. In order to assess the significance of this, it is necessary to have an estimate of the likely moisture content which can occur in the element under consideration. Arnold stated that from measurements obtained from heated buildings a moisture content value of 5 per cent by volume should be used for the outer leaf of a brick or concrete wall which was exposed to rain. For the inner leaf (i.e. where the material is protected from the rain) a value of 1 per cent for brick and 3 per cent for lightweight concrete should be used. In that paper it was pointed out that the French and German Building Specifications did consider the effect of moisture content and that the proposals which were being put forward for the value of k gave good agreement with those published in the German specification, but were slightly lower than those in the French specification.

Many of the proposals discussed by Arnold are now included in the *IHVE Guide* and are current British practice. The procedure for adjusting the k-value to allow for moisture contents varying between 1 and 25 per cent is described in *Building Research Establishment Digest No. 108* [3]. The method is to multiply the published k-value, which is based upon a moisture content of 1 per cent, by an appropriate 'moisture factor', the latter depending upon the assumed moisture content of the exposed element.

The following example will illustrate this method, the appropriate values for the 'moisture factor' being taken from *Building Research Establishment Digest No. 108* [3].

Fig. 5.1 Relationship between bulk density and thermal conductivity for concrete (from data given in *IHVE Guide*).

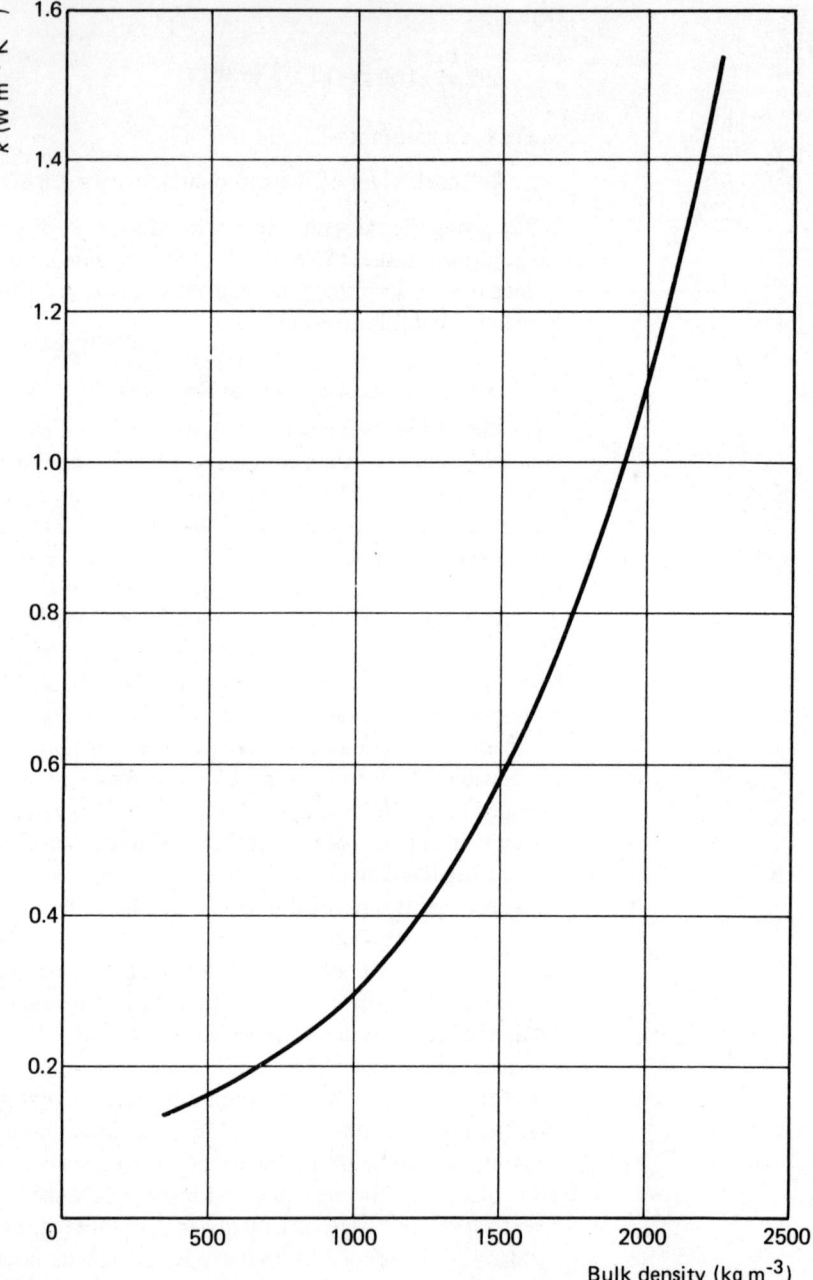

Example 5.1   A brick wall in a very exposed situation is assumed to have a moisture content of 10 per cent by volume. Thermal conductivity of brickwork at 1 per cent moisture content = 0.71 W m^{-1} K^{-1}; moisture factor for 1 per cent moisture content = 1.3; moisture factor for 10 per cent moisture content = 2.1. Hence,

Increase in k-value = 2.1/1.3 = 1.62.

Therefore, k-value for 10 per cent moisture content = 0.71 × 1.62 = 1.15 W m^{-1} K^{-1}.

5.2.2 Thermal Resistivity

Thermal resistivity is the reciprocal of thermal conductivity, i.e. $1/k$ m K W^{-1}.

5.3 Thermal resistance

The product of the thickness of the element (l) multiplied by the resistivity ($1/k$) is a measure of the resistance of the element to the flow of heat. Therefore,

Thermal resistance, $R = l/k$ m^2 K W^{-1}.

Hence, rate of heat flow per unit area through an element whose surface temperatures are t_1 and t_2 is

$$Q/A = (k/l)(t_1 - t_2) \quad \text{Wm}^{-2}.$$

5.3.1 Thermal Resistance of a Compound Element

Consider a building element composed of a number of different layers each of a different material.

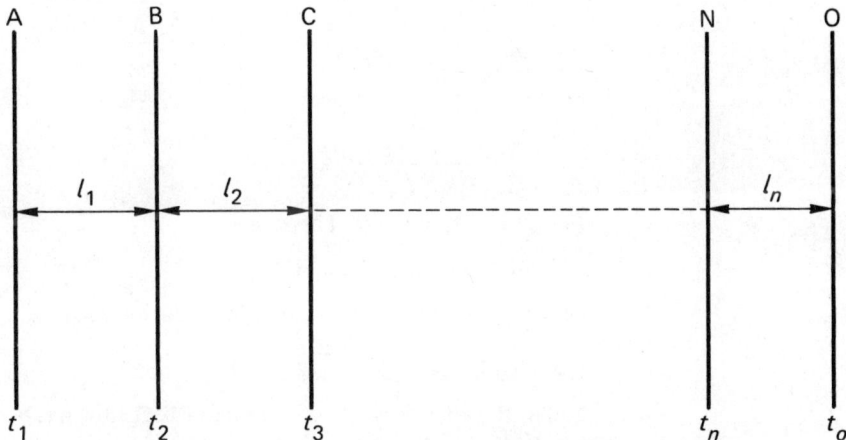

Let the innermost leaf be of thickness l_1 and conductivity k_1, the next leaf thickness l_2 and conductivity k_2, etc. At A, let the inner surface temperature be t_1. At B, let the temperature between the two layers be t_2. At C, let the temperature be t_3. At O, let the temperature on the outside face be t_0. Then, rate of heat flow per unit area between surfaces A and B is

$$\frac{Q_{AB}}{A} = \frac{k_1}{l_1}(t_1 - t_2) = \frac{1}{R_1}(t_1 - t_2) = \frac{t_1 - t_2}{R_1};$$

rate of heat flow per unit area between B and C is

$$\frac{Q_{BC}}{A} = \frac{k_2}{l_2}(t_2 - t_3) = \frac{1}{R_2}(t_2 - t_3) = \frac{t_2 - t_3}{R_2};$$

rate of heat flow per unit area between N and O is

$$\frac{Q_{NO}}{A} = \frac{k_n}{l_n}(t_n - t_0) = \frac{1}{R_n}(t_n - t_0) = \frac{t_n - t_0}{R_n}.$$

Let $\bar{R}$ = total resistance of entire element. Then, rate of heat flow per unit area between surfaces A and O is

$$\frac{Q}{A} = \frac{1}{\bar{R}}(t_1 - t_0). \tag{5.1}$$

But, for steady-state conditions, the rate of heat flow per unit area between each surface must be the same, i.e.

$$\frac{Q_{AB}}{A} = \frac{Q_{BC}}{A} = \frac{Q_{NO}}{A} = \frac{Q}{A}$$

Hence

$$\frac{Q}{A} = \frac{t_1 - t_2}{R_1} = \frac{t_2 - t_3}{R_2} = \frac{t_n - t_o}{R_n}.$$

If

$$\frac{a}{b} = \frac{c}{d} = \frac{e}{f} = \frac{a + c + e + \dots}{b + d + f + \dots},$$

then

$$\frac{Q}{A} = \frac{(t_1 - t_2) + (t_2 - t_3) + \dots (t_n - t_o)}{R_1 + R_2 + \dots R_n}$$

or

$$\frac{Q}{A} = \frac{t_1 - t_o}{R_1 + R_2 + \dots + R_n}.$$

But $Q/A = (t_1 - t_o)/\bar{R}$. Therefore,

$$\bar{R} = R_1 + R_2 + \dots + R_n,$$

i.e. the total resistance = sum of individual resistances.

5.3.2 Heat Transfer between Surface and Air

So far, the consideration of the rate of heat flow has been concerned with *conduction* and with the difference between surface temperatures. In order to deal with the air-to-air temperature differences in a building it is necessary to consider the heat exchange that occurs between the external and internal surfaces of an element and the external and internal air. In these situations the heat exchange will be by *radiation* and by *convection*.

5.3.2.1 Internal surface

If t_{ai} = internal air temperature and t_{si} = internal surface temperature, then the rate of heat flow per unit area by convection is given by the approximate formula

$$Q_C/A = h_c (t_{ai} - t_{si})$$

and the rate of heat flow per unit area by radiation is given by the approximate formula

$$Q_R/A = Eh_r (t_{ri} - t_{si}),$$

where h_c = convection coefficient, E = emissivity factor, h_r = radiation coefficient. Hence,

$$\text{Total heat flow} = Q_R/A + Q_C/A$$
$$= Eh_r (t_{mrti} - t_{si}) + h_c (t_{ai} - t_{si}),$$

where t_{mrti} = mean radiant temperature as seen by inside surfaces. For most situations it is sufficiently accurate to assume that $t_{mrti} = t_{ai}$. Therefore,

Rate of heat flow per unit area at internal surface

$$= Eh_r (t_{ai} - t_{si}) + h_c (t_{ai} - t_{si})$$
$$= (Eh_r + h_c)(t_{ai} - t_{si})$$
$$= (1/R_{si})(t_{ai} - t_{si}),$$

where R_{si} = internal surface resistance = $1/(Eh_r + h_c)$.

The emissivity factor for most building materials can be assumed to be 0.9 and for normal room temperatures $Eh_r = 5.13$ W m^{-2} K^{-1} would be suitable. The value of h_c will depend upon the direction of the heat flow. Appropriate values are:

Heat flow upwards, $h_c = 4.3$ W m^{-2} K^{-1};
Heat flow downwards, $h_c = 1.5$ W m^{-2} K^{-1};
Heat flow horizontally, $h_c = 3.0$ W m^{-2} K^{-1}.

From the above, the values of R_{si} can be found, the values adopted in current British practice being:

Heat flow upwards, $R_{si} = 0.106$ m^2 K W^{-1};
Heat flow downwards, $R_{si} = 0.15$ m^2 K W^{-1};
Heat flow horizontally, $R_{si} = 0.123$ m^2 K W^{-1}.

5.3.2.2 External surface

In a similar manner to that used for the internal surface it can be shown that the external surface resistance $R_{so} = 1/(Eh_r + h_{co})$, where Eh_r can be taken as 4.14 W m^{-2} K^{-1} and h_{co}, the external convection coefficient, has a value depending on the external wind speed, i.e. $h_{co} = 5.8 + 4.1\,v$ where v is in metres per second.

It is seen that the wind speed can have an important effect upon the rate of heat flow from an element and, hence, the degree of exposure of a building (in relation to wind flow) has to be taken into consideration.

British practice is to consider the exposure under three categories:

(i) sheltered   (ii) normal   (iii) severe.

Sheltered are low-rise buildings or the lower floors of buildings in urban areas. Normal are the 4th to 8th floors of buildings in urban areas. Severe are upper floors or buildings on exposed sites. Taking these categories and inserting suitable wind speeds it is possible to calculate values for R_{so} as shown in Table 5.1.

Table 5.1   *Values for R_{so}*

Surface	Exposure	Wind speed (m s^{-1})	h_{co} (W m^{-2} K^{-1})	$R_{so} = 1/(Eh_r + h_{co})$ (m^2 K W^{-1})
Roof	Sheltered	1.0	9.9	0.07
	Normal	3.0	18.1	0.045
	Severe	9.0	42.7	0.02
Walls	Sheltered	0.7	8.7	0.08
	Normal	2.0	14.0	0.055
	Severe	6.0	30.4	0.03

5.4 Thermal transmittance — U-values

Having obtained values for the surface resistance it is possible to calculate the rate of heat flow due to the difference between an inside air temperature and an external air temperature.

As was shown earlier, the rate of heat flow per unit area for a composite element due to difference of surface temperatures was

$$\frac{Q}{A} = \frac{(t_1 - t_2)}{R_1 + R_2 + \ldots + R_n}.$$

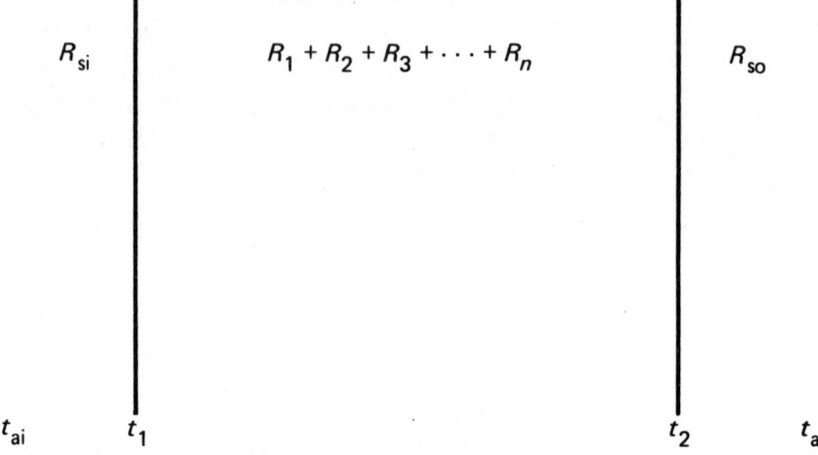

$$R_{si} \qquad\qquad R_1 + R_2 + R_3 + \cdots + R_n \qquad\qquad R_{so}$$

$$t_{ai} \qquad t_1 \qquad\qquad\qquad\qquad\qquad t_2 \qquad t_{ao}$$

Considering the temperature difference between the internal and external air,

$$\frac{Q}{A} = \frac{(t_{ai} - t_{ao})}{R_{si} + R_1 + R_2 + \ldots\ldots R_n + R_{so}}$$
$$= U(t_{ai} - t_{ao}),$$

where U = thermal transmittance and is given by

$$U = \frac{1}{\text{Sum of resistances}} = \frac{1}{\Sigma R}\ \text{W m}^{-2}\ \text{K}^{-1}. \tag{5.2}$$

Hence,

$$Q/A = U(t_{ai} - t_{ao})\ \text{W m}^{-2}, \tag{5.3}$$

i.e. the rate of heat flow per unit area through an element is equal to the thermal transmittance multiplied by the air-to-air temperature difference.

Alternatively the relationship can be written as

$$Q = A U(\Delta t)\text{W}$$

where Δt = temperature difference.

5.4.1 Effect of Cavity or Air Space

The thermal resistance of an air space or cavity depends upon the heat exchange between the two parallel surfaces on either side of the cavity, this heat exchange being by radiation and convection.

The main factors which affect the thermal resistance of the cavity are:

(i) the emissivity of the two surfaces facing each other;
(ii) the distance between the two surfaces, i.e. width of cavity;
(iii) the rate of air flow in the cavity;
(iv) the direction of heat flow.

The effects of the first two factors are as shown in Figs. 5.2 and 5.3. Typical values for the thermal resistance for an unventilated air space or cavity between building materials having a high emissivity are as shown in Table 5.2.

Table 5.2   *Standard thermal resistance of unventilated air-spaces* [3]

Type or thickness of air-space	Surface emissivity	Thermal resistance* $(m^2 \ K \ W^{-1})$	
		Heat flow horizontal or upwards	Heat flow down-wards
5 mm	High	0.11	0.11
	Low	0.18	0.18
20 mm or more	High	0.18	0.21
	Low	0.35	1.06
High-emissivity planes and corrugated sheets in contact		0.09	0.11
Low-emissivity multiple-foil insulation with air-space on one side		0.62	1.76

*Including internal boundary surface

Where surfaces have a high emissivity (e.g. foil insulation) then a higher value for the resistance is obtained.

5.4.2 Calculation of U-value

The following examples will illustrate the procedure for calculating U-values.

Example 5.2   Calculate the U-value for a 220 mm brick wall with 16 mm plaster on the inside face. Assume normal exposure.
For brick, $k = 0.84$ W m^{-1} K^{-1}; for plaster $k = 0.5$ W m^{-1} K^{-1}.

Internal resistance, $R_{si} = 0.123$ m^2 K W^{-1},

Plaster resistance $= l/k = 0.016/0.5 = 0.032$ m^2 K W^{-1},

Brick resistance $= 0.22/0.84 = 0.262$ m^2 K W^{-1},

External resistance, $R_{so} = 0.055$ m^2 K W^{-1}.

Hence,

Total resistance $= 0.123 + 0.032 + 0.262 + 0.055 = 0.472$ m^2 K W^{-1}.

Therefore,

$$U = 1/\Sigma R = 2.12 \ \text{W m}^{-2} \ \text{K}^{-1}.$$

Fig. 5.2 The variation of air-space conductance with air-space width (after Robinson *et al.* [4]).

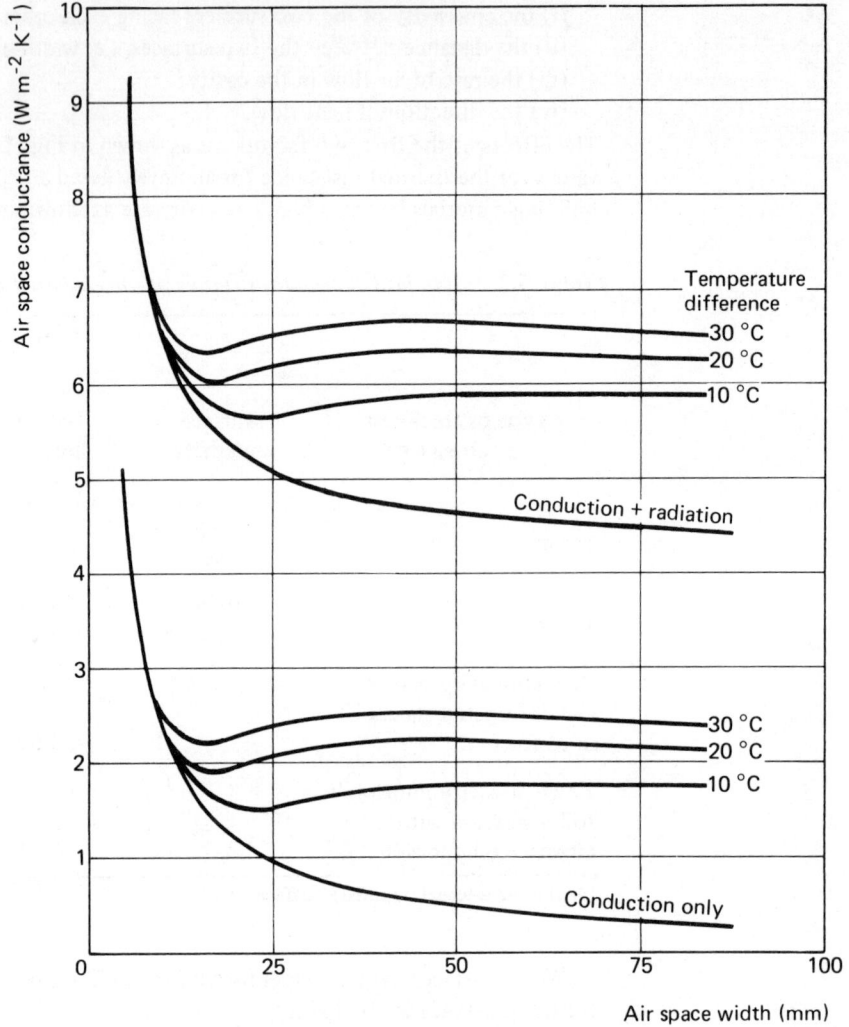

Note that in calculating the resistances for the materials, the thickness *l* has to be expressed in metres.

Example 5.3   Calculate the *U*-value for a brick cavity wall made up as follows: 105 mm brick outer leaf, 50 mm unventilated air space, 105 mm inner brick leaf, 16 mm plaster on inner surface. For brick outer leaf, $k = 0.84$ W m^{-1} K^{-1}; for brick inner leaf, $k = 0.62$ W m^{-1} K^{-1}. Note that the difference in the value of k for the inner and outer leaves is to allow for the increase in the moisture content of the outer leaf, since it will normally be exposed to rain.

Internal resistance, $R_{si} = 0.123$ m^2 K W^{-1},

Plaster resistance $= 0.016/0.5 = 0.032$ m^2 K W^{-1},

Brick inner leaf resistance $= 0.105/0.62 = 0.169$ m^2 K W^{-1},

Cavity resistance $= 0.18$ m^2 K W^{-1},

Brick outer leaf resistance $= 0.105/0.84 = 0.125$ m^2 K W^{-1},

External resistance $= R_{so} = 0.055$ m^2 K W^{-1}.

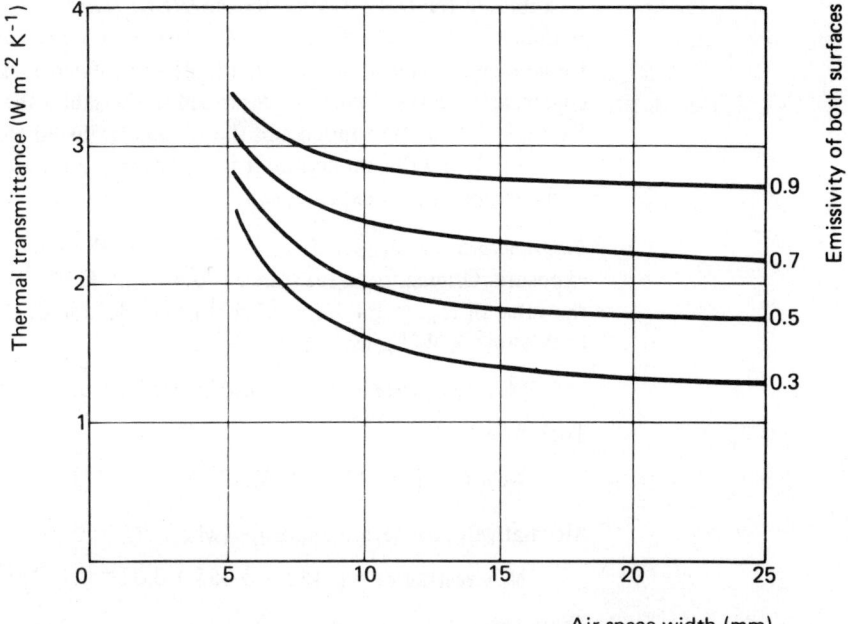

Fig. 5.3 The effect of surface emissivity on the radiant component of the heat transfer across an air space (from Turner [5]).

Hence,

$$\text{Total resistance} = 0.123 + 0.032 + 0.169 + 0.18 + 0.125 + 0.055$$

$$= 0.684 \text{ m}^2 \text{ K W}^{-1}.$$

Therefore,

$$U = 1/\Sigma R = 1/0.684 = 1.46 \text{ W m}^{-2} \text{ K}^{-1}.$$

Example 5.4   As Example 5.3 but with foam insulation in the cavity. For foam insulation, $k = 0.026$ W m^{-1} K^{-1}.

In this type of problem it is not necessary to recalculate all the values. If the original U-value is known, then all that is required is to obtain the original total resistance, adjust this for any changes and, hence, obtain the new U-value.

U-value of original wall = 1.46 W m^{-2} K^{-1}.

Hence,

$$\text{Original total resistance} = 1/U = 1/1.46 = 0.684 \text{ m}^2 \text{ K W}^{-1}.$$

$$\text{Resistance of foam} = 0.05/0.026 = 1.923 \text{ m}^2 \text{ K W}^{-1}.$$

Therefore, new total resistance will be given by the original total resistance combined with the resistance of the foam-filled cavity less the resistance of the previous air space, i.e.

$$\text{New total resistance} = 0.684 + 1.923 - 0.18 = 2.427 \text{ m}^2 \text{ K W}^{-1}.$$

Therefore,

$$\text{New } U = 1/2.427 = 0.41 \text{ W m}^{-2} \text{ K}^{-1}.$$

Comparing this with the original U-value, the effect of the foam insulation is clearly evident.

Tables in the *IHVE Guide*, the *ASHRAE Handbook of Fundamentals* and *Building Research Establishment Digest No. 108* give conductivity and U-values for a range of typical building materials and elements. Where the desired construction varies from that described in the tables the procedure as set out in Example 5.4 can be applied and the U-value adjusted to meet the required situation. Using this procedure it is interesting to note the effect which a change in the exposure (i.e. external resistance) can have on a wall.

Example 5.5   Consider Example 5.2 with a 'sheltered' exposure and a 'severe' exposure. Original total resistance = 0.472 m² K W⁻¹. Hence, by deduction of the value of R_{so} (= 0.055 m² K W⁻¹) and addition of the sheltered exposure R_{so} (= 0.08 m² K W⁻¹), we obtain

New resistance = 0.472 − 0.055 + 0.08 = 0.497 m² K W⁻¹.

Therefore,

New U = 1/0.497 = 2.0 W m⁻² K⁻¹.

Alternatively, for severe exposure (where R_{so} = 0.03),

New resistance = 0.472 − 0.055 + 0.03 = 0.447 m² K W⁻¹.

Therefore,

New U = 1/0.447 = 2.24 W m⁻² K⁻¹

Percentage increase over 'sheltered' value = $\dfrac{0.24}{2.0} \times 100$ = 12 per cent.

Repeating this procedure for Example 5.4 the following values were obtained:

Sheltered exposure U = 0.41 W m⁻² K⁻¹,

Severe exposure U = 0.42 W m⁻² K⁻¹,

Percentage increase over 'sheltered' value = 2.4 per cent.

It will be seen that a change in exposure conditions from sheltered to severe for a well insulated wall has a very small effect, but for a poorly insulated wall it has a noticeable effect. This is simply due to the fact that in the case of the well insulated wall the total resistance was quite large and hence it would require a considerable change in the external resistance value to make a major difference.

5.4.3 Windows

The thermal resistance of glass is assumed to be zero. Hence, the total resistance for a single sheet of glass is the addition of the external and internal resistance. For example, for normal exposure,

R = 0.123 + 0.055 = 0.178 m² K W⁻¹.

Therefore,

U = 1/0.178 = 5.6 W m⁻² K⁻¹.

For double glazing the effect of the air space has to be added:

R = 0.123 + 0.18 + 0.055 = 0.358 m² K W⁻¹,

U = 1/0.358 = 2.8 W m⁻² K⁻¹.

Metal frames have a U-value similar to single glass in normal exposures, but where timber frames or other exposures exist then the above values should be changed. *U*-values for windows in timber frames are given in the *IHVE Guide* and reproduced below.

Table 5.3   *U-values for typical windows (from IHVE Guide)*

Window type	Fraction of area occupied by frame (per cent)	U-values for stated exposure (W m^{-2} K^{-1})		
		Sheltered	Normal	Severe
Single glazing				
Wood frame	30	3.8	4.3	5.0
Metal frame	20	5.0	5.6	6.7
Double glazing				
Wood frame	30	2.3	2.5	2.7
Metal frame with thermal break	20	3.0	3.2	3.5

Note: Where the proportion of frame differs appreciably from the above tabulated values, particularly with wood or plastic, the *U*-values should be calculated (metal members have a *U*-value similar to glass).

5.4.4 Walls with Windows

Consider an element composed of a number of units, such that area A_1 has value U_1, A_2 has value U_2, A_n has value U_n.

Then the overall *U*-value for the entire element is given by

$$U = (A_1 U_1 + A_2 U_2 + \ldots + A_n U_n)/(A_1 + A_2 + \ldots + A_n)$$

This method can be used to prepare a simple design guide for calculating the overall *U*-value of an external wall with a window.

Let A = total external wall area, A_g = area of window, A_w = net area of external solid wall = $A - A_g$, U_g = *U*-value of window, U_w = *U*-value of wall, r = ratio window to solid wall = A_g/A; then $A_g = rA$.

$$\text{Overall } U\text{-value for external wall} = [A_g U_g + A_w U_w]/(A_g + A_w)$$
$$= [A_g U_g + (A - A_g)U_w]/A$$
$$= [rA U_g + (A - rA)U_w]/A$$
$$= rU_g + (1-r)U_w.$$

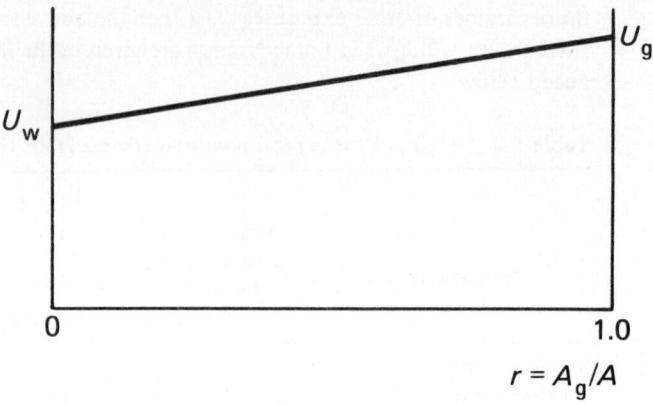

$$r = A_g/A$$

To prepare design graph, draw a base line representing the value of r from 0 to 1.0, mark off the appropriate values of U_w and U_g on the two vertical axes at $r = 0$ and $r = 1.0$, join the two points.

This method can be used to solve the following example.

Example 5.6   A wall has a U-value of 1.0 W m^{-2} K^{-1}. (a) What would be the overall U-value of the external wall if the window area was 50 per cent of the wall surface? (U-value for window = 5.6 W m^{-2} K^{-1}.) (b) What would be the improvement if the window area was reduced to 25 per cent of the wall surface? (c) Would there be any improvement over case (b) if the U-value of the wall was improved to 0.5 W m^{-2} K^{-1} but the window area was increased to 40 per cent?

Fig. 5.4 shows the required design graph. Values corresponding to $U = 1.0$ and 5.6 were marked off on the vertical axes corresponding to $r = 0$ and $r = 1.0$ and the points joined.

(a) A vertical line was drawn from $r = 0.5$ (50 per cent window) to cut the sloping line at X, giving combined $U = 3.3$ W m^{-2} K^{-1}.

(b) Process repeated using a vertical line from $r = 0.25$, combined $U = 2.15$ W m^{-2} K^{-1}. Therefore,

$$\text{Improvement} = \frac{3.3 - 2.15}{3.3} \times 100 = 35 \text{ per cent.}$$

(c) A new sloping line was drawn for $U = 0.6$ at $r = 0$. Vertical line from $r = 0.4$ gave combined $U = 2.54$ W m^{-2} K^{-1}. The value is greater than for case (b) and so there is no improvement. In fact it will be seen that in order to keep the same combined U-value of 2.15 W m^{-2} K^{-1} the value of r should be 0.32.

Example 5.7   If the wall has a U-value of 0.5 W m^{-2} K^{-1}, what is the area of (a) single glazing ($U_g = 5.6$ W m^{-2} K^{-1}) and (b) double glazing ($U_g = 2.8$ W m^{-2} K^{-1}) required to give a combined U-value of 1.5 W m^{-2} K^{-1}?

From Fig. 5.5, (a) $r = 0.2$ (20 per cent wall area); (b) $r = 0.43$ (43 per cent wall area).

5.4.5 Ground Floors

Building Research Establishment Digest No. 145 [6] states that 'for ground floors, either solid or suspended, it is not possible to calculate U-values from first

Fig. 5.4 Graphs showing combined U-value for single glazing and wall, where wall has $U = 1.0$ W m^{-2} K^{-1} or $U = 0.5$ W m^{-2} K^{-1}.

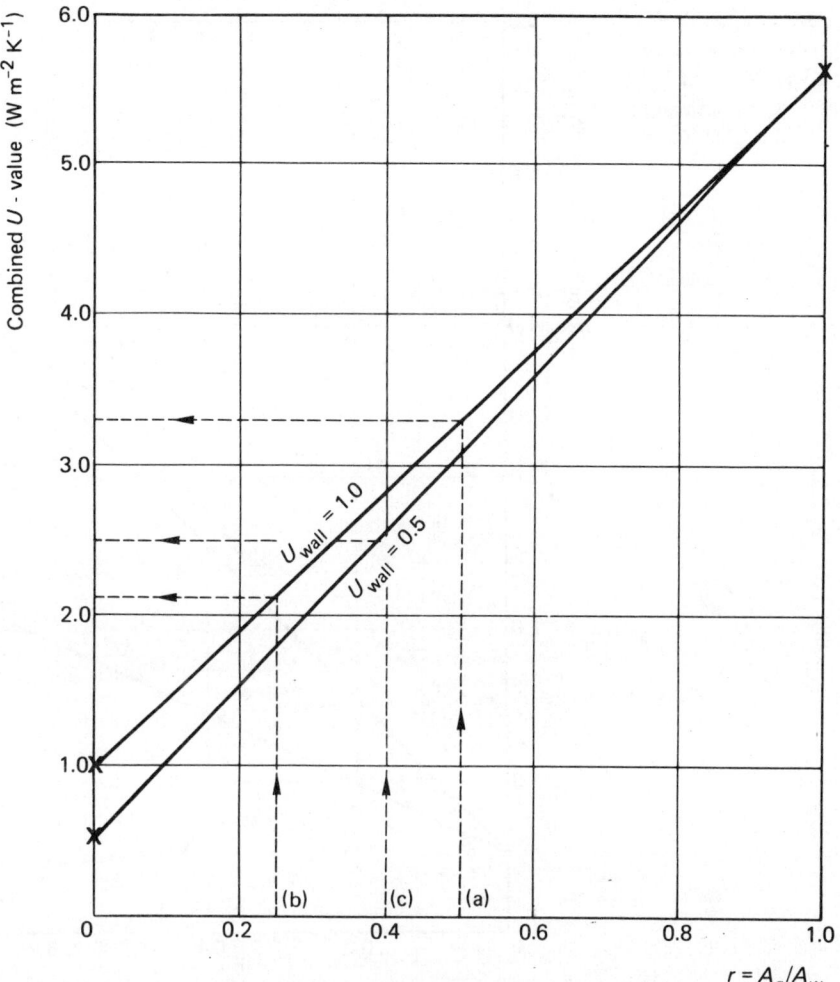

principles.' The reason for this statement is that the heat flow through a solid floor is as shown in Fig. 5.6. The greater the length of the heat flow path the smaller is the rate of heat loss, hence the U-value to be used for the floor must be based upon the dimensions of the floor and the edge conditions.

Tables of U-values for ground floors are given in *Building Research Establishment Digest No. 145* [6] and also in the *IHVE Guide*. The original investigation which formed the basis of these tables was published by Billington [7].

Figs. 5.7 and 5.8 are curves based upon the published values and show the influence that the edge conditions and floor area has upon the U-value.

If the ratio of floor perimeter to the floor area is plotted against floor area, as in Fig. 5.9, a similar curve is obtained to those shown in Figs. 5.7 and 5.8. From these curves it is evident that the ratio of floor perimeter to floor area is of prime importance and that as the area of the floor increases the rate of heat flow per unit area of floor decreases.

5.5 Temperature gradient through an element

It has been shown that

$$\frac{t_{ai} - t_1}{R_{si}} = \frac{t_1 - t_2}{R_1} = \frac{t_2 - t_3}{R_3} = \frac{t_{ai} - t_{ao}}{\Sigma R}.$$

Fig. 5.5 Graphs showing combined U-value for a wall ($U = 0.5$ W m^{-2} K^{-1}) with single and double glazing.

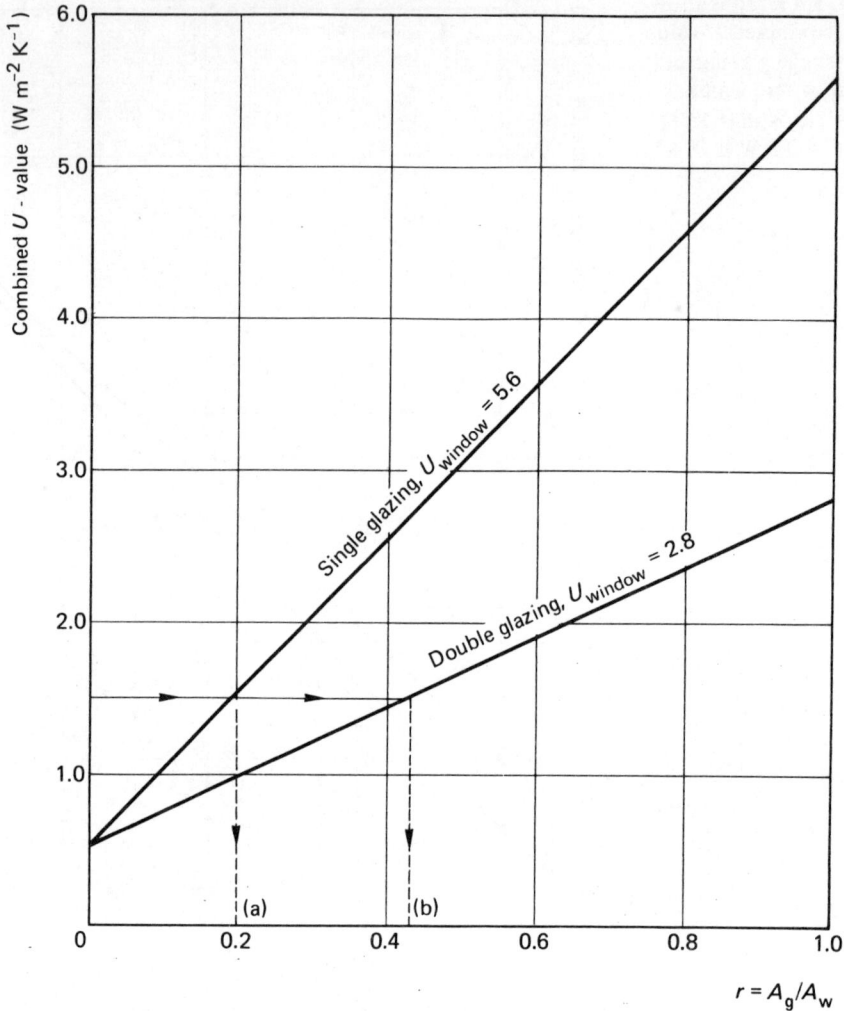

Fig. 5.6 Heat flow through ground slab (from *BRE Digest No. 145* [6]).

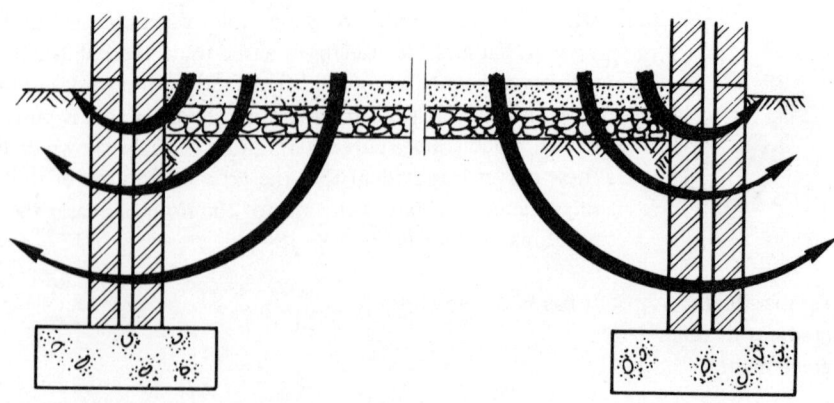

Fig. 5.7 *U*-values for solid floors on soil (from data in *IHVE Guide* and *BRE Digest No. 145* [6].)

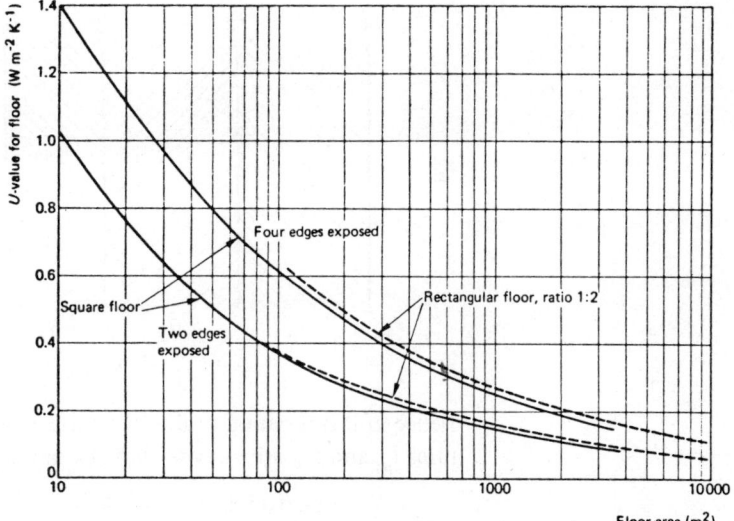

Fig. 5.8 *U*-values for suspended timber floor above ground (from data in *IHVE Guide* and *BRE Digest No. 145* [6]).

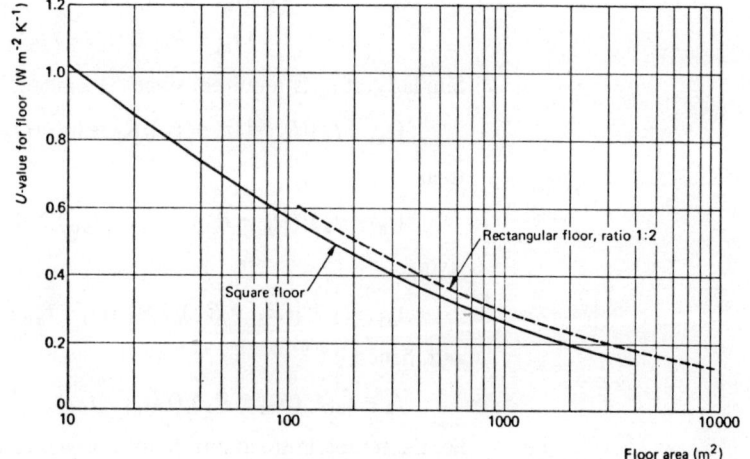

Fig. 5.9 Relationship between floor area and the ratio of floor perimeter to floor area.

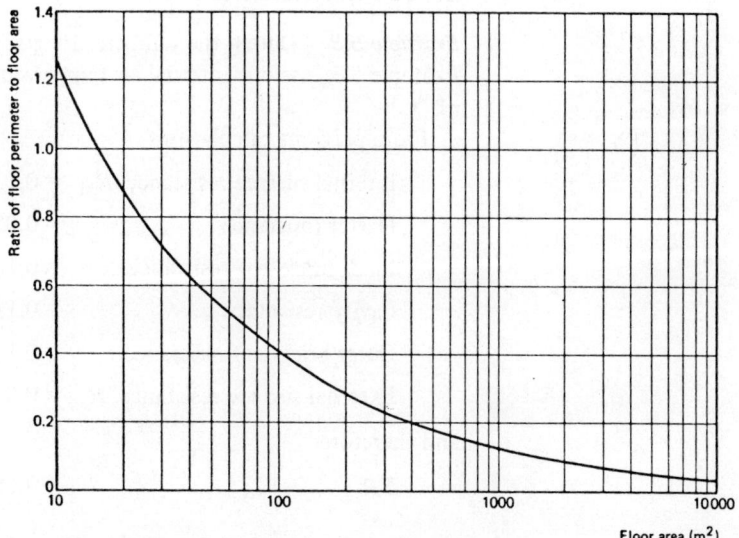

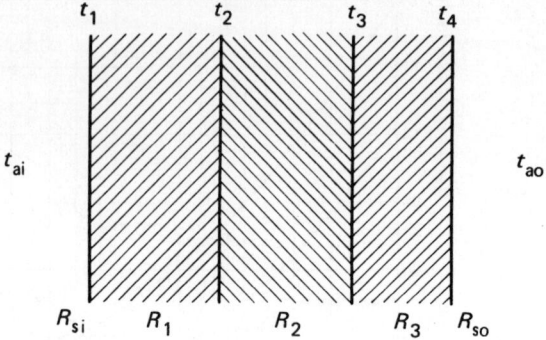

Hence, if it is required to find the surface temperature t_1 when the air temperatures t_{ai} and t_{ao} are known, then, from the above relationship,

$$(t_{ai} - t_1)/R_{si} = (t_{ai} - t_{ao})/\Sigma R,$$
$$t_{ai} - t_1 = (R_{si}/\Sigma R)(t_{ai} - t_{ao}),$$
$$t_1 = t_{ai} - (R_{si}/\Sigma R)(t_{ai} - t_{ao})$$
$$= t_{ai} - R_{si} U(t_{ai} - t_{ao}).$$

Similarly, if t_2 is required, since

$$(t_{ai} - t_1)/R_{si} = (t_1 - t_2)/R_1 = (t_{ai} - t_{ao})/\Sigma R,$$

then

$$(t_{ai} - t_2)/(R_{si} + R_1) = (t_{ai} - t_{ao})/\Sigma R,$$

giving,

$$t_{ai} - t_2 = [(R_{si} + R_1)/\Sigma R](t_{ai} - t_{ao})$$

and, hence,

$$t_2 = t_{ai} - (R_{si} + R_1) U(t_{ai} - t_{ao}), \tag{5.4}$$

i.e. the temperature at any point is equal to the internal air temperature minus the sum of resistances to that point multiplied by the thermal transmittance and air-to-air temperature difference.

Example 5.8   Obtain the temperature gradient for the wall described in Example 5.3. Assume internal air temperature, 20 °C; external air temperature, −1 °C.

From previous calculations,

Internal surface resistance, R_{si} = 0.123 m² K W⁻¹,

Plaster resistance   = 0.032 m² K W⁻¹,

Inner brick leaf resistance   = 0.169 m² K W⁻¹,

Cavity resistance   = 0.18 m² K W⁻¹,

Outer brick leaf resistance   = 0.125 m² K W⁻¹,

External surface resistance, R_{so} = 0.055 m² K W⁻¹

and therefore

ΣR = 0.684 m² K W⁻¹.

Hence,

$$U = 1/0.684 = 1.46 \text{ W m}^{-2} \text{ K}^{-1}.$$

Now, $t_{ao} = -1\ ^{\circ}\text{C}$ and $t_{ai} = 20\ ^{\circ}\text{C}$, so

$$t_{ai} - t_{ao} = 20 - (-1) = 21\ ^{\circ}\text{C}.$$

At plaster face,

$$t_1 = t_{ai} - R_{si}\ U(t_{ai} - t_{ao})$$
$$= 20 - [0.123 \times 1.46 \times 21]$$
$$= 20 - 3.8 = 16.2\ ^{\circ}\text{C}.$$

At inner brick face,

$$t_2 = 20 - [(0.123 + 0.032) \times 1.46 \times 21]$$
$$= 20 - 4.8 = 15.2\ ^{\circ}\text{C}.$$

At inner face of cavity,

$$t_3 = 20 - [(0.123 + 0.032 + 0.169) \times 1.46 \times 21]$$
$$= 20 - 10 = 10\ ^{\circ}\text{C}.$$

At outer face of cavity,

$$t_4 = 20 - [(0.123 + 0.032 + 0.169 + 0.18) \times 1.46 \times 21]$$
$$= 20 - 15.5 = 4.5\ ^{\circ}\text{C}.$$

At outer face of wall,

$$t_5 = 20 - [(0.123 + 0.032 + 0.169 + 0.18 + 0.125) \times 1.46 \times 21]$$
$$= 20 - 19.3 = 0.7\ ^{\circ}\text{C}.$$

The temperature gradient is as shown in Fig. 5.10(a).

Fig. 5.10(b) shows the temperature gradient for the wall with foam insulation in the cavity (as in Example 5.4). The changes in the surface temperatures are clearly evident and, since the internal surface temperature affects the mean radiant temperature, which has a bearing on the sensation of comfort, as explained in Chapter 3, it will be seen that this can also be influenced by the use of insulation.

5.6 Condensation

5.6.1 Humidity

At any given temperature the air can contain only a certain amount of water vapour. When the air cannot contain any more moisture, it is said to have reached its *saturation point*. The amount of moisture that the air can contain before it reaches its saturation point increases with temperature.

The relative humidity (RH) can be expressed as

$$RH = \frac{\text{Vapour pressure}}{\text{Saturated vapour pressure at same temperature}} \times 100 \text{ per cent}$$

or

$$RH = \frac{\text{Amount of water vapour in the air}}{\text{Amount of water vapour for air to be saturated at same temperature}}$$
$$\times 100 \text{ per cent.}$$

Fig. 5.10 Temperature gradient through a wall: (a) as in Example 5.3 and (b) as in Example 5.4.

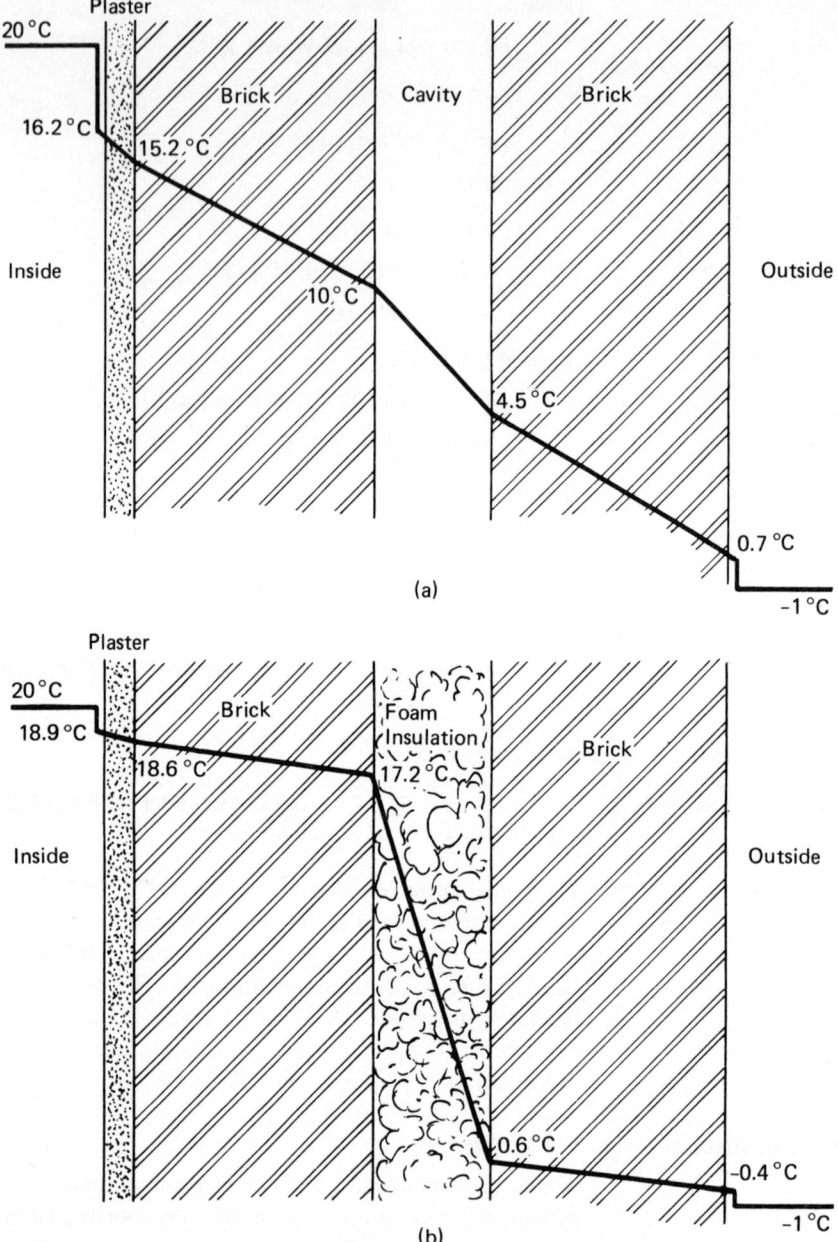

Vapour pressure is measured in pascals (Pa), but it is also convenient to express the amount of moisture in the air as a mixing ratio, i.e. mass of water vapour per unit mass of dry air, measured as grammes of water vapour per kilogramme of dry air. Fig. 5.11 shows the relationship between relative humidity, temperature and vapour pressure and the following example will demonstrate the use of the graph.

Fig. 5.11 Relationship between relative humidity, temperature and vapour pressure.

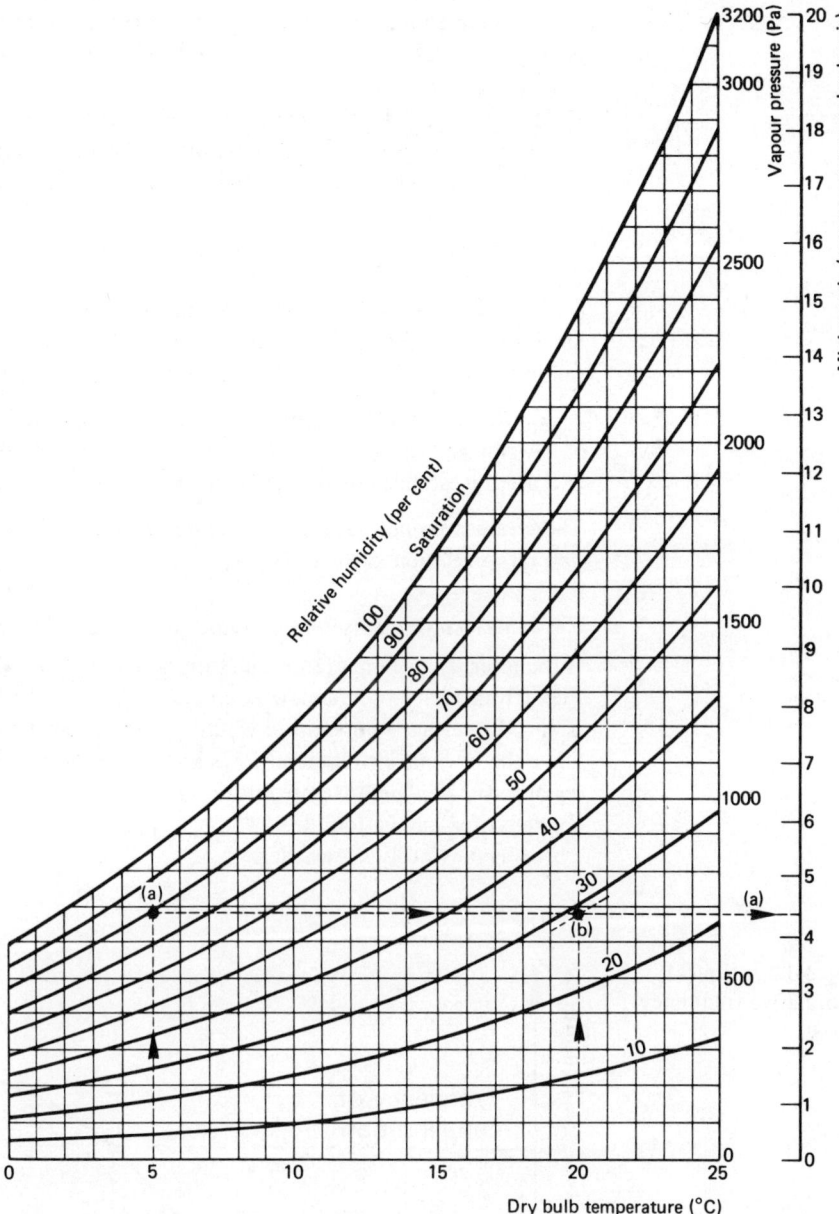

Example 5.9   (a) What is the mixing ratio when the temperature is 5 °C and RH = 80 per cent? (b) What would be the relative humidity if the temperature was increased to 20 °C and the mixing ratio kept the same?

(a) From Fig. 5.11, mixing ratio = 4.3 g water vapour per kg dry air.
(b) From Fig. 5.11, RH = 29.5 per cent.

It will be seen from the graph that if the mixing ratio is kept constant, but the temperature reduced, the relative humidity will continue to increase until it reaches the 100 per cent value, any further reduction in the temperature will cause the moisture in the air to condense. The stage at which this occurs is the *dew point*.

From the above it will be seen that if the surface temperature of a building element is equal to or falls below the dew point then condensation will occur on that surface.

However, in order to calculate the dew point it is necessary to know the vapour pressure or amount of moisture in the air at a given temperature. For the purpose of checking whether condensation will occur for a winter condition, the external air temperature can be assumed to be at 0 °C and the air saturated, i.e. RH = 100 per cent, corresponding to a mixing ratio of 3.8 g water vapour per kg dry air.

The indoor air will have an excess moisture content in relation to the outdoor air. *Building Research Establishment Digest No. 110* [8] gives values of the mixing ratio which can be used for estimating this and these are as follows:

Shops, offices, classrooms,   1.7 g water vapour per kg dry air;
Dwellings,   3.4 g water vapour per kg dry air;
Catering establishments and workshops, 6.8 g water vapour per kg dry air.

These values should be added to the mixing ratio of the external air (assuming natural ventilation in the buildings).

5.6.2 Surface Condensation on Windows

If the internal air temperature, mixing ratio and relative humidity are known, then (from Fig. 5.11) the dew point can be found. For surface condensation to occur, the surface temperature would have to be at the dew point temperature. Since the internal air temperature is known, by putting the surface temperature equal to the dew point temperature, the outside temperature necessary to cause condensation can be found.

It was previously shown that

$$t_{si} = t_{ai} - R_{si}U(t_{ai} - t_{ao}). \tag{5.5}$$

Fig. 5.12 A typical cumulative frequency curve.

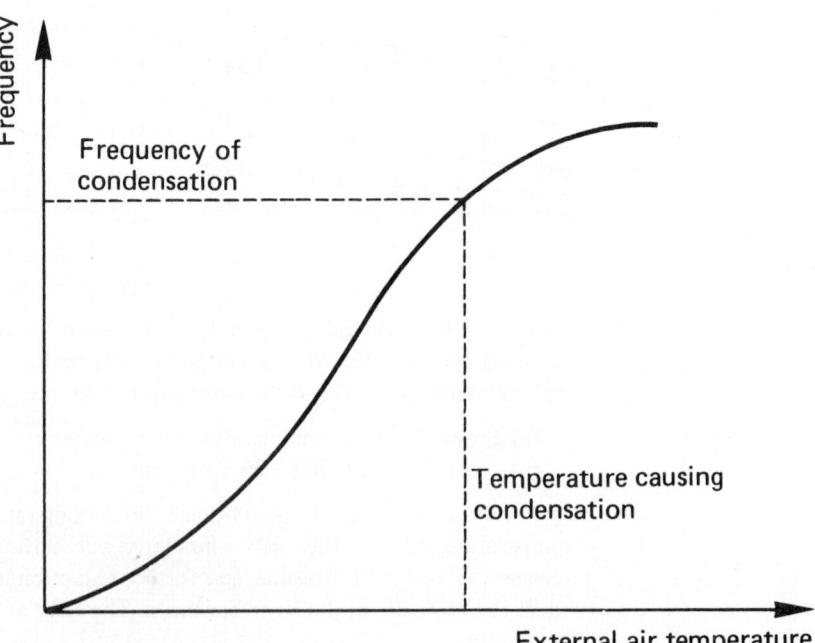

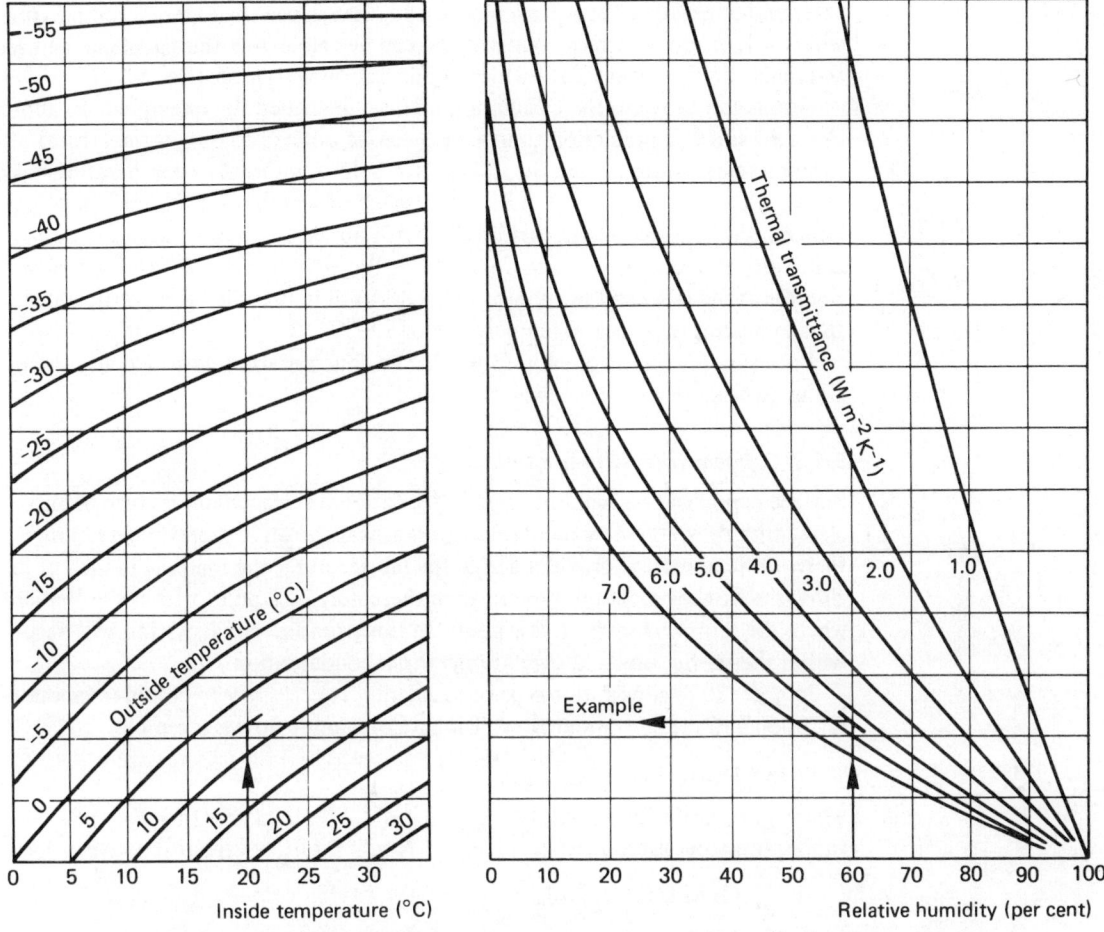

Fig. 5.13 Condensation prediction chart (from Turner [5]).

For a window (single glazing, metal frame), $U = 5.6$ W m^{-2} K^{-1} and $R_{si} = 0.123$ m^2 K W^{-1}. Then,

$$t_{si} = t_{ai} - (0.123 \times 5.6)(t_{ai} - t_{ao})$$

$$= t_{ai} - 0.69(t_{ai} - t_{ao})$$

$$= 0.69 t_{ao} + 0.31 t_{ai},$$

giving

$$t_{ao} = (t_{si} - 0.31 t_{ai})/0.69 = 1.45 t_{si} - 0.45 t_{ai}. \tag{5.6}$$

Example 5.10   If the internal air temperature is 20 °C and the internal relative humidity is 60 per cent, what is the outside temperature that will cause condensation on the inner face of a single-glazed window?

From Fig. 5.11, dew point = 12.3 °C. Therefore $t_{si} = 12.3$ °C. From equation (5.6),

$$t_{ao} = (1.45 \times 12.3) - (0.45 \times 20)$$

$$= 17.84 - 9 = 8.84 \text{ °C.}$$

If a cumulative frequency curve (as described in Chapter 4) is drawn for the external temperature for a particular period, then, since the external temperature which will produce surface condensation can be calculated, this curve can be used to predict the frequency with which condensation will occur (Fig. 5.12).

As an alternative to the calculation method described for Example 5.10 above, Fig. 5.13 shows a prediction chart which can be utilized to obtain the critical external temperature. From the values used before, internal air temperature = 20 °C, relative humidity = 60 per cent, U-value of window = 5.6 W m^{-2} K^{-1}. Hence, using the right-hand part of Fig. 5.13, obtain the point where the 60 per cent vertical line cuts the curve for $U = 5.6$. Project a horizontal line from this point into the left-hand portion of Fig. 5.13 until it cuts the 20 °C vertical line, thus indicating an external temperature of 8.8 °C.

Both Fig. 5.13 and equation (5.5) contain four variables. Provided any three are known, the fourth can always be found.

5.6.3 Condensation within Fabric

Surface condensation will not occur if the internal surface temperature of an element is above the dew point. However, as was shown in a previous section, there is a temperature gradient across the fabric, and if the material is such as to allow the flow of moisture vapour, then there may be a point within the element where the temperature is at dew point. In this situation condensation will occur within the fabric; this is known as *interstitial* condensation.

In order to deal with this type of problem it is necessary to consider vapour diffusion and rate of vapour flow. The rate of vapour flow is given by

$$G = (v_p/l)\,(P_{v1} - P_{v2})\text{ ng m}^{-2}\text{ s}^{-1},$$

where v_p = vapour permeability (ng m N^{-1} s^{-1}), l = thickness (m), $P_{v1} - P_{v2}$ = vapour pressure difference (P_a) (1 Pa = 1 N m^{-2}), $1/v_p$ = vapour resistivity. Then

$$G = (1/R_v)\,(P_{v1} - P_{v2}),$$

where R_v = vapour resistance = l/v_p and, for a composite element,

$$G = (1/\Sigma R_v)\,(P_{v1} - P_{v2}).$$

Note the similarity with the heat flow equation

$$Q/A = (1/\Sigma R)\,(t_1 - t_2).$$

This indicates that vapour pressure gradients can be obtained in the same way as temperature gradients. It was shown in a previous section that the temperature at any point in an element was given by

$$t_x = t_{ai} - (R/\Sigma R)(t_{ai} - t_{ao}).$$

So, in a similar manner, the vapour pressure at any point can be found from the following:

$$P_{vx} = P_{v1} - (R_v/\Sigma R_v)\,(P_{v1} - P_{v2}). \tag{5.7}$$

The *IHVE Guide* uses the units as given in the above equations, but in *BRS Digest No.* 110, the pressure difference is expressed in millibars (1 mbar = 100 N m^{-2} = 100 Pa) and the vapour resistance in MN s g^{-1}. The latter unit for vapour resistance will be used in the following examples.

Table 5.4 *Comparative values of thermal and vapour resistivity for various building materials* [8]

Materials	Thermal resistivity $(m\ K\ W^{-1})$	Vapour resistivity $(MN\ s\ g^{-1}\ m^{-1})$
Brickwork	0.69–1.38	25–100
Concrete	0.69	30–100
Rendering	0.83	100
Plaster	2.08	60
Timber	6.93	45–75
Plywood	6.93	1500–6000
Fibre building board	15.2–18.7	15–60
Hardboard	6.93	450–750
Plasterboard	6.24	45–60
Compressed strawboard	9.7–11.8	45–75
Wood-wool slab	3.66	15–40
Expanded polystyrene	27.72	100–600
Foamed urea-formaldehyde	27.72	20–30
Foamed polyurethane (open or closed cell)	27.72	30–1000
Expanded ebonite	27.72	11 000–60 000

Example 5.11   (a) A brick wall is 220 mm thick with 16 mm of plaster on its inside face; the internal air temperature is 20 °C, the external air temperature is 0 °C; assume that the outside air is saturated and check if condensation will appear. (b) What would be the effect of replacing the plaster with 25 mm of fibreboard? (c) What would be the effect in (b) if the internal air temperature was reduced to 18 °C and then to 15 °C? (d) What would be the effect of an air space between two brick leaves and a vapour barrier behind the fibreboard?

Material	Thermal conductivity $k(W\ m^{-1}\ K^{-1})$	Vapour resistivity, $1/v_p\ (MN\ s\ g^{-1}\ m^{-1})$
Brick	0.83	25
Plaster	0.5	60
Fibreboard	0.055	60

Since the outside air temperature is 0 °C and it is saturated, then (from Fig. 5.11) the vapour pressure is 600 Pa and the mixing ratio is 3.8 g water vapour per kg dry air. Hence, adding 3.4 g water vapour per kg dry air to allow for the excess of the internal moisture over the external moisture, we have

Total mixing ratio on the inside = 3.8 + 3.4 = 7.2.

From Fig. 5.11, a mixing ratio of 7.2 g water vapour per kg dry air corresponds to a vapour pressure of 1140 Pa = P_{v_1}. Thus,

$$P_{v_1} - P_{v_2} = 1140 - 600 = 540 \text{ Pa}.$$

(a) For 16 mm of plaster on the internal face, we have

Internal thermal resistance, $R_{si} = 0.123$ m^2 K W^{-1},

Plaster thermal resistance $= 0.016/0.5 = 0.032$ m^2 K W^{-1},

Brick thermal resistance $= 0.22/0.83 = 0.265$ m^2 K W^{-1},

External thermal resistance, $R_{so} = 0.055$ m^2 K W^{-1}.

Therefore,

Total thermal resistance $= 0.123 + 0.032 + 0.265 + 0.055$

$$= 0.475 \text{ m}^2 \text{ K W}^{-1}.$$

Fig. 5.14 Temperature and dew point gradients – Example 5.11(a).

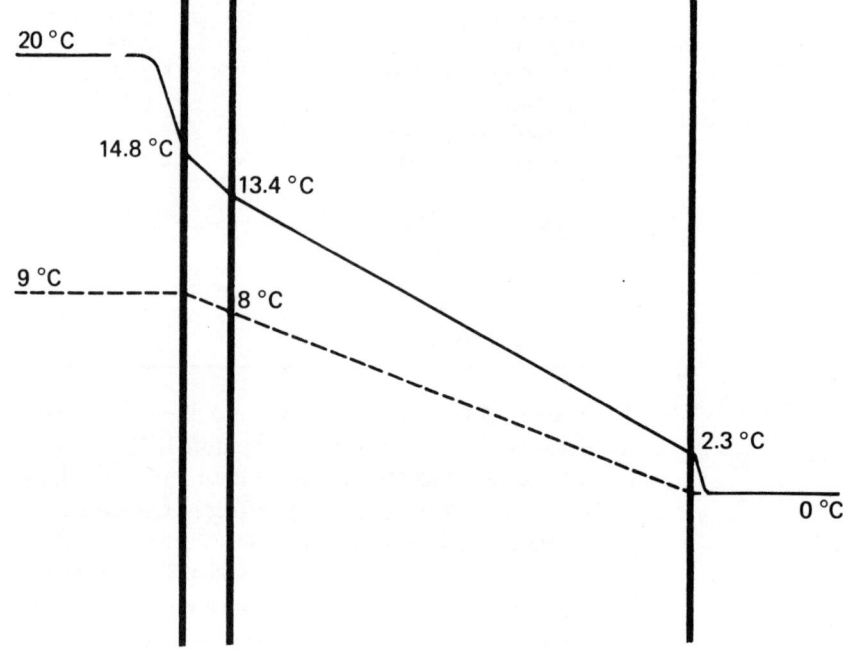

The temperature gradient is as shown in Fig. 5.14. In addition,

Plaster vapour resistance $= l/v_p = 0.016 \times 60 = 0.96$ MN s g^{-1},

Brick vapour resistance $= 0.22 \times 25 = 5.5$ MN s g^{-1}.

Therefore,

Total vapour resistance $= 0.96 + 5.5 = 6.46$ MN s g^{-1}.

Hence,

Vapour pressure at internal brick face $= P_{v1} - (R_v/\Sigma R_v)(P_{v1} - P_{v2})$

$$= 1140 - (0.96/6.46) \times 540$$

$$= 1060 \text{ Pa}.$$

Position	Vapour pressure (Pa)	Dew point (°C)
At inside face	1150	9
At inner brick face	1060	8
At outside face	0	0

(b) When the plaster is replaced by 25 mm of fibreboard, we have

Internal thermal resistance, R_{si} = 0.123 m² K W⁻¹,

Fibreboard thermal resistance = 0.025/0.055 = 0.455 m² K W⁻¹,

Brick thermal resistance = 0.022/0.83 = 0.265 m² K W⁻¹,

External thermal resistance, R_{so} = 0.055 m² K W⁻¹.

Therefore,

Total thermal resistance = 0.123 + 0.455 + 0.265 + 0.055

= 0.898 m² K W⁻¹.

Similarly,

Fibreboard vapour resistance = 0.025 × 60 = 1.5 MN s g⁻¹,

Brick vapour resistance   = 0.22 × 25 = 5.5 MN s g⁻¹.

Therefore,

Total vapour resistance = 1.5 + 5.5 = 7.0 MN s g⁻¹.

The appropriate temperature and dew point gradients are as shown in Fig. 5.15. If the actual temperature falls below the dew point, condensation will take place. This is seen to occur where the broken line (dew point gradient) crosses the continuous line (actual temperature gradient).

(c) Figs. 5.16 and 5.17 show the situation when the internal temperature is 18 °C and 15 °C, respectively.

(d) With an air space between two brick leaves and a polythene vapour barrier behind the fibreboard we have

Fibreboard vapour resistance = 1.5 MN s g⁻¹,

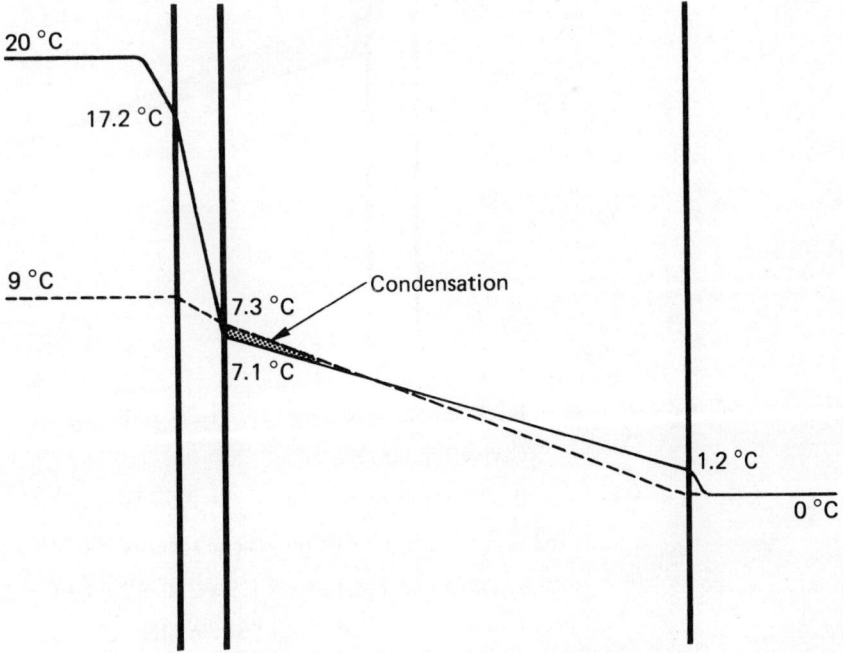

Fig. 5.15 Temperature and dew point gradients – Example 5.11(b).

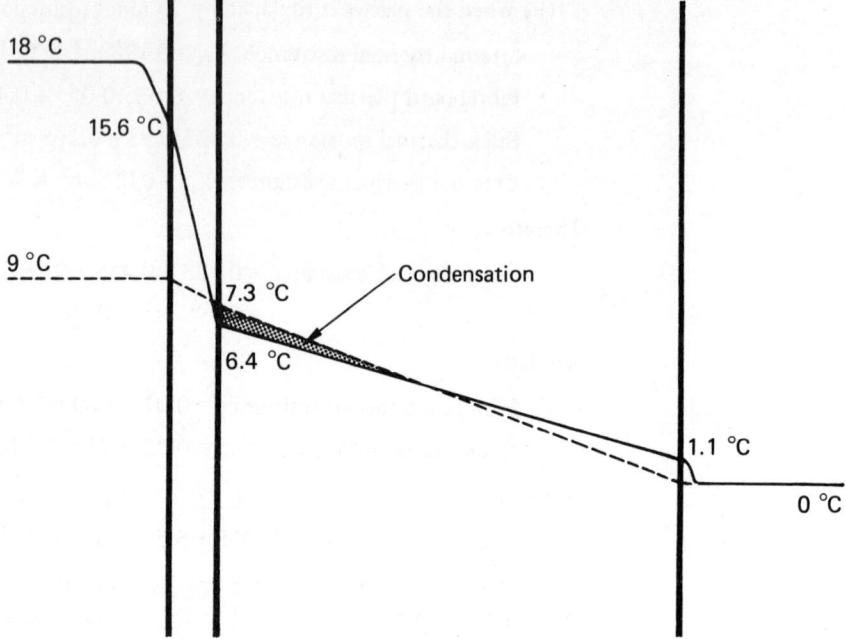

Fig. 5.16 Temperature and dew point gradients – Example 5.11(c), 18 °C.

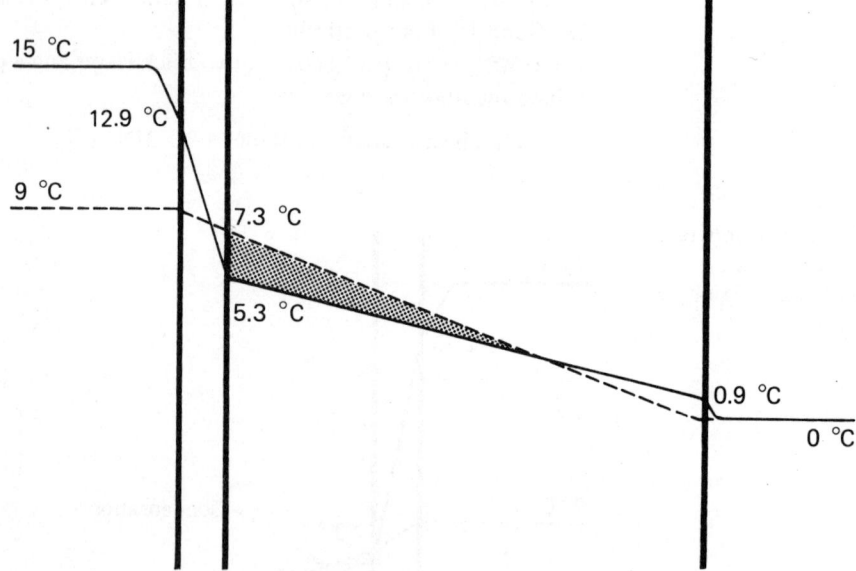

Fig. 5.17 Temperature and dew point gradients – Example 5.11(c), 15 °C.

Brick vapour resistance = 2.63 MN s g⁻¹,
Cavity vapour resistance = 0,
Brick vapour resistance = 2.63 MN s g⁻¹.

If the vapour resistance of polythene sheet is 250 MN s g⁻¹, then we have

Total vapour resistance = 1.5 + 250 + 2.63 + 0 + 2.63

= 256.76 MN s g⁻¹.

Hence,

$$\text{Vapour pressure at outer face of fibreboard} = 1140 - (1.5/256.76) \times 540$$
$$= 1137 \text{ Pa}$$

and the dew point is approximately 9 °C;

$$\text{Vapour pressure at outer face of polythene} = 1140 - (251.5/256.76) \times 540$$
$$= 611 \text{ Pa}$$

and the dew point is approximately 0 °C. Fig. 5.18 shows the appropriate gradients.

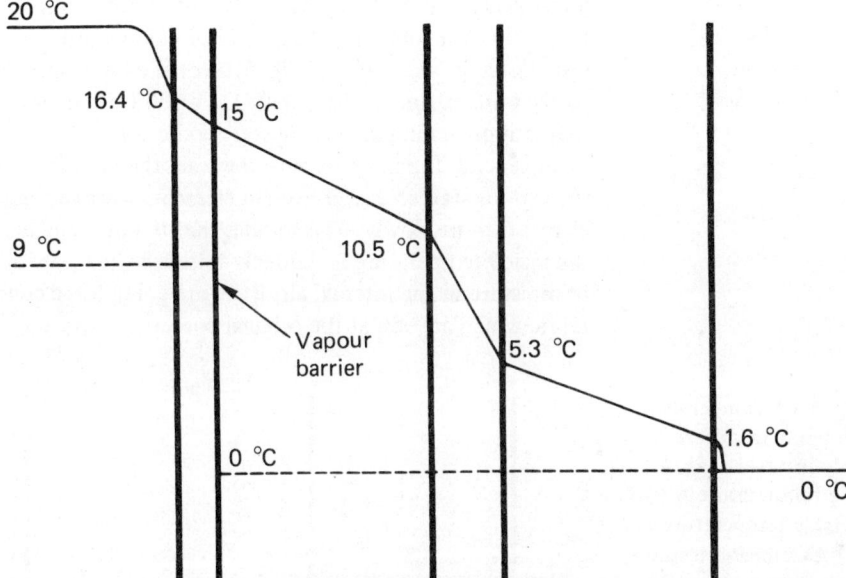

Fig. 5.18 Effect of polythene vapour barrier – Example 5.11(d).

From these examples it is seen that in case (b) where the fibreboard is used, although it has an improved thermal insulation in relation to the plaster (case (a)), it has the same value for vapour diffusance as the plaster. As a result there is an increase in the surface temperature, an improvement in the thermal performance and the actual temperature gradient is changed by a considerable amount, but there is not any significant change in the dew point gradient – resulting in condensation taking place.

In case (c) it is seen that as the internal temperature decreases, the temperature gradient is depressed downwards and the risk of condensation increases.

Finally, in case (d), the risk of condensation is removed by the insertion of the air space and vapour barrier, but it is evident that the vapour barrier would not have had any effect if it had been placed on the other side of the wall, i.e. on the cold face. Hence, vapour barriers should always be placed on the warm side.

It must be noted that all the temperature gradients shown in these examples are for steady-state conditions.

Loudon [9] comments upon the importance of the U-value, and the energy requirements of a house in relation to condensation. He examines a typical house and shows that for the unheated bedroom in this particular house where the U-value of the external walls is 1.7 W m^{-2} K^{-1} and the roof is 1.5 W m^{-2} K^{-1} the relative humidity cannot be kept below 70 per cent. However, when the U-value of the walls and roofs were reduced to 0.5 W m^{-2} K^{-1}, then it was possible to achieve a lower relative humidity. This paper illustrates how important it is to consider the risk of condensation and the need to provide adequate thermal insulation. However, due attention must be paid to the problem of the correct positioning of the insulation.

Although the analysis of transient heat flow is treated in a later chapter, it is worthwhile at this stage to consider its implication in relation to condensation. Fig. 5.19 shows the probable temperature gradients in a wall at different time intervals. In Fig. 5.19 (a) the inside and outside temperatures are the same; in Fig. 5.19(b) at some time θ_0, the inside temperature is raised but the wall has just started to warm up. In Fig. 5.19(c) at a later time, $\theta_0 + \Delta\theta_1$ the wall is partly warmed and in Fig. 5.19(d) at a still further time interval $\theta_0 + \Delta\theta_2$, the wall is approaching the steady-state condition.

In general, the more massive the wall, the greater is the time interval between the various stages, i.e. lightweight elements warm up quickly, heavyweight elements more slowly. This implies that if a building has cooled down, and then the inside temperature is suddenly raised, with a possible increase in the amount of moisture in the internal air, there are going to be considerable parts of the fabric which are still at the original cooler temperature and where there is a risk

Fig. 5.19 Temperature gradients in different time intervals. (a) Inside temperature t_i = outside temperature t_o. (b) At time θ_0, inside temperature raised to t_i'. (c) At time $\theta_0 + \Delta\theta_1$. (d) At time $\theta_0 + \Delta\theta_2$.

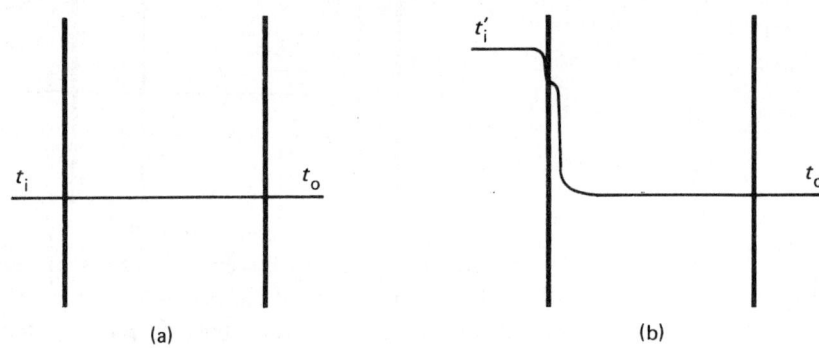

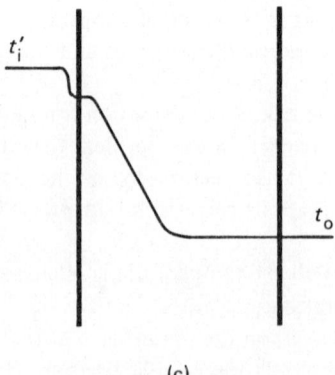

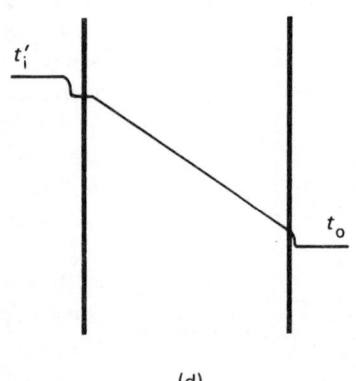

of condensation. Since it has been stated that heavyweight elements take a long time to warm up, the period during which condensation might occur will tend to be greater in these elements. *Building Research Establishment Digest No. 110* [8] draws attention to this problem and refers to heavyweight solid floors without insulation on the internal surface. It makes the point that in this type of situation it can take a considerable period for the floor to warm up and an equally long period during which condensation could be taking place on the face of the slab.

Where considerable variations in the internal temperature are likely to occur, e.g. where the heating is intermittent and the building is allowed to cool down in between the heating periods, then the use of lightweight elements on the inside face of the wall or floor will result in a quicker thermal response (*see* Chapter 7). Heavyweight elements on the inside will be the converse, taking a long time to warm up and could result in surface condensation. It should be noted that a light-weight element which is vapour permeable and placed on the inside may result in interstitial condensation (similar to Example 5.11(b) and Figs. 5.15 to 5.17).

In tropical conditions, where a building is air-conditioned, the internal environment may be cool, the external environment warm. This situation is the reverse of those previously described and the temperature gradients of walls, etc., will be the opposite of those shown.

5.7 Heat loss by fabric

It has been shown that for steady state the rate of heat flow through the fabric is given by

$$Q_f = AU(t_{ai} - t_{ao}),$$

where t_{ai} = internal air temperature and t_{ao} = external air temperature.

As was shown earlier, the surface temperature of an element is not the same as the internal air temperature. Hence t_{ai} and the mean radiant temperature (t_{mrt}) can differ. It was pointed out by Loudon [10] that the effect of this is to cause heat to be transferred to the exposed surfaces by radiation from other surfaces. As a result, the above equation for Q_f is not universally valid and current British practice is to allow for this by replacing the internal air temperature by the environmental temperature t_{ei}, i.e.

$$Q_f = AU(t_{ei} - t_{ao}), \tag{5.8}$$

where

$$t_{ei} = \frac{1}{3} t_{ai} + \frac{2}{3} t_{mrt}. \tag{5.9}$$

It should also be noted that the environmental temperature, as other temperature indices which include radiation, gives a more accurate assessment of comfort than does the internal air temperature, and is a simpler index than the thermal comfort index given in Chapter 3.

If the enclosed area under consideration has several external surfaces (e.g. walls, roof, ground floor, etc.) then the total fabric loss is given by

$$Q_f = \Sigma AU(t_{ei} - t_{ao}). \tag{5.10}$$

5.8 Heat loss by ventilation

The rate of heat transfer by ventilation is given by

$$Q_v = c\rho V(t_{ai} - t_{ao}),$$

where t_{ai} = internal air temperature, t_{ao} = external air temperature, c = specific heat capacity of air (J kg^{-1} K^{-1}), ρ = density of air (kg m^{-3}), V = ventilation rate (m^3 s^{-1}). The normal value for $c\rho$ is 1.2 kJ K^{-1} m^{-3}.

Let Vol = volume of enclosed space, n = number of air changes per hour (ach). Then,

$$\text{Volume to be heated per second} = Vol \times n/3600.$$

Therefore,

$$Q_v = \frac{1.2 \times 10^3 \times Vol \times n}{3600} (t_{ai} - t_{ao}) \text{ J s}^{-1}$$

$$= \frac{Vol \times n}{3} (t_{ai} - t_{ao}) \text{ J s}^{-1} \text{ or W.}$$

The total rate of heat loss from the building is then given by

$$\Sigma Q = Q_f + Q_v$$

$$= \Sigma AU(t_{ei} - t_{ao}) + \frac{Vol \times n}{3} (t_{ai} - t_{ao}).$$

It will be noted that the fabric and ventilation heat loss rates are not based on the same temperature differences. However, if the building is well insulated (i.e. elements have a low U-value) and there is a relatively small area of external surface, then it will be found that there is little variation between the values of t_{ai} and t_{ei}. In this situation it is appropriate to base all the calculations on t_{ei}, i.e.

$$\Sigma Q = \left[\Sigma AU + \frac{Vol \times n}{3} \right] (t_{ei} - t_{ao}). \tag{5.11}$$

Where a difference between t_{ei} and t_{ai} does occur, e.g. with convective heating, then an alternative method has to be used. The method as set out in the *IHVE Guide* and discussed in the paper by Loudon [10] is to assume that there is a conductance h_a between t_{ei} and t_{ai}.

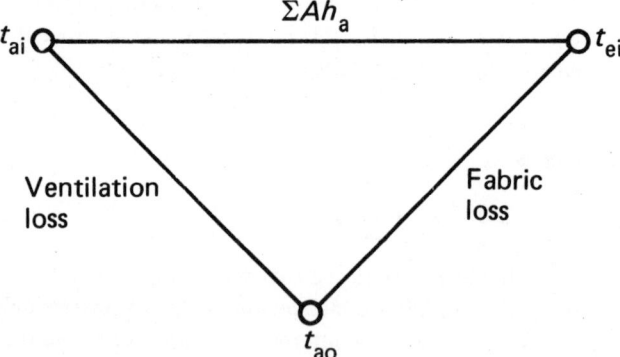

It can be shown that

$$\frac{1}{h_a} = \frac{1}{h_c} - R_{si}.$$

Putting $h_c = 3$ W m^{-2} K^{-1} and $R_{si} = 0.123$ m^2 K W^{-1} gives

$$h_a = 4.8 \text{ W m}^{-2} \text{ K}^{-1}.$$

For convective heating it is assumed that the input is to t_{ai}; hence, there is a heat exchange from t_{ai} to t_{ei} and then from t_{ei} to t_{ao} as shown.

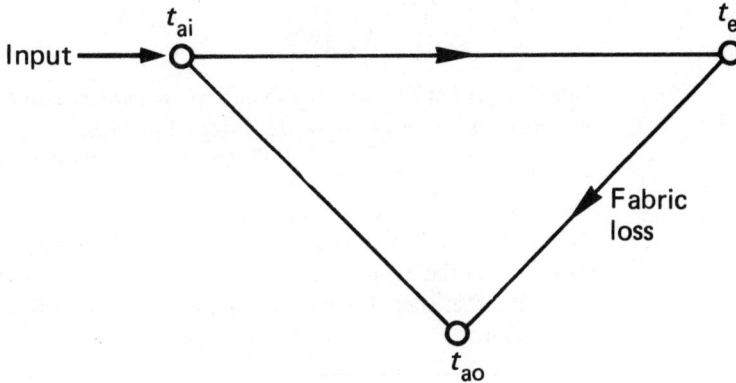

For steady-state conditions, the rate of heat flow from t_{ai} to t_{ei} must be the same as from t_{ei} to t_{ao}, i.e.

$$\Sigma A h_a (t_{ai} - t_{ei}) = \Sigma A U (t_{ei} - t_{ao}).$$

Therefore,

$$t_{ai} - t_{ei} = [(\Sigma A U)/(\Sigma A h_a)] \, (t_{ei} - t_{ao})$$

$$= \Sigma A U (t_{ei} - t_{ao})/4.8 \, \Sigma A = Q_f/4.8 \, \Sigma A. \qquad (5.12)$$

For radiant heating it is assumed that the input is at t_{ei}. Then in a similar manner to above it can be shown that

$$t_{ei} - t_{ai} = Q_v/4.8 \, \Sigma A.$$

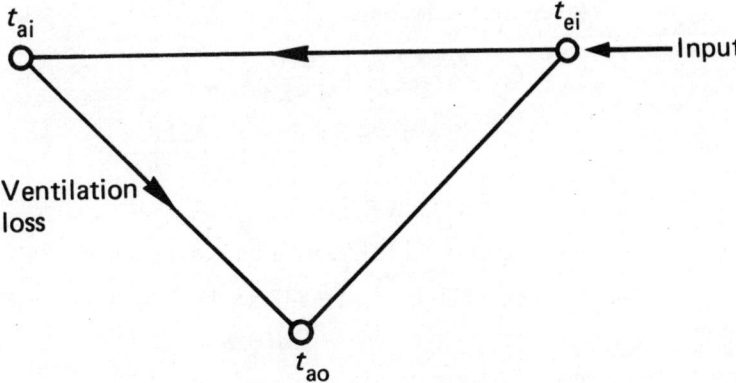

So that the entire heat loss calculation (fabric and ventilation) can be based upon the same temperature difference $(t_{ei} - t_{ao})$, the expression for Q_v can be modified and rewritten as

$$Q_v = C_v (t_{ei} - t_{ao}), \qquad (5.13)$$

where C_v = ventilation conductance and, for convective heating,

$$C_v = \frac{Vol \times n}{3} (1 + \frac{\Sigma A U}{4.8 \, \Sigma A}), \qquad (5.14)$$

and, for radiant heating,

$$\frac{1}{C_v} = \frac{3}{Vol \times n} + \frac{1}{4.8 \, \Sigma A} .$$

(5.15)

Note that ΣA is the sum of *all* surfaces (i.e. external and internal surfaces) whereas ΣAU refers only to the external surfaces.

The following example will illustrate the method of working.

Example 5.12   Calculate the heating load for a small workshop 12 m × 6 m × 4.5 m when it is to be heated by (a) convective heating, (b) radiant heating. Assume that the external air temperature is − 1 °C, environmental temperature 18 °C and that there is a ventilation rate of 6 ach. Additional data as in the table below.

Surface	Area (m^2)	U(W m^{-2} K^{-1})	AU(W K^{-1})
External wall	121	1.0	121
Window	36	5.6	201.6
Door	5	2.9	14.5
Floor	72	0.7	50.4
Roof	72	0.9	64.8
	$\Sigma A = 306$		$\Sigma AU = 452.3$

From equation (5.10),

Fabric loss, $Q_f = \Sigma AU \, (t_{ei} - t_{ao}) = 452.3 \, (18 + 1)$

$= 8594$ W.

From equation (5.14), under conditions of

(a) convective heating,

$$C_v = \frac{Vol \times n}{3} (1 + \frac{\Sigma AU}{4.8 \, \Sigma A})$$

$$= \frac{12 \times 6 \times 4.5 \times 6}{3} (1 + \frac{452.3}{4.8 \times 306})$$

$$= 847.5 \text{ W K}^{-1}$$

From equation (5.13), ventilation loss is given by

$Q_v = C_v (t_{ei} - t_{ao}) = 847.5 \times 19$

$= 16103$ W.

Therefore,

Total heating load $= Q_f + Q_v$

$= 8594 + 16103$

$= 24697$ W

$= 24.7$ kW;

(b) radiant heating, from equation (5.15),

$$\frac{1}{C_v} = \frac{3}{Vol \times n} + \frac{1}{4.8 \, \Sigma A} = \frac{3}{324 \times 6} + \frac{1}{4.8 \times 306}$$

$$= 0.002 \, 22 \text{ K W}^{-1},$$

$$C_v = 450.5 \text{ W K}^{-1}.$$

Hence,

Ventilation loss $= 450.5 \times 19 = 8560$ W,

Total heating load $= 8594 + 8560$

$$= 17154 \text{ W}$$

$$= 17.15 \text{ kW}.$$

Example 5.13   As Example 5.12 but ventilation rate reduced to 1.5 ach.

Fabric loss, $Q_f = \Sigma A U (t_{ei} - t_{ao}) = 452.3 (18 + 1)$

$$= 8594 \text{ W}$$

(a) Convective heating,

$$C_v = \frac{Vol \times n}{3} (1 + \frac{\Sigma A U}{4.8 \, \Sigma A})$$

$$= \frac{12 \times 6 \times 4.5 \times 1.5}{3} (1 + \frac{452.3}{4.8 \times 306})$$

$$= 211.9 \text{ W K}^{-1}.$$

Ventilation loss, $Q_v = C_v (t_{ei} - t_{ao}) = 211.9 \times 19$

$$= 4026 \text{ W}$$

Hence,

Total heating load $= Q_f + Q_v$

$$= 8594 + 4026$$

$$= 12620 \text{ W}$$

$$= 12.62 \text{ kW}.$$

(b) Radiant heating,

$$\frac{1}{C_v} = \frac{3}{Vol \times n} + \frac{1}{4.8 \, \Sigma A} = \frac{3}{324 \times 1.5} + \frac{1}{4.8 \times 306}$$

$$= 0.006 \, 85 \text{ K W}^{-1},$$

$$C_v = 145.9 \text{ W K}^{-1}.$$

Ventilation loss $= 145.9 \times 19 = 2772$ W.

Hence,

Total heating load $= 8594 + 2772$

$$= 11366 \text{ W}$$

$$= 11.37 \text{ kW}$$

Comparing the heating loads for these two examples:

	6 ach	1.5 ach
Convective heating	24.7 kW	12.26 kW
Radiant heating	17.15 kW	11.37 kW

In both cases the convective heating load is larger than the radiant heating load, but the difference between them is not as significant when the ventilation rate is 1.5 ach.

In this latter case, if C_v had been assumed to be

$$C_v = \frac{Vol \times n}{3} = \frac{324 \times 1.5}{3} = 162 \text{ W K}^{-1},$$

then

Ventilation loss = $162 \times 19 = 3078$ W.

Hence,

Total heating load = 8594 + 3078

$$= 11672 \text{ W}$$

$$= 11.67 \text{ kW}.$$

This indicates that, for low ventilation rates, it is sufficiently accurate to assume that

$$C_v = \frac{Vol \times n}{3}.$$

However, for high ventilation rates, equations (5.13) and (5.14) have to be used. Further consideration of this aspect is given in Chapter 6.

5.9 Energy consumption during heating periods

So far, in our calculations for a heat loss where we have used the expression $Q = \Sigma AU + C_v(t_{ei} - t_{ao})$, a design external temperature has been inserted for t_{ao}. As was explained in Chapter 4, this design external temperature is appropriate for estimating the size of plant required. However, if we wish to calculate the energy consumed over a specified time, then we have to use a value for t_{ao} which is the average temperature for the particular period.

Example 5.14   Calculate the energy required during October to heat a small building in Glasgow. Assume mean environmental temperature for the building (over a 24-h period) = 15 °C. Average external temperature for October = 9.44 °C. $\Sigma AU + C_v = 300$ W K^{-1}.

Energy (in kilowatt-hours) consumed during month is

($\Sigma AU + C_v$) × Temperature difference for month ×

Number of days in month × 24 × 10^{-3}.

Note that 24 = number of hours in day and that 10^{-3} is required to convert watts to kilowatts. Therefore,

Energy consumed for month = 300 × (15 − 9.44) × 31 × 24 × 10^{-3}

$$= 1241 \text{ kW h}.$$

In order to calculate the energy required to heat the building during the entire heating period, the procedure in Example 5.14 would be repeated for each month (or part of month) and then totalled. An allowance should be made for casual gains, e.g. solar gains, heat from lights, etc., and this should be deducted from the total.

A useful approximate method which can be used as an alternative is the degree day described in Chapter 4. This includes an allowance for casual gains but is related to a fixed base temperature.

Example 5.15   Calculate the energy required over the heating period to heat the building in Example 5.14 if it is situated in the Thames Valley.

From Table 4.3, degree-day for Thames Valley = 2012 (base temperature = 15°C).

$$\text{Energy required} = (\Sigma A U + C_v) \times \text{Number of degree days} \times 24 \times 10^{-3}$$
$$= 300 \times 2012 \times 24 \times 10^{-3}$$
$$= 14\ 486\ \text{kW h}$$

It should be observed that in Examples 5.14 and 5.15 it is assumed that the heating is continuous for 24 h every day. If the heating is to be intermittent, then an allowance has to be made for this in the calculations.

References

1   Loudon, A. G., *U*-values in the 1970 Guide. *Building Research Station Current Paper 79/68,* 1968.
2   Arnold, P. J., Thermal conductivity of masonry materials. *Building Research Station Current Paper 1/70,* 1970.
3   *Standard U-values. Building Research Establishment Digest No. 108.* HMSO, London, 1975.
4   Robinson, H. E., Powlitch, F. J. and Dill, R. S., The thermal insulating value of air-spaces. *Washington Housing and Home Finance Agency Research Paper No. 32,* 1954.
5   Turner, D. P. (ed.), *Windows and Environment.* Pilkington Bros., St. Helens, 1969.
6.   *Heat Losses through Floors. Building Research Establishment Digest No. 145.* HMSO, London, 1972.
7   Billington, N. S., Heat loss through solid ground floors. *Journal of the Institution of Heating and Ventilating Engineers,* **19**, 351–372, 1951.
8   *Condensation. Building Research Establishment Digest No. 110.* HMSO, London, 1969.
9   Loudon, A. G., The effect of ventilation and building design factors on the risk of condensation and mould growth in dwellings. *Building Research Station Current Paper 31/71,* 1971.
10   Loudon, A. G., Summertime temperatures in buildings. *Building Research Station Current Paper 47/68,* 1968.

APPENDIX 5: Tables of *U*-values (pages 304–309)

These have been taken from *IHVE Guide.*

U-Values for External Walls: Masonry Construction

Construction	Thickness	U value (W m⁻² K⁻¹)			Material	Thermal Properties	
		Sheltered	Normal (Standard)	Severe		Density (kg m⁻³)	Conductivity k (W m⁻¹ K⁻¹)
Brickwork							
1. Solid wall, unplastered	105	3.0	3.3	3.6	Brick	1700	0.84
	220	2.2	2.3	2.4			
	335	1.6	1.7	1.8			
2. Solid wall, with 16mm plaster on inside face							
(*a*) With dense plaster	105	2.8	3.0	3.2	Plaster	1300	0.50
	220	2.0	2.1	2.2			
	335	1.6	1.7	1.8			
(*b*) With lightweight plaster	105	2.3	2.5	2.7	Plaster	600	0.16
	220	1.8	1.9	2.0			
	335	1.4	1.5	1.6			
3. Solid wall, with 10 mm plasterboard lining fixed to brickwork with plaster dabs	105	2.6	2.8	3.0	Plasterboard	950	0.16
	220	1.9	2.0	2.1			
	335	1.5	1.6	1.7			
4. Cavity wall (unventilated) with 105 mm outer and inner leaves with 16 mm plaster on inside face							
(*a*) With dense plaster	260	1.4	1.5	1.6	Brick (outer leaf)	1700	0.84
(*b*) With lightweight plaster	260	1.3	1.3	1.3	Brick (inner leaf)	1700	0.62
5. As 4, but with 230 mm outer leaf and 105 mm inner leaf							
(*a*) With dense plaster	375	1.2	1.2	1.2	Plaster	1300	0.50
(*b*) With lightweight plaster	375	1.1	1.1	1.1	Plaster	600	0.16

Brickwork/lightweight concrete block

No. / Description	Thickness (mm)				Material	Density	Conductivity
6. Cavity wall (unventilated), with 105 mm brick outer leaf 100 mm lightweight concrete block inner leaf and with 16 mm dense plaster on inside face	260	0.93	0.96	0.98	Concrete block	600	0.19
7. As 6, but with 13 mm expanded polystyrene board in cavity		0.69	0.70	0.71	Expanded polystyrene	25	0.033
Lightweight concrete block							
8. Solid wall, 150 mm aerated concrete block, with tile hanging externally and with 16 mm plaster on inside face		0.95	0.97	1.0	Aerated concrete block	750	0.22
9. Cavity wall (unventilated) with 75 mm aerated concrete block outer leaf, rendered externally, 100 mm aerated concrete block inner leaf and with 16 mm plaster on inside face 50 mm cavity		0.82	0.84	0.86	Aerated concrete block (outer leaf) (inner leaf)	750 750	0.24 0.22
Concrete							
10. Cast	150 200	3.2 2.9	3.5 3.1	3.9 3.4	Concrete	2100	1.40
11. Cast, 150 mm thick, with 50 mm woodwool slab permanent shuttering on inside face finished with 16 mm dense plaster		1.1	1.1	1.1	Woodwool slab	450	0.09
12. As 11, but 200 mm thick		1.1	1.1	1.1			
13. Pre-cast panels, 75 mm thick		3.9	4.3	4.8			
14. As 13, but with 50 mm cavity and sandwich lining panels, composed of 5 mm asbestos-cement sheet, 25 mm expanded polystyrene and 10 mm plasterboard					Asbestos-cement sheet	1500	0.36
15. Pre-cast sandwich panels comprising 75 mm dense concrete, 25 mm expanded polystyrene and 150 mm lightweight concrete		0.79	0.80	0.82	Concrete Lightweight concrete	2100 1200	1.4 0.38
16. Pre-cast panels 38 mm on timber battens and framing with 10 mm plasterboard lining and 50 mm glass-fibre insulation in cavity (Assumed 10% area of glass fibre bridged by timber)		0.71 0.61	0.72 0.62	0.73 0.63	Glass fibre Timber	25 650	0.035 0.14

U-Values for External Walls: Curtain Wall Construction

Construction	U value (W m⁻² K⁻¹)			Material	Thermal properties	
	Sheltered	Normal (Standard)	Severe		Density (kg m⁻³)	Conductivity, k (W m⁻¹ K⁻¹)
Composite cladding panels						
1. Comprising 25 mm expanded polystyrene between 5 mm asbestos-cement sheets set in metal framing, 50 mm cavity, 100 mm lightweight concrete block inner wall, finished with 16 mm plaster rendering on inside face	0.79	0.81	0.83	Expanded polystyrene	25	0.033
(Assumed 5 per cent area of expanded polystyrene bridged by metal framing)						
2. Obscured glass, 38 mm expanded polystyrene cavity 100 mm lightweight concrete back-up wall, dense plaster	0.51	0.51	0.52	Lightweight concrete	800	0.23
3. Stove-enamelled steel sheet, 10 mm asbestos board, cavity, 100 mm lightweight concrete back-up wall, dense plaster	1.1	1.1	1.1	Asbestos board	700	0.11
Curtain walling panelling with 5 per cent bridging by metal mullions, 150 mm × 50 mm wide						
4. With mullion projecting outside, flush inside:						
Panel construction 2	0.8	0.9	0.9			
Panel construction 3	1.4	1.4	1.5			
5. With mullion projecting inside and outside:						
Panel construction 2	1.3	1.5	1.8			
Panel construction 3	1.9	2.1	2.4			
Curtain walling panelling with 10 per cent bridging by metal mullions 150 mm × 50 mm wide						
6. With mullion projecting outside, flush inside:						
Panel construction 2	1.2	1.2	1.3			
Panel construction 3	1.7	1.7	1.8			
7. With mullion projecting inside and outside:						
Panel construction 2	2.2	2.5	3.0			
Panel construction 3	2.7	3.1	3.6			

U-Values for External Walls: Framed Construction

Construction	U value (W m⁻² K⁻¹)			Material	Thermal properties	
	Sheltered	Normal (Standard)	Severe		Density (kg m⁻³)	Conductivity, k (W m⁻¹ K⁻¹)
Tile hanging						
1. On timber battens and framing with 10 mm plasterboard lining, 50 mm glass-fibre insulation in the cavity and building paper behind the battens (Assumed 10 per cent area of glass fibre bridged by timber)	0.64	0.65	0.66	Clay tiles	1900	0.84
Weatherboarding						
2. On timber framing with 10 mm plasterboard lining, 50 mm glass-fibre insulation in the cavity and building paper behind the boarding (Assumed 10 per cent area of glass fibre bridged by timber)	0.61	0.62	0.63	Weatherboarding	650	0.14
Corrugated sheeting						
3. 5 mm thick asbestos-cement (No allowance has been made for effect of corrugations on heat loss)	4.7	5.3	6.1	Asbestos-cement sheeting	1500	0.36
4. As 3, but with cavity and aluminium foil-backed plasterboard lining	1.7	1.8	1.9			
5. Double-skin asbestos-cement with 25 mm glass-fibre insulation in between	1.1	1.1	1.1			
6. As 5, but with cavity and aluminium foil-backed plasterboard lining	0.76	0.78	0.79			
7. Aluminium:						
(a) Bright surface outside and inside	2.4	2.6	2.9			
(b) Dull surface outside bright surface inside	2.6	2.8	3.0			
8. As 7, but with cavity and aluminium foil-backed plasterboard lining:						
(a) Bright surface outside	1.7	1.8	1.9			
(b) Dull surface outside	1.8	1.9	2.0			
9. Plastic-covered steel	5.0	5.7	6.6			
10. As 9, but with cavity and aluminium foil-backed plasterboard lining	1.8	1.9	2.0			

U-Values for Flat Roofs

Construction	U value (W m⁻² K⁻¹)			Material	Thermal properties	
	Sheltered	Normal (Standard)	Severe		Density (kg m⁻³)	Conductivity, k (W m⁻¹ K⁻¹)
1. Asphalt 19 mm thick or felt/bitumen layers* on solid concrete 150 mm thick (treated as exposed)	3.1	3.4	3.7	Asphalt Concrete	1700 2100	0.50 1.4
2. As 1, but with 50 mm lightweight concrete screed and 16 mm plaster ceiling	2.1	2.2	2.3	Lightweight concrete Dense plaster	1200 1300	0.42 0.50
3. As 2, but with screed laid to falls, average 100 mm thick	1.7	1.8	1.9			
4. Asphalt 19 mm thick or felt/bitumen layers* on 150 mm thick autoclaved aerated concrete roof-slabs	0.87	0.88	0.89	Aerated concrete	500	0.16
5. Asphalt 19mm thick or felt/bitumen layers* on hollow tiles 150 mm thick	2.1	2.2	2.3	Hollow tile	$R = 0.27$	
6. As 5, but with 50 mm lightweight concrete screed and 16 mm plaster ceiling	1.5	1.6	1.7			
7. As 6, but with screed laid to falls, average 100 mm thick	1.4	1.4	1.5			
8. Asphalt 19 mm thick or felt/bitumen layers* on 13 mm cement and sand screed, 50 mm woodwool slabs on timber joists and aluminium foil-backed 10 mm plasterboard ceiling, sealed to prevent moisture penetration	0.88	0.90	0.92	Cement/sand Woodwool slab Plasterboard	2100 560 950	1.28 0.10 0.16
9. As 8, but with 25 mm glass-fibre insulation laid between joists	0.59	0.60	0.61	Glass fibre	25	0.035
10. Asphalt 19 mm thick or felt/bitumen layers* on 13 mm cement and sand screed on 50 mm metal edge reinforced woodwool slabs on steel framing, with vapour barrier at inside	1.4	1.4	1.5			

Note: Other flat roof values can be found in the *IHVE Guide*.

U-Values for Pitched Roofs (35° Slope)

Construction	U value (W m^{-2} K^{-1})			Material	Thermal properties	
	Sheltered	Normal (Standard)	Severe		Density (kg m^{-3})	Conductivity, k (W m^{-1} K^{-1})
1. Tiles on battens, roofing felt and rafters, with roof space and aluminium foil-backed 10 mm plaster-board ceiling on joists	1.4	1.5	1.6	Tiles	1900	0.84
				Roofing felt	960	0.19
2. As 1, but with boarding on rafters	1.3	1.3	1.3	Timber	650	0.14
3. As 2, but with 50 mm glass-fibre insulation between joists	0.49	0.50	0.51			
4. Corrugated asbestos-cement sheeting	5.3	6.1	7.2	Asbestos-cement sheeting	1500	0.36
5. As 4, but with cavity and aluminium foil-backed 10 mm plasterboard lining	1.8	1.9	2.0			
6. Corrugated double-skin asbestos-cement sheeting with 25 mm glass-fibre insulation between (No allowance has been made for effect of corrugations on heat loss)	1.1	1.1	1.1	Glass fibre	25	0.035
7. As 6, but with cavity and aluminium foil-backed 10 mm plasterboard lining; ventilated air space	0.79	0.80	0.82			
8. Corrugated aluminium sheeting	3.3	3.8	4.3			
9. As 8, but with cavity and aluminium foil-backed 10 mm plasterboard lining	1.8	1.9	2.0			
10. Corrugated plastic-covered steel sheeting	5.7	6.7	8.1			
11. As 10, but with cavity and aluminium foil-backed 10 mm plasterboard lining; ventilated air space	1.9	2.0	2.1			

6

HEAT GAINS DUE TO SOLAR RADIATION—STEADY-STATE AND CYCLIC CONDITIONS

6.1 Influence of solar radiation

Before considering how a building reacts to solar radiation, it is necessary to take into account the manner in which the radiation will enter the building. Radiation striking a surface may be

    (i) absorbed;   (ii) reflected;   (iii) transmitted.

If a = proportion of radiation absorbed, r = proportion of radiation reflected, τ = proportion of radiation transmitted, then

    $a + r + \tau = 1.0.$

The values of a, r and τ will depend upon the physical characteristics of the surface receiving radiation.

6.2 Absorption

A body which is a perfect emitter of radiation is termed a 'black body'. A body which absorbs radiation will also emit radiation and it is possible to measure experimentally the radiation at different wavelengths emitted by a black body. When these values are plotted for different temperatures a set of curves, as shown in Fig. 6.1, is obtained.

It can be shown that the area under the curve is proportional to the fourth power of the absolute temperature. Since the area under the curve is equal to the total power radiated, this can be expressed as

    Total power radiated = $\sigma A T^4$,   (6.1)

Fig. 6.1 Spectral distribution of black-body radiation.

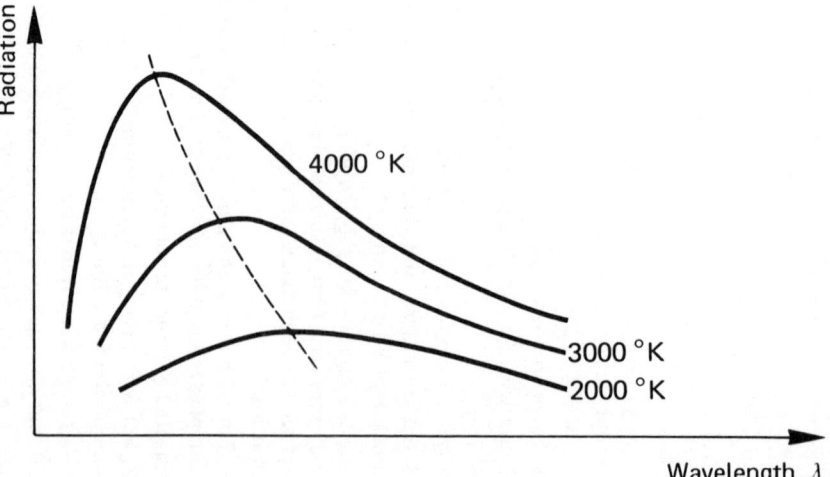

where A = area (in square metres), T = absolute temperature (in kelvins), σ = Stefan's constant = 5.7×10^{-8} W m^{-2} K^{-4}, the above equation being the Stefan–Boltzmann law.

The significance of the temperature being raised to the fourth power in the above equation is demonstrated in Table 6.1, where the radiation intensity from the various sources are expressed as a ratio of the first example.

Table 6.1

Example	Source	Temperature ($^\circ$C)	Temperature (K)	(Temperature)^4 (K^4)	Ratio
(i)	–	0	273	55.5×10^8	1.0
(ii)	Wall surface temperature	20	293	73.7×10^8	1.33
(iii)	Human skin temperature	34	307	88.8×10^8	1.6
(iv)	Central heating radiator	70	343	138.4×10^8	2.5
(v)	Sun	–	5800	1131.6×10^{12}	203 900

Another important aspect of the influence of the temperature should be noted. From the curves shown in Fig. 6.1, it is seen that the wavelength at which the maximum radiation occurs changes with the temperature, the wavelength becoming shorter as the temperature rises. Hence, a high-temperature source will radiate at a short wavelength and conversely a low-temperature source will radiate at a long wavelength. This change in wavelength with temperature has to be taken into account when considering the transmission of solar radiation through glass, an aspect which is discussed in a later section.

6.3 Emissivity

At a given wavelength, the maximum amount of radiation which can be emitted will be that from a black body, i.e. the emissivity of a black body = 1.0. It follows that a non-black body will have an emissivity less than 1.0.

The emissivity of any body at a given wavelength is the ratio of its emission to that of a black body at the same wavelength.

$$E_\lambda = \frac{\text{Total power emitted per unit area of body}}{\text{Total power emitted per unit area of black body}}.$$

Within the temperature range normally met in practice, most building materials have a high emissivity (0.9 to 0.95) whereas polished metals have a low emissivity (e.g. polished aluminium having a value 0.05).

Example 6.1   Calculate the rate of radiation emitted per square metre by a body at 50 $^\circ$C having an emissivity value of 0.3. What is the amount of energy radiated during a period of 30 min?

Temperature = 50 + 273 = 323 K.

From equation (6.1),

Black body radiation = $5.7 \times 10^{-8} \times (323)^4$

$= 620.4$ W m^{-2}.

For a body with emissivity = 0.3,

Radiation = 0.3×620.4

$= 186.1$ W m^{-2}

$= 186.1$ J m^{-2} s^{-1}

Therefore, for a period of 30 min,

$$\text{Energy radiated} = 186.1 \times 30 \times 60$$
$$= 335 \times 10^3 \text{ J m}^{-2}$$
$$= 335 \text{ kJ m}^{-2}.$$

Mention has been made of the following important aspects regarding wavelength:

(i) the value of the absorptivity and emissivity are influenced by the wavelength;

(ii) the wavelength at the peak radiation depends upon the temperature of the radiating source.

The sun, being a high-temperature source, will emit radiation in the short waveband while a building, being a low-temperature source, will radiate at a long wavelength. In order to consider how a building will behave in relation to solar radiation it is necessary to consider the absorptivity and emissivity values at different wavelengths.

Beckett [1] measured the absorption values of some building materials at different wavelengths and Groundwater [2] describes the apparatus and method used.

Although the range of solar radiation with which we are concerned extends from 300 to 3000 nm, Beckett confined his investigation to the range 500 to 1780 nm. However, he decided that for practical purposes absorption values based upon a wavelength of 500 to 600 nm were appropriate for assessing the effect of short-wave solar radiation.

Table 6.2 gives typical values appropriate to long- and short-wavelength radiation.

Table 6.2   *Emissivity and absorptivity values (based on data in IHVE Guide)*

Surface	Emissivity of low-temperature radiation	Absorptivity of solar radiation
Aluminium	0.05	0.2
Asbestos sheets	0.9	0.6
Asphalt	0.95	0.9
Brick (dark)	0.9	0.65
Brick (red sand lime)	0.9	0.55−0.7
Concrete	0.9	0.65
Paint − white	0.9	0.3
− black	0.9	0.9
Slate	0.9	0.9
Tiles (red clay)	0.9	0.4−0.8
Whitewashed roof	0.9	0.3−0.5

A simple way to demonstrate the effect of different absorption values in relation to solar radiation is to feel the roofs of parked cars in an open-air car park during a sunny day. The roof surface of a black or dark-coloured vehicle will be found to be hotter to the touch than that of a white or light-coloured car.

In the same way, any dark surface or tarred area adjacent to a building, and subjected to solar radiation, will tend to become hotter than a similar white or pale-coloured area. The hotter area, in turn, will then re-radiate its heat to its surroundings. Thus, the choice of the materials surrounding a building can have a noticeable effect on the microclimate of that building.

6.4 Sol-air temperature   In determining the rate of heat flow due to solar radiation acting on the fabric of a building it is convenient to base the calculations on a temperature difference.

When the surfaces of a building are subjected to solar radiation, a rise in the internal temperature is produced. A similar rise in the internal temperature could occur if there was no solar radiation but if the external air temperature was increased. This increased external air temperature which is producing the same internal temperature rise as was obtained with the solar radiation acting in conjunction with the actual external air temperature is termed the *sol-air temperature*. Hence,

Rate of heat flow due to sol-air temperature = Rate of heat flow due to solar radiation + Actual external air temperature.

An expression for the sol-air temperature can be derived as follows. If t_{so} = external surface temperature, t_{ao} = external air temperature, R_{so} = external surface resistance, then

Rate of heat flow at surface of fabric due to temperature difference per unit area = $(1/R_{so}) (t_{ao} - t_{so})$.

Let I_G = global solar irradiance on surface of fabric (i.e. direct + diffuse), a = solar absorptivity of surface, then solar radiation absorbed by fabric per unit area = aI_G. Hence,

Heat flow at surface per unit area = Flow due to actual temperature difference + Gain due to solar radiation = $(1/R_{so}) (t_{ao} - t_{so}) + aI_G$.

In addition to this heat flow, the fabric will radiate heat to the sky and surroundings by long-wave radiation. Therefore,

Heat loss by long-wave radiation per unit area = EI_L,

where I_L = long-wave radiation and E = emissivity. Hence,

Net heat flow rate per unit area at surface = $(1/R_{so}) (t_{ao} - t_{so}) +$
$$+ aI_G - EI_L.$$

Let t_{eo} = sol-air temperature, then the heat flow rate per unit area at surface due to the sol-air temperature is given by

$(1/R_{so}) (t_{eo} - t_{so})$.

But,

Rate of heat flow due to sol-air temperature = Rate of heat flow due to actual temperature difference + Solar radiation effect,

$$(1/R_{so})(t_{eo} - t_{so}) = (1/R_{so}) (t_{ao} - t_{so}) + aI_G - EI_L.$$

Multiply each side by R_{so}, then,

$$t_{eo} - t_{so} = t_{ao} - t_{so} + R_{so}(aI_G - EI_L),$$

$$t_{eo} = t_{ao} + R_{so}(aI_G - EI_L). \tag{6.2}$$

The *IHVE Guide* gives a value of 100 W m^{-2} for the long-wave radiation from horizontal roofs to a clear sky. In the case of vertical surfaces, the *Guide* states that EI_L can be taken as zero, since it is assumed that the long-wave radiation which a wall emits is approximately balanced by that which it receives from the ground.

Since the sol-air temperature may be used for checking whether overheating will occur in a building during summer conditions or to calculate a cooling load, the external air temperature t_{ao} has to be appropriate to a period when there is constant sunshine. The *IHVE Guide* gives values of typical average external air temperatures for 5 per cent of days of highest solar radiation for 51.7°N during the period March to September. This has been discussed in detail in Chapter 4. It adds the comment that these temperatures are fairly typical of most populous areas within the United Kingdom.

Hottel [3] has given the following simple method for estimating the average temperature for a sunny day in a particular month. If t_{max} = average monthly maximum daily temperature and t_{mean} = average monthly mean daily temperature, then

Average monthly temperature for sunny day = 0.3 t_{max} + 0.7 t_{mean}.

Example 6.2   Calculate the sol-air temperature for a vertical wall facing east using the following data: $I_{GV} = 135$ W m^{-2}, $R_{so} = 0.05$ m^2 K W^{-1}, $a = 0.7$, $t_{ao} = 23.5$ °C.

From equation (6.2),

$$t_{eo} = t_{ao} + R_{so}(aI_G - EI_L).$$

For a vertical surface, EI_L is ignored, $I_G = I_{GV}$, and so

$$t_{eo} = 23.5 + (0.05 \times 0.7 \times 135)$$

$$= 23.5 + 4.73 = 28.23 \text{ °C}.$$

It should be noted that the time when the maximum value of the sol-air temperature occurs on a particular orientation may not be the same time as that for the maximum external air temperature.

The sol-air temperature on a vertical surface can be considered as consisting of two components, *viz.*

External air temperature = t_{ao}

(independent of orientation with peak value in afternoon)

Temperature increase over external air temperature due to solar

radiation = $R_{so}aI_{GV}$

(time of peak value depends on orientation).

The variation of the value of the two components with time is illustrated in Examples 6.3 and 6.4.

Example 6.3   Consider a wall facing (a) east, (b) south. Let $R_{so} = 0.05$ m^2 K W^{-1}; $a = 0.6$. Summer condition in Britain. Calculate the sol-air temperature for the period 06.00 to 18.00 hours.

Table 6.3

	True solar time												
	6	7	8	9	10	11	12	13	14	15	16	17	18
Irradiance on east face (W m^{-2})	525	665	695	630	505	330	135	130	120	105	90	70	45
Irradiance on south face (W m^{-2})	45	70	200	345	465	540	570	540	465	345	200	70	45
$R_{so}aI_{GV}$ (east face) ($^\circ$C)	15.8	20.0	20.9	18.9	15.2	9.9	4.1	3.9	3.6	3.2	2.7	2.1	1.4
$R_{so}aI_{GV}$ (south face) ($^\circ$C)	1.4	2.1	6.0	10.4	14.0	16.2	17.1	16.2	14.0	10.4	6.0	2.1	1.4
External air temperature, t_{ao}($^\circ$C)	14.3	15.6	17.2	18.9	20.6	22.2	23.5	24.6	25.2	25.4	25.1	24.6	23.5
Sol-air temperature (east face), $t_{ao} + R_{so}aI_{GV}$	30.1	35.6	38.1	37.8	35.8	32.1	27.6	28.5	28.8	28.6	27.8	26.7	24.9
Sol-air temperature (south face), $t_{ao} + R_{so}aI_{GV}$	15.7	17.7	23.2	29.3	34.6	38.4	40.6	40.8	39.2	35.8	31.1	26.7	24.9

Note. The irradiance values were obtained from tables in the *IHVE Guide*, but for a particular situation the methods described in Chapter 4 could be used.

The values are shown in Table 6.3 and in graphical form in Fig. 6.2(a) and (b).

Example 6.3 was for conditions pertaining to Britain, which has a temperate climate; however, the same procedure can be used for any other geographical position provided the hourly external air temperature and solar irradiance are known. The latter can be obtained by using the techniques described in Chapter 4. Petherbridge [4] has published tables of air temperatures and irradiances suitable for use for locations in West Africa, appropriate for a tropical arid climate, and additional tables for an equatorial humid climate – in all cases the values relate to the period May to July. (However, Petherbridge has stated that these tables are only put forward as tentative proposals.)

Using data from these tables the sol-air temperature has been recalculated for the same conditions as in Example 6.3, but for a tropical arid climate. This is shown in graphical form in Fig. 6.3. It will be observed that the curves are of a similar form to those obtained for the British temperate climate; however, in the case of the south-facing wall it will be seen that the increase in the temperature due to the solar radiation in relation to the external air temperature is much less for the tropical arid climate than for that in Example 6.3, this being due to the difference in Latitude. A better comparison can be made with the north-facing wall (Fig. 6.3(c)).

Another very important aspect of the sol-air temperature is the actual surface of the element under consideration. This can be illustrated by considering a horizontal flat roof subjected to solar radiation in a tropical arid climate.

Example 6.4   Calculate the sol-air temperature at noon (true solar time) for a flat roof under the following conditions: external air temperature, $t_{ao} = 36.2$ $^\circ$C; solar irradiance, $I_{GV} = 1170$ W m^{-2}; surface resistance, $R_{so} = 0.045$ m^2 K W^{-1}; long-wave radiation, $I_L = 100$ W m^{-2}; surface of roof (a) whitewashed, $a = 0.3$, $E = 0.9$, (b) asphalt, $a = 0.9$, $E = 0.9$.

In the case of a roof, the long-wave radiation loss has to be included; hence,

Fig. 6.2 The variation of temperature with time in Example 6.3. (a) East-facing wall. (b) South-facing wall.

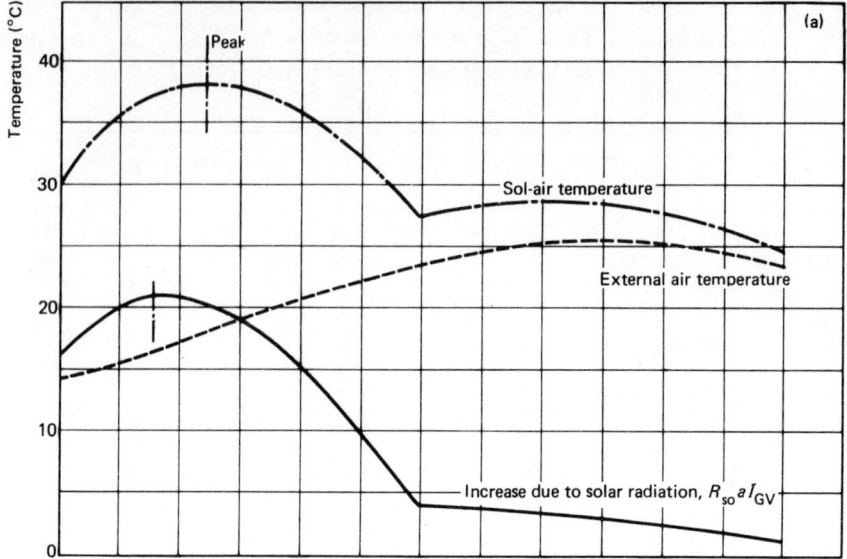

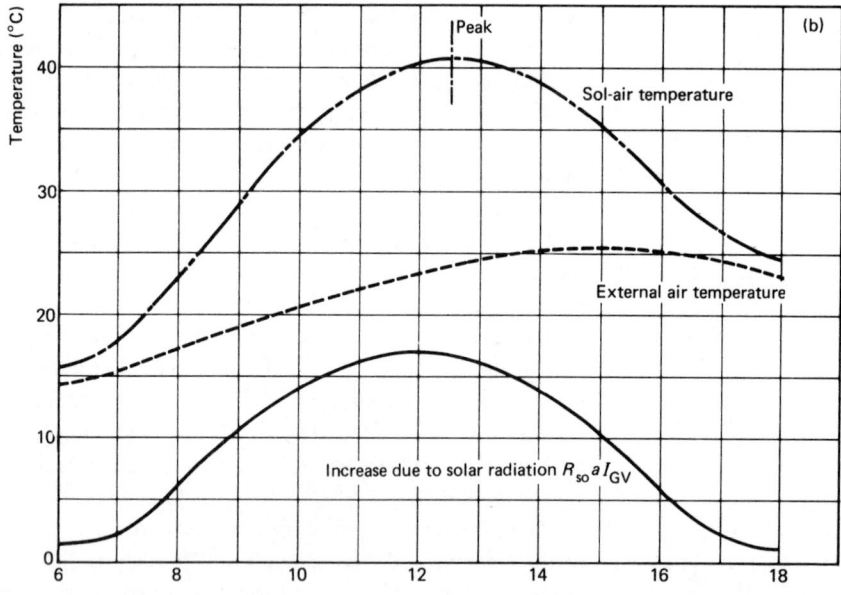

the sol-air temperature is given by

$$t_{eo} = t_{ao} + R_{so}(aI_{GV} - EI_L)$$

(a) Whitewashed:

$$t_{eo} = 36.2 + 0.045\,[(0.3 \times 1170) - (0.9 \times 100)]$$
$$= 47.95\,^{\circ}C.$$

Fig. 6.3 Sol-air temperatures for a tropical arid climate at Latitude 5°N during the period May to July. $R_{so} = 0.05 \text{ m}^2 \text{ K W}^{-1}$ and $a = 0.6$. (Based on data in *BRS CP7/74* [4].)
(a) South-facing wall.
(b) East-facing wall.

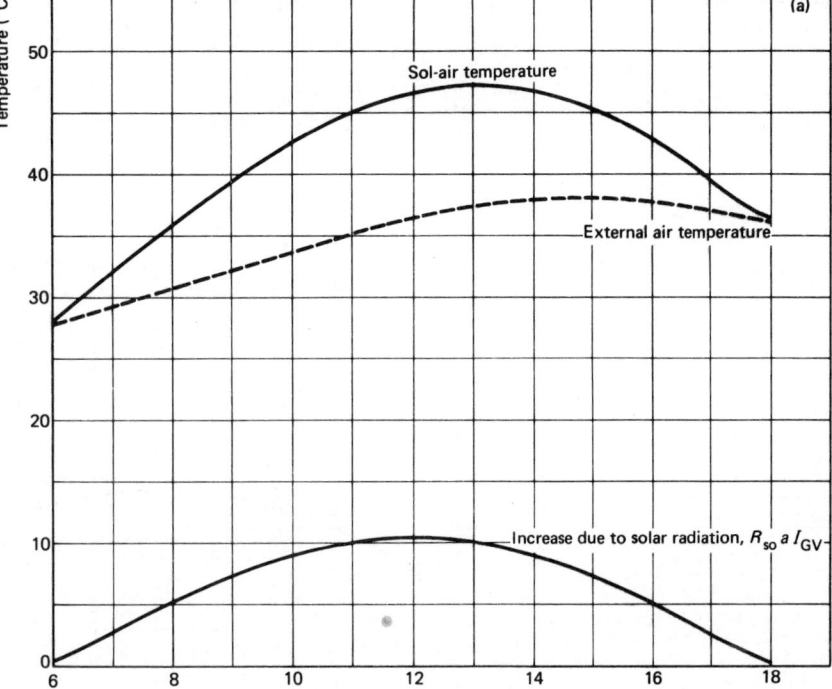

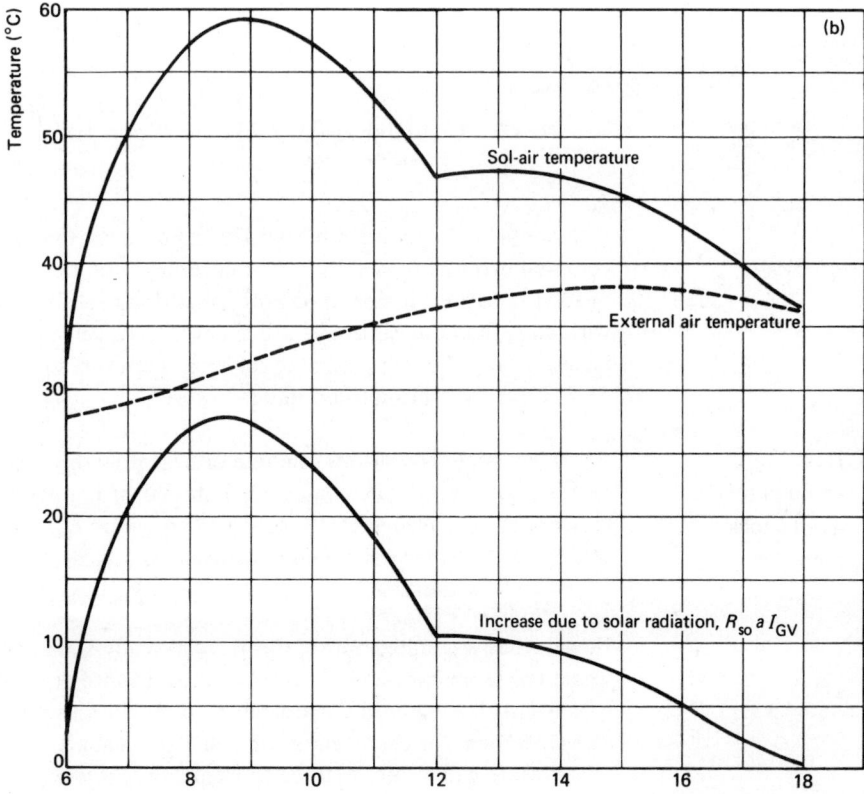

Fig. 6.3 (c) North-facing wall.

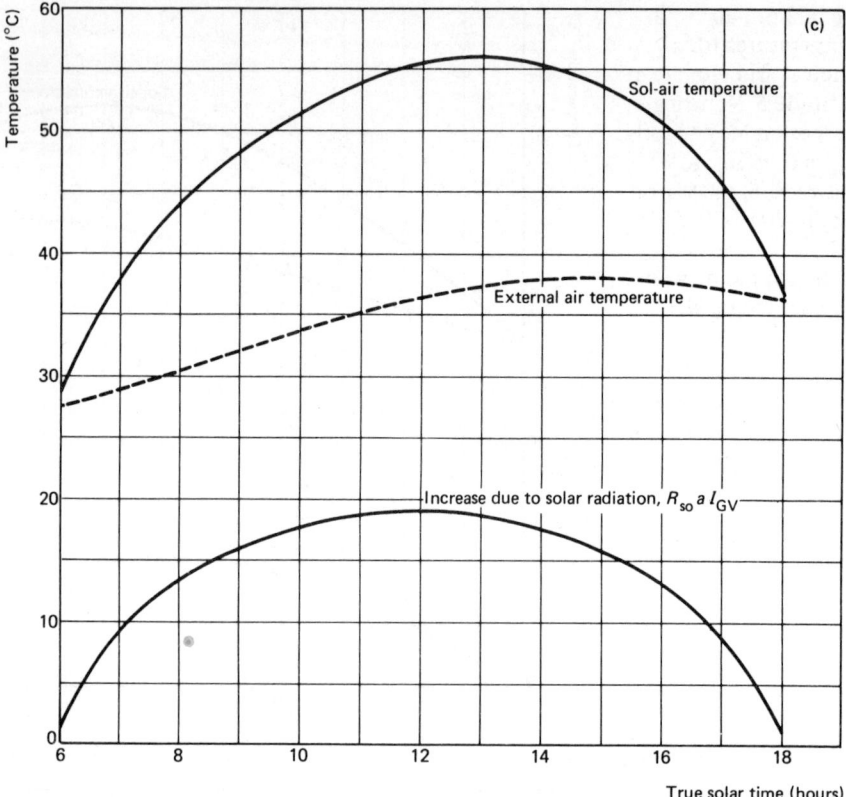

(b) Asphalt:

$$t_{eo} = 36.2 + 0.045 \; [(0.9 \times 1170) - (0.9 \times 100)]$$
$$= 79.53 \; ^{\circ}C.$$

Example 6.4 demonstrates the kind of problem that can arise if a dark-coloured material is used for a roof covering in an area where there is a high level of solar radiation. It should be noted that if the roof becomes dirty or covered with dust, then the value of a will change, and a value of 0.5 should be used instead of 0.3. For this case, the sol-air temperature in the example will become 58.5 $^{\circ}C$ for the whitewashed roof.

6.5 Heat Flow through fabric due to solar radiation

For steady-state conditions, the rate of heat flow through a wall is given by $Q/A = U(t_{ei} - t_{ao})$, where t_{ao} is the external air temperature. If the external air temperature is replaced by the sol-air temperature t_{eo}, then the rate of heat flow through an external wall could be written as

$$Q/A = U(t_{ei} - t_{eo}).$$

However, as was stated above, this is for a steady-state condition, i.e. the situation where the temperature difference between the internal and external temperatures is constant. If the internal temperature, or environmental temperature, is kept constant, then, for the steady-state equation to apply, the external or sol-air temperature will also have to be constant. But, as was shown in Example 6.3 and from the graphs in Fig. 6.2, the sol-air temperature does not remain constant; on the contrary, it varies with time; hence, the temperature difference $(t_{ei} - t_{eo})$ also varies with time.

When considering the problem of condensation in Chapter 5, reference was made to intermittent heating, and the diagrams in Fig. 5.19 illustrated the variations in the temperature gradient across the wall at different time intervals. It was stated that, in general, there was a more rapid thermal response with a lightweight structure than with a heavyweight one. Applying this to the case where the sol-air temperature is varying with time, this would imply that the time lag between the instant when the sol-air temperature changes to the instant when this change has been transmitted through the fabric will depend upon the type of structure, i.e. whether it is lightweight or heavyweight.

In addition to the time lag, the actual rate of heat flow will be influenced by the type of structure; this is illustrated in Fig. 6.4.

Fig. 6.4 Effect of (a) lightweight and (b) heavyweight structure on heat flow variation.

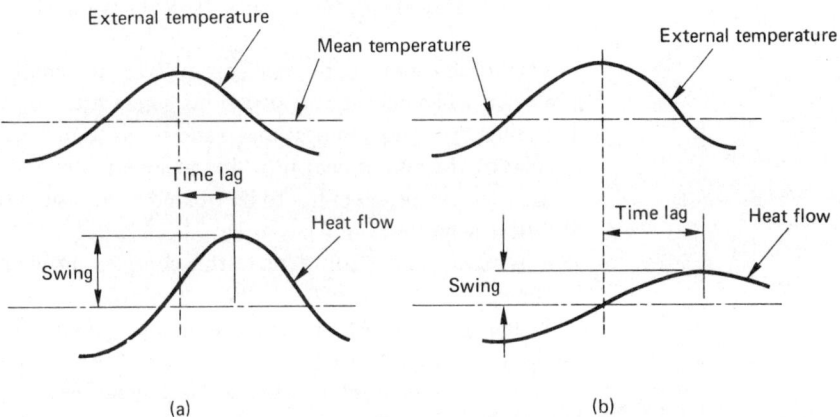

(a)   (b)

It is seen that in Fig. 6.4(b), heavyweight structure, the time lag is increased but the amplitude or 'swing about the mean' heat flow is reduced or damped. This is termed the 'decrement'. This increase in time lag and damping effect is related to the heat storage effect, i.e. the thermal capacity of the element.

Thermal capacity measured in joules per kelvin can be expressed as

Thermal capacity = Volume × Density × Specific heat.

The specific heats of some typical building materials are given in Table 6.4.

Table 6.4   *Specific heats of typical building materials* [5]

Material	Specific heat $(J\ kg^{-1}\ K^{-1})$	Density $(kg\ m^{-3})$
Brick	800	1700
Concrete	840	2100
Lightweight concrete block	1000	600
Fibreboard	1000	300
Plaster	1000	1300
Timber	1210	600

Example 6.5   Calculate the thermal capacity for each square metre of (a) a

brick wall 220 mm thick, (b) lightweight concrete blocks 75 mm thick, (c) a concrete slab 150 mm thick.

(a) Thermal capacity of brick wall = Volume × density × specific heat

$$= 0.22 \times 1 \times 1700 \times 800$$

$$= 299.2 \times 10^3 \text{ J K}^{-1}.$$

(b) Thermal capacity of lightweight concrete blocks

$$= 0.075 \times 1 \times 600 \times 1000$$

$$= 45 \times 10^3 \text{ J K}^{-1}.$$

(c) Thermal capacity of concrete slab = $0.15 \times 1 \times 2100 \times 840$

$$= 264.6 \times 10^3 \text{ J K}^{-1}.$$

Note that, although the concrete slab in (c) is twice as thick as the lightweight concrete blocks in (b), the thermal capacity is almost six times as great.

The influence of the thermal capacity, i.e. the ability to store heat, is very important when considering situations where there are variations in temperature difference or changes in heat input and it has to be taken into account when calculating the rate of heat flow due to sol-air temperature.

This type of problem has to be treated as 'transient heat flow' and a number of different methods of analysis have been proposed. A comprehensive survey of various mathematical solutions to this complex problem is given by Givoni and Hoffman [6].

In addition to this type of solution, approximate methods have been put forward. One such procedure is discussed by Groundwater [2], where a worked solution based upon the method of Mackey and Wright is given. Groundwater gives the equation for the heat gain due to the sol-air temperature as

$$Q/A = U(\bar{t}_{eo} - t_{ai}) + \lambda U(t_{eo} - \bar{t}_{eo}),$$

where $\bar{t}_{eo}$ = average sol-air temperature for 24-h period, λ = amplitude decrement factor, depending on thickness, material, orientation, t_{eo} = sol-air temperature at time earlier than time for which heat gain is being calculated.

Billington [7] deals with the variable flow of heat and refers to the work of Mackey and Wright, Danter and others.

Jones [8] also describes the method of Mackey and Wright and points out that the procedure given in the *ASHRAE Handbook of Fundamentals* is based upon the work of Mackey and Wright and also of J. P. Stewart, whereas the method described in the British *IHVE Guide* is based upon the work of E. Danter. Jones states that the latter method is claimed to be more accurate. He gives a worked example with calculations based upon the Mackey and Wright method and the *IHVE* procedure and comments upon the solutions.

The method set out in the *IHVE Guide* is very simple to use and will now be considered. The mean heat flow through the fabric is given by

$$\bar{Q}_f/A = U(\bar{t}_{eo} - \bar{t}_{ei}),$$

where $\bar{t}_{eo}$ = mean sol-air temperature for 24-h period, $\bar{t}_{ei}$ = mean environmental temperature.

If the sol-air temperature did not vary, i.e. steady-state condition, then the above equation would apply. Similarly, if the sol-air temperature did fluctuate, but the thermal capacity of the fabric was so large that the amplitude of the heat flow swing about the mean became zero, i.e. there was no corresponding heat flow fluctuation, the above equation would apply.

Alternatively, if the sol-air temperature fluctuated and the fabric had no thermal capacity, then the fluctuation in the heat flow would be of the same form as those in the sol-air temperature and be instantaneous. In this case; the rate of heat flow through the fabric at any given time θ is

$$Q_f/A = U(t_{eo} - \bar{t}_{ei})$$

where t_{eo} = sol-air temperature at time θ and Q_f/A = instantaneous rate of heat flow.

The true condition for an element will be somewhere between these two extremes and also will be subject to a time lag ψ. This means that the fluctuation in heat flow corresponding to a fluctuation in the sol-air temperature at time θ will occur at time $(\theta + \psi)$.

If $\bar{Q}_f/A$ = mean rate of heat flow through the fabric and $\widetilde{Q}_f/A$ = variation from the mean rate of heat flow through the fabric at time $\theta + \psi$, then the actual rate of heat flow through the fabric at time $\theta + \psi$ is given by

$$(Q_f/A)_\psi = \bar{Q}_f/A + \widetilde{Q}_f/A,$$

where

$$\bar{Q}_f/A = U(\bar{t}_{eo} - \bar{t}_{ei}), \tag{6.3}$$

$$\widetilde{Q}_f/A = fU(t_{eo} - \bar{t}_{eo}), \tag{6.4}$$

f = decrement factor, t_{eo} = sol-air temperature at time θ. Values of the decrement factor, f, and the time lag, ψ, are given in the *IHVE Guide* and shown in Figs. 6.5 and 6.6. Therefore,

$$(Q_f/A)_\psi = U(\bar{t}_{eo} - \bar{t}_{ei}) + fU(t_{eo} - \bar{t}_{eo}).$$

It is interesting to compare the above expression with Groundwater's.

The following example demonstrates the use of the *IHVE* procedure.

Example 6.6   Calculate the heat flow through a south-facing concrete wall (use data from Example 6.3). Mean sol-air temperature $\bar{t}_{eo}$ = 23.9 °C. Mean environmental temperature = 21 °C. (a) Wall 300 mm thick, no insulation, U = 2.5 W m^{-2} K^{-1}. (b) Wall 200 mm thick, no insulation, U = 3.1 W m^{-2} K^{-1}. (c) Wall 200 mm thick, insulation on inside, U = 1.1 W m^{-2} K^{-1}.

(a) Maximum sol-air temperature occurs at 13.00 hours (true solar time),

$$t_{eo} = 40.8 °C.$$

From Fig. 6.5, time lag ψ = 8.5 h and from Fig. 6.6 decrement factor f = 0.22. From equation (6.3), mean heat flow through wall is given by

$$\bar{Q}_f/A = U(\bar{t}_{eo} - \bar{t}_{ei})$$
$$= 2.5(23.9 - 21) = 7.3 \text{ W m}^{-2}.$$

From equation (6.4), peak-to-mean heat flow through wall is given by

$$\widetilde{Q}_f/A = fU(t_{eo} - \bar{t}_{eo})$$
$$= 0.22 \times 2.5(40.8 - 23.9)$$
$$= 9.3 \text{ W m}^{-2}.$$

Fig. 6.5 Values of time lag, ψ (from *IHVE Guide*).

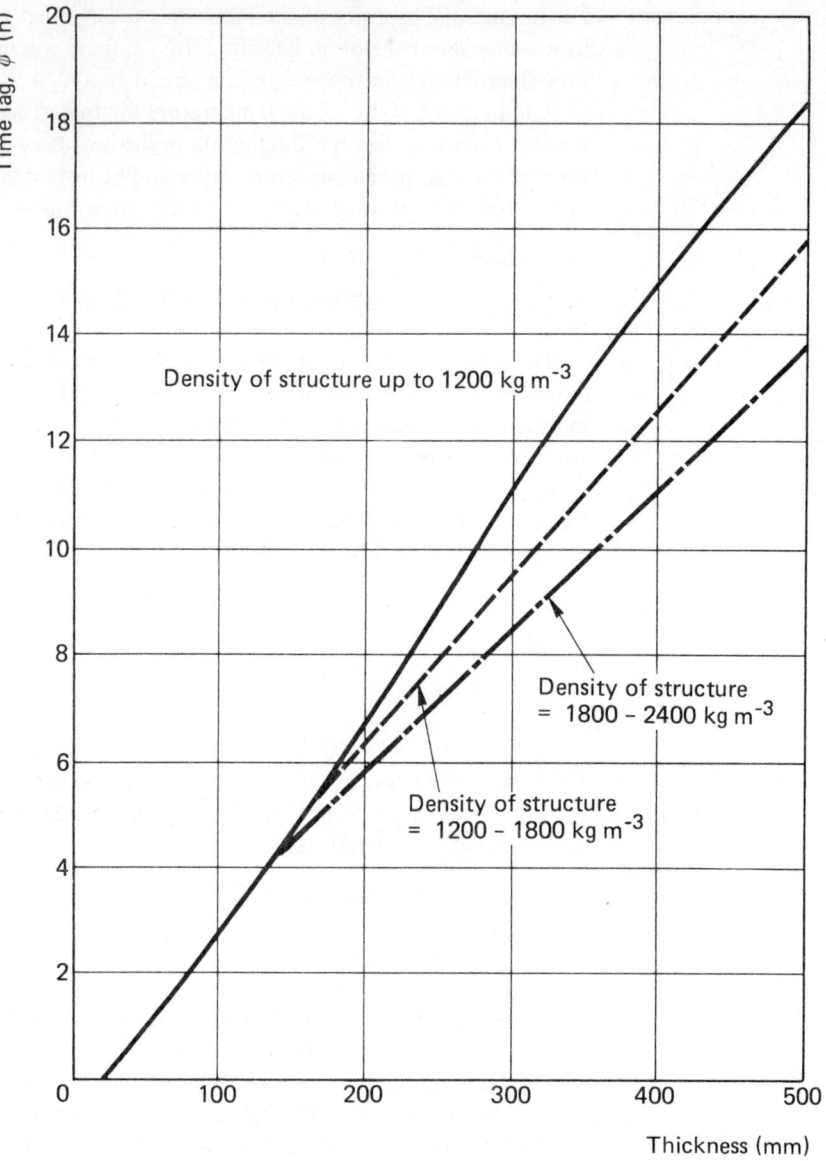

Therefore,

Peak heat flow = 7.3 + 9.3 = 16.6 W m^{-2}.

The peak heat flow occurs at 13.00 + ψ hours = 13.00 + 8.30 = 21.30 hours.

(b) From Figs. 6.5 and 6.6, f = 0.48, ψ = 6 h.

Mean heat flow = $\bar{Q}_f/A$ = 3.1(23.9 − 21) = 9.0 W m^{-2}.

Peak-to-mean heat flow = $\widetilde{Q}_f/A$ = 0.48 × 3.1(40.8 − 23.9) = 25.1 W m^{-2}.

Hence,

Peak heat flow = 34.1 W m^{-2}, occurs at 19.00 hours.

It will be observed that in case (b) the peak heat flow is much larger than in case (a) and occurs at an earlier time, i.e. the time lag is shorter. These differences

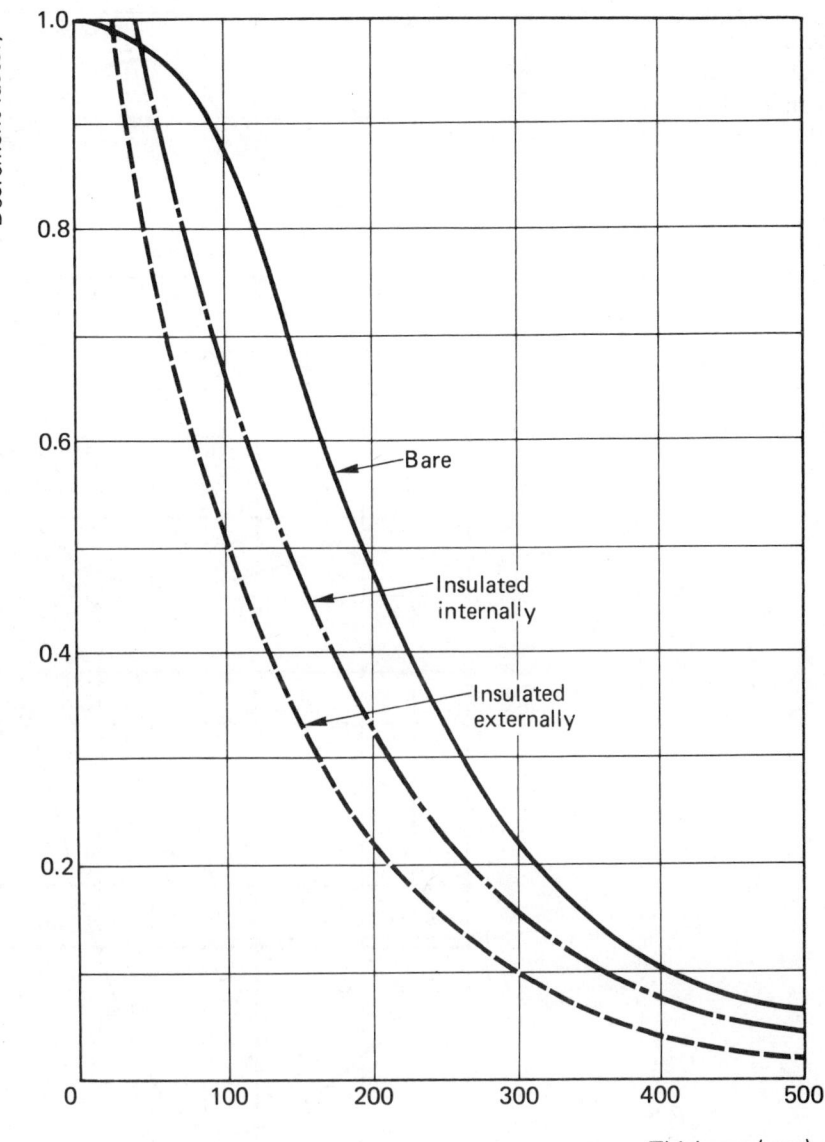

Fig. 6.6 Values of decrement factor, f (from *IHVE Guide*).

are due to the thermal capacity of the 200-mm wall being less than that for the 300-mm wall. Since thermal capacity was defined as volume × density × specific heat, any change in thickness will result in a corresponding change in volume and hence a different thermal capacity.

(c) In this case, where insulation is added, the *IHVE Guide* gives a suitable allowance for this, depending upon the position and thermal resistance of the insulation. The resistance of insulation is greater than 0.4 m² K W⁻¹ and it is placed on the inside; the addition to the time lag = 1 hour. Therefore

$$\psi = 6 + 1 = 7\,\text{h}.$$

From Fig. 6.6, $f = 0.33$.

Mean heat flow = $\bar{Q}_f/A = 1.1(23.9 - 21) = 3.2\,\text{W m}^{-2}$.

Fig. 6.7 Graphical representation of rates of heat flow from Example 6.6.

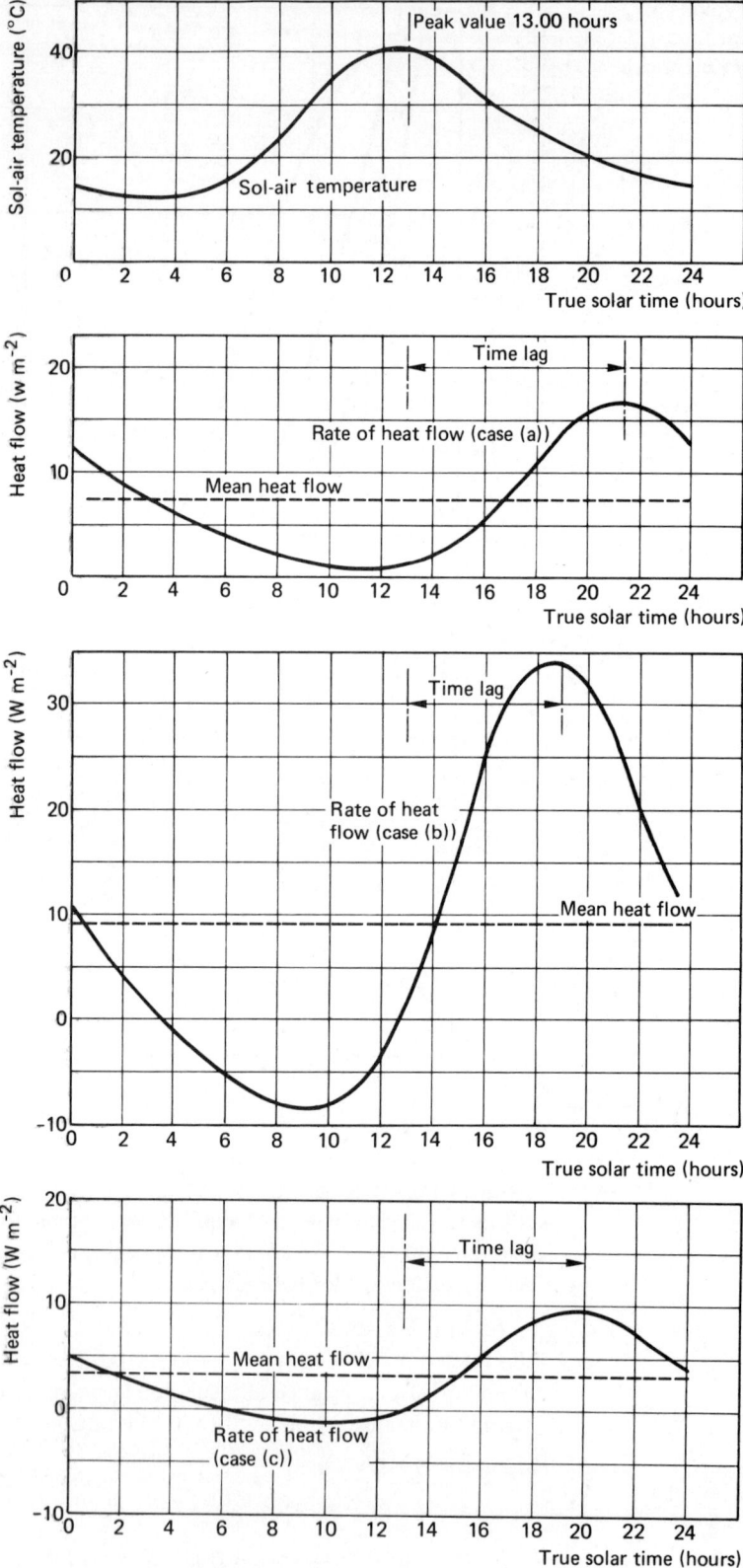

Peak-to-mean heat flow = $\widetilde{Q}_f/A$ = 0.33 × 1.1(40.8 − 23.9)

$$= 6.1 \text{ W m}^{-2}.$$

Therefore,

Peak heat flow = 3.2 + 6.1 = 9.3 W m^{-2}.

Peak heat flow occurs at 20.00 hours.

The calculations for the values of the heat flow for each case over a 24-h period are shown in Table 6.5 and in graphical form in Fig. 6.7.

As a further example in the use of this method of calculation consider the case of similar wall constructions but facing east and located in a tropical arid climate.

Example 6.7   Calculate the heat flow through an east-facing wall (construction as in Example 6.6) located in a tropical arid climate. Mean sol-air temperature = 38.8 °C. Maximum sol-air temperature at 9.00 (true solar time) = 59.2 °C. Assume same mean internal environmental temperature as in Example 6.6, 21 °C.

(a) Wall 300 mm thick.

Mean heat flow = 2.5(38.8 − 21) = 44.5 W m^{-2}.

Peak-to-mean heat flow = 0.22 × 2.5(59.2 − 38.8) = 11.2 W m^{-2}.

Peak heat flow = 44.5 + 11.2 = 55.7 W m^{-2}

and it occurs at 17.30 hours.

(b) Wall 200 mm thick.

Mean heat flow = 3.1(38.8 − 21) = 55.2 W m^{-2}.

Peak-to-mean heat flow = 0.48 × 3.1(59.2 − 38.8) = 30.3 W m^{-2}.

Peak heat flow = 55.2 + 30.3 = 85.5 W m^{-2}

and it occurs at 15.00 hours.

(c) Wall 200 mm thick with insulation on the inside.

Mean heat flow = 1.1(38.8 − 21) = 19.6 W m^{-2}.

Peak-to-mean heat flow = 0.33 × 1.1(59.2 − 38.8) = 7.4 W m^{-2}.

Peak heat flow = 19.6 + 7.4 = 27.0 W m^{-2}

and it occurs at 16.00 hours.

As is to be expected, the rate of heat flow through the walls is very much higher for the situations in a tropical arid climate than in the British temperate climate, but in both examples the influence of the insulation and the lower *U*-value is clearly demonstrated.

In Example 6.7 (where the wall is facing East) note that the peak heat flow is now tending to occur in the afternoon, corresponding to the time of day when the external air temperature is approaching its peak value.

These points are also extremely important when considering the heat flow due to solar radiation acting on a flat roof. Petherbridge has made similar comments for the case of roofs in warm climates and shows that the roofs of buildings in areas near the equator receive more solar radiation than any other surface of the building. He points out that the decrement factor and time lag

Table 6.5   *Heat flow through concrete wall due to solar radiation*

						True solar time, θ							
	0	2	4	6	8	10	12	14	16	18	20	22	24
t_{eo}	14.3	12.6	12.6	15.7	23.2	34.6	40.6	39.2	31.1	24.9	20.6	17.2	14.3
$t_{eo} - \bar{t}_{eo}$	−9.6	−11.3	−11.3	−8.2	−0.7	10.7	16.7	15.3	7.2	1.0	−3.3	−6.7	−9.6
Case (a)													
Time, $\theta + \psi$	8.30	10.30	12.30	14.30	16.30	18.30	20.30	22.30	0.30	2.30	4.30	6.30	8.30
$\bar{Q}_f/A \doteq U(\bar{t}_{eo} - \bar{t}_{ei})$	7.3	7.3	7.3	7.3	7.3	7.3	7.3	7.3	7.3	7.3	7.3	7.3	7.3
$\tilde{Q}_f/A = fU(t_{eo} - \bar{t}_{eo})$	−5.3	−6.2	−6.2	−4.5	−0.4	5.9	9.2	8.4	4.0	0.6	−1.8	−3.7	−5.3
$(Q_f/A)_\psi$	2.0	1.1	1.1	2.8	6.9	13.2	16.5	15.7	11.3	7.9	5.5	3.6	2.0
Case (b)													
Time, $\theta + \psi$	6	8	10	12	14	16	18	20	22	24	2	4	6
$\bar{Q}_f/A$	9.0	9.0	9.0	9.0	9.0	9.0	9.0	9.0	9.0	9.0	9.0	9.0	9.0
$\tilde{Q}_f/A$	−14.3	−16.8	−16.8	−12.2	−1.0	15.9	24.8	22.8	10.7	1.5	−4.9	−10.0	−14.3
$(Q_f/A)_\psi$	−5.3	−7.8	−7.8	−3.2	8.0	24.9	33.8	31.8	19.7	10.5	4.1	−1.0	−5.3
Case (c)													
Time, $\theta + \psi$	7	9	11	13	15	17	19	21	23	1	3	5	7
$\bar{Q}_f/A$	3.2	3.2	3.2	3.2	3.2	3.2	3.2	3.2	3.2	3.2	3.2	3.2	3.2
$\tilde{Q}_f/A$	−3.5	−4.1	−4.1	−3.0	−0.3	3.9	6.1	5.6	2.6	0.4	−1.2	−2.4	−3.5
$(Q_f/A)_\psi$	−0.3	−0.9	−0.9	0.2	2.9	7.1	9.3	8.8	5.8	3.6	2.0	0.8	−0.3

depend on material thickness and, since increased thickness also results in reduced U-values, a double benefit is obtained [4].

The difference between the thermal behaviour of lightweight and heavyweight structures and the effects of insulation in relation to transient heat flow due to solar radiation are discussed by van Straaten [9]. Although he is considering these aspects mainly in relation to warm arid climates, the graphs which he shows clearly illustrate the increased time lag which occurs with heavyweight structures and the reduction in the internal temperature when insulation is used. It is interesting to compare the curves obtained in the worked example (Fig. 6.7) with those given by van Straaten as it will be observed that they follow the same trends.

6.6 Transmission of solar radiation through glass

Glass transmits radiation within the range 300 to 2800 nm, its spectral distribution being as shown in Fig. 6.8. An important feature of glass is that it is opaque to long-wave radiation from low-temperature emitters and it is this phenomenon which gives rise to what is termed the 'greenhouse effect' (Fig. 6.9).

Radiation emitted by the sun and received by the glass is of short wavelength, i.e. radiation from a high-temperature source. The glass is transparent at this wavelength and the radiation is transmitted into the interior of the structure. This energy is absorbed by the surfaces, etc., inside the building which in turn rise in temperature and become low-temperature emitters. The radiation emitted by these surfaces will be of long wavelength to which the glass is opaque and as a consequence this energy is contained within the structure with a corresponding rise in temperature.

It is this effect which can give rise to overheating in summer due to solar heat gains and hence an appreciation of the probable solar radiation intensities and the transmission characteristics of the glass are necessary for estimating summer cooling loads.

6.6.1 Transmission Characteristics of Glass

In the case of radiant energy striking a surface it was stated that it could be transmitted, absorbed or reflected. Consideration of how this would apply to

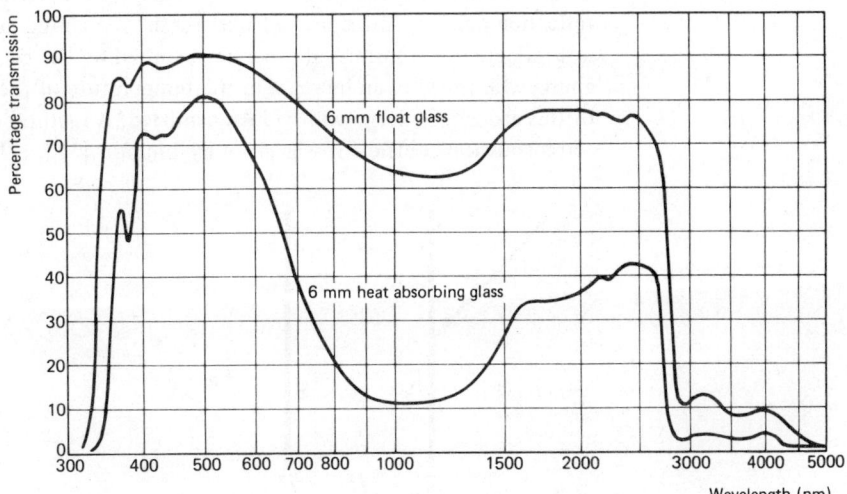

Fig. 6.8 The spectral transmission characteristics of glasses (from Turner [10]).

Fig. 6.9 The 'greenhouse effect'.

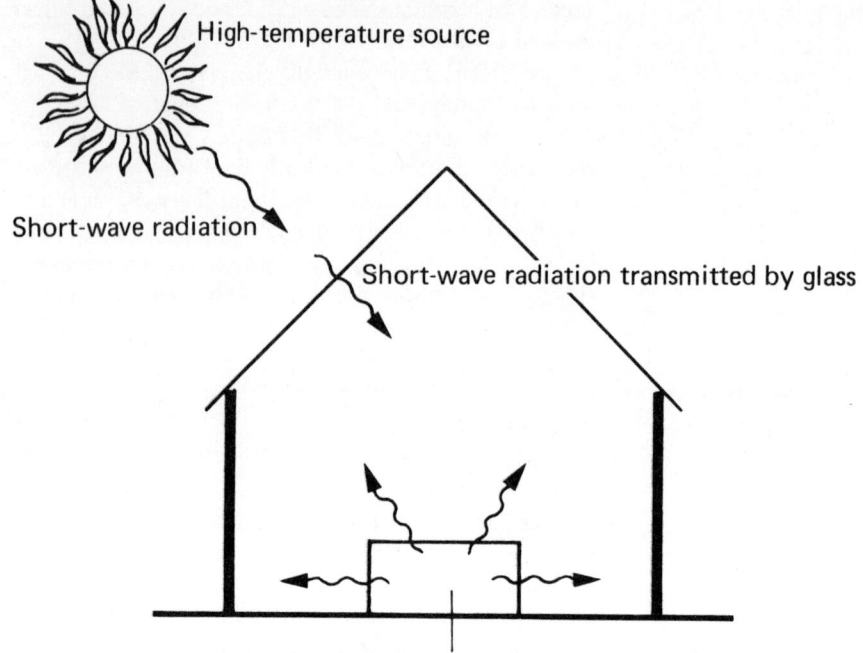

High-temperature source

Short-wave radiation

Short-wave radiation transmitted by glass

Radiation absorbed, rise in temperature
Low-temperature emitter, long-wave radiation

glass when subjected to solar radiation implies that:

(i) The energy transmitted through the glass at any given wavelength = Incident solar energy on glass × Transmission coefficient;

(ii) The energy reflected by the glass = Incident solar energy on glass × Reflection coefficient.

The reflection coefficient changes with angle of incidence and this is illustrated in Fig. 6.10.

For clear glass the reflection factor varies from 0.08 at normal incidence up to 1.0 at 90° angle of incidence.

From the statement that $a + r + \tau = 1.0$ (where a, r and τ are the absorption, reflection and transmission coefficients) the remaining radiant energy which is not reflected or transmitted must be absorbed by the glass. This absorbed energy will result in an increase in the temperature of the glass and a proportion of this absorbed energy will be retransmitted. A method of obtaining the retransmission coefficient was given by Loudon [11] as follows.

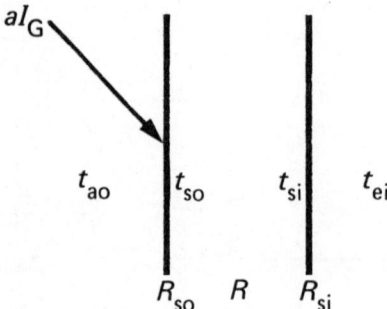

aI_G

t_{ao} t_{so} t_{si} t_{ei}

R_{so} R R_{si}

Fig. 6.10 The change of reflection coefficient with angle of incidence (from Turner [10]).

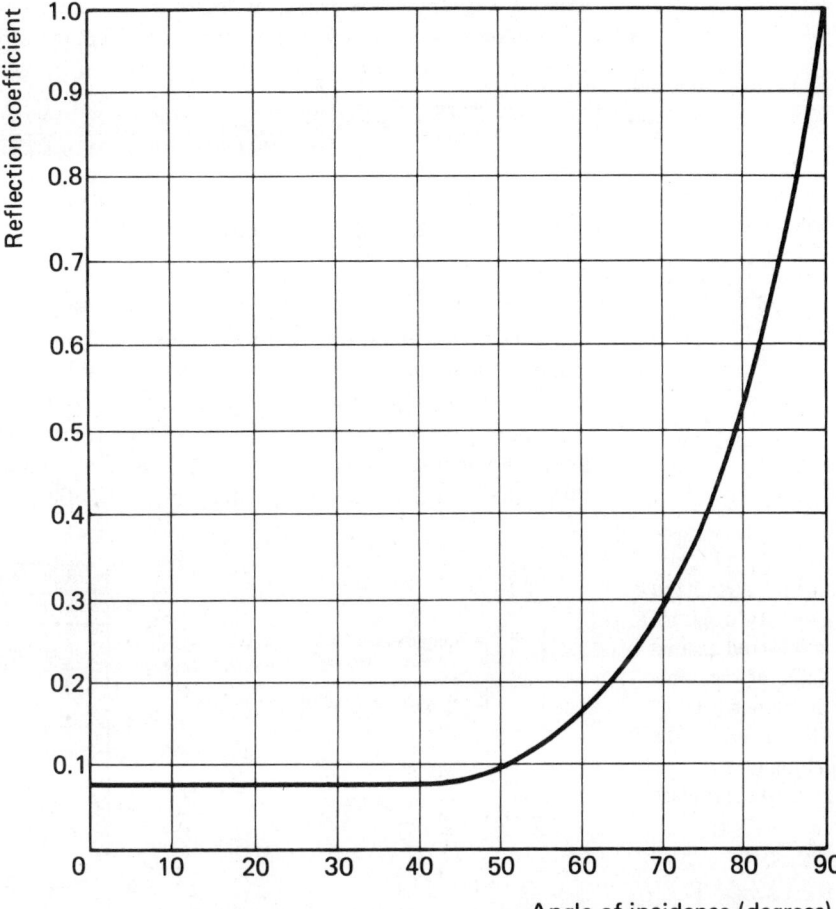

Let aI_G = absorbed radiant energy, t_{ao} = external air temperature, t_{ei} = environmental temperature, t_{so} = external surface temperature, t_{si} = internal surface temperature, R_{so} = external surface resistance, R_{si} = internal surface resistance, R = resistance of material.

Then, for steady-state conditions, rate of heat flow per unit area is given by

$$Q/A = (t_{ei} - t_{si})/R_{si},$$

$$Q/A = (t_{si} - t_{so})/R$$

and

$$Q/A + aI_G = (t_{so} - t_{ao})/R_{so}.$$

Hence,

$$Q/A = (t_{so} - t_{ao})/R_{so} - aI_G$$
$$= (t_{ei} - t_{ao})/(R_{si} + R + R_{so}) - aI_G R_{so}/(R_{si} + R + R_{so}).$$

But $U = 1/(R_{si} + R + R_{so})$. Therefore,

$$Q/A = U(t_{ei} - t_{ao}) - UR_{so} aI_G$$
$$= U(t_{ei} - t_{ao}) - f_r aI_G$$

where $f_r = UR_{so}$ = retransmission factor.

Loudon shows that where heat inputs are generated partway through a structure they have to be multiplied by the factor f_r, which he defines as

$$f_r = \frac{\text{Thermal resistance from outside to point where heat is generated}}{\text{Total thermal resistance of structure}}.$$

Example 6.8 Calculate the retransmission coefficient for single glazing given $U = 5.6 \text{ W m}^{-2} \text{ K}^{-1}$ and $R_{so} = 0.055 \text{ m}^2 \text{ K W}^{-1}$.

$$f_r = U \times R_{so} = 5.6 \times 0.055 = 0.3.$$

Knowing the amount of energy absorbed and, hence, retransmitted, the total radiation being transmitted through the glass can be obtained. Fig. 6.11 shows typical transmission, absorption and reflection curves for different types of glass.

In order to calculate the total energy being transmitted through the glass, the direct and diffuse irradiances have to be considered separately. The reason for this is that at a given time the incident direct irradiance will strike the glass

Fig. 6.11 Total solar radiation transmitted for a variety of glazing types, plotted against the angle of incidence (from Turner [10]). (a) Float glass. (b) Heat-absorbing glass. (c) Coated clear glass.

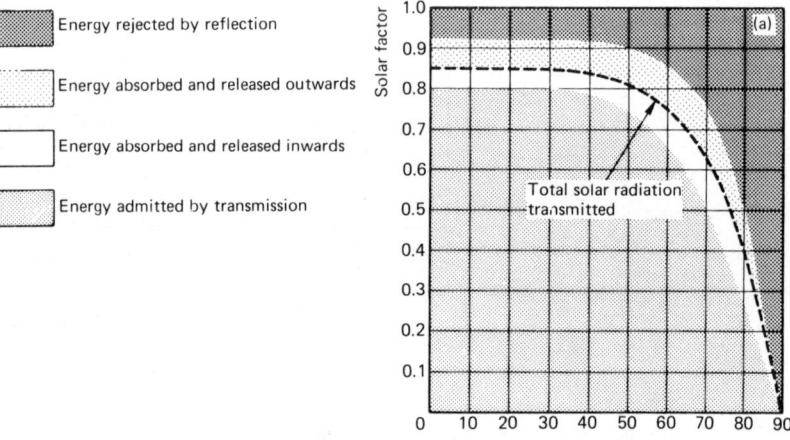

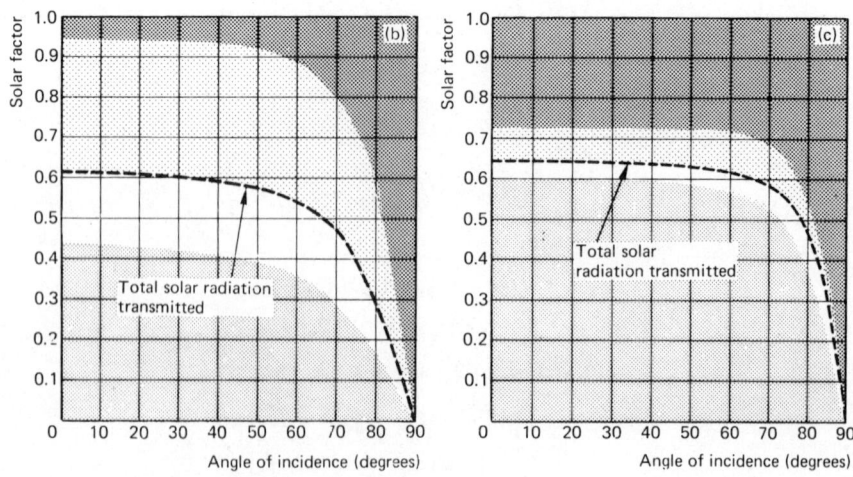

surface at a particular angle, with a corresponding transmission coefficient for that angle. On the other hand the diffuse irradiance will be striking the glass surface at all angles from $0°$ to $180°$ and will consequently be multiplied by a different transmission coefficient to that used for the direct irradiance.

6.6.2 Solar Gain Factor

A method for obtaining the total radiation transmitted through a window is given by Petherbridge [12]. A series of overlays are given which, when used in conjunction with the stereographic sunpath projections described in Chapter 4, enable the hourly and daily total transmitted radiation to be computed. The procedure and use of the overlays are fully described by Petherbridge.

However, where the mean daily transmitted radiation is required or a less accurate value than that obtained from the overlays is appropriate, then it may be more convenient to use an overall 'solar gain factor' for the glass. This concept was used by Loudon [11] who pointed out that this factor depends upon the angle of incidence of the radiation. In addition, an allowance has to be made for inter-reflection between different window surfaces in the window system. Loudon published values for various types of glazing and sun controls which he stated are average values for August for orientations south of east-west and which can be used without serious error for the summer months. Similar values are published in the *IHVE Guide* and are reproduced in Table 6.6.

Table 6.6   *Solar gain factors (S) for various types of glazing and shading (strictly accurate for UK only, approximately correct world wide) (from IHVE Guide)*

Position of shading and type of sun protection		Solar gain factors* (S) for the following types of glazing	
Shading	Type of sun protection	Single	Double
None	None	0.76	0.64
	Lightly heat absorbing glass	0.51	0.38
	Densely heat absorbing glass	0.39	0.25
	Lacquer coated glass, grey	0.56	—
	Heat reflecting glass, gold (sealed unit when double)	0.26	0.25
Internal	Dark green open weave plastic blind	0.62	0.56
	White venetian blind	0.46	0.46
	White cotton curtain	0.41	0.40
	Cream holland linen blind	0.30	0.33
Mid-pane	White venetian blind	—	0.28
External	Dark green open weave plastic blind	0.22	0.17
	Canvas roller blind	0.14	0.11
	White louvred sunbreaker, blades at 45°	0.14	0.11
	Dark green miniature louvred blind	0.13	0.10

* All glazing clear except where stated otherwise. Factors are typical values only and variations will occur due to density of blind weave, reflectivity and cleanliness of protection.

Fig. 6.12 Radiation transmitted through glass (based upon data in *BRS CP47/68* [11]).

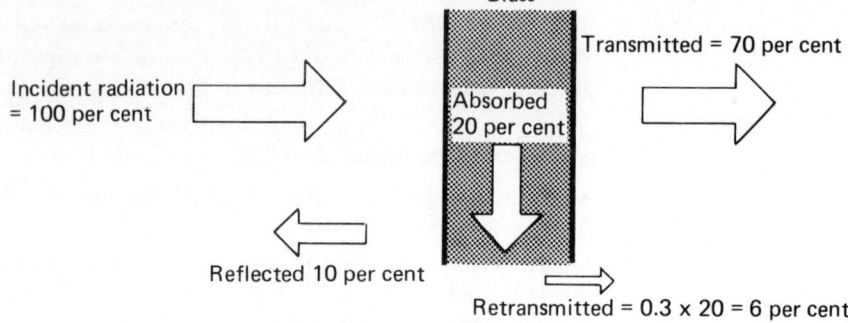

As was mentioned, the solar gain factor has to be based upon angles of incidence, but an appreciation of the components which are combined to form this factor can be obtained by a consideration of the following approximate values for single glazing (*see* Fig. 6.12). Assume incident radiation = 100 per cent, then

Total transmitted + retransmitted = 70 + 6 = 76 per cent.

Therefore,

Solar gain factor = 0.76.

The use of the solar gain factor is demonstrated in Examples 6.9 to 6.11.

Example 6.9   A room is 6 m × 5 m × 3 m high with one external wall on the long axis and has a single-glazed window 4.5 m × 2 m facing south. Calculate the mean environmental temperature for the following conditions: mean external air temperature, $\bar{t}_{ao}$ = 17 °C, mean global irradiance on window, $\bar{I}_{GV}$ = 180 W m^{-2}, mean sol-air temperature, $\bar{t}_{eo}$ = 25 °C, U-value of wall = 0.7 W m^{-2} K^{-1}, U-value of window = 5.6 W m^{-2} K^{-1}. Assume two air changes per hour and that adjacent rooms are at the same environmental temperature.

Solar gain = $S\bar{I}_{GV}A_g$.

S = solar gain factor = 0.76 and A_g = area of glass = 9 m^2. Therefore,

Heat gain due to solar radiation = 0.76 × 180 × 9

$$= 1231.2 \text{ W.}$$

Heat loss by ventilation = $C_v(\bar{t}_{ei} - \bar{t}_{ao})$.

Where the ventilation rate is large then C_v has to be obtained from

$$\frac{1}{C_v} = \frac{3}{Vol \times n} + \frac{1}{4.8\,\Sigma A},$$

where ΣA = total surface area of room. The use of this expression for C_v was discussed in Chapter 5. However, for a small number of air changes C_v can be taken as $Vol \times n/3$, where Vol = volume, and n = number of air changes per hour. Therefore,

$$C_v = 6 \times 5 \times 3 \times 2/3 = 60 \text{ W K}^{-1}.$$

Hence,

Ventilation loss = $60(\bar{t}_{ei} - 17)$.

$$\text{Fabric loss due to window} = A_g U_g(\bar{t}_{ei} - \bar{t}_{ao})$$
$$= 9 \times 5.6 \, (\bar{t}_{ei} - 17)$$
$$= 50.4 \, (\bar{t}_{ei} - 17).$$

Fabric loss due to opaque portion of external wall $= A_w U_w \, (\bar{t}_{ei} - \bar{t}_{eo})$.
Note that the sol-air temperature is used in the calculation of the heat flow through the opaque portion of the wall.

$$A_w = 18 - 9 = 9 \text{ m}^2,$$
$$A_w U_w(\bar{t}_{ei} - \bar{t}_{eo}) = 9 \times 0.7 \, (\bar{t}_{ei} - 25) = 6.3 \, (\bar{t}_{ei} - 25).$$

But Heat gain = Heat loss. Therefore,

Solar radiation gain = Heat loss due to (ventilation + window + opaque portion of wall)

$$1231.2 = 60(\bar{t}_{ei} - 17) + 50.4(\bar{t}_{ei} - 17) + 6.3(\bar{t}_{ei} - 25)$$
$$= 116.7 \, \bar{t}_{ei} - 2034.3$$

Therefore,

$$\bar{t}_{ei} = 28 \, °\text{C}.$$

Example 6.10   As Example 6.9, but window double-glazed (glass only).

$$\text{Heat gain} = S\bar{I}_{GV}A_g = 0.64 \times 180 \times 9$$
$$= 1036.8 \text{ W}.$$

Heat loss by ventilation and opaque portion of wall, as before, is

$$= 60(\bar{t}_{ei} - 17) + 6.3 \, (\bar{t}_{ei} - 25).$$
$$\text{Heat loss by window} = 9 \times 2.8 \, (\bar{t}_{ei} - 17) = 25.2 \, (\bar{t}_{ei} - 17).$$

Therefore,

$$1036.8 = 60 \, (\bar{t}_{ei} - 17) + 25.2 \, (\bar{t}_{ei} - 17) + 6.3 \, (\bar{t}_{ei} - 25).$$

Hence,

$$\bar{t}_{ei} = 29.2 \, °\text{C}.$$

Note that although the double glazing has reduced the solar radiation gain, the improved insulation of the window has resulted in a lower heat loss with a resulting overall rise in the mean environmental temperature.

Example 6.11   As Example 6.9 but window area reduced to half previous size, i.e. $A_g = 4.5 \text{ m}^2$.

Solar gain $= 0.76 \times \cdot 180 \times 4.5 = 615.6$ W.

Ventilation loss $= 60 \, (\bar{t}_{ei} - 17)$,

Fabric loss due to window $= 4.5 \times 5.6 \, (\bar{t}_{ei} - 17)$
$$= 25.2 \, (\bar{t}_{ei} - 17),$$

Fabric loss due to opaque portion of wall $= 13.5 \times 0.7 \, (\bar{t}_{ei} - 25)$
$$= 9.45 \, (\bar{t}_{ei} - 25).$$

Therefore,

$$615.6 = 60 \, (\bar{t}_{ei} - 17) + 25.2 \, (\bar{t}_{ei} - 17) + 9.45 \, (\bar{t}_{ei} - 25),$$

giving

$$t_{ei} = 24.3 \,°C.$$

As an alternative method, the various steps in the solutions to these three examples can be combined to give a single expression for $\bar{t}_{ei}$ as follows:

Heat gain = $S\bar{I}_{GV}A_g$,

Total heat loss = $C_v(\bar{t}_{ei} - \bar{t}_{ao}) + U_gA_g(\bar{t}_{ei} - \bar{t}_{ao}) + U_wA_w(\bar{t}_{ei} - \bar{t}_{eo})$.

Therefore,

$$S\bar{I}_{GV}A_g = (C_v + U_gA_g)(\bar{t}_{ei} - \bar{t}_{ao}) + U_wA_w(\bar{t}_{ei} - \bar{t}_{eo})$$
$$= (C_v + U_gA_g + U_wA_w)\bar{t}_{ei} - (C_v + U_gA_g)\bar{t}_{ao} - U_wA_w\,\bar{t}_{eo}.$$

Hence,

$$\bar{t}_{ei} = \frac{S\bar{I}_{GV}A_g + (C_v + U_gA_g)\bar{t}_{ao} + U_wA_w\bar{t}_{eo}}{C_v + \Sigma AU}. \tag{6.5}$$

6.7 Effect of solar radiation on the building — cyclic heat inputs

In considering the heat flow through the fabric of a building it has been assumed that the difference between the external and internal temperatures did not vary with time, i.e. 'steady-state' conditions. However, it will be appreciated that this is an ideal condition and that due to fluctuations in the external temperature, effect of solar radiation, variations in the internal heat input etc., both the external and internal temperatures can change and, hence, the temperature difference can vary with time.

There have been a number of analytical solutions proposed for this type of situation and mention has been made of the review by Givoni and Hoffman [6]. A considerable amount of work on this type of problem has been carried out at the Building Research Station by Danter, Loudon and others and has resulted in a simplified approach which, although an approximation, is sufficiently accurate for practical use. For this analysis a 24-h period is used and the energy input into the building is assumed to be of sinusoidal form. Danter investigated the effects of the sinusoidal heat inputs by using an electrical analogue and observed the variation in the internal temperature. He found that the fluctuation in the internal temperature in a room (i.e. the temperature swing) was controlled by a property of the room which he termed the 'room admittance'.

The room admittance is a function of the admittance (Y) of the individual elements. This is defined by Milbank and Harrington-Lynn [5] as the reciprocal of the thermal resistance or impedence of an element to cyclic heat flow from the environmental temperature point and has the same units as U-value (W m^{-2} K^{-1}), i.e.

$$Y = \tilde{q}/\tilde{t},$$

where $\tilde{q}$ = heat input per unit area = $\tilde{Q}/A$ and $\tilde{t}$ = temperature swing. Hence,

$$\tilde{t} = \tilde{Q}/AY.$$

This means that for a given energy input the temperature swing is inversely proportional to the admittance, i.e. the greater the admittance, the smaller the temperature swing.

The factors which influence the admittance value of a particular material are the thermal diffusivity and thickness. The diffusivity (D) is the thermal conductivity divided by the volume specific heat, i.e.

$$D = k/c\rho.$$

For thick homogeneous slabs it can be shown that the admittance is constant and does not vary with an increase in thickness, whereas for very thin units (e.g. glass) the admittance becomes the same as the U-value. Since it was stated that the admittance was affected by the thermal diffusivity, this implies that dense materials will have a larger admittance value than those for a less dense material. In addition, since the temperature swing varies inversely as the admittance, it follows that dense, heavyweight structures will have small temperature swings, and lightweight structures larger temperature swings.

In the case of composite units, e.g. a concrete slab with insulation on the surface receiving the variable heat input, it is the layer of insulation which will influence the value of the admittance.

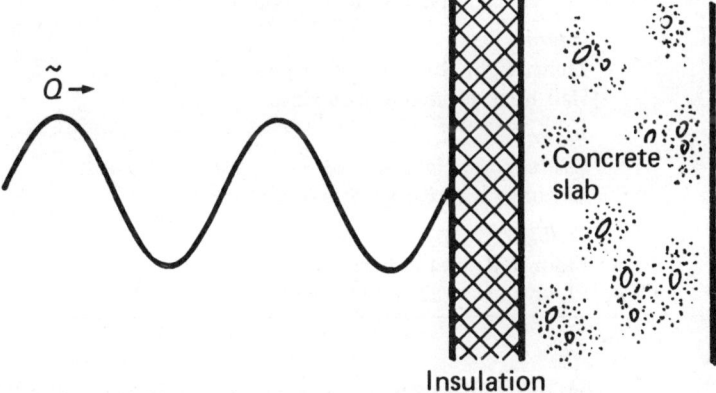

Since the insulation layer has a high thermal resistance it is preventing the variable heat energy from getting into the heavyweight slab. As a result, the slab is tending to have a relatively small damping effect and the composite element is reacting in a similar manner to a lightweight unit.

Loudon [11] published some typical admittances and similar values are given in the *IHVE Guide*. A more comprehensive list is given by Milbank and Harrington-Lynn [5] from which the data in Table 6.7 are taken.

Loudon shows that when the temperatures and rates of input are changing slowly the ventilation heat flow can be added to the fabric heat flow thus giving a simple equation for the environmental temperature swing, i.e.

$$\widetilde{t}_{ei} = \widetilde{Q}/(\Sigma A Y + C_v). \tag{6.6}$$

Considering the alternating heat input due to solar radiation, if I'_G = peak solar irradiance and $\overline{I}_G$ = mean solar irradiance over a 24-h period, then

$$\text{Alternating intensity} = \widetilde{I}_G = I'_G - \overline{I}_G.$$

In the case of steady-state input, the radiation transmitted by the window was given by $Q = S\overline{I}_{GV}A_g$, where S = mean solar gain factor. However, for an alternating input, an alternating solar gain factor S_a has to be used. This factor

Table 6.7   *Admittance values* [5]

Element	Admittance, Y $(\text{W m}^{-2}\text{ K}^{-1})$
Walls	
Cavity wall, 105 mm brick inner and outer leaves. Dense plaster on inside face	4.3
As above but lightweight plaster on inner face	3.3
Cavity wall brick outer leaf, lightweight concrete block inner leaf. Dense plaster on inside face	2.9
As above but with 13 mm polystyrene in cavity	3.0
Roofs	
Asphalt on 75 mm lightweight concrete screed on 150 mm dense concrete	5.1
Asphalt on fibre insulation board on hollow asbestos cement decking	1.9
Asphalt on cement/sand screed on woodwool slab on steel framing with plasterboard ceiling	1.45
Internal walls	
Lightweight concrete block plastered both sides	2.55
Half brick plastered both sides	4.53
Floors	
Cast concrete with screed	5.6
As above with carpet or wood block	3.1
Ceiling	
Floor unit: cast concrete with screed	5.6
Floor unit: as above with carpet or wood block	5.8

has different values for heavyweight and lightweight buildings. The alternating heat input due to solar radiation that is transmitted by the window $\widetilde{Q}_g$ is given by

$$\widetilde{Q}_g = S_a \widetilde{I}_{GV} A_g. \tag{6.7}$$

Typical values for S_a are given in Table 6.8, reproduced from the *IHVE Guide*.

Calculations based upon 'steady-state' equations will give the mean environmental temperature, but in order to be able to obtain the peak environmental temperature (or the minimum) due to an alternating heat input it is necessary to calculate the temperature swing $\widetilde{t}_{ei}$, i.e. the peak-to-mean value.

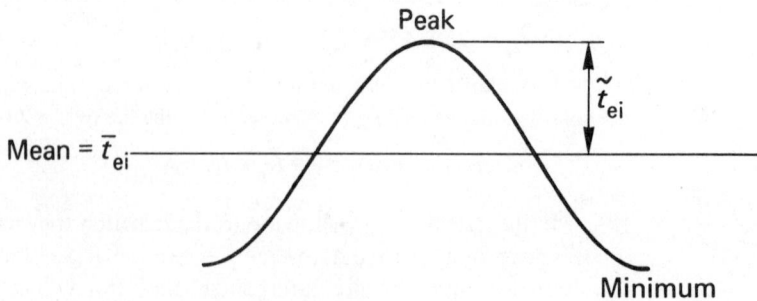

Table 6.8 *Alternating solar gain factors (S_a) for various types of glazing and shading and for heavyweight and lightweight buildings (strictly accurate for UK only; approximately correct world wide) (from IHVE Guide)*

Position of shading and type of sun protection		Alternating solar gain factors* (S_a) for the following building and window types			
		Heavyweight building		Lightweight building	
Shading	Type of sun protection	Single	Double	Single	Double
None	None	0.42	0.39	0.65	0.56
	Lightly heat absorbing glass	0.36	0.27	0.47	0.35
	Densely heat absorbing glass	0.32	0.21	0.37	0.24
	Lacquer coated glass, grey	0.37	–	0.50	–
	Heat reflecting glass, gold (sealed unit when double)	0.21	0.14	0.25	0.20
Internal	Dark green open weave plastic blind	0.55	0.53	0.61	0.57
	White venetian blind	0.42	0.44	0.45	0.46
	White cotton curtain	0.27	0.31	0.35	0.37
	Cream holland linen blind	0.24	0.30	0.27	0.32
Mid-pane	White venetian blind	–	0.24	–	0.27
External	Dark green open weave plastic blind	0.16	0.13	0.22	0.17
	Canvas roller blind	0.10	0.08	0.13	0.10
	White louvred subreaker, blades at 45°	0.08	0.06	0.11	0.08
	Dark green miniature louvred blind	0.08	0.06	0.10	0.07

*All glazing clear except where stated otherwise. Factors are typical values only and variations will occur due to density of blind weave, reflectivity and cleanliness of protection.

The following examples demonstrate the procedure for obtaining the peak environmental temperature due to the effects of solar radiation and show the use of the admittance method.

Example 6.12   Consider a room 6 m × 5 m × 3 m high with data as in Example 6.11: A_g = 9 m^2, U_g = 5.6 W m^{-2} K^{-1}, A_w = 9 m^2, U_w = 0.7 W m^{-2} K^{-1}, $\bar{t}_{ao}$ = 17 °C, C_v = 60 W K^{-1}, $\bar{I}_{GV}$ = 180 W m^{-2}. Floor, cast concrete with screed and carpet. Internal walls, lightweight concrete plastered both sides. Assume peak external air temperature 22 °C.

The *IHVE Guide* suggests that a 1 h time lag should be allowed so that if the peak occurs at 13.00 hours, then the irradiance at 12.00 hours should be used. Let irradiance at 12.00 hours = I'_{GV} = 600 W m^{-2}. Hence,

Peak-to-mean intensity, $\tilde{I}_{GV} = I'_{GV} - \bar{I}_{GV} = 600 - 180 = 420$ W m^{-2}

Alternating solar gain factor for single glazing, S_a = 0.42. Therefore,

Alternating solar irradiance gain = $S_a \tilde{I}_{GV} A_g$

$$= 0.42 \times 420 \times 9 = 1587.6 \text{ W}.$$

Additional alternating heat input due to the opaque portion of the external wall is given by $fAU(t_{eo} - \bar{t}_{eo})$. The derivation and use of this expression was considered in Section 6.5. However, the *IHVE Guide* states that, in most cases in the UK, this component of the heat gain is very small and can be ignored.

Additional heat gain due to variation in external air temperature transmitted by the window is given by $A_g U_g \tilde{t}_{ao}$, where

$\tilde{t}_{ao}$ = Diurnal air temperature swing

$$= \text{Peak} - \text{Mean} = 22 - 17 = 5 \text{ °C}$$

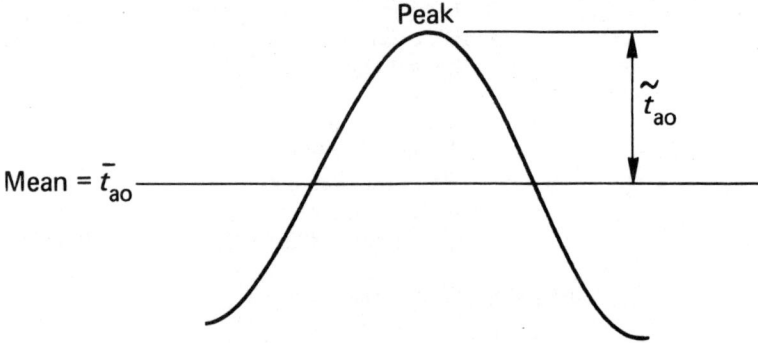

Therefore,

$$A_g U_g \tilde{t}_{ao} = 9 \times 5.6 \times 5 = 252 \text{ W}.$$

Additional heat gain due to variation in external air temperature introduced by ventilation is given by

$$C_v \tilde{t}_{ao} = 60 \times 5 = 300 \text{ W}.$$

Therefore,

Total alternating gain = 1587.6 + 252 + 300 = 2139.6 W

$$= \tilde{Q}.$$

Environmental temperature swing, $\tilde{t}_{ei} = \tilde{Q}/(\Sigma AY + C_v)$.

Element	$A(\text{m}^2)$	$Y(\text{W m}^{-2} \text{ K}^{-1})$	$AY(\text{W K}^{-1})$
External wall	9	3.0	27.0
Window	9	5.6	50.4
Ceiling	30	5.8	174.0
Floor	30	3.1	93.0
Internal walls	48	2.55	122.4
		$\Sigma AY =$	466.8

Therefore,

$$\tilde{t}_{ei} = 2139.6/(466.8 + 60) = 4.1 \,°C.$$

Peak environmental temperature = $\bar{t}_{ei} + \tilde{t}_{ei}$ = 28 + 4.1 = 32.1 $°C.$

Example 6.13   As Example 6.12, but window with double glazing.

Solar irradiance gain = $S_a \tilde{I}_{GV} A_g$

$$= 0.4 \times 420 \times 9 = 1512 \text{ W}.$$

Additional heat gains:

$$A_g U_g \tilde{t}_{ao} = 9 \times 2.8 \times 5 = 126 \text{ W};$$
$$C_v \tilde{t}_{ao} = 60 \times 5 = 300 \text{ W}.$$

Therefore

$$\tilde{Q} = 1512 + 126 + 300 = 1938 \text{ W}.$$

Element	$A(\text{m}^2)$	$Y(\text{W m}^{-2}\,\text{K}^{-1})$	$AY(\text{W K}^{-1})$
External wall	9	3.0	27.0
Window	9	2.8	25.2
Ceiling	30	5.8	174.0
Floor	30	3.1	93.0
Internal walls	48	2.55	122.4
		$\Sigma AY =$	441.6

Hence,

$$\tilde{t}_{ei} = \tilde{Q}/(\Sigma AY + C_v) = 1938/(441.6 + 60) = 3.9 \,°C$$

and

Peak environmental temperature, t'_{ei} = 29.2 + 3.9 = 33.1 $°C.$

Note that although the use of double glazing did not result in a reduction in the mean environmental temperature when compared with the same room having single glazing, the temperature swing is very slightly lower.

These examples were for assumed summer conditions in Britain and were calculated for a ventilation rate of two air changes per hour. It is interesting to note what occurs when the external air temperature is much higher, as would be the case in a tropical area, and if the air change rate is increased.

Example 6.14   Calculate the mean environmental temperature and peak environmental temperature at 15.00 hours for a room having the same dimensions as before but for a tropical area. The window area is 4.5 m^2 situated on an east-facing wall, fitted with a suitable solar shading device, such as an external perforated screen which shields the window from the sun. Assume that there is no solar radiation entering through the window. The mean external air temperature = 32 $°C$. The peak external air temperature = 38 $°C$ which occurs at 15.00 hours (true solar time). The mean sol-air temperature on vertical surface (a = 0.6) = 38.8 $°C$. Ventilation rate = 10 ach. U-value for wall = 0.7 W m^{-2} K^{-1}; U-value for window = 5.6 W m^{-2} K^{-1}.

As was mentioned before, for low ventilation rates it is sufficiently accurate to assume that

$$C_v = Vol \times n/3 \quad \text{(or } 0.33 \; Vol \times n\text{)}$$

and, hence, the ventilation loss is expressed in the form

$$Q_v = (Vol \times n/3) \, (t_{ei} - t_{ao}).$$

However, for high ventilation rates, the conductance h_a between the environmental temperature and the air temperature has to be included and, as was shown in Chapter 5, the expression for C_v becomes

$$\frac{1}{C_v} = \frac{3}{Vol \times n} + \frac{1}{4.8 \Sigma A}.$$

This can be rewritten as

$$\frac{1}{C_v} = \frac{1}{0.33 \; Vol \times n} + \frac{1}{4.8 \; \Sigma A} = \frac{4.8 \Sigma A + (0.33 \; Vol \times n)}{(0.33 \; Vol \times n) \times 4.8 \Sigma A}$$

or

$$C_v = \frac{4.8 \Sigma A \times (0.33 \; Vol \times n)}{4.8 \Sigma A + (0.33 \; Vol \times n)}$$

which is the form given by Petherbridge for C_v [4].

Inserting the dimensions of the room, C_v is obtained as follows:

$$4.8 \Sigma A = 4.8 \; [(2 \times 5 \times 3) + (2 \times 6 \times 3) + (2 \times 5 \times 6)]$$

$$= 604.8 \; \text{W K}^{-1};$$

$$0.33 \; Vol \times n = 0.33 \times 90 \times 10 = 300 \; \text{W K}^{-1}.$$

Hence,

$$C_v = \frac{604.8 \times 300}{604.8 + 300} = 200.5 \; \text{W K}^{-1}.$$

The ventilation loss is given by

$$C_v(\bar{t}_{ei} - \bar{t}_{ao}) = 200.5 \; (\bar{t}_{ei} - 32).$$

Fabric loss due to the window is given by

$$A_g U_g (\bar{t}_{ei} - \bar{t}_{ao}) = 4.5 \times 5.6 \; (\bar{t}_{ei} - 32)$$

$$= 25.2 \; (\bar{t}_{ei} - 32).$$

Fabric loss due to the external wall is given by

$$A_w U_w (\bar{t}_{ei} - \bar{t}_{eo})$$

$$= 13.5 \times 0.7 \; (\bar{t}_{ei} - 38.8)$$

$$= 9.45 \; (\bar{t}_{ei} - 38.8).$$

Therefore,

$$200.5 \; (\bar{t}_{ei} - 32) + 25.2 (\bar{t}_{ei} - 32) + 9.45 (\bar{t}_{ei} - 38.8) = 0,$$

Hence,

$$\bar{t}_{ei} = 32.3 \; ^\circ\text{C}.$$

Assume that the wall is insulated on the outside, then, from Figs. 6.5 and 6.6, the decrement factor f is found to be 0.22 and the time lag ψ is 6½ h.

In order to calculate the peak-to-mean, or alternating, heat flow through the wall at 15.00 hours the sol-air temperature at $(\theta - \psi)$ hours has to be obtained, i.e. at $15.00 - 6.30$ hours = 8.30 hours.

From temperature and irradiance data, and using the procedure described in Example 6.2, the sol-air temperature for this particular time was found to be 58.1 °C.

$$\text{Alternating heat flow through the external wall} = fAU(t_{eo} - \bar{t}_{eo})$$

$$= 0.22 \times 13.5 \times 0.7(58.1 - 38.8) = 40.1 \text{ W.}$$

$$\text{Diurnal temperature swing, } \widetilde{t}_{ao} = \text{Peak temperature} - \text{Mean temperature}$$

$$= 38 - 32 = 6 \text{ °C.}$$

Alternating heat flow through window (due to temperature differences)

$$= A_g U_g (\widetilde{t}_{ao}) = 4.5 \times 5.6 \times 6 = 151.2 \text{ W.}$$

$$\text{Alternating heat input due to ventilation} = C_v(\widetilde{t}_{ao})$$

$$= 200.5 \times 6 = 1203 \text{ W.}$$

Therefore,

$$\text{Total alternating heat input, } \widetilde{Q} = 40.1 + 151.2 + 1203$$

$$= 1394.3 \text{ W.}$$

Element	$A(\text{m}^2)$	$Y(\text{W m}^{-2}\text{ K}^{-1})$	$AY(\text{W K}^{-1})$
External wall	13.5	3	40.5
Window	4.5	5.6	25.2
Ceiling	30	5.8	174.0
Floor	30	3.1	93.0
Internal walls	48	2.55	122.4
		$\Sigma AY =$	455.1

Hence,

$$\text{Peak-to-mean environmental temperature, } \widetilde{t}_{ei} = 1394.3/(455.1 + 200.5)$$

$$= 2.1 °\text{C,}$$

$$\text{Peak environmental temperature} = 32.3 + 2.1 = 34.4 °\text{C.}$$

Example 6.14 illustrates two interesting features. In the case of the wall, if the insulation had been placed on the inside instead of the outside, the decrement factor would have been 0.33 instead of 0.22, thus showing that the positioning of the insulation is important in controlling the alternating heat input through the fabric (i.e. the insulation having the greatest effect when placed on the side nearest the alternating heat input).

The second feature to note is the effect of the ventilation. It will be observed that with a ventilation rate of 10 ach, the mean environmental temperature of 32.3 °C is not much greater than the mean external air temperature of 32.0 °C. This application of ventilation for cooling can be used to reduce the heating

load due to solar radiation acting on a roof. Petherbridge has shown that the
most effective way of dealing with solar gains through roofs is by using shading
devices and has suggested a form of construction with an air space between the
roof covering and the ceiling. He comments that when air spaces are freely
ventilated to the external air, then the temperature in the space tends to
approach that of the external air.

Van Straaten [9], Groundwater [2] and Koenigsberger *et al.* [13] deal with
the problem of heat flow through roofs in warm countries, illustrate different
ways in which this can be controlled and comment upon the use of ventilation.
However, care must be taken not to assume that by making further increases in
the ventilation rate for buildings in tropical areas additional cooling can
always be obtained. This last point can be demonstrated by recalculating
Example 6.14 but with the ventilation rate increased to 20 ach.

Example 6.15   For $n = 20$ ach,

$$0.33 \; Vol \times n = 600 \text{ W K}^{-1}$$

and

$$C_v = \frac{604.8 \times 600}{604.8 + 600} = 301.2 \text{ W K}^{-1}.$$

Ventilation loss = $301.2 \; (t_{ei} - 32)$,

Fabric loss = $25.2 \; (\bar{t}_{ei} - 32) + 9.45 \; (\bar{t}_{ei} - 38.8)$,

giving,

Mean environmental temperature, $\bar{t}_{ei} = 32.2 \; °\text{C}$.

Alternating heat gain due to ventilation = $301.2 \times 6 = 1807.2$ W

Alternating heat gain through fabric   = 191.3 W.

Therefore,

Total alternating heat gain = 1998.5 W,

Peak-to-mean environmental temperature = $1998.5/(455.1 + 301.2)$

$$= 2.6 \; °\text{C}$$

Hence,

Peak environmental temperature = $32.2 + 2.6 = 34.8 \; °\text{C}$.

It is seen that the increased ventilation rate has resulted in a slight decrease in
the mean environmental temperature, but this is offset by a rather larger increase
in the peak-to-mean environmental temperature, resulting in an overall increase in
the peak environmental temperature. This effect is due to the following. Since the
value of C_v has to be obtained from

$$C_v = \frac{4.8 \Sigma A \times (0.33 \; Vol \times n)}{4.8 \Sigma A + (0.33 \; Vol \times n)}$$

it is found that when the value of n is doubled (i.e. from 10 to 20 ach) then the
corresponding value of C_v is only increased by about 1.5 times (i.e. from 200.5
to 301.2), with the result that the ventilation loss $C_v(t_{ei} - t_{ao})$ is not as large as
might have been expected.

With regard to the peak-to-mean environmental temperature, an increase in the ventilation rate and C_v also results in an increase in the alternating ventilation heat input and, hence, in the total alternating heat input.

References

1 Beckett, H. E., Reflecting power of rough surfaces at solar wavelengths. *Proceedings of the Physical Society Part 3,* **43** (238), 227–241, 1931.

2 Groundwater, I. S., *Solar Radiation in Air Conditioning.* Crosby Lockwood, London, 1957.

3 Hottel, H. C., Performance of flat-plate solar energy collectors. In *Space Heating with Solar Energy,* M.I.T. Press, Cambridge, Mass., 1954, 58–71.

4 Petherbridge, P., Limiting the temperatures in naturally ventilated buildings in warm climates. *Building Research Station Current Paper 7/74,* 1974.

5 Milbank, N. O. and Harrington-Lynn, J., Thermal response and the admittance procedure. *Building Research Establishment Current Paper 61/74,* 1974.

6 Givoni, B. and Hoffman, E., *Critical Review of Scaled Mathematical Models for Prediction of Transient Heat Flow and Indoor Temperature in Buildings.* Technion, Haifa, 1969.

7 Billington, N., *Building Physics: Heat.* Pergamon Press, Oxford, 1967.

8 Jones, W. P., *Air Conditioning Engineering,* 2nd ed. Edward Arnold, London, 1973.

9 van Straaten, J. F., *Thermal Performance of Buildings.* Elsevier Publishing Co., Amsterdam, 1967.

10 Turner, D. P. (ed.), *Windows and Environment.* Pilkington Bros., St. Helens, 1969.

11 Loudon, A. G., Summertime temperature in buildings. *Building Research Station Current Paper 47/68,* 1968.

12 Petherbridge, P., Sunpath diagrams and overlays for solar heat gain calculations. *Building Research Station Current Paper 39/65,* 1965.

13 Koenigsberger, O. H., Ingersoll, T. G., Mayhew, A. and Szokolay, S. V., *Manual of Tropical Housing and Building, Part I: Climatic Design.* Longman, London, 1974.

7
INTERMITTENT HEATING OF A BUILDING– WINTER CONDITIONS

It has been demonstrated by Milbank and Harrington-Lynn [1, 2], Billington [3] and others that the admittance procedure can be applied to the case of intermittent heating for winter conditions.

Billington has considered the temperature swing in buildings and has shown that it can be related to a characteristic which we shall term the thermal damping factor T_{df}. His derivation for T_{df} is as follows:

$$\bar{Q} = (\Sigma AU + C_v)(\bar{t}_{ei} - \bar{t}_{ao}),$$

$$\tilde{Q} = (\Sigma AY + C_v)\tilde{t}_{ei},$$

where $\bar{Q}$ = steady or average flow of heat, $\tilde{Q}$ = cyclic flow, $\bar{t}_{ao}$ = average external air temperature, $\bar{t}_{ei}$ = average environmental temperature, $\tilde{t}_{ei}$ = temperature swing (i.e. peak-to-mean), A, U, Y and C_v are as defined in previous chapters. Hence,

$$\frac{\bar{Q}}{\tilde{Q}} = \frac{\bar{t}_{ei} - \bar{t}_{ao}}{\tilde{t}_{ei}} \frac{(\Sigma AU + C_v)}{(\Sigma AY + C_v)} = \frac{\bar{t}_{ei} - \bar{t}_{ao}}{\tilde{t}_{ei}} T_{df},$$

where

$$T_{df} = \frac{\Sigma AU + C_v}{\Sigma AY + C_v}. \tag{7.1}$$

Therefore,

$$\tilde{t}_{ei} = T_{df}(\tilde{Q}/\bar{Q})(\bar{t}_{ei} - \bar{t}_{ao}).$$

But $(\bar{t}_{ei} - \bar{t}_{ao})$ = average temperature difference = $\Delta \bar{t}_{ei}$. Therefore,

$$\tilde{t}_{ei} = T_{df}(\tilde{Q}/\bar{Q}) \Delta \bar{t}_{ei}.$$

$\Delta \bar{t}_{ei}$ is obtained from a consideration of the desired environmental temperature and the external microclimate. The ratio $\tilde{Q}/\bar{Q}$ is dependent on the heating cycle. For an 'on–off' situation this ratio is related to the period when the heating is on.

If Q_x = heat output when heating is on, then, for a 24-h period with heating

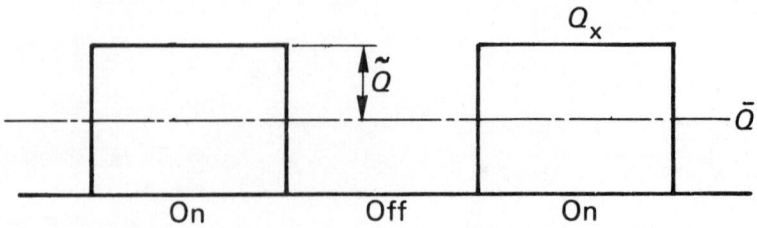

on for 12 h, off for 12 h,

$$\bar{Q} = \tfrac{1}{2} Q_X, \qquad \tilde{Q} = \tfrac{1}{2} Q_X.$$

Therefore,

$$\tilde{Q}/\bar{Q} = \tfrac{1}{2} Q_X / \tfrac{1}{2} Q_X = 1.0.$$

With $\Delta \bar{t}_{ei}$ and $\tilde{Q}/\bar{Q}$ known, T_{df} defines the temperature swing. This enables a direct comparison to be made between different buildings when subject to the same values of $\Delta \bar{t}_{ei}$ and $\tilde{Q}/\bar{Q}$.

The calculation of Billington's characteristic T_{df} is demonstrated in the following examples.

Example 7.1   (a) An upper-floor room in a building is 5 m × 4 m × 3 m high with one external wall on the long axis. The external wall is of brick with cavity fill, and 50 per cent of the area glazed. The floors are of concrete with screed and covered with carpet. The internal walls are brick, 105 mm thick, plastered both sides. Assume ventilation loss $C_v = 30$ W K^{-1} (corresponding to approximately 1.5 ach. Calculate damping factor T_{df}).

Element	A (m^2)	U (Wm^{-2}K^{-1})	AU (W K^{-1})	Y (Wm^{-2}K^{-1})	AY (W K^{-1})
Window	7.5	5.6	42.0	5.6	42.0
External wall	7.5	0.7	5.25	3.0	22.5
Floor	20	–	–	3.1	62.0
Ceiling	20	–	–	5.8	116.0
Internal walls	39	–	–	4.5	175.5
			$\Sigma AU = 47.25$		$\Sigma AY = 418.0$

From equation (7.1),

$$T_{df} = \frac{\Sigma AU + C_v}{\Sigma AY + C_v} = \frac{47.25 + 30}{418.0 + 30} = 0.17.$$

(b) What would be the value of T_{df} if the ventilation loss C_v is increased to 40 W K^{-1} (corresponding to approximately 2 ach)?

$$T_{df} = \frac{47.25 + 40}{418 + 40} = 0.19.$$

(c) What would be the value of T_{df} if the ventilation loss C_v is reduced to 20 W K^{-1} (corresponding to approximately 1 ach)?

$$T_{df} = \frac{47.25 + 20}{418 + 20} = 0.15.$$

Note that decreasing the ventilation rate resulted in a reduction in T_{df} and, hence, in the temperature swing.

Example 7.2   Room as in Example 7.1 but lightweight construction, floors, suspended timber covered with carpet. Internal walls of lightweight concrete blocks plastered both sides. What are the new values of T_{df} for conditions (a), (b), and (c)?

Element	A (m^2)	U (Wm^{-2}K^{-1})	AU (W K^{-1})	Y (Wm^{-2}K^{-1})	AY (W K^{-1})
Window	7.5	5.6	42.0	5.6	42.0
External wall	7.5	0.7	5.25	3.0	22.5
Floor	20	–	–	1.5	30.0
Ceiling	20	–	–	3.0	60.0
Internal wall	39	–	–	2.5	97.5
			$\Sigma AU = 47.25$		$\Sigma AY = 252.0$

Note that the change from heavyweight to lightweight construction in the interior of the building does not affect the value of ΣAU.

(a) $C_v = 30$ W K^{-1}, therefore,

$$T_{df} = \frac{47.25 + 30}{252 + 30} = 0.27.$$

(b) $C_v = 40$ W K^{-1}, therefore,

$$T_{df} = \frac{47.25 + 40}{252 + 40} = 0.30.$$

(c) $C_v = 20$ W K^{-1}, therefore,

$$T_{df} = \frac{47.25 + 20}{252 + 20} = 0.25.$$

Example 7.3   If the room has to have a ventilation loss $C_v = 20$ W K^{-1}, what is the required change in ΣAU such that the lightweight room will have the same temperature swing as the heavyweight room?

$$\Sigma AY = 252 \text{ W K}^{-1}, \qquad C_v = 20 \text{ W K}^{-1}, \qquad \text{Required } T_{df} = 0.15.$$

Therefore,

$$0.15 = \frac{\Sigma AU + 20}{252 + 20},$$

$$\Sigma AU = [(252 + 20) \times 0.15] - 20$$

$$= 20.8 \text{ W K}^{-1}.$$

Example 7.3 shows that, for the same temperature swing, the lightweight building has to have a much lower value of ΣAU, i.e. smaller area of glazing and better insulation. Billington makes a similar comment, stating that 'light structures need to have better insulation than heavy structures.' He also draws attention to the fact that if the same maximum cooling is to be allowed in an area with a different external temperature, then $T_{df} \Delta \bar{t}_{ei}$ has to be constant, i.e. 'better insulation and/or higher thermal capacity is required in colder climates'; this is demonstrated later in this chapter.

In obtaining T_{df} it is seen that it consists of three components:

ΣAU, insulation;

ΣAY, thermal capacity;

C_v, ventilation.

Changing any one of these has an effect on T_{df}, but it is of interest to consider their interaction and to assess their relative significance.

Let

$x = \Sigma AY/\Sigma AU$, then $\Sigma AY = x \Sigma AU$.

Similarly, let

$y = C_v/\Sigma AU$, then $C_v = y \Sigma AU$.

Hence,

$$T_{df} = \frac{\Sigma AU + C_v}{\Sigma AY + C_v} = \frac{\Sigma AU + y \Sigma AU}{x \Sigma AU + y \Sigma AU}$$

$$= \frac{\Sigma AU(1 + y)}{\Sigma AU(x + y)} = \frac{1 + y}{x + y}.$$

Inserting values of $x = 5.0$ to $x = 10.0$ and $y = 0.2$ to $y = 1.6$, Table 7.1 was obtained.

Table 7.1   *Values of T_{df}*

| | | | x | | | |
y	5	6	7	8	9	10
0.2	0.23	0.19	0.17	0.15	0.13	0.12
0.4	0.26	0.22	0.19	0.17	0.15	0.14
0.6	0.29	0.24	0.21	0.19	0.17	0.15
0.8	0.31	0.27	0.23	0.20	0.18	0.17
1.0	0.33	0.29	0.25	0.22	0.20	0.18
1.2	0.35	0.31	0.27	0.24	0.22	0.20
1.4	0.38	0.32	0.29	0.26	0.23	0.21
1.6	0.39	0.34	0.30	0.27	0.25	0.22
1.8	0.41	0.36	0.32	0.29	0.26	0.24
2.0	0.43	0.38	0.33	0.30	0.27	0.25

From Fig. 7.1, it is seen that for a given insulation, the lowest value of T_{df} occurs with a low ventilation loss (C_v) and a high thermal capacity (ΣAY). Conversely, the highest value of T_{df} is obtained with a high ventilation loss and a low thermal capacity.

It will be noted that the sloping lines which represent constant values of T_{df} are further apart towards the lower right of the graph and closer together towards the upper left. This implies that the rate of change of T_{df} with changes in C_v and ΣAY is slower with low values of T_{df} and more rapid with high values. In addition the slope of the radiating lines varies, those towards the left

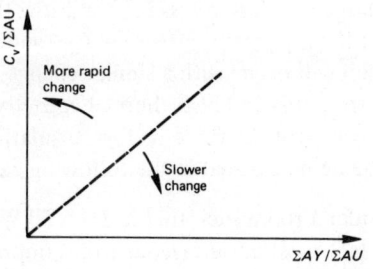

Fig. 7.1 Values of T_{df}.

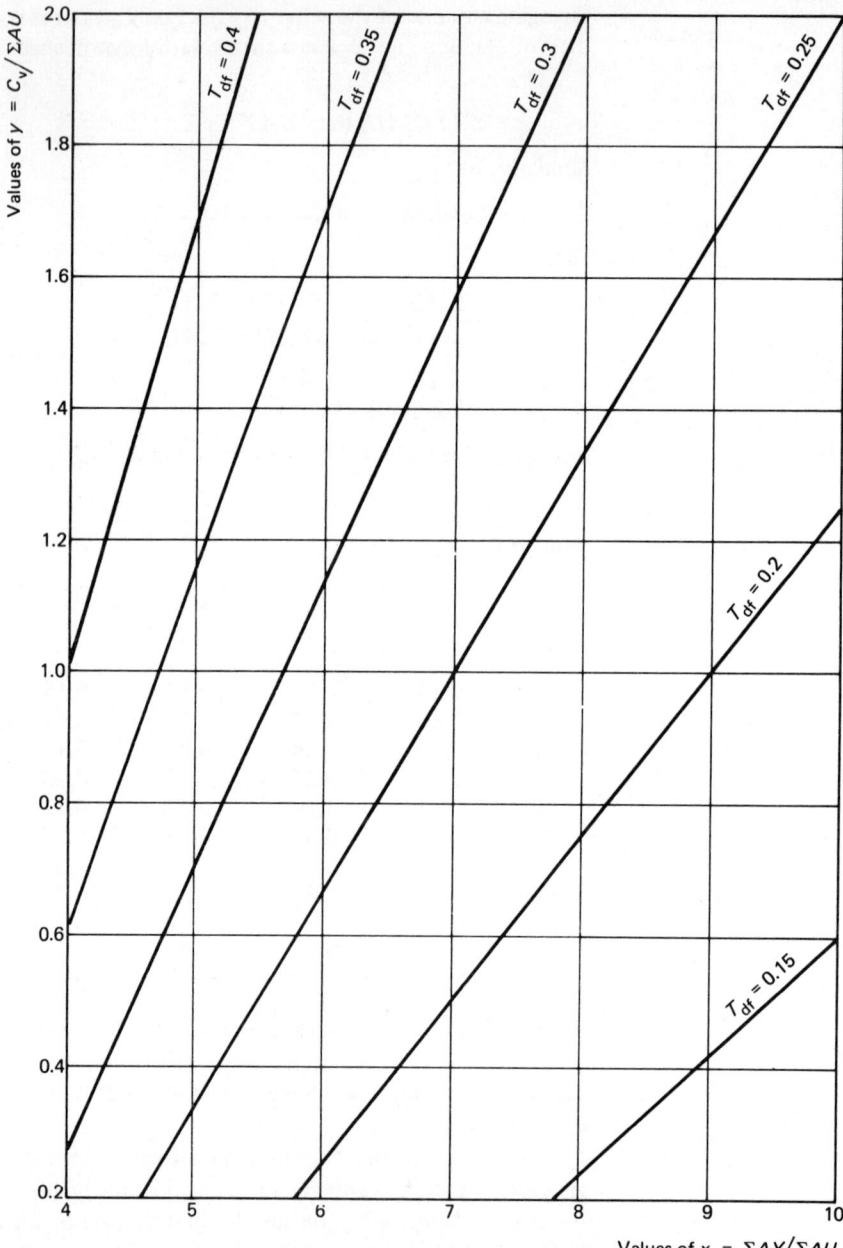

approaching the vertical, those to the right, the horizontal. This indicates that in a building with a large ventilation loss (C_v) and low thermal capacity ($\Sigma A Y$), a change in C_v or $\Sigma A Y$ has a greater effect on T_{df} (and, hence, the temperature swing) than that which will occur with a similar change in C_v or $\Sigma A Y$ in a building with a low ventilation loss and high thermal capacity.

The relative importance of the three factors, insulation, thermal capacity and ventilation loss can be demonstrated in the following examples.

Example 7.4   Consider a room such that $\Sigma A U = 50$ W K^{-1}, $\Sigma A Y = 400$ W K^{-1} and $C_v = 30$ W K^{-1}. Is it most advantageous to (a) improve insulation by 25 per cent, (b) increase thermal capacity by 25 per cent, (c) decrease ventilation rate by 25 per cent?

Existing values are

$$x = (\Sigma AY/\Sigma AU) = 400/50 = 8.0, \qquad y = C_v/\Sigma AU = 30/50 = 0.6.$$

From Fig. 7.1, $T_{df} = 0.19$.

(a) ΣAU decreased by 25 per cent = 37.5 W K^{-1}. Therefore,

$$x = \frac{400}{37.5} = 10.7, \qquad y = \frac{30}{37.5} = 0.8 \quad \text{and so } T_{df} = 0.16.$$

(b) ΣAY increased by 25 per cent = 500 W K^{-1}. Therefore,

$$x = \frac{500}{50} = 10.0, \qquad y = 0.6 \qquad \text{and so } T_{df} = 0.15.$$

(c) C_v decreased by 25 per cent = 22.5 W K^{-1}. Therefore,

$$x = 8.0, \qquad y = \frac{22.5}{50} = 0.45 \qquad \text{and so } T_{df} = 0.17.$$

Hence, an increase in the thermal capacity produces the lowest value of T_{df}.

Example 7.5   Using the same data as in Example 7.4, what will produce the least change in T_{df}: (a) Reduce insulation by 25 per cent, (b) Reduce thermal capacity by 25 per cent, (c) Increase ventilation loss by 25 per cent?

(a) $\Sigma AU = 62.5$ W K^{-1}. Therefore,

$$x = \frac{400}{62.5} = 6.4, \qquad y = \frac{30}{62.5} = 0.48 \qquad \text{and so } T_{df} = 0.22.$$

(b) $\Sigma AY = 300$ W K^{-1}. Therefore,

$$x = \frac{300}{50} = 6.0, \qquad y = 0.6 \qquad \text{and so } T_{df} = 0.24.$$

(c) $C_v = 37.5$ W K^{-1}. Therefore,

$$x = 8.0, \qquad y = \frac{37.5}{50} = 0.75 \qquad \text{and so } T_{df} = 0.2.$$

Reductions in the insulation and the thermal capacity produce greater changes than does an increase in the ventilation rate.

Putting $\Sigma AU = 50$ W K^{-1}, $\Sigma AY = 250$ W K^{-1} and $C_v = 30$ W K^{-1} and repeating the procedure as in Examples 7.4 and 7.5, gave the same rank order:

	Change	T_{df}
(a)	Reduce ΣAU by 25 per cent	0.24
(b)	Increase ΣAY by 25 per cent	0.23
(c)	Reduce C_v by 25 per cent	0.27
(a)	Increase ΣAU by 25 per cent	0.33
(b)	Reduce ΣAY by 25 per cent	0.37
(c)	Increase C_v by 25 per cent	0.30

Fig. 7.2 Relationship between C_v, $\Sigma A Y$ and $\Sigma A U$ at $T_{df} = 0.2$.

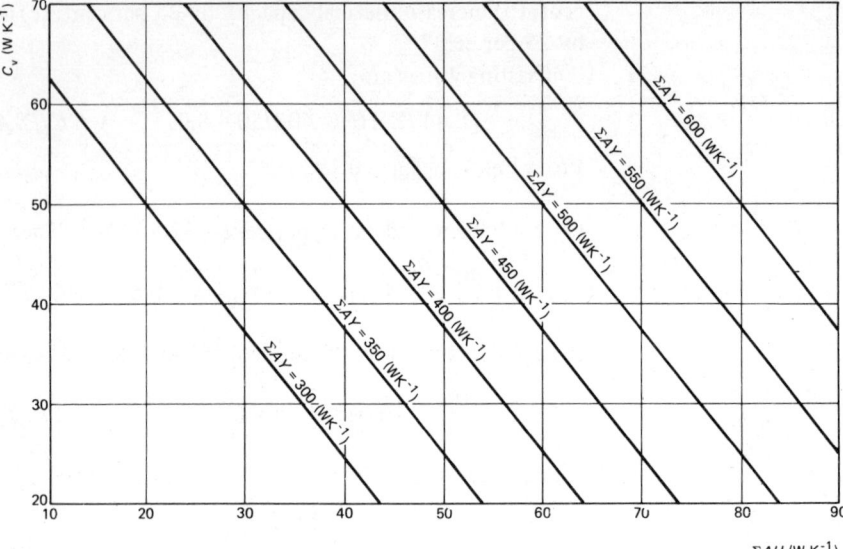

Fig. 7.3 Relationship between C_v, $\Sigma A Y$ and $\Sigma A U$ at $T_{df} = 0.25$.

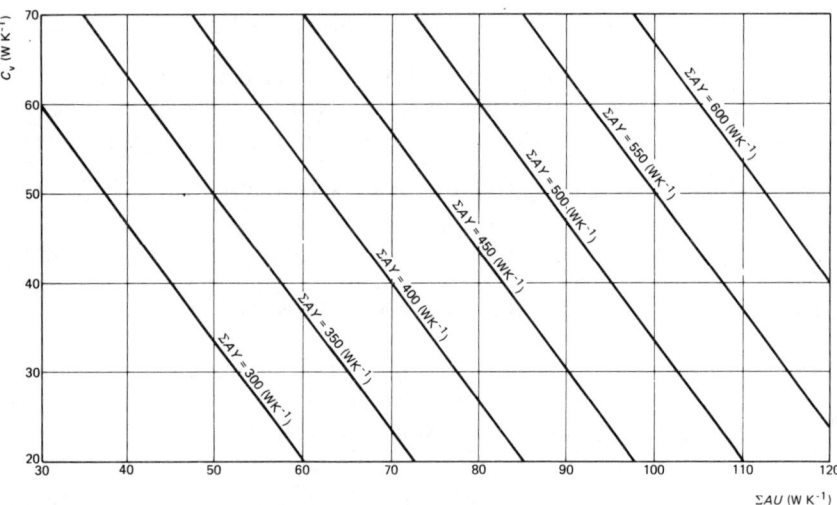

Fig. 7.4 Relationship between C_v, $\Sigma A Y$ and $\Sigma A U$ at $T_{df} = 0.3$.

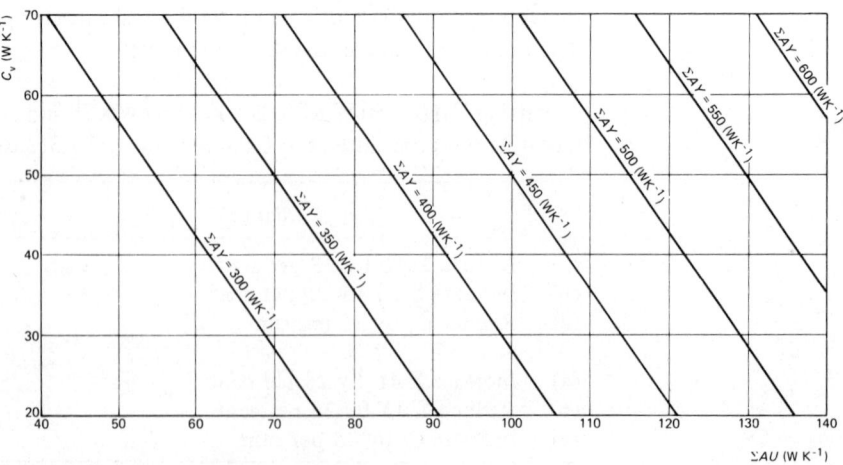

The effects of insulation (ΣAU) and ventilation loss (C_v) are illustrated in Fig. 7.2. Taking the case when $T_{df} = 0.2$, the ventilation loss C_v has been plotted against ΣAU for different values of ΣAY. It is seen that for any particular value of ΣAY, as C_v increases, then ΣAU can be reduced. Figs. 7.3 and 7.4 show similar sets of graphs for $T_{df} = 0.25$ and 0.3. For the given values of T_{df}, these graphs can be used to find any of the variables ΣAU, ΣAY or C_v when any two are known.

Example 7.6   When $T_{df} = 0.2$ and $\Sigma AY = 500$ W K^{-1}, find the percentage reduction in insulation which can be obtained in a room when the ventilation loss is reduced from 40 W K^{-1} to 25 W K^{-1} such that the temperature swing will be the same.

From Fig. 7.2, when $C_v = 40$ W K^{-1}, $\Sigma AU = 68$ W K^{-1} and when $C_v = 25$ W K^{-1}, $\Sigma AU = 80$ W K^{-1}. Therefore,

$$\text{Change in } \Sigma AU = \frac{12}{68} \times 100 = 17.6 \text{ per cent.}$$

Example 7.7   What would be the percentage change in ΣAU if $\Sigma AY = 350$ W K^{-1}. From Fig. 7.2, when $C_v = 40$ W K^{-1}, $\Sigma AU = 38$ W K^{-1} and when $C_v = 25$ W K^{-1}, $\Sigma AU = 50$ W K^{-1}. Therefore,

$$\text{Change in } \Sigma AU = \frac{12}{38} \times 100 = 31.6 \text{ per cent.}$$

Note that in this case, where the admittance value is smaller signifying a room with a lower thermal capacity, the insulation has to be greater (ΣAU less), and that the ventilation change produces a larger percentage alteration in ΣAU.

7.2 Intermittent heating — energy consumption

For the case of 'on–off' intermittent heating, with the heating on for 12 h, off for 12 h, during a 24-h period, it was shown in the previous section that

$$\bar{Q} = \tfrac{1}{2} Q_x \text{ and } \widetilde{Q} = \tfrac{1}{2} Q_x,$$

where Q_x is the maximum heating input.

If the heating period is less than 12 h, then $\bar{Q}$ will be less than $\tfrac{1}{2} Q_x$ and $\widetilde{Q}$ greater than $\tfrac{1}{2} Q_x$. Billington points out that this situation results in greater temperature swings but lower energy consumption.

However, in considering the case of a 12-h on-off cycle, Billington proposes that the square wave input be replaced by a sinusoidal input for a 24-h period and his method of analysis is as follows.

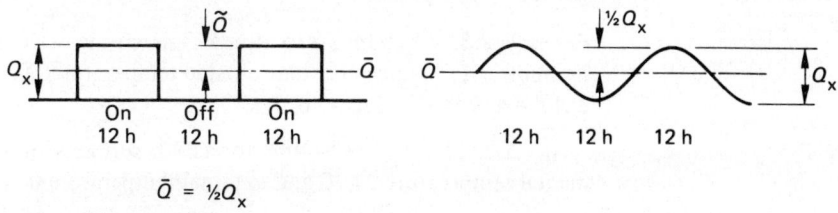

Square wave form   Assumed sinusoidal form

Since $\bar{Q} = (\Sigma AU + C_v) \Delta \bar{t}_{ei}$ and for a 12-h on-off cycle $\bar{Q} = \tfrac{1}{2} Q_x$, then

$$\Delta \bar{t}_{ei} = \bar{Q}/(\Sigma AU + C_v) = \tfrac{1}{2} Q_x/(\Sigma AU + C_v). \tag{7.2}$$

Also, $\widetilde{Q} = (\Sigma AY + C_v)\widetilde{t}_{ei}$ and $\widetilde{Q} = \frac{1}{2} Q_x$. Therefore,

$$\widetilde{t}_{ei} = \frac{1}{2} Q_x/(\Sigma AY + C_v) \qquad (7.3)$$

It is assumed that the environmental temperature will also form a sinusoidal curve.

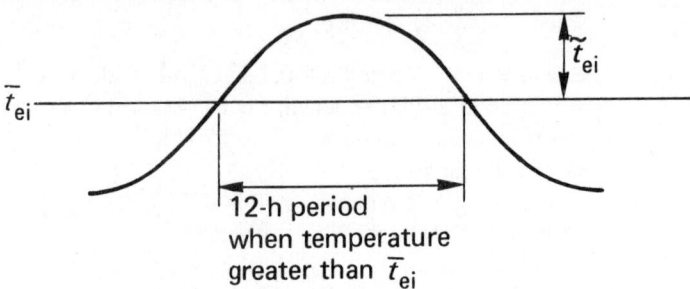

12-h period
when temperature
greater than $\overline{t}_{ei}$

Billington considers the portion of the curve for the 12-h period when the temperature exceeds the 24-h mean value $\overline{t}_{ei}$. The mean temperature during this 12-h period $\overline{t}_{12}$ is given by

$$\overline{t}_{12} = \overline{t}_{ei} + 0.64\,\widetilde{t}_{ei}. \qquad (7.4)$$

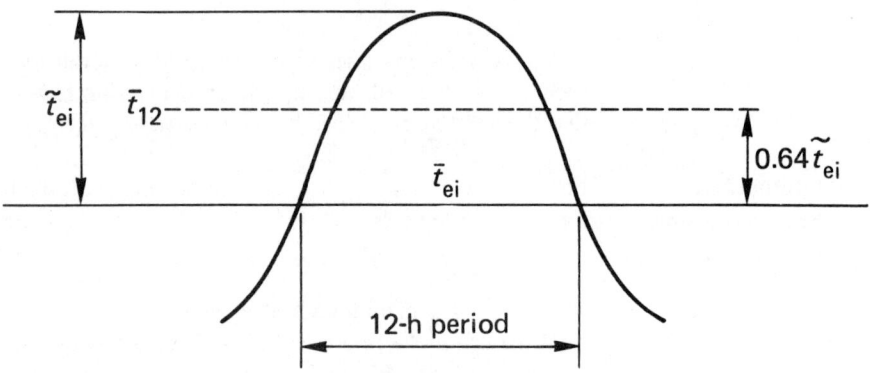

By specifying a value for $\overline{t}_{12}$, i.e. the required mean environmental temperature during the 12-h period when the building is to be in a 'heated' condition, it is possible to obtain $\overline{t}_{ei}$, $\widetilde{t}_{ei}$ and, hence, Q_x. This procedure can be demonstrated in the following example.

Example 7.8   A room 5 m × 4 m × 3 m with construction as specified in Example 7.1. Assume constant outside temperature. $\Sigma AU = 47.25$ W K^{-1}, $\Sigma AY = 419$ W K^{-1}, $C_v = 30$ W K^{-1}.

(a) Assume constant heating for a 24-h period with required mean environmental temperature 21 °C and external temperature 0 °C.

$$\Delta \overline{t}_{ei} = \overline{t}_{ei} - \overline{t}_{ao} = 21 - 0 = 21\ ^\circ C,$$
$$\overline{Q} = (\Sigma AU + C_v)\,\Delta \overline{t}_{ei} = (47.25 + 30)\,21$$
$$= 1622\ W.$$

(b) Assume intermittent heating, 12-h on–off cycle and mean environmental

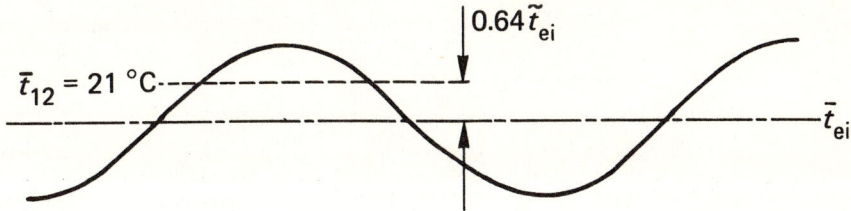

temperature during 12-h heating period to be 21 °C. Note that in this situation $\bar{t}_{ei}$ does not equal 21 °C. $\bar{t}_{ei}$ is the mean environmental temperature for the 24-h period and, since the heating is only on for 12 hours, $\bar{t}_{ei}$ will be less than 21 °C. Since it is $\bar{t}_{12}$ which is to be 21 °C, then, from equation (7.4),
$\bar{t}_{12} = \bar{t}_{ei} + 0.64\,\tilde{t}_{ei} = 21$. From equation (7.2),

$$\Delta \bar{t}_{ei} = \tfrac{1}{2} Q_x / (\Sigma AU + C_v) = \tfrac{1}{2} Q_x / 77.25$$

also

$$\Delta \bar{t}_{ei} = \bar{t}_{ei} - \bar{t}_{ao} = \bar{t}_{ei} - 0.$$

Therefore,

$$\bar{t}_{ei} = \Delta \bar{t}_{ei} = \tfrac{1}{2} Q_x / 77.25.$$

From equation (7.3),

$$\tilde{t}_{ei} = \tfrac{1}{2} Q_x / (\Sigma AY + C_v) = \tfrac{1}{2} Q_x / 449.$$

Combining these equations, i.e.

$$\left.\begin{aligned} \bar{t}_{ei} + 0.64\,\tilde{t}_{ei} &= 21, \\ \bar{t}_{ei} &= \tfrac{1}{2} Q_x / 77.25, \\ \tilde{t}_{ei} &= \tfrac{1}{2} Q_x / 449, \end{aligned}\right\}$$

gives

$$(\tfrac{1}{2} Q_x / 77.25) + 0.64\,(\tfrac{1}{2} Q_x) / 449 = 21.$$

Therefore,

$$\tfrac{1}{2} Q_x = 1461 \text{ W}.$$

Substituting the value of $\tfrac{1}{2} Q_x$,

$$\tilde{t}_{ei} = \frac{1461}{449} = 3.3 \text{ °C}$$

and

$$\bar{t}_{ei} = \frac{1461}{77.25} = 18.9 \text{ °C}.$$

(c) Same conditions as for (b) but with lightweight construction, $\Sigma AY = 252$ W K^{-1} (*see* Example 7.2). Repeating the procedure as above gives

$$\left.\begin{aligned} \bar{t}_{ei} + 0.64\,\tilde{t}_{ei} &= 21, \\ \bar{t}_{ei} &= \tfrac{1}{2} Q_x / 77.25, \\ \tilde{t}_{ei} &= \tfrac{1}{2} Q_x / 282. \end{aligned}\right\}$$

Hence $\tfrac{1}{2} Q_x = 1380$ W, $\tilde{t}_{ei} = 4.9$ °C, $\bar{t}_{ei} = 17.9$ °C.

The values obtained from the three solutions are compared in Table 7.2.

Table 7.2

	Continuous heating	Intermittent heating Heavyweight $\Sigma AY = 419 \text{ W K}^{-1}$	Lightweight $\Sigma AY = 252 \text{ W K}^{-1}$
Mean environmental temperature for 24-h period, $\bar{t}_{ei}$	21 °C	18.9 °C	17.9 °C
Temperature swing, $\tilde{t}_{ei}$	0 °C	3.3 °C	4.9 °C
Maximum temperature, $\bar{t}_{ei} + \tilde{t}_{ei}$	–	22.2 °C	22.8 °C
Minimum temperature, $\bar{t}_{ei} - \tilde{t}_{ei}$	–	15.6 °C	13.0 °C
Maximum heat input, Q_x	1622 W	2922 W	2760 W
Daily heat input = $Q_x \times$ duration of heating	38.9 kW h	35.1 kW h	33.1 kW h

It should be observed that the calculation for Q_x where there was continuous heating was based upon the 'steady-state' equation and, as a result, was not affected by thermal capacity or mass. In other words, the difference between heavyweight and lightweight construction is not evident when continuous heating is being considered.

In addition to demonstrating the application of the admittance method and the difference between the heavyweight and lightweight structures, this example illustrates another very important feature regarding intermittent heating.

It will be observed that in the two situations where the intermittent heating is used there is a saving in the energy used over the 24-h period when compared with the continuous (or steady-state) condition. This is to be expected, since the intermittent heating is only being used for half of the 24-h period. However, although the total energy has become less, in order to achieve the desired mean environmental temperature of 21 °C when the heating is on, it is necessary to have a much higher maximum heat input, i.e. larger plant.

	Change in relation to continuous heating (per cent) Heavyweight	Lightweight
Increase in maximum input	80	70
Reduction in daily input over 24 h	10	15

Note that although the heating is only on for 50 per cent of the time, there is not a saving of 50 per cent in energy.

The increase in maximum input when intermittent heating is being used is noted in the *IHVE Guide*. The *IHVE Guide* gives data for obtaining heating loads for a constant environmental temperature and includes factors to be applied to allow for the effect of intermittent heating.

Another important aspect of intermittent heating is the preheating period. A concise analysis of the influence of preheating is given by Billington [4] and it is pointed out that in order to achieve a rapid rise in the temperature in the building, the heating plant must be several times as large as that required to keep a steady internal temperature.

Comparing the heavyweight and lightweight buildings in Example 7.8, it is seen that the minimum amount of energy for the 24-h period occurs with the lightweight structure. On the other hand the lightweight structure has the lowest mean temperature for the 24-h period, a large temperature swing and a correspondingly low minimum temperature. Attention was drawn to the significance of low internal temperatures in Chapter 5 dealing with condensation and this important factor has to be borne in mind when considering temperature swings and acceptable minimum temperatures.

It is interesting to observe the effect on the temperatures and energy demand in the lightweight structure when the ventilation loss is reduced to 20 W K^{-1}, the insulation is improved by reducing the window area and by using double glazing.

Element	A	U	AU	Y	AY
Window	6	2.8	16.8	2.8	16.8
External wall	9	0.7	6.3	3.0	27.0
Floor	20	–	–	1.5	30.0
Ceiling	20	–	–	3.0	60.0
Internal wall	39	–	–	2.5	97.5
			$\Sigma AU = 23.1$		$\Sigma AY = 231.3$

$$\Sigma AU + C_v = 23.1 + 20 = 43.1 \text{ W K}^{-1},$$
$$\Sigma AY + C_v = 231.3 + 20 = 251.3 \text{ W K}^{-1}.$$

Hence,

$$\left. \begin{array}{l} \bar{t}_{ei} + \tilde{t}_{ei} = 21, \\ \bar{t}_{ei} = \tfrac{1}{2} Q_x / 43.1, \\ \tilde{t}_{ei} = \tfrac{1}{2} Q_x / 251.3. \end{array} \right\}$$

Solving, gives $\tfrac{1}{2} Q_x = 816$ W, $\bar{t}_{ei} = 18.9$ °C, $\tilde{t}_{ei} = 3.3$ °C. Therefore,

Mean environmental temperature for 24-h period	= 18.9 °C,
Maximum temperature, $\bar{t}_{ei} + \tilde{t}_{ei}$	= 22.2 °C,
Minimum temperature, $\bar{t}_{ei} - \tilde{t}_{ei}$	= 15.6 °C,
Maximum heat input, Q_x	= 1632 W,
Daily heat input	= 19.6 kW h.

The calculated temperatures in this last example are the same as those for the heavyweight structure with the original area of window, insulation and ventilation loss. The change in ΣAY is relatively small in comparison to the major alterations in ΣAU and C_v; in other words, the main change occurs in the two factors which are used for the steady-state calculation. This example illustrates the important point that, in the case of intermittent heating, for a lightweight building to have similar internal temperatures to those in a heavyweight building, then the steady-state heat loss of the lightweight structure has to be much less than that for the heavyweight one. This is similar to the statement by Billington, referred to earlier, that 'light structures need to have better insulation than heavy structures.'

Billington [5] has commented that because of the different behaviour between lightweight and heavyweight structures and the importance of the thermal capacity in relation to temperature swings, the U-value of the different elements of the building should be related to the mass. He points out that in most European countries the regulations do take this into account and quotes the following example from the Italian requirements:

Horizontal roof: $U = 1.16$ W m^{-2} K^{-1} for element of 300 kg m^{-2};

$$U = 0.35 \text{ W m}^{-2} \text{ K}^{-1} \text{ for element of 20 kg m}^{-2}.$$

This aspect was discussed in Chapter 1.

Another important aspect which has to be considered when analysing the effects of intermittent heating is the influence which the external air temperature has upon the temperature swing. This can be demonstrated by recalculating the original example of the heavy- and lightweight room but with the external air temperature at 7 °C instead of 0 °C. As before,

$$\bar{t}_{ei} + 0.64\, \tilde{t}_{ei} = 21.$$

For the heavyweight structure,

$$\tilde{t}_{ei} = \tfrac{1}{2} Q_x / (\Sigma A Y + C_v) = \tfrac{1}{2} Q_x / 449,$$
$$\Delta \bar{t}_{ei} = \tfrac{1}{2} Q_x / (\Sigma A U + C_v) = \tfrac{1}{2} Q_x / 77.25.$$

But with $\bar{t}_{ao} = 7$ °C,

$$\Delta \bar{t}_{ei} = \bar{t}_{ei} - \bar{t}_{ao} = \bar{t}_{ei} - 7.$$

Hence,

$$\bar{t}_{ei} = \Delta \bar{t}_{ei} + 7 = (\tfrac{1}{2} Q_x / 77.25) + 7.$$

The three equations become

$$\left. \begin{array}{l} \bar{t}_{ei} + 0.64\, \tilde{t}_{ei} = 21, \\ \qquad \bar{t}_{ei} = (\tfrac{1}{2} Q_x / 77.25) + 7, \\ \qquad \tilde{t}_{ei} = \tfrac{1}{2} Q_x / 449, \end{array} \right\}$$

which gives $\tfrac{1}{2} Q_x = 974$ W, $\bar{t}_{ei} = 19.6$ °C, $\tilde{t}_{ei} = 2.2$ °C.

Repeating the procedure for the lightweight building, gives $\tfrac{1}{2} Q_x = 920$ W, $\bar{t}_{ei} = 18.9$ °C, $\tilde{t}_{ei} = 3.3$ °C.

The two examples are compared in Table 7.3.

As would be expected, the energy demands are less when there is a higher external air temperature. In addition it will be noted that the temperature swings, or range of temperatures, have become less and the minimum temperatures higher; this is particularly noticeable in the case of the lightweight building. This indicates that the requirement that a lightweight building should have a

Table 7.3

	External air temperature $\bar{t}_{ao} = 0\,^{\circ}C$		External air temperature $\bar{t}_{ao} = 7\,^{\circ}C$	
	Heavyweight	Lightweight	Heavyweight	Lightweight
Mean environmental temperature, $\bar{t}_{ei}$	18.9 $^{\circ}$C	17.9 $^{\circ}$C	19.6 $^{\circ}$C	18.9 $^{\circ}$C
Maximum temperature, $\bar{t}_{ei} + \tilde{t}_{ei}$	22.2 $^{\circ}$C	22.8 $^{\circ}$C	21.8 $^{\circ}$C	22.2 $^{\circ}$C
Minimum temperature, $\bar{t}_{ei} - \tilde{t}_{ei}$	15.6 $^{\circ}$C	13.0 $^{\circ}$C	17.4 $^{\circ}$C	15.6 $^{\circ}$C
Energy used over 24-h period (12-h on–off cycle)	35.1 kW h	33.1 kW h	23.4 kW h	22.1 kW h

better standard of insulation than a heavyweight one when intermittent heating is being used is of considerable importance in areas having a cold climate.

It was probably this aspect which led Billington to make the following proposals for maximum U-values for dwellings:

	Design external air temperature ($^{\circ}$C)					
	−4		−1		2	
Type of building	Heavy	Light	Heavy	Light	Heavy	Light
Maximum U-value (W m^{-2} K^{-1})	0.5	0.4	0.6	0.5	0.6+	0.6+

It is important to note that the calculations shown in this chapter for intermittent heating have been based upon the case of a 12-h on, 12-h off heating regime. For different heating regimes, equations (7.2), (7.3) and (7.4) do not apply and the reader should refer to the work of Billington [3] and Harrington-Lynn [2].

References

1   Milbank, N. O. and Harrington-Lynn, J., Thermal response and the admittance procedure. *Building Research Establishment Current Paper 61/74*, 1974.
2   Harrington-Lynn, J., The admittance procedure: intermittent plant operation. *Building Services Engineer*, **42**, 219–221, 1974.
3   Billington, N. S., Thermal insulation and thermal capacity of buildings. *Building Services Engineer*, **43**, 226–233, 1976.
4   Billington, N. S., *Building Physics: Heat*. Pergamon Press, Oxford, 1967.
5   Billington, N. S., Thermal insulation of buildings. *Building Services Engineer*, **42**, 63–67, 1974.

8

AIR INFILTRATION INTO BUILDINGS BY NATURAL MEANS

8.1 Air infiltration

In the calculations for the heat losses from a building in winter or the heat gains due to solar radiation in the summer described in the previous chapters an allowance was made for the effect of ventilation. The estimation of this ventilation effect was based upon an assumed number of air changes per hour, but in this chapter we shall consider the calculation for air infiltration by natural means into the building in greater detail.

Air entering a building can be due to

(i) infiltration through cracks round windows, doors, etc.;

(ii) air flow through ventilation openings;

caused by wind-flow or variation between the internal air temperature and external temperature producing what is termed 'stack effect'.

In all cases the actual amount of air flowing into the building will depend upon the pressure difference between the inside and outside and also on the resistance that any openings give to the flow of air. In the first cause mentioned above the pressure difference is produced by the action of the wind flow around the building whereas in the second case (temperature variation) the pressure is caused by a difference in the density of the internal and external air, this difference in pressure being due to the phenomenon that warm air is less dense than cold air.

8.2 Calculation of infiltration

The *ASHRAE Handbook of Fundamentals* [1] states that there are two methods of estimating the air infiltration into buildings:

(i) calculations based upon the leakage characteristics of the structure and pressure differences (the 'crack method');

(ii) calculations based upon an assumed number of air changes per hour.

The latter method of calculation has already been used in many of the previous examples in this book and it has been demonstrated that it is very simple to use. Down [2] has commented that more exact calculations would not be justified for small simple buildings. Both the *ASHRAE Handbook of Fundamentals* and the *IHVE Guide* publish tables giving suitable ventilation rates which can be used, the following data in Table 8.1 for domestic buildings being taken from the *ASHRAE Handbook of Fundamentals*.

The *IHVE Guide* quotes a range of ventilation rates for various types of buildings of typical construction appropriate for normal British winter use. These published values are for normal exposure and for an average ratio of 25 per cent of openable area (windows and doors) to the external wall area. The

Table 8.1 *Ventilation rates (from ASHRAE Handbook of Fundamentals)*

Kind of room	Number of air changes per hour*
Rooms with no windows or exterior door	$\frac{1}{2}$
Rooms with window or external door on one side	1
Rooms with window or external door on two sides	$1\frac{1}{2}$
Rooms with window or external door on three sides	2
Entrance halls	2

*For rooms with weather-stripped windows use two-thirds of these values.

IHVE Guide also gives some ventilation rates for offices and rooms appropriate to summer conditions. These latter rates are much higher than those which are given for the winter conditions, this being due to the assumption that large areas of the fenestration will be kept open.

However, two points regarding the air change rate method of calculation are worth noting. First, recent research work at the Building Research Establishment has indicated that for modern domestic buildings with closed well-fitting windows very low air change rates may occur. In *BRE Digest No. 190* [3] it is stated that

> 'for typical dwellings on sheltered and exposed sites the ventilation rate can be taken as 1 and 2 ach respectively. In houses without flues ventilation rates will be lower and rates of 0.5 ach are not uncommon.'

However, for situations where there is considerable sunshine and a warm external air temperature the windows may be kept open. The *IHVE Guide* proposes that where the windows are open for 24 h then, for a room with windows on one wall, the ventilation rate can be taken as 10 ach.

Secondly, the *ASHRAE Handbook of Fundamentals* states that it is not advisable to use the air change method for factories or industrial buildings because of the considerable variation in the types and relative areas of fenestration.

8.3 Pressure due to wind flow

Before dealing with the rate of air infiltration due to pressure differences between the inside and outside of the building it is necessary to consider how this pressure difference is caused.

The relationship between wind pressure and wind velocity can be obtained from Bernoulli's equation:

$$\text{Wind pressure, } P_{\text{w}} = \frac{\rho v^2}{2},$$

where ρ = air density, v = wind velocity. *Building Research Establishment Digest No. 119* [4] gives this equation in SI units as

$$P_{\text{w}} = 0.613\, v^2 \text{ Pa}$$

where v is in metres per second.

The *Digest* gives a conversion chart which enables P_{w} to be obtained in newtons per square metre, kilogrammes-force per square metre and pounds-force per square foot, where v is given in knots, miles per hour and metres per second.

The British Meteorological Office records hourly wind speeds measured at a height of 10 m above an open level site. However it has been observed in Chapter 4 that local factors such as ground topography, height of the building, interaction with other buildings, etc., affect the wind velocity and the manner in which it acts upon a given building and as a consequence must be taken into account. Although *Building Research Establishment Digest No. 119* [4] is concerned with the structural wind loading on buildings, it does indicate the manner in which these factors can influence the wind velocity and contains much useful information and guidance.

The *IHVE Guide* proposes appropriate wind velocities for different locations to be used for estimating the pressure on a building for the purposes of air infiltration calculations. These are:

9   m s^{-1} for isolated buildings in open country;

5.5 m s^{-1} for buildings in suburban areas;

3   m s^{-1} for buildings in city centres.

However, two important points have to be noted. First, wind velocity increases with height; hence, greater wind speeds have to be used when considering the pressures acting on buildings whose height is in excess of 10 m. Second, we are concerned with the wind pressure acting over the entire face of the building and it will be a mean pressure difference which will be used in the calculation for the rate of air infiltration. Fig. 8.1, which is based upon data in the *IHVE Guide*, shows the variation of the mean pressure difference with height for buildings in the three different locations.

Fig. 8.1 Pressure differences due to wind effect (based upon values in the *IHVE Guide*).

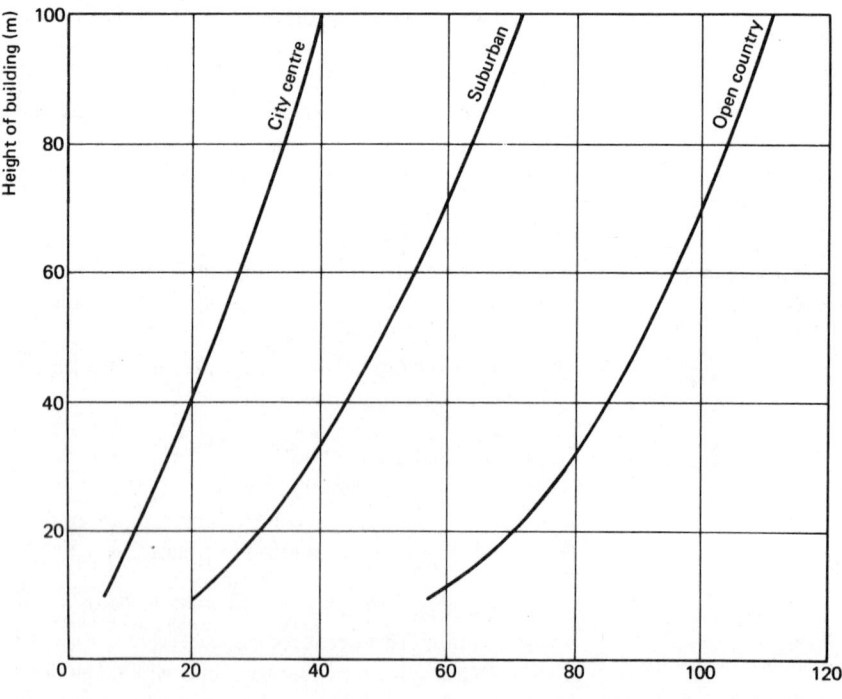

When the wind blows at right angles to a building it is stopped by the face of the building and as a result produces a pressure on the windward face. The wind is deflected over the top and round the sides of the building which gives areas of suction on these other faces as indicated in Figs. 8.2 to 8.5.

Fig. 8.2 Wind pressure and suction on a building.

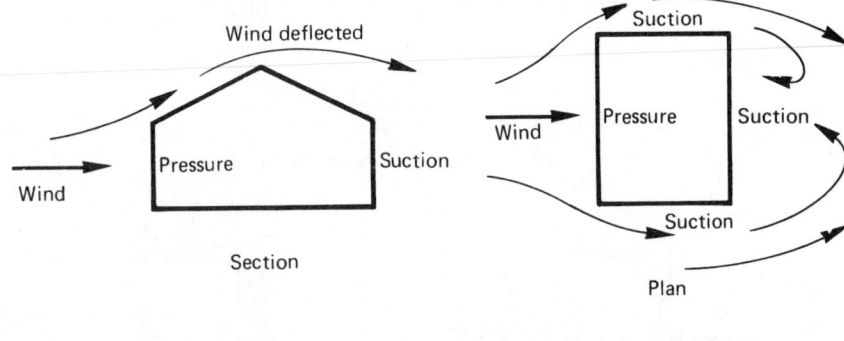

Fig. 8.3 Wind flow round buildings (from Newberry and Eaton [5]).

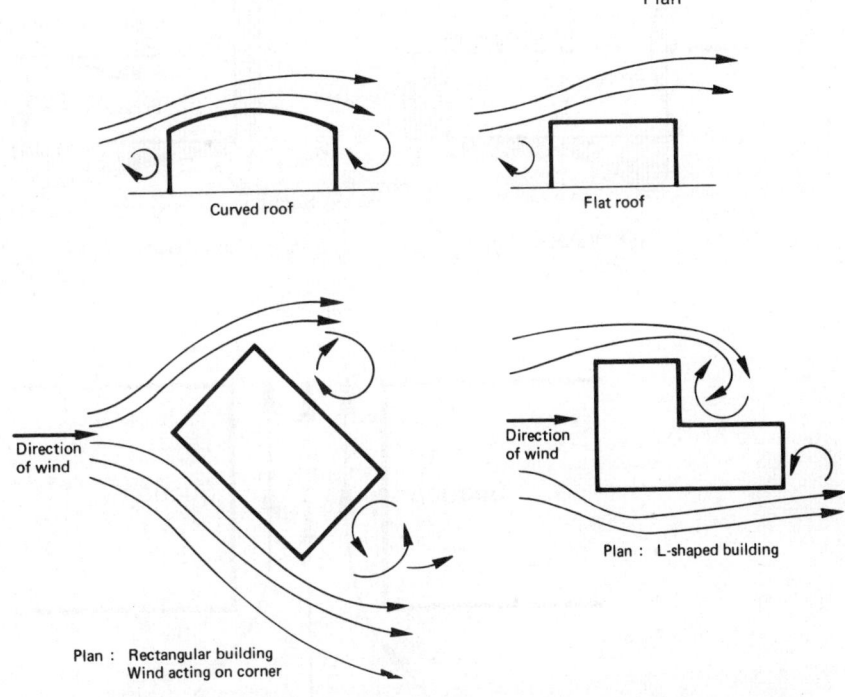

Similar diagrams to Fig. 8.2 are to be found in *Building Research Establishment Digest No. 119* [4], where it is explained that the wind pressure tends to be greatest near the centre on the windward face with the most severe suction at the edges and corners. The *IHVE Guide* states that the pressure on the windward face varies from 0.5 to 0.8 times the velocity pressure of the free wind, while on the leeward side the suction is from 0.3 to 0.4 the velocity pressure of the free wind, somewhat similar values being given in the *ASHRAE Handbook of Fundamentals*.

As was stated earlier, since pressure is proportional to the square of the velocity, an increase in wind velocity produces a considerable increase in suction. *Building Research Establishment Digest No. 119* draws attention to this and shows how the channelling of wind between two buildings can result in an increase in velocity and hence a large suction effect on the sides facing the gap.

In addition, the interaction of high and low rise buildings (Fig. 8.6) can cause

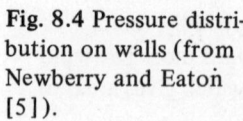

Fig. 8.4 Pressure distribution on walls (from Newberry and Eaton [5]).

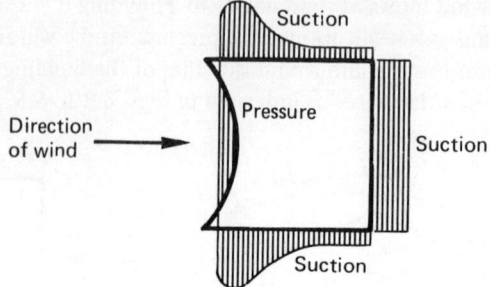

Direction of wind →

Suction

Pressure

Suction

Suction

Plan : Rectangular building

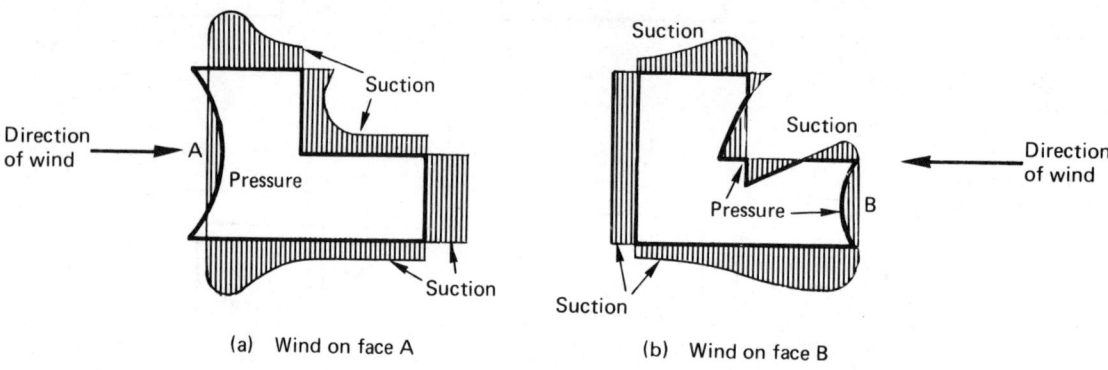

Direction of wind →

A

Pressure

Suction

Suction

(a) Wind on face A

Suction

Suction

Pressure →

B

Direction of wind ←

Suction

(b) Wind on face B

Plan : L-shaped building

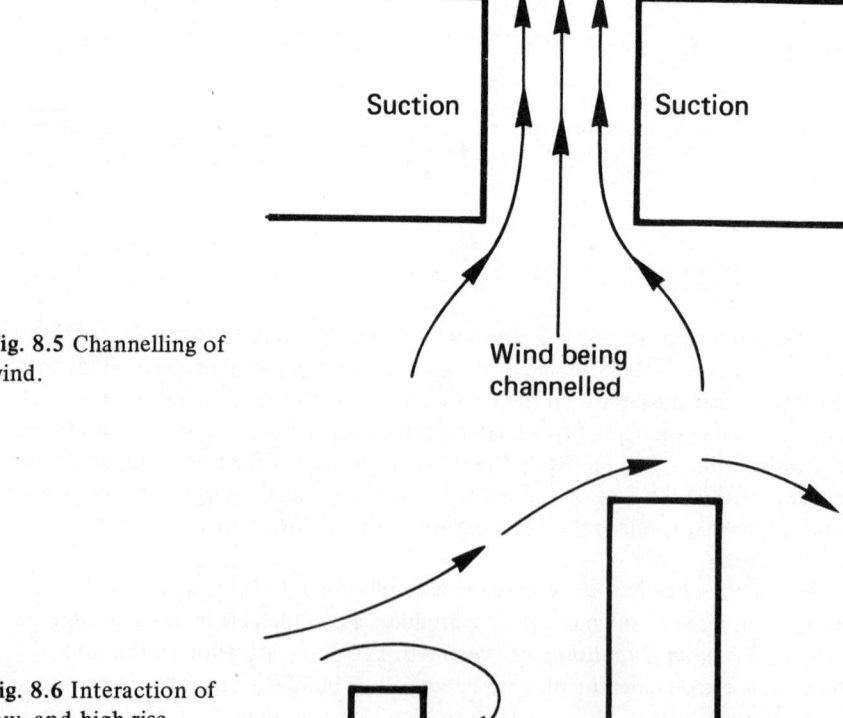

Suction

Suction

Wind being channelled

Fig. 8.5 Channelling of wind.

Fig. 8.6 Interaction of low- and high-rise buildings.

considerable wind turbulence producing a speeding up of the wind velocity with resulting large increases in the wind pressures. This latter point is considered by Penwarden and Wise [6].

If the ratio of the wind speed at pedestrian height to the free wind speed at pedestrian height on open site is considered, then for the situation previously mentioned, i.e. a low rise building in front of a high rise block, the values of the ratio shown in Table 8.2 have been obtained.

Table 8.2   (*From Penwarden and Wise* [6])

Position	Ratio
Vortex, between buildings	1.3
Corner stream	2.5
Through flow, under high rise block	3.0

Fig. 8.7 Wind flow under buildings (from Penwarden and Wise [6]).

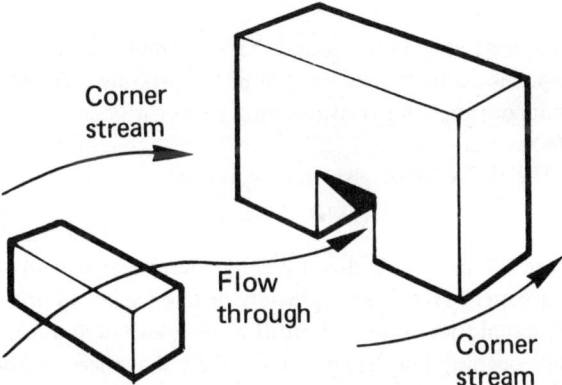

Other cases of increased wind speeds due to the interaction of high and low rise buildings are illustrated in the *BRE* publication quoted and this indicates the care that is required when considering this particular form of building layout.

The actual areas where a wind pressure or suction occurs are of considerable importance in relation to natural ventilation, since openings placed on the face of a building subjected to wind pressure will act as air inlets while those positioned on a face where there is suction will perform as air outlets.

Chapter 4 shows that the sheltering effect of buildings should not be overlooked. Where one requires a pedestrian zone, courtyard or garden, the sheltering effect of buildings may be advantageous. However, if it is desired to use the wind flow to produce natural ventilation for the purpose of cooling a building, then if that particular building is positioned within the 'leeward shadow' or suction zone of another structure the air inlets will not function adequately (Fig. 8.8).

Fig. 8.8 Shadow effect (after Koenigsberger *et al.* [7]).

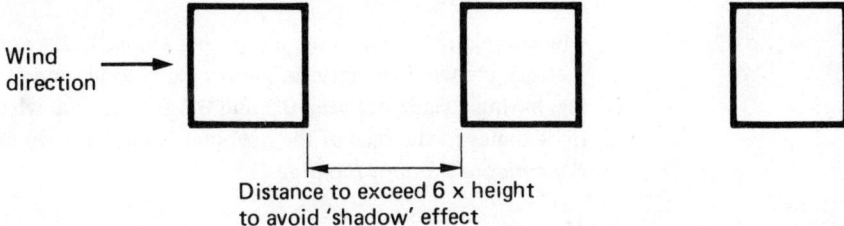

Koenigsberger [7] has reported on tests which showed that this 'shadow' effect extended for a considerable distance behind the building and that in order to avoid its effect the buildings had to be spaced at a distance of six times their height. However, as Koenigsberger points out, a staggered layout will help to overcome this type of problem (Fig. 8.9).

Fig. 8.9 Layout to avoid shadow effect (after Koenigsberger *et al.* [7]).

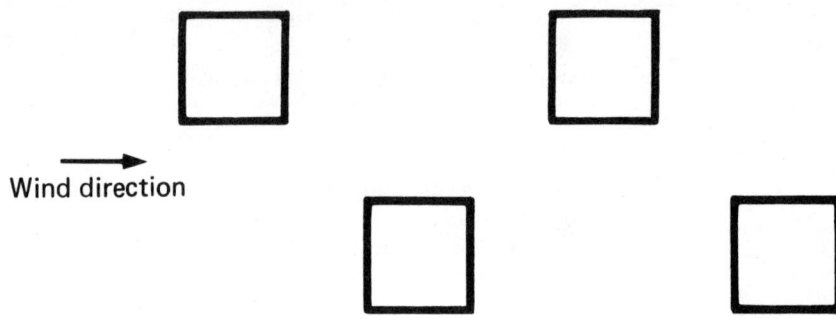

Wind direction

8.4 Air flow through openings

From tests, it has been found that the rate of air flow is approximately proportional to the square root of the pressure difference and the *IHVE Guide* points out that this relationship is sufficiently accurate for establishing the main effects of air infiltration.

The *IHVE Guide* gives the expression as

$$V = 0.827 \, A \, (\Delta p)^{0.5}$$

where V = rate of air flow (in cubic metres per second), A = area of orifice (in square metres) and Δp = pressure difference across orifice (in pascals). However, it is stated that in practice infiltration does not as a rule take place through a single opening but that it is more likely that there will be a number of openings.

Where the openings are in parallel, the above equation is changed to the form

$$V = 0.827 \, (\Sigma A) \, (\Delta p)^{0.5} \; \mathrm{m^3 \, s^{-1}}, \tag{8.1}$$

and where the openings are in series, the expression becomes

$$V = 0.827 \, [A_1 A_2 /(A_1{}^2 + A_2{}^2)^{0.5}] \, (\Delta p)^{0.5} \; \mathrm{m^3 \, s^{-1}}. \tag{8.2}$$

Since it was shown that there was a relationship between wind pressure and velocity, i.e. $P_\mathrm{w} = \rho v^2 /2$, then it follows that the pressure difference can be expressed as a function of the wind velocity squared. Also, as was shown above, the flow of air through an opening is proportional to the square root of the pressure difference, then by combining these two relationships it is possible to obtain an expression for the flow of air in terms of the wind velocity, i.e.

$$V = \text{constant} \times A \times v.$$

The *ASHRAE Handbook of Fundamentals* gives an equation of the form

$$V = EAv \tag{8.3}$$

where V = air flow (in cubic metres per second), A = area of inlet (in square metres), v = wind velocity (in metres per second) and E = effectiveness of opening, having a value between 0.5 and 0.6 for the case where the wind is acting at right angles to the face of the opening. A similar form of equation is given in *Principles of Modern Building* [8].

Fig. 8.10 Factor for case in which the area of outlet differs from the area of inlet (based on data in *Principles of Modern Building* [8]).

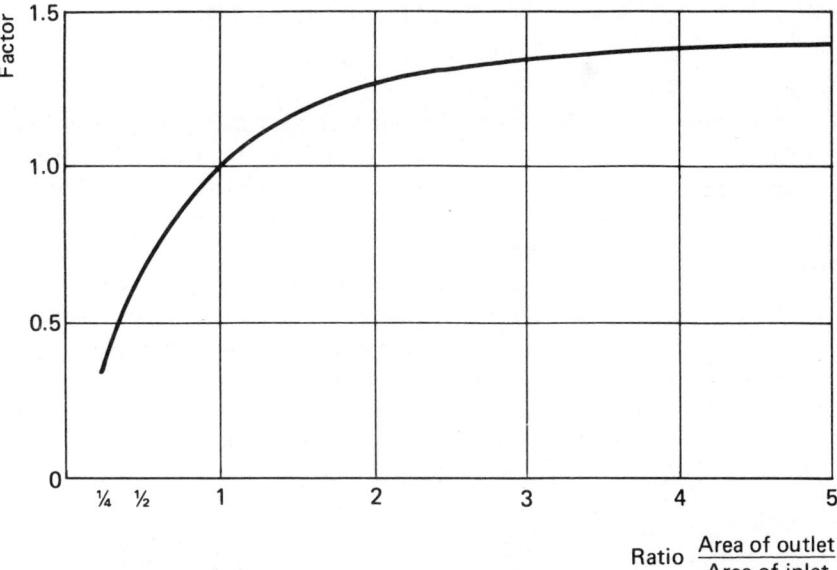

Equation (8.3) applies for the case where the area of inlet is the same as the area of outlet. Where they are different then a correct factor has to be applied. The correction factor is shown in graphical form in Fig. 8.10.

Where the wind is blowing at 45° to the inlet face then both the *ASHRAE Handbook of Fundamentals* and *Principles of Modern Building* propose that the value of V should be reduced by 50 per cent.

Example 8.1   A building is subjected to a wind velocity of 3 m s^{-1} with the wind blowing at right angles to one face. A total inlet area of 1 m^2 is situated on the windward face and a total outlet area of 1 m^2 is on the leeward face. Calculate the ventilation rate. Assume $E = 0.6$.
From equation (8.3)

$$V = 0.6\,Av = 0.6 \times 1 \times 3 = 1.8 \text{ m}^3 \text{ s}^{-1}.$$

Example 8.2   A building is situated in a city centre and is 20 m high. A total inlet area of 1 m^2 is situated on the windward face and a similar outlet area on the leeward face. Calculate the ventilation rate.
From Fig. 8.1, pressure difference $\Delta p = 11$ Pa. From equation (8.2),

$$V = 0.827\,[A_1 A_2/(A_1{}^2 + A_2{}^2)^{0.5}]\,(\Delta p)^{0.5}.$$

But $A_1 = A_2 = 1$ m^2. Therefore,

$$V = 0.827\,[1/\sqrt{2}]\,(11)^{0.5} = 1.93 \text{ m}^3 \text{ s}^{-1}.$$

Example 8.3   What would be the ventilation rate if the building in Example 8.2 was situated in open country?
From Fig. 8.1, $\Delta p = 70$ Pa. Therefore,

$$V = 0.827\,[1/\sqrt{2}]\,(70)^{0.5} = 4.89 \text{ m}^3 \text{ s}^{-1}.$$

Example 8.4   What would be the effect if in Example 8.3 the outlet area was decreased to 0.5 m^2?

$$V = 0.827 \ [1 \times 0.5/(1 + 0.25)^{0.5}] \ (70)^{0.5}$$
$$= 0.827 \ [0.5/\sqrt{1.25}] \ (70)^{0.5} = 3.09 \ \text{m}^3 \ \text{s}^{-1}.$$

8.5 Temperature difference — stack effect

The phenomenon of warm air tending to rise is well known and convection currents set up by this process are used to advantage in gliding. The reason for the warm air rising is due to the fact that heated air is less dense than cold air, the variation in air density being directly proportional to the absolute temperature of the air.

Since the temperature inside a building is likely to be different from that outside, this implies that the internal and external air will have different densities. Where there are openings in the building at different levels this variation in air density can produce a flow of air.

The effect of the flow of air due to a temperature difference is very noticeable in a chimney flue and this particular situation can be used to demonstrate the principle involved.

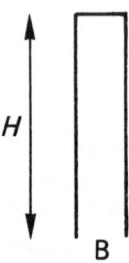 

H

B   A

Consider two positions in a building, A and B, with a chimney at B of height H. There will be a column of warm air of height H at B and a similar column of colder air at A. The density of air at 0 °C (= 273 K) = 1.293 kg m^{-3}. Hence 1 m^3 of air at 273 K has a mass of 1.293 kg. But, since density of air is proportional to absolute temperature, then at some other temperature T K the mass of the same volume of air will have changed by the ratio of the temperature, i.e.

Mass = $1.293 \times 273/T$ kg.

Let absolute temperature of column of air at A = T_0 K and absolute temperature of column of air at B = T_1 K. Then, mass of column of air at A per unit cross-sectional area is given by

Mass at A = $[1.293 \times 273/T_0] \ H$ kg

and mass of column of air at B per unit cross-sectional area is given by

Mass at B = $[1.293 \times 273/T_1] \ H$ kg.

But, since pressure = force per unit area,

Pressure at base of column of air at A = $9.81 \ [1.293 \times 273/T_0] \ H$ Pa,

Pressure at base of column of air at B = $9.81 \ [1.293 \times 273/T_1] \ H$ Pa.

(Note that the factor 9.81, the gravitational acceleration, must be utilized to convert masses to forces, and, hence, kilogrammes to newtons.)

Let pressure difference between A and B = Δp. Therefore,

$$\Delta p = 9.81 \ H \ [(1.293 \times 273/T_0) - (1.293 \times 273/T_1)]$$

$$= 9.81 \, H \times 1.293 \times 273 \left(\frac{1}{T_0} - \frac{1}{T_1} \right)$$

$$= 3463 \, H \left(\frac{1}{T_0} - \frac{1}{T_1} \right) \text{Pa}. \tag{8.4}$$

The above general expression is given in the *IHVE Guide*. If the temperatures are given in degrees Centigrade, i.e. t_1 and t_0, then the expression can be rewritten as

$$\Delta p = 3463 \, H \left(\frac{1}{t_0 + 273} - \frac{1}{t_1 + 273} \right)$$

$$= \frac{3463 H}{(t_0 + 273)(t_1 + 273)} (t_1 - t_0) \text{ Pa}.$$

The *IHVE Guide* states that when the temperatures t_1 and t_0 are not greatly different from 10 °C, then the above equation is approximately

$$\Delta p = \frac{3463 \, H}{(283)^2} (t_1 - t_0) = 0.043 \, H(t_1 - t_0) \text{ Pa}. \tag{8.5}$$

Consider a building with two openings, one at low level the other at a higher level. When the internal air temperature in the building is greater than the external air temperature, the cooler air will tend to be drawn in at the low level with a corresponding outward flow of the warm air at the upper level.

It will be observed that the inlet and outlet openings, although at different heights, can be considered as acting in series and equation (8.2) can be applied to this situation.

Example 8.5   A building has openings totalling 1 m^2 in area at low level and openings of the same area at a higher level, the distance between them being 20 m. If the mean internal air temperature is 21 °C and the external air temperature is 5 °C, calculate the ventilation rate due to stack effect.

Temperature difference, $t_1 - t_0 = 21 - 5 = 16$ °C.

From equation (8.5),

Pressure difference, $\Delta p = 0.043 \, H(t_1 - t_0) = 0.043 \times 20 \times 16$

$$= 13.76 \text{ Pa}$$

From equation (8.2), for openings in series,

$$V = 0.827 \, [A_1 A_2 / (A_1^2 + A_2^2)^{0.5}] \, (\Delta p)^{0.5}$$

$$= 0.827 \, [1/\sqrt{2}] \, (13.76)^{0.5} = 2.17 \text{ m}^3 \text{ s}^{-1}.$$

Instead of relating the stack effect to a pressure difference it is possible to obtain an equation for the flow of air through an inlet due to temperature difference which is of the general form

$$V = \chi A \, [H(t_1 - t_0)]^{0.5}$$

where V = volume flow, A = area of inlet = area of outlet, H = difference in height between openings and χ = constant. A number of sources are available for values of χ [1, 8, 9, 10].

By combining equations (8.2) and (8.5)

$$V = 0.827 \ [A_1 A_2 /(A_1{}^2 + A_2{}^2)^{0.5}] \ (\Delta p)^{0.5}, \ . \Big\}$$
$$\Delta p = 0.043 \ H(t_1 - t_0),$$

then,

$$V = 0.827 \ [A_1 A_2 /(A_1{}^2 + A_2{}^2)^{0.5}] \ [0.043 \ H(t_1 - t_0)]^{0.5}$$
$$= 0.827 \ [A_1 A_2 /(A_1{}^2 + A_2{}^2)^{0.5}] \ 0.2073 \ [H(t_1 - t_0)]^{0.5}$$
$$= 0.171 \ [A_1 A_2 /(A_1{}^2 + A_2{}^2)^{0.5}] \ [H(t_1 - t_0)]^{0.5} \ \mathrm{m^3 \ s^{-1}}.$$

This expression is similar to that given by Croome-Gale and Roberts [11].
Where the areas of two openings are equal, i.e. $A_1 = A_2 = A$, then

$$V = 0.171 \ (A^2 / \sqrt{2} A) \ [H(t_1 - t_0)]^{0.5}$$
$$= 0.121 \ A \ [H(t_1 - t_0)]^{0.5} \ \mathrm{m^3 \ s^{-1}}. \tag{8.6}$$

8.6 Combined wind and stack effect

When the wind and stack effect act together the resultant flow rate through the openings is *not* the sum of the two flow rates.

Since it has been shown that the air flow rate is proportional to the square root of the pressure difference (both for wind and stack effect) it is seen that it is the individual pressure differences which have to be added together, and it is this combined pressure difference which is then used for calculating the air flow rate.

This means that, if the pressure difference due to the stack effect was the same as the pressure difference due to the wind action, then, adding these two pressures together and using the square root of this to obtain V', the resultant flow rate,

$$V' = (\sqrt{2}) \times \text{Individual flow rate},$$

i.e.

$$V' = 1.4 \times \text{Flow rate of either wind or stack effect acting alone.}$$

Similarly, it can be shown that where the flow rate of either the wind action or the stack effect is much larger than the other, then the combined flow rate will be approximately the same as the larger flow rate acting by itself.

8.7 Air infiltration around windows

Both the *IHVE Guide* and the *ASHRAE Handbook of Fundamentals* give an equation for the air leakage through cracks around closed windows as

$$V = X(\Delta p)^n,$$

where V = flow rate, X = constant, Δp = pressure difference and n = exponent of flow.

The *ASHRAE Handbook of Fundamentals* gives the value of n as being between 0.5 and 1.0, while the *IHVE Guide* gives n as 0.63 and publishes different values of X depending upon the type of window. The *IHVE Guide* also publishes a graph which enables V to be obtained directly for a given building height, location and window type. The first two factors, building height and location, are required in order to establish the appropriate wind velocity and hence the pressure difference. The infiltration rate, V, obtained from this graph is expressed in litres per second per metre run of window opening joint. Further correction factors (f) are given in the *IHVE Guide* to allow for the effect of the internal room resistance which is related to the proportion of openable area and to the internal structure. Hence, the basic infiltration rate becomes

$$V_b = V \times f, \tag{8.7}$$

where f = internal correction factor. If L_R = crack length, then

Room infiltration rate, $V_R = V_b \times L_R$.

This equation applies to the situation where there are windows on one external wall. For the case of a corner room with windows on two adjacent walls, the *IHVE Guide* gives the expression as

$$V_R = 1.5 \, V_b \times L_R. \tag{8.8}$$

The *ASHRAE Handbook of Fundamentals* gives a table of infiltration rates expressed in cubic feet per hour per foot of crack for various types of windows for a number of pressure differences. The pressure difference has to be calculated in Imperial units.

Example 8.6   Using data from the *IHVE Guide*, calculate the room infiltration rate for an office which has metal windows without weather stripping. The building is in an urban area and the infiltration rate is $0.6 \, l \, s^{-1} \, m^{-1}$, the window crack length = 20 m, the internal correction factor $f = 0.8$.

Basic infiltration rate, $V_b = V \times f = 0.6 \times 0.8$

$$= 0.48 \, l \, s^{-1} \, m^{-1},$$

Room infiltration rate, $V_R = V_b \times L_R = 0.48 \times 20$

$$= 9.6 \, l \, s^{-1}.$$

This room infiltration rate can be compared with the fresh air requirements per person given in Table 3.4. Assuming that the above value was obtained for an office room 5 m × 4 m × 3 m being used by a single occupant, then the air infiltration rate would be adequate. It must be noted that if a window or door is opened then very much higher rates would occur.

8.8 Total infiltration rate

In calculating the heat load due to the total air infiltration rate for a building, care must be taken to note that this total is not simply the sum of the individual room infiltration rates.

The reason for this can be seen by considering the air entering and leaving a building as shown in Fig. 8.11. Air entering the building on the windward side due to natural ventilation will be at the same temperature as the external air; it will then have to change its temperature to that of the room internal air temperature (producing either a heating or cooling load) and will then leave the building on the leeward side at this room temperature. In other words it is only the air entering the building on the windward side which has to be changed in

Fig. 8.11 Air flow temperature.

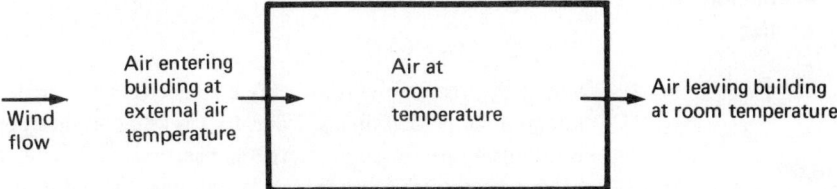

temperature; the air leaving the building does not add anything to the heating load.

The total infiltration rate can be obtained from the formula in the *IHVE Guide* as follows:

$$V_{tot} = V_b \times \text{Crack length per unit area of glazed facade} \times A_{rep}, \qquad (8.9)$$

where V_b = basic infiltration rate and A_{rep} = representative area.

The *IHVE Guide* defines the representative area as the area through which the air passes from one side of the building to the other (Fig. 8.12). For a building with windows on the two opposite long walls of length a, and no windows on

Fig. 8.12 Representative area.

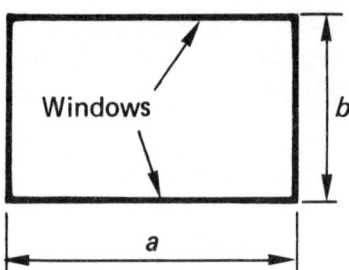
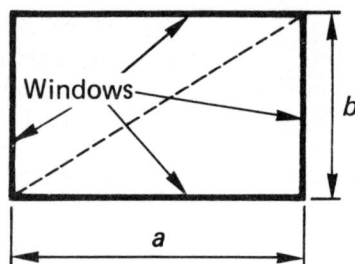

the short walls, dimension b, and having a height H, the representative area is given by

$$A_{rep} = a \times H.$$

Where the building has windows on all four walls, the *IHVE Guide* states that the representative area is that of the vertical diagonal plane.

Length of diagonal = $(a^2 + b^2)^{0.5}$.

Hence,

$$A_{rep} = (a^2 + b^2)^{0.5} H. \qquad (8.10)$$

Example 8.7   An office block is 40 m long × 18 m wide × 45 m high and the crack length per unit area of glazed facade is 1 m m^{-2}. If the basic infiltration rate is 0.5 l s^{-1} m^{-1}, calculate the total infiltration when the building has windows on (a) all four faces (b) two long walls only.

(a) $A_{rep} = (a^2 + b^2)^{0.5} H = (40^2 + 18^2)^{0.5} \, 45 = 1973.9 \text{ m}^2$,

$V_{tot} = 0.5 \times 1.0 \times 1973.9 = 987 \text{ l s}^{-1}$.

(b) $A_{rep} = aH = 40 \times 45 = 1800 \text{ m}^2$,

$V_{tot} = 0.5 \times 1.0 \times 1800 = 900 \text{ l s}^{-1}$.

8.9   Use of ventilation for cooling

It was shown in Chapter 5 that the heat flow due to ventilation could be expressed as

$$Q_v = c\rho V (\Delta t)$$

where Q_v = heat flow (in watts), c = specific heat capacity of air (in joules per kilogramme per kelvin), ρ = density (in kilogrammes per cubic metre), V = ventilation rate (in cubic metres per second) and Δt = temperature difference (in kelvins or degrees Centigrade). It was stated that the accepted value of $c\rho$ for most room conditions was 1.2×10^3 J K^{-1}, which leads to the expression being written as

$$V = Q_v/[1.2 \times 10^3 \ (\Delta t)] \ \text{m}^3 \ \text{s}^{-1}. \tag{8.11}$$

If it is desired to express the ventilation rate as a number of air changes per hour, then if Vol = volume of air space and n = number of air changes per hour,

$$Vol \times n = Q_v \times 3600/[1.2 \times 10^3 \ (\Delta t)] = 3Q_v/(\Delta t)$$

or

$$Q_v = \frac{Vol \times n}{3} \ \Delta t,$$

which is the form that has been used in the previous chapters.

Example 8.8 A small building has a heat gain input of 4250 W. The desired internal air temperature is to be 21 °C and the air can be introduced into the inlets at 18 °C. If the pressure difference across the building is 15 Pa, calculate the area of inlets assuming that the total inlet and outlet areas are the same.

Temperature difference = $21 - 18 = 3$ °C.

From equation (8.11),

$$V = Q_v/[1.2 \times 10^3 \ (\Delta t)] = 4250/[1.2 \times 10^3 \times 3] = 1.18 \ \text{m}^3 \ \text{s}^{-1}.$$

From equation (8.2),

$$V = 0.827 \ [A_1 A_2/(A_1{}^2 + A_2{}^2)^{0.5}] \ (\Delta p)^{0.5} \ \text{m}^3 \ \text{s}^{-1}.$$

Since area of inlets = area of outlets, put $A_1 = A_2 = A$. Then,

$$V = 0.827 \ (A^2/A\sqrt{2}) \ (\Delta p)^{0.5}$$
$$= 0.827 \ (A/\sqrt{2}) \ (15)^{0.5} = 2.26 \ A.$$

Hence,

$$1.18 = 2.26 \ A.$$

Therefore,

$$A = 0.52 \ \text{m}^2.$$

Note that in Example 8.8 the temperature difference was related to air temperatures, i.e. the difference between the incoming air temperature and the desired internal air temperature. Where the environmental temperature is used then care must be taken to use the appropriate expression, i.e.

$$C_v = Q_v/(t_{ei} - t_{ao}).$$

The procedure for calculating C_v when there is a high ventilation rate is as described in Chapter 6.

References

1 *ASHRAE Handbook of Fundamentals.* American Society of Heating, Refrigeration and Air-Conditioning Engineers, New York 1972.

2 Down, P. G., *Heating and Cooling Load Calculations.* Pergamon Press, Oxford, 1969.

3   *Heat Losses from Dwellings. Building Research Establishment Digest No. 190.* HMSO, London, 1976.

4   *Assessment of Wind Loads. Building Research Establishment Digest No. 119.* HMSO, London, 1974.

5   Newberry, C. W. and Eaton, J. K., *Wind Loading Handbook.* HMSO, London, 1974.

6   Penwarden, A. D. and Wise, A. F. E., *Wind Environment around Buildings.* HMSO, London, 1975.

7   Koenigsberger, O. H., Ingersoll, T. G., Mayhew, A. and Szokalay, S. V., *Manual of Tropical Housing and Building. Part I: Climatic Design.* Longman, London, 1974.

8   Building Research Station, *Principles of Modern Building,* Vol. I. HMSO, London, 1959.

9   Billington, N., *Building Physics: Heat.* Pergamon Press, Oxford, 1967.

10   van Straaten, J. F., *Thermal Performance of Buildings.* Elsevier Publishing Co., Amsterdam, 1967.

11   Croome-Gale, D. J. and Robinson, B. M., *Air-Conditioning and Ventilation of Buildings.* Pergamon Press, Oxford, 1975.

9
SHAPE OF BUILDING

9.1 Variables

The rate of heat loss from a building for steady-state conditions can be written as

$$Q = Q_f + Q_v$$

where Q_f = fabric loss = $\Sigma A U \Delta t_1$ and Q_v = ventilation loss = $(Vol \times n/3) \Delta t_2$ (volume being measured in cubic metres). Δt_1 and Δt_2 are the appropriate temperature differences.

The variables which affect this rate of heat loss could be considered as being

(i) $\Sigma A U$, i.e. fabric;
(ii) $Vol \times n/3$, i.e. ventilation rate or volume of air to be heated;
(iii) Δt, i.e. temperature difference.

It is clear that the designer of the building can influence the first variable simply by making changes in the choice of materials and the form of construction. These changes would affect the U-value and the method of construction (in particular the design of window frames) could also influence the number of air changes per hour and hence the ventilation loss.

However, a further consideration of the variables listed above indicates that the designer is able to have an influence on them all. For any given enclosed volume there are numerous ways in which the actual dimensions of height, length and breadth can vary, resulting in different total surface areas. Thus two buildings, both having the same volume and built of the same materials, may have quite different surface areas and hence different rates of fabric heat loss.

In addition, it has been shown that in certain cases the temperature difference used for calculating the rate of fabric heat loss can be based upon the sol-air temperature. Since this temperature is related to orientation, the last variable listed is dependent on the relative position and layout of the building.

Hence, in order to design a building which will have a minimum thermal energy demand pattern, all these variables must be considered and their interaction taken into account.

9.2 Relationship between surface area and volume

The ventilation loss $(Vol \times n/3) (t_{ai} - t_{ao})$ can be expressed in terms of the environmental temperature difference as $C_v(t_{ei} - t_{ao})$. It has been stated that where there are low ventilation rates then C_v can be taken as being approximately equal to $Vol \times n/3$, and in this case $t_{ei} \simeq t_{ai}$. Considering the case of a winter condition, where the fabric loss is related to the temperature difference $(t_{ei} - t_{ao})$, and assuming that the same temperature difference applies to the ventilation loss, then by dividing each side of the basic equation by Δt, it can be written as Q per degree Centigrade = $\Sigma A U + Vol \times n/3$.

However, when considering the factors which will result in a minimum heat loss, care must be taken to relate Q per degree Centigrade to the size of the building. Failure to do so merely results in stating that for similar conditions a large building has a greater heat loss than a small one. An analogy can be made with a two-seater car and a 70-seater bus. For the same length of journey the bus will consume far more fuel than the car, but a far better comparison of their performance is obtained when the amount of fuel consumed is related to the number of passengers which each vehicle can carry. A similar situation arises with the heat loss for a building; the value of Q per degree Centigrade has to be related to the capacity of the building, i.e. volume. A new relationship begins to emerge when each side of the heat loss equation is divided by Vol:

$$Q \text{ per cubic metre per degree Centigrade} = \frac{\Sigma AU}{Vol} + \frac{n}{3}.$$

Two important features can be seen from this:

(i) the term $\Sigma AU/Vol$ is dependent not only on the U-value but upon the ratio 'surface area/volume';

(ii) if the term $\Sigma AU/Vol$ is less than $n/3$ then the ventilation loss is greater than the fabric loss.

The ratio 'surface area/volume' is now seen to be an important factor and the relationship between them will be considered.

This ratio is dependent both upon the dimensions for height, length and breadth, and also upon the actual size of the building. The latter point is illustrated by considering a cube of side x.

Table 9.1

Dimension = x	Surface area $= 6 x^2$	Volume = x^3	Ratio 'surface area/volume' = $6/x$
1	6	1	6
5	150	125	1.2
10	600	1000	0.6
20	2400	8000	0.33

From Table 9.1 it is seen how quickly the volume increases relatively to the surface area as the dimensions of the cube increase and also the way in which the ratio 'surface area/volume' changes with the size of cube.

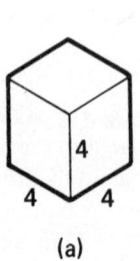

(a)

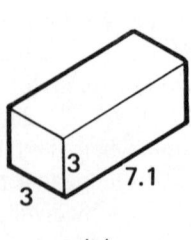

(b)

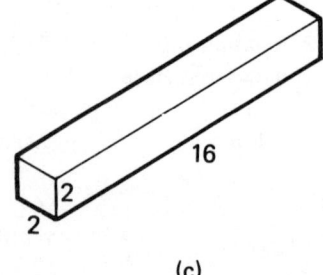

(c)

The ratio of the individual sides of the enclosed space is also important; this is demonstrated by the following example. Consider three solids shown at the bottom of page 374: (a) all sides equal, (b) and (c) two sides equal.

Table 9.2

Solid shape type	Surface area	Volume	Ratio 'surface area/volume'
a	96	64	1.5
b	103.2	64	1.61
c	136	64	2.13

In each case the volume was the same but the surface area was different, thus giving different values for the 'surface area/volume' ratio. It will be noted that the lowest value for this ratio occurs with the cube.

It is possible to derive an expression which will indicate how much the 'surface area/volume' ratio for a particular shape will vary from that obtained for a cube of the same volume.

Consider a building of height H, breadth B and length L. Let $\alpha = B/H$, $\beta = L/B$. Thus,

$$B = \alpha H, \qquad L = \beta B = \alpha\beta H.$$

$$\text{Surface area} = 2(B + L)H + 2BL$$
$$= 2H(\alpha H + \alpha\beta H) + 2\alpha^2\beta H^2$$
$$= 2\alpha H^2(1 + \beta) + 2\alpha^2\beta H^2$$
$$= 2\alpha H^2[(1 + \beta) + \alpha\beta].$$

$$\text{Volume} = BLH = \alpha^2\beta H^3.$$

Therefore,

$$\text{Ratio 'surface area/volume'} = 2\alpha H^2[(1 + \beta) + \alpha\beta]/\alpha^2\beta H^3$$
$$= \frac{2}{\alpha\beta H}[(1 + \beta) + \alpha\beta]$$
$$= \frac{2}{H}\left[\left(\frac{1 + \beta}{\alpha\beta}\right) + 1\right]$$
$$= \frac{2}{H}\gamma,$$

where

$$\gamma = \left(\frac{1 + \beta}{\alpha\beta}\right) + 1.$$

Hence, as H increases, 'surface area/volume' ratio decreases; this is due to the volume being dependent on H^3 whereas the surface area depends on H^2.

The factor γ is dimensionless, based entirely on the shape of the envelope, and does not vary with size. Table 9.3 gives values of γ.

Table 9.3   *Values of* γ

α	β						
	0.25	0.5	1.0	2.0	3.0	4.0	5.0
0.25	21	13	9	7	6.33	6.0	5.8
0.5	11	7	5	4	3.67	3.5	3.4
1.0	6	4	3	2.5	2.33	2.25	2.2
2.0	3.5	2.5	2	1.75	1.67	1.63	1.6
3.0	2.67	2	1.67	1.5	1.44	1.42	1.4
4.0	2.25	1.75	1.5	1.38	1.33	1.31	1.3
5.0	2.0	1.6	1.4	1.3	1.27	1.25	1.24

However in order to compare the 'surface area/volume' ratio of different shapes of buildings, the volume of the buildings must be the same. It has been shown that the best 'surface area/volume' ratio occurs with a cube; hence, this can be used as a reference.

Consider a cube of side H_0. Then

Volume of cube = $H_0{}^3$.

Now consider some other shape, such that dimensions are L, B and H; then, using previous notation,

Volume of other shape = $LBH = \alpha^2 \beta H^3$

But the volumes have to be the same, i.e.

$$H_0{}^3 = \alpha^2 \beta H^3$$

or

$$H_0/H = \sqrt[3]{(\alpha^2 \beta)}. \tag{9.1}$$

Having obtained the above relationship it is now possible to compare different shapes of buildings, using the 'surface area/volume' ratio as a criterion.

Surface area/volume of cube = $6/H_0$,

Surface area/volume of other shape = $\dfrac{2}{H}\gamma$,

Ratio of change = $\dfrac{2}{H}\gamma \div \dfrac{6}{H_0} = \dfrac{2\gamma}{H} \times \dfrac{H_0}{6} = \dfrac{\gamma}{3}\dfrac{H_0}{H}$

$$= \dfrac{\gamma}{3}\sqrt[3]{(\alpha^2 \beta)},$$

which is independent of actual size. Values of this ratio for different values of α and β are given in Table 9.4 at top of page 377.

The use of Table 9.4 enables a direct comparison to be made between different building shapes with reference to the 'surface area/volume' ratio.

Example 9.1   A building is to have the breadth twice the height, and the length four times the breadth. (a) By how much is the 'surface area/volume' ratio worse than that for a cube? (b) Would the situation improve if the breadth was increased to five times the height but the length decreased to twice the breadth?

Table 9.4 *Values of* $\dfrac{\gamma}{3}\sqrt[3]{(\alpha^2\beta)}$

α	β						
	0.25	0.5	1.0	2.0	3.0	4.0	5.0
0.25	1.75	1.37	1.19	1.17	1.21	1.26	1.31
0.5	1.46	1.17	1.05	1.06	1.11	1.17	1.22
1	1.26	1.06	1.0	1.05	1.12	1.19	1.25
2	1.17	1.05	1.06	1.17	1.27	1.37	1.45
3	1.17	1.1	1.16	1.31	1.44	1.56	1.66
4	1.19	1.17	1.26	1.46	1.61	1.75	1.87
5	1.27	1.24	1.36	1.6	1.79	1.93	2.07

(a) $\alpha = B/H = 2,\qquad \beta = L/B = 4.$

From Table 9.4, ratio = 1.37, i.e. 'surface area/volume' ratio for building is 37 per cent greater than that for a cube.

(b) $\alpha = B/H = 5,\qquad \beta = L/B = 2.$

From Table 9.4, ratio = 1.6, i.e. situation is now worse.

9.3 'Thermal cube'

When the U-values for the various surfaces are taken into account, the 'surface area/volume' ratio in itself does not give sufficient information with regard to the fabric heat loss.

The aim is to optimize the building shape so that the fabric heat loss will be a minimum. This aspect was considered by Page [1] who derived an expression for the fabric heat loss in terms of N, where N = number of floors or storeys in the building. By differentiating with respect to N and equating the resulting expression to zero, he was able to calculate the ideal storey height for a given set of conditions.

This form of approach can be applied to the analysis of the 'surface area/volume' ratio of the previous section. Consider a building such that A_W = area of walls with U-value = U_W, A_R = area of roof with U-value = U_R, A_G = area of ground floor with U-value = U_G.

Fabric heat loss per degree Centigrade = Q_f per degree Centigrade

$$= A_W U_W + A_R U_R + A_G U_G.$$

Assume that roof area = ground floor area, i.e. $A_R = A_G$. Then,

$$Q_f \text{ per degree Centigrade} = A_W U_W + A_R(U_R + U_G).$$

Let $\bar{U} = \tfrac{1}{2}(U_R + U_G)$. In order that all the surfaces may be considered to have an equal thermal performance, the wall area has to be 'weighted' by the ratio $U_W/\bar{U}$. Put

$$r = U_W/\bar{U} = U_W/\tfrac{1}{2}(U_R + U_G),$$

i.e. $U_W = r\bar{U}$. Then,

$$Q_f \text{ per degree Centigrade} = A_W r\bar{U} + 2A_R \bar{U}.$$

Assume that all the walls have the same U-value, the building is square on plan and that the temperature difference for each surface is the same.

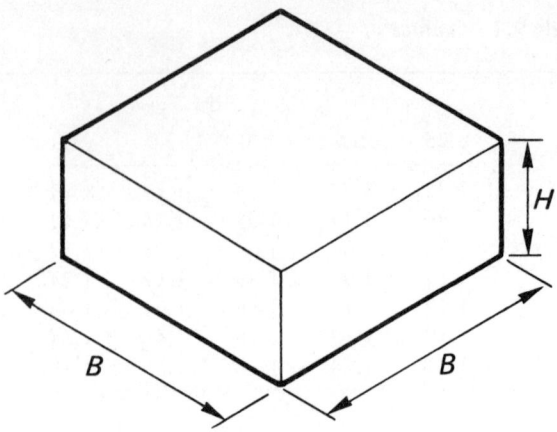

Let $\alpha_1 = B/H$ or $B = \alpha_1 H$, then

$$A_W = 4BH = 4\alpha_1 H^2; \qquad A_R = B^2 = \alpha_1{}^2 H^2.$$

Therefore,

$$Q_f \text{ per degree Centigrade} = 4\alpha_1 H^2 r\bar{U} + 2\alpha_1{}^2 H^2 \bar{U}.$$

Volume $= B^2 H = \alpha_1^2 H^3$. Therefore,

$$Q_f \text{ per unit volume} = \frac{4\alpha_1 H^2 r\bar{U} + 2\alpha_1{}^2 H^2 \bar{U}}{\alpha_1{}^2 H^3} = \frac{\bar{U}}{H}\left[\frac{4r}{\alpha_1} + 2\right].$$

But for cube of side H and having a U-value of $\bar{U}$,

$$Q_f \text{ per unit volume} = 6\,\bar{U}/H.$$

Therefore

$$\frac{\bar{U}}{H}\left[\frac{4r}{\alpha_1}\right] + 2 = \frac{6\bar{U}}{H},$$

$$(4r/\alpha_1 + 2) = 6,$$

$$4r/\alpha_1 = 4.$$

Hence,

$$\alpha_1 = r.$$

It was shown that the minimum 'surface area/volume' ratio was obtained with a cube. Hence, if the product $A\bar{U}$ is considered as a 'thermal surface', then the best shape to minimize $\Sigma AU/Vol$ will be obtained with a 'thermal cube'. From the analysis above this occurs when $\alpha_1 = r$. Therefore, a 'thermal cube' is a building of height H and sides Hr. Since $Vol =$ Volume $= H^3 r^2$, then, if the volume of the building is known, the appropriate height and width can be obtained from

$$H = \sqrt[3]{(Vol/r^2)} \tag{9.2}$$

and

$$B = Hr.$$

Example 9.2   A building has to have a volume of 360 m^3. The U-values of the surfaces are, walls $U_W = 1.5$ W m^{-2} K^{-1}, roof $U_R = 0.6$ W m^{-2} K^{-1}, ground floor $U_G = 0.7$ W m^{-2} K^{-1}. Calculate the optimum dimensions for the building for a minimum fabric heat loss.

$$r = U_W/\tfrac{1}{2}(U_R + U_G) = 1.5/\tfrac{1}{2}(0.6 + 0.7) = 2.3.$$

From equation (9.2), height of 'thermal cube' is given by

$$H = \sqrt[3]{(Vol/r^2)} = \sqrt[3]{(360/2.3^2)} = 4.08 \text{ m}.$$

Hence,

$$B = Hr = 4.08 \times 2.3 = 9.4 \text{ m}$$

and so the optimum dimensions for the building are 9.4 m × 9.4 m × 4.08 m high.

There will be many situations where a square plan is not suitable but a similar form of analysis can be used to obtain optimum dimensions where a restriction is placed upon the plan shape. For a rectangular plan the following analysis is used. Let

$$L = \beta_1 B = \alpha_1 \beta_1 H.$$

Then,

$$A_W = 2\alpha_1 H^2 + 2\alpha_1\beta_1 H^2 = 2\alpha_1 H^2(1 + \beta_1),$$
$$A_R = \alpha_1{}^2\beta_1 H^2.$$

Thus,

$$Q_f \text{ per degree Centigrade} = 2\alpha_1 H^2(1 + \beta_1)\bar{U}r + 2\alpha_1{}^2\beta_1 H^2\bar{U}.$$

Volume $= LBH = \alpha_1{}^2\beta_1 H^3$ and so

$$Q_f \text{ per unit volume} = \frac{2\alpha_1 H^2(1 + \beta_1)\bar{U}r + 2\alpha_1{}^2\beta_1 H^2\bar{U}}{\alpha_1{}^2\beta_1 H^3} = \frac{2\bar{U}}{H}\left[\frac{(1 + \beta_1)r}{\alpha_1\beta_1} + 1\right].$$

But Q_f per unit volume for cube $= 6\bar{U}/H$. Therefore,

$$\frac{2\bar{U}}{H}\left[\frac{(1 + \beta_1)r}{\alpha_1\beta_1} + 1\right] = \frac{6\bar{U}}{H},$$

$$\frac{(1 + \beta_1)r}{\alpha_1\beta_1} + 1 = 3,$$

$$\frac{(1 + \beta_1)r}{\alpha_1\beta_1} = 2.$$

Hence,

$$\alpha_1 = \frac{(1 + \beta_1)r}{2\beta_1}. \tag{9.3}$$

Inserting values of β_1, the following expressions for α_1 are obtained:

$\beta_1 = 1,$ $\alpha_1 = r$ ('thermal cube' as before);

$\beta_1 = 2,$ $\alpha_1 = 0.75r;$

$\beta_1 = 3,$ $\alpha_1 = 0.67r;$

$\beta_1 = 4,$ $\alpha_1 = 0.625r;$

$$\beta_1 = 5, \qquad \alpha_1 = 0.6r.$$

Volume of building $= \alpha_1{}^2\beta_1 H^3$. Therefore,

$$H = \sqrt[3]{(Vol/\alpha_1{}^2\beta_1)}, \qquad\qquad (9.4)$$

where α_1 has value as above and

$$B = \alpha_1 H, \qquad L = \beta_1 B.$$

Example 9.3   What are the ideal dimensions for the building described in Example 9.2 if the length is to be twice the breadth?

As before: $Vol = 360$ m^3, $r = 2.3$, $\beta_1 = 2.0$ and, hence, $\alpha_1 = 0.75r$.
From equation (9.4),

$$H = \sqrt[3]{\frac{Vol}{\alpha_1{}^2\beta_1}} = \sqrt[3]{\frac{360}{(0.75 \times 2.3)^2 \times 2.0}}$$

$$= \sqrt[3]{60.5} = 3.92 \text{ m}$$

Therefore,

$$B = 0.75 \times 2.3 \times 3.92 = 6.76 \text{ m}, \qquad L = 13.52 \text{ m},$$

and so ideal dimensions are 6.76 m × 13.52 m × 3.92 m high.

It is of interest to note the rate of increase of the fabric heat loss when the dimensions vary from the ideal values. This is illustrated in the following example.

Example 9.4   Consider a building having a volume of 500 m^3 and with the length = three times the breadth. The U-value of the walls = twice mean U-value of roof and ground floor. (a) Calculate the ideal dimensions. (b) Calculate the effect with regard to the fabric heat loss if the length to breadth ratio is kept constant but the breadth is made (i) three times height; (ii) twice the height; (iii) equal to the height; (iv) half the height.

(a) $Vol = 500$ m^3, $\beta_1 = 3.0$, $r = 2.0$. Therefore,

$$\alpha_1 = 0.67r = 1.34,$$

$$H = \sqrt[3]{\frac{Vol}{\alpha_1{}^2\beta_1}} = \sqrt[3]{\frac{500}{1.34^2 \times 3}} = 4.54 \text{ m}$$

Therefore,

$$B = \alpha_1 H = 1.34 \times 4.54 = 6.08 \text{ m},$$

$$L = 3B = 3 \times 6.08 = 18.16 \text{ m}.$$

(b) By defining the ratio of breadth to height, the value of α_1 is fixed, i.e. $\alpha_1 = B/H$.

Case	α_1	
(i)	3.0	
(ii)	2.0	In each case $\beta_1 = 3.0$.
(iii)	1.0	
(iv)	0.5	

The required value of H can be found from $H = \sqrt[3]{(Vol/\alpha_1{}^2\beta_1)}$ and, hence, B and L. Since

$$Q_f/\bar{U} = 2H(B + L)r + 2BL,$$

the appropriate values can be inserted and the results compared. This is shown in Table 9.5.

Table 9.5

Case		α_1	H(m)	B(m)	L(m)	$Q/\bar{U}(\text{m}^2)$	Expressed as a percentage of case (a)
(a)		1.33	4.54	6.08	18.16	661.6	100
(b)	(i)	3.0	2.65	7.95	23.85	716.2	108.2
	(ii)	2.0	3.47	6.94	20.82	674.2	101.9
	(iii)	1.0	5.5	5.5	16.5	665.5	100.6
	(iv)	0.5	8.74	4.37	13.11	725.5	109.7

Page [1] has suggested that the thermal efficiency of a building could be assessed by means of a thermal shape performance index. He defined this as the ratio 'minimal possible conduction heat loss/actual heat conduction loss'. The last column in Table 9.5 could be considered in this way.

Yaneske [2] has produced a table and a procedure for obtaining a similar form of index. This procedure can be applied to buildings where the opposite external walls have the same U-value, but the adjacent external walls may differ. The index proposed by Yaneske is defined as the ratio

Actual convection heat loss/Minimum convection heat loss

and can be used as an indication as to how much worse a particular shape of building is from the optimum shape. The procedure is as follows.

(i) Find the overall U-value for each external building surface. Add U-values of opposing surfaces. Let U_{RF} = sum of floor U-value and roof U-value, U_{12} = sum of U-values of one pair of opposing walls and U_{34} = sum of U-values of other pair of opposing walls. Then evaluate

$$r_{12} = U_{12}/U_{RF}; \qquad r_{34} = U_{34}/U_{RF}.$$

(ii) From the required volume = Vol, or the required total floor area = A, find the representative dimension L_r such that

$$L_r = \sqrt[3]{Vol} \quad \text{or} \quad L_r = \sqrt[3]{AH_m}$$

where H_m is the height module.

(iii) The optimum building height, H_0', is given by

$$H_0' = L_r/\sqrt[3]{(r_{12}r_{34})}. \tag{9.5}$$

(iv) The optimum plan dimensions are $L_0' = r_{34}H_0'$, $B_0' = r_{12}H_0'$, where L_0' is the dimension of separation between the pair of walls with U-value sum U_{34}.

(v) If these dimensions are unsuitable, choose new dimensions L', B', H'. Set

$$r_0 = r_{12}/r_{34}, \qquad r_x = B'/L'$$

and then

$$\alpha' = H'/H_0', \qquad \beta' = r_x/r_0.$$

Table 9.6

β'	$\frac{1}{16}$	$\frac{1}{8}$	$\frac{1}{4}$	$\frac{1}{2}$	1	2	4	8	16
					α'				
$\frac{1}{16}$	5.69	3.17	2.04	1.67	1.75	2.17	2.92	4.05	5.69
$\frac{1}{8}$	5.60	3.04	1.86	1.42	1.39	1.67	2.20	3.04	4.26
$\frac{1}{4}$	5.54	2.96	1.75	1.26	1.17	1.35	1.75	2.40	3.35
$\frac{1}{2}$	5.51	2.92	1.69	1.17	1.04	1.17	1.50	2.04	2.85
1	5.50	2.90	1.67	1.14	1.00	1.11	1.42	1.93	2.69
2	5.51	2.92	1.69	1.17	1.04	1.17	1.50	2.04	2.85
4	5.54	2.96	1.75	1.26	1.17	1.35	1.75	2.40	3.35
8	5.60	3.04	1.86	1.42	1.39	1.67	2.20	3.04	4.26
16	5.69	3.17	2.04	1.67	1.75	2.17	2.92	4.05	5.69

Look up the values of α' and β' in Table 9.6, or interpolate between values, and read off the ratio of the new heat loss to the minimum heat loss possible, Q_0, where

$$Q_0 = 3 \times U_{RF} \times L_r^2 \times \sqrt[3]{(r_{12}r_{34})}.$$

Add ventilation loss, $Vol \times n/3$ W K^{-1}, to obtain total heat loss.

(vi) If the new heat loss is unsatisfactory, either change the dimensions or the U-values and then recheck the heat loss.

(vii) Note that for buildings of non-rectangular plan, but which can be conveniently subdivided into rectangular plan areas, e.g. 'L' and cruciform shapes, treat each subdivision as a separate block using the above method. One can then assess what heat load is involved when the 'pieces' are put back together into a single built form. Where a length is, or is part of, an internal subdivision, a U-value contribution of zero should be given to the internal length as shown.

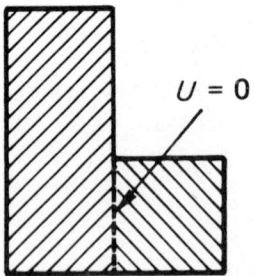

The effect of surface area has been considered by Hardy [3], who commented that there was a relationship between plan area, glazing area and roof area. He shows that the most thermally inefficient is the single-storey building; for a building having a plan area of 500 m^2, two storeys gave a slight improvement, for 1000 m^2 a significant improvement was obtained with two storeys. A 2000 m^2 plan area should have three storeys but it was pointed out that the thermal performance was reduced if the storey height was increased beyond this, while for a 6000 m² plan area, four storeys was proposed.

It is interesting to note how these values compare with those which are obtained using equation (9.4) with the proviso that $r = U_W/\bar{U} = 2.5$.

Example 9.5   (a) Assume the building has a square plan and that the storey height is 2.8 m.

	Total floor plan area (m²)	Volume (m³)
(i)	500	1400
(ii)	1000	2800
(iii)	2000	5600
(iv)	6000	16800

$H = \sqrt[3]{(Vol/\alpha_1{}^2\beta_1)}$ and $\alpha_1 = r$; $\beta = 1.0$. Therefore,

$$H = \sqrt[3]{(Vol/2.5^2)}$$

Inserting the appropriate value for *Vol*, the following heights are obtained:

(i) $H = 6.08$ m (2 storeys),
(ii) $H = 7.66$ m (2 storeys),
(iii) $H = 9.64$ m (3 storeys),
(iv) $H = 13.9$ m (4 storeys).

(b) If the building is rectangular on plan, with the length = three times breadth, then

$$\alpha_1 = 0.67\, r = 1.675,$$

$$H = \sqrt[3]{(Vol/\alpha_1{}^2\beta_1)} = \sqrt[3]{(Vol/8.42)}.$$

Hence,

(i) $H = 5.5$ m (2 storeys),
(ii) $H = 6.9$ m (2 storeys),
(iii) $H = 8.7$ m (3 storeys),
(iv) $H = 12.6$ m (4 storeys).

The difference between the heights in case (a) and case (b) of Example 9.5 is not as marked as is the difference in the plan shape, i.e. a square and a rectangle with the length three times the breadth. Hardy makes a similar comment in his paper, drawing attention to the fact that provided the plan shape was a simple rectangle, the actual plan ratio was of minor importance. However, he does draw attention to the case of a complex shape with numerous re-entrant angles. In this situation the external surface area will tend to become greater and, since it has been shown that the 'surface area/volume' ratio is of prime concern in dealing with the fabric heat loss, it is evident that this type of plan will result in a lower thermal performance.

Fig. 9.1 shows various plan shapes and the appropriate formulae for obtaining the height of the building for a minimum fabric heat loss per unit volume. The relationship between the height of the building, volume and plan shape is shown in graphical form in Figs. 9.2 and 9.3; in these graphs the height is plotted

Fig. 9.1 Values of α_1 for various plan shapes and expressions for the height of the buildings. In all cases $\alpha_1 = B/H$ and $r = U_W/\frac{1}{2}(U_R + U_G)$.

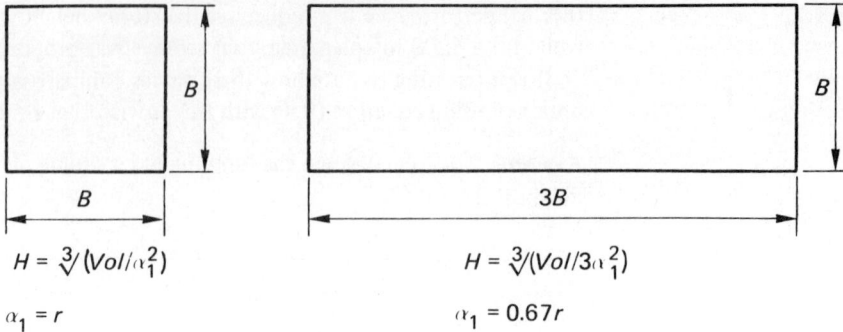

$$H = \sqrt[3]{(Vol/\alpha_1^2)}$$

$$\alpha_1 = r$$

$$H = \sqrt[3]{(Vol/3\alpha_1^2)}$$

$$\alpha_1 = 0.67r$$

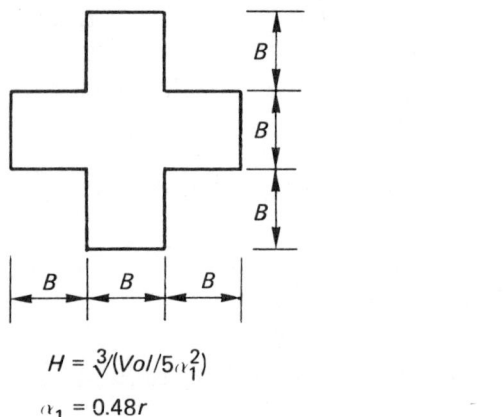

$$H = \sqrt[3]{(Vol/5\alpha_1^2)}$$

$$\alpha_1 = 0.48r$$

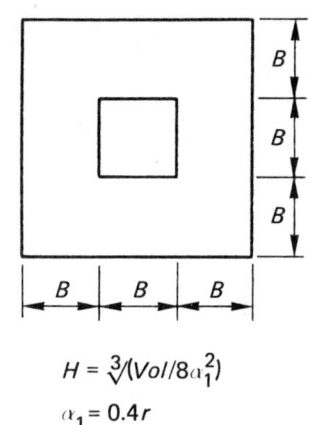

$$H = \sqrt[3]{(Vol/8\alpha_1^2)}$$

$$\alpha_1 = 0.4r$$

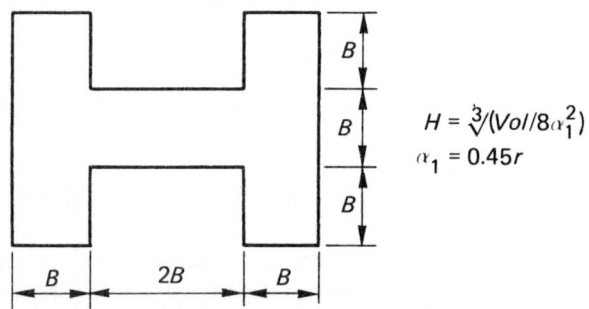

$$H = \sqrt[3]{(Vol/8\alpha_1^2)}$$

$$\alpha_1 = 0.45r$$

against the volume for different plan shapes but the U-value ratio, r, is kept constant. It will be noted that the height increases rapidly with changes in volume when the building is small, but when the building is large the rate of increase of height with increase in volume is much less. In addition it will be observed that the less compact the building, i.e. departing from a 'thermal cube', then the smaller the ideal height becomes.

Fig. 9.4 shows curves obtained for a rectangular plan shape where the length is three times the breadth. As before, the height is plotted against volume, but the plan shape is kept constant and the U-value ratio, r, is changed. In this graph it is now seen that there is a considerable difference between the curves, indicating the major effect which the U-value ratio has on the calculation of the optimum height.

Fig. 9.2 Relationship between height and volume of building. $B = \alpha_1 H$, $r = 1.0$.

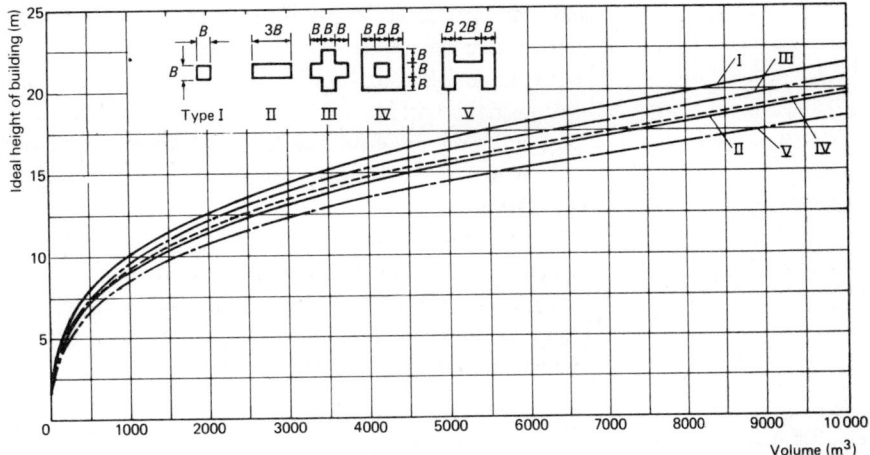

Fig. 9.3 Relationship between height and volume of building. $r = 2.0$ and 3.0.

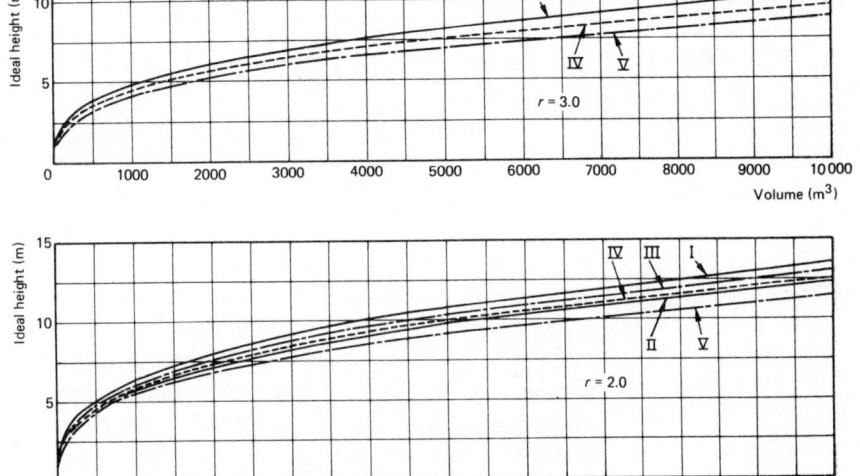

Fig. 9.4 Relationship between height, volume and U-value ratio for a building of rectangular plan area. $L = 3B$.

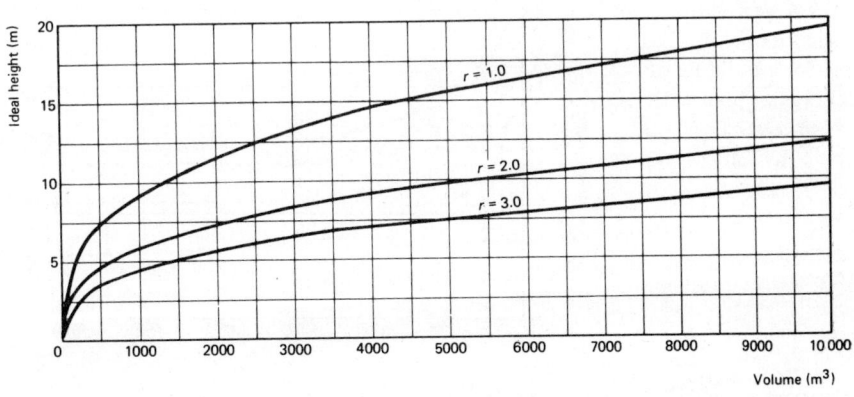

9.4 Fabric heat loss, ventilation loss and volume

It was stated earlier that the heat loss per unit volume could be expressed as

$$Q/Vol = \frac{\Sigma A U}{Vol} + \frac{n}{3} \text{ (where equation in SI units)}$$

and that when $\Sigma A U/Vol = n/3$ then the fabric loss and the ventilation loss per unit volume were equal and each contributed one half of the total heat loss per unit volume. This situation will be examined in the following example.

Consider a building having a rectangular plan shape such that the length is three times the breadth. The average U-value for the roof and ground floor $= 0.7$ W m^{-2} K^{-1}, U-value for walls $= 1.4$ W m^{-2} K^{-1} ($r = U_W/\bar{U} = 1.4/0.7 = 2.0$). Ventilation rate $= 1$ air change per hour.

Fig. 9.5 shows how the fabric heat loss per unit volume and the ventilation loss per unit volume change with the volume of the building. From the graph it is seen that for buildings having a volume in excess of 3000 m^3 the ventilation loss is approaching the fabric loss; for those having a smaller volume, then the fabric loss becomes the major factor in the total heat loss.

Fig. 9.5 Ventilation and fabric loss per unit volume for a building of rectangular plan with $L = 3B$, $r = 2.0$, $\bar{U} = 0.7$ W m^{-2} K^{-1} and $n = 1$ ach.

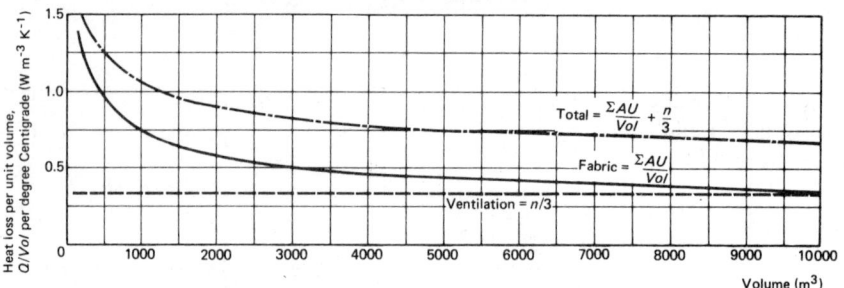

A similar trend occurs when the ventilation rate is increased to 2 ach (Fig. 9.6). In this case it will be noted that the point where the fabric heat loss curve crosses the ventilation loss line is the situation where the two heat losses are equal, i.e. $\Sigma A U/Vol = n/3$. This occurs when the building has a volume of 1300 m^3. Where the volume exceeds this value, the fabric loss per unit volume continues to decrease and hence the ventilation loss per unit volume becomes the major source of heat loss for the building. On the other hand, where the volume is less than 1300 m^3, then the fabric loss per unit volume increases rapidly with a reduction in volume and is the major source of heat loss.

Fig. 9.6 Ventilation and fabric loss per unit volume for a building of rectangular plan with $L = 3B$, $r = 2.0$, $\bar{U} = 0.7$ W m^{-2} K^{-1} and $n = 2$ ach.

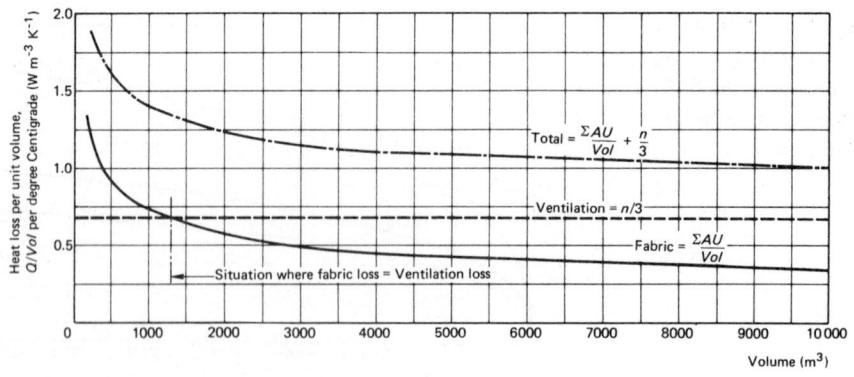

It is interesting to compare Fig. 9.6 with Figs. 9.2 and 9.3, showing height plotted against volume for a similar plan shape. In these diagrams the portion of the graph where the volume was less than 1300 m^3 corresponded to the portion where the height was changing most rapidly.

9.5 Relationship between heat flow, window area and orientation for buildings in a temperate climate

In calculating the heat load for a building the heat losses and also the heat gains have to be taken into account. A major source of heat gain can be that due to solar radiation transmitted through the windows. Hence, the net heat flow can be expressed as

$$Q = Q \text{ (loss)} - Q \text{ (gain)}.$$

For steady-state conditions, and assuming that the only heat gain is from solar radiation, then

$$Q = (A_g U_g + C_v)(\bar{t}_{ei} - \bar{t}_{ao}) + A_w U_w (\bar{t}_{ei} - \bar{t}_{eo}) + S\bar{I}_{GV} A_g,$$

where A_g = area of glass with U-value U_g, A_w = area of opaque portion of external wall with U-value U_w. C_v = ventilation loss, $\bar{t}_{ei}, \bar{t}_{ao}, \bar{t}_{eo}$ = mean environmental, external air and sol-air temperatures, S = solar gain factor and $\bar{I}_{GV}$ = mean global solar irradiance on vertical surface.

From the above equation it might be thought that there would be an advantage in having large areas of glazing on the facades of a building facing south of an east–west axis so as to take full benefit of the solar radiation gain and thus reduce the total heat flow. However, it must be noted that in the UK, and similar areas, the highest external air temperatures tend to occur in summer, when heating is not required, and coincide with the period of maximum solar radiation on vertical surfaces south of an east–west axis. Hence, solar gains in summer may result in excessive cooling loads and large areas of glazing can be a considerable disadvantage.

The effect of summertime overheating due to solar radiation has been investigated in some depth by Loudon [4].

Reference has been made to the fact that the time of day when the peak irradiance and, hence, the summertime peak environmental temperature occurs depends on the orientation. This is also mentioned in the *IHVE Guide*, where it states that, although the time changes, the actual peak environmental temperatures are very similar for any orientation south of the east–west axis.

The procedure for calculating the peak summertime environmental temperature using the admittance method is described in Chapter 6. This method is based upon the work of Loudon and is quoted in the *IHVE Guide*. Examples 6.12 to 6.15 demonstrated this method and this type of calculation can be used to investigate the influence of glass area and room shape on the peak and mean summertime environmental temperatures.

9.5.1 Ratio of Glazing to External Wall Surface

Consider a room 8 m × 5 m × 3 m high with the external window wall on the long axis, 2 air changes per hour, and assume that the adjacent rooms are at the same temperature (i.e. no heat transfer through internal walls, etc.).

The summertime environmental mean and peak temperatures were calculated for the room for single and double glazing when the percentage of glazing was 25, 50 and 75 per cent. This is shown in graphical form in Fig. 9.7.

The *IHVE Guide* states that the procedure for calculating the mean and peak environmental temperatures can be extended to cover the case where two rooms on either side of a corridor receive different amounts of solar radiation. The *IHVE Guide* publishes a set of graphs for generalized solutions, showing peak temperatures plotted against proportion of glazing. These graphs are applicable

Fig. 9.7 Calculated environmental temperatures in a heavyweight building during summer conditions with two air changes per hour and heat flow through the external wall only.
(a) Single glazing.
(b) Double glazing.

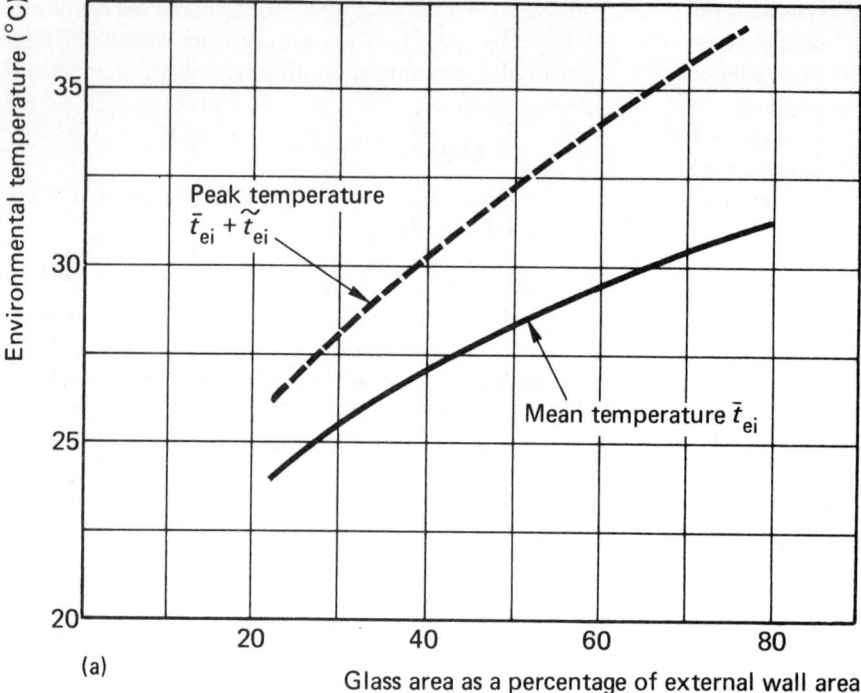

(a)

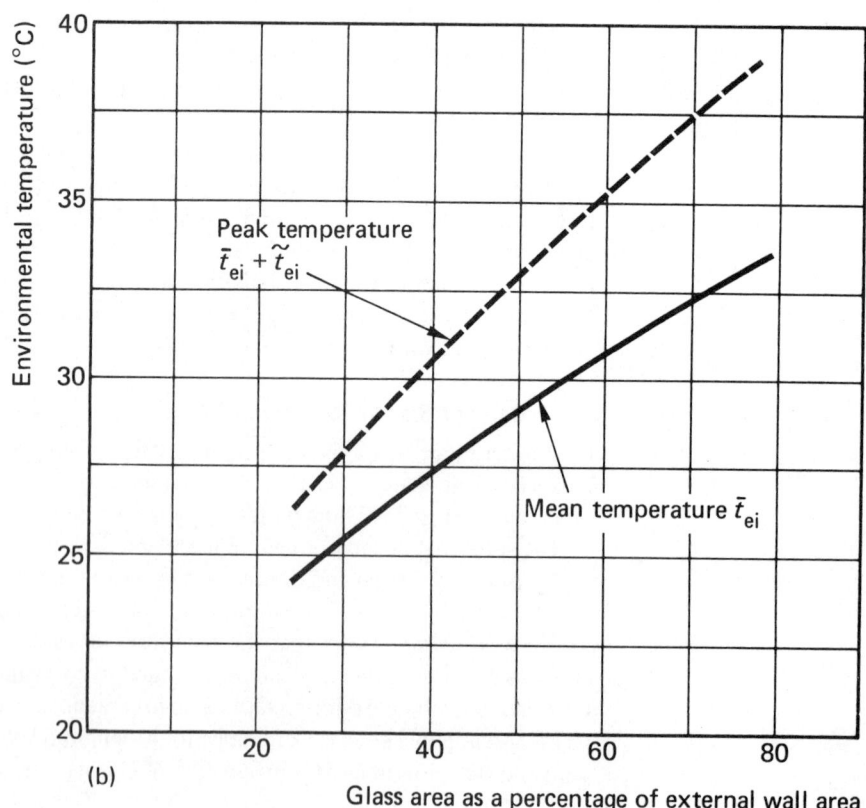

(b)

to rooms facing south of an east–west axis and backed by similar rooms. The curves are similar in form to those shown in Fig. 9.7 but give rather lower values (approximately 2 °C less).

Inspection of these curves indicates the consequences of the use of large areas of glazing in relation to summertime overheating.

9.5.2 Room Shape and Area

9.5.2.1 Width of room

If the width of the room is increased by a factor of two, but depth, height and the proportion of glazing to external wall surface kept constant, then the area of external wall is increased by a factor of two. So also is the area of glazing (A_g), the opaque portion of the wall (A_w) and, hence, the products $A_g U_g$ and $A_w U_w$. In addition the ventilation loss (C_v) depends on the room volume, which is width × height × depth, so this also is increased by the same factor. Since

$$\bar{t}_{ei} = \frac{S\bar{I}_{GV}A_g + (A_g U_g + C_v)\bar{t}_{ao} + A_w U_w \bar{t}_{eo}}{\Sigma AU + C_v},$$

all the terms in both the top and bottom lines of the right-hand side of the equation are increased by the same factor; hence, $\bar{t}_{ei}$ will not change with room width, provided the proportion of glazing is kept constant.

In the case of the peak-to-mean temperature,

$$\tilde{t}_{ei} = \frac{S_a\tilde{I}_{GV}A_g + (A_g U_g + C_v)\tilde{t}_{ao}}{\Sigma AY + C_v},$$

the term ΣAY will increase with width, but not by the same factor. However, the error in assuming that $\tilde{t}_{ei}$ will remain independent of width will be small and the

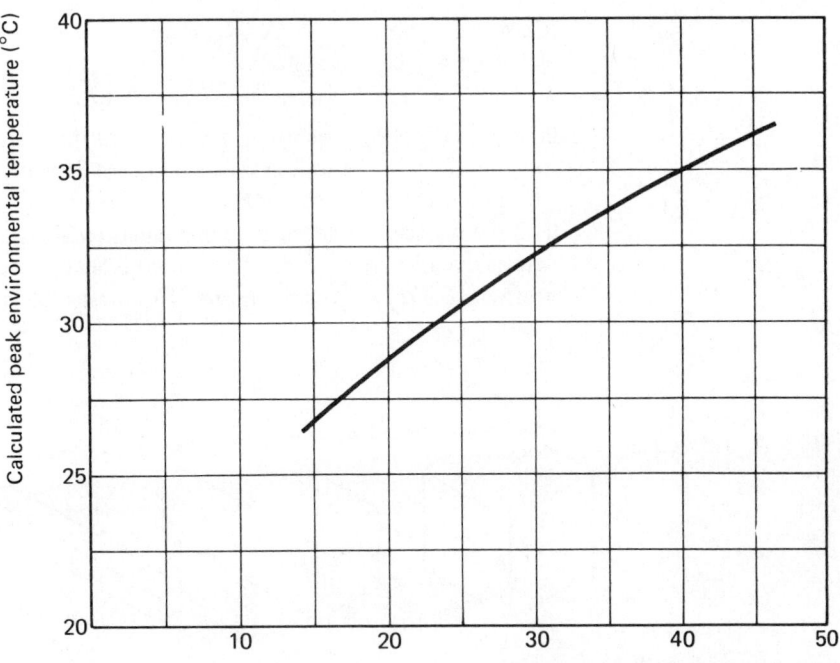

Fig. 9.8 Calculated peak environmental temperatures in a heavyweight building during summer conditions with two air changes per hour. The room is 8 m wide, single glazed and heat flows only through the external wall.

values of the peak temperature $t_{ei} = \bar{t}_{ei} + \tilde{t}_{ei}$ shown in Fig. 9.7 and in the *IHVE Guide* can be assumed to be valid for any width of room.

9.5.2.2 Depth of room

If the depth of the room is increased by a factor of two, but the other dimensions are kept constant, then the only terms in the equations for $\bar{t}_{ei}$ and $\tilde{t}_{ei}$ which will change will be C_v and $\Sigma A Y$.

In this situation, the top and bottom lines of the right-hand side of the equations are not being affected by the same amounts and, hence, $\bar{t}_{ei}$ and $\tilde{t}_{ei}$ will be affected by an alteration in the room depth.

A convenient way of analysing the influence of the room depth is to relate the area of glazing to the floor area, since floor area is a function of room width and depth. Considering a similar room to that used in the previous analysis, width 8 m, height 3 m, single glazing, 2 air changes per hour, and making the same assumptions regarding heat flow, the mean and peak environmental temperatures were calculated for room depths of 4 m, 5 m and 6 m. The values are shown plotted in Fig. 9.8. Recalculating these values for a room 4 m wide but with the other dimensions as before, gave similar values for the mean environmental temperature but peak temperatures lower by about 0.6 °C although the curve follows the same trend as for the 8 m wide room.

9.6 Relationship between shape of building and solar radiation heat gain

Earlier in this chapter it was shown how an 'ideal' theoretical shape could be calculated in order to obtain a minimum heat loss for a given volume. A similar treatment can be used for the converse situation, i.e. an 'ideal' shape in order to obtain a minimum heat gain due to solar radiation – the type of problem that can arise in warm climates.

The building can be considered as consisting of three components which can transmit radiation: the opaque portion of the walls, the windows, and the roof. The mean radiation gains for these components are:

(i) walls, $Q_w = \Sigma A_w U_w (R_{so} a \bar{I}_{GV})$;
(ii) windows, $Q_g = \Sigma A_g (\bar{I}_{GV} S)$;
(iii) roof, $Q_R = A_R U_R R_{so} (a \bar{I}_{GV} - E I_L)$.

In each of the above equations it is seen that the radiation gain is obtained by multiplying an area by a function which in turn depends upon the irradiance. Let this function be denoted by F.

If all the surfaces produced the same radiation heat gain they would all have the same value of F and, hence, the minimum heat gain per unit volume would occur when $(\Sigma A)F/V$ was a minimum. This means that for a given value of F,

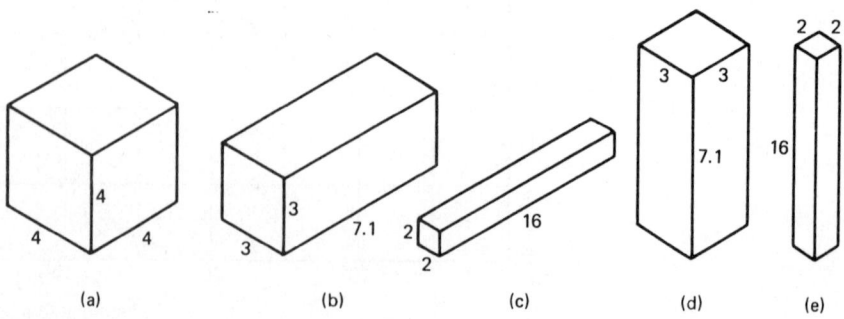

(a)   (b)   (c)   (d)   (e)

the minimum would occur when the 'surface area/volume' ratio was a minimum, the same situation as applied when the heat loss from the building was being considered.

With regard to the radiation heat gain, only five faces of the building are affected (four walls and roof), but again it can be shown that a cube produces the minimum surface area/volume ratio.

Solid shape type	Surface area (5 faces)	Volume 1	'Surface area/volume' ratio
(a)	80	64	1.25
(b)	81.9	64	1.28
(c)	104	64	1.63
(d)	94.2	64	1.47
(e)	132	64	2.01

Consider a wall receiving a daily mean global solar irradiance $= \bar{I}_{GV}$. Let $A_1 =$ total area of wall, $A_w =$ area of opaque portion of wall and $A_g =$ area of windows. Mean radiation transmitted through opaque portion is given by

$$A_w(U_w R_{so} a \bar{I}_{GV}) = A_w F_w,$$

where $F_w = U_w R_{so} a \bar{I}_{GV}$. Mean radiation transmitted through windows is given by

$$A_g \bar{I}_{GV} S = A_g F_g$$

where $F_g = \bar{I}_{GV} S$ and $S =$ solar gain factor. Therefore,

Total mean irradiance transmitted through wall of area $A_1 = A_w F_w$

$$+ A_g F_g.$$

Let

$$r_f = \text{proportion of fenestration} = \frac{\text{Window area}}{\text{Total wall area}} = \frac{A_g}{A_1}.$$

Therefore,

$$A_g = r_f A_1 \quad \text{and} \quad A_w = A_1 - A_g = A_1(1 - r_f).$$

Hence,

Mean radiation transmitted through wall $= A_w F_w + A_g F_g$

$$= A_1(1 - r_f) F_w + A_1 r_f F_g$$

$$= A_1 [(1 - r_f) F_w + r_f F_g] = A_1 F_1$$

where

$$F_1 = \text{Irradiance factor for wall } A_1 = (1 - r_f) F_w + r_f F_g.$$

Consider an entire rectangular building such that $F_2 =$ irradiance factor for wall A_2, F_3 for A_3, F_4 for A_4 and F_R for A_R.

Then

Total mean irradiance being transmitted into building

$$= A_1 F_1 + A_2 F_2 + A_3 F_3 + A_4 F_4 + A_R F_R.$$

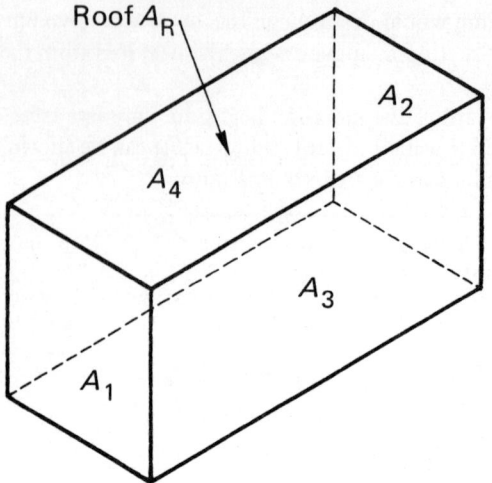

But it can be assumed that $A_1 = A_2 = A_{12}$ and $A_3 = A_4 = A_{34}$. Also let

$$F_{12} = (F_1 + F_2)/2 \text{ and } F_{34} = (F_3 + F_4)/2,$$

then,

Total mean irradiance $= 2F_{12}A_{12} + 2F_{34}A_{34} + F_R A_R$.

This is very similar to the form of heat loss equation where the walls have different U-values and which was considered by Yaneske (*see* equation (9.5)). In order to derive an expression for an ideal shape, the general form of analysis given for equations (9.3) and (9.4) can be applied.

Using similar notation as before,

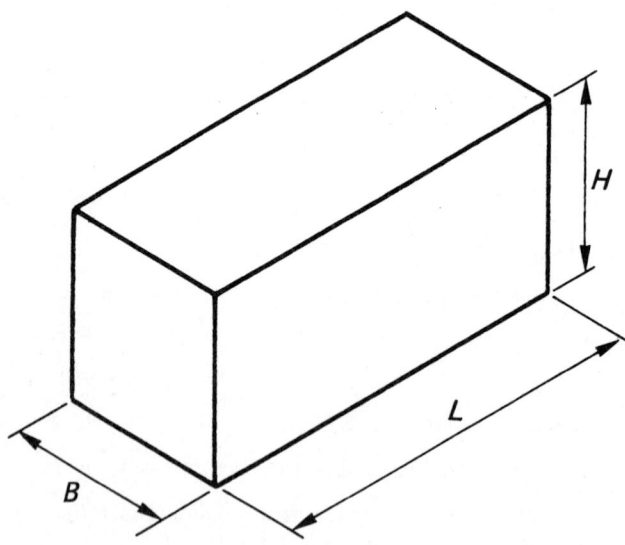

$$B = \alpha_2 H, \qquad L = \beta_2 B = \alpha_2 \beta_2 H;$$

then

$$A_{12} = \alpha_2 H^2, \qquad A_{34} = \alpha_2 \beta_2 H^2, \qquad A_R = \alpha_2^2 \beta_2 H^2.$$

Let $r_{12} = F_{12}/F_R$ and $r_{34} = F_{34}/F_R$ then

$$\text{Mean irradiance gain} = 2F_R r_{12} \alpha_2 H^2 + 2F_R r_{34} \alpha_2 \beta_2 H^2 + F_R \alpha_2{}^2 \beta_2 H^2$$

$$= F_R \alpha_2{}^2 \beta_2 H^2 \left[\frac{2r_{12}}{\alpha_2 \beta_2} + \frac{2r_{34}\beta}{\alpha_2 \beta_2} + 1 \right]$$

Volume of building $= \alpha_2{}^2 \beta_2 H^3$. Therefore,

$$\text{Mean irradiance gain per unit volume} = \frac{F_R}{H} \left[\frac{(2r_{12} + 2r_{34}\beta_2)}{\alpha_2 \beta_2} + 1 \right]$$

But if all the surfaces had the same irradiance factor F_R, the ideal shape would be a cube; hence, for this case, the mean irradiance gain per unit volume $= 5F_R/H$. Therefore for ideal situation,

$$\frac{F_R}{H} \left[\frac{(2r_{12} + 2r_{34}\beta_2)}{\alpha_2 \beta_2} + 1 \right] = \frac{5F_R}{H}$$

$$(2r_{12} + 2r_{34}\beta_2)/\alpha_2 \beta_2 = 4,$$

$$\alpha_2 = (r_{12} + r_{34}\beta_2)/2\beta_2. \tag{9.6}$$

Note that if $r_{12} = r_{34} = r$, then the expression for α_2 becomes the same as that given in equation (9.3) for α_1.

Since volume of building $= Vol = \alpha_2{}^2 \beta_2 H^3$, then as before,

$$H = \sqrt[3]{Vol/\alpha_2{}^2 \beta_2}, \tag{9.7}$$

where α_2 is obtained from equation (9.6).

Looking at this analysis it is seen that the factor F is very important in arriving at an ideal theoretical shape. As F for any particular surface area becomes larger, then, in order for the building to function as a 'thermal cube', that particular area will have to become smaller in relation to the other areas. A good example of this situation is to be found when one considers the fenestration. If the windows are not provided with shading, then, since the amount of solar radiation being transmitted through the windows will be far greater than that which is transmitted through the opaque portion of the external wall, the aim will be to make the window area as small as possible. In addition it would be desirable to position the windows in such a way that they were on the facade that received the least amount of radiation. In other words, an attempt would be made to relate the area to the inverse of the factor F.

An indication of how the orientation of the building can affect the factor F and, hence, the shape, can be obtained by considering the example of a building in a tropical area and using the data given by Petherbridge for a West African location [5].

Example 9.6   The building has windows on only one external wall and the proportion of windows to overall wall area for that particular facade is 15 per cent. Let U-value for walls and roof $= 1.0$ W m^{-2} K^{-1} and absorption coefficient for walls and roof $= 0.4$. Calculate values of factors F_{12}, F_{34} and F_R.

(a) Assume that windows are fitted with suitable shading devices and do not transmit any radiation.

(i)

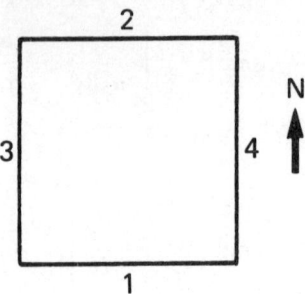

Building on N–S axis

	Windows on facade number			
Factor	1	2	3	4
F_{12}	2.2	2.03	2.29	2.29
F_{34}	3.28	3.28	3.04	3.04

(ii)

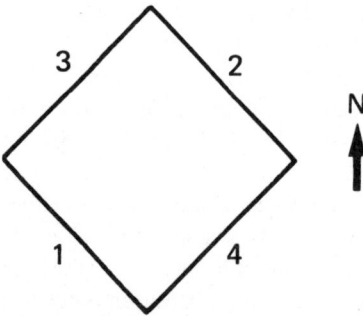

Building on NE–SW axis

	Windows on facade number			
Factor	1	2	3	4
F_{12}	2.59	2.47	2.74	2.74
F_{34}	2.74	2.74	2.47	2.59

In all cases $F_R = 1.37$.

(b) Assume that windows are not shaded and receive radiation.

(i)

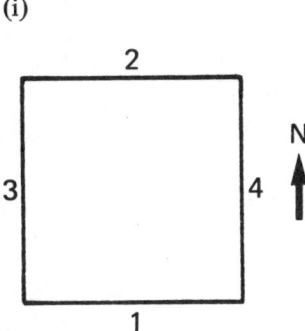

Building on N–S axis.

Factor	Windows on facade number			
	1	2	3	4
F_{12}	5.13	10.95	2.29	2.29
F_{34}	3.28	3.28	11.51	11.51

(ii)

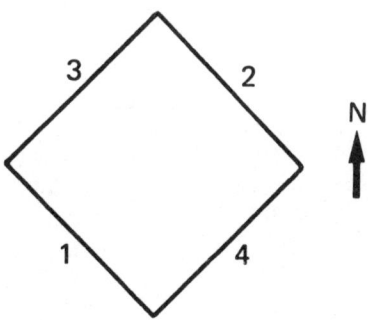

Building on NE–SW axis

Factor	Windows on facade number			
	1	2	3	4
F_{12}	7.54	11.7	2.74	2.74
F_{34}	2.74	2.74	11.7	7.54

In all cases $F_R = 1.37$.

Where there is no radiation being transmitted by the windows and only the opaque portion of the wall is to be considered, it is seen that the lowest value of F occurs for walls 1 and 2 with the building on a N–S axis. This indicates that if a rectangular plan is to be used then the long walls should face N–S and the short walls E–W. Where the windows receive radiation a similar situation occurs, the lowest value of F for a window wall occurs when the building is on a N–S axis and the windows face south.

Petherbridge makes a similar comment regarding the long walls facing N–S and also states that 'since these orientations receive direct sunlight only when the sun is high in the sky, it is also much easier to use structural shading to protect them from the sun.' [5]

The tables used in this example were appropriate for a West African location; similar tables can be calculated for other locations and will enable the effect of orientation and positioning of windows to be assessed.

References

1   Page, J. K., Optimization of building shape to conserve energy. *Journal of Architectural Research,* Vol. 3, No. 3, 20–28, 1974.

2   Yaneske, P., Design guide to the optimisation of built forms to conserve energy. Internal Report, Department of Architecture and Building Science, University of Strathclyde, 1975.

3   Hardy, A. C., Architecture and building science. *Royal Institute of British Architects Journal,* Electricity Council Supplement, November 1971.

4   Loudon, A. G., Window design criteria to avoid overheating by excessive solar heat gains. *Building Research Station Current Paper 4/68,* 1968.

5   Petherbridge, P., Limiting the temperatures in naturally ventilated buildings in warm climates. *Building Research Establishment Current Paper 7/74,* 1974.

10
EXPERIMENTAL METHODS

10.1 Data required

The previous chapters have dealt with mathematical models and computation methods for the analysis of the thermal performance of a building. However, in certain circumstances it may be advantageous or desirable to use an experimental technique to obtain measured data, e.g. air temperature, mean radiant temperature, air velocity. This information may be used as a check on previously calculated values or may be an unknown quantity which is needed in order to make further predictions.

The most likely data which will be required and are relatively simple to measure are:

(i) air temperature;
(ii) surface temperature;
(iii) mean radiant temperature;
(iv) humidity;
(v) air velocity.

All of the above have an influence on comfort conditions (*see* Chapter 3) and items (i), (ii) and (iii) are used in heat flow calculations (*see* Chapter 5).

Fig. 10.1 Different types of thermistor.

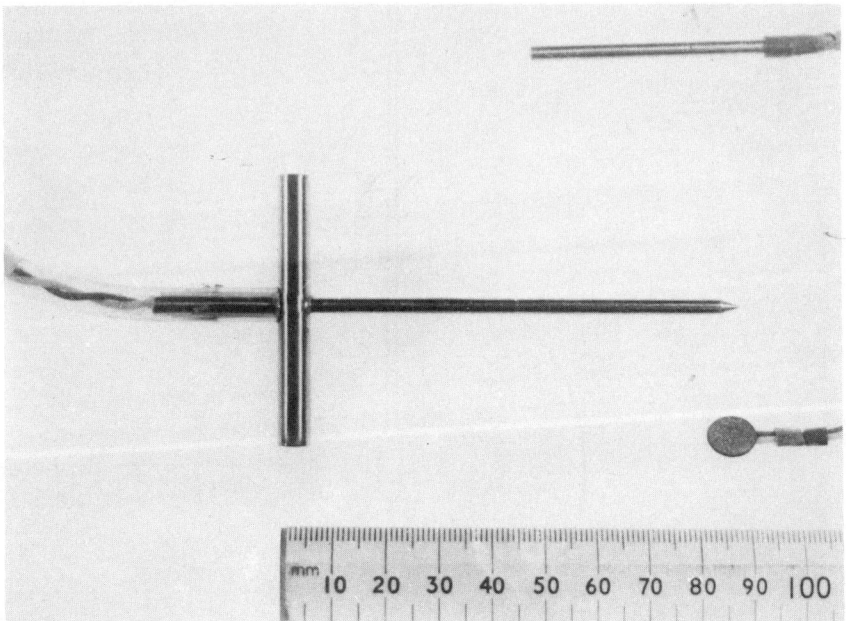

10.2 Temperature measurement

The measurement of temperature can be achieved by using

(i) mercury or alcohol thermometers;
(ii) thermistors.

Mercury and alcohol thermometers are suitable for measuring the temperature of the air and liquids and in certain conditions can be inserted into solids. Thermistors can be described as sensitive resistors whose resistance varies inversely as the temperature rise. A critical review of their use and application was given by O'Sullivan [1]. They can be obtained in the form of short probes suitable for measuring air temperature, as pointed probes for inserting into materials or as small flat discs which can be fixed to surfaces for the measurement of surface temperatures (Fig. 10.1). Suitable recorders are available which are calibrated so that the data appear as actual temperature readings and are capable of recording the output of several probes in graphical form.

When using a glass thermometer for measuring air temperature, Bedford [2] has pointed out that care has to be taken to ensure that the thermometer is protected from radiant heat and suggests that the bulb of the thermometer should be surrounded by a cylindrical shield of polished metal. If this is not done then the readings will be affected by the radiation from the surroundings.

For obtaining the mean radiant temperature the most convenient procedure is an indirect method involving the use of a globe thermometer (Fig. 10.2).

The globe thermometer consists of a hollow sphere painted black into which is placed a thermometer such that the bulb of the thermometer is at the centre of the sphere. As an alternative a thermistor can be inserted instead of the thermometer.

Fig. 10.2 Globe thermometer.

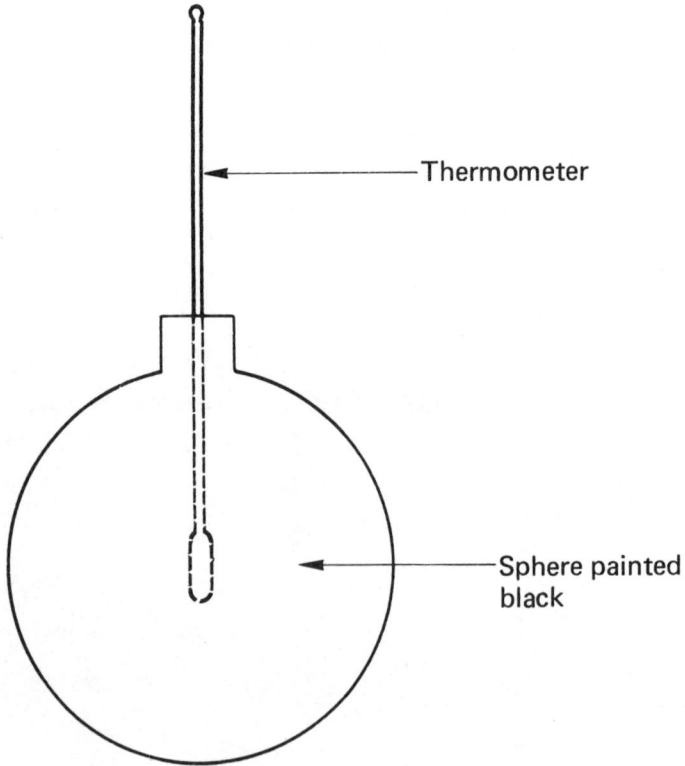

Thermometer

Sphere painted black

The relationship between globe thermometer temperature (t_g), air temperature (t_a), mean radiant temperature (t_{mrt}) and air velocity (v) as given by Humphrey [3] was shown in Chapter 3, equation (3.10) to be

$$t_g = t_a + f_g(t_{mrt} - t_a).$$

This expression can be derived as follows:

Radiation exchange of globe thermometer $= h_r(t_{mrt} - t_g)$,

Convection exchange $= h_c(t_g - t_a)$.

For equilibrium,

$$h_r(t_{mrt} - t_g) = h_c(t_g - t_a)$$

which gives

$$t_g = \frac{h_r t_{mrt} + h_c t_a}{h_r + h_c}$$

$$= \frac{t_{mrt} + (h_c/h_r)t_a}{1 + h_c/h_r}$$

$$= \frac{t_a(1 + h_c/h_r) - t_a + t_{mrt}}{1 + h_c/h_r}$$

$$= t_a + \frac{t_{mrt} - t_a}{1 + h_c/h_r}$$

$$= t_a + \frac{h_r}{h_r + h_c}(t_{mrt} - t_a)$$

$$= t_a + f_g(t_{mrt} - t_a)$$

where $f_g = h_r/(h_r + h_c)$.

As was explained in Chapter 3, the value of f_g depends upon the air velocity and the diameter of the globe thermometer (see Fig. 3.2). The following examples will demonstrate its application.

Example 10.1   Calculate the mean radiant temperature for a room if the air temperature $= 18\ ^\circ$C, velocity of the air $= 0.1$ m s^{-1} and the reading on a globe thermometer of 40 mm diameter $= 20\ ^\circ$C.

From Fig. 3.2, $f_g = 0.49$.

$$t_g = t_a + f_g(t_{mrt} - t_a),$$
$$20 = 18 + 0.49(t_{mrt} - 18),$$

and so

$$t_{mrt} = 22.1\ ^\circ\text{C}.$$

Example 10.2   If the air temperature, mean radiant temperature and air velocity are as in Example 10.1 what would be the reading on a globe thermometer of 150 mm diameter?

From Fig. 3.2, $f_g = 0.62$. Therefore,

$$t_g = 18 + 0.62(22.1 - 18)$$
$$= 20.5\ ^\circ\text{C}.$$

Example 10.3   What is the mean radiant temperature in the room if the air and globe thermometer temperatures are as in Example 10.1, but the air velocity is increased to 0.3 m s^{-1}?

From Fig. 3.2, f_g = 0.33. Therefore,

$$20 = 18 + 0.33(t_{mrt} - 18),$$

$$t_{mrt} = 24.1 \ ^\circ C.$$

Example 10.4   Calculate the mean radiant temperature for a room if the air temperature = 18 $^\circ$C, velocity of air = 0.3 m s^{-1} and the reading from a globe thermometer of 40 mm diameter = 19.4 $^\circ$C.

From Fig. 3.2, f_g = 0.33. Therefore,

$$19.4 = 18 + 0.33(t_{mrt} - 18),$$

$$t_{mrt} = 22.2 \ ^\circ C.$$

Compare this Example with Example 10.1.

10.3 Humidity

Chart recorders are available which will record humidity levels at regular intervals over a period of several days. However, for obtaining an individual reading a suitable instrument is the whirling or sling hygrometer (Fig. 10.3). This instrument consists of two thermometers mounted on a frame which can be rotated rapidly. One of the thermometers has its bulb exposed to the air (dry bulb) the other has its bulb inserted into a wick which is kept moist (wet bulb). As was pointed out in Chapter 3, evaporation of moisture causes cooling; hence, as the wick loses moisture the wet bulb will be cooled, will give a lower temperature reading than the dry bulb thermometer, and the difference between the two readings will give an indication of the relative humidity. To carry out the measurement the instrument should be whirled rapidly through the air and the readings on the two thermometers noted. Tables are normally provided with the hygrometer which enable the relative humidity to be obtained from the wet and dry bulb readings.

Fig. 10.3 Whirling hygrometer.

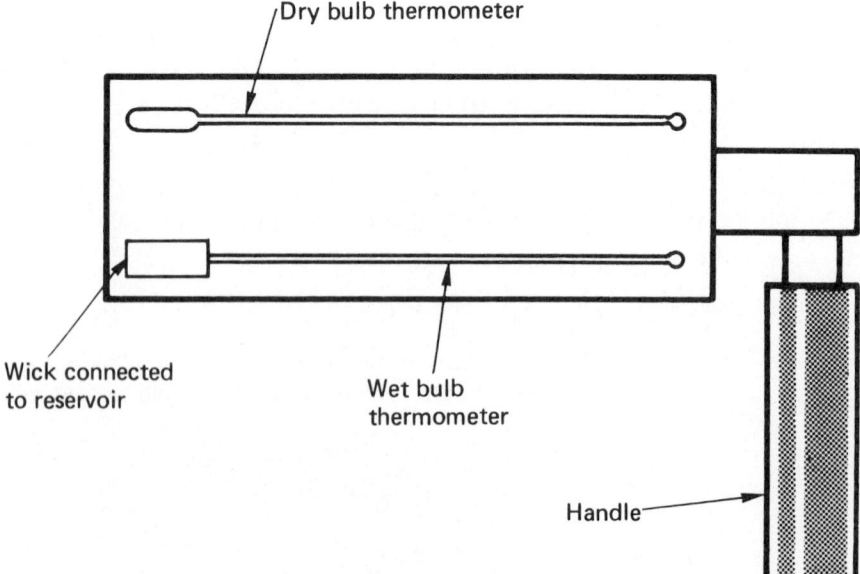

10.4 Air velocity

Measurements of the air velocity in a room will normally be for low speeds; a suitable procedure for this situation is to use the Kata thermometer. This instrument was devised by Sir Leonard Hill [4] and used to measure ventilation. It consists of a thermometer with a large bulb filled with red spirit and has a cooling range of 37.8 °C to 35 °C.

To measure the air velocity, the thermometer is heated by placing the bulb in hot water until the thermometer gives a reading greater than 37.8 °C; it is then suspended in air and the time taken for the thermometer to cool from 37.8 °C to 35 °C is noted. Reference has been made to the influence of air velocity upon heat loss by convection; hence, alterations in air velocity will result in changes in the cooling power of the Kata thermometer. Knowing the time taken for the temperature to drop by the specified amount the air velocity can be obtained from charts usually supplied with the thermometer and which are published in *British Standard 3276* [5]. The Kata thermometer, having a cooling range 37.8 °C to 35 °C, is not suitable for use in a hot environment. In this situation a Kata thermometer with a silvered bulb and having a cooling range 65.5 °C to 62.5 °C should be used. *British Standard 3276* contains charts which are appropriate for use with Kata thermometers having silvered bulbs and cooling ranges 37.8 °C to 35 °C, 54.5 °C to 51.5 °C and 65.5 °C to 62.5 °C.

An alternative procedure is to use a hot wire anemometer. This instrument has an exposed fine resistance wire which is electrically heated by a small battery or cell; air flowing over the wire affects its temperature and this is recorded on a gauge calibrated to give a direct reading of the air velocity. Hot wire anemometers are available for measuring air velocities within the range 0 to 30 m s^{-1}.

So far we have been describing experimental techniques and instruments for obtaining environmental data for a real situation; however, there may be occasions where a scale model may be appropriate. Reviews of the use of experimental models in architecture and building science have been given by Page [6] and Cowan [7], but in this chapter we shall confine our attention to two specific applications, i.e.

(i) use of a heliodon for the study of the areas of insolation and shadows;
(ii) use of an electrical analog for the study of steady and transient heat flow.

10.5 The heliodon

It has been shown that the heating effect of solar radiation may be considerable and that there may be many situations where measures have to be taken to ensure that windows or portions of the building are in the shade. Conversely, for a winter condition in Northern Europe, it may be beneficial to design a structure so that the windows are going to allow solar radiation to enter the building in order to reduce the heating load. In both of the situations mentioned, in order to be able to compare the merits of alternative designs or layouts, it is important to be able to assess the areas of insolation.

A technique for predicting shadow angles and areas of insolation has been given in Chapter 4, but this procedure may be found to be rather tedious if a number of alternative solutions are being investigated. A most useful device which enables the shadows and sunlit areas to be observed on a model of the building or layout is the heliodon. This apparatus was developed at the Building Research Station by Dufton and Beckett [8] and uses a lamp to represent the sun. In this experimental technique a lamp is fitted into a holder which can slide up and down a vertical staff which is marked off in months. At a fixed distance

Fig. 10.4 Position of
earth and sun.

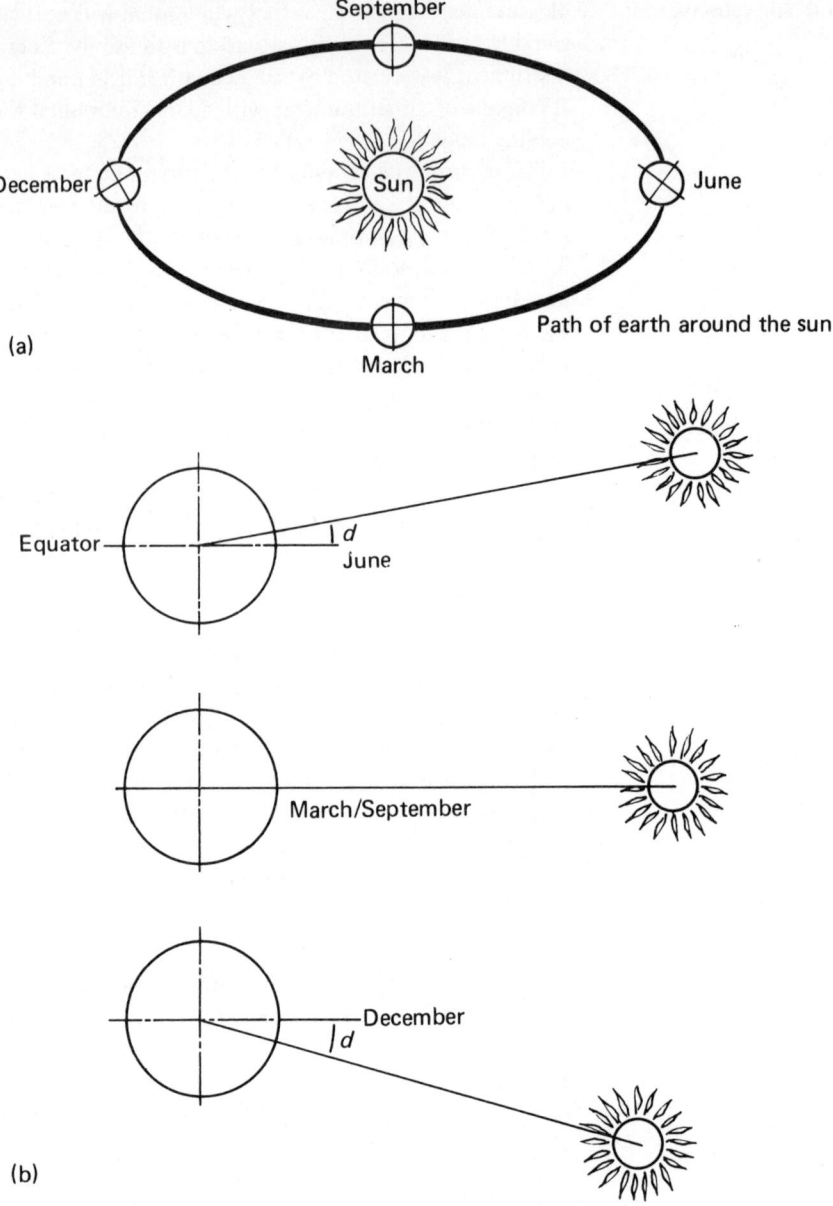

(a)

(b)

from the vertical staff, a small-scale model of the building or layout is placed
upon a board which is set at an angle to the horizontal so as to represent the
Latitude of the particular location. The board upon which the model has been
placed is capable of rotating on a vertical axis so that a complete rotation of the
model through 360° will reproduce the effect of the earth's rotation during a
24-h period.

The general principle upon which the apparatus is based is as follows.

Due to the tilt of the earth's axis, at noon in June the sun appears to be
above the equator, at noon in March/September the sun appears to lie on an
axis passing through the equator, and at noon in December the sun is below the
equator (Fig. 10.4(b)).

Fig. 10.5 Arrangement for heliodon.

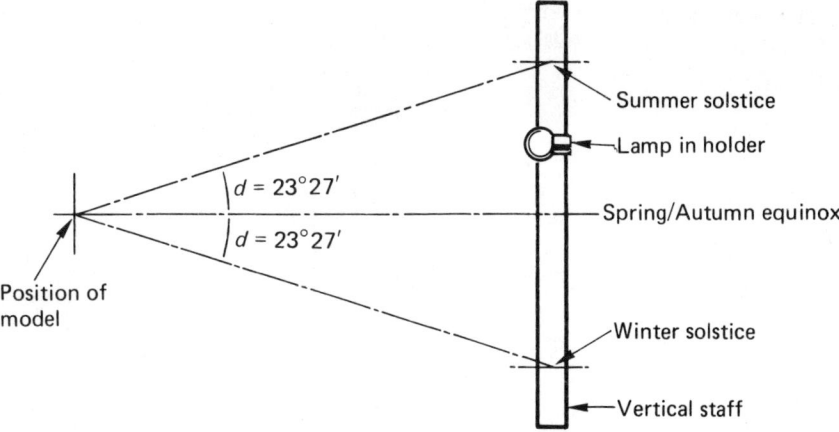

The angular displacement above or below an axis passing through the equator is the angle of declination (d). In the heliodon this apparent movement of the sun is represented by the lamp sliding up and down the vertical staff. An arrangement for a location in the northern hemisphere is as shown in Fig. 10.5.

By positioning the vertical scale at a fixed distance from the model, e.g. 2.5 m, the relative positions of the winter and summer solstice on the staff can be obtained:

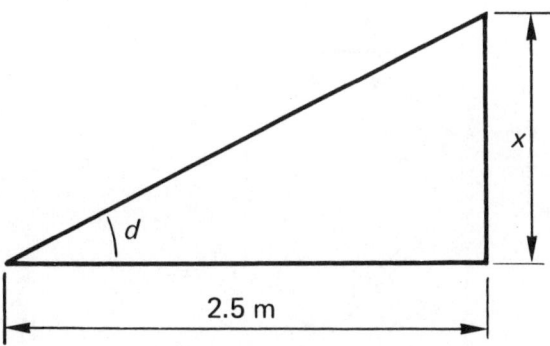

$$x = 2.5 \tan d = 2.5 \times 0.4338 = 1.085 \text{ m.}$$

Hence the total height of the staff will have to be 2.17 m.

By inserting the appropriate value of d for other times of the year, e.g.

January 31st, $d = -17° \, 36'$;

February 28th, $d = -8° \, 24'$;

etc.

a complete scale can be constructed (*see* Fig. 10.6).

In order to be able to adjust the position of the lamp the top of the scale should not be much higher than 2 m, otherwise it is getting beyond reach. Since the height of the staff is related to its distance from the model this implies that the distance between the staff and the model cannot be more than 2.5 m.

The base upon which the model is placed is pivoted horizontally and vertically.

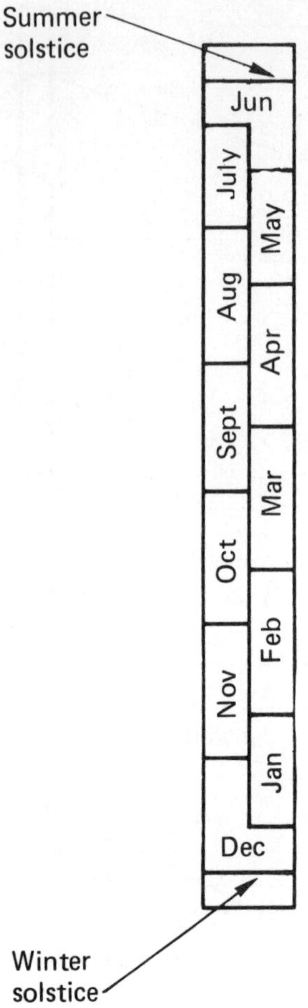

Fig. 10.6 Vertical staff for heliodon (northern hemisphere).

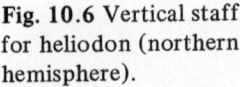

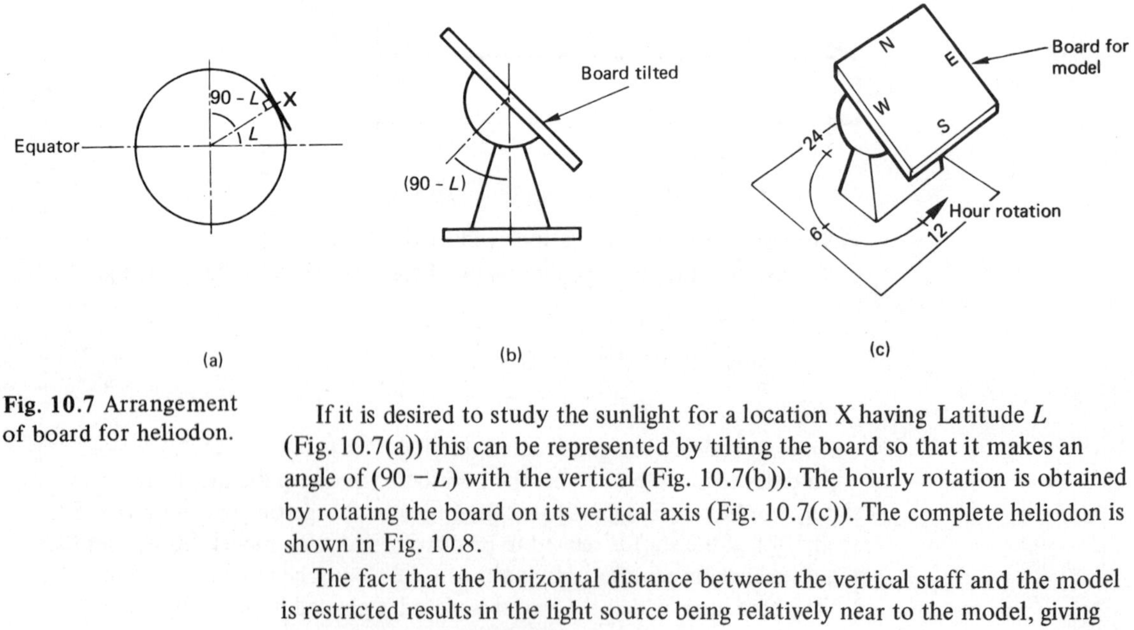

Summer solstice

Jun

July

May

Aug

Apr

Sept

Mar

Oct

Feb

Nov

Jan

Dec

Winter solstice

Fig. 10.7 Arrangement of board for heliodon.

(a)

(b)

(c)

Equator

$90 - L$ X

L

Board tilted

$(90 - L)$

N

E

W

S

24

6

12

Board for model

Hour rotation

If it is desired to study the sunlight for a location X having Latitude L (Fig. 10.7(a)) this can be represented by tilting the board so that it makes an angle of $(90 - L)$ with the vertical (Fig. 10.7(b)). The hourly rotation is obtained by rotating the board on its vertical axis (Fig. 10.7(c)). The complete heliodon is shown in Fig. 10.8.

The fact that the horizontal distance between the vertical staff and the model is restricted results in the light source being relatively near to the model, giving rise to shadow distortion.

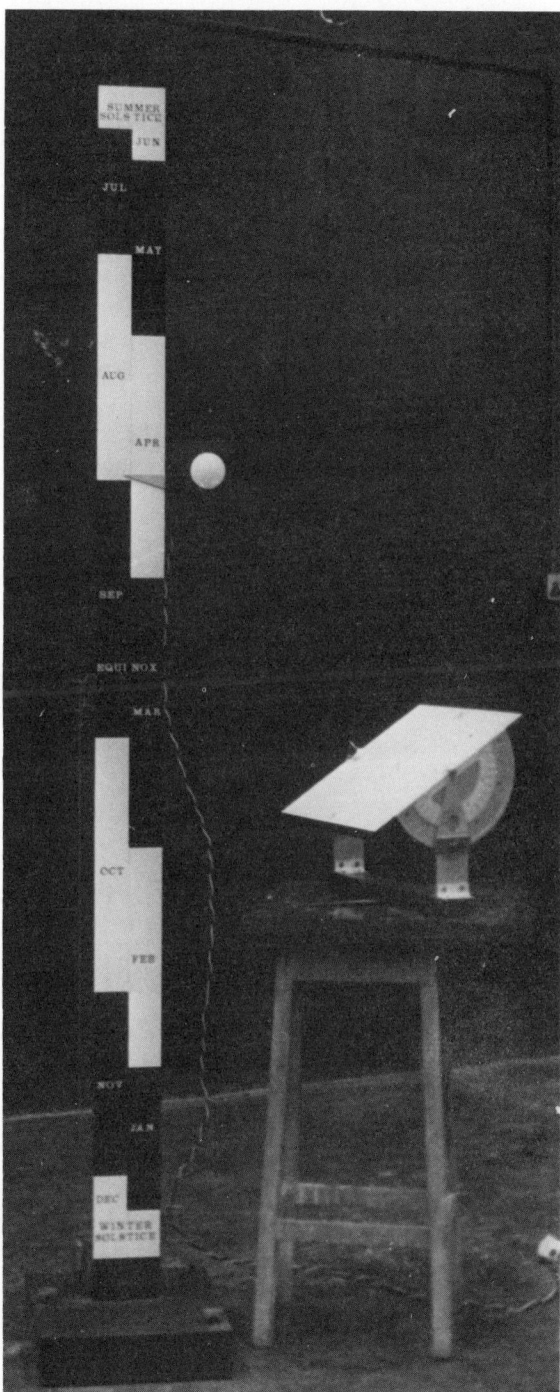

Fig. 10.8 Heliodon.

Fig. 10.9 Revised type of heliodon (based upon Shelliodon).

In order to overcome this an improved version of the heliodon was devised by the Scottish Development Department [9] termed the Shelliodon. In this apparatus the model is placed upon a board which can be moved to represent the Latitude of the location and can rotate about a vertical axis to give the hours of the day. This arrangement is mounted on another board or platen which can be adjusted for the months of the year (i.e. moved according to the appropriate angle of declination). The advantage of this system is that the lamp representing the sun does not require to be moved up and down and hence can be positioned much further away from the model. Fig. 10.9 shows a modified heliodon based upon this principle.

The experiments which can be performed with a heliodon involve the use of scale models. Now we wish to consider another type of experimental model where use is made of the fact that an electrical system can be shown to be analogous to a thermal system.

10.6 Use of electrical analogs

The flow of heat through a structure can be studied by means of experimental models and one very convenient method is to use an electrical analog. This particular experimental method has been used for many years, an early report of this procedure being given by Paschkis and Baker [10] in 1941.

In the first instance, consider a steady-state heat transfer condition such as the rate of heat flow between the inside and outside surfaces of a composite element.

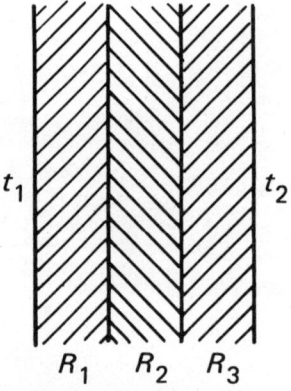

If the resistances of the individual components of the element are R_1, R_2 and R_3, then (as was shown in Chapter 5) the total resistance of the composite unit is $R_1 + R_2 + R_3$.

Rate of heat flow per unit area is

$$Q/A = (t_1 - t_2)/(R_1 + R_2 + R_3)$$

$$= \frac{\text{Temperature difference}}{\text{Total resistance}} = \frac{\Delta t}{\Sigma R}.$$

A similar situation occurs when one considers electrical resistances which are connected in series:

$$\text{Total resistance} = R_1 + R_2 + R_3.$$

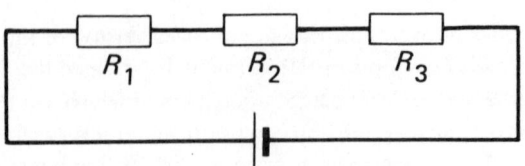

If V = voltage and I = current (measured in amperes), then, from Ohm's Law,

$$I = V/R.$$

But since total resistance = $R_1 + R_2 + R_3$,

$$I = V/(R_1 + R_2 + R_3).$$

This indicates that the two systems are analogous and that it is possible to construct an electrical model of a structure and to represent temperature by voltage.

Example 10.4   Construct an electrical model for a cavity wall having the following properties:

Element	Thermal resistance (m^2 K W^{-1})
Internal resistance	0.123
Plaster	0.032
Inner leaf	0.27
Air space	0.18
Outer leaf	0.123
External resistance	0.055

The above values can be considered as unit thermal resistances, i.e. the thermal resistance for an element having an area of 1 m^2. Hence, the table can be rewritten as:

Element	Unit thermal resistance (K W^{-1})
Internal resistance	0.123
Plaster	0.032
Etc.	

Using an analog scale, let 1 °C (= 1 K) be represented by 1 V and 1 W be represented by 200 μA = 200 × 10^{-6} A. Therefore,

$$1 \text{ K W}^{-1} = 1 \text{ V}/(200 \times 10^{-6} \text{ A}) = V/I.$$

But $V/I = R$ and so

$$1 \text{ K W}^{-1} = 1/(200 \times 10^{-6}) = 5000 \ \Omega.$$

So far the area of the wall has not been taken into account. Let the wall have a surface area = 5 m^2. The values of the unit thermal resistances corresponded to elements having an area of 1 m^2; hence, for elements having an area of 5 m^2, the appropriate resistances can be obtained by dividing the previous values by 5, e.g.

Surface resistance of wall for an area of 5 m^2 = 0.123/5

$$= 0.0246 \text{ K W}^{-1};$$

Resistance of plaster for an area of 5 m^2 = 0.032/5 = 0.0064 K W^{-1}.

The appropriate electrical resistances required for constructing the analog can be calculated by repeating this procedure for the other elements and then multiplying them by the analog scaling factor, as shown in the table below.

Element	Thermal resistance for 5 m² area (K W⁻¹)	Electrical resistance (Ω)
Internal surface resistance	0.0246	0.0246 × 5000 = 123
Plaster	0.0064	0.0064 × 5000 = 32
Inner leaf	0.054	0.054 × 5000 = 270
Air space	0.036	0.036 × 5000 = 180
Outer leaf	0.0246	0.0246 × 5000 = 123
External surface resistance	0.011	0.011 × 5000 = 55

The analog can be used to demonstrate the difference between adding resistances and adding U-values.

Fig. 10.10 Resistances in series.

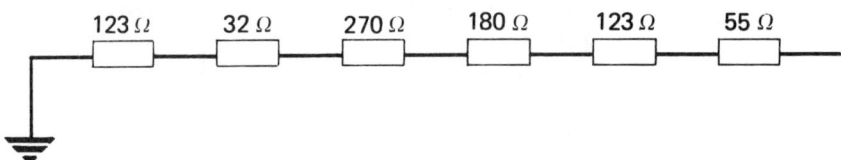

In the above example the electrical resistances would be connected in series (Fig. 10.10) to represent the wall unit, each resistance corresponding to a particular element of the wall. If we wish to consider the fabric heat loss (steady state) for a room or a building this can be represented on the electric analog by connecting the resistances of the various structural units in parallel (Fig. 10.11).

Fig. 10.11 Resistances in parallel.

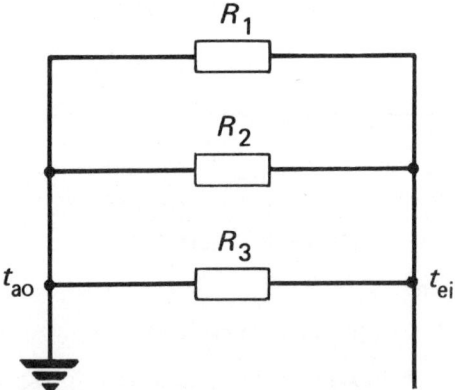

If R_1 = total resistance of floor, R_2 = total resistance of roof or ceiling, R_3 = total resistance of external walls, then, when a current is applied, the voltage drop across the circuit will represent the temperature difference $t_{ei} - t_{ao}$.

The reason for connecting the resistances in parallel can be demonstrated as follows.

If I = current and V = voltage, then $I = V/R$, which is analogous to

$$Q = \frac{A \times \text{Temperature difference}}{\text{Resistance}}.$$

But for electrical resistances in parallel,

$$\frac{1}{R} = \frac{1}{R_1} + \frac{1}{R_2} + \frac{1}{R_3}.$$

Hence,

$$I = \frac{V}{R} = V\left(\frac{1}{R}\right) = V \times \left(\frac{1}{R_1} + \frac{1}{R_2} + \frac{1}{R_3}\right) = V\Sigma\left(\frac{1}{R}\right)$$

As was stated earlier in this section, the total resistance for a particular area was obtained by dividing the unit resistance by the area, i.e.

$$\text{Total resistance of wall} = \frac{\text{Unit resistance of wall}}{\text{Area}} \text{ K W}^{-1}.$$

But $1/U$ = unit resistance and, hence,

$$\text{Total resistance of wall} = 1/(U_\text{w} \times \text{Area of wall})$$

or

$$A_\text{w} U_\text{w} = \frac{1}{\text{Total resistance of wall}}.$$

Therefore,

$$\text{Sum of } U\text{-values} \times \text{Areas of various elements} = \Sigma AU$$

$$= \frac{1}{\text{Total resistance of floor}} + \frac{1}{\text{Total resistance of roof}}$$

$$+ \frac{1}{\text{Total resistance of walls}}.$$

But total resistance of floor is represented in the analog by R_1, total resistance of roof is represented in the analog by R_2, etc. Hence, ΣAU is represented by

$$\frac{1}{R_1} + \frac{1}{R_2} + \frac{1}{R_3} = \Sigma \frac{1}{R}$$

So far we have used the analog to represent the steady-state heat flow condition; however, it is in the consideration of cyclic heat inputs that the electrical analog can be used to its best advantage.

When dealing with cyclic heat inputs in Chapter 6 it was shown that the effects of thermal capacity and time had to be taken into account; hence, in order to be able to deal with this type of energy input on the analog it is necessary to show that there is a similar relationship between capacity, (the term in electrical engineering is 'capacitance'), resistance and time for the thermal and electrical systems.

10.6.1 Relationship between Capacity (Capacitance), Resistance and Time.

10.6.1.1 Thermal system

$$\text{Unit thermal capacity} = \text{Specific heat capacity} \times \text{Mass}$$

$$= \text{Specific heat capacity} \times \text{Density} \times \text{Volume}$$

$$= \text{J kg}^{-1} \text{ K}^{-1} \times \text{kg m}^{-3} \times \text{m}^3$$

$$= \text{J K}^{-1};$$

$$\text{Unit resistance} = \text{Resistance/Area} = m^2 \ K \ W^{-1} \times m^{-2}$$
$$= K \ W^{-1}.$$

But the watt is a rate of energy flow:

$$1 \ W = 1 \ J \ s^{-1}.$$

Therefore,

$$\text{Unit resistance, } K \ W^{-1} = K \ s \ J^{-1}.$$

Multiplying unit capacity by unit resistance gives

$$J \ K^{-1} \times K \ s \ J^{-1} = s \ (\text{time})$$

10.6.1.2 Electrical system

Electrical capacitance, farads = coulombs/volts. By Ohm's law,

$$\text{Resistance, } R = V/I.$$

But

$$\text{Current, } I = \text{coulombs/time}.$$

Therefore,

$$R = \text{volts} \times \text{time/coulombs}.$$

Multiplying capacitance by resistance gives

$$\frac{\text{coulombs}}{\text{volts}} \times \frac{\text{volts} \times \text{time}}{\text{coulombs}} = \text{time}.$$

Hence, it is seen that in both systems (thermal and electrical)
Capacity (Capacitance) × Resistance = Time
The analogy between the two systems is shown in the table below.

Quantity	Units	Quantity	Units
Heat flow rate	$W \ (J \ s^{-1})$	Electric current	A
Unit thermal resistance	$K \ W^{-1}$	Electrical resistance	Ω
Unit thermal capacity	$J \ K^{-1}$	Electrical capacitance	F
Temperature	$^{\circ}C$	Voltage	V
Time	s	Time	s

10.6.2 Analog Scale Ratios

From the table it is seen that there are five quantities; hence, in order to construct an analog it is necessary to obtain five scale ratios. However, by deciding upon three ratios the other two can be obtained.

Let the analog scale ratios for the heat flow rate, temperature and time be a, b and c, respectively, i.e. let $1 \ W = a \ A$, $1 \ ^{\circ}C = b \ V$ and $1 \ s$ (real time) $= c \ s$ (analog time). The analog scale ratio for unit resistance

$$1 \ K \ W^{-1} = (b \ V)/(a \ A) = b/a \ \Omega. \tag{10.1}$$

The analog scale ratio for unit capacity is obtained from the relationship

$$\text{Capacity (Capacitance)} \times \text{Resistance} = \text{Time}.$$

Hence,

$$\text{Capacity (Capacitance)} = \text{Time/Resistance}.$$

Therefore,

$$1 \text{ J K}^{-1} = \frac{\text{Time scale}}{\text{Resistance scale}} = \frac{c}{b/a} = \frac{ac}{b}. \text{ F} \qquad (10.2)$$

Example 10.5   Calculate the analog scale ratios for the case where $1 \, {}^{\circ}\text{C} = 1$ V, $1 \text{ W} = 0.05 \, \mu\text{A} = 0.05 \times 10^{-6}$ A and 1 h real time is to be represented on the analog by 5 s, i.e.

$$1 \text{ h (real time)} = 3600 \text{ s} = 5 \text{ s (analog time)},$$

and so

$$1 \text{ s (real time)} = \frac{5}{3600} = \frac{1}{720} \text{ s (analog time)}.$$

Thus,

$$a = 0.05 \times 10^{-6}, \qquad b = 1.0, \qquad c = \frac{1}{720}$$

and the scale for unit resistance, equation (10.2), is

$$1 \text{ K W}^{-1} = \frac{b}{a} = \frac{1}{0.05 \times 10^{-6}} = 20 \times 10^6 \, \Omega = 20 \text{ M}\Omega.$$

The scale for unit capacity, equation (10.3), is

$$1 \text{ J K}^{-1} = \frac{ac}{b} = \frac{0.05 \times 10^{-6} \times 1/720}{1.0}$$

$$= 0.000\,07 \times 10^{-6} \text{ F}$$

$$= 0.000\,07 \, \mu\text{F}.$$

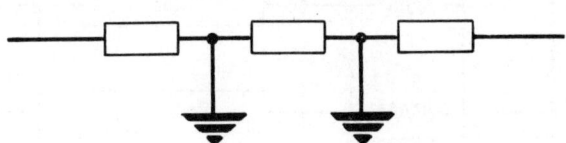

In constructing the analog the various elements should be subdivided into small units similar to the Greek letter π.

Example 10.6   Design a portion of an analog to represent a solid brick wall, 105 mm thick, having an area of 5 m^2. Thermal conductivity $k = 0.84$ W m^{-2} K^{-1}; density = 1700 kg m^{-3}; specific heat = 800 J kg^{-1} K^{-1}

From the previous example, the analog scale factors are

$$1 \text{ K W}^{-1} = 20 \text{ M}\Omega,$$

$$1 \text{ J K}^{-1} = 0.000\,07 \, \mu\text{F}.$$

$$\text{Thermal resistance} = \frac{\text{Thickness}}{\text{Conductivity} \times \text{area}} = \frac{0.105}{0.84 \times 5}$$

$$= 0.025 \text{ K W}^{-1};$$

Resistance (analog) = 0.025 × 20 MΩ   = 0.5 MΩ

= 500 kΩ;

Thermal capacity = Specific heat × Density × Volume

= 800 × 1700 × 0.105 × 5

= 714 000 J K^{-1};

Capacitance (analog) = 714 000 × 0.000 07 = 50 μF.

Divide the 'wall' into five sections as shown in Fig. 10.12.

Fig. 10.12 Analog circuit for a wall.

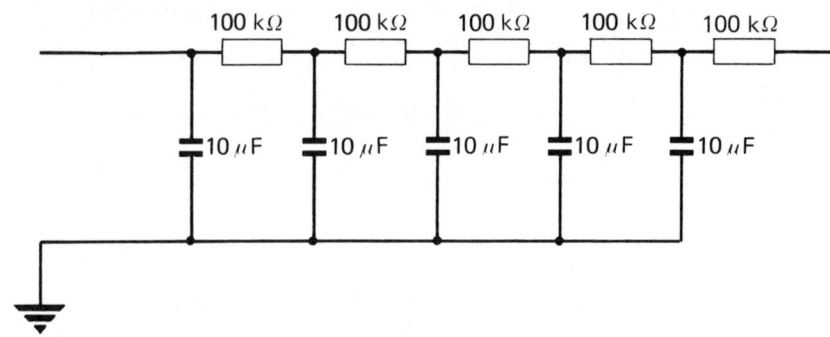

Fig. 10.13 Analog circuit for a room.

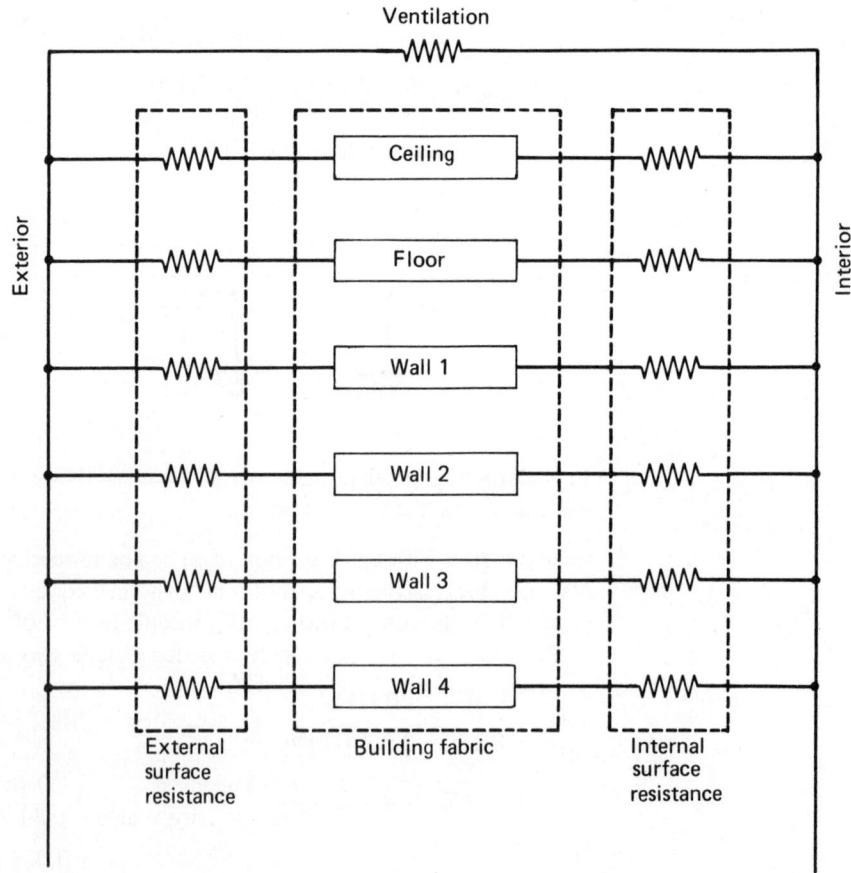

Fig. 10.14 Analog circuit for a room with radiation transfers.

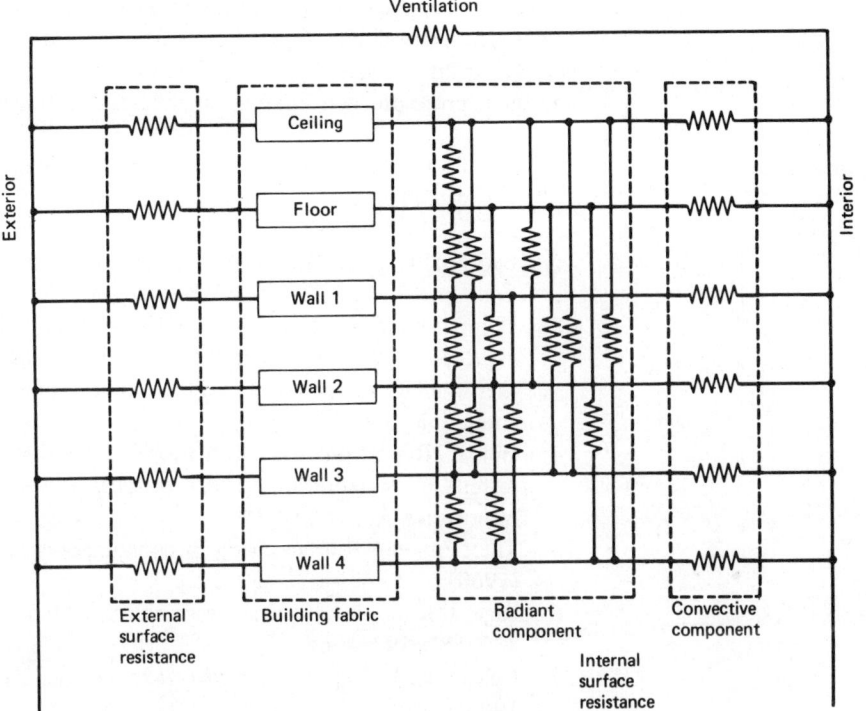

A suitable circuit for a constant current generator for use with electrical analogs is illustrated by Bassett and Pritchard [11] together with descriptions of a number of different electrical analogs for carrying out various thermal experiments. Fig. 10.13 shows an analog which could be used for analysing a room; this particular circuit could be extended to include windows, heat inputs, etc.

If it is desired to consider the radiation transfer between the various surfaces then the analog circuit as shown in Fig. 10.13 should be modified to that in Fig. 10.14. Burberry [12] illustrated this latter type of circuit and published some of the experimental data which was obtained from its use.

The type of analog illustrated can be used to investigate the energy required to heat a room or building to a specified temperature. Alternatively, by measuring the voltage at a particular point in the circuit, the analog can be used to predict air, environmental or surface temperatures. Temperature gradients across the fabric can be measured and the problem of surface or interstitial condensation (as described in Chapter 5) can be studied.

10.7 Use of models

There are many other types of problem where scale models can be used with success. For example, model buildings placed in a wind tunnel with a suitable smoke generator can be used to investigate wind flow conditions. The smoke patterns produced will indicate the influence that a certain shape of building or particular layout will have upon the wind flow and an area where there is turbulence or an increase in wind velocity will become evident.

It is possible to make measurements of the actual wind pressures on the models but for this type of experiment attention has to be paid to scale effects. A similar situation can arise with models used for structural analysis and a detailed consideration of scale effect and structural measuring techniques is given by Cowan [7].

A further application of experimental model techniques is in the investigation of daylight in a building. For this type of study a model of the room or building is placed in an artificial sky. Descriptions of the construction of an artificial sky and the appropriate instrumentation are given by Walsh [13] and Lynes [14].

References

1   O'Sullivan, P., Thermistors – their theory and application to building science and environmental physics. *Architectural Science Review*, **9**, 28–35 and 91–98, 1966.

2   Bedford, T., *Basic Principles of Ventilating and Heating*. Lewis, London, 1974.

3   Humphrey, M. A., The optimum diameter for a globe thermometer. *Building Research Establishment PD 30/75*, 1975; and Adjustment to globe-thermometer temperature to allow for air movement. Private communication.

4   Hill, L., Report on ventilation and the effect of open air and wind on the respiratory metabolism. *Report of Local Government Board on Public Health, New Series, No. 100*. 1914.

5   Thermometers for measuring air cooling power. *British Standard 3276* (1960).

6   Page, J. K., Environmental Research using Models. *The Architects' Journal*, **139**, 587–593, 1964.

7   Cowan, H. J., *Models in Architecture*. Elsevier Publishing Co., Amsterdam, 1968.

8   Sun planning by means of models. The Dufton–Beckett Heliodon. *Royal Institute of British Architects Journal*, **38** 509–510, 1931.

9   Ministry of Housing and Local Government, *Planning for Daylight and Sunlight. Planning Bulletin 5*. HMSO, London, 1966.

10   Paschkis, V. and Baker, H. D., A method for determining unsteady-state heat transfer by means of an electrical analogy. *Transactions of the American Society of Mechanical Engineers*, **64**, 105–112, 1942.

11   Bassett, C. R. and Pritchard, M. D., *Heating*. Longman, London, 1969.

12   Burberry, P., Conserving energy in buildings. *The Architects' Journal*, **160**, 615–628, 1974.

13   Walsh, J. W. T., *The Science of Daylight*. Macdonald, London, 1961.

14   Lynes, J. A., *Principles of Natural Lighting*. Elsevier Publishing Co., Amsterdam, 1968.

11
ENGINEERING SERVICES

11.1 Flow systems

In one chapter it is not possible to deal with individual building services in the degree of detail necessary to the engineering practitioner; for this he is referred to standard textbooks on space heating and cooling and ventilation. Rather, what is attempted is to construct a framework for an understanding of the general principles involved, such as is required by the building designer and project manager.

We need, therefore, to extract from the multiplicity of building services and their different technologies some common basis between them. What we recognize is that they are all made up of parts connected together, with an overall function (the maintenance of one or more of the conditions for comfort). Building services, therefore, conform to any reasonable definition of a *system*, and the approach of this chapter is, therefore, systemic. The reader will already have met the important systems concepts and terminology in Chapter 2; in this introductory section the aim is to define these more precisely and to extend them as a basis for what follows. The treatment here is necessarily condensed, and it is recommended that the reader should refer back to this section as the need arises, and perhaps again at the end of the chapter as a convenient summary of its argument.

The generalized system diagram (Fig. 11.1) in which a system is defined by the relation between its inputs and outputs permits, given sufficient dexterity in the definition of these variables, unlimited application; indeed at this level of generalization the systems concept is of no more than introductory interest. For

Fig. 11.1 Generalized system diagram.

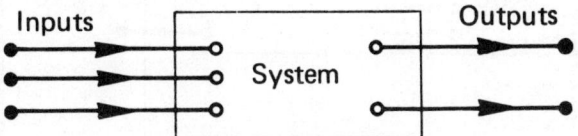

this chapter, however, we will require that the input and output variables are measurable quantities of matter, energy or information. This concept of a system is then paralleled by the mathematical concept of a function; in particular by a function between sets of real numbers (Fig. 11.2).

We may familiarly extend the concept of function to the system itself: the *function* of a system is to transform available inputs to required outputs, where inputs and outputs have the nature described. Such systems are called *flow systems*; the building services with which we are concerned here are all flow systems.

Fig. 11.2 The function $x \to x^2$ ($x \in \{1, 2, 12\}$).

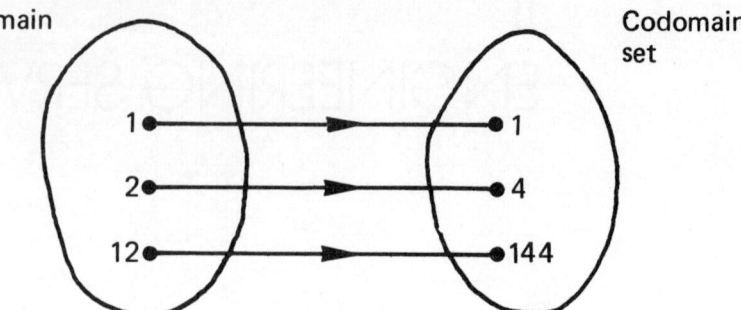

That which is not the system is its environment. In Fig. 11.3, the environment is shown as unenclosed, i.e. non-systemic. However, certain parts of the environment are more intimately associated with the system than the rest. These are the *resource environment*, from which the system draws its inputs, and the *controlled environment*, into which the system discharges its outputs (Fig. 11.4).

Fig. 11.3 System and environment.

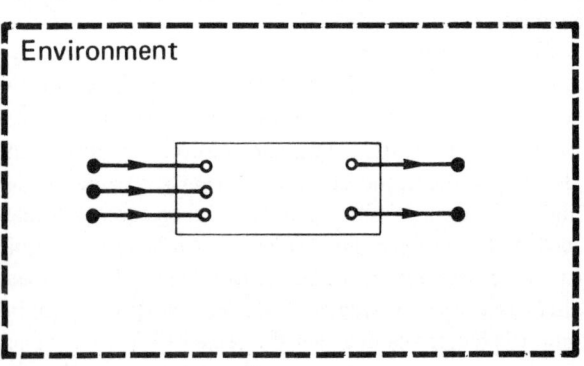

Fig. 11.4 The resource environment (RE) and controlled environment (CE).

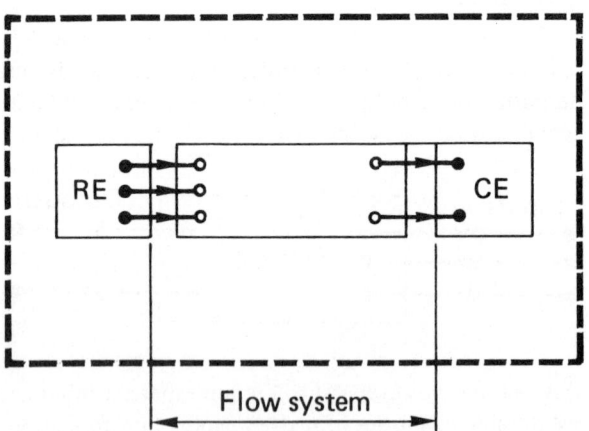

The state of the controlled environment is maintained, within the limits dictated by comfort, by the system outputs. The systems nature of these environments is implied by their enclosure; they correspond respectively to the domain and codomain sets of a mathematical function. The drawing of these boundaries around parts of the environment must, to some extent, be arbitrary; and, consequently, so is the boundary of the flow system operating between them.

The non-specific environment will henceforth disappear from our diagrams, but it is always to be implied by the vacant space around them. Thus, products of the transformation that do not contribute to the output required in the controlled environment, such as smoke from a boiler, are shown as secondary outputs – to the environment (Fig. 11.5).

Fig. 11.5 Secondary outputs to the environment.

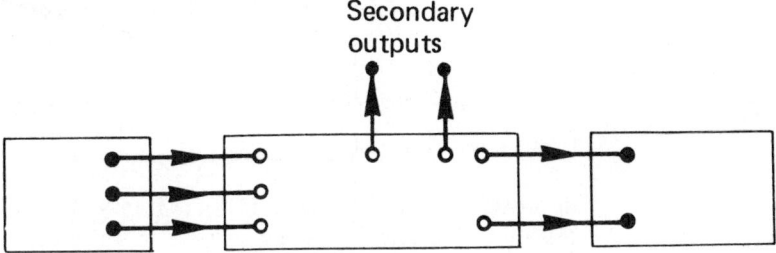

Variations in the environment may take the form of secondary inputs, which we will call disturbances, to the controlled environment (Fig. 11.6). In the context of this book, climatic temperature variation is an obvious example of a disturbance.

Fig. 11.6 Disturbances to the controlled environment.

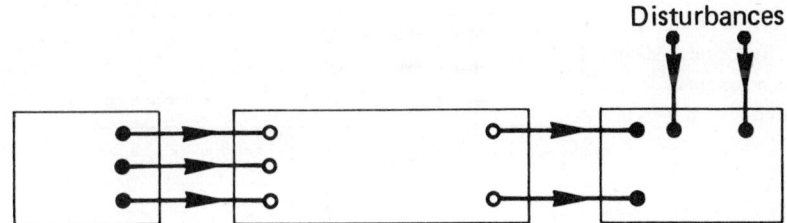

Rarely can a system be considered in isolation. Commonly, systems with different controlled environments have resource environments that overlap, partially or completely (Fig. 11.7). This is the case with *competitive systems*. The car and washing-machine industries compete for raw materials such as steel. The way by which such competition is reconciled characterizes the political state in which the industries operate. The ordering of priorities between systems implies that they are *sub-systems* of a higher-order system. Thus, a building designer must allocate the resources represented by the client's capital between the various building sub-systems, possibly according to some recognized ordering principle.

Two systems may also connect in that a secondary output from one acts as a

Fig. 11.7 Overlapping resource environments.

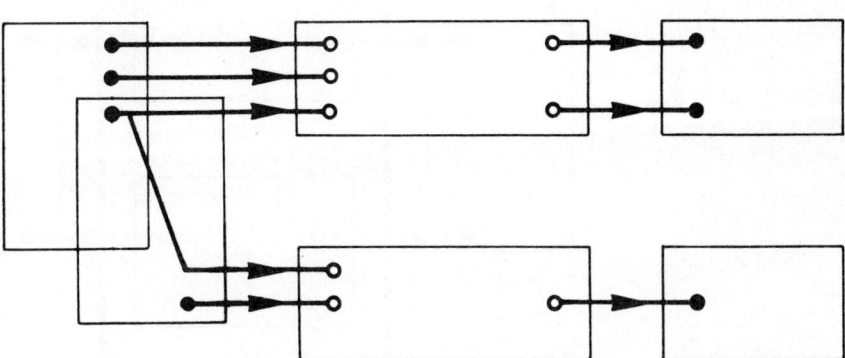

Fig. 11.8 A secondary output from one system acting as a disturbance to the other.

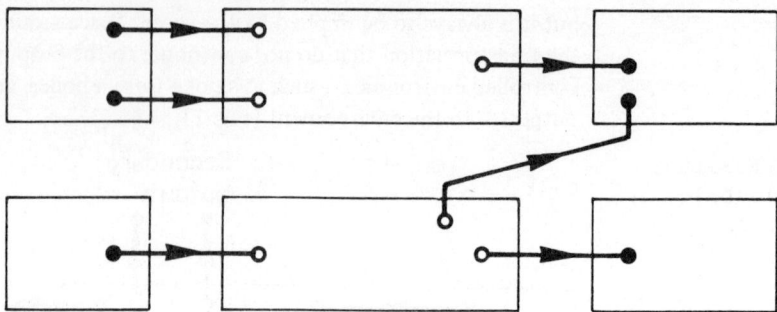

disturbance to the other (Fig. 11.8); or it may affect the resource environment of the other. This effect is usually adverse, in which case we would consider it as *pollution*; the affected system, to function properly, must then include *filtration* among its processes. It may be, however, that the waste products of one system are useful to the other; and geographical grouping of such *complementary systems* would be indicated (Fig. 11.9). The waste heat from electrical generation is now frequently used for space-heating.

Fig. 11.9 A secondary output from one system acting as a resource to the other.

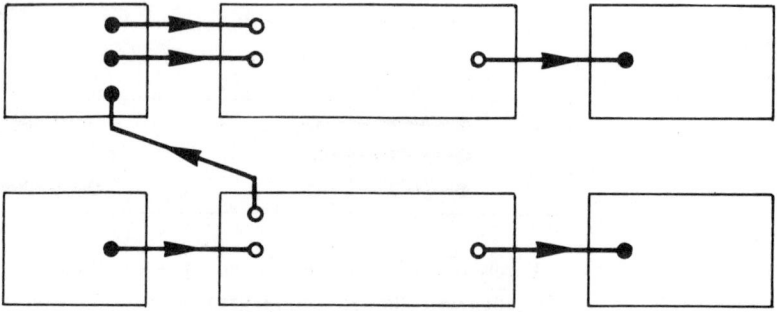

Where two systems have the same resource environment and also the same controlled environment either we have extreme competition (such as between two car manufacturers catering for identical markets) or we have *supplementary systems* in which one system is, apparently, redundant. In the latter case the two systems are properly considered as one (Fig. 11.10); redundancy (or standby) is a feature of any system that bears an appreciable cost of failure.

Fig. 11.10 Supplementary systems.

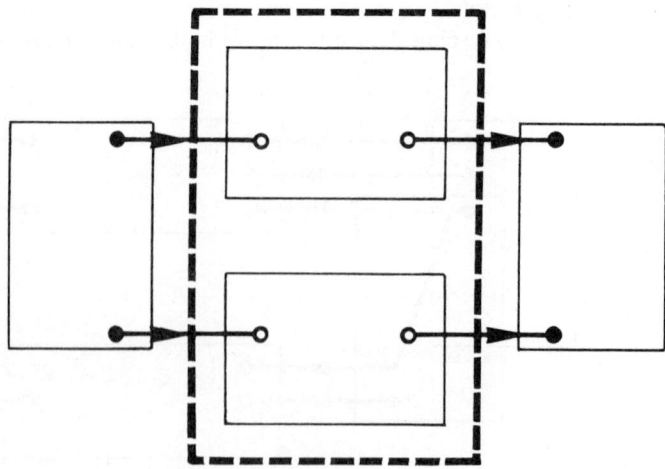

Flow systems are made up of *components* with linkages between them. Sub-systems may share components (Fig. 11.11).

Fig. 11.11 Sub-systems
with shared
components.

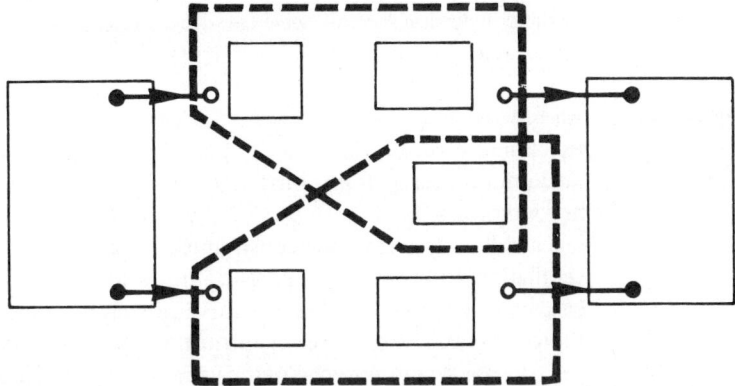

As we have seen, the controlled environment is likely to be subject to disturbances which result in variation in demand on the flow system. The system, therefore, needs to be continuously informed about the state of this environment so that there is appropriate regulation of output (Fig. 11.12). The means by which this information is generated and interpreted, and appropriate action is taken, comprise the *control* mechanism of the flow system. We see that this feedback from the controlled environment establishes a symmetrical relationship between it and the system (Fig. 11.13); the input and output of one being, respectively, the output and input of the other.

Fig. 11.12 Feedback of
information.

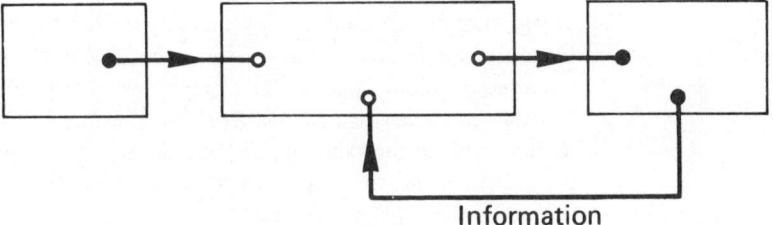

Information

Fig. 11.13 Symmetrical
relationship between
the system and the
controlled environment.

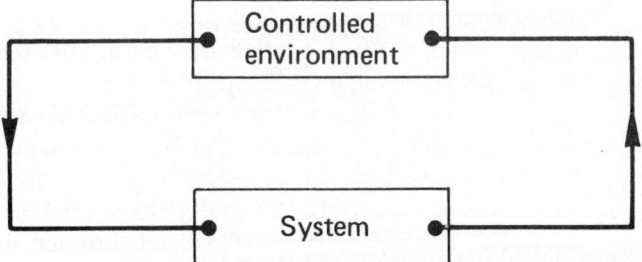

Controlled
environment

System

The function of a flow system has been described generally as the transformation of inputs to outputs. More precisely, three kinds of transformation may be involved: a transformation in space from a point of supply to a demand point; an energy transformation; a transformation in time between supply and demand levels. We will refer to these, respectively, as the distribution, conversion and storage functions of a system and identify components by these functions.

Sections 11.2, 11.3 and 11.4, therefore, are concerned with distribution, conversion and storage in flow systems, respectively. We then progress, in Sections 11.5 to 11.7, to deal with important aspects of systems as a whole and, in the concluding section, we extend our consideration of services into the three-dimensional problems of building design.

11.2 Distribution in systems

All flow systems contain at least one distribution component. This transport function substitutes for labour in the movement of matter (which may be a medium for energy or information); it permits the extension of organizations beyond the limits imposed by our physique. Consequently we can, and do, plan our buildings free from the constraints of providing natural lighting and ventilation, of keeping circulation routes within walking or climbing distances, of keeping our functional spaces small enough to be heated from a few point sources. We can inhabit basements or the tops of towers without physical (but perhaps not without psychological) strain. We will colonize hostile environments: the deserts, the poles, the sea, outer space. In each case we depend upon the movement into the environment of all the necessities of life, and the removal of its waste products. Flow systems operate over distance.

Flow is effected through *channels*; all channels exert a *resistance* to flow which is some function of channel size (cross-sectional area and length); the resistance of a channel may be constant (or nearly so) or it may vary.

We associate with a falling body two variable quantities that, in total at a given time, constitute the energy state of the body. One, the kinetic energy, is a function of its motion; the other, the potential energy, is a function of its position above some datum (usually ground). Similarly, associated with the movement of a fluid through a channel are two variables which measure the energy state of the fluid. At any time, θ, one has the same value at each end of the channel, and this we call the *through-variable, $T(\theta)$*; it is a rate of flow. The other has different values at the channel terminals, and the difference at time θ is known as the *across-variable, $A(\theta)$*, for the channel. In relation to some datum we may refer to the value of $A(\theta)$ at a point in the channel; the value will vary progressively along its length when there is flow. For example, with water flow through a pipe $T(\theta)$ is measured as the rate at which mass enters and leaves it (in kilogrammes per second). There is a difference in the water pressure at each end of a length of the pipe, and this is the across-variable (measured in newtons per square metre). The corresponding variables for an electrical conductor are electrical current, $I(\theta)$, and voltage difference, $V(\theta)$; for a thermal conductor they are heat flow and temperature difference.

For any channel there will be a relationship, empirically determined, between the through- and across-variables, and the channel resistance. For electrical flow the relationship is linear and is described by Ohm's Law, $V(\theta) = I(\theta)R$, where R is the constant value of the electrical resistance; and the isomorphism between this and the equation for thermal conduction permits the construction of electrical analogs for thermal systems described in Chapter 10. The isomorphism may be extended to other physical and mechanical systems [1].

Not all flow in channels can be described by such convenient linear equations. We are commonly concerned with the distribution of water or air, either as primary commodities or as secondary media for the distribution of thermal energy. Resistance to such fluid flow is made up of viscous and turbulent effects and varies (but not directly) with flow velocity. The general equation for fluid flow is

$$\Delta p = F(v^x/d^y)\rho L, \qquad\qquad (11.1)$$

where Δp = pressure difference, F = configuration factor, v = velocity, d = diameter of (circular) channel, ρ = density of fluid, L = length of channel, and x and y are constants. By substitution we find that the ratio $A(\theta)/T(\theta)$ is proportional to a power of v.

Typical distribution problems, therefore, involve for each channel three variables: channel resistance per unit length (usually measured as a cross-sectional area), through-flow rate, and across-difference.

Generally, the flow through the channel is a requirement on the system (e.g. current required at an electrical outlet, mass flow rate of water at a tap, volume flow rate of air in a duct); if the value of $A(\theta)$ is fixed outside the system (as with the voltage of grid-supplied electricity or with an available head of water) then the only unknown is the resistance of the channel. For systems (such as electrical systems) in which this resistance is constant, it is readily determined by formula; and for a given length of conductor the resistance is inversely proportional to cross-sectional area. Hence, a suitable gauge for the conductor is determined. The analogous problem in water supply is solved by resource to tables such as those in the *IHVE Guide*. $A(\theta)$ is the pressure drop in the pipe (measured in newtons per square metre per metre run of pipe); $T(\theta)$ is the mass flow rate (in kilogrammes per second) and the resistance is measured indirectly through the pipe diameter.

In ventilation systems and in heating or cooling systems that use water or air as a secondary medium, the across-difference is usually generated within the system − by pumps or fans. The problem in three variables now has two unknowns and permits a range of solutions limited only by availability of equipment.

Consider fan-generated ventilation of a room through a duct. For low-velocity systems we may reasonably take the through-flow as a volume flow rate (in cubic metres per second); $A(\theta)$ is again a pressure difference (in newtons per square metre); and again the cross-sectional area is a measure of resistance (although there is also a dependence on cross-sectional *shape*). As before, the required flow rate is a demand on the system, and this is commonly expressed in terms of a number of air changes per hour for the serviced space. If *Vol* is the volume of the room (in cubic metres) and n is the number of air changes per hour, the volume flow rate in the duct must be $(n \times Vol)/3600$ m^3 s^{-1}. The unknowns are the cross-sectional area of the duct, A (in square metres), and the velocity of the air in the duct, v (in metres per second). We have

$$Av = (n \times Vol)/3600 \qquad\qquad (11.2)$$

If there is some restriction on the system, the equation may become determinate. We frequently find that a limit is imposed on the size of ducts by openings in the structure or by some planning consideration. This limit will determine the least value of the velocity. There may be an upper limit to the velocity for acoustic reasons, which will determine a minimum duct area. If the velocity and duct area are determined, the system designer can proceed to select a fan that will raise the appropriate across-difference for the channel. Again, he may have recourse to tables or a nomogram such as Fig. C4.3 in the *IHVE Guide*, simplified here as our Fig. 11.14. From this the reader should confirm that for a round

Fig. 11.14 Air flow in round ducts (after Fig. C4.3 in *IHVE Guide* [2]).

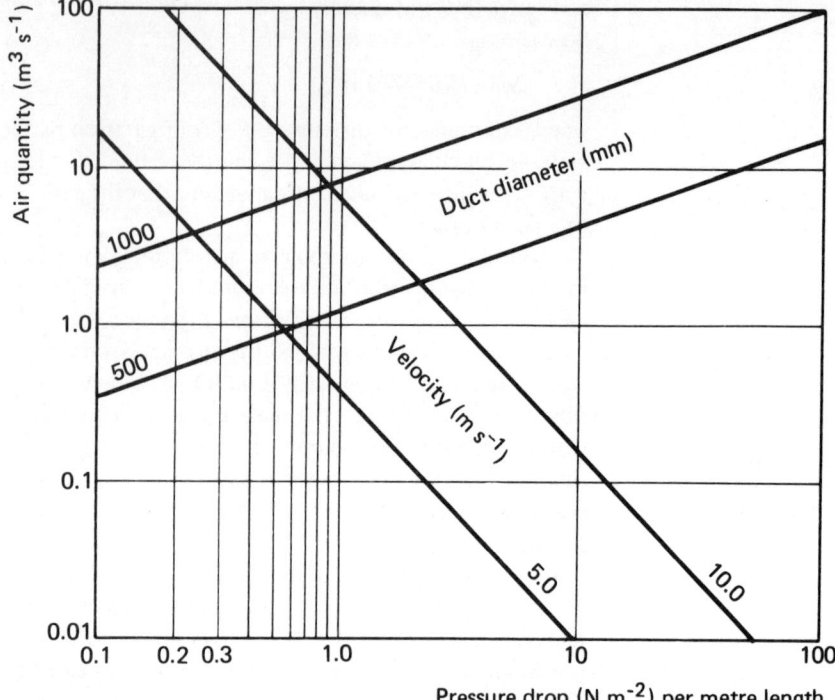

duct 500 mm in diameter and in a straight length of one metre, a velocity of 5.0 m s^{-1} requires a pressure difference at the duct terminals of 0.55 N m^{-2}.

The *power* of a fluid in flow is defined as the product of its through- and across-variables ($p(\theta) = T(\theta)A(\theta)$) and is measured in watts. Hence, the *air power* (which is expended in overcoming energy losses in the duct) is the product: (volume rate in cubic metres per second) (pressure drop in newtons per square metre). The units are therefore newton-metres per second, joules per second or,

Fig. 11.15 Equivalent resistance of fittings in equal metres (after Stokes [3]).

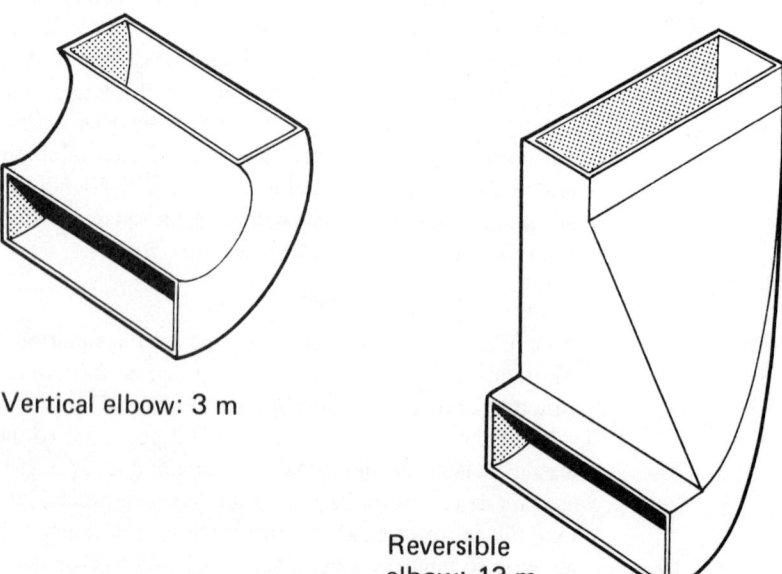

Vertical elbow: 3 m

Reversible elbow: 13 m

as we would expect, watts. For our 1 m duct, the volume flow rate is about 1.0 m^3 s^{-1}; so the air power is 0.55 W. This is the power the fan must deliver; a suitable fan may be selected from manufacturers' catalogues.

The resistance of an electrical conductor depends on its length, but not on a particular route through a building. For flow in pipes and ducts, however, every bend, junction, grille and transition from one shape to another increases resistance, and appropriate allowance must be made in the calculation. One method is to express the resistance of such fittings as the equivalent resistance of a length of straight duct, determined empirically, and to use in calculations the overall *effective length* of the duct. Fig. 11.15 illustrates some equivalent resistances for a warm-air heating system; more sophisticated approaches to problems of configuration are dealt with in the standard textbooks on ventilation engineering.

So far we have been limited to a single channel between a point of supply (or *source*) and a point of demand (or *sink*). If we are to consider combinations of channels, or *networks*, between multiple sources and sinks, we need systems laws that govern the distribution of through- and across-variables in a network. These laws are, respectively, the laws of *continuity* and *compatibility*.

At its simplest, the law of continuity states that the flow into a node equals the total flow from it. Hence, for Fig. 11.16, we have:

$$i_1 = i_2 + i_5,$$
$$i_2 + i_4 = i_3,$$
$$i_5 + i_6 = i_4 + i_7.$$

At its most general the law tells us that if we draw a boundary around part or all of a system then the total sum of $T(\theta)$ entering the boundary equals the total sum of $T(\theta)$ leaving it. If this continuity is not observed then the boundary contains one or more sources or sinks. So, for the boundary indicated, we have:

$$i_1 + i_6 = i_3 + i_7$$

which may also be deduced from the previous set of equations.

The law of compatibility concerns circuits in a network, such as that comprising channels AC, CB, BA. Provided that a circuit is traversed in a consistent

Fig. 11.16.

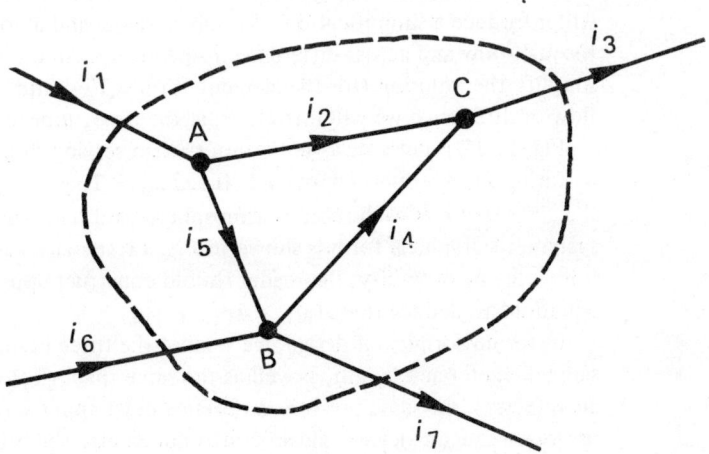

direction then the total sum of across-variable differences within the circuit is zero. Hence for our network:

$$A(\theta)_{AC} + A(\theta)_{CB} + A(\theta)_{BA} = 0, \text{ where } A(\theta)_{AC} = -A(\theta)_{CA}.$$

In appropriate contexts the continuity law is a statement of the conservation of charge (Kirchhoff's Current Law); the conservation of momentum; the conservation of matter; and the conservation of energy. Kirchhoff's voltage law is merely a special case of the law of compatibility.

We now introduce a graphical representation in which

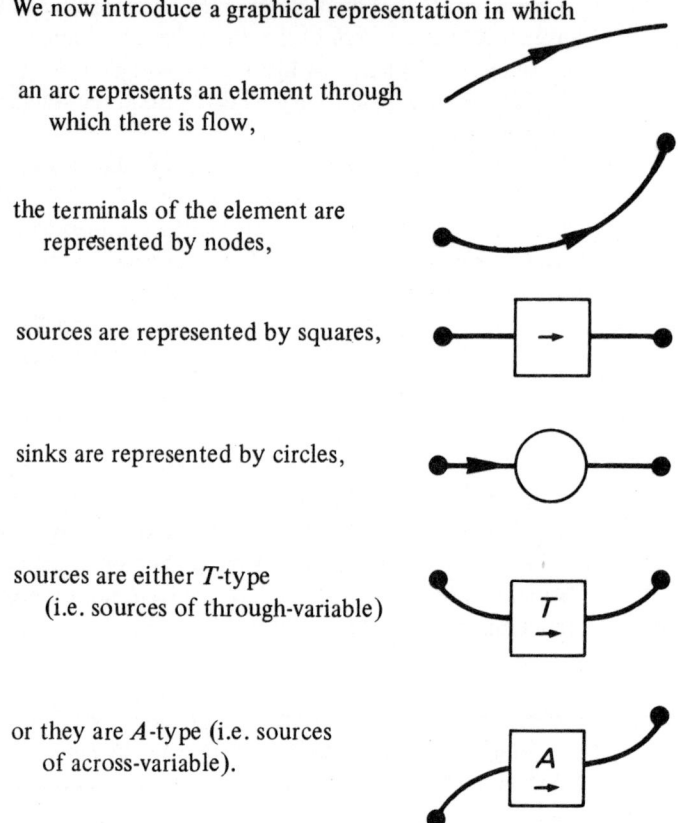

an arc represents an element through
   which there is flow,

the terminals of the element are
   represented by nodes,

sources are represented by squares,

sinks are represented by circles,

sources are either T-type
   (i.e. sources of through-variable)

or they are A-type (i.e. sources
   of across-variable).

Since for what immediately follows we will assume steady-state conditions, we will introduce a simplification: through-variable and across-variable as *constant* through-flow and across-difference, respectively. And we will, correspondingly, simplify the notation (for the element XY) to T_{XY} and A_{XY}. To particularize a flow or difference we will introduce, at the time, appropriate symbols.

Fig. 11.17 represents a ventilation system serving three identical rooms, each requiring air at a rate of $V \, \text{m}^3 \, \text{s}^{-1}$; (i.e. $T_{BB'} = T_{CC'} = T_{DD'} = V$). If we assume the air pressure in each room is atmospheric and take this as ground (G) for the system, its graphical form is shown in Fig. 11.18. The values of through-flows follow from continuity; the reader should construct appropriate across-difference equations to deduce that $A_{BG} > A_{CG} > A_{DG}$.

If, for uniformity of design, we require the three branch ducts to have the same diameter and length, as well as the same through-flow (and, hence, the same air velocity), the same pressure-difference must apply across their lengths. Hence pressure-reducing devices must be introduced into the branches; pressure-

Fig. 11.17 Representation of a ventilation system serving three identical rooms.

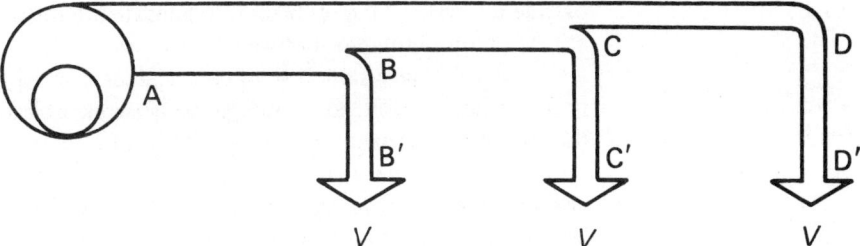

Fig. 11.18 Graphical representation of the system shown in Fig. 11.17.

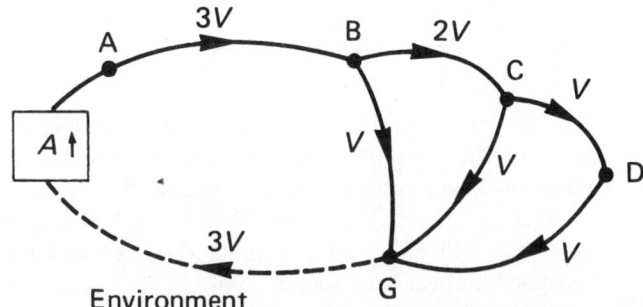

reduction would normally be effected by dampers at B, C and D or at the outlet grilles to the rooms. Their adjustment to achieve uniformity of across-difference for the three ducts would be part of the tuning process required in the commissioning of any complex ventilation or air-conditioning system. Fig. 11.19 is a revised graph for the system, with pressure adjustment at the outlet grilles (B'B'', C'C'', D'D'') so that $A_{BB'} = A_{CC'} = A_{DD'}$. Since $A_{B''G} = A_{C''G} = A_{D''G} = 0$ the graph could be simplified by identifying B'', C'' and D'' with G.

Fig. 11.19 A revised graphical representation of the system shown in Fig. 11.17.

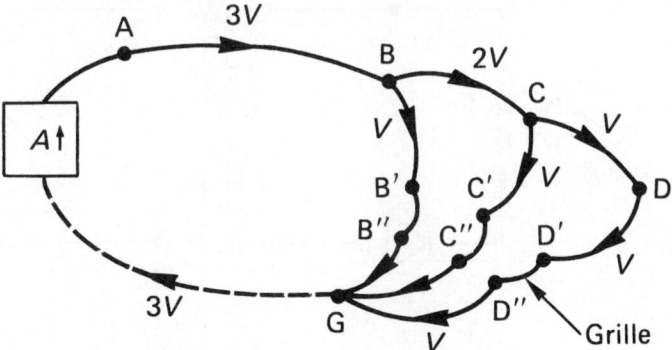

Each route through the system begins at the pressure level of A and ends at atmospheric pressure, but this overall pressure drop will be determined by the necessary pressure-difference for a particular route (which given the conditions in our case will be the route ABCDG). This route is called the index run; its total resistance to the required flows will determine the fan size for the system.

This system is one that supplies a single material commodity, namely air. Essentially the same principles apply to the sizing of pipes for hot or cold water supply, though here the overall pressure-difference (head) is often established outside the system; the problem is to allocate intermediate pressure levels to achieve an optimum pipe network.

In a ventilation system it is, of course, duct-sizing that is of particular interest to the architect. Flow rates through the network are established by continuity; it is usually sufficient for his purpose to ascribe approximate velocities to the various channels and thereby deduce cross-sectional areas. Velocities are increased towards the source since this is the direction of increased volume flow. Duct velocities are gauged against the general noise level of their environment. In an office building, for example, suitable values for a low-velocity system are:

through ceiling grilles,	$1.5 - 3 \text{ m s}^{-1}$;
through branches to grilles,	$2 - 4 \text{ m s}^{-1}$;
through main horizontal branches,	$5 - 7 \text{ m s}^{-1}$;
through main vertical ducts,	$6 - 10 \text{ m s}^{-1}$.

Apart from their life-supporting functions, air and water find common use as media for the distribution of thermal energy. Consider now the heating needs of a suite of three rooms, B, C and D; suppose that calculations of heat loss by conduction and ventilation show that the heat to be supplied in each case, from a common source, A, is at a rate of Q watts. A *material* network is used to transport this heat from source. Typically it comprises pipe- or duct-work connecting heat exchangers in a circuit. At one exchanger, connected to the source, heat is transferred to the medium; at the others it is discharged to the controlled environments. The medium is then recycled to the heat source where its initial energy content is restored.

There are basically two ways in which these exchangers may be connected: in series and in parallel (Figs. 11.20 and 11.21).

We will assume that the system to be used is a conventional pumped hot-water system, in which the dissipating heat exchangers are 'radiators' which, of course,

Fig. 11.20 Exchangers in series.

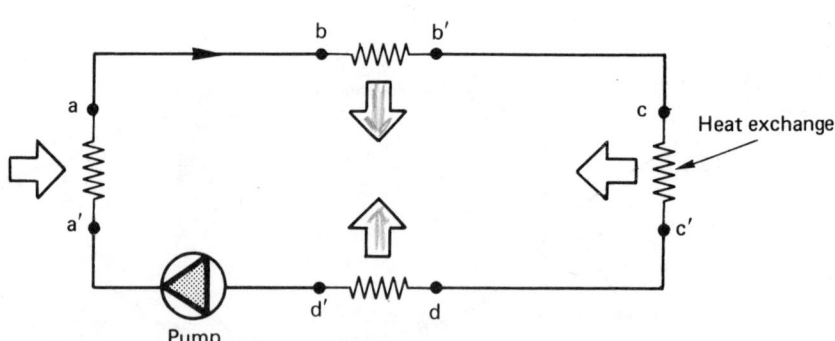

Fig. 11.21 Exchangers in parallel.

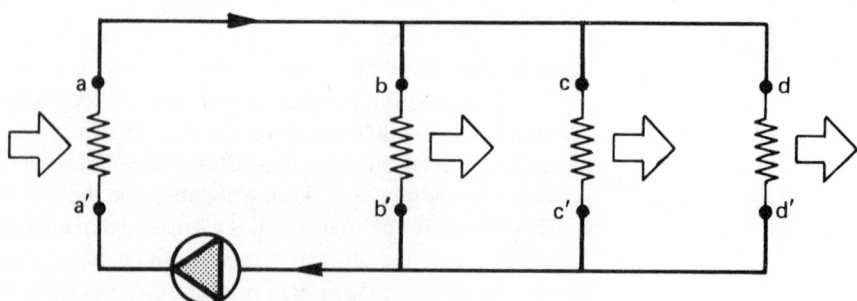

give up their heat by both convection and radiation. The heat flow into a room depends upon the differences between the surface temperature of the radiator and the temperatures of its surroundings.

In terms of the previous discussion the energy source is T-type (through-flow is heat); across-differences are temperature-differences. Assuming that there are no thermal losses in the distribution between the heat exchangers we have as

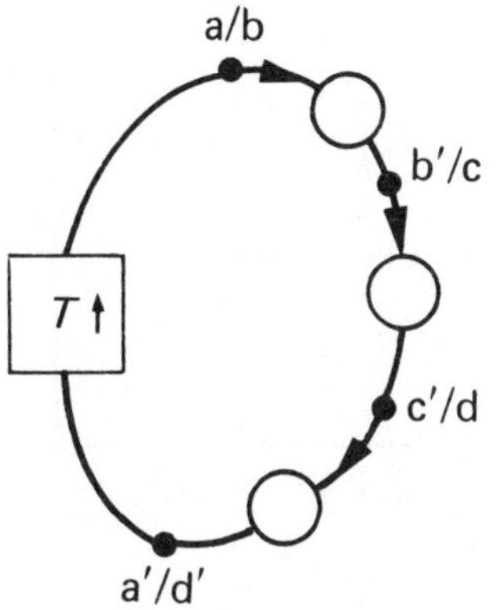

Fig. 11.22 Graphical representation of system shown in Fig. 11.20.

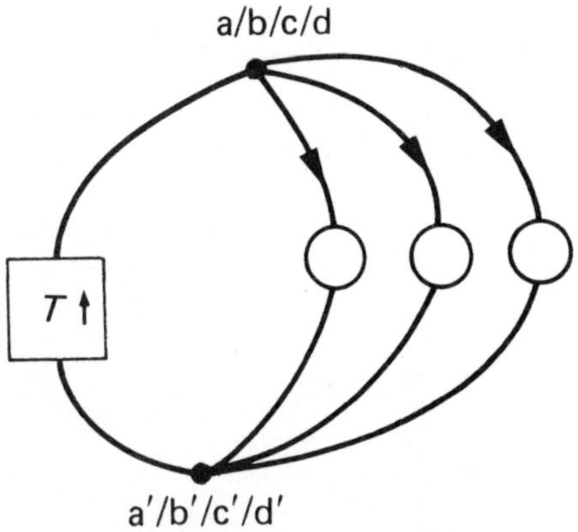

Fig. 11.23 Graphical representation of system shown in Fig. 11.21.

Figs. 11.22 and 11.23 the respective thermal graphs for the two systems.

Notice that the radiators are represented as heat sinks; connecting pipework would be shown similarly if heat losses in it were taken into account. The reader should construct the temperature-difference equations for each network; from these he or she will see that in series-connection the temperatures across the radiators decrease progressively; heat output from similar radiators, series-connected, will decrease through the circuit. In parallel-connection the input temperatures to all radiators can be similarly high; so this must be preferred. The reader should construct the thermal graph for the parallel-connected system that takes into account (as sinks) heat losses in connecting pipework, and should again deduce all the temperature-difference equations.

Although we have one system (Fig. 11.24), we can conceptualize it as two superimposed networks, a thermal energy network and a fluid network (Fig. 11.25). In the former, as we have seen, through-flow and across-difference are, respectively, heat flow and temperature-difference; the source is T-type. In the latter through-flow is fluid-flow; across-difference is pressure-difference, and the source is A-type — a pump.

The fluid-flow rate (q) through a radiator, and the rate of heat emitted by it

Fig. 11.24 A heating system.

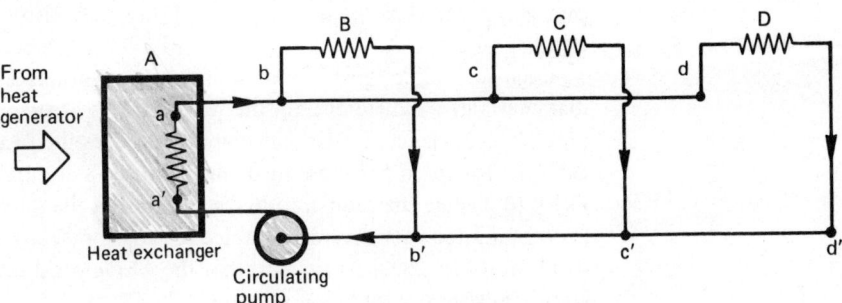

Fig. 11.25 Conceptualization of the system shown in Fig. 11.24 as two superimposed networks.

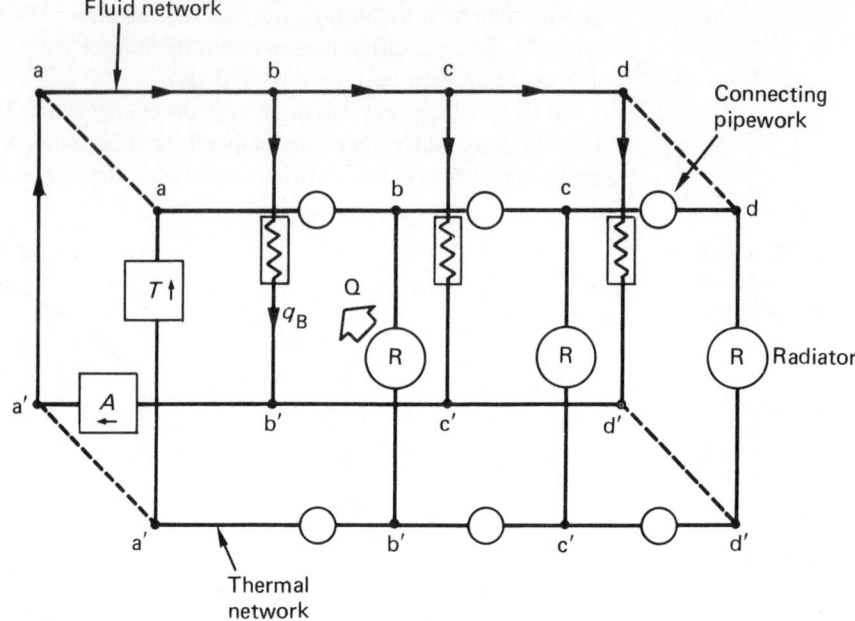

(*Q*) are related through the thermal capacity of the fluid. For if the temperature drop across the radiator at B is $t_{bb'}$, and the rate at which water flows through the unit is q_B kg s^{-1}, then in one second the heat lost at the radiator is $q_B s t_{bb'}$, where s is the specific heat of water. This must be the heat emitted by the radiator in one second $-Q$ W. Hence,

$$Q = q_B s t_{bb'}. \tag{11.3}$$

This is the basic relationship that links the two networks: the heat emitted at each segment (radiator or connecting pipework) is proportional to the product of fluid flow through the segment and the temperature-difference across it. Since both factors of the product are to be determined, the design process is iterative.

Radiators suitable to provide heat at the required rate (*Q*) are selected from manufacturers' catalogues, which also specify the operating mean surface temperatures for the components. From these values is made an appropriate initial distribution of temperatures around the network, taking into account assumed heat losses from connecting pipework. For the assumed temperature-difference across the terminals of a radiator, there is a corresponding fluid flow through it, determined by equation (11.3). Hence, all flows for the fluid network may be established, using continuity. For these flow rates a choice of pipe diameters and a pump is made using principles already described; note that since pipe and pump sizes are interdependent they may also be determined by an iterative procedure.

Engineers' tables give heat losses from pipework as a function of pipe diameter and the difference in the temperatures of the environment and of the pipe surface. Hence, for the calculated pipe sizes the heat losses from pipework can be substituted for those made in the initial assumption. It is because this is likely to change the temperature distribution in the network, and because there is no guarantee that the initial choice of radiator (from which all else follows) will lead to the cheapest system, that the whole process is iterative; it is, of course, best performed by computer.

Fig. 11.26 A combined heating and ventilation system.

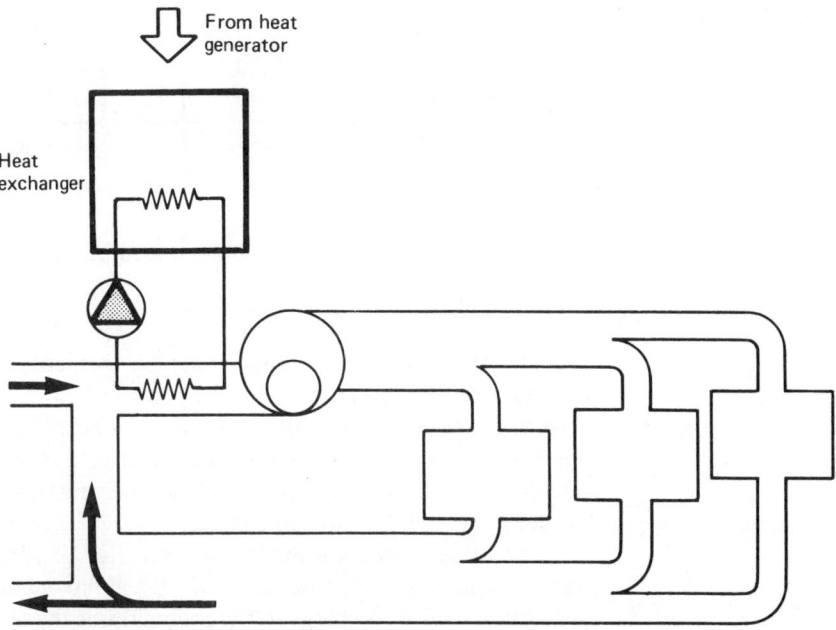

The design of other secondary-media systems is conducted analogously.

We have considered, separately, a ventilation system and a heating system for a suite of three rooms; it is an obvious development to combine the ventilation and heating in one system (Fig. 11.26). This system should be compared with that represented by Fig. 11.24. The heat exchanger and pump of the latter now correspond, respectively, to a heat exchanger (which usually involves an intermediate medium such as water to transfer heat to the air) and fan. The heat transfer that occurred at a radiator now takes place in the room itself through the intimate contact of surfaces and circulating air. There may be heat sources as well as heat sinks in the rooms. To conserve energy the air is recycled; but the ventilation needs are met by rejecting a proportion of the returned air to the environment. Generally duct-sizing is based upon the ventilation needs and proceeds as previously described; the air temperatures at grilles will be calculated to produce comfortable levels after discharge and mixing within the rooms. It may be, of course, that the calculated rate of heat loss from the rooms exceeds the possible rate of heat supply by air, with its low thermal capacity, at these temperatures and ventilation rates. Rather than compensate for heat losses by increasing the heated-air supply rate (which may, in any case, lead to disturbing air-flow effects in the rooms) it would be better, from the point of energy conservation, to reduce losses by fabric or other design changes; and, similarly, cooling should not be used to compensate for avoidable heat gains.

Analogs of the systems represented in Figs. 11.24 and 11.26 may be used for space-cooling. Heat is *withdrawn* at each exchanger and ultimately rejected to the environment through the cooling plant. In the analog to Fig. 11.24 the transfer of cooling to the controlled environment is effected by fan-blowing room air and fresh air over cooling coils (Fig. 11.27). This is called, for obvious reasons, a fan–coil system.

Limited cooling of the controlled environment may be achieved without recourse to mechanical heat transfer if the external air temperature is below

Fig. 11.27 A fan–coil system.

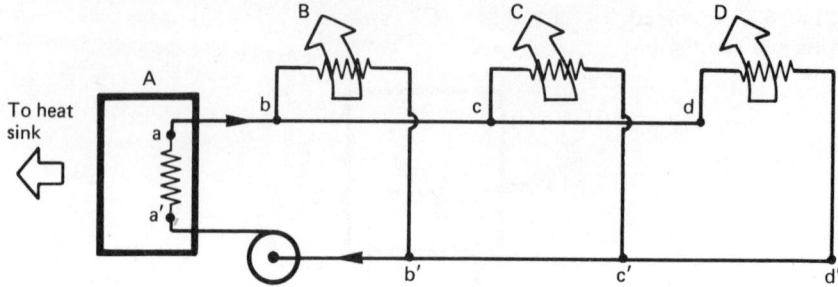

room temperature, simply by increasing the ventilation rate. This would be effected by opening dampers at the air inlet.

A single air-ducted system may be used for heating, cooling and ventilation, but its operation will depend upon a sophisticated control mechanism which monitors conditions in the controlled environment. Control systems are the subject of Section 11.7 of this chapter.

Clearly, any specified room temperature may be achieved by distributing warm air and cool air in separate channels and mixing them in appropriate proportions before discharge to the room. This is the principle of the dual-duct system which, though expensive, is the best way to meet a requirement for a variety of environmental conditions within a building.

If to the system which combines heating, cooling and ventilation we add filtration and the facility to vary the humidity of the distributed air, we have a full air-conditioning system. Mechanisms for humidity control, together with those for raising heat and for cooling are discussed in the following section.

11.3 Conversion in systems

Rarely is the energy in the resource environment available in the form in which it will be used in buildings; an exception of increasing interest is solar energy, and its use as a source is the subject of Chapter 13. Energy may also be available in a directly usable form if one system is complementary to another; this will be amplified in Section 11.5. Our primary sources of energy are the chemical energy of fossil fuels, from which heat is generated by combustion, and the thermal energy liberated in nuclear-fission processes. Since buildings do not normally, as yet, incorporate their own nuclear reactors, our interest in these is restricted here to their place in the centralized generation of electricity.

The conventional generation of electricity necessitates first the raising of heat, then the conversion of this thermal to mechanical energy by some form of heat engine or prime mover, and, finally, the transfer of this motion to an electrical conductor located in a magnetic field. Since all three processes are pertinent to the present study, they will be discussed in some detail.

Fundamental to all energy conversion processes are the laws of thermo-dynamics, of which the first states that energy is conserved – it may be converted but not destroyed – and the second that the energy available for use is continuously being diminished. This is not the only form in which the second law is expressed; another, of importance in considerations of heat transfer, is that heat will not flow contrary to a temperature gradient without expenditure of work.

A designer, seeking to make the best use of his resources, must be concerned with the *performance* of his system; performance may be loosely defined as the ratio of the usefulness of the system outputs to the cost of the system inputs. Unless usefulness and cost can be expressed in common units the ratio is without meaning; in choosing between systems, however, it is often adequate to assume that they are of equal effect and to select the system of least total cost. Where systems are of significantly different effect a cost-benefit analysis may be the best basis for design decision. For a more sophisticated discussion of the evaluation of systems the reader is referred to Chapter 12.

Fortunately for the present discussion, for components of energy conversion the ratio is expressible in common units of energy: the useful amount of energy output by the component to the corresponding amount of energy input to the component. This performance of the component is usually referred to as its *efficiency* and is measured as a percentage. It is a consequence of the second law that this efficiency is always less than 100 per cent. It is important to note that nothing in this definition implies that the efficiency of a component is constant.

It remains to be stated that energy is useful when it could be the means for work, specifically to raise a mass against gravity. From the second expression of the second law it follows that a quantity of heat at a high temperature is more useful than the same quantity of heat at a lower temperature; by extension we can think of the level of energy in any form according to its potential for work. The alternative expression of the second law refers to the diminishing of the work potential of the energy of the universe.

Still of principle interest to us as a high-level resource is chemical energy. Chemical reactions comprise changes in molecular configuration; when the total internal energy of the molecules is thereby reduced, heat is given out. This process is said to be exothermic. Chemical processes that absorb energy are termed endothermic. The endothermic reaction of supreme significance to all life forms is the formation of carbohydrates from water and atmospheric carbon dioxide by plants, in which the energy absorbed is solar. Ultimately carbo-hydrates were the source of our hydrocarbon fossil fuels: coal, oil and gas. The oxidation of carbohydrates and hydrocarbons to form carbon dioxide and water are exothermic reactions which complete the carbon cycle. This oxidation is most frequently by combustion in air.

The main convenience of a fossil fuel as an energy source is that it is easily transported and stored. The conversion to thermal energy may be achieved where and when it is required; it may be localized. However, in this chapter we are not concerned with the coal fire, the paraffin stove or bottled gas. It is assumed that there will be some centralization of combustion and a distribution of the energy raised to various demand points on principles already discussed; we will, however, be returning to discussion of localization and centralization in other sections of this chapter. For the moment it should be noted that localization does not contradict the earlier statement that all flow systems include distribution, since this function has now been shifted to the transport network.

For non-localized space-heating systems the heat raised in the combustion of fossil fuels is transferred to a distribution medium, generally air, water or steam. The transfer takes place in a heat exchanger — a boiler, if the medium is water or steam. It is not part of the purpose of this chapter to discuss the design of system components; we are, however, very much concerned with their operating efficiencies. For consistency with subsequent discussion, Fig. 11.28 is redrawn from its source; it shows performance curves for typical boilers.

Notice here that performance is represented as a *percentage of the maximum*

Fig. 11.28 Typical part-load performance of space-heating boilers (after Robertson *et al.* [4]).

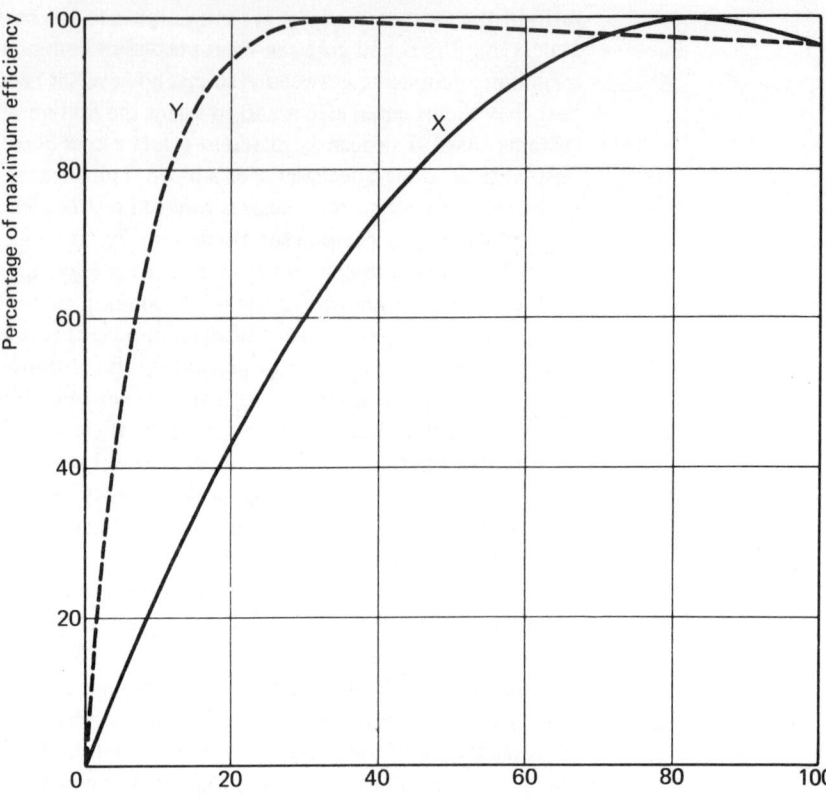

efficiency of the boiler, and this is expressed as a function of the output of the boiler as a percentage of its maximum load-capacity. Curve X gives the performance of a sectional cast-iron boiler and shows a marked decline from maximum efficiency with loads below 80 per cent. For example, at 40 per cent load the boiler operates at only 75 per cent of its maximum efficiency. Curve Y illustrates modern improvements in boiler design in this respect, and is for a packaged shell boiler. Maximum efficiency is reached at as low as 30 per cent of the maximum load and is more or less constant at higher loads. Clearly, and as we will later elaborate, the shapes of efficiency curves are of prime importance in choosing conversion equipment to meet demand profiles. For the moment we will simply note that, in general, efficiencies of conversion components vary with load, and that at low loads these efficiencies are also low.

The conversion of thermal energy to mechanical energy utilizes the expansion of gases in a heat engine. Consider a cylinder of cross-sectional area A in which a gas is enclosed by a frictionless piston (Fig. 11.29). Let the pressure (i.e. force per unit area) of the gas on the piston be P. If we supply heat to the gas we increase its internal energy; if the pressure remains constant the gas must expand. The force on the piston throughout the expansion then remains at PA; the distance moved by the piston is x, so the work done on the piston is $PAx = P\Delta Vol$, where ΔVol is the increase in volume of the gas. Generalizing (and noting that practical heat engines do not operate at constant pressure), the work done by a gas during a process of expansion or contraction is given by

Fig. 11.29 A heat engine.

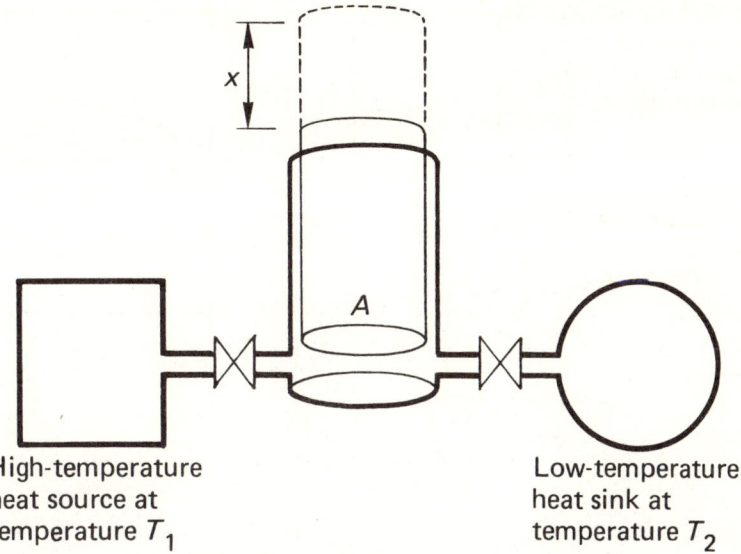

High-temperature heat source at temperature T_1

Low-temperature heat sink at temperature T_2

$\int P\,\mathrm{d}\,Vol.$ To complete the cycle, that is to bring the piston back to its original position and thereby prepare the engine for more work, heat must be extracted from the gas and discharged to a heat sink. If the work done, the heat input, and the heat rejected to the sink per cycle are, respectively, Wk, Q_1 and Q_2, then, by the first law of thermodynamics $Wk = Q_1 - Q_2$; and the efficiency of the engine, η, is given by

$$\eta = Wk/Q_1 = (Q_1 - Q_2)/Q_1. \tag{11.4}$$

It follows from the second law that the heat source must be at a higher temperature than the heat sink. If the temperatures of the source and sink are, respectively, T_1 and T_2, it can be shown that

$$\eta = (T_1 - T_2)/T_1. \tag{11.5}$$

What we have described is a very simple, and in the thermodynamic sense an ideal, closed-cycle reciprocating heat engine, in which the motion of the piston is to-and-fro in a straight line. By a system of cranks it may be converted into rotary motion.

From equation (11.5) it can be seen that even for an ideal engine the efficiency may never be 100 per cent. If T_2 is taken to be constant, we can show efficiency as a function of source temperature, as in Fig. 11.30.

We see that for a sink temperature of 15 °C and a source temperature of 600 °C (which are typical temperatures in conventional electricity generation systems), the maximum possible efficiency is about 60 per cent; but most power stations operate at a figure nearer 30 per cent. Consequently, the reconversion of the electrical energy thereby generated to thermal energy for space-heating would appear to be an extravagant use of fossil-fuel resources, which is, or should be, a matter for political concern.

If we reverse the heat engine, that is if we apply work to it, we may achieve a flow of heat from a source at a temperature T_2 to a sink at a *higher* temperature T_1 (Fig. 11.31).

Fig. 11.30 Efficiency of an ideal heat engine as a function of source temperature, with the sink temperature constant at 15 °C.
The graph is diagramatic and must not be used for calculations.

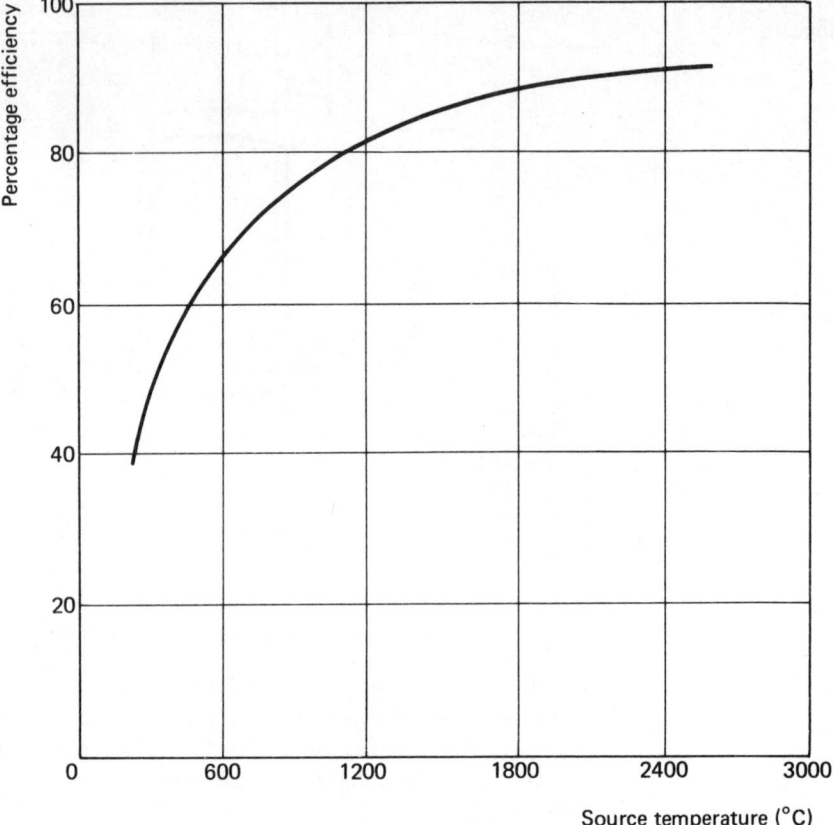

Fig. 11.31 A reversed heat engine.

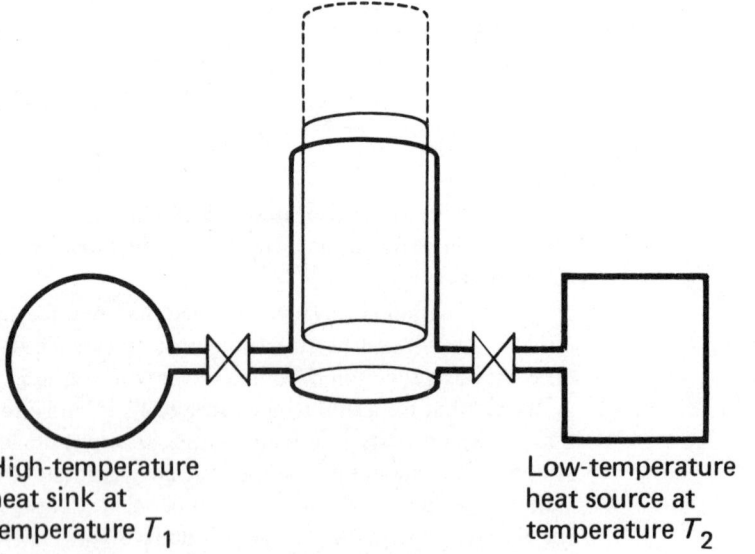

High-temperature heat sink at temperature T_1

Low-temperature heat source at temperature T_2

In practice, this flow is usually effected using a medium that readily changes state over the range of pressures applied throughout the cycle, thereby utilizing the more effective latent heat transfers of evaporation and condensation. Fig. 11.32 represents such a vapour-compression machine.

Fig. 11.32 A refrigerator or a heat pump.

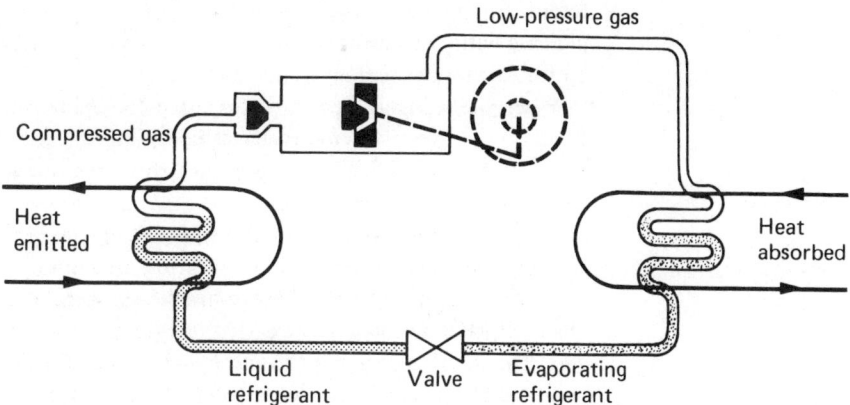

When it is used to achieve cooling of the source the machine is termed a *refrigerator*; when it is used to provide heat at a sink it is called a *heat pump*. The difference is one of function, not of thermodynamic principle. But there is a difference in the measure of performance, as reference to our earlier definition will show. If, per cycle, Q_2 is the quantity of heat absorbed from the source at temperature T_2, Q_1 the quantity of heat transferred to the sink at temperature T_1, and Wk the work done on the machine, then for the refrigerator and the heat pump the *coefficients of performance* are, respectively, Q_2/Wk and Q_1/Wk. Between Figs. 11.31 and 11.32 we have moved from an ideal and reversible heat pump to a practical and irreversible machine. For the former, the coefficient of performance is the reciprocal of its efficiency when acting as a heat engine, that is $1/\eta$ or $T_1/(T_1 - T_2)$. For the corresponding reversible refrigerator, the coefficient of performance is given by $T_2/(T_1 - T_2)$ or $(1/\eta) - 1$. Whereas the efficiency of a heat engine increases with the difference between source and sink

Fig. 11.33 The three components of a cooling system.

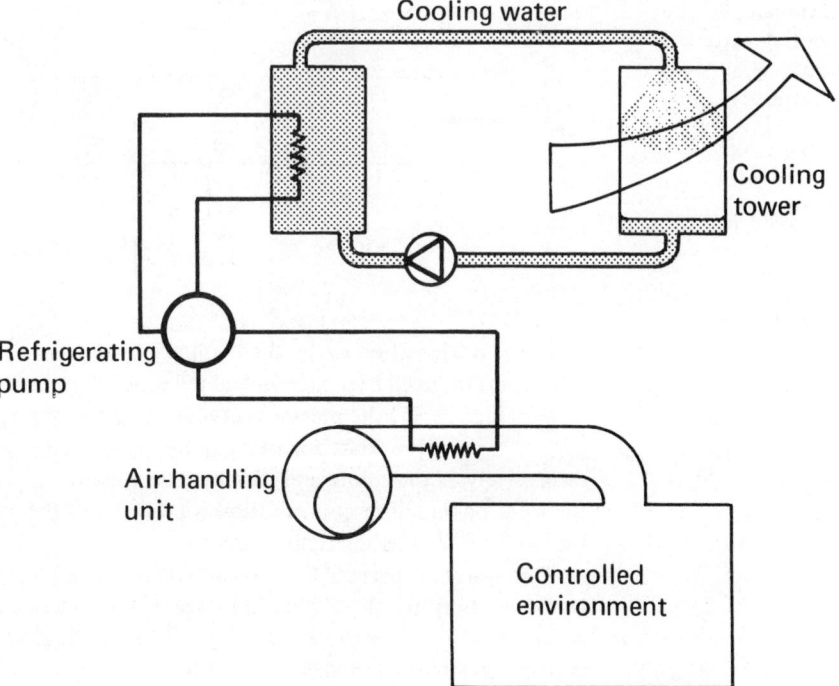

temperatures, the coefficients of performance of a heat pump and a refrigerator increase with decreasing temperature difference. The reader is referred to Chapter 13 for further discussion on this matter.

When the refrigerator is used for space-cooling we may identify in the system three types of component, as suggested by Fig. 11.33. Central to the process is a *pump*, usually electrically operated, which on the one hand compresses and condenses the refrigerant, and on the other decompresses and evaporates it, respectively giving up heat, usually to the atmosphere through a *cooling tower,* and absorbing heat from some distribution medium by which the cooling is transferred to the controlled environment. At some stage in this distribution there will be a mechanically assisted transfer of cooling to air at an *air-handling unit*. The figure represents this mechanical transfer of heat through and from a building; but it must be borne in mind for later discussion that nothing in this description limits the numbers of each type of component comprising the cooling system.

The facility to cool an air stream also offers the opportunity of controlling its humidity. As moist air is cooled its relative humidity increases until it is 100 per cent at and below its dew point. The technique is therefore to cool the air stream to a specified temperature, t_1, and then to saturate it by spraying it with water at the same temperature. It is then heated to the temperature, t_2, required in the controlled environment. As the temperature rises to this value the relative humidity will fall to its required level, RH. The relationship between t_1, t_2, and RH, is embodied in the psychometric chart, as shown in Appendix 3B. From this a suitable value for t_1 is selected. Fig. 11.34 represents such a rudimentary *air-conditioning plant*.

Fig. 11.34 A simple air-conditioning unit.
1, Dampers; 2, filter; 3, cooling battery; 4, water spray; 5, heating battery; 6, fan.

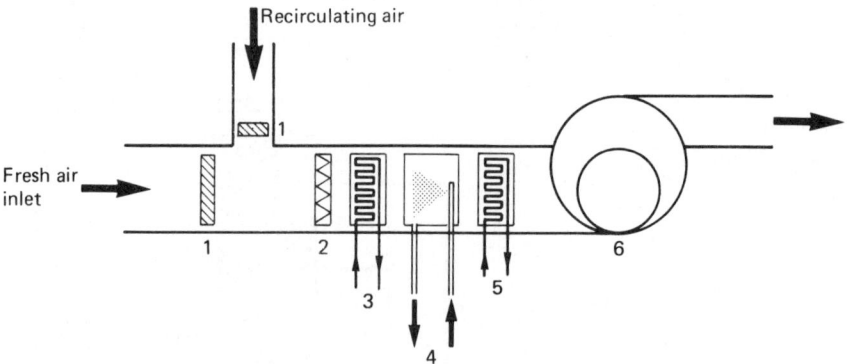

In the refrigeration cycle, the cooling is a result of the evaporation of the refrigerant induced by a mechanical reduction in pressure. In the *absorption chiller* (Fig. 11.35) the pressure is reduced by the absorption of refrigerant vapour in an appropriate solvent; commonly ammonia and water are used respectively as the solute and solvent. The volatile solute is then distilled from the solution and after condensation is returned to the evaporator, through which the medium for cooling is circulated.

This system is particularly appropriate as a complement to another which has heat (necessary for the distillation stage of the process) as a secondary output given, of course, that there is also a need for cooling. Such complementary systems are considered in Section 11.5.

Fig. 11.35 Absorption chiller.

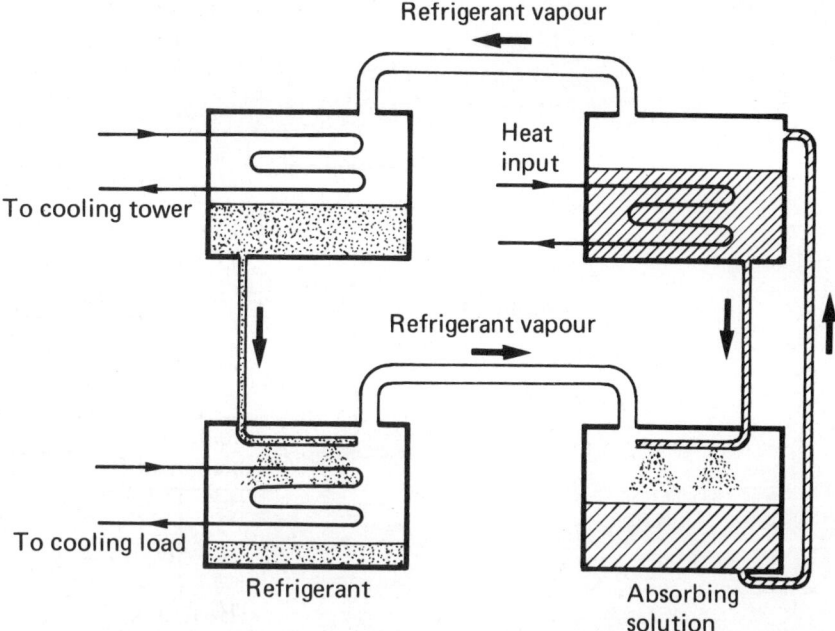

When an electrical conductor is moved to cut across a magnetic field, an electromotive force is induced across its terminals; current will flow through a circuit connected across these terminals. Most electricity-generating authorities produce alternating current from an *alternator* in which it is the magnetic field that is rotated within the heavy conductor windings. The rotary motion is generally derived from some form of heat engine.

Apart from the small-scale and standby use of diesel and petrol engines, the heat engines now used in electricity generation are non-reciprocating.

In a *turbine* the kinetic energy of fluid flow is converted directly into rotary motion, through impact on blades attached to a shaft, or rotor. The traditional water wheel is a primitive impulse turbine. In more sophisticated machines, the flow is directed through a cylinder containing alternating sets of fins fixed to the casing and fins attached to the movable rotor, all profiled to achieve maximum conversion of the available kinetic energy into rotary motion. Hydroelectric power, generated through water-turbines, is a valuable resource for mountainous countries which permit the catchment of rainwater and its storage at levels of high potential energy. In recent energy-conscious times we have seen the principle extended to the relatively small potential differences of tidal levels. Globally, however, hydroelectric generation satisfies only a small proportion of the demand for electrical power; the greater part of the world's electrical energy is produced from thermal plant.

Like the water-turbine, steam- and gas-turbines are operated by fluid flow; but the kinetic energy is a consequence of the expansion of vapour or gas following transfer of heat from a source.

In the *closed-cycle gas-turbine* the fluid remains in a gaseous state throughout the process (Fig. 11.36). Under pressure at 1 it is fed into heat exchanger A to which energy is supplied from an external combustion chamber (the products of combustion at a high temperature enter the exchanger and pass through its tubes to exhaust). The high-pressure, high-temperature gas (at 2) is then fed into the

Fig. 11.36 Closed-cycle gas-turbine.

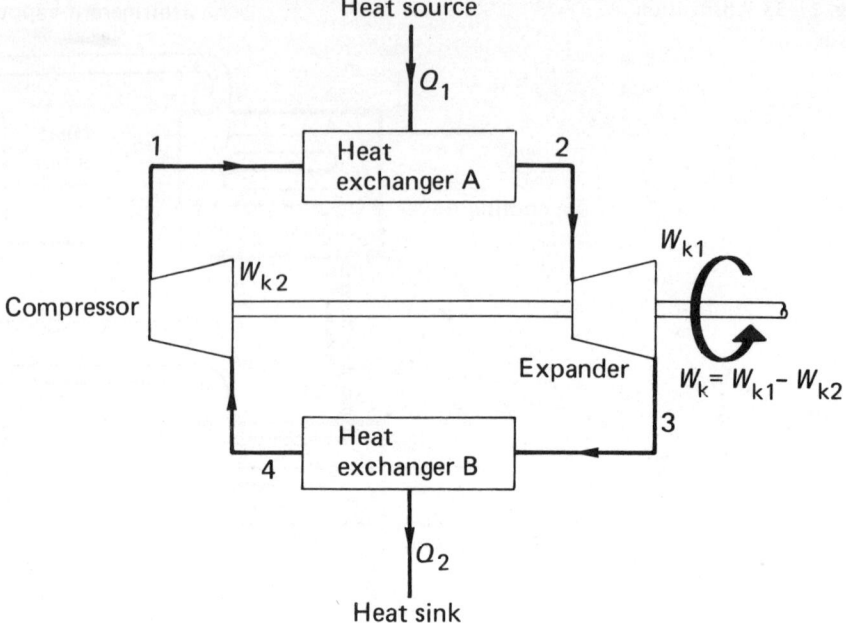

turbine; the expansion is adiabatic (no heat is given up or absorbed), but there is a loss in the energy of the fluid between 2 and 3 which may be observed as a drop in its temperature and pressure. The gas then passes into heat exchanger B which is in thermal contact with a low-temperature sink. From 4 to 1 the fluid passes through an adiabatic compressor which restores its pressure and temperature to its original state at 1. If, per cycle, Wk_1 is the work produced by the expansion and Wk_2 the work required for compression, the work available for use is $Wk_1 - Wk_2 = Wk$. The efficiency of the operation is, as before, Wk/Q_1. In the *steam-turbine* heat exchanger A is a boiler; steam at high pressure and temperature is fed into the expander; heat exchanger B is a condensor and the change of state of the fluid here maintains a high pressure differential across the expander. The compressor is a pump which carries water back to the boiler.

It would be possible in the steam-turbine to exhaust steam at 3 to the atmosphere and supply fresh water to the boiler. We would then have an *open-cycle* engine – the cycle is closed through the environment. We might use this form of

Fig. 11.37 Open-cycle gas-turbine.

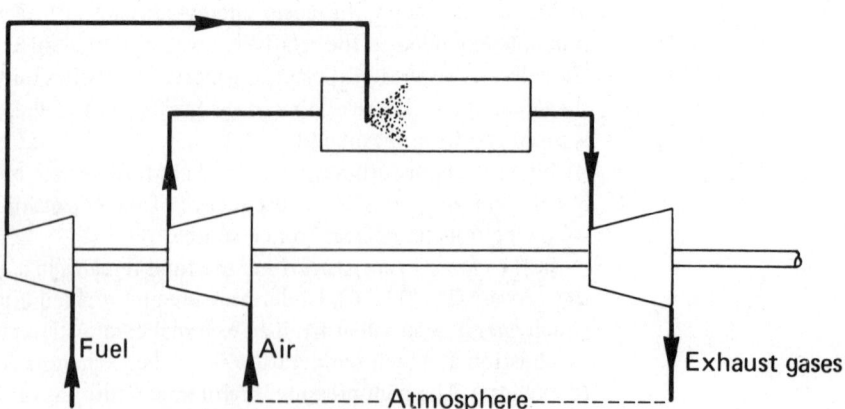

engine if we have a subsequent use for the exhaust steam. The closed-cycle gas turbine involves a secondary fluid, such as the products of combustion, to supply energy to the working fluid. The heat exchanger for this transfer may be very large, and it is common instead to combine the heater with the combustion chamber (Fig. 11.37).

The fuel (oil or natural gas) is injected into the working fluid (air) and takes the oxygen required for combustion from it. Obviously, this system, like the common internal combustion engine, cannot be closed, and the exhaust gases are taken to atmosphere.

The rotors of the turbine and the electrical alternator are connected; usually the one is the extension of the other. The mechanical-electrical conversion may be achieved with efficiencies as high as 95 per cent; but it must be remembered that where the mechanical energy is derived from a heat engine, such as the gas- or steam-turbine, the efficiency of this particular exchange is limited not only by energy degradation arising in any technological process, but also by the theoretical considerations exemplified in Fig. 11.30.

Fig. 11.38 represents the typical part-load performance of an open-cycle gas turbine; this should be compared with the corresponding curves for space-heating boilers (Fig. 11.28).

Fig. 11.38 Typical part-load performance of an open-cycle gas-turbine (after Craig [5]).

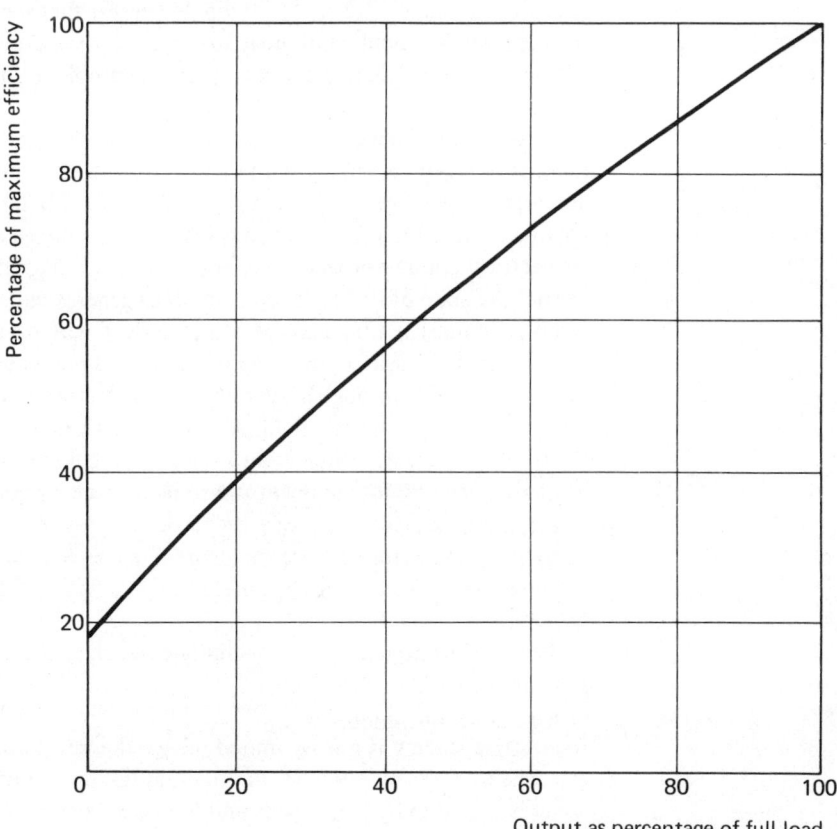

Output as percentage of full load

In summary, the generation of electricity from fossil fuels involves a chain of conversions: chemical to thermal energy by combustion; thermal to mechanical energy using a heat engine; mechanical to electrical energy in an alternator.

The most significant development in this industry in recent years has been the introduction of nuclear fuel for heat generation. It is a consequence of Einstein's Theory of Relativity that mass and energy are equivalent and that, therefore, the law of energy conservation is of restricted validity; the equivalence was demonstrated with momentous effect in the fission bombs of the last World War and in the even more powerful fusion weapons developed since. It is the fission process that is commercially exploited today; the peaceful use of nuclear fusion remains a matter for very expensive research of which some have doubted the probability of a fruitful outcome.

Fission involves the breakdown of the nucleus of a heavy unstable element; the instability is induced by bombarding suitable nuclei with neutrons, and since the products of fission include free neutrons we have a self-sustained chain reaction. Fission is accompanied by a loss in mass which is liberated as energy, mainly in the form of radiant energy and the heat generated from the kinetic energy of the products. The technology of the process resides principally in the shielding and control of the chain reaction, the disposal of its radioactive products, and the extraction of the heat for useful purposes. This last is achieved by circulating a gas, such as carbon dioxide, through the reactor and then through a heat exchanger. The temperature of the process is very high, over 2000 °C. Reference to Fig. 11.30 would suggest that such a high temperature of the heat source would be of great advantage for the efficiency of a heat engine, but unfortunately there are several practical problems in the operation of machinery at temperatures much above 600 °C.

Consequently, devices have been developed which effect direct conversion of thermal to electrical energy without the utilization of moving parts. One such development has been in magnetohydrodynamic (MHD) generation. We have previously noted that an electromotive force is induced across the terminals of an electrical conductor when it is moved across a magnetic field. We did not restrict the state of the conductor; in MHD generation the conductor is a gas (such as helium) at a high temperature, derived perhaps from nuclear processes, and seeded with easily ionized elements such as potassium. The gas is passed at supersonic speeds through a duct lined with electrodes, and across which is directed a strong magnetic field. An electromotive force is induced between the electrodes, which are connected to the external circuit. The emerging gases may be at a sufficiently low temperature to be utilized by conventional generating plant; when coupled in this way the device is known as a 'topper'. The increased operating temperature-difference afforded by such a combination significantly improves the efficiency of the generating process and, hence, the utilization of resources.

MHD generation, like other techniques (such as thermoelectric and thermionic generation) which utilize thermal energy to raise electricity, is limited in efficiency by the implications of Fig. 11.30. Direct conversion of chemical energy to electrical energy is not so limited; hence the interest in such devices as the fuel cell. The hydrox cell operates, in effect, as the reverse of hydrolysis in which water is split into hydrogen ions and hydroxyl ions by the passage of an electrical current.

Oxygen and hydrogen are diffused through permeable electrodes immersed in an electrolyte (potassium hydroxide solution). In the presence of a catalyst the gases are ionized; the ions combine to form water with the liberation of free electrons at the hydrogen electrode. This passage of electrons constitutes an electric current. Since electrical energy can be utilized for the reverse process of hydrolysis which generates the original gases, and since these can be stored and recycled, we have a technique for the indirect storage of electricity. Electricity derived from fuel cells has been used to drive vehicles and is used in manned spacecraft where the waste product, water, is used for drinking. Many fuel cells have been developed, using all manner of fuels and catalysts. A cell run on inputs of natural gas and oxygen (from air) is feasible; this would permit on-site generation of electricity from a piped gas source, without the loss of efficiency involved in thermal and mechanical processes.

This brief survey of conversion processes has been structured around the production of electrical energy; it remains to consider the uses for electricity in building, and in particular those concerned with the thermal environment. Electricity is of prime importance as an energy form because of its versatility, the ease with which it is distributed and its supply is controlled. Its chemical, magnetic, thermal and luminous effects may all be readily achieved where and as required. Its disadvantages are that it is expensive, because of the inefficiency of its generation, and that it is difficult to store in any quantity. Hence, electrical costs to a consumer must, in general, take into account not only his total but also his peak demand on the supply system, and the period when this peak occurs compared with that of other consumers.

The chemical effects of electricity are primarily of industrial significance, although in the context of buildings we have just noted a possible future application in reversing the action of the fuel cell; and electricity has similar use in recharging batteries for standby supply. Our interest in electric lighting in this book is confined to its thermal consequence; so our main concern now is with the magnetic and thermal effects of electrical energy.

When a current flows in a conductor, it forms a magnetic field around the conductor; if two current-carrying conductors are placed in proximity then the two magnetic fields will react to move the conductors relatively. This is the principle of the electric motor by which, in general, all mechanical movement in buildings – of goods, of people and of services – is effected. The efficiency of the electrical–mechanical conversion varies from 50 per cent for small motors to over 90 per cent for large motors.

The across-type energy sources of the previous section, that is pumps and fans, are motor-driven, and their presence in a system implies the need for electrical connection. So, too, since a pump is the heart of the refrigeration cycle, is an electrical input implied generally when there is mechanical cooling. The circulations inside the absorption chiller may, on a small scale, be achieved through convection effects; but on a large scale they are also pump-dependent.

It is the fact that heat pumps are usually electrically driven that may undermine their apparent economic benefit. In immediate energy terms, coefficients of performance of the order of 5 or so seem very favourable; but, as we have seen, the electrical input may be derived from a process which is itself highly inefficient. Even in a country where this inefficiency is masked by subsidies, the cost of heating a building by heat pump from a freely-available low temperature source may well exceed that of a conventional fossil-fuelled heating system. This argument may not, of course, apply where there is available a direct source of mechanical energy, such as the wind or a fast-flowing stream. (Even here the energy is usually converted to electrical energy because of easier distribution, the storage facility afforded by batteries, and the other uses to which electricity can be put.) All of the issues raised in this paragraph are amplified substantially in Chapter 13.

The reader will recall from Section 11.2 that with any flow through a channel work has to be done to overcome resistance to flow, and that the instantaneous rate at which this work is expended (i.e. the applied power consumed) is the product of the corresponding across- and through-variables: $p(\theta) = A(\theta) T(\theta)$. For electrical channels we have $p(\theta) = V(\theta) I(\theta)$; the units of the variables being, respectively, watts, volts and amps. We also know that for electrical flow $V(\theta)$ and $I(\theta)$ are linearly related through the constant channel resistance: $V(\theta) = I(\theta)R$. Since the power required to overcome resistance to flow is dissipated as heat, we have $q(\theta) = (V(\theta))^2/R$. If the voltage has a constant or some mean value V, then the total heat, Q (in joules), emitted over a period of time Θ (in seconds) is given by $Q = (\Theta V^2)/R$. Electrical resistance of a conductor is proportional to its length and inversely proportional to its cross-sectional area; so $Q = \Theta V^2 kr^2/L$ where k is a constant, r the radius of the conductor, and L its length. If we wish to use this thermal effect for space-heating, then to deliver the same quantity of heat we have the choice between an element of which the radius and length are both relatively large, or one in which they are both relatively small. Now it can be shown that the temperature rise of the element is inversely proportional to its surface area and, hence, to its radius. So the first element will have a lower temperature than the second. The common electric fire, in which the short fine-gauge conductor is wound on a ceramic form, is an example of a high-temperature unit. Longer, thicker low-temperature electrical elements are employed in underfloor and in ceiling heating.

An electrical element may be the heat source in secondary-medium systems such as that illustrated in Fig. 11.24. Invariably such a system incorporates thermal storage, primarily because of the preferential tariffs offered by electricity suppliers to off-peak customers. Underfloor heating set in a floor (such as concrete) with high thermal capacity also offers this advantage; as do factory-made off-peak thermal storage units.

On page 440 mention was made of the thermoelectric or *Seebeck* effect, which is a method for converting heat energy directly to electrical energy. Seebeck found that if two wires of dissimilar metals are joined at one end and the junction heated, then a small voltage difference appears across the cooler unjoined ends. This effect is used for temperature measurement in thermo-couples; perhaps more significantly it also has potential for solar-energy generated electricity. It can be reversed: if a current is passed through a loop made from two dissimilar metallic wires, then the temperature of one junction is raised, and the other junction is cooled. This is known as the *Peltier* effect, discovered as long ago as 1834. It is, however, a phenomenon of renewed interest following the development of semiconducting materials, since these also display the same property. They offer the possibility of solid-state heating and cooling, and modules have already been developed commercially for refrigeration.

11.4 Storage in systems

Storage is used to even out fluctuations in the supply to a system or in the demands made on it, or both.

A storage component is placed between two consecutive components in a flow system when the second is subject to variable demand and there are operational reasons for not matching this with supply from the first (Fig. 11.39).

Fig. 11.39 Storage component in a system.

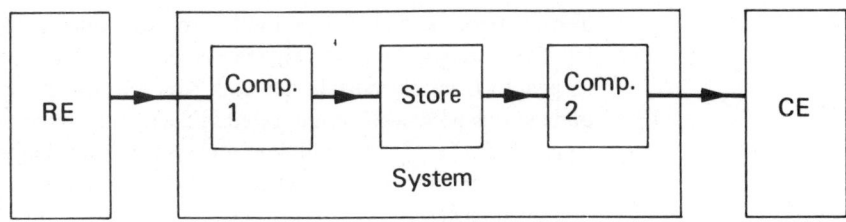

There are consequent economies in the costs of distribution channels and conversion plant that *precede* the storage component. In general these savings increase with increased storage, but so too does the cost of the storage component. This section, based on the work of Maver [6, 7], develops graphical techniques by which the optimum combination of costs may be determined.

Hot-water supply systems will exemplify the argument. These must comprise at least two components; a heat source incorporating a heat exchanger, and a distribution network to demand points (Fig. 11.40).

Fig. 11.40 A hot-water supply system.

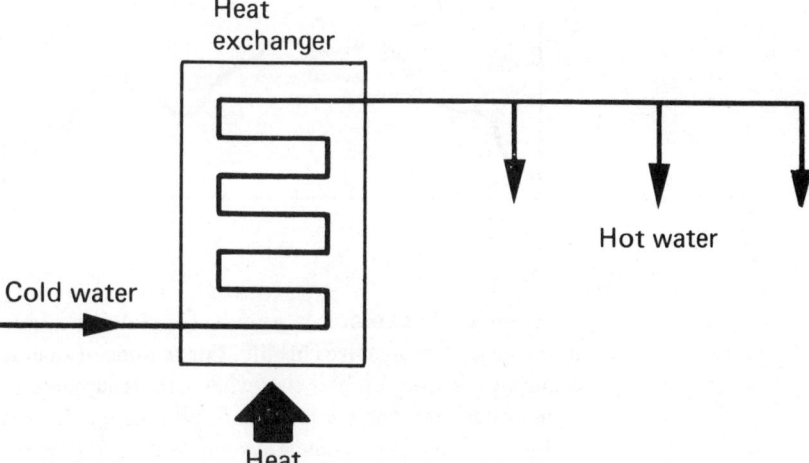

The energy supply to such a system must be readily controlled, since it is turned on or off according to the flow of water through the exchanger, i.e. according to the demand for hot water. Gas and electricity are commonly used. The main variable in the system is the rate at which heat is supplied to it, that is the size of the heating element-exchanger; and this is determined by some expectation of the simultaneity of demand at hot-water outlets. In fact, simple systems like this are all small in scale, often domestic, and it is usually assumed that there will rarely be demand for hot water at more than one point at a time; i.e. that when there is demand for heat it is at a constant rate. The heating element-exchanger is sized accordingly. In this system then the heat demand and supply profiles are assumed to be identical. When more demand points are supplied by the system the less appropriate is this assumption likely to be, and the greater the risk of failure in supply. Notice that there is also a limitation on scale imposed by the draw-off before there is hot water at the most remote outlet.

It would be possible for the supply of hot water where there are many and dispersed points, such as in a hotel, to provide one of these systems at each outlet. There are good reasons why this is rarely a preferred strategy. First, there is no benefit from diversity in demand from multiple systems each serving single outlets; this point will be amplified in Section 11.6. Second, if there are other demands for heat in the building, such as for space-heating, it is an advantage to share the conversion plant. It should also be noted that although for the strategy of individual systems distribution of hot water is minimized, there must be an extensive distribution of cold water and gas or electricity to each unit. This exemplifies the problem of balance between primary and secondary distribution networks to which we will return in Section 11.8.

With centralization of supply, we must expect that demand may vary continuously over time. Let Fig. 11.41 represent the way that demand rate for hot water varies, typically.

Fig. 11.41 Variation of the rate of demand for hot water.

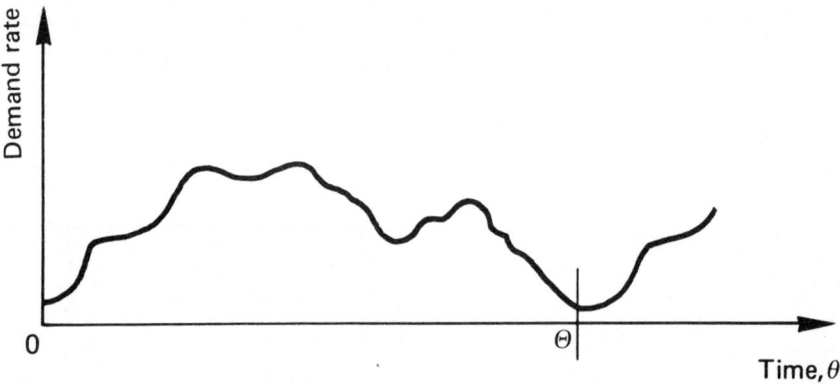

As we would expect it is periodic (of period Θ), corresponding to the cycles into which man organizes his life. For reasons of operational efficiency and economy we would prefer that when heat is supplied to the system it should be at a constant rate, below the rate of peak demand.

Fig. 11.42 shows a typical system. Notice that distribution is in the form of a ring around which hot water is pumped continuously, thereby avoiding draw-off delays, and heat loss from hot water left standing in pipes after each use. The calorifier has the double function of a heat exchanger and hot-water store. Cold water is fed into the bottom of the calorifier on demand, passing over the heating element; the heated water rises by convection and is stored in the upper part of the cylinder. The two variables are the storage volume of the calorifier, and the

Fig. 11.42 A hot-water supply system.

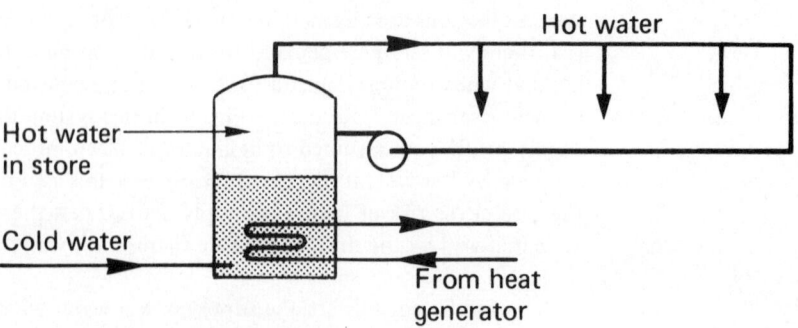

rate at which heat is supplied from the boiler; the latter determines the size of the heating element.

So that supply and demand may be compared directly we will treat both in terms of a volume rate of hot water. This supply rate is directly proportional to the rate of heat supply from the boiler; for if the hot water supply rate is Vol m^3 s^{-1}, and the water is raised t °C at the heating element, then the heat supply rate is s_v Vol t watts, where s_v is the (volumetric) specific heat of water.

Over the period of demand we require that the total volume supplied to it must at least equal the total volume of demand on it. If $d(\theta)$ and $s(\theta)$ are, respectively, the rates of demand and supply as functions of time, we require

$$\int_0^\Theta d(\theta)\,\mathrm{d}\theta \leqslant \int_0^\Theta s(\theta)\,\mathrm{d}\theta. \qquad (11.6)$$

If

$$\int_0^\Theta d(\theta)\,\mathrm{d}\theta < \int_0^\Theta s(\theta)\,\mathrm{d}\theta,$$

we have overflow; this condition prevails in the not uncommon circumstance where room temperature is adjusted by opening and closing windows while the heating system is maintained at full bore, and in the old domestic back boiler. Overflow is always wasteful of resources, but it is unavoidable if supply cannot be controlled.

Selection of a continuous and constant rate of supply such that

$$\int_0^\Theta d(\theta)\,\mathrm{d}\theta = \int_0^\Theta s(\theta)\,\mathrm{d}\theta$$

would only be practicable if the profile of demand itself showed no variation from period to period; and this is highly improbable. To ensure that

$$\int_0^\Theta d(\theta)\,\mathrm{d}\theta = \int_0^\Theta s(\theta)\,\mathrm{d}\theta$$

we require a rate of supply greater than this over which we have some form of control. Different modes of system control are discussed in Section 11.7. For this analysis, we will assume that there is some regulating switch on the heat supply from the boiler. A switch is either fully open or fully closed, and never in between. This on–off control is activated by a thermostat which turns off the heating when the calorifier is full of hot water.

From the demand profile we construct the graph of cumulative demand over the period. Fig. 11.43 demonstrates the analysis when supply is continuous but without overflow.

The initial and terminal values of cumulative demand and supply must be the same. This establishes the straight line of cumulative supply, the gradient of which is the (constant) supply rate. This is represented by a continuous horizontal line on the graph of demand and supply rates; the differentially shaded areas must, in total, be equal. For $0 < \theta < \theta_2$ the cumulative demand is less than the cumulative supply; hot water is added to store. This addition reaches a maximum value, A, at θ_1. At θ_2 the cumulative supply and demand are

Fig. 11.43 Storage analysis for constant supply, without control and without overflow.

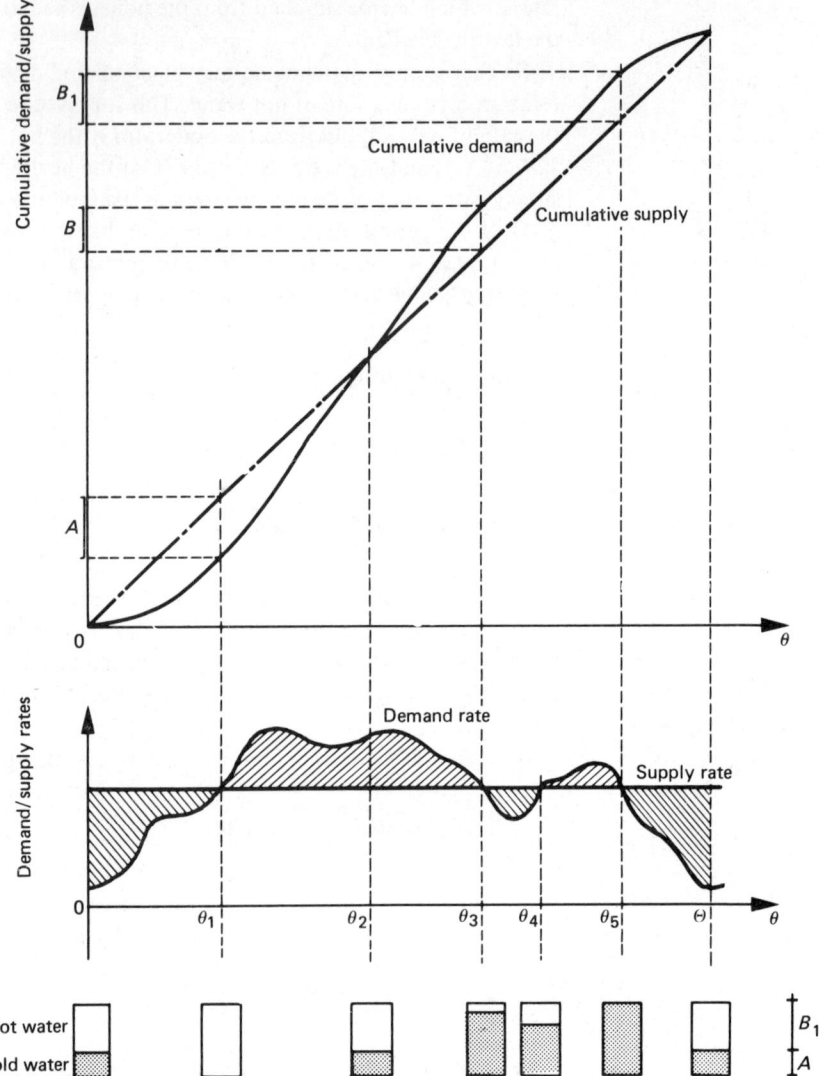

equal; all the additional stored hot water has been withdrawn. For $\theta_2 < \theta < \Theta$ the cumulative demand is greater than the cumulative supply, and extra demand is made on the store. The maximum value of this demand is the maximum vertical distance between the cumulative graphs and occurs at θ_3 (value B) or θ_5 (value B_1) or at similar points in time (i.e. when supply and demand rates coincide after demand rate has exceeded supply rate[*]). Then the total storage

[*]Formally, let

$$y(\theta) = \int_0^\theta d(\theta)\,\mathrm{d}\theta - \int_0^\theta s(\theta)\,\mathrm{d}\theta;$$

then

$$\frac{\mathrm{d}y}{\mathrm{d}\theta} = d(\theta) - s(\theta).$$

Hence, $\mathrm{d}y/\mathrm{d}\theta = 0$ when $d(\theta) = s(\theta)$. For values of θ when $\mathrm{d}y/\mathrm{d}\theta = 0$, if $d(\theta - \Delta\theta) > s(\theta - \Delta\theta)$ and $d(\theta + \Delta\theta) < s(\theta + \Delta\theta)$, then $y(\theta)$ is a local maximum.

Fig. 11.44 Storage analysis for minimum supply rate when supply is controllable.

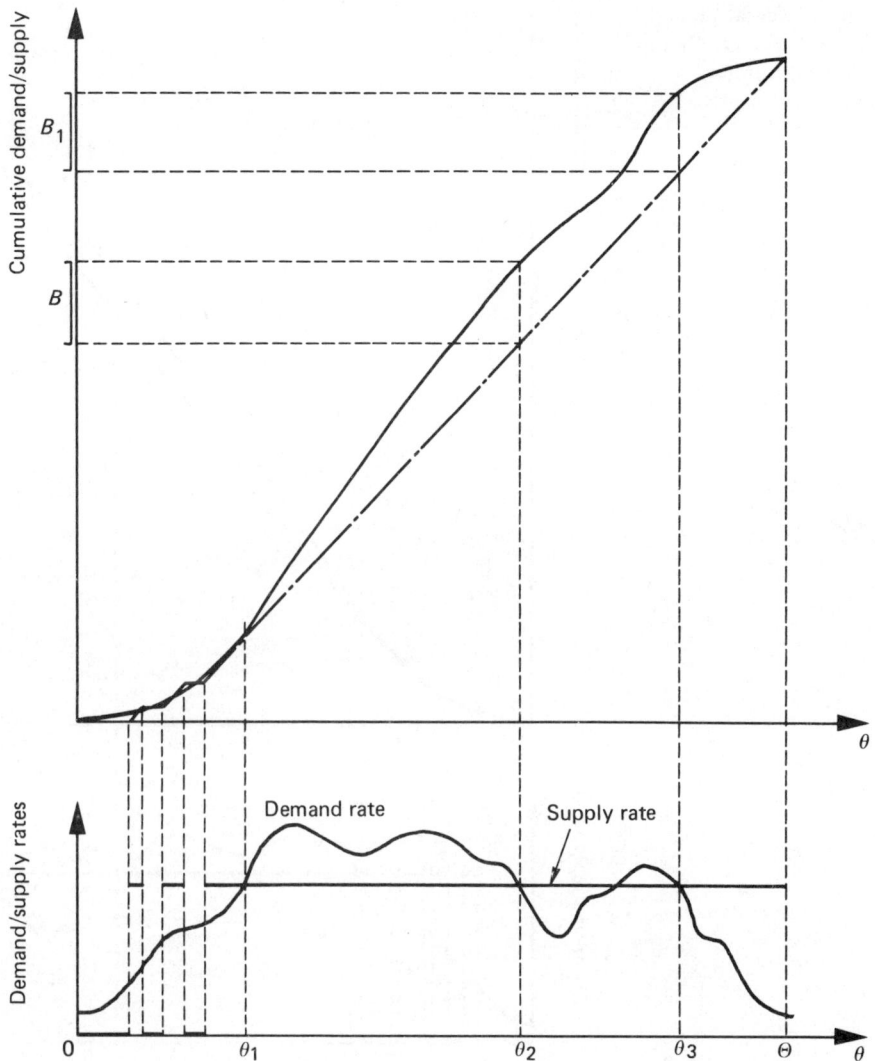

required in the system is $A + \max(B, B_1, B_2, \ldots)$. In this example $B_1 > B$ and the storage capacity required is $A + B_1$.

The supply rate assumed in this analysis is the minimum constant rate of supply that will satisfy the demand on the system. If on–off control is introduced to avoid overflow, the supply must be at a higher rate since it does not operate for the whole period, but must satisfy the same cumulative demand. The minimum rate of supply with on–off control that will satisfy the demand on the system is given by the gradient of the line which is tangential to the graph of cumulative demand and passes through its terminal point (Fig. 11.44).

From time 0 to time θ_1 the rate of demand is less than this rate of supply; the storage level is maintained over short intervals of supply determined by the operating differential of the control mechanism (*see* Section 11.7). At θ_1 the store is full; from θ_1 to Θ there are periods in which the rate of demand falls below the rate of supply, but cumulative supply only catches up on cumulative demand at Θ. Hence, from θ_1 to Θ supply is continuous. The maximum

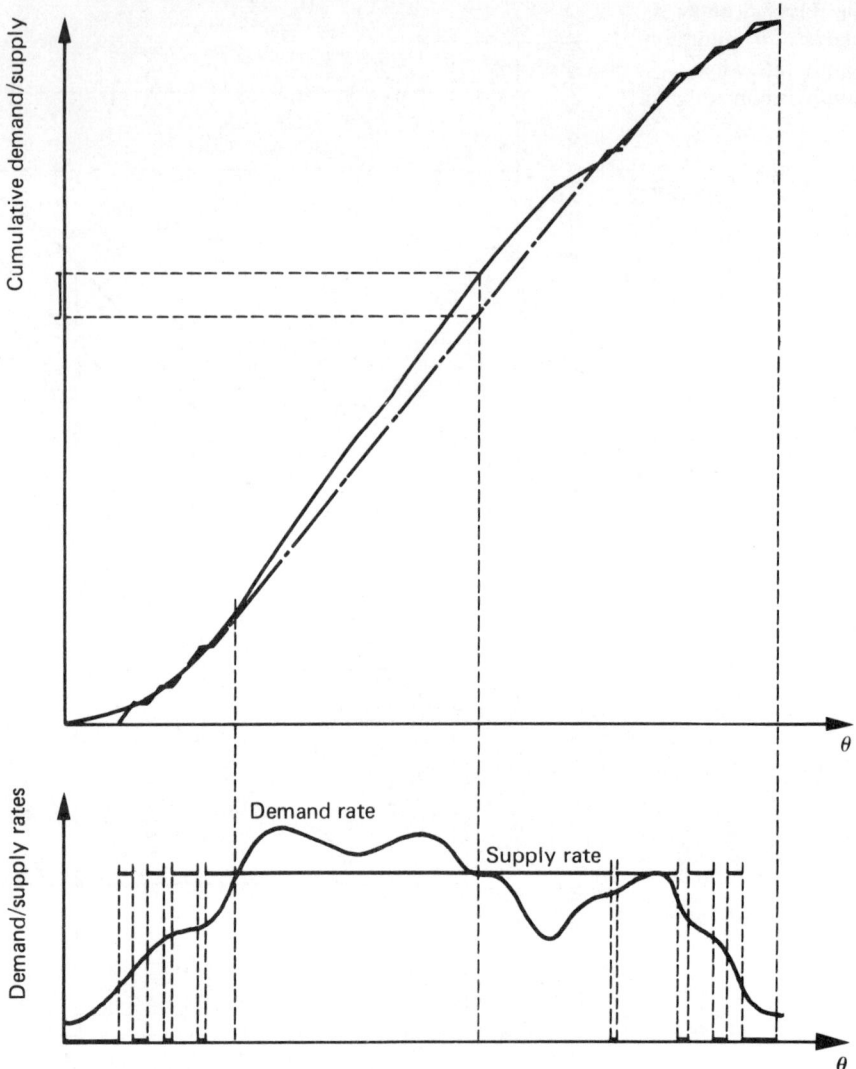

Fig. 11.45 Storage analysis for supply rate above minimum.

difference between the two cumulative graphs occurs at θ_2 or θ_3. It is the amount to be stored in the system for this rate of supply. In the example its value is given by B.

With control, however, it is not necessary to supply at this minimum rate. If the rate of supply is increased (Fig. 11.45), the amount of storage is decreased.

So we have a range of suitable supply rates, and with each rate is associated a corresponding storage requirement. For each combination of supply rate and storage volume there is a corresponding capital cost. It comprises the cost of storage, that is of the appropriate calorifier, and the cost of supply. Remember that the rate of supply of hot water is proportional to the rate of heat supply, and that the latter determines boiler size. So the cost of supply is, principally, the cost of a suitable boiler.

It is a well-known optimization technique, for problems that involve two variables, to compare sets of combinations of equal effect with sets of combinations of equal cost. The independent variables are represented along the

Fig. 11.46 Coordinate system plotting storage against supply.

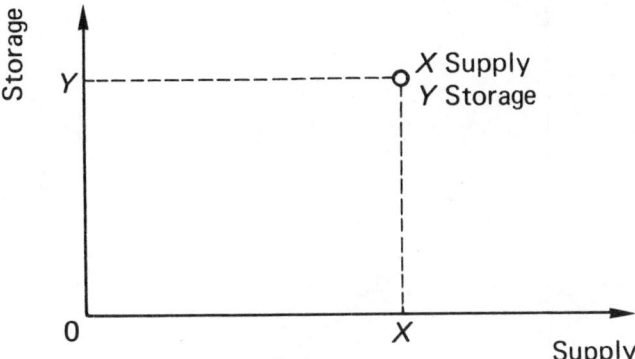

Fig. 11.47 A set of components of equal effect.

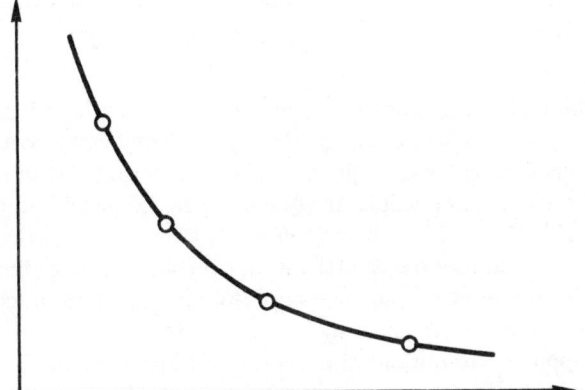

axes of a coordinate system (Fig. 11.46). Then, the coordinates of a point in the plane represent the values of the variables in a particular combination. *Sets* of combinations may be identified as collections of points; these may form a line or a region in the plane. One such set comprises those combinations which precisely satisfy demand on the system, determined by our method. This is the set of equal effect (Fig. 11.47). We seek that member of this set that costs least, i.e. that has the best performance. Another set may be defined that comprises all combinations that cost the same amount, say £X. A series of such equal cost lines may be generated. If these are of the form shown in Fig. 11.48 the optimum

Fig. 11.48 A series of equal cost lines.

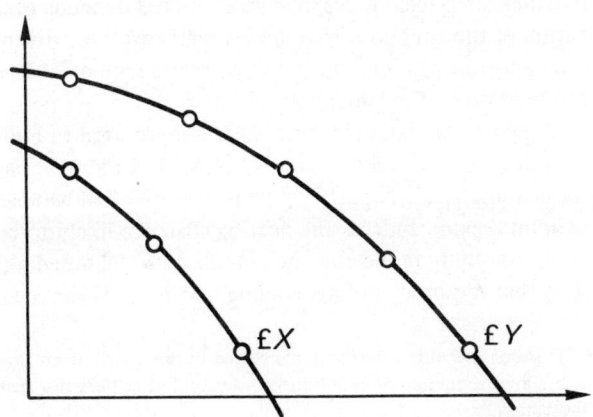

Fig. 11.49 The optimum component (x_1, y_1).

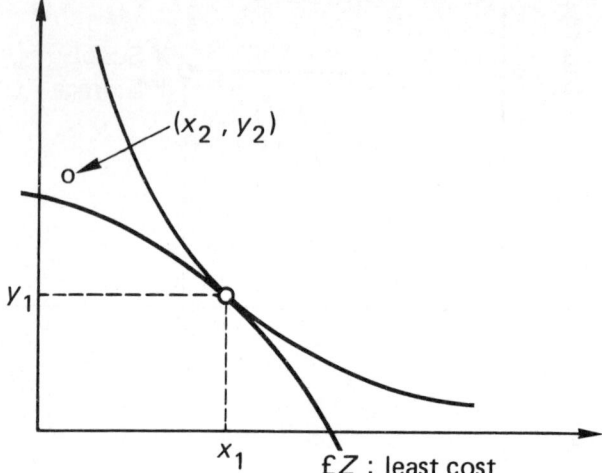

(x_2, y_2)

y_1

x_1 £Z : least cost

solution to the problem is that combination represented by a point of tangency to both the curve of equal effect and *a* line of equal cost (Fig. 11.49). This combination has a supply rate of x_1, a storage capacity of y_1, and a cost of £Z. Note that it is possible to pay more than £Z and still not satisfy demand on the system (e.g. with combination x_2, y_2).*

To optimize the capital cost of supply and storage implies that they are both directly borne by the same organization. This is not usually the case where the supply is of a resource, such as fuel oil. A resource is stored on site because supply is intermittent or as a safeguard against failure of supply. In either case the volume of a resource stored will be decided from data on the consumption of the resource. The statistical techniques applied to this sort of decision-making will be discussed in Section 11.6, when we will also consider the problem of 'representative' demand profiles.

11.5 Complementary systems

Two systems are complementary if a secondary output from one contributes to the resource environment of the other (Fig. 11.9). The exploitation of this dependence between systems is, therefore, important for the conservation of resources; that two systems are complementary implies that they are sub-systems of some higher-order system. Although this section is concerned only with the mechanics by which systems may be made complementary, the degree to which such techniques may be exploited depends fundamentally on the nature of the functions that are brought together within a building. Basically the opportunities for resource conservation are afforded at the stages of brief formulation and organization.

Suppose, for example, that there is a proposal to build a recreational complex providing sports facilities. In colder climates there would certainly be a demand for heating: space-heating for some activities and water-heating if there is to be a swimming pool. Indeed, the heating costs are likely to be high, and these could be substantially reduced if the complex also included a facility, such as an ice rink, that required cooling; cooling, as we have seen, necessitates the rejection of

* It should be noted that water is stored in the distribution ring of Fig. 11.42, and that with a low frequency of simultaneous demand at outlets this storage may be adequate for the system.

heat. The technical feasibility of using this rejected heat would depend upon heating and cooling demands of similar magnitude occurring simultaneously, although limited displacement in time could be afforded by thermal storage. The heat energy would probably be transferred by means of a heat pump; the ice rink would be the low temperature source from which the heat demands of the rest of the complex would, at least in part, be satisfied. The energy costs of the system would be those of supply to the heat pump; this is likely to be electrical, and the economic feasibility of the proposal will therefore be strongly influenced by comparative energy tariffs. In the UK the integration by mechanical transfer of thermal energy from areas with a cooling demand to those requiring heating has been stimulated, understandably, by the Electricity Council.

All machinery generates heat; some mechanical processes, such as electronic computation, require that this heat be promptly removed from the environment. It is possible, therefore, that it be used for heating other parts of the building, such as offices and canteens. A simple system would duct air directly between these areas; but where this does not achieve sufficient cooling, or where the mechanical process is polluting, transfer by a heat pump will be more efficacious.

Closely associated with this concept is that of heat recovery. However well the tenets of this book are observed in the design of building fabric, there must still be energy losses through ventilation, and in a mechanical ventilation system these losses will be substantial if, for reasons of pollution, no air is recirculated. The intention to consider the resource and controlled environments as systems was made in the introduction to this chapter. The primitive diagram (Fig. 11.4) may, therefore, be interpreted as a chain of three systems, the middle of which is the mechanical system. Heat losses, including ventilation losses, are secondary outputs of the controlled environment to the environment at large. If the mechanical system is for heating, its resource environment encompasses energy convertible to thermal energy, or thermal energy itself. Hence, if by some means heat lost from the controlled environment is channelled to the resource environment, the two may properly be considered, within the terms of this section, as complementary. The system by which this linkage is effected is a heat recovery system. Heat recovery and its appropriate techniques are considered more fully in Chapter 13.

It will be recalled from Section 11.3 that heat is a waste product in most techniques for electrical generation and that this accounts substantially for the low efficiencies of these processes and, hence, the relatively high cost of electricity. The utilization of this waste heat in complementary systems has long attracted engineering attention. At the largest scale, district heating schemes have been coupled to generating power stations, with intervening thermal storage to accommodate fluctuations in heat supply and demand. Although older power stations are often located conveniently for this application, new stations, for environmental or other reasons (including the availability of cooling water!) are usually too remote. The absence of a convenient power station does not, of course, preclude the use of a district heating system. Some schemes are fuelled by a district's own rubbish; but more frequently they are fossil-fuelled, in which case the main motivation for centralization is the benefit of economy in scale to be considered in Section 11.6. Heating is not the only purpose to which waste heat from electricity generation (or any other mechanical process) may be put; for with the absorption chiller it may be converted for cooling. As with district heating, district cooling may be complementary to a waste-heat producing system, or it may be independent. There are combined district heating and district cooling systems [8].

It is generally true that the customer for electricity from some centralized generating authority must bear the costs of an intrinsically inefficient process; and few are located conveniently enough to benefit directly through district schemes dependent upon its waste products. The prospect, therefore, of localized complementary systems for the generation of electricity and the use of its waste heat is an increasingly attractive, but not always feasible, alternative. This concept is the core of a *total energy installation*; specifically this is a system by which all of the energy requirements of a building or building complex are met from the resource of a single fuel. Since almost all buildings require electricity, a total energy system involves its on-site generation and the recovery and utilization of waste heat from the generation process. Supplementary heat generation may be necessary if there are times when waste heat is not sufficient to meet the heat demand (Fig. 11.50).

Fig. 11.50 The principle of total energy.

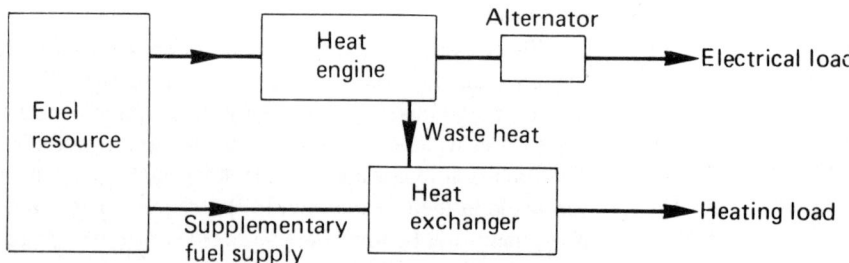

Essential to the design of these systems is familiarity with the principles and techniques of energy conversion and distribution described in Sections 11.2 and 11.3. The techniques of Section 11.4 may be used to test the possibility of thermal storage as an alternative (perhaps in part) to supplementary firing.

Compared with the alternative of buying electricity from the national grid and heating by (say) an oil-fired system, a total energy installation involves high capital expenditure on plant. The first necessary condition for a system to be feasible is, therefore, that the plant be highly utilized; it must not lie idle or be used much below maximum capacity for long periods. It is, therefore, most likely to be considered for industrial processes with shift work, or for building complexes with diverse functions and spread demands. The efficient operation of a total energy system could, therefore, be influential in strategic planning decisions. The increased capital expenditure must be offset by significantly lower running costs. This suggests three further necessary conditions:

(i) a relatively cheap fuel must be available; much of recent interest in the UK has been stimulated by developments in natural gas supply;

(ii) there must be maximum recovery and utilization of waste heat − this has important implications for building form and fabric;

(iii) the different kinds of energy demand must be reasonably balanced for some appropriate heat engine − this very important condition is amplified immediately below.

It will be clear from the summary of conversion processes in Section 11.3 that there will be many technically possible routes by which a fossil fuel input may be converted to meet the various kinds of energy demand in a building. But not all of these, nor any, may be economically feasible. A quick check on feasibility may be made by comparing *heat–power ratios* for the building and various forms of engine. For an engine this ratio is that of recoverable heat to the electricity generated; for a building it is a demand ratio of the sum of all energy demands that can be met from a heat source to the electrical demand. For engines the ratio varies with load, but for steam-turbines, gas-turbines and reciprocating Diesel engines it is, respectively, of the order of 12:1, 3:1 and 1:1. The building demand ratio will therefore indicate which (if any) is to be preferred in a total energy installation. But it is unlikely that demand ratio is constant, and great variation would indicate an almost certainly uneconomic combination of engines; and even if the demand levels, and *not* the ratio, vary there may be significant operational inefficiency. Hence, a proposal for a total energy installation is likely to be feasible only if neither the heat–power demand ratio nor the individual energy demand levels vary greatly, and if the first matches reasonably the heat–power ratio of an engine. For a sufficiently large scheme variation in the demand levels, but not in the demand ratio, may be met by modularization of plant, as discussed in Section 11.7.

Although the four conditions are, at least in the particular resource environment of the United Kingdom, necessary for the feasibility of a total energy installation, they are not sufficient, and any proposal must be subjected to detailed scrutiny. The main features of a feasibility study are best illustrated by hypothetical example.

Suppose the installation is to meet the following loads: electrical, mechanical, space-heating, space-cooling, hot-water. It is likely that the mechanical load (from, say, lifts and machinery) will be met through electrical motors; and other demands will be met from recovered heat. If the heat–power demand ratio is favourable for the utilization of a gas-turbine, Fig. 11.51 represents a possibly suitable total energy installation.

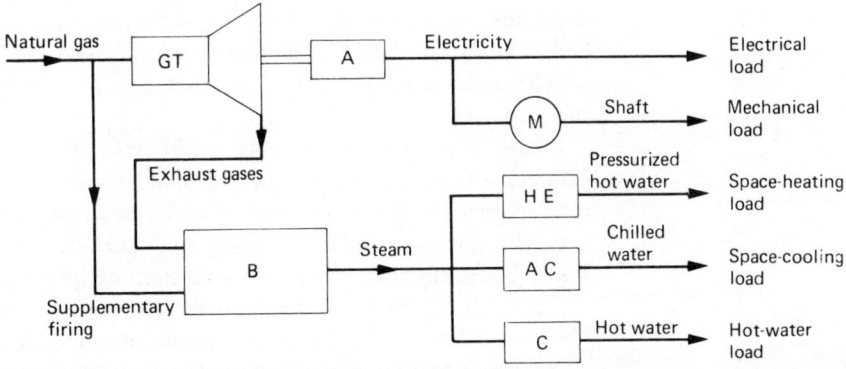

Fig. 11.51 A total energy installation. A, alternator; AC, absorption chiller; B, boiler; C calorifier; GT, gas turbine; HE, heat exchanger; M, motor.

To test this hypothesis, we must have estimated demand profiles for each type of load over days representative of seasonal variation. The study comprises an assessment of capital and running costs. Each piece of plant is sized to meet the peak demand made on it. Hence, the motor, heat-exchanger, absorption chiller and calorifier are sized directly from the demand profiles; suitable components are selected and priced from manufacturers' catalogues. These will also give the efficiencies with which each piece of plant operates at its maximum loading, and, hence, the corresponding energy input to it is determined. The process is continued back through the system to the boiler. Its size and cost are determined from the maximum *simultaneous* sum of the inputs to the three dependent systems; notice that the space-heating and space-cooling peak loads are unlikely to coincide. A similar process is conducted for the electrical and mechanical loads. Although the gas turbine is to supply exhaust gases to the boiler, it, and the alternator, are sized only to meet the demands from the electrical branch of the installation. The exhaust gases are secondary products; any deficiency in heat is made good by supplementary gas firing to the boiler. The capital cost of the system will be the sum of all the plant capital costs, the costs of distribution channels and the costs of associated building work including flues. The running costs will comprise the costs of natural gas supply to the turbine and the costs of supplementary firing, and recurring items such as maintenance. Whereas plant costs are determined from peak demand values, the fuel costs will depend upon daily demand profiles. If the estimated profile of electrical demand on the turbine-alternator has a stepped form, the 24-h period may be divided into N time intervals during any one of which the rate of demand is constant. If over the time interval θ_x the demand rate is d_x and the efficiency (obtained from the manufacturer's manual) at that load is η_x, the energy consumed over the interval will be $(\theta_x d_x)/\eta_x$; and for the whole day the consumption will be the sum given by:

$$\sum_{x=1}^{N} (\theta_x d_x)/\eta_x \qquad (11.7)$$

The manufacturer's manual will also show the rate of recoverable heat as a function of the electrical demand. So a profile of the available waste heat may be built up over the period. From deficiencies between this and the profile of the required energy input to the boiler (it is left to the reader to deduce how this is constructed) the energy required for supplementary firing may be calculated. This added to the energy input to the turbine will give the total fuel consumption for the day. The consumption is then summed over the season for which the day is representative, and then season by season to yield an annual fuel cost.

If alternative systems are being considered, they may best be compared by combining their different capital and running costs in present-worth sums. If the only comparison is with a system in which electricity is bought from a generating authority it is useful to know the *pay-back period*; that is the time over which the savings accumulated in running expenditure of the total energy installation will compensate for its inevitably higher plant costs. The reader is referred to Chapter 12 for these and other techniques of economic appraisal.

The condition for energy balance has restricted interest in independent total energy installations; but this condition is relaxed if surplus secondary output may be disposed of profitably. This possibility has prompted research into the development of small total energy plant, suitable for domestic use.[*] In this the

---

[*] I am indebted to Mr P. Agnew, Department of Mechanical Engineering, University of Glasgow, for bringing this to my attention, and for providing details of a technically feasible system.

primary output is heat, and the generating plant is sized to meet central heating and hot water demand; its secondary output is electricity. When electrical supply is deficient, electricity would be bought from the national grid; this external supply of electricity is analogous to supplementary gas-firing in the more orthodox total installation. But the important innovatory idea is that at times when surplus electricity is being generated it should be fed, for profit, *into* the national grid. A diesel or a spark ignition engine would appear to be a suitable prime mover for domestic demand. The latter, a modified petrol engine, could be fuelled by natural gas. For seasonal climates, the proposition has the great attraction that surplus electricity would be generated locally in winter, when there is maximum load on the grid.

The reader will recall that the only direct conversion of chemical into electrical energy described in Section 11.3 utilized the fuel cell. There is continuing research into its use for domestic-scale electrical supply and, since the process generates heat, there is the possibility of attaching to it a complementary heating system. The heat produced is unlikely to satisfy a space-heating requirement, but could be sufficient for hot-water supply. Because of the small scale of the system it is likely to suffer relatively high peak loads; and it would then be necessary to include storage for both electricity (in batteries) and hot water. The reader is invited to extend to these complementary systems the techniques of storage-supply optimization outlined in Section 11.4.

11.6 Sizing of systems

Our discussion of systems has not yet adequately recognized the very important observation that the demand on them is variable. In Section 11.2 the distribution network of the space-heating system (Fig. 11.24) was designed to supply heat at a constant rate of Q W from each radiator; and even though the storage analyses in Section 11.4 and the sizing of conversion plant in Section 11.5 acknowledge that demand varies over daily and seasonal periods, the calculations are based on *single* demand profiles. These should, therefore, be representative in some way of the infinitely many different profiles that may occur when the system is commissioned.

This section and the next are concerned with this variation in demand. Respectively, they are addressed to the questions:

(i) Given that there is variation in demand, what is the level of demand that a system and its components should be designed for?

(ii) How may a system be designed to respond to variation in demand up to that level?

Consider again the heating system of Fig. 11.24, which we will suppose to be oil-fired. The demand on the system will vary for reasons adequately conveyed in earlier chapters, and the system will be sized to meet some demand level (Q W at each radiator) in accordance with the methods they describe for calculating heat loss. But, because of climatic and other variation, the system will not operate continuously at this level; and consequently there will be variation in its demand for fuel oil. Site storage of this resource is introduced between the supply organization and the system since supply is intermittent; we will assume it to be at fixed, say monthly, intervals. The problem is to decide what volume is to be stored.

One solution is to use some rule of thumb or consult a design guide, but this is only the indirect application of more fundamental approaches carried out by others. These are, ultimately, statistical. Where other systems operate in closely similar contexts, data may be collected on their varying demand for the resource. If a system is without such precedent it must be modelled (often with a set of mathematical equations) and the model subjected to varying demands likely to be experienced by the system itself; this *simulation* is best conducted by computer, and its output could include estimates of the corresponding fuel consumptions. For either approach we have a collection of values showing consumption of fuel oil during intervals between supply. These values may be displayed as a *frequency distribution* (Fig. 11.52).

Fig. 11.52 Frequency distribution of fuel oil consumption.

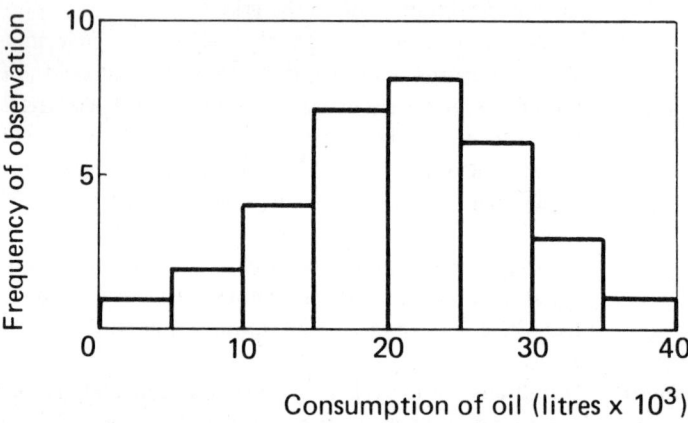

Consumption of oil (litres x 10^3)

From this data the designer or his client must decide what storage is to be provided. The answer must depend on the cost of failure to supply oil to the system and, since failure may mean no heating at all, the client may ask for guaranteed supply. This is, however, impossible to provide. It is certainly not adequate to size storage to meet the maximum observed or estimated value of consumption, since our observations or simulation runs must be finite in number and others are quite likely to include a greater maximum. The upper limit to storage would assume that combustion plant is continuously and maximally in operation throughout an interval; and, if the cost of storage is low compared with the cost of failure, this will be the preferred strategy. But even this storage value cannot preclude failure due, for example, to a breakdown in delivery; and indeed the component cannot be sized to meet the maximum possible demand on it, since this cannot be quantified. The best that can be done is to meet demand with an estimated probability of success.

In making decisions based on a collection of data, it is helpful if it can be assumed that it conforms to one or other of the standard statistical distributions; certain characteristics of the data will indicate which distribution, if any, to apply. A *normal distribution* is the most frequently applicable to natural phenomena (and to services data), and it is the only one which we have space to consider here. Strictly, it should be assumed only if the observed variable may take any value within infinite limits; and this condition does not apply to the frequency distribution of Fig. 11.52, since the lower limit on consumption is 0. But the mean of the distribution, which measures its central tendency, has the value 21, and this is sufficiently far from the lower limit for the assumption of normality to be a reasonable approximation.

Fig. 11.53 Standard
normal distribution
curve.

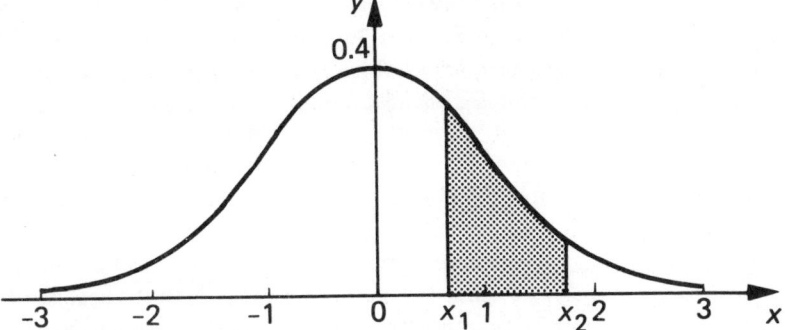

A normal distribution is uniquely defined by the parameters of its standard
deviation, which measures its dispersion, and its mean. The *standard* normal
distribution has a mean of 0 and a standard deviation of 1; the area under its full
curve (Fig. 11.53) sums to 1; and the proportion of this area between value x_1
and x_2 measures the *probability* of the variable having some value between
these limits.

We are assuming that our empirical distribution belongs to the normal family.
Through its parameters (it has a standard deviation of 8) it is transformed to the
standard normal distribution. Statistical tables which display proportions of area
under the standard normal curve then enable us to make probability statements
about the empirical distribution. So, for example, storage of 29.3×10^3 litres
has 0.85 probability of meeting demand for fuel, or 0.15 probability of failure.
For probabilities of failure of 0.10, 0.05 and 0.01 the corresponding storage
requirements are 31.2×10^3, 34.2×10^3 and 39.6×10^3 litres. Fig. 11.54
demonstrates that at these levels investment against failure shows rapidly
diminishing marginal returns.

Fig. 11.54 Probabilities
of failure of system as a
function of storage
capacity.

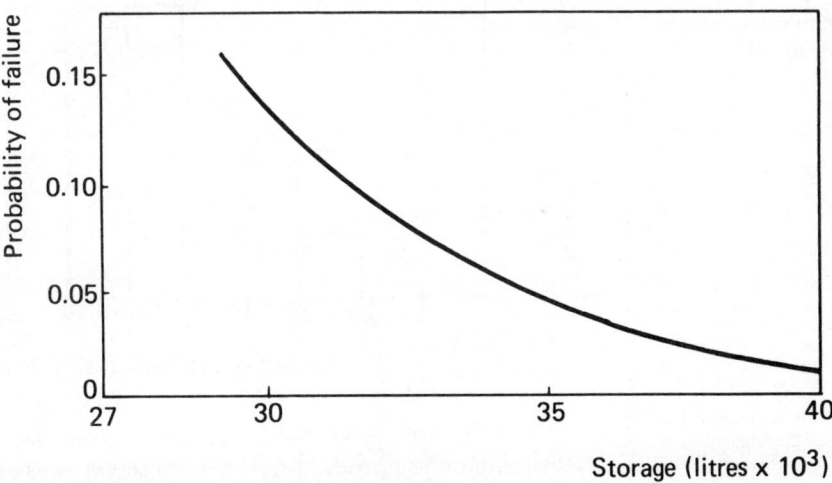

The techniques of statistical inference introduced in this section offer an
approach to the problem of demand profiles raised in Sections 11.4 and 11.5.
The selection of a single profile as characteristic of a collection is a problem
because it is very difficult to define precisely how one irregular *shape* may be
representative of a group. We may avoid the problem if we conduct an analysis

for *each observed profile*. Suppose, in the example of hot-water supply and storage of Section 11.4, that there were 50 observed demand profiles; then for any one rate of hot-water supply there would be up to 50 values for corresponding storage. The distribution of these values would be analysed statistically (again assuming normality), and for each supply rate a storage volume likely to meet demand with an estimated probability would be determined. These would then be the supply-rate and storage-volume combinations used in the optimization procedure described in that section.

There is yet another and important aspect of variability in demand that we must consider. We return for example to the heating system of Fig. 11.24. In each of the three rooms (B, C and D) there is to be a radiator, capable of supplying heat at a rate of Q W. If all three rooms are normally in use throughout the design day, then the heating plant must be big enough to supply heat at a rate of $3Q$ W (as well as to compensate for any heat losses in distribution). Suppose, however, that simultaneous use is rare, and that heating in a room is switched off when a room is not in use. There would then be a case for smaller plant because of this *diversity* in demand. This is the fundamental concept to be considered in the remainder of this section.

Although in special circumstances the occupancy of rooms and, hence, the coincidence of demand for heating, could be accurately predicted, say from a time-table, it is more likely to be estimated probabilistically from observations of a similar organization in operation.

It is unlikely that there would be much diversity in the occupation of the three rooms of our example; but it could be considerable in, say, a 100-room hotel. Fig. 11.55 is a hypothetical frequency distribution of 100 observations on simultaneous use of bedrooms in such an example.

Fig. 11.55 Frequency distribution of simultaneous use of bedrooms.

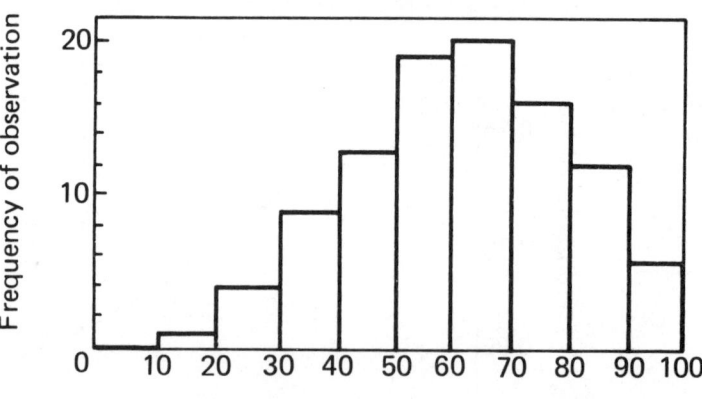

Given this data, decisions for a designer and his client would concern levels of satisfaction to be provided from all of the services in a new hotel. Should provision be for 100 per cent occupancy (which as we see has not occurred more than six times in a hundred observations) or, for economy, should the provision be less than this? These are not only decisions about building services such as heating, but also about hotel services such as catering; and they will be reflected in the size of kitchens, dining-rooms and so on. As we have noted, the level of satisfaction selected for a service will be related to the cost of failure to meet a demand for it; but we must remember that by failure we may simply mean, for example, occasional thermal discomfort in bedrooms or a queue for a dining place. Design guides for different building types frequently recommend a *diversity factor*, expressed as a percentage of the maximum occupancy, that may be applied to the provision of a service.

If, again, we assume that the empirical frequency distribution of Fig. 11.55 belongs to the normal family (even though not only has it a lower limit, zero, but also the variable may take only discrete values), we can apply the statistical techniques already described to deduce that a service provision to 85 bedrooms has 0.90 probability of satisfying demand for it. For this level of satisfaction of 90 per cent, the diversity factor is 85 per cent. Since it is the client organization that has to bear the cost of failure, it has to decide on the levels of satisfaction to be provided by the various services. For a hotel, high levels of satisfaction are reflected in the hotel's tariffs.

Exploitation of diversity is a fundamental principle in systems design. To illustrate this we return to the hypothetical data of fuel-oil consumption displayed in Fig. 11.52. Suppose now that it is proposed to construct a complex of *two* blocks, each similar in scale and operation to the building from which the data were collected, so that it can be assumed that the data are equally valid for both. If each block has its own heating system, including fuel storage, two tanks each of 29.3×10^3 litres capacity are required to meet demand with 0.85 probability of satisfaction. As an alternative strategy, we might consider centralization of fuel storage. Now it can be shown that if the mean and standard deviation of one set of n identical frequency distributions are, respectively, $\bar{x}$ and s_x, then the mean of the complete set is $n\bar{x}$, and its standard deviation is $s_x\sqrt{n}$. So the distribution of fuel consumption data for the two blocks combined has a mean of 42 and a standard deviation of 11.3. Notice, compared with the distribution for one block, that although the mean is doubled, the standard deviation is increased by a factor of only $\sqrt{2}$. The combined data is more centrally distributed because there is some probability that the maximum demands in the two blocks will not coincide. We find that, for the same probability of 0.85 satisfaction, the required centralized storage is 53.75×10^3 litres, compared with a total of 58.6×10^3 litres for the two localized stores. Although the mathematical relationships are more complex when dissimilar distributions are combined, we may safely make the generalization that *diversity in demand favours centralization of conversion and storage plant.*

It is economy of scale arising from diversity in demand that is the prime justification for district heating and the centralization of electricity supply. Indeed, a supply authority is likely to structure its tariffs to promote diversity, i.e. the non-coincidence of peak demands from its customers.

There are, however, important influences against centralization within a system. The greater the degree of centralization the longer will be the distribution channels from plant to demand points; failure of centralized plant may mean the failure of the whole system, whereas with decentralization at least some part of the system may continue to function; different *kinds* of demand (for example, in humidity) are more easily satisfied by at least some decentralization (or zoning); and localized plant is more easily controlled to respond to local variations in demand. Systems control is the subject of the next section, and we will be returning to the more general issues of centralization and localization in systems in the final section of this chapter. For now we will simply note that in any reasonably large system we would expect to find varying degrees of centralization of the conversion and storage functions.

11.7 Control of systems

This book is about environments designed economically so that human activity may be pursued in comfort; the function of a relevant system is to provide inputs to such an environment so that some comfort criterion may be achieved and maintained. We have thought of such an environment as the controlled environment of the system. Hence, an environmental variable, such as temperature, which is incorporated in the comfort measure is called a *controlled variable* for the system. The value of the controlled variable required for comfort is termed, variously, its *design value* or *desired value* (both abbreviated as DV).

The variability of the environment will be due to disturbances such as heat losses or gains through the fabric with changes in external climate, and variation in incidental heat gains with changes in occupancy. If the system is to respond to deviations from the design value there must be some manipulation of its throughput; for economy of resources this is usually effected by some switch or valve located between the system and its resource environment. The flow which is thereby varied is called the *manipulated variable* for the system; for example, a manipulated variable for a gas-fired central heating system is the rate of flow of gas to the boiler. This term may also be extended to the setting of the switch or valve.

Control of a system means control over the inputs to it.

Control may be *open-loop* or *closed-loop*, and either may be *manual* or *automatic*. In open-loop control the manipulated variable is in no way affected by the controlled variable. A caretaker turning a heating system on and off at specified times is an example of open-loop manual control; if his instructions are to observe room temperatures and to switch the system on and off according to some temperature criterion, then the control, still manual, is closed-loop; if the switch to the system is governed by some external temperature-sensing device the control is open-loop but automatic; control by a similar device, but which senses internal temperature, is automatic and closed-loop. Notice that it is closed-loop control that requires *feedback* from the controlled environment of information as to the state of the controlled variable (Fig. 11.12). A control system may comprise combinations of any form of control, but in this section we will consider only systems that are automatic.

The first of the above examples demonstrates *open-sequence* control; this may be made automatic if the caretaker is replaced by a clock-operated device. Open-sequence control over space-heating or cooling systems is common in buildings with intermittent use. Ideally we would like to operate these systems only when the building is in use, bringing, on demand, the controlled variable immediately to its design value (Fig. 11.56); but, largely because of the thermal capacity of the building fabric and its contents, this is not possible. Hence, the controlled variable is brought to the design value before the hours of use, the system being activated by a time switch; and, again because of thermal capacity, the controlled variable decays gradually from the design value when the system is switched off (Fig. 11.57).

When the building is occupied the system is governed by closed-loop control. The generalized closed-loop control system (Fig. 11.58) comprises:

(i) sensing devices, which generate signals as to the state of controlled variables;

Fig. 11.56 Ideal open-sequence control.

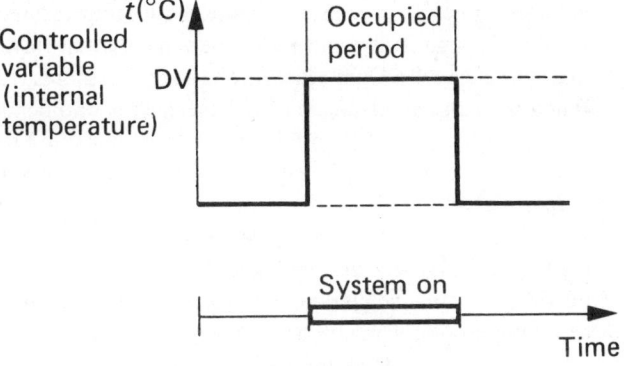

Fig. 11.57 Practical open-sequence control.

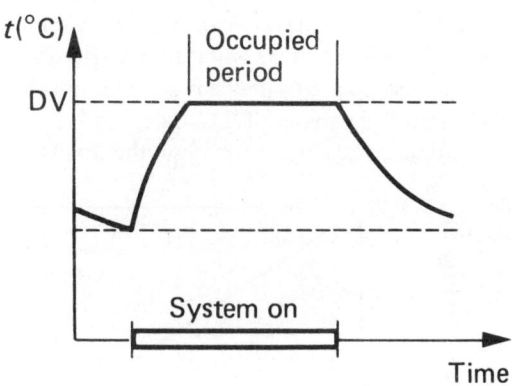

Fig. 11.58 A generalized closed-loop control system.

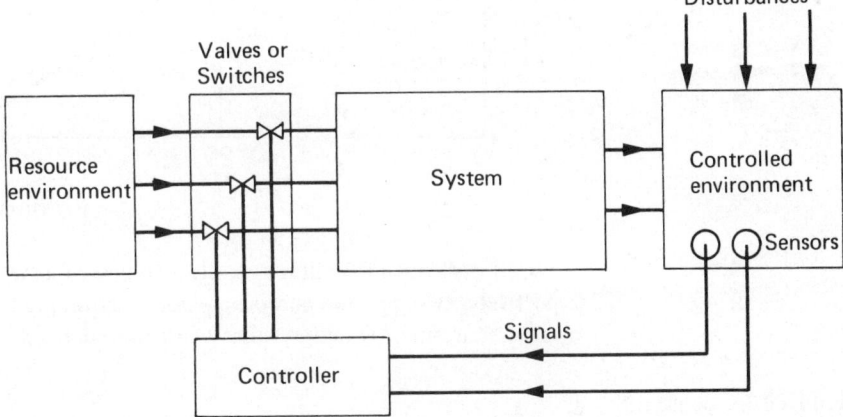

(ii) a controller, which receives these signals, interprets them and, if necessary, takes corrective action on the system inputs;

(iii) valves or switches, the means of control on the input channels.

A wide range of environmental sensors is available. Temperature-sensing devices include the bimetallic strip and the thermistor. The first is composed of two fused strips of different coefficients of expansion. The bending of the strip as its temperature changes is used to make or break an electric circuit. The thermistor is a semiconductor of which the electrical resistance changes with temperature. It is connected in series with a fixed resistance, R, and a constant voltage source. As its resistance varies with temperature, so too does the current flowing through it. By continuity the same current flows through R, and hence, in accordance with Ohm's law, the voltage across this resistance varies as some function of the temperature of the thermistor, and hence of the environment in which it is located. This voltage signal is the signal fed to the controller.

Notice that whereas the signal produced from the movement of the bimetallic strip has only two states, the signal derived from the thermistor may take any value from a continuous range. Movement may, however, be converted to a continuously variable voltage signal by a potentiometer; and this is utilized in humidity sensors which depend on a change of dimension with humidity in certain hygroscopic materials.

With a switch, the manipulated variable may assume only one of two values, with full flow or with no flow. A switch-control system, therefore, has an on–off (or two-position) *mode of control*. A valve permits between its extreme open and closed positions any intermediate flow rate. Within these limits the value of the manipulated variable is a continuous function of the deviation of the controlled variable. The simplest and cheapest continuous mode of control is proportional action, i.e. when the function is linear (Fig. 11.59).

Fig. 11.59 Proportional action mode of control

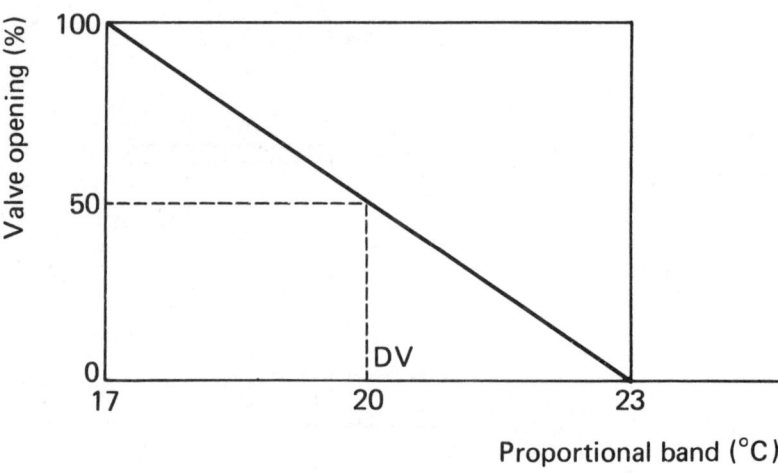

Figs. 11.60 and 11.61 illustrate the response of a system to deviation with, respectively, two-position and proportional action modes of control. Notice that in the first around the design value is introduced an *operating differential* within

Fig. 11.60 Response of a system to deviation with a two-position mode of control.

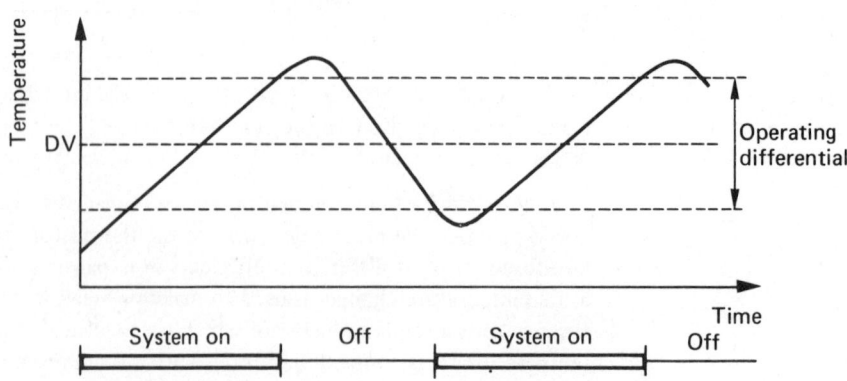

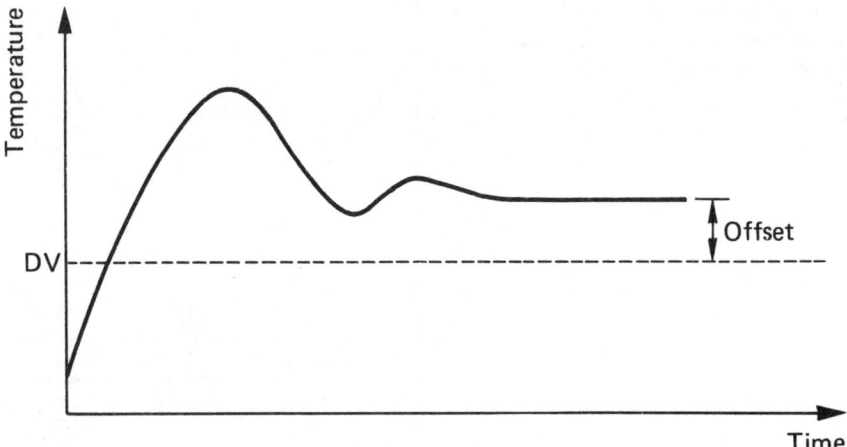

Fig. 11.61 Response of a system to deviation with a proportional action mode of control.

which the control system will not respond to changes in the controlled variable. This differential is necessary to avoid excessive switching and consequent wear on system mechanisms. It follows that the controlled variable is only momentarily at its design value.

In proportional action the valve setting (and, hence, the heat flow into the controlled environment) is calculated on an assumed heat loss and, therefore, on an assumed climatic temperature. It follows that, with this mode of control, generally there is sustained deviation or *offset* from the design value. There are more sophisticated (and more expensive) modes of control which reduce or eliminate offset.

Sensors should be carefully located to give the best information about the controlled environment. Consider an environment heated or cooled by a single air-duct system (Fig. 11.62). A sensor at A tells nothing about room conditions or heat gains or losses; nor can it detect lagging due to thermal capacity. A sensor at B or C is to be preferred; at B care must be taken to shield it from spurious local effects; at C the space conditions are averaged out. Where one system serves many environments they should, if possible, be zoned so that within a zone the environments are exposed to comparable disturbance (it is difficult, for example,

Fig. 11.62 Location of sensors.

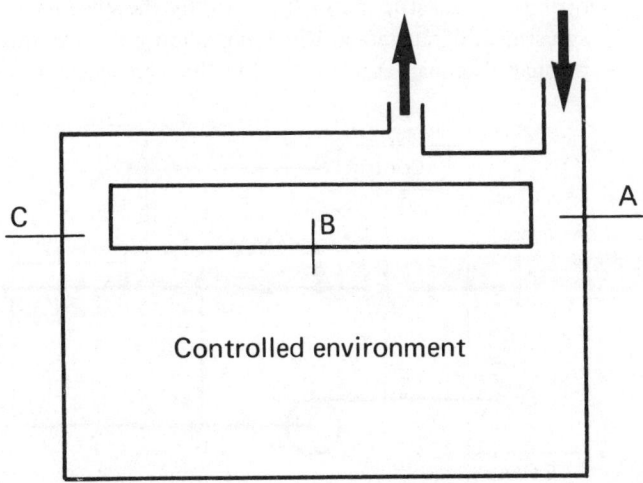

Fig. 11.63 Sequenced proportional control. *PB* is the proportional band.

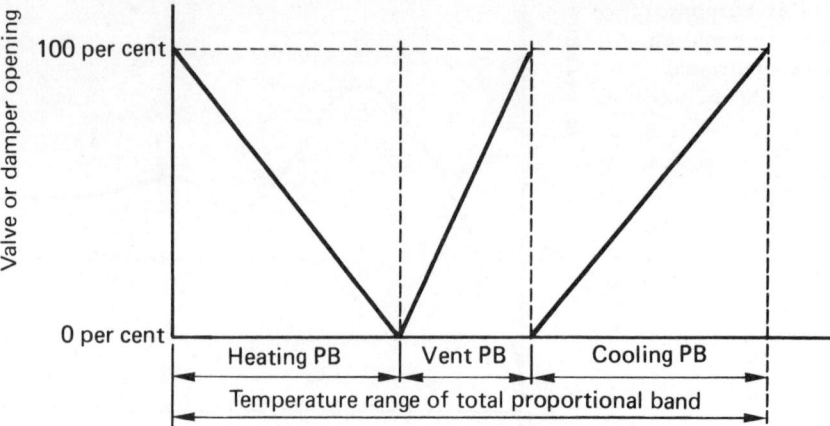

to design a system to respond adequately through the same distribution channel to the very different variations that may occur in north- and south-facing rooms); and within a zone the environment chosen for sensor location should be 'typical'.

For an air-ducted system, proportional control could be sequential over heating batteries, air inlet damper and cooling batteries (Fig. 11.63). Of course, cooling by ventilation will depend on external air temperature, and the control system will require a sensor at the air inlet.

Let us now consider the application of control to the space-heating system of Fig. 11.24. B, C and D are three environments and we will take C as the average environment in which to locate a temperature sensor. A two-position mode of control implies switching of heat supply, which is more suitable for fluid than for solid fuels. Although this mode of control is common for gas- or oil-fired domestic heating systems, it is rarely used in large systems since, not only does it lack centralized manipulation of the rate at which heat is supplied, it also involves repeated operation of boilers at low efficiency (*see* Fig. 11.28). For proportional-action or some other continuous mode of control, the sensor in C must provide a continuous signal; a thermistor is suitable.

Generally, control is achieved by maintaining the water from the exchanger at a constant high temperature, mixing it with cooler water from the return channel, and varying the proportion of the mix at a mixing valve (Fig. 11.64). The valve is operated by electric motor, governed by the system controller. Final local adjustment of the rate at which hot water circulates through individual radiators is usually manual (at b, c or d); but there are available automatic control valves

Fig. 11.64 Control by mixing-valve.

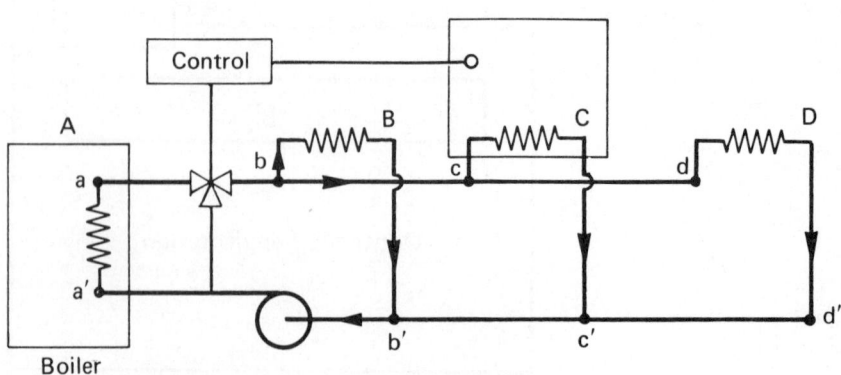

(with sensors either built-in or remote) for this purpose. (But beware ! The combination of individual and centralized control may cause problems if the average environment does not have an average occupant.)

The control system of Fig. 11.64 is particularly suitable when a building is zoned, that is when within it are grouped environments which make similar demands on the system. The grouping may be due to similarity in function or in exposure to disturbance. Fig. 11.65 shows a system with three zones, with zonal control by mixing. In the terms of the previous section we have centralized conversion, with the benefits of diversity, together with a degree of decentralization of control.

Fig. 11.65 Zonal control.

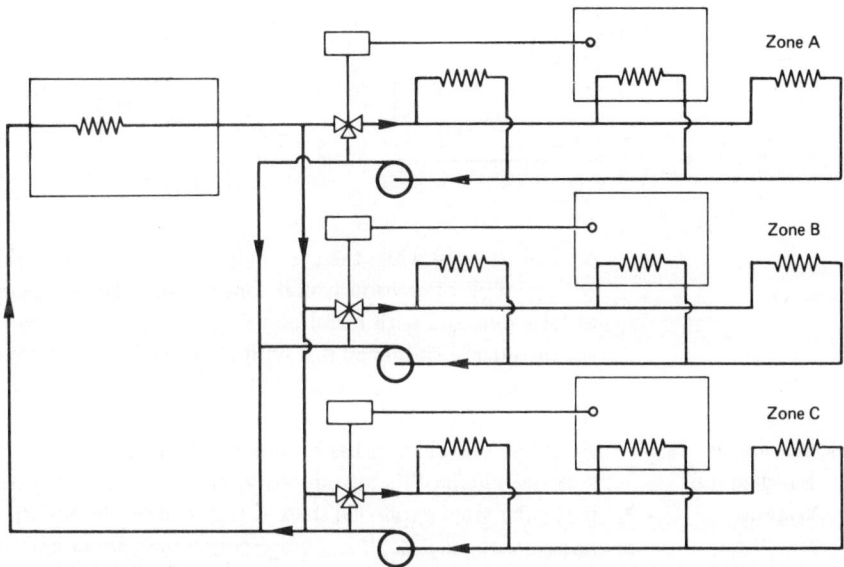

Although the peak/average demand ratio should be smaller for centralized than for localized plant, it may still be significantly high if the pattern of zonal occupation is unfavourable. The reader should remind himself of the typical boiler efficiency curve (Fig. 11.28). If the pattern of demand on the plant is such that it will operate for substantial periods at low loads, i.e. with poor efficiency, the capital benefits of centralization will rapidly be offset by high running costs. In this circumstance, centralized plant should be made up of smaller units (i.e. it should be modularized) that can operate efficiently in combination according to the load (Fig. 11.66).

It should be noted that modularization reduces substantially the risk of total system failure, and that, without interruption to supply, it permits repair and maintenance work on plant during intervals of low demand.

A large modern building may contain many systems each with a quite complex control mechanism. At the heart of each control system is a controller, an analogue or digital device that transforms a signal into action according to a set of rules. The controller is the most expensive component in a control system, and a change of control strategy may mean a change of controller. For these reasons there is increasing interest in the centralization, in the form of a mini-computer, of all the controllers in a building complex. The computer as controller would permit, merely by a change in its program, experiment in

Fig. 11.66 Centralized plant made up of modular units.

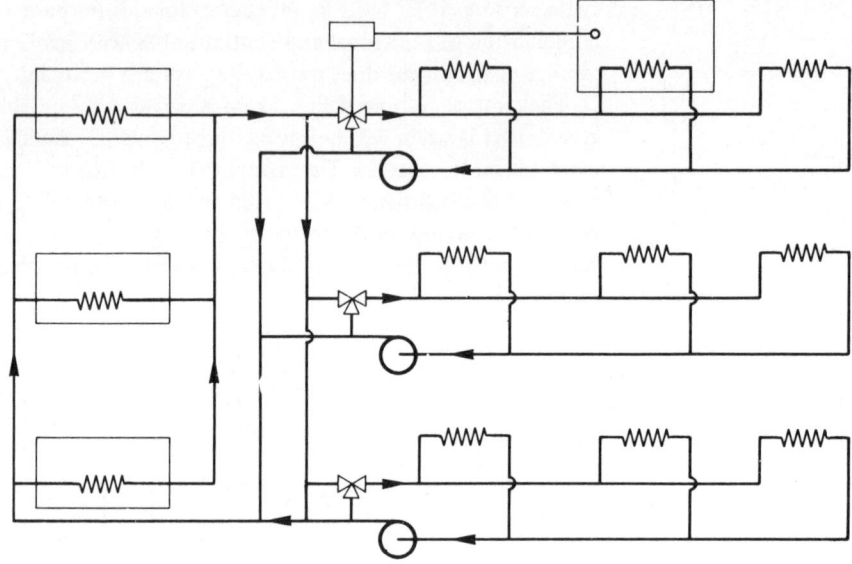

control strategy while the system is in operation. It could be associated not only with systems of environmental control, but also, for example, with lift installations and with manufacturing or other processes which are the function of the organization. Indeed it is with organizations that are already dependent on the computer that we are most likely to find this extension of its role.

11.8 Services as building sub-systems

Although this chapter has been concerned with the special category of flow systems, much of its introductory section applies to systems in general. The particular view expressed there is that systems boundaries are defined by *function* or purpose; it is a usage consciously inconsistent with the general in that, for example, it could not as yet encompass a *planetary system*. Until recent years it was not common even to think of our earth as a system. It was generally considered to be the infinite environment in which all man-made systems prospered more-or-less independently. With the growth of these systems consequent on increasing population and expectation, there has been a progressive enmeshing of their resource and controlled environments, and this has forced into our consciousness the finite boundary around human activity; the boundary is the earth, and the only input is of energy at a constant rate from space. So, out of our necessity, we have given to the earth the function of sustaining and enriching human life; only then have we recognized it as a system, and we now explore the connections between its sub-systems, seeking thereby to direct the system as a whole.

In this book we hope to contribute to that exploration; the awareness of the systems context for buildings as consumers of resources, in particular resources of energy, is its motivation. In Chapter 2 the function which, for this purpose, defines a building as a system is made quite explicit: it is to achieve a satisfactory thermal environment for those human activities that require shelter. Hence, the building is seen as a complex *energy-flow system*. For this function the measure of building performance is direct: that solution is best that provides the required environment with the least consumption of finite energy resources. This measure then disciplines all decision-making in the progress of design. It conditions the compactness of the building envelope; the construction of the building fabric; the choice of structure; and it has consistently informed the discussion of building services in this chapter.

While the aims of this book require this particular definition of building function, the full diversity of architecture, a consequence of the richness of life itself, does not permit a single definition that is both sufficiently comprehensive, and, at the same time, useful as a criterion for total design. A building is designed to meet a *set* of objectives.

It may still, therefore, be properly considered, in totality, as a system. So viewed, an assessment of its performance may be attempted by comparing the measure to which it consumes resources and the degree to which it fulfils its separate aims [9]. However, it must be admitted that there are two important limitations to such a systems approach to building design: except when particular circumstances — such indeed as energy scarcity — give one priority over others, there is no clear ordering principle to be applied between the satisfaction of all the different objectives; and for some objectives, including perhaps the most important, satisfaction is not quantifiable. But even though these limitations — which some may claim merely to be in our present understanding — preclude a resolution of all design problems according to objective systems criteria, each designer will have his own not fully articulated values by which he balances (rather than optimizes) satisfaction of different and possibly conflicting aims; and he is well aware when his design begins to meet all of its multifarious objectives to some sufficient degree, that is when it begins to 'work' as a whole — as a system. It is as sub-systems of the now admittedly imprecisely defined system that is a building that our interest in services is extended in this last section.

A flow system has a *topological structure*. It can clearly be recognized that the two systems of Fig. 11.67 are in some important essence the same, although it is true that the distribution channels of each will be of different dimension and that, therefore, there will be differences in the sizing and costs of the systems. But they both comprise the same numbers of conversion and storage components, linked in the same order by a distribution network. We say that the structures of the systems are topologically identical.

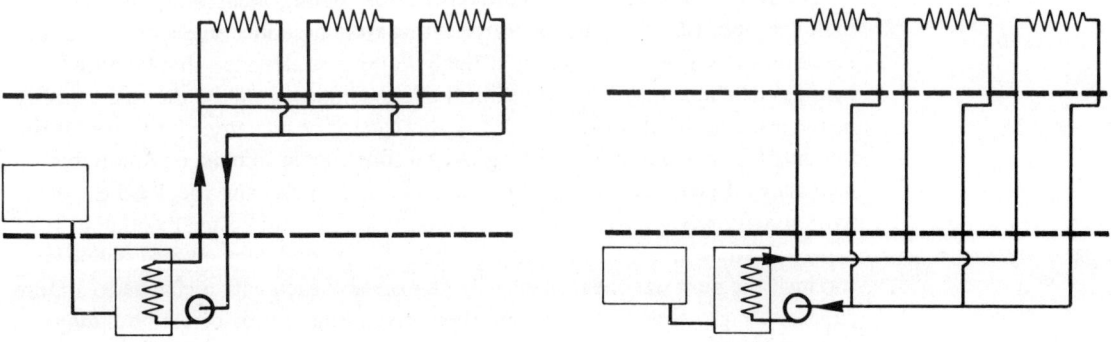

Fig. 11.67 Topologically identical systems.

We will consider first what, in a given context, makes one service topology more appropriate than another. We have seen in preceding sections how this may be decided to some extent on energy considerations alone; consequently we may have, for example, modularized plant or zoned control. But the influences we are interested in here are spatial. At an early stage in the progress of a design spatial relationships are also topological. Associations between activities are used to relate them without particular reference to dimension in space; the activities become fixed in space as the design crystallizes. So too do the points at which demands are made on services.

The extension of demand points in space is of particular significance to the topology of secondary-medium systems because the medium has a limited energy-carrying capacity. Since the point will perhaps be clearer if it is made specific we will consider how it applies to the particular problems of space-cooling (and, by extension, space-heating and air-conditioning) by means of mechanical transfer of energy to air. The reader will recall that, as summarized in Fig. 11.33, three types of component comprise the conventional cooling plant of buildings: refrigerating pump, air-handling unit and cooling tower. We begin with the situation where there is one component of each type, located in a *services centre*; in all but the simplest contexts the chilled air must be distributed through a network of ducts (Fig. 11.68, cf. Fig. 11.26).

Fig. 11.68 Space-cooling with centralized plant.

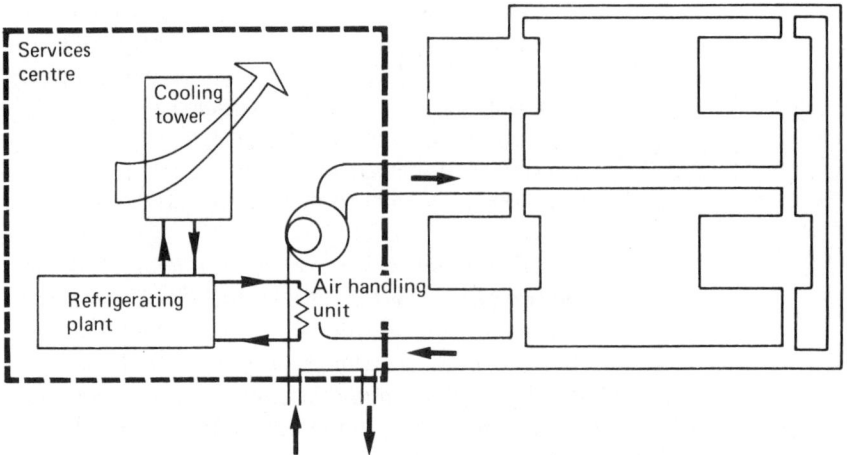

The system will satisfy ventilation as well as cooling needs; and the approximate methods for sizing such a network that were described in Section 11.2 are based on the former, assuming that the building is so designed that cooling (or heating) demands may be met within the limits imposed by the thermal capacity of the distributing air medium. Clearly this cannot be guaranteed, for even if the building fabric and ductwork linings are so constructed to reduce undesirable heat gains, these cannot be totally eliminated and so we cannot extend the network indefinitely without the air, at some stage, critically losing its cooling capacity. There are other problems of scale: if the total demand for cooling is too high the duct sizes near plant may be excessive even with a change to a more expensive high-velocity system, and these may mean high associated building costs and inconvenience in planning; the required fan power for long distribution runs may be greater than is readily available commercially.

The usual solution is to change to a distributing medium that has greater thermal capacity, say water, and to effect the transfer to air at various points throughout the complex (Fig. 11.69). We have then moved from the topology of

Fig. 11.69 A system with sub-centres for energy transfer.

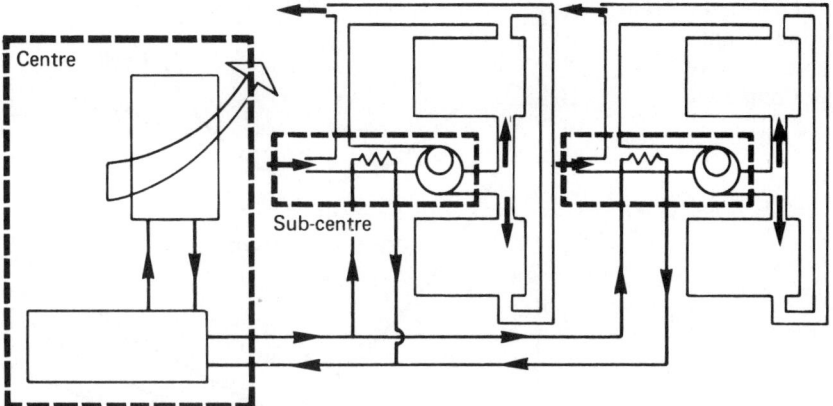

a single services centre to one in which, while some plant is still centralized, there are *sub-centres* for energy transfer. We may think of a transfer unit as connecting two distribution networks; one (water-medium) originating in the refrigerator and the other (air-medium) terminating in the controlled environment. These are, respectively, the primary and secondary networks of the unit. For a given distribution of demand points in space, as we increase the number of sub-centres we reduce the total secondary network and increase the primary (Fig. 11.70), and correspondingly reduce and increase their costs.

Fig. 11.70 Variation in primary and secondary networks.

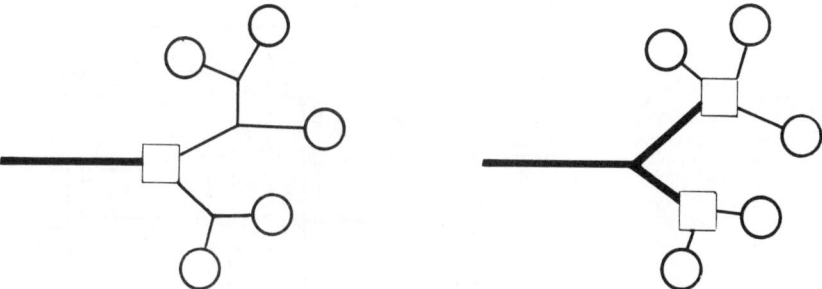

But these are not the only cost effects. For it follows from Section 11.6 that if there is any diversity in demand within a system it will favour centralization of plant; and, moreover, it is generally true that one piece of plant is cheaper than two combined to meet the same extreme demand.* From both aspects it follows that plant *capital* costs are usually increased by decentralization. In Fig. 11.71 the first costs for a varying number of sub-centres in a system for a hypothetical building complex are summed to produce an optimum.

Notice that it is suggested that associated building costs increase with the number of sub-centres since the costs of provision of space for sub-centres are likely to be more influential than savings on building costs associated with changes in distribution medium. It is clear that, unless the cost of secondary distribution is substantially reduced as the number of sub-centres is increased then, on the basis of first costs, there can be no case for decentralization.

*This statement is undermined if there are easily available, appropriate and cheap mass-produced packaged units.

Fig. 11.71 First costs as
functions of the
number of sub-centres
(after Copple and
Murray [10]).

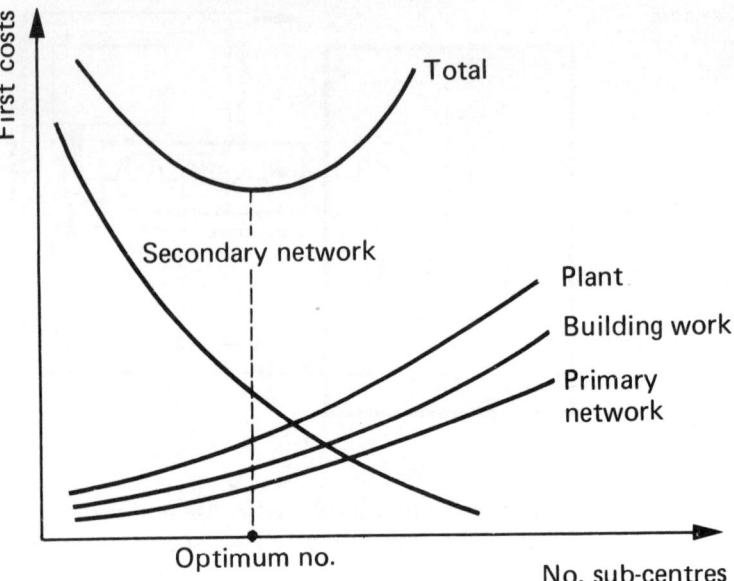

Fig. 11.72 A system
with centralized plant
and zonal after-cooling.

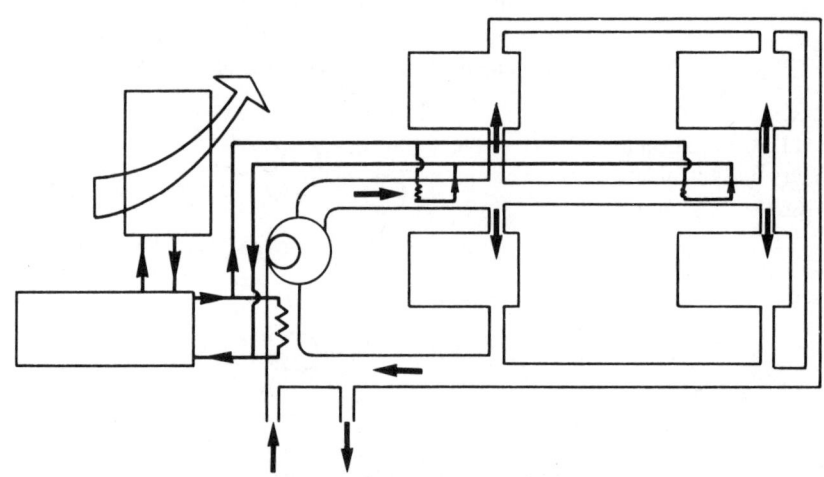

Fig. 11.73 Decentralization of refrigeration.

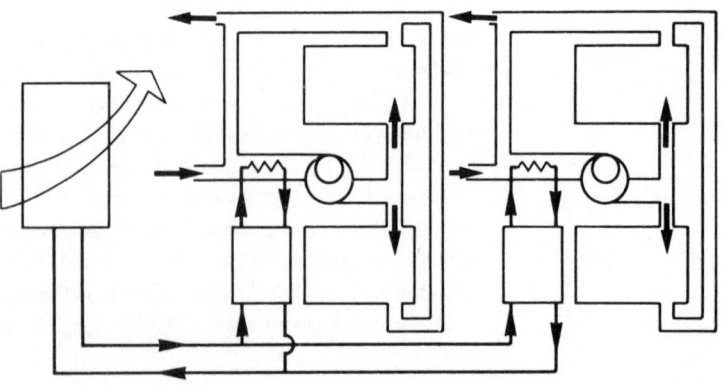

Fig. 11.74 Decentralization of refrigeration and heat rejection.

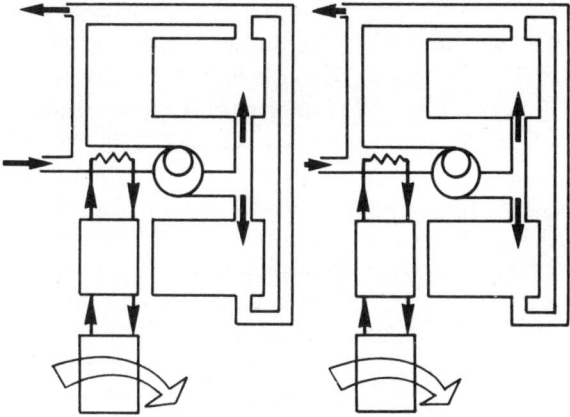

Fig. 11.75 The fully-localized system.

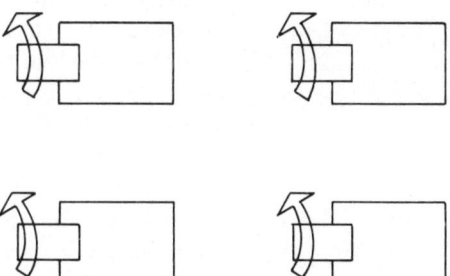

Fig. 11.72 represents a compromise between the two systems thus far compared. It maintains the centralization of plant, including fans, but the cooling capacity of the distributed air is boosted locally through water-chilled batteries. The process of decentralization may be continued by the localization of refrigeration (Fig. 11.73), and then of heat-rejection (Fig. 11.74); first as shown in zones and ultimately in small mass-produced units fixed through external walls of individual rooms (Fig. 11.75).

Between the extremes represented by Figs. 11.68 and 11.75 there are systems in which while cooling is centralized the exchange of air is effected in room units. One is the fan–coil system described in Section 11.2 and illustrated in Fig. 11.27; another is the induction system in which sufficient air to refresh the controlled environment is ducted to a unit where its emission at very high velocity drags room air over a cooling coil. It is not likely, however, that the choice of a high degree of decentralization will be motivated by the preceding logic, but by factors of zoning and control discussed in Section 11.7.

Recognition of the general in the particular is one of the intended benefits of systems thinking. It is important that the application by analogy of Fig. 11.24, and the heating concepts to which it refers, to the water-cooled circuit of Fig. 11.69 be appreciated; and, similarly, that the present arguments are not restricted to space-cooling. So too, the necessity to balance primary and secondary distribution costs does not apply merely to energy transfer units, but to all plant. A primary network may comprise, for example, an access road for delivery of fossil fuel, and a corresponding secondary network may be that of a space-heating system; the intervening plant will be for fuel storage and conversion. Notice that to produce the primary and secondary distribution cost curves in Fig. 11.71 there must be some assumption about *location* of services sub-centres. By summing the costs of alternative proportions of primary and secondary network it would be possible to arrive at the optimum location of each piece of plant within a system. But here, as with most services decisions, other factors (such as restrictions on access) are likely to be influential. Where the costs of primary network may safely be ignored, the location of plant near the centre of demand (analogous with centre of gravity) is a good, but not infallible, guide, as this should keep the total cost of secondary network near to its minimum.

As we have seen, the important influence on secondary-medium systems topology is the energy-carrying capacity of the distribution medium. Suppose the medium, with specific heat c J kg^{-1} K^{-1}, circulates through the supply exchanger at a rate of q kg s^{-1}, and its temperature is thereby raised t °C; then the rate at which heat is supplied at the exchanger is qct W. So one obvious way to increase the heat content of the medium is to raise its temperature; but there are limitations on this. If the medium is air, since q and c are both low, the temperature has to be raised considerably to achieve a significant increase in heat content; possibly well above the temperature appropriate to the required ventilation rate. If the medium is water, the limitations are the temperatures at which it changes state. Steam itself can, of course, be used as a heating medium, but it requires a more complicated technology; it is now more common to use water under pressure, which elevates its boiling point. For any of the larger water-medium systems that we have previously described, such as that of Fig. 11.66, the circulating medium is likely to be under pressure so that its temperature may be in excess of 100 °C. Similarly, the freezing point of water may be depressed by the addition of solute, and brine is a common cooling medium.

We have assumed that the appropriate topology of a services system is determined by the location in space of the points of demand on the system. But, since design is an iterative process, it may well be that a possible topology stimulates the designer in his spatial organization and, indeed, in the formal expression he gives to it; it is, therefore, important for him to be equipped with alternative systems strategies in his early exploration of his client's brief.

We now progress to that stage of design beyond abstract topological relationships when the designer begins to locate in space all the various components which comprise the building system. The components belong to functionally defined sub-systems, of which for our present purpose we will limit consideration to three: those with, respectively, structural, space-enclosing and service functions (Fig. 11.76).

We must remember that systems may share components: they need not be spatially distinct. A sharing of components is indicated by overlapping of systems; there is a clear parallel here with Venn diagrams of sets. Thus, in Fig. 11.77, components which are both structural and space-enclosing but not services (such as load-bearing walls) would be represented in the shaded overlap between the sub-systems.

Fig. 11.76 Three sub-systems of a building system.

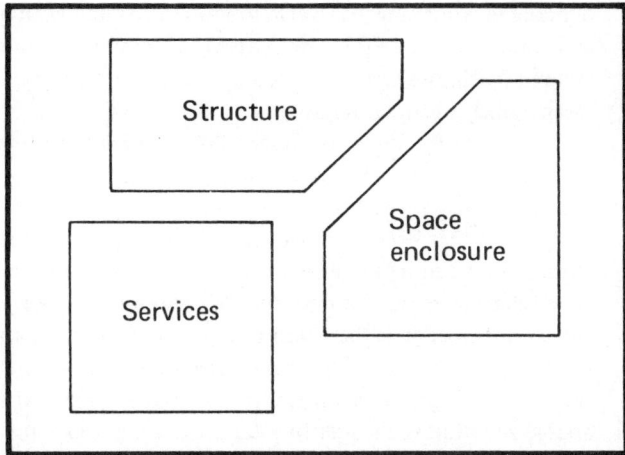

Fig. 11.77 Sub-systems overlap.

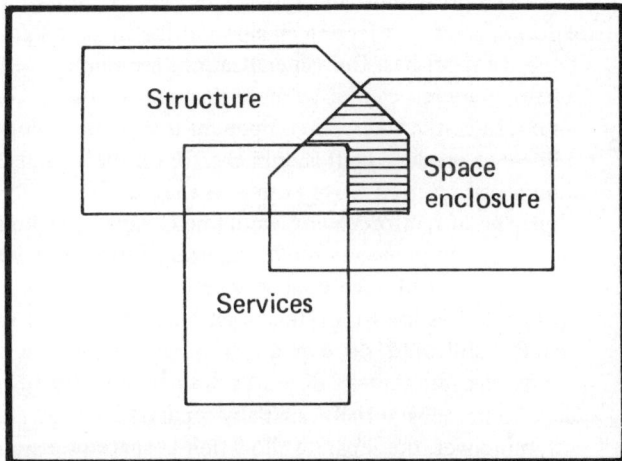

Fig. 11.78 Near-identity of sub-systems.

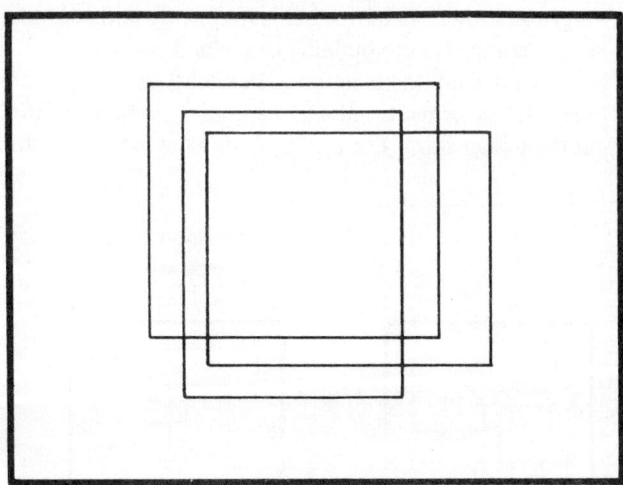

As other examples of shared components we may instance the early industrial hollow cast-iron columns also intended as distribution channels for steam, as mentioned in Chapter 2; and there has recently been completed a library building in which mechanical ventilation is routed within precast concrete beams and columns. Fig. 11.78 represents an almost total identity of the three sub-systems, such as is approximated by the traditional brickwork house, and in recent times, by the inflatable.

The degree to which sub-systems overlap may be dictated by objectives of the building system. It may, for example, be that the system must be responsive to significant changes of function. Now, if a change requires modification of a component that belongs to two sub-systems, then obviously the effect of that change will be more widespread, and probably more expensive, than if the component were part of only one. We may generalize from this argument as long as we remember that there will be exceptions to prove the rule: the degree to which sub-systems overlap is an inverse indication of the *flexibility* of the total system. Let us generalize further: if we can assume that a component that has a double function is cheaper in total than two corresponding single-function components, then it would follow that flexibility, as we have described it, is bought at a price in initial capital. This cost would have to be balanced against the future costs of effecting change and the total compared with the costs of alternative strategies. Our generalizations are summarised in Fig. 11.79. The diagram, however, cannot be more than an hypothesis to be tested in a given context, since the cost of a component is very much dependent on industry's readiness to produce it. It is unlikely, for example, that the hollow concrete columns just referred to, requiring, as they would, greater precision in formwork and placing of reinforcement, would be cheaper than conventionally independent columns and ducts; unless a contractor were geared to mass-produce them. Although the cost interpretation of Fig. 11.79 can, therefore, only be a suggestion for particular analysis, the flexibility implication is more generally valid. And, since modification prior to change requires access to com-ponents, the functionally disjoint sub-systems of the highly flexible building must also be, substantially, spatially separate.

If, moreover, the separate allocation in space of disjoint sub-systems is made the *principle* upon which the total system (that is the building) is to be organized, then we have what is frequently and confusingly referred to as the systems approach to building design and construction. To this approach should accrue not only the benefits of flexibility-in-use, in accordance with the preceding argument, but also a speedier discharge of professional responsibilities at the design stage. For just as, during the life of a building, the effects of a

Fig. 11.79 Flexibility and cost of systems.

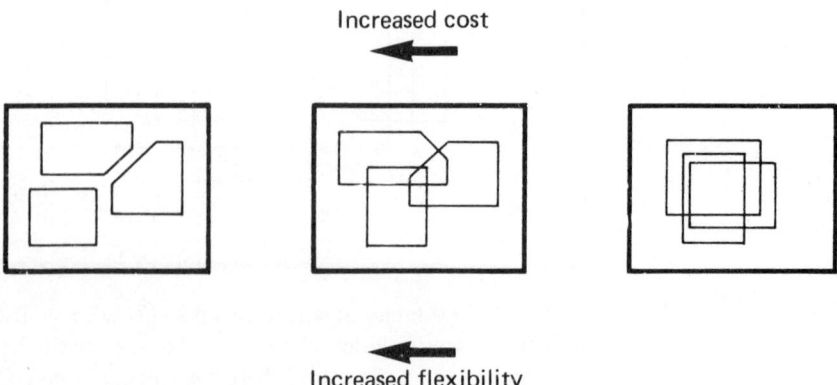

Increased cost

Increased flexibility

modification to a sub-system would be localized to it, so too, during the process of design, would be the effects of a change in decision concerning a sub-system. Hence, in theory, it should be possible to optimize the design of any sub-system with little reference to the others; and communications between the various decision-makers (and notice how closely the three sub-systems we have defined correspond to the separate interests of the structural engineer, the services engineer and the architect) could be correspondingly simplified. It cannot be claimed, however, that this approach permits optimization of the system as a whole, unless the objectives of speed in design and construction, and flexibility-in-use have very heavy weighting. This would seem to have been the case in the example to which the reader is referred [11].

It is important, by the way, to avoid even further confusion in terminology by not mistaking this approach to the *building as a system* for a proprietory *building system* comprising prefabricated construction components; although, of course, use of the latter may be adopted within the former.

The flexibility implication of Fig. 11.79 assumes that the alternative systems have the same life. The systems approach described immediately above assumes the building to have a conventional life span during which it may suffer significant change-in-use. An alternative strategy is to choose a short-life system (such as the inflatable) that is disposed of when it becomes obsolete. For such a system the economic hypothesis would suggest an integration of sub-systems.

The degree of flexibility offered by spatial separation of sub-systems is not required in most buildings; more typically the designer juxtaposes components from the different sub-systems or even, as we have seen, shares components between them. To a large extent it is the manner in which these component relationships are manipulated that gives to a building its architectural quality. In services it is distribution networks permeating a building that present the designer with this particular challenge and opportunity. This chapter is, therefore, concluded as it began, with consideration of distribution channels, but now in the context of the total building system.

In order not to compromise the use of space, distribution is usually effected through a network of horizontal and vertical channels. Where the cost of horizontal and vertical runs differ there will be, for a particular service and for a

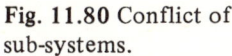

Fig. 11.80 Conflict of sub-systems.

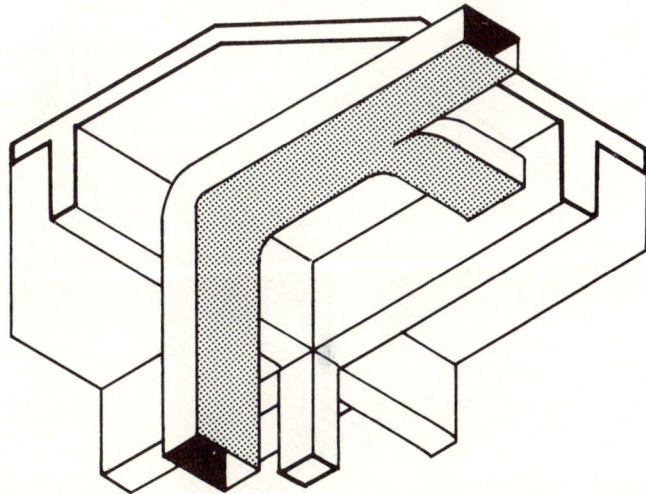

given location of its sinks in space, an optimum number of vertical risers. However, this number is not likely to be the same for one service (say, ventilation) as for another (say, hot-water supply). Now, in a multi-storey building every continuous vertical element is a constraint on planning; the fewer the better. So it is usual to make intuitive departures from dimly recognized optima and to group vertical service risers into a few ducts, even just one. But the argument may be carried further: a structural system usually also contains continuous vertical elements; it is common, therefore, to attempt to include these in the grouping.

This attempt has an inherent difficulty, particularly in framed buildings: near column heads are places of maximum shear force, and these are not the best to be perforated by service risers; the junction of column and beams is often near to horizontal branching from vertical runs, and the beam system may interfere with the routing of horizontal ducts (Fig. 11.80).

It is, of course, possible to run horizontal ducts freely below the structural beams, in which case the network is often concealed by suspended ceilings. It will be appreciated that this solution is bought at the cost of increased building volume. A spatially more economical answer is to treat each column as a pair of elements placed either side of the duct (the pairing may, in fact, increase structural stiffness). The corresponding beam system, with a shallow connection between the vertical elements, permits a free run of horizontal ducts in one direction within the overall structural depth. Figs. 11.81, 11.82 and 11.83 illustrate this concept and its progressive elaboration that allows duct runs in two horizontal directions and then into the structural bay itself. Figs. 11.82 and 11.83 represent the fully developed *tartan-grid* plan, in which narrow service bands alternate in two directions with broad serviced areas; if adequately dimensioned, the narrow bays may also be used for circulation. These grids have in the UK been the bases of master plans for highly-serviced and phased building complexes [12].

The tartan grid is a discipline most suitable for low-rise development. It is motivated by the need for horizontal circulation or services routes to deep within a site, and the comparative restriction in number of vertical structural-

Fig. 11.81 Compatibility of sub-systems.

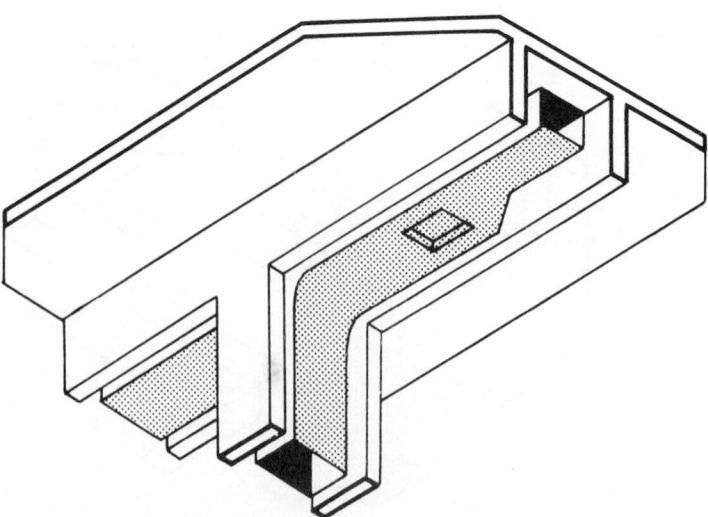

Fig. 11.82 The tartan-grid (1).

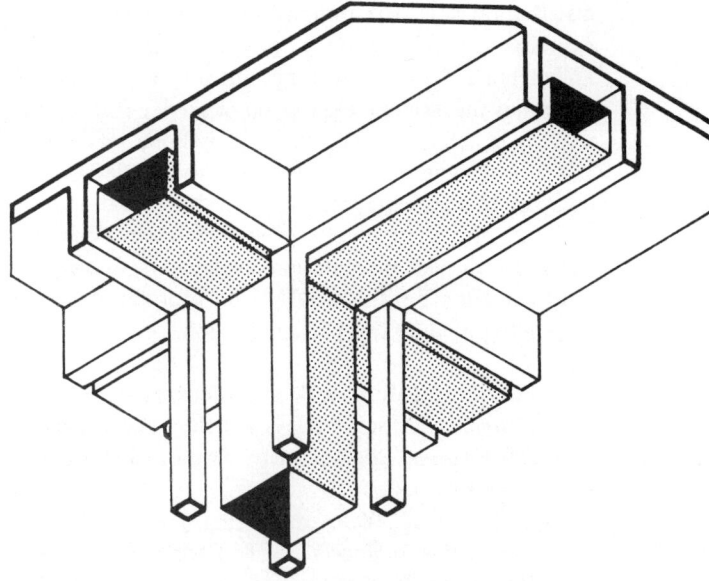

Fig. 11.83 The tartan-grid (2).

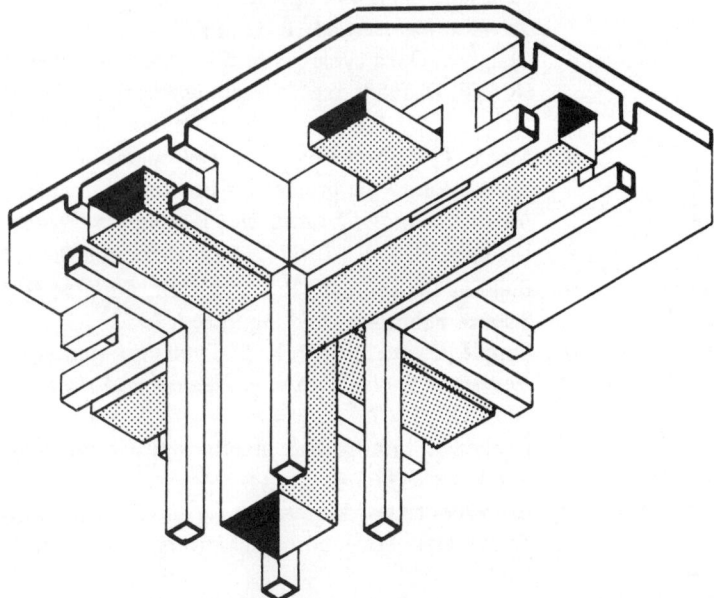

services elements. In high-rise building other vertical features − stairwells and lift shafts − assume greater significance, and the core in which are packed lifts, escape stairs, service risers and closely associated rooms has long been a feature of such constructions. The core has frequently been used for structural stiffening against wind forces, and its structural potential has been dramatically extended in recent immense American towers. In these the requirement for natural lighting is relaxed, and the consequent very deep structures are stiffened according to the hull-core principle.

A vertical stacking of services elements need not be located centrally, though it is still convenient to call it a services core. Clearly, the further it is from the geometric centre of a building complex the longer must be the horizontal distribution runs. The grouping of served spaces around service cores may be exploited for architectural effect, as in Kahn's Richards Laboratories in Philadelphia. Less monumental, but similarly motivated as an organizing formal system, is the external expression of service towers (frequently containing little more than escape stairs) connected by horizontal bands of perimeter ducting; this is now something of a cliché of modern design. It would be interesting to compare the aesthetic intention of this integration of services, circulation and structure into a few simple articulated design elements with the quite different image of sub-system separation displayed, for example, in the recent Pompidou Centre in Paris; but this would lead us too far outside the boundary of the system imposed by this particular book.

References

1 Shearer, L., Murphy, A. and Richardson, H., *Introduction to Linear Systems*. Addison-Wesley, Reading, Mass., 1967.

2 *IHVE Guide, Book C*. Institution of Heating and Ventilating Engineers, London, 1970.

3 Stokes, R. W., Warm air heating. *Journal of the Institution of Heating and Ventilating Engineers,* **38**, 1–10, 1970.

4 Robertson, P., McKenzie, E. and Ravenscroft, R., A new approach to the economic sizing and operation of space heating boiler plant. *Building Services Engineer,* **41**, 1–11, 1973.

5 Craig, H., Open-cycle gas turbines and total energy. In *Total Energy* (R.M.E. Diamant, ed.). Pergamon Press, Oxford, 1970, Chapter 5.

6 Maver, T. W., *Building Services Design*. RIBA Publications, London, 1971.

7 Maver, T. W., Some techniques of operational research illustrated by their application to the problem of hot and cold water plant sizing. *Journal of the Institution of Heating and Ventilating Engineers,* **33**, 301–313, 1965.

8 Diamant, R. M.E., *Total Energy*. Pergamon Press, Oxford, 1970, Chapter 10.

9 Building Performance Research Unit, *Building Performance*. Applied Science Publishers, Barking, Essex, 1972.

10 Copple, C. and Murray, K. I., Total cost approach to hospital design. *Journal of the Institution of Heating and Ventilating Engineers,* **37**, 303–319, 1967.

11 Weekes, J., Intermediate architecture. *Transactions of the Bartlett Society,* **2**, 83–106, 1963-4;

12 Arup Associates, *Master Plan for the Loughborough University of Technology*. Loughborough University of Technology, Loughborough, 1966.

12
ENERGY ACCOUNTING–
METHODS OF ANALYSIS

12.1 Introduction

This chapter examines the methods used to evaluate energy at global, national and individual consumer levels within the system boundaries of a building resource allocation model. (*Note*: in the context of this Chapter, unless otherwise stated, energy is taken to mean the energy required to control and maintain the internal environment of buildings.)

12.2 Measurement of resources

Historically, money, as a method of facilitating barter, has always been accepted as the ultimate measure of the availability of a resource. The use of money implies scarcity, since we only barter one scarce thing for another. In turn, the fact of scarcity makes it necessary for us to economize, i.e. to achieve the best use of limited resources.

Recently, however, there has been an increasing tendency to challenge the reliability of money, in the form of market prices, as a suitable method of measuring energy resources. *Building Research Establishment Current Paper 56/75* 'Energy conservation: a study of energy consumption in buildings and possible means of saving energy in housing' [1] demonstrates an attempt to modify market prices to take account of national as well as individual consumer interests by using a technique called national or prime energy accounting.

Prime energy accounting, whilst still using currency as a method of measuring energy resources, replaces the metered price of energy paid by the individual consumer with the estimated cost to the nation of the prime energy resource which is consumed to deliver a given quantity of energy to the consumer. The calculations involve estimates of the energy expended in running power stations, in transportation and distribution: as well as the energy losses which occur upon conversion, particularly from fossil fuel to electricity [1, 2]. A more radical approach to energy economics has recently been developed, called energy analysis. Based on the laws of thermodynamics, rather than economics, energy analysis does not rely on money as a unit of measurement but attempts to quantify the resultant reduction from the global stock of energy caused by the provision of a commodity or service at a chosen point in the economic system. Energy analysis is not an alternative theory of value to money but is based on the premise that energy, like time, can be used only once, i.e. energy is unique, in that, unlike any other resource, it cannot be recycled. Thus, the unit of measurement used in energy analysis is a unit of energy, normally the joule [3].

The use of the word 'energy' in the context of energy analysis means not only the energy required to maintain and control the built environment, but also the energy required to produce the built environment.

To summarize, the energy required to control and maintain the internal environment of buildings can be measured at different levels in the economic system:

(i) individual consumer level, using market prices;
(ii) national level, using prime energy accounting;
(iii) global level, using energy analysis.

Energy analysis, level (iii), attempts to measure not only the energy consumed by a building throughout its life, but also the energy expended in producing the building.

All three methods of measurement, irrespective of their methodology, can be prescribed by a single model with clearly defined boundaries which describes the allocation of resources required to produce a building and to control and maintain its internal environment throughout its life span.

12.3 Building resource allocation model

Clearly, any durable, be it a building, washing machine or motor car, involves the allocation or expenditure of resources throughout its life. In a building this resource allocation could range from stripping turf on a green field site in preparation for the erection of a new building, to spreading top soil and sowing grass seed 60 years hence after the building has been demolished.

It is normal practice when considering the allocation of resources in a building to group these resources into four main elements:

(i) construction;
(ii) maintenance;
(iii) running (energy);
(iv) demolition.

The percentage distribution of resources among the elements will vary widely depending on building type and use patterns of the occupants of the building. The four elements are closely interdependent; for example, by expending a large amount of resources at the construction stage it would be possible to construct an extremely robust building with a high-quality durable finish which would have low maintenance demand characteristics requiring a small resource

Fig. 12.1 Graph of durability of initial building provision against cost.

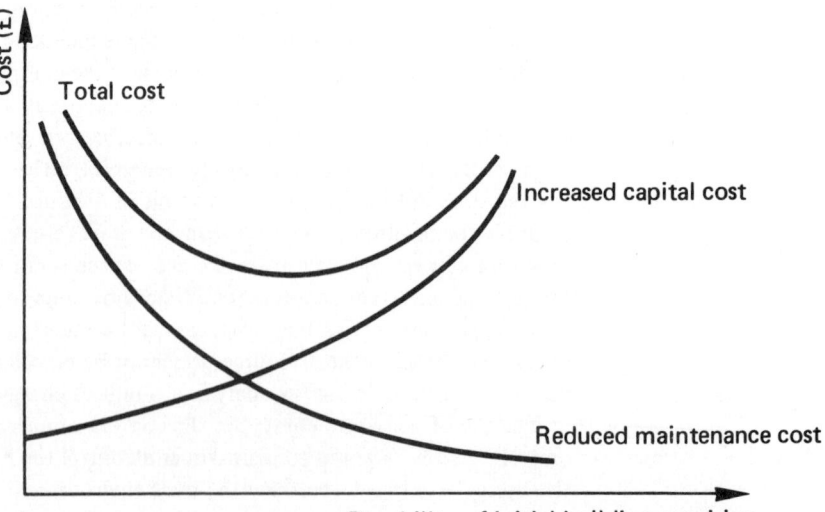

allocation throughout the life of the building. The converse of this example is also true, in that it is equally possible to construct a building of similar area to that given in the first example with high maintenance demand characteristics coupled with a smaller construction resource allocation (Fig. 12.1). Thus it can be said that maintenance allocation is simply a deferred form of construction allocation [4, 5, 6, 7, 8].

The resources required to run a building are also closely related to construction resource allocation; for example, the energy required for heat, light and power during a building's life will clearly depend on the initial resource allocation on the building's envelope and environmental support system (Fig. 12.2).

The resources required to demolish a building are also closely related to the building's constructional form. Frequently a large constructional resource allocation results in a large demolition resource requirement.

Fig. 12.2 Graph of quality of thermal provision against cost.

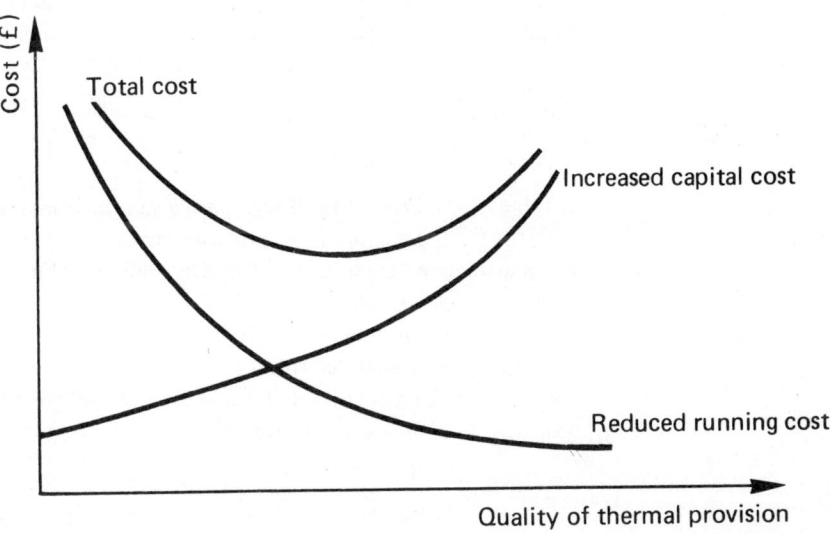

A family of cost prediction techniques has been derived from the building resource allocation model. These techniques are fundamentally identical but have been given a variety of titles ranging from cost-in-use, life-cycle costing and value engineering to terotechnology. The term life-cycle costing will be used in this chapter, on the premise that life-cycle costing is the most self-descriptive title of those in current use.

12.4 Life-cycle costing

Life-cycle costing attempts to apply a quantitative analysis to the building resource allocation model.

The main problem, in terms of quantitative analysis, which is immediately encountered is the time element of resource allocation. Since resources are expended in varying amounts at different periods of time throughout a building's life, the basic task of life-cycle costing, whether applied at individual consumer level, national level, or global level, is to reduce the time stream of resource flows to a single base.

12.5 Life-cycle costing using market prices

If market prices are used to measure resources, the normal method of reducing these resource flows to a common time base is to apply the technique known as discounted cash flow (DCF).

12.5.1 Discounted Cash Flow

DCF is based on the simple premise that future outflows of cash are worth less than their present face value. It is a premise which is instinctively understood by anyone with outstanding debts. For example, faced with the prospect of paying a bill for £500 today or in 5 years time one would naturally choose to pay the bill in 5 years time since this would allow the investment of £500 capital for a period of 5 years. Thus, when payment of the bill becomes due, the £500 bill could be cleared leaving the payee with 5 years accumulation of compound interest.

The single compound amount formula is as follows:

$$F = P(1 + i)^N \qquad (12.1)$$

where P = a present sum of money, F = a future sum of money (equivalent to P at the end of N periods of time at an interest rate of i), i = interest rate and N = number of interest periods. Thus F, the future sum of money equivalent to £500 at the end of 5 years at 10 per cent interest can be calculated as follows:

Example 12.1

$$F = 500 \ (1 + 0.1)^5 = £805$$

It follows, therefore, that if one were given the opportunity of purchasing an IOU for £500 payable in 5 years time, that the purchase of this IOU would only be an attractive proposition if the IOU could be obtained for less than its face value.

The precise amount which should be paid for the IOU for any given rate of interest can be calculated using the standard discounting formula, normally called the single present worth (or present value) formula. The single present worth formula, is the reciprocal of the single compound amount formula, i.e.

$$P = F \frac{1}{(1 + i)^N}. \qquad (12.2)$$

Thus, P the present worth of £500 payable in 5 years time at 10 per cent interest can be calculated as follows:

Example 12.2

$$P = 500 \times \frac{1}{(1 + 0.1)^5} = £310.$$

The single present worth formula is the central formula in discounted cash flow calculations, representing the concept that the present worth of outflows of cash diminishes as these cash flows advance from present to future time, the rate of diminution being determined by the rate of interest. Tabular solutions for the present worth formula are available (see Appendix 12A) for a range of values of the parameters i and N, thus simplifying DCF calculations

Example 12.3   From Appendix 12A the single present worth of £1 payable in 5 years at 10 per cent interest is 0.6209. Thus, the single present worth of £500 payable in 5 years at 10 per cent interest is:

$$500 \times 0.6209 = £310$$

To summarize, the single present worth formula can be used to convert specific cash sums occurring at different points in time to a single time base, e.g. replacement of a heating system after 15 years, or demolition of an entire building after 30 years.

A problem frequently encountered in energy accounting calculations is the conversion of annually recurring costs to a single cash sum, e.g. a domestic fuel bill of £250 per annum for 25 years. This calculation can be carried out using the uniform present worth formula, which is derived from the single compound amount formula. The uniform present worth formula is

$$P = A \frac{(1 + i)^N - 1}{i(1 + i)^N}, \tag{12.3}$$

where A = an end-of-period payment (or receipt) in a uniform series of payments (or receipts) over N periods at i interest rate, usually annually. Thus P, the present worth of £250 per annum for 25 years at an assumed interest rate of 10 per cent can be calculated as follows:

Example 12.4

$$P = 250 \times \frac{(1 + 0.1)^{25} - 1}{0.1(1 + 0.1)^{25}} = £2269$$

The tabular solution (from Appendix 12B) is

$$250 \times 9.077 = £2269.$$

A simple example of the use of single and uniform present worth formulae is given in Example 12.5, a life-cycle costing of a crude building resource allocation model using market prices discounted to a common time base.

This example illustrates the value of applying life-cycle costing to a building resource allocation model. Whilst Design Proposal B has a higher initial capital cost than Design Proposal A, in terms of total present worth Proposal B is lower than Proposal A due to B's lower running and maintenance costs. Another important point to note from the example is the use of life-cycle costing in a comparative situation. The main purpose of a market price life-cycle costing is not to predict with absolute certainty the total monetary expenditure throughout a building's life, but is rather to establish the rank ordering, in terms of price, of alternative strategies.

The comparative nature of life-cycle costing cannot be overstressed, since the process of comparison allows the elimination of influential variables, e.g. inflation.

12.5.2 Inflation

Undoubtedly the most difficult obstacle to overcome in arriving at an understanding of a market price life-cycle costing is in resolving the apparent conflict between the concept of discounted cash flow and the concept of inflation. Discounted cash flow states that the present worth of an item diminishes as the requirement to purchase that item is postponed, whereas in an inflationary situation the price of the same item will increase over time.

There are two main reasons why the effects of inflation do not necessarily invalidate the results of life-cycle costing using market prices:

Example 12.5   Life-cycle costing of total building costs for two alternative hotel design proposals (A and B) based on market prices assuming a discount rate of 10 per cent.

Date	Cost category	Description	Expenditure		Discount procedure	Present worth	
			A	B		A	B
1977	Capital	Labour, machinery and materials required to produce complete building	1 000 000	1 200 000	None	1 000 000	1 200 000
1982, 87, 92 … 2037	Maintenance	Part continuous, part cyclical (continuous costs included in running costs)	80 000 (every 5 years)	60 000 (every 5 years)	A$^{(1)}$ 80 000 × 1.6293 B 60 000 × 1.6293	130 344	97 758
1977, 78, 79 … 2037	Running	Annual cost, mainly energy, but also including continuous maintenance costs	70 000	50 000	A$^{(2)}$ 70 000 × 9.967 B 50 000 × 9.967	697 690	498 350
2037	Demolition	Labour and machinery required to demolish complete building	40 000	40 000	A$^{(3)}$ 40 000 × 0.0033 B 40 000 × 0.0033	132	132
					Total present worth	1 828 166	1 796 240

(1) Obtained by aggregation from single present worth table, i.e. Appendix 12C.
(2) Uniform present worth (Appendix 12B).
(3) Single present worth (Appendix 12A).

(i) It is normal to assume that, as prices inflate or deflate, revenues or incomes will also inflate or deflate at the same rate, i.e. price rises are offset by similar increases in income; thus, the real price of an item remains relatively constant. This is obviously a rather sweeping statement which is open to challenge and will be dealt with in greater depth later in the chapter.

(ii) As stated previously, life-cycle costing is best used as a comparative technique; thus, it is normally assumed that inflation will act equally on the alternative proposals, i.e. that inflation is a constant factor and, as such, can be excluded from the calculations. If the alternative proposals were to vary widely in terms of labour intensity or fuel consumption then theoretically inflation cannot be taken as a constant factor.

It is possible, however, to adapt DCF calculations to take account of items which are subject to differential rates of inflation, i.e. items which inflate or deflate at a different rate than the general price level of other commodities. Historically, fuel costs and maintenance costs (which are labour intensive) have shown a tendency to inflate at a faster rate than the general level of other commodities. Provided that differential rates of inflation can be predicted with some degree of certainty, and this of course is a very big proviso, the discounting procedure is simple and straightforward.

The formula for calculating the price of an item expected to increase at a faster, but constant, rate than general price levels is as follows:

$$P = F \frac{(1 + e)^N}{(1 + i)^N}, \tag{12.4}$$

where e = fixed rate of price escalation. It should be noted, however, that in principle, no single major commodity can, in the long term, rise in real cost faster than the test discount rate, since this would simply imply that the discount rate selected was inappropriate.

Differential rates of inflation are of most use when used to test the sensitivity of DCF calculations to changes in test discount rates.

12.5.3 Discount Rates

All the DCF examples in this chapter assume a discount rate of 10 per cent. This is the rate currently used for all public sector accounting in the UK and all Federal Government Agencies in the USA.

The selection of an appropriate discount rate in the private sector will depend largely on the financial background of each private company or individual, which in turn will be influenced by prevailing market conditions, and will vary in different economies. For example, in the UK, maintenance and running costs are treated as a charge against Corporation Tax. Thus, all maintenance and running costs in the private sector should be modified by multiplying by a factor of less than 1 (the extent of this reduction will depend on the current rate of Corporation Tax). This factor should be further modified to take account of Fiscal Drag, i.e. the delay between a tax liability being incurred and payment of the tax (in the UK there is normally an 18-month tax delay period).

Private companies will also be influenced by their sources of finance, i.e. whether a project is financed from retained profits (unborrowed funds) or debt-financed (borrowed funds) and the relationship of these finance sources to depreciation for tax purposes.

The subject of company taxation and its influence on running and maintenance costs is extremely complex and is beyond the scope of this chapter. (The interested reader is advised to consult references [9] and [10].) The selection of an appropriate discount rate for a private individual or set of individuals is perhaps less complex, but no less difficult than for a private company. Since the discount rate is a measure of the opportunity cost of tying up capital, the availability and cost of finance is a very important factor to an individual and will vary widely depending on an individual's personal financial circumstances.

Given that the selection of an appropriate discount rate is extremely uncertain, it is advisable to apply a sensitivity analysis to life-cycle costings using discounted market prices.

12.5.4 Sensitivity Analysis

There are two variables in the standard discounting formula, i (the rate of interest) and N (the number of interest periods, i.e. the investment life). Fig. 12.3 illustrates that the rate of interest effectively governs the maximum period of time over which an investment can be considered. For example, the present worth of annual payments of £1000 at 15 per cent 'flattens out' at 25 years, i.e. the present worth of 25 payments of £1000 at 15 per cent is approximately £6500; similarly the present worth of 100 payments of £1000 at 15 per cent is also approximately £6500. Thus, in terms of sensitivity, it is pointless to discount high interest rates in the region of 15 per cent for periods of longer than 25 or 30 years. However, as interest rates reduce, the slope of the curve takes longer to 'flatten out'. For example, the present worth of annual payments of £1000 at 5 per cent does not 'flatten out' until year 50. Thus, as interest rates reduce, the period over which these rates can be effectively discounted, is extended. This is a useful feature of the discounting technique, since if one equates high interest rates with risk and uncertainty, and low interest rates with a more stable, predictable economic situation, then DCF has an in-built control mechanism which reduces the effective investment period as interest rates rise, i.e. one is forced to make predictions over a shorter period.

Since market price life-cycle costing is best used on a comparative basis to establish a rank ordering of alternatives, it is advisable (as previously stated) to

Fig. 12.3 Graph indicating the effective control of interest rate over the maximum period of time over which an investment can be considered.

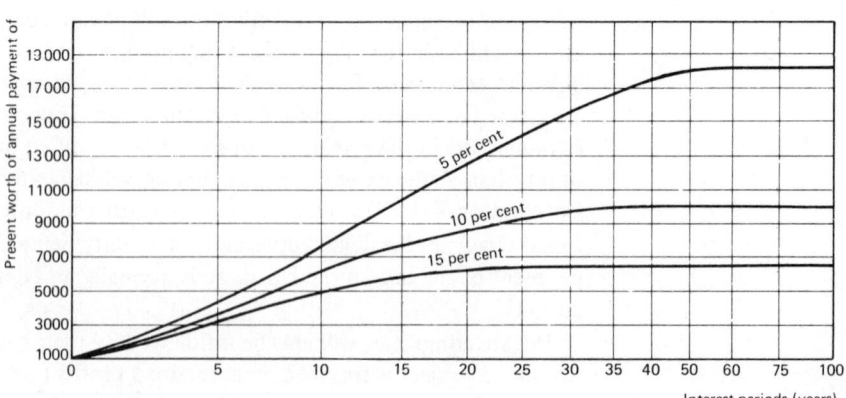

test the sensitivity of this rank ordering to changes in interest rate with associated changes in investment periods.

From the foregoing discussion, it should be clear that, as interest rates increase, the sensitivity of DCF calculations is reduced, e.g. a fuel bill of £1000 per annum discounted at 15 per cent has a present worth of £6500 after 25 years and has the same present worth after 60 years, whereas a fuel bill of £1000 per annum discounted at 5 per cent has a present worth of £14 090 after 25 years and has a present worth of £18 930 after 60 years.

12.5.5 Examples of Life-cycle Costing Based on Market Prices

Example 12.6   The following data refer to three house types A, B and C, each house having the same internal plan of 95 m^2 gross floor area. The house types have differing standards of thermal insulation and different heating systems, resulting in differing capital, maintenance and running cost characteristics.

House type	Capital cost	Maintenance cost	Running cost
A	£6613	£15 per annum, £180 every 10 years	£336 per annum
B	£7057	£20 per annum, £180 every 10 years	£200 per annum
C	£7702	£20 per annum, £680 every 10 years	£180 per annum

The problem is to reduce the various maintenance and running cost cash flows to a single base to allow an intelligible comparison to be made between the life-cycle costs of A, B and C.

Assume an interest rate of 10 per cent and a life-cycle period of 60 years. Present worth calculations are as follows

	A	B	C
Capital costs (in £)	6613	7057	7702
Maintenance costs			
A £15 × 9.967 (from Appendix 12B)	150		
£180 × 0.6221 (from Appendix 12C)	112		
B £20 × 9.967		199	
£180 × 0.6221		112	
C £20 × 9.967			199
£680 × 0.6221			423
Running costs			
A £336 × 9.967	3349		
B £200 × 9.967		1993	
C £180 × 9.967			1794
Total present worth	10 224	9361	10 118

An alternative method to the use of total present worth calculations is to use annual equivalent costs. This method converts capital and maintenance costs into annual equivalents which can then be added to annual recurring costs, e.g. fuel costs. It should be stressed that the annual equivalent method is simply a variation in terms of presenting DCF results and is in no way a departure from the basic DCF concept. Thus, the rank order of total life-cycle costs established in Example 12.6 (B, C, A from low to high) should be confirmed by annual equivalent costs based on the same data.

Example 12.7   Using annual equivalent cost calculations and the data given in Example 12.6.

		A	B	C
Capital costs				
A	£6613 × 0.100 33 (from Appendix 12D)	663		
B	£7057 × 0.100 33		708	
C	£7702 × 0.100 33			773
Maintenance costs				
A	£15 per annum	15		
	£180 × 0.062 75 (from Appendix 12E)	11		
B	£20 per annum		20	
	£180 × 0.062 75		11	
C	£20 per annum			20
	£680 × 0.062 75			43
Running costs				
A	£336 per annum	336		
B	£200 per annum		200	
C	£180 per annum			180
	Annual equivalent costs	1025	939	1016

Life-cycle costing need not necessarily be applied to buildings as a whole, but can be applied to the component parts of a building. Life-cycle costings are frequently carried out on heating and air-conditioning systems to investigate the relationship between capital and running costs, as illustrated in the following example.

Example 12.8   The following data refer to two air-conditioning systems, types A and B, each producing identical environmental conditions, but having differing capital and running costs.

	System A	System B
Capital cost	£57 800	£79 400
Life of plant	20 years	30 years
Annual fuel costs and maintenance costs (after deduction of appropriate tax allowances)	£18 900	£14 100
Salvage value of plant	£1500	£3500

Assume an interest rate of 10 per cent and an investment period of 60 years. The present worth calculations are then:

	A	B
Capital costs (in £)	57 800	79 400

Replacement costs

A   System life 20 years. Therefore assume
replacement at year 20 and year 40*
£(57 800 − 1500) × 0.1707   9610
(from Appendix 12C)

B   System life 30 years. Therefore, assume
replacement at year 30
£(79 400 − 3500) × 0.0573   4349

Running costs
A   £18 900 × 9.967 (from Appendix 12B)   188 376
B   £14 100 × 9.967   140 535

	A	B
Total present worth	255 786	224 284

The above example illustrates two important aspects of life-cycle costing using discounted market prices:

(i) Whereas system A is £21 600 less than system B in terms of the capital cost of the installation, in terms of overall life-cycle costs system B is approximately £31 500 less than system A.

(ii) Although system A has a plant replacement cost of £56 300 and system B a cost of £75 900, because system A has a shorter life than system B, the discounted replacement costs of systems A and B are £9610 and £4349, respectively.

Example 12.9   Sensitivity analysis   In Example 12.8, the results are liable to be influenced by three factors:

(a) choice of interest rates;
(b) predicted system lives;
(c) length of investment period.

Attempts to deal exhaustively with the simultaneous effects of (a), (b) and (c) could lead to a laborious mathematical task. However, as previously stressed, life-cycle costing is best used in a comparative situation to provide an approximate answer to the precise question of rank ordering, thus it is normally possible to test the sensitivity of life-cycle costing results by means of a series of spot checks.

(a) *Choice of interest rate*. The total present worth at 8 per cent for 60 years is as follows:

	System A	System B
Capital costs (in £)	57 800	79 400

---

* It could be argued that a replacement should also be taken at year 60; it is, however, highly unlikely that this replacement would have any influence on the outcome of the calculations.

	System A	System B

Replacement costs
A   System life 20 years
    £56 300 × 0.2606 (from Appendix 12C)

	System A	System B
£56 300 × 0.2606 (from Appendix 12C)	14 672	
B System life 30 years £75 900 × 0.0994		7545

Running costs

	System A	System B
A £18 900 × 12.377 (from Appendix 12B)	233 925	
B £14 100 × 12.377		174 516
	306 397	261 461

Similarly, the total present worth at 10 per cent for 60 years (from Example 12.8) is

	System A	System B
	255 786	224 284

Finally, the total present worth at 14 per cent for 60 years is

	System A	System B
Capital costs (in £)	57 800	79 400

Replacement costs

	System A	System B
A System life 20 years £56 300 × 0.0781 (from Appendix 12C)	4397	
B System life 30 years £75 900 × 0.0196		1489

Running costs

	System A	System B
A £18 900 × 7.140 (from Appendix 12B)	134 946	
B £14 100 × 7.140		100 674
	197 143	181 563

The total present worth of system B is lower than system A throughout the range of interest rates 8, 10 and 14 per cent. As interest rates increase, the total present worth of each system diminishes, this in turn reduces the difference in present worth between the two systems.

(b) *Predicted system lives.* From the preceding calculations it can be seen that the replacement costs of the two systems is unlikely to be a significant component (in this instance) of the total life-cycle costs assuming that the relative difference in the life of systems A and B remains constant. The following calculations confirm this statement.

The total present worth at 10 per cent for 60 years is given by

	System A	System B
Capital costs (in £)	57 800	79 400
Running costs (in £)	188 376	140 535

	System A	System B

Replacement costs

A   System life 10 years (5 replacements)
     £56 300 × 0.6221 (from Appendix 12C) — **35 024**

B   System life 15 years (3 replacements)
     £75 900 × 0.3104 — **23 559**

	System A	System B
	281 200	243 494

From Example 12.8,

	System A	System B

A   System life 20 years (2 replacements)

B   System life 30 years (1 replacement)   **255 786**   **224 284**

	System A	System B
Capital costs (in £)	57 800	79 400
Running costs (in £) as before	188 376	140 535

Replacement costs

A   System life 30 years (1 replacement)
     £56 300 × 0.0573 (from Appendix 12C) — **3226**

B   System life 45 years (1 replacement)
     £75 900 × 0.0137 (from Appendix 12C) — **1040**

	System A	System B
	249 402	220 975

(c) *Investment period*. As previously mentioned in the commentary on 'choice of interest rates' the difference in total present worth of the two systems is at its lowest when discounted at the highest interest rate. Since high interest rates effectively reduce the period over which investments can be considered (*see* Fig. 12.3) then, in this example, it is unlikely that even a substantial reduction of the given investment period of 60 years will reverse the results obtained in Example 12.8. If an investment period of 20 years is assumed (the predicted life of system A, eliminating the need for replacements) then the calculations are as follows.

The total present worth at 14 per cent for 20 years is

	System A	System B
Capital costs (in £)	57 800	79 400

Running costs

A   £18 900 × 6.623 (from Appendix 12B)   **125 175**

B   £14 100 × 6.623   **93 384**

	System A	System B
Replacement costs	Nil	Nil
	182 975	172 784

In conclusion, we can see that the calculations show that system B has a lower total present worth than system A throughout all the conditions tested.

The above example of a sensitivity analysis is specific to the conditions given in Example 12.8. It is not possible to give a clear-cut set of instructions on the application of sensitivity analyses, since the subjects under analysis are capable of infinite variety. The form which a sensitivity analysis takes is at the discretion of the analyst. In Example 12.8 the solution was shown to be an extremely robust one. It was, therefore, a simple task to apply a sensitivity analysis as confirmation of the results. It is outside the scope of this chapter to deal with the multiplicity of conditions imposed by systems and subsystems which the analyst is liable to encounter in the 'real life' situation, where pay-back periods, capital rationing and taxation exert powerful influences [10].

Example 12.10   This example tests the sensitivity of life-cycle costing using discounted market prices by using differential rate of inflation to give a speculative cost profile. The data given in Example 12.6 is used as the basis of a speculative cost profile which assumes an annual rise in the real cost of energy of 4 and of 7 per cent with a base discount rate of 10 per cent over 60 years. The formula for calculation of differential rates of inflation has already been given in the text (equation (12.4)). The following tabular solution of this formula is taken from a Building Research Establishment publication [1].

Table 12.1

Cash flow per annum	Present value (£)		
	0 per cent	4 per cent	7 per cent
£1 (60 years)	9.967	16.735	28.879
£1 (40 years)	9.779	15.495	23.866
£1 (30 years)	9.427	14.112	20.107
£1 (15 years)	7.606	9.860	12.109
£1 (10 years)	6.145	7.441	8.616

From Example 12.6 we have:

House type	Capital cost	Maintenance cost	Running cost
A	£6613	£15 per annum, £180 every 10 years	£336 per annum
B	£7057	£20 per annum, £180 every 10 years	£200 per annum
C	£7702	£20 per annum, £680 every 10 years	£180 per annum

Note that the values for capital and maintenance costs are identical to those in Example 12.6; only the values for running (energy) costs are affected, in this instance, by differential rates of inflation.
    The running costs are

	0 per cent	4 per cent	7 per cent
A	336 × 9.967 = 3349	336 × 16.735 = 5623	336 × 28.879 = 9703
B	200 × 9.967 = 1993	200 × 16.735 = 3347	200 × 28.879 = 5776
C	180 × 9.967 = 1794	180 × 16.735 = 3012	180 × 28.879 = 5198

and so, in summary:

	Capital	Maintenance	Running	Present worth
A	6613	262	3349 (0 per cent)	10 224
			5623 (4 per cent)	12 498
			9703 (7 per cent)	16 578
B	7057	311	1993 (0 per cent)	9361
			3347 (4 per cent)	10 715
			5776 (7 per cent)	13 144
C	7702	622	1794 (0 per cent)	10 118
			3012 (4 per cent)	11 336
			5198 (7 per cent)	13 522

In this instance the speculative cost profile confirms the rank order established by the base discount rate. The assumption that energy prices will rise at a faster uniform rate than general price levels accentuates the difference between low and high energy demand solutions.

12.6 Life-cycle costing using prime energy accounting

Prime energy accounting has been previously defined in this chapter as 'the estimated cost to the nation of the prime energy resource which is consumed to deliver a given quantity of energy to the consumer' [1].

Since prime energy accounting also uses money as a method of measurement, albeit as a modified market price, the *rationale* of market price life-cycle costing, is applicable. In terms of the four main elements of the building resource allocation model, three of the elements, construction, maintenance and demolition costs are dealt with identically in market price and prime energy accounting. It is only in the element, 'running costs' that there is a difference between market price and prime energy accounting techniques.

12.6.1 Running Costs Based on Prime Energy Accounting

The terms used in this section are based on those given by the Building Research Establishment [1] and are defined as follows:

(i) 'Primary energy' is that contained in fossil fuel in the form of coal, oil or natural gas, or in nuclear energy or hydroelectricity.

(ii) 'Secondary energy' is that contained in coke, coal-gas or other manufactured fuels or in electricity.

(iii) 'Gross energy' is the amount of primary energy that is consumed in the course of producing and distributing net energy.

(iv) 'Net energy' is the energy consumed by any particular set of consumers and is the energy actually received by them.

(v) 'Energy overhead' is the difference between gross energy and net energy.

The four primary energy sources in Table 12.2 are either used directly as an energy supply to individual consumers, or are used as a gross energy input in the manufacture of electricity or manufactured fuels as shown in Table 12.3.

Table 12.2   *Primary energy: UK energy supply and consumption in 1972* [1]

Source	Energy (GJ) ($\times 10^9$)
Oil	4.23 (48 per cent)
Coal	3.22 (37 per cent)
Natural gas	1.07 (12 per cent)
Nuclear and hydro power	0.31 (3 per cent)
Total	8.83 (100 per cent)

Table 12.3   *Gross energy: electricity and manufactured fuels (1972)* [1]

Gross energy input to industry (GJ) ($\times 10^9$)			
Electricity			
	Coal	1.61	
	Oil	0.89	
	Nuclear and hydro	0.31	
	Natural gas	0.06	2.87
Manufactured fuels			
	Coal	0.77	
	Natural gas	0.34	
	Oil	0.11	
	Public electricity	0.04	1.26
		Total	4.13

Tables 12.2 and 12.3 illustrate the relative importance of the four primary energy sources in terms of their current usage both as direct suppliers of energy to the individual consumer and also as gross energy inputs in the production of electricity and manufactured fuels.

Prime energy accounting is, however, more concerned with estimating the *efficiency* of conversion and distribution of prime energy sources, than with recording the total amounts of prime energy resources consumed.

Table 12.4 illustrates the *efficiency* of conversion and distribution of prime energy in terms of the ratio between the energy received by the individual consumer and the prime energy which is used in production.

Table 12.4   *Efficiency of conversion and distribution of primary energy* [1]

Final energy	Primary energy input per unit of final energy
Electricity	3.73
Manufactured fuels	1.40
Oil	1.08
Natural gas	1.06
Coal	1.02

The following calculations demonstrate the use of prime energy accounting as a method of calculating running costs. These calculations allow not only for the efficiency of conversion and distribution of prime energy (as illustrated in Table 12.4) but also take account of the efficiency with which the final form of the energy can be utilized. The energy prices* used are those given by the Building Research Establishment [1].

12.6.2 Example of Prime Energy Accounting

Example 12.11   Running costs of a five-apartment terraced house, calculated on the basis of prime energy accounting and market prices. (The market price calculations are given to allow a basis of comparison with the prime energy accounting calculations.) Data is taken from Building Research Establishment statistics [1].

Market price	Gas:	£1.23/GJ net (Substitute natural gas £1.31/GJ net)
	Electricity:	£3.89/GJ net (Off-peak £2.78/GJ net, on-peak £4.17/GJ net).
	Coal:	£0.95/GJ net
	Oil:	£1.52/GJ net
Prime energy accounting	Gas:	£1.04/GJ gross
	Electricity:	£1.05/GJ gross
	Coal:	£0.93/GJ gross
	Oil:	£1.40/GJ gross

Weighting the costs of energy in the proportion in which they are consumed in the domestic sector gives an average cost of energy of £1.05/GJ (gross).

Energy requirements	Method of energy supply	Net energy (GJ)	Primary energy (Gross) (GJ)	
Space heating	Gas (warm air system)	198.9 ‡	198.9 × 1.06†	210.8
Cooking	Gas	10.0	10.0 × 1.06†	10.6
Lights, TV, etc.	Electricity	3.0	3.0 × 3.73†	11.2
Hot water	Electricity	12.0	12.0 × 3.73†	44.8
	Total	223.9	Total	277.4

* Energy prices are subject to frequent and rapid changes, and are also subject to regional variations. Thus it is difficult to establish a precise figure at any point in time. For many purposes, the relative difference in energy prices is more important than the precision of any particular figure at a specific point in time.

‡ Values based upon gas operating at 60 per cent seasonal efficiency.

† Primary energy input per unit of final energy in Table 12.4.

Energy costs	Market prices (£)		Prime energy accounting (£)	
Space heating	198.9 × 1.31*	260.56		
Cooking	10.0 × 1.31*	13.10	277.4 × 1.05 ‡	291
Lights, TV, etc.	3.0 × 4.17†	12.51		
Hot water	12.0 × 4.17†	50.04		
	Total	336	Total	291

In Example 12.11, the prime energy accounting calculations have produced a lower per annum value than the market price calculations. If, however, electricity were used to provide space heating, then the differences in values between market price and prime energy accounting would be reversed.

Per annum figures (whether prime energy or market price) can be converted to a present worth, using the discounting techniques previously discussed.

12.7 Energy analysis

This section is concerned with the application of energy analysis in the context of life-cycle costing. It is not proposed to give here a detailed critique of the origins and methodology of energy analysis. However, a brief description of the development of energy analysis is given below; this description is based on work by the International Federation of Institutes of Advanced Study [3].

12.7.1 Description

Although various attempts have been made over a long period of time to describe energy in the context of world economy, in physical rather than money terms, it was only as recently as 1971 that the first papers using energy values were published. A source of stimulus for many of the early workers in the energy field was the publication of a book by Odum [11] which highlighted the importance of energy in terms of world economy.

In 1974 it was generally agreed that the term 'energy analysis' should be used in preference to the many other terms currently in use at that time. Energy analysis was defined as 'the determination of the energy sequestered in the process of making a good or service within the framework of an agreed set of conventions or applying the information so obtained'. An important aspect of this definition is the use of the word 'framework', since all analyses or costings must be carried out within a frame of reference. Clearly, if analyses are to be comparable, they must be based on identical sets of constraints and boundary conditions. However, these constraints and boundary conditions should not necessarily be considered as barriers, but simply as a framework or envelope as perceived from a certain viewpoint.

In terms of this chapter, the system boundary ranges from the mining of ores from the ground to the final fixing or placement of the finished product in a building. This system boundary holds good for market prices, modified market prices, or energy units.

---

* Substitute natural gas.
† On-peak electricity.
‡ Average cost of energy (gross).

12.7.2 Energy Units

As previously stated, the currency of energy analysis is the joule. Although the joule is a physically definable unit, as opposed to money which is not, it would be quite wrong to assume that the concept of energy units is inherently more simple than the concept of monetary costs. An important qualification in the use of energy units is to distinguish between enthalpy and 'free energy'. The calorific value of a fuel, or enthalpy of combustion of the fuel, is a definition of that fuel in terms of heat. However, it is more important to the energy analyst to be able to identify the usefulness, i.e. thermodynamic potential, of a fuel source rather than the total calorific value of that fuel. This thermodynamic potential, which is a measure of the attractiveness of energy sources, is known as 'free energy'. 'Free energy', then, is the unit which best expresses the *objectives* of energy analysis. For many processes, however, it is difficult, and in some cases not yet possible, to calculate the 'free energy' content of goods or services. In other cases, e.g. most intensive fuels (high free energy potential per unit mass, i.e. oil, coal, etc.), the error in using enthalpy rather than free energy is approximately 10 per cent.

In this chapter the energy unit of account used is the gross energy requirement (GER); the value of GER is the gross enthalpy released at a standard rate of all the naturally occurring energy sources which must be consumed to make a good or service available, and is normally expressed as megajoules per kilogramme or gigajoules per tonne of the delivered product. The GER of most products used in the construction of buildings is available in published reports.

Before proceeding to the consideration of energy analyses in the context of life-cycle costing, one further general aspect on the methodology of energy analysis will be briefly dealt with, i.e. the implications of labour.

12.7.3 Labour/Manpower

Energy analysis divides manpower into two distinct categories: industrialized economies and low-intensity agricultural economies.

In this chapter we are concerned with industrialized economies and their use and depletion of energy sources. Thus, we are concerned with the quantity of energy sources consumed to furnish the life support system of labour employed in the industrialized processes, i.e. the gross energy requirement of the work force. In an industrial context it will almost invariably be found that the GER of the life support system of the work force will be so insignificant in terms of the GER of the industrial process itself that it can be disregarded. Moreover, the GER of the life support system of an individual will be more or less constant irrespective of whether or not that individual is in employment.

To summarise, 'where energy analysis refers to developed or industrialised economies it is not necessary to consider the energy for life-support of manpower' [3].

12.8 Life-cycle costing using energy analysis

As stated at the outset, the main problem in life-cycle costing is manipulation of the time element of resource allocation. In market price life-cycle costing the normal method of reducing these resource flows to a common time base is to use discounted cash flow.

In energy analysis it is not accepted practice to discount energy units. There are two reasons for this. First, the *quality* of energy resources is tending to decline. On the other hand, the technology used to extract these resources is expected to improve, thus it could be argued that one trend will counteract the other, leaving the GER of energy resources unchanged over time.

The second reason for not discounting energy units, is that research has shown that on the basis of modern technology, much of the potential improvement in energy use for production has already been carried out, there being thermodynamic limits on further improvements. This again suggests that future GER values will remain similar to present day values.

Both reasons tend to suggest that, on balance, if discounting were to be applied to energy analysis, a negative discount rate should be applied, the effect of which would be to increase the future value of energy resources; this, of course, is the opposite of the current discounted cash flow techniques which converts future resource flows into a reduced present worth.

The following examples illustrate the fundamental difference in the approaches adopted by market price and energy analysis to the time element of resource allocation.

12.8.1 Examples of Energy Analysis

Example 12.12   A heating unit requires to be replaced every 10 years throughout the 60-year life of a building (i.e. five replacements). Calculate the present worth and lifetime GER of the system (excluding the initial installation cost and initial GER). The capital cost of unit is £180 and the GER of unit is 35.9 GJ.

From Appendix 12C, the present worth may be calculated from the market price assuming a 10 per cent interest rate, i.e.

Present worth = 180 × 0.6221 = £112.

By energy analysis we can calculate the lifetime GER as

Lifetime GER = 35.9 × 5 = 179.5 GJ.

Example 12.13   Calculate the present worth and the lifetime GER of the following yearly fuel expenditure for the next 60 years.

Per annum metered fuel consumption:

	Electricity	15.0 GJ
	Gas	208.9 GJ

Per annum gross (prime) energy requirement (from Table 12.4):

	Electricity	15.0 × 3.73 = 56.0 GJ
	Gas	208.9 × 1.06 = 221.4 GJ

The present worth of the annual fuel bill (market price) may be calculated as follows:

Electricity	15.0 × 4.17 =	62.55
Gas	208.9 × 1.31 =	273.66
	Total	£336 per annum

(The values of 4.17 and 1.31 are taken from Example 12.11.) Hence,

Present worth of annual fuel bill = 336 × 9.967 = £3349,

where 9.967 is 10 per cent for 60 years uniform present worth (from Appendix 12B).

The lifetime GER (Energy analysis) is

$(56.00 + 221.4) \times 60$ years $= 16\,644$ GJ.

12.9 General summary

The continuing energy crisis has highlighted the need to conserve and manage the use of energy resources in a responsible manner. One of the prerequisites of any budgetary control or housekeeping system is the ability to measure and monitor the various parts of the system and the interaction of these parts upon each other and upon the system as a whole. The main emphasis of this chapter has been concentrated on methods of measuring and monitoring energy resources within a system; the system in this instance being a building and the system boundaries being those imposed by a building. The methods of measurement investigated, whilst not exhaustive in themselves, cover the major areas of energy resource measurement currently in use. Although current criticism of the reliability of the market price system was noted, it was not intended to give the impression that other methods should be used in preference to the market price system. The formulation of energy strategies is an extremely complex subject which requires maximum use of all available decision-making tools. Therefore, where at all possible, all three techniques described in this chapter should be used collectively. In addition, sensitivity analyses should also be applied whenever the robustness of a solution is in doubt.

Throughout this chapter, no mention has been made of the term 'cost effectiveness', which is often used in connection with energy accounting. The reason for this omission is that this chapter is concerned with general rather than specific applications of measurement principles. For a cost effectiveness analysis to be of any practical use it must of necessity be applied to a clearly specified system with well-defined boundary conditions. The first question which should be asked of a cost effectiveness analysis is 'to whom is the solution cost effective?', i.e. a single individual, a group of individuals, a local community, a nation, or the community at large. For example, it could be argued that the most cost effective solution in terms of fuel costs for a region could be to supply each schoolchild with additional winter woollens rather than increase the internal temperature of school buildings during cold periods. However, although this may appear to be the most cost effective solution in terms of the region's fuel bills, it may not be cost effective in terms of national economy due to increased fuel bills for cleaning and also the capital cost of replacement and administrative costs of the proposed solution. Thus, it can be seen from this example that the main difficulty in cost effectiveness analysis, is not in the use of measurement techniques, but in being able to satisfactorily describe a system in a comparatively static partial equilibrium form, i.e. being able to perform before and after comparisons of two situations, each of which reflects a full adjustment of the immediately affected parts of the economic system to a stable (or at any rate unaffected) general environment [12]. The problem of describing appropriate system boundaries which are neither so narrow that they preclude significant variables, nor so wide that they prejudice the assumptions which, *ceteris paribus*, partial equilibrium analysis requires, is the central problem of energy accounting.

References

1   Energy conservation: a study of energy consumption in buildings and possible means of saving energy in housing. *Building Research Establishment Current Paper 56/75, 1975.*

2   Phipps, H. H., The resource utilization factor concept as an energy measurement tool. *American Society of Heating, Refrigeration and Air-Conditioning Engineers Journal,* May 1976.

3   Methodology and conventions of energy analysis. *International Federation of Institutes of Advanced Study Report No. 6, 1974.*

4   Building Performance Research Unit, *Building Performance.* Applied Science Publishers, Barking, Essex, 1972.

5   O'Neill, D., Determinants of housing cost. Part 3: Cost-in-use. *Architects Journal,* **159**(5), 753–755, 1974.

6   Stone, P. A., *Building Design Evaluation, Costs-in-use.* Spon, London, 1975.

7   Noble, V., Economic life of buildings. *Construction No. 9,* 1974.

8   *Building Maintenance Cost Information Service.* Royal Institution of Chartered Surveyors, London.

9   Drake, B. E., The economics of maintenance. *Quantity Surveyor,* July/August 1969.

10   Solar heating and cooling in buildings: methods of economic evaluation. *National Bureau of Standards COM-75-11070, 1975.*

11   Odum, H. T., *Environment, Power and Society.* Wiley-Interscience, New York, 1970.

12   Walsh, H. G. and Williams, A., Current issues in cost-benefit analysis. *Centre for Advanced Study Occasional Papers No. 11, 1971.*

APPENDIX 12A

Single Present Worth of a Payment of £1 Payable in n Years

Years	\multicolumn{11}{c}{Rate of interest (per cent)}
	5	6	7	8	9	10	11	12	13	14	15
1	.9524	.9434	.9346	.9259	.9174	.9091	.9009	.8929	.8850	.8772	.8696
2	.9070	.8900	.8734	.8573	.8417	.8264	.8116	.7972	.7831	.7695	.7561
3	.8638	.8396	.8163	.7938	.7722	.7513	.7312	.7118	.6931	.6750	.6575
4	.8227	.7921	.7629	.7350	.7084	.6830	.6587	.6355	.6133	.5921	.5718
5	.7835	.7473	.7130	.6806	.6499	.6209	.5935	.5674	.5428	.5194	.4972
6	.7462	.7050	.6663	.6302	.5963	.5645	.5346	.5066	.4803	.4556	.4323
7	.7107	.6651	.6227	.5835	.5470	.5132	.4817	.4523	.4251	.3996	.3759
8	.6768	.6274	.5820	.5403	.5019	.4665	.4339	.4039	.3762	.3506	.3269
9	.6446	.5919	.5439	.5002	.4604	.4241	.3909	.3606	.3329	.3075	.2843
10	.6139	.5584	.5083	.4632	.4224	.3855	.3522	.3220	.2946	.2697	.2472
11	.5847	.5268	.4751	.4289	.3875	.3505	.3173	.2875	.2607	.2366	.2149
12	.5568	.4970	.4440	.3971	.3555	.3186	.2858	.2567	.2307	.2076	.1869
13	.5303	.4688	.4150	.3677	.3262	.2897	.2575	.2292	.2042	.1821	.1625
14	.5051	.4423	.3878	.3405	.2992	.2633	.2320	.2046	.1807	.1597	.1413
15	.4810	.4173	.3624	.3152	.2745	.2394	.2090	.1827	.1599	.1401	.1229
16	.4581	.3936	.3387	.2919	.2519	.2176	.1883	.1631	.1415	.1229	.1069
17	.4363	.3714	.3166	.2703	.2311	.1978	.1696	.1456	.1252	.1078	.0929
18	.4155	.3503	.2959	.2502	.2120	.1799	.1528	.1300	.1108	.0946	.0808

Years	5	6	7	8	9	10	11	12	13	14	15
19	.3957	.3305	.2765	.2317	.1945	.1635	.1377	.1161	.0981	.0829	.0703
20	.3769	.3118	.2584	.2145	.1784	.1486	.1240	.1037	.0868	.0728	.0611
21	.3589	.2942	.2415	.1987	.1637	.1351	.1117	.0926	.0768	.0638	.0531
22	.3418	.2775	.2257	.1839	.1502	.1228	.1007	.0826	.0680	.0560	.0462
23	.3256	.2618	.2109	.1703	.1378	.1117	.0907	.0738	.0601	.0491	.0402
24	.3101	.2470	.1971	.1577	.1264	.1015	.0817	.0659	.0532	.0431	.0349
25	.2953	.2330	.1842	.1460	.1160	.0923	.0736	.0588	.0471	.0378	.0304
26	.2812	.2198	.1722	.1352	.1064	.0839	.0663	.0525	.0417	.0331	.0264
27	.2678	.2074	.1609	.1252	.0976	.0763	.0597	.0469	.0369	.0291	.0230
28	.2551	.1956	.1504	.1159	.0895	.0693	.0538	.0419	.0326	.0255	.0200
29	.2429	.1846	.1406	.1073	.0822	.0630	.0485	.0374	.0289	.0224	.0174
30	.2314	.1741	.1314	.0994	.0754	.0573	.0437	.0334	.0256	.0196	.0151
31	.2204	.1643	.1228	.0920	.0691	.0521	.0394	.0298	.0226	.0172	.0131
32	.2099	.1550	.1147	.0852	.0634	.0474	.0355	.0266	.0200	.0151	.0114
33	.1999	.1462	.1072	.0789	.0582	.0431	.0319	.0238	.0177	.0132	.0099
34	.1904	.1379	.1002	.0730	.0534	.0391	.0288	.0212	.0157	.0116	.0086
35	.1813	.1301	.0937	.0676	.0490	.0356	.0259	.0189	.0139	.0102	.0075
36	.1727	.1227	.0875	.0626	.0449	.0323	.0234	.0169	.0123	.0089	.0065
37	.1644	.1158	.0818	.0580	.0412	.0294	.0210	.0151	.0109	.0078	.0057
38	.1566	.1092	.0765	.0537	.0378	.0267	.0190	.0135	.0096	.0069	.0049
39	.1491	.1031	.0715	.0497	.0347	.0243	.0171	.0120	.0085	.0060	.0043
40	.1420	.0972	.0668	.0460	.0318	.0221	.0154	.0107	.0075	.0053	.0037
41	.1353	.0917	.0624	.0426	.0292	.0201	.0139	.0096	.0067	.0046	.0032
42	.1288	.0865	.0583	.0395	.0268	.0183	.0125	.0086	.0059	.0041	.0028
43	.1227	.0816	.0545	.0365	.0246	.0166	.0112	.0076	.0052	.0036	.0025
44	.1169	.0770	.0509	.0338	.0226	.0151	.0101	.0068	.0046	.0031	.0021
45	.1113	.0727	.0476	.0313	.0207	.0137	.0091	.0061	.0041	.0027	.0019
46	.1060	.0685	.0445	.0290	.0190	.0125	.0082	.0054	.0036	.0024	.0016
47	.1009	.0647	.0416	.0269	.0174	.0113	.0074	.0049	.0032	.0021	.0014
48	.0961	.0610	.0389	.0249	.0160	.0103	.0067	.0043	.0028	.0019	.0012
49	.0916	.0575	.0363	.0230	.0147	.0094	.0060	.0039	.0025	.0016	.0011
50	.0872	.0513	.0339	.0213	.0134	.0085	.0054	.0035	.0022	.0014	.0009
55	.0683	.0406	.0242	.0145	.0087	.0053	.0032	.0020	.0012	.0007	.0005
60	.0535	.0303	.0173	.0099	.0057	.0033	.0019	.0011	.0007	.0004	.0002

APPENDIX 12B

Uniform Present Worth of Regular Annual Payments of £1 for n Years

	Rate of interest (per cent)										
Years	5	6	7	8	9	10	11	12	13	14	15
0 to:											
1	0.952	0.943	0.935	0.926	0.917	0.909	0.901	0.893	0.885	0.877	0.870
2	1.859	1.833	1.808	1.783	1.759	1.736	1.713	1.690	1.668	1.647	1.626
3	2.723	2.673	2.624	2.577	2.531	2.487	2.444	2.402	2.361	2.322	2.283
4	3.546	3.465	3.387	3.312	3.240	3.170	3.102	3.037	2.974	2.914	2.855
5	4.329	4.212	4.100	3.993	3.890	3.791	3.696	3.605	3.517	3.433	3.352

Years	5	6	7	8	9	10	11	12	13	14	15
6	5.076	4.917	4.767	4.623	4.486	4.355	4.231	4.111	3.998	3.889	3.784
7	5.786	5.582	5.389	5.206	5.033	4.868	4.712	4.564	4.423	4.288	4.160
8	6.463	6.210	5.971	5.747	5.535	5.335	5.146	4.968	4.799	4.639	4.487
9	7.108	6.802	6.515	6.247	5.995	5.759	5.537	5.328	5.132	4.946	4.772
10	7.722	7.360	7.024	6.710	6.418	6.145	5.889	5.650	5.426	5.216	5.019
11	8.306	7.887	7.499	7.139	6.805	6.495	6.207	5.938	5.687	5.453	5.234
12	8.863	8.384	7.943	7.536	7.161	6.814	6.492	6.194	5.918	5.660	5.421
13	9.394	8.853	8.358	7.904	7.487	7.103	6.750	6.424	6.122	5.842	5.583
14	9.899	9.295	8.745	8.244	7.786	7.367	6.982	6.628	6.302	6.002	5.724
15	10.380	9.712	9.108	8.559	8.061	7.606	7.191	6.811	6.462	6.142	5.847
16	10.838	10.106	9.447	8.851	8.313	7.824	7.379	6.974	6.604	6.265	5.954
17	11.274	10.477	9.763	9.122	8.544	8.022	7.549	7.120	6.729	6.373	6.047
18	11.690	10.828	10.059	9.372	8.756	8.201	7.702	7.250	6.840	6.467	6.128
19	12.085	11.158	10.336	9.604	8.950	8.365	7.839	7.366	6.938	6.550	6.198
20	12.462	11.470	10.594	9.818	9.129	8.514	7.963	7.469	7.025	6.623	6.259
21	12.821	11.764	10.836	10.017	9.292	8.649	8.075	7.562	7.102	6.687	6.312
22	13.163	12.042	11.061	10.201	9.442	8.772	8.176	7.645	7.170	6.743	6.359
23	13.489	12.303	11.272	10.371	9.580	8.883	8.266	7.718	7.230	6.792	6.399
24	13.799	12.550	11.469	10.529	9.707	8.985	8.348	7.784	7.283	6.835	6.434
25	14.094	12.783	11.654	10.675	9.823	9.077	8.422	7.843	7.330	6.873	6.464
26	14.375	13.003	11.826	10.810	9.929	9.161	8.488	7.896	7.372	6.906	6.491
27	14.643	13.211	11.987	10.935	10.027	9.237	8.548	7.943	7.409	6.935	6.514
28	14.898	13.406	12.137	11.051	10.116	9.307	8.602	7.984	7.441	6.961	6.534
29	15.141	13.591	12.278	11.158	10.198	9.370	8.650	8.022	7.470	6.983	6.551
30	15.372	13.765	12.409	11.258	10.274	9.427	8.694	8.055	7.496	7.003	6.566
31	15.593	13.929	12.532	11.350	10.343	9.479	8.733	8.085	7.518	7.020	6.579
32	15.803	14.084	12.647	11.435	10.406	9.526	8.769	8.112	7.538	7.035	6.591
33	16.003	14.230	12.754	11.514	10.464	9.569	8.801	8.135	7.556	7.048	6.600
34	16.193	14.368	12.854	11.587	10.518	9.609	8.829	8.157	7.572	7.060	6.609
35	16.374	14.498	12.948	11.655	10.567	9.644	8.855	8.176	7.586	7.070	6.617
36	16.547	14.621	13.035	11.717	10.612	9.677	8.879	8.192	7.598	7.079	6.623
37	16.711	14.737	13.117	11.775	10.653	9.706	8.900	8.208	7.609	7.087	6.629
38	16.868	14.846	13.193	11.829	10.691	9.733	8.919	8.221	7.618	7.094	6.634
39	17.017	14.949	13.265	11.879	10.726	9.757	8.936	8.233	7.627	7.100	6.638
50	17.159	15.046	13.332	11.925	10.757	9.779	8.951	8.244	7.634	7.105	6.642
41	17.294	15.138	13.394	11.967	10.787	9.799	8.965	8.253	7.641	7.110	6.645
42	17.423	15.225	13.452	12.007	10.813	9.817	8.977	8.262	7.647	7.114	6.648
43	17.546	15.306	13.507	12.043	10.838	9.834	8.989	8.270	7.652	7.117	6.650
44	17.663	15.383	13.558	12.077	10.861	9.849	8.999	8.276	7.657	7.120	6.652
45	17.774	15.456	13.606	12.108	10.881	9.863	9.008	8.283	7.661	7.123	6.654
46	17.880	15.524	13.650	12.137	10.900	9.875	9.016	8.288	7.664	7.126	6.656
47	17.981	15.589	13.692	12.164	10.918	9.887	9.024	8.293	7.668	7.128	6.657
48	18.077	15.650	13.730	12.189	10.934	9.897	9.030	8.207	7.671	7.130	6.659
49	18.169	15.708	13.767	12.212	10.948	9.906	9.036	8.301	7.673	7.131	6.660
50	18.256	15.762	13.801	12.233	10.962	9.915	9.042	8.304	7.675	7.133	6.661
55	18.633	15.991	13.940	12.319	11.014	9.947	9.062	8.317	7.673	7.137	6.664
60	18.929	16.161	14.039	12.377	11.048	9.967	9.074	8.324	7.689	7.140	6.665

APPENDIX 12C

Present Worth of Periodic Payments of £1 (Aggregation of Single Present Worths from Appendix 12A)

Investment life (years)	Life of components (years)							
	1	2	5	10	15	20	30	45
Rate of interest = 5 per cent								
10	7.1078	3.1528	0.7835					
20	12.0853	5.7022	1.8785	0.6139	0.4810			
30	15.1411	7.2674	2.5506	0.9908	0.4810	0.3769		
40	17.0170	8.2282	2.9633	1.2222	0.7124	0.3769	0.2314	
50	18.1687	8.8181	3.2167	1.3642	0.8237	0.5189	0.2314	0.1113
60	18.8758	9.1803	3.3722	1.4514	0.8237	0.5189	0.2314	0.1113
Rate of interest = 6 per cent								
10	6.8017	3.0145	0.7473					
20	11.1581	5.2561	1.7229	0.5584	0.4173			
30	13.5907	6.5078	2.2677	0.8702	0.4173	0.3118		
40	14.9491	7.2068	2.5719	1.0443	0.5914	0.3118	0.1741	
50	15.7076	7.5971	2.7418	1.1415	0.6640	0.4090	0.1741	0.0727
60	16.1311	7.8150	2.8367	1.1958	0.6640	0.4090	0.1741	0.0727
Rate of interest = 7 per cent								
10	6.5152	2.8847	0.7130					
20	10.3356	4.8595	1.5838	0.5083	0.3624			
30	12.2777	5.8633	2.0264	0.7668	0.3624	0.2584		
40	13.2649	6.3737	2.2515	0.8981	0.4938	0.2584	0.1314	
50	13.7668	6.6331	2.3659	0.9649	0.5414	0.3252	0.1314	0.0476
60	14.0219	6.7650	2.4240	0.9989	0.5414	0.3252	0.1314	0.0476
Rate of interest = 8 per cent								
10	6.2469	2.7628	0.6806					
20	9.6036	4.5057	1.4590	0.4632	0.3152			
30	11.1584	5.3130	1.8196	0.6777	0.3152	0.2145		
40	11.8786	5.6870	1.9866	0.7771	0.4146	0.2145	0.0994	
50	12.2122	5.8602	2.0640	0.8231	0.4459	0.2606	0.0994	0.0313
60	12.3667	5.9404	2.0998	0.8445	0.4459	0.2606	0.0994	0.0313
Rate of interest = 9 per cent								
10	5.9952	2.6482	0.6499					
20	8.9501	4.1893	1.3469	0.4224	0.2745			
30	10.1983	4.8403	1.6413	0.6008	0.2745	0.1784		
40	10.7255	5.1152	1.7656	0.6762	0.3499	0.1784	0.0754	
50	10.9482	5.2314	1.8182	0.7081	0.3706	0.2103	0.0754	0.0207
60	11.0423	5.2804	1.8404	0.7215	0.3706	0.2103	0.0754	0.0207
Rate of interest = 10 per cent								
10	5.7590	2.5404	0.6209					
20	8.3649	3.9054	1.2459	0.3855	0.2394			
30	9.3696	4.4317	1.4868	0.5342	0.2394	0.1486		
40	9.7570	4.6346	1.5797	0.5915	0.2967	0.1486	0.0573	

Investment life (years)	Life of components (years)							
	1	2	5	10	15	20	30	45
Rate of interest = 10 per cent								
50	9.9063	4.7128	1.6155	0.6136	0.3104	0.1707	0.0573	0.0137
60	9.9639	4.7430	1.6293	0.6221	0.3104	0.1707	0.0573	0.0137
Rate of interest = 11 per cent								
10	5.5370	2.4389	0.5935					
20	7.8393	3.6501	1.1546	0.3522	0.2090			
30	8.6501	4.0766	1.3523	0.4762	0.2090	0.1240		
40	8.9357	4.2268	1.4219	0.5199	0.2527	0.1240	0.0437	
50	9.0362	4.2797	1.4464	0.5353	0.2618	0.1394	0.0437	0.0091
60	9.0717	4.2984	1.4550	0.5407	0.2618	0.1394	0.0437	0.0091
Rate of interest = 12 per cent								
10	5.3282	2.3432	0.5674					
20	7.3658	3.4197	1.0721	0.3220	0.1827			
30	8.0218	3.7662	1.2346	0.4256	0.1827	0.1037		
40	8.2330	3.8778	1.2869	0.4590	0.2161	0.1037	0.0334	
50	8.3010	3.9138	1.3037	0.4698	0.2222	0.1144	0.0334	0.0061
60	8.3229	3.9253	1.3092	0.4732	0.2222	0.1144	0.0334	0.0061
Rate of interest = 13 per cent								
10	5.1317	2.2529	0.5428					
20	6.9380	3.2112	0.9972	0.2946	0.1599			
30	7.4701	3.4935	1.1311	0.3814	0.1599	0.0868		
40	7.6268	3.5767	1.1706	0.4069	0.1855	0.0868	0.0256	
50	7.6730	3.6012	1.1822	0.4145	0.1895	0.0943	0.0256	0.0041
60	7.6866	3.6084	1.1856	0.4167	0.1895	0.0943	0.0256	0.0041
Rate of interest = 14 per cent								
10	4.9464	2.1677	0.5194					
20	6.5504	3.0222	0.9292	0.2697	0.1401			
30	6.9830	3.2526	1.0398	0.3425	0.1401	0.0728		
40	7.0997	3.3148	1.0696	0.3621	0.1597	0.0728	0.0196	
50	7.1312	3.3316	1.0776	0.3674	0.1625	0.0781	0.0196	0.0027
60	7.1397	3.3361	1.0798	0.3689	0.1625	0.0781	0.0196	0.0027
Rate of interest = 15 per cent								
10	4.7716	2.0871	0.4972					
20	6.1982	2.8502	0.8673	0.2472	0.1229			
30	6.5509	3.0388	0.9587	0.3083	0.1229	0.0611		
40	6.6380	3.0855	0.9813	0.3234	0.1380	0.0611	0.0151	
50	6.6596	3.0970	0.9869	0.3271	0.1399	0.0648	0.0151	0.0019
60	6.6649	3.0998	0.9883	0.3280	0.1399	0.0648	0.0151	0.0019

APPENDIX 12D

Annual Equivalent of Initial Payments of £1.

Years	5	6	7	8	9	10	11	12	13	14	15
					Rate of interest (per cent)						
1	1.05	1.06	1.07	1.08	1.09	1.10	1.11	1.12	1.13	1.14	1.15
2	.537 80	.545 43	.553 09	.560 76	.568 47	.576 19	.583 93	.591 70	.599 48	.607 29	.615 12
3	.367 20	.374 10	.381 05	.388 03	.395 05	.402 11	.409 21	.416 35	.423 52	.430 73	.437 98
4	.282 01	.288 59	.295 22	.301 92	.308 67	.315 47	.322 33	.329 23	.336 19	.343 20	.350 27
5	.230 97	.237 39	.243 89	.250 45	.257 09	.263 80	.270 57	.277 41	.284 31	.291 28	.298 32
6	.197 01	.203 36	.209 79	.216 31	.222 92	.229 61	.236 38	.243 23	.250 15	.257 16	.264 24
7	.172 81	.179 13	.185 55	.192 07	.198 69	.205 41	.212 22	.219 10	.226 09	.233 20	.240 38
8	.154 72	.161 03	.167 46	.174 01	.180 66	.187 44	.194 32	.201 28	.208 37	.215 56	.222 85
9	.140 69	.147 02	.153 48	.160 07	.166 80	.173 64	.180 60	.187 68	.194 85	.202 18	.209 55
10	.129 50	.135 86	.142 37	.149 02	.155 81	.162 73	.169 80	.176 99	.184 29	.191 71	.199 24
11	.120 38	.126 79	.133 35	.140 07	.146 95	.153 96	.161 10	.168 40	.175 83	.183 38	.191 05
12	.112 82	.119 27	.125 90	.132 69	.139 64	.146 75	.154 03	.161 44	.168 97	.176 67	.184 46
13	.106 45	.112 96	.119 65	.126 52	.133 56	.140 78	.148 14	.155 66	.163 34	.171 17	.179 11
14	.101 02	.107 58	.114 34	.121 29	.128 43	.135 74	.143 22	.150 87	.158 67	.166 61	.174 70
15	.096 34	.102 96	.109 79	.116 82	.124 05	.131 47	.139 06	.146 82	.154 75	.162 81	.171 02
16	.092 26	.098 95	.105 85	.112 97	.120 29	.127 81	.135 51	.143 38	.151 42	.159 61	.167 95
17	.088 69	.095 44	.102 42	.109 62	.117 04	.124 65	.132 46	.140 44	.148 61	.156 91	.165 37
18	.085 54	.092 35	.099 41	.106 70	.114 20	.121 93	.129 83	.137 93	.146 19	.154 63	.163 18
19	.082 74	.089 62	.096 75	.104 12	.111 73	.119 54	.127 56	.135 75	.144 13	.152 67	.161 34
20	.080 24	.087 18	.094 39	.101 85	.109 54	.117 45	.125 58	.133 88	.142 34	.150 98	.159 76
21	.077 99	.085 00	.092 28	.099 83	.107 61	.115 62	.123 83	.132 24	.140 80	.149 54	.158 42
22	.075 97	.083 04	.090 40	.098 03	.105 90	.113 99	.122 30	.130 80	.139 47	.148 30	.157 25
23	.074 13	.081 27	.088 71	.096 42	.104 38	.112 57	.120 97	.129 56	.138 31	.147 23	.156 27
24	.072 47	.079 67	.087 18	.094 97	.103 01	.111 29	.119 78	.128 46	.137 30	.146 30	.155 42
25	.070 95	.078 22	.085 81	.093 67	.101 80	.110 16	.118 73	.127 50	.136 42	.145 49	.154 70
26	.069 56	.076 90	.084 56	.092 50	.100 71	.109 15	.117 81	.126 64	.135 64	.144 80	.154 05
27	.068 29	.075 69	.083 42	.091 44	.099 73	.108 26	.116 98	.125 89	.134 97	.144 19	.153 51
28	.067 12	.074 59	.082 39	.090 48	.098 85	.107 44	.116 25	.125 25	.134 39	.143 65	.153 04
29	.066 04	.073 57	.081 44	.089 61	.098 05	.106 72	.115 60	.124 65	.133 86	.143 20	.152 64
30	.065 05	.072 64	.080 58	.088 82	.097 33	.106 07	.115 02	.124 14	.133 40	.142 79	.152 29
31	.064 13	.071 79	.079 79	.088 10	.096 68	.105 49	.114 50	.123 68	.133 01	.142 45	.151 99
32	.063 28	.071 00	.079 07	.087 45	.096 09	.104 97	.114 03	.123 27	.132 66	.142 14	.151 72
33	.062 49	.070 27	.078 40	.086 85	.095 56	.104 50	.113 62	.122 92	.132 34	.141 88	.151 51
34	.061 75	.069 59	.077 79	.086 30	.095 07	.104 06	.113 26	.122 59	.132 06	.141 64	.151 30
35	.061 07	.068 97	.077 23	.085 80	.094 63	.103 69	.112 93	.122 30	.131 82	.141 44	.151 12
36	.060 43	.068 39	.076 71	.085 34	.094 23	.103 33	.112 62	.122 07	.131 61	.141 26	.150 98
37	.059 83	.067 85	.076 23	.084 92	.093 87	.103 02	.112 35	.121 83	.131 42	.141 10	.150 85
38	.059 28	.067 35	.075 79	.084 53	.093 53	.102 74	.112 12	.121 63	.131 26	.140 96	.150 73
39	.058 76	.066 89	.075 38	.084 18	.093 23	.102 49	.111 90	.121 46	.131 11	.140 84	.150 64
40	.058 27	.066 16	.075 00	.083 86	.092 96	.102 25	.111 71	.121 30	.130 99	.140 74	.150 55
45	.056 26	.061 70	.073 49	.082 58	.091 90	.101 38	.111 01	.120 72	.130 53	.140 39	.150 28
50	.054 77	.063 44	.072 45	.081 74	.091 22	.100 85	.110 59	.120 42	.130 29	.140 19	.150 12
55	.053 66	.062 53	.071 73	.081 17	.090 79	.100 53	.110 35	.120 23	.130 15	.140 11	.150 06
60	.052 82	.061 87	.071 22	.080 79	.090 51	.100 33	.110 20	.120 13	.130 08	.140 05	.150 03

APPENDIX 12E

Annual Equivalent of Periodic Payments of £1

Years	Rate of interest (per cent)										
	5	6	7	8	9	10	11	12	13	14	15
1	1.000 00	1.000 00	1.000 00	1.000 00	1.000 00	1.000 00	1.000 00	1.000 00	1.000 00	1.000 00	1.000 00
2	.487 80	.485 44	.483 09	.480 77	.478 47	.471 69	.473 93	.471 69	.469 48	.467 28	.465 11
3	.317 21	.314 11	.311 05	.308 03	.305 05	.302 11	.299 22	.296 38	.293 51	.290 69	.288 01
4	.232 01	.228 59	.225 23	.221 92	.218 67	.215 47	.212 31	.209 24	.206 18	.203 21	.200 28
5	.180 98	.177 40	.173 89	.170 46	.167 09	.163 80	.160 56	.157 40	.154 32	.151 28	.148 32
6	.147 02	.143 35	.139 80	.136 32	.132 91	.129 61	.126 37	.123 22	.120 14	.117 15	.114 23
7	.122 82	.119 14	.115 55	.112 07	.108 69	.105 41	.102 21	.099 11	.096 10	.093 19	.090 35
8	.104 72	.101 04	.097 47	.094 01	.090 67	.087 44	.084 32	.081 30	.078 38	.075 56	.072 84
9	.090 69	.087 02	.083 49	.080 08	.076 80	.073 64	.070 60	.067 67	.064 86	.062 16	.059 57
10	.079 50	.075 87	.072 38	.069 03	.065 82	.062 75	.059 80	.056 98	.054 28	.051 71	.049 25
11	.070 39	.066 79	.063 36	.060 08	.056 95	.053 96	.051 12	.049 86	.045 84	.043 39	.041 06
12	.062 83	.059 28	.055 90	.052 70	.049 65	.046 76	.044 02	.041 43	.038 98	.036 66	.034 48
13	.056 46	.052 96	.049 65	.046 52	.043 57	.040 78	.038 15	.035 67	.033 35	.031 16	.029 11
14	.051 02	.047 58	.044 34	.041 30	.038 43	.035 75	.033 22	.030 87	.028 66	.026 60	.024 68
15	.046 34	.042 96	.039 79	.036 83	.034 06	.031 47	.029 06	.026 82	.024 74	.022 80	.021 01
16	.042 27	.038 95	.035 86	.032 98	.030 30	.027 82	.025 51	.023 39	.021 42	.019 61	.017 94
17	.038 70	.035 44	.032 43	.029 63	.027 05	.024 66	.022 47	.020 45	.018 60	.016 91	.015 36
18	.035 55	.032 36	.029 41	.026 70	.024 21	.021 93	.019 84	.017 93	.016 20	.014 62	.013 18
19	.032 75	.029 62	.026 75	.024 13	.021 73	.019 55	.017 56	.015 76	.014 13	.012 66	.011 33
20	.030 24	.027 18	.024 39	.021 85	.019 55	.017 46	.015 57	.013 37	.012 35	.010 98	.009 76
21	.028 00	.025 01	.022 29	.019 83	.017 62	.015 62	.013 83	.012 24	.010 81	.009 54	.008 41
22	.025 97	.023 05	.020 41	.018 03	.015 91	.014 01	.012 31	.010 81	.009 47	.008 30	.007 26
23	.024 14	.021 28	.018 71	.016 42	.014 38	.012 57	.010 97	.009 55	.008 31	.007 23	.006 27
24	.022 47	.019 68	.017 19	.014 98	.013 02	.011 30	.009 78	.008 46	.007 30	.006 30	.005 42
25	.020 95	.018 23	.015 81	.013 68	.011 81	.010 17	.008 74	.007 49	.006 42	.005 49	.004 69
26	.019 56	.016 90	.014 56	.012 51	.010 72	.009 16	.007 81	.006 65	.005 65	.004 80	.004 06
27	.018 29	.015 70	.013 43	.011 45	.009 73	.008 26	.006 98	.005 90	.004 97	.004 19	.003 52
28	.017 12	.014 59	.012 39	.010 49	.008 85	.007 45	.006 25	.005 24	.004 38	.003 66	.003 05
29	.016 04	.013 58	.011 45	.009 62	.008 06	.006 73	.005 60	.004 66	.003 86	.003 20	.002 65
30	.015 05	.012 65	.010 59	.008 83	.007 34	.006 08	.005 02	.004 14	.003 41	.002 80	.002 30
31	.014 13	.011 79	.009 80	.008 11	.006 69	.005 50	.004 50	.003 68	.003 00	.002 45	.001 99
32	.013 28	.011 00	.009 07	.007 45	.006 10	.004 97	.004 04	.003 28	.002 65	.002 14	.001 73
33	.012 49	.010 27	.008 41	.006 85	.005 56	.004 50	.003 62	.002 92	.002 34	.001 87	.001 50
34	.011 76	.009 60	.007 80	.006 30	.005 08	.004 07	.003 25	.002 86	.002 07	.001 64	.001 30
35	.011 07	.008 97	.007 23	.005 80	.004 64	.003 69	.002 92	.002 31	.001 82	.001 44	.001 13
36	.010 43	.008 39	.006 72	.005 34	.004 24	.003 34	.002 63	.002 06	.001 61	.001 26	.000 98
37	.009 84	.007 86	.006 24	.004 92	.003 87	.003 03	.002 36	.001 83	.001 42	.001 10	.000 85
38	.009 28	.007 36	.005 80	.004 54	.003 54	.002 75	.002 12	.001 63	.001 26	.000 96	.000 74
39	.008 76	.006 89	.005 39	.004 19	.003 24	.002 49	.001 91	.001 46	.001 11	.000 85	.000 64
40	.008 28	.006 46	.005 01	.003 86	.002 96	.002 25	.001 71	.001 30	.000 98	.000 74	.000 56
45	.006 26	.004 70	.003 49	.002 59	.001 90	.001 30	.001 01	.000 73	.000'53	.000 38	.000 27
50	.004 78	.003 44	.002 46	.001 74	.001 23	.000 86	.000 59	.000 41	.000 28	.000 20	.000 13
55	.003 67	.002 53	.001 74	.001 17	.000 79	.000 53	.000 35	.000 23	.000 15	.000 10	.000 06
60	.002 83	.001 88	.001 22	.000 64	.000 51	.000 32	.000 21	.000 13	.000 08	.000 05	.000 03

13

NATURAL SOURCES, HEAT PUMPS AND HEAT RECOVERY

13.1 Solar power and buildings

Of all the potential alternatives to fossil fuels, it is solar energy that has captured the imagination of both scientists and laymen, with its promise of a non-polluting, inexhaustible, source of energy in vast quantities. While it has generated enormous publicity and interest, it has also generated much that is naive, technically incompetent and hopelessly optimistic, not least in the popular press and the brochures of some solar energy collector manufacturers, and most countries are only just beginning to draft standards and codes of practice in this field. Solar energy may be free, but the means for utilizing it are not and involve many technical problems yet to be satisfactorily resolved before the 'Solar Age' can be said to have arrived in an economic and commercial sense.

The use of solar energy to provide domestic hot water has reached, or is reaching, cost effectiveness in a number of countries with favourable solar radiation levels such as Japan and Australia, and, in these countries, there is a widespread and increasing use of solar water heaters. It is anticipated that the next cost breakthrough will come with the widespread use of solar energy to provide partial space heating in buildings, since heating systems can operate at the relatively low temperatures, say 38 °C to 60 °C, that can be achieved with simple, flat plate collection devices in favourable conditions. Solar-powered cooling may become economically viable by the mid 1980's.

The effectiveness with which solar energy can be harnessed varies considerably from country to country, depending on such things as climate, building standards, competing fuel supplies, energy consumption and the fact that the great majority of buildings now standing were designed without solar energy in mind, either as to orientation, built form, shading or systems. New buildings designed to use solar energy strongly reflect the needs of optimum orientation and, possibly, of the solar plant itself in their architecture as, for example, in the Shenandoah Community Centre, Georgia, USA, currently one of the largest and most advanced applications of solar heating and cooling in the world [1].

To put matters in perspective, the USA confidently expects some 5 to 10 per cent of its national heating and cooling needs to be met eventually by solar energy. The UK can expect some 1 to 2 per cent of its national energy consumption to be so met since, with its less favourable climate and the present state of technology, only domestic water heating has potential for application to suitable buildings [2]. If partial space heating by solar energy could also be provided in the UK, the percentage savings would increase by an order of magnitude [3, 4].

13.1.1 The Flat Plate Collector

The flat plate collector is the device most widely used to collect solar energy at modest temperatures and has been the device used, almost without exception, for domestic water heating applications. It is also the most frequently considered device for use in the heating and cooling of buildings by solar energy.

The essential element of such a device is a flat plate, normally of copper, aluminium or steel, with a black frontal surface which absorbs solar radiation and converts it to sensible heat. This heat is then transmitted by conduction to a fluid which circulates from one edge of the plate to the other by means of pipes, channels, etc., which may be attached to or be integral with the plate. The heat transfer fluid may be water, air or some other fluid such as an antifreeze. A very large number of absorber plate designs for solar water and air heaters have been tried with varying degrees of success [4, 5].

To reach the temperatures required for heating and cooling applications in buildings, the heat losses from the absorber plate must be controlled. Thermal insulation is installed behind and at the edges of the absorber plate and one or more layers of transparent material are placed above its frontal surface, mainly to prevent convection losses. Some of the heat loss is also due to long-wave infra-red radiation from the heated absorber plate and can be reduced by using glass, which is opaque to long-wave infra-red radiation, as the cover material. Plastics are generally poorer in this respect than glass. The radiant heat loss can be further reduced by treating the frontal surface of the absorber plate with a selective black surface which has a high absorptivity in the solar spectrum but a low emissivity in the long-wave infra-red region. It is generally thought that a good selective coating can be equivalent to one layer of glass cover, provided at least one layer of glass is present to prevent weathering.

Proprietary flat plate collectors are delivered in a case or container, ready to be rigidly fastened in a fixed position that will yield either maximum annual heat output or maximum seasonal heat output. In the northern hemisphere, collectors should be oriented southwards for maximum effect, though orientations 20° or so east or west of south will not significantly impair performance. For maximum annual heat output, collectors should be tilted with respect to the horizontal at an angle equal to the angle of Latitude. Reducing the tilt by some 15° or so, increases summer output at the expense of winter output, while increasing the tilt by a similar amount produces the opposite result. Both its ability to function at a fixed angle and to accept diffuse solar radiation are potential advantages of the flat plate collector, especially in temperate climates with large amounts of diffuse radiation.

The performance of a flat plate collector is limited by its heat losses, which increase with increasing difference between the collector temperature and ambient temperature. When temperature rises of only a few degrees above ambient are required, as in heating swimming pools, no transparent cover is needed. To obtain the moderate temperature rises above ambient useful in space and domestic water-heating applications, a single layer cover is normally required. Two or even three layer covers have been used to obtain reasonable efficiencies at higher operating temperatures above ambient, as also have selective coatings of the absorber plate. A comprehensive, technical description of the behaviour of flat plate collectors has been given by Duffie and Beckman [6].

13.1.2 Domestic Water Heating

This is by far the most understood, developed and economically viable application of present solar energy technology; well over a million solar water-heating systems are now in operation in countries with favourable radiation levels such as Israel, Japan and Australia. Nevertheless, designs, results and operating experience cannot be unquestioningly transferred from one climatic zone to another. For example, north-western Europe, and the UK in particular, has generally milder winters than the USA, but only about half the sunshine hours. This area of Europe also has a lower energy requirement per capita than the USA and experience with solar heating systems of any kind is very limited.

The components of a typical solar water-heating system are a flat plate collector, storage tank, piping, circulating pump and controls as shown in Fig. 13.1. Whenever the temperature of the water at the top of the collector rises a preset number of degrees above the water in the bottom of the storage tank, the pump is switched on and water is circulated between the collector and tank until the temperature difference is equalized, either as a consequence of the tank heating up or the solar radiation level falling. In countries where freezing is a possibility, an indirect storage tank is used so that antifreeze can be circulated through the collector and indirect coil circuit, separately from the water in the tank. Alternatively, provision for draining the system down can be included.

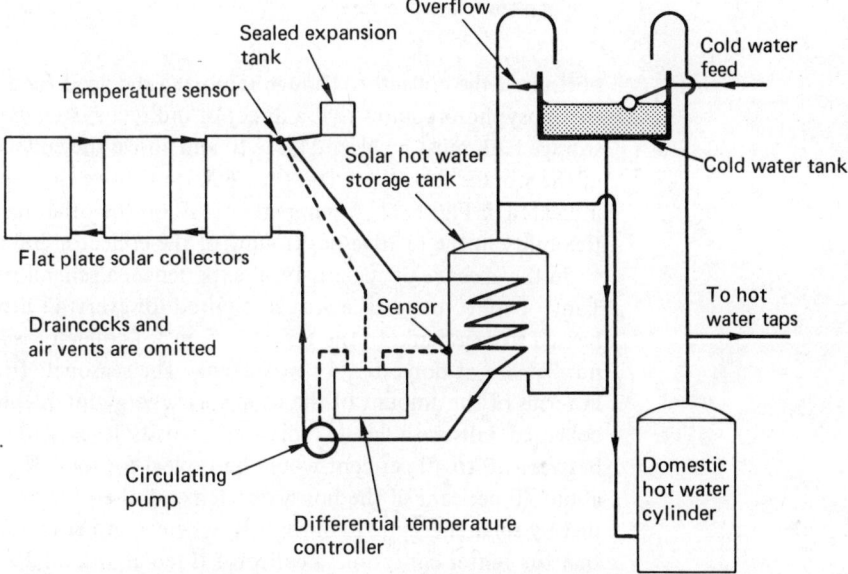

Fig. 13.1 Indirect forced circulation system (after McVeigh [7]).

Wherever the domestic hot water tank contains provision for auxiliary heating, it is advantageous to use a second tank of similar size which is then heated by solar energy and acts as a preheat to the hot water supply tank. Such an arrangement increases the chance of useful solar energy gains, since it is impossible to introduce heat into a storage tank where the temperature is above that of the collector fluid. In the case of a tank with auxiliary heating its temperature may be very high relative to the collector fluid temperature.

In some countries, notably Australia and Israel, there is widespread use of systems employing natural circulation. Such thermosyphons rely on the change in density of water with temperature so that water heated in the collector rises into the upper half of a storage tank placed above the collector, while cooler, denser water from near the bottom of the tank flows downwards and enters the

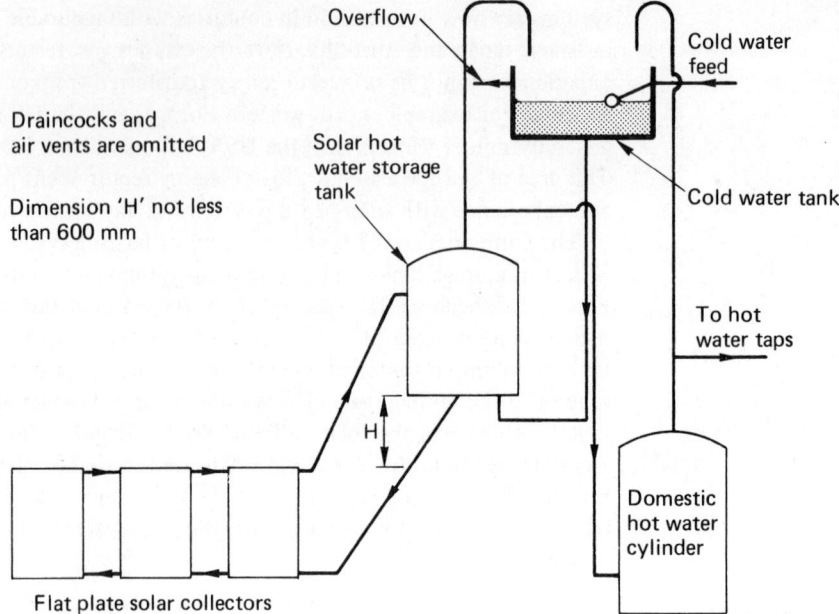

Fig. 13.2 Direct natural thermosyphon system (after McVeigh [7]).

Overflow

Cold water feed

Draincocks and air vents are omitted

Solar hot water storage tank

Cold water tank

Dimension 'H' not less than 600 mm

To hot water taps

H

Domestic hot water cylinder

Flat plate solar collectors

bottom of the collector. Though removing the need for a pump and controls, a thermosyphon requires that a direct or indirect system be used in which the storage tank must be placed close to and above the collector, so that the bottom of the storage tank is not less than 600 mm above the top of the collector, as indicated in Fig. 13.2. A pumped circuit, on the other hand, gives considerable flexibility in the relative positioning of the collector and tank.

In the absence of specific local experience, a general rule of thumb is that 1 m² of collector surface area is required for every 45 litres of water in the solar-heated storage tank. In the UK, 4 to 5 m² of collector is appropriate with a normal size of domestic hot water tank. The seasonal efficiency of such systems, in terms of the amount of the total solar energy intercepted that is usefully collected, falls with falling radiation intensity levels and a seasonal efficiency of between 30 to 40 per cent would be typical for the UK [4]. As a result, only about 40 per cent of the hot water demand of an average UK household could be met by solar energy [3]. In the UK, where summer radiation greatly outweighs that for winter collection, a collector tilted at around 30° to the horizontal would not only perform acceptably well but would present less of a problem in being integrated aesthetically and structurally with normal roof lines than a collector tilted at a steeper angle for winter operation.

13.1.3 Solar Space Heating

Before 1972, experience with solar space heating was limited to a handful of buildings, virtually all single-family dwellings, built mostly as the result of individual enthusiasm and largely in the USA. Of the 20 or so buildings in the USA at that time, only one was a commercial building. Beyond proving the technical feasibility of solar heating, there was little of general validity that could be drawn from these, often very diverse, examples as to the likely economic and commercial implications of a widespread application of solar heating to buildings of all kinds.

Most of these space-heating systems employed large arrays of flat plate collectors in conjunction with large storage tanks to supply heated water for partial space heating. Typical collector areas have been around 0.5 of the heated floor area and storage volumes around 50 l m^{-2} of heated floor area [7]. A few houses have employed flat plate solar air heaters with a warm-air distribution system and thermal storage provided by rock-filled bins, through which air can be circulated [8]. Collector:floor area ratios and equivalent storage volume:floor area ratios are similar to those of water heating systems. Apart from water and rock, no other commercially feasible form of heat storage exists except perhaps in the structure of the building itself. A well-known example of this form of solar heating is to be found in the UK in the annexe of St George's School, Wallasey, which is a structurally massive building with a high thermal inertia and derives some 30 per cent of its heating through a south-facing wall composed of glazing. This principle is limited to situations where the net heat balance across the glazing is favourable during the heating season [9].

After the establishment of the Energy Research and Development Administration/Solar Division and as a result of the Solar Heating and Cooling Demonstration Act of 1974, the number of solar-heated buildings in the USA has enormously increased as part of a research and development effort to reduce system costs, increase systems performance and to produce economically viable systems that are both socially and environmentally acceptable for widespread use. The great majority of these projects have used banks of roof-mounted, flat plate collectors and large storage tanks to provide hot water for partial space heating, with a conventional auxiliary system sized to meet the design heat load. An account of more than 300 solar-heated buildings has been given by Shurcliff [8]. While experience gained in the USA cannot be transferred whole-sale to northern Europe and other areas where climate and fuel resources differ, a considerable amount of potentially useful information has emerged, more so since the comparatively small-scale European research programmes are, by and large, just beginning [4, 7]. An assessment of some of the major US projects from a north European point of view is given by Keller [10].

The most common problems encountered have been associated with freeze protection, the expansion and contraction of large liquid volumes and the flow characteristics in complex piping systems. Other general problems to be high-lighted are that building inspectors and planning departments with little relevant experience will take a conservative line in response to proposals; that few people are experienced in solar technology; that there are no generally recognized performance standards and that solar heating systems, in requiring auxiliary energy at times of peak heating demand, can produce a very unfavourable load characteristic on the conventional power supply network. Some examples of particular problems are: that at the Towns Elementary School in Atlanta, Georgia, the cost of pipes, fittings, and valves was three times that of the 930 m^2 collector; that at the New England Telephone Company Exchange Building in North Chelmsford, Massachusetts, the erection of the collectors cost as much as the entire solar plant because of storm risk; and that at the Timonium Elementary School, Maryland, maintenance costs have exceeded savings.

The two major improvements needed appear to be the production of a low-cost collector system and of a convenient, efficient and low-cost method of thermal storage, other components of solar heating systems being largely standard items.

The distribution temperatures available from solar heating systems are lower than provided by conventional systems. In solar water-heating systems, unless a large radiant surface in the form of ceiling radiant panels or underfloor heating is available, units employing forced convection, probably with oversized coils and fans, will be needed. Solar air-heating systems will require correspondingly large ducts to carry an increased volume of the relatively low-temperature air to meet heating demands. In consequence, solar air-heating systems are only suitable for small buildings, particularly dwellings, where cooling is not required and where their simplicity, lack of corrosion and leakage problems can be exploited. Their immunity to freezing might make air-heating systems suitable for use in northerly climates like the UK, but little research has been carried out.

In any new building, heat losses should be minimized at the outset. The lay-out of duct work, piping, collector manifolding, location of controls, heater units, fans and heat exchangers should be considered at the preliminary design stage. Provision for thermal storage is usually less expensive when designed into the building from the start. Retrofitting a building is a more difficult task, but a necessary one if solar heating is to have any great impact. Low-rise buildings give a better ratio of roof area to volume for collector mounting; buildings that are used continuously make better use of the installed solar system; and buildings with low heating demands minimize the need for supplementary energy. Considerable problems can be met in trying to interface an existing heating system with a solar heating system because of the lower distribution tempera-tures of the latter.

How much of our current experience and technology will prove to be applicable to northern Europe is impossible to say at present; and as yet we do not know whether flat plate collector systems or passive systems (as embodied in St George's School, Wallasey) will prove to be practicable. The potential for the solar heating of buildings in the UK has been reviewed by the UK section of the International Solar Energy Society with some attention to north European projects, which highlights our considerable lack of knowledge in this area [4]. In this regard, it has been stated that space-heating systems using solar water heaters are unlikely to succeed in the UK until the technology of long-term (i.e. inter-seasonal) thermal storage is vastly improved [3].

One interesting aspect of a number of past and present north-west European projects is the use of heat pumps in combination with some form of solar collection. There is also considerable interest in this area in the USA, particularly for northern areas. Whether the future of European solar heating lies in this direction or not, one fact that is certain is that energy conserving design is the prerequisite of a successful solar heating application.

13.1.4 Solar Space Cooling

Unlike solar heating, solar cooling has the advantage of being required at times of high solar radiation levels but the disadvantage of having been the subject of comparatively little research and development. This situation is rapidly changing owing to the considerable effort now being concentrated on solar cooling systems particularly in the USA [11].

As will be discussed further in Section 13.3, air-conditioning systems designed to handle cooling loads have employed refrigeration units of one of two kinds: vapour compression chillers or absorption chillers. Though less efficient, it is the absorption chiller which has first found application in solar cooling systems since, in some forms, it can be directly energized by hot water at temperatures attainable by flat plate collectors. More technical information is given by Duffie and Beckman [6].

Small absorption chiller units for use in dwellings are usually designed to be powered directly by gas or oil heating and, therefore, are designed to operate at high energizing temperatures. Domestic units that can be powered directly by solar heating await the result of future research and development [11].

Large, commercial absorption chillers, on the other hand, have been much more highly developed and their performance over a wide range of energizing temperatures and operating conditions is known. Most often designed to run off steam, conversion to hot water is readily accomplished and is a standard conversion offered by many manufacturers. Given the range of water temperatures available from a flat plate collector system, only units employing lithium bromide and water as the absorbent/refrigerant pair are currently available for solar cooling purposes. All such units are designed to reject the heat they remove into a water circuit which, in turn, usually rejects this heat to the atmosphere via a cooling tower.

The cooling capacity of a conventional lithium bromide/water chiller unit can be reduced by either throttling the supply of steam or hot water, or by lowering the supply temperature. In solar-powered systems, for reasons of performance, it is preferable to reduce capacity by lowering the temperature of the hot water supply, not by reducing its flow rate [12].

While any cooling plant has to deal with a variable demand and a variable heat rejection temperature, that of ambient air, a solar-powered system also has to cope with a variable hot water supply temperature from the collector array which, during cloudy weather or at night, is too low for operation. Hot water storage is normally needed to enable the chiller unit to be powered at these times. Since maximum cooling loads occur relatively infrequently and solar collectors operate more efficiently at low temperatures, it is advantageous to store only a portion of the water at a high temperature, sufficient to meet periods of high demand, and to store the bulk of the water at a lower temperature sufficient for operation at reduced capacity [12]. In some cases, it may also be possible to store chilled water to offset peak cooling loads [13]. As yet, however, no general guidelines exist for the design of such systems.

An evaporative cooling technique has been successfully developed and applied to a number of buildings, including schools, in Australia [14, 15]. Known as the Rock Bed Regenerative system, it employs two identical beds of rock screenings, some 127 mm deep and approximately 5 m^2 in area, through which exhaust air, cooled by evaporation, is passed, in alternation, chilling the beds. Every 5 min the direction of air flow is reversed so that fresh air is passed through one of the beds and cooled before entering the building.

Other methods of providing solar-powered cooling are also under active investigation. One of these is the development of a large vapour compression machine driven by a solar-powered engine, which will require temperatures well above the boiling point of water for efficient operation. Another is the development of a solar desiccant dehumidifier. Since the latent heat load is a significant part of the total cooling load for warm, humid, air, then if it could be removed by a desiccant material which could be regenerated by solar heat, the load on the chiller unit would be significantly reduced.

13.1.5 Economic Considerations

The use of solar water-heating, space-heating or cooling systems in buildings will largely depend on their economic performance in relation to competing conventional systems. In virtually all applications of solar energy to buildings, a conventional auxiliary system has to be installed and sized to carry full load when necessary, so that solar systems generally involve a large extra investment. There are a number of economic analyses by which the cost effectiveness or cost benefit of a system can be evaluated, but since a solar system involves savings spread out over the life of the system, it is appropriate to use a method of economic evaluation such as life-cycle costing, a technique discussed in Chapter 12. Various approaches to the economic assessment of solar systems are discussed by Duffie and Beckman [6], McVeigh [7] and Courtney [16].

Whatever method of economic analysis is used, it should be remembered that for solar space heating, and even more so for solar cooling, a considerable amount of system detail yet remains to be resolved. Again, the performance of any solar system cannot be properly evaluated unless good solar radiation and other relevant meteorological data are available in sufficiently detailed form, for example as hourly values, for the site in question. Chapter 4 outlines available prediction methods. Conditions often change significantly between sites 80 km or less apart but no measuring network yet exists anywhere recording detailed data at this scale.

Where suitable data is available, computer simulation of system performance over a number of years can be run using the kind of system modelling techniques described by Duffie and Beckman [6]. In the absence of real hourly radiation data, hourly values for an average day for each month of the year can be generated using the techniques described in Chapter 4. Simulations run using such average hourly data are thought to indicate long-term performance and, by the result of such simulations, Klein *et al.* have been able to deduce a performance chart for solar heating systems where the water-heating load is small relative to the space-heating load [17]. Another approach, partly graphical and partly by calculation, has been given by Swanson and Boehm [18]. Nevertheless, the performance of solar heating and of solar cooling systems yet remains to be well established in practice.

As domestic water heating is likely to be the first widespread use of solar energy in many countries and as there are no agreed performance prediction methods, two simple methods by which the annual energy receipts of such a system can be reasonably estimated will be given. The first method involves calculating or otherwise deriving the monthly average daily clear sky total radiation intensity, I_{Gs} (in watts per square metre), incident upon the collector surface as is discussed in Section 4.4.2.1(e). The monthly solar energy receipt for the system is given by

$$Q_m = 0.024 \times I_{Gs} \times \bar{n}/\bar{N}_0 \times \eta \times A \times m,$$

where $\bar{n}/\bar{N}_0$ is the monthly mean ratio of actual to possible sunshine hours for the site, η is the instantaneous collector efficiency at design (working) conditions, A is the exposed collector area in square metres and m is the number of days in the month [19].

The second method involves calculating the monthly average daily total and diffuse irradiation on a horizontal surface from sunshine hour figures and then calculating the monthly average daily total irradiation on the collector surface by means of the techniques given in Section 4.4.2.2(c). The monthly receipts of solar energy can then be derived, multiplied by the system seasonal efficiency factor, and totalled to give the annual receipt.

Both methods were applied to two UK sites very close to $52°N$ and $56°N$ respectively for a solar collector of 4 m^2 area, facing due south and mounted integrally with a roof slope of $25\frac{1}{2}°$. An instantaneous efficiency of 50 per cent, which corresponds to a single cover collector typically designed to operate at a water temperature of 30 $°C$ above ambient under 600 W m^{-2} irradiance [4, 7, 19], was assumed in the first method and a seasonal efficiency of 35 per cent was assumed in the second [4].

The results are given in tabular form in Table 13.1. It can be seen that while the estimated monthly total energy receipts differ between the methods as might be expected, the annual totals are in good agreement with each other and with the estimate of 1400 kW h given by Courtney on the basis of Kew data for a south-facing collector of 4 m^2 area, tilted at $30°$ to the horizontal [16].

Table 13.1 *Solar energy collected (in kilowatt hours) calculated by two different methods for Latitudes $52°N$ and $56°N$, respectively*

Month	52°N		56°N	
	Method 1	Method 2	Method 1	Method 2
January	31.8	45.1	27.5	38.9
February	53.2	60.5	59.2	61.6
March	129.1	121.5	101.6	99.8
April	155.9	143.1	149.3	137.2
May	237.4	196.2	193.8	172.3
June	245.6	207.7	199.2	179.1
July	221.6	191.6	168.7	163.0
August	205.6	182.6	156.6	151.9
September	156.0	149.3	102.5	109.6
October	93.2	103.7	67.4	78.8
November	36.1	53.0	26.8	42.0
December	24.3	48.4	18.7	29.7
Totals	1590	1503	1271	1264

13.2 Wind power and buildings

Although the history of the windmill use goes back some 4000 years, here we are concerned only with those modern windmills designed to produce electricity, which began to appear at the turn of the century. Such windmills or aerogenerators typically employ two or three specially designed aerofoil blades, mounted on a horizontal axis, as shown in Fig. 13.3, and which rotate at a high speed, quite unlike the more familiar multiblade windmills used for pumping water and employed all over the world. A useful account of the history of aerogenerators and their present state of development has been given by Tagg [20].

The output of aerogenerators depends on:

(i) the cube of the wind speed;

Fig. 13.3 The modern, small aerogenerator (after Rayment [24]). D = rotor diameter, P_R = rated output.

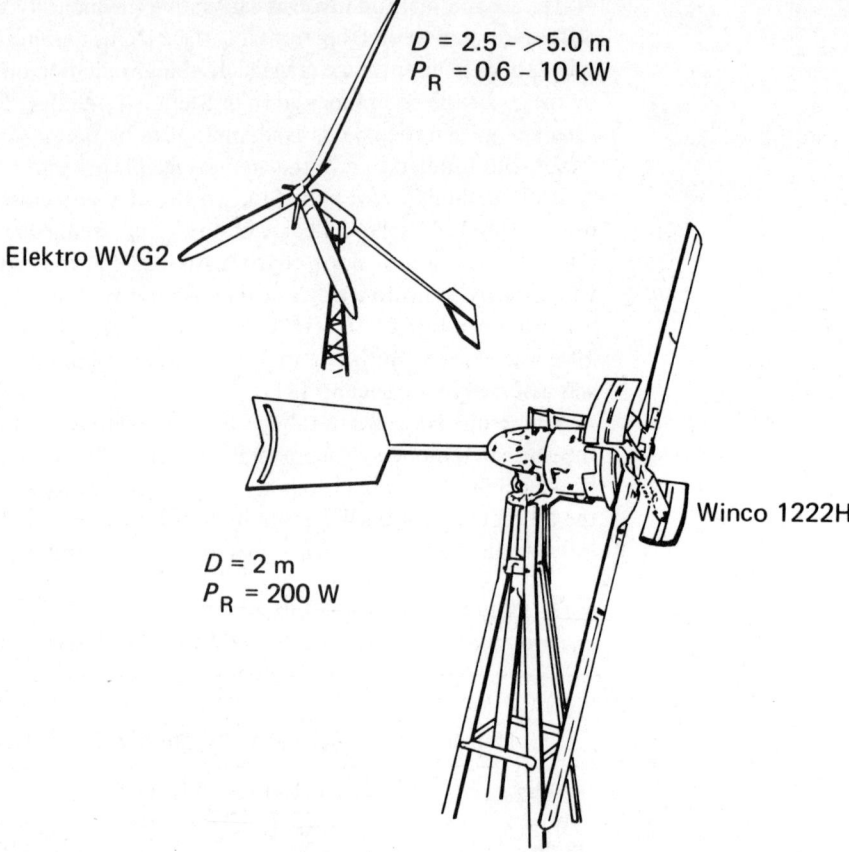

Elektro WVG2

$D = 2.5 - {>}5.0$ m
$P_R = 0.6 - 10$ kW

Winco 1222H

$D = 2$ m
$P_R = 200$ W

   (ii) air density and turbulence;
   (iii) the square of the rotor diameter, i.e. the area swept by the blades;
   (iv) propellor and generator efficiency;
   (v) the starting wind speed and the rated wind speed at which full output is reached;
   (vi) the rated output.

The first two items are affected by the choice of site. An ideal site has a high continuous wind speed with no turbulence. In practice, the energy in the wind is both intermittent, because the wind speed at any particular time is unpredictable, and dilute, because the density of air is low. The effect of topography upon wind speed has been discussed by Putnam [21] and Golding [22] and more recently by Caton [23] and by Rayment [24] who give wind speed and wind energy correction factors both for height and terrain. Such corrections are normally necessary since most measurements of wind speed are taken at meteorological stations on exposed, open sites and are not directly applicable to built-up areas. Wind velocity profiles over three types of terrain are shown in Chapter 4.

    The next three items on the above list are functions of the aerogenerator design. The rotor diameter is usually restricted by practical considerations whereas the combined propellor-generator efficiency is limited fundamentally to no more than 60 per cent in terms of the energy extractable from the wind energy arriving at the rotor and, in practice, reaches about 40 per cent. Rayment has shown that, when all three items are taken into consideration, a suitable estimate of the extractable electrical energy, E_e, available per unit swept area is

$$E_e = 0.0148\, v_{50}^3 \text{ GJ m}^{-2} \text{ per annum}$$

where v_{50} is the site windspeed exceeded 50 per cent of the time [24]. If v_{50} is not known, the mean annual windspeed will generally provide a close approximation.

The final item on the list is also a design parameter of the aerogenerator. By convention, aerogenerators are rated according to their maximum potential output, but the actual output power at any particular instant depends on the instantaneous wind speed and is, in consequence, unpredictable and unreliable. Again the value of E_e given above is considerably less than the value that would obtain if the aerogenerator produced its rated output whenever the wind blew. More information on this aspect has been given by Warne [25]. For convenience, we can break down aerogenerator rating according to three scales of operation as follows:

(i) large-scale operation, rating around 1000 kW;
(ii) medium-scale operation, rating around 100 kW;
(iii) small-scale operation, rating around 10 kW.

13.2.1 Large-scale Operation

Machines of this size would normally be envisaged as part of a national generating network, with their output feeding directly into a national or large-scale electrical supply grid. The largest machine of this type was erected in 1941 at Grandpa's Knob in Vermont, USA, and had a rating of 1250 kW. The project, which has been described by Putnam [21], ended when the machine failed.

Generally, such machines would be sited in remote areas of continuous high wind, and, while having an impact on the environment as a whole, would not be expected to have any significant effect upon the built environment in particular.

13.2.2 Medium-scale Operation

Most of our knowledge of machines at this scale was obtained after the Second World War. Of particular note was the work started in the UK in 1947 at the Electrical Research Association by a team headed by E. W. Golding, who later summarized much of this work in a book [22]. By the early 1960's, interest in such machines had largely evaporated, due to mechanical failures in many of the machines tested, but mainly because of their poor economic return. With rising fuel costs, interest has now revived, and in Ohio, USA, a 100 kW aerogenerator has been built at NASA's Lewis Research Center [26]. The windmill has two 18.9 m long aluminium blades and is situated on a 30.5 m high steel tower.

The 1950's work in the UK indicated that medium-scale operation only had potential in remote districts, where one machine served several buildings [27]. A much more recent analysis reaches similar conclusions in that only a medium-scale machine, both large enough to serve several households and located in a windy district, has a chance of proving cost effective [24].

It appears, then, that medium-scale aerogenerators might be suitable for servicing groups of buildings in windy locations and remote or other areas where fuel costs are high. Such a machine would normally be sited reasonably close to the buildings it served to lower transmission losses and costs, and, as we can see from the dimensions given above, it would have considerable impact on the local environment.

13.2.3 Small-scale Operation

By 1910 several hundred machines, of 5 to 25 kW rated output, were successfully supplying village dwellings in Denmark with electrical power. The operation of these machines reached a peak around the First World War due to fuel shortages, but then declined as cheap supplies of fuel for generating sets became available. During the interwar years, some small, high quality aerogenerators became available, such as those produced by Jacobs [28] which supplied thousands of mid-west farms in the USA with electrical power, and the Lucas Freelite [22] which similarly supplied many isolated and rural dwellings in North Britain.

A largely successful demonstration of small-scale wind power was carried out in the UK using an Allgaier machine of 7.5 kW rated output and 10 m rotor diameter. The installation has been described by Walker [29] and the aerogenerator by Tagg [30]. The aerogenerator was sited near Aviemore in Scotland, on a moderately windy site, and supplied all the domestic electrical needs of a forestry worker's house, while also running power tools and providing soil warming for growing plants. However, despite the fact that the technical problems of conventional small-scale aerogenerators seem largely solved, other serious problems remain.

Satisfactory siting demands that the aerogenerator be at least 3 m in height above any object within 450 m of its mounting point and that it be as close to the building it serves as possible to minimize transmission losses. In built-up areas, where the majority of people in developed countries live, each dwelling would require an adjacent, high tower. Alternatively, the aerogenerator might be erected on the roof of a building or incorporated into the design of a new building. Rayment [24] suggests a maximum practicable rotor diameter of 3 m for roof-mounted aerogenerators, and of 6 m if mounted on a back garden tower, which will severely restrict the amount of power available on sheltered urban sites. Problems of visual impact, noise, vibration, and safety all militate against a widespread use of small-scale aerogenerators.

A further serious problem is that of cost, to which we will return later. Small-scale aerogenerators involve the highest cost per unit installed output and it seems unlikely that conventional, horizontal axis machines will be cost effective now or in the foreseeable future for the majority of locations.

13.2.4 The Utilization of Wind Power in Buildings

The output from any aerogenerator will reflect the intermittent and unpredictable nature of the wind, so that some form of energy storage is essential if the full potential of a wind-powered system is to be realized.

At large-scale operation, the distribution grid to which the aerogenerator is linked will provide an essentially infinite sink for the electrical energy generated, so dispensing with any need for storage. The only form of electrical energy storage commonly available at the other scales of operation is afforded by such rechargeable batteries as the familiar lead–acid battery found in motor cars. The application of this form of storage to medium-scale operation is quite impractical and even at small-scale will double or even treble the initial costs of the system [31], unless only a trivial amount of electrical energy is stored, suitable, say, for a few lights.

Since virtually all buildings require space and water heating, a sensible approach to the energy storage problem at medium and small-scale operation is to convert the electrical energy from the aerogenerator directly to heat and to employ some form of cheap thermal storage.

The most effective way to use a medium-scale aerogenerator would, therefore, appear to be, not to supply several buildings with electrical energy, but to supply them with heat via a district heating scheme [24]. The optimum sizing of the storage system and of any conventionally fuelled auxiliary system can be decided by application of the method outlined in Chapters 11 and 12.

The conclusion of a study carried out into the application of small-scale aerogenerators on rural premises in Ireland [32], and supported by a study of the Orkney Islands off Scotland [33], was that the simplest, most efficient and cheapest system consisted of a free-running propellor-driven alternator feeding directly to resistance heaters in a thermal store. This store could take the form of a tank of water with immersion heaters or could be in solid form, either free-standing, as in the case of a conventional electrical storage heater, or as part of the building structure, such as a floor or wall of solid construction with embedded resistance wiring.

13.2.5 Economic Considerations

The cost effectiveness of aerogenerators has always been marginal and critically dependent on the detailed behaviour of the wind at the proposed site and upon the way the generated energy is utilized.

The capital cost of an aerogenerator, C, in pounds sterling, can be expressed as

$$£C = C_1 \times (\text{swept area}) + C_2$$

and the cost of the wind-generated energy, assuming a 20 year life, as

$$£ \text{ per GJ} = \frac{0.117}{E_e} \left\{ C_1 E_e / 0.0148 v_{50}^3 + C_2 \right\}$$

where, at 1976 prices, according to Rayment [24], C_1 and C_2 are, respectively, £55 m^{-2} and £1100 for small-scale aerogenerators and £40 m^{-2} and £825 for medium-scale aerogenerators and E_e is the extractable electrical energy as defined in page 517. Since the price of the aerogenerator is only part of the cost of the total installation, any other costs should be added in to the aerogenerator capital cost. The cost effectiveness or otherwise of any wind-power system then depends on the local costs of any competing energy such as oil, gas or mains electricity.

Considerable reductions in capital costs have been predicted for a vertical axis aerogenerator, generally referred to as a 'catenary' or 'Darrieus' mill (as shown in Fig. 13.4), which has been brought to prominence notably by the work of South and Rangi [34]. Rayment [24] has projected values for C_1 and C_2 of £15 m^{-2} and £300, respectively, for such machines. If achieved, such a cost reduction could radically and favourably alter the cost effectiveness of wind-generated energy, even at small-scale operation.

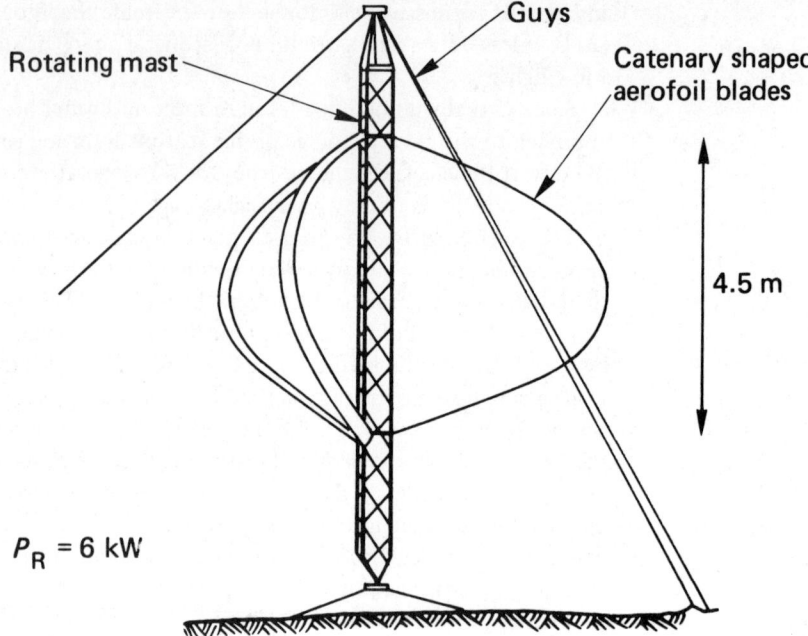

Fig. 13.4 The catenary-mill (after Rayment [24]).

Rotating mast

Guys

Catenary shaped aerofoil blades

4.5 m

$P_R = 6$ kW

The complementary nature of high winter wind speeds and high summer radiation levels has been noted in many areas. Attempts to make use of combined wind-solar energy systems have been reported [35, 36] and it may be that such schemes will succeed as a result of the potential cost benefits due to the reduction of energy storage capacity required.

13.3 Heat pumps

A heat pump is a machine which can extract heat from a low temperature source, such as outside air, and upgrade or 'pump' it to a higher temperature level so that it becomes suitable for space- and water-heating purposes. The principle is similar to that of the domestic refrigerator, but there the emphasis is on the refrigeration effect, i.e. on the efficiency with which heat can be removed from a low temperature source. In contrast, heat pumps are usually described in terms of their heating capability, that is, the efficiency with which heat can be upgraded.

The efficiency of a heat pump is measured as a coefficient of performance (COP) and, since a heat pump can be used for either heating or cooling depending, simply, on which way round it is used, ambiguity can arise between the COP for heating and the COP for refrigeration. In this text COPh refers to the COP for heating, and it can be useful to know, as is explained in Section 11.3, that for any heat pump COPh = refrigeration COP + 1.

The COPh of a heat pump is defined as the ratio of the heat output supplied at the higher temperature, i.e. 'what you get', to the net energy supplied to operate the machine, i.e. 'what you pay for'. The attraction of the heat pump is that it will always produce more energy as heat output than is used directly in driving it.

Commercial heat pumps are based on either an absorption or a vapour compression refrigeration cycle, details of which can be found in Section 3 of Chapter 11. Absorption cycle machines are driven directly by heat and, except for small circulating pumps, have no moving parts. However, their COPh is much lower than for vapour compression machines, which is why they have found only limited application for refrigeration purposes, in some air-conditioning systems and domestic refrigerators.

Most machines are based on the more efficient vapour compression cycle which, as the name suggests, requires the use of a motor-driven compressor. Commercial models are always powered by electricity, but a few examples of machines powered by other fuels do exist. As is discussed in Section 11.3, the theoretical COPh for a vapour compression cycle machine is given by

$$\text{COPh} = \frac{\text{Heat energy output}}{\text{Net driving energy input}} = \frac{T_1}{T_1 - T_2},$$

where T_1 and T_2 are the absolute temperatures of the heat output and low grade heat source, respectively.

Some important properties of heat pumps are revealed by this relation. First, that the COPh is always greater than unity so that, as previously mentioned, a heat pump will always produce more energy for heating than is used directly in driving it. Second, however, that this advantage decreases the larger the difference between the supply and source temperatures, T_1 and T_2. Finally, it shows that, for a fixed supply temperature T_1 and driving power, the output will vary with the source temperature, which is exactly what happens in practice. As a consequence, heat pumps are rated according to their output at a specific temperature, typically 7 °C.

According to the above equation, a heat pump working between a source temperature of 0 °C (273 K) and a supply temperature of 50 °C (323 K) ought to have a COPh of about 6.5, but, unfortunately, the values achieved by real machines fall short of such theoretical predictions due to practical problems [37]. Even so, manufacturers tend to quote COPh values which can be misleading if interpreted naively, since their data is usually derived from tests on heat pumps operating steadily under laboratory conditions. Under practical conditions, heat pumps typically operate intermittently and use extra energy to run fans or pumps and to defrost their heat extraction coils. The net effect of all this is to reduce the seasonal average COPh of a typical heat pump to between 2 and 3 [38]. There is evidence to show that larger machines tend to be more efficient than small ones [39].

If, in addition, any auxiliary energy is used to supply heating should the heat pump output fall below demand, a very marked reduction in the net COPh of the heat pump installation can occur.

13.3.1 Air as a Heat Source and Sink

Outside air is available everywhere and is by far the most commonly used heat source. Its main disadvantage is that it has a variable temperature so that at times when air temperatures are falling and heat loads are rising, the heat pump COPh and its output are falling. Conversely when air temperatures rise and heat loads fall, the heat pump increases its output.

As a result of this characteristic of air-source heat pumps, if the heat pump is sized to peak demand, it will work at only a fraction of its capacity during much of the heating season, leading to unsatisfactory operating conditions. Thermal storage, for instance in the form of hot water, could be used to give a smoother load characteristic, but practical considerations of size and cost have meant that the solution adopted in practice has been to size the heat pump to, say, 40 per cent of peak demand and to use auxiliary direct electric heating when necessary. The penalty incurred by using auxiliary heating has already been mentioned. Other disadvantages of air are that its low thermal capacity per unit volume results in the need to handle large volumes of air in order to extract heat without an excessive temperature drop and, at outside temperatures near freezing point, water vapour condenses as ice on the heat extraction coils, which must then be periodically defrosted.

Where a heat pump installation has been designed to provide cooling, air is again the most readily and commonly used heat sink for the rejected heat. Since peak cooling loads tend to coincide with maximum summer air temperatures, occasional problems can be encountered in rejecting heat into outside air at high temperatures.

13.3.2 Ground as a Heat Source and Sink

Although the ground is as universal as air, its exploitation as a heat source or sink is much more difficult. Its main advantage as a heat source is that its temperature varies less than that of outside air so that a superior heating performance can be obtained compared to an air source system.

The availability of heat in the ground for winter heating depends, not on the trickle of heat from the Earth's interior, but rather on the heat that has flowed into the subsoil from the surface and adjoining soil during periods of high radiation. Some soil temperature conditions at various seasons are shown in Section 4.5.2. In order to extract this heat, a network of pipes, normally carrying an antifreeze solution and not expensive refrigerant, is usually buried to a depth of between one and two metres over a sufficient area to avoid undue cooling or even freezing of the soil. Apart from the extra installation costs incurred as compared to using air, thermal capacity and heat transmission characteristics vary widely with soil type and moisture content, so that no single set of guidelines, applicable to all localities, is available. Again, should maintenance to the buried piping be required, access could be a problem and in built-up areas there may be insufficient ground area per building to provide for a large enough network.

As a sink of rejected heat for cooling purposes, the ground is not very satisfactory. The soil surrounding the buried pipes tends to dry out so, increasing its thermal resistance and preventing the required transfer of heat.

Generally, then, the ground does not provide a satisfactory source of or sink for heat for heat pump applications, except in a few locations where particularly favourable, wet, soil conditions exist. Such conditions are found at Aachen in Germany where an experimental house has been built which includes a heat pump heating and cooling system that makes use of a buried heat exchanger consisting of 120 m of plastic tubing laid under a basement of 150 m² area [40].

13.3.3 Water as a Source and Sink of Heat

Water can be an excellent source of low grade heat for heat pump applications, but it suffers from the considerable drawback that its use is confined to those relatively few locations where buildings are found close to a supply of cheap, reasonably pure water. Water from rivers, lakes and even the sea can be used provided that the water either flows sufficiently quickly or belongs to a big enough reservoir to prevent it freezing under working conditions. It may also be possible to make use of waste warm water from industrial processes and generating stations in some circumstances [38].

In certain areas with a high water table, such as exist in Belgium and Germany, use has been made of ground water [41]. Artesian wells are sunk, from which water is pumped to the heat pump unit, the heat extracted and the cooled water returned to the ground to prevent disturbance to the soil. Since ground water has a temperature of around 7 to 10 °C, and this is both more stable and higher than average winter air temperature, it enables a good performance to be obtained in comparison to air or ground source systems. So much so, in fact, that at the time of writing, the West German government is offering grants to encourage the installation of such systems.

A suitable supply of water can also act as an excellent sink of heat for cooling purposes.

13.3.4 Heat Distribution

Whether air or water is chosen as a heat transfer medium, it should be realized that, in order to keep the heat pump COPh at a reasonable value, supply temperatures have to be kept at lower values than is the case with conventional heating systems. Distribution temperatures of 35 °C for air and 45 °C for water are typical.

A water-medium distribution system has the advantage of using compact pipework and the potential to take advantage of existing pipework. However, the low distribution temperature means that normal-sized radiators cannot be used, but that either very large surface area emitters or fan convector units must be used, adding to the cost and complexity of the system. Whole walls can be used as radiating surfaces and direct advantage taken of any existing underfloor heating system which employs embedded hot-water pipes.

Air is much the most common heat transfer medium used, but, because of the low distribution temperature, a greater volume flow of air is required than with a conventional warm air system of comparable capacity, normally necessitating the use of larger size ductwork. Some care needs to be taken to ensure comfort for the room occupants during heating, and cooling if provided, so that a fully ducted air distribution system is desirable, preferably with room perimeter outlets at floor level.

The advantages of such a system are those of any warm air system, namely fast response giving rapid flexibility in space use, and the ability to prevent condensation by air movement.

13.3.5 Heat Pump Applications in Large Buildings

Serious development of heat pumps began in the 1950's in the USA, where interest lay primarily in their ability to provide cooling. Reliable vapour compression machines with heat extraction rates from tens to hundreds of kilowatts have been available for some time for use in air-conditioning systems. Such chiller units normally take the form of non-reversible, i.e. one-way, heat pumps designed to produce either a chilled water or cool air supply, and are available in package forms suitable for both internal and external installation. Roof mounted units can be difficult to integrate architecturally with the roof design.

It has been common practice to employ an entirely separate heating system of conventional form alongside such cooling plant, and to simply jettison the upgraded heat output from the chiller unit to the outside air by one means or another. Clearly, such a practice is wasteful in energy terms and, as a consequence of rising energy prices, attention has been focused on means to minimize such waste.

During winter operation, where a simultaneous demand for heating and cooling can arise in different building zones, the heat rejected from the chiller units can be used to preheat the return water of a heat distribution loop before it re-enters the boiler, so reducing the required capacity of the boiler [42]. Where the cooling load exceeds the heating load, another possibility is to operate the cooling plant at a sufficient capacity for the rejected heat to meet the heating demand, and to make up any excess cooling demand by use of cold outside air [43]. In other circumstances it may be possible for the heat extracted during the day to be rejected into a thermal store in the form of a tank of water for use later in night-time heating [44].

The above are examples of the recovery of heat that would otherwise have been wasted, a subject to which we shall return in Section 13.4. However, only a relatively simple technical step is involved in turning to truly reversible heat pumps, suitable for both heating and cooling. A typical system employs roof-mounted units capable of extracting heat from internal air and rejecting it to outside air for cooling purposes and vice versa for heating purposes. The system would normally be sized to meet the summer cooling load and, in UK conditions for instance, would only supply a proportion of the design heat loss so that an auxiliary heating system is required to meet any excess demand.

Absorption cycle chillers are also quite widely used in the USA to provide cooling within air-conditioning systems. They have few moving parts and can be expected to need less maintenance than vapour compression machines. They also avoid the need to use electricity since they can be driven directly by any suitable source of heat. Their main disadvantage lies in their low COPh, which usually lies between 1.2 and 1.7, smaller than that for a vapour compression machine operating under similar conditions. However, their potential for use in conjunction with solar water-heating systems is likely to encourage their use in areas of high insolation and associated cooling demand.

Apart from the large cooling plant so far mentioned, smaller vapour compression cycle machines are available in units suitable for wall or ceiling mounting in individual rooms. Typical heat extraction rates range from 0.3 to 14 kW, with each unit incorporating fans to ensure an adequate distribution of cool air.

Few large installations of heat pumps designed to provide heating, rather than cooling, have been reported. Two examples from the UK have been the installations at the Royal Festival Hall, London and at Nuffield College, Oxford. The Festival Hall heat pump, installed in 1949, made use of the River Thames as its low grade heat source and was driven by Merlin aero-engines converted to run on town gas [45]. The Nuffield College heat pump, installed in 1961, was designed to use sewage as its heat source and to be driven by a diesel engine [46].

Both systems were sized to meet about one third of the design heat loss, this being some 7600 kW and 450 kW for the Festival Hall and Nuffield College, respectively. In practice, the heating requirement for the Festival Hall turned out to be vastly overestimated and the heat pump grossly oversized, with the result that the system proved uneconomic and was replaced by a conventional heating system. The Festival Hall heat pump was also designed to provide a degree of summer cooling, and it was concluded, at the time, that a more favourable situation would have existed had the heat pump been designed to have an output based on the cooling load rather than the heating load [45] as, indeed, is modern practice.

Both these installations represent individual examples from which few conclusions of general validity can be drawn apart, perhaps, from the fact that the economics of any heat pump system designed for heating purposes are critically dependent on its sizing with respect to the design heat loss and the auxiliary heating system. This follows from the fact that the output from current heat pumps is either all or nothing, and that a heat pump designed to meet too large a fraction of the heat load will spend considerable periods of time cycling on and off when output exceeds demand, leading to a poor load factor and poor operating conditions.

13.3.6 Heat Pumps for Use in Dwellings

The development of heat pumps for domestic use has also taken place largely in the USA, stimulated by a need for summer cooling. To make an economically attractive installation, the potential of the heat pump to supply heating was also exploited. The result has been the production of air-to-air, electrically powered, reversible heat pumps of the vapour compression type, primarily designed to provide cooling in summer. A typical package unit is complete in a single casing, and is designed to be fitted externally, adjacent to the dwelling it serves. Flow and return ducts are provided to carry indoor air between the dwelling and the unit. Split machines are also available in which the heat output unit is fitted indoors, separately from the outdoor heat extraction unit; the two units are connected by a pair of extended refrigerant lines and wiring. Direct-acting electric resistance heating is provided as standard to boost the warm air output when necessary for winter heating purposes.

Early machines proved unreliable and, during the 1960's, research was undertaken to determine the major causes of heat pump failure and how their design might be improved. As a result of improvements, it was possible to conclude by 1973 that American air-to-air heat pumps were of sufficient reliability and performance to encourage their more general exploitation [47]. Despite their high capital cost, the sacrifice in COPh required to obtain reversibility and the need for expensive electric boost heating, the attraction of a combined heating and cooling system for domestic use led to over one million units being installed in the USA by the end of 1974 [37].

Currently available heat pumps are almost exclusively of American origin, and the application of such machines in countries where different conditions apply has problems. In the UK, for example, mild humid winter conditions cause a much greater frequency of defrosting than expected in the USA, adding some 5 per cent to the annual energy requirements for heating [48]. A high starting current is also required, so much so that unacceptable voltage fluctuations can be produced in the supply network where only a 240 V, single phase supply is available, as in UK domestic premises. Again, the noise level of these machines is such that in quiet areas, or where denser housing conditions exist than in the USA, annoyance may be caused if the unit is located externally. If the unit is fitted internally, commonly in the roof space, both sound and vibration isolation will be required. Finally, in countries which do not have a domestic cooling requirement, the need is not for a compromised reversible heat pump, but for a non-reversible machine optimized for heating under local conditions.

There are a number of other points to note in connection with the installation of a domestic heat pump. If fitted internally, provision must be made to drain off the water that will condense from the air on the heat extraction coils. Attention should be given to the fact that while defrosting will remove ice formed on the heat extraction coils, under adverse conditions it may not melt ice that has formed in the drip tray which may cause blocked drain holes and flooding.

The installation and commissioning of a heat pump requires the attention of a specialist refrigeration engineer and, in particular, if a split machine is used, then the extended refrigerant lines have to be installed, connected and charged on site, which requires a very high standard of workmanship and cleanliness.

Fig. 13.5 Balance between dwelling heating requirement and heat pump capacity as a function of ambient air temperature.

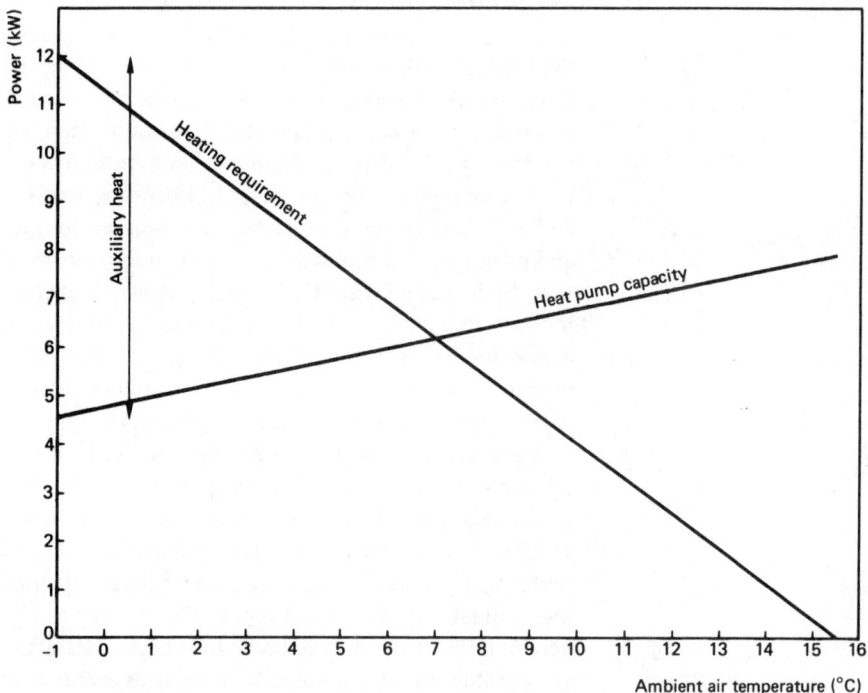

As already noted, unlike conventional systems, a heat pump can only supply full output when it is on. In addition, the COPh of an air-to-air heat pump will vary with outside air temperature, but in the opposite sense to the heat loss. A typical situation is shown in Fig. 13.5 for a balance point temperature of 7 °C, where the heat pump has been selected to provide 40 per cent of the total heat load at an ambient air temperature of −1 °C. If the heat pump is oversized, it will spend considerable periods cycling on and off when its output exceeds demand. Short cycling not only reduces efficiency, because operating conditions need a finite time to be re-established, but reduces the life expectancy of the machine.

Undersizing requires the increased use of boost heating which, if electrical, involves a considerable penalty in running costs and effective system COPh.

13.3.7 Economic Considerations

Air-conditioning systems employing chiller units have been successfully used in many large buildings including schools, commercial office blocks and shopping centres. Wherever there is a demand for cooling it is likely that the capital cost of a heat pump can be justified, since it can also provide a substantial amount of heating. Whether a demand for cooling is itself justified is not altogether a simple matter of climate, comfort, and energy costs, but also of such less tangible matters as standard of living and attitude. Cooling can be 'essential' for prestige city centre offices and cooling is becoming increasingly important to shopping centres and supermarkets where good energy management means providing good selling conditions all year round rather than simple energy conservation. Cooling can increase industrial morale and productivity by improving working conditions. On the other hand, UK hotels, faced with large bills in coming up to new fire regulations standards in a period of economic restraint, have given the installation of cooling plant a very low priority.

The cost effectiveness of cooling plant can be increased if otherwise wasted heat is recovered and put to good use, although, in general, the high capital cost of heat pumps militates against their economic use for heating only. It would appear, however, that the scope for individual initiative and ingenuity is large in this respect. The complexity and sophistication of thermal storage systems, both for chilled or heated water, that can be employed with chiller or heat pump systems, has limited their use so far to large buildings where the energy savings can justify the extra costs of equipment.

The introduction of domestic, air-to-air heat pumps in the USA has also been largely a result of their cooling capability. In the UK, where domestic cooling is not required, the performance of the present generation of reversible machines is not good enough to enable them to compete in running costs with non-electric forms of heating, especially in the case of natural gas; and their capital costs of around £100 kW^{-1} of heat delivered at 1977 prices are much higher than for conventional plant of similar output. However, should the COPh of future machines be improved and, perhaps, fossil-fuelled machines become available, both likely possibilities, the domestic heat pump could have a very bright future and its integration into new or existing buildings would be considerably easier than that of solar- or wind-power systems.

13.4 Heat recovery within buildings

While the potential for the recovery of low grade heat before it escapes from buildings is enormous, the economic return from the actual quantities of energy saved in any particular building have caused heat recovery techniques to have been developed mainly for application in large buildings [49]. For example, office blocks, schools and factories often exhaust large amounts of heat as warm air in order to balance incoming fresh air, and to keep people and processes cool. Opportunities for further energy savings exist wherever there is wastage of process heat, for example, as hot water or hot flue gases.

It is often advantageous for heat recovery systems to include thermal storage to reduce peak loads and to provide smoother operation at light loads. In multi-zone buildings, where a simultaneous heating and cooling demand can exist, the concept of heat balance can be employed, where heat removed from zones with a cooling demand can be transferred by a heat recovery system to zones requiring heat. Only the difference need be supplied by imported energy.

The purpose of this section is not to present an exhaustive survey of the application and technology of heat recovery, but to present a sufficient picture to awaken the reader to the possibilities, and limitations, of heat recovery applications in buildings. Nevertheless, it should be clear that much of the technology described below is adaptable to other forms of heat recovery, and that the scope for ingenuity is large.

13.4.1 The Heat Pump as a Heat Recovery System

The potential of the heat pump to extract heat from the external environment to provide internal heating and from the internal environment to provide cooling has been dealt with in the previous section. The opportunity for heat recovery in the latter case was also mentioned and, in response to a growing demand, some manufacturers now supply a range of vapour compression chiller units complete with the necessary equipment to produce warm water, usually at about 40 °C, from the rejected heat. One application of this technique has been to swimming pools, where air extracted from the pool hall is normally discharged directly from the building, taking with it a considerable amount of heat. A chiller unit, acting as a heat pump, can be used to recover this heat from the air before it is expelled and the heat is then reused to heat incoming fresh air and pool water.

In air-handling systems, the air-to-air heat pump can be employed to extract heat from warm exhaust air and to reuse it to heat incoming make-up air. Another application has been to produce cool air in one zone of a building with a cooling demand, and to use the extracted heat to provide warm air in another zone with a heating demand, by means of a split machine with extended refrigerant lines.

The electro-hydronic heat pump system provides another, very flexible, method of transferring heat from zones requiring cooling to others requiring heat. In this system, room perimeter units employing water-to-air heat pumps are connected in parallel to a single water distribution loop throughout the building. Each heat pump is reversible and can use the loop as a heat source or sink to provide heating or cooling as required. The water in the loop is kept at 20 to 30 °C all year round by a central plant which only has to supply the net thermal balance required to keep the loop within the required temperature range.

Among the advantages that can be obtained by employing a heat pump to perform heat recovery within the internal environment are: separation of recovery and supply points; no pollution or cross-contamination; high COPh; and ease of control. Among the likely disadvantages are cost and the fact that each application will require considerable analysis and may border on unknown territory.

13.4.2 Heat Recovery from Exhaust Air

Though increased thermal insulation and optimized control of plant can result in major energy savings, the law of diminishing returns applies to these two measures unless attention is also paid to ventilation heat loss. Wherever mechanical ventilation is necessary to control ventilation rates at design levels, the opportunity exists for some form of heat recovery from the exhaust air. The following is a description of some of the technology available for this purpose [50].

13.4.2.1 Plate type exchanger

These exchangers consist of a stack of fixed plates, separated so that the exhaust and supply air streams can pass between them in alternation, and can be made from a range of materials including metals and plastics. Only sensible heat is exchanged between the air streams unless the temperature of one air stream falls below the dew point temperature of the other and there is condensation on the plates. Preheating can be used to prevent such condensation which, otherwise, can lead to corrosion, icing and a high pressure drop across the unit.

For flexibility in connection, both cross- and counter-flow models are made, though counter-flow gives the better heat transfer. Sensible heat recovery efficiencies generally lie between 40 and 60 per cent, and the amount of heat recovery can be controlled by arranging to bypass some of the supply air past the exchanger.

A variation of this type of exchanger, which has recently become available and is suitable for use in textile, paper and laundry industries, is designed to convert both sensible and latent heat, or total heat, from very humid exhaust air into sensible heat in the incoming fresh air supply. The unit contains removable heat recovery packs made of corrugated aluminium foils arranged in layers, which the supply and exhaust air streams, completely separated by aluminium walling and seals, enter through the upper openings and pass diagonally down through the module to leave at the lower openings, so forcing the condensate down to drain pans beneath. Such a unit is claimed to be capable of recovering more than 70 per cent of the total heat from the exhaust air stream.

These types of heat exchangers have the advantages of relative cheapness, reduced maintenance since there are no moving parts, no cross-contamination since the two air streams are physically separated, and of requiring no energy except that to overcome the static pressure drop across the unit.

13.4.2.2 Heat pipe exchanger

A heat pipe usually takes the form of a metal tube which is lined with a compatible wick material and contains a working fluid, such as a refrigerant. Heat applied to one end of the pipe causes the working fluid to evaporate, and the resulting vapour then flows to the other, cooler, end of the pipe, where it condenses giving up its latent heat of evaporation. The condensed fluid moves through the wick by capillary action until it returns to be revapourized and the cycle is repeated. In some forms, gravity rather than a wick is used to return the condensed fluid, so that the cool end must always be uppermost. A heat pipe of either kind can transfer up to one thousand times more heat than a solid copper rod of the same dimensions [51].

A typical heat exchanger consists of a bundle of heat pipes passing through a centre-dividing partition which seals off the exchanger into two sections. Fins are usually added to enhance heat transfer. The supply air is ducted to one side of the exchanger, the exhaust air to the other. In wick types, heat is transferred in the appropriate direction whenever there is a temperature difference between the two ends, so that recovery of both winter heating and summer cooling will occur naturally. With gravity types, the air flows must be interchanged to obtain all year round operation.

Apart from higher sensible heat recovery efficiencies of between 58 and 78 per cent and, also, of higher capital costs, the problems and advantages of this type of exchanger are similar to those of the plate type exchanger.

13.4.2.3 Run-around system

In this system, one standard, finned-tube water coil is situated in each of the supply and exhaust air streams. A pump circulates water or an antifreeze solution in a closed circuit between the two coils, transferring heat between the two air streams.

As with the previous two exchangers, this system provides sensible heat recovery, which is seasonably reversible, at typical efficiencies of 40 to 60 per cent. Its advantage over the other two systems is that the supply and exhaust air ducts can be separated since only piping is required to complete the interconnection of the coils; otherwise, apart from having an essential moving part in the pump, it has similar problems and advantages.

13.4.2.4 Rotary heat exchanger

A rotary heat exchanger consists of a motor-driven cylindrical drum or wheel which rotates slowly through counterflows of supply and exhaust air in adjacent ducts. Air seals help minimize cross-contamination, which can be further reduced by purging the wheel with fresh air just before it rotates from the exhaust air stream to the supply air stream.

Metallic sheets of aluminium or stainless steel mesh provide sensible heat recovery only, except when the temperature of one air stream falls below the dew point temperature of the other causing water vapour to condense. The supply air is usually preheated when temperatures below freezing point are encountered to prevent ice forming.

Hygroscopic rotary exchangers are treated with a desiccant salt so that water vapour can be absorbed from the more humid air stream and be desorbed to the drier air stream as the wheel rotates between them. In this way the supply air can be heated and humidified in winter and cooled and dehumidified in summer.

Non-hygroscopic rotary exchangers have typical sensible heat recovery efficiencies of 70 to 80 per cent and total heat efficiencies of 40 to 60 per cent. Hygroscopic exchangers typically recover 70 to 80 per cent of the total heat.

Apart from the possible limitations of cross-contamination and the need for adjacency in the exhaust and supply air streams, rotary heat exchangers have the advantages of low capital cost, low operating cost and high recovery efficiencies. Hygroscopic exchangers present maintenance difficulties in that they lose their desiccant salt when washed.

13.4.2.5 Run-around, multiple tower, desiccant spray exchanger

In this run-around circuit, two towers containing extended, packed surfaces rather than coils are used and a liquid desiccant salt solution is sprayed through them, rather than a water or antifreeze solution. Two pumps are required to complete the flow round the circuit. Unlike the run-around, coil and pump exchanger, this system provides for recovery of total, not just sensible, heat and, like the hygroscopic rotary exchanger, will heat and humidify the supply air in winter and cool and dehumidify it in summer. Total heat recovery efficiencies generally lie in the range 55 to 70 per cent.

Some of the advantages of this system are that there is no leakage between air flows, that the exhaust and supply air streams can be separately located and that the solution spray can act as an air washer. Precautions should be taken to prevent the salt solution from solidifying and clogging the system in conditions when the air streams become very dry.

13.4.3 Heat Recovery from Lights

The heat from light fittings can be a prime source of internal heat gain and may be recovered and redistributed to advantage. The recovery of such heat at source will also reduce the space-cooling load and may eliminate the need for otherwise costly air-conditioning [52].

Water-cooled luminaires can be made with aluminium reflector housings containing integral water channels. Water pumped through them absorbs some 70 per cent of the 'lighting heat'. The warm water can be used, for instance, as a heat pump source in winter or, in its own separate distribution system, to warm incoming air.

Ducted air systems are suitable for the control and redistribution of heat from lights. Light fixtures with slots allow the induction of return air up and around the lamps, ballasts and metal housings, picking up to some 80 per cent of the total energy supplied to the fitting [53]. The warmed air can be used in a dual duct system or mixed with incoming air in a single duct system. As a side effect, some light sources are up to 13 per cent more efficient when cooled.

13.4.4 Heat Recovery from Combustion Gases

Hot combustion gases are produced wherever fuel is burnt to provide process heat, mechanical and electrical work, carrying anything up to 80 per cent of the available energy as waste heat. As a result, package heat recovery boiler units have been designed which can provide heating for offices and workshops associated with such processes [54]. These units have found application in recovering heat from the exhausts of gas turbine and diesel power plants and from the flue gases of foundries and heat treatment plants.

Heat recovery boilers have to present a large, extended surface area to the hot gas to be effective because the temperature difference that exists between a hot exhaust gas and fluid being heated is only a fraction of that produced in a conventional boiler system. Despite relatively high first costs, such a system can often be designed to recover its capital outlay in fuel saved within two years.

13.4.5 Cost Effectiveness

That heat recovery can save both energy and money is proven beyond doubt, but economic success depends on a thorough and careful analysis being carried out for each particular application. The use of heat recovery systems can add substantially to plant installation costs, depending on the degree of complexity, sophistication or difficulty involved in the heat recovery process.

As a general rule, the urge to recover every last joule should be curbed and consideration first given to the simplest system that can perform reasonably well in the circumstances. In this respect, the actual quantity of heat available for recovery is important. For instance, the amount of heat energy lost by the domestic sector through waste hot water and ventilation is considerable, but the actual amount lost by an individual dwelling is relatively very small, which militates against cost-effective heat recovery on this scale. However, in a well insulated dwelling, ventilation heat loss is a proportionately larger part of the total heat loss and it is here that domestic heat recovery is likely to find a future, profitable, application [2].

Finally, it is wise to remember that systems are run and maintained by real people and that simplicity in design and operation leads to better understanding and maintenance of equipment, which, in turn, will result in a greater proportion of any potential energy saving being achieved in practice.

References

1   Bruning, S. F. and George, M. S., The Shenandoah Community Center: a total solar design concept. *American Society of Heating, Refrigeration and Air-Conditioning Engineers Journal,* **18**(11), 53–56, 1976.

2   Energy conservation: a study of energy consumption in buildings and possible means of saving energy in housing. *Building Research Establishment Current Paper 56/75,* 1975.

3   Courtney, R. G., Solar energy utilisation in the UK: current research and future prospects. *Building Research Establishment Current Paper 64/76,* 1976.

4   *Solar Energy – A U.K. Assessment.* UK Section of the International Solar Energy Society, London, 1976.

5   Yellot, J. I., Utilization of sun and sky radiation for heating and cooling of buildings. *American Society of Heating, Refrigeration and Air-Conditioning Engineers Journal,* **15**(12), 31–42, 1973.

6   Duffie, J. A. and Beckman, W. A., *Solar Energy Thermal Processes.* John Wiley & Sons, New York, 1974.

7   McVeigh, J. C., *Sun Power: An Introduction to the Applications of Solar Energy.* Pergamon, Oxford, 1977.

8   Shurcliff, W. A., *Solar Heated Buildings, A Brief Survey,* 13th ed. Shurcliff, Cambridge, Mass., 1976. Available from the author at 19 Appleton Street, Cambridge, Mass., USA.

9   Davis, M. G., Heating buildings by winter sunshine. *Building Science Supplement, Energy and Housing,* 53–66, 1975.

10 Keller, G., Solar study project by CCI. *Heating and Ventilating Review,* **17**(12 and 13), 1976.

11 Solar activated cooling projects for solar heating and cooling applications. *ERDA Request for Proposals RFP No. EG-77-R-03-1439,* 1977.

12 Newton, B. A., Optimizing solar cooling systems. *American Society of Heating, Refrigeration and Air-Conditioning Engineers Journal,* **18**(11), 26–31, 1976.

13 Duncan, R. T. and Doering, E. R., Solar heating for Atlanta School. *American Society for Heating, Refrigeration and Air-Conditioning Engineers Journal,* **17**(7), 35–39, 1975.

14 Read, W. R., The use of RBR systems in South Australian schools. *Australian Refrigeration, Airconditioning and Heating,* **26**(12), 20–27, 1972.

15 Hogg, F. G., A switched bed regenerative cooling system. Paper to the 13th International Congress on Refrigeration, Washington, D.C., 1971.

16 Courtney, R. G., An appraisal of solar water heating in the UK. *Building Research Establishment Current Paper 7/76,* 1976.

17 Klein, S. A., *et al.,* A design procedure for solar heating systems. *Solar Energy,* **18**(2), 113–125, 1976.

18   Swanson, S. R. and Beohm, R. F., Calculation of long term solar collector heating system performance. *Solar Energy*, **19**(2), 129–138, 1977.

19   *Solar Energy for Engineers, Architects and Designers, Proceedings of the Joint IIRS and IHVE Conference, 31st March – 3rd April 1976. Dublin.* Institution of Heating and Ventilating Engineers, London, 1976.

20   Tagg, J. R., Brief survey of the history and present state of knowledge of the use of windpower. In *Energy and Humanity*. Peter Peregrinus, Stevenage, 1974.

21   Putnam, P. C., *Power from the Wind.* Van Nostrand, London, 1948.

22   Golding, E. W., *The Generation of Electricity by Wind Power.* Spon, London, 1955.

23   Caton, P. G. F., *Meteorological Office Climatological Memorandum No. 79*, 1976.

24   Rayment, R., Wind energy in the UK. *Building Services Engineer,* **44**, 63–69, June 1976.

25   Warne, D. F., Usable energy from the wind. In *Proceedings of the Conference on Ambient Energy and Building Design at the University of Nottingham, 21st and 22nd April 1977.*

26   Plans and status of the NASA-Lewis Research Center Wind Energy Project. *NASA Technical Memorandum TMX-71701*, 1975.

27   Gimpel, G. and Stodhart, A. M., Windmills for electricity supply in remote areas. *ERA Technical Report C/T 120*, 1958.

28   Jacobs, M. L., Experience with Jacobs wind-driven electric generating plant 1931–1957. United Nations Conference on New Sources of Energy, Rome, 1961. Paper W/22.

29   Walker, J. G., The automatic operation of a medium-sized wind driven generator running in isolation. *ERA Technical Report C/T 122*, 1960.

30   Tagg, J. R., Wind-driven generators: the difference between the estimated output and the actual energy obtained. *ERA Technical Report C/T 123*, 1960.

31   Smith, G. E., Economics of solar collectors, heat pumps and wind generators. *University of Cambridge Department of Architecture, Autonomous Housing Study Working Paper No. 3*, 1973.

32   Frost, L. N., Wind power in Ireland. *Technology in Ireland*, 13–17, December 1974.

33   Yaneske, P. P. and Ogilvie, C., Considerations on the utilisation of wind power for domestic (small scale) purposes in Orkney. *Internal Report,* Department of Architecture and Building Science, University of Strathclyde, May 1975.

34   South, P. and Rangi, R. S., A wind tunnel investigation of a 14' diameter vertical axis windmill. *National Research Council of Canada Report LTR-LA 105*, 1972.

35   Andrews, J. W., Energy storage requirements reduced in wind–solar generating systems. *Solar Energy,* **18**(1), 73–74, 1976.

36   McVeigh, J. C. and Pontin, W. W., A wind/solar project in local authority housing. In *Proceedings of the Conference on Ambient Energy and Building Design at the University of Nottingham, 21st–22nd April, 1977.*

37   Goodall, E., Problems arising with the application of heat pumps in the domestic market. *Heating and Ventilating Engineer*; **49**, 13–16, May 1975.

38   Freund, P., Heat pumps for use in buildings. *Building Research Establishment Current Paper 19/76*, 1976.

39   Heap, R. D., Domestic heat pump operation. In *Proceedings of the Heating, Ventilating and Air-Conditioning Seminar, Imperial College, London, 25th June 1975.*

40   Horster, H., *The Philips Experimental House.* Philips Research Laboratory, Aachen, West Germany, 1975.

41   New Markets for domestic heat pumps. *Heating and Ventilating Review,* **17**, 40, January 1977.

42   Austerweil, L., Optimized data for heat pump systems. *Building Systems Design,* **71**, 13–18, June/July 1974.

43   Henderson, J. K., A balanced heat recovery system. *American Society of Heating, Refrigeration and Air-Conditioning Engineers Journal,* **17**(4), 56–57, 1975.

44   Cuplinskas, E. L., Sizing and application of thermal storage systems. *American Society of Heating, Refrigeration and Air-Conditioning Engineers Journal,* **17**(7), 31–32, 1975.

45   Montagnon, P. E. and Ruckley, A. L., The Festival Hall heat pump. *Journal of the Institute of Fuel,* **27**, 170–192, April 1954.

46   Kell, J. R. and Martin, P. L., The Nuffield College heat pump. *Journal of the Institution of Heating and Ventilating Engineers,* **30**, 333–356, January 1963.

47   Cole, M. H. and Pietsch, J. A., Qualification of heat pump design. *American Society of Heating, Refrigeration and Air-Conditioning Engineers Journal,* **15**(7), 43–47, 1973.

48   Heap, R. D., Heat pumps for British houses? In *Proceedings of the 1976 International Symposium held at the British Building Research Establishment.* Construction Press/CIB, London, 1976.

49   Greiner, P. C., Designing sophisticated hivac systems for optimum energy use. *American Society of Heating, Refrigeration and Air-Conditioning Engineers Journal,* **15**(2), 27–31, February 1973.

50   Bowlen, K. L., Energy recovery from exhaust air. *American Society of Heating, Refrigeration and Air-Conditioning Engineers Journal,* **16**(4), 49–57, April 1974.

51   Dunn, P. D. and Reay, D. A., The heat pipe. *Physics in Technology,* **4**(3), 187–201, 1973.

52   *IES Code for Interior Lighting.* Illuminating Engineering Society, London, 1977, Part 1, Section 4.3.

53   *IHVE Guide,* 5th ed. Institution of Heating and Ventilating Engineers, London, 1977, Sections A7 and B9.

54   Smith, P. R., Heat recovery boilers. *Building Services Engineer,* **44**(4), A32–A33, July 1976.

INDEX

Aberdeen, cold weather data, 147
Absorption chiller units, 436, 513, 524
Absorption coefficient, 328
Acclimatization effect, 67–8
Admittance, 334, 335, 344, 351, 354
Aerogenerator, 517, 518
  choice of site, 516
  cost effectiveness, 519
  design, 516
  distribution grid, 518
  economic considerations, 519–20
  energy storage problem, 519
  history, 515
  large-scale operation, 517
  medium-scale operation, 517
  modern, small, 516
  output, 515–16
  small-scale operation, 518
  vertical axis, 519
Air changes per hour, 371
  see also Ventilation rate
Air conditioning, 68, 69, 430, 436
Air flow
  in ducts, 422
  through openings, 210, 364–5
Air flow temperature, 369–70
Air-handling unit, 436
Air infiltration
  around windows 368–9
  by natural means, 358–72
  calculation of, 358
  total, 369–70
Air movement, 62–4
Air power, 422
Air velocity, 62, 401
Alhambra, 24
Alternator, 437
Analog circuits, 406–13
Analog scale ratios, 410
Analog scaling factor, 408

Angular momentum, 166
Anthropotoxin theory, 38
Arab-Israeli conflict, 1
Artificial sky, 414
Asymmetry, 64–5
Australia, 507, 509

Baghdad, courtyard houses, 155–60
Bernoulli's equation, 359
Bimetallic strip, 461
Bioclimatic chart, 25
Biological analysis, 22
Black body, 310, 311
Black globe, 38
Boilers, 431, 432, 448, 454, 531
Building resource allocation model, 479–83

Capital costs, 453, 469
Catenary mill, 519
Chemical energy, 431, 455
Chimney flue, temperature differences in, 366
China, 13
Chiswick house (1725), 7
Climate, 140–267
  effects on dwelling characteristics, 141
  effects on materials, 141
  effects on thermal design, 141
  elements of, 165–207
  external, 24
  general concepts, 142–55
  global, 143, 144
  interaction with built form, 155–65
  physical forces, 140
  probability aspects, 144–5
  satellite information, 144
  scale effect, 142–4
  spatial systems, 143

  Standard Effective Temperature (SET), 154–5
  thermal design data selection, 146
  thermal design information, 144–55
  time scales, 143
  urban, 214–15
  see also Microclimate
Climate modification, 28–31
Climatic analysis, 3, 4
Climatic determinism, 140
Climatic differentiation theories, 8
Climatic system, 3
Clothing effects, 44, 45, 47, 59, 64, 67, 71, 73
Combustion gases, heat recovery, 531
Comfort requirements, 34
Comfytest meter, 39
Compatibility law, 423
Competitive systems, 417
Complementary systems, 418, 450–55
Computers, 144–5, 151, 514
Condensation, 285–97
  interstitial, 290
  on windows, 288–90
  within fabric, 290–97
Conduction, 272
Conductivity
  See Thermal conductivity
Connected systems model, 23
Construction resource allocation, 481
Continuity law, 423
Control systems, 31, 460–66
  automatic, 460
  closed-loop, 460
  manual, 460
  open-loop, 460
  sequenced proportional, 464
  zonal, 465

Controlled environment, 27, 416–19
Controllers, 461, 465
Convection, 46, 272
Convection coefficient, 272
Convection heat loss, 381
Convective heating, 298–301
Cooling effect of ventilation, 370–71
Cooling load, 182
Cooling tower, 436
Coordinate system plotting storage against supply, 449
Corbusier, Le, 8
Coriolis acceleration, 166
Coriolis force, 167
Corrected Effective Temperature (CET), 25, 39, 162–4
Cost analysis, 146
Cost effectiveness, 499
Courtyard houses, 23–4, 155–60
Cumulative frequency curves, 55
Cumulative frequency distribution, 144
Curtain walls, 306

Daly, César, 15, 19
Darrieus mill, 519
Daylight, continued enjoyment of, 4
Daylight investigations, 414
Degree days, 151–3, 204, 216
Demand diversity, 458, 459
Demand profiles, 453, 458
Demolition resource requirement, 481
Developing countries, 2
Dew point, 287, 292–5
Direct natural thermosyphon system, 510
DISC, 50, 51, 55–9, 145
Discount rates, 485–6
Discounted Cash Flow (DCF), 481–3
Disease patterns, 71
Distribution network, 467
District cooling, 452
District heating, 451
Diversity exploitation, 459
Diversity factor, 459
Dry respiration heat loss, 44
Duct-sizing, 429
Ducted systems, 422, 430, 531

Economic factors, 35, 72
Effective temperature scale, 38
Efficiency, 431, 433
Electrical elements, 442
Electrical energy, 441, 455
Electrical resistance, 406, 408, 409, 442, 461
Electrical system, 410

Electricity generation, 430, 437, 439, 452, 455
Emissivity, 272, 273, 275
Endo-skeleton, 22
Energy accounting, 479–506
Energy analysis, 479, 480
  application of, 496
  development of, 496
  examples, 498–9
  labour/manpower, 497
  life-cycle costing using, 497–9
  objectives of, 497
  use of term, 496
Energy balance, 454
Energy conservation, 1–2
Energy consumption, 3, 214
  during heating period, 302–303
  in intermittent heating, 351–7
  prediction of, 151–3, 182
Energy conversion, 430–42, 494
Energy costs, 73, 495, 496
Energy crisis, 499
Energy-flow system, 466
Energy resources, measuring, 479
Energy services, 19
Energy system, 3
Energy units, 497
Engineering services, 415–78
Enthalpy, 497
Environment
  secondary outputs to, 417
  thermal. See Thermal environment
Environment index 57–9
Environmental factors, 2, 36, 66
Environmental gradients, 29–30
Environmental states, 26
Environmental temperature, 318, 336–43, 352
Equal cost lines, 449
Equation of time, 169, 170
Equivalent temperature, 39
Eskimo igloo, 141, 164–5
Etruscan cosmological creation rites, 26
Eupatheoscope, 39
European Common Market, 4
Evaporation, 43, 59
Evaporative cooling technique, 513
Exhaust air, heat recovery, 528–32
Exo-skeleton, 22
Experimental methods, 397–414

Fabric heat loss, 297, 298, 300, 301, 333, 373, 377, 383, 385, 386
Failure cost, 146
Failure probability, 146, 457
Feasibility study, 453
Feedback, 460

Feng Shui system, 13
Filtration, 418, 430
Fiscal drag, 485
Flat plate collector, 507–508
Flexibility of systems, 474–5
Floor temperatures, 65
Flooring materials, 66
Flow systems, 415–20
  components and linkages, 419
  control mechanism, 419
  definition, 415
  distribution components, 420–30
  distribution problems, 421
  function of, 419
  in pipes and ducts, 423
  power of fluid, 422
  through channels, 421
  topological structure, 467
Fluid flow, 427
Fluid network, 427
Fossil fuels, 431, 439, 441, 451
Free energy, 497
Freeze protection, 511
Frequency distributions, 144, 456, 458, 459
Fresh air requirements, 68–9
Freshness concept, 61
Frost hollows, 204, 210
Fuel cell, 455
Fuel oil consumption, 456, 459
Function of a system, 415

G-coefficient, 4
Gas-turbine
  closed-cycle, 437, 439
  open-cycle, 439
Generalized system diagram, 415
Glazing
  and external wall surface, 387–9
  effect in intermittent heating, 355
  solar radiation transmission through, 327–34
  thermal resistance, 278–80
  transmission characteristics, 327–31
Globe temperature correction factor, 49
Greenhouse effect, 327
Gropius layout principles, 8
Gross Energy Requirement (GER), 497–9
Ground floors, U-values for, 280–81

Health requirements, 35, 71
Heat balance, 40, 41
Heat balance equation, 40, 42, 46, 76
Heat conduction through clothing, 44
Heat engines, 432, 433, 437

Heat exchangers, 426, 427, 429, 431
  heat pipe, 529
  hygroscopic, 530
  non-hygroscopic, 530
  plate type 529
  rotary, 530
  run-around, 530
Heat flow, 406, 427
  between two surfaces, 268
  due to sol-air temperature, 313
  due to solar radiation, 313
  due to temperature difference,
    274
  effect of heavyweight or light-
    weight structure, 319
  relationship with window area
    and orientation, 387-90
  through concrete wall, 321, 325,
    326
  through fabric, 297, 318-27
  through roof, 342
  through solid floor, 281
  transient, 296, 320
Heat gain, 69, 387, 390-96
  see also Solar radiation
Heat island, 215
Heat loss, 41-6, 69, 165, 387, 428,
  451
  by fabric. See Fabric heat loss
  by ventilation. See Ventilation
    loss
  seasonal, 151
  under steady-state conditions,
    268-309
  variables affecting, 373
Heat pipe exchanger, 529
Heat-power ratios, 453
Heat pumps, 435, 441, 520-27
  absorption cycle, 520
  advantages, 528
  air-source, 521-2
  balance between heating require-
    ment and heat pump capacity
    as function of ambient air
    temperature, 526
  commercial, 520
  commissioning, 526
  cooling use, 527
  cost effectiveness, 527
  currently available, 525
  distribution temperatures, 523
  economic considerations, 527
  effective installations, 527
  efficiency, 520
  electro-hydronic, 528
  failures, 525
  ground-source, 522
  heat distribution, 523
  heat recovery system, 528

  in dwellings, 525-7
  in large buildings, 523-5
  installation, 526
  large installations, 524
  load factor, 525
  noise level, 525-6
  performance, 520-21
  potential of, 528
  practical problems, 521
  principle of, 520
  properties of, 521
  short cycling, 526
  theoretical predictions, 521
  vapour compression, 521
  water-service, 522-3
Heat recovery, 451, 454, 524,
  527-32
  combustion gases, 531
  cost effectiveness, 531
  exhaust air, 528-32
  heat pump, 528
  light fittings, 531
  opportunities for, 527
Heat sinks, 427, 435
Heat transfer, 24, 42, 406
  between surface and air, 272-3
    external surface, 273
    internal surface, 272-3
Heathrow, wind speed and
  temperature, 148, 150
Heating load, 148, 300-302, 387
Heating system, 423, 429
Heliodon, 401-6
  arrangement for, 403, 404
  general principle of, 402
  improved version of, 405-6
  vertical staff for, 403
Homeostasis, 22, 34, 40
Hour angle, 171
Human adaptability, 73
Human system 27-9
Humidity and humidity effects, 16,
  38, 39, 49, 51, 59-60, 162, 203,
  207, 211-14, 285-8, 296, 400
Hydroelectric power, 437
Hygrometer, 400
Hypocaust, 19
Hypothermia, 34, 71

Illumination angle, 9
Indirect forced circulation system,
  509
Inflation, 483-5
Information feedback, 419
Interest rates, 486-92, 500-506
Intermittent heating, 344-57
  effect of external air temperature
    on temperature swing, 356
  energy consumption, 351-7

  glazing effect, 355
  preheating period, 355
  temperature swings, 344-51
  window area effect, 355
Internal heat production, 42
Isotherms, 203, 215
Israel, 509

Japan, 13, 507, 509

Kata thermometer, 38, 401, 420, 437
Kirchhoff's current law, 424
k-value, 269, 270
  see also Thermal conductivity

Laboratory studies, 66
Latent respiration heat loss, 44
Legislation, 4
Lévi-Strauss, 14
Life-cycle costing, 481
  based on market prices, examples
    of, 487-93
  comparative nature of, 483
  using discounted market prices,
    492
  using energy analysis, 497-9
  using market prices, 481-93
  using prime energy accounting,
    493-6
Light fittings, heat recovery, 531
Lithium bromide/water chiller unit,
  513
Local Apparent Time (LAT), 169
London, 215
Los Angeles Hall of Records, 10

Magnetic field, 441
Magnetohydrodynamic (MHD)
  generation, 440
Maintenance allocation, 481
Malay timber house, 23-4, 160-64
Manipulated variable, 460
Materials shortages, 2, 3
Mean radiant temperature, 38
Mean solar time, 170
Mechanical energy, 432
Mechanical systems, 451
Metabolic energy, 42
Metabolic rate, 66
Metaphysical symbols, 15
Microclimate, 4, 24, 28, 29, 143,
  144, 207-25
Mixing value, 464-5
Model techniques, 413-14
Modular units, 465
Mongolian yurt, 141
Monumental buildings, 16

Nature conservation, 2

Navajo Hogan, 12
Networks, 423
New effective temperature (ET*), 40, 49
Normal distribution, 456–7
Nuclear fission, 440
Nuclear fuel, 440
Nuffield College, Oxford, 524

Office blocks, 10
Ohm's law, 420, 462
Operating differential, 462
Operative temperature, 39, 48
Operative temperature charts, 78–83
Orientation
    and heat flow, 387–90
    and solar radiation, 393–6
Orientation rules, 13
Overlay charts, 173, 179, 237–61
Oxidation, 42

Panopticon, 19
Participation, 2, 3
Pay-back period, 454
Peltier effect, 442
Performance, 430, 431
Performance coefficient, 435, 436
Performance criteria, 70–71
Performance requirements, 34
Pipework, heat losses from, 428
Planetary system, 466
Plant costs, 146, 454
Plant design, 146
Plant growth, 214
Plant type exchanger, 529
Pollution, 2, 3, 31, 418
Potential energy, 420
Predicted Mean Vote (PMV), 55, 60
Predicted Percentage of Dissatisfied
    (PPD), 55, 73
Preheating, influence of, 355
Pressure differentials, 69, 359–64
Primitive settlements, 3, 5, 11
Probability, 457
Probability aspects of climate,
    144–55
Psychological factors, 35, 72, 73
Psychometric charts, 59
Peublo Indian group dwelling, 12, 16

Radiant heating, 299–301
Radiation, 37, 45, 215, 272
    global, 165
    long-wave, 165
Radiation coefficient, 272
Radiators, 427, 428
Rapoport, A., 11, 13, 16
Reflectance, 165
Reflection coefficient, 328

Reflectivity, 215
Reform Club, 15, 19
Refrigerator, 435, 436
Resource environment, 27, 28,
    416, 417
Rights of light, 4
Room admittance, 334
Room depth, 390
Room shape and area, 389
Room width, 389
Royal Festival Hall, 524
Run-around system, 530
Running costs, 453, 454, 493
R-values, 192, 262–7

Saturation point, 285
Seebeck effect, 442
Semiconductors, 442, 461
Sensitivity analysis, 486, 489, 491,
    492
Sensors, 460, 463–5
Service towers, 478
Services as sub-systems, 466–78
Services centre, 468
Services system, 472
Severity index, 204
Shading and shading devices, 10, 174,
    179, 182, 342
Shadow angles, 172–4
Shadow effect, 363–4
Shadow pattern, 214
Shape of building, 373–96
Shelter concepts, 1–18
Sheltering effect of buildings, 363
Shivering, 41
Sizing of systems, 455
Skin diffusion, 43
Skin temperature, 41, 46, 49, 50, 60,
    64
Skin wettedness, 49, 50
Sleep conditions, 65–6
Social factors, 35, 72
Sol-air temperature, 155, 313–19,
    341
    calculation of, 314–18
    heat flow due to, 313
Solar altitude, 168, 171–3, 184, 187,
    188
Solar angles, 8, 172, 173
Solar azimuth, 168, 171, 173
Solar constant, 165
Solar control, 10
Solar declination, 170
Solar desiccant dehumidifer, 513
Solar energy, 182, 507, 520
    economic considerations, 514–17
    performance prediction, 514–15
Solar gain factor, 331–5, 337, 338,
    391

Solar geometry, 11
Solar movement, 168–82, 214
Solar radiation, 6, 165, 168,
    182–200, 214, 310, 387, 390–96
    absorption, 310, 312
    air mass effect, 185
    altitude above sea level, 186
    atmospheric absorption and
        scatter, 184
    calculation examples, 195–9
    clear sky diffuse and reflected
        ground irradiance on surfaces
        other than horizontal, 189
    clear sky diffuse irradiance and
        reflected ground irradiance, 187
    cyclic heat inputs, 334–43
    direct irradiance on surfaces other
        than normal, 186
    direct normal incidence
        irradiance, 182
    effect on building, 334–43
    emissivity, 311–13
    global clear sky irradiance on any
        surface, 189
    global clear sky irradiance using
        overlays, 195
    global clear sky irradiance using
        tables, 195
    global irradiation on sloping
        surface, 197
    graphical plots, 199–200
    heat flow due to, 313, 318–27
    heat gains due to, 310–43
    hourly irradiation values, 193–4
    hourly mean global irradiation on
        horizontal surface. 198
    hourly mean global irradiation on
        sloping surface, 198
    influence of temperature, 311
    maximum values under clear sky
        conditions, 182–9
    mean diffuse irradiation on hori-
        zontal surface, 190
    mean global irradiation on hori-
        zontal surface, 189
    mean irradiation on tilted
        (including vertical) surface, 192
    monthly mean daily diffuse
        irradiation on horizontal
        surface, 197
    monthly mean daily global
        irradiation on horizontal
        surface, 197
    monthly mean daily global
        irradiation on sloping surface,
        197
    monthly mean daily values of
        clear sky irradiation, 189–92
    overcast sky irradiation, 194–5

Solar radiation (*contd*)
    prediction of, 173
    transmission through glass,
        327–34
    turbidity effect, 186
    turbidity values, 188
    wavelength effect, 312
    see also Sol-air temperature
Solar space cooling, 512–14
Solar space heating, 510–12, 514
Solar spectrum, 182
Solar water-heating, 507–10, 514
Space continuity concept, 25
Space-cooling, 429, 436, 468
Spatial mobility of people, 23
Specific heats of building materials,
    319
Squatter housing movement, 1
Stack effect, 69, 366–8
Standard deviation, 457
Standard Effective Temperature
    (SET), 27, 40, 46, 48, 50–52,
    56–9, 63, 66, 154–5, 203
Standard normal distribution, 457
Steam turbine, open-cycle, 438
Stefan Bolzmann radiation, 45
Stereographic projection, 173–82
Storage, 442–50
Storage analysis for supply rate above
    minimum, 448
Stuffiness, 61
Sub-centres for energy transfer, 469
Sub-systems, 417, 419, 466–78
    compatibility of, 476
    overlapping, 474
Sun
    apparent movement of, 168–82
    earth's orbit around, 168–9
    position of, 168
Sunlight patterns, 214
Sunpath diagrams, 173–82, 214,
    219–36
Supplementary systems, 418
Surface area effects, 382
Surface area/volume ratio, 373–8,
    391
Survival requirements, 34, 40–46
Sweat rate, 60
Sweat secretion, 41, 43, 46
Sweating, 68
Swimming pools, 508
System concept, 19–32
    point in open shelter, 29
    point in serviced building, 30
    point in space, 27
    point in unserviced building, 30
    point in urban setting, 31
    point near ground, 28
System sizing, 455

Tartan-grid plan, 476
Taxation, 485, 486
Temperature
    air, 149
    design, 202
    microscale-variation of, 210
    variation in time, 203
    vertical gradient with height
        above earth's surface, 204
Temperature data, 202
Temperature difference, 168
    heat flow due to, 274
    internal and external, 204, 366
Temperature distribution, 203
Temperature effects, 200–204,
    210–11
Temperature gradients, 210, 281–5,
    295, 296, 413
Temperature index, 48
Temperature measurement, 398–400
Temperature requirements, 40
Temperature-sensing devices, 461
Temperature swings, 61, 344–51
Thermal capacity, 215, 319–21, 323,
    348, 349, 351, 409, 412
Thermal comfort, 38, 46–9, 200
    and behaviour, 69
    factors affecting, 24
    history of early theoretical and
        experimental work, 37
    mental work, 37
    prediction of, 51
Thermal comfort charts, 48, 50, 66,
    84–139
Thermal comfort equation, 46–8, 77
Thermal condition, prediction of,
    145
Thermal conductivity, 268–71, 278
    coefficient of, 269
    factors affecting, 269
Thermal cube, 377–86, 393
Thermal damping factor, 344
Thermal diffusivity, 335
Thermal discomfort, 38, 47, 52–7,
    145
Thermal efficiency, 381
Thermal energy, 431, 432
Thermal energy network, 427
Thermal environment
    basic principles and requirements,
        33–7
    earlier work, 37
    human response to, 72–3
    quality of, 34
    related to function, 35
    response to, 33–139
    specification of, 33
Thermal gradient, 24
Thermal index, 48–51

Thermal radiation, 38
Thermal resistance, 271–3, 293, 323,
    330, 335, 407, 408
    air space or cavity, 274–5
    compound element, 271
    glazing, 278–80
    unventilated air-spaces, 275
Thermal resistivity, 271, 291
Thermal response, 33, 72–3, 214
Thermal sensation scales, 53, 56
Thermal systems, 409
Thermal transients, 33, 60–62
Thermal transmittance, 274–81
    see also U-values
Thermistors, 398, 461
Thermodynamics, laws of, 25, 430
Thermoelectric effect, 442
Thermometers, 398, 400
Thermoregulatory processes, 41, 46
Thermosyphons, 509, 510
Timber houses, 23–4, 160–64
Topkapi Palace, 24
Topologically identical systems, 467
Topology of services system, 472
Total energy system, 452–5
Trade winds, 167
Transmission coefficient, 328
Transmittance, 149
Troposphere, 204
True solar time, 169–71
TSENS, 53, 56, 57
Turbines, 437

United Kingdom, 507, 510, 515,
    524, 525, 527
United States of America, 507,
    510–12, 518, 523–5, 527
Urban blight, 2
U-value ratio, 384
U-values, 204, 205, 295, 296, 327,
    335, 356, 357, 377, 381, 384,
    392, 408, 409
    calculation of, 275–8
    external walls
        curtain wall construction, 306
        framed construction, 307
        masonry construction, 304–305
    flat roofs, 308
    ground floors, 280–81
    pitched roofs (35° slope), 309
    solid floors on soil, 283
    suspended timber floor above
        ground, 283
    windows, 279–80

Vapour barrier, 293, 295
Vapour-compression machine, 434
Vapour diffusion, 290
Vapour flow rate, 290

Vapour pressure, 285–6, 288, 292, 295
Vapour resistance, 292–4
Vapour resistivity, 291
Vasoconstriction, 41
Vasodilation, 41
Venn diagrams, 472
Ventilation loss, 297–302, 332, 340, 342, 345–8, 351, 355, 370–71, 373, 382, 386
Ventilation rate, 68, 69, 302, 340–43, 358, 359, 367, 371
Ventilation systems, 421, 424, 426, 429
Vernacular settlements, 1, 3, 5, 11, 34
Vitruvius, 1, 5, 7, 19, 26

Wall solar azimuth, 172
Washington D.C., annual temperature record, 215

Waste heat, 451, 452, 454
Wastes, 2, 3
Water heating systems, 443
Water vapour pressure stratification, 212
Wind channelling, 362
Wind direction, 206, 207
Wind effects, 204–207, 208, 368
Wind flow
    pressure differences due to, 359–64
    round buildings, 361
    under buildings, 363
Wind funnels, 214
Wind patterns, 166
Wind power, 515–20
    economic considerations, 519–20
    large-scale operation, 517
    medium-scale operation, 517
    small-scale operation, 518
    utilization of, 518

Wind pressure, 359
    and suction on building, 361
    distribution on walls, 362
Wind rose, 207
Wind scoop, 160
Wind tunnels, 413
Wind turbulence, 21
Wind velocity, 149, 203, 205, 207, 208, 214, 359, 360, 363
Winchill index, 64
Windmill. See Aerogenerator
Windows
    air infiltration around, 368–9
    area effects, 355, 387–90
    condensation on, 288–90
    metaphysical elements, 13
    thermal resistance, 278–80
    total radiation transmitted through, 331
    U-values 279–80

Extension worksheet 1

✏ Think and write.

12 t w e l v e   15 _ _ _ _ _ _ _ _   19 _ _ _ _ _ _ _ _ _

r _e_ d   purpl _   fi _ teen
_ leven   yel _ ow   _ hirteen
blu _   se _ enteen   gr _ y
_ en   nine _ een   pi _ k
gree _   s _ xteen   _ ourteen
e _ ghteen   orang _   _ hite
brow _   tw _ lve   twe _ t y

Colours	Numbers
• red	•
•	•
•	•
•	•
•	•
•	•
•	•
•	•
•	•
•	•
	•

   Read and match. Listen.

Let's play a game. What's this colour? B-l-u-e. ☐

Three. I've only got three pencils! ☐

Are pencils your favourite food, Trevor? ☐

I know. That's four. Here are four pencils! My turn. ☐

a,b,c,d,e,f,g … 1

No, Trevor. It's purple. Your hair's purple. ☐

Unit 1

Song worksheet

 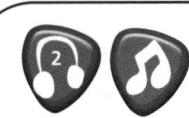 Listen and match. Sing.

a b c d

e f g

h i j k

l m n o p

q r s

t u v

w x y z

c _ _ _   _ _ _ _

_ _ _ _   _ _ _

© Cambridge University Press 2009   Primary Kid's Box Teacher's Resource Pack 2

Reinforcement worksheet 1

- Pupils look at the pictures and read the speech bubbles, then match them by writing the correct number in each answer box.

Key: 1 I can play football, 2 I can't play basketball, 3 I can ride a bike, 4 I can play the guitar, 5 I can't swim, 6 I can play tennis.

- *Optional follow-up activity:* Pupils work in pairs, A and B. Pupils study the pictures for a minute. Pupil B puts his/her worksheet face down on the desk. Pupil A says the name of a character, e.g. *Maskman.* Pupil B has to remember what the character can/can't do and says *I can play the guitar.* Pupils A and B exchange roles.

Reinforcement worksheet 2

- Pupils look at the pictures and complete the sentences.

- Monitor and help pupils with spelling as necessary.

Key: My father can play football. He can't ride a horse. My mother can play the guitar. She can't sing. My brother can swim. He can't ride a bike. My sister can play basketball. She can't play tennis.

- *Optional follow-up activity:* Pupils work in pairs, A and B. They think of a person in their family and write a sentence about him or her, e.g. *My mother can swim.* They show and read their sentence to their partner.

- Fast finishers can write additional sentences and draw pictures to illustrate them.

Extension worksheet 1

- Pupils look at the code. They complete the sentences by using the code. They draw a picture in box number 3 to illustrate the third sentence.

Key: 1 I can play the guitar, 2 I can't ride a bike, 3 Can you swim?

- *Optional pairwork activity:* Pupils work in pairs, A and B. They write three sentences using the code. They exchange their sentences, then decode them.

Extension worksheet 2

- Pupils cut out the pictures from the story and place them in order.

- Pupils listen to the story (track 3) and check their work. Then they number the pictures 1–6.

Key: 2, 3,
     1, 5,
     6, 4.

- *Optional follow-up activity:* Pupils make a zig-zag book. They fold a piece of A4 card in half lengthwise, then fold it again into three sections. They stick the pictures on each side in order.

- You may like to prepare a model in advance to show pupils the finished book.

Song worksheet

- Pupils listen to the song (track 4). They complete the song by choosing and copying the correct words. Then they draw in the missing details in the pictures.

Key: bike, tennis, basketball, swim, football, guitar.

- *Optional follow-up activity:* Pupils work in pairs, A and B. Pupil A mimes doing a sport. Pupil B names the sport. Pupils A and B exchange roles.

  Look, read and match.

1

I can ride a bike.

☐

2

I can play football.

1

3

I can't swim.

☐

4

I can play tennis.

☐

5

I can play the guitar.

☐

6

I can't play basketball.

☐

 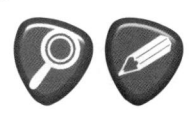 Look and write.

My father can <u>play</u> <u>football</u>.
He can't <u>ride</u> a <u>horse</u>.

My mother can _____ the _____. She can't _____.

My brother can _____.
He can't _____ a _____.

My sister can _____.
She can't _____.

Extension worksheet 1

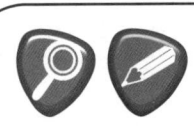 Look, write and draw.

☆	■	○	▬	◆	◧	●	★	◈	△	▼	⌣	◐
a	b	c	d	e	f	g	h	i	j	k	l	m

◿	✦	◤	◇	▲	⌣	▽	□	▬	◡	▽	▭	◸
n	o	p	q	r	s	t	u	v	w	x	y	z

1

I / c a n / _ _ _ _ _ /

_ _ _ _ / _ _ _ _ _ _ .

2

_ _ _ / _ _ _ _ ' _ /

_ _ _ _ / _ / _ _ _ _ .

3

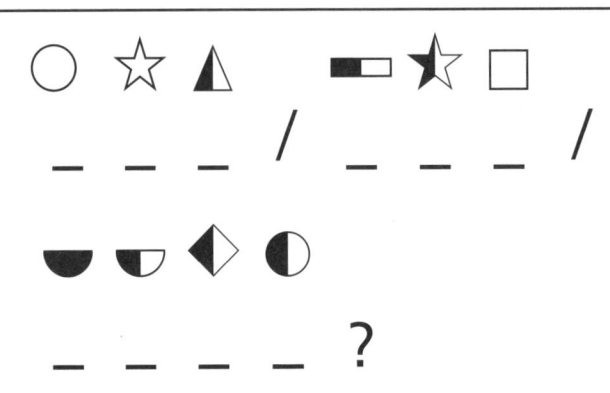

_ _ _ / _ _ _ _ /

_ _ _ _ ?

 © Cambridge University Press 2009   Primary Kid's Box Teacher's Resource Pack 2

Extension worksheet 2

   Cut and order. Listen.

Primary Kid's Box Teacher's Resource Pack 2 © Cambridge University Press 2009 **PHOTOCOPIABLE**

Song worksheet

4 ♪ Listen, write and draw. Sing.

football	basketball
tennis	guitar
~~bike~~	swim

Do the Maskman song,

Do the Maskman song,

Let's all do the Maskman song …

Ride a _____bike_____.

Play _____, _____.

Play, play, play.

Do the Maskman song,

Do the Maskman song,

Let's all do the Maskman song …

Now let's _____.

Play _____, the _____.

Play, play, play.

Do the Maskman song,

Do the Maskman song,

Let's all do the Maskman song …

© Cambridge University Press 2009   Primary Kid's Box Teacher's Resource Pack 2

3 Teacher's notes

Reinforcement worksheet 1

- Pupils choose one of the colours in the word pool for each item and colour in each picture. They label each picture by copying one word from each word pool, e.g. *A black lorry*.

- *Optional follow-up activity:* Pupils work in pairs, A and B. Pupil A looks at his/her worksheet, Pupil B turns his/her worksheet face down on the desk. Pupil A says a word, e.g. *helicopter*. Pupil B spells it, e.g. *H E L I C O P T E R*. Pupils A and B exchange roles.

Reinforcement worksheet 2

- Pupils look at the pictures and complete each speech bubble by copying the correct phrase from the word pool, e.g. *I'm riding a motorbike*.

- *Optional follow-up activity:* Pupils work in pairs, A and B. They both choose a speech bubble and copy it, in secret, onto a slip of paper. Pupil A has three guesses to find out what Pupil B has written on his/her paper, e.g. *walking*. Pupil B then has three guesses about Pupil A's paper. If pupils guess correctly, they win a point. They choose another speech bubble and continue the game. The pupil with the most points at the end of the game wins.

Extension worksheet 1

- Pupils make a word from the letters in each star. They write the word next to the star. They draw a picture of each word in the box.

Key: 1 lorry, 2 helicopter, 3 boat, 4 plane, 5 bus, 6 motorbike.

- *Optional follow-up activity:* Pupils work in pairs, A and B. Pupil A chooses one of the words and writes it on Pupil B's back. Pupil B guesses the word. Pupils A and B exchange roles.

Extension worksheet 2

- Pupils look at the story and identify where the missing pictures should go. They write the number of the frame each missing picture belongs to in the answer box beside it, then draw the picture in the correct place in the story.

- Pupils listen to the story (track 5) and check their work.

Key: 3, 5, 1, 4, 6, 2.

- *Optional follow-up activity:* Say a line from the story to the class. Ask *Maskman? Boy? Trevor? Monty? Marie?* The first pupil to put their hand up and say which character says the line has the next go.

Song worksheet

- Pupils listen to the song (track 6). They number the strips 1 to 10 in the correct order as they listen. Play the song as many times as necessary.

Key: 1 I'm walking, … favourite shoes.
2 I'm walking.
3 I'm driving, … long white lorry.
4 I'm driving.
5 I'm sitting, … big green boat.
6 I'm sitting.
7 I'm riding, … motorbike.
8 I'm riding.
9 I'm flying, … helicopter.
10 I'm flying.

- *Optional follow-up activity:* Pupils work in pairs, A and B. Pupil B turns his/her worksheet face down on the desk. Pupil A says one of the actions from the song, e.g. *I'm flying*. Pupil B says the corresponding line from the song, e.g. *I'm flying in my helicopter*. Pupils A and B exchange roles.

 Colour and write.

blue	green	yellow	red	~~black~~	purple

boat	~~lorry~~	helicopter	bus	motorbike	plane

a ....black....... ...lorry....

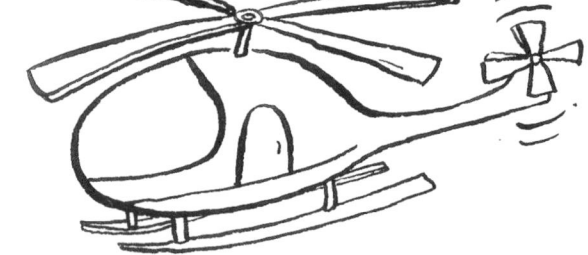

a ....

a ....

a ....

a ....

a ....

Reinforcement worksheet 2

Look and write.

flying a helicopter	driving a bus	walking	flying a plane
~~riding a motorbike~~	driving a lorry		

> What are you doing?

1

> I'm riding a motorbike.

2

3

4

5

6

Primary Kid's Box Teacher's Resource Pack 2   © Cambridge University Press 2009   **PHOTOCOPIABLE**

Unit 3 Extension worksheet 1

  **Write and draw.**

1  l o r r y

2 _ _ _ _ _ _ _ _ _ _

3 _ _ _ _

4 _ _ _ _ _

5 _ _ _

6 _ _ _ _ _ _ _ _ _

Star letters: star1: l r o r y / star2: e l p r i c h o t / star3: o t b a / star4: n l a p e / star5: s b u / star6: r o t o b e i k m

Extension worksheet 2

  Write and draw. Listen.

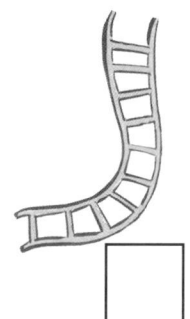     

		1			

🎧6 🎵 Listen, read and number. Sing.

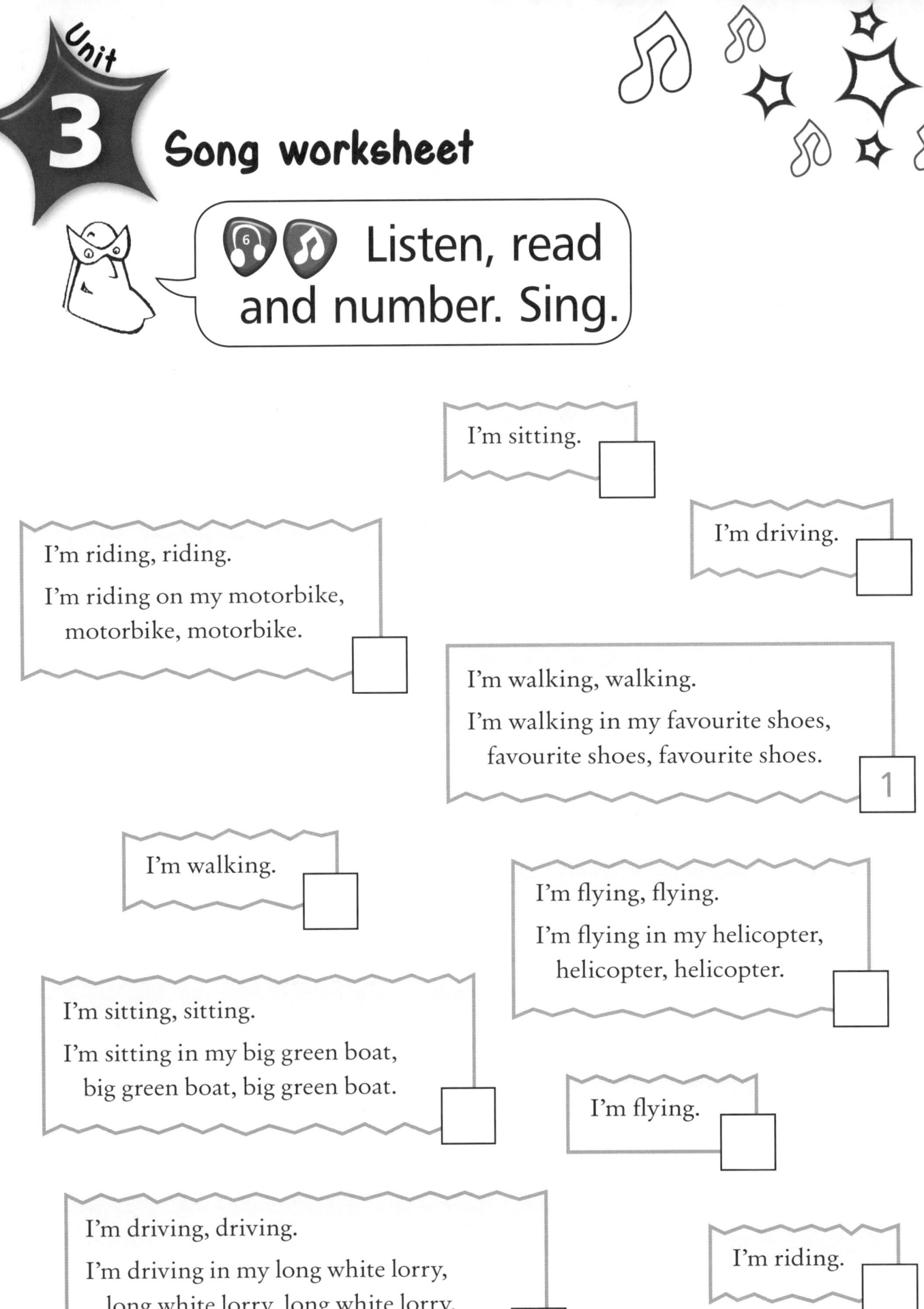

I'm sitting. ☐

I'm driving. ☐

I'm riding, riding.
I'm riding on my motorbike,
motorbike, motorbike. ☐

I'm walking, walking.
I'm walking in my favourite shoes,
favourite shoes, favourite shoes. 1

I'm walking. ☐

I'm flying, flying.
I'm flying in my helicopter,
helicopter, helicopter. ☐

I'm sitting, sitting.
I'm sitting in my big green boat,
big green boat, big green boat. ☐

I'm flying. ☐

I'm driving, driving.
I'm driving in my long white lorry,
long white lorry, long white lorry. ☐

I'm riding. ☐

Reinforcement worksheet 1

- Pupils look at the house and read the sentences. They complete each sentence by copying the correct word from the word pool.

Key: 1 living room, 2 bedroom, 3 kitchen, 4 hall, 5 bathroom, 6 dining room.

- *Optional follow-up activity:* Pupils work in pairs, A and B. They take turns to ask and answer a question about the house, e.g. *Where's the doll? In the kitchen*.

Reinforcement worksheet 2

- Pupils find and circle six words in the wordsearch. They look at the pictures and complete each sentence by copying the correct word from the wordsearch.

Key: 1 reading, 2 eating, 3 watching, 4 drawing, 5 listening, 6 sitting.

- *Optional follow-up activity:* Pupils work in pairs, A and B. Pupil A mimes one of the six actions. Pupil B guesses, e.g. *You're reading a book!* Pupils A and B exchange roles.

Extension worksheet 1

- Pupils look at the pictures and the anagrams, then match them by writing the correct number in the box. Pupils then write the word under the anagram.

Key: 1 bedroom, 2 living room, 3 dining room, 4 bathroom, 5 kitchen, 6 hall.

- *Optional follow-up activity:* Pupils work in pairs, A and B. They prepare their own anagrams, using the words on Extension worksheet 1. They exchange their work and solve their partner's word puzzles.

Extension worksheet 2

- Pupils match the two halves of each frame of the story.
- Pupils listen to the story (track 7) and check their work.

Key: 1 – 4, 2 – 3,
  3 – 2, 4 – 1,
  5 – 6, 6 – 5.

- *Optional follow-up activity:* Pupils work in pairs, A and B. Pupil A describes a frame from the story, e.g. *Suzy's got 10 pencils*. Pupil B says the number of the frame. Pupils A and B exchange roles.

Song worksheet

- Pupils listen to the song (track 8). As they listen, they match the questions and answers by writing the correct number in the box. Play the song as many times as necessary.

Key: 1 In the dining room, 2 He's eating fish, 3 In the living room, 4 He's watching TV, 5 In the bathroom, 6 She's having a bath, 7 In her bedroom, 8 She's reading a book, 9 In the hall, 10 Opening the door.

- *Optional follow-up activity:* Pupils work in pairs, A and B. They write down the five names in the song on a piece of paper. They place the worksheet face down on the desk. Pupil A chooses a name and asks Pupil B two questions from memory: *Where's Grandpa? / What's he doing?* Pupil B answers, from memory: *In the dining room. / He's eating fish*. They look at the worksheet to check. Pupil A ticks off the name from his/her list. Pupils A and B exchange roles.

Read and write.

| kitchen | hall | bathroom | dining room | bedroom | ~~living room~~ |

❶ The fish is in the .... living room ....

❷ The computer is in the ....

❸ The doll is in the ....

❹ The bike is in the ....

❺ The book is in the ....

❻ The ball is in the ....

© Cambridge University Press 2009   Primary Kid's Box Teacher's Resource Pack 2

 Find and circle. Match and write.

1 He's ....reading.... a book.　　**2** The cat's _____ a fish.

```
d  r  e  a  d  i  n  g  s
r  a  i  l  i  i  i  s  e
a  l  m  a  t  r  u  p  a
w  a  t  c  h  i  n  g  t
i  q  u  i  s  i  r  e  i
n  w  a  l  n  g  u  c  n
g  e  s  i  t  t  i  n  g
l  i  s  t  e  n  i  n  g
```

3 He's _____ TV.　　**4** He's _____ a picture.

5 She's _____ to music.　　**6** The dog's _____ under a table.

Extension worksheet 1

 Look, match and write.

1

hamotorb ☐

_ _ _ _ _ _ _ _

2

gdinin oomr ☐

_ _ _ _ _ _ _   _ _ _ _

3

cenktih ☐

_ _ _ _ _ _ _

4

medobor 1

<u>b e d r o o m</u>

5

lahl ☐

_ _ _ _

6

inlgvi moro ☐

_ _ _ _ _ _   _ _ _ _

© Cambridge University Press 2009   Primary Kid's Box Teacher's Resource Pack 2   27

  Match. Listen.

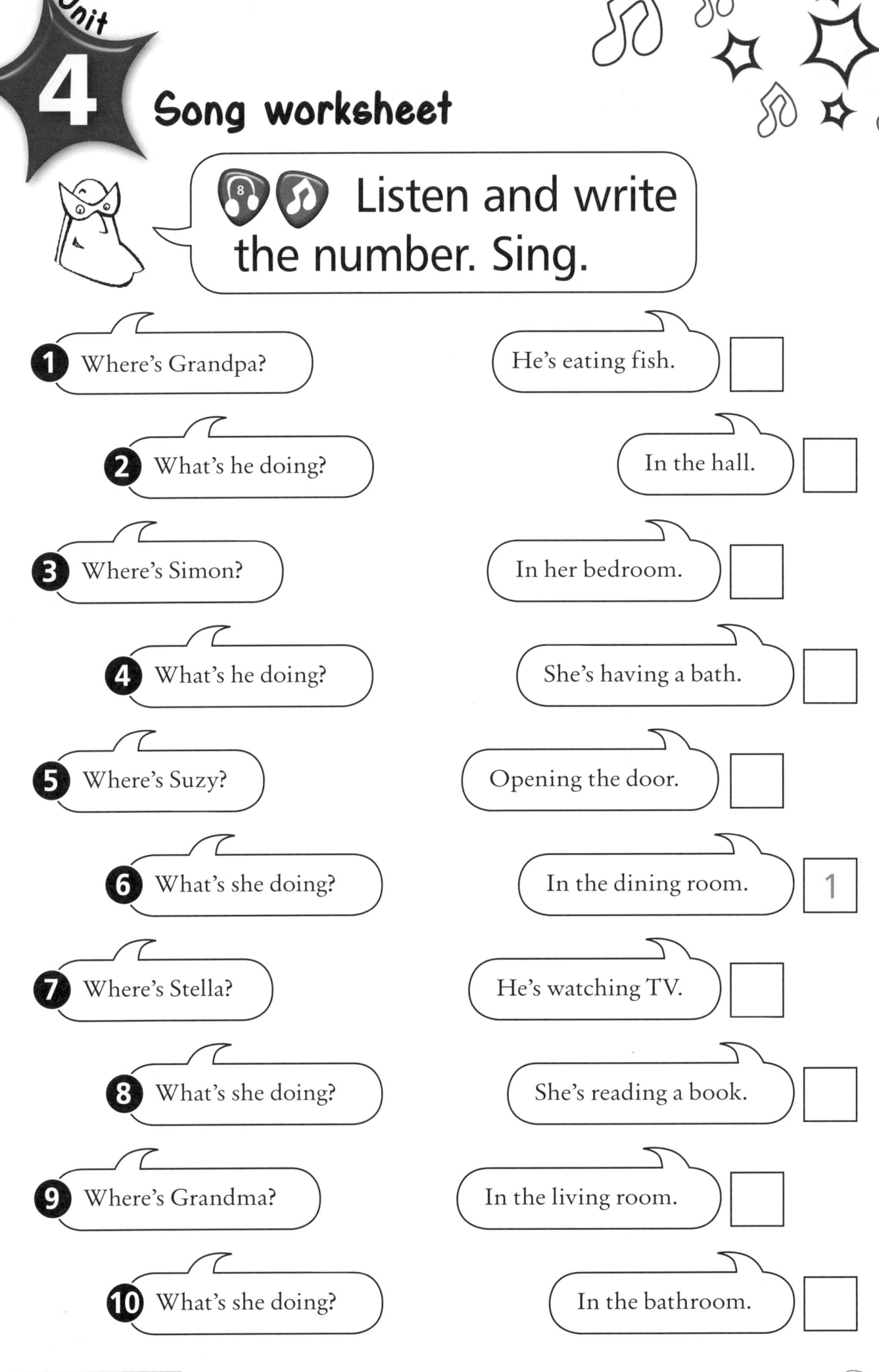

Unit 4 Song worksheet

Listen and write the number. Sing.

1 Where's Grandpa? — He's eating fish. □

2 What's he doing? — In the hall. □

3 Where's Simon? — In her bedroom. □

4 What's he doing? — She's having a bath. □

5 Where's Suzy? — Opening the door. □

6 What's she doing? — In the dining room. 1

7 Where's Stella? — He's watching TV. □

8 What's she doing? — She's reading a book. □

9 Where's Grandma? — In the living room. □

10 What's she doing? — In the bathroom. □

Primary Kid's Box Teacher's Resource Pack 2

Reinforcement worksheet 1

- Pupils complete each picture, then label them by copying the correct word from the word pool.

Key: 1 cake, 2 banana, 3 burger, 4 apple, 5 chocolate, 6 ice cream.

- *Optional follow-up activity:* Pupils work in pairs, A and B. They both make a word puzzle. They choose three food words and write them in pencil on a piece of paper. In each word they erase two or three letters and replace them with a small line, e.g. c _ k _. They exchange papers and solve their partner's word puzzles.

- Fast finishers can be encouraged to try this activity to revise other vocabulary sets.

Reinforcement worksheet 2

- Pupils look at the pictures and complete the speech bubbles by writing the correct word(s), *like/don't like*. They match each speech bubble to the correct food by drawing a line.

Key: 1 I don't like chocolate, 2 I like bananas, 3 I like ice cream, 4 I don't like apples, 5 I like cake, 6 I don't like burgers.

- *Optional follow-up activity:* Pupils work in pairs, A and B. Pupil A chooses a food item and asks Pupil B a question, e.g. *Do you like ice cream?* Pupil B points to the item on the worksheet and answers *Yes!* or *No!* Pupils A and B exchange roles.

Extension worksheet 1

- Pupils look at the food items and work out the next item in each sequence. They draw the item and label it.

Key: 1 cake, 2 chocolate, 3 apple, 4 banana, 5 burger, 6 ice cream.

- *Optional follow-up activity:* Pupils turn over their worksheet and make their own sequences with the food words. They give them to their partner to complete.

Extension worksheet 2

- Pupils cut out the pieces of the jigsaw, try to remember the story, and put the jigsaw together so that the story is in order.

- Pupils listen to the story (track 9) and check their work.

Key: See Pupil's Book, page 35.

- *Optional follow-up activity:* Pupils stick the jigsaw pictures in order onto coloured card, or into their notebooks.

Song worksheet

- Pupils listen to the song (track 10) and draw the food words. Then they listen and write the words from the word pool in the correct place.

Key: 1 bananas, 2 fish, 3 ice cream, 4 apples, 5 chocolate, 6 burgers.

- *Optional follow-up activity:* Pupils work in pairs, A and B. They write some more verses for the song using other food items that they know, e.g. *cake* and *oranges*. Personalise the activity by asking pupils to tell you what their favourite food is in L1 if necessary. Translate the new words. The class sings the song again with the new verses.

Draw and write.

| burger | chocolate | ice cream | banana | ~~cake~~ | apple |

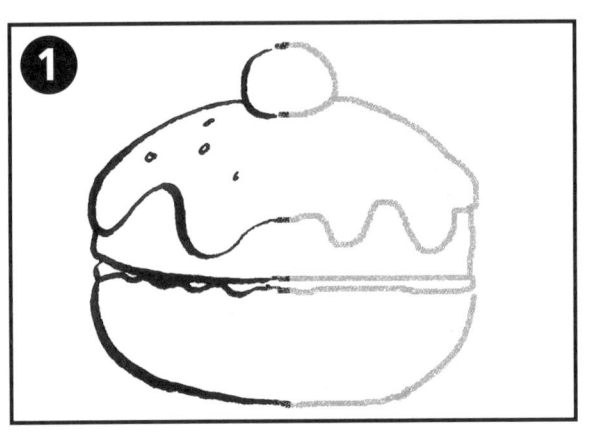

1

.... cake ....

2

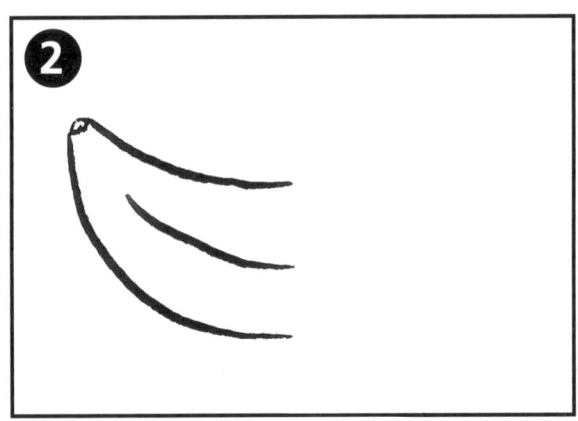

3

4

5

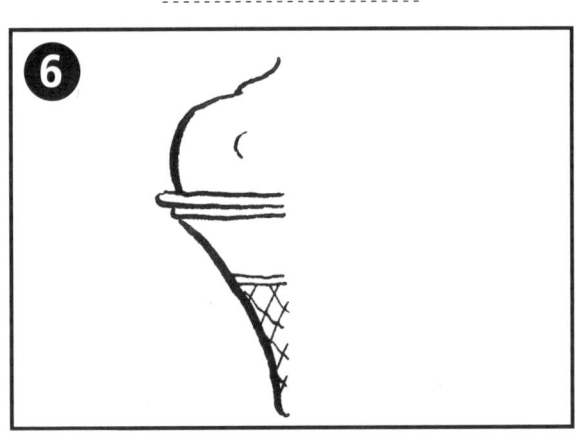

6

© Cambridge University Press 2009   Primary Kid's Box Teacher's Resource Pack 2

Look, write and match.

1  I _don't like_ chocolate.

2  I _____like_____ bananas.

3  I _____ ice cream.

4  I _____ apples.

5  I _____ cake.

6  I _____ burgers.

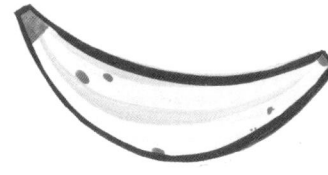

Primary Kid's Box Teacher's Resource Pack 2   © Cambridge University Press 2009   **PHOTOCOPIABLE**

Unit 5

Extension worksheet 1

 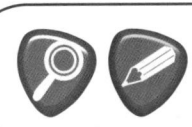 Look, complete and write.

1

...... cake ......

2

3

4

5

6

5 Extension worksheet 2

  Cut and order. Listen.

Primary Kid's Box Teacher's Resource Pack 2 © Cambridge University Press 2009 **PHOTOCOPIABLE**

Song worksheet

**Listen and draw.
Listen and write. Sing.**

burgers   fish   apples   ~~bananas~~   ice cream   chocolate

1

Do you like ..bananas..?

   Yes, yes, yes.

2

Do you like ....?

   Yes, yes, yes.

3

Do you like ....?

   Yes, yes, yes.

4

Do you like ....?

   Yes, yes, yes.

5

Do you like ....?

   Yes, yes, yes.

6

Do you like ....?

   No, no, no.

 © Cambridge University Press 2009   Primary Kid's Box Teacher's Resource Pack 2

Reinforcement worksheet 1

- Pupils look at the picture and spell the word in order to complete each sentence. They then answer the questions. They will need to count the number of objects in the classroom to give an accurate answer.

Key: 1 desk, 2 bookcase, 3 board, 4 ruler, 5 cupboard, 6 teacher.

- *Optional follow-up activity:* Pupils turn over their worksheets and write questions about different classroom objects. Pupils then swap worksheets and answer the questions.

Reinforcement worksheet 2

- Pupils use the pictures to help them follow the letter trail in the word maze from *in* to *out*. Pupils then write the words below the pictures.

Key: 1 cupboard, 2 teacher, 3 desk, 4 bookcase, 5 ruler, 6 board.

- *Optional follow-up activity:* Pupils work in pairs, A and B. Pupil A spells aloud one of the words from the worksheet. Pupil B says the word. Pupils exchange roles.

Extension worksheet 1

- The code gives the colour of each book. Words with an initial letter 'b' are coloured grey, those with an initial letter 'c', blue, etc. Pupils look at the picture on each book, write the name of the object under the correct heading and colour in the book.

Key: 1 book, 2 board, 3 bookcase, 4 bag, 5 cupboard, 6 computer, 7 desk, 8 pencil, 9 pen, 10 table, 11 teacher, 12 ruler, 13 eraser.

- *Optional follow-up activity:* Pupils write as many words as possible (from any lexical set) beginning with the initial letters used in the exercise. They then compare their lists by taking it in turns to read them.

Extension worksheet 2

- This can be done as a listening exercise (track 11) or a reading exercise. Pupils match the scenes from the story with the missing text.

Key: 5, 4, 2, 6, 1, 3.

- *Optional follow-up activity:* Pupils work in pairs and play *Pelmanism*. They cut out the cards and join the two packs. Then they place the cards face down on the desk and turn over two cards at a time. If the cards show a scene and the missing text, they form a pair. When a pupil finds a pair, he/she reads the text and then has another go. When the cards do not form a pair he/she puts the cards face down on the desk once more. The winner is the pupil with the most pairs at the end of the game.

Song worksheet

- Pupils cut out the cards and place them in a row under the classroom scene. You may wish to ask pupils to fold the page so that the lyrics are hidden. Pupils listen to the song (track 12) and place the objects in the correct position.

- *Optional follow-up activity:* Pupils work in pairs, A and B. Pupil A says a sentence, e.g. *The teacher is on the bookcase.* Pupil B places the card accordingly. Pupils exchange roles.

 Look, write and answer.

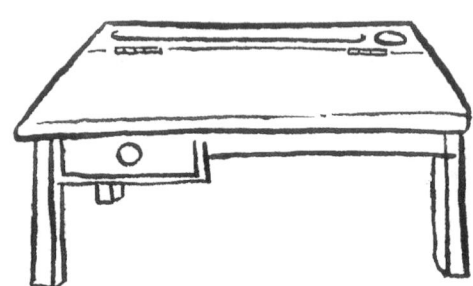

1 How many d e s k s are there in your classroom? ......

2 How many _ _ _ _ _ _ _ _ _ s are there in your classroom? ......

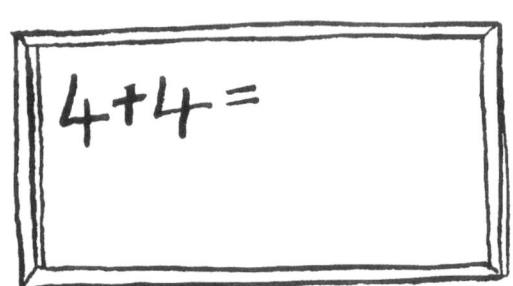

3 How many _ _ _ _ _ _ s are there in your classroom? ......

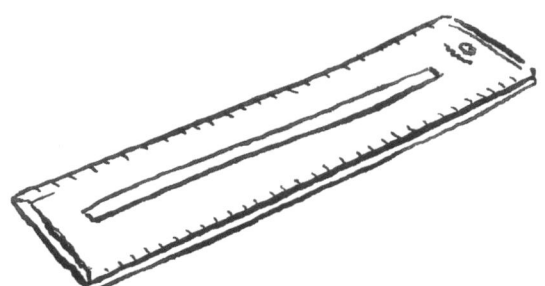

4 How many _ _ _ _ _ s are there in your classroom? ......

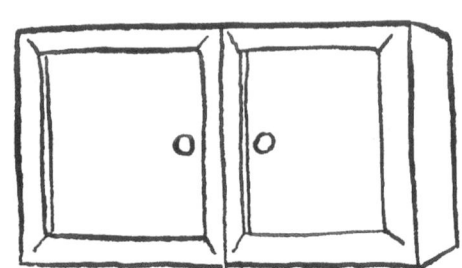

5 How many _ _ _ _ _ _ _ _ _ s are there in your classroom? ......

6 How many _ _ _ _ _ _ _ s are there in your classroom? ......

Look, follow and write.

1 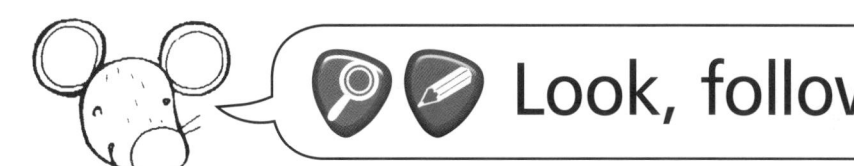 **2** **3** **4** **5** **6**

cupboard _____ _____ _____ _____ _____

In ➔

c	u	b	p	i	o	v	r	w	i	e	a
a	p	d	t	e	a	c	s	q	t	f	z
t	b	r	m	d	c	u	k	d	x	o	r
v	o	a	j	e	h	s	b	s	w	k	d
w	g	c	d	r	g	f	y	p	o	i	h
d	z	v	e	u	t	m	e	r	b	v	g
l	t	k	s	z	v	p	l	q	o	a	r
b	h	b	o	i	e	r	u	v	x	q	d
x	m	y	o	n	s	k	w	i	h	u	f
e	q	u	k	c	a	x	g	o	l	j	t

➔ Out

Primary Kid's Box Teacher's Resource Pack 2 © Cambridge University Press 2009 **PHOTOCOPIABLE**

Unit 6

Extension worksheet 1

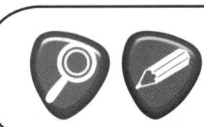 Look, write and colour.

b = grey   c = blue   d = green

1 b <u>o</u> <u>o</u> k   **5** c _ _ _ _ _ _ _ _   **7** d _ _ _

2 b _ _ _ _   **6** c _ _ _ _ _ _ _

3 b _ _ _ _ _ _ _

4 b _ _

p = yellow   t = purple   r = red   e = brown

8 p_ _ _ _ _   **10** t _ _ _ _   **12** r _ _ _ _   **13** e _ _ _ _ _

9 p_ _   **11** t _ _ _ _ _ _

Extension worksheet 2

 Match and play. Listen.

1

Now, how many pencils are there?

There are 9, 10, 11 pencils.

☐

2

Now there's an eraser in the bag, Marie.

Good! Thank you, Monty.

☐

3

Hmm. Is there a ruler?

Yes, there is. It's a 'Maskman' ruler.

☐

4

11 pencils! Where's the pencil? Trevor?!!!

Sorry. Here you are. Pencils are my favourite food.

☐

5

OK, everybody. This bag is for school. Let's look.

OK, Marie!

1

6

Look, Marie. Here's an eraser.

Good! Can you put it in the bag, please, Monty?

☐

Song worksheet

 Listen and place. Sing.

fold- fold - - -

There are pencils in the classroom, yes there are.

There's a cupboard on the pencils, yes there is.

There's a ruler on the cupboard,

There's a bookcase on the ruler,

There's a teacher on the bookcase, yes there is ...

© Cambridge University Press 2009   Primary Kid's Box Teacher's Resource Pack 2

 **7** **Teacher's notes**

Reinforcement worksheet 1

- Pupils unjumble the words.

Key: 1 camera, 2 robot, 3 lorry, 4 kite, 5 watch, 6 computer game.

- *Optional follow-up activity:* Pupils work in pairs, A and B. Pupil A names one of the toys on the spinner. Pupil B spins the spinner. If it lands on the toy Pupil A has chosen, Pupil A gets a point. Pupils exchange roles. After a set amount of time, stop the activity and check who has the most points.

Reinforcement worksheet 2

- Pupils begin by tracing the toy on each child. They then fill in the gaps.

Key: 1 ball, Anna, 2 robot, Ben, 3 camera, Nick, 4 lorry, Kim, 5 watch, Sue, 6 kite, Tony.

- *Optional follow-up activity:* Pupils work in pairs and play *Snap!* They cut out the individual cards and shuffle them, each keeping their own pack. On the word *Go!* they each turn over their top card. If they are the same, the first pupil to say *Snap!* wins the cards (plus any others that haven't been won). If the cards are different, they each turn over the next card and play continues. The winner is the pupil who has the most cards at the end of the game.

Extension worksheet 1

- Pupils look at the pictures of clothing and toys and match the item(s) with the pattern favoured by each character. They then use the information to write the appropriate questions and answers.

Key: 1 Whose is this? It's Maria's. 2 Whose are these? They're Daniel's. 3 Whose are these? They're Mark's. 4 Whose is this? It's Sara's. 5 Whose are these? They're Daniel's. 6 Whose is this? It's Sara's. 7 Whose is this? It's Maria's. 8 Whose is this? It's Mark's.

- *Optional follow-up activity:* Pupils work in groups of three. Pupil A draws another item with one of the four patterns, Pupil B asks the question and Pupil C answers. Pupils exchange roles.

Extension worksheet 2

- This can be done as a listening exercise (track 13) or a reading exercise. Pupils look at the jumbled sentences and rewrite them below in the correct order.

Key: See Pupil's Book, page 49.

- *Optional follow-up activity:* Pupils work in groups and play *Bingo!* They each draw a four by two grid in their notebooks and write eight of the words that they used in the sentence-ordering activity (without using any word more than once). One pupil acts as bingo caller (decided by throwing a six on a dice). The winner of the first game is the caller in the second game, etc.

Song worksheet

- You may wish to ask pupils to fold the page so that the lyrics are hidden. Pupils listen to the song (track 14) and draw lines between the characters and the corresponding items of clothing. They then listen again to complete the answers and, finally, colour the clothes accordingly.

- *Optional follow-up activity:* Pupils work in groups. They think of an item of clothing and each draw and colour it. They show each other the pictures and Pupil A collects them all in, shuffles them and turns over the top picture. He/she asks Pupil B *Whose is this/are these ... (item of clothing)?* Pupil B answers *It's/they're ...'s,* then turns over the next picture and asks Pupil C. When all pupils have answered, they decide on a new item of clothing.

Reinforcement worksheet 1

 Look and write.

a a e c r m   o t r o b   r o r y l

1 c a m e r a   **2** _ _ _ _ _   **3** _ _ _ _ _

k e t i   t h c w a

4 _ _ _ _   **5** _ _ _ _ _

e c r m p o t u   m g e a

6 _ _ _ _ _ _ _ _   _ _ _ _

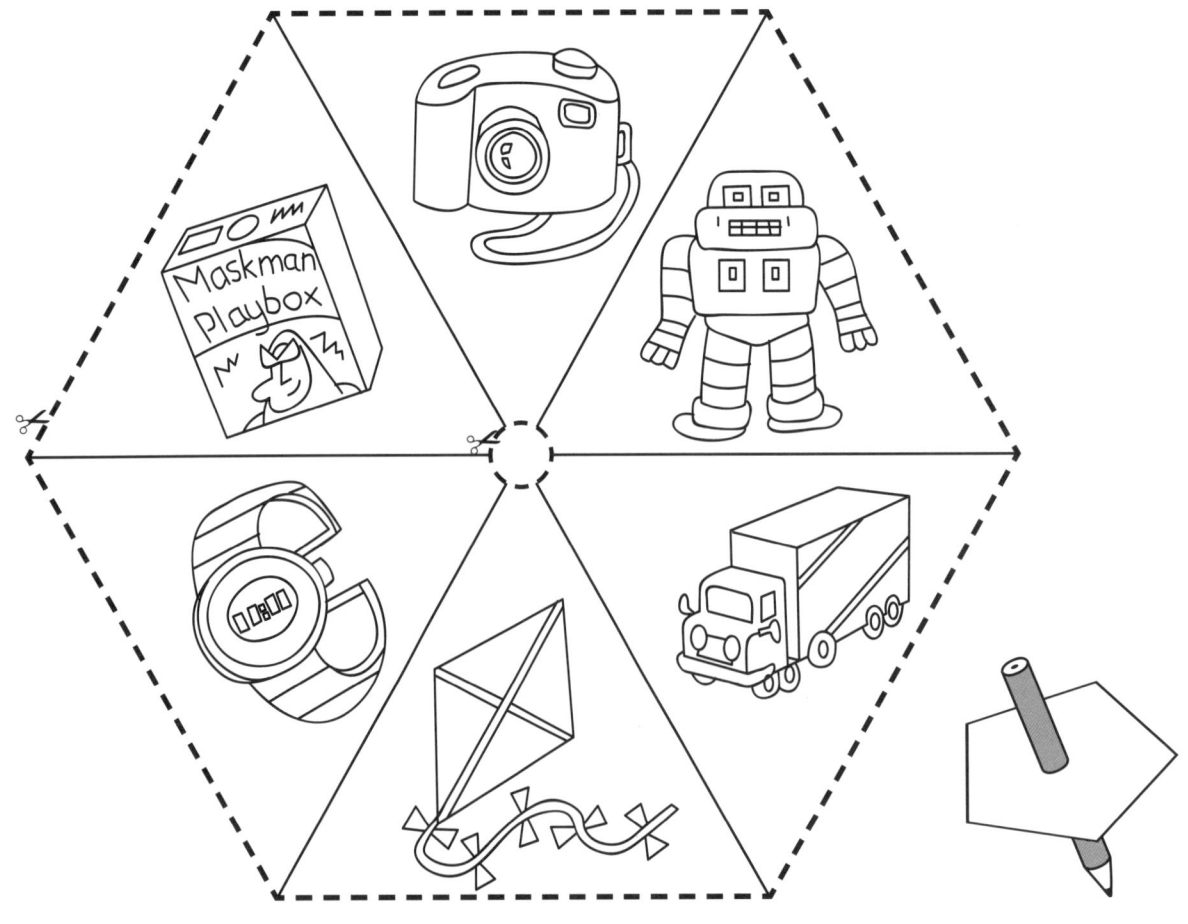

Trace and write.

1 The b a l l
is A n n a 's.

2 The _ _ _ _ _
is _ _ _ 's.

3 The _ _ _ _ _ _
is _ _ _ _ 's.

  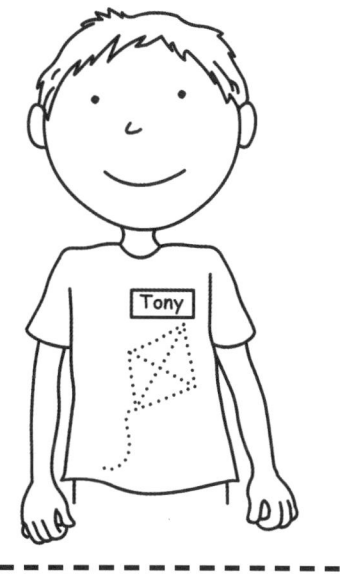

4 The _ _ _ _ _
is _ _ _ 's.

5 The _ _ _ _ _
is _ _ _ 's.

6 The _ _ _ _
is _ _ _ _ 's.

Unit 7

Extension worksheet 1

 Match and write.

 Sara

 Daniel

 Maria

 Mark

Whose is this?   Whose are these?

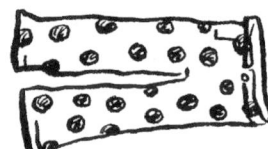

1 ....It's Maria's........   **2** They're ....   **3** ....

4 ....   **5** ....   **6** ....

7 ....   **8** ....

Extension worksheet 2

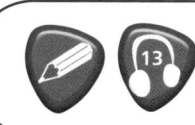 Sort and write. Listen.

1   this   robot?   Whose   is

Whose is this robot? ....

2   your   name?   Hello.   What's

....

3   talk.   walk   I   I   can   can   and

....

4   I   can   I   spell.   and   talk   can

....

5   it   and   can't   Yes,   fly.   it   is ...

....

6   'sorry',   Maskman!   please.   Say

....

Primary Kid's Box Teacher's Resource Pack 2   © Cambridge University Press 2009

Unit 7

Song worksheet

   Listen, write and colour. Sing.

What colour is the skirt?
The skirt is .... purple ....

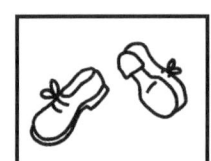
What colour are the shoes?
The shoes are _____

What colour is the jacket?
The jacket is _____

What colour are the trousers?
The trousers are _____

fold --- fold

Whose is this jacket? ...
What? That black jacket?
Yes, this black jacket.
Whose is this jacket?
It's John's.
Oh!

Whose are these shoes? ...
What? Those blue shoes?
Yes, these blue shoes.
Whose are these shoes?
They're Sheila's.
Oh!

Whose is this skirt? ...
What? That purple skirt?
Yes, this purple skirt.
Whose is this skirt?
It's Sue's.
Oh!

Whose are these trousers? ...
What? Those brown trousers?
Yes, these brown trousers.
Whose are these trousers?
They're Tom's.
Oh!

 © Cambridge University Press 2009   Primary Kid's Box Teacher's Resource Pack 2

Reinforcement worksheet 1

- Pupils locate the furniture vocabulary in the wordsearch. Words are written horizontally, vertically and diagonally. They write the words under the corresponding pictures.

Key: 1 phone, 2 mirror, 3 clock, 4 sofa, 5 mat, 6 lamp.

- *Optional follow-up activity:* Pupils work in pairs, A and B. They cut out the picture cards, shuffle them and place them face down on the table. Pupil A turns over two cards. If they are different, play passes to Pupil B. If they are the same, Pupil A says *The* (items of furniture) *are mine* and has another go. The winner is the player with the most pairs at the end of the game.

Reinforcement worksheet 2

- Pupils read the words and draw the furniture. They then look at the picture of the house and match the furniture to the correct room.

Key: bedroom: lamp. **kitchen:** clock, mat. **living room:** sofa, phone. **bathroom:** mirror.

- *Optional follow-up activity:* Pupils work in pairs. They decide on a room and then take it in turns to name all the items they know that are normally found in that room. The pupil who runs out of ideas or repeats a word that has already been said loses, and the other pupil gets a point. They then repeat the process with items found in another room.

Extension worksheet 1

- Pupils look at the two houses and compare them to spot the differences. They use their knowledge to complete the sentences. In the first four sentences the pieces of furniture are given, but in the other sentences, pupils will need to realise which pieces of furniture, not already named, are present in house B but not in house A.

Key: House A: 1 bedroom, 2 bathroom, 3 living room, 4 kitchen. House B: 1 mirror, 2 phone, 3 clock, lamp, 4 sofa, mat.

- *Optional follow-up activity:* Pupils take it in turns to read the sentences. One pupil describes where the lamp is in house A and the other in house B, etc.

Extension worksheet 2

- Pupils use the shape code to help them complete the sentences. They then check their answers either by listening (track 15) or by comparing with the text in the Pupil's Book. Discuss with the class which alternative answers are valid and which are not.

Key: 1 play, 2 close, count, 3 are, is, tail, under, chair, 4 feet, see, next, 5 in, cupboard, hair, 6 horse.

- *Optional follow-up activity:* Pupils cut out the characters and sentences and stick them in their notebooks according to who says what in the story. Pupils work in groups. They each choose a character and act out the story. Pupils exchange roles.

Song worksheet

- Pupils listen to the song (track 16) and number the verses.

Key: See Pupil's Book, page 53.

- *Optional follow-up activity:* Pupils work in groups of three. Each pupil cuts out the shoe outlines. Pupil A puts his/her set face down in a pile whilst B and C put their sets face down on the table in front of them. Pupil A turns over the first shoe and sings the verse. Pupils B and C each turn over one of their shoes and whoever finds the corresponding verse takes over the role of singing the lyrics by turning over the next shoe on the pile. If neither B nor C turns over the verse, Pupil A sings the next verse.

  Find and write.

l	m	c	l	o	c	k
a	m	s	a	b	r	t
m	t	i	l	e	e	o
p	i	a	r	b	f	d
c	m	a	t	r	j	l
m	s	o	f	a	o	e
v	p	h	o	n	e	r

1 p h o n e

2 _ _ _ _ _ _

3 _ _ _ _ _

4 _ _ _ _

5 _ _ _

6 _ _ _ _

🔍✏️ Read and draw. Look and match.

clock

mirror

mat

bedroom

kitchen

bathroom

living room

sofa

phone

lamp

Unit 8

Extension worksheet 1

Look and write.

A

B

A

1 There's a mat and a lamp in the ....bedroom........ .

2 There's a mirror in the ....

3 There's a sofa and a phone in the ....

4 There's a clock in the ....

B

1 There's a ....mirror.......... in the bedroom.

2 There's a .... in the bathroom.

3 There's a .... and a .... in the living room.

4 There's a .... and a .... in the kitchen.

51

Unit 8

Extension worksheet 2

 Write and stick. Listen.

●	see count ~~play~~ is are close
■	arm chair horse cupboard tail hair feet
▲	in next under

1 Let's ● ......play...... hide and seek.

2 Trevor, ● .... your eyes and ● .... to 20.

3 Where ● .... they?

Whose ● .... that ■ .... ?

I can see you, Monty. You're ▲ .... the ■ ....

4 Look. Whose ■ .... are those? Come out, Maskman.

We can ● .... you ▲ .... to the bookcase.

5 Marie's ▲ .... the ■ ....

Look! That's her ■ ....

6 It's a toy ■ ....

Song worksheet

16 ♫ **Listen and write. Sing.**

Whose are these shoes? ...
Stella! Are they yours? ...
No, they aren't mine! ...

Hmm. Which shoes are Simon's? ...
Which, which, which, which?
Which shoes are Simon's?
The grey ones are his ...

Hmm. Which shoes are Suzy's? ...
Which, which, which, which?
Which shoes are Suzy's?
The red ones are hers ...

SO! Whose shoes are those? ...
Whose, whose, whose, whose?
Whose shoes are those?
Those are Grandpa's ...
Grandpa's?
GRANDPA!

Look at this!
Look at this!

1

© Cambridge University Press 2009   Primary Kid's Box Teacher's Resource Pack 2   53

Festivals

Halloween

The following cultural notes describe both the origins and the current traditions of this festival. Explain as much as you feel is relevant to the class and ask pupils to point to the relevant items on the worksheet that you use first.

■ Halloween is celebrated on 31 October in the United Kingdom, the United States, Canada, Australia and New Zealand and many other countries around the world. It is not a public holiday, but it is a very important celebration for children. The word *Halloween* originally came from *All Hallows' Eve*, which means the evening before the Day of the Holy Ones or All Saints' Day, 1 November. The tradition is that on this night, spirits, ghosts and witches wander the earth. People used to make lanterns out of pumpkins and place them in the window to scare away these frightening creatures.

■ Nowadays, on the night of Halloween, children get dressed up as witches, ghosts, vampires, and other scary monsters and have a fancy dress party. Items that are traditionally associated with Halloween are pumpkin lanterns, bats, spiders and black cats. Children often play a traditional game called 'apple bobbing'. In this game, you have to bite an apple that is floating in water or hanging on a string. Typical party food would be cakes and pizza decorated with horrible faces.

■ At Halloween, children love to play *Trick or Treat*. Children knock on neighbours' doors and ask *Trick or Treat?* If the neighbour chooses a treat, he/she must offer the children sweets, chocolate or fruit. If not, the children will play a naughty trick, such as using a water pistol. It's always a good idea to have treats ready for visitors on Halloween!

Halloween worksheet 1

- Pupils count how many examples there are of each Halloween character/object and write the number in the answer box. Pupils colour the Halloween scene.

Key: 1 two pumpkin lanterns, 2 one ghost, 3 one cat, 4 one witch, 5 four spiders, 6 six bats, 7 eight cakes, 8 seven sweets, 9 three apples.

- *Optional follow-up activity:* Pupils work in pairs, A and B with their worksheets face up in front of them. Pupil A names a colour that he/she can see on the worksheet. Pupil B points to it. Pupils A and B exchange roles.

Halloween worksheet 2

- Pupils need scissors, string, card, glue and a drinking straw. Pupils colour, cut out and mount the Halloween items onto card.

- They cut the string into different lengths and attach a short piece to each item. They tie the items along the straw. They attach a piece of string to each end of the straw and hang the mobiles around the classroom.

- As pupils work, circulate and ask them questions about the items, e.g. *What's this? What colour is your pumpkin?*

- You may like to prepare a model in advance to show pupils the finished mobile.

- *Optional follow-up activity:* In turn, pupils point and name the items on their mobiles.

 **Festivals**

Christmas

The following cultural notes describe both the origins and the current traditions of this festival. Explain as much as you feel is relevant to the class.

■ Christmas Day is celebrated in countries around the world on 25 December, to commemorate the birth of Jesus. In the weeks before Christmas, people decorate a Christmas tree with ornaments. They usually put a star on the top to remind them of the story of the birth of Jesus and the Three Wise Men. People also like to send each other Christmas cards with typical Christmas scenes and a Christmas message. Younger children write a letter to Father Christmas, or Santa Claus as he is sometimes called, to tell him what they would like for Christmas. On Christmas Eve, 24 December, they hang a Christmas stocking at the end of their bed or by the fireplace, if they have one. This stocking is similar to a very big sock. Traditionally Father Christmas arrives in his sleigh pulled by reindeer. He flies through the air, lands on the roofs of children's houses and delivers the presents by climbing down the chimneys with a huge sack of presents!

■ On Christmas Day, families come together to eat a traditional midday meal. This consists of roast turkey, with vegetables. Dessert is a rich fruit pudding served with a brandy sauce that is set alight! The table is decorated with candles and brightly coloured crackers. Everyone pulls the crackers which make a loud bang. Children love to look inside the crackers to find a colourful paper Christmas hat, a small toy and a Christmas joke.

Christmas worksheet 1

- Pupils need scissors, coloured card, glue and sticky tape.

- Pupils colour and mount the Santa Claus and chimney onto card. They then cut along the dotted lines.

- They fold a piece of A4 coloured card in half. They open the card, and place the Santa Claus behind the chimney, and tape the sides of the chimney to the front of the card so that the Santa can slide up and down easily.

- Write *Merry Christmas!* on the board. Pupils copy the message inside the card and sign their name.

- They illustrate the inside of the card with presents, Christmas trees, candles, etc.

- While pupils are working, circulate and ask questions, e.g. *What's this? What colour is the Christmas tree?*

- *Optional follow-up activity:* Pupils give the card to a member of their family and say *Merry Christmas!* They then name all of the things they have drawn on their card.

Christmas worksheet 2

- Pupils colour the four pictures and read the words. Ask them to cut out the four pictures. Staple the four pictures together to make a book making sure that the half-way lines coincide. The children then cut along the horizontal line of the pictures stopping before the stapled strip. By turning the different pages of the book, they can invent new Christmas characters.

- *Optional follow-up activity:* Pupils work in pairs, A and B. Pupil A makes up a new Christmas character without showing Pupil B. He/she names it, and Pupil B must make up the same character. They swap roles.

Festivals

Easter

The following cultural notes describe both the origins and the current traditions of this festival. Explain as much as you feel is relevant to the class and ask pupils to point to the relevant items on the worksheet that you use first.

■ Easter is a Christian festival which celebrates Jesus rising from the dead. As Easter always falls in spring, some people associate it more widely with new life, which is why images of chicks and eggs, lambs, baby rabbits and spring flowers are also traditional. The date is fixed according to the lunar calendar and therefore differs slightly every year. In the weeks before Easter, people send Easter cards to their friends and family, and they buy chocolate Easter eggs and Easter bunnies for their children. Many children like to boil real eggs and then paint them with bright colours. Children often have egg rolling competitions or hold Easter egg hunts looking for the colourful eggs around the garden. Baskets are also associated with Easter. People make and fill them with Easter eggs and spring flowers to decorate their houses.

■ In the United Kingdom, people like to eat hot cross buns, a type of sweet bread with dried fruit in it. These buns are marked with the Christian symbol of the cross and are traditionally eaten during Lent (the 40 days leading up to Easter). In the Middle Ages, the bakers sold these buns in the streets.

■ Easter is an important church festival and Good Friday and Easter Monday are public holidays.

Easter worksheet 1

- Pupils need scissors, glue and two pieces of different coloured card.

- Pupils cut out the rectangles. They mount the pictures on one piece of coloured card and the words on the other piece of coloured card.

- Pupils work in pairs, A and B. They shuffle their cards together and lay them face down on the desk. Pupil A turns over two cards, one of each colour, and names each card. If the cards are the same, Pupil A keeps them. If not, Pupil A turns the cards face down again. Pupils A and B exchange roles. The pupil with the most cards at the end of the game is the winner.

- *Optional follow-up activity:* Call out the four Easter items in random order. Pupils hold up the corresponding picture and word card. Pupils can work in pairs and continue this activity.

Easter worksheet 2

- Pupils need scissors, glue and card.

- Pupils colour, cut out and mount the basket and Easter eggs on card. They stick the reverse of the sides of the basket together and fold the flaps outwards so the basket stands up. Finally pupils stick their eggs inside the top of the basket.

- Ask pupils to say all the Easter words they know.

- *Optional follow-up activity:* Pupils show their parents their Easter basket and tell them in L1 about Easter traditions in English-speaking countries. They can try and teach their parents the Easter words they know.

Halloween worksheet 1

  Count. Write the number.

1. 2
2.
3.
4.
5.
6.
7.
8.
9.

© Cambridge University Press 2009   Primary Kid's Box Teacher's Resource Pack 2

Halloween worksheet 2

 Colour, cut and make.

Primary Kid's Box Teacher's Resource Pack 2   © Cambridge University Press 2009   **PHOTOCOPIABLE**

Christmas worksheet 1

  Make a Christmas card.

© Cambridge University Press 2009   Primary Kid's Box Teacher's Resource Pack 2

Christmas worksheet 2

  Colour and play.

snow

man

Father

Christmas

rein

deer

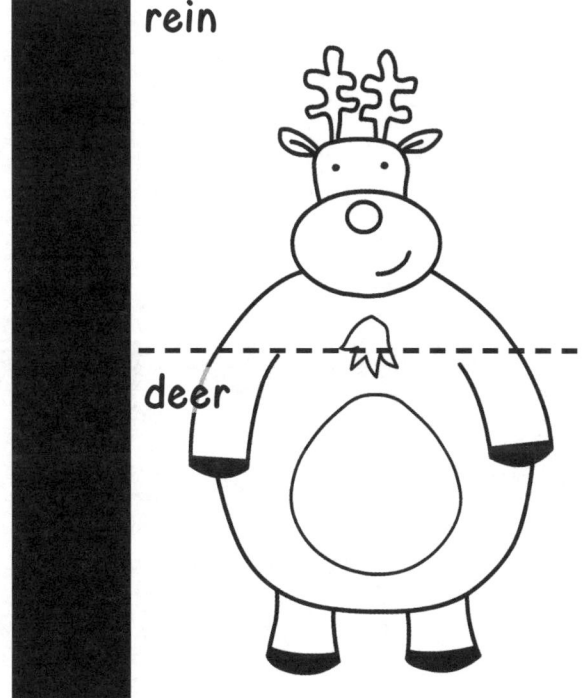

Christmas

tree

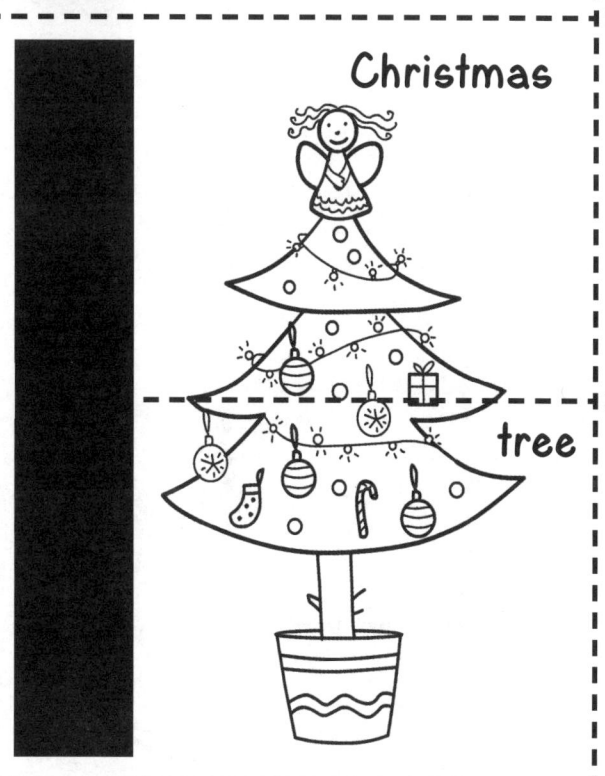

Easter worksheet 1

  Cut and play.

Easter egg

hot cross bun

Easter bunny

flower

© Cambridge University Press 2009   Primary Kid's Box Teacher's Resource Pack 2

Easter worksheet 2

  Colour, cut and make.

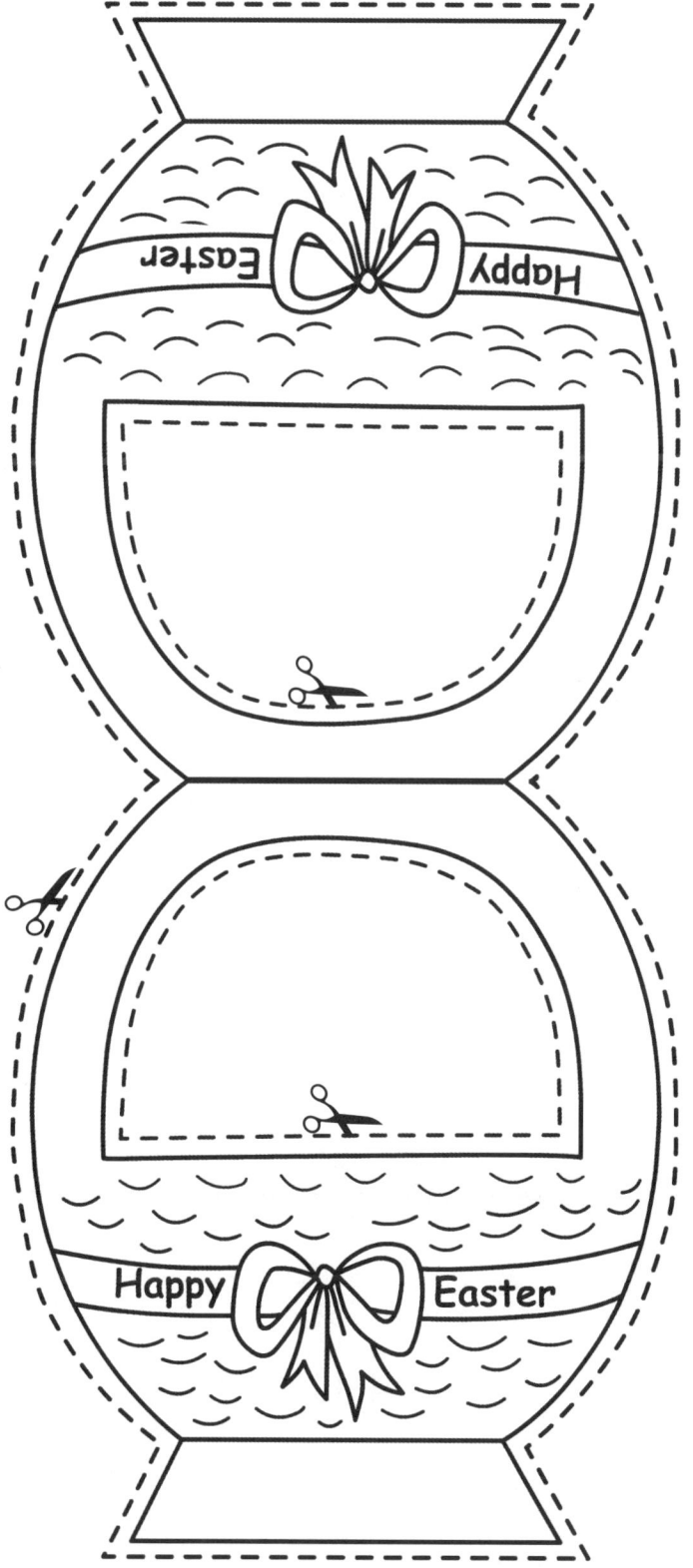

Happy **Easter**

Happy Easter

Primary Kid's Box Teacher's Resource Pack 2 © Cambridge University Press 2009 **PHOTOCOPIABLE**

Word cards: alphabet

a	b	c	d
e	f	g	h
i	j	k	l
m	n	o	p
q	r	s	t
u	v	w	x
y	z		

© Cambridge University Press 2009   Word cards   Primary Kid's Box TRP 2

Word cards: colours

pink

green

orange

purple

blue

black

brown

grey

white

Primary Kid's Box TRP 2   Word cards   **PHOTOCOPIABLE**

Word cards: numbers

eleven

twelve

thirteen

fourteen

fifteen

sixteen

seventeen

eighteen

nineteen

twenty

play football

play basketball

play tennis

play the guitar

play the piano

swim

ride a bike

 Primary Kid's Box TRP 2   Word cards   © Cambridge University Press 2009   **PHOTOCOPIABLE**

Word cards: At the funfair

a bus

a lorry

a motorbike

a helicopter

a plane

a boat

 © Cambridge University Press 2009 Word cards   Primary Kid's Box TRP 2

a bathroom

a bedroom

a dining room

a hall

a kitchen

a living room

Word cards: Party time!

an apple

a banana

a burger

cake

chocolate

ice cream

a board

a bookcase

a cupboard

a desk

a ruler

a teacher

Word cards: Play time!

a camera

a watch

a kite

a robot

a lorry

a computer game

a mat

a lamp

a clock

a phone

a mirror

a sofa

Primary Kid's Box TRP 2   Word cards   © Cambridge University Press 2009   **PHOTOCOPIABLE**